James Duff Brown

Biographical Dictionary Of Musicians

James Duff Brown

Biographical Dictionary Of Musicians

ISBN/EAN: 9783741152054

Manufactured in Europe, USA, Canada, Australia, Japa

Cover: Foto ©Angelika Wolter / pixelio.de

Manufactured and distributed by brebook publishing software (www.brebook.com)

James Duff Brown

Biographical Dictionary Of Musicians

Biographical Dictionary

OF

Musicians:

With a Bibliography of English Writings on Music.

BY

JAMES D. BROWN,
MITCHELL LIBRARY, GLASGOW.

ALEXANDER GARDNER,
PAISLEY; AND 12 PATERNOSTER ROW, LONDON.
1886.

PREFACE.

THE following explanatory remarks and acknowledgments are offered by way of Introduction.

This work is intended for students of Music or persons interested in the art, and while not claiming a great degree of completeness in any department, may nevertheless be found interesting and useful as a supplement to larger and more ambitious works of the same class. It aims at conciseness in every particular, and each notice is so arranged that any fact of a biographical or bibliographical character may be readily found. All anecdotal and gossipy matter has been suppressed, the intention of the Editor being merely to put forth a work of utility, especially in view of the fact that so many works in musical literature exist to which readers can turn for pastime. The endeavour has been to present a series of brief notices of Musicians in which every important fact likely to be of use has been noted. Prominence has naturally been given to British Musical Biography, and no one whose life or works seemed of interest has been knowingly omitted. The Bibliographical character of the work accounts for the presence of many names of minor importance, and accordingly no apology is offered for the comparative insignificance of any name mentioned throughout the book. The notices of Foreign Musicians are confined to such as claim attention by their acknowledged eminence, or by their connection in any way with Britain. The Critical Remarks occurring here and there throughout the work are generally digests from a collation of opinions by writers of authority. It should also be further remarked that the nationalities of biographical subjects are, with certain exceptions, fixed by parentage and not by birthplace.

The Bibliographical Appendix forms a brief Subject-Index to the work itself, and in a general way to the English Literature of Music. No pretence is made to an exhaustive or even accurate treatment of this division of the work, and the only plea which can be recorded on its behalf is its almost complete novelty. To be a Bibliography in the strict meaning of the word would make it needful to record every particular of publication, which has been found impossible in the present case, as a personal examination of only a small number of the books indexed could be made. For its imperfections both in regard to accuracy and detail the compiler can only apologize. With a view to the compilation of a complete Bibliography of the English writings on Music and Collections of all kinds, the Author would be obliged if possessors of musical books would communicate titles and dates to him.

To Mr. Stephen S. Stratton, of Birmingham, the Author desires to express most grateful acknowledgment for willing and valuable assistance in every department of the work. The book is indebted to him for dates, facts, and suggestions of every kind, and to him is due many of the corrections of chronological errors in musical biography which have been perpetuated in work after work. His valuable services in connection with the revisal for the press are also thankfully acknowledged. Thanks are also warmly accorded to Mr. James Love, of Falkirk, N.B.; Major G. A. Crawford, of London; Mr. W. H. Dana, of Warren, Ohio; Mr. W. H. Daniell, of Boston, Mass.; and Messrs. Karl Merz, W. B. Gilbert, J. C. Fillmore, David Baptie, C. E. Stephens, and many others, for services rendered in connection with British and American Biography and Bibliography. The notices of many of the living musicians noticed throughout the work are indebted to themselves for revision and correction in the biographical sections, and the Author desires to acknowledge much assistance freely rendered in this respect.

In conclusion the Author would invite additions, suggestions and corrections of all kinds, which may be sent for him to the care of the publisher, and of these, acknowledgment will gladly be made.

LANGSIDE, GLASGOW, 1886.

ABBREVIATIONS.

Words omitted to shorten titles.
[ ] Dates within brackets, are approximations or doubtful.
B.—Born.
C—Circa (about).
Cantab.—Cambridge University.
Cantuar.—Canterbury (Lambeth Musical Degree).
Cath.—Cathedral.
'Cello.—Violoncello.
Ch.—Church.
Chap.—Chapel.   Chap. Roy.—Chapel Royal.
Chor.—Chorister, Chorus.
Coll.—College.
Comp.—Composer, Composed, Composition, or other forms.
Cond.—Conductor, Conducted, etc.
Cons.—Conservatory, Conservatoire.
D.—Died.
Ed.—Editor, Edited, Edition.
F.C.O.—Fellow of College of Organists.
Gent.—Gentleman (Gent. of Chap. Royal).
Mem.—Member.
Mus. Bac. or Mus. Doc.—Bachelor or Doctor of Music.
N.D.—No date.
Op.—Opus (work).
Orch.—Orchestra, Orchestral.
Org.—Organ, Organist.
Oxon.—Oxford University.
Pf.—Pianoforte.
R.A.M.—Royal Academy of Music, London.
S.—Studied, Saint.
Vn., Vnst.—Violin, Violinist.

Attention is drawn to the Appendix of Additions and Corrections at the end of the Book.

DICTIONARY OF MUSICIANS.

AARON. Scottish writer, B. towards close of 10th cent. Abbot of St. Martin Cologne, 1042. D. 1052.

WORK.—"De Utilitate Cantus vocalis et de Modo cantandi atque psallendi." Aaron points out the advantages to be derived from chanting psalms, and other vocal music, in public worship.

AARON (Pietro). See Aron (Pietro).

ABACO (Evaristo F. Dall'). Italian comp. and violinist, B. Verona, 1662. Concert-master to the Kurfürst Max. Emanuel of Bavaria. D. Feb., 1726.

WORKS.—Sonatas for violin and bass, and for two violins, 'cello, and bass. Six concertos for four violins, tenor, bassoon, 'cello, and bass, op. 5. He also composed a great quantity of ch. music.

ABBATINI (Antonio Maria). Italian comp., B. Tiferno. [1595.] Chap. master of the Lateran, 1626-28; of the Ch. of the Gesù; of the Ch. of Maria Maggiore, 1645; of S. Lorenzo in Damaso, 1646; of the Ch. of Maria Maggiore (2nd time), 1649-57; of the Loretto, 1657; and of the Ch. of Maria Maggiore (3rd time), 1672-77. D. 1677.

WORKS.—Four Books of Psalms, Rome, 1630. Five Books of Motets, Rome, 1636-38. Three Books of Masses, Rome, 1638-50. Del Male in Bene, Opera, produced 1654. Antifone for twenty-four voices, Rome, 1677.

In conjunction with Kapsberger and Carissimi he assisted Kircher with the compilation of his "Musurgia Universalis."

ABBÉ (Joseph B. St.-S.). French violoncellist and comp., B. Agen, June 11, 1727. D. 1787. Comp. works for 'cello, etc.

ABBEY (John). English organ-builder, B. Whilton, Northamptonshire, Dec. 22, 1785. He went to Paris in 1826 and established there a firm which extended its operations over Europe and Gt. Britain, besides parts of S. America, etc. D. Versailles, Feb. 19, 1859. He built organs for the Cathedrals of Rheims, Nantes, Amiens, Evreaux, Rochelle, Rennes, Tulle, Versailles, Viviers, Bayreaux, and numerous churches and theatres. Abbey invented no improvements in organ mechanism, but his general workmanship was good.

ABBOT (Henry). English ch. clergyman, flourished about the middle of the 18th cent. Lecturer at St. John's the Baptist, Bristol. Author of "The Use and Benefit of Church Music, towards quickening our Devotion," 1724.

ABBOTT (Thomas Moreton). English violinist, B. Bilston, Staffordshire, Aug. 13, 1843. S. under Henry Hayward. Resident in Birmingham as violinist and teacher. Is well known in the Midland Counties as an admirable performer and leader.

ABEILLE (Johann C. Ludwig). German comp. and org., B. Bayreuth, Feb., 1761. S. at Stuttgart. Mem. of Duke of Wurtemberg's Band. Org. at Court

A

Chap. of Duke of Würtemberg, 1803-32. Concert-master to the same, 1802. Received Royal gold medal and pension, 1832. D. 1832.

WORKS.—Poems by Hubner, set to music, 1788; Do., second part, 1793; Idylles de Florian, 1793; Cantata pour le mercredi des Cendres, 1798; Chansons for the piano, 1790; Four sonatas for the piano, 1789; Sonata for Pf., with variations, 1790; Fantasia for the Pf., 1790; Concerto for the Pf.; Grand concerto for Pf. duet, 1793; Songs and Elegies, with Pf. accomp., 1809; Polonaise for Pf.; Valses, etc., for Pf.; L'Amour et Psyche, opera, 1801. Pierre et Annette, operetta, 1810.

ABEL (J. E.). German pianist and comp., B. Ludwigslust, 1795. Teacher at a German court. Seized with a painful disease. Went to America, 1819. Came to England, 1820. Teacher in London of Pf. and 'cello. He is author of a few unimportant pieces for the Pf., etc.

ABEL (Karl Friedrich). German comp. and viol.-da-gamba player, B. Köthen, 1725. Played under Hasse at the Court of Dresden, 1748-58. Visited London, 1759. Appointed chamber musician (violinist) to Queen Charlotte, 1765. Gave concerts in conjunction with J. C. Bach, 1762-82. Returned to Germany, 1783. Returned permanently to London, and gave concerts, 1785-87. Further history unknown. Supposed to have D. London, June 22, 1787.

WORKS.—Op. 1. six overtures in 8 parts for orch.; op. 2. six sonatas for clavichord, with accomp. for violin or flute; op. 3. six concertos for 2 violins, flute, 'cello, and bass; op. 4. six overtures in 8 parts for orch; op. 5. six sonatas for clavichord and violin; op. 6. six solos for flute, with bass accomp.; op. 7. six overtures, etc., for orch.; op. 8. six quartets for strings; op. 9. six trios for strings; op. 10. six overtures for orch.; op. 11. six sonatas for clavichord, violins and bass; op. 12. six quartets for strings; op. 13. six sonatas for clavichord and violin; op. 14. six overtures for orch.; op. 15. six quartets for strings; op. 16. six trios for strings; op. 17. six overtures for orch., in 4 pts.; op. 18. six sonatas for clavichord and violin.

Abel's instrumental compositions are marked by refinement and skill in manipulation; but this, again, is marred by lack of energy and a languid flow of ideas.

ABELA (Carl Gottlob). German comp., B. Borna, Saxony, April 29, 1803. D. April 22, 1841. Writer of Lieder and Part-songs.

ABELL (John). English comp. and vocalist, B. [1660.] Gent. extraordinary Chap. Roy., 1679. Sent to Italy to study by Charles II. Returned to England, 1683. Re-entered Chap. Roy., and remained till 1688, when he was dismissed on account of his being an adherent to the Roman Catholic faith. Went abroad and sung in Germany and Poland with success. Returned to England about 1701. D. Cambridge, 1724.

WORKS.—A Collection of Songs in several Languages, 1701. A Collection of Songs in English, 1701. Two songs in Pills to Purge Melancholy. Les Airs d'Abell," etc.

ABENHEIM (Joseph). German violinist and comp., B. Worms, 1804. Mem. of Chap. Roy., Stuttgart. Mem. of orch. of the theatre, Stuttgart, 1825.

WORKS.—The greater portion of this composer's works are in MS. His principal pieces include:—Six songs for voice and Pf., op. 2; Six do., op. 5. Songs from works of Schiller, with Pf. accomp; Nocturnes and Polonaises for Pf.; Music to "Hariadan," a drama, produced in 1842, Chamber music, etc.

ABERT (Johann Josef). Bohemian comp., B. Kachowitz, 1832. S. at Prague, etc. Entered service of King of Würtemberg as double-bass player, 1852. Chap.-master to do., 1867.

WORKS.—Columbus, Musikalisches Seegemälde, in Form einer Symphonie, für grosses Orchester, op. 31, 1864; Symphony in C minor, for orch., 1853; Symphony in A minor, for orch., 1856; Anna von Landskorn, opera, 1859; Le Roi Enzio, opera, 1862; Astorga, opera, 1866; String quartets; Vocal quartets; Pf. music; Songs; Bac fugues arranged for orch.; Ekkhard, opera, etc.

ABINGDON (Willoughby, Earl of). English amateur comp. and flute-player, B. Jan. 16, 1740, D. Sept. 26, 1799. Established concerts in London, etc.
WORKS.—Twelve sentimental catches and glees, for three voices; a Representation of the Execution of Queen Mary of Scots, in seven views; the music composed and adapted to each view by the Earl of Abingdon. Songs, Duets, Flute music, etc.

ABOS (Geronimo). Italian comp., B. Malta, beginning of 18th century. Teacher at Cons. of " La Pietà," Naples. Visited London in 1756. Trained several musicians who have attained eminence: among others Aprile, the vocalist. D. Naples, 1786.
WORKS.—La Pupilla e 'lTutore, opera; La Serva Padrone; L'Ifigenia in Aulide; L'Artaserse, 1746; L'Adriano, 1750; Tito Manlio, 1756; Creso, 1758. Masses. Litanies, etc., preserved in MS. at Naples, Rome, Paris and Vienna.

ABRAM (John). English comp. and org., B. Margate, Aug. 7, 1840. Org. of S. John's, Torquay, 1864. Org. of S. Peter and Paul, Wantage, 1865. Org. of S. Paul's Ch., St. Leonards-on-Sea, 1869. Mus. Bac. Oxon., May 27, 1868. Mus. Doc. Oxon., April 22, 1874. F. C. O., Lond.
WORKS.—Jerusalem, a Sacred Cantata. The Widow of Nain, an Oratorio. Anthems, Services, Pianoforte Music, etc.

ABRAMS (Harriet). English soprano vocalist and comp., B. 1760. S. under Dr. Arne. Début at Drury Lane, London, in Arne's "May Day," 1775. Sang at Handel Commemoration, 1784. Appeared also at principal London concerts. D. in first half of present century.
WORKS.—Collection of Scotch Airs harmonized for three voices, 1790. Collection of Songs, 1787. Set of Glees. Songs, Crazy Jane, The Orphan's Prayer, and others.
"Miss Abrams, though not possessed of great power of voice, sang with much sweetness and delicacy ('Georgian Era'). Her sisters, Theodosia and Eliza, were also vocalists, the former a contralto of much ability, who afterwards became Mrs. Garrow."

ABT (Franz Wilhelm). German comp., B. Eilenburg, in Saxony, Dec. 22, 1819. Cond. of Philharmonic Soc., Zurich, 1841. Entered staff of Hoftheater, Brunswick, 1853. Cond. at Hof-theater, Brunswick, 1858-80. Visited America and cond. at the "Gilmore Jubilee," 1872.
WORKS.—His works extend to over op. 500, comprising over 3000 pieces. Among the principal are:—1. *Cantatas:* Cinderella; Little Red Ridinghood; Richard Cœur de Lion; Snow Maidens; The Water Fairies; The Silver Cloud; The Wishing Stone. 2. *Concerted Vocal Music:* Quartets, Trios, etc., A Rose in Heaven: Alpine Horn is Sounding; Ave Maria; O Fatherland; Merry May; Evening; Joy; Morning; Our Native Land; A Winter Song; The Minstrels; The Rovers; The Boat Song; Night Song; Vineta; Thuringian Volkslied; Eventide; The Wanderer's Song; Home; etc. 3. *Songs:* Agathe, or, When the Swallows homeward fly; Irene; Louise; Devotion; May Song; Ever Thine; Flora; How dear thou art to me; My Mother's Voice; Oh! ye Tears (C. Mackay); A Sound fills the Wood; Oh early morn; The Exile; Songs for Children; Solemn Night. 4. Pianoforte Music, Dances, Drawing-Room Pieces, etc. Orchestral Music, Chamber Music, Choruses for Male voices, etc.
Abt's melodies are catching, albeit oftentimes tinged with melancholy, generally in sympathy with the subject, and invariably marked with those characteristics which distinguish the cultivated musician.

ABYNGDON (Henry). English comp., B. during 15th cent. Sub-centor of Wells, 1447-97. Master of Song, Chap. Roy., Lond., 1465. Master of St. Catherine's Hospital, Bristol, 1478. D. Sept., 1497.
The works of this musician are unknown, but it is generally supposed that he wrote extensively for the church.

ACHARD (Leon). French tenor vocalist, B. Lyons, 1831. Début at Lyons,

Oct., 1862. S. at Milan. Married to Mdlle. Le Poitevin, July, 1864. Has appeared in Paris in several important *rôles.*

ACLAND (A. H. D.) English writer, wrote "Letters on Musical Notation," Lond., 8vo, 1841.

ACLAND (T. G.) English writer, published "Chanting Simplified." Lond., 12mo, 1843.

ADAM de la HALE. See Hale.

ADAM (Adolphe Charles). French comp. and pianist. B. Paris, July 24, 1803. Entered Paris Cons. and S. under Boieldieu, 1819. Went to London, 1832. Received Cross of Legion of Honour, 1836. Mem. of Institute de France, 1844. Established and directed the Theatre National, 1847. Prof. of Comp., Paris Cons., 1849. D. Paris, May 6, 1856.

WORKS.—1. *Operas:* Pierre et Catherine, 1829; Danilowa, 1830; Le Chalet, 1834; La Marquise, 1835; Micheline, 1835; Le Postillon de Longjumeau, 1836; Le Brasseur de Preston, 1838; Le Fidèle Berger, 1838; Régine, 1839; La Reine d'un Jour, 1839; La Main de fer, ou le Secret, 1841; La Rose de Péronne, 1841; Le Roi d' Yvetot, 1842; Lambert Simnel, 1843; Cagliostro, 1844; Richard en Palestine, 1844; Giralda, 1850; Les Nations, 1851; Le Farfadet, 1852; La Poupée de Nuremberg, 1852; Si j'étais Roi, 1852; La Sourd, 1853; La Favridondaine, 1853; Le Roi des Halles, 1853; Le Bijou perdu, 1853; Mam' zelle Geneviève, 1853; Le Muletier de Tolede, 1854; A Clichy, 1854; Le Houzard de Berchiny, 1855; Falstaff, 1856; Les Pantins de Violette, 1856. 2. *Ballets.* Faust, 1832; La Fille du Danube, 1836; Les Mohicans, 1837; La jolie fille de Gand, 1839; Giselle, 1841; Griselidis, 1848; Orfa, 1852; Le Corsaire, 1856; La Filleule des Fées. 3. *Cantatas:* Le Premiers Pas, 1847, composed for the inauguration of the Opera National; La Fête des Arts, 1852; Chant de Victoire, 1855; Cantata, 1856. 4. Two Masses, 1847-1850. 5. Pianoforte music, consisting of Fantasias, Rondos, Dances, and Morceaux de Salon, etc.

Adam was one of those clever, flippant, and brilliant writers with which the world—but particularly France—abounds. His talent was a commodity easily handled, since continued and thoughtful effort was unnecessary to what he wrote. His writings possess no depth, and are marked by those features which betoken an easy command of surface dexterity in shaping materials. The work which may be noted as his best is "Le Postillon de Longjumeau," in which he has followed Boieldieu in general style. His later works are influenced by Auber, but have neither the powerful emotional characteristics, nor the refined method of expression shown by the composer of " La Muette de Portici."

ADAM (Carl F.) German comp. and org., B. Zadel, nr. Meissen, 1770. D. [Saxony, 1810.]

Writer of Pf. music, organ music, choruses for male voices, etc.

ADAM (J. Louis). Father of A. C. Adam, B. Miettershelz, Alsace, 1758. Prof. Paris Cons., 1797-1842. D. Paris, 1848.

WORKS.—Sonatas for the Pianoforte. Two Symphonies for orch., produced, 1798. Arrangements of Haydn's and Pleyel's quartets for Pf. Two works on Pianoforte playing, Paris, 1798. Pieces for Harp and Violin, Piano and Violin, etc., etc.

ADAM (Josef August.) German comp. and cond., B. Vienna, 22nd April, 1817.

Writer of military and orchestral music.

ADAMBERGER (Valentin). German tenor vocalist, B. Munich, 6th July, 1743. S. under Valesi, and in Italy. Sang in London, 1777. Appeared in Vienna, 1780. Teacher and singer in Vienna. D. Vienna, Aug., 1804.

ADAMS (Abraham). English org. and comp. Flourished at end of 18th and beginning of 19th cent. Org. of ch. of St. Mary-le-bone, 1810. Compiled " The Psalmist's New Companion," Lond., n.d.

ADAMS (Rev. F.A.) See Root, G. F.

ADAMS (John S.) English writer, compiled a work entitled "Five Thousand Musical Terms." Lond., 1861.

ADAMS (Sara Flower). See Flower, Sara.

ADAMS (Stephen). See Maybrick, Michael.

ADAMS (Thomas). English org. and comp., B. 5th Sept., 1785. S. under Busby. Org. Carlisle Chap., Lambeth, 1802-14. Org. St. Paul's, Deptford, 1814. Org. ch. of St. George, Camberwell, 1824. Org. St. Dunstan Ch., 1833. D. Sept. 15, 1858.

WORKS.—Fugues, Fantasias, Voluntaries, Interludes, etc., for Organ. Anthems. Hymns. Pianoforte Pieces, etc.

Adams was one of the finest organists Britain has yet produced. His performance was uniformly good, but he excelled in extempore playing. His compositions are masterly, and are coming into general repute.

ADAMS (Thomas Julian). English comp. and cond., B. London, Jan., 1825. S. under Moscheles. Cond. of orchestras in various towns and watering-places in England and Scotland. Comp. some pieces of dance music. Has done much to introduce good orchestral music in towns where its cultivation was neglected.

ADCOCK (James). English comp., B. Eton, 1778. Chorister, St. George's Chap., Windsor, 1786. Lay-clerk, do., 1797. Mem. of Trinity, St. John's, and King's Colleges, Camb. D. Cambridge, April, 1860.

WORKS.—Three glees for 3 and 4 voices, dedicated to Sir Patrick Blake [c. 1815]. Hark how the Bees, glee for 4 voices. Welcome Mirth, glee for 3 voices. The Rudiments of Music, etc.

ADCOCK (John). English writer, author of "The Singers' Guide to Pronunciation, with an Appendix consisting of a Pronouncing Dictionary of Musical Terms, etc." Nottingham [1873].

ADDISON (John). English comp. and double-bass player, B. London, 1770. Played 'cello at Vauxhall Gardens. Double-bass player at the Italian opera, and at the "Ancient" and "Vocal" Concerts. Married to Miss Williams, 1793. Latterly speculated in mills, and was nearly ruined. D. London, 30th January, 1844.

WORKS.—"Elijah," a sacred drama. Music to the dramas of "The Sleeping Beauty," 1805; "The Russian Imposter," 1809; "My Aunt," 1813; "Two Words," 1816; "Free and Easy," 1816; "My Uncle," 1817; "Singing Practically treated in a series of Instructions," Lond., n.d. [1836]. His other works consist of songs, glees, etc.

Addison was a teacher of some celebrity, and was the instructor of A. Lee, Pearman, and others. His compositions are now forgotten, though they are tuneful and were popular. His wife (*née* Miss Williams) made her *début* in "Love in a Village," in 1796. She was a favourite singer at Vauxhall gardens and other places in London.

ADDISON (Joseph). English poet and essayist, B. Milston, Wilts, 1672. D. London, 1719.

Addison wrote the book of "Rosamund," an opera, which was originally adapted to music by Clayton, and had a run of *three nights*. Arne subsequently wrote music to it, and produced it with success in 1733. Addison is noticed here chiefly on account of his attacks on the Italian opera. These appeared in the *Spectator*, and ridiculed the whole concern. There certainly existed many incongruities in these performances—chiefly in matters of detail—and Addison, though scarcely qualified to play the musical critic, made fun out of a serious exhibition spoiled by ignorance.

ADDISON (R.) English music-publisher, B. 1797. Was successively in partnership with several publishers of note. While chief of the firm, Addison and Beale, he published many important works. D. Jan. 17, 1868.

ADELBURG (August von). Hungarian violinist and comp., B. Constantinople, 1833. Writer of an Opera, Music for String insts., Pf., etc.

ADHEMAR (Comte Abel d'). French song-writer, B. Paris, 1812. Commenced comp. in 1836. D. 1851.

WORKS.—Songs, principally for male voices, with such titles as the following:— "The Bravo," "The Brigand," "The Kabyle," "The Torréador," etc.

ADLER (Georges). French violinist and comp., B. Buda, [Hungary, 1806. Comp. for violin and Pf.

ADLER (Vincent). French comp. and pianist, B. 1828. D. Geneva, 1871.

WORKS.—Op. 1. Thème Hongrois, for 2 vns., alto and bass. Op. 2. Variations for Pf. solo. Op. 3. Sonata for Pf. and Vn. Op. 4. Variations for Pf. Op. 6. First Polonaise for Violin. Op. 7. Rondo, for Pf. Op. 8. Thème (original), for Pf. Op. 10. Four Songs. Op. 11. "Libera me, Domine," for 4 voices and organ. Op. 12. Songs for male quartet. Op. 13. Three songs for male quartet. Op. 15. Cantata for one and more voices, with Pf. accomp. Op. 18. Nouvelle Scene de Bal, for Pf. Op. 19. Thème Styrien, for Pf. Op. 20. Idylle for Pf. Op. 22. Idylle for Pf. Op. 23. Scene Pastorale, for Pf. Op. 24. Grand March for Pf. Op. 27. Sonata for Pf. duet. Two Prayers for 4 voices, orch. and organ. Songs, etc.

His compositions are of the same school as those of Ascher and Heller; light, pleasing efforts, with some originality and much careful, as well as skilful, elaboration.

ADLINGTON (William). English pianist and teacher, B. Southwell, near Nottingham, 1838. S. at R. A. M. Associate R. A. M., 1865. Principal of the Edinburgh Institution for Music, etc. Cond. of Aberdeen University Orch. Soc., etc. Author of "Elementary Principles of Music, and Elements of Harmony, adapted for those studying the Pianoforte." Edin., 8vo., 1881.

ADLUNG (Jacob). German writer, B. near Erfurt, Jan. 14, 1699. S. at School of St. Andrew, Erfurt, 1711. Org. of Evangelical Ch., Erfurt, 1727. Prof. at the Raths-gymnasium, Erfurt, 1741. D. Erfurt, Jan. 5, 1762.

WORKS.—Anleitung zu der musikalischen Gelahrtheit, Erfurt, 1758, Dresden ed., 1783. Musica Mechanica Organœdi, etc., Berlin, 1768. Musikalisches Siebengestirn, Berlin, 1768.

ADRIANI (Francisco). Italian comp., B. Santo Severino, 1539. D. Aug. 16, 1575. Writer of Psalms, Chansons, etc.

ADRIEN (Martin Joseph). Belgian comp., B. Liége, May 26, 1767. D. 1822. Writer of Dramatic Music, etc. His brother was a comp. of Songs and Romances, B. Liege, 1767.

ADYE (Willett). English amateur musician and violin virtuoso, has published "Musical Notes," Lond., 1869. This is a work on the subject of violinists.

AELSTERS (Georges J.) Belgian comp., B. Ghent, 1770. Carilloneur of Ghent, 1788-1839. Music director of the Ch. of S. Martin, Ghent, 1839-49. D. April, 1849.

WORKS.—Chiefly church music, and consisting of Motets, Masses, Litanies, a Miserere, Hymns, etc.

AERTS (Egidius). Belgian flute-player and comp., B. Boom, 1822. S. flute and comp. at Brussels Cons., 1834. Travelled through France and Italy, concert-giving, 1837-48. Prof. of flute, Brussels Cons., 1847. Gave concerts in Brussels, etc., till 1852. D. Brussels, 9th June, 1853.

WORKS.—Symphonies for orch. Concertos for flute. Fantasias, etc., for flute. Overtures, etc.

AFRANIO. Italian ecclesiastic and inventor, was Canon of Ferrara about commencement of the 16th cent. Said to be the inventor of the bassoon on the authority of woodcuts occurring in a work by Albonesi on the Chaldean Language. 1539.

AGABEG (Madame E.) See Wynne (Edith).

AGAZZARI (Agostino). Italian comp., B. Sienna, Dec. 2, 1578. Master of Chap. at German Coll., Rome, 1603. Master of Sienna, Cath. 1630-40. D. 1640.
WORKS.—Il Primo Libro di Madrigali a cinque voci, Venice, 1600. Madrigali Armoniosi a cinque o sei voci, Venice, 1600. Sacræ Cantiones, 5, 6, 7, 8 voci, Liber primus, 1602. Do., Liber Secundus, 1603. Do., Third Book, 1603. Three Books of Motets, 1608-9. Sacræ Cantiones, 2, 3, 4 voices and organ, 2 Books, 1603. Sacræ Laudes de Jesu, 4, 5, 6, 7 and 8 voices and organ, 1603. Il primo libro di Motteti, for 2 and 3 voices, 1604. Sacræ Laudes, 2nd. Book, 1603. Psalmi, 1618. Eucharisticum, 1625. Litanie, 1639. La Musica Ecclestica, 1636. Eumelio, a pastoral drama, 1614.

AGNESI (Louis F. L.) French bass vocalist, B. Erpent, 1833. D. London, Feb., 1875. S. Brussels Cons. Celebrated as an operatic singer.

AGOSTINI (Ludovico). Italian comp. and poet, B. Ferrara, 1534. Chap.-master to Duke Alfonso II. d'Este. D. Sept. 20, 1590.
WORKS.—Il primo libro di Madrigali, a 5 voci, Venice, 1570. Madrigali, a 4 voci, Venice, 1572. L'Eco ed enigmi musicali, 6 voci, 1581. Messe, Vespri, Mottetti, Madrigali et Sinfonie, Ancona, 1588.

AGOSTINI (Paolo). Italian comp., B. Vallerano, 1593. Pupil of B. Nanini. Master of Vatican Chap., Rome, Feb., 1629. Chap.-master and org. of S. Maria, Trastevere. Do. S. Lorenzo, in Damaso. D. Rome, 1629.
WORKS.—Two Books of Psalms, Rome, 1619. Two Books of Magnificats, for 1 2, and 3 voices, Rome, 1620. Books of Masses, Rome, 1624-28. Motets, Masses, etc., preserved in the Vatican Library, Rome.

"For invention he is said to have surpassed all his contemporaries. His composition for four, six, and eight choirs are said to have been the admiration of all Rome."—*Hawkins.*

AGRELL (Johann). Swedish comp., B. Löth. Lived at Cassel and Nuremberg during 18th cent. D. Jan. 19, 1769. Writer of instrumental music, published during 1723-1761.

AGRELLI (Salvatore). Italian comp., B. Palermo, 1817. S. Naples Cons. under Zingarelli, Donizetti, etc.
WORKS. — *Operas:* I due Pedanti, 1834; Il Lazzarone Napolitano, 1838; Una Notte di Carnevale, 1838; I Due Gemelli, 1839; I Due Forzati, 1839; La Locandiera, 1839; La Sentinella Notturna, 1840; L'Omicido Immaginario, 1841; I Due Pulcinelli simili, 1841; Il Fantasma, 1846; La Jacqurie, 1849; Léonore de Médicis, 1855; Les Deux Avares, 1860; Calisto; Blanche de Naples; La Rose. Ballets, etc.

AGRICOLA (Alexandre). Belgian comp., B. 1470. Entered service of Philip, Duke of Austria. Went to Castile, 1506, where he D. 1530 [1526-27].
WORKS.—Motets, Masses, etc. Chiefly preserved in manuscript.
He was accounted one of the greatest among the musicians of his day.

AGRICOLA (Georg L.) German comp. and org., B. Thuringia, Oct. 25, 1643. Chap.-master at Gotha, 1670. D. Gotha, Feb. 22, 1676.
WORKS.—Madrigals; Sonatas for Violin, etc.; Songs (Lieder), etc.

AGRICOLA (Johann Friedrich). German comp. and org., B. Saxony, Jan. 4, 1720. S. under J. S. Bach, and at University of Leipsic. Resided at Berlin, 1741. Chap.-master and comp. to Frederick the Great, on death of Graun, 1759. D. Nov. 12, 1774.
WORKS. — *Operas:* Il Filosofo convinto, 1750; La Ricamatrice divenuta damma; Il Re pastore, 1752; Cleofide, 1754; Il Tempio d'Amore, 1755; Psyche, 1756; Achille in Sciro, 1758; Ifigenia in Tauride, 1765. Cantatas. Pamphlets on musical subjects (satirical). A work on the precedence of Melody over Harmony. A work on the Elements of Singing, etc.

AGRICOLA (Martin). German theoretical writer, B. Sorall, Silesia, 1486

[1500]. Teacher of Music in Protestant School, Magdeburg, 1524-56. Chanter in Ch. of Magdeburg. D. June, 1556.

WORKS.—Ein Kurtz Deutsche Musica, 1528. Musica Instrumentalis Deudsch, etc., Wittemberg, 1529-45. Musica Figuralis Deudsch, etc., 1532. Rudimenta Musices, etc., 1539, etc.

"The works of Agricola seem intended for the instruction of young beginners in the study of music; and, though there is something whimsical in the thought of a scientific treatise composed in verse, it is probable that the author's view in it was the more forcibly to impress his instructions on the memory of those who were to profit by them. His "Musica Instrumentalis" seems to be a proper supplement to the "Musurgia" of Ottomarus Luscinius, and is perhaps the first book of directions for the performance on any musical instrument, ever published."—*Hawkins*.

AGTHE (Carl Christian). German comp. and pianist, B. Kettstaedt, 1739. D. Nov. 27, 1797.

Writer of Operas, Songs, Pf. music, etc.

AGUADO (Dionisio). Spanish comp. and guitar-player, B. Madrid, April, 1784. S. Paris under Garcia, 1825. Returned to Madrid, 1838. D. Madrid, Dec., 1849.

WORKS.—New Method for the Guitar, 1825. Three Rondos for the Guitar, 1822. Collection of Andantes, Valses and Minuets, for Guitar. Solos. Transcriptions, etc.

He was one of the greatest performers on the guitar, and his feats on it are spoken of as remarkable.

AGUILAR (Emanuel). English comp. and pianist, B. Clapham, London, Aug. 23, 1824. Son of E. Aguilar, a West Indian of Spanish extraction. Has given concerts of high-class music in London and the provinces.

WORKS.—1. The Bridal of Triermain, a Dramatic Cantata, founded on the poem of Sir Walter Scott, produced by the Bedford Musical Society, Oct., 1880. 2. A Summer Night, Cantata for treble voices. 3. Goblin Market, a Cantata for treble voices. 4. The Bridal Wreath, an Opera (manuscript). 5. *Pianoforte Music:* Six Pieces, op. 27; War March; Couleur de Rose, galop, op. 29; Reveries; Mélodie; Boléro, op. 20; Serenade, op. 23; Galop, and Tyrolienne, op. 24; Deux Morceaux; Nocturne; Leonore, mazurka; Ophelia, romance; Aréthuse, melodie; Transcriptions, etc. 6. Fantasia for Organ, 2 Pianofortes, and Violin, produced at the Musical Artists' Association, March, 1881. 7. *Songs:* The Appeal, The stars are brightly beaming; In a wood on a windy day; Sympathy; Farewell; Break, Break; Hope Alway. 8. Little Book about Learning the Pianoforte. Lond. [1866]. 9. Symphonies, overtures, trios, sonatas, etc. in MS., which have been performed at concerts.

AGUJARI (Lucrezia). Italian soprano vocalist, B. Ferrara, 1743. D. Parma, May, 1783. Chiefly celebrated for the extraordinary upward range of her voice.

AHLE (Johann Rudolf). German comp. and org., B. Mühlhausen, Thuringia, Dec. 1625. Org. at Erfurt and Mühlhausen, 1644-73. D. 1673.

Composer of church and instrumental music.

AHLSTROEM (A. J. R.) Swedish org. and comp., B. Stockholm, 1762. D. there in first part of present century. Known only by a few songs.

AIBLINGER (Joseph Caspar). German comp., B. Bavaria, Feb. 23, 1779. S. in Italy, 1803-11. Recalled to Germany, and appointed Chap.-master to King of Bavaria, 1826. Returned to Italy, and compiled collection of ancient music, 1833. D. Munich, May, 1867.

WORKS.—Op 1. Requiem for 4 voices, org. and orch. Op. 2. Litanies for 4 voices and orch. Op. 3. Latin Mass for 4 voices and orch. Op. 4. Graduel and Offertoire for 4 voices, orch. and organ. Op. 5. Requiem for 4 voices, orch. and organ. Op. 6. Litanies for 4 voices and orch. Op. 7. Two Latin Masses. Op. 8. Two do. do.; Op. 11. Ave Regina. Op. 12. Seventeen Psalms for 4 voices, orch. and organ. Op. 13. Six Offertoires, etc. Opera, Rodrigues et Chimène.

AICHINGER (Gregor). German comp., B. [1565]. S. music, and became a priest. Org. at Augsburg. Visited Rome, 1599. Returned to Augsberg, 1601. D. [1614.]
WORKS.—1. Sacrarum Cantionum, 1590. 2. Liturgica, 1593. 3. Book II., do., 1595. 4. Sacræ Cantiones, 1597. 5. Tricinia Mariana, 1598. 6. Divinæ Laudes, 1602. 7. Vespertinum Virginis Canticum, 1604. 8. Ghirlanda di Canzonette, 1604. 9. Fasciculus sacrarum harmoniarum quatuor vocum, 1609. 10. Solemnia corporis Christi in sacrificio missæ, 1606. 11. Cantiones Ecclesiasticæ, 1607. 12. Virginalia, 1608. 13. Teutsche Gesenglein, 1609. 14. Sacræ Dei Laudes, 1609. 15. Odaria Lectissima, 1611. 16. Corona Eucharistica, 1611. 17. Vulnera Christi, etc.
One of the greatest musicians of the sixteenth century. His writings abound with passages wherein may be found examples of profound contrapuntal knowledge, together with much inspiration and loftiness of expression.

AÏDÉ (Hamilton). Greek poet, novelist, dramatist, and musical comp., B. Paris, 1830. Educated in England, and at University of Bonn. Entered army as officer of 85th Regiment. Left army in 1853—*Biograph.*
WORKS.—*Novels:* Rita; Confidences; Carr of Carrlyon; Mr. and Mrs. Faulconbridge; The Marstons; Penruddoche. Philip, a drama, 1872. Poems. *Songs:* Alone on the Shore; At my feet; Babe, good night; Come Again; The Fisher; In Autumn; Little May; The Music of the Sea; Spanish Boat Song; Winter is Past. *Operettas,* etc.

AIKIN (John). English writer, author of 1. Essays on Song-writing, Dublin, 1777; 2. Vocal Poetry, or a Select Collection of English Songs: to which is prefixed an Essay on Song-writing, London, 1810.
The " Essay " which is prefixed to No. 2 is of no historical value.

AIMON (Esprit). French 'cellist and comp., B. Lisle, 1754. D. Paris, 1828. Writer of string quartets, opera, Pf. music, and songs.

AIMON (Pamphile L. F.) French comp. and violoncellist, B. near Avignon, 1779. Cond. of theatre orch., Marseilles, 1776. Cond. at " Gymnase Dramatique," Paris, 1821. Cond. at Théâtre Française, 1822. D. Paris, Feb., 1866.
WORKS.—*Operas:* Jeux Floraux, 1818; Michel et Christine, 1821; Velleda; Abufar; Alcide et Omphale; Les Cherusques; Les Deux Figaros. Quintet for strings. Op. 4. Three Quartets for strings. Op. 6. Three do. Opp. 7, 8, 9. Nine do. Op. 43, 46, 47. Nine do. Concertos for bassoon. Airs and solos for violin and clarinet. Writings on harmony. Violoncello Music.

AINSWORTH (Henry). English musician and theologian. B. about middle of 16th cent. Lived in Holland from 1593. D. Amsterdam, 1622. Published a collection of Psalms, Amsterdam 1612. An American edition of this was issued with the title " The Book of Psalms: Englished both in Prose and Metre," etc.

AIRD (James). Scottish music-seller engaged in business in Glasgow. Published in the 18th cent. " A Selection of Scots, English, Irish, and Foreign Airs, adapted for the Fife, Violin, and German Flute." 6 vols, n.d.

AIRETON (Edward). English violin-maker, B. 1727. D. 1807.
This maker worked under Wamsly of London, and received instruction from him. His instruments are pale yellow in colour, and the model is that of N. Amati. Violins and violoncellos were the instruments on which he principally worked.

AIRY (Sir George B.) English mathematician and writer, B. Alnwick, Northumberland, June 21, 1801. Educated at Hereford, Colechester, and Cambridge. B.A. Cambridge, 1823. M.A. Cambridge, 1826. Delivered lectures on Experimental Philosophy, 1827-1836. Plumian Prof. at Cambridge, 1828. Astronomer Royal, 1835. D?
WORKS.—On Sound and Atmospheric Vibrations, with the Mathematical Elements of Music, Lond., 1868. Mathematical Tracts. Treatise on Errors of Observation. Treatise on Magnetism, 1870.

AKEROYDE (Samuel). English comp., B. Yorkshire about end of 17th cent. D. early in 18th cent. Comp. of many songs in the "Theater of Musick,' 1685, 86, 87. "The Banquet of Music," 1688; and in many other of the collections published during that period.

He is briefly noticed by Hawkins.

ALA (Giovanni Battista). Italian comp., B. Monza, Milan, in latter part of 16th century. D. after 1612. Wrote Canzonets, madrigals, motets, and other church music.

ALARD (Delphin). French violinist and comp., B. Bayonne, March 8, 1815. Went to Paris, and S. at the Cons., 1827. Gained two prizes (1st. and 2nd.) for violin-playing. Made first appearance as performer in Public, 1831. Prof. of violin at Paris Cons., 1843. Chevalier of Legion of Honour, 1850.

WORKS.—Op. 1. Fantasia for violin; op. 2. Six studies for violin solo; op. 3. Twenty-nine variations for violin; op. 4. Second fantasia for violin; op. 5. Third fantasia for violin; op. 6. First nocturne for violin and Pf.; op. 7. Élégie, Caprice for violin; op. 8. First quartet for strings; op. 9. Fantasia (Norma) for violin and Pf.; op. 10. Ten studies for violin; op. 11. Fantasia (Donizetti) for violin; op. 12. Do. on Donizetti's Linda; op. 13. Second nocturne for violin and Pf.; op. 14. Tarantella for two violins; op. 15. First concerto for violin and orch., in E.; op. 16. Ten studies for violin; op. 17. Fantasia for violin; op. 20. Fantasia for violin; op. 21. Fantasia (Mozart) for violin and orch.; op. 22. Three easy duets for violins; op. 23. Three do.; op. 24. Fantaisie Caractéristique for violin and orch.; op. 25. Duet for Pf. and violin; op. 26. Barcarolle and Saltarello for violin and Pf.; op. 27. Three duets for 2 violins; op. 28. Fantasia for violin and orch.; op. 29. Villanelle for violin and Pf.; op. 30. Fantasia (Beethoven) for violin and orch.; op. 31. First symphony for 2 violins and orch.; op. 32. Fantasia (Verdi) for violin and orch.; op. 33. Second symphony for 2 violins and orch., in D.; op. 34. Second concerto for violin and orch., in A.; op. 34a. Third symphony for 2 violins and orch., in A.; op. 35. Fantasia (Rossini) for violin and orch.; op. 36. Fantasia (Auber) for violin and orch.; op. 37. Do. (Verdi); op. 38. Do. (Verdi); op. 39. Eight easy Fantasias for violin and Pf.; op. 40. Fantasia (Verdi) for violin and Pf.; op. 41. Twenty-four studies; op. 42. Valse for violin and Pf.; op. 43. Mélodie for Pf. and violin; opp. 44, 45, 46, 47, 48. Fantasias for violin and Pf. (Meyerbeer, Rossini, Verdi, Gounod, and Halevy). Fantasias, Transcriptions, etc.

The playing of Alard is described as being similar in object to that of Ole Bull, Paganini, etc. He endeavours to make impressions more by a clever display of technical ability than by legitimate and sympathetic treatment of his subject. His compositions are light, brilliant, and effective in character.

ALARY (Giulio E. A.) French comp., B. Mantua, 1814. Educated at Milan Cons. Went to Paris, 1833. Librarian to Society for Religious and Classic Music, Paris, 1841. Accompanist at Imperial Chap., 1853. Music-director at Theatre Italien.

WORKS.—Redemption, a Mystery, 1850. *Operas:* Le Tre Nozze, 1851; Sardanaple, 1852; L'Orgue de Barbarie, 1856; La l'eauté du Diable, 1861; Le Brasseur d'Amsterdam, 1861; La Voix Humaine, 1861; Locanda gratis, 1866. Songs. Duets. Quartets (vocal). Dance Music. Masses, etc.

ALBANI (Mdlle. E.) *See* La Jeunesse, Marie Emma.

ALBANI (Mathias). German violin-maker, B. Botzen, 1621. Pupil of N. Amati at Cremona and Jacob Stainer (?) D. Botzen, 1673. The violins of this maker, though well modelled and beautifully finished, are still considerably inferior to those of Jacob Stainer. This, chiefly because of defective construction.

There are several other makers of this name, but none of them appear to have gained any great degree of fame.

ALBENIZ (Pedro). Spanish org. and comp., B. Logrono, 1795. Prof. of Pf. at Madrid Cons. D. Madrid, 1855. Comp. pf. music, vocal music, and author of a Method for the Pf., etc.

ALBERGATI (Count Pirro C.) Italian Amateur comp. Flourished at end of 17th and beginning of 18th centuries.
WORKS.—*Operas:* Gli Amici, 1699. Il Principe selvaggio, 1712. Op. 1. Baletti, Correnti, Sarabande, etc., 1682. Op. 2. Sonata for 2 violins, with organ and bass, 1683. Op. 3. Cantate Morali a voce sola, 1685. Op. 4. Messa e Salmi, 1687. Op. 5. Plettro Armonico, 1687. Op. 6. Cantate da Camera, 1687. Op. 8. Motetti e Antifone, 1691. Op. 9. Concerti (vocal), 1702. Op. 10. Cantate Spirituali, 1702. Giobbe, oratorio, 1688, etc.

ALBERT (Charles D'.) French [?] dance-music comp., B. near Hamburg, 1815. He is a dancing-master in England.
WORKS.—Dance-music, consisting of Polkas, Quadrilles, Waltzs, Valses, etc., etc., chiefly based on melodies in popular operas.
His son, EUGENE, was B. at Glasgow, 10th April, 1864. S. under Sir A. Sullivan, Prout, and Pauer. First appeared at the Crystal Palace, 5th Feb., 1881, and has since appeared as a pianist on the Continent with great success. His works include a Pf. Concerto in A (1881) and a Pf. suite (1883).

ALBERT (Emile). French comp. and pianist, B. Montpellier, 1823. D. 1865.
WORKS.—Jean le Fol, opera, 1865. Les Petits du Premier, operetta, 1864. Symphonies; Trios for strings; Sonatas for violin and pf.; Pf. solos, etc-

ALBERT (Heinrich). German poet and comp., B. Lobenstein, June 28, 1604. D. Königsberg, 1657. His psalms and chorales are in use, while his writings greatly influenced contemporary opinion on music.

ALBERT (Johann Frederic). German comp., B. Thuningen, Jan. 11, 1642. D. 14th June, 1710. Writer of music for the organ and church.

ALBERT (H.R.H. Prince Francis C. A. A. E.) German amateur musician, B. Rosenau, Coburg, August 26, 1819. Married to Queen Victoria of Britain, Feb., 1840. D. Dec. 14, 1861.
WORKS.—1. Vocal Compositions of H.R.H. the Prince Consort, Lond., 1862. 2. Songs and Ballads, arranged by E. J. Loder. 3. Anthems, Services, etc.
Prince Albert did much in every way to encourage music in Britain. He took a lively interest in everything pertaining to the art, and was known and respected for the patronage which he extended to all the struggling British musical institutions. The members of his family exhibit a similar regard for music, and evince much concern in all matters touching its development.

ALBERTAZZI (Emma), *née* **HOWSON.** English soprano vocalist, B. London, May 1, 1814. S. under Sir M. Costa. *Début* at Argyle Rooms, 1829. Sung at King's Theatre, London, 1830. Went to Italy, and married Signor Albertazzi, 1831. *Début* at Milan, 1831. Sung in Spain and Paris, 1835. Returned to London, and appeared at several concerts, etc., 1837. Sung on Continent, and again in London, 1846. D. 1847.
"In execution, Madame Albertazzi has little to acquire. . . Her face and figure are more than pleasing—her action tame, but still not inappropriate. On the whole, she is an acquisition to our opera of the highest value."—*Athenæum*, April 22, 1837.

ALBINONI (Tomaso). Italian comp., B. Venice at end of 17th century. D. [1745.] Nothing relative to his career has been handed down,
WORKS.—Op. 1. Magnificat for 4 voices. Op. 2. Sinfonie, 1700. Op. 3. Dieci e due balletti ossia sonate da camera a tre. Op. 4. Twelve cantatas for solo voice and bass. Op. 5. Twelve concertos for six instruments. Op. 6. Twelve cantatas for solo voice and bass. Op. 7. Twelve concertos for oboe and violin. Op. 8. Twelve ballets for 2 violins, 'cello, and bass. Op. 9. Twelve concertos for 2 oboes, alto, 'cello, and organ. 10. *Operas:* Palmerini, 1694; Il Prodigo dell' innocenza, 1695; Zenone, 1696; Tigrane, 1697; Radamisto, 1698; Primislas I., 1698; L'Ingratudine castigata, 1698; Diomede, 1701; L'Inganno innocente, 1701; L'Arte in gara con l'arte, 1702; La Fede tra gli inganni, 1707; Astarte, 1708; Il Tradimento tradito, 1709; Ciro, 1710; Giustina, 1711; Il Tiranno Eroe, 1711; Le Gare generose, 1712; Eumene, 1717;

Il Meleagro, 1718; Gli Eccessi della gelosia, 1722; Ermingarda, 1723; Marianna, 1724; Laodicea, 1724; Antigono tutore, 1724; Scipione nelle Spagne, 1724; Didone abandonata, 1725; Alcina, 1725; Il Trionfo d'Armida, 1726; L'Incostanza schernita, 1727; La Griselda, 1728; Il Concilio dei pianetti, 1729; L'Infedelta delusa, 1729; Engelberta (written in conjunction with Gasparini); I due Rivali in amore, 1728; Statira, 1730; Gli Stratagemmi amorosi, 1730; Elenia, 1730; Ardelinda, 1732; Gli avvenimenti di Ruggiero, 1732; Candalide, 1734; Artamene, 1741.

Albinoni was formerly regarded as one of the lights of the Venetian school, and his works appear to have been received with moderate success during his day, though they are now forgotten.

ALBONI (Marietta). Italian contralto vocalist, B. Cesena, Forli, 10th March, 1824. S. under Rossini. *Début* as contralto at Milan, 1843. Appeared successively at Bologna, Brescia, Vienna, Hamburg, Leipzig, Dresden, and Rome, 1845-47. *Début* in London as Arsace, in "Semiramide," 1847. Sang in London in opposition to Jenny Lind during 1849-51-56-57-58. Sung in America, 1852. Married to Count Pepoli, 1853. Sang in Brussels, Paris, Italy, and Spain. Last appeared and retired, 1863. She has since sung for charitable purposes, and appeared in London in 1871. Married again, 1877, to Captain Ziegler, Paris.

Alboni was esteemed the greatest contralto of the nineteenth century. Her voice exceeded two octaves in register, and was rich and mellow in quality.

ALBRECHT (Johann Lorenz). German poet and comp., B. 1732. D. 1773.

ALBRECHTSBERGER (Johann Georg). German writer, comp., and teacher, B. Klosterneuburg, near Vienna, Feb. 3, 1736. Org. in church at Melk, and at Raab, in Hungary. Court org. at Vienna, 1772-92. Director of music at Ch. of St. Stephen, Vienna, 1792. Married to Rosalie Weiss, 1769. Mem. of Academy of Music, Vienna, 1793. Mem. of Academy of Music, Stockholm, 1798. Instructor of Beethoven, Hummel, Weigl, Eybler, Mosel, Preindl, Seyfried, etc. D. Vienna, March 7, 1809.

WORKS.—1. Twenty-six Masses for 6 and 4 voices, organ and orch. 2. Forty-three Graduels, for voices and organ. 3. Thirty-four Offertoires. 4. Five Vespers, for choir, orch., and organ. 5. Four Litanies. 6. Four Psalms. 7. Four Te Deums. 8. Six Motets. 9. Five Salve Regina. 10. Six Ave Regina. 11. Two Tantum Ergo. 12. Eighteen Hymns. 13. *Oratorios:* The Pilgrims of Golgotha; The Invention of the Cross; The Birth of Christ; The Nativity; The Passion of Christ. 14. Nine Sacred songs or cantiques. 15. An opera. 16. Forty-four fugues for organ. 17. Forty-two sonatas and quartets for various instruments. 18. Thirty-eight quintets for 2 violins, 2 violas, and 'cello. 19. Seven sextets for 2 violins, 2 violas, 'cello, and D. Bass. 20. Twenty-eight trios for 2 violins and 'cello. 21. Six concertos for Pf., harp, organ, mandoline, and trombone. 22. Four symphonies for full orchestra. 23. *Theoretical Works:* Gründliche Anweisung zur Composition, etc., Leipzig, 1790; Kurzgefasste Methode den Generalbass zu erlernen, Vienna, 1792; Klavierschule für Anfænger (Pianoforte School), Vienna, 1800; Collected Works in 3 vols., published in Vienna, 1826.

A large portion of these works remain unpublished. His works on harmony and composition have been published in English by Messrs. Novello & Co., and Messrs. R. Cocks & Co.

The profound contrapuntal learning of this composer is reflected in the larger portion of his published works. His organ music is well known among English organists, and is chiefly noted for its massive, and oftentimes heavy, character. The theoretical works of Albrechtsberger which have been translated are remarkable for their extreme lucidity and detailed exposition of every matter connected with the subject.

ALBRICI (Vincenzo). Italian comp., B. Rome, June 26, 1631. D. Prague, about 1682. Writer of Masses, Psalms, etc.

ALCOCK (John). English comp. and org., B. London, April 11, 1715. Chor. St. Paul's. Pupil of Stanley, the blind organist, 1729. Org. successively of Allhallows Ch., London, 1735. St. Andrew's, Plymouth, 1737. St. Andrew's, Holborn, London, 1742. St. Laurence's Ch., Reading, 1742. Org. and Choir-master of Lichfield Cath., 1749. Mus. Bac. Oxon, June,

1755. Mus. Doc. Oxon, 1761. Resigned post of org. and choir-master at Lichfield, retaining only that of lay-vicar, 1760. Org. at Sutton-Coldfield, 1761; and Tamworth, 1765. Gained prize medal at Catch Club, 1770. D. Lichfield, March, 1806.

WORKS.—Six-and-twenty select Anthems in score, for 1, 2, 3, 4, 5, 6, and 8 voices, to which are added a Burial Service for 4 voices, and part of the last verse of the 150th Psalm, for 8 voices and instruments, in 21 parts, London, 1771. Six Canzonets or Glees, in three parts (1770). Harmonia Festi, or a Collection of canons, cheerful and serious glees, and catches for 4 and 5 voices, Lichfield, 1791. Morning and Evening Service in E minor. Six Suites of Lessons for the Harpsichord. The Harmony of Sion, a collection of Psalm tunes, 1802. Divine Harmony; or, a Collection of fifty-five double and single chants. Lichfield, 8vo, 1752. Hail, ever pleasing solitude, a glee; gained prize medal (Catch club) in 1770. Life of Miss Fanny Brown, a novel. etc.

A most agreeable composer. His concerted vocal music (glees and catches) is perhaps most suited to the present taste, although his anthems are very fair specimens of sacred writing, and might command a hearing. His son, John (1740-91), was also an org. and comp. of vocal music.

ALDOVRANDINI (Giuseppe A. V.) Italian comp., B. Bologna, 1665. D. early in 18th century. Wrote operas, motets, instrumental music, oratorios, etc.

ALDRICH (Henry). English comp. and divine, B. Westminster, 1647. S. at Westminster School, and at Christ Church, Oxford, 1662. B.A. Oxon, May 31, 1666. M.A. Oxon, April 3, 1669. Canon of Christ Church, Feb., 1681. D.D. Oxon, 1682. Dean of Christ Church, Oxon, June, 1689. D. Oxford, Dec. 14, 1710.

WORKS.—1. Artis Logicæ Compendium. A work on Logic. 2. Service in G. 3. Service in A. 4. *Anthems:* I am well pleased. Not unto us, O Lord (adapted). Out of the deep. O give thanks. O praise the Lord. Thy beauty, O Israel. We have heard with our ears. 5. A Catch on Tobacco. 6. Hark, the bonny Christ Church bells, glee for 3 voices. 7. *Miscellaneous Treatises:* Theory of Organ-building. On the Construction of the Organ. Principles of Ancient Greek music. Fragment of a Treatise on Counterpoint. Memorandums made in reading ancient authors, relative to several parts of music and its effects. Excerpta from Père Menestrier; proportion of instruments; exotic music. Argument of Ancient and Modern performance in music. Theory of modern musical instruments, etc.

Aldrich was a man of varied accomplishments, in all of which he excelled, and in addition to his skill in logic and music, was a good architect. His anthems are still occasionally sung in the provinces.

ALESSANDRI (Felice). Italian comp., B. Rome, 1742. S. at Naples. Went to Dresden and produced an opera, 1773. Appeared in London, 1769-74. Married Guadagni the vocalist. Went to Russia. Returned to Italy, 1788. D. [after 1792].

WORKS.—*Operas:* Ezio, 1767; Il Matrimonio per concorso, 1767; L'Argentino, 1768; La Moglie fedele, Lond., 1769; Il Re alla caccia; L'Amore Soldato, 1773; Creso, 1774; La Sposa Persiana, 1775; La Contadina, 1778; Venere in Cipro, 1779; Attalo, 1780; Il Vecchio Geloso, 1781; Demofoonte, 1783; Il marito geloso, 1784; Artaserse, 1774; I Puntighi gelosi, 1784; I due Fratelli, 1785; Dario, 1791, etc.

ALEXANDRE ET FILS. French Harmonium-makers, established, 1829. Received the prize medal for excellence of workmanship at Paris exhibition, 1855. Have since patented several inventions applicable to harmonium mechanism.

To Messrs. Alexandre is due the present effective condition of the harmonium. Their inventions, chiefly in connection with tone and mechanism, have rendered the harmonium a fit instrument for the concert-room.

ALFORD (John). English lutenist, published, " A Briefe and Easye Introduction to learne the tableture, to conduct and dispose the hands unto the Lute," London, 1568.

This is a translation of a work by a Frenchman named Le Roy.

ALFORD (Marmaduke). English vocalist and comp., B. Somersetshire, 1647. D. May, 1715. He was successively a Yeoman and Sergeant of the Vestry of the Chapel Royal.

ALKAN (Charles Henri V.) French comp. and pianist, B. Paris, 1813. S. at Paris Cons., 1819-1830. Visited London, 1833. Gained first prize of Institute of France, for comp., 1831. Resides in Paris as concert-giver and teacher.

WORKS.—Etude caprice for Pf., opp. 12, 13, 15, 16. Le Preux, concert study, op. 17. Duet for violin and Pf., op. 21. Nocturne for Pf., op. 22. Saltarelle for Pf., op. 23. Gigue for Pf., op. 24. Alleluja for Pf., op. 25. Transcription from Mozart, op. 26. Etude for Pf., op. 27. Bourée d'Auvergne, op. 29. Trio for Pf., violin and 'cello, op. 30. Twenty-five preludes for Pf. or organ, op. 31. Collection of Impromptus for Pf., op. 32. Sonata for Pf., op. 33. Twelve studies for Pf., op. 35. Three Marches for Pf., op. 37. Two books of Chants (Songs without words) for Pf., op. 38. Twelve Studies for Pf., op. 39. Three Marches for Pf. duet, op. 40. Three Fantasias for Pf., op. 41. Reconciliation, Caprice for Pf., op. 42. Paraphrase for Pf., op. 45. Sonata for Pf. and 'cello, op. 47, etc.

The works of this composer abound with technical difficulties of every description. His studies are especially extravagant in construction, and require close attention from even the best performers to warrant adequate interpretation.

ALLAN (James). English piper and adventurer, B. Rothbury, March, 1734. Known as the "celebrated Northumberland Piper." D. Durham, 13 Nov., 1810, in jail. Allan was famous as a strolling vagrant, half gipsy, half itinerant musician. His adventures are detailed in the "Life of James Allan, the celebrated Northumberland Piper, detailing his surprising adventures, etc." By James Thompson. Newcastle, 1828. He is also the hero of a hundred chapbooks, hailing from Newcastle, Glasgow, etc. His performance on the pipes is mentioned as having been extraordinary.

ALLAN (James). Scottish cond. and barytone vocalist, B. near Falkirk, 27 July, 1842. Well known in Scotland as cond. of the "Glasgow Select Choir," a post which he has held since 1880. The choir itself is perhaps without equal in Scotland, and has a high reputation in London and some of the larger English towns.

ALLCHIN (William Thomas Howell). English org. and comp., B. 1843. Mus. Bac. Oxon., 1869. Cond. of Oxford Choral Soc., 1869. Org. of St. John's Coll., Oxford, 1875. Local Examiner for the R. A. M., 1881. D. Oxford, Jan. 8, 1883.

WORKS.—The Rebellion of Korah, a Sacred Dramatic Cantata, for Tenor Solo, chorus, and full orchestra (manuscript). Produced and composed for the degree of Mus. Bac., June, 1869. *Songs:* A Shadow; A Rainy Day; A Lament for the Summer; A Song for November; A Christmas greeting; Prythee why so pale? A Sea song; The Wrecked Hope; O but to see her face again; The Forsaken, etc.

ALLEGRANTI (Madalena). Italian soprano vocalist, B. Venice, 1754. Flourished during last century, and appeared in London in 1781. D. after 1799.

ALLEGRI (Gregorio). Italian comp., B. Rome, 1580. Priest and comp. at Cath. of Fermo. Pupil of G. Nanini. Chorister in Chap. of Pope Urban VIII., 1629-1652. D. Rome, Feb., 1652.

WORKS.—Il primo Libro di concerti a due, tre, e quattro voci, Rome, 1618; A second book of concertos, Rome, 1619; First book of motets, &c., Rome, 1620; Motecta duarum, trium, quatuor, quinque, sex vocum, liber secundus, 1621; Various pieces of sacred music preserved in church libraries in Italy.

Allegri is the composer of a "Miserere" frequently used in the papal chapel at Rome, and which is said to be one of the finest specimens of this form of composition.

ALLEN (Alfred Benjamin). English comp. and pianist, B. Kingsland, Middlesex, Sept. 4, 1850. Commenced study of the Pianoforte, 1855. S. at London Academy of Music, 1868. Teacher of Music near London.

WORKS.—*Songs:* Sweet Birdie, mine, 1868; God speed the Galatea, with chorus, 1869; She sang to her harp, 1869; She answered, yes, 1870; How sweetly chime those evening bells; Eily's Reply; Row, Boatie, Row; Lead, kindly Light; Dream on, my Heart; He was very good to me; A widow bird sate mourning; The Castaway; Does he love me? A Sea-shell; It was a lover and his lass. Marche Grotesque, for orch., 1874. Festival Gavotte. Egyptian Court Dance, 1877. Orchestral music. Organ music. Other works to the amount of 100, and including a secular cantata, remain in MS.

ALLEN (George). American writer, author of "The Life of Philidor, Musician and Chess-Player." Philadelphia, 1863. This book is notable as having been the first work printed on vellum in America.

ALLEN (George Benjamin). English comp. and vocalist, B. London, April 21, 1822. Chor. at St. Martin's-in-the-fields, 1830. Chor. in Westminster Abbey, 1832. Deputy for Mr. Clark, St. Paul's Cath., and Mr. J. B. Sale, Westminster Abbey. Established the "Abbey Glee Club," 1841. Chor. (bass) Armagh Cath., Ireland, 1843. Married in London. Cond. of Classical Harmonists' Soc., Belfast. Originated and executed the scheme for the building of the "Ulster Hall," Belfast. Bac. Mus. Oxon, 1852. Resigned appointment at Armagh, 1862. Org. and choir-master of All Saints' Ch., Kensington. Established suburban academies, for music, in London. Org. at Toorak, Melbourne, Australia. Cond. of Lyster's opera company, Australia. Organized opera company and visited the principal towns of Australia, New Zealand, and India, with great success; this being greatly due to the efforts of his pupil, Miss Alice May. Returned to England. Established a comedy opera company (limited), and produced "The Sorcerer," "H.M.S. Pinafore," and "The Pirates of Penzance," comic operas by W. S. Gilbert and Sir A. S. Sullivan.

WORKS.—*Operas:* Castle Grim, 2 Acts, London, 1865. The Viking, 5 acts, Danish subject (not produced owing to the failure of the English opera company). The Wicklow Rose, Manchester, 1882. Two others remain in MS. *Cantatas:* Harvest Home, 1863. The Vintage of the Rhine, 1865; Ministering Angels, 1884. *Te Deums* in D and F. Introits and the Office of the Holy Communion. *Anthems:* A Book of Fifteen Anthems, 1853; Listen, O Isles; In the beginning was the Word; Now is Christ risen; O God, the rock of ages; O come let us worship; Praise the Lord; The Lord is King; Awake, thou that sleepest. *Concerted Vocal Music:* Six four-part Songs [1861]; Far from din of Cities; I love my love in the morning; The Shepherd's Song; Swiss-Lakers' Festival Song; Morning; May; Down in yon Green Vale; See the Shepherd Swains; The Wind on the Tree-tops. *Serenade:* Soft may thy Slumbers be; When lovely Spring; Lovely Spring; A Game of Croquet; Out among the Summer Meadows; Oberon, trio; The three plagues of life, do.; To a Robin, do.; Voice of Moonlight, do.; Loving Voices, do. *Songs:* A Shadow; Arrow and the Song; Angels' Gift; Adeline; Boyhood's Dream; The Bridge; The Brooklet; The Bird is on the Tree-top; The Baby Song; The Barque that bears thee; Bessie; Who can tell; Little bird so sweetly singing; The Fisherman's Wife; Denis; Katty; The Bridge; The Old Mill; The Sea King; Carillon; The Children's Hour; Whither away? Unrest; Goat-bells; Beware; Marita; In Silence and Tears; 'Twas long long since in the Springtime; Settings of many of Longfellow's Songs, and others, amounting in all to about 300. *Pianoforte* and *organ* music. The Scales in Music and Colours—their Analogy, from *The Musical World*. New Pianoforte Tutor and School. London, n. d.

Allen is one of the best and most thoroughly English composers now living. His works abound in bright melody and agreeable harmony, and are in every respect worthy of attention. He is a good vocalist, and was capable, when only about twelve years old, of taking Miss Clara Novello's part at first sight at a concert at which she could not attend. His church music is stamped with more than mere cleverness; while his songs and part-music are admittedly among the best of any produced within recent years.

ALLEN (Henry Robinson). Irish vocalist, B. Cork, 1809. Sung in opera at Drury Lane Theatre, and gave concerts at London. D. London, Nov. 27, 1876.

"He retired early from an active professional career, and devoted himself to tuition and quiet study. He was undoubtedly a man of very considerable powers."—*Era*.

ALLEN (Richard). English writer, flourished at end of 17th and beginning of 18th centuries. Author of "An Essay to prove Singing of Psalms with conjoined voices a Christian duty," London, 1696.

ALLISON (Horton Claridge). English comp., org., and pianist, B. London, July 25, 1846. Entered R. A. M., 1856. Received instruction in music from W. H. Holmes, Sir G. A. Macfarren, Garcia, Plaidy, E. F. Richter, Reinecke, Hauptmann, and Moscheles. S. at Leipzig Cons., 1862-1865. Gained first prize at Leipzig for general proficiency, 1865. Played at Gewandhaus Concerts, Leipzig, during his stay there. Commenced concert-giving in London, July, 1865, and has since appeared in the principal towns of the provinces. Org. of St. James', Westminster St., London (Rev. H. R. Haweis), 1867. Married in 1869. A. R. A. M., 1862. Examiner (Manchester) for R. A. M. Mus. Bac., Cambridge, 1877. Mus. Doc., Dublin, 1877. M. R. A. M., 1880. Examiner to Soc. of Professional Musicians, and one of H.M. Examiners, 1884.

WORKS.—Cantata for 4 solo voices, chorus and orch., composed in 1874 (MS.). Sacred Cantata for 4 solo voices, chorus and orch., 1871 (MS.), performed in 1877. Symphony for full orchestra, 1875 (MS.). Suite for orchestra (MS.). Concerto for Pf. and orch., composed in 1870, performed in 1877 (MS.). War March, Le Champ de Mars, for orch., 1873. Sonata for organ, composed in 1865, published in 1879. String quartet, composed and performed in 1865. Concert duet for 2 pianofortes, 1865. The Oxford Concert Pieces, for Pf. solo, 1872. The Cambridge Concert Studies, for Pf. solo, 1873. Melodious and Characteristic Pianoforte Studies (in two books, consisting of 19 numbers in all), 1874. Lyrics in Three Sets, for Pf., 1874. Other Pieces for Pianoforte, including the Marathon March, Tarantella in A minor, Valse (1869), etc. The 110th, 117th, and 134th Psalms, for solo voices, chorus, and string orchestra, composed in 1876 (MS.). Behold, bless ye the Lord, anthem. O Praise ye the Lord, do., 1873. Boaz and the Reapers, 4-part song. The Four Friends, do. Sigh no more, Ladies, do., 1871. *Songs:* A Song of Welcome; Again the Woods, 1860; Lovely Flowers, 1872; The Meeting; Philomèle, 1868. Lord Wolseley's March, 1883.

ALLISON (Richard). English comp., flourished in the 16th cent. D. early in 17th century.

"He was one of the ten persons who composed parts to the common psalm tunes printed by Thomas Est in 1594." Also composer of 1. "The Psalmes of David in Meter, the Plaine Song being the common tunne to be sung and plaide vpon the lute, or pharyon, citterne, or base violl, severally or altogether, the singing part to be either tenor or treble to the instrument, according to the nature of the voyce, or for foure voyces," etc., London, fo. 1599. 2. An Hour's Recreation in Musick, apt for Instruments and Voyces, London, 1606.

ALLON (Rev. Henry, D.D.) English writer, B. Welton, near Hull, Oct. 13, 1881. Editor of the *British Quarterly Review*. Author of 1. Church Song in its Relations to Church Life, Lond., 1862. 2. The Psalmody of the Reformation, Lond., 8vo, 1864. 3. Congregational Psalmist (with Dr. Gauntlett), Lond., 1868. Other Editions, 1875, 1883. 4. Book of Chants, 1860. 5. Book of Church Anthems, 1872. 6. Children's Worship Hymns, 1878; Tunes, 1879. 7. The Worship of the Church (in Reynold's Ecclesia), 1870.

ALMENRÆDER (Charles). German bassoon player and comp., B. Ronsdorf, near Dusseldorf, Oct. 3, 1786. D. Bieberich, Sept. 14, 1843. Composed music for the bassoon, a method for the bassoon, and other instrumental works.

ALTENBURG (Michael). German comp., B. Trcchtelborn, Thuringia, 1583. D. 12 Feb., 1640. Wrote psalms, chants, motets, etc.

ALTÈS (Joseph Henri). French comp. and flute-player, B. Rouen, 18 Jan., 1826. Instrumental music.

ALTÈS (Ernest Eugene), brother of above. French violinist, B. Paris, 28 March, 1830. Works for his instrument.

AMADEI (Roberto). Italian comp. and org., B. Loreto, Nov. 29, 1840. Comp. operas, motets, etc.

AMAT (Paul Leopold). French comp. of romances, songs, and operettas. Flourished in the present century. B. Toulouse, 1814. D. Nice, Oct. 31, 1872.

AMATI (Andrea). Italian violin-maker, B. Cremona [1520]. D. [1577]. The founder of the "Cremona" school of violin-making. Connoisseurs affect to distinguish this maker's instruments, which are very rare, by their small build.

AMATI (Antonio). Son of above, Italian violin-maker, B. 1550. D. 1635. This maker worked some time with his brother Hieronimo. His instruments are small in size, but possess a pleasantly sweet tone.

AMATI (Hieronimo). Son of Andrea, Italian violin-maker, B. ? D. 1638. The instruments of this maker are generally superior to those of Antonio or Andrea. The tone which they are capable of producing is more powerful, and of a better quality.

AMATI (Nicolo). Italian violin-maker, son of Hieronimo Amati, B. Cremona, Sept. 3, 1596. D. Aug 12, 1684. The most celebrated maker of this family. His violins are accounted superior to those of Joseph Guarnierius, and are highly valued.

AMBROS (August Wilhelm). Hungarian comp., writer, and pianist, B. Mauth, near Prague, Nov. 17, 1816. D. Vienna, June, 28, 1876. Author of several important works on musical history and criticism. Prof. of music at the University of Prague, 1869. Mem. of the University of Vienna, 1872. He spent the years 1860 till 1868 in collecting material for his "History of Music," the publication of which is now completed.

Works.—Die Gränzen der Poesie und Musik, Prague, 1856; Bunte Blätter, Skizzen und Studien für Freunde der Musik und der bildenden Kunst, 2 vols; Die Musik als Culturmoment in der Geschichte; Robert Franz, eine Studie; Geschichte der Musik, Breslau, 1862-8. Kinderstücke; Wanderstücke, and other pieces for the Pf. A Stabat Mater; Two Masses; Songs, etc.

His history is written in a very readable and agreeably brilliant style, and is a most valuable contribution to recent musical literature. His ideas on English music require revision.

AMBROSE (St.) Eminent Father of the Christian Church, was B. in Gaul, 340 A.D. Studied at Rome. D. [397].

Ambrose introduced into the church service the practice of antiphonal singing. This usage originated in the Eastern Church, and was subsequently transplanted by S. Ambrose into the church at Milan, of which he was bishop. The composition of the "Te Deum laudamus" has been ascribed, erroneously, to him.

AMICIS (Anna Lucia de). Italian vocalist, B. Naples, 1740. *Début* in London, 1763. Date of death unknown.

AMMON (Antoine Blaise). French comp., B. Imot in the Tyrol, Jan. 2, 1572. D. Munich, 9 April, 1614. Composer of Masses, Motets, Psalms, etc.

AMNER (John). English comp. and org., B. towards end of 16th century. Org. and choir-master at Ely Cath., 1610-41. Mus. Bac. Oxon, 1613. D. 1641.

Works.—A Sacred Collection of Hymns, of three, foure, five, and six Parts, for voices and vyols, 1615; Anthems, etc.

AMNER (Ralph). English bass vocalist, son of the above, was a lay clerk at Ely in 1604, and Gent. of H.M. Chapels Royal. D. Windsor, 1644.

AMON (Johann Andreas). German comp., B. Bamberg. 1763. Director of music at Heilbronn, 1789. Chap.-master to the Prince of Wallerstein, 1817-1825. D. Mar. 29, 1825.

B

WORKS.—Op. 1. Duets for violin and tenor; op. 8. Three trios for violin, tenor and bass; op. 10. First concerto for violin and orch. ; op. 11. Three sonatas for Pf. and violin; op. 15. Three quartets for strings; op. 19. Three sonatas for Pf. and violin; op. 20. Three quartets for horns; op. 26. Six songs for voice and Pf. ; op. 30. ; Symphony in B flat for orch.; op. 33. Six songs for voice and Pf. ; op. 34. Concerto for Pf. and Orch. ; op. 36. Six songs for voice and Pf. ; op. 39. Three quartets for flutes; op. 40. Six Pieces for Pf. ; op. 42. Three quartets for flutes; op. 43. Six songs for voice and Pf. ; op. 44. Concerto for flute and orch., in G ; op. 48. Three sonatas for flute and 'cello; op. 50. Six variations for violin and orch ; op. 51. Six songs for voice and Pf. ; op. 53. 54. Do. ; op. 55. Sonata for flute and Pf. ; op. 58. Three trios for Pf., violin, and 'cello ; op. 59. Sonata for flute and Pf. ; op. 60. Symphony in 16 parts, for orch; op. 62. Six Songs for voice and Pf. ; op. 63. Three sonatas for Pf. solo ; op. 64. Six songs for voice and Pf. ; op. 67. Sonata for Pf. duet ; op. 71. Sonata for flute and Pf. ; op. 72. Twelve pieces for Pf. ; op. 76. Three sonatas for Pf., violin and 'cello; op. 83. Sonata for Pf. ; op. 86. Nine songs for voice and Pf. ; op. 92. Three sonatas for flute quartet ; op. 95. Sonata for harp and flute ; op. 99. Two sonatas for do. ; op. 106. Two quartets for clarinets; op. 109. Three quartets for oboes ; op. 110. Quintet for flute, horn, viola, and bass; op. 113. String quartet ; op. 123. Three serenades for Pf. and guitar. Le Sultan Wampou and another opera. A Requiem and several cantatas.

The music of Amon is in use in Germany at the present time, but we are not certain that any of it has been publicly given in Britain. The instrumental works are immeasurably superior to the vocal pieces, and are compactly and clearly designed.

AMOTT (John). English comp. and org., was org. of Abbey Ch., Shrewsbury, 1822-32. Org. of Gloucester Cath., 1832-65. D. Goucester, Feb. 3, 1865.
He conducted the Gloucester Musical Festival, and wrote a work entitled, "The Annals of the Three Choirs," 1864 [2nd ed. of work by D. Lysons]; as well as services, anthems, kyries, etc. He was a good organist, and trained a number of musicians of wide celebrity.—*Musical Standard*, Jan. 7, 1882.

ANACKER (August F.) German comp., B. Freiberg, Oct. 17, 1790. S. at Freiberg and Leipzig. Appointed teacher of music in Normal School of Freiberg, 1822. Established music school at Freiberg, 1823. Established annual concerts and a choral soc. at Freiberg. D. there, Aug. 21, 1854.

WORKS.—*Overture:* Goetz de Berlichingen ; Concert Overture ; *Cantata:* Lebensblume und Lebensunbestand ; Part Songs ; Songs ; Pianoforte music.

Anacker was universally known throughout Germany for his efforts to promote the study of music in a district which had been neglected previous to his advent. The fact that his choral society was composed of singers drawn from dwellers in a mining district is sufficient to prove his courage and perseverance.

ANCOT (Jean). Belgian comp. and violinist, B. Bruges, Oct. 22, 1779. Received first instructions in music in choir of ch. of S. Donat, Bruges. Went to Paris and S. violin under R. Kreutzer and Baillot, and harmony under Catel. Returned to Bruges, 1804, and occupied himself with concert-giving, teaching, and composing. D. Bruges, July 12, 1848.

WORKS.—Four concertos for violin and orch. ; Three quartets for strings ; Two masses for 3 voices and organ ; Six Tantum Ergo, for 3 and 4 voices and organ ; Four Ave Maria for 4 voices ; Airs with variations for violin and orch. ; Two overtures for fifteen instruments ; Two fantasias for fifteen instruments ; Marches, and other instrumental music ; Dance music, songs, etc.

ANCOT (Jean). Belgian comp. and pianist, brother of above, B. Bruges, July 6, 1799. S. at Paris under Berton and Pradher. Went to London, 1823. Pianist to Duchess of Kent, etc. Left London, 1825. D. Boulogne, June 5, 1829.

WORKS.—Six overtures for full orch. ; Amelia, dramatic scene, for chorus and orch. ; Marie Stuart, do. ; La Resolution, do. ; La Philosophie d'Aracréon, do. ; Eight fantasias for Pf. duet. : Sonata for Pf., op. 4 ; Nocturne for Pf. and violin, op. 8 ; Grand sonata for Pf. and violin, op. 14 ; Fantasias for Pf. and orch. ; Concertos for Pf. and orch.; Five concertos for violin and orch. ; Numerous pieces for Pf. solo, consisting chiefly of fantasias, variations, etc.; Twelve fugues for organ, etc.

ANDER (Aloys). Bohemian tenor vocalist, B. Liebitz, Aug. 24, 1821. *Début* at Vienna in "Stradella." Sang in various parts of Europe till 1864. D. Dec. 11, 1864.

ANDERSON (George Frederick). English violinist, B. London, 1793. Cond. of Royal private Band. Hon. Treasurer to Philharmonic Soc. Do. to Royal Soc. of Musicians. Married to Miss Lucy Philpot (the pianist), 1820. D. Dec. 14, 1876.

Anderson was the governing power in the Philharmonic Society, and exercised much influence on every institution with which he had connection. He wrote "Statement of Mr. G. F. Anderson, in Reply to Calumnious Charges against him as Director of Her Majesty's Private Band," Norwich [1855]. Privately printed.

ANDERSON (Lucy), *née* Philpot. English pianist, B. Bath, 1789 [1797]. Instructed in Music by Windsor. Appeared in London at Philharmonic Soc. Concert, April 29, 1822, and gained great applause by her playing. Married G. F. Anderson, July, 1820. Teacher of Queen Victoria and several other members of the royal family. D. London, Dec. 25, 1878.

Mrs. Anderson played before the Philharmonic Society, being the first lady pianist who ever did so, and was acknowledged in her day to be the best pianist in England.

ANDERSON (John). Scottish comp., who flourished in Edinburgh in 18th century. He published "A Selection of the most approved Highland Strathspeys, Country Dances, English and French Dances. with a Harpsichord or Violoncello Bass," Edinburgh, n. d.

ANDERSON (Josephine). English vocalist, B. 1808. D. 1848. Well-known in her day as a singer of surpassing merit. She appeared in London and the provinces.

ANDERSON (William). Scottish writer, Author of "Remarks on Congregational Psalmody," Aberdeen, 1855.

ANDERSON (Rev. William). Scottish divine and musician. B. Kilsyth, 1800. He was a great enthusiast in musical matters, and his able "Apology for the Organ as an assistance of Congregational Psalmody," Glasgow, 1829, thoroughly exposes the weak basis on which the arguments of the school of Begg and Candlish were founded. His "Exposure of Popery" is a standard work. D. Glasgow, Sept. 15, 1872.

ANDERTON (Thomas). English amateur comp., B. Birmingham, April 15, 1836. Editor of the *Midland Counties Herald,* Birmingham.

WORKS.—*Cantatas:* The Song of Deborah and Barak (Solihull, 1871); The Wreck of the Hesperus; John Gilpin; The Three Jovial Huntsmen, 1881. *Operettas:* Gentle Gertrude, Alexandra Theatre, Liverpool, Feb. 21, 1881; The Chiltern Hundreds, by J. E. Pemberton, Liverpool, April 17, 1882; Artaxominous ye Great. Symphony for orch.; Quartet for strings, in F, 1884; Overtures, various, and an oratorio (MS.). Part songs, numerous. *Songs:* Blossoms; Be with me still; Come to me, O ye children; Crocus-gathering; Dreaming and waking; Felling of the Trees; Household Fairies; Ivied Cottage; Little Fishermaiden; One Summer Time; Time of Roses; Vespers, etc. *Pf. Music:* Allemande; Play hours; Seaside sensations; Satyr's dance; Three sketches, etc.

Mr. Anderton is one of the most successful amateur composers of recent times, and it is only needful to point to his cantatas, part-songs, and some of his songs in support of this. "The Wreck of the Hesperus" has been frequently performed by choral societies, and a number of his songs are very popular. His music is tuneful and bright, without undue straining or scientific display, and the whole of his productions are of high general merit. His brother, John Anderton, is a clever librettist, and has furnished more than one "book" for the composer.

ANDRÉ (Johann). German comp., B. Offenbach, Mar. 28, 1741. Established a large silk factory, and published music. Director of Music at the Dobblin Theatre, Berlin. D. Offenbach, June 18, 1799.

WORKS.—*Operas:* Der Tœpfer ; Erwin und Elmire ; Herzog Michel ; Der Alte Freyer ; Peter und Hannchen ; Der Fürst im hœchsten glanze ; Laura Rosetti ; Claudine ; L'Alchemist ; Das Tartarisch Gesetz ; Das Friedens Feyer ; Die Schaden freude ; Kurze Thor heit ist die beste ; Das Wüthende Heer ; Das Automat ; Der Barbier von Bagdad. Songs. Trios for Pf., vn., and 'cello, 1786.
His melody is spontaneous, and has an easy flow, quite in keeping with the graceful originality of his style. "Der Tœpfer" (the Potter) is a fair specimen of his style, and is no less simple and unaffected in melody than rich and appropriate in harmony.

ANDRÉ (Johann Anton). German comp. and violinist, son of above, B. Offenbach, Oct. 6, 1775. Educated at Jena. Succeeded to his father's business, 1799. Issued a complete list of Mozart's works (thematic). D. Offenbach, April 5, 1842.

WORKS.—Twenty-one symphonies for full orchestra ; Three concertos for violin ; Seven concertos for wind instruments ; Seven books of quartets for strings. Two masses. Rinaldo et Alcina, opera, 1799. Lehrbuch der Tonkunst, 6 vols., 1823 ; Thematisches Verzeichniss sammtlicher compositionen von W. A. Mozart, 1829 ; Anleitung zum violéns pielen, etc.

ANDRÉ (Johann B.) Son of above, German comp. and pianist, B. Offenbach, 1823. Wrote Studies for the Pianoforte, Fantasias for the Pf., Duets for violin and Pf., and 'cello and Pf., etc. D. Offenbach, Dec. 9, 1882.

ANDRÉ (Peter Friedrich Julius). German org. and comp., brother of above, B. Offenbach, 1808. Org. and Prof. at Frankfort-on-the-Maine. D. there, April, 1880.

WORKS.—Method for the organ, theoretical and practical ; Anleitung zum Selbstunterricht im Pedalspiel, 1834, Trans. into English by J. A. Hamilton, Lond., n. d. ; Songs for voice and Pf. ; Twelve pieces for the organ, op. 9 : Do., op. 26 ; Valses and Nocturnes for Pf. ; Organ music, consisting of fugues, voluntaries, fantasias, sonatas, etc.

ANDREOZZI (Gaetano). Italian comp., B. Naples, 1763. S. at Cons. of Naples under Jommelli. Went to Russia, 1784. Returned to Italy, 1785. D. Italy, 1826.

WORKS.—*Operas:* La Morte di Cesare, 1779 ; Il Bajazet, 1780 ; L'Olimpiade, 1780 ; Agesilao, 1781 ; Theodolinda, 1781 ; Catone in Utica, 1782 ; Il Trionfo d' Arsace, Rome, 1782 ; La Vergine del Sole, 1783 ; Angelica e Medoro, 1783 ; Dido, 1784 ; Giasone e Medea, 1784 ; Argentina, 1786 ; Sofronia e Olindo, 1789 ; Il finto cieco, 1790 ; La Principessa filosofa, 1790. *Oratorios:* Saul, 1789 ; La Passione di Giesù Christo, 1790. Six quartets for 2 violins, viola, and 'cello, 1786. Songs, etc.

ANDREVI (Francesco). Italian comp., B. near Lerida, 1785. D. Barcelona, Nov. 23, 1844. Wrote church music, etc.

ANDREWS (Richard Hoffman). English writer and comp., B. 1803. Author of "Music as a Science," 1865 ; "Sacred Music, adapted for Public and Private Devotion," Manchester, 8vo, n.d. "The Family Vocalist ;" "Songs of the Hearth ;" "Handel's Songs ;" "The German Choral Harmonist." He has also published numerous pieces for the Pf., glees, duets, songs, etc. His sons, RICHARD HOFFMAN (B. Manchester, 1831), and EDWARD HOFFMAN (B. Manchester, 1836), are both successful composers and teachers in the United States.

ANDROT (Albert Auguste). French comp., B. Paris, 1781. S. Paris Cons. Gained prize for comp., 1803. S. under Guglielmi. D. Rome, Aug. 19, 1804. Comp. operas, church music, etc.

ANERIO (Felice). Italian comp., B. Rome, 1560. Pupil of G. M. Nanini. Chap.-master at Papal Chap., 1594. D. ?

WORKS.—Three books of madrigals, 1585 ; Book of madrigals for 5 voices, 1587 ;

Two books of concertos for use in the church, for 4 voices, 1593; Book of hymns, songs, and motets for 8 voices, 1596; Second book of hymns and motets for 5, 6, and 8 voices, 1602; Books of madrigals for 6 voices; Litanies; Miscellaneous works, as psalms, masses, Ave Regina, etc., are preserved in many church libraries in Italy.

ANERIO (Giovanni Francesco). Brother of above, Italian comp., B. Rome, 1567. Chap.-master to Sigismund III., King of Poland. Do. of Cath. of Verona. Chap.-master of Ch. of the Madonna di Monti. Do. of Lateran Chap., 1600-13. D. [unknown.]

WORKS.—Il Libro primo de motetti a una, due e tre voci, Rome, 1609; Il libro secondo de' motetti, con le litanie a le quattro antifone maggiori dopo il vespero, a sette e otto voce, 1611; Il libro terzo, do., 1613; Il Libro quarto, do., 1617; Il Libro quinto, do., 1618; Sacri concenlus qualuor, quinque, sex vocibus una cum basso ad organum, 1619; Ghirlanda di sacre rose, motetti a cinque voci, 1613; Selva armonica, etc., 1617; Diporti musicali, madrigali ad una, due, tre, quattro voci, 1617; Antifone sacri concerti per una, due, tre voci, 1613; Libro de' Responsori, 1619; Litanie for 7 and 8 voices, 1626; Messa di morti, 1620; Libro de salmi a tre e quattro voci, 1620; Antifonæ, vesperæ, etc., 1620; La Recreazione armonica, madrigali ad una e due voci, 1611; Teatro armonico spirituale de madrigali a cinque, sei, sette e otto voci, 1619; La bella clori armonica, canzonette e madrigala a una, due e tre, voci, 1619; Ghirlanda di sacre Rose a 5 voci, 1619; Dialogo pastorale, a tre voci con l' intovolatura di cembalo e del luito in rame, 1600. Other works of this composer are masses, motets, magnificats, etc. Several of Anerio's madrigals are published in English collections, but the most of his works are unknown to the present age.

ANFOSSI (Pasquale). Italian comp., B. Naples, 1729 [1736]. Pupil of Piccinni. Resided in London for a time. Visited France, 1780. Returned to Italy, 1784. Chap.-master at the Lateran Chap., 1791-97. D. Rome, Feb., 1797.

WORKS.—*Operas:* Cajo Mario, 1769; La Clemenza di Tito, 1769; I Visionari 1771; Il Barone di Rocca, 1772; L'Incognita persequitata 1773; Antigono, 1773; Demofoonte, 1773; Lucio Silla, 1774; La Finta Giardiniera, 1774; Il Gelosa in Cimento, 1775; La Contadina in Corte. 1775; L'Avaro, 1775; Isabella e Rodrigo, 1776; La Pescatrice fedele, 1776; I.'Olimpiade, 1776; Il Curioso indiscreto, 1778; Lo Sposo disperato, 1778; Cleopatra, 1778; Il Matrimonio per inganno, 1779; La Forza delle donne, 1780; I Vecchi burlati, London, 1781; I Viaggiatori felici, London, 1782; Armida, 1782; Gli Amanti canuti, 1784; Il Trionfo d' Ariana, 1784; Il Cavaliere per Amore, 1784; Chi cerca trova, 1784; La Vedova scaltra, 1785; 'I'Imbroglio delle tre spose, 1786; La Pazzia de' Gelosi, 1787; Creso, 1787; La Villanella di Spirito, 1787; Didone abbandonata, 1785; Artaserse, 1788; L'Orfanella Americana, 1788; La Maga Circe, 1788; Le Gelosie fortunate, 1788; La Gazetta, 1789; Zenobia, 1790; Issifile, 1791; Il Zottico incivilito, 1792; L'Americana in Olanda; La Matilda ritrovata; Gli Artigiani. *Oratorios:* La Fiera del Ascensione; L'Assalone. Il Figlinol prodigo, cantata. Masses, etc. The works of Anfossi attained great popularity in their day, but are now unknown save to musical antiquaries and curious students.

ANGEL (Alfred). English org. and vocal comp., B. 1816. Org. Exeter Cath., 1842-76. D. Exeter, May 24, 1876.

ANGELET (Charles F.) Belgian com., B. Ghent, Nov. 18, 1797. D. Ghent, Dec. 20, 1832. Wrote symphonies, Pf. music, etc.

ANGELO DA PICITONE. Italian comp. and writer of 16th century. Author of "Fior Angelico di Musica." Venice, 1547, etc.

ANGELUCCI (Angelo). Italian violin-maker of 18th century. D. 1765.

ANGER (Ludwig). German comp., org. and pianist, B. Andreasberg, Hanover, Sept. 5, 1813. D. Luneberg, Jan. 18, 1870. Writer of Pf. music, Lieder, overtures, etc.

ANGUS (John). Scottish ecclesiastic and comp., B. about middle of 16th century. Attached to Dunfermline Monastery. Embraced the Protestant faith, and became chaplain at Stirling. D. 1596.

He is mentioned in the "Wood MSS." as a composer of sacred music, but we are not aware of any of his compositions being extant. He is one of a number of other composers mentioned in the same work.

ANIMUCCIA (Giovanni). Italian comp., B. Florence at end of 15th century [1505]. S. under Goudimel. Chap.-master at the Vatican, 1555-71. D. Rome, 1571.

WORKS.—Il primo libro di madrigali a tre voci, 1565; Joannis Animucciæ magistri capellæ sacro sanctæ basilicæ vaticanæ Missarum libri, 1567; Il primo libro de' madrigali a quattro, cinque e sei voci, 1567; Canticum B. Mariæ Virginis, 1568; Il secondo libro delle laudi, etc., 1570; Credo Dominicalis quatuor vocum, 1567; Magnificat ad omnes modos, liber secundus, 1568; Masses, Agnus Dei, Motets, etc.

Animuccia was one of those composers who, in conjunction with S. Filippo Neri, first employed music as a means of attracting audiences to the orations delivered in the New Church of Rome. He composed the first *laudi* or hymns employed for this purpose, and may reasonably be accredited with the foundation of the modern oratorio.

ANIMUCCIA (Paolo). Brother of above, Italian comp., B. about commencement of 16th century. Chap.-master at the Lateran, 1550-52. D. Rome, 1563.

WORKS.—Madrigals and motets. These are preserved in many private libraries, and some are published in collections which appeared in his time.

ANNIBALI (Domenico). Italian vocalist (soprano), who flourished during the 18th century. He appeared originally in Germany, and was engaged by Handel for the Italian opera at London in 1736. He sang in Handel's operas till about 1737, when he disappeared. No record appears to have been kept of his subsequent doings.

ANSANI (Giovanni). Italian tenor vocalist, B. Rome, middle of 18th century. Appeared at London in 1780 and in 1781. Sung at various towns throughout Italy, etc. D. [after 1815].

He wrote vocal music and an opera entitled "La Vendetta di Minos," 1791. The latter years of his life were spent in training young vocalists for the stage.

ANSCHÜTZ (Karl). German comp., B. Coblentz, Feb. 1813. Musical Director at Coblentz till 1848. Went to United States of America, 1857. Established German opera at New York, 1862. D. New York, Dec. 30, 1870.

This composer wrote several operas and minor works. American writers speak in high terms of his efforts to propagate a taste for music in New York at a time when sensation in everything was the rule of the day.

ANTHIOME (Eugène Jean B.) French operatic comp. and pianist, B. Lorient, Aug. 19, 1836.

ANTON (M.T.) *See* PARADIS (M. T.)

ANTONIOTTI (Giorgio). Italian violinist and writer, B. Milan, 1692. D. Milan, 1776. Resided for a time in England, where he published "L'Arté Armonica; or, a Treatise on the Composition of Musick. . . With an Introduction on the History and Progress of Musick from its beginning to this time." London, 1760, 2 v.

ANTONY (Francois Joseph). German writer and org., B. Feb. 1, 1790. D. Münster, 1837.

Wrote on Ecclesiastical music, the organ, etc.

APELL (Johann David A. D'). German comp., B. Cassel, 1754. D. 1833. Wrote masses, operas, cantatas, symphonies, etc.

APOLLONI (Giuseppe). Italian comp., B. Vicenza, A living writer of operas, etc.

WORKS.—*Operas:* L'Ebreo, 1856; Pietro d'Albano, 1856; Adelchi, 1856; Il Conte di Kœnigsberg, 1866; Gustavo Wasa, 1872.

APRILE (Guiseppe). Italian vocal teacher, B. Bisceglia, 1738. Author of a treatise on vocalization trans. and published in London as "The Modern Italian Method of Singing." Ed. by Cooke. D. between 1792-1800.

APTOMMAS. (Thomas.) Welsh harper, B. Bridgend, Glamorgan, 1826. Known all over Britain as a harpist of great execution and ability.

ARAJA (Francesco). Italian operatic comp., B. Naples, 1700. D. 1770.

ARANAZ (Don Pedro). Spanish comp., B. Soria. D. Cuença, at an advanced age, 1825. Org. and writer of sacred music.

ARANGUREN (Jose'). Spanish pianist and comp., B. Bilbao, May 25, 1821, Professor of music at Madrid Cons. Writes Pf. music, songs, etc.

ARBAN (Joseph Jean Baptiste Laurent). French comp. and cornet-player, B. Lyons, Feb., 1825. S. at Lyons from 1841. Gained second prize for cornet-playing, 1844. Professor of the Sax-horn, etc., at the school for the education of military bands, 1857-69.

WORKS.—Grand Methode complète de cornet-à-pistons et de sax-horn, Paris. Pieces for the Pianoforte, consisting of airs from operas, shop-pieces on topics of current interest, etc. ; Dance music for orchestra and military band ; Fantasias, etc., for cornet.

ARBUCKLE (Matthew). American writer and bandmaster, B. 1828. D. New York, May 23, 1883. Author of "Arbuckle's Complete Cornet Method. (Boston : Ditson, n. d.)" Compiled partly from the works of Jones, Koenig, and Levy.

ARCADELT (Jacob) or ARKADELT. Dutch comp., B. about end of 15th century [1490]. Pupil of Josquin, Singing-master at St. Peter's, Rome, 1539. Mem. of Coll. of Papal singers, 1540. Private musician to Cardinal, Charles of Lorrain, Duke of Guise, 1555. D. Paris, in latter part of 16th century, [1575].

WORKS.—Il Primo Libro de' madgali a più voci, Venice, 1538 ; Il secondo libro de' madrigali a quattro voci, etc., Venice, 1539 ; Il terzo libro de' madrigali, etc. ; Il quatro libro de' madrigali d' Archadelt a quattro voci, 1539 ; Il quinto libro de' madrigali d'Archadelt a cinque voci, 1556. Masses ; Motets, etc.

One of the most popular composers of his time. His madrigals are fine examples of contrapuntal skill, and have been reprinted at several different periods. We are informed by historians that his motets held such repute in Italy that publishers never scrupled to attach his name to works of an inferior order by way of securing their sale. The claim laid by the French to Arcadelt as a countryman is founded on error.

ARCHAMBEAU (Jean Michel d'). Belgian org. and comp., B. Herve, Liège, 1823. Writer of masses, organ music, etc.

ARCHAMBEAU (Edouard d'). Brother of above, B. Herve, 1834. Pianist and comp.

ARCHER (Frederic). English comp. and org., B. Oxford, June 16, 1838. Chorister of Margaret Chap., London. Org. at Royal Panopticon, after Dr. Chipp, till its close. Org. of Merton Coll. Org. at the Alexandria Palace, London. Director of an English Opera Company. Cond. for a season (1878-80) of Glasgow Select Choir. Resident in America, as org. in H. Ward Beecher's Ch., Brooklyn etc., and as editor of the *Keynote*.

WORKS.—The Organ : A Theoretical and Practical Treatise intended to assist the Student in acquiring a sound knowledge of the Instrument and its proper manipulation, with a series of Original Exercises and Illustrative Compositions written specially for this work, London : Novello & Co., n.d. ; The Collegiate Organ Tutor, London, Weekes & Co., n.d. ; Adagio Maestoso for organ ; Fugue for organ, in D minor ; Grand Fantasia in F, for organ ; Andantes for organ, in D, F, and A ; Concert Variations for organ ; Marche Triomphale for organ ; Set of twelve organ pieces, intended chiefly for church use ; Two Gavottes for Pf. in D, and E flat ; Polka de Salon, for Pf. ; Three Impromptus for Pf. ; Bourée in C, for Pf. ; Requited Love, part song ; Night, part song ; The Chase, part song ; O give thanks, anthem ; The glorious majesty, anthem. *Songs*: My Lady's Face ; I'm

sister to the cure (comic) ; King Witlaff's drinking horn ; Arrangements for organ, Pf., choir, etc.
Archer is a very good organist, a successful conductor, and a moderately good composer. His organ playing is marked by much technical ability and a careful observance of the composer's leading meaning. In many respects—and this by reason of his careful regard for the production of legitimate effects—he may be said to rank among the foremost of living organists. His compositions display cleverness, but are neither inspired nor inspiring. He is most successful when writing for his adopted instrument, the organ.

ARCHILACHUS. Greek musician, who flourished 700 B.C. He is accredited with the invention of dramatic music and the epode. This dramatic music probably belonged to that class of composition described in such flattering language by historians, although its actual existence is only a matter of conjecture.

ARDITI (Luigi). Italian comp. and cond., B. Crescentino, Piedmont, July 16, 1825. S. Milan Cons,. *Début* as violin-player. Director of Italian Opera at Vercelli, 1843. Member of Academia Filarmonice, Vercelli. Went with Bottesini, the double-bass player, to America, 1846 ; remained till 1857 ; cond, and produced operas in New York, Philadelphia, and other parts of America. Settled in London, 1857. Musical Director at H. M. Theatre, (Italian opera), 1857. Cond. Italian opera at St. Petersburg, 1871-73. Has visited America several times with the Royal Italian opera company.

WORKS.—*Operas:* I Briganti, 1841 ; Il Corsaro, 1846 ; La Spia, N. Y., 1856. *Vocal Music:* Kellogg Valse ; L'Ardita ; L'Orfanella ; La Farfalletta ; Vuole amor un giovin cor ; For ever thine, duet ; Let me love thee ; Love's presence ; They ask me why I love her ; The Clock ; L'Orologio ; A kiss for your thought ; The Page's song ; True ; Il Bacio, vocal valse ; Garibaldi ; Song of Joy, *Pf. Music:* L'Estasi ; Hymne Turc; Ilma, valse ; La Stella ; Forosetta ; Vocal valses, above noted, arranged for Pf. ; Transcriptions, etc.

Arditi is celebrated as a conductor of operatic music, in which capacity he has appeared at the principal towns in Britain. His compositions are brilliant, and his "vocal valses" require great flexibility of voice on the part of the performer. Some of them, as "Il Bacio," have obtained great success among vocalists and concert-goers.

ARETINO. See Guido de Arezzo.

ARIENZO (Nicola D'). Italian comp., B. Naples, Dec. 24, 1843. Prof. of Harmony in Coll. of S. Pietro, Naples. Obtained second prize from the "Societa del Quartetto," for 4 vocal nocturnes, 1869.

WORKS.—*Operas:* Monzù Gnazio, 1860 ; I due Mariti, 1866 ; Le Rose, 1868 ; Il Cacciatore della Alpi, 1870 ;. Il Cuoco, 1873 ; Rita di Lister, MS. ; I Viaggi, MS. Il Cristo sulla croce, cantata, MS. Songs. Trio for strings, in C., 1864, etc.

ARIOSTI (Attilio). Italian comp., B. in Italy, [1660]. Originally a priest of the order of S. Dominick. Obtained the papal dispensation. Chap-master to Electress of Hanover, 1690-1716. Appeared in London, 1716. Produced operas in London in opposition to Handel, 1716-1727. D. [unknown].

WORKS.—1. *Operas:* Dafne, 1696 ; Erifile, 1697 ; La Madre de' Maccabei, 1704 ; La Festa d'Imenei, 1700 ; Atys, 1700 ; Nabucodonosor, 1706 ; La più gloriosa fatica d'Ercole, 1706 ; Amor tra nemici, 1708 ; Ciro, London, 1721 ; Mucius Scevola, London, 1721 (1st act only) ; Coriolan, Lond., 1723 ; Vespasian, Lond., 1724 ; Arastere, Lond., 1724 ; Dario, Lond., 1725 ; Lucius Verus, Lond., 1726 ; Tenzone, Lond., 1727. 2. *Cantatas.* 3. S. Radegonda, regina di Francia, oratorio, 1693. 4. Lessons for the viol d'amore, 1728.

Ariosti was for some time a rival of Händel in London, and was associated with him and Buononcini in the composition of "Mucius Scevola." He left England about 1728, and was afterwards unknown to fame.

ARKADELT. See Arcadelt.

ARKWRIGHT (Mrs. Robert). English song-writer, authoress of numerous lyrical pieces which had some favour in their day. Among them the "Sailor's Grave," "Repentance," "Zara's Ear-rings," and other songs. D. 1849.

ARMES (Philip). English comp. and org., B. Norwich, 1836. Chor. in Norwich Cath., 1846-48. Do. Rochester Cath., 1848-50. Articled pupil of J. L. Hopkins, Rochester, 1850-55. Org. of Trinity Ch., Milton, Gravesend, 1855-57. Org. of St. Andrew's Ch., Wells St., Lond., 1857-61. Mus. Bac. Oxon., 1858. Org. of Chichester Cath., 1861-62. Org. of Durham Cath., 1862. Mus. Doc. Oxon., 1864. Degrees also conferred by University of Durham in 1863 and 1874. Lecturer on Harmony and counterpoint at the Newcastle Branch of Trinity College, Lond. Examiner for Do.

WORKS.—Hezekiah, an oratorio, produced at Worcester festival in 1878. St. John the Evangelist, an oratorio, produced at York, in 1881. Communion Service in A; Communion Service in B flat; Te Deum in G. I will sing a new song, verse anthem ; O send out Thy light, anthem ; We wait for Thy loving kindness, anthem. Morning and Evening Service, in G.

ARMINGAUD (Jules). French violinist and comp., B. Bayonne, May 3, 1824. Writer of Fantasias, etc. for his instrument.

ARMSDORFF (Andreas). German comp., B. Muhlberg, Sept. 9, 1670. D. June 31, 1699. Compositions for the Church exist in MS.

ARMSTRONG (W.G.) American writer, author of "A Record of the Opera in Philadelphia." Philad., 1884.

ARNE (Michael). English comp., natural son of Dr. T. A. Arne, B. London, 1741. Educated by his aunt, Mrs. Cibber, for the stage. *Début* as vocalist in 1751. Married Elizabeth Wright, a vocalist, November 5, 1766. Director of music at theatre in Dublin, 1779. Director of oratorios at London, 1784. Devoted himself to alchemy, and lost a fortune in an endeavour to discover "the philosopher's stone." D. London, Jan. 14, 1786. [The date, 1806, sometimes given, is wrong.]

WORKS.—The Flow'ret, a new Collection of English Songs ; Songs and Ballads sung at Vauxhall. Music for the Dramas of The Fairy Tale, 1763 ; Almena, 1764 (with Battishill); Cymon, 1767 ; The Positive Man ; Hymen, 1764 ; The Father, 1778 ; The Belle's Stratagem, 1780; The Choice of Harlequin, 1781 ; Tristram Shandy, 1783. Songs, Glees, etc.

Arne's single songs possess much grace, though not the refinement of his father's, and are well worthy of being preserved, if only as specimens of pure melody. Arne embraced the doctrines inculcated by the learned Dr. Dee, and was a follower of Paracelsus in two manners, inasmuch as he practised his philosophy and imbibed his invention.

ARNE (Thomas Augustine). English comp., B. in King Street, Covent Garden, London, May 28, 1710. Educated at Eton Coll. Designed for study of the Law. Practised privately the spinnet, and learned musical theory. S. violin under Festing. Instructed his sister in music. Married Cecilia Young, daughter of Charles Young, organist, 1736. Comp. to Drury Lane Theatre, 1738. Resided in Dublin, 1742-44. Returned to London and became comp. to Vauxhall Gardens, 1745. Mus. Doc. Oxon, July 6, 1759. D. London, Mar. 5, 1778, buried in St. Paul's Cathedral.

WORKS.—*Operas:* Rosamond (Addison), Lond., Mar. 7, 1733 ; The Opera of Operas or Tom Thumb, Lond., 1733; Dido and Æneas, Lond., 1734; Comus, a masque, Lond., 1738 ; The Judgment of Paris, a masque, Lond., 1740 ; Alfred, a masque, Lond., 1740 ; Britannia, a masque, Dublin, 1743 ; Eliza, opera, Dublin, 1743 ; Artaxerxes, opera, London, 1762 ; The Fairies, 1762 ; Olimpiade, 1765. *Music to the following plays :* The Fall of Phaeton, Lond., 1736 ; Zara, 1736 ; The Blind Beggar of Bethnal Green, 1741 ; Thomas and Sally, Dublin, 1743 ; The Temple of Dulness, 1745 ; King Pepin's Campaign, 1745 ; Neptune and Amphitrite, 1746 ; Don Saverio, 1749 ; The Prophetess, 1759 ; The Sultan, 1759 ; Love in a Village (compiled), 1762 ; The Birth of Hercules (never produced), 1763 ; The Guardian Outwitted, 1764 ; The Ladies' Frolic, 1770 ; The Fairy Prince, 1771 ; The Cooper, 1772 ; Elfrida (Mason), 1772 ; The Rose, 1773 ; The Contest of Beauty and Virtue, 1773 ; Achilles in Petticoats, 1773 ; May Day, 1775 ; Phœbe at Court, 1776 ; Caractacus (Mason), 1776 (MS. lost); As you Like it, 1740 ; Twelfth Night, 1741 ; The Merchant of Venice, 1742; The Tempest, 1746 Romeo and Juliet, 1750.

Collections of Songs: Lyric Harmony, for voice, harpsichord, and violin; The Syren, a Collection of Favourite Songs; The Vocal Grove; Summer Amusement; The Winter's Amusement; Vocal Melody, 1753; The Agreeable Musical Choice; Six Cantatas for a voice and instruments; The Monthly Melody . . . Collection of . . . Music, 1760. Ode on Shakspeare, composed for the Stratford Jubilee, 1769. Songs and Glees for 2, 3, and 4 voices (composed for the Catch Club). Eight Sonatas for the Harpsichord; Glees, catches, and canons in Warren's Collection. Organ music, consisting of lessons, concertos, &c.. Overtures for Orch.; Sonatas for violin. *Oratorios:* Abel, Mar. 12, 1755; Judith, Feb. 29, 1764. The Compleat Musician, Lond., fo. n. d.

The compositions of Arne, generally—but more particularly his songs—are marked by limpid sweetness of melody, great refinement and grace, spontaneity and propriety in ideas, and a fresh and thoroughly English character which should endear them to every admirer of genuine melody. The freshness of his songs is a feature which must be apparent to even the casual observer, and their merits as agreeable compositions will not readily be excelled. In several respects he resembles Purcell, but in one he is entirely different. While he is occasionally energetic in a marked degree, as in "Rule Britannia" (a familiar instance), it must be allowed that deeply felt and vigorously powerful melodies are scarce throughout the body of his works. Purcell exhibits fire, grandeur of conception, and a continual flow of energy, conjoined with a faithful perception of the emotional requirements of his text, Arne rarely reaches the summit of dramatic illustration. Briefly, Arne is one of those musicians who seem adapted to illustrate the more domestic and pleasing traits of every-day experience, by means of songs set to fine melodies, which readily appeal with a refining influence to the most unmusical.

His position as an English composer is high in the school of Henry Purcell, though he has been also subject to Händel's influence. Other composers, notably O. Gibbons, Boyce, Tallis, and Greene, have surpassed him in dignity and loftiness of expression, but none ever exceeded him in purity of style and popularity among his own countrymen. The following lines from Churchill's "Rosciad" would seem to indicate that, to a certain extent, Arne was regarded in an unfavourable or jealous light by contemporary writers:—

> "Let Tommy Arne, with usual pomp of style,
> Whose chief, whose only merit's to compile,
> Who, meanly pilfering here and there a bit,
> Deals music out as Murphy deals out wit,
> Publish proposals, laws for taste prescribe,
> And chant the praise of an Italian tribe."

He, whose only merit was to compile, has been more fondly cherished in the memories of musicians, than the once formidable satirist has been among poets. The extent to which Arne stole from the Italian school was not so great as to be broadly evident. Arne was in a very wide sense a thoroughly *English* composer.

ARNOLD (Carl), German comp. and pianist, B. Neukirchen, May 6, 1794. Resided in London as teacher. Went to reside at Christiana in 1849. D. there, 11 Nov., 1873. Writer of Opera, Concertos, Sonatas, Valses, Fantasias, Quartets, and "The Art of Singing, or Complete Instructions for Acquiring the Elementary Parts of the Science." Lond., 1828.

ARNOLD (George Benjamin). English comp. and org., B. Petworth, Sussex, Dec. 22, 1832. S. under Dr. S. S. Wesley. Org. of St. Columba's Coll., 1852. Org. of St. Mary's Ch., Torquay, 1856; Org. of New Coll., Oxford, 1860. Org. of Winchester Cath., 1865. Mus. Bac. Oxon., 1854. Mus. Doc., Oxford, 1861.

WORKS.—Ahab, oratorio, Exeter Hall, London, 1863; The Second Coming of Our Lord, oratorio (manuscript); The Song of David (MS. cantata); Sennacherib (cantata), Gloucester, 1883. Communion Service in G major; Te Deum in C, and Te Deum and Jubilate, in D; Magnificat and Nunc Dimittis, in D; and Sanctus, Kyrie and Credo, in B minor; 43rd Psalm. *Anthems and Motets:* Praise the Lord; The Lord is my Shepherd: Let the Righteous be glad; The Night is far spent; The Eyes of all wait upon Thee; Give Sentence. *Concerted Vocal Music:* Thou soft Flowing Avon; Live like the Rose; Farewell; No Jewell'd Beauty; Music when soft voices die; Tricks of Love; Oh heart of deep unrest, trio; A Widow Bird, duet; The Sweet West Wind, do. *Songs:*

Go, sit by the Summer Sea; The Colour from the Flow'r is gone; Hope; Orphan hours the year is dead; The sea hath its Pearls; Night Winds; Harmony (Lancashire Choral Union Prize Glee), for 5 voices; My Dainty Chloris, madrigal; O Queen of Love, do. *Pianoforte Music:* Sonata in F minor; Sonata in D; Minuet and Trio; Prelude and Fugue; Andante; Air varied, etc.

Arnold is one of the leading composers of English church music, and his services and anthems possess that solidity and sacredness of character with which English cathedral music has always been identified. His songs and concerted vocal music are well worked out examples of modern English composition, and his powers as an organist are reckoned great.

ARNOLD (Johann Gottfried). German comp. and violoncellist, B. Niedernhall in Würtemberg, 1773. Commenced study of 'cello, 1785. 'Cellist at Theatre of Wertheim, 1789. S. under Willmann and Romberg. Travelled in Germany as 'cellist. First 'cellist at Theatre of Frankfort-on-the-Maine, 1798. D. Frankfort, July 26, 1806.

WORKS.—Five concertos for violoncello, and orch. in C, G, F, E, and D; Symphony concertante for 2 flutes and orchestra; Six themes with variations for 2 violoncellos, op. 9; Duets for guitar; Variations for flute and strings; Music for string instruments, etc.

ARNOLD (John). English comp., B. Essex [1720]. D. 1792. Compiler of " Essex Harmony : being a choice Collection of the most celebrated Songs, Catches, Canons, Epigrams, Canzonets, and Glees, for 2, 3, 4 and 5 voices," 2 vols., 8vo, 1767 and 1774. "The Complete Psalmodist : or, the Organist's, Parish-Clerk's, and Psalmodist's Companion." Various editions.

ARNOLD (Samuel). English comp. and org., B. London, August 10, 1740. Educated in the Chap. Roy. under Bernard Gates. Comp. to Covent Garden Theatre, 1763. Purchased Marylebone Gardens and produced several dramatic entertainments (the librettos of two being by Thomas Chatterton), 1769. Retired from management with pecuniary loss, 1771. Married Miss Napier, 1771. Mus. Doc. Oxon., 1773. Succeeded Dr. Nares as comp. and org. to Chap. Roy., 1783. Sub-director of Handel Commemoration, 1784. Issued an edition of Handel's works in 36 vols. Cond. of Academy of Ancient Music, 1789. Org. of Westminster Abbey, 1793. Cond. the annual musical performances at St. Paul's Cath. for benefit of the Sons of the Clergy, 1796. Established the Glee Club, in conjunction with Dr. Callcott. D. London, Oct. 22, 1802.

WORKS.—*Music for Dramas, etc.:* The Maid of the Mill, 1765; Rosamond, 1767; The Portrait, 1770; Mother Shipton, 1770; The Son-in-Law, 1779; Summer Amusements, 1779; Fire and Water, 1780; The Wedding Night, 1780; The Silver Tankard, 1780; The Dead Alive, 1781; The Castle of Andalusia, 1782; Harlequin Teague, 1782; Gretna Green, 1783; Hunt the Slipper, 1784; Two to One, 1784; Turk and no Turk, 1785; Siege of Cuzzola, 1785; Inkle and Yarico, 1787; The Enraged Musician, 1788; The Battle of Hexham, 1789; New Spain, 1790; The Basket Maker, 1790; The Surrender of Calais, 1791; Harlequin and Faustus, 1793; The Children in the Wood, 1793; Auld Robin Grey, 1794; Zorinski, 1795; The Mountaineers, 1795; Love and Money, 1795; Who Pays the Reckoning? 1795; The Shipwreck, 1796; Bannian Day, 1796; The Italian Monk, 1797; False and True, 1798; Cambro-Britons, 1798; Throw Physic to the Dogs, 1798; Obi, 1800; The Review, 1801; The Corsair, 1801; The Veteran Tar, 1801; The Sixty-third Letter, 1802; Fairies' Revels, 1802; The Revenge; The Woman of Spirit. *Oratorios:* The Cure of Saul, 1767; Abimelech, 1768; The Prodigal Son, 1773; The Resurrection, 1777; Redemption (compiled from the works of Handel), 1786; Elijah, 1795. Cathedral Music; a collection in score of the most valuable and useful compositions by the English masters of the 17th and 18th centuries, London, 1790. Two Services for the Church, in A (continuing Boyce) and B flat; Ode for the Anniversary of the London Hospital. Songs composed for Vauxhall Gardens, several sets. Concertos; Overtures, Lessons and Sonatas for the Harpsichord or Pf. Anthems, various. Anacreontic Songs, for 1, 2, 3 and 4 voices, London, 1785.

This composer furnishes a remarkable instance of the oblivion into which men of

talent fall, who write merely for money and their own generation. Of the whole
body of Arnold's works scarcely one number is now performed. The exceptions
consist of anthems ; one of which, in A, is a beautiful piece of sacred music. Had
Arnold bent his talents in a higher direction, confining his efforts to church music,
the result would have been more creditable to himself and his period. His
oratorios, according to Busby, are injudicious efforts, and would better have
remained unwritten ; since comparison with Handel's works displays them in an
aspect anything but favourable to their inspired character. His songs are faithful
imitations of those of Dr. Arne, but are pretty, and seem to have been received with
favour by Vauxhall audiences of about a century since. His collection of Cathedral
music is the most substantial monument he has to perpetuate his memory.

ARNOLD (Youry von). German comp. and writer, B. St. Petersburg, Nov.
1, 1811. Prof. in Moscow Cons.

ARNOULD (Madeleine Sophie.) French soprano vocalist and actress, B.
Paris, Feb., 1744 *Début*, Dec. 15, 1757. She was the original "Iphigena"
in Gluck's opera, 1779. Retired from the stage, 1778. D. 1803.

ARON (Pietro). Italian writer, B. Florence, about end of 15th cent., [1480].
Canon of Rimini, 1516. Founder of a School of Music at Rome [1516].
D. 1533.

WORKS.—I tre libri dell' Istituzione armonica, Bologna, 1516 ; Toscanello in
Musica, Venice, 1523 [2nd. ed., 1529; scarce ed., 1532] ; Trattato della natura et
cognitione di tutti gli tuoni di canto figurato non da altrui più scritti, Venice, folio,
1525 ; Lucidario in Musica di Alcune opinioni antiche et moderne, Venice, 1545 ;
Compendiolo di molti dubbi segreti et figuratio, Milan.

This description of the two principal works of Aron is taken from Busby's "History of Music," vol. 2, p. 69 :—" The first book of the *Toscanello*, after recognising
the divisions of music by Boetius and others, into mundane, humane, and instrumental, abruptly proceeds to the exposition of the principles of the *Cantus Mensurabilis*,
including the doctrine of the ligatures ; all which, however, candour must acknowledge Gafforio and his predecessors had, already, quite as well explained." The
second book treats of the intervals, consonances, and genera of the ancients ;
musical proportion, and the tuning of instruments. The "Lucidario" discusses
"The use of extraneous, or accidental semitones, forbidden by the pure scales of
canto fermo," and recommends their adoption ; and also asserts the legitimacy of
the false fifth, formerly interdicted by Gafforio. "This, it is justice to allow, opened
the door to modern refinement, and introduced intervals and modulations, which,
though then deemed licentious, have, long since been sanctioned by general
adoption."

ARQUIER (Joseph). French comp. and 'cellist, B. 1763. D. 1816.

ARRIAGA (Juan Chrysostome de). Spanish comp., B. Bilbao, 1808. D.
1826. Comp. church music, symphony, overtures, songs, etc.

ARRIETA (Don Juan Emilio). Spanish comp., B. 1823. S. at Milan under
Cagnoni from 1842. Prof. of comp. at Madrid cons., 1857.

WORKS.—35 operas, of which the following are the principal :—Ildegonda,
1847 ; Marina, 1855 ; El Sonámbulo, 1856 ; El Conjuro, 1866 ; La Tabernera de
Londres, etc. Songs and other vocal music.

ARRIGONI (Carlo). Italian comp. of 18th century. [1708-1738.]

ARTARIA (Dominico). Italian publisher, B. Blevio, Tuscany, Nov. 20, 1775.
He established that famous publishing house at Vienna from which issued
many of the principal works of Mozart, Haydn, Beethoven, Moscheles, etc.
The founder D. July 5, 1842, at Vienna.

ARTEAGA (Stefano). Spanish writer on music and Italian drama, who
flourished during the 18th century, B. Madrid [1750]. D. Paris, Oct. 30,
1799. Wrote Le Rivoluzioni del teatro Musicale Italiano, etc. Venice,
1783-8. 3 v.

ARTHUR (J.) English writer, author of "The Modern Art of Flute Playing..."
etc. Lond., 1827.

ARTÔT (Alexandre Joseph Montagny d'). Belgian violinist and comp., B. Brussels, 1815. D. near Paris, July 20, 1845.

ARTÔT (Marguerite J. De'sire'e Montagny d'). French soprano vocalist, B. Paris, July 21, 1835. Niece of A. J. Artot. S. under Pauline Viardot-Garcia. Appeared with much success in London and Paris, 1857. Appeared after 1860 successively in Brussels, Amsterdam, St. Petersburg, London, Vienna, etc. Married to Padilla the vocalist, 1869. Her repertory includes parts in operas by Mozart, Rossini, Verdi, Donizetti, Gounod, etc.

ARTUSI (Giovanni Maria). Italian writer, B. Bologna. Canon of St. Saviour. Flourished in the 16th century. Author of L'Arte del Contrapunto, 1586. L'Artusi overo delle impetufettioni della moderna musica, 1660; and other works.

ASANTSCHEWSKY (Michel von). Russian comp., B. Moscow, 1838. S. at Leipzig. Director of St. Petersburg Cons. Comp. of music for orchestra, Pf., and voice, etc.

ASCHENBRENNER (Christian Heinrich). German comp., B. Stettin, Dec. 29, 1654. D. Jena, Dec. 13, 1732. Writer of sonatas, preludes, etc., for Harpsichord.

ASCHER (Joseph). German comp. and pianist, B. Lond., 1831. S. under Moscheles. Went to Paris, where he chiefly resided, and became pianist to the Empress Eugenie. D. London, June, 1869.

WORKS.—*Pianoforte:* op. 1. Tarentella; op. 2. Valse; op. 3. Nocturne; op. 4. Valse; op. 5. Caprice; op. 6. Danse; op. 7. La Fileuse; op. 8. Rêverie; op. 9. Polka; op. 10. Poëme; op. 11. Mazurka; op. 12. Impromptu; op. 13. Polka; op. 14. Barcarolle; op. 15. Les Hirondelles; op. 16. Thème russe; op. 17. Caprice; op. 18. Valse; op. 19, 20. Trans; op. 21. L'Orgie; op. 22 Capriccio; op. 23. Dozia; op. 24. Danse (Spanish); op. 25. March; op. 26. Impromptuvalse; op. 27, 28. Trans.; op. 29. Idylle; op. 30. Caprice; op. 31. Galop; op. 32. Le Papillon; op. 33-34, 36-7. Trans.; op. 35. Styrienne; op. 38. Souvenir; op. 39. Idylle; op. 40. Fanfare; op. 41. Mazurka; op. 42. Prière; op. 43. March; op. 44, 45. Trans.; op. 46. Valse; op. 47. Dans ma Barque; op. 48. Les Clochettes; op. 49. Galop; op. 50. Trans.; op. 51. La Sevillana; op. 52. La Fanchonette; op. 53. Trans.; op. 54. Three Morceaux; op. 55, 56. Trans.; op. 57. La Sylphide; op. 58. Tyrolienne; op. 59. Feuilles et Fleurs; op. 60. Trans.; op. 61. Dance; op. 62. March; op. 64. Souvenir; op. 65. Impromptu; op. 66. Ave Maria; op. p. 63, 67-71, 75-77. Trans.; op. 72. March; op. 73. La Zingara; op. 74. La Favorite; op. 78. Rêverie; op. 79. Trans.; op. 80. La Cascade de Roses; op. 81, 82. Impromptus; op. 83. Galop; op. 84, 85, 86, 87. Trans.; op. 88. Berceuse; op. 89. Meditation; op. 90. Fantasia; op. 91. Polka; op. 92. Serenade; op. 93. Le Phalène; op. 94. Le Chalet; op. 95. Chant; op. 96. Galop; op. 97. Gardez cette Fleur; op. 98. Mazurka; op. 99. Impromptu; op. 100. Valse; op. 101. Trans.; op. 102. Rhapsodie; op. 103. Trans.; op. 104. La Ronde des Elfes; op. 105. Impromptu; op. 106. La Cloche du Couvent; op. 107. Mazurka; op. 108. Valse; op. 109. Caprice; op. 110. Rêverie; op. 111. Caprice; op. 112. I Lazzaroni; op. 113. Caprice; op. 114, 115, 116, 117, 118. Trans.; op. 119. Le Sylphes des Bois; op. 120. Vision; op. 121. Volhynia; op. 122. Trans.; op. 123. Invocation; op. 124. Pensée; op. 125. Nocturne; op. 126. Marinilla; op. 127. Rêverie; op. 128. Idylle. *Songs:* Bygone Love; A twilight dream; Alice, where art thou?; Mélanie; I'll think of thee, etc.

A composer who, had he been more careful in his worldly relations, might have proved one of the greatest among recent musicians. As it stands, his music is more than commonplace, and many of his single pieces evince genius of a decidedly original turn. The numerous pieces which he has produced for the Pf. are in general brilliant and effective in character; while several of them show tokens of real genius inspiration.

ASHDOWN EDWIN, a music-publishing firm in London, established originally by Wessel & Co. in 1825. Messrs. Ashdown & Parry succeeded to the business in 1860, and have since worked it with considerable success. The publications of the firm consist of music of every description, instrumental and vocal. The catalogue of vocal music contains the names of Abt, Balfe, Barnett, Benedict, Calkin, Glover (S.), Hatton, Knight, Linley, Loder, Macfarren, Salaman, Smart, Sullivan, Wallace, etc. The catalogue of Pianoforte music contains works by F. E. Bache, Bennett, Calkin, Heller, Kullak, Lott, Macfarren, Osborne, Oury, Richards, Silas, Smith, etc. Besides these the firm publishes an enormous quantity of other music, chiefly arrangements of popular works, fantasias, brilliant *morceaux de salon*, and the usual amount of light music. Of large important works published by this firm we may specify "The Singer's Library of Concerted Music," edited by John Hullah, a very valuable publication; "The Devil's Opera," and "Helvellyn," operas by G. A. Macfarren; Concerted instrumental music by Beethoven, Weber, Spohr, Oberthür, Mozart, and others; and several important collections, mostly all copyright.

Messrs. Ashdown & Parry issued for a time a monthly magazine of instrumental and vocal music, edited by L. Sloper, called "Hanover Square." This contained compositions by eminent living and recent composers, and was a good idea well executed. The sole business is now [1884] carried on by Mr. Edwin Ashdown.

ASHE (Andrew). Irish flute-player, B. Lisburn, Ireland, 1758 [1756?] Educated at Woolwich, where he learned the violin. Adopted by General Bentinck, with whom he went to the Island of Minorca. Travelled with Bentinck through Spain, Portugal, France, Germany, and Holland. Commenced study of flute at Hague, receiving instructions from Wendling. Went to Brussels and became family musician to Lord Torrington. Competed with Vanhall for place of first flute-player at the Brussels opera-house, and gained, 1779. Went to Dublin, 1784, remained till 1791. Played concerto for flute, of his own composition, at Saloman's second concert in 1792. Became principal flutist at Italian opera. Married Miss Comer, a singer of some note, 1799. Director of Bath concerts, 1810-1822. D. Dublin, April, 1838.

His compositions consist of concertos and other music for the flute, none of which survive.

ASHLEY (Charles Jane). English violoncellist, B. 1773. One of the founders of the Glee club, Secretary to Royal Soc. of Musicians. Mem. of Philharmonic Soc. Was a prisoner for debt nearly twenty years, in King's Bench prison, London. Proprietor of Tivoli Gardens, Margate, 1843. D. August 20, 1843.

Ashley played in the band organized by his father, John Ashley. Contemporary accounts speak highly of his excellence as a performer on the violoncello. No compositions by him have come down to this period.

ASHLEY (John), father of above, English bassoon-player and cond., B. first quarter of the 18th century. Assistant cond. under Joah Bates, of Handel Commemoration, 1784. Director of oratorio performances at Covent Garden Theatre, 1795. Organizer of the band (in which his sons, C., *General*, J. J., and Richard played) which travelled throughout the provinces of England giving concerts of instrumental music. D. about beginning of 19th century.

His sons were *General*, a violin-player, who died in 1818; John James [1771, London, Jan., 1815], an org. and teacher of vocalization, who instructed Mrs. Salmon, Mrs. Vauchan, and others; and Richard, a violinist who played in provincial orchestras.

ASHLEY (Josiah or John), of Bath. English comp., vocalist, and bassoon-player, B. Bath, 1780. He resided chiefly in Bath, where he was a teacher of music and concert vocalist. D. Bath, 1830.

WORKS.—Songs. Reminiscences and Observations respecting the origin of our National Anthem, 1827 (an answer to Clark's work). A Letter to the Rev. W. L. Bowles, supplementary to the Observations, etc., 1827.

ASHTON (Hugh) or ASHTAN. English comp., flourished during the 16th century. Comp. of several masses and anthems, which are preserved in the Music School of Oxford.

ASHWELL (Thomas). English comp., flourished during first half of 16th century. His works, consisting of motets, etc., are preserved in MS. in the Music School at Oxford.

ASHWORTH (Caleb). English writer, B. Northampton, 1721. Director of Theological Institution founded upon Coward's bequest, Northampton. D. Daventry, 1775.

Works.—Introduction to the Art of Singing, London, 1787; Collection of Tunes and Anthems, London, n. d.; Sermons; A Hebrew Grammar; etc.

ASIOLI (Bonifacio). Italian comp. and writer, B. Correggio, April 30, 1769. S. under Crotti, an org., and Morigi. Resided successively at Turin, Venice, and Milan. Censor at Milan Cons. Director of Music to Viceroy of Italy. D. Correggio, May 26, 1832.

Works.—Cinna, opera; Cantatas; Motets and other church music; Theoretical works, etc.

Of these, "A Compendious Musical Grammar" was translated by Jousse, Lond., 1825; and "Introductory Exercises to the Art of Singing" was translated by T. Rovedino, 1826.

ASPA (Edwin). Italian comp., B. London, May, 1835. D. Lincoln, August 17, 1883.

Works.—The Gipsies, cantata; Endymion, cantata; Songs; Pf. pieces, etc.

"The composer has evidently much feeling for that important element in a Cantata obviously written to catch the public ear, which we should perhaps rather call 'tune' than 'melody;' and throughout his composition (The Gipsies) he has liberally used this power . . . ."—*Musical Times.*

ASPA (Mario). Italian comp., uncle of preceding, B. Messina, 1799. D. there, Dec., 1868.

Works.—*Operas:* Giovanni Banier, 1830; Il Carceu d' Ildegonda, 1831; La Burla, 1832; Il Litigante senza lite, 1833; La Finta grega; Il Marinaro, 1839; Guglielmo Colman, 1843; Paolo e Virginia, 1843; La Verga majica; Werther, etc.

ASPA (Rosario). Italian comp., brother of Edwin, B. Messina, Januay, 1827. Is engaged as a Pianoforte dealer at Leamington.

He has written a large number of songs, pianoforte pieces, and an opera entitled, "The Artist's Stratagem;" also a work entitled, "Exercises and Observations intended to assist in the Cultivation of the Voice," N. D.

ASPELMAYER (Franz). German comp., ballet-master to Emperor of Austria, D. 1786.

ASPULL (George). English pianist, B. Manchester, 1813. He displayed a precocity in musical matters only equalled by Dr. Crotch, and on appearing in London, was hailed as a pianist of the first rank. This favourable opinion was afterwards indorsed by Rossini, who pronounced him one of the most remarkable persons in Europe. His works, published after his death, consist of a volume of Pianoforte music, and a few songs. His age and education considered, Aspull was certainly one of those inspired geniuses who occasionally astonish the world with the exceptional brilliancy of their attainments. Accepting contemporary accounts of his playing as correct, England never produced one who would have made a greater pianist. D. Leamington, Aug. 20, 1832.

ASSMAYER (Ignaz). Austrian comp., B. Salzburg, Feb. 11, 1790. Org. S. Peter's, Salzburg, 1808. D. Vienna, Aug. 31, 1862. Comp. oratorios, masses, and much secular, vocal music, etc.

ASTON. See Ashton (Hugh).

ASTORGA (Emanuele, Baron d'). Italian comp., B. Palermo, 1681. Educated and instructed in music in Spain. Member of the Italian diplomatic body, under title of Baron d' Astorga, 1705. Visited England, Spain, etc. Went to Prague, Bohemia, and D. there, Aug. 21, 1736.

Works.—Stabat Mater, Oxford, 1713; Dafne, opera, 1709; Cantatas, etc.

ASTRUA (Giovanna). Italian soprano vocalist, B. 1725. D. 1758.

ATKINSON (Frederick Cook). English comp. and org., B. Norwich, Aug. 21, 1841. S. under Dr. Z. Buck. Assistant to do. Org. of Manningham Ch., Bradford. Mus. Bac., Cantab., 1867. Org. of Norwich Cath., 1881.

WORKS.—Services, Anthems, volume of masonic music, Songs, Part-Songs, Pianoforte pieces, etc.

ATKYNS (B. K.) English writer. Author of "Choir-master's Manual; containing full instructions for Training a Choir," 8vo, n. d.

ATTERBURY (Luffman). English comp., B. London, in first half of 18th century, [circa, 1735-40]. Musician in ordinary to George III. Obtained several prizes from the Catch Club about 1780. D. London, June 11, 1796.

WORKS.—Glees and catches, contained in Warren's collection; Goliah, oratorio, produced in 1773; A collection of glees, etc., op. 3, 1790. Collection of catches and glees, Lond. [1777].

ATTEY (John).—English comp. [159?-1640], flourished during the commencement of 17th century. Wrote a work entitled "First Booke of Ayres of Four Parts, with Tableture for the Lute, so made that all the parts may be plaid together with the Lute, or one voyce with the Lute and bass viol." London, 1622.

ATTWOOD (Thomas). English comp., and org., B. Lond., 1767 [1765]. Chorister in the Chap. Roy., 1776. S. under Nares and Ayrton, 1776-1781. Sent to Italy by George IV. (then Prince of Wales) to study, 1783. Received instruction from Latilla, Mozart, etc., 1783-87. Returned to England. Org. of St. George the Martyr's Ch., Lond. Mem. of Prince of Wales' chamber band. Instructor (musical) of several members of the Royal family, 1791-95. Org. of St. Paul's Cath., June, 1796. Comp. to Chap. Roy., 1796. Org. to George IV., 1821. Mem. of Philharmonic Soc., 1813. Org. of Chap. Roy., 1836. D. London, March 24, 1838.

WORKS.—*Music to Dramas, &c.*: The Prisoner, 1792; The Mariners, 1793; Caernarvon Castle, 1793; The Adopted Child; The Poor Sailor, 1795; The Smugglers, 1796; The Devil of a Lover, 1798; The Mouth of the Nile, 1798; A Day at Rome, 1798; The Red Cross Knight, 1799; The Castle of Sorrento, 1799; The Magic Oak, 1799; The Old Clothesman, 1799; The Dominion of Fancy, 1800; True Friends, 1800; The Escapes, or the Water Carrier (from Cherubini), 1801; The Curfew, 1807. *Services* in F, A, D, and C. *Anthems*: Come, Holy Ghost; Enter not into judgment; Grant, we beseech Thee; I was glad when they said unto me; Let the words of my mouth; O God, who by the leading of a Star; O Lord, we beseech thee; Teach me, O Lord; Teach me Thy way, O Lord; They that go down to the Sea; Turn Thee again, O Lord; Turn Thy face from my sins; Withdraw not Thou Thy mercy. Nine Glees for 3, 4, 5, and 6 voices (Lond., 1828). *Songs*: Soldier's Dream; Young Lochinvar; The Spacious Firmament; The Sigh; Dear Vale, whose green retreats; and numerous others.

Dismissing the music which Attwood wrote for the plays above enumerated as forgotten and consequently non-existant, we find that his fame rests entirely on his compositions for the church, his glees, songs, and other detached pieces. While it can not be admitted that Attwood is ever sublime in his conceptions, yet his anthems and services will be found to contain passages in which are united nobility and dignity, with science and that finished grace which is usually the attribute of an artistic mind. While he occasionally affects the manner of the modern school in straining after dramatic effect, he rarely omits to infuse into his compositions that lofty and sacred character which is admittedly the special feature of English church music. His concerted vocal music (glees, etc.) is remarkable for melody and careful finish, and in such works is chiefly noticeable that clear method of writing which was no doubt the fruits of Mozart's preceptorship.

AUBER (Daniel François Esprit). French comp., B. Caen, Jan. 29, 1782. Intended for commercial life, Auber was sent to London in 1802, where he remained for a time as clerk in a merchant's office. He subsequently returned to Paris, where he remained till his death. He never held any public appointments, but devoted his time to the production of operas. Mem. of the "Institut," 1829. Commander of the Legion of Honour, 1847. Grand Officer of the Legion of Honour, 1861. D. Paris, May 13, 1871.

WORKS.—*Operas:* Le Séjour militaire, 1813; Le Testament et les Billets-doux, 1819; La Bergère châtelaine, 1820; Emma, 1821; Leicester, 1822; La Neige, 1823; Vendôme in Espagne, 1823; Les Trois Genres, 1824; Le Concert à la cour, 1824; Léocadie, 1824; Le Maçon, 1825; Le Timide, 1826; Fiorella, 1826; La Muette de Portici (Masaniello), 1828; La Fiancee, 1829; Fra Diavolo, 1830 (London 1831); Le Dieu et la Bayadère, 1830; La Marquise de Brinvilliers (with others), 1831; Le Philtre, 1831; Le Serment, 1832; Gustave III., 1833; Lestocq, 1834; Le Cheval de Bronze, 1835; Actéon, 1836; Les Chaperons blancs, 1836; L'Ambassadrice, 1836; Le Domino Noir, 1837; Le Lac des Fées, 1839; Zanetta, 1840; Les Diamants de la couronne, 1841; Carlo Broschi, 1842; Le Duc d'Olonne, 1842; La Part du Diable, 1843; La Sirène, 1844; La Barcarolle, 1845; Haydee, 1847; L'Enfant prodigue, 1850; Zerline, 1851; Marco Spada, 1852; Jenny Bell, 1855; Manon Lescaut, 1856; Le Reve d'Amour, 1869; Le premier jour de bonheur, 1869. Concertos for violin, and violoncello and orchestra; Detached Pianoforte pieces; Overture for the London International Exhibition, 1862.

The production of a succession of works almost equally original, brilliant, and catching in character, is undoubtedly the outcome of a properly economised *genius*. We emphasize the last word because of our intention of applying it to Auber and his works, and because of certain unjust strictures which a number of writers of a recent school have passed upon him, and which may be regarded as the result of that professional feeling which is cherished by different *schools* against the methods and means employed by each other in affecting certain results. The amount of dramatic or pleasing effect gained by Auber, considering the comparatively humble means he employs, is greatly in excess of what many more recent composers, with an apparatus unparelleled in magnitude, have readily achieved. We see on one hand a huge array of combined scenic, mechanical, musical, and histrionic efforts, working to affect a certain end, that end being dramatic effect. On the other hand we see the ordinary efforts which an intelligent musician would practise, combined with musical illustration clear enough to be easily comprehended. On these grounds Auber is entitled to the respect of the large body of musicians who prefer comprehensible music of an agreeable character, to music which repels by its complication, and failure to make the advertised impression.

AUBÉRY DU BOULLEY (Prudent Louis). French comp. and writer, B. Verneuil, Dec. 9, 1796. D. Verneuil, Feb. 1870.

Writer of masses; quartets, etc., for various instruments; sonatas; theoretical works, etc.

AUDRAN (Edmond). French comp., B. Lyons, April 11, 1842. Composer of operas, church music, Pf. music, etc. Among his operas may be named "La Mascotte" and "Olivette," both among the recent operatic successess in Britain.

AUER (Leopold). Hungarian violinist, B. Veszprem, Hungary, May 28, 1845. Pupil of Dont and Joachim. Appeared in London in 1863.

AUGENER & CO. German firm of music-sellers and publishers established in London, 1853. Their catalogues contain many good writers names, and their publications are remarkable for a high standard of excellence where engraving, paper, and typography is concerned. They publish the arrangements of Ernst Pauer, and Pianoforte pieces by Ascher, Beethoven, Brahms, Chopin, Scotson Clark, Clementi, Gade, Haydn, Liszt, Mendelssohn, Mozart, Reinecke, Scharwenka, Schumann, Weber, etc. Their publications for the organ are represented by Bach, Best, Clark (S.), F. E. Gladstone, Händel, Lefébure-Wely, Mendelssohn, Prout, Rinck, etc. Among the composers of vocal music may be mentioned Abt, Arne, Beethoven, Bishop, Brahms, Goldschmidt, Hatton, Hullah (valuable editions of English classical songs), Mendelssohn, Reinecke, Schubert, Schumann, Weber, and many others. "The Monthly Musical Record" (1870) published by them is a well conducted magazine, worked on German lines.

AUMONT (Henri Raymond). French comp. and violinist, B. Paris, July 31, 1818. Writer of violin music.

AUSTIN (W. Frank). English musician, author of "A National School of Opera for England; the Substance of a paper read before the Licentiates of Trinity College, 1882," Lond., 8vo, 1883. Songs and Pf. music.

AUSTIN (G. L.) American writer, author of "Life of Franz Schubert." Boston, 12mo, 1873.

AUSTIN (John). Scottish writer, B. Craigton, near Glasgow. Wrote "A System of Stenographic Music," London, 4to, n. d.

"The principal object of the author was to simplify the prevailing method of notation. In place of five lines, his system consisted of only one, written upon by certain characters (six in number) which, reversed and inverted, were held capable of expressing every variety in music." For the purpose quoted the work is useless. However good theoretically it may be, it is impossible in practice. The writer, who was also an inventor of some note in connection with machinery for use in the manufacture of textile fabrics, is mentioned, and a portrait of him given, in "Kay's Original Portraits," vol. ii., p. 376. Edinr. 1838.

AUSTIN (Walter). English comp. of present time, has written "The Fire King," a cantata; "The Stepmother," an operetta; Overtures for orchestra; Songs, Pianoforte Pieces, etc.

AUTRIVE (Jacques F. de). French comp. and violinist, B. St. Quentin, 1758. D. Mons, Belgium, Dec. 1824. Good violinist and comp. for his instrument.

AUVERGNE (Antoine d'). French comp., director of R. A. M., Paris, B. 1713. D. 1797.

AVENARIUS (Mathæus A.) German comp. of church mus., B. 1625. D. 1692.

AVERY (John). English org. builder, B. about middle of 18th century. D. Carlisle, 1808.

Erected organs at Carlisle, Winchester, Cambridge, and other places throughout England.

AVISON (Charles). English writer, comp., and org., B. Newcastle, 1710. S. in Italy. S. in England under Geminiani. Org. of St. Nicholas Ch., Newcastle, 1736. D. Newcastle, May 10. 1770.

WORKS.—An Essay on Musical Expression, London, 8vo, 1752 (other editions, with reply to Hayes, 1753; Third edition, 1775; German edition, Leipzig, 1775); Marcello's Psalms, edited by Avison and Garth, 1759; Sonatas for violin; Concertos for organ or harpsichord, op. 9, etc.; Concertos for strings and harpsichord, op. 2, 3, 4, and 6, 1740-58; Songs, etc.

This writer's chief work is the "Essay on Musical Expression." It is evidently intended to present in this work an exposition of musical æsthetics, as well as to fix a standard of criticism whereby works of abiding interest may be judged. This design, however, is partly destroyed by a number of comparisons which the author has chosen to institute between composers of such diverse genius as Handel, Marcello, Rameau, etc.

AXT (Friedrich Samuel). German comp. of sacred music, B. 1684. D. 1745.

AYLWARD (Theodore). English comp. and org., B. [1731]. Gained prize medal from Catch Club, 1769. Prof. of music in Gresham Coll., June, 1771. Assistant Director at Handel Commemoration, 1784. Org. and choir-master at St. George's Chap., Windsor, 1788. Mus. Bac. Oxon, Nov., 1791. Mus. Doc., Oxon, 1791. D. London, Feb. 27, 1801.

WORKS.—Op. 1. Six Lessons for the Harpsichord, Organ, or Pianoforte; op. 2. Elegies and Glees [1785]; Music for Dramas of—Harlequin's Invasion, Midsummer Night's Dream, etc.; Eight Canzonets for 2 soprano voices; Glees, various single; Church Music in MS.

AYRTON (Edmund). English comp. and org., B. Ripon, Yorkshire, 1734. Pupil of Dr. Nares. Org. of Collegiate Church, Southwell. Gent. of

Chap. Roy., 1764. Vicar-choral, St. Paul's Cath., London. Lay-clerk of Westminster Abbey. Master of Children of Chap. Roy., 1780-1805. Mus. Doc. Oxon, 1784. Assistant director of Handel Commemoration, 1784. D. London, May, 1808.

WORKS.—Two Services for the Church; Anthems; "Begin unto my God," Degree Anthem, 1784, etc.

AYRTON (William). English writer and editor, son of above, B. London, Feb. 24, 1777. Married to a daughter of Dr. S. Arnold. Unsuccessful candidate for Gresham Professorship, 1801. Mem. of Royal Soc.; Antiquarian Soc.; Athenæum Club; the Philharmonic Soc., etc. Critic of *Morning Chronicle*, 1813-26. Do. of *Examiner*, 1837-51. Editor of *Harmonicon*, 1823-33. D. London, May, 1858.

WORKS.—Critiques in Journals; Editor of Knight's Musical Library, 1834, 8 vols; Editor of Sacred Minstrelsy: a collection of sacred music by the Great Masters of all Ages and Nations ..with Biographies. 2 vols. fo., 1835; etc.

Ayrton was the founder of that healthy school of criticism which is now practised almost universally by living English writers. The "Harmonicon" was a most admirably conducted magazine, and furnished readers with a perfect storehouse of interesting facts and speculations concerning music and musicians. The criticisms were uniformly just, and reflect great honour on the integrity of their writers.

AZAÏS (Pierre Hyacinthe). French comp., B. 1743. D. 1796.

AZPILCUETA (Martin D'). Spanish theoretical writer, B. Verasoin, Navarre, 1491. D. Rome, 1586.

B.

BAAKE (Ferdinand Gottfried). German org., pianist, and comp., B. Hendeleer, April 15, 1800. S. under Hummel. Comp. much music for Pf. and voice.

BABBINI (Matteo). Italian tenor vocalist, B. Bologna, 1754. S. medicine. *Début* in [?] Engaged for the opera of Frederick the Great. Sang in Russia, and entered employment of Catherine II. Sang at Vienna, 1785. Sang in London, 1786-87. Sang on Continent from 1789 till 1802. D. Bologna, Sept. 21, 1816.

BABELL (William). English violinist and comp., B. 1690. S. under Dr. Pepusch. Mem. of Royal Band of Music. Org. of All Hallows Ch., Bread Street, London. D. 1723.

WORKS.—Twelve solos for violin or oboe; Twelve solos for flute or oboe, op. 2; Six concertos for the piccola flute and violins, etc.; Suits of the most celebrated Lessons collected and fitted to the Harpsichord or Spinet, fo. n.d.; Arrangements for Harpsichord, etc.

BACCELLI (Padre Matteo). Italian comp. of church music, etc., B. Lucca, 1680. D. Lucca, 1756.

BACCHINI (Cesare). Italian comp., B. Florence, 1846. Writer of songs, operas, etc.

BACCUSI (Ippolito). Italian priest and comp. of 16th century. Chap. master at Cath. of Verona. Comp. masses, psalms, madrigals, etc. Flourished 1550-96.

BACH (Alberto B.) German writer and teacher, author of "Musical Education and Vocal Culture," Edin., 8vo, 1880; 2nd ed., 1881; 3rd ed., 1883.

BACH. This name is one of the most important in Musical history. The family consists of fourteen principal members; but only the historical four noticed below are worthy of attention as having influenced musical art.

BACH (Johann Christian). German comp. ... ..g., ..eve...n son of J. S. Bach, B. Leipzig, 1735. S. under his father. Lived with K. P. E. Bach at Berlin on death of his father in 1750. S. under K. P. E. Bach. Org. of Milan Cath., 1754. Married to Cecilia Grassi, 1759. Went to London, 1759. Established concerts in conjunction with K. F. Abel, which lasted between 1764-84. D. London, 1782.

WORKS.—*Operas:* Catone, 1758 [London 1764]; Orione, 1763; Zanaida, 1763; Berenice (with Galuppi and Hasse), 1764; Adriano in Seria, 1764; Carattaco, 1767; L'Olimpiade, 1769; Ezio; Orfeo, 1770; Temistocle; Silace; Lucio Silla; La Clemenza di Scipione. [Produced mostly in London.] *Oratorio:* Gioas re di Giuda. Magnificats; Glorias; Laudates; and other ch. music. Cantatas. Fifteen symphonies for 8 instruments. Eighteen concertos for clavichord. Six quintets for flutes and violins. Thirty trios for clavichord, violin, and bass. Quartets for clavichord, 2 violins, and bass. Sonatas for the clavichord. Songs, etc.

This composer, sometimes called *English* Bach, was received with much enthusiasm on his first appearance in London. The concerts which he gave along with Abel were very successful, and latterly were denominated *Professional* Concerts. Of his works little can be said, as, with a few exceptions, all of them are now forgotten. His chief claim to notice lies in the fact that he greatly raised the quality of instrumental music in his day, by introducing works which were considered advanced in tendency. His compositions are in general sound in character, but by no means are they similar to those of his father, either in skilful construction or inspiration.

BACH (Johann Sebastian). German comp. and org., B. Eisenach, March 21, 1685. Taught violin by his father, Johann Ambrosius Bach, a violinist. Self-taught to a considerable extent. S. under his brother, Johann Cristoph, at Ohrdruff, from 1693. Chor. in Coll. of St. Michael at Lüneburg, 1700. Mem. of band of Prince Johann Ernst of Weimar. Org. of Arnstadt Ch., 1703. Went to Muhlhausen as org. of St. Blasius Church, 1707. First married Oct. 17, 1707. Court Org. at Weimar, 1708. Court concertmaster at Weimar, 1714. Went to Dresden, 1717. Chap.-master at Köthen, 1717. First wife died, 1720. Competed for Organist's place at the "Jacobi Kirche," Hamburg, unsuccessfully, 1721. Married to his second wife, Dec. 3, 1721. Cantor of the Thomas-Schule, Leipzig, 1723. Court comp. to Elector of Saxony, 1736. Chap.-master to Duke of Weissenfels, 1736. D. Leipzig, July 28, 1750.

WORKS. — *Church Music:* Grosse Passionsmusik nach dem Evangelium Matthei (Passion according to St. Matthew), 1729; Passionsmusik nach dem Evangelium Johannis (Do. St. John), 1729. Two other passion-oratorios are ascribed to him, one being on St. Luke; but both are disputed, and one is entirely lost. Cantatas for the Church, scored for solo voices and chorus, organ and orchestra. Of those works 230 only survive, out of an estimated total of 400. Motets. Masses in B minor, G. minor, A, G, F. C, etc. Christmas Oratorio, 1734. Magnificats in various keys. Psalms, the 7th, 117th, 149th, etc., for double choirs, organ, and orch. Litanies. Offertoires. Kirchengesænge für solo und chorstimmen mit Instrumental begleitung. Miscellaneous pieces, as psalms, hymns, chorales, etc. *Organ Music:* Die Kunst der Fuge (The art of fugue), 1749; Clavierübung, bestehend in verschiedenen Vorspielen über die Cathechismus und andere Gesænge vor die Orgel, Leipzig. 1739; Sechs Chorœle verschiedener Art. auf einer Orgel mit zwei Clavieren und Pedal vorzuspielen, 1740; Canonische Veraenderungen über das Weinachtslied, 1747; Choral-Vorspiele für die Orgel mit einem und zwei Clavieren und Pedal; 44 Kleine Choral-Vorspiele; 15 Grosse-Choral-Vorspiele; 52 Choral-Vorspiele verschiedener Form; 18 Choral-Vorspiele mit den 5 variationem; Prakische Orgelschule, enthaltend 6 sonaten für 2 Manuale und oblig. Pedal, Zurich; Passacaglia für Orgel, 1736. Miscellaneous pieces consisting of Pastorals, Preludes, Fugues, Themes, etc. *Music for the Clavichord:* Das Wohltemperirte Clavier (The well-tempered clavichord), 48 fugues and 48 preludes, v. 1, 1725, v. 2, 1740. Clavierübungen, bestehend in Præludien Allemanden, etc., Leipzig, 1728-31; Part two, do., 1735; Part three, do., 1739; Part four, do., 1742. Chromatische Fantaisie. Toccattos. Fifteen inventions. Fifteen symphonies in 3 parts. Fantasias. Six Suites. Suites Angloises. Six sonatas for clavier with violin oblig. Miscellaneous pieces. *Concerted Instrumental Music:* Three sonatas for violin ; Five duets for 2 violins ; Six sonatas for violoncello ; Six concertos for various instruments ; Overtures in B. minor, D, etc. ; Symphonies in D, D minor, etc. ; Caprices for lute ; Concertos for violin and orch. A great quantity of miscellaneous pieces. *Secular Vocal Music:* Secular Cantatas, various. Two of those cantatas were introduced to the London musical public for the first time by Mr. S. Reay of Newark-on-Trent, in 1879; their titles were "The Coffee Cantata," and "The Peasant's Cantata." Odes, Choruses, Songs, etc.

It is remarkable that Bach should have attained such eminence as he now occupies when the quiet, unvarying, domestic nature of his life is considered. With very few exceptions—and Bach is one—men of genius pass lives of great bustle and activity ; their minds are more or less strongly exercised by many outward circumstances ; their whole lives are in continual and ever changing relation to the many exciting circumstances which crowd everyday experience ; and destiny seems to have conspired to augment the bitterness attendant on a moiling journey through life. Indeed, it may be truly said that a life of homely or domestic felicity is highly incongenial to artistic development, and prejudicial to the ambitious aspirations of genius. Comparatively few men of genius are blessed during their sojourn on earth with any surprising degree of happiness ; Mozart, Burns, Beethoven, Scott, and Milton occur as familiar examples of those who have had their aspirations clouded by misfortune and annoyance in various forms. But this, far from deterring them from the active pursuit of their chosen study, seems to have spurred them to continued and greater efforts.

On this argument is based the belief that Bach was not only a great genius, but recognising the untoward conditions of his career, a great example of direct musical inspiration ; qualified, however, to a vast extent by education. His life was as appears by the chronicles of his biographers, one of the direst monotony, unrelieved by those stirring events which direct and qualify the efforts of genius. His occasional appearances at different courts, and the unfortunate state of impoverishment which clogged his latter days, had no direct influence on the artistic quality of his works. Indeed he is always spoken of as having been quite indifferent to contemporary applause, and the poverty which eventually overtook him could have had no effect on his works, since they were mostly composed previous to the advent of bad circumstances. The whole tenor of his career was that of a dull, monotonous, homely content, which fact alone is sufficient to prove that his works were the outcome of intense inward impulse, neither governed nor inspired by the passing events of his time. Domestic life is entirely opposed to artistic ideals, and the instinctive feeling shown by Bach for what was truly poetical in art would seem to place him in the first rank of nature-born artists. The deeply devotional tone which pervades most of his church music is obviously the result of heartfelt emotions, and an intuitive perception of what was appropriate and beautiful.

Coming directly to his works, the first thing that will strike the student is the polyphonic texture of his concerted writings, whether vocal or instrumental, and the surprising dexterity with which he interweaves the various independent melodies which constitute the score. Careful examination will further reveal that this method of making each part an independent melody is in many instances destructive to perspicuity. On the other hand there is abundance of earnest purpose and loftiness of endeavour to counterbalance this defect. The whole body of his music is in advance of his period, and a considerable portion of it is even now beyond the discerning capacities of many amateurs and no small number of professional musicians. Until the musical knowledge of amateurs, and the musical public generally, has been extended in many directions, his music will continue to be disliked, and regarded as dry unsympathetic exercises in counterpoint. A superficial knowledge of composers and their works will not enable anyone to grow enthusiastic over the compositions of this master. To be enjoyed Bach must be conscientiously studied, and patiently followed throughout his several ramifications.

The instrumental music of Bach when examined side by side with that of his contemporaries exhibits an immense degree of difference in the method of orchestration employed. The string band, occasionally strengthened by trumpets, oboes and flutes, constituted Handel's sole means of instrumental colouring. For many succeeding years this method was employed by every musician except Bach, and until the appearance of Haydn the method was thought unsurpassable.

Turning to Bach's scores we find that almost constant use is made of the wind instruments which Handel employed, together with a number of others now obsolete. This fact, coupled with the skilful manner in which he treated the orchestra, proves that he was so far in advance of his time; and though his instrumentation was widely different from that of Haydn or Mozart, his general constructive method was not less perfect than that of the composers mentioned, nor less an advance on the productions during and anterior to his time. His instrumental music is a great source of enjoyment to every one who can take pleasure in quaint and pretty forms, and original and beautifully worked out periods. To say nothing of his fugues, which are universally known, the pianist has an unfailing supply of sterling music in his other pieces, which, if continually practised, will be very profitable as a means of refining his taste, and giving strength and consistency to his style of performance. His organ music is too well known to need much comment, but his fugues, preludes, etc. are generally allowed to be unrivalled. His other instrumental works are becoming more and more known as each succeeding season passes, and they are bidding fair to earn more attention than is readily accorded similar works of the same period.

The general characteristics of Bach's vocal music are deep religious feeling, careful and intricate elaboration of parts, refined and beautiful melody, and an ever fresh and original thematic treatment. Many of his pieces present difficulties of an extraordinary character; the parts being obviously written without the least regard for the executive abilities of the performers. Indeed, it seems to have been a leading idea with the composer never to deviate from his original design for the mere sake of securing an adequate interpretation. This feature is apparent in the writings of many other composers whose works are equally unpopular, though much less deserving of notice than those of Bach. Before quitting the subject of his vocal music we may say that beautiful editions of these works are issued by the Bach Society of Leipzig.

As time advances more attention will be given Bach and his productions. In the past his music was cultivated in a most desultory fashion, its present advance in public esteem being due to the efforts of Wesley in England and Mendelssohn in Germany. The latter, indeed, may fairly be accounted the originator of the present favourable feeling which is manifested, and quietly but surely spreading, in Bach and his music. Numbers of musicians now exist in Britain where formerly there was but a few, who cherish the most affectionate regard for Bach and his works; who know, appreciate and can afford to make earnest endeavours in promoting a general knowledge of his compositions.

In conclusion we may say that Bach is one of the great masters whose influence has been long and forcibly exercised on succeeding epochs of musical history. He shares with other composers the honour of being one of the fountainheads of musical thought. His importance in musical art cannot be overvalued, since the whole body of his works is a lasting monument of profound, beautiful, and withal pleasing musical imagery, unequalled in its peculiar style. There is no plea of immediate recognition to urge on his behalf, as a large body of the musical public are conscious of his manifold merits, and strive to extend the general knowledge of his powers; while we have also a substantial assurance of his vitality and coming popularity in his steady onward progress in the past, and extensive cultivation in the present.

BACH (Karl Philipp Emanuel), German comp., third son of the above, B. Weimar, Mar. 14, 1714. S. at the Thomas School, Leipzig. S. at Leipzig University and at Frankfort-on-the-Oder, for the Law. Appeared in Berlin, 1737. Chamber musician and accompanist to Court at Berlin, 1746. Went to Hamburg as Choirmaster, 1751. Director of Music in succession to Telemann at the Court, Hamburg, 1767. D. Hamburg, Dec. 14, 1788.

WORKS.—Solos for the Clavichord; Trios for Clavichord, violin and 'cello; Eighteen Symphonies for orchestra, 1741-1776; Sonatas for the Clavichord; Solos for Flute, Oboe, Harp, etc.; Quartets for Clavichord, Flute, Alto, and 'cello, 1788. Church music, consisting of Motets, Services (3 for the Fête of S. Michael, 1756-78-81), Sanctuses, Litanies, Magnificats, 22 Cantatas (1768-1788), etc. Philis et Tircis, cantata, 1766; Der Wirth und die Gaste, do., 1796. Die Israeliten in der Wüste, oratorio, 1779. Versuch über die wahre Art das Klavier zu spielen, mit

Exemplen und 18 Probstücken in 6 Sonaten, 1752-1762 (Treatise on clavichord playing); A work on Counterpoint, 1757; Memoir of his Father, J. S. Bach, etc.

This musician is placed by authorities next to his great father, by reason of the uniformly excellent character of his works and their value as marking a historic development in instrumental music. His vocal music is by no means of such good quality as his instrumental music would seem to warrant. There exists in it a decided want of those salient features which in vocal music should command instant attention, these being spontaneity and melody. His church cantatas are not worthy of resuscitation. His instrumental music—of which considerable quantities survive—is perhaps equal to anything produced during the same period. The form is strictly pure, and the ideas are not lacking of a certain grace which at all times has been a recommendation. We miss, however, the fancy and powerful expression of Haydn and Mozart. Bach lived at a time when artificial forms were made subservient to every form of Art. This has been most strikingly exposed where painting is concerned by Hogarth in his "Analysis of Beauty." The same cold, unsympathetic features which are apparent in much of the poetry of the period are observable in the music. Very few composers, excepting, of course, Handel, J. S. Bach, and others, had during K. Bach's time surmounted the contrapuntal severity of the former age; but the effort once made to escape the trammels of distorted polyphony, the whole character of the music became entirely changed until the transition to Mozart and Beethoven became a matter easy to understand. With the development of Pianoforte music K. Bach had much to do. He brought chamber music to a certain height of refinement which was never attained so completely before; but he introduced no radical reforms either as regards style or form, and cannot therefore be regarded as a great light in history. His music is elegant, not inspiring, and for this feature he received in an elegant period marks of approval which were not accorded men of greater mental powers in other branches of art who were his contemporaries. It remains only to be said that at one period of his career Bach studied for the Law, but that like other musicians, his ardent love for music compelled him to relinquish the dry-bones of jurisprudence for the more congenial study of harmony. As a whole, his compositions are creditable to his period and his education.

BACH (Wilhelm Friedemann). German comp. and org., B. Weimar, 1710. Educated by his father, J. S. Bach. Org. of the Ch. of S. Sophia, Dresden, 1733. Choirmaster and org. of S. Mary's Ch., Halle, 1747-67. D. Berlin, 1784.

WORKS.—Sonatas, Polonaises, Concertos, Fugues, Fantasias, etc., for the Clavichord; Symphonies for 2 vns., viola, 2 flutes, and bass; Trios for 2 flutes and bass; Cantatas; Church music, etc., chiefly in manuscript.

Bach was, as judged by contemporary opinion, the greatest organ-player of his time. How far he influenced the art cannot now be fixed, but it seems evident that in many respects his good example has been followed by many organists down to the present time. We have no means of determining whether or not W. Bach excelled his father, but popular opinion would seem to decide in favour of the Cantor of Leipzig. His compositions are now almost unknown, with perhaps the exception of a few transcribed pieces for the organ. Their claims to immortality need not be disturbed. In his private relations Bach was a drunkard and a profligate.

BACH (Otto). German comp., B. Vienna, 1833. Writer of symphonies, quartets, songs, Pf. music, etc. "Lenore," opera, Augsburg, 1884.

BACHE (Francis Edward). English comp. and pianist, B. Birmingham, 14th Sept., 1833. Gave early tokens of musical precocity. S. under Alfred Mellon. Played violin at Birmingham Festival, under Mendelssohn, 1846. S. under W. S. Bennett at London from 1849. S. under Hauptmann and Plaidy at Leipzig, 1853. S. under Schneider at Dresden, 1854. Returned to London, 1855. Went to Algeria for his health, 1856. Visited Leipzig, 1856. Returned to England, 1857. D. Birmingham, Aug. 24, 1858.

WORKS.—Which is Which, an opera, 1851; Rübezahl, an opera, 1853; Six songs for voice and Pf., op. 16; Trio for Pf. and strings, op. 25; Four mazurkas for Pf., op. 13; Five Characteristic Pieces for Pf.; Drinking Song; Beloved;

Forsaken; Barcarolle; A village merry-making; Two Romances for Pf.; Deux Morceaux caractéristiques for Pf.; La Penserosa e l'Allegra; Two Polkas for Pf., in E and E flat; Transcriptions and Miscellaneous pieces for Pf.; Andante and Rondo Polonaise for Pf. and orch; Concerto for Pf. and orch., in E. Morceau de Concert for Pf. and orch.; Trio for Pf., vn., and 'cello. Songs, etc.

Bache is an example of one of the many highly talented artists who have been cut off in the midst of a most promising career. It seems to be universally acknowledged that, had he attained to full maturity, he would have been an honour and an ornament to English musical art. The existing specimens of his powers must of course be regarded as the initial efforts of an aspiring genius and not as examples of what might have been. His Pianoforte music is brilliant and highly wrought, but in other respects does not evince much greatness of conception. Like his brother Walter, he was a remarkable performer on the Pianoforte, and equally expert at interpreting works by masters old and new.

BACHE (Walter). English pianist, B. Birmingham, June 19, 1842. Fourth son of the Rev. Samuel Bache. Lived at Birmingham, studying at the Proprietary School till 1858. S. the Pianoforte and theory of music under James Stimpson, org. of Birmingham Town Hall. S. at Leipzig under Plaidy, Moscheles, Hauptmann, and Richter, Aug., 1858, till 1861. Visited Milan and Florence, 1861. S. under Liszt at Rome, 1862-65. Gave first concerts and commenced teaching, 1862-65. Returned to London in May, 1865, where he has since resided as a teacher of the Pianoforte and concert-giver.

Mr. Bache is a musician of the advanced school, who, being imbued with an intense regard for the compositions of Liszt, endeavours assiduously to extend the public knowledge of them whenever a suitable opportunity occurs. His efforts have been the principal means of introducing to the London public the works of that remarkable though unquestionably whimsical composer; and around the concerts at which those works are brought forward is centered the most lively interest. The works—instrumental and choral—which he has brought forward comprise, among others, the following:—"The Legend of S. Elizabeth;" "A Faust Symphony;" "Mazeppa," symphony (twice performed); "Orpheus," symphony (twice performed); "Tasso," symphony (twice); "Festklänge" (twice) "Les Préludes" (thrice); "The 13th Psalm" (twice); Concertos for Pianoforte in E flat and A. All of the foregoing works, excepting "Mazeppa" and the Pianoforte concerto in A, were produced in England for the first time by Mr. Bache.

Although Mr. Bache has shown himself zealous in the cause of Liszt and modern music, he has not been indiscreet in the matter of selection; his programmes, as a rule, being composed of music of many schools and periods. Mr. Bache has not yet composed or edited any music, but he is one of the foremost among British pianists. His school is essentially modern or romantic in principle, but his training and catholic taste may easily enable him faithfully to interpret the great classics of bygone times. While Mr. Bache has become in England the acknowledged exponent of Liszt's music, he must also be credited with having boldness enough to produce side by side works of ancient and present fame; thereby challenging comparison of their respective merits.

BACHMANN (Gottlob). German comp. and org., B. Bornitz, Mar. 28, 1763. Org. at Zeitz from 1791. D. (?) Writer of Cantatas. *Operas:* Phædon et Naïde, Orfeo, etc. Songs; Odes. Symphonies; Quintets and Quartets for strings, etc.; Organ music; Pf. music; Theoretical works, etc.

This very prolific composer is now almost unknown, save by a few fine songs.

BACHOFEN (Johann Caspar). Swiss comp., B. Zurich, 1692. Singing-master and choir-master at Zurich. D. Zurich, 1755.

Bachofen has written numerous pieces for the church service, but is chiefly known by his hymns and psalms, a few of which still remain popular.

BACHSMIDT (Anton). Austrian comp. and trumpeter, B. Moelk, 1709. D. 1780. Writer of symphonies, masses, concertos, operas, songs, etc.

BACK (Sir George). English naval officer and collector. B. Stockport, 1796. D. 1878. Published "Canadian Airs collected by Lieut. Back, R.N., during the late Arctic Expedition under Captain Franklin. With Symphonies and Accompaniments by E. Knight, jun., the words by George Soane. Lond., 1823."

BACKUS (A.) American writer, author of a treatise entitled, "History, Theory, and Analysis of Music." Troy, U.S.A. 8vo, 1839.

BACON (Richard Mackenzie). English writer and teacher, B. Norwich, 1776. D. Norwich. 1844.

WORKS.—The Science and Practice of Vocal Ornament, Lond., n.d. Elements of Vocal Science; being a Philosophical Enquiry into some of the Principles of Singing. Lond., 8vo, 1824. Art of Improving the Voice and Ear, and of increasing their Musical Powers on Philosophical Principles. 8vo, 1825.

A critic, and writer of many useful musical and other works. Editor of the "Quarterly Musical Magazine and Review."

BADARZEWSKA (Thecla). Polish female comp. and pianist, B. Warsaw, 1838. D. 1862. Writer of many meritorious works for the pianoforte, including the well-known "Maiden's Prayer," or "La Prière d'une Vierge."

BADIA (Luigi). Italian comp., B. Tiramo, Naples, 1822. Writer of Operas and Songs.

BADIALI (Cesare). Italian bass vocalist, B. 1800. *Début* at Trieste in 1827. Sang in Italy, Spain, England, France, and America. D. Imola, Nov. 18, 1865.

Badiali has written a few songs. He is written of as having been a great singer: one of the best of his day.

BAEHR (Johann). German ecclesiastic, writer, comp., and vocalist, B. 1652. D. 1700.

BAERMANN. See Bärmann.

BAGGE (Selmar). German critic and comp., B. Coburg, June, 1823. S. at Prague, under D. Weber, 1837. S. under Sechter. Prof. of comp. at Vienna Cons., 1851. Org. at Vienna, 1853-55. Edited journal at Leipzig, 1863. Director of Music School at Basle, 1868.

WORKS.—Instrumental music, consisting chiefly of music for Pf., and combinations of stringed and other instruments.

Bagge is a conservative and has attacked Wagner with a vehemence worthy of a thorough Teuton. He adores Beethoven, Schumann, and other masters, and his writings are remarkable for acumen and clearness. His compositions are not so good as those of Wagner or Raff, but are, for educational purposes, all that can be desired.

BAI (Tommaso), or **Baj.** Italian comp., B. Bologna, in latter half of 17th century [1680]. D. Rome, 1714. Comp. of a famous miserere, popularly believed to be one of the finest specimens of this class of devotional music; also of masses, motets, etc.

BAILDON (Joseph). English comp. and vocalist, B. 1727. Gent. of the Chap. Roy. Lay-vicar of Westminster Abbey about middle of 18th century. Gained a first prize given by the Catch Club, 1763. Gained another prize, 1766. Org. of St. Luke's Ch., Old Street, London. Org. of All-Saints' Ch., Fulham. D. London, May 7, 1774.

WORKS.—Collection of Glees and Catches, Lond. [1768]. Catches. "The Laurel," a collection of Songs. Songs in "Love in a Village." Ode to Contentment.

BAILEY (Thomas and Daniel). American music publishers and composers. Established about 1755. They issued various collections of psalmody, including "A Complete Melody in Three Parts" [from Tansur], 1755. They also put forth "New and Complete Introduction to the Grounds and Rules of Music," 1764.

BAILLIE (Peter). Scottish comp. and violinist, B. Libberton, Mid-Lothian, 1779. Educated by his Parents. Learned to be a Mason. Mem. of the private bands of several noble families. D. after 1825.

WORKS.—"A Selection of Original Tunes for the Pianoforte and Violin," Edinburgh, fo., 1825. Scotch dance music, etc.
The contents of No. 1 consist of Reels, Jigs, and Strathspeys, named after various persons. Other pieces in manuscript are still in existence.

BAILLOT (Pierre Marie Francois de Sales). French comp. and violinist, B. Passy, Oct. 1, 1771. Gave early signs of a love of music. S. under Polidori and Sainte-Marie. Sent to Rome by M. de Boucheporn, a Frenchman who had adopted him, where he was further instructed in violin-playing, by Pollani, 1783. Played in the orchestra of the Paris opera, 1791. Received Government appointment in Finance department. Joined Army, 1793. Returned to Paris, and became a teacher, 1795. Mem. of Napoleon's private band, 1802. Travelled with Lemare in Russia, 1805-8. Established chamber concerts in Paris, 1814. Played in England, etc., during 1815-16. Leader of.orch. at Paris Opera, 1821-31. Leader of Royal Band, 1825. Prof. of violin in Paris Cons. D. Paris, Sept. 15, 1842.

WORKS.—"Methode de Violon adoptee par le Conservatoire," 1824 (written in conjunction with Rode and Kreutzer). Six duets for 2 violins. Fifteen trios for 2 violins and 'cello. Twelve caprices and studies for solo violin. Nine concertos for violin and orchestra. Thirty airs with variations for violin and orchestra. Three nocturnes for 5 instruments. Three quartets for 2 violins, tenor, and 'cello, Sonata for Pf. and violin. Twenty-four preludes. Fantasias, etc. Contributions to periodical literature.

During his various tours, Baillot was received with enthusiasm, and audiences took a wholesome delight in listening to his legitimate playing. His whole style was more noble in purpose than that of Paganini, and he did not descend to trickery. This is greatly in his favour, and places him with Joachim and F. David as a truly artistic violinist. Baillot's compositions are not of much value considered as music, but as violin practice they are invaluable; the "Methode" and the "Studies" being especially useful. Baillot was a thorough master of his instrument, and showed to every advantage in works demanding dignified and refined interpretation.

BAIN (John). Scottish musician and teacher in Glasgow. Published "The Vocal Musician, being a Collection of Select Scots and English Songs, adapted to two, three, or four Voices," Glasgow, 1774.

BAINI (Giuseppe, Abbe). Italian comp. and writer, B. Rome, Oct. 21, 1775. Chorister in Pontifical Chapel, 1802. S. under Jannaconi. Admitted to holy orders. D. Rome, May 21, 1844.

WORKS.—Memorie storico-critiche della vita e delle opere di Giovanni Pierluigi da Palestrina, Rome, 2 v., 4to, 1828. Saggio Sopra l'identità de'ritmi Musicale e poetico, Florence, 8vo, 1820. Church Music, including a famous Miserere, etc.

His biography of Palestrina is the most trustworthy one written. It has been translated into German (Leipzig, 1834), and is a standard, though one-sided, work of individual musical biography.

BAITZ (Heinrich Hartmann). Dutch organ builder of Utrecht, flourished 1708-1770.

BAKER (Benjamin Franklin). American writer and comp., B. Wenham, Mass, July 10, 1811. S. music in Salem, 1831; and under J. Paddon at Boston. Director of Music in Dr. Channing's Ch., 1839. Vice-President of Handel and Haydn Soc. Editor of Boston *Musical Journal*. Principal of Boston Music School, etc.

WORKS.—Theoretical and Practical Harmony, Boston (Ditson), n. d. Vocal Method, with L. H. Southard (Do.) Elementary Music Book (Do.) School Music Book (Do.) Church Chorals (collected). The Burning Ship, a Cantata. The Storm King, a Cantata. Normal School Teacher, with McTrimmer (Brainard's, Cleveland, n. d.) Songs, etc.

BAKER (George). English comp., B. Exeter, 1768 [1750]. Instructed in music by Jackson of Exeter and Hugh Bond. Entered family of the Earl of Uxbridge, 1775. Placed by Earl of Uxbridge under W. Cramer and Dussek for instruction. Org. at Stafford. Mus. Doc., Oxon., 1801. D. Rugeley, Feb., 1847.

WORKS.—"The Caffres," musical entertainment, London, 1802. Sonatas for the Pf. Organ Voluntaries. Six Anthems, for 4, 5, and 6 voices. Glees, for 3 and 4 voices. Songs, etc.

BAKER (Sir Henry Williams, Bart.) English divine and musician, B. London, May 27, 1821. Educated at Cambridge. B.A., 1844. M.A., 1847. Vicar of Monkland, near Leominster, 1851. D. near Leominster, Feb. 1877.

He was one of the principal compilers of "Hymns, Ancient and Modern," for which he wrote original hymns.

BAKER (James Andrew). English org. and comp., B. Birmingham, Nov. 8, 1824. Comp. vocal and instrumental music.

BALART (Gabriel). Spanish operatic comp., B. Barcelona, June 8, 1824.

BALATKA (Hans). Austrian cond. and comp., B. Hoffnungsthal, Moravia, March 5, 1827. Chor. in Olmütz Cath. S. at Vienna under Proch and Sechter, 1843. Director of the "Academa" choir at Vienna, 1844. Went to New York in June, 1849. Settled at Milwaukee, 1850. Established the Milwaukee Musical Society, 1850. Resided at Chicago as Teacher and Cond. from 1860. Established at Chicago "The Philharmonic Society," "The Musical Union," "The Liederkranz," and the "Orpheus Society." Director of the "Chicago Sängerfest," or Musical Festival.

WORKS.—"The Power of Sound," Cantata, 1856. Pf. Concertos. Songs. Pianoforte Music, etc.

Balatka has a wide reputation throughout the Northern States of America for his great organising powers. He has done much to promote the study and taste for good works in Chicago and district, and has produced among other works "The Creation;" "Masaniello;" "Der Freischütz;" Symphonies by Beethoven, Mozart, and Haydn; Instrumental works by Wagner and others. He has also conducted numerous Festivals in different parts of the United States.

BALBASTRE (Claude). French org. and comp., B. Dijon, Dec. 8, 1729. D. Paris, April 9, 1799. Writer of organ music, etc.

BALDENECKER (Johann Bernard). German comp. of chamber music, B. [?] D. 1849.

BALDENECKER (Johann Bernard), the younger, B. Mayence, Aug. 23, 1791. D. June 25, 1855. Pianist and comp. for his instrument.

BALDENECKER (Nicolas), brother of the above, B. Mayence, March 27, 1782. D. [?] Writer of organ and Pf. music.

BALDEWEIN (Johann Christian). German comp. of songs and Pf. music, B. Cassel, 1784. D. [?]

BALDWIN (W.) English writer, author of "The Science of Music," London, 12mo, 1829.

BALFE (Victoire). Irish soprano vocalist, daughter of M. W. Balfe, B. Paris, Sept. 1, 1837. S. under W. S. Bennett, Balfe, and Garcia. Début as "Amina" in "La Sonnambula," May 28, 1857. Sang in Ireland and Italy. Married to Sir John F. Crampton. Divorced from him. Married to the Duke de Frias, a Spanish noblemen. D. Madrid, Jan. 22, 1871.

Miss Balfe sang in the "Bohemian Girl," "Don Giovanni," and other operas, but was by no means suited for heavy parts. Her voice was light and pleasant in quality, but not powerful.

BALFE (Michael William). Irish comp. and vocalist, B. in Pitt Street, Dublin, May 15, 1808. S. in Ireland under C. E. Horn, O'Rourke (Rooke) and Lee. Taken to England by Horn. Violinist at Drury Lane Theatre, 1824. Début as vocalist, London and the provinces, 1824. Adopted by Count Mazzara, 1825. Taken to Italy by Mazzara. Married to Mdlle Lina Roser, vocalist. Sang in Italy, and in Paris, 1827. Remained on the Continent till

1835. Appeared in London as vocalist, 1835. Manager of Lyceum Theatre, 1839. Cond. National Concerts at Drury Lane, 1850. Appeared in Russia, 1852. Cond. at H. M. Theatre, 1845-52. Engaged as Composer, 1852-70. D. Rowney Abbey, Herts, Oct. 20, 1870.

WORKS.—*Operas:* I Rivali di se Stessi, Palermo, 1829; Un Avertimento di Gelosi, Pavia, 1830; Enrico Quarto al passo della Marno, Milan, 1831; Siege of Rochelle, Lond., 1836; The Maid of Artois, Lond., 1836; Catherine Grey, do., 1837; Joan of Arc, do., 1837; Diadeste, do., 1838; Falstaff, do., 1838; Keolanthe, do., 1841; Le Puits d'Amour, Paris, 1843; The Bohemian Girl, London, Nov. 27, 1843; The Daughter of St. Mark, Lond., 1844; Les Quarte Fils Aymon, Paris, 1844; The Enchantress, Lond., 1845; L'Etoile de Séville, Paris, 1845; The Bondman, Lond., Dec. 11, 1846; The Devil's in It, Lond., 1847; The Maid of Honour, Lond., 1847; The Sicilian Bride, do., 1852; Pittore e Duca, do., 1856; (revived as "The Painter of Antwerp," 1881); The Rose of Castille, Lond., 1857; Satanella, do., 1858; Bianca, do., 1860; Blanche de Nevers, do., 1860; The Puritan's Daughter, do., 1861; The Armourer of Nantes, do., 1863; The Sleeping Queen, Lond., 1863; Il Talismano, do., June 11, 1874. *Cantatas:* Mezeppa, Lond. [?]; The Page [?]; one produced at Bologna, one produced at Paris. Moore's Irish Melodies harmonised, 1859 (Novello). Six new Songs and a Duet, Longfellow, 1856. Trio for Pf., vn., and 'cello, in A. *Glees, Part-Songs, etc.:* Hark! 'tis the Hunter's jovial horn; Trust her not; Excelsior. *Songs and Ballads:* The Angels call me; Annie of Tharaw; The Arrow and the Song; As the sunshine to the flower; A home in the heart; Ah, would that I could love thee less; Anabel Lee; A Simple Rose; Bird of the twilight; Beneath a Portal; The Bells; Bridal Ballad; Come into the Garden, Maud (Tennyson); Daybreak; The day is done; Fortune at her Wheel; Fandango; The First Kiss; Fairy and the Flowers; Flowers, sweet flowers; Good night, beloved; The Green trees whispered; Hidden voices; Long ago; Once more; That last light of sundown; The Lonely Rose; The joy of Tears; I'd rather be a Village Maid; Maureen; Merry and Free; Merry May; Noble Foe; Sea hath its Pearls; Sing, Maiden, sing; Spirit of Light; The Happiest Land; Margaretta; Nelly Grey; The Power of Love; The Rainy Day; Scenes of Home; Stars of the Summer Night; What does little Birdie say; I love you; Mary; Fresh as a Rose; Phœbe the Fair; Old Friends; Zillah; Killarney; Defence, not Defiance; The Three Fishers; Lady Hildred; Maggie's Ransom; O let the solid ground; Kathleen Machree; Rose of the Heath; The Evening chime is sounding. Vocal Duets. New Universal Method of Singing without the use of Solfeggi, Lond., fo. n.d. Miscellaneous Instrumental Music.

If lovely melodies, appropriate orchestration, and good dramatic illustration can constitute a claim on the sympathies of musicians, Balfe is fairly entitled to a considerable amount of popularity. Always rising to the general level of his book, and palpably improving lame situations, he seems to have been successful in his treatment of whatever fell to his lot. The librettos which he set were almost invariably puerile; their poetical merits were commonplace; and they abounded in unskilfully devised situations. The "Bohemian Girl," his most popular, but not most artistic work, is a fair specimen of what he could do with absolutely absurd poesy. Witness:—

> "In the Gipsy's life you read
> The life that all would like to lead
> Sometimes under roof, and sometimes thrown
> Where the wild wolf makes his lair,
> For he who's no home to call his own
> Will find a home somewhere."

Shade of Dryden! The sentiment of this lovely lyric, to say nothing of its rhythm, is entirely wrong. Gipsies even in the 16th century preferred to sleep in barns. The attraction of a "wild wolf's lair" seems somewhat at variance with the details narrated in Fielding's veracious history of "Joseph Andrews," of the doings of modern Egyptians in the last century. The above rhyme is a very favourable sample of the style of libretto which not only Balfe, but Barnett, Wallace, and Macfarren, had to contend against. The good music which has been lavished on the trash called operatic poetry warrants the assertion that English composers have invariably raised their themes to a height of excellence immeasurably superior to the quality of their books. Sufficient allowance has rarely been made by British

...ers for the shortcomings of such librettos, and it remains a surprising fact that they still maintain that the musical faculty was denied native composers of thirty odd years ago.

Balfe's genius is exclusively lyrical, and he is most successful in those melodies which colour and enforce passages of human interest. "The Bondman," "The Bohemian Girl," "The Talisman," "The Daughter of St. Mark," "The Siege of Rochelle," and "Satanella," are his finest creations; and in point of melody need bow to no other English work. They are exquisite musical works when regarded in their proper aspect as relaxing and amusing entertainments for the public, and they should not be judged or measured by the absolute standards of more pretentious works. Many of his songs are still in vogue among cultivated musicians, and at least two of his operas, "The Bohemian Girl" and "The Rose of Castille" (one of his worst), are constantly being performed in the English provinces.

A life of Balfe written by C. L. Kenny was published in 1876, and contains an account of his last opera, "Il Talismano," written by Desmond Ryan. In other respects the book is chiefly remarkable for much gossipy writing, and a great absence of dates. Mr. Ryan seems to consider this last work (Il Talismano) of Balfe's as being quite superior in merit to anything else he produced. Although a more artistic, better elaborated, and certainly more musicianlike work than any of his others, it does not contain those elements of popularity which are now required to ensure success with the public. French light opera has made the public adverse to any melody not catchy, and although Balfe has shown himself in former works possessed of this virtue to a great extent, he does not appear in the present instance to have desired to sacrifice his good name to popularity. Should English Opera ever be established on a thoroughly national footing, it will be necessary to draw largely on the many works which Balfe has produced. Of those works, "The Bondman," "The Daughter of St. Mark," "The Siege of Rochelle," "The Talisman," and, of course, "The Bohemian Girl," appear most likely to prove acceptable. It would be truly gratifying to see such operas mounted with all the elaborate stage accessories now deemed necessary for works of even fourth-rate merit. We have formerly mentioned his songs as being possessed of many attractive features, and would reproduce that statement with the additional remark that they seem to be embued with considerable vitality, despite many unfavourable critiques which greeted their original appearance. As a vocalist Balfe was considered of a high order of merit, and it has been asserted that he was one of the leading barytones of his time. His acting was of only medium quality, and was only balanced by the surpassingly fine quality of his voice. He played the violin in the earlier part of his career, but like Wallace, never attained to first-rate ability.

Regarded as a whole, Balfe's career seems romantic when read in conjunction with the ordinarily prosaic records of concerts and appointments which comprise the general substance of other musicians' lives. The life endeavour of Balfe was one great struggle to establish English opera on a secure foundation; and to a small degree he succeeded. Since his time there has always existed a company more or less national in character which has been accepted by the public as a standard institution, and at the present date a warm and increasing interest is manifested in the operatic productions of living Englishmen,

BALL (William). English writer and adapter, B. 1784. D. London, May 14, 1869.

Ball was the writer of the English version of Mendelssohn's "St. Paul," Rossini's "Stabat Mater," and several Masses by Mozart, Haydn, and Beethoven, and others. He also contributed to the musical press, and wrote the verses of many songs.

BALTZAR (Thomas). German violinist. B. Lübeck, 1630. Appeared in England in 1656. Mem. of the King's private band, 1663. D. [1664].

The best violinist of his period, famed alike in England and on the Continent for the vigour and purity of his style. Baltzar, though unknown in general musical history, was nevertheless one of the founders of classical violin-playing.

BALTZARINI. Italian violinist of 16th century. First came into notice as leader of the band of Italian violinists, brought from Piedmont to the Court of

Catharine de'Medecis, by Marshal de Brissac. He is commonly credited with the introduction of the Ballet into France; the work usually regarded as the first being "Circe," produced in 1581 for the nuptials of the Duke of Joyeuse with Mdlle. de Vaudemont, sister of Catharine de'Medecis.

BAMFORD (H. A.) English musician, author of "The Rudiments of the Theory of Music, Designed for the use of pupil-teachers and students in Training Colleges," Manchester, 8vo, 1881.

BANASTER (Gilbert). English poet and musician who flourished in latter half of 15th century. His works are "The Miracle of Saint Thomas," in verse, contained in Stone's "History of the Monks of Christ Church (Canterbury);" "The Story of Guiscard and Sigismond," trans., in verse; and numerous prophecies. These latter, however, are said by Warton to have emanated from a William Bennett.

Banaster received in 1482, 40 marks yearly as "Master of the Song assigned to teach the children of the King's Chapel." His musical attainments, spoken of as great, are not known beyond his contributions in the Fairfax MS.

BANCHIERI (Adriano). Italian comp. and writer, B. Bologna, 1567. S. under Guami. Org. of Ch. of Imola. Org. of S. Maria, Regola. Org. of Ch. of S. Michael, Bosco, near Bologna, 1603. D. 1634.

WORKS.—Primo libro di Madrigali a 5 voci, 1593; Tanie et Concerti a otto voci; Il primo libro di madrigali a 3 voci, 1594; Salutazione loretane a otto voci, 1594; Primo Libro di Canzonette a quattro voci, 1595; Secondo Libro di Canzonette a 4 voci, 1595; Terzo libro di Canzonette a 4 voci, 1596; Il quarto libro di canzonette a 4 voci, 1597; Il quinto libro di Canzonette a 4 voci, 1598; La Pazzia senile, raggionamenti vaghi e dilettevoli, composti e dati in luce colla musica a tre voci, 1598; Salmi a quattro voci, 1598; Missa Solenne a otto voci, 1599; Secondo libro di Madrigali a 5 voci, 1600; Sinfonie Ecclesiastiche ossia canzoni francesi per cantare et sonare a 4 voci, 1601; Terzo libro di Madrigali a 5 voci, 1602; Fantasi e Canzoni, 1603; Conclusioni nel suono dell' organo, novellamente tradotte et dilucidate in scrittori musici ed organisti celebri, op. 20, 1609 (second edition); Motetti a due voci, op. 21, 1609; Li Metamorfosi musicali, quarto libro delle canzonette a tre voci, 1606; Carta di Sacre Lodi a 4 voci, 1605; L'Organo suonarino, opera ventesima quinta, Venice, 1605; La Prudenza Giovenile (musical comedy), 1607. Cartella musicale nel canto figurato (2nd ed.), 1610; Concerti moderni a 2 voci,...1617; A number of single masses and madrigals; other collections of church music and madrigals.

This composer, at one time greatly admired, is now known only to the curious antiquary. His music, if melodious is also extremely learned, and on this account would not accord with present tastes. His madrigals are not equal to those of the English school, nor is his sacred music, though profound, marked by much devotional expression.

BANCK (Carl). German comp., B. Magdeburg, 1804. S. under Schneider, Zelter, and Klein. Writer of Lieder and Pf. music, of which a number of pieces are issued by Breitkopf and Härtel.

BANDERALI (Davide). Italian vocal instructor, B. Palazzo, Jan. 12, 1789. D. Paris, June 13, 1849. Prof. solfeggi at Paris Cons. Wrote songs and vocal exercises.

BANISTER (Henry Charles). English comp., pianist, and writer, B. London, June 13, 1831. Son of H. J. Banister, noticed below. S. under his father, originally, but principally self-taught. Gained the King's Scholarship at R. A. M., Dec., 1846. S. at the R. A. M. under C. Potter, Jan., 1847—Dec., 1848. Gained King's Scholarship again, and S. at the R. A. M. till 1850. Assistant Prof. of Harmony and Comp. at R. A. M., Jan., 1851. Appointed Prof. of Harmony and Comp. (full post) at the R. A. M., 1853, a position which he now (1885) holds. Gave First Concert, Nov,, 1855. Prof. of Harmony at Guildhall School of Music, London, 1880. Prof. of Harmony at the Royal Normal College for the Blind.

WORKS.—Op, 1. Canzonet—Lay a garland on my hearse, 1846; op. 2. Three Bagatelles for the Pf., 1st set; op. 3. Canzonet—Go, you may call it madness, folly; op. 4. Three Bagatelles for the Pf., 2nd set; op. 5. Seven Variations on an original air. Dedicated to Cipriani Potter; op. 6. Three Bagatelles for the Pf., 3rd set; op. 7. Sonata in F sharp minor, for Pf. duet, produced 1852; op. 8. Gather ye rosebuds, part song; op. 9. Second air with variations for Pf.; op. 10. Trifles for Pf.; op. 11. Tarantella (No. 1) in B flat, for Pf.; op. 12. Song—The Hemlock Tree; op. 13. Mazurka—Coralie, for Pf.; op.14. Barcarolle—La Gondoletta, for Pf.; op.15. Trio—A Morning in May, for female voices; op. 16. Three Songs—Rose and Violet, Maiden wrap thy Mantle round thee, O Heart, my Heart; op. 17. The Wind goes by, sacred song; op. 18. Capriccietto for Pf.; op. 19. Felice, ma non gajo, for Pf.; op. 20. Two Winter Songs; op. 21. Trio—Summer Days, female voices; op. 22. Good Wishes, piece for Pf.; op. 23. Song—Bonnie wee Thing; op. 24. Song—The Lark and the Nightingale; op. 25. Anthem—O satisfy us early; op. 26. Souvenirs, for Pf., composed for Miss C. E. Burr; op. 27. Ricordanza, for Pf.; op. 28. Low dies the Day, part song; op. 29. Farewell, for Pf.; op. 30. Part song—Hail! bright Springtime, 5 voices; op. 31. Andante with Variations for Pf. duet, in F major; op. 32. Sacred Song—My voice shalt Thou hear in the Morning; op. 33. Sacred Song—I will lay me down in peace; op. 34. Allegretto alla Marcia for Pf. 35. Chants: contained in "The Psalter and Canticles, edited by W. H. Monk. 36. *MSS. Works*: Sonata in E, for Pf.; First Symphony in D, for orchestra, 1847; Second Symphony in E flat, for orchestra, 1848; First Quartet for Strings, in F sharp minor, 1848; First Overture in E flat, for orchestra, 1849; Third Symphony for orchestra, in A minor, 1850; Second Pf. duet, Sonata, in G minor, 1850; Second Quartet for Strings, in D, 1850; Sacred Cantata for chorus, solo voices and orchestra, April, 1851; Second Overture—Cymbeline, July, 1852; Andante and Rondo for Pf. and orchestra, in E flat, March, 1852; Third Overture in E minor, for orchestra, June, 1852; Fourth Symphony in A, for orchestra, April, 1853; Third Sonata for Pf. duet, in A flat; Fourth Sonata for Pf. duet, in A minor; Capriccio in A minor, for Pf. and orchestra; Fourth Overture—The Serenade, in E, for orchestra; Fantasia in D, for Pf. and orch., Musical Soc., 1863; Intermezzo in E, for orch., Alexandra Palace, 1875; Fifth Overture—From Sorrow to Joy, in B flat, 1876; Sonatas for Pf. in B flat, F sharp minor ([a]), F minor, F sharp minor ([b]); Fantasia in F minor, for Pf., 1874; String Quartet in E. minor; Cantata—The Sea Fairies, words by Tennyson, for female voices and orch., R.A.M., 1861; Cantata—The Maiden's Holiday, for female voices (composed for private choir of Madame Bassano). 37. Text-book of Music, London, Dec., 1872, 12mo, and other editions. Numerous Songs, Part-Songs, etc.

Number 37 of the foregoing list is perhaps that work by which Mr. Banister is most widely known. The neat, clear, and concise language in which it is written, makes it a refreshing and agreeable study for musical students. The fact that an eleventh edition has been called for is a sufficient witness to its importance and widespread popularity among musicians. Mr. Banister has likewise lectured on "Some of the underlying principles of Structure in Musical Composition," before the Musical Association of London; a subject on which he is an eminent authority; and on "Some Musical Ethics and Analogies," published London, 1884, 12mo.

BANISTER (Henry Joshua). English violoncellist, father of above, B. London, 1803. D. London, 1847. Wrote a work entitled "Domestic music for the wealthy; or a Plea for the Art and its Progress," London, 8vo, 1843. Banister was one of the best of English instrumentalists, and played violoncello at many of the principal concerts. He published the "Tutor's Assistant for the Violoncello;" "Lessons on Double-notes" (cello); and "Exercises on the use of the Thumb." His father, CHARLES WILLIAM [1768-1831], was a comp., and published a "Collection of Vocal Music," London [1803], hymns, songs, etc,

BANISTER (John). English comp. and violinist, B. London, 1630. Sent by Charles II. to France, where he studied the violin. Returned to England and became leader of the King's band. Established and carried on concerts in the "Musick School," Whitefriars, 1672-78. Dismissed from the King's band for upholding the superiority of English over French violin-players. D. London, Oct., 1679.

Works.—Mu.... ..or Sir William Davenant's "Circe" (with P. Humphrey), 1676. Music for Shakespeare's "Tempest," 1676. Songs. New Ayres and Dialogues composed for voices and viols of two, three, and four parts, Lond., 1678 (with Thomas Low). Lessons for viols or violins, etc.

Banister's songs are good specimens of vocal writing, and are thoroughly English in style. He was regarded as one of the most capable performers on the violin living in the 17th century in England, and was evidently bold in his expressions of opinion, when he could uphold, in the face of a royal patron, the superior powers of his countrymen as violinists.

BANISTER (John, *Junior*). English violinist, son of above, one of the musicians in the private bands of Charles II., James II., and Anne. Principal violinist at the Italian opera, London.

BANKS (Benjamin). English violin-maker, B. Salisbury, July 14, 1727. Worked chiefly at Salisbury. D. Salisbury, Feb. 18, 1795.

This maker, who is one of the greatest among the English, copied Amati, and produced violins, violas, and 'cellos of very fine quality and good tone. These instruments are now rare, and command good prices.

BANKS (James and **Henry).** Sons of the above, worked together and produced many fine instruments. Benjamin Banks, junior (1754-1818) worked with his father, and produced a number of fair copies of Amati. The general characteristics of the work of Banks' family are pure, sweet tone ; pale yellow colouring ; high Amati model ; and general excellent finish.

BANNISTER (Charles). English comp. and vocalist, B. Gloucestershire, 1760. Joined travelling theatrical company as actor, and played "Romeo," "Richard," etc., 1778. Appeared in London as actor in Foote's "The Orators." Sang at Ranelagh and Mary-le-bone Gardens. Sang at the "Royalty," London, and in the English provinces. D. Lond., Oct., 1804.

Bannister was a fair actor and a better vocalist, excelling in buffo pieces. His imitations of Champness, Tenducci, and other vocalists were at one period features in the entertainments at which he appeared. Shield composed for him "The Wolf."

BANTI (Brigitta Giorgi). Italian soprano vocalist, B. Crema, Lombardy, 1759. Appeared in London, 1779-80, and again in 1799, as "Semiramide" in Bianchi's opera of that name. This vocalist was originally a street singer, and made her *début* on the operatic stage at Paris in 1779. D. Bologna, Feb. 18, 1806.

BANWART (Jacob). Swedish comp. who flourished during the 17th century. D. about 1657. Wrote music for church and chamber.

BAPTIE (David). Scottish comp. and writer, B. Edinburgh, Nov. 30, 1822. Self-taught in music. Music-seller in employment of Swan & Pentland, Glasgow, etc.

Works.—Descriptive Catalogue of upwards of 23,000 Secular part-songs, consisting of Glees, Madrigals, Elegies, Trios, Quartets, etc. (MS.); commenced about 1846. Harmonium Tune Book, 1867-68 (edited with Wm. Hume). Harmonium Chant Book, 1868-69 (do.) Union Song-Garland, 1874 (do.) The Scottish Book of Praise (with Lambeth), 1876. Academy Vocalist (selected), 1879. Richard Werner's Hymn Book (revised), 1881. Moody and Sankey's Hymn Book, 1881. Vocal Compositions :—*Glees and Part-songs (Original)*: A rosy gift I twine for thee ; Evening (It is the hour) ; Soft pity never leaves ; Gratitude (Sweet is the breath) ; The Haaf Fishers ; Jolly Shepherd ! ; The hour is lovely ; When pleasure sparkles ; Beautiful Spring ; Breathe softly, flutes ; Come away, come away, Death ! ; Come, gentle Peace ; Come to the sunset tree ! ; Glide along, our bonny boat ; The Lark (Lo ! the blithesome lark) ; Let not dull sluggish sleep ; May song (Beautiful flow'rs) ; Morning (Hark ! the lark begins) ; Now the bright morning star ; The Shepherd's Holiday ; Spring Morning (See ! the Spring) ; The murmur of the merry brook ; The sun's bright orb ; By dimpled brook ; Call the loves around ; Come from the cloud of night ! ; Hark ! the speaking strings ;

Martilmasse Day; Soft thro' the woodland; Sweetly, sweetly tune the Lyre; Wind thy horn, my hunter boy! *Glees, harmonized or adapted:* Banks of the Yarrow; Bells of Aberdovey; Bells of St. Michael's Tower; Down the burn, Davie; Waters of Elle!; Erl-King; Fair Flora decks; Hark! Apollo strikes the Lyre!; Hence, gloomy care!; Hope told a flatt'ring tale; It was a friar of orders grey; Kelvin Grove; Pretty Fairy! when I view; Rosabelle (O listen, listen); Row, gently row; Rule Britannia; The Storm; Winds gently whisper; The midges dance aboon the burn; The Maid of Islay. *Anthems:* Calm on the bosom of thy God; My soul truly waiteth; Sing aloud unto God; The Prodigal Son (I will arise) *adapted;* also, hymn tunes, chants, school songs harmonized, rounds, etc.; Handbook of Musical Biography. London, 12mo, 1883.

BAPTISTE (Ludwig Albert Friedrich.) French comp., B. Attingen, Swabia, Aug. 8, 1700. D. Cassel, 1764. Composer of instrumental music.

BARBA (Jozé). Spanish comp., B. Barcelona, April 15, 1804. Writer of church music. D. Barcelona, 1883.

BARBAJA (Domenico). Italian impresario, B. Milan, 1778. D. Posilippo, Oct. 16, 1841. Produced operas by Rossini, Bellini, and Donizetti, and brought forward a number of famous vocalists.

BARBANDT (Charles). German org. and comp., was org. of Chap. of Count Haslang, the Bavarian Ambassador, London, 1764. Writer of symphonies for orchestra, and sonatas for harpsichord, etc. Teacher of Samuel Webbe, and compiler of "Sacred Hymns, Anthems, and Versicles,"...1766.

BARBARA (Pierre Henri). French pianist and comp., B. Orleans, April 28, 1823. D. Libourne, May 9, 1863.

BARBARINO (Bartolomeo). Italian comp. of motets and madrigals, issued during 1609-1617.

BARBATI (Aniello). Italian professor and comp., B. Naples, Sept. 4, 1824. Writer of masses, operas, etc.

BARBEDETTE (Henry). French writer, B. 1825. Author of works on Beethoven, Chopin, Weber, Schubert, Mendelssohn, Heller, etc. The work on Heller has been translated into English by the Rev. R. Brown-Borthwick.

BARBER (Abraham). English comp. of this name wrote a "Book of Psalm Tunes, in four parts," 1686: which in 1715 had reached a 7th edition. Barber was a bookseller in Wakefield.

BARBEREAU (Mathurin Auguste B.) French comp., B. Paris, Nov. 14, 1799. S. at Paris Cons. from 1810. Gained "Grand Prix de Rome" (with "Agnes Sorel," cantata), 1824. Leader at Théâtre des Nouveautés, Paris. D. Paris, 1879.

Barbereau's works consist of some orchestral pieces and a number of vocal pieces of varying extent. He is principally known in France as a theorist, while in England he is scarcely known at all. He travelled in Germany and Italy after gaining the *Grand Prix,* and while there, laid the foundation of that profound theoretical knowledge for which he has been made famous. His compositions are not numerous, and they do not seem to possess any of those features which claim popularity.

BARBIER (Frederic Étienne). French comp., B. Metz, Nov. 15, 1829. Resided in Paris, where he lived as teacher and leader at the Théâtre International.

WORKS.—*Operas:* Le Mariage de Colombine; Une Nuit à Séville, 1855; Rose et Narcisse, 1855; Le Pacha, 1858; Francastor, 1858; Le Page de Mme. Malbrough, 1858; Le Faux Faust, 1858; Le Docteur Tam-Tam, 1859; Monsieur Deschalumeaux, 1859; Le Grand Roi d' Yvetot, 1859; Le Loup et l'Agneau, 1862; Simon Terre-Neuve, 1863; Deux Permissions de dix heures, 1864; l'anne aux Airs; Les Amours d'un Shah, 1861; Flamberge au vent, 1861; Versez, marquis, 1862; La Cigale et la Fourmi, 1862; La Gamine du Village, 1863; Les Trois Normandes, 1863; Achille chez Chiron, 1864; Le Bouqetière de Trianon, 1864; Mme.

Pygmalion, 1865; Un Congrès de Modistes, 1865; Une Femme qui a perdu sa clef, 1866; Gervaise, 1867; Les Oreilles de Midas, 1866; Les Légendes de Gavarni, 1867; Le Soldat malgré lui, 1868; Mam 'zelle Pierrot, 1869; Mam 'zelle Rose, 1874; Le Souper d' Arlequin. Ballets, Duets, Romances, etc.

A typical French composer of the school of A. C. Adam, M. Barbier has produced a number of light operas, each with a sufficiency of evanescence to render them acceptable to the Parisian public. Their sparkling lightness is the only recommendation they possess.

BARBIERI (Francisco A.) Spanish comp. B. Madrid, Aug. 3, 1823. S. Madrid Cons. Cond. of Italian opera company. Mem. of numerous Spanish societies, etc.

WORKS.—*Operas:* Gloria y Peluca, 1850; Tramoya, 1850; La Jacara, ballet, 1851; Jugar con fuego, 1851; La Hechicera, 1852; La Espada de Bernardo, 1853; Don Simplicio Bobadilla, 1853; Galanteos en Venecia, 1853; El Sargento Federico, 1855; El Barberillo de Lavapiés, 1874. Other ballets, operas, etc., to the number of 51. Instrumental music and songs.

Barbieri's operas have been favourably received, but will not outlive their gifted composer.

BARBIROLLI (Lorenzo). Italian operatic comp., B. Rovigo, 1813.

BARCROFT (Thomas). English comp. and org., flourished in the 16th century. Org. of Ely Cath., 1535. Anthems, and a Te Deum and Benedictus in F are contained in the Tudway MSS., British Museum.

BARGIEL (Woldemar). German comp. and pianist. B. Berlin, Oct. 3, 1828. S. under Dehn. S. at Leipzig Cons., 1846. Returned to Berlin, and resided there as a teacher, 1850-59. Professor at Cons. of Cologne, 1859-65. Chap.-master and musical director at Rotterdam School of Music, 1865-74.

WORKS.—Three Notturnos for Pf., op. 3; Six Bagatelles, do., op. 4; Three Fantasiestücke for Pf., op. 9; Octett for 4 violins, 2 violas, and 2 'cellos, op. 15a; Third Quartet in A minor, for strings, op. 15b; Suite for Pf. and violin, op. 17; Suite for Pf., op. 21; Drei Tänze, for Pf. (4 hands), violin and 'cello, op. 24. Suite for Pf., op. 31; Eight Pianofortestücke, op. 32; Sonata for Pf., in C, op. 34. Third Trio in B flat for strings, op. 37; Adagio for violin and Pf., op. 38. 61st Psalm, Höre, Gott, mein geshrei, for chorus, barytone solo, and orch., op. 43; Allemanden, for Pf., op. 71; A Symphony; 2 Overtures—Médee, and Prometheus.

A polished dulness may be said to be the peculiar characteristic of this composer's works, which are thoroughly inspired by Schumann.

BARKER (Charles Spackman). English organ-builder and inventor, B. Bath, Oct. 10, 1806. Resided chiefly on the Continent; having failed to receive encouragement from English organists in the furtherance of his invention. D. Maidstone, Nov. 26, 1879.

Barker invented the pneumatic lever (which is also claimed for David Hamilton) and electric action for the organ, both of which, after being worked by a French firm, have been adopted by all the leading organ-builders.

BARKER (George Arthur). English tenor vocalist and comp., B. 1812. Sang in opera in the English provinces and in Scotland. D. Mar. 2, 1876. Composed a number of popular songs, of which the following is a representative list:— Blossoms of Spring; Cease your funning; Do not leave me; Dream of life; Emigrant's child; Eva, my darling; Excelsior; Gallant men of old; I cannot smile, dear mother; I dream of thee; I know that we have parted; Lesson of the Water Mill; Mary Blane; My skiff is on the shore; O how much more doth beauty; Only me; On to conquest; Roses of Youth; Sands of gold; Soldier's farewell; Song of the silent land; Take back the ivy leaf; White squall. The last named is by far the most popular of this composer's songs.

BARKER (Laura Wilson). *See* TAYLOR (Mrs. Tom).

BÄRMANN., German family of instrumentalists, consisting of Heinrich J. (Feb., 1784-1847); Karl (1782-1842); and Karl, son of Heinrich (1820 —).

H. J. Barman and Karl, his son, were reckoned among the foremost clarinet players of their time. Heinrich's brother, Karl, was a bassoon player of considerable ability.

BARNARD (Charles). American writer, has compiled a series of biographical hand-books entitled the "Tone Masters." The volumes published are—"Bach and Beethoven," Boston, 1871; "Handel and Haydn," do.; and "Mozart and Mendelssohn," 1870.

BARNARD (Mrs. Charles) "Claribel." English song-writer, B. 1834. D. Dover, Jan. 30, 1869.

WORKS.—*Songs:* All along the valley; Although the day; Answer to the dream; The Bell's whisper; Blind Alice; Blue Ribbon; The Broken Sixpence; The Brook; By the blue Alsatian mountains; Children's voices; Come back to Erin; Do you remember?; Dreamland; The dressmaker's thrush; Drifting; Farewell to Erin; Far away in bonnie Scotland; Five o'clock in the morning; Friends for ever; Friendship and love; Golden days; Half-mast high; Hidden voices; Hope; Hussar's parting; I cannot sing the old songs; I leaned out of the window; I remember it; Jamie; Janet's bridal; Janet's choice; Kathleen's answer; The life-boat; Little bird on the green tree; Lowland Mary; Maggie's secret; Maggie's welcome; Milly's Faith; My brilliant and I; Norah's treasure; The old house on the hill; Only a year ago; Out at Sea; Riding thro' the Broom; The Sailor Boy; Silver Chimes; Spring-time; Susan's story; Tell it not; Through the Jessamine; Walter's wooing; When I was young and fair; Won't you tell me why, Robin? Vocal duets, trios, quartets. Pianoforte pieces, etc.

The wide-spread popularity of the majority of the songs above noted, was principally due to the homely events which they were intended to illustrate, and the pretty and extremely vocal melodies to which they were set. It is a mistake to suppose that the popularity of these effusions was due to bad taste on the part of the public, for the truth of the matter is that the people prefer songs which contain an element of humanity, however distorted, and of necessity must accept the efforts of those who will deign to write to their level. Great composers, as a rule, do not strive to elevate the taste of the people by first writing music easy of comprehension and afterwards raising the tone of their efforts, but uniformly confine themselves to the production of works calculated to please the learned. The songs of Mrs. Barnard lay no claim to be considered works of art, but they are certainly healthy and fairly interesting.

BARNARD (Rev. John). English divine, published a "Book of Psalms, together with Fifty Tunes to sing them, neatly engraven on copper-plates." 1727. Also "A New Version of the Psalms of David, fitted to the Tunes used in the Churches." Boston (U.S.A.), 1752, 12mo.

BARNARD (Rev. John). English divine, lived during the 16th and 17th centuries. Minor-canon of St. Paul's cath., temp. Charles I.

Barnard is famed as having been the first to issue a collection of cathedral music. His collection of "Cathedral Music" appeared in 1641, and contains services, anthems, etc., by Tallis, Gibbons, Mundy (W.), Parsons, Bird, Morley, Tye, Bull, etc. The only perfect copy of this work is contained in the library of Hereford Cathedral. The title of this most valuable work is, "The First Book of Selected Church Music, consisting of Services and Anthems, such as are now used in the cathedral and collegiate churches of this kingdom; never before printed, whereby such Books as were heretofore, with much difficulty and charges, transcribed for the use of the Quire, are now, to the saving of much Labour and Expense, published for the general good of all such as shall desire them either for public or private exercise. Collected out of divers approved Authors, 1641."

BARNBECK (Friedrich). German violinist and comp., B. Westfälisch-Minden, Nov. 17, 1807. Writer of lieder, violin and Pf. music, etc.

BARNBY (Joseph). English comp., org., and cond., B. York, Aug. 12, 1838. Chor. in York Minster. S. at R.A.M., London. Org. of S. Andrew's Ch., Wells Street, London, 1863-71. Precentor and Choir-master, S. Anne's, Soho, 1871; Precentor and director of musical instruction of Eton Coll., 1875;

Cond. of Barnby's Choir, the Oratorio Concerts, London Musical Soc., and the Royal Albert Hall Choral Soc.

WORKS.—Rebekah, a Sacred Idyll, written by Arthur Matthison; The Lord is King, for soli, chor. and orch., Leeds Festival, 1883. Service in E; The Offertory Sentences; Canticles in Chant form; Te Deum in B flat (unison); Te Deum in D (unison); Benedictus in E; Magnificat and Nunc dimittis in D; Service (2nd) in E; Original Tunes to Popular Hymns, for use in Church and Home (142 numbers). *Anthems:* As we have borne the image of the earthy; Behold, I bring you good tidings; Come, ye blessed; Drop down, ye heavens; Grant to us, Lord, we beseech Thee; Have mercy upon me; I bow my knee; I will give thanks unto Thee, O Lord; I will lift up mine eyes; It is a good thing to give thanks; It is high time to awake out of sleep; Let the words of my mouth; Let Thy merciful kindness; Let your light so shine; Make me a clean heart, O God; Not unto us, O Lord; O Father blest, Thy name we sing; O how amiable are Thy dwellings; O Lord God, to whom vengeance belongeth; O Lord, how manifold; O praise the Lord; O risen Lord; Sing and Rejoice; Sweet is Thy mercy; The Grace of God that bringeth salvation; Thy mercy, O Lord; King All Glorious, motet for Ascension day, for chorus, organ, and orch. *Part-songs:* Home they brought her warrior dead; It was a lover (madrigal) Norwich Fest., 1884; Lullaby, a Cradle Song; Sleep, the bird is in its nest; Luna; Phœbus; Carmen Etonense; Annie Lee; A wife's song; Starry crowns of heaven; The Skylark; The wind; Sweet and low; To daffodils; Welcome; Silent night. *Songs:* Daybreak; Forget me not; How fades the light; I sit alone; In spring-time; Light; My golden ship; My summer-time. The rainy day; The rose and the nightingale; The wrecked hope; The Bells of St. Ethelred; Thou whom my heart adoreth; Vesper Music; When the tide comes in; Beggar Maid (in Cusins' "Songs from the published writings of Alfred Tennyson"). Organ Music. Hymns, etc.

Mr. Barnby is one of the ablest conductors of vocal music now living. With Mr. H. Leslie he shares the honour of being the most successful cultivator of choral music; and like him, his choir is of universal renown. He was the first to introduce the modern orchestra into the church, by conducting Bach's "Matthew" Passion music in Westminster Abbey. To him also belongs the merit of having introduced more new and great works to the English public than any other musician. Among such may be named Dvoraks "Stabat Mater," and Wagner's "Parsifal." As a composer of concerted vocal music Barnby is highly esteemed, his lovely part-song "Sweet and Low" being a favourite throughout Europe and America. Of his larger work, "Rebekah," it is impossible to speak in terms of unqualified praise; for despite numerous good points, the work is marred by a laborious manner. Mr. Barnby is connected with the publishing house of Novello & Co., for whom he has edited many works. He has also contributed to periodical musical literature. Of his powers as an organist it is unnecessary to speak, his capabilities in the art being universally recognised. His church music is well represented in the services of the principal churches and cathedrals, and is highly deserving of the notice bestowed on it.

BARNES (Frederick Edwin). English comp. and org., B. London, 1858. S. under Helmore in Chap. Roy. S. at the R.A.M. from 1872. Org. of All Saints' Ch., Norfolk Square, London, 1872. Org. of S. Margaret's Ch., Prince's Square, Liverpool, 1876. Org. of the Cath. of Montreal, Canada, 1878-9. Assistant org. at Trinity Ch., New York. Cond. of Montreal Philharmonic Soc. Married to Miss Leonora Braham. D. Sept. 21, 1880.

WORKS.—An opera, libretto by Mrs. G. L. Craik (MS.); An Operetta (German Reed); The 23rd Psalm for solo voices, chorus and orch.; Songs; Organ and Pf. music, etc.

BARNES (Robert). English violin-maker, flourished towards the end of the 18th century. He worked with Norris, and Thomas Smith in London. His violins are of average merit, but their fame is very obscure.

BARNETT (John). English comp., B. Bedford, July 15, 1802. Articled to S. J. Arnold, proprietor of the Lyceum Theatre. S. under C. E. Horn, Price, and Ries. Married Miss Lindley, daughter of the violoncello player, 1837. S. Vogler's system of harmony at Frankfort under Schnyder von Wartensee. Returned to London, 1838. Opened S. James' Theatre for English opera,

1839. Retired to Cheltenham, where he established himself as a vocal teacher,
1841. Resided in Leipzig and in Italy for a short time, superintending the education of his children. Has since remained at Cheltenham.

WORKS.—*Operettas and Operas:* Before Breakfast, a Musical Farce, written by Richard Peake, Lyceum, 1828; Music in M'ss Mitford's "Rienzi," Drury Lane, 1828; Monsieur Mallet, operetta, written by Thomas Moncrieff, Adelphi Theatre, 1828; The Two Seconds, operetta, written by R. Peake, Lyceum, 1829; Carnival at Naples, opera, Covent Garden, 1830; Robert the Devil, musical drama, Covent Garden, 1830; The Picturesque, operetta, written by Thomas Haynes Bayley, Lyceum, 1830; Baron Trenck, operetta, written by T. Morton, sen., destroyed in the fire at Covent Garden Theatre, 1830; Country Quarters, musical farce, Covent Garden, 1831; Court of Queen's Bench, operetta, Olympic Theatre (Vestris), 1832; The Paphian Bower, operetta, written by Planché and C. Dance, Olympic Theatre, Dec., 1832; Harlequin Pat, operetta, Covent Garden, 1832; Married Lovers, musical farce, Lyceum, 1832; Promotion, musical farce, Lyceum, 1833; Pet of the Petticoats, operetta, Sadler's Well, Aug., 1832; Win Her and Wear Her, opera, Drury Lane, Dec., 1832; The Soldier's Widow, musical drama, written by E. Fitzball, English opera company, Adelphi, 1833; Two songs and a march in "Nell Gwynne," Covent Garden, 1833; Song in Planché's "Charles the Twelfth," Drury Lane, 1833; The Deuce is in her, operetta, 1833; Olympic Revels, 1833; Blanche of Jersey, 1834; The Mountain Sylph, opera, written by Thackwray, Lyceum, Aug. 25, 1834; Fair Rosamond, opera, written by C. Z. Barnett, Drury Lane, March 30, 1837; Farinelli, opera, written by C. Z. Barnett, Drury Lane, Feb. 8, 1837; Kathleen, opera (never produced), composed in 1840; Marie, opera, composed in 1845 (unfinished). *Oratorios:* The Omnipresence of the Deity, published in 1829 (never performed); Daniel, unfinished, composed in 1841. A Symphony, unfinished, composed in 1840; Two string quartets, MS., composed in 1840. Twelve Russian Melodies, with words by Harry Stoe van Dyk, Goulding [1822]; Six Bohemian Melodies, with words by Sir (then Mr.) John Bowring, London, 1824; Twenty-four songs in imitation of the music of various nations, with words by Van Dyk, Leon Lee, and Mayhew, 1824; Twelve Songs from Fairy Land, written by Thomas Haynes Bayley, Cramer & Co., 1827; Lyric Illustrations of the Modern Poets, 1834, Reprinted in 1877. School for the Voice, a Theoretical and Practical Treatise on Singing. Lond., fo. [1860], since reprinted several times. Twelve Part-songs, mostly published in 1870; Chamber Madrigals, London, 1861. *A selection from Mr. Barnett's Concerted vocal pieces and Songs which have been published, the total number of such works being about 2000, issued between 1816 and 1880—Part-songs:* It is summer, it is summer; Bend down from thy chariot; Haste not; Farewell to the Flowers; Tic-tac of the mill; Dear peaceful valley; Evening drum; Merrily, merrily sounds the horn; In the merry greenwood; Wrong not, sweet mistress (madrigal); Chamois Hunter; O Lord, our governor. *Duets:* A smile, a tear; A spring song; Come where the flowers are blooming; Dear maid, my heart is thine; Down in the dell; The Gleaner's Bell; Good night; The Hungarian to his bride; I'll follow thee; Moonlight, music, love, and flowers; My gondola glides; No more, no more; Oh! give to me; Oh! 'tis sweet to meet again; Spring; The twilight hour; There's not a breeze; When at night; Where are the mountains; Wilt thou tempt the wave? *Songs:* Adieu to thee, fair Rhine; Ask me no more; A day-dream; Banks of Brooms-grove; Break, break, break; Bride's farewell; Chase the falling tear; Clansman's bride; Come to me, thou gentle child; Dear Napoli; Days of Chivalry; Days that ne'er return; Flower of my life; Fill up the wine-cup; Flowers of summer; Go, thou art free; Highlander's bride; Her heart is mine; Highland soldier; Highland minstrel boy; Hark, the fairy bells; Hope for the best; Here's a health to merry England; The Holly; Hark, hark to the sound; I have been to the woods; Is the reign of fancy over?; Knight of the golden crest; Light Guitar; Light of heart am I; Lord, I believe; List to my wild guitar; My home beside the Quadalquiver; Minstrel's lament; Mermaid's song; Maid of Athens; My native land, good night; Maiden of Sicily; Now the lamp of day has fled; Normandy maid; Rock me to sleep; Rose of Lucerne, 1823; Rise, gentle moon; Swiss shepherd; Sing, nightingale, sing; Sailor boy's song; Spirit of love; There sits a lovely maid; The opal ring; The ship; Vesper hour; Up to the Forest; Village bells; Young moss rose; Year's last hours. Systems and Singing Masters, a Comment upon the

Wilhem System and Remarks upon Mr. J. Hullah's Manual. Lond., 1842, another edition, 1877.

Barnett, like Balfe, made one great effort to establish English opera on a firm footing. He sought to make it independent of the jealousies of artists, and the hostility of the press which had all along shown little favour for works not of foreign origin; and, but for one unfortunate circumstance, would have succeeded. Here follows his account of the matter:—"In 1833 both Drury Lane and Covent Garden Theatres were only opened for the performance of German and Italian operas; at the other theatres comedies and farces were done; consequently there was at that period no field for English composers. I published a letter in *The Times* setting forth the situation. My letter was approved of, and read in Green Rooms of theatres, and amongst musicians. I called together the chief composers of the day, Sir Henry Bishop (then Mr. Bishop), Mr. Rodwell, and others, to consult as to the best means of establishing an English Opera House: nothing, however, was found practicable. I was on intimate terms at that period with Capt. Arbuthnot -one of King William the Fourth's Gentlemen-in-waiting: he had the ear of the King, who was very partial to him. He promised to present a memorial from me to the King, asking for a patent for English Opera. The memorial was presented, and the King promised to grant me the patent, when shortly after, he died—and there was an end of my hopes." Had Mr. Barnett effected his purpose, English opera would no doubt have been enriched by many contributions from his pen, as well as by the works of other composers, whom he would have been enabled to encourage and bring before the public.

Previous to the production of the "Mountain Sylph" there had not been brought out in Britain any work written in strict opera form. The so-called operas of Bishop, Kelly, Braham, King, Shield, and others, were nothing more or less than plays interspersed with songs and concerted pieces, and occasionally garnished with instrumental pieces in the form of overtures and pantomine music. Barnett had long considered this point, and in 1834 brought out the first English opera which was modelled on the accepted operatic form current among great continental writers like Weber, and which was accordingly the archetype and precursor of modern English opera. This work was received with much enthusiasm, and had a successive run of upwards of one hundred nights; and on it are modelled the more recent works of Balfe, Wallace, and their followers. This work, produced at a period when English operatic music was at its lowest ebb, is an honour to its composer, and remains to this day one of the freshest and most genuinely-inspired English works of its class.

His four operas are among those which will doubtless form part of the repertory of future English opera companies; granted that such companies are managed with a regard to the interests of native composers. "The Mountain Sylph," "Farinelli," and "Fair Rosamond," are works which would discredit no composer or school; being, as they are, creations of great beauty, finish, and dramatic power; abounding in melodies of exquisite sweetness and lofty fancy; rich and compact harmonies; and instrumentation of a skilful and appropriate contrivance. Many of his songs have acquired great popularity owing to their pleasing and fanciful character. His "Lyrical Illustrations of the Modern Poets"—originally published in 1834--when reprinted in 1877, received such commendations from the press as clearly demonstrated their intrinsic value as works of art; at the same time showing that revivification is only necessary to make his works widely appreciated. Mr. Barnett's retirement from active life was due to the disgust he conceived at the "intrigues of all connected with theatres," and a desire for relaxation from the fatiguing excitements attending his appearance before the public. He was frequently called by the press to return, but his beautiful home at Lickhampton Hill possessed for him the united charms of rural quietness and natural beauties, which were sufficiently binding to render a return to the bustling life of a public composer most undesirable. We must, however, express regret that Mr. Barnett should not have consented to the production of his MS. opera, "Kathleen," which, according to Mr. C. Salaman, is a work of the greatest beauty. The members of Mr. Barnett's family are all musically inclined, his eldest son being chief pianoforte-teacher at the Lady's College, Cheltenham, and his two daughters singers of much ability. Miss Clara Barnett, who married an American barrister of distinction, a friend of the poet Longfellow, was a member of the "Carl Rosa" opera company during its visit to America. His eldest daughter is married to Mr. Robert Francillon the well-known novelist.

Barnett's works are among the finest examples of English opera, and the public only require to be made cognizant with the fact to fully endorse it. The Press of late years have manfully asserted the right of Englishmen to obtain a hearing, and we trust that their efforts will be terminated in a manner as speedily to bring the best English works to the front. Charity begins at home, and Englishmen must be illiberal, narrow-minded, and insular with regard to everything springing from an exotic source, till her own musical institutions are firmly established.

BARNETT (John Francis). Nephew of the preceding, English comp. and pianist, B. London, Oct. 16, 1837. Commenced study of the pianoforte, 1843. S. under Dr. Wylde, 1849. Gained Queen's scholarship at the R.A.M., 1850. Gained it again, 1852. First appeared as pianist, New Philharmonic Concerts, 1851. S. at Leipzig under Hauptmann, Rietz, Plaidy, and Moscheles, 1856-1859. Returned to London, 1859. Appeared at the Philharmonic Society's Concerts, 1861. Cond. the performance of "The Good Shepherd," cantata, at Brighton Musical Festival, 1876. Do. "The Building of the Ship," cantata, at Leeds Festival, Oct., 1880. Prof. at Royal College of Music, 1883.

WORKS.—The Raising of Lazarus, an oratorio, Hereford, 1876 ; The Ancient Mariner, a cantata, Birmingham, 1867 ; Paradise and the Peri, cantata, Birmingham, 1870 ; The Good Shepherd, a sacred cantata, Brighton, 1876 ; The Building of the Ship (Longfellow), a cantata, Leeds, Oct., 1880. The Lay of the Last Minstrel, orchestral work, Liverpool Festival, 1874 ; Symphony in A minor, for orchestra, Musical Society, 1864 ; Ouverture Symphonique, 1868 (MS.), Philharmonic Soc. ; Overture to Shakespeare's "Winter's Tale," 1873 (MS.), British Orchestral Soc. ; Concerto in D minor, for Pf. and orch., 1868 ; String Quartet in D minor ; Trio in C minor, for Pianoforte, vn., and 'cello (MS.) ; Sonata for Pf. and violin in E minor (MS.) ; Quintet in G minor, for strings (MS) ; Sonata in E minor, for Pf., op. 45 ; The Harvest Festival, Symphonic Poem, for orchestra, written for Norwich Festival ; Elfland, pizzicato for orchestra ; Six Studies for Pf. (MS.); L'Espérance, morceau élégant, for Pf. ; A Pastoral Scene for Pf. ; Rosalind, romance, for Pf. ; The Ebbing Tide, piece for orch., transcribed for Pf., op. 36 ; Passepied, No. 1 of Ancient Dances for Pf. ; The Chapel by the Sea, descriptive piece for Pf. ; Six Sketches, for Pf., dedicated to H. F. Broadwood, Esq. ; Gavotte, for Pf. ; Valse des Saisons, for Pf. ; Mountain Echoes, for Pf. ; Mount S. Bernard, for Pf. ; Sunrise and Sunset, two pastorals ; Three Impromptus, for Pf., dedicated to Ferdinand Hiller ; Chanson d'Amour, for Pf. ; Return of Spring, for Pf., dedicated to Arabella Goddard ; Caprice Brilliant, for Pf., op. 1. Nocturne for Pf. *Vocal Music, Part-songs:* Come thou Holy Spirit, anthem ; It is not always May ; 'Midst grove and dell; If I had but two little wings, madrigal. *Songs:* The minstrel ; The Indian girl ; He is all to me ; I love, I love thee ; The Rock of Ages ; The golden gate ; Star of the morn ; The violet girl's song ; Into the World ; Outside ; Star of Home ; The sea fairies, duet ; The parting hour, duet.

J. F. Barnett is one of the leading English composers of the present time. His works are bright, tuneful, and skilfully constructed, while their popularity is such as to place beyond all doubt the place which they hold in the estimation of the public. His minor works, songs, and pianoforte music, possess less merit in an artistic sense than his cantatas, but are not less popular. Of his cantatas "The Ancient Mariner" is probably the most popular, though all of them are frequently performed by different societies throughout the country. The orchestral works possess much merit, and have been warmly commended by various writers.

BARNETT (Robert). English pianist and comp., B. Macclesfield, 1818. D. Slough, near Windsor, Nov., 1875.

BARNHILL (James, M.A.) English writer, author of "The Statics of Harmony, with an Appendix on Anticipations, Suspensions, and Transitions, illustrated by Examples from the Great Masters." London, 12mo, 1865. A reprint from the *Choir.*

BARNI (Camille). Italian comp. and violoncellist, B. Como, Jan. 18, 1762. Writer of operas, songs, chamber music, etc. D. [?]

BARON (Ernst T.) German lute-player and comp., B. Breslau, Feb. 27 1696. D. Berlin, April 12, 1760. Sonatas and other pieces for the lute are the principal works of this once-celebrated performer. Author of a work on the Lute, 1727.

BARONI-CAVALCABO (Julie). Italian pianist and comp. B. Vienna, 1805. Writer of Pf. music.

BARR (James). Scottish minor musician, B. Tarbolton, Ayr, 1781. Employed by J. Stephen, music-publisher, Wilson Street, Glasgow, 1812. Music teacher in Glasgow. Resided in Canada as farmer, 1832-1855. The "blithe Jamie Barr, frae St. Barchan's toun, who when wit gets a kingdom, he's sure o' the crown," of Tannahill. Composer of a few melodies. D. Kilbarchan, Feb. 24, 1860.

BARR (Samuel). Scottish comp. and writer, B. Glasgow, 1807. Self-taught. Teacher in Glasgow, and Precentor in Dr. Wardlaw's (Independent) Church. Prof. of Music in the Mechanic's Institute, Glasgow. D. Glasgow, May 16, 1866.

WORKS.—The Theory and Practice of Harmony and Composition, Lond., 1861 ; Singing at Sight Simplified, Glasgow, 1859. Anthems ; Psalms. Hurrah ! for the Highlands, song ; The warning, song ; The land for me, song ; The bridal gem, song ; Naebody kens ye, song. Part-songs ; Miscellaneous writings.

Barr was well known in Glasgow and the West of Scotland as a teacher of great merit, and is generally supposed to have introduced class music teaching into the West of Scotland. His work on Harmony, so far as it goes, is a good, plain exposition of the elementary rules, carefully and clearly written. Both of his theoretical works were popular. His compositions are not distinguished by any remarkable flow of melody, and, except "Naebody kens ye," are plainly and unassumingly commonplace.

BARRET (Apollon Marie Rose). French oboe-player, B. 1804. D. Paris, March 8, 1879. Author of the best "Method for the Oboe" extant. S. under Gustav Vogt.

BARRETT (John). English violin-maker, flourished about beginning of 18th century. His workshop was the "Harp and Crown" in Piccadilly, London. His violins, which are very rare, are modelled on those of Jacob Stainer, but are only of average merit. Barrett may be regarded as a second-rate maker of the so-called "London school."

BARRETT (John). English org. and comp., B. 1674. Pupil of Dr. Blow. Music teacher at Christ's Hospital [1710]. Org. at Ch. of S. Mary at Hill, 1710. D. London, 1735.

WORKS.—Music for "Love's Last Shift," 1696 ; Tunbridge Walks, 1703; Mary, Queen of Scots, 1703. Songs, etc.

BARRETT (William Alexander). English writer and org., B. Hackney, Middlesex, Oct., 15, 1836. Chorister in St. Paul's Cath., 1846-49. Pupil of W. Bayley and George Cooper, and Sir John Goss for comp. Org. at St. Andrew's, Wales Street, London, 1858-1861. Clerk of Magdalen Coll., Pentonville, 1855. Principal alto. Oxford, 1861-67. Matriculated at St. Mary's Hall, Oxford, 1866. Mus. Bac.Oxon., 1870. Assistant Vicar-choral, S. Paul's Cath., 1867-1876. Vicar-choral, do., 1876. Assistant Examiner in Music under Dr. John Hullah, 1873. Fellow of the Coll. of Org., 1871. Mem. of the Council, do., 1871. Fellow of the Royal Soc. of Literature, 1876. Mem. of the Council, do. 1879. Musical Editor of the *Morning Post*, 1869. Do. of the *Globe*, 1874-5. Editor of the *Monthly Musical Record*, 1877 and 1885. Editor of the *Orchestra and the Choir*, 1881 ; Musical Examiner to the Council of Military Education, 1883.

WORKS.—Dictionary of Musical Terms (with Dr. Stainer), London, large 8vo, 1875 ; Etymons of Musical Terms, do., London, 1876 ; English Glee and Madrigal Writers, Lond., 8vo, 1877 ; Introduction to form and Instrumentation for Beginners in Composition, 1879 ; The Chorister's Guide, 1874 ; Flowers and Festivals,

or Directions for the Floral Decoration of Churches, 1868 ; Christ before Pilate, oratorio ; Anthems ; Songs ; Papers in Musical Journals ; English Church Composers, 1882 ; Balfe—his Life and Work. Lond., 8vo, 1882.
Mr. Barrett has translated the librettos of several operas, and is otherwise well known as a lecturer and writer on musical subjects. His works on the "English Glee and Madrigal writers," and "Balfe," are most interesting, and contain just estimates of the composers noticed. The monument to Balfe in Westminster Abbey was erected through his exertions. His contributions to periodical literature are numerous, and consist of leading articles, criticisms, and notes on events of current interest. He has lectured on English Organ Music, English Anthems, Madrigals and Glees, History of the Sonata, Bishop, Mozart, Balfe, English Folk Songs, Negro Hymnology, Irish Folk Songs, etc.

BARRINGTON (Hon. Daines). English writer on Law, Music, and Natural History, B. London, 1727. Judge on Welsh Circuit, 1757. Second Justice at Chester. Retired from the Law and resided in the Temple. D. 1800.

Barrington wrote a standard work on the Statutes, a work on the possibility of reaching the North Pole, and several papers dealing with Crotch, the Wesleys, Mornington, and Mozart. See his "Miscellanies," 1781, and the Philosophical Transactions, 1780. Also author of "Experiments and Observations on the Singing of Birds," Lond., 4to, 1773.

BARROILHET (Paul). French barytone operatic vocalist, B. Bayonne, Sept. 22, 1810. D. Paris, April, 1871. Appeared in operas of Rossini, Halévy, Adam, Donizetti, Mercadante, etc.

BARRY (Charles Ainslie). English comp., org., and writer, B. Lond., June 10, 1830. Educated at Rugby and Trinity Coll., Cambridge. Instructed in music by T. A. Walmisley at Cambridge. Graduated at Cambridge. S. for the ministry, by his father's wish, and passed the voluntary Theological Examination at Cambridge. Resolved to study music in preference to theology. S. at Cologne Cons. under F. Weber (organ), E. Frank (pianoforte), and F. Hiller (composition). S. at Leipzig under Moscheles, Plaidy, and Richter, 1856-7. Married, Sept., 1857. Resided for a time at Dresden, where he received valuable hints from Reissiger. Returned to London, 1858. Org. and Choir-master at the Forest School, Leytonstone, 1858-1860. Devoted himself to musical and literary composition from 1859. Contributed under the initials "C. A. B." to the *Guardian*, *The Monthly Musical Record*, *The Athenæum*, the *Musical World*, and to the Analytical programme-books of the Crystal Palace, Philharmonic, Richter, and Bache Concerts, etc., during 1863-1885.

WORKS.—Echoes from the Old Church Aisle, andante Religioso, for the Pf. (Novello) ; Mazurka, Vivien, for Pf. (Novello) ; Tarantella, for Pf. ; Menuetto grazioso, e Barcarolle, for Pf. ; Birthday March, for Pf. ; Theme, with variations, Pf. duet ; Andante from Tschaikowsky's Quartet in D, transcribed for Pf. (Lucas & Co) ; Overture, Beatrice and Benedict, Berlioz, transcribed for Pf. duet ; Te Deum (Berlioz) arranged for voices and Pf. *Vocal Music:* Six songs with English and German words ; Come to me in my dreams, canzonet ; Sleep, little birdie, baby song (Tennyson) ; Flow, softly flow (Tennyson), song ; Elizabeth's Songs from "The Saint's Tragedy" (Kingsley) ; Four songs by Charles Kingsley ; Sweet and low ; Good night and good morning ; Father's Lullaby ; To England, song ; Beware, song ; O holy night, five-part song. The Child's Book of Praise (Novello) ; Choral Hymns for Four Voices ; The Story of the Resurrection, a cycle of hymns ; The Christmas Story, do. ; Two Hymns.—Macedon, and Annunciation, in "Hymns Ancient and Modern ;" Three Hymns, No. 132, Capstone,—No. 169, Adoration,—and No. 195, Chesterfield, in the "New Mitre Hymnal." *Works in MS.:* A Symphony for full orchestra ; Two overtures for orchestra ; Marches for orchestra ; A quartet for stringed instruments. An operetta. Several Cantatas, sacred and secular, etc.

A residence, combined with a musical education, in Germany, has infused the compositions of Mr. Barry with what is commonly known as the *advanced* or Wagnerian character ; and his writings are distinguished by their keen advocacy of the "Music of the Future." He wrote prefaces to the authorised English versions of the librettos of Wagner's "Meister-singer," and "Tristan und Isolde." His music is scholarly and well constructed, and possesses not a few original features. Mr. Barry is a highly esteemed professor of music, and his vocal music has qualities which should recommend it to the public.

BARRY (William Vipond). Irish pianist, comp. and writer, B. Bandon, March, 1827. Appeared in Belfast as pianist, 1846. Founded the Belfast Classical Harmonist Soc. Resided for a time in the "Potteries," England. He S. under Liszt, and was M.A. and Ph.D. of Göttingen University *honoris causi*. Org. of the Cath., Port of Spain, Trinidad. D. there, March 13, 1872. He comp. music for the Pf., and wrote a work entitled "Dissertation upon the Emotional Nature of Musical Art," dedicated to the late king of Hanover. His son, William II. Barry, B. Belfast, April, 1858, is a comp. and concert-giver in Dublin.

BARSANTI (Francesco). Italian musician, B. Lucca, 1690. Lived for a time in Scotland, where he published "A Collection of Old Scots Tunes, with the Bass for Violoncello or Harpsichord." Edin., 1742. He composed also concertos for violin, etc. D. [?]

BARSOTTI (Tommaso G. F.) Italian comp. and pianist, B. Florence, Sept. 4, 1786. D. Marseilles, April, 1868. Composer of light Pf. music.

BARTA (Josef). Bohemian comp., B. 1744. D. after 1803. Writer of operettas, instrumental music, lieder, etc.

BARTHE (Grat Norbert). French comp. and pianist, B. Bayonne, June 7, 1828. Writer of operas and Pf. music.

BARTHEL (Johann Christian). German comp., B. Plauen, April 19, 1776. D. Altenburg, June 10, 1831. Org. and comp. of organ, pianoforte, and vocal music.

BARTHELEMON (Francois Hippolite). French comp., B. Bordeaux, July 27, 1741. Was an officer in the Irish brigade. S. music at the request of the Earl of Kellie. Appeared in England in 1765. Leader of band of Italian opera, London. Married to Miss Mary Young. Leader at Vauxhall Gardens, 1770. Visited Dublin in 1784. D. London, July 23, 1808.

WORKS.—Jefte in Masfa, oratorio, Florence, 1776. Music for The Enchanted Girdle; The Judgment of Paris, 1768; The Election, 1774; The Maid of the Oaks, 1774; Belphegor, 1778; Orpheus, 1768; Pelopida, opera, London, 1766. String quartets; Concertos; Songs, etc.

BARTHOLDY. See MENDELSSOHN-BARTHOLDY, Felix.

BARTHOLOMEW (Ann Sheppard Mounsey, nee Mounsey). English comp. org., and pianist, B. London, April 17, 1811. Pupil of Logier, from 1817. Noticed by Spohr (in his diary) as evincing remarkable precocity, 1820. Org. at Clapton, 1828. Org. at S. Michael's, Wood Street, 1829. Org. at S. Vedast's, Foster Lane, from 1837. Associate of the Philharmonic Society, 1834. Mem. of the Royal Soc, of Musicians, 1839. Married to Mr. W. Bartholomew, April 28, 1855. Gave series of Classical Sacred Concerts, for one of which Mendelssohn comp. "Hear my Prayer," 1843 Presently engaged in teaching the organ, piano, and harmony.

WORKS.—The Nativity, an Oratorio, produced by Hullah at S. Martin's Hall, Lond., 1855; Sacred Harmony, hymns, etc., edited by Ann and Elizabeth Mounsey, 1839; The Christian Month—30 original hymns and anthems, 1842; Original Sanctuses, Kyries, and Chants, 1853; Sacred cantata, Supplication and Thanksgiving, dedicated to H.R.H. The Princess of Wales, 1864; The Young Vocalist, arranged from classical authors, 1867; Hymns of Prayer and Praise, edited and partly composed by Mrs. Mounsey Bartholomew and Miss Mounsey; Holy Thoughts, arranged as juvenile sacred songs, 1875; Thirty-four Original Tunes (hymns), London, 1883. *Part-Songs:* Six four-part songs, op. 37; Shun delays; Take care; Tell me, where is Fancy bred; Before thine eyelids close; Three 4-part songs, in Tonic Sol-fa notation, 1870; A wreath for Christmas. *Songs:* A Farewell; Mary, meet me there; When day has fled; The bridesmaid; The warrior's love; When should lovers breathe their vows?; The northern star; Gently will I glide; The wedding day; The maid who vowed to love me; Enchanting maid; Lady mine; Six Songs of Remembrance. Six vocal duets in canon, 1836; The Erl King; Fair Daffodils; The Daguerrotype; The Nautilus cradle; Lyrics for Youth—six songs; Six Songs, composed for the Royal Society of Female Musicians; Life is full of perils; The winds are sleeping; The castanet's gay sound; Now I am thine; Moonlight; Lily of the vale; The soul's release; The uncertainty of life; The Rose; Stars of the summer night; Charming maiden; Constancy; I hear his horn; Speak gently; The praise of a country life; If all the world; One by one; Days gone by; The Cherry Earrings; Nearer my God to Thee; Flow, murmuring stream; The fountain; Angry words; Questions; Yesterday and to-morrow; Ten years ago; The Merry Beggars; The water rushing; The fortune-teller; If I could only say; Dreaming and waking; Only a day; Song of a sprite; Together; The tambourine player; O say, fond heart; Six Songs [from Shakespeare, Mackay, Heber, Poe, Hood, etc.], London, 1882. Org. and Pf. works.

It is somewhat remarkable that music, as a means of emotional expression, should have found so few exponents among women. That an art so graceful in itself and so eminently suited to the refined capabilities of women should find less favour with them than the sister art of poetry seems phenomenal, and indicative to a considerable extent of the disadvantages presented by the technical requirements of musical composition. Poetry has been graced by many female writers of rare merit, and can boast of numerous lights who take foremost places in the second rank of poesy. From Sappho to Mrs. Browning there have flourished many female writers who have sweetened the art with their productions, and earned the applause of posterity. In music, we can only record the names of a very few females who take high rank as composers; and of these Mrs. Bartholomew may be placed with the most eminent. Mrs. Bartholomew is a fairly good example of the first-rate class of female talent in musical composition, and she exhibits in her works all the beauties and defects incident to such class. Her part-songs are well-written pieces, and many of her ballads are conceived in that trivial-pretty fashion so common in the works of female writers. We are inclined, on the whole, to base her claim to recognition on her many really meritorious concerted vocal pieces. These are written in a graceful, but withal able manner, and are effective without requiring a great degree of skilful interpretation.

BARTHOLOMEW (William). English chemist, writer, and violinist. B. London, 1793. Married to Miss Ann S. Mounsey, April 28, 1853. Chiefly known as the adapter of the librettos of Mendelssohn's works. D. London, Aug. 18, 1867.

WORKS.—English version of the words of Mendelssohn's Antigone, Athalie, Ædipus, Lauda Sion, Walpurgisnacht, Loreley, Elijah, Christus; Spohr's Jessonda; Costa's Eli and Naaman; Bartholomew's The Nativity, etc., etc.

Mr. Bartholomew is better known for his connection with Mendelssohn than for any eminence gained by works of his own production. His intercourse with Mendelssohn was friendly and intimate, and he was mentioned by him in terms of respect. His careful selection of scripture passages for "Elijah" is highly creditable to his good taste. Mr. Bartholomew has written, in addition to the works above mentioned, many hymns of considerable merit.

BARTLEMAN (James). English bass vocalist, B. Westminster, Sept. 19, 1769. S. under Dr. B. Cooke. Bass chorister at the Ancient Music Concerts, 1788-91. Principal bass at the Vocal Concerts, 1791. Do. at the Concert of Ancient Music, 1795. D. London, April 15, 1821.

This vocalist should have his name enshrined among the benefactors of Music. He revived, and by his magnificent performance, created an interest in the music of Henry Purcell which lived for many years. Bartleman was possessed of a magnificent bass voice, and rendered Purcell's music in a style then considered unsurpassable.

BARTLETT (John). English comp., B. in latter half of 16th century. Wrote a "Book of Ayres, with a Triplicitie of Musicke, whereof the First Part is for the Lute or Orpharion, and the Viole de Gamba, and 4 Parts to Sing: the

Second Part is for 2 Trebles to sing to the Lute and Viole ; the Third Part is for the Lute and one Voice, and the Viole de Gamba," London, 1606. Bartlett was a Bachelor of Music, Oxford, in 1610, but his biography is unknown.

BARTOLI (Padre, Erasmo). Italian comp., B. near Naples, 1606. D. Naples, July 14, 1656. Writer of oratorios, cantatas, masses, motets, psalms, etc.

BASEVI (Abramo). Italian theoretical and historical writer, B. Livorno, Dec, 1818. Has comp. operas, and owns *Boccherini*, an Italian musical journal.

BASILI (Francesco), or Basily. Italian comp., B. Loretto, Ancona, Feb., 1766. S. under Jannaconi. Chap.-master at Foligno. Chap.-master at Macerata. Do. at S. Peter's, Rome, 1837. Director of Milan Cons., 1827. Was for a short time an opera vocalist; *début*, Milan, 1787. D. Mar. 25, 1850.
WORKS.—La Sansone, oratorio, 1824. *Operas :* La Locandiera ; D'Achille nell' assedio di Troja, 1798 ; Il Ritorno d'Ulysse, 1799 ; Lo Stravagante e il Dissipatori, 1802 ; L'Ira d'Achille, 1817 ; L'Orfana egiziana, 1817 ; Gl' Illenesi, 1818 ; Il Califfo e la Schiava. Requiem for Jannaconi, 1816. Psalms ; Miserere ; Motets. Organ Music ; Quartets for stringed instruments ; Miscellaneous Church Music.

BASSANI (Giovanni Battista). Italian comp. and violinist, B. Padua, 1657. Chap.-master at Bologna Cath. Chap.-master at Ferrara. Mem. of the "Accademia delle Morte," Ferrara. Director of Accademia dei Filarmonici, Bologna, 1682. D. Ferrara, 1716.
WORKS.—Op. 1. Sonata da Camera, for stringed insts., 1693 ; op. 2. L'Armonia delle Sirene, cantata amorose musicali a voce solo, 1692 ; op. 3. Cantata for solo voice, 1698 ; op. 4. La Moralita Armonica, cantata for 2 and 3 voices, 1700 ; op. 5. Sonata for 2 violins and bass ; op. 6. Affetti canori, cantate ed ariette, 1697 ; op. 7. Eco armonica delle muse, cantata for solo voice, 1694 ; op. 8. Resi Armonici in Motteti a voci sola con violini, 1691 ; op. 9. Armonici Entusiasmi di Davide, 1695-1698 ; op. 10. Salmi di Completa, a tre e quattro voci, 1691 ; op. 11. Concerti Sacri (Motets), 1697 ; op. 12. Motets for solo voices, 1700 ; op. 13. Armonie Festive, 1696 (English edition, Harmonia Festiva, etc., Lond., fo. n. d.) ; op. 14. Amorosi sentimenti di cantate a voce solo, 1696 ; op. 15. Armoniche Fantasie di cantate amorose a voce sola ; op. 16. La Musa Armonica, cantata for solo voice, 1695 ; op. 17. La Sirena Amorosa, cantata for voice and violin, 1699 ; op. 18. Three masses for 4 and 5 voices, 1698 ; op. 19. Languidezza Amorosa, cantata for solo voice, 1698 ; op. 20. Mass for 4 voices, 1698 ; op. 21. Psalms for 2, 3, 4, and 5 voices, 1699 ; op. 22. Lagrime armoniche, ossia il Vespero de defunti, for 4 voices, 1699 ; op. 23. Le Notti lugubri concertate ne' responsori dell' uffezio de' morti, 1700 ; 24. Davide Armonico espresso ne' salmi di mezzo, for 2 and 3 voices, 1700 ; op. 25. Compietori correnti a quattro voci concertate, 1701 ; op. 26. Antifone Sacre, for solo voice, 1701 ; op. 27. Motetti sacre a voce solo con violini, 1701 ; op. 28. Cantata Amorose a voce solo, 1701 ; op. 29. Corona di fiori musicali . . . 1702 ; op. 30. (?) ; op. 31. Cantata Amorose a voce sola con violini, 1705 ; op. 32. Mass for 4 voices, 1710, Falaride, opera, 1684 ; Amorosa preda di Paride, opera, 1684 ; Alarico, opera, 1685 ; Ginevra, 1690 ; Il Conte di Bacheville, 1696. Church music in MS , etc.

The general characteristics of Bassani's music—or rather the small portion known —are extreme delicacy in the management of pathetic effects, careful construction, and uniform religious feeling. We are unable correctly to state the degree to which his music is now cultivated in Italy or anywhere.

BASSANTIN (James). Scottish astronomer of the 16th century, D. 1568. Author of " Musica Secundum Platonem," in his collected writings.

BASSI (Luigi). Italian barytone vocalist, B. Pesaro, 1766 ; S. under Morandi. *Début* as sopranist, 1779. *Début* at Prague in Paisiello's " Re Teodoro," 1784. Resided at Vienna, 1806-14. Returned to Prague, 1814. Manager of the opera at Dresden, 1815. D. Dresden, Sept. 13, 1825.

Bassi was one of the finest singers of his time, and was selected by Mozart as a suitable vocalist for the part of Don Giovanni, if, indeed, the part was not written to suit his voice.

BASSINI (Carlo). Italian teacher and violinist, B. Piedmont, 1812. Appeared in South America as violinist with an opera company. Settled in New York as a teacher. D. at Irvington, New Jersey, Nov. 26, 1870.

WORKS.—The Art of Singing, 1857 ; Method for the Barytone, 1868 ; Method for the Tenor, 1866; Melodic Exercises, 1865. Songs.

BASTIAANS (J. G.) Dutch org. and comp., B. Wilp, 1812. D. 1874. Writer of organ music, chorales, motets, etc.

BASTON (Josquin). Flemish comp. of 16th century, comp. chansons, motets, and other vocal music.

BATCHELDER (John C.) American org. and pianist, B. in Topsham Vt., 1852. S. at Berlin under Haupt, Ehrlich, and Loeschhorn for four years. Teacher of organ and piano in the Detroit Cons. of Music, and Org. of S. Paul's Episcopal Ch.

He has given between thirty and forty organ recitals in Detroit, and played also publicly in many large cities, Philadelphia, Pittsburg, Toledo, and at other points.

BATES (Joah). English musician, and one of the founders of the Handel Commemoration, B. Halifax, 1740. Instructed in music by Hartley, org. at Rochdale ; and R. Wainwright, org., Manchester. Resided for a time at Eton and Cambridge. Private Secretary to the Earl of Sandwich. Established the Concert of Ancient Music, 1776. Cond. of the Ancient Concerts. Founded Handel Commemoration (with Sir W. W. Wynn and Viscount Fitzwilliam), 1783. D. London, June 8, 1799.

The "Handel Commemoration" with which Bates is chiefly identified was, in its time, a much talked of enterprize. No such gathering of a large body of musicians had ever before taken place, and the extensive arrangements undertaken in connection with it caused sufficient stir to assure its success. The vocalists who held the principal parts on the occasion of the first public performance were—Miss Cantelo, Miss Abrams, Mdlle. Mara, Miss Harwood, Sig. Bartolini and Tasca ; and Messrs. Harrison, Dyne, Champness, Bellemy, Corfe, Norris, Knyvett, Clerk, Reinhold, and Matthieson. Bates conducted, and the affair took enormously. The first performance was in Westminster Abbey, on May 26, 1784. Second and third performances were given on May 27 and 29. The programme included "The Messiah," The Dettingen Te Deum, a Coronation Anthem, and miscellaneous selections from Handel's works.

As regards Bates it can be said that he was a famous conductor, and in every respect a musician of great knowledge and administrative ability. He did not compose anything so far as we can learn, but appears to have been widely known among musicians of every grade during his lifetime. He is somewhat roughly handled by the Scotch poet, A. Macdonald, in " Monitory Madrigals to Musical Amateurs," Nos. 3 and 4, contained in his Miscellaneous Works, 1791.

BATES (Sarah). See HARROP (Sarah).

BATES (William). English comp., B. about the beginning of the 18th century. Connected during his life with Marylebone Gardens. Instructed Ann Cately in music and singing, 1760. Fined and accused, together with a Sir Francis Blake Delaval, of using illegal means of disposing or selling the person of Ann Cately, 1763. (See CATELY.) Date of death unknown.

WORKS.—Glees ; Songs sung at Marybone Gardens, 1768 ; Music for several farces as the " Theatrical Candidates ;" Catches and Canons, etc.

BATESON (Thomas). English comp. and org., B. [?] Org. of Chester Cath., 1599. Resided in Ireland for many years, from 1608 (?). Org. of Christ Ch. Cath., Dublin, 1608 (?). Mus. Bac., Dublin. (The first on whom the degree was conferred by the University). D. [unknown.]

WORKS.—First Set of Madrigals, 1604 ; Second Set of Madrigals, 1618 ; Two Madrigals in the "Triumphs of Oriana."

This composer, who was a madrigal writer of great power, is unfortunately shrouded in much gloom where his life is concerned. His two books of madrigals are the chief memorials we possess of a writer who can be classed with such men as Wilbye and Weelkes without detracting greatly from their honour by such association. His madrigals are not many, but they are beautifully worked out pieces; being no less well constructed than very melodious. His first book of madrigals was reprinted by the Musical Antiquarian Society in 1846.

BATHE (William). Irish Jesuit and writer, B. Dublin, 1564. Professor of Languages at the University of Salamanca. D. Madrid, June 17, 1614. Wrote "A Brief Introduction to the true Arte of Musicke," Lond., 4to, 1584. Another edition was issued with title of "A Briefe Introduction to the Skill of Song, etc." Lond., n. d.

BATISTE (Antoine Edouard). French org., Prof., and comp., B. Paris, March 28, 1820. S. at Paris Cons. under Leborne, Bienaimé, Le Couppey, Halévy, and Benoist. Gained second prize for solfeggi, 1832. Gained first do., 1833. Gained second prize for harmony and accomp., 1836. First prize do, 1837. Second prize for counterpoint and fugue, and second prize for the organ, 1838. First prizes for both, 1839. Gained Second Grand Prix de Rome, 1840. Prof. of singing at the Cons. from 1836. Org. of the Ch. of St. Nicholas des Champs, 1842. Org. of St. Eustache, Paris, 1855. D. Paris, Nov. 9, 1876.

WORKS.—Instruction Books for Singing. Pf. music. Organ music, consisting of Offertoires, Sonatas, Fugues, Fantasias, Voluntaries, etc. Songs. Church music, etc.

This organist was accounted among the best of modern performers in the brilliant style. His compositions are, on the whole, good and serviceable if somewhat showy pieces for the organ. His andante movements are no doubt the most adapted for church use, and they are not only very melodious but also very skilfully constructed. Batiste endeavoured to procure from his instrument effects which can only be said to belong legitimately to the orchestra. The success with which orchestral effects are imitated on the organ is marvellous. Skilful organists seem to produce the more broad orchestral colourings with the greatest ease. Overtures are transcribed and rendered in a style combining neatness with fulness, but the delicate gradations of light and shade are not with the present mechanism perfectly attainable. Batiste's organ music is noisy, brilliant, and not so sacred and dignified as church music is expected to be.

BATISTIN (Johann B.) *or Struck.* German comp., B. Florence [?]. D. Paris, Dec. 9, 1755. Writer of operas, etc.

BATTAILLE (Charles Amable). French bass vocalist, B. Nantes, Sept. 20, 1822. D. Paris, May 2, 1872.

BATTANCHON (Felix). French comp. and violoncellist, B. Paris, April 9, 1814. Writer of Studies, duets, rondos, and other pieces for 'cello, with accomp.

BATTEN (Adrian). English comp. and org., B. in latter portion of 16th century (1585-90). S. under Holmes of Winchester Cath. Vicar-choral of Westminster Abbey, 1614. Vicar-choral of S. Paul's Cath., 1624. Org. do., 1624. D. middle of the 17th century (1640?).

WORKS.—*Anthems:* Hear my Prayer; O Praise the Lord; Deliver us, O Lord (in Boyce's Cathedral Music); Te Deum, Benedictus, Jubilate, Kyrie, etc., in D (Novello); Thirty-four Anthems (words only—Clifford); Twenty-four Anthems in Barnard's Cathedral Music.

Batten was an inferior composer, and can by no means be classed with such men as Lawes, Hilton, Gibbons, or others who were his contemporaries. The anthems published in "Boyce" (and by Messrs. Novello) are favourable examples of his style.

BATTISHILL (Jonathan). English comp., B. London, May, 1738. Chor. in S. Paul's Cath., 1747. Articled to W. Savage, by whom he was ill treated. Wrote for Sadler's Wells Theatre. Deputy org., under Boyce, at the Chap.-

Royal. Cond. and accompanist at Covent Garden Theatre. Married to Miss Davies (the original " Madge " in " Love in a Village"), 1763. Org. of United parishes of S. Clement, Eastcheap, and S. Martin Orgar, 1764. Org. of Christ Church, Newgate Street, 1764. Resigned cond. of Covent Garden. Devoted himself to teaching and composition. Presented with gold medal by the Nobleman's Catch-club, 1771. Lost taste for music and became addicted to drink, on the death of his wife, 1777. D. Islington, Dec. 10, 1801.

WORKS.—Almena, an opera (with M. Arne), Drury Lane, 1764 ; The Rites of Hecate, a musical entertainment, 1764. Collection of Twelve Songs. Set of Sonatas for the Harpsichord. 2 Collections of Glees, 1776. *Anthems:* Behold, how good and joyful ; Call to remembrance ; I will magnify Thee, O God ; O Lord, look down from heaven; Six Anthems and ten Chants, ed. by Page, 1804. *Glees:* Amidst the myrtles ; Come, bind my hair ; Again my mournful sighs. Music for Charles Wesley's Hymns. Chants. Collection of Catches. Music (with Baildon) for Lee's Dramatic Entertainments, 1777. Songs for 3 and 4 voices, Lond., 1783; Miscellaneous songs, anthems. glees, etc.

The foregoing list of works does not represent one-third of Battishill's compositions. His anthems are now only occasionally sung, and then only in provincial churches. The simple grace of this composer has long since given way to the more laboured works of modern times.

Battishill was an organist of most sterling qualities, and was specially good at extemporaneous playing. Handel's music also drew out his powers to their fullest extent, and Dr. Busby speaks of him as equalling Handel himself in his exquisite rendering of the organ concertos, etc. The following estimate of his powers is taken from Dr. Busby's "History of Music," vol. ii. Speaking of "The Rites of Hecate" :—"In the airs of this piece he demonstrated a strength and originality of imagination, and, in the adjustment of his score, an elegance and mastery that delighted the general ear, and excited the admiration of every musical critic. . . . In the composition of catches and glees, this master exhibited great resources of imagination, and an abundant store of science and ingenuity. . . . The productions of this ornament of his day are marked by a peculiar strength of conception, considerable originality and sweetness, and fine harmonical adjustment. His anthems are characterized by the learning and sober majesty of Boyce's best cathedral compositions ; and his choruses in *Almena* may be compared with those in the celebrated serenata of his early friend and favourite master."

BATTISTA (Vincenzo). Italian comp., B. Naples, Oct. 5, 1823. D, Naples, Nov. 14, 1873. Operatic writer.

BATTMAN (Jacques Louis). French org., pianist, and comp., B. Massevaux, Aug. 25, 1818. Composer of over 200 works of medium quality for organ, piano, etc.

BATTON (Désiré Alexandre). French comp., B. Paris, Jan. 2, 1797. S. under Cherubini at the Cons., 1806-17. Travelled in Germany and Italy, 1818-23. D. Paris, Oct. 16, 1855.

WORKS.—Operas, Cantatas, etc., now for the most part unknown or forgotten.

BATTU (Pantaleon). French violinist and comp., B. Paris, 1799. D. Paris, Jan. 17, 1870.

BAUDIOT (Charles Nicolas). French violoncellist and comp., B. Nancy, March 29, 1773. Performer in the King's Chapel, 1816. Prof. of 'cello at the Cons., 1822. D. Sept. 26, 1849.

WORKS.—Two Concertos for 'cello, and orch., opp. 19, 20 ; Trio for strings, op. 3 ; Duets for 2 'cellos, op. 5 and 7 ; Fantasias, Pot-pourri, etc., for 'cello ; Sonatas for 'cello ; Trios for Pf., 'cello, and horn ; Méthode de Violoncello pour l'usage du Conservatoire, etc.

BAUDRON (Antoine Laurent.) French violinist and comp., B. Amiens, May 16, 1743. D, 1834.

BAUERSACHS (Carl Friedrich). German violoncellist and basset-horn player, B. at Pegnitz, June 4, 1770. D. Dec. 14, 1845.

BAULDUIN (Noel) *Balduin*. Belgian comp., B. towards latter part of 15th century. D. 1529. Writer of church music.

BAUMANN (Emanuel). German comp. and pianist, B. 1825. Writer of Pf. music, operettas, songs, etc.

BAUMBACH (Friedrich August). German comp. and writer, B. 1753. D. Leipzig, Nov. 30, 1813. Composer of Pf. music, collector of songs, etc.

BAUMFELDER (Friedrich A. W.) German comp. and pianist, B. Dresden, May 28, 1836. Writer of overtures, concertos, Pf. music, etc.

BAUMGARTEN (Carl Friedrich). German org. and comp., B. 1754. Appeared in London about the end of the 18th century. Org. in Lutheran Chap. in the Savoy, London. Leader at the opera, Covent Garden Theatre. Leader of Duke of Cumberland's private band. D. London, 1824.

Baumgarten wrote music for several pantomimes, etc.,'as also a work on musical theory.

BAYLEY (William). English org. and comp., B. [1810] Vicar choral, S. Paul's. Org. of S. John's, Southwark. D. London, 1858. Comp. a number of songs, cavatinas, and other vocal music, and was an organist of some ability.

BAYLY (Rev. Anslem),) English writer and divine, B. 1719. Matriculated at Exeter Coll., Oxford, 1740. Lay vicar at Westminster Abbey, 1741. Gent. Chap. Roy., 1741. Priest, do., 1744. B. C. L., 1749. D. C. L., Oxford, 1764. Sub-dean of Chap. Roy., 1764. D. 1792.

WORKS.—Practical Treatise on Singing and Playing with just expression and real elegance, London, 1771 ; The Alliance of Musick, Poetry, and Oratory, 1789; The Sacred Singer, containing an Essay on Grammar, the requisites of singing cathedral compositions, etc., Lond., 8vo, 1771. Collection of Anthems used in His Majesty's Chapel . . . 8vo, 1769. Sermons, etc.

BAYLY (Thomas Haynes). English lyrical poet, B. London, 1798. D. April 22, 1829.

The life of this latterly unfortunate poet seems to have been of a nature sufficiently varied to furnish him with the various themes, melancholy and cheerful, on which he expended so much careful finish. As he is the founder of a style or departure in English ballad writing, it will be necessary to notice him at more length than, as an ordinary poet, he would have been entitled to. The departure in ballad writing spoken of is that in which the poet deals closely with events in every-day life which are personal in character. The domestic side of man is taken up, his social and homely feelings are appealed to in what are known as *vers de société*. Though Bayly has had numerous imitators, we think that on the whole he has been more successful than any of his followers in the treatment of such subjects. This school of poetry, which was born, but has not died, with the *Annuals*, has been greatly instrumental in lowering the artistic tone of our national songs. The style of the poetry, originally healthy enough, has gradually been degenerating into an empty, glittering sentimentality. Bayly's songs were originally set by himself, Bishop, J. P. Knight, A. Lee, Loder, and others of sound attainments. The poetry was good, and the music often so. Such collections as—"Songs of the Old Chateau," "Songs for Winter Nights," "Songs of the Grave and Gay," were really good. In our day this has been reversed ; the poetry is sickly and the music dolorous. The melancholy side of Bayly, as displayed in " Long, long ago," " She wore a wreath of roses," etc., has in present times been carried to excess, and the market is deluged with productions of the most effete nature, having for subject matter such stories as the ascent to heaven of departed souls, *via* a sunbeam, or the death-scenes of pauper children, either in cathedrals or on the gutter. Bayly also wrote plays and some novels, all long since forgotten.

BAYR (Georg). Bohemian flute-player and comp., B. 1773. D. Vienna, 1833. Wrote concertos, etc. for his instrument.

BAZILLE (August Ernest). French comp., B. Paris, May 27, 1828. Writer of operettas, songs, etc.

BAZIN (Francois Emanuel Joseph). French operatic comp., B. Marseilles, Sept. 4, 1816. D. Paris, July 2, 1878.

BAZZINI (Antonio). Italian violinist and comp., B Brescia, Nov. 24, 1818. Played throughout Italy, France, Germany, and Belgium. Prof. of Comp. at Milan Cons., 1876.
WORKS.—Concertos, Variations, and Transcriptions for the Violin, etc.
Bazzini was long a favourite with the more vulgar portion of the musical public on the Continent, and succeeded in persuading them, as he had persuaded himself, that he was a fiddle-god. Like Paganini and others of that school, he contrived to delight his audiences more by mechanical means than by those usually regarded as highly academic.

BEALE (John). English comp. and pianist, B. London, [1676 ?]Pupil of J. B. Cramer. Mem. of Phil. Soc., 1720. Prof. of Pf. at R A. M. Teacher in London, and Director of Music at Argyle Rooms. D. [?]
Beale was a most respectable professor, and wrote a large quantity of indifferent songs and Pianoforte music, none of which is now in existence. He wrote " Complete Guide to the Art of Playing the German Flute,"...fo. n. d.

BEALE (Thomas Willert) *Walter Maynard.* English comp. and writer, B. London, 1831. Called to the bar at Lincoln's Inn, 1863. Mem. of firm of Cramer & Co.
WORKS.—The Enterprising Impresario, London, 1867 ; Articles in *Gentleman's Magazine, Once a Week,* etc. *Songs:* Ah ! would that I could weep ; I think of thee still ; In the silence of the night ; 'Tis home where'er thou art ; The Carabineers ; Let me stay ; Lover's vows ; Macbeth, dramatic scena ; O, say once more, I love thee ; Regret ; Thy voice in tender accents ; 'Twas but a word ; When those bright hours ; Why did we meet, etc., etc. ; Concerted vocal music : Pf. music, etc.

BEALE (Thurley). English bass vocalist, B. Royston, Hertfordshire, April 23, 1840. Joined J. Hullah's Choral Soc. in London, 1864. Chor. in S. Andrew's, Wells Street, London. S. under Joseph Barnby. Chor. at S. Paul's Cath.
Beale has sung at nearly every town of importance in England and Scotland, and is justly regarded as one of the leading English basses.

BEALE (William). English comp., B. Landrake, Cornwall, Jan. 1, 1784. S. under Dr. Arnold and R. Cooke. Gained prize cup from Madrigal Soc. 1813. Engaged in London as teacher of music, 1813-54. D. London, May 3, 1854.
WORKS.—Madrigals, etc., for 3, 4, and 5 voices, Lond., 1815 ; Collection of Glees and Madrigals, 1820. *Madrigals:* Awake, sweet muse (prize), 1813 ; What ho ! what ho ! 1816 ; Come let us join the roundelay ; This pleasant month of May. *Glees* (edited by E. Plater, S. Lucas & Co.) : I'll enjoy the present time ; How soft the music ; By the side of a grove ; Scenes of woe ; Lo ! the Pride of the Village is dead ; How often from the sleep ; Oh ! by yonder mossy seat ; The humble tenant ; Ode to the memory of Samuel Webbe ; Thou herald of the blushing morn ; When Fanny, blooming fair ; Again the balmy zephyr (round) ; Sing unto the Lord (canon), etc. [1879]. Songs, etc.
Beale was one of the last of the long roll of eminent English glee composers. The glee, as a thoroughly English species of composition, is daily receiving less attention, and it is very probable that Beale and Bishop will never be succeeded. The glees of Beale are fresh and agreeable compositions, graced with all the refine-

ment and artistic skill usually found in such works, and they are in many respects worthy to be named with the best creations of the older writers.

BEARD (John). English tenor vocalist, B. 1716. Chor. in Chap. Roy. under B. Gates. *Début* at Covent Garden in 1736. Sang at Drury Lane, 1737. Married to Lady Henrietta Herbert, widow of Lord Edward Herbert, 1739. Afterwards married to Miss Rich (daughter of Rich of Covent Garden Theatre), 1759. One of the proprietors of Covent Garden Theatre, 1761. Retired from public life, 1768. D. Hampton, London, February 4, 1791.

Beard was for long the leading English tenor vocalist, and was, together with Harrison, one of the leading exponents of Handel's music. He was also famous as a ballad vocalist.

BEARDMORE (Mrs.) See PARKE (Maria H).

BEATTIE (James, LL.D.) Scottish poet and writer, B. Laurencekirk, Oct. 25, 1735. S. at Aberdeen University. Schoolmaster in Kincardine, 1753-58. Prof. of Moral Philosophy, Marischal Coll., Aberdeen, 1760. Married to Miss Mary Dun, 1767. D. Aberdeen, Aug. 18, 1803.

WORKS.—Essays on Poetry and Music as they affect the Mind, etc., London, 1776; second edit., 1779. Letter to the Rev. Hugh Blair, D.D., on the Improvement of Psalmody in Scotland, 8vo, 1778; another edit., Edin., 12mo, 1829; Poems, Ethical works, etc.

The essay on "Poetry and Music" was translated into French. His eldest son, JAMES HAY BEATTIE (B. Aberdeen, 1768—D. 1790) was a violinist, and amateur musician of great promise.

BEAULIEU (Marie Désiré), or *Martin*. French comp. and writer, B. Paris, April 11, 1791. Received first instructions in music when 7 years old. S. at the Cons. under R. Kreutzer and Méhul. Gained second prize for comp. at Cons. D. Paris, Dec., 1863.

WORKS.—*Operas:* Anacreon; Psyché et l'Amour, 1833; Philadelphie, 1855. *Cantatas, oratorios, etc.:* Sapho, 1813; Jeanne d'Arc, 1817; L' Hymne du Matin, oratorio, 1843; L'Immortalité de l'âme, 1851. Church music—Miserere, 1812; Laudate Dominum, for 2 choirs, 1813; Domine Salvum, for 5 voices, 1814; Requiem Mass, solo, chorus and orch., 1819; Masses, etc. Pf. music, consisting of rondos, fantasias, sonatas, etc. Mémoire sur ce qui reste de la Musique de l'ancienne Grèce dans les premiers chants de l'Eglise. 8vo, 1856. Mémoire sur le caractère que doit avoir la musique d'Eglise...8vo, 1858. Mémoire sur l'origine de la Musique. Niort, 8vo, 1859.

BEAUHARNAIS (Hortense Eugenie). See HORTENSE.

BEAUMARCHAIS (Pierre Augustin Caron de). French dramatist, B. Paris, Jan. 24, 1732. D. Paris, May 17, 1799.

Beaumarchais is noticed here as having written the comedies of "The Barber of Seville" and "The Marriage of Figaro," from which were drawn the librettos of two most successful operas, written respectively by Rossini and Mozart. Was music-master to the daughters of Louis XV.

BEAUMONT (John). English musician, published "The New Harmonic Magazine, or Compendious Repository of Sacred Music, in full Score." Lond., fo. 1801.

BECHER (Alfred Julius). German comp.. B. Manchester, 1803. Educated at Universities of Heidelberg, Berlin, etc. Resided at Vienna as Editor of the "Radikale," a democratic sheet, which was filled with seditious articles by Becher. Shot at Vienna for sedition, Nov. 23, 1848.

WORKS.—Op. 1. Songs for solo voice and Piano; op. 2. Lyrical pieces for the Pf. ; op. 3. Six poems for voice and Pf. ; op. 5. Rondo for the Pf. ; op. 6. Six songs for voice and Pf. ; op. 7. Three sonatas for Pf. solo ; op. 8. Original theme for Pf. ; op. 9. Monologue for Pf. ; op. 10. Six Songs for voice and Pf. ; op. 11.

Sonata for Pf. ; op. 18. Nine pieces for the Pf. A Symphony ; String Quartets ; Writings on various musical subjects, etc.

BECHSTEIN (Friedrich Wilhelm Carl). German piano-maker, B. Gotha, June, 1826. One of the most extensive Pf. manufacturers on the Continent. The instruments of this firm have long taken a leading place among those of recent makers, and have been awarded not a few prizes at various exhibitions.

BECK (Franz). German comp., B. Mannheim, 1731. Resided chiefly in Paris and Bordeaux, where he was a teacher of some note. D. Bordeaux, 1809.

WORKS.—Symphonies ; Pandore, a melodrama, 1786; Quartets for strings; Church music.

BECKEL (J. C.) American pianist and writer, has published the following works :—Amateur's School for the Piano (Ditson, Boston, n.d.) ; New and Improved Operatic Instruction-Book for the Pianoforte (Do.) ; Amateur's Organ School (Do.); Amateur Melodeon or Reed Organ School (Do.); Church Manual, a Collection of Psalms, etc. (Do.) ; The Psalter, a Collection of Sacred Music (Do.) ; Philadelphia Anthem Book (Do.), etc.

BECKER (Carl Ferdinand). German writer and teacher, B. Leipzig, 1804. S. under Schneider and Schicht. Org. of the Nicolai-Kirche, Leipzig. Prof. at Leipzig Cons. D. Leipzig, October 26, 1877.

WORKS.—Systematisch-chronologishe Darstellung der musikalischen Literatur von der fruhesten bis auf die neueste zeit, Leipzig, 1836; Die Hausmusik in Deutschland in dem 16-ten, 17-ten, and 18-ten Jahrhunderte, Materialien zu einer Geschichte desselbenes, etc., 1840 (Materials for a history of chamber music in Germany in the 16th, 17th, and 18th centuries); Die Tonwerke des XVI. und XVII. Jahrhunderts, oder Systematisch-chronologische zusammenstellung der in diesen zwei Jahrhunderten gedruckten Musikalien, Leipzig, 4to, 1847 (Catalogue of music printed during the 16th and 17 h centuries) ; Alphabetisch und chronologisch geordnetes Verzeichniss einer samml ng von musikalischen Schriften ein Beitrag zur Literatur-Geschichte der Musik, 1847 (Catalogue of the works contained in his own collection) ; Die Tonkünstler des neunzehnten Jahrhunderts, ein Kalendarisches Handbuch zu Kunzt-geschichte, 1849, etc.

The foregoing works are valuable contributions to musical literature, and are marked by much painstaking industry and veracity. Becker was notable as being a skilled bibliographer, and his collection of music was extensive, and contained many rarities.

BECKER (Constantin Julius). German comp,, B. Freiberg, Feb. 3, 1811. S. under Anacker. Resided at Leipzig as assistant editor (with Schumann) of the "Neue Zeitschrift für Musik," 1835. Teacher of singing at Dresden, 1843. D. Oberlössnitz, Feb. 26, 1859.

WORKS.—The Siege of Belgrade, opera, Leipzig, 1848 ; Collections of Lieder, opp. 2, 5. 6, 8, 14, 17 ; Symphony, 1843 ; Serenade for violin and 'cello, op. 34 ; A vocal school for men, and Duets for female voices ; Music for Pf., etc. ; A work on Harmony, trans. into English as " A Concise Treatise on Harmony, Accompaniment, and Composition." Lond., 1845.

BECKER *(Johann). German violinist, B. Mannheim, 1836. S. under Kettenus and Alard. Début as violinist in 1847. Leader of Mannheim orch. Appeared at Paris with some success, 1859. Played at Monday Popular Concerts, London. Cond. the Philharmonic Concerts. Settled at Florence, 1866.

Since about 1866 Becker has been a member of the celebrated string quartet party, located at Florence, and named the "Florentiner Quartet," whose playing of music for stringed instruments is announced as superb. The other members of the party are Masi, Chiostri, and Hilpert. Becker has comp. music for the violin.

BECKER (Paul). German pianist and comp., presently residing in Chicago, where he settled about 1858. His works consist principally of arrangements and transcriptions. He is best known in America as a pianist of much ability.

BECKET (Thomas a'). American org. and teacher, B. Philadelphia, Pa., 1843. Teacher in Girard Coll., Philadelphia. Charter Member of the American Coll. of Musicians. Best known as an accompanist, in which capacity he has travelled with some of the leading artists in America. Comp. music for Pf. and org., and songs.

BECKWITH (John Christmas). English comp. and org., B. Norwich, Dec. 25, 1759. S. under Philip Hayes. Org. of Norwich Cath., 1780. Org. of S. Peter's Mancroft, Norwich, 1780. Mus. Bac., Oxon., 1803. Instructed Thomas Vaughan, the vocalist, in singing. D. Norwich, June 3, 1809.

WORKS.—The First Verse of every Psalm of David, with an ancient or modern chant in score, adapted as much as possible to the sentiment of each Psalm. Lond., 1808. *Anthems*: The Lord is very great ; My soul is weary of life ; Six Anthems in Score, for 1, 2, 3, 4, and 5 voices (Clementi). *Glees*: Hark, o'er the waves ; The Chimney Sweepers. Pianoforte Music and Songs ; Concertos and other pieces for the organ.

Beckwith was one of the best organists of his time, and a highly esteemed vocal instructor. Some of his secular vocal music is melodious in character, but otherwise his music is dull. He was succeeded by his son, John Charles Beckwith [1788-1819] at Norwich Cathedral. The book of chants contains an introductory article on chanting.

BECWARZOUSKY (Anton Franz). Bohemian org. and comp., B. 1750. D. Berlin, May 17, 1823.

BEDFORD (Arthur). English divine and writer, B. Tiddenham, Gloucester, September, 1668. S. at Oxford. D. London, 1745.

WORKS.—The Temple of Musick, or an Essay concerning the Method of Singing the Psalms of David in the Temple before the Babylonish Captivity, wherein the Musick of our Cathedrals is vindicated...Bristol, 8vo, 1706 ; The Great Abuse of Musick, containing an account of the use and design of Musick among the Antient Jews, Greeks, Romans, etc., Lond., 8vo, 1711 ; The Excellency of Divine Musick, Lond., 1733 ; Scripture Chronology demonstrated by Astronomical Calculations, Lond., 1730 ; The Present State of the Republick of Letters, Lond., 1730 ; Serious Reflections on the Scandalous Abuse and Effects of the Stage, Bristol, 1705 ; The Evil and Danger of Stage Plays, etc.

BEER (Jacob). See MEYERBEER (Jacob).

BEER (Johann). German comp. and writer, B. 1652. D. 1700.

BEER (Joseph). German clarinet-player, B. Grünwald, 1744. D. Potsdam, 1811.

BEERALTHER (Aloys). German clarinet-player, B. 1800. D. Stuttgart, Mar. 21, 1850.

BEETHOVEN (Ludwig van). German comp., B. Bonn, Dec. 17, 1770. Commenced study of music under his father, 1775. Instructed further by Pfeiffer, a vocalist, 1779. Learned organ-playing from Van den Eeden, org. of the Court-Chap., Bonn. S. under Neefe, successor to Van den Eeden as court organist, 1781. Deputy-org. in Court-chap., 1782. Cond. of theatre orchestra at Bonn, 1783. Visited Vienna for first time, 1787. Sent by the Elector to Vienna, where he S. under Haydn and Salieri, 1792. His father died, 1792. Took lessons from Albrechtsberger, 1794. Visited successively Prague, Nuremberg, and Berlin, 1796. First troubled with deafness, 1806. Hopelessly attacked with deafness, 1810. Made acquaintance of Goethe at Toplitz, 1812. Undertook charge of Carl, his brother Caspar-Carl's son, 1815. Latter years of his life passed in great seclusion. D. Vienna, March 26, 1827.

WORKS.*—Op. 1. Three Trios for Pf., vn., and 'cello, in E flat, G, and C minor, 1795 ; op. 2. Three Sonatas for Pf., in F minor, A, and C, 1796 ; op. 3.

---

* The dates given are those of composition or publication.

Trio in E flat for vn., tenor, and 'cello, 1787 ; op. 4. Quintet in E flat for 2 violins, 2 tenors, and 'cello, 1796 ; op. 5. Two Sonatas for Pf. and 'cello, in F and G min., 1796 ; op. 6. Sonata for Pf. duet, in D minor, 1796 ; op. 7. Sonata for Pf., in E flat, 1797 ; op. 8. Serenade for vn., tenor, and 'cello, in D, 1786 (?); op. 9. Three trios for vn., tenor, and 'cello, in G, D, and C min., 1797-8 ; op. 10. Three sonatas for Pf. in C min., F, and D, 1797-8 ; op. 11. Grand trio for Pf., clarionet, and 'cello, 1798 ; op. 12. Three Sonatas for Pf., in D, A, and E flat, 1799 ; op. 13. Sonata (pathetic) for Pf., in C min., 1799 ; op. 14. Two Sonatas for Pf., in E and G, 1799 ; op. 15. First Concerto for Pf. and orch., in C, 1795 ; op. 16. Grand Quintet for Pf., oboe, clarinet, horn, and bassoon, in E flat, 1797 ; op. 17. Sonata for Pf. and horn, in F, 1798 ; op. 18. Six Quartets for 2 vns., tenor, and 'cello, in F, G, D, C min., A, and B flat, 1800 ; op. 19. Second Concerto for Pf. and orch., in B flat, 1795 ; op. 20. Septet for vn., tenor, horn, clarinet, bassoon, 'cello, and bass, in E flat, 1800 2 ; op. 21. First grand symphony for orchestra, in C, 1800 ; op. 22. Grand Sonata for Pf., in B flat, 1802 ; op. 23. Sonata for Pf. and vn., in A min., 1801 ; op. 24. Sonata for Pf. and vn., in F ; op. 25. Serenade for Flute, vn., and tenor, in D, 1802 ; op. 26. Grand Sonata for Pf., in A flat, 1802 ; op. 27. Two Sonatas for Pf., in E flat, and C sharp min. (popularly known as the "Moonlight Sonata"), 1802 ; op. 28. Grand Sonata (Pastorale) for Pf., in D, 1802 ; op. 29. Quintet for 2 vns., 2 tenors, and 'cello, in C, 1802 ; op. 30. Three Sonatas for Pf. and vn, A, C min., and G, 1802 ; op. 31. Three Sonatas for Pf. in G, D min., and E flat, 1803 ; op. 32. Six Songs (cantiques) of Gellert for voice and Pf., 1803 ; op. 33. Bagatelles for Pf., 1792 ; op. 34. Six variations on an original theme, for Pf., 1803 ; op. 35. Fifteen variations with one Fugue, for Pf., in E flat, 1803 ; op. 36. Second Symphony for orch., in D, 1804 ; op. 37. Third concerto, for Pf. and orch., in C min., 1805 ; op. 38. Grand Trio, for Pf., clarinet, and 'cello, in E flat (arranged from op. 20), 1803 ; op. 39. Two Preludes on the major and minor scales for Pf. or organ, 1803 ; op. 40. Romance for vn. and orch, in G, 1803 ; op. 41. Serenade for Pf. and flute, in D (arranged from op. 25), 1804 ; op. 42. Nocturne for Pf. and tenor, in D (arranged from op. 8), 1804 ; op. 43. Die Geschöpfe des Prometheus, Ballet, 1801 ; op. 44. Fourteen variations for Pf., vn., and 'cello, in E flat, 1804 ; op. 45. Three Grand Marches for Pf. duet, in C, E flat, and D, 1804 ; op. 46. "Adelaide," cantata for tenor solo and Pf. (Poem by Matthison), in F 1797 ; op. 47. Sonata for Pf. and vn., in A (Kreutzer), 1803 ; op. 48. Scene and Air—"Ah! Perfido," for soprano voice and orch., 1803 ; op. 49. Two Sonatas (easy) for Pf., in G min., and D, 1796 ; op. 50. Romance for vn and orch., in F, 1804 ; op. 51. Two Rondos for Pf., in C and G ; op. 52. Eight Songs (or Lieder) for solo voice and Pf., 1791 ; op. 53. Grand Sonata for Pf., in C, 1803 ; op. 54. Sonata for Pf., in F, 1805-6 ; op. 55. Third Symphony for orchestra ("Eroica"), in E flat, 1802-4 ; op. 56. Concerto for Pf., vn., and 'cello, with orch., in C, 1807 ; op. 57. Grand Sonata (Appassionata) for Pf., in F min., 1803-7 ; op. 58. Fourth concerto for Pf. and orch., in G, 1806 ; op. 59. Three Grand Quartets for strings, in F, E min., and C, 1806 ; op. 60. Fourth Symphony for orch., in B flat, 1809 ; op. 61. Concerto for vn. and orch., in D, 1806 ; op. 71. Sextet for 2 clarinets, 2 horns, and 2 bassoons, in E flat, 1810 ; op. 72. Leonore ("Fidelio"), opera in 2 acts, produced Vienna, Nov., 1805 ; London, 1832 ; in English, 1835 ; op. 73. Fifth Concerto for Pf. and vn., in E flat, 1811 ; op. 74. Quartet for strings, in E flat, 1810 ; op. 75. Six Songs by Goethe, for solo voice and Pf. ; op. 76. Variations for Pf., in D, 1810 ; op. 77. Fantasia for Pf., in G minor ; op. 78. Sonata for Pf., in F sharp, 1810 ; op. 79. Sonata for Pf., in G, 1810 ; op. 80. Fantasia for P, chorus, and orch., in C minor (Choral Fantasia), 1811 ; op. 81. Sonata (Les Adieux) for Pf., in E flat, 1811 ; op. 81a. Sextet for 2 vns., tenor, 'cello, and 2 horns, oblig., in E flat, 1811 ; op. 82. Four Ariettas, and one duet, for voice and Pf. ; op. 83. Three Songs by Goethe, for voice and Pf. : op. 84. Overture and Entr'actes to "Egmont" (Goethe), 1810 ; op. 85. The Mount of Olives, oratorio for solo voices, chorus, and orchestra,

1800; op. 86. Mass, in C, for 4 voices and orch., 1810; op. 87. Trio for 2 oboes and cor anglais, in C (arranged from op. 53), 1806; op. 88. "Das Gluck der Freundschaft," song; op. 89. Polonaise for Pf, in C, 1815; op. 90. Sonata for Pf., in E flat, 1815; op. 91. The Victory of Wellington, or the Battle of Vittoria, for orchestra, 1816; op. 92. Seventh Symphony for orch., in A, 1812-16; op. 93. Eighth Symphony for orch., in F, 1812-16; op. 94. An die Hoffnung, song for solo voice and Pf.; op. 95. Quartet for 2 vns., tenor, and 'cello, in F minor, 1816; op. 96. Sonata for Pf. and vn., in G, 1816; op. 97. Grand Trio for Pf., vn., and 'cello, in B flat, 1816; op. 98. An die ferne Geliebte, song for voice and Pf., 1816; op. 99. Der Mann vorn Wort, for solo voice and Pf.; op. 100. Merkenstein, ballad for solo voice and Pf.; op. 101. Sonata for Pf. in A; op. 102. Two Sonatas for Pf. and 'cello, in C and D; op. 103. Grand Octet for 2 clarinets, 2 oboes, 2 horns, and 2 bassoons, in E flat; op. 104. Quintet for 2 vns, 2 tenors, and 'cello (arranged from op. 1); op. 105. Six themes with variations for Pf., vn., and flute; op. 106. Sonata for Pf., in B flat (Hammer-Clavier), 1819; op. 107. Ten themes for Pf., vn., and flute; op. 108. Twenty-five Scottish Songs, arranged for voice, with Pf., vn., and 'cello accompt., 1815; op. 109. Sonata for Pf., in E, 1822; op. 110. Sonata for Pf., in A flat, 1823; op. 111. Sonata for Pf, in C, 1823; op. 112. Meerestille und Glückliche—Fahrt (Goethe), "Calm sea and a prosperous voyage," for 4 voices and orch., 1823; opp. 113, 114. The Ruins of Athens (cantata or secular oratorio), for solo voices, chorus, and orch., 1812; op. 115. Grand Overture for orch., in C; op. 116. Trio for Soprano, Tenor, and Bass, with orch. accomp.; op. 117. Overture, King Stephen, in E flat, 1812; op. 118. Chant Elégiaque for 4 voices, with accomp. for 2 vns., tenor, 'cello, and Pf.; op. 119. Twelve Bagatelles for Pf, 1822; op. 120. Thirty-three variations on a valse by Diabelli, in C; op. 121. Adagio, variations, and rondo, for Pf. in G; op. 121a. Opferlied, by Matthison, for solo voice, chorus, and orch.; op. 122. Bunderslied (Song of Federation), by Goethe, for solo voices, and small chorus and orch.; op. 123. Second Mass for 4 voices and orch., in D, 1822-24; op. 124. Overture for orch., in C, 1822; op. 125. Ninth Symphony (Choral Symphony) on Schiller's "Ode an die Freude" for chorus and orchestra, in D minor, 1822-23; op. 126. Six Bagatelles for Pf, 1822; op. 127. Quartet for strings, in E flat; op. 128. Der Kus, arietta for solo voice and Pf.; op. 129. Rondo a Capriccio for Pf., in G (posthumous); op. 130. Quartet for strings in B flat; op. 131. Quartet, in C sharp minor, for strings, 1825; op. 132. Quartet for strings, in A minor, 1825; op. 133. Grand Fugue in B flat, for string quartet, 1825; op. 134. Do., arranged for Pf. duet, 1825; op. 135. Quartet for strings, in F, 1825; op. 136. Der Glorreiche Augenblick, cantata on poem of Weissenbach's, for 4 voices and orch., 1814; op. 137. Fugue for 2 vns., 2 tenors, and 'cello, Nov., 1817; op. 138. Second Overture to "Leonore," for orch., in C, 1807. *Principal Unnumbered Works:* 139. Three Quartets for Pf. and stringed instruments, in E flat, D, and C; 140. Third Overture to "Leonore," in C, for orch., 1806; 141. Rondino for 2 clarinets, 2 oboes, 2 bassoons, and 2 horns, in E flat; 142. Three Sonatas for Pf., in E flat, F minor, and D, 1780; 143. Variations (various) for Pf.; 144. Numerous Dances and Marches; 145. Songs (various). *Summary—vocal and instrumental:* 1 Oratorio, 1 opera, 2 Masses, 2 Cantatas, 1 Ballet. *Instrumental:* 9 Symphonies; 8 Overtures, 1 vn. Concerto, 5 Pf. Concertos, 1 Octet, 1 Septet, 1 Sextet, 4 Quintets, 17 Quartets, 18 Trios (various), 38 Pf. sonatas, Songs (many single), etc.

In reviewing Beethoven's array of magnificent works, the handy classification of the three styles will be discarded for the more convenient one of groups; these will consist of:—

    1. Orchestral and Symphonic Works.
    2. Chamber Music.
    3. Vocal Music; and
    4. Pianoforte Music.

The examination will be confined to the body of music in each group, not to each single work in detail.

The vast difference in regard to emotional colouring apparent between the works of Haydn and Beethoven is indicative to some extent of the great change which, at the end of last century, passed over every art. In literature we find the formal scholasticism of Gray and his school giving place to the more natural and genial school of which Scott and Byron are representative. The strict diction of the school of Dryden and Pope, as in music that of Bach and the classical writers, had been succeeded by one of a more human and passionate order. In painting, the rigidity of West, Opie, Fuseli, and Barry had been supplanted by the naturalness of Wilkie and Landseer. So in music do we now find, in composers from Beethoven till now, a greater degree of warmth in the treatment of poetical subjects; a more manifest effort to sympathetically illustrate the general tendency of a chosen subject.

Beethoven is probably the first composer who attempted to express in instrumental music the feelings which perhaps a poem would be expected to engender. He was the first to give his symphonic writings the character and consistency of epic poems. In them, apart from the mechanical manipulation of sweet sounds, is to be found the various degrees of light and shade corresponding to the fluctuating events in an epic. There is fire, energy, dignity, depth, and many other varying forms of expression to be found in the writings of both Haydn and Mozart, but that consistency of purpose which enabled Beethoven in the course of a symphony to impart a definite idea of unity in his treatment of emotional elements is wanting in both. A strict adherence to form, corresponding to the literature of their period, robs the music of Haydn and Mozart of much of that passionate natural character which is so noticeable a characteristic in Beethoven. On the one hand, we have correct, melodious, and genial writing; on the other, strength of conception and beauty of execution in those subjects which express, so far as music can, the varying feelings of man. The expressional powers of Beethoven's symphonies are greatly superior to anything which has ever been produced in the form of instrumental music. The whole of the symphonies from No. 3 to 9 are more powerfully conceived than any others. Their character is more elevated and noble than the most ambitious efforts of his followers. Beethoven regarded the orchestra as a means of conveying a certain amount of his own feelings and aspirations to others. That he looked upon it as a medium whereby pictorial representations of certain subjects could be produced, is not entertained. The orchestra is not of itself capable of stimulating the imagination to the realization of events of any nature. Beethoven wrote for the orchestra having in his mind a subject or *programme*, which he tried to colour and illustrate. He did not pretend, as composers now do, to create pictorial representations of events, or the substantial idea of them by means of absolute music and a *programme*.

Beethoven having left no definite clue to the event or passion which he endeavoured to illustrate in his symphonic works, it is useless at this distant period trying to compound a programme to fit the general tone of any one of them, excepting, of course, the "Pastoral." To this he himself indicated in a slight way the general impression which the music was to illustrate; but beyond a few bird calls, his account does not extend to details connected with the aspects of nature, strips of blue sky, or so forth. It has been said that too romantic a standpoint cannot be taken when considering Beethoven's works. To this be added the reservation that the romantic vapourings descend not to the depths of the nonsensical. The following criticism from the pen of G. F. Graham, and appearing in the 8th edition of the *Encyclopædia Britannica*, may be taken as the general opinion on Beethoven which was current forty or fifty years ago :—

"As a composer Beethoven stands in the foremost rank. He possessed a powerful, inventive, and original mind. In respect of regularity of design, purity of harmonic combination, and skilful management of all his materials, he is, generally speaking, inferior to Haydn and Mozart. But still, all his best compositions are pervaded by an enthusiastic spirit of inspiration, a wild and masculine energy, relieved by frequent touches of tender beauty and melancholy, which stamp the superior genius of the man, and may, perhaps, be said to render his music analogous in character to the poetry of Dante. His earlier works and those of the second period of his artistic development are his best. His deafness may in a great measure account for the dry, crude, and unmelodious style of many of his later works. In vocal composition he was not in general greatly successful." This decision has been almost reversed at the present period. His third period, usually counted from op. 81, being now regarded as that in which his originality and powers of poetic treatment were most manifested.

Beethoven's chamber music, like his other instrumental works, is highly original, and an advance on anything achieved by his predecessors. This is said, not with regard to proportion or form, but with regard to a consistent and impassioned treatment of poetic themes. Haydn is the more pleasing and genial quartet writer of the two, but he did not carry the expressive capabilities of the quartet to the height achieved by Beethoven. Schubert and Mendelssohn equal Beethoven in this respect more than Haydn; but none of their writings will ever be so popular with the masses as those of Haydn. The genial warmth, almost *personal* tunefulness of Haydn has never been equalled by any writer up to the present time. Beethoven, in trying to make the quartet a means of giving orchestral expression to his themes, laid the foundation of the present school of music for stringed instruments. The endeavour of composers since Beethoven's time has been to expand the sphere of the string quartet; to place it on a level with the symphony as an artistic musical form; and to give it a somewhat more compact form than was the practice with the older writers.

Of his vocal music it will be unnecessary to speak at length. His masses are for the concert-room rather than for the cathedral; because he has expressed in them his artistic ideas of musical combinations for effect, rather than assisted the devout song-offerings of Christian worshippers. By straining after dramatic effect he has utterly destroyed the sacred character of his music, and rendered it unfit for the church service. They are stupendous experiments in musical colouring, suited only to the perceptions of trained musicians. His opera is wedded to a libretto almost "Bunnish" in absurdity. The instrumental portions are beautiful, as likewise are many of the vocal numbers, but it is dull so far as purely dramatic interest is concerned. He has failed to seize the extremely few opportunities given him of intensifying the emotional situations. A musician can enjoy the ideal beauty of the music abstractly; but as a drama it fails to interest. It is, more than any other opera of pretension, a collection of variously wrought-out forms of music strung together without the least appearance of dramatic continuity or organic uniformity. "The Mount of Olives" is semi-sacred throughout, and does not compare favourably with Mendelssohn's "Elijah," or Handel's "Messiah;" nevertheless, it is a musical work of the greatest beauty, containing passages of striking grandeur, and showing here and there its writer's vast individuality. "The Ruins of Athens" and the incidental music to Goethe's "Egmont" display in a much greater measure the peculiar character of his style. But it is chiefly in the orchestral aids that the full grandeur of his genius is manifested. The general character of his vocal music is unspontaneous, and he fails to obtain the same effects from it that other composers, inferior to him in many respects, gain with seeming ease. Intricacy and straining in vocal music is invariably destructive to its character, and this is often made painfully manifest in most of Beethoven's larger works.

His pianoforte sonatas stand among the greatest and most original monuments to the capabilities of that instrument. Since their production the art of playing the pianoforte has advanced in immense strides. The compositions of Schumann, Mendelssohn, Brahms, and Liszt have given an entirely fresh turn to its powers; and their proper performance entails a degree of perfect technique which was formerly only possessed by a few. That the great modern school of Pianoforte playing was founded by the requirements of Beethoven's sonatas is indisputable. The works of Haydn, Mozart, Clementi, Cramer, and Czerny do not present great difficulty to the pianist of moderate culture, while those dating after Beethoven and Schumann require skilful interpretation to produce the intended effect. Beethoven's reputation as a composer for this instrument will always rest on his sonatas and concertos. While the latter have been equalled by composers of a more recent date, it is certain that the sonatas have not yet been touched in their poetical and lovely natures, though they have been surpassed where mere construction is concerned. His sonatas have been so often analysed, and efforts so often made to prove that each was invested with some underlying principle closely bearing on their author's life, that it is unnecessary to dilate on the subject.

There is but a short space left for a brief summary of the great revolution which Beethoven effected in instrumental music. It is well known that previous to Beethoven's advent the endeavour of composers was to carefully develop and embellish certain themes within the academic rules of strict form. We do not find in the works of either Haydn and Mozart any great degree of those emotional characteristics which form so distinguishing a line of demarcation between them and Beethoven. They followed closely the form of the symphony as had been accepted by others, though Haydn made the most important additions to the instrumental resources and methods of treatment, and sought only to develop in a pleasing and beautiful manner lovely melodic phrases. Beethoven, on the contrary, developed, so to say, a thought of more or less power throughout his whole work. He attached important significance to phrases which his predecessors only regarded as essential but not inseparable portions of the entire structure. Each movement of the work was with them a distinct piece, never altogether in accordance with the sentiment of the others; while in Beethoven's works each movement must be taken with the others as necessary adjuncts of an organic structure. Beethoven carried the expressive capabilities of the orchestra far beyond anything ever achieved. Schubert, Schumann, Mendelssohn, and Brahms, though each marked by a distinct individuality, are nevertheless followers in the lines which Beethoven so powerfully laid down.

The following list of works may be profitably consulted by persons desirous of obtaining a full knowledge of Beethoven's life and works :—Biographische Notizen über L. van Beethoven. Wegeler und Ries, 1838; French edit. by Legentil, Paris, 1862—Biographie von L. van Beethoven. A. Schindler, Münster, 1840; English ed. by Moscheles, Lond., 2 vols., 1841—Beethoven et ses trois styles. Lenz. 2 vols, 1855—Beethoven eine Kunst-studie. Lenz. Cassel. 5 vols., 1855-60—Beethoven; ses critiques et ses glossateurs. Oulibicheff. Paris, 1857—L. van Beethoven Leben und Schaffen. Marx. 2 vols., 1863—Chronologisches Verzeichniss der Werke L. van Beethoven's. Thayer, 1865—L. van Beethoven's Leben. Thayer, 1866-79. 3 vols.—Beethoven's Leben. L. Nohl. 2 vols., 1867; English ed. by J. Lalor, 1883—Letters from Collections of Nohl and Köchel, trans. by Lady Wallace. 2 vols, 1866—Beethoven, sa Vie et ses Œuvres. Barbedette, 1870—Beethoven, a Memoir by E. Graeme, 1870—Beethoven nach den Schilderungen seiner Zeitgenossen, 1877; English Trans. by E. Hill, 1880—Beethoven by Wagner, trans. by Dannreuther, 1880—Ein Skizzenbuch von Beethoven aus dem Jahre, 1803. Nottebohm, Berlin, 1880—Beethoven's Symphonies Critically and Sympathetically Discussed, by A. T. Teetgen. Lond., 1879—Beethoven's Clavier Sonaten für freunde der Tonkunst. E. von Elterlein. Leipzig, 1856; trans. by E. Hill. Lond., 8vo, 1879.—Also articles in Fétis' Dictionnaire, Mendel's Lexikon, Grove's Dictionary of Music, and the following PERIODICALS :—Westminster Review, 1839 (vol. 32); Colburn's New Monthly Magazine (by Geo. Hogarth), 1840 (vol. 62); Boston Quarterly Review, 1840; Tait's Edinburgh Magazine, 1841 and 1858; North American Review, 1841 (vol. 53); Bentley's Miscellany, 1847; Atlantic Monthly, 1858; Journal of Speculative Philosophy, 1868; Contemporary Review, 1866; Appleton's Journal, 1870; Argosy, 1870; British Quarterly Review, 1871; Fortnightly Review, 1872; Edinburgh Review, 1873 (vol. 138); Macmillan's Magazine, 1876 (vol. 34); and Musical Journals generally.

BEGG (Rev. James, D.D.) Scottish divine, B. 1809. D. Edinburgh, 1883. Author of "The Use of Organs and other Instruments of Music in Christian Worship Indispensible." Glasgow, 12mo, 1866. Instrumental Music unwarrented in the Worship of God." Edin., 8vo, n. d. His father, the Rev. James Begg, D.D., minister of New Monkland, Lanarkshire, wrote a tract entitled "Treatise on the Use of Organs and other Instruments of Music in the Worship of God." Glasgow, 8vo, 1808.

BEGNIS (Guiseppe de). Italian barytone vocalist, B. Lugo, 1793. Sopranist at Lugo till 1808. Début at Modena in 1813. Début at Paris in 1819. Appeared with his wife in London, 1822. Undertook the direction of opera at Bath from 1823. D. Aug., 1849.

BEGNIS (Claudin Ronzi de). Wife of above, B. Paris, Jan. 11, 1800. Début at Paris, 1819. Appeared with her husband in London, 1822. D. July 3, 1853.

BEGREZ (Pierre Ignace M.) French tenor vocalist, B. Namur, Dec., 1787. D. Dec., 1863. Sang at King's Theatre, London, 1822.

BEHNKE (Emil). German writer and teacher, B. Stettin, 1836. Teacher of Voice Production to singers, speakers, and speech-sufferers. Lecturer on Vocal Physiology. Author of "The Mechanism of the Human Voice." Lond., 1880. Co-Author with Mr. Lennox Browne, F.R.C.S., of "Voice, Song, and Speech, London (1883); and Co-author with Mr. Charles W. Pearce, Mus. Doc., of "Voice Training Exercises," Lond., 1884. "The Child's Voice," Lond., 1885.

Mr. Behnke has, for many years, made the physiological laws of voice-production his special study, and he has been so successful in the application of scientific principles to the practical work of teaching, and more particularly to the restoration of voices impaired by false training, as to have established an entirely new profession. He lectures at the foremost musical and scientific institutions of the country, and is universally accepted as a leading authority on all matters relating to the voice.

BEHRENS (Christoph Heinrich Theodor). German comp., B. Erckerode, Brunswick, Mar. 27, 1808. Writer of lieder, etc.

BEKKER (Johann Heinrich). Dutch violinist and org., B. Windschoken, Groningen, Jan. 5, 1826. Writer of org. music, sacred music, songs.

BELCHER (J.) English writer, author of "Lectures on the History of Ecclesiastical Music," 8vo, 1872.

BELCHER (William Thomas). English comp. and org., B. Birmingham, Mar. 8, 1827. Org. of Great Barr Ch., Staffordshire, 1856. Org. and Choirmaster of St. Silas' Lozells, Birmingham, 1861. Org. and Choir-master of S. George's Parish Ch., Birmingham, 1864-78. Org. and Choir-master of Handsworth Parish Ch., 1878-81. F.C.O., 1867. Mus. Bac., Oxon., 1867. Mus. Doc., do., 1872. Org. and Choir-master, Holy Trinity Ch., Bordesley, 1884.

WORKS.—Oratorio, The Sea of Galilee (MS.), Oxford, 1872; opera, Estelle (MS.); cantata, The Fates (performed at the Music School, Oxford, July, 1867), 1868; cantatina, Excelsior. *Four-part Songs:* The Holly Tree and the Misletoe; Sweet spring is coming; Crowned with blushing roses; The ripe fruits mellow in the sun; Give me the lusty winter time; I wish you a merry Christmas. *Church Music:* Sabbath Harmonies; Four Hymns; Six Hymns; Full Anthem for Double Choir, from Psalm 122; Service in C; Anthems from Psalms 13, 27; Chants, etc. *Glees:* Wake, wake, each instrument of sound; The Shipwreck; Happy hearts in gladness met; Hark! the syren strikes the lyre; Arise and go forth; Merry Harvest. The Clarion, 6 org. pieces. *Songs:* Songs of the Convent; The Bridegroom's Serenade; The Death of Wellington; My home is on the mountain steep; The brave and the bereaved; 'Tis lovely May; Come, then, join our soldier band; Our village Bells; Ever mine! ever thine; 'Tis not when smiles are brightest; Polkas and Quadrilles for Pf.

BELCKE (Friedrich August). German trombone player and comp., B. Lucka, Saxony, May 27, 1795. Mem. of Gewandhaus orch., Leipzig. Principal Trombone player in Royal Band, Berlin. D. Berlin, Dec. 10, 1874.

WORKS.—His composition, over 100 in number, consist of music for the trombone, concerted vocal music for male voices, Pianoforte music, and a few orchestral pieces. The trombone music is among the best of its class.

BELLAMY (Thomas Ludford). English bass vocalist, B. Westminster, 1770. S. as Chor. in Westminster Abbey under Cooke. S. under Tasca. Concert vocalist in London till 1794. Stage manager of theatre in Dublin, 1794-97. Part-proprietor of Chester, Lichfield, Manchester, and Shrewsbury theatres, 1800. Proprietor of Belfast, Londonderry, and Newry theatres, 1803. Sang in Covent Garden Theatre, 1807-12. Do. in Drury Lane Theatre, 1812-17. Choir-master at Chap. of Spanish Embassy, London, 1819. Bass at Concert of Ancient Music. D. London, Jan 3, 1843.

WORKS.—Songs and Part-songs. Lyric Poetry of Glees, Madrigals, Catches, Rounds, Canons, and Duets. Lond., 8vo, 1840.

Bellamy was for long one of the best English bass singers, and kept before the public for a period of nearly half a century. His voice was powerful in tone and of a round, full quality.

BELLAMY (Richard). English comp. and org., father of preceding, B. about middle of 18th century. He was a Bachelor of Music, and composed a "To Deum, for a full orchestra; also a set of anthems," 1788. His other works were anthems, songs, and "Six Glees for 3 and 4 voices," 1789. D. London, Sept., 1813.

BELLASIS (Edward). English writer, B. Jan. 28, 1852. *Lancaster Herald*, 1882. Author of "Cherubini: Memorials Illustrative of his Life." Lond., 8vo, 1874. "The Law of Arms," etc. Comp. *Songs:* Alone I wander'd; Ministering Spirits; The Haven; Consolation; Waiting for the Morning; The Two Worlds; Tyre; Marionette Pantomime, etc.

BELLETTI (Giovanni). Italian barytone vocalist, B. Lunigiana, 1813. *Début* in Rossini's "Il Barbiere," at Stockholm, 1837. Appeared in London, 1848. Sang with Jenny Lind, under Sir Julius Benedict, in the United States. Sang in London up till 1863. Appeared afterwards in several parts of Italy.

BELL'HAVER (Vincenzo). Italian comp. of madrigals, etc., B. Venice, 1530. D. [1589.]

BELLI (Giulio). Italian comp., flourished in 16th and 17th centuries, and wrote Masses, Psalms, and other church music, and two books of madrigals, 1589-92.

BELLINI (Vincenzo). Italian comp., B. Catania, Sicily, Nov. 3, 1802. S. under his father, an organist. S. under Zingarelli at Naples Cons. Went to Paris, 1834. Mem. of the Legion of Honour. S. in Paris. D. Puteaux, near Paris, Sept. 23, 1835.

WORKS.—*Operas:* Adelson e Salvino, 1825; Bianca e Fernando, Naples, 1826; Il Pirata, Milan, 1827, London, 1830; La Straniera, Milan, 1828, Lond., 1832; Zaira, Parma, 1829; Il Capuletti ed i Montecchi, Venice, 1830, Lond., 1833; La Sonnambula, Milan, 1831, Lond., 1831, English version, 1833; Norma, Milan, 1832, Lond., 1833, English version, 1837; Beatrice di Tenda, Venice, 1833, Lond., 1836; I Puritani, Paris, 1834, Lond., 1835.

That school of opera which depended for effect on melody has now almost entirely disappeared, leaving in its place one which pretends to more powerful dramatic character. The pure Italian school of opera once so influential has now almost departed from the stage, leaving for its representatives Rossini, Verdi, Donizetti, and occasionally Bellini. This applies, of course, only to the British stage. We find that Bellini and Donizetti are fast dying out of the current musical programmes, and that they who were reigning favourites twenty or thirty years ago are now comparatively neglected. This would seem to denote that culture in music is quickly obliterating the taste for simple melodies. Musicians who are not altogether one-sided in their leanings appear to delight in music that exercises the reflective faculties rather than that which passes time off in an agreeable fashion.

The numberless lovely melodies of which Bellini was author, are not in the least hampered by the text of the opera. They are spontaneous creations which can be sung with an entire disregard to the poetry from which it is supposed they spring; so meagre is the element of dramatic continuity possessed by them. They are, moreover, only thoroughly relished by denizens of the sunny south, to whom mere outward beauties are most grateful. It is possible that, had Bellini lived long enough, he would have proved an ornament to modern Italian music, but rather in the school of Verdi than of Cherubini. As it is, he has proved himself a more graceful melodist than the former, though in every respect he is much less robust in his manner of colouring emotional passages. His theoretical knowledge was also limited, as may readily be perceived from the numerous guitar passages with which his works abound.

See also articles in the Westminster Review, 1838 (vol. 31); the Art Journal, 1858; and in the Musical Times, Musical World, etc. A. Pougin has issued a biography entitled "Bellini, sa vie, ses Euvres." Paris, 1868.

BELLMAN (Carl Gottfried). German bassoon-player and manufacturer, B. Schellenberg, Saxony, Aug. 11, 1760. D. Dresden, 1816.

BELOCCA (Anna de). Italian (?) mezzo-soprano vocalist, B. St. Petersburg, Jan., 1854. Has appeared in London and the English provinces, and been everywhere received with favour.

BEMETZRIEDER (?) French writer, B. Alsace, 1743. Lived in London, 1781-1810. Wrote instruction books for singers and instrumentalists. "Leçons de Clavecin et Principes d' Harmonie," Paris, 4to, 1771; "New Guide to Singing," London, etc.; "New Lessons for the Harpsichord, containing the

Principles of Melody and of Harmony," etc., Lond., 1783 ; Music made easy to every capacity, in a series of Dialogues...Trans. by Giffard Bernard, M.A., London, 1778.

BENDA (Franz). German violinist and comp., B. Nov. 25, 1709. S. under Graun and others. Concert-director to Frederick the Great, 1771. D. Potsdam, Mar. 7, 1786.

WORKS.—Solos, Exercises, and Studies for the Violin.

Benda was one of the founders of classical violin-playing, and was himself esteemed a great exponent. His son Friedrich (1745-1814) was also a violinist and comp.

BENDA (Friedrich Ludwig). German comp., B. Gotha, 1746. D. Königsberg, Mar. 27, 1792. Writer of operas, violin-music, etc. Son of Georg Benda, and at one time music-director at Hamburg.

BENDA (Georg). German comp. and oboe player, B. 1721. Music-director to Duke of Gotha. D. Thuringia, 1795.

WORKS.—*Operas:* Ariadne auf Naxos, 1774 ; Medea ; La Foire de Village, 1776 ; Walder, 1777 ; Le Bücheron, 1778 ; Pygmalion, 1780. Sonatas for Harpsichord ; Concertos for Clavecin ; Cantatas, etc.

BENDALL (Wilfred Ellington). English comp., B. London, April 22, 1850. S. harmony and comp. under Charles Lucas and E. Silas. S. also at Leipzig Cons., 1872-74.

WORKS.—*Operettas:* Lovers' Knots, St. George's Hall, 1880 ; Opera Comique, 1881. Quid pro Quo, 1880. *Cantatas:* Parizädeh, produced at St. James' Hall, by Willing's Choir, April, 1884 ; The Lady of Shalott, for female voices ; The Rosière, for female voices. Part-songs and trios ; Numerous songs and duets ; Pianoforte pieces, various.

BENDEL (Carl). Bohemian comp., B. Prague, April 16, 1838. Writer o masses, an opera, songs, Pf. music, etc.

BENDEL (Franz). Bohemian comp. and pianist, B. Bohemia, Mar. 3, 1833. A popular pianist and composer. D. Berlin, 1874.

WORKS.—A large quantity of miscellaneous Pianoforte music principally of the drawing-room kind. These are characterized by great brilliancy, and many of them are spirited and taking in so far as rhythm and melody are concerned.

BENDER (Jacob). German comp., B. Worms, 1798. D. Antwerp, August 9, 1844. Writer of instrumental music.

BENDER (Valentin). Brother of the above, B. Bechtheim, Worms, 1800. Writer of military music, etc.

BENDIX (Carl). Swedish operatic comp., B. Stockholm, 1818.

BENDIX (Otto). Danish pianist and teacher, B. Copenhagen, 1850. Son of Emanuel Bendix, merchant and amateur musician. S. in Copenhagen under A. Rée and N. W. Gade. S. in Berlin under Kullak ; in Weimar under Liszt. Teacher of Pf. in Copenhagen Cons., and oboe player in the Royal Theatre orch. Settled in Boston, 1880. Teacher of Pf. in the New England Cons. of Music. Has comp. a few pieces for Pf. and other instruments. "With... brilliancy of execution and a clearness of interpretation, he combines what not all artists do—rare fitness as a teacher." Has played in Europe and America with great success. [*Musical Herald*, Boston.]

BENEDICT (Sir Julius). German comp. B. Stuttgart, Nov. 27, 1804. S. under Hummel and Weber. First works published, 1821. Musical-Director of Kärntner Thor Theatre, Vienna, 1824. Cond. at Naples. Went to Paris, 1835. Settled in London, 1835. Musical-Director of the Lyceum Theatre, 1836. Travelled in America with Mdlle. Jenny Lind, 1850. Cond. at H.M. Theatre. Knighted by Queen Victoria, 1871. Knight-Commander of the orders of Francis and Joseph (Austria), 1871. Do. of order of Frederic (Wurtemberg), 1871. Cond. Liverpool Musical Festival, 1874. Has been twice married. President of the Schubert Soc. Prof. of Pianoforte at Trinity Coll., London. Prof. at the R.A.M. Mem. of Royal Soc. of Musicians; the Philharmonic Soc. Presented with a Testimonial, 1884.

WORKS.—*Operas:* Un Anno ed un Giorno, 1836; The Gipsey's Warning, 1838; Giacinta ed Ernesto, 1827; I Portoghesi in Goa, 1830; The Brides of Venice, 1846; The Crusaders, 1846; The Lily of Killarney, by Boucicault and Oxenford, London, 1862; The Bride of Song, 1864. *Oratorios:* The Legend of St. Cecilia, Norwich Festival, 1866; St. Peter, Birmingham, 1870. *Cantatas:* Undine. op. 70, Norwich Festival, 1860; Richard Cœur de Lion, Norwich Festival, 1863; Graziella, Birmingham Festival, 1882; Recitatives for Weber's "Oberon," 1860. Symphony, 1873. *Pianoforte Music:* Concerto for Pf. and orch., op. 89; Do. in C minor, op. 45; Nocturnes; Rondos; Instructions in the Art of Playing the Pianoforte; Exercises, Studies, Scales, Lessons, etc.; Idylles, Reveries, Impromptus, Marches, Souvenirs, etc., for Pf. solo and duet, published between 1821 and 1880 by Ricordi, Milan; Hofmeister, Leipzig; Steiner, Vienna; Schott, Peters, and London publishing firms. *Anthems:* Try me, O God; The Lord be a lamp; Praise the Lord; etc. *Part-Songs:* Home; Summer is nigh; Old May day; A night song; Sylvan pleasures; The wreath; The hunting song; Sweet repose is reigning now; Homeward bound; May, etc. *Songs:* Dreamy Eyes; England yet; Come where the willows; By the sad sea waves; Sleep on, sad heart; The gipsy and the bird; Alone; Lost; The bird that came in spring; While the wood grows; As weeping on my heart she lay; Medora's song; Morning; Thoughts at eve; Little Willie; A spring thought; Mine, thou art mine; When my thirsty soul I steep; The echo song; The parting; Love at sea; Rock me to sleep; Sighing for thee; Angel adored; Come to our fairy bower; O do not scorn my love; Welcome to our Prince; Alma adorata. Lectures on various subjects. "Weber" (Great Musicians), Lond., 8vo, 1881. Contributions, chiefly didactic, to musical periodicals.

"The Lily of Killarney," "St. Peter," and "St. Cecilia" are Benedict's finest and most popular works. The first is an especial favourite, and when rendered, rarely fails in securing well-merited success. The melodies are fine, the orchestration is scholarly, and the general construction of the music is highly dramatic and well adapted to the nature of the situations. His sacred music is less successful. This is depending greatly on a somewhat secular treatment of sacred subjects. The music in "St. Peter" is, from a musician's point of view, beautiful and refined, but it is lacking in tender sacred spirit. Died Lotsw, June 5, 1885.

BÉNÉDIT (Pierre Gustave). French writer and comp., B. Marseilles, April 7, 1802. D. Dec. 8, 1870.

BENELLI (Antonio Peregrino). Italian comp., B. at Forli, Rome, Sept. 5, 1771. D. Aug. 6 1830. Writer of Pf. music, church music, cantatas, songs, etc.

BENESCH (Josef). Austrian comp.. B. Battelau, Moravia, 1795. D. Feb. 11, 1873. Comp. Pf. music, songs, etc.

BENEVOLI (Orazio). Italian comp., B. Rome, 1602. Chap.-master of Vatican, 1646. D. Rome, June, 1672.

WORKS.—Masses for 8 voices, motets, magnificats, etc.

BENINCORI (Angelo Maria). Italian comp., B. Brescia, 1779. S. under Cimarosa. D. Paris, Dec. 30, 1821. Comp. operas and instrumental music.

BENJAMIN (J.) American musician, of Northampton, Mass., issued "Harmonia Cœlestis, 1799. A collection of church music in which, for the first time in America, use is made of accompaniments for harpsichord or organ.

BENKERT (George F). American comp., B. Germantown, Penn., April 11, 1831. S. under J. F. Duggan at Philadelphia, and Lindpainter in Germany. Teacher in America. Comp. miscellaneous vocal and instrumental music.

BENNET (John). English comp., flourished at the end of 16th and beginning of 17th centuries [1570-1615].

Works.—Madrigals to four voyces, being his first works, 1599; Madrigal, "All creatures now are merry minded," in the "Triumphs of Oriana," 1601; Songs in a collection published by Ravenscroft; O God of Gods, verse anthem, Sacred Harmonic Society's Library; Anthems and Madrigals in MS.

"His madrigals are finely studied, and abound with all the graces and elegance of vocal harmony." Bennet was one of the ornaments of the Madrigalean period, and will doubtless descend to posterity bearing a name for fine, melodious writing. Nothing as to his biography appears to have been chronicled. His book of madrigals was re-published in 1845 by the Musical Antiquarian Society.

BENNET (Saunders). English org., pianist, and comp., B. in last quarter of 18th century. Org. of Ch. at Woodstock. D. 1809.

Wrote some vocal music (glees and songs), and a number of rondos, sonatas, variations, etc., for the organ and Pf.

BENNETT (Alfred). Son of Thomas Bennet, org. and comp., B. 1805. S. under his Father. Org. of New Coll., Oxford, 1825. Mus. Bac. Oxon. D. Oxford, 1830.

Works.—Church Services and Anthems; Chants, 1829; Songs; Instructions for the Pianoforte, with popular National Airs arranged as Lessons. Lond. [1825].

BENNETT (James). English comp. and writer, author of "A Practical Introduction to Part and Sight-singing," London, 1843; "Elementary Exercises for the Cultivation of the Voice," London fo. n.d.

BENNETT (Thomas). English org. and comp., B. 1779. Chor. in Salisbury Cath. S. under Joseph Corfe. Org. of St. John's Chap., Chichester. Do. of Chichester Cath., 1803. D. Chichester, March 21, 1848.

Works.—Introduction to the Art of Singing, London, fo. n.d.; Songs and organ pieces; Sacred Melodies—a collection of Psalms and Hymns, composed, selected, and adapted for Divine Worship, London, 8vo, n.d.; Cathedral Selections, Anthems, Chants, etc., n.d.

BENNETT (Joseph). English writer and musician, B. Berkeley, Gloucestershire, Nov., 1831. Musical critic successively in connection with the *Sunday Times*, *Musical Standard*, *Daily Telegraph*, *Pall Mall Gazette*, *Graphic*, and *Musical Times*. To the *Daily Telegraph* and the *Musical Times* most of his important writings have been contributed. Editor of *Concordia*, 1874, and of the *Lute*, 1884. Author of "The Musical Year" [1883], London, 1884; Biographies of Musicians (Berlioz, Chopin), 1884, reprinted from *Musical Times*, and numerous analyses for festival and concert use.

BENNETT (William). English org. and comp., B. near Teignmouth, 1767. S. under Jackson of Exeter, and J. C. Bach and Schroeter, London. Org. of St. Andrew's Ch., Plymouth. D. [?]

Works.—Six Songs and a Glee, London [1799]; Anthems and organ music, etc.

BENNETT (William Cox). English lyrical author, B. Greenwich, 1820. Has written a number of good songs, and some long poems, chiefly on domestic subjects, of much merit. He wrote "Songs for Sailors," in conjunction with J. L. Hatton, and numerous lyrics which have been set by various composers.

BENNETT (Sir William Sterndale). English comp. and pianist, B. Sheffield, April 13, 1816. S. as chor. in choir of King's Coll., Cambridge, under his grandfather, John Bennett. Received subsequent instruction from Charles Lucas, Dr. Crotch, Cipriano Potter, and W. H. Holmes. S. at Leipzig Cons., under Moscheles, at expense and on suggestion of Messrs. Broadwood & Sons, Pianoforte makers, 1836-40. Appeared in England as concert-giver, 1843-1856. Unsuccessful candidate for Music Professorship at Edinburgh University, 1844. Married to Miss Mary Ann Wood, 1844. Founded (with others) the Bach Society, 1849. Cond. the Philharmonic Soc. Concerts, 1856-66. Cond. the Leeds Musical Festival, 1858. Prof. of Music at Cambridge, 1856. Mus. Doc., Cambridge, 1856. M.A., Cambridge, 1857. Principal of the R.A.M., 1866. D.C.L., Oxford, 1870. Knighted, 1871. Presented with Testimonial, 1872. D. London, Feb. 1, 1875.

WORKS.—Op. 1. First Concerto for Pf. and orch., in D minor, 1832; op. 2. Capriccio for Pf, in D; op. 3. Overture for full orch., Parisina, 1834-35; op. 4. Second Concerto for Pf. and orch., in E flat; op. 8. Sestet for Pf. and strings, 1844; op. 9. Third Concerto for Pf. and orch., in C minor, 1834; op. 10. Three Musical Sketches for Pf.; op. 11. Six Studies for the Pf.; op. 12. Three Impromptus for Pf.; op. 13. Sonata for Pf., 1842; op. 14. Three Romances for Pf.; op. 15. Overture for full orch., The Naiads, 1836; op. 16. Fantasia for Pf., 1842; op. 17. Three Diversions for Pf. duet; op. 18. Allegro Grazioso for Pf.; op. 19. Fourth Concerto for Pf. and orch., in F minor, 1836-1849; op. 20. Overture for full orch., The Wood Nymph, 1840; op. 22. Caprice in E. for Pf. and orch., 1840; op. 23. Six Songs for solo voice with Pf. accomp.; op. 24. Suite de Pieces, for Pf., 1843; op. 25. Rondo Piacevale for Pf.; op. 26. Trio for Pf., vn., and 'cello, 1844; op. 27. Scherzo for Pf.; op. 28. Rondino for Pf., 1853; op. 29. Two Studies for Pf.; op. 30. Four Sacred Duets; op. 31. Tema e Variazione for Pf.; op. 32. Sonata for Pf. and 'cello, 1852; op. 33. Sixty Preludes and Lessons for Pf., 1853; op. 34. Rondo for Pf.; op. 35. Six Songs (second set) for voice and Pf.; op. 36. Flowers of the Month; op. 38. Toccato for Pf.; op. 39. The May Queen, a Pastoral, by H. F. Chorley (cantata) for solo voices, chorus, and orch., Leeds Musical Festival, 1858; op. 40. Ode, written for the opening of the International Exhibition, 1862, by (Lord) Alfred Tennyson, 1862; op. 41. Cambridge Installation Ode, 1862; op. 42. Fantasie-overture, Paradise and the the Peri, for full orch., 1862; op. 43. Symphony for full orch. in G minor; op. 44. The Woman of Samaria, an oratorio, for solo voices, chorus, and orch., Birmingham Festival, 1867; op. 45. Music to Sophocles' Ajax; op. 46. Pianoforte Sonata, The Maid of Orleans.

In addition to the above he wrote overtures (The Merry Wives of Windsor, etc.), songs, part-songs, Pf. music, and collections of chants, etc., most of which have been published.

Bennett holds a unique position in English musical history. No other modern Englishman has attained equal prominence as a composer of instrumental music; nor has any one of the recent composers achieved more universal fame. His works are chiefly remarkable on a first examination for their exquisite finish and air of refinement—a characteristic peculiar to Bennett above all Englishmen. The works best known to the general public are his overtures, his cantata, and oratorio. The symphony in G minor and the Pianoforte concertos are of less frequent occurrence in concert programmes, from which it may be inferred that they are less appreciated or less known. The overtures are among the finest specimens of imaginative writing ever produced in Britain. We say nothing of their grandeur, for no pretence is made in that direction, but as purely fanciful pieces of writing they are among the foremost. The "Naiads" is a most lovely work, graceful and melodious in character, and entirely free from constructional defect. "The Parisina" overture is also of great beauty and, considering its author's experience when written, a gem among concert overtures, and is thoroughly deserving of its popularity.

The G minor symphony does not really receive the amount of attention which its merits claim. Though not a work of the greatest power, nor one which displays the highest degree of imagination, it is still a superior work, and one which excites considerable interest in performance. The "May Queen," cantata, shares with Macfarren's "May Day" the greatest popularity among provincial choral societies. It is thoroughly English in style, and is full of pleasant melody and charming harmony. It is a work which never fails in pleasing, and conclusively shows that Bennett had the art of writing well, even to a popular level. It is frequently given in England, and is well deserving of the attention bestowed on it. His finest choral work is least often given of all. "The Woman of Samaria," though crowded from beginning to end with beauties of every variety, appears to receive less favour from musical societies than its surpassing merits would seem to warrant. At any rate, it appears much less frequently in the prospectuses of choral societies than it should. Its difficulty may be an obstacle; but the neglect is none the less shameful.

The pianoforte compositions are beautiful and valuable contributions to this important branch of musical art, and his concertos, if less given than they ought, are perhaps amply counterbalanced for their neglect by the popularity of the minor pieces. Many of them have vast popularity both in Britain and America, and frequently appear in the programmes of the best performers in the latter country.

Bennett must ever be known as one of Britain's men of mark, and his name will always be mentioned with respect. No more conscientious artist ever lived in England, nor one who has done more to raise the musical taste of the British people. His influence over that important institution, the Royal Academy of Music, was felt to be great, and it is owing to him that much of its present success is due. His influence in developing the higher forms of musical art in England has continued with strengthening power from year to year, and though it is not presently very widely recognised, it must still stand to his credit that to his impulse may be attributed much of the present manifestations of popular interest in music. His works are among the most beautiful creations in the whole range of musical art, and what they lack in power and vigour is amply made up in polish and refinement. An interesting article on this musician will be found in *Fraser's Magazine*, v. 91-92.

BENOIST (Francois). French comp., org., and writer, B. Nantes, Sept. 10, 1794. S. at Paris Cons. under Catel and Adam. Org. of Chap. Roy., Paris, Prof. of Org., Paris Cons , 1819. Chevalier of Legion of Honour, 1851. D. Paris, May, 1878.

WORKS.—Felix et Leonore, opera, 1821 ; Diable Amoureux, ballet, 1848 ; Other ballets, etc. ; Organ music, fugues, etc.

Benoist is chiefly famous as a teacher and organist. Among his more famous pupils may be named Lefébure-Wely, Chauvet, Batiste, Vilbac, Bazin, Bizet, Duvernoy, Salomé, Dubois, and Paladilhe.

BENOIT (Pierre Léonard Léopold). Belgian comp., B. Harelbeker, August 17, 1834. S. under Fétis at Brussels from 1851. Gained prizes for harmony, etc. Violinist in theatre at Brussels. Director of Music School at Antwerp.

WORKS.—*Operas:* De Belgische Natie, 1856 ; Het dorp in't gebergte, 1857 ; Isa, 1867. Lucifer, oratorio, 1866. Instrumental and church music.

BENONI (Giulio). Italian comp., B. Vienna, 1835 (or Strelohostic, Bohemia, 1833). Writer of operas, songs, etc.

BENTAYOUX (Frederic). French comp., B. Bordeaux, June 14, 1840. Writer of operettas, etc.

BENTLEY (John Morgan). English comp. and org., B. Manchester, Sept. 3, 1837. Org. of S. Philip's, Salford, 1855 ; S. Stephen's, Manchester, 1860 ; S. Saviour's, Manchester, 1866 ; Bowdon Parish Ch., 1868 ; Cheadle Abbey Ch., 1877. Mus. Bac. Cantab., 1877. Mus. Doc., do., 1879. Local Examiner for R.A.M., 1881. Established the Academy of Music, S. Ann's, Manchester, 1870. Cond. successively the following musical societies :—S. Philip's Choral, S. Stephen's do. ; S. Saviour's do. ; Lea Choral ; Bowdon Musical ; S. Cecilia, Winsford ; S. Cecilia, Blackburn ; Eccles Choral ; Cheadle Choral. Prov. Gr. Organist of East Lancashire, 1881.

WORKS.—Gethsemane, dramatic cantata, 1877 (Mus. Bac. Exercise) ; What is Life ? oratorio, 1879 (Mus. Doc. Exercise) ; Yuletyde, cantata for mixed voices (Hutchings & Romer) ; The Golden Butterfly, cantata for female voices (Hutchings) ; Horæ Sacræ, a series of sacred pieces for Violin and Piano ; The Two Violinists, a series of duets for Violins with Pf. accompaniment ; Vesper Canticles (Novello) ; Psalter pointed and Psalter chants (Heywood, Manchester) ; Symphony for full orchestra (MS.), and other orchestral works ; numerous songs published by Metzler & Co., Hutchings & Romer, Duff & Stewart, Novello & Co., etc.

BENVENUTI. (Tommaso). Italian operatic comp., B. 1834.

BÉRANGER (Pierre Jean de). French lyrical author, B. Paris, Aug. 19, 1780. D. Paris, July 16, 1857. His songs have been often set by various composers, and are well adapted for musical treatment. A collection of them has been published with the music.

BÉRAT (Eustache). French comp., B. Rouen, Dec. 4, 1791. Writer of songs and Pf. music. D. Neuilly, January, 1885.

BERBIGUIER (Benoit Tranquille). French comp. and flute-player, B. Caderousse, Vaucluse, Dec. 21, 1782. S. at Paris Cons. Served in the Army,

1813-19. Teacher and concert-giver from 1830. D. near Blois, January 29, 1838.

WORKS.—Op. 1. Three solos for flute ; op. 2. Three duets for flutes ; op. 3. Duets for Flute ; op. 4. Three duets for flute ; opp. 5, 6, 7, Duets for flute ; opp. 8, 9, 10, 11, 12, 13, 14, 15, 16, 17. Solos, trios, etc., for flute and other instruments ; op. 18. Concerto for flute and orch., in B minor ; op. 22. Three duets for flute, in E minor, C and D ; op. 23. Three sonatas for flute and 'cello ; opp. 26, 27. Concertos for flute and orch., in E min. ; opp. 29, 30. Concertos for flute and orch., in G minor, and E flat ; op. 33. Three trios for flutes, in G, E, and A ; op. 37. Three trios for flute, violin, and alto, in E flat, F, and D ; op. 44. Concerto for flute and orch., in D ; op. 50. Symphony concertante for 2 flutes and orch., in A ; op. 54. Concerto for flute and orch., in D ; op. 74. Concerto for flute and orch., in D ; op. 86. Quartet for flute, violin, viola, and 'cello. Method for the Flute. The op. numbers omitted in the foregoing list are chiefly solos, duets, fantasias, etc., for the flute and other instruments.

Berbiguier's writings for the flute possess much that is eminently suitable to its character and powers of expression, and they are in constant use among flute players all over the world.

BERCHEM (Jachet). Flemish comp., B. Berchem, near Antwerp, in first quarter of 16th century [or about 1500]. Musician in service of the Duke of Mantua. Supposed to have died in 1580.

WORKS.—Libro primus, vocum quinque, Vigenti Motetos, 1539 ; Il primo libro di Motetti di Jachet, a cinque voci, 1540 ; Il primo libro di Motetti a quattro voci, 1545 ; Il primo libro de madrigali a quattro voci, 1556 ; Capriccio di Jachetto Berchem con la musica da lui composta sopra le stanze del Furioso, a quattro voci, 4to, 1561 (3 books) ; Orationes complures ad offic—Hebdom—Sanctæ pertinentes quatuor et quinque vocum, 1567 ; Messe dei Fiore a cinque voci, libro primo, 1561 ; Messe di Jachetto a cinque voci, Libro 2, 1555.

Berchem's works are marked by a simplicity of construction rarely found in works of the polyphonic period in which he lived. His part-songs from Ariosto's "Orlando Furioso" are ingenious in construction and clear in design. He is regarded as one of the leading Flemish composers of the 16th century.

BERENS (Hermann). German comp., B. Hamburg, 1826. Cond. of theatre in Stockholm. Teacher and cond. there. D. May 9, 1880.

WORKS.—Operas: Song of a Night ; Lully und Quinault, 1859 ; Riccardo, 1869. Org. and Pf. music: Fantasia for org., op. 25 ; Mazurka di Bravura, op. 35 ; Two Studies, op. 36 ; Caprice Humoristique, op. 37 ; Dorfgeschichten, op. 40 ; Nocturne, op. 41 ; Le Zephyr, op. 43 ; Grand Caprice, op. 54 ; Boléro, op. 57 ; Neue Dorfgeschichten, op. 82 ; Idylle, op. 34 ; Etudes de la Vélocité (Pf.), op. 61 ; Six easy Sonatas (Pf.) op. 81. Quartets and Trios for stringed instruments ; Overtures for orch. Songs and Part-songs, etc.

Berens is well known among modern composers for the Pianoforte by many graceful contributions to the general store.

BERG (Adam). German music publisher who flourished between the years 1540-1590. He is supposed to have died early in the 17th century.

"Patrocinium Musices," 1573-1589 is his principal publication, and is a collection of sacred music containing pieces by Lassus, Amon, Sale, etc.

BERG (Conrad M). German comp. and pianist, B. Colmar, April 27, 1785. S. at Paris Cons., 1806-7. Resided at Strasburg from 1808. Visited Paris during successive years 1810, 1818, 1835, 1851. D. Strasburg, Dec. 7, 1852.

WORKS.—First Concerto, Pf. and orch. ; Second, op. 21 ; Third, op. 32 ; Rondo, Pf. and orch., op. 24 ; Sonatas for violin and Pf., opp. 9, 23, 25 ; Three Trios for Pf., vn., and 'cello, op. 11 ; Two do., op. 15 ; Three do., op. 20 ; Three quartets for strings, op. 26 ; Quartet for Pf., vn., viola, and 'cello, op. 33 ; Sonatas for Pf. solo, opp. 5 and 30 ; Exercises, Fantasias, Variations, etc., for Piano ; Method for the Piano. Wrote also a history of the musical doings in Strasburg during 50 years, published in 1840.

F

BERG (Georg). German comp. [B. 1730], who lived in England during last century. S. under Dr. Pepusch. Gained 3 prizes from Catch Club for Glees. Was org. and teacher in London, 1771. His works consist of glees, songs, 12 Sonatinas or Lessons for the Harpsichord (op. 3), and miscellaneous instrumental works.

BERGER (Emile). French pianist and arranger. Resides in Glasgow as teacher of music. Arranger of numerous pieces for the Pianoforte, which exhibit some degree of talent. Berger is a pianist of ability.

BERGER (Francesco). German comp. and pianist. B. London, June 10, 1835. Educated in Germany. S. music in Italy under Luigi Ricci, and Carl Lickl. First works published in London, 1850. S. at Leipzig under Hauptmann and others. Settled in London as teacher and comp., 1855. Married to Miss Lascelles, the English contralto vocalist, 1864. Established an Amateur Society for the practice of concerted Pianoforte music, 1869. Has conducted several choral societies. Director of the Philharmonic Soc. for some years, and now its Hon. Secy.

WORKS.—An opera and a mass, produced in Italy ; Music for the private theatricals organised by Charles Dickens. Drei lieder, op. 18; Mondnacht, op. 19 ; Funf Lieder, op. 20. *Part-Songs*: Hurrah for merry England ; Arise, arise, the sunbeams hail ; Childhood's melody ; Essay, my heart ; Night, lovely night ; Now ; Song to Spring ; Sunset ; The dawn of May ; Echoes ; The Tritons ; Excelsior. *Songs*: Amor timido ; Fair, but fleeting ; Books ; An old fashion ; Is it not strange ? Birds of the flickering wing ; Thou still art left to me ; At last ; The blue heaven ; Faith in Spring ; I weep alone ; The song of evening ; There's rest for thee in heaven ; Sunshine o'er my soul ; The friends we love ; Thy will be done ; 10 two-part songs to Longfellow's poems. Numerous Pianoforte pieces, etc.

BERGER (Johann Anton). German org. and comp., B. 1719. D. 1777. Was org. at Cath. of Grenoble.

BERGER (Ludwig). German pianist and comp., B. Berlin, April 18, 1777. S. under Clementi. Visited London, where he practised as teacher, 1812-15. Returned to Germany and resided in Berlin as teacher and concert-giver, 1815-1839. D. Berlin, Feb. 16, 1839.

WORKS.—*Pianoforte*: Op. 1 ; Sonata pathétique, in C minor ; Sonatas, opp. 7, 9, 10, 18 ; Sonata, Pf. Duet, op. 15 ; Preludes and Fugues, op. 5 ; Preludes à la turque, op. 8 ; Twelve studies, op. 11 ; Rondo Pastoral ; Three Marches, op. 16. Several collections of songs for voice, with Pf. accomp. Cantatas. "Oreste," opera (MS.), never produced.

Berger was one of the connecting links binding the stately legato style of Clementi with the more modern development of Hummel, Moscheles, and Chopin. He was acknowledged by his contemporaries to be in the foremost rank as a pianist and teacher, while his works were popular. Among his works op. 11 will doubtless be the most durable. He was teacher of a number of musicians who have attained eminence ; among others may be mentioned Mendelssohn, Taubert, and Henselt.

BERGERRE (Alexandre Basile). French comp., violinist, and writer, B. Sep. 26, 1803. Author of "Nouvelle Classification des demi-tons," Paris, 8vo, 1833. "Méthode de Violon,...1837," etc.

BERGGREEN (Andreas Peter). Danish comp., B. Copenhagen, Mar. 2, 1801. D. 1880. Writer of cantatas, songs, prose works ; a Psalmebog, 1853 ; and a standard collection of Danish national melodies, entitled "Folke sange og Melodier, faedrelandske og fremmede, Samlede og udsatte," for Pf., 1869. He was an organist, and one of the teachers of Niels W. Gade.

BERGMANN (Josef). Bohemian comp., B. July 26, 1822. Writer of Pf. music, songs, etc.

BERGMANN (Karl). German cond. and violoncello player, B. Eisenach, Saxony, 1821. Settled in America, 1850. Resided in New York as teacher and cond., 1857-1877. D. New York, Aug. 10, 1876.

BERGONZI (Carlo). Italian violin-maker, flourished between the years 1716-1755. Learned under Antonio Stradivarius. His violins are beautifully modelled, and have a sweet and powerful tone. Other members of this family are Nicolo and Michele (1720-60), both makers of medium ability.

BERGSON (Michel). Polish comp., B. Warsaw, May, 1820. Writer of Pf. music, lieder, etc. A brilliant pianist, and comp. of much taste.

BERGT (Christian Gottlob August). German org. and comp., B. Freiberg, June 17, 1771. Org. of Ch. of St. Peter, Bautzen. D. Bautzen, Feb. 10, 1837.

WORKS.—La Passion, oratorio, op. 10. *Operas:* Laura et Fernando; Die Wunderkur; List gegen List; Erwin und Elmira; Das Stændchen. Symphony for orch., op. 12. Collections of Songs for voice and Pf.; Cantatas; Pianoforte and Organ music, church music, etc.

BERINGER (Oscar). German pianist and comp., B. Baden, 1844. First appeared as pianist at the Saturday Concerts of the Crystal Palace, Sydenham, 1861; S. at Leipzig Cons. under Moscheles, Reinecke, and Richter, 1864; S. at Berlin under Carl Tausig and F. Weitzmann. Resided in London since 1871. Established the "Academy for the Higher Development of Pianoforte Playing," 1873. Has given concerts in London and played at provincial festivals.

WORKS.—*Pianoforte:* Three series of six pieces for small hands; From blush to bloom; Gavotte; Allegretto; Transcription from Serenade by G. Weber; Three fairy Tales; Queen Mab; Gnome's wedding; Undine; Two Sonatinas, in F and, B flat; Andante and Presto Agitato, Pf. and orch., produced at Crystal Palace Concerts, and F. H. Cowen's Orchestral Concerts, 1880. Songs, etc.

BERINGER (Robert), brother of the above. German pianist and comp., B. Furtwangen, in the Black Forest, June 14, 1841. Pianist at the Crystal Palace, Sydenham, from 1861. Has played at numerous London and Provincial concerts, and is cond. of several Choral Societies. Lectured on the History of Pianoforte music and literature.

WORKS.—Songs; Choruses; Two orchestral pieces, both performed; Works for the Pianoforte, etc.

BERIOT (Charles Auguste de). Belgian violinist and comp., B. Louvain, Feb. 20, 1802. S. under Baillot and Viotti at Paris, 1821. *Début* in Paris. Appeared in London, at Philharmonic Soc. Concert, May, 1826. Solo violinist to King of the Netherlands, 1826-30. Travelled on Concert-tour with Mdlle. Malibran in England, France, Belgium, and Italy, 1830-1835. Married to Mdlle. Malibran, 1835. Prof. of violin in Brussels Cons., 1843-52. Retired, 1852. D. Brussels, April 8, 1870.

WORKS.—op. 1-3. Airs with variations, for violin and orch., in D minor, D, and E; opp. 7, 12, 15. Airs varied for vn. and orch.; op. 9. Ten studies for violin solo; op. 14. Variations for vn. and Pf., in A; op. 19. Duet for 2 vns., in E flat; op. 25. Duet on an original theme, in B flat; op. 26. First concerto for vn. and orch., in D; op. 27. Six Studies for vn. and Pf.; op. 32. Second concerto for vn. and orch., in B minor; op. 33. Nocturne (Rossini), vn. and Pf.; op. 35. Le Fruit de l'etude—six easy duets for 2 vns; op. 37. Three characteristic studies for vn. and Pf.; op. 39. Souvenirs d'Auber, violin duet; op. 41. Le Progrès, duets for 2 vns.; op. 42. Air with variations for vn. and orch., in D; op. 43. Three grand studies for 2 vns.; op. 44. Third concerto for violin and orch., in E; op. 45. Six Morceaux de Salon on original themes for vn, and Pf.; op. 46. Fourth concerto for violin and orch., in D min.; op. 48. Souvenir de Boulogne, duets for 2 vns.; op. 50. La Soirée de Boulogne, do.; op. 52. Air with variations for vn. and Pf.; op. 54. Duet for 2 vns.; op. 55. Fifth concerto for vn. and orch, in D; op. 58. First trio for Pf., violin, and 'cello; op. 59. Valses, vn., and Pf.; op. 67. Three duets, concertante, for 2 vns.; op. 68. First sonata concertante for vn. and Pf.; op. 69. Air with variations, vn. and Pf., in D; op. 70. Sixth concerto for violin and orch., in A; op. 71. Second trio for Pf., vn., and 'cello; op. 72. Duet, Pf. and vn.; opp. 73, 74. Duets, vn. and Pf.; op. 75. Guide des Violonistes, studies in 2 parts; op. 76. Seventh concerto for violin and orch., in G; op. 77-98. Minor works for violin and other instruments; op. 99. Eighth concerto for violin and orch., in G; op. 100.

Fantasia for violin and orch. ; op. 122. Overture for Pf. and vn. ; op. 127. Tenth concerto for vn. and orch., in A minor. Methode de Violon, en trois parties, Paris, 1858. A number of minor works consisting of variations and arrangements of operatic airs constitute the remaining portion of de Beriot's works.
Beriot was a prolific composer, and as bright and clever in one work as in another. His compositions are moderately easy, brilliant, and always pretty. The airs and concertos are of especial value to the violinist. In them will be found a wealth of bright ideas, and exercise of benefit alike to the fingers and the mind. As a violinist de Beriot is generally classed along with the school of which Paginini is the chief. This school aims at securing popular applause by the practice of various tricks tending to mystify by their seeming complexity. That Beriot was a follower in this school cannot be doubted. But that he was superior as an artist to Paganini is also true. His compositions are not whimsical nor eccentric, and can be appreciated by any one. His dexterity, if inferior to that of Paganini, was counterbalanced by his less frequent indulgence in mechanical trickery.

BERIOT (Charles Wilfrid de). French pianist and comp., son of the above, B. Paris, Feb. 12, 1833. Comp. Pf. music, songs, etc.

BERLIN (Johann Daniel). German comp. and org., B. Memel, 1710. D. 1775. Writer on music, and comp. of chamber music. "Anleitung zur Tonometrie,..." 1767, is his chief work.

BERLIOZ (Hector). French comp., B. Côte-Saint-André, Isère, December 11, 1803. Sent to Paris to study medicine, 1821. S. music under Lesueur and Reicha at the Cons. Gained second prize for comp. Gained the Grand "Prix d Rome," 1830. Travelled in Italy, Germany, and Russia. Married to Miss Smithson, an Irish actress. Librarian to the Paris Cons., 1839. Decorated with the Cross of the Legion of Honour, 1839. Cond. New Philharmonic Concerts, London, 1852; cond. his " Benvenuto Cellini," at Covent Garden Theatre, London, June 25, 1853. D. Paris, March 8 [9], 1869.

WORKS.—Op. 1. Overture—Waverley, for full orch. [c. 1828]; op. 2. Irlande : Melodies for one and two voices, choruses and Pf. accomp.; op. 3. Overture—Des Francs-Juges for full orch.; op. 4. Overture—King Lear, for full orch.; op. 5. Messe des Morts (Requiem), for solo voices, chorus and orch., Paris, 1837; op. 6. Le cinq Mai, Chant for Death of Napoleon I., for bass solo, chorus and orch.; op. 7. Les Nuits d' eté : Six songs for solo voice and Pf.; op. 8. Rêverie et Caprice, for violin and orch.; op. 10. Traité d' Instrumentation; op. 11. Sara la baigneuse, ballade for three choruses and orch.; op. 12. La Captive : Rêverie for contralto voice and orch.; op. 13. Fleurs des Landes : Five songs for solo voice and Pf.; op. 14. Episode sur la vie d'un artist : Symphonie-fantastique, for full orch.; op. 14 a. Le Retour à la vie, Mélalogue, for solo voices, chorus and orch., Paris, 1832; op. 15. Symphony : Symphonie Funèbre et Triomphale, with an orch. of string instruments and a choir ad libitum ; op. 16. Symphony : Harold in Italie, for full orch., in four parts, with an alto-principal part, Paris, 1834, London, 1855; op. 17. Symphony : Romeo et Julietta, for full orch., with solos and chorus, Paris, 1839, Vienna, 1856 ; op. 18. Tristia, Meditation Religieuse, for three choirs and orch.; op. 19. Feuillets d' Album, three pieces for Pf.; op. 20. Vox Populi, Hymn for two choirs and orch.; op. 21. Overture : Le Corsaire, for full orch.; op. 22. Te Deum for three choirs and organ ; op. 23. Opera : Benvenuto Cellini, in three acts, Paris, 1838, London, 1853 ; op. 24. La Damnation de Faust, Legend in four parts, for full orch., solo voices and chorus, Paris, 1846 ; op. 25. L'Enfance du Christ : Trilogie Sacrée, for solo voices, chorus and orch. (Part I., Le Songe d' Hérode ; Part II., La Fuite en Egypte ; Part III., L' Arrivée à Sais), Paris, 1854 ; op. 26. L' Imperiale : Cantata for two choruses and orch. *Unnumbered Works:* La Belle Isabeau, chorus and orch. ; Le Temple universel, for chorus and organ ; Prière du Matin, for chorus and Pf.; Le Chasseur danois, for bass voice and Pf.; L' Invitation à la valse (Weber), arranged for orch.; March Marocaine (L. de Meyer), arranged for orch.; Recitatives for Der Freischütz (Weber) ; Beatrice et Bénédict, opera in 2 acts, Paris, 1862 ; Les Troyens à Carthage, opera in 5 acts, and a prelude, Paris, 1864 ; La Prise de Troie, opera in three acts. *Literary Works:* 'A travers chants, études musicale, adorations, boutades et critiques, Paris, 12mo, 1862 ; Voyage Musical en Allemagne et en Italie : études sur Beethoven, Gluck et Weber, Paris, 2 vols., 8vo, 1844 ; Les Soirées de l'Orchestre, Paris, 1853 ; Les Grotesques de la Musique, Paris, 8vo, 1859; Mémoires d' Hector Berlioz, comprenant ses voyages en Italie, en Allemagne en Russie et en Angleterre, 1803-1865, Paris, 8vo, 1870. In addition to the foregoing works, Berlioz wrote a large number of contributions to periodical literature.

Only within recent times has the genius of Berlioz been fully admitted. In his own day he received but scant attention, and, it may be said, less than justice; but now a complete revulsion of feeling has taken place among musicians, and we see as the result Berlioz elevated to the highest place among instrumental composers. His works are of a bold and original stamp, and strike the ordinary and non-partizan observer as being on the whole whimsical, and marked by an undue straining after impressive effect. His admirers, on the other hand, discern nothing in them which does not discover some profound wrinkle of an incomprehensible mind. It may safely be said, however, be the merits of the works ever so high, that without the printed *programme*, their value as works of art would be very questionable. A great array of forces managed with skill denotes an ambitious mechanic rather than an inspired architect; and when we see conjoined to this display a continual effort to be vast, profound, or terror-inspiring, the reflection is forced upon us that there must be some considerable weakness to hide beneath all this weight of the machinery of genius. His works have been repeatedly performed in Britain within recent years, and the result has been considerably to modify the impressions formed of the supernatural power of the composer. He has been found to be merely human, but also ambitious, and one who strove to force the orchestra into the *delineation* of scenes and events which are quite beyond the graphic powers of musical art, and certainly beyond the capabilities of instrumental resource. A long time must pass before his place is thoroughly fixed, and in the meantime it is only just to admit that, when considered apart from their trappings of instrumental trickery, some of his works are of the most dignified and noble nature. "The Damnation of Faust," the "Requiem," the operas, and certain other works are most striking and inspired creations. Others, again, though picturesque and full of variety, seem overweighed by a superfluity of orchestral colouring.

Much has been written in recent years anent Berlioz and his works, and among works of interest may be named:—"Autobiography of Hector Berlioz from 1803 to 1865; comprising his Travels in Italy, Germany, Russsia, and England. Trans. by Rachel and Eleanor Holmes." Lond., 2 vols., 8vo, 1884. "Correspondence inédite, avec notice biographique par D. Bernard." Paris, 1879, 2nd ed. "L'Œuvre Dramatique de H. Berlioz, par A. Ernst." Paris, 1884. "Berlioz, l'homme et l'artiste d'après des documents nouveaux, par E. Hippeau." Paris, 1883, with portrait. "Berlioz," by Joseph Bennett, London, 1883. "Lettres intimes." Paris, 1881. "Life and Letters of Berlioz, Trans. by H. M. Dunstan." Lond., 2 vols., 8vo, 1882—from Bernard's work. In addition to the foregoing reference should be made to the following magazine articles:—Fraser's Magazine, 1848 (vol. 38), and 1851 (vol. 45); Eclectic Magazine, v. 15; All the Year Round, 1868 (vol. 21); London Society (vol. 39); Edinburgh Review, 1870 (vol. 133); Atlantic Monthly, 1877 (vol. 41); Appleton's Journal, 1880 (vol. 24), etc. An edition of his literary works was published in German by R. Pohl, Leipzig, 1865, in 4 vols. under the title, "Gesammelte Schrifte."

BERLYN (Anton W.) Dutch comp., B. Amsterdam, May 2, 1817. D. Amsterdam, Jan. 20, 1870. Writer of operas, symphonies, cantatas, oratorios, concertos, quartets, songs, etc.

BERNABEI (Giuseppe Ercole). Italian comp., B. Caprarola, 1620. S. under Benevoli. Chap.-master St. John, Latern, and at Munich. D. Munich, 1690. He comp. "Concerto madrigalesco a tre voci," 1669; "Madrigali a cinque e sei voci," 1669; "Opus Motettorum," 1690; Magnificats, etc. His son, GIUSEPPE ANTONIO, B. Rome, 1659, D. Munich, March 9, 1732, comp. masses, operas, and instrumental music.

BERNACCHI (Antonio). Italian soprano vocalist, B. Bologna [1690]. S. under Pistocchi. Sang in London in Handel's "Rinaldo," 1717. Returned to Italy. Vocalist in service of the Elector of Bavaria. Re-appeared in London, where he sang in Italian opera, 1729. Settled at Bologna as teacher, 1730.

Principal of the Società Filarmonica, Bologna, 1748-49. D. Bologna, March, 1756.

This vocalist enjoyed much success in his time, and was regarded as a good exponent of the music of Handel.

BERNARD (Paul). French comp. and writer, B. Poitiers, Oct. 4, 1827. S. under Halévy. Writer of Pf. music, critical miscellanies, etc. D. 1879.

BERNARDIN (Bernard) or *Courtois*. French comp. and violinist, B. 1826. D. Paris, 1870. Wrote dramatic music, violin pieces, etc.

BERNASCONI (Antonia). Italian soprano vocalist who flourished during last century. She made her *début* in Gluck's "Alceste," Vienna, 1764. Sang in London, 1768, and throughout Europe with some success.

BERNER (Friedrich Wilhelm). German comp. and org., B. Breslau, March 16, 1780. Studied under his father, an org., and Reichardt. Org. of Church of S. Elizabeth, Breslau. Compiled a catalogue of the music in suppressed monasteries. D. Breslau, May, 1827.

WORKS.—Cantata, libretto by S. G. Bürde, for four voices and orch. ; Three songs for 2 sopranos, tenor and bass, op. 26 ; Der Here is Gott, Hymn for 4 male voices and orch. of wind instruments ; Le Maître de Chapelle, comic interlude ; Three Choruses for a Tragedy ; Numerous pieces for the Pf. ; Preludes and Offertoires for the organ ; Songs ; Church music, etc. Grundregeln des Gesanges, nach Hiller entwarfen, Breslau, 1815 ; Theorie der Choralzwischenspiele, 1819 ; Die Lehre der Musikalischen Interpunktion, 1821. His biography was published in 1821.

BERNHARD (Christoph). German comp., org., and writer, B. Dantzig, 1612. D. 1692.

BERNHARDT (J. W.) Author of "Music and Mind, and Musical Physics." Lond. [1878].

BERNIER (Nicolas). French Comp., B. Mantes-sur-Seine, June 28, 1664. D. Paris, 1734. Writer of church music, "Motets," 1703, 1713, etc.

BERNSDORF (Eduard). German writer and song comp., B. Dessau, March 25, 1825. S. under F. Schneider and Marx. Edited the "Neues Universal-Lexikon der Tonkunst," Dresden, 3 vols., 1855. This writer has gained considerable notoriety in Germany as a species of Hazlitt or Jeffery in musical criticism.

BERRÉ (Ferdinand). Belgian comp., B. Ganshoren, Feb. 5, 1843. Writer of operas, Pf. music, etc.

BERSELLI (Matteo). Italian tenor vocalist, who flourished at the beginning of last century. Sang in London in Buononcini's "Astartus," Nov. 19, 1720. Biography unknown. Disappeared about 1721.

BERTALI (Antonio). Italian comp., B. Verona, 1605. D. [?] Wrote masses, sonatas, etc.

BERTELMAN (J. G.). Dutch comp. and pianist, B. Amsterdam, 1782. D. 1854. Wrote masses, cantatas, overtures, songs, etc.

BERTELSMANN (Carl August). German comp., B. Gütersloh, Westphalia, Aug 3, 1811. D. Amsterdam, Nov. 30, 1861. Writer of part-songs, lieder, organ music, etc.

BERTEZEN (Salvatore). Italian writer, author of "Principi della Musica," London, 8vo, 1781. Trans. as "Extract of the Work entitled Principles of Music," London, 8vo, 1782.

BERTHA (Alexander). Hungarian comp. and celebrated pianist. B. Pesth. Pupil of Moscheles and Bülow. Comp. for the Pf. and writer of songs.

BERTHAUME (Isidore). French comp. and violinist, B. Paris, 1752. D. S. Petersburg, March 20, 1802.

BERTHOLD (Carl Friedrich Theodor). German comp., B. Dresden, Dec. 18, 1815. Wrote masses, symphonies, oratorios, etc. D. Dresden, April 28, 1882.

BERTIN (Louise Angelique). French pianist and comp., B. near Paris, 1805. Has sung successfully in public. She has also composed three operas, Le Loup garou, 1827 ; Faust, 1831 ; and Notre-Dame de Paris, 1836. D. Paris, April, 1877.

BERTINI (Auguste). French writer. Author of "Phonological System for Learning and Acquiring extraordinary Facility on all Musical Instruments in a very short space of time,"...Lond., fo, 1830. [Other editions.] "Stigmatographie ou l'art d'ecrire avec des points,"...Paris, 8vo, n. d.

BERTINI (Domenico). Italian comp., B. Lucca, June 26, 1826. Writer of cantatas, masses, etc.

BERTINI (Henri Jérome). French comp. and pianist, B. London, Oct. 28, 1798. S. under his father, etc. Travelled through Germany and Holland. Travelled in England and Scotland. Resided in Paris as teacher and concert-giver from 1821. D. Meylan, near Grenoble, Oct. 1, 1876.
WORKS.—Studies for the Pf., opp. 29, 32, 66, 86, 94, 100, 133, 134, 134a, 137, 142, 147, 166, 175, 176, 177, 178, 180 ; Trios for Pf., violin, and 'cello ; Sextets for Pf., 2 violins, viola, 'cello, and bass, opp. 79, 85, 90, 114 ; Sonatas for Pf. and violin, opp. 152, 153, 156 ; Nonetto for Pf. and wind instruments.
The series of "Studies" in the foregoing list are the works by which Bertini will continue to be known. He was a renowned pianist in his day, and contributed not a little to the development of the brilliant school of execution. Like Heller and Ascher, to whose school he belonged, he excelled in music of a light and dashing character.

BERTINI (Salvatore). Italian comp., B. Palermo, 1721. S. under Pozzuolo. D. Dec. 16, 1794. Comp. church music, sonatas, etc. His son, GIUSEPPE, ABBE', B. Palermo, 1756, D. after 1847, wrote a "Dizionario Storico-critico degli Scrittori di Musica," Palerm," 4 vols., 4to, 1814-15.

BERTINOTTI (Teresa). Italian soprano vocalist, B. Savigliano, Piedmont, 1776. Sang in London, Paris, Germany, Spain, and Italy with much success. Married to Felice Radicati. D. Bologna Feb. 12, 1854.

BERTOLLI (Francesca). Italian contralto vocalist who flourished in the 18th century. Sang in Handel's operas during 1729-37. D. [unknown].

BERTON (Henri Montan). French comp. and writer, B. Paris, Sept. 17, 1767. S. under Rey and Sacchini. Violinist in orch. of the Opera, Paris, 1773. Formed connection with Mdlle. Maillard, by whom he had an illegitimate son, François, 1782. Prof. of Harmony at Paris Cons., 1795. Cond. of Italian Opera, Paris, 1807. Mem. of the Institut, 1815. D. Paris, April 22, 1844.
WORKS.—*Operas:* Le Premier Navigateur, 1786 ; Les Promesses de Mariage, 1787 ; La Dame invisible. 1787 ; Cora, 1789 ; Les Brouilleries, 1789 ; Les Deux Sentinelles, 1790. Les Rigueurs du Cloître, 1790 ; Le Nouveau d'Assas, 1791 ; Les Deux Sous-lieutenants, 1791 ; Eugène, 1792 ; Viala, 1792 ; Tyrtée, 1793 ; Ponce de Léon, 1794 ; Le Souper de Famille, 1796 ; Le Dénouement in attendu, 1798 ; Montano et Stephanie, 1799 ; L'Amour bizarre, 1799 ; Le Délire, 1799 ; Le Nouvelle au camp, 1799 ; Le Grand Deuil, 1801 ; Le Concert interrompu, 1802 ; Aline, Reine de Golconde, 1803 ; La Romance, 1804 ; Delia et Verdikan, 1805 ; Le Vaisseau amiral, 1805 ; Les Maris-garçons, 1806 ; Le Chevalier de Sénanges, 1807 ; Ninon chez Madame de Sévigné, 1807 ; Françoise de Foix, 1809 ; Le Charme de la voix, 1811 ; Valentin, 1814 ; Feodor, 1816 ; Roger de Sicile. 1817 ; Corisandro, 1820 ; Virginie, 1823 ; Les Mousquetaires, 1824 ; La Mère et la Fille ; Les Petits Appartements, 1827. *Cantatas:* various. *Oratorios:* Absalon, 1786 ; Jephté ; David dans le temple ; Les Bergers de Bethléem. Ballets. Romances for voice and Pf. Traité d'Harmonie...Paris, 4to [1815] ; De la Musique mécanique et de la Musique philosophique, Paris, 1822 ; Writings against Rossini and other literary works.

Like other French composers, Berton has only enjoyed a temporary success. His works are now unknown outside historical books, and may be said to be dead to the musical world.

BERTON (Francois). French comp., B. Paris, May 3, 1784. Natural son of H. M. Berton and Mdlle. Maillard. S. at Paris Cons., 1796. D. [?] Wrote several operas and ballets.

BERTON (Pierre Montan). French comp., B. Paris, 1727. Leader at the Paris Opera House. D. Paris, 1780. Father of Henri M. Berton.

WORKS.—*Operas:* Deucalion et Pyrrha, 1755 ; Erosine, 1768 ; Sylvie, 1766 ; Théonis, 1767 ; Adèle de Ponthieu, 1773, etc.

BERTONI (Ferdinando Giuseppe). Italian comp. and org., B. Venice, 1727. S. under Padre Martini. Org. of S. Mark's, Venice, 1750. Choirmaster of Cons. dei Mendicanti, 1757-97. Appeared in London as comp., 1778. Choir-master of S. Mark's, Venice, 1785. D. 1810.

WORKS.—*Operas:* Orinzio e Curiazio, 1746 ; La Vedova Accorta, 1746; Cajetto, 1747 ; Ipermestra, 1748 ; Le Pescatrici, 1752 ; Geneura, 1753 ; La Moda, 1754 ; Le Vicenda amorose, 1760 ; La Belle Girometta ; Amore in Musica, 1763; Achille in Sciro, 1764 ; L'Ingannatore ingannato, 1764 ; L'Olimpiade, 1765 ; Alessandro nell Indie, 1770 ; L'Anello incantato, 1771 ; Andromacea, 1772 ; Aristo e Temira, 1774 ; Orfeo, 1776 ; Ezio, 1777 ; Telemacco, 1777 ; Quinto Fabio, 1778 ; Tancredi, 1778 ; Artaserse, London, 1780 ; Armida, 1781 ; Eumene, 1784 ; La Nitteti, 1789 ; Ifigenia in Aulide, 1790. Cantatas ; Ballets ; String Quartets, etc.

BERTUCH (Karl Volckmar). German org., B. Erfurt, 1730. D. Berlin, 1776.

BERWALD (Johann Friedrich). Swedish comp., B. Stockholm, July 23, 1788. Travelled as an infant prodigy till 1817. Cond. and choir-master at Stockholm, 1819-68. D. Stockholm, Sept., 1861.

WORKS.—Op. 1. Three Polonaises for Pf. and violin, 1798 ; Symphony for orch., 1799 ; Three quartets for stringed instruments, 1808 ; Sonata for Pf., op. 6. ; Songs, etc.

This musician did much for the propagation of musical taste in Sweden as a conductor, although none of his works, save the songs, are of much value. His cousin FRANZ (B. Stockholm, 1796. D. there, April 3, 1868), comp. much instrumental music.

BESLER (Samuel). German comp., B. Silesia, Dec. 15, 1574. D. Breslau, July 19, 1625. Wrote church music, etc.

BESOZZI (Alessandro). Italian oboe-player, B. Parma, 1700. Oboist to the King of Sardinia. D. Turin, 1775. One of a most famous family of instrumentalists, of whom ANTONIO, his brother (B. Parma, 1707 ; oboist to King of Sardinia, 1775-1781 ; D. 1781); CARLO, son of Antonio, oboist (B. Dresden, 1745 ; D. (?) ; and HIERONIMO, his brother, basson-player (B. Parma, 1713 ; D. Turin [?];) were the chief members, forming one of the most remarkable groups of wind instrument performers known to musical history.

BESSEMS (Antoine). Belgian comp. and violinist. B. Antwerp, April 4, 1806. D. Paris, Oct. 19, 1868. Wrote concertos for violin, masses, Pf. music, songs, etc.

BESSON (Gustave Auguste). French maker of wind instruments. Has gained several prizes in Exhibitions of 1851, 1855, etc., for excellence of manufacture. The manufactory is in Paris with branches.

BEST (William Thomas). English org. and comp., B. Carlisle, Aug. 13, 1826. S. under Young of Carlisle Cath. Org. successively of Pembroke Chap., Liverpool, 1840 ; the Church for the Blind, Liverpool, 1847 ; Liverpool Philarmonic Soc., 1848 ; Panopticon of Science and Art, London, 1852 ; Church of S. Martin's-in-the-Fields, 1852 ; Lincoln's Inn Chap., 1854 ; St. George's Hall, Liverpool, 1855 ; Parish Church of Wallasay, Birkenhead, 1860 ; Holy Trinity Church, near Liverpool, 1863 ; Musical Soc. of Liverpool, 1868 ; Royal Albert Hall, 1871 ; West Derby Parish Church, 1879. Has played frequently in Paris, Rome, the English provinces, London, and in Scotland and Ireland.

WORKS.—*Organ:* Arrangements for the Scores of the Great Masters, 5 vols.; The Art of Organ Playing, in 4 parts, London, n. d.; Collection of Pieces expressly Composed for Church Use, 6 Books; Sonata for Org., in G; Thirty Progressive Studies for the Use of Young Students; Handel Album, 20 vols.; Four Concert Fantasias; Christmas Fantasy on Ancient English Carols; Modern School for the Organ (Cocks), Lond. 1855; Handel's Six Organ Concertos (edited) 2 series; and opera and oratorio songs; Hommage à Handel, by I. Moscheles, arranged for org.; Three Preludes and Fugues; Six Concert Pieces; Andante with vars.; Introduction and Fugue (ded. to Hesse); Collection of Italian org. comps., edited; "Cecilia," a collection of org. pieces in diverse styles; Overture for orch., Festival, in C; and Marche Triomphale. *Pianoforte Music:* Marche Militaire; Romanesca, op. 16; Notturno, op. 27; Marche Triomphale, op. 21; Serenade from Don Juan. *Church Music:* Morning and Evening Service, composed for the Parish Church, Leeds, op. 40; A Morning, Communion, and Evening Service in simple chant form; A Morning and Evening Chant Service; A Communion Service, consisting of Kyrie, Nicene Creed, Sanctus, and Gloria; An Evening Service adapted to the Ancient Gregorian Plain Chant; Benedicite omnia opera; Te Deum in C; The Athanasian Creed. *Anthems, etc.:* Behold I bring you glad tidings; I will magnify Thee, O God, my King; Praise the Lord, call upon His name; The Lord is great in Sion; While shepherds watched their flocks by night; Abide with me (hymn); Jesus Christ is risen (hymn); Dies Iræ (hymn). What mournful thoughts. Glee for 5 voices.

Mr. Best is generally acknowledged to be the greatest master of the organ now living in Britain. He belongs to that school of modern development which endeavours to make the organ the exponent of orchestral works. That the organ is in itself capable of producing orchestral effects in an adequate manner is indisputable, and the excellent manner in which it has been proved should be sufficient to reconcile those who imagine that it is performing out of its function and lending its powers to trickery. Best's technical knowledge of the instrument is great, while he possesses the utmost command over its various features. His recitals at Liverpool are among the most interesting items of the musical season in that city, and he has played with the greatest success throughout the provinces of England and in Scotland. He is great in every style, from Bach to Guilmant, and is particularly grand in his rendering of the divine fugues of the former master. His compositions for the Church Service are also highly deserving of praise, and are frequently produced in cathedrals and churches throughout England. Many of his anthems are in constant use in English churches. His didactic works are among the standard instruction books of the period, and are remarkable for the clearness of their explanations and the practical character of their descriptions.

BETTINI (Alessandro). Italian tenor vocalist, B. Rome, 1830. S. under Sgatelli. *Début* at Madrid in 1853. *Début* in England at H.M. Theatre, London, 1862. Sang in St. Petersburg. Married to Mdlle. Trebelli, 1863.

Signor Bettini is allowed to be a most useful tenor, and his voice is of an agreeable quality.

BETTS (Arthur). English violinist and comp. of end of 18th and beginning of 19th centuries. B. in Lincolnshire. S. under Hindmarsh, Votti, Dussek, and Steibelt. Comp. sonatas, duets for vn. and 'cello; arrangements, etc.

BETTS (Edward). English musician and writer of 18th century. He compiled "An Introduction to the Skill of Musick;" Anthems, Hymns, and "Psalm Tunes in several parts." Lond., 8vo, 1724.

BETTS (John). English violin-maker, B. Stamford, Lincolnshire, 1755. Pupil of Richard Duke. Carried on business in shop in Royal Exchange, London. D. London, 1823. The quality of his violins is admired by some judges but depreciated by others. His nephew, EDWARD BETTS, also a pupil of Duke's, copied Amati with great success. He died [1815-20].

BEUMER (Henri). French comp. and violinist, B. Leuwarden, 1831. Writer of violin music, ballets, overtures, songs.

BEVIN (Elway). Welsh comp. and org., B. about middle of 16th century [1560-70]. S. under Tallis. Org. of Bristol Cath., 1589. Gent. Extraordinary, Chap.-Roy., 1605. Lost both places on being discovered a Roman Catholic, 1637. D. [1640].

WORKS.—A Briefe and Short Introduction to the Art of Musicke, to teach how to make Discant of all Proportions that are in use : very necessary for all such as are desirous to attaine to knowledge in the Art ; and may, by Practice, if they can sing, soon be able to compose three, four, and five parts ; and also to compose all sorts of Canons that are usuall, by these Directions, of two or three parts in one, upon a Plain Song, 1631 ; A Short Service in D minor, and "Praise the Lord," anthem, in Barnard's Collection. Other anthems exist in manuscript.

Bevin was the teacher of Dr. Child. "Though the accent of his compositions is not always correct, and his modulation partakes of the antique, the fulness of his harmony, and general dignity of his style, compensate for those defects, and demand the indulgence due to a man of acknowledged science and genius."—*Busby*. Bevin is usually credited with having been the first in England to systematise the rules for the composition of canons.

BEXFIELD (William Richard). English comp. and org., B. Norwich, April 27, 1824. S. under Dr. Zachariah Buck. Org. of Boston Ch., Lincoln. Mus. Bac, Oxon., 1846. Unsuccessful candidate for the Music Professorship of Oxford University. Org. of St. Helen's Church, Bishopgate Street, Lond., 1848. Mus. Doc. Cantab., 1849. D. London, Oct. 29, 1853.

WORKS.—Israel Restored, oratorio, Sept. 22, 1852 ; reproduced, 1879 ; Church Anthems, in score, with portrait, Lond., n. d. ; A Set of Fugues for the Organ, Lond., n. d. ; songs and part-songs ; organ music, etc.

The revivification of this composer's oratorio in 1879 gave rise to much favourable criticism among competent writers, and it was allowed that had Bexfield lived he would have proved an ornament to the English school of church music. "Israel Restored" is a work of much promise, but cannot be said to be a mature work of genius.

BEYER (Ferdinand). German comp. and pianist, B. Querfurt, Saxony, July 25, 1803. Was arranger and editor in employment of Messrs. Schott and Co., Mayence. D. Mayence, May 14, 1863.

WORKS.—*Pianoforte :* Des Hausesletzte Stunde, Fantasia, op. 31 ; Les Charmes de l'opera, op. 33 ; Répertoire des Jeunes Pianistes, op. 36 ; Bouquets de Mélodies, op. 42 ; Six Morceaux Elégants sur des Airs allemands favoris, op. 80 ; Le Premier Début, 24 pieces arranged for Pf., op. 83 ; Fleurs Italiennes, op. 87 ; Heures de loisir, dances, op. 92 ; Fantasias and minor arrangements without number. Berger's works possess considerable value as teaching pieces, but their artistic merits are not much above the average.

BEYLE (Marie Henri). French writer, B. Grenoble, 1783. D. Paris, 1842. He published, under the *nom de plume* of L. A. C. Bombet, "Lettres écrites de Vienne en Autriche sur le célèbre compositeur Joseph Haydn, suivies d' une vie de Mozart, et de considérations sur Métastase et l'état présent de la Musique en France et en Italie," Paris, 8vo, 1814. Re-issued as "Vies de Haydn, et de Métastase," Paris, 8vo, 1854. This work was stolen from a similar book issued by Carpani. It was translated into English as "The Lives of Haydn and Mozart with Observations on Metastasio..." Lond., 8vo, 1817 ; 2nd edit., 1818. Under the name of M. de Stendhal he also published a "Vie de Rossini," Paris, 1823. English translation, anonymous, 1824. Second edition, Paris, 1854. This is also a plagarism of a work by Carpani. Beyle's other writings are very numerous, and comprise many other subjects besides music.

BEZDECK (Friedrich Wenzel). Bohemian comp. and violinist, B. Prague, Sept. 24, 1804. Writer of quartets, Pf. music, violin music, songs, etc.

BIAGGI (Gerolamo Alessandro), *Ippolito d' Albano.* Italian writer and critic, B. Milan, 1815. S. music at Milan Con. He acted as musical critic for the *Gazetta d' Italia,* and wrote a work entitled "Della Musica Religiosa e delle questioni inerenti discorso," Milan, 8vo, 1856. He has also contributed largely to periodical literature.

BIAL (Carl). German comp. of Pf. music and songs. B. Habelschwerdt, near Glatz, July 14, 1833.

BIANCHI (Francesco). Italian comp., B. Cremona, 1752. Chap.-master at Cremona. Mem. of Italian opera orch. at Paris, 1775. Assistant cond. at Ch. of S. Ambrogio, Milan, 1784. Second org. of S. Mark's, Venice, 1785. Came to London, 1793. Married to Miss Jackson, 1800. Teacher and comp. in London. Committed suicide, Hammersmith, London, Nov. 27, 1810.

WORKS.—*Operas:* La Réduction de Paris, 1777 ; Castor a Polluce, 1780; Trionfo della Pace, 1782 ; Demofoonte, 1783 ; Brisside, 1784 ; La Caccia d' Enrico iv., 1784; Asparde principe Battriano, 1784 ; Il Dissertoro, 1785; La Villanella rapita, 1785 ; Piramo et Tisbe, 1786 ; La Vergine del Sole, 1786; Scipione Africano, 1787 ; La Secchia rapita, 1787 ; L' Orfano della China, 1787 ; Pizarro, 1788 ; Mesenzio, 1788 ; Alessandro nell' Indie, 1788 ; Tarara, 1788 ; Il Ritratto, 1788 ; L' Inglese stravagante, 1789 ; Il Gatto, 1789 ; La Morte di Giulio Cesare, 1789 ; L' Arminio, 1790 ; La Dame bizzaria, 1790 ; Cajo Ostilio, 1791 ; La Capriccioso ravveduta, 1793 ; L'Olandese, 1794 ; La Stravagante, 1795 ; Zenobia, Lond.; Inez de Castro ; Aci e Galatea ; La Semiramide, 1798. *Oratorios:* Agar, 1791 ; Joas, 1791. Songs and other vocal music.

Bianchi was the teacher of Sir H. R. Bishop and other musicians who have attained eminence. His operas were pleasing but not original. They are now completely forgotten.

BIBER (Heinrich Johann Franz von). Bohemian violinist and comp. B. Wartenberg, 1638. Vice chap.-master at Court of Bishop of Salzburg. D. Salzburg, 1698.

WORKS.—Fidicinium Sacro profanum, 1681 ; Harmonico artificioso-ariosa ; Vesperae longiores ac breviores, una cum litaniis Lauretanis a quatuor vocibus, Salzburg, 1693 ; Sonatas for violin and bass, etc.

He was esteemed an excellent performer and composer in his day, and introduced several effects into the style of violin playing practised in his time.

BIBL (Andreas). Austrian comp., B. Vienna, April 8, 1797 (1807). Org. at the Ch. of S. Stephen, Vienna, from 1818.

WORKS.—Twelve preludes for org., op. 3 ; Salvi Regina for 4 voices and org., op. 5 ; Three Ave Maria, do., op. 6 ; Two Tantum Ergo, for 4 voices and org., op. 8 ; Graduel, for 4 voices, strings, and org., op. 9 ; Cadences for the org., op. 10 ; Thirty-two Versels for org., op. 7 ; Three Prelude for org., op. 12. ; Do., op. 13 ; Do., op. 15 ; Twenty Preludes for organ, op. 16 ; Fugue for the organ, in C, op. 17 ; Offertoire for tenor voice, chorus, small orch., and org., op. 18 ; Graduel for 4 voices, small orch., and org., op. 19 ; Mass for 4 voices, small orch., and org., op. 20 ; Tantum Ergo, for soprano voice, chorus and orch., op. 21 ; Tantum Ergo for contralto solo, chorus, and orch., in E flat, op. 22 ; Prelude and Fugue for org., op. 23, etc.

BIBL (Rudolph). Son of the above, B. Vienna, 1832. He has written a number of works for organ and Pianoforte, and is a good performer on the former instrument.

BICKHAM (George). English engraver and penman, flourished in the first part of the 18th century. He published "The Musical Entertainer," 2 vols. fo. [c. 1750], a collection of songs of some value. He died in 1769.

BICKING (Alfred). German comp. and vocalist, B. Berlin, 1840. D. 1864. Wrote an opera, songs, etc.

BICKNELL (John Laurence). English writer and barrister-at-law, and reputed author of "Musical Travels through England, by Joel Collier, Licenciate in Music." Lond., 12mo, 1774 (various editions). In 1818 appeared "Redivivus, an entirely edition of that celebrated Author's Musical Travels." The work is a satire on Burney, and is an amusing production, now getting very scarce. It has also been ascribed to Peter Beckford, a writer and musical amateur of last century.

BIDDLE (Horace P.) American theoretical writer, has published the "Musical Scale," a scientific treatise on the tones of the scales, etc. (Ditson, Boston, n.d.)

BIENAIMÉ (Paul Emile). French comp., teacher, and writer, B. Paris, July 6, 1802. Prof. of accompaniment and harmony in Paris Cons. from 1828. D. Paris, Jan. 17, 1869. He was chiefly celebrated as a successful teacher. He wrote "l'Histoire du Piano depuis son origine, etc." Paris, 3 vols., 1863; "Cinquante études d'harmonie pratique." Paris, 1844.

BIERY (Gottlob Benedict). German comp., B. Dresden, July 25, 1772. S. under Weinlig. Music director of opera at Vienna, 1807; ditto at Breslau, 1824. D. Breslau, May 5, 1840.

WORKS.—Numerous operettas and cantatas, a complete list of which is contained in the "Dictionnaire" of Fétis.

A few of his cantatas still survive, but are not generally known.

BIGGS (Edward Smith). English glee comp. and pianist, B. during latter half of 18th century. D. about [1820]. Was a celebrated teacher of music in London.

WORKS.—*Pianoforte:* Twenty-eight Waltzes; Rondos and and Marches. *Glees:* Ah! me, with that false one; A poor soul sat sighing; Beneath this stone lies Catherine Gray; Bring the song; Cease sorrow (from Jommelli); Hark! what sound; Here beneath this willow sleepeth; Here's lawn as white as driven snow; In my cot, tho' small's my store; Lost is my quiet for ever; Now ev'ning's come; O! synge unto mie Roundelaie; Tho' ruthless war; Under the greenwood tree; Where feeds your flock; Will you buy any tape?. *Songs:* Six English Songs...the words from Mrs. Opie; The suicide; Come, my lads, time posts away; Ha! what is this?; Fox and the crow; I once rejoiced; Barbara Allan; Whar hae ye been a' day, my boy Tammy?; Where are you going my pretty maid?. Duets; Sets of Welsh and Russian Airs.

BIGGS (Rev. L. C.) English writer of "English Hymnology" (a series of articles reprinted from the "Monthly Packet").

BIGLIANI (Vincenzo). Italian comp. and writer, B. Alexandria, 1801. D. Turin, 1876. Writer of church music, etc.

BIGNON (Louis). French org. and comp., B. Paris, July 12, 1827. D. Marseilles, 1874.

BIGOT (Marie), *née* Kiene. German pianist, B. Colmar, 1786. Resided at Paris, where she was married to M. Bigot in 1804. D. Paris, Sept. 16, 1820.

She was a fine performer of the music of Mozart, and excelled in interpreting Beethoven and others of the classical school.

BILLERT (Karl Friedrich August). German comp. and cond., B. Stettin, Sept. 14, 1821. Has composed a number of symphonies, overtures, and other instrumental music of considerable merit. His songs and sacred compositions are also of great repute. D. Berlin, Jan. 2, 1876.

BILLET (Alexandre Philippe). French comp. and pianist. B. S. Petersburg, Mar. 14, 1817. S. at Paris Cons. Travelled in Italy and resided in London as teacher and comp. for the pf.

BILLINGS (William). American comp., B. Boston, Oct. 7, 1746. D. Boston, Sept. 26, 1800.

WORKS.—The New England Psalm Singer, 1700; The Singing Master's Assistant, 1778 (arranged from number 1); Music in Miniature, 1779; The Psalm Singer's Amusement, 1781; The Suffolk Harmony, 1786; The Continental Harmony, 1794; Single anthems, etc.

Billings, who was at one time a tanner, is regarded as the first American comp. of any note. His psalms are pretty, and laid the foundation no doubt of the modern style of sentimental psalmody affected in the States.

BILLINGTON (Elizabeth), *née* Weichsell. German soprano vocalist, B. [1765] or London, [1768]. Married to James Billington, a double-bass player, 1784. Made *début* at Dublin in "Orpheus and Eurydice." *Début* in London, Feb. 13, 1786, as Rosetta in "Love in a Village." Went to Italy with her husband,

1794. Sang at Naples, 1794. Her husband died, 1794. Appeared at Venice, 1796. Married to a M Felissent, 1798. Separated from him, 1798. Returned to England, and appeared at different times at Drury Lane and Covent Garden Theatres, the Ancient and Vocal Concerts, etc., 1801-17. Reconciled to her husband (M. Felissent) and retired with him to Venice, 1818. D. Venice, Aug. 28, 1818.

This vocalist, said to be one of the most handsome and dissolute women of her time, was classed among the greatest of living singers. Her voice was of extreme compass and remarkable for its sweetness. Her acting was inferior, and was only compensated for by the great beauty of her person. Her letters were published towards the commencement of this century, and created a great scandal. Some biographies of recent date hold that her manner of life was not so bad as has been represented, and that the cruelty of her French husband was a sufficient excuse for any little failing. Full details of her career will be found in Hogarth's "Memoirs of the Musical Drama," and in "Memoirs of Mrs. Billington, from her Birth ; containing a variety of matter, ludicrous, theatrical, musical, and with copies of several original letters written by Mrs. Billington to her Mother," Lond., 8vo, 1792. A suppressed book.

BILLINGTON (Thomas). English pianist, harpist, and comp., B. about end of 18th century. He lived in London as a teacher of the piano and harp. The dates of his birth and death are unknown. [Supposed to have been the husband or brother-in-law of above.]

WORKS.—Music to Gray's Elegies ; Pope's Eloisa to Abelard ; Prior's Garland ; Petrarch's Laura ; The Children in the Wood, Morton ; Twelve canzonets for 2 voices ; Six songs for voice and Pf.; Sonatas, various, for Pf.; Music to Young's Night Thoughts ; Music to Pope's Elegy to the Memory of an Unfortunate Lady ; Numerous Glees ; Songs ; Miscellaneous Pf. music ; Scotch airs, etc., harmonized, Lond. [1785].

BILSE (Benjamin). German comp. and cond., B. Liegnitz, Aug. 17, 1816.

He has composed a great amount of popular dance-music, and conducts a famous orchestra of 70 performers at Berlin.

BIMBONI (Giovacchino). Italian trumpet-player, B. Florence, Aug. 19, 1810.

BINCHOIS (Egidius) or *Gilles*. French comp. of church music, B. in Picardy [1406]. Chap.-master in service of the Duke of Bourgogne. D. [1465]. Comp. masses, chansons, etc.

BING (Jacob). German pianist and comp., B. Eschenbach, July 16, 1821. D April 17, 1841. Wrote Pf. music, etc.

BINGLEY (Rev. William, M.A.) English writer, B. Doncaster, 1774. S. at Cambridge. D. London, March 11, 1823. Author of "Musical Biography, or Memoirs of the Lives and Writings of the most Eminent Musical Composers and Writers who have flourished in the different countries of Europe during the last Three Centuries," London, 1814, 2 vols. 8vo ; 2nd edit., Lond., 1834, 2 vols. ; an imperfect and inaccurate work. Animal Biography, 1802, 3 vols., etc.

BINNEY (Thomas). English writer, author of "The Service of Song in the House of the Lord." Lond., 1849.

BIRCH (Rev. Edward). English author, wrote "A Tract on Responding, with a Postscript on Singing." Manchester, 1862.

BIRCH (Samuel). English comp., B. London, Nov. 8, 1757. Served as Lord Mayor in 1815. D. London, 1840.

WORKS.—The Mariners, musical entertainment, 1793 ; "The Packet Boat, or a Peep behind the Veil," a masque, Covent Garden, May 13, 1794 ; The Adopted Child, 1795 ; The Smugglers, musical drama, 1796 ; Fast Asleep, do., 1795 Albert and Adelaide, do., 1798. Glees ; songs, etc.

BIRCH (William Henry). English org. and comp., B. Uxbridge, May, 1826. S. under Elvey, Blagrove and R. Barnett. Org. of S. Mary's Ch., Amersham.

Prof. Music at Caversham, near Reading. Comp. of a number of operettas, anthems, songs, etc.

BIRCHALL (Robert). English music publisher, was business manager of the Ancient Concerts and one of the first to establish a Circulating Musical Library. He was originally in the employment of Randall and was succeeded by Lonsdale and Mills. He published works by Beethoven, Mozart, Haydn, and others. D. 1819.

BIRD (Horace). American teacher and writer, author of "Bird's Singing School Companion" (with Joseph Bird), Boston, n. d.; Songs, etc.

BIRD (Joseph). American teacher and writer, has published "Bird's Vocal Music Reader (Ditson, Boston, n. d.), and edited, with Horace Bird, a number of useful collections of music adopted for use in Schools. He has also published "Gleanings from the History of Music." Boston, 8vo, 1850.

BIRD (H. D.). American org. and comp., B. 1837. Is presently located in Chicago, where he is a teacher and organist of ability. His compositions are not known in England.

BIRD (William Hamilton). English collector. Author of "The Oriental Miscellany, a Collection of the most favourite Airs of Hindoostan, adapted for the Harpsichord," Calcutta, fo. 1789.

BIRD (William). See BYRD (William).

BIRKENSHA (John). Irish (?) writer. Lived in London as teacher of the viol in the first half of the 17th century.

He translated the "Templum Musicum" of Johannes Henricus Alstedius, and published it in 1664. For particulars of Birkensha see Busby's History, vol. ii., p. 246, and the "Imperial Dictionary of Biography."

BIRKENSTOCK (Julius Adam). German violinist and comp., B. Alsfeld, Feb. 19, 1687. D. Feb. 26, 1733.

BISCACCIANTI (Eliza Ostinelli). American vocalist, B. Boston, Mass., 1825. Sang with success in America and Europe.

BISCHOFF (Carl Bernard). German comp., B. Nieder-Rœblingen, Weimar, Dec. 24, 1807. Writer of oratorios; "Christus," "Joas," etc.; also motets, and other vocal music.

BISCHOFF (Gaspard Josef). German comp., B. Ausbach, April 7, 1823. Writer of church music, an opera, songs, Pf. music, etc.

BISCHOFF (Ludwig Friedrich Christoph). German comp. and teacher, B. Dessau, Nov. 27, 1794. S. at Berlin University from 1812. Pro. at Berlin, and Director of the Gymnasium at Wesel, 1823-49. Founded several musical societies. D. Cologne, Feb. 24, 1867.

BISHENDEN (Charles James). English writer and bass singer, B. 1848. Author of "The Voice, and how to use it," "How to Sing," etc.

BISHOP (Anna), *née* Rivière, wife of the undernoted. A French soprano vocalist, B. London, 1812 [1814-15]. S. under Moscheles at the R. A. M. Married Bishop, 1832. *Début* at London, 1837. Sang at the Musical Festivals of Gloucester, York, and Hereford. Travelled with Bochsa in Europe, 1839. Appeared in Copenhagen, 1839. Sang in Stockholm, 1840. St. Petersburg, 1840. Sang in Russia with great success, 1840-1. Appeared in Austria, etc., 1842. Visited Italy, 1843. Went to America, 1846. Travelled in America, Australia, etc., 1853-8. Married to Martin Schultz, of New York, 1858. Returned to England in 1858. Returned to America, 1859. Travelled round the world concert-giving, 1865-69, and again in 1873-76. Between the years 1839 and 1843 she sang at 260 concerts. She was a cultivated vocalist and member of many musical societies. D. New York, March 18 [20], 1884.

BISHOP (Sir Henry Rowley). English comp., B. London, Nov. 18, 1786. S. music under F. Bianchi. Musical Director at Drury Lane Theatre, 1810-

11. Founded (with others) the Philarmonic Soc., 1813. Visited Dublin, 1820. Cond. at Drury Lane Theatre, 1825. Musical director at Vauxhall Gardens, 1830. Mus. Bac. Oxon., 1839. Musical director at Covent Garden Theatre, 1840-41. Cond. of the Ancient Concerts, 1840-48, Prof. of Music at Edinburgh University (in succession to John Thomson), 1841-43. Knighted, 1842. Prof. of Music at Oxford University (in succession to Dr. Crotch), 1848. Mus. Doc. Oxon., 1853. D. London, April 30, 1855.

WORKS.—*Operas and Musical Dramas:* Angelina, farce, 1804; Tamerlan et Bajazet, ballet, 1806; Narcissa et les Graces, grand anacreontic ballet, 1806; Caractacus, ballet, 1806; Love in a Tub, a pastoral ballet, 1806; The Mysterious Bride, 1808; The Circassian Bride, 1809; Mora's Love, ballet, 1809; The Vintagers, 1809; The Maniac, or, Swiss Banditti, 1810; The Knight of Snowdoun, 1811; The Virgin of the Sun, 1812; The Æthiop, or Child of the Desert, 1812; The Renegade, 1812; Haroun Alraschid (altered from The Æthiop), 1813; The Brazen Bust, 1813; Harry Le Roy, 1813; The Miller and His Men, 1813; For England Ho! 1813; The Farmer's Wife (with Reeve and Davy), 1814; The Wandering Boys, or The Castle of Olival, 1814; Sadak and Kalasrade, or The Waters of Oblivion, 1814; The Grand Alliance, 1814; The Forest of Bondy, or Dog of Montargus, 1814; The Maid of the Mill, comic opera, 1814; The Noble Outlaw, 1815; Telemachus, 1815; A Midsummer Night's Dream (Shakespere), 1816; Guy Mannering, or The Gypsey's Prophecy (from Scott), (with Whittaker), 1816; The Heir of Vironi, or Honesty the Best Policy, 1817; Don Juan, or The Libertine (compiled from Mozart), 1817; The Duke of Savoy, or Wife and Mistress, 1817; The Barber of Seville (compiled from Rossini), 1818; The Marriage of Figaro (compiled from Mozart), 1819; The Heart of Midlothian (from Scott), 1819; A Roland for an Oliver, 1819; The Gnome King, or The Giant Mountains, 1819; The Comedy of Errors (Shakes.), 1819; The Antiquary (from Scott), 1820; The Battle of Bothwell Brigg, 1820; Henri Quatre, or Paris in the Olden Time, 1820; Twelfth Night (Shakes.), 1820; Don John, or The Two Violettas, 1820; The Two Gentlemen of Verona (Shakes.), 1821; Montrose, or The Children of the Mist (from Scott), 1820; The Law of Java, 1822; Maid Marian, or The Huntress of Arlingford, opera 1822; Clari, or The Maid of Milan, opera in three acts (J. H. Payne), 1823; The Beacon of Liberty, 1823; Cortez, or The Conquest of Mexico, 1823; Native Land, or Return from Slavery, 1824; Charles the Second, operetta, 1824; The Fall of Algiers, opera, 3 acts, 1825; Hofer, The Tell of the Tyrol (compiled from Rossini), 1825; Edward the Black Prince, 1825; Aladdin, or The Wonderful Lamp, opera (by J. R. Planché), London, 1825; The Knights of the Cross, opera, 1826; Under the Oak, opera, 1830; Adelaide, or The Royal William, opera, 1832; Home, Sweet Home, operatic drama, 2 acts, 1832; The Magic Fan, or The Fillip on the Nose, operetta, 1832; Yelva, musical drama, 2 acts, 1833; The Rencontre, operatic comedy, 1833; The Doom Kiss, opera, 1836; The Slave, opera in 3 acts, by J. R. Planché, 1816; As You Like It (Shakes.); Aurora, ballet; Brother and Sister, 1814; Cymon (from M. Arne), 1815; Comus, 1815; Dr. Sangrado, ballet, 1814; December and May; Don Pedro, tragedy (2 glees); Der Freyschutz (compiled from Weber), 1824; Englishman in India, comic opera, 1827; Faustus, 1825; Fortunatus and his Sons, 1819; John of Paris (from Boieldieu), 1814; John du Bart (incidental music), 1815; Ninetta, opera, 3 acts; The Bottle of Champagne, operetta; The Czar of Muscovy, opera; The Humorous Lieutenant, 1817; The Romance of a Day, operatic drama; Zuma, or The Tree of Health, comic opera, 1818. The Fallen Angel, oratorio; The Seventh Day, cantata, 1833. *Glees:* Six original English glees; Poetry by Hemans, Baillie, etc.; Twelve original English glees; Complete collection of glees, 8 vols., 1839 (other collections have since appeared, one—Novello's—with orch. accompaniments). *Songs:* Songs for the seasons, by T. H. Bayly; Select and rare Scottish melodies, Poetry by Hogg; Songs of the old chateau, Poetry by Bayly; Lays and legends of the Rhine, J. R. Planché; Do. of the Upper Rhine; Melodies of various nations, Bayly; Songs for leisure hours, W. Walton; Edition of Handel's Trios, choruses, etc.; Grand triumphal ode, Accession of the King; Funeral Ode; The Jolly Beggars, cantata by Robert Burns; Single songs in great numbers. Pf. music, and various pieces of instrumental music. English national melodies, Poetry, edit. by Chas. Mackay. Syllabus of a course of six lectures on the origin and progress of the lyric drama, or opera...to be delivered in the Manchester Athenæum, 8vo, 1845

It is believed that, had Bishop earnestly endeavoured to regenerate English opera, he would have succeeded. He possessed high attainments in musical knowledge, and was possessed of a fine imagination and much dramatic perception. His vocal music is especially fine, and certainly not inferior to that of any English operatic composer. What he most lacked was consistency. Having a personal knowledge of his powers he seems to have produced work after work without the slightest regard to care. He sinned in wasting rather than in economising his genius, and produced a vast number of pieces, some of which possessed very little merit.

The works which may be noted as Bishop's best are—"The Knight of Snowdoun," "Clari," "Cortez," "Fall of Algiers," "Oberon," and "The Slave," with, perhaps, his music to Shakespeare's plays. They are not in the strict operatic form made classical by Mozart, Weber, etc., containing expressive instrumental aids and making use of the recitative, but are simply in that form of musical drama known as English ballad opera. Bishop wrote with fluency and refinement, if carelessly, and showed on every possible occasion a strong feeling for the truly artistic.

It is in his vocal music that Bishop shows in his full powers, and his glees are still frequently performed and stand high in public esteem. These works—many of which appeared in operas—are, in the highest sense of the word, art-songs. They are conceived and shaped conformably to the purest art principles, and must be known as classics equally with the work of other composers. Such works as "Blow gentle gales," "Where art thou, beam of light?," "Up, quit thy bower;" "Sleep, gentle lady," etc., are musical gems from whatever standpoint they may be viewed.

Bishop is one of the best among English lyrical composers. He lacks to a certain extent that quaint unaffected style which is so admirable a feature in the older composers, but on the other hand some of his concerted vocal music is unsurpassed in variety. Had he concentrated his powers on the production of dramatic music wholly his own, the record of his life would have been rich in works of lasting value.

BISHOP (John). English org. and writer, B. Cheltenham, July 31, 1817. Org. of S. Paul's Ch., Cheltenham, 1831. Org. at Blackburn, Lancashire, 1838-9. Org. of S. James' Ch., Cheltenham; Roman Catholic Chap., do; St. John's Church, do. Org. appointments all resigned, 1852.

WORKS.—Remarks on the Causes of the Present generally degraded state of Music in our Churches, 1860; Brief Memoir of George Frederick Handel, fo., 1856; Selection of favourite Pieces by the Great Masters, adapted as solos for the organ, with pedal obbligato; Repertorium Musicæ Antiquæ, a Miscellaneous collection of classical compositions by the greatest masters of Italy, Germany, etc. (edited with Joseph Warren), London, 1848. Translator of Czerny's School of Practical Composition (Cocks); Reicha's Course of Musical Composition (edited only); G. Weber's Theory of Musical Composition (edited from Warner's American edit., with additions); Otto's Treatise on the Violin; Czerny's Art of Playing the Ancient and Modern Pianoforte Works; Campagnoli's Method for the Violin; Spohr's Violin School; Duport's Violoncello School; Hamilton's Dictionary of Musical Terms, edited. Remarks on the Singing of the Daily Psalms, prefixed to 2 Collections of Chants, 1852-1857. Anthems; organ music; songs, etc.

Mr. Bishop has enriched the educational resources of England by his admirable translations of standard foreign theoretical works. They have long been established as part of our musical literature, and are useful class-books. As an organist Mr. Bishop has earned fame, and is known over the greater portion of England as an authority on church music and psalmody.

BISHOP (John). English org. and comp., B. 1665. D. 1737. Org. of Winchester Cath.

BISSET (Catherine). English pianist, B. London, 1795. Eldest daughter of Robert Bisset, LL.D., author of the "Life of Burke," etc. Early exhibited talent for music. S. under J. B. Cramer. Appeared at New Musical Fund Concert, 1811. Played in Paris, with success, 1823. D. Barnes, Feb., 1864. Miss Bisset was almost exclusively engaged at private concerts given by the nobility, and was a performer of first-rate ability. Her early ability as a pianist, and the promise she gave, induced her instructor (Cramer) to teach her without emolument. Her younger sister, ELIZABETH ANNE, B. London, 1800, was a harpist and comp. of great talent, who S. under F. Dizi, and became widely known by her performance and compositions. Among the latter may be named "Fantasia on C. E. Horn's air, 'Through the Wood,'" 1840; "Fantaise brillante pour la Harp," 1840; "The Sailor's Adieu," ballad, 1842. The date and place of her death has not been ascertained.

BITTER (Carl Hermann). German writer, B. Schwedt-on-the-Oder, Feb. 27, 1813. Employed in Government of Prussia. Chiefly known to musicians by his "Johann Sebastian Bach," Berlin, 2 vols., 1865; his "Carl Philipp Emanuel und Wilhelm Friedeman Bach und deren Brüder," Berlin, 2 vols, 8vo, 1898; and by his organisation of several large musical festivals. Recent publications by Bitter are—"Beitrag. zur Geschichte des Oratoriums," Berlin, 1872; and "Eine Studie zum Stabat mater." Leipzig, 1883. And Berlin, Sep. 12, 1885.

BIZET (Alexander César Leopold or Georges). French comp., B. Paris, Oct. 25, 1838. S. under Halévy. Gained the "Prix de Rome" at Paris Cons., 1857. Married to Mdlle. Halévy. Lived in Paris as teacher and composer. D. Paris, June 3, 1875.

WORKS.—*Operas and Operettas:* Docteur Miracle, 1857; Vasco de Gama, 1863; Les Pêcheurs de Perles, 1863; Le Jolie Fille de Perth, 1867; Djamileh, 1872; L'Arlésienne, 1872; Carmen, opera in 4 acts, Paris, March 3, 1875; Noah, opera, unfinished work of Halévy's, Carlsruhe, 1885. Overture for orch., Patrie. Songs, etc.

The renown of Bizet rests solely on "Carmen," a work which has attained the greatest popularity, despite a somewhat savoury libretto. It is a clever and original work and seems destined to maintain a place on the stage for some time. Bizet's other works are rarely if ever produced.

BLACKWELL (Isaac). English comp., flourished during latter part of 16th century. Comp. "Choice Ayres, Songs, and Dialogues to the theorbo-lute and bass-violo," Lond., 1657.

BLAES-MEERTI (Elisa), née Meerti. German vocalist, B. Antwerp, 1820. Married to Arnold Joseph Blaes, Prof. in Brussels Cons. Sang at the Gewandhaus Concerts, Leipzig, 1839. Sang with success in various Continental towns. Resides in Brussels as a teacher of music.

BLAGROVE (R. M.) English violinist and teacher. Author of "A New and Improved System to the Art of Playing the Violin"...Lond., 1828.

BLAGROVE (Henry Gamble). English violinist, B. Nottingham, Oct., 1811. Son of above. First appeared in public, 1816. Taken to London by his Father, 1817. Played at Drury Lane Theatre, 1817. S. under Spagnoletti, 1821. Pupil at the R.A.M., 1823. Gained silver medal, R.A.M., for violin-playing, 1824. Mem. of Queen Adelaide's private band, 1830-1837. S. under Spohr in Germany, 1833-34. Played at London Concerts and Provincial Festivals. D. London, Dec. 15, 1872.

Blagrove was one of the best among the small array of first-rate English violinists. He had a great reputation throughout the provinces of England, and was well-known in Scotland. His tone was pure, if not remarkably powerful, and he had perfect command over the mechanical requirements of the instrument.

BLAHETKA (Leopoldine). Austrian pianist and comp., B. Guntramsdorf, Vienna, Nov. 15, 1809. Wrote an opera, lieder, Pf. music, etc.

BLAINVILLE (Charles Henri). French violinist and comp. B. Tours, 1711. D. Paris, 1769. Wrote on the science of music and composed various pieces.

BLAKE (Benjamin). English comp., B. Kingsland, 1751. S. by himself. Learned the violin, 1760. Mem. of orch. of Italian opera, Lond., 1768. Prof. of music in Public School at Kensington, 1789-1810. D. Lond., 1827.

WORKS.—Three Books of Six Duets for violin and viola. Six Sonatas for Pf. and violin. Collection of Sacred Music for voices and organ. Three Solos for

G

viola, with bass accomp. Glees and Songs. A Musical Dialogue between Master and Scholar.

BLAKE (Rev. Edward, D.D.) English comp., B. 1708. Prebendary of Salisbury Cath. Rector of S. Thomas' Church, Salisbury. D. June, 1765. Composed Anthems and instrumental duets.

BLAMONT (Francois Colin de). French comp. and writer, B. Versailles, Nov. 22, 1690. D. Paris, Feb. 14, 1760. Wrote numerous cantatas, ballets, and other works, of which the following list is representative :— Les Fêtes Grecques et Romaines, 1723 ; Les Fêtes de Thétis ; Diane et Endymion, 1731 ; Les Caracteres de l'Amour, 1738 ; Jupiter vainqueur des Titans, 1745 ; Les Amours du Printemps ; Les Fêtes du Labyrinthe, 1728 ; Zéphire et Flore, 1739 ; Il Pastor Fido. Also Motets, Songs, and an "Essai sur les goûts anciens et modernes de la musique Française," Paris, 1754.

BLANC (Adolph). French comp., B. Manosque, June 24, 1828. Writer of chamber music, trios, quartets, quintets, etc.

BLANCHARD (Henry Louis). French comp. and writer, B. Bordeaux, 1778. D. Paris, 1858.

BLANCKS (Edward). English comp., flourished during 16th cent. Comp. tunes in Este's "Whole Booke of Psalmes."

BLAND (Maria Theresa), *née* Romanzini. Italian vocalist, B. London, 1769. First appeared at Royal Circus, London, 1773. Sang at Dublin Theatre. *Début* at Drury Lane Theatre, Oct. 24, 1786. Married Mr. Bland, brother to Mrs. Jordan. Sang at Haymarket Theatre, 1791. Sang in London till 1824. D. insane (?)

She was a magnificent ballad vocalist, and earned most of her success on the operatic stage.

BLAND (John). English music-publisher, issued among other works "The Ladies Collection of Catches, Glees, Canons, Canzonets, Madrigals, etc," Lond., fol. 3 vols. [1720]; also the "Gentleman's Collection" about same time.

He published a "Collection of Sonatas, Lessons, Overtures, etc., for Harpsichord or Pianoforte," Lond., n.d. Continued by F. Linley in 5 vols.

BLANDFORD (George, Marquis of), Fourth Duke of Marlborough, B. Jan. 26 [1738]. D. Jan. 30, 1817. Musical amateur comp., was connected with many of the musical enterprises of the end of last and the beginning of the present century. He published "Twelve Glees for three and four Voices." Lond. [1798]; and a Collection of Vocal Music. Also Sonatas, various, for Pianoforte, opp. 1, 2, 3.

BLANGINI (Giuseppe Marco Marie Felice). Italian tenor vocalist, teacher, and comp., B. Turin, Nov. 18, 1781. S. as chor. in Turin Cath., 1789. Went to Paris, 1799. Resided at Munich from 1805. Chap.-master to Princess Borghese at Munich, 1806. Music-director to King Jerome at Cassel, 1809. Music-director at Paris, to the Emperor, 1814. D. Paris, Dec. 18, 1841.

WORKS.—*Operas:* La Fausse Duègne, 1802 (work left unfinished by Dellamaria) ; Zélie et Terville, 1803 ; Chimère et Réalité, 1803 ; Encore un tour de Calife, 1805 : Nephtali, ou les Ammonites, 1806 ; Inès de Castro ; Les Fêtes Lacédémoniennes, 1810 ; Les Femmes vengées, 1811 : L'Amour Philosophe, 1811 ; Le Naufrage comique, 1812 ; La Fée Urgèle, 1812 ; La Princesse de Cachemire, 1812 ; Trajano in Dacia, 1814 ; La Sourde-Muette, 1815 ; La Comtesse de Lamark, 1817 ; Le Jeune Oncle, 1820 ; Marie Thérèse, 1820 ; Le Duc d'Aquitaine, 1823 ; Le Projet de Pièce, 1825 ; La Saint-Henri, 1825 ; L'Intendant, 1826 ; Le Coureur de Veuves, 1827 ; Le Jeu de Cache-Cache, 1827 ; Le Morceau d'ensemble, 1825 ; L'Anneau de la Fiancée, 1827 : Le Chanteur de Société, 1830 ; La Marquise de Brinvilliers, 1831 (with Cherubini, Carafa, etc.) ; Un Premier pas, 1831 ; Les Gondoliers, 1833 ; Le Vieux de la Montagne. Romances for solo voice and Pf. to the number of upwards of 100. Nocturnes for 2 voices. Collections of Canzonets for voice and Pf. Motets and Masses for 4 voices and orch. Notturnos for 3 voices. Lond., n. d.

The great popularity of Blangini's Italian and French songs, or romances, was chiefly due to their agreeable character. Their reputation, like that of his operas, is fading. His life was published by Villemarest in 1834, under title of "Souvenirs de F. Blangini maitre de chapelle du roi de Bavière, membre de la Légion d'honneur et de l'Institut historique de France," 1797-1834.

BLASERNA (Pietro). Author of "The Theory of Sound in its Relation to Music," Lond., 8vo, 1876. (International Scientific Series.)

BLASIS (Francesco Antonio de). Italian comp., B. Naples, 1765. D. Florence, Aug. 22, 1851. Comp. operas, ballets, oratorios, masses, overtures, and theoretical works. His son Carlo was a writer on music; and his daughter, Virginia (B. Marseilles, 1804. D. Florence, May 11, 1838), a soprano vocalist of note.

BLASIUS (Matthieu Frédéric). French violinist and comp., B. 1758. D. 1829.

BLASSMAN (Adolf Josef Maria). German comp. and pianist, B. Dresden, Oct. 27, 1823.

BLAZE (Henri Sebastien). French comp., B. Cavaillon, 1763. D. May 11, 1833.

Wrote duets for Harp and Pianoforte; Sonatas for Pf.; Songs; and a Romance entitled "Julien, ou le Prétre," Paris, 1805.

BLAZE (Francois Henri Joseph), or *Castil-Blaze.* French writer, son of above, B. Cavaillon, Dec. 1784. S. for the Law. S. at Paris Cons., 1799. Sous-préfet in Department of Vaucluse, 1820. Musical critic to Journal des Débats, 1822-32. D. Paris, Dec. 11, 1857.

This writer, otherwise known as Castil-Blaze, contributed to the periodical literature of his time many articles on musical subjects. He also wrote "De l'Opera en France," Paris, 2 vols., 1820; "Dictionnaire de musique moderne," Paris, 2 vols., 1821;" "Chapelle-musique des Rois de France," 1832;" "Molière musicien notes sur les œuvres de cet illustre maitre..." 2 vols., 1852; "Théâtres Lyriques de Paris," 2 vols., 1855; "L'opera Italien de 1548 à 1856," Paris, 1856. His son, HENRY BLAZE, BARON DE BURY, B. Avignon, 1813, wrote articles on musicians in the "Revue des Deux Mondes" and elsewhere, reprinted as "Musiciens Contemporains," Paris, 1856; "Meyerbeer, et son Temps," Paris, 1865, etc.

BLEW (William Charles Arlington). English writer and Barrister-at-Law, B. London, 1848. Called to the Bar, 1876. Author of "Organs and Organists in Parish Churches; a Handbook of the Law relating to the Custody, Control, and Use of Organs, and the Duties, Rights, and Disabilities of Organists .." Lond., 8vo, 1878.

BLEWITT (Jonas). English comp. and org., B. in first half of 18th century. Held important organ appointments now untraceable. Performed publicly at festivals, etc. D. 1805.

WORKS.—Treatise on the Organ, with explanatory voluntaries, op. 4, London, n. d.; Ten Voluntaries, or preces for the organ, in easy and familiar style, equally adapted for the church or chamber with organ, proper directions for the use of the stops, etc., op. 5; Twelve easy and familiar movements for the organ, op. 6.

Blewitt was one of the greatest organists of last century, and was famed for his powerful and effective style. His work on the organ is now superseded, and his compositions are antiquated, but both possess many good points.

BLEWITT (Jonathan or John). Son of above, English comp. and org., B. London, 1782, S. under his father and Battishill. Deputy org. to his father, 1793. Org. at Haverhill, Suffolk; do. at Brecon; do. at Sheffield; do. of St. Andrew's Church, Dublin, 1811. Comp. and cond. at Theatre Royal, Dublin, 1811. Grand Org. to the Masonic Soc. of Ireland. Returned to

London, 1826 Musical director at Sadler's Wells Theatre, 1828-29. Teacher of vocal music and org. in London. D. London, Sept. 4, 1853.
WORKS.—*Music to Plays, etc.:* Harlequin, or the Man in the Moon, 1826 ; The Talisman of the Elements ; Auld Robin Gray ; My Old Woman ; The Corsair ; The Magician ; The Island of Saints ; Rory O'More ; Mischief Making, etc. *Instrumental:* Concerto for Pf. and orch. ; Sonatas and Duets for Pf. ; Caprices, fugues, and sonatas for the organ. The Vocal Assistant, treatise on singing, Lond., n.d. *Songs:* A nice little man ; Adieu my moustachios ; Barney Brallaghan ; England, merry England ; Let us drink to old friends ; My hopes are fixed upon thee ; Emerald Isle ; The White Cliffs of England ; Good bye ; Groves of Blarney ; Hamlet ; I saw him but once ; New cries of London ; O for a cot ; Our jolly stout jackets of blue ; Phillis, have you seen my love ? ; Pic-nic ; When crowned with summer roses.

BLISS (Mrs. J. W.) See LINDSAY (Miss).

BLITHEMAN (William). English comp. and org., flourished in latter half of 16th century. Org. of the Chap. Royal. Mus. Bac. Cantab., 1586. Mus. Doc. do. [15 ?]. D. 1590.

Blitheman was the preceptor of Dr. John Bull, and was succeeded by him at the Chapel Royal in 1591. His biography is unknown, but it is believed that he composed church music and had much celebrity in his time.

BLOCKLEY (John). English comp., writer, and publisher, B. 1800. Engaged in music-publishing business in London. D. London, Dec. 24, 1882.

WORKS.—The Sabbath Minstrel [collection of sacred music]. Lond., 8vo, n. d. ; The Singer's Companion, Lond., fo., n.d. *Songs:* My childhood's home : I remember thy voice ; We have been friends together ; The absent one ; A blessing on thine eyes ; The Arab's farewell to his favourite steed ; The friend of our early days ; Love not ; Love on (reply) ; The Englishman ; and numerous other songs written to words of the Hon. Mrs. Norton, etc.

BLODEK (Wilhelm). Bohemian flute-player and comp., B. Oct. 14, 1834.

BLOW (John). English comp. and org., B. North Collingham, Nottingham, 1648. One of Children of Chap. Roy., 1660. S. under Captain Cook, Hingeston, and Christopher Gibbons. Org. of Westminster Abbey, 1669-80. Gent. of Chap.-Roy., Mar., 1674. Master of the Children, do., July, 1674. Org. of Chap.-Royal. Private Musician to King James II., 1685. Almoner and master of the choristers of St. Paul's Cath., 1687. Re-appointed org. of Westminster Abbey, 1695-1708. Married Elizabeth Braddock. Comp. to Chap.-Royal, 1699. D. London, Oct. 1, 1708.

WORKS.—Amphion Anglicus, a work of many compositions for one, two, three, and four voices, with several accompagnements of Instrumental Musick, and a Thorow-Bass to each song, figur'd for an Organ, Harpsichord, or Theorboe-Lute, Lond. fo. [1700]. *Odes:* A Second Musical Entertainment, performed on St. Cecilia's Day, November 22, 1684, words by John Oldham, London, 1684 ; Great Quire of Heaven, St. Cecilia's Day, 1691 ; Te Deum and Jubilate, composed for St. Cecilia's Day, 1695 ; Triumphant Fame, St. Cecilia's Day, 1700 ; Arise, Great Monarch, New Year's Day, 1681 ; New Year's Day Ode, 1683 ; Hail, Monarch, do., 1686 ; Is it a Dream?, do., 1687 ; Ye Sons of Phœbus, do, 1688 ; others in 1689 and 1693-94 ; Appear in all thy pomp, appear, do., 1700 ; Ode on the Death of Mr. Henry Purcell, the words by Mr. Dryden, London, 1696 ; Three Elegies upon the much lamented loss of our late most Gracious Queen Mary,—sett to Musick by Dr. Blow and Mr. Henry Purcell, Lond., fol., 1695. Church Services in A, G, and E minor, one in triple measure and 10 unedited. Anthems, numbering about 100, published in Boyce's Collection, Clifford's Collection, Page's Harmonia Sacra, Novello's Series; others existing in MS. A choice Collection of Lessons for the Harpsichord, Spinnet, etc., containing four Setts, as grounds, almands, corants, sarabands, minuets, and jiggs, 1698. A Choice Collection of Lessons, being excellently sett to the Harpsichord, etc., by Blow and Purcell, 1705. Catches in the "Pleasant Musical Companion," published in various editions ; Do. pub. in The Catch Club, or Merry Companions ; Songs in D'Urfey's collections, and in others of the same period ; Organ music ; various.

Dr. Blow was one of those musicians of whom England has so many—dry, severe, and scholastic, but often grand and dignified. His works are, on the whole, more suggestive of learning than of fancy, though many of his songs and some of his anthems are very fine, both as regards melody and construction.

BLOXSOME (Charles). English writer, author of "Elementary Practice for the Vocal Student," Lond., 1857; "Elements of Singing, Chord and Scale Exercises to Develop the Voice," Lond., n. d.

BLUM (Karl). German org., comp., and poet, B. Berlin, 1788. D. Berlin, July 2, 1844.

BLUMENTHAL (Jacob). German comp. and pianist, B. Hamburg, Oct. 4, 1829. S. under Sechter, Grund, and Bocklet. S. at Paris Cons. from 1846 under Halévy. Settled in London, 1848, as pianist and piano teacher. Presently residing there.

WORKS.—Trio for Pf., violin, and 'cello, op. 26. *Pianoforte:* Op. 1. La Source, caprice; op. 2. Two Caprices; op. 3. Three Melodies; op. 4. Fête Cosaque, caprice; op. 5. Three Mazurkas; op. 7. Fantasia; op. 8. Les deux Anges; op. 10. Two Nocturnes; op. 11. Caprice; op. 14. Ballade; op. 15. Reverie-Nocturne; op. 16. Fantasia; op. 17. Two Marches; op. 18. Fantasia; op. 19. Nocturne-Impromptu; op. 20. Three Mazurkas; op. 21. Three Pieces; op. 27. March; op. 28. Third Nocturne; op. 30. Elegie; op. 31. Tyrolienne; op. 33. L'Exaltation; op. 34. Chanson; op. 36. Fantasia; op. 37. Souvenir; op. 38. Nocturne; op. 39. La Caressante; op. 40. Barcarolle; op. 41. Rondo-Galop; op. 42, 43, 44, 45, 46, 47, 48. Morceaux de Salon, various; Le Parfum, op. 60; op. 66. Nocturne; op. 67. Adagio Sostenute; op. 73. Chant Religieux; op. 81. L'Appasionata; Valses and Salon pieces innumerable. Six Part-songs (Novello). *Songs:* The Message; My Queen; Bend of the River; Boatman's Song; Clear and Cool; Comrades, send the flagon round; Gondoliera; Good night; Hebe; Leoline; Love the Pilgrim: Sweet is true love; Thinking of thee; The wedding day; Yes; The Requital; Days that are no more; Life; My Palace; Her Name; Arise and follow me!; Chemin du Paradis.

BLUMMER (Martin). German comp., B. Fürstemberg, Nov. 21, 1827. Writer of lieder, cantatas, Columbus, 1853, etc.; oratorios, Abraham, 1860; Fall of Jerusalem, 1881.

BOCCABADATI (Luigia). Italian soprano vocalist, B. Parma. *Début* in 1817. Appeared in London in Rossini's "Cenerentola," Feb., 1833. Married to M. Gazzuoli. D. Turin, Oct., 1850.

"Her voice, like most flexible voices, is of a thin quality; her intonation is generally perfect, and her style is purely Italian; rather meretricious in ornament perhaps, but expressive. Her species of voice is properly denominated, *voce di testa*, and we observed, that some melodies were not only transposed, but disguised by inversion. However, altogether it was a respectable performance, and her reception was very flattering."—*Athenæum*, 1833, p. 124.

BOCCHERINI (Luigi). Italian comp., B. Lucca, Jan. 14, 1740. S. music at Rome. Travelled through Italy and France with Manfredi. Played at the "Concerts Spirituels," Paris, 1768. Played in Spain by invitation without success. Chamber musician to the King of Prussia, Frederich Wilhelm II., 1785-97. D. in impoverished circumstances, Madrid, May 28, 1805.

WORKS.—Op. 1. Sei Sinfonie o sia quartetti per dui violoni, alto e 'cello, Paris; op. 2-3. Two sets of six trios for 2 vns. and 'cello; op. 4. Six symphonies (quartets) for 2 vns., viola, and 'cello; op. 5. Six duets for 2 vns.; op. 6. Six sonatas for harpsichord and violin, 1768; op. 6a. Six quartets for 2 vns., viola, and 'cello, 1769; op. 7. Six conversazioni (or trios) for 2 vns. and 'cello; op. 8. Concerto for 2 vns., oboe, viola, 'cello, and D-bass; op. 9. Six Terzetti for 2 vns. and 'cello; op. 10. Six quartets for strings, 1770; op. 11. Six Divertissements for 2 vns., viola, and bass; op. 12. Six quintets for 2 vns., viola, and 2 'cellos, 1771; op. 13. Six quintets for 2 vns., viola, and 2 cellos, 1771; op. 14. Six Terzetti for vn., viola, and 'cello, 1772; op. 15. Six Divertissements for 2 vns., flute oblig., viola, 2 'cellos and bass, 1773; op. 16. Six symphonies for various instruments, 1771; op. 17. (?) Six quintets for 2 vns., viola, and 2 'cellos, 1774 ; op. 20. Six quintets for strings ; op. 21. Six quintets for flute, 2 vns., viola, and 'cello; op. 22. Six symphonies for 2 vns., viola, and bass, oboe, flute, and horn, 1775 ; op. 23. Six quintets for 2 vns., viola, and 2 'cellos, 1775 ; op. 24. Six sestets concertanti for 2 vns., 2 violas, and 2 'cellos, 1776 ; op. 25. Six quintets for flute, 2 vns., viola, and 'cello, 1774 ; op. 26. Six quartets for strings, 1775 ; op. 27. Six do., 1777 ; op. 27a. Concerto for flute ; op. 28. Six trios for 2 vns. and 'cello; op. 29, 30, 31. (?) op. 32. Six quartets for strings, 1778 ; op. 33. Six do., 1780; op. 34. Concerto for 'cello ; op. 35. Six trios for 2 vns. and 'cello, 1781 ; op. 36 ; Three quintets for 2 vns., alto, and 2 'cellos, 1788 ; op. 37. Six duets for 2 vns. ; op. 37a. Twenty-four quintets for 2 vns., alto, and 2 'cellos ; op. 38. Six trios for violin, alto, and 'cello, 1793 ; op. 39. Twelve quartets for strings; op. 40. Six quartets (short) for strings, 1796 ; op. 41. Symphony for eight instruments, 1797 ; op. 42. Sextet for 2 vns., viola, horn, and 2 'cellos ; Do., for violin, viola, oboe, or flute, bassoon, horn, and bass, 1797 ; op. 43. Overture for full orch., 1790 ; op. 44. Six trios for 2 vns. and 'cello, 1796 ; op. 45. Six quintets for flute or oboe, 2 vns., viola, and 'cello, 1797 ; op. 46. Six duets for 2 vns. ; op. 46a. Six quintets for Pf., 2 vns., alto, and 'cello, 1797 ; op. 47. Twelve quintets for strings; op. 48. Six do. ; op. 49. Six do. ; op. 50. Six string quartets, 1788 ; op. 51. Six do., 1779 ; op. 52 to 57 (?) op. 58. Six quartets for strings, 1799. Unnumbered works consisting of Sonatas, Trios, Symphonies, Quintets, Quartets, Concertos for Violoncello, a Stabat Mater, etc.

The numerous delicious bits of melody and harmony which this composer has given the world, to say nothing of his invention of the string quartet, should secure for him the favour of posterity. The amount of Boccherini's compositions though great, is not such as had a damaging influence on his originality of idea or flow of melody. The reproach of vulgarity as common-placeness is also inapplicable to his works. There is a brightness of style and a simplicity of structure about his music which is extremely refreshing. The absence of laboured phrases and construction is also very pleasing. Boccherini was a noted violoncellist, and played music of his own composition.

BOCHSA (Robert Nicolas Charles). French harp-player and comp., B. Montmédi, 1789. Appeared as pianist at an early age. Resided at Bordeaux till 1806. S. at Paris Cons. under Catel and Méhul, 1806. S. harp under Marin and Nadermann. Harpist to the Emperor Napoleon I., 1813. Harpist to Louis XVIII. Do. to the Duc de Berri. Discovered in connection with some forgeries, 1817. Came to England (London), 1817. Cond. the Lenten Oratorios with Sir George Smart, 1822-23. Prof. of Harp at R.A.M., Secretary do. Dismissed from the R.A.M. on his character becoming known, 1827. Cond. at King's Theatre, London, 1826-32. Travelled with Madam Anna Bishop in America, Europe, and Australia. D. Sydney, Australia, Jan. 7, 1856.

WORKS.—*Oratorio:* Le Deluge Universel. *Operas:* Les Héritiers de Paimpol, 1813 ; Alphonse d'Aragon, 1814 ; Les Héritiers Michau, 1814 ; Les Noces de Gamacle, 1815 ; Le Roi et la Ligue, 1815 ; La Lettre de change, 1815; La Bataille de Denain, 1816 ; Un Mari pour étrenne, 1816. Method for the Harp. *Ballets:* Beniowsky ; or, the Exiles of Kamschatka ; Le Corsaire, etc. Fantasias, Studies, Variations, Concertos and Arrangements for Harp. Bohemian Melodies, harmonised, Lond., n. d. Songs, etc.

Bochsa was the leading harpist of his time, and was one of the most influential teachers of that instrument. His compositions for the harp still survive, but his memory is best kept green through his pupils or their descendents. Parish-Alvars and J. B. Chatterton were his best-known English pupils. Of his private character nothing need be said. His harp compositions are brilliant in style, and afford ample scope for performers.

BOCKMÜHL (Robert Emil). German violoncellist and comp., B. Frankfort-on-the-Maine, 1820. Is still living as a 'cellist and teacher.

WORKS.—Didactic work on the Violoncello. Fantasias, Divertissements, Caprices, Concertos, Sonatas, etc. for the violoncello, with accompaniments for piano or orchestra,

These works possess some value for those who are studying the instrument.

BOCQUILLON-WILHEM, See WILHEM.

BODDA. See PYNE (Louisa).

BODENSCHATZ (Erhard). German comp. and collector, B. Lichtenberg [1570]. D. Querfurt, 1638. Famed for his collections of ancient sacred music, especially "Florilegium Portense. Pars prima continens cxv. cantiones selectissimas, 4, 5, 6, 7, 8 vocum," Lipzig, 1603. Second part, 1606. "Psalterium Davidis," Leipzig, 1605. "Harmonia Angelica," 1608, etc.

BOEHM (Carl Leopold.) Austrian comp. and violoncellist, B. Vienna, Nov. 4, 1806. Writer of concertos, etc.

BOEHM (Joseph). Bohemian violinist, B. Pesth, 1798. S. under Rode. Début at Vienna, 1815. Prof. at Vienna Cons., 1819-48. Mem. of Imperial band, Vienna, 1821. Retired in 1868. D. Vienna, Mar., 1876.

WORKS.—op. 1. Polonaise for violin, with quartet accomp. ; op. 2. and 3. Variations for violin ; op. 4. Two polonaises for violin and quartet accomp ; Five variations for violin and orch., op. 8 ; Four variations (Rossini) for vn. and orch., op. 9 ; Concertino for vn. and orch., op. 10. Quartets for strings, etc.

This professor has the honour of having taught more musicians who have attained eminence as violinists than perhaps any other master. Ernst, Joachim, Singer, Helmesberger, and L. Strauss are among the more noted. Personally he was an able performer and composed some serviceable music for his instrument.

BOEHM (Theobald). German flute-player and inventor, B. Munich, Bavaria, 1802. Chap.-master at Munich. Perfected his system of fingering for flutes, oboes, clarionets, etc., 1831. Received Prize medal at Exhibition of 1851, London. D. Dec., 1881.

WORKS.—Fantasias for the Flute, opp. 8, 21, 23, 24, etc. Variations. Polonaises. Rondos. Studies. "Ueber den Flötenbau und die neuesten Verbesserungen desselben," Mayence, 1847, etc.

Boehm patented the well-known system of fingering for keyed instruments, which is named after him. See History of the Boehm Flute, by Christopher Welch, M.A., Lond., 1883. It makes easy the performance of difficult solos, but as mechanism, adds much to the weight and detracts from the tone of the instrument. Recent improvements have modified its defects and perfected its capabilities as a solo-performing instrument. The invention has been adopted by many makers. His work on the flute has been translated as "An Essay on the Construction of Flutes, giving a History and Description of the most recent Improvements, with an Explanation of the Principles of Acoustics, applicable to the Manufacture of Wind Instruments," by W. S. Broadwood, Lond., 1882.

BOEHNER (Johann Ludwig). German comp. and pianist, B. Toesselstadt, Gotha, Jan. 8, 1787. A good teacher and capable performer. D. 1860.

WORKS.—*Pianoforte, etc.:* Variations, op. 3. Quartet for Pf., vn., alto, and 'cello ; Variations, op. 6. *Concertos:* Pf. and orch., in E flat, op. 7 ; in D, op. 8 ; in C, op. 11. Serenade for orch. in F, op. 9. Concertos for Pf., op. 13 and 14. Sonata, op. 15. Fantasias, op. 19 and 20. Fantasia for clarinet and orch. in C, op. 21. Fantasia, Pf., op. 22. Variations for horn and string accomp., op. 24. Fantasia, Pf. duet, op. 60. *Overture:* Der Dreiherrenstein, for orch. Twelve quartets for stringed instruments. Motets. Songs, and other vocal music.

BOËLY Alexandre Pierre Francois). French org., pianist, and comp., B. Versailles, April 19, 1785. D. Paris, Dec. 27, 1858. Comp. much Pf. and org. music, duets, trios, etc.

BOERS (J. C.) Dutch violinist and comp., B. Nimeguen, 1812. Writer of symphonies, psalms, songs, Pf. music, etc.

BOHRER (Maximilian). German comp. and violoncellist, B. Munich, 1785. S. 'cello under A. Schwartz. 'Cellist in Court band at Munich. S. under Romberg. Resided in Paris till 1830. Principal 'cellist at Court of Stuttgart. Travelled in Russia and America, 1838-43. Travelled in Holland, Belgium, and England, 1847. Composed music for the violoncello, etc. D. 1867.

Other members of this family were talented musicians, but notably ANTON BOHRER (1783-1852), who composed much good music for the violin. His works extend over 100 op. numbers, and include concertos, etc. CASPAR BOHRER, father of the foregoing (B. Mannheim, 1744. D. Munich, 1809,) was a famous trumpet-player. Anton's daughter SOPHIE (1828-1849) was a pianist of some ability.

BOIELDIEU (Francois Adrien), French comp., B. Rouen, Dec. 16, 1775. Chorister in Rouen Cath. S. under Broche, the org. there, till 1791. Went to Paris, 1794. Prof. of Pf. at Paris Cons., 1800. Married to Mdlle. Mafleuroy, 1802. Was unhappy in this union. Went to S. Petersburg to avoid his wife, 1802. Appointed Chap.-master to Emperor of Russia, 1802. Returned to Paris, 1811. Accompanist to the King's Band, 1815. Married to Mdlle Philis, his first wife having died, 1816. Member of the Institut, 1817. Prof. of Comp. at Paris Cons., 1817. Mem. of Legion of Honour, 1821. D. Grosbois near Bordeaux, Oct. 8, 1834.

WORKS.—*Operas:* La Fille coupable, Rouen, 1793; Rosalie et Myrza, 1795; La Famille Suisse, Paris, 1797; l'Heureuse Nouvelle, 1797; Le Pari, 1797; Zoraïme et Zu'nare, 1798; La Dot de Suzette, 1798; Les Méprises Espagnoles, 1799; Emma, ou la Prisonnière (with Cherubini), 1799; Beniowski (by Duval), 1800; Le Calife de Bagdad (by St. Just Dancourt), Paris, Sept. 16, 1800; Ma Tante Aurore, Jan. 13, 1803; Le Baiser et la Quittance (with Méhul, Kreutzer, and Nicolo), 1803; Aline, reine de Golconde, St. Petersburg, 1804; Amour et Mystère; Abderkhan; Un Tour de Soubrettle; La Jeune Femme colère, 1805 (Paris, 1812); Télémaque, 1806; Les Voitures versées (by Dupaty), 1808; La Dame invisible, 1808; Rien de trop, 1810; Jean de Paris, Paris, April 4, 1812 (in English by Bishop, London, 1814); Le Nouveau Seigneur de Village, 1813; Bayard à Mézières (with Cherubini, Catel, and Nicolo), 1814; Les Béarnais (with Kreutzer), 1814; Angéla (with S. Gail), 1814; Fa Fête du Village voisin, 1816; Charles de France, ou Amour et Gloire (with Hérold), 1816; Le Petit Chaperon rouge, 1818; Blanche de Provence (with Berton, etc.), 1821; Les Trois Genres (with Auber) 1824; Pharamond (with Berton and Kreutzer), 1825; La Dame blanche (from Sir W. Scott's "Monastery" and "Guy Mannering"), Opéra Comique, Dec. 10, 1825, London. Covent Garden, Jan. 2, 1837; Les Deux Nuits (by Bouilly and Scribe), 1829; La Marquise de Brinvilliers (with Auber, etc.), 1831. Instrumental music, church music, etc.

Boieldieu was the founder of modern French opera, and himself an excellent composer of comic operas. His music is beautiful. fresh, and rarely trivial, and he seems to have been in possession of a great command over the more cheerful capabilities of instrumental expression. The adaptability of his music to the comic situations constantly occurring in his works is so obvious and apt as to do away with the feeling of incongruity which arises when consideration is given to the stupidity of a libretto and the beauty of its music. The genial character of the music to "Jean de Paris" is typical of most of his works. Boieldieu's instrumentation is always effective, though scored for a smaller orchestra than is now considered necessary; and some of his overtures are occasionally heard in concert rooms; while those to "La Dame Blanche" and "Le Calife de Bagdad" are in constant use in small orchestras all over the world. The pieces by which he is best known in France and elsewhere are those named "Le Calife de Bagdad," "Jean de Paris," and "La Dame Blanche," which latter is especially deserving of praise, as much for the agreeable melodies interspersed throughout course, as for the never-flagging spirit and freshness of its general treatment. "Jean de Paris" was adapted to the English stage by Bishop, and with other operas of Boieldieu was very successful. "The Califé de Bagdad" overture alone survives, but not a few of Boieldieu's minor pieces are constantly in use on the Continent. The best works on Boieldieu are the following :—" Boieldieu sa vie, ses œuvres, son caractère, sa correspondance," by A. Pougin, Paris, 1875.

His son, ADRIEN L. V., B. Paris, November 3, 1816. S. under his father, and obtained considerable success as a composer. D. Combs-la Ville, near Paris, July, 1883. Among his operas may be named Marguerite, 1838; L'Aïeule, 1841; Le Bouquet de l'Infante, 1847; La Butte des Moulins, 1852; La Fille Invisible, 1854; La Halte du Roi, 1875. He also comp. masses, cantatas, etc.

BOISMORTIER (Joseph Bodin de). {French comp., B. Perpignan, 1691. D.

Paris, 1765. Writer of operas, cantatas, motets, sonatas, concertos, serenades, string music, etc.

BOISSELOT (Xavier). French comp. and Pf. manufacturer, B. Montpellier, Dec. 3, 1811. Writer of cantatas, operas, Pf. music, etc.

BOÏTO (Arrigo). Italian comp. and poet, B. [Milan, February 24], Padua, 1842. S. at Milan Cons. from Sept., 1853 Visited London, 1880.
 WORKS.—Mefistofele, opera, Milan, Sep., 1868; Bologna, Oct. 4, 1875; London, July 6, 1880. Ero, e Leandro, opera (MS.) Le Sorelle d'Italia, Allegory, libretto only. Poetical works, various. Marcello—one of the "Great Musicians" Series, edited by Hueffer.
 The work by which Boïto has suddenly become known to the musical world is "Mefistofele," an opera which owes much of its success to the music and legend so skilfully blended. Boïto has endeavoured to transfuse his opera with an interest wholly apart from the conventional musical and dramatic elements. How far he is justified in making use of an additional motive cannot be now entered into, but it may be pointed out that Wagner has in a different fashion furnished a precedent. The psychological opera is a novelty in many respects, but it does not follow that the idea of embodying the principles of good and evil in the action of a theatrical entertainment is by any means new. We find in the mediæval miracle plays and mysteries, characters which are intended to typify not only the primary elements of good and evil, but their numerous sub-divisions. In them evil, or the devil, assumed a tangible shape; appearing as a tailed and hornéd monster. The Mefistofele of Boïto's opera, as in Gounod's, is also a tangible devil, representing evil, but shorn of certain appendages which formerly carried terror into the hearts of old world audiences.

BOLCK (Oskar). German comp. and pianist, B. Hohenstein, Mar. 4, 1839. Presently a conductor and teacher in Germany.
 WORKS.—Pierre Robin, opera, Altenburg, 1874; Der Schmied von Gretna Green, opera, Leipzig, 1882, Paris, 1884; Six Lieder for voice and Pf., op. 5; Mädchens Geständnisse, for voice and Pf., op. 7; Sechs Charakterbilder in 2 books, for Pf., op. 46; Herbstklänge, Five songs for barytone or contralto voice and Pf., op. 51. Two anthems published by Messrs. Novello & Co.

BOMBET. See BEYLE (Henri).

BOMTEMPO (Joãs Domingos). Portuguese comp. and pianist, B. Lisbon, 1775. Settled in Paris, 1795. Visited London. Director of Lisbon Cons. Knight of the Order of Christ, Portugal. Director of Court Band, etc. D. Lisbon, Aug., 1842. He comp. Operas, Church Music, Pf. Music, etc., and wrote a Method for the Pf.

BONA (Valerio). Italian ecclesiastic and comp., flourished at end of 16th cent. Wrote a work on counterpoint (1595), masses, motets, madrigals, etc.

BONAWITZ (Johann Heinrich). German comp., B. Durkheim-on-the Rhine, Dec. 4, 1839. S. at Liège Cons. Resided for a time in the United States. Teacher and comp in London. Comp. The Bride of Messina, opera, Philadelphia, 1874. Ostrolenka, opera, 1875. Irma, Lond., 1885. Requiem Mass, Lond., 1881. Concertos, sonatas, etc., for Pf. Songs and other vocal music.
 As a pianist Herr Bonawitz has given "Beethoven Recitals" and "Historical Concerts" in Germany, Austria, France, etc., and has been on concert tours with Dr. J. JOACHIM in Germany, Italy, Russia, etc., in 1880-82.

BONAZZO (Giuseppe). Italian double-bass player and comp, B. 1824. D. Trieste, 1880.

BOND (Capel). English comp. and org., lived in Coventry during middle of last century. The dates of his birth and death are unknown. He was org. and cond. of the first Birmingham Musical Festival, 1768.
 WORKS.—Six Anthems in Score, one of which is for Christmas Day, 1769. Six Concertos for 4 violins, tenor, and 'cello, with thorough bass, 1766. Glees and Songs.

BOND (Hugh). English org. and comp., B. Exeter, beginning of 18th century. Lay-vicar Exeter Cath., 1762. Org. of Ch. of S. Mary Arches. D. 1792.
WORKS.—Twelve Hymns and four Anthems, for four voices, Lond., n. d. Glees and Songs.

BONFICHI (Paolo). Italian comp., B. Livraga, Lodi, Oct. 16, 1769. D. Dec., 1840. Wrote oratorios, etc.

BONMARCHE (Jean). Belgian comp. of church music, B. Ypres, 1520. D. (?)

BONNYBOOTS. An English singer and dancer of much fame in the reign of Queen Elizabeth bore this nickname.
Noticed in Hawkins' "History of Music."

BONOLDI (Claudio). Italian tenor vocalist and comp., B. Piacenza, 1783. D. 1846. Comp. Pf. music and songs.

BOOM (Johann Van). Dutch comp., B. Utrecht, Oct 15, 1807. D. Stockholm, 1872. Wrote music for the Pianoforte, on which he was a performer. His father and brother were composers.

BOOSEY & CO. English music publishers, established about 1819 by Thomas Boosey. Published originally valuable copyright works by Hummel, Romberg, De Beriot, Rossini, and a number of popular Italian operas. In 1854 they were deprived of the exclusive right of publishing Italian operas by a decision of the House of Lords.
They publish a large amount of vocal music, and their publications include songs by Abt, G. B. Allen, Balfe, Benedict, Blumenthal, Claribel, F. Clay, F. H. Cowen, Miss Dolby, Virginia Gabriel (March), A. S. Gatty, Hatton, G. Linley, J. L. Molloy, Pinsuti, Richards, Sullivan, and J. Thomas. The instrumental publications include compositions by Beethoven, Benedict, Cowen, Favarger, Gollmick, Kuhe, Mozart, Oury, Richards, Rubinstein, Thalberg, Schumann, etc. Among their Series of publications may be also mentioned the "Royal Edition of Operas," edited by Messrs. Sullivan and Pittman; the "Musical Cabinet," comprising Operas arranged for Pf. solo, Albums of Vocal Music, etc.; their Royal Edition of Song Books and Operatic Albums; "The Cavendish Music Books;" Collections of Standard Songs and Pf. Music, etc. In addition to the works already mentioned they publish the large choral works of Bach, Handel, Mendelssohn, Beethoven, Sullivan, Webbe, Cowen, Boyce, etc. "The Choralist" is the collective title of a large body of concerted vocal music issued in good style in penny numbers. They also issue a great number of popular tutors for various instruments, and publish some standard theoretical works. Their "Military Journal," established in 1845, is an important annual collection of band music. In addition to their publications, Messrs. Boosey manufacture an improved class of military band instruments.

BOOTH (Karl Edmund Otto von). German comp., violonist, org., and pianist, B. Schloss Weinheim, Weinheim, Baden, March 13, 1842. S. music at Carlsruhe Cons. S. violin under Concert-meister Will, a pupil of Spohr. *Début* as violinist in Town Hall, Birmingham, 1853. Settled permanently in London, 1856. S. composition under B. Molique; organ under Dr. Steggall. Org. at St. Matthew's, Bayswater, 1868-75.
WORKS.—Symphony in C minor (MS.); Operetta, Prizes and Blanks (MS.); A Cantata (MS); Overture, Godiva, for orch. (MS.); Marchia Funèbre, for orch. (MS.) A Te Deum in D; Anthems and Church Services. Sonata Quasi Fantasia, for organ; Offertoires for org.; Quartets and Quintets for stringed instruments (MS.); Victoria March for orch.; Sonata in A minor for violin and Pf.; Do. in D for violin and Pf.; Romance in F for vn. and Pf.; Morceaux Faciles: Ten Easy pieces for violin and Pf.; Wanderlieder—sketches for Pf.; Gavotte and Bourée for Pf. *Songs:* Fancies; The Star Angel; Break, break, break; Autumn Leaflets; The Broken Tryst; Greeting; Pretty little Warbler, stay; The Fisher; Beautiful May, four-part song, etc.

BORDE. See LABORDE.

BORDÈSE (Luigi). Italian comp., B. Naples, 1815. S. at Naples Cons. Went to Paris, 1834. Resided there from 1834.

He has composed a number of light operas, such as Zelimo e Zoraide, 1834; La Mantille, 1837; L'Automate de Vaucanson, 1840; Jeanne de Naples, 1840; Les Deux Bambins, 1848, which have achieved temporary popularity.

BORDOGNI (Marco). Italian comp. and vocal teacher, B. Bergamo, 1788. S. under Simon Mayr. *Début* in opera at Milan, 1813. Appeared in Paris, 1819. Prof. of Singing in Paris Cons., 1820. Chevalier of Legion of Honour. D. Paris, July, 31, 1856.

Bordogni trained a large number of vocalists who have attained to eminence in the profession, and wrote a great quantity of vocal exercises, solfeggi, and other works of great use to teachers of vocalisation.

BORDONI. See HASSE (Faustina B.)

BORGHI (Luigi). Italian violinist and comp., B. (?) S. under Pugnani. Teacher in London about 1780. Violinist at Handel Commemoration, 1784. D. (?)

WORKS.—Op. 1. Six Sonatas for the violin; op. 2. Three concertos for the violin; op. 3. Six solos for the violin; op. 4. Six duets for 2 violins; op. 5. Six duets for 2 vns.; op. 6. Six duets for violin and viola; op. 7. Six duets for violin and 'cello. Symphonies for full orch. Italian canzonets, songs, etc.

BORNACCINI (Giuseppe). Italian comp., B. Ancona, 1805. Writer of cantatas, masses, motets, operas, etc.

BORREMANS (Joseph). Belgian comp., B. Brussels, Nov. 25, 1775. D. Dec. 15, 1858. Writer of operas, masses, etc.

BORTNIANSKY (Dmitri Stepanovitch). Russian comp. and writer, B. Gloukoff, Ukraine, 1751. S. at Moscow and St. Petersburg under Galuppi. Do. at Rome, Naples, and Bologna. Director of Empress's Choir, 1779. D. Sept. 28 (Oct. 9), 1825.

WORKS.—Psalms, masses, operas, etc.

BOSANQUET (R. H. M.) Contemporary English writer, and Fellow of S. John's College, Oxford, has written a work entitled "An Elementary Treatise on Musical Intervals and Temperament," Lond., 8vo, 1876.

BOSCHI (Giuseppe). Italian bass vocalist, B. at end of 18th century. Appeared in London, 1711 and 1720. Sang in London at Italian opera till 1728, when he disappeared. He sang principally in operas by Handel, and was considered one of the greatest bass vocalists of his period.

BOSIO (Angiolina). Italian vocalist, B. Turin, Aug. 22, 1830. S. at Milan Cons. *Début*, July, 1846, in I Due Foscari," at Milan. Sang in Italy, Spain, Paris, and America with much success. Married to a Greek gentleman, 1851. Appeared in London, July, 1852, in "L'Elisir d'Amour." Reappeared again at different periods. D. St. Petersburg, April 12, 1859.

BOSSENLIENGER (Heinrich Jacob). German comp., B. Cassel, Oct. 27, 1838. Writer of operettas, lieder, etc.

BOTTESINI (Giovanni). Italian double-bass player and comp., B. Crema, Lombardy, Dec. 24, 1823. S. at Milan Cons. Cond. of orchestra at the Havannah theatre, 1846. Travelled in Britain and Europe as contra-bassist. Leader of orchestra at Italian opera, Paris, 1856. Travelled in Germany, Holland, Belgium, France, and England, 1857-58. Returned to Italy, 1859. Teacher and composer there.

WORKS.—*Operas:* Christope Colomb, Havannah, 1846; L'Assedio di Firenze, 1856; Santa Radegonda; Il Diavolo della notte, 1859; Marion De Lorme, 1862; Vinciguerra, 1870; Ero e Leandro, 1879; La Regina del Nepal, 1880. Methode Complete de Contre-basse, Paris, n. d.; English translation, Lond., n. d. Songs, chamber music, etc.

To a powerful and fine tone Bottesini adds great powers of execution and delicacy of phraseology. His rendering of many difficult pieces of violin music is superior to that of a number of violinists, while it cannot be doubted that in chamber music he is unsurpassed. His school for the double bass is the best ever penned. His other compositions are unknown in Britain, but they are highly spoken of in authoritative biographical works.

BOTTOMLEY (Joseph). English comp., org., and pianist, B. Halifax, Yorkshire, 1786. S. under Grimshaw, Watts, Yaniewicz, Lawton, and Woelfl. Org. of Parish Ch. of Bradford, 1807. Org. of Parish Ch., Sheffield, 1820. D. [?]

WORKS.—A Dictionary of Music, London, 1816. New System of Practising and Teaching the Pianoforte..., Sheffield, 4to, n. d. Six Exercises for the Pf. Rondos and airs for Pf. Divertissements for Pf. and Flute. Twelve Sonatinas for Pf. Songs, Glees, etc.

BOUCHER (Alexandre Jean). French violinist and comp., B. Paris, April 11, 1770. D. Paris, Dec. 29, 1861.

This performer travelled extensively in Spain, France, Germany, and Italy, and was everywhere received with much enthusiasm consequent on his extraordinary powers as a mechanical violinist. He composed concertos and sonatas for his instrument.

BOUFFET (Jean Baptiste). French comp. and Professor of Singing, B. Amiens, Oct. 3, 1770. D. Paris, Jan. 19, 1835. Wrote operas, church music, songs, etc.

BOULANGER (Ernest Henri Alexandre). French comp., B. Paris, Sept. 16, 1815. S. at the Cons. under Alkan and Halévy, 1830. Gained first prize for comp., with "Achille," a cantata. Prof. of Singing at Paris Cons., 1871. Mem. Legion of Honour, 1869.

WORKS.—*Operas:* Le Diable à l' école, 1842 ; Les Deux Bergères, 1843 ; Una Voix, 1845 ; La Cachette, 1847 ; Les Sabots de la Marquise, 1854 ; L' Eventail, 1860 ; Le Docteur Magnus, 1864 ; Don Quichotte, 1869 ; Don Mucarade, 1875. Cantatas, Pf Music, etc.

BOURGAULT-DUCOURDRAY (Louis Albert). French comp., B. Nantes, Feb. 2, 1840. S. at Paris Cons. Gained "Grand Prix de Rome," with "Louise de Mézières," cantata, 1865. S. at Rome till 1868. Returned to Paris, 1868. Founded an Amateur Choral Soc. in Paris for performance of works by great masters. Lectured on Musical history, etc.

WORKS.—Louise de Mézières, cantata, 1865 ; Stabat Mater, for chorus, org., and orch., 1868 ; Dieu notre divin père, sacred cantata ; Fantasia in C. minor for orchestra, 1874 ; Gavotte and Minuet for Pf. ; Cantata, written in honour of Sainte Françoise d' Amboise, duchesse de Bretagne, 1876. Souvenir d' une mission musicale en Grèce et en Orient, 1876. Trente mélodies populaires de Grèce et d' Orient. Conférence sur la modalité dans la Musique Grècque, Paris, 1879.

This composer is an eminent antiquary, and his collection of Greek and Eastern melodies is valuable, as also are his remarks thereon. A number of his compositions have been given in London, while in Germany and France he is generally well known. His compositions are spoken of in terms of much approval by both British and Foreign writers.

BOURGES (Jean Maurice). French operatic comp. and writer, B. Bordeaux, Dec. 2, 1812. D. Paris, April, 1881. Comp. "Sultana," an opera, 1846, etc.

BOURNE (C. E.) English writer, author of " The Great Composers ; or, Stories of the Lives of Eminent Musicians," London, 8vo, 1884.

BOUSQUET (Georges). French comp., B. Perpignan Mar. 12, 1818.

WORKS.—*Operas:* L' Hôtesse de Lyon, 1844 ; Le Mousquetaire, 1844 ; Tabarin, 1852. Critical writings, etc.

BOWIE (John). Scottish musician of Perth, published about the end of last century " A Collection of Strathspey Reels and Country Dances, with a Bass, etc. Dedicated to the Countess of Kinnoul," Edin., n. d.

BOWLEY (Robert K.) English musician. B. London, May, 1813. D. August, 1870. Author of "Grand Handel Musical Festival at the Crystal Palace in 1857, a Letter." Lond., 1856. "The Sacred Harmonic Society, a Thirty-five Years Retrospect," Lond., 1867. This musician was connected with the Sacred Harmonic Society, and he assisted in establishing the Great Handel Celebrations at the Crystal Palace, London.

BOWMAN (Edward M.) American comp. and org., B. Barnard Vt., July 18th, 1848. Org. of Second Baptist Church, St. Louis, Mo. Associate of the London Royal College of Organists. S. at Berlin under A. Haupt and E. Rohde for organ, Franz Bendel for piano, and C. F. Weitzman in theory, composition, etc. Also spent a portion of the years abroad in study with Batiste at Paris, and Drs. MacFarren, Bridge, and E. H. Turpin, of London. Twice elected Pres. of the Music Teachers National Association.

WORKS.—Bowman's Weitzman's Manual of Musical Theory. Delivered the following addresses, which have appeared at various times in the published reports of the M. T. N. A.:—Harmony: Historic points and Modern Methods; Formation of Piano Touch; Relation of Musicians to the Public; Relation of the Professional to the Amateur Teacher, etc.

Mr. Bowman is well known as a musician and organist of ability, and as the projector of the "National College of Teachers" has a name and place in the hearts of America's musicians. His Weitzman's theory is one of the leading works on the subject in the country. He was the first American who won the distinction of "Associate of the College of Organists." He is a painstaking and conscientious student, and in the midst of his professional duties finds time for a moderate amount of excellent composing. He is recognised throughout the country as an eminent organist and teacher.

BOWMAN (Henry). English comp., flourished during latter half of 17th cent. Wrote "Songs for one, two, and three voyces to the Thorow-Bass. With some short Symphonies. Collected out of some of the Select Poems of the incomparable Mr. Cowley, and others, and composed by Henry Bowman, Philo-Musicus," Oxford, 1677.

BOX (Charles). English writer, author of "Church Music in the Metropolis; its Past and Present Condition, with Notes, Critical and Explanatory," Lond., 8vo, 1884.

BOXBERG (Christian Ludwig). German comp., B. Sondershausen, April 24, 1670. D. [?] Writer on the organ. Comp. of operas, etc.

BOYCE (William). English comp. and org., B. London, 1710. Chor. in S. Paul's Cath. under Charles King. Articled Pupil to Maurice Greene, org. of S. Paul's. Org. of Oxford Chap., Cavendish Sq. S. under Dr. Pepusch. Org. (in succession to Kelway) of St. Michael's, Cornhill, 1736. Comp. to Chapel Royal and the King, June, 1736. Cond. at Meetings of Choirs of Gloucester, Hereford, and Worcester, 1837. Org. of Ch. of Allhallows the Great and the Less, Thames Street, 1749. Bac. and Doc. of Music, Cambridge, 1749. Master of Royal Band of Music, 1775. One of the org. to Chapel Royal, 1758. D. Kensington, Feb. 7, 1779.

WORKS.—Peleus and Thetis, masque, by Lord Lansdowne, 17 ?; Solomon, serenata by Dr. Edward Moore, 1747; The Chaplet, a musical drama, Lond., fo., 1745; David's Lamentation over Saul and Jonathan, oratorio, by Lockman, 1736; Ode for St. Cecilia's Day, by Lockman; Music to the Shepherd's Lottery, 1750; Ode for the Installation of the Duke of Newcastle as Chancellor of Cambridge University, 1749; Fifteen Anthems and a Te Deum and Jubilate, 1780; Twelve Anthems and a Service, 1790; Ode to Charity; Pindar's First Pythian Ode, 1749; Masque in the Tempest. Cathedral Music, being a Collection in score of the most valuable and useful compositions for that service, etc., [containing examples of Aldrich, Batten, Bevin, Byrd, Blow, Bull, Child, Jer. Clark, Creyghton, Croft, Farrant, Gibbons, Goldwin, Humphreys, King Henry VIII., Lawes, Locke, Morley, Purcell, Rogers, Tallis, Turner, Tye, Weldon, and Wise]; London, 3 vols. fo., 1760; second edit., 1778. Eight symphonies for various instruments; Twelve sonatas for 2 violins and bass, 1749; Ode for St. Cecilia's Day, by Rev. Mr. Vidal; An organ concerto; Two odes in Home's "Agis," 1758; Lyra Britannica .. collection of songs, duets, and cantatas, fo., n. d.; Various overtures; Songs, duets, etc., in the collections of the period, as The British Orpheus, etc.; A Collection of Services and Anthems, published in 4 vols. by Novello, Ewer & Co. (modern).

Of the many great composers of church music whom England has produced, Boyce is held in especial reverence. Sabbath after Sabbath his anthems and services are being heard in churches of importance throughout England. This is owing chiefly to the great suitability of his music for use in public worship; but a certain amount of traditional regard for his works is also in vogue. His anthems are for the most part admirable specimens of sacred music, being impressed with these characteristics of majesty and devout feeling which are universally allowed to be appropriate attributes of Christian song-offerings. It is almost impossible to discover in the whole range of Boyce's writings a slovenly or flippant passage. There is not the slightest appearance of any endeavour to gain applause by the introduction of astounding progressions or flashy melodies, and the impression made by his broad and powerful harmonies is healthy, inspiring, and legitimate in the highest degree.

BRADBURY (William B.). American comp. and writer, B. York, Maine, U.S.A., 1816. Self-taught on many instruments. Went to Boston and became an org., 1830. Settled at New York as teacher, 1836. S. at Leipzig under Hauptmann, 1847. Established a Pianoforte manufactory, 1854 Editor of the "New York Musical Review." D. at Montclair, New Jersey, Jan. 7, 1868.

WORKS.—Esther, the Beautiful Queen, cantata; Daniel, cantata (with G. J. Root). *Collections:* The Young Choir, 1841; School Singers, 1843; Flora's Festival, 1845; Young Melodist; Musical Gems; Sabbath School Melodies; Young Shawm, 1855; Psalmata, or Choir Melodies; Alpine Glee Book, 2 vols., 1850-54; Metropolitan Glee Book; The Golden Chain; Golden Shower; Fresh Laurels; The Jubilee; The Key Note; The Temple Choir; Songs, etc.

The productions of this musician are marked by a plainness and wealth of familiar reminiscence which make them easy for performance by aspiring Sunday school choirs. He is said to have done much for music in New York; but whether in an artistic or popular sense is not known. He collected a very valuable musical library.

BRADE (William). English comp. and viol-player, flourished about commencement of 17th century. Published Paduanen, Galliarden, Canzonetten, etc., 1609; Neue Paduanen und Gagliarden mit stimmen, 1614; Neue Lustige Volten Couranten, Balletten, etc. D. at Frankfort, 1647.

BRADFORD (Jacob). English comp. and teacher, is a Mus. Bac. Oxon., 1873, and Mus. Doc., do., 1878. Principal of the South London Music Training College.

BRADSKY (Theodor Wenzel). Bohemian comp., B. Raknovik, Jan. 17, 1833. Prof. in the Real-Schule, Berlin. D. Berlin, Aug. 9, 1881. Comp. operas, "Christian von Schweden," 1872, etc.; songs, and instrumental music.

BRADY (Nicholas). Irish divine and poet, B. Bandon, 1659. D. Richmond, Surrey, 1726. Associated with Tate in the production of the metrical version of the Psalms of David, now in general use. He also wrote "Church Music Vindicated, a Sermon," Lond., 1697.

BRAGA (Gaetano). Italian comp. and violoncellist, B. Giulianuova, June 1829.

BRAHAM (John). English tenor vocalist and comp., B. London, 1774. S. under Leoni. *Début* at Royalty Theatre, Wellclose Square, London, 1787. Appeared at Covent Garden Theatre, April 21, 1787. Sang in Bath, 1794. S. under Rauzzini at Bath, 1794. Sang at Drury Lane Theatre, 1796, Travelled in Italy, and sang at Florence, Rome, Naples, Milan, Genoa. Venice, etc., occasionally with Mrs. Billington. S. under Isola in Italy. Returned to London, 1801. Re-appeared at Covent Garden Theatre, 1801. Married to Miss Bolton of Ardwick, 16, Appeared as "Huon," in Weber's

"Oberon," 1826. Lost his fortune by failure of several speculations, 1851. D. London, Feb. 17, 1856.

WORKS.—*Music to Dramas:* The Cabinet, 1801; Family Quarrels, 1802; The English Fleet, 1802 (containing "All's Well," duet, etc.); Thirty Thousand, 1804; Out of Place, 1805; False Alarms, 1807; Kais, or Love in a Desert, 1808 (with Reeve); The Devil's Bridge (with C. E. Horn), 1812; The Paragraph; Narensky, or, The Road to Yarostaf; The Americans; The Magicians (with M. P. King), Single songs, glees, etc.

Braham lived in a period when the naval achievements of Britain were the subjects of universal comment. The popular feeling ran high in the direction of the maintenance of a supremacy on the seas, and the writers who appeared in response to the national manifestations were warmly received. Among those, however, Charles Dibden and John Braham were undoubtedly supreme. The former wrote and the latter sang a number of ballads highly suited to the prevailing taste of the time. Braham possessed a voice of considerable compass and remarkable quality. He excelled in ballad singing, but was also successful in the more exacting dramatic music of Weber and others. In songs of his own composition, as the "Death of Nelson," Braham excelled all others. This work is a very respectable specimen of the class of song patronised in the first part of this century, and with Davy's "Bay of Biscay" and Dibdin's "Tom Bowling," it is among the most popular of English naval songs. The cabinet opera, "The Americans," contains also some melodious music, but its merit is not of a first-class order.

BRAHMS (Johannes). German comp., B. Hamburg, Mar. 7, 1833. S. under Marxsen. Noticed by Schumann. Travelled in Germany as pianist. Went to Vienna, 1861. Cond. of the Sing-Akademie, 1863-73. Director of the Gesellschaft der Musikfreunde Concerts, 1872-1875. Mem. of Academy of Arts, Berlin, 1874.

WORKS.—Op. 1. Sonata for Pf. in C; op. 2. Sonata for Pf. in F Sharp minor; op. 3. Six Gesänge für Tenor oder Sopran mit Pianoforte; op. 4. Scherzo for Pf. in E flat minor; op. 5. Sonata for Pf. in F minor; op. 6. Six Songs for voice and Pf.; op. 7. Do.; op. 8. Trio in B for Pf., vn., and 'cello; op. 9. Variations for Pf. on theme by Schumann; op. 10. Balladen für Pf.; op. 11. Serenade for orch. in D; op. 12. Ave Maria, for female voices, org., and orch.; op. 13. Funeral Hymn for chorus and orch. of wind instruments; op. 14. Eight Songs and Romances; op. 15. Concerto for Pf. and orch., in D; op. 16. Serenade for small orch., in A; op. 17. Four part songs for female voices, 2 horns and harp; op. 18. Sextet for strings, in B flat; op. 19. Five Songs for voice and Pf.; op. 20. Three duets for soprano and alto voices with Pf.; op. 21. Two variations for Pf.; op. 22. Seven Marienlieder for mixed choir; op. 23. Variations for Pf. (Schumann); op. 24. Variations and Fugue for Pf. (Handel); op. 25. Quartet for Pf. and strings in G minor; op. 26. Do. in A; op. 27. Psalm xliii for female voices and organ; op. 28. Four duets for alto and barytone voices and Pf.; op. 29. Two motets for 5 voices; op. 30. Giestliches Lied von Paul Flemming, for 4 voices and organ; op. 31. Three quartets for S. A. T. B.; op. 32. Nine Songs by Platen and Daumer, for voice and Pf.; op. 33. Fifteen Romances from Tieck's Magelone, for voice and Pf.; op. 34. Quintet for Pf. and strings in F. minor; op. 34a. Sonata for Pf. duet, trans. from the Quintet; op. 35. Twenty-eight variations for Pf. [Paginini]; op. 36. Sextet for strings, in G; op. 37. Three sacred choruses for female voices; op. 38. Sonata for Pf. and 'cello, in E minor; op. 39. Sixteen waltzes for Pf. duet; op. 40. Trio for Pf., violin, and horn or 'cello; op. 41. Five part songs for Men's voices; op. 42. Three songs for chorus; op. 43. Four songs for solo voice and Pf.; op. 44. Twelve Songs and Romances for female chorus; op. 45. "Ein Deutscher Requiem," German Requiem, for solo voices, chorus, and orch., 1868; op. 46. Four songs for voice and Pf.; op. 47. Four do.; op. 48. Seven do.; op. 49. Five do.; op. 50. "Rinaldo," cantata by Goethe, for solo, chorus, and orch.; op. 51. Two Quartets for strings in C minor, and A minor; op. 52. Liebeslieder, Waltzes for Pf. duet and voices; op. 53. Rhapsodie: Fragments from Goethe's "Harzreise," for alto-solo, male chorus, and orch.; op. 54. "Schicksalslied." Song of Destiny by F. Holderlin, for chorus and orch; op. 55. Triumphlied for 8 part chorus and orch.; op. 56. Variations on theme by Haydn, for orch.; op. 56a. Do. for Pf. duet; op. 57. Eight songs by Daumer for voice and Pf.; op. 58. Eight songs for voice and Pf.; op. 59; Eight do.; op. 60. Quartet for Pf. and strings, in C minor; op. 61. Four duets for soprano and alto; op. 62. Seven songs for mixed choir; op. 63. Nine Lieder and Songs for voice and Pf.; op. 64. Four Quartets for 4 voices; op. 65. Neue Liebeslieder, Waltzes for Pf. duet; op. 66. Five vocal duets; op. 67. Quartet for strings, in B flat; op. 68. First Symphony for full orch., in C minor, 1876; op. 69. Nine songs for voice and Pf.; op. 70. Four do.; op. 71. Five do.; op. 72. Five do.; op. 73. Second Symphony for full orch., in D, 1877; op. 75. Four vocal duets; op. 76. Eight Pianoforte pieces in 2 books; op. 77. Concerto for violin and orch., in D; op. 80. Akademische Fest-Ouverture, for full orch., 1880; op. 81. Tragische Ouverture, for full orch., 1880. Concerto for Pf. and orch., 1881. Third Symphony for orch., in F, op. 90, etc.

Hailed from the very outset of his career as a coming genius, Brahms had small difficulty in gaining a hearing for his works. Praised in a general way by every class of musicians, because he did not in any great measure depart from the standard methods of composition, and made no endeavour to imitate a school to be for ever identified with his name, Brahm may fitly be described as one of those genuises who neither retard nor advance contemporary art. He rises far above the genteel mediocrity of the average German professor, but the general tone of his writings is more learned than inspired. He is neither accounted extraordinary and eccentric like Berlioz, Liszt, or Wagner, nor very staid and dull; but he is remarkably ponderous and massive. Massive is perhaps the fittest appellation which can be applied to his class of genius. The truly legitimate manner in which he gains his effects is one of the features which redeems his music in a large degree from heaviness. The honesty by which he rules his artistic method is so evident as to banish all notions as to quackery or undue assumption in his music.

His most representative works are his symphonies, which have gained a certain amount of approval wherever produced. They are grand and dignified works, entirely free from sensation, and pervaded with a fervour of manner which raises them far above the average concert works of recent times. At the same time it must be admitted that the beauty of a large portion of his works is somewhat marred by a pedantic manner which repels all but the most earnest student.

BRAINARD (Silas and Sons). An American music-publishing firm established in Cleveland, Ohio, in 1836. Was originally a shop known as "Brainard's Bazaar," and subsequently as the "Melodeon." The founder of the firm, Silas Brainard, B. at Lempster, N. Y., Feb. 14, 1814, D. in 1871, and was succeeded by his sons, Charles S. and Henry M., who in February, 1876, opened a large store in Euclid Avenue. Their publications, commenced to be issued in 1845, are many, numbering about 16,000 different pieces, and consisting of songs, choral music, instruction books, cantatas, pianoforte music, and a monthly magazine named "Brainard's Musical World." This journal is well conducted, and gives many valuable articles on musical topics, as well as a selected amount of music of varying quality. Among the music books issued by the firm may be mentioned the Dollar Musical Library, The Crystal Glee Book; Brainard's Musical Albums; The Golden Chord; Anthems of the Church; and a great number of song and chorus books bearing as a rule fanciful titles.

BRAINARD (George W.) American musician and writer, author of a "New Method for the Pianoforte," Cleveland, n. d.

BRAMBACH (Carl Josef). German comp., B. Bonn, July 14, 1833.
WORKS.—*Cantatas:* Die Mach des gesanges; Velleda. Das Lied vom Rhein, for male chorus and brass orchestra, op. 40; Four Clavierstücke, op. 1; Vier Frühlingslieder, for 2 soprano voices and Pf., op. 2; Sonata for Pf., in G, op. 3; Six Lieder for voice and Pf., op. 4; Sextet for Pf., 2 violins, 2 violas, and Pf., op. 5; Concerto for Pf. and orch., in D minor, op. 39; Two Romances for Violoncello and Pf., op. 41; Two Sonatas for Pf., op. 20; Three Fantasiestücke for Pf., op. 34; Songs, etc.

BRANDL (Johann). German comp., B. Rohr, near Ratisbon, Nov. 14, 1760. S. under Valesi, and at Schools of Rohr, Munich, and Neuburg. Musical director to Prince Hohenlohe Bartenstein, 1784. Music-director to Bishop of Bruchsal, 1789. Do. to the Archduke of Baden, 1806. D. Carlsruhe, May 26, 1837.

WORKS.—Symphony for orch., in D, op. 25, 1790; Serenades for small orch., op. 4, 1792, and op. 7, 1796; Six quartets for strings, op. 8; Three sets of six quintets for strings, op. 8; op. 10; and op. 11, 1797; Symphony for orch. in E flat, op. 12; Quintet for Pf., vn., viola, bassoon, and 'cello, op. 13, 1798; Quintet for violin, 2 violas, bassoon, and 'cello, op. 14; Sextet for various insts., op. 16; Six String Quartets, op. 17, 1799; Quartet for strings in D minor, op. 18, 1799; Nocturne for 2 vns. and 'cello, op. 19; Symphony concertante for violin, 'cello, and orch., op. 20, 1801; Germania, opera, in 3 acts, 1800; Three quartets for strings, op. 23, 1803; Hermann, opera, etc.

BRANDUARDI (Enrico). Italian pianist and comp., B. in Italy, 1846. Has composed a number of brilliant salon pieces, and has played with considerable success throughout Italy, etc.

BRASSIN (Louis), or BRASSINE. German comp. and pianist, B. Aix-la-Chapelle, June 24, 1836. S. at Leipzig Cons. under Moscheles, etc., and also at Cologne. Prof of Pf. at Berlin Cons. Prof. of Pf. at Brussels Cons. Has played in various parts of Europe. Prof. at St. Petersburg Cons., 1878-84. D. St. Petersburg, May 17, 1884.

WORKS.—*Operettas:* Der Thronfolger; Der Missonär. L'Ecole moderne du Piano; Bluette for Pf., op. 4; Valse-Caprice for Pf., op. 6; Grand Galop Fantastique, for Pf., op. 5; Le Chant du Soir, for Pf., op. 7; Le Ruisseau, Morceau de Salon, op. 8; Nocturne for Pf., op. 9; Prière for Pf., op. 10; Second Valse-Caprice for Pf., op. 11; Grandes Etudes de Concert for Pf., op. 12; Rêverie Pastoral for Pf., op. 13; Mazurka de Salon, for Pf., op. 14; Les Adieux for Pf., op. 15; Second Galop Fantastique for Pf., op. 16; Nocturne for Pf., op. 17; Second Grand Polonaise for Pf., op. 18; Six Morceaux de Fantaisie for Pf., op. 21; Concerto for Pf. and orch., op. 22; Third Grand Polonaise for Pf., op. 22; Transcription (Gounod), op. 27; Scherzo for Pf., op. 24; Works for Pf. and orch., various. Songs, part-songs, etc.

BRAY (Mrs. Anna Eliza), *née* Kempe. English writer, B. St. Mary, Newington, Surrey, Dec. 25, 1790. D. London, Jan. 21, 1883. Wrote a number of novels and miscellaneous works, and "Handel : his Life, Personal and Professional, with Thoughts on Sacred Music," Lond., 8vo, 1857.

BREAKSPEARE (Eustace John). English writer and comp., B. Birmingham, April 22, 1854. S. under Mr. S. S. Stratton. Correspondent of the "Musical Standard," 1879. Author of Papers on "Musical Aesthetics" (Musical Assoc., 1880); "Songs and Song Writers," 1882; "Musical Expression" (Coll. of Organists), 1883; "Notes on Musical Tuition and Study," reprinted from the *Musical Standard*, 1881. Translator of Hanslick's "Vom Musikalisch Schönen," 1854; and Ehrlich's "Die Musik-Aesthetik," 1882, both preparing for publication. Breakspeare has comp. a number of Songs, and is well known as a writer who has done much to awaken an interest in the subject of musical aesthetics.

BRECHIN (William). Scottish Teacher, and inventor of "Brechin's Stave Sol-fa Notation," B. Brechin, Forfar, 1824. Held appointments as precentor in Montrose, Forfar, Perth, Leith, and Edinburgh. The principal feature of his system is the employment of letters, as in the ordinary Tonic Sol-fa, to represent the notes, together with certain signs to mark the duration. The notes are written on the staff. In addition to the invention of the Stave Sol-fa Notation, Brechin has edited and compiled "Vocal Exercises, Rounds, etc., in the Stave Sol-fa Notation, forming a short course of Lessons in Sight Singing in the key of F." "Congregational Music, Psalms, Hymns, etc., in in Stave Sol-fa Notation." "The Standard Scottish Psalmody (compiled from the foregoing. "Exercises in Sight Singing." School Song Books. The Stave Sol-fa Journal (publishing in parts) containing pieces by Croft, Beethoven, Mason, Stevenson, Blow, Handel, etc. Two Books of Swedish Songs.

BREE (Johann Bernard Van). Dutch comp., B. Amsterdam, Jan. 29, 1801. A prominent musician in Amsterdam, and Musical Director there, 1821-1857. D. Amsterdam, Feb. 14, 1857.

WORKS.—*Cantatas:* St. Cecilia's Day; Lord Byron. Overtures for orch,

Masses. Chamber Music. Symphonies for orch. Sappho, lyric drama. Mimm dich in Acht, opera, etc. Masses, Motets, etc.

BREKELL (John). English divine, author of "A Discourse on Music, chiefly Church Music; occasioned by the opening of the new Organ at St. Peter's Church in Liverpool...Sermon," Lond., 8vo, 1766.

BREITKOPF and HÄRTEL. German Music-publishing firm, founded in 1719 by B. C. Breitkopf. He was born in 1695, and died 1777. Other members were his sons J. G. I. Breitkopf (1719-1794), and G. C. Härtel (Jan., 1763-1827), together with the present representatives of the house.

The publications by which they are best known are their great editions of the complete works of Palestrina, Bach, Mozart, Beethoven, Mendelssohn, Schumann, Schubert, etc., some of which are in course of issue. These editions are the most lasting and monumental tributes which could possibly be raised to the memory of the great composers represented. Their catalogue, which extends to nearly 500 pages, contains the name and some work of nearly every continental musician of eminence, as well as a few English works. The following list of musicians, whose works the firm issue, will give some idea of the vastness of the firm's operations:— Abert, Auber, Bargiel, Benedict, Bertini, Blumenthal, Brahms, Bruch, Burgmüller, Carulli, Cherubini, Chopin, Clementi, Cramer, Czerny. David (Ferd.), Dotzauer, Dupont, Dussek, Duvernoy, Eckert, Field, Franz, Gade, Gernsheim, Gluck, Halévy, Handel, Hauptmann, Heller, Henselt, Hiller (F.), Hünten, Kalkbrenner, Köhler, Kuhlau, Kummer, Lefébure-Wély, Liszt, Lobe, Lortzing, Lumbye, Marschner, Meyerbeer, Neukomm, Onslow, Paër, Raff, Reichardt, Reinecke, Rietz, Rode, Rossini, Rubinstein, Scarlatti, Scharwenka, Schubert, Schumann, Spohr, Steibelt, Street, Taubert, Thalberg, Tours, Viotti, Voss, Wagner, Weber, Winter, Wölfl, Zumsteeg. Here every school is represented, from the most frivolous to the most profound.

The connection of this firm with the musical progress on the continent has ever been close, and the ready recognition by the firm of rising composers has been as beneficial to the art as it certainly has been honourable to themselves. Of their productions it may be said that the engraving, paper, and style are in the highest artistic taste, and that the prevailing correctness of their editions of standard works has given them a widespread name.

BREMER (Johann Bernhard). Dutch pianist, org., and comp., B. Rotterdam, 1830. Comp. of "Judith," an oratorio, quartets, Pf. music, etc.

BREMNER (Robert). Scottish publisher and writer, B. in Scotland, 1720. Teacher of singing in Edinburgh, and kept the music shop at the sign of the Harp and Hoboy. Settled in London, with same sign, as music-seller. D. Kensington, London, May 12, 1798.

WORKS.—Rudiments of Music; or a Short and Easy Treatise on that Subject, to which is added a Collection of the best Church Tunes, Canons, and Anthems. Edin., 12mo, 1756; 2nd edit., Edin.; 3rd edit. also with Psalms, London, 1763. Thoughts on the Performance of Concert Music, Lond., fol., n. d. Instruction for the Guitar. The Vocal Harmonist's Magazine; being a Collection of Catches, Glees, Canons, and Canzonets, fo. Lond., n.d. The Songs in the Gentle Shepherd adapted to the Guitar, 1759; Thirty Scots Songs for a Voice and Harpsichord. Edinburgh, 1749; A Second Set of Scots Songs for a Voice and Hpsd., Edin.; Twelve Scots Songs for a voice and guitar, with a thorough Bass adapted for that instrument, Edin., 1760; A Collection of Scots Reels or Country Dances, also Twelve Scots Songs for a voice or guitar, with a Bass for the violoncello or harpsichord, Edin., n. d., also Lond, 1764; A Curious Collection of Scots Tunes with variations for the violin and a Bass for the violoncello or harpsichord, Lond., 1759; Thirty Scots Songs adapted for a voice and harpsichord (the words by Allan Ramsay), Lond., n. d. [1760]; The Freemasons' Songs, with Choruses, in three and four parts, and a Bass for the organ or violoncello, 1759; A Second Collection of Scots Reels or Country Dances, 1761.

BRENDEL (Carl Franz). German writer and critic, B. Stollberg in the Harz, Nov. 25, 1811. Educated at Freiberg, Leipzig, and Berlin. Delivered historical lectures on Music. Resided at Leipzig as editor (in succession to Schumann) of the *Neue Zeitschrift für Musik*. D. Leipzig, Nov. 25, 1868.

WORKS.—Grundzüge der Geschichte der Musik ; Geschichte der Musik in Italien, Deutschland und Frankreich, von den erster christlichen Zeiten bis auf die Gegenwart, Leipzig, 8vo, 1852 ; 2nd edit., 2 vols. 1855 ; 4 editions to 1875 ; Die Musik der Gegenwart und die Gesammtkünst der Zükünst, Leipzig, 8vo, 1854 ; Anregungen für Künst, Leben und Weissenchaft (with R. Pohl), Leipzig, 6 vols, 1856.

BRENT (Miss). See PINTO (Mrs).

BREWER (Thomas). English comp.; flourished during the 17th century [1610-80]. Educated at Christ's Hospital. He was a performer on the viol. Dates of birth and death unknown.

WORKS.—Seven fantasias for the viol ; Rounds and catches in Hilton's "Catch that catch can" ; Turn, Amaryllis, to thy Swain, part-song in Playford's Musical Companion.

The biography of this composer is unknown. "Turn, Amaryllis," is a well known and pretty piece.

BREWER & CO. An English firm of music-publishers, established in London by Samuel Brewer (B. 1817. D. Brighton, 1879). They publish a great number of standard songs and concerted vocal music by all the principal English composers, as well as instrumental music of various kinds.

BREWSTER (Henry). English writer. Author of a "Concise Method of Playing Thoroughbass," Lond., 1797.

BRIAN. See BRYNE.

BRICCIALDI (Giulio). Italian flute-player and comp., B. Terni, March 1, 1818. S. at Rome. Teacher and comp. at Milan. D. Florence, Dec. 17, 1881.

WORKS.—Notturno, for flute and Pf., op. 32 ; Morceau de concert for Pf. and flute, op. 61 ; Andante and Polonnise, do., op. 62 ; Deux Fleurs, do., op. 63 ; Caprice for flute and Pf., op. 64 ; Concerto for flute and orch., op. 65 ; Cavatina for flute and Pf., op. 70 ; Il Carnevale di Venezia, flute and orch., op. 77 ; Concertino, flute, and Pf., op. 104 ; Capriccio for flute and Pf., op. 105 ; Fantasias on themes from operas. A Method for the Flute, etc.

This composer's works are justly esteemed by all flute players, alike for their brilliancy and neatness. Briccialdi is one of the greatest flute-players of recent times. His works number over 200, but consist principally of Fantasias. He aided in the improvement of flute mechanism.

BRIDGE (Frederick Albert). English org., vocalist, lecturer, and writer, B. London, 1841. Choir-master and solo-bass of St. Andrew's Undershaft. Org. of St. Martin's, Ludgate, 1873-78. Choir-master S. Martin-in-the-Fields, 1878-82. Do. S. John's, Lewisham. Has composed some music, and is author of a "Brief History of Mr. Henry Leslie's Choir from its formation to its dissolution." London, 1880. He was married to Miss Elizabeth Stirling, the gifted composer, in 1862. First commenced his Musical Monologue Lecture Entertainment in 1872.

BRIDGE (Mrs. Frederick A.) See STIRLING (Elizabeth).

BRIDGE (John Frederick). English comp., org., and writer, B. Oldbury, Dec. 5, 1844. Educated under his Father, John Bridge, Lay Clerk of Rochester Cath. Org. of Trinity Ch., Windsor, 1865. Bac. Mus. Oxford, 1868. Org. of Manchester Cath., 1869. Doc. Mus., Oxford, 1874. Org. of Westminster Abbey, 1875-81. Prof. of Harmony and Comp. at Royal Coll. of Music.

WORKS.—Mount Moriah, oratorio, 1874 ; Boadicea, cantata, 1880 ; Magnificat and Nunc Dimittis, in D. *Anthems:* Give unto the Lord the glory ; Harvest Hymn to the Creator (motet) ; It is a good thing to give thanks ; The Lord hath chosen Zion ; Seek ye the Lord ; We declare unto you glad tidings ; Hope thou in the Lord ; Magnificat and Nunc dimittis in G. *Part-songs:* Christmas Bells ; Flowers ; Loose the sail, rest the oar ; Peace, a Fable ; When the sun sinks to rest ; With thee, sweet hope ; Hurrah ! hurrah ! for England. *Songs:* Forget me not ; Tears. Counterpoint (Music Primer), London, 8vo, 1880 ; Double Counterpoint and Canon (do.), London, 8vo, 1881. The Offertory Sentences as used in

Westminster Abbey, 1884. Rock of Ages, Latin and English words, for barytone solo, chorus, and orch., 1885, for Birmingham Festival.

"Boadicea" is frequently performed, and, no doubt, being a skilful and well-constructed work, deserves all success. Dr. Bridge's theoretical writings are useful elementary works, and form part of Novello's Music Primer Series. His minor compositions evince much of that scholarly treatment which is so marked in his cantata and oratorio. As an organist Dr. Bridge is widely known and justly famed.

BRIDGE (Joseph Cox). English comp. and org., brother of above, B. Rochester, Kent, Aug. 16, 1853. S. at Rochester Cath. Assistant org. in do. Assistant to his brother at Manchester Cath. Org. of Exeter Coll., Oxford, 1871. B.A., Oxford, 1875. B. Mus., Oxon., 1876. Org. of Chester Cath., 1877. M.A., Oxford, 1878. F.C.O., 1879. Mus. Doc., Oxon, 1884.

WORKS.—Service for voices and orchestra, Chester Festival, 1879. String Quartet in G minor, 1879; Greek War Song, for male voices, with accomp. of brass instruments; Bourée for Pf.; Sonata for violoncello and Pf.; Part-songs; Songs, etc. Daniel, oratorio, Chester Festival, 1885.

BRIDGETOWER (George Augustus Polgreen). African violinist, B. Bisla, Poland, 1780. Played at Drury Lane Theatre and at various concerts in London, 1790. S. for a time under Attwood and Giornovichi. Played at the Salomon concerts. Returned to Germany and travelled as a concert-giver, 1802. D. England after 1840.

WORKS.—Jubilee Quintet for strings; String duets, trios, and quartets; Songs, etc.

He was a good performer, but his compositions are not of any merit.

BRIDGMAN (Frederick William). English pianist, B. London, Jan., 1833. Well known in Scotland, and particularly in Edinburgh and Glasgow as a pianist and teacher.

BRIDSON (John). English barytone singer. B. Liverpool. Holds a foremost place among living vocalists. He sings with much artistic ability and refinement, and displays a strong degree of dramatic feeling. He is a pupil of Mr. J. B. Welch, and has sung at the principal provincial Festivals and London concerts.

BRIEGEL (Wolfgang Karl). German comp. and org., B. 1626. Org. at Stettin. Music-director to Prince Friedenstein, Gotha. Do. to the Duke of Saxe-Gotha, 1660. Do. to the Landgrave of Darmstadt, 1670. D. 1710. A very voluminous composer of concertos, airs, dance music, lieder, sonatas, madrigals, psalms, etc., published between 1652 and 1709.

BRIGGS (Thomas F.) American writer, author of "Briggs' Banjo Instructor." (Ditson, Boston, n. d.)

BRIND (Richard). English org. and comp. of 17th century. Educated at St. Paul's Cath. Org. of St. Paul's Cath. Comp. a thanksgiving anthem, etc., but is best known as the teacher of Greene.

BRINKERHOFF (Clara), *née* ROLPH. English soprano vocalist, B. London. Taken to the United States about 1834-5 by her parents, and taught music and singing by her mother and Herr Derwort, a German musician. She S. afterwards under Madame Arnault. *Debut* at a concert in Apollo Hall, Broadway, New York, when sixteen years of age. Married to Mr. C. E. L. Brinkerhoff, 1848. Appeared at the principal concerts in New York, Boston, and in many of the States. She appeared in London in 1861, and has appeared in Belgium, France, etc. She has comp. a few songs, and is mistress of four or five languages.

BRINSMEAD & SONS (John). English firm of pianoforte makers, established by John Brinsmead in 1836. The founder was born at Wear Gifford on the Torridge, North Devon, in 1814. He was originally a cabinet-maker, but becoming a workman in a pianoforte manufactory, he learned there the practical details of his business. Having a thorough knowledge of the principles of his work, Mr. Brinsmead early made endeavours to improve upon the existing mechanism of the pianoforte, and in 1862 was awarded a first-class medal at the London Exhibition for his sostenente instruments. In these the tone was more sustained and full than that which formerly had been attained by manufacturers. Other medals and prizes were gained at Paris in 1867; Amsterdam, 1869; Paris, 1870; Philadelphia, 1876; South Africa, 1877; and again at Paris in 1878. In 1868 Mr. Brinsmead took out a patent for that improvement which has so widely extended the firm's name: we refer to the "Perfect Check Repeater Action." This action is described in the following extract from the *Engineer* :—

"The improvements in pianoforte actions invented by John Brinsmead & Sons, of 18 Wigmore Street, Cavendish Square, possess the following advantages :—The hammer being held firmly by the check after it has struck the blow on the string allows the string to vibrate freely, producing a perfectly pure and sustained tone, and as there is no tremulous recoil of the hammer (which so quickly wears out the action and impedes the tone by touching the string a second time), greater power. When this has been even partially attained previously, the repetition has been sacrificed, as it was necessary when the hammer was held 'in check' to raise the finger completely off the key, allowing it to rise to a level with the others, before the action was completely reinstated and ready for a second blow. In this action, however, a repetition of the note can be obtained even when the key is pressed down to within an eighth of an inch of its utmost limit. The top of the 'hopper' being bevelled allows it to 'escape' freely, and assists in readjustment of the action. This also obviates the necessity of having a space between the hopper and hammer which, through striking against the leather on the butt of the hammer, in a very short time produces that 'rattling' which is so disagreeable to pianoforte players; this action having no space between the hopper and hammer, the hopper simply *presses* against the butt, and having no sharp corners to scrape against it, the friction is reduced to a minimum, the blow is rendered direct and uniform, and intermediate percussion between the finger on the key and the blow of the hammer on the string is entirely avoided, whilst the almost entire absence of friction of working surfaces ensures good wear even with the hardest work. The spring is at one end fastened into the bottom of the hopper, and at the top (the hook end) is held by a silk loop which passes through a slot in the top of the hopper, where it is attached to the under part of the hammer butt; its peculiar position, with the aid of the bevel, causes the hammer and hopper to be drawn into their respective positions, serving all the purposes that three, sometimes four, springs are often used for. This renders the use of a complication of pieces and centres quite unnecessary. The stroke of the hammer on the string is so direct from the key, and the escapement so instantaneous, that a far more powerful blow (and consequently greater volume and richness of tone) is produced than in the ordinary piano. It is impossible for the hammer to remain against the string and stop the tone after the blow has been struck (termed blocking), as the button against which the arm at the bottom of the hopper presses *forces* the sticker quite clear of the hammer butt. This is an important improvement, as the ordinary action has many hinges and coverings of vellum, cloth, and leather, which attract moisture, and in a damp room soon become so stiff and swollen as to render it quite impossible to play upon the piano, at all events with any degree of pleasure."

This action has long ago been highly appreciated by the leading pianists, and is therefore in need of no recommendation. In addition to this invention, the firm must also be credited with the improvements achieved in the "Tone sustaining pedal," and the "Upright grand construction," with other standard inventions too numerous to mention.

The other prizes gained by the firm are two gold medals from the Melbourne International Exhibition; a first prize from the Queensland Exhibition; and the two first prizes, with the special diploma above all competitors, at the Sydney Exhibition of 1880; two first class medals and diplomas of honour, Calcutta, 1884; and the diploma of honour and gold medal, London International Exhibition, 1884. Mr. Brinsmead is a Chevalier of the Legion of Honour (1878), and is assisted in business by his sons Thomas and Edgar. Mr. Edgar Brinsmead (B. London, March, 1848) is author of a work on the "History of the Pianoforte, with an Account of Ancient Music and Musical Instruments," Lond., n. d.; another ed., 1879, which is a useful and well-written work.

BRION D'ORGEVAL (Edouard Barthélemy). French comp., B. Saint Etienne, Loire, May 13, 1833. Writer of operas, "Ivan IV.," 1876; "Duc et Paysan," 1877, etc.

BRISSON (Francois). French comp. and pianist, B. Angoulême, Charente, Dec. 25, 1821. Teacher in Paris.

WORKS.—Reverie for Pf., op. 17; Arabesque, op. 19; Caprice-étude, op. 25; L'Américaine, Caprice-étude, op. 30; L'Espagnol—Boléro, op. 32; Galop de Concert, op. 36; Fantaisie brillante, op. 40; Hymne triomphale, op. 41; Makouba, Danse Arabe, op. 42; Caprice-Nocturne, op. 44; Rêverie fantastique for Pf., op. 50; Valse de Concert, op. 59; Caprice-Elegante for Pf., op. 51; Caprice Imitatif, op. 55; Three Concert Pieces, op. 46. Fantasias, etc., from operas.

BRISTOW (George French). American comp. and pianist, B. Brooklyn, N. Y., Dec. 19, 1825. S. under his father. Alto singer at Cincinnati, U.S. Cond. of Männerchor Choral Society. Teacher and cond. in New York.

WORKS.—Rip Van Winkle, opera, 1855; Praise to God, an oratorio, 1860; Two Symphonies; Andante et Polonaise for Pf., op. 18; Orchestral overtures; Pf. music; Songs and church music; Mass, 1884; etc.

Bristow is one of the best known American composers, and has shown himself one of the most ambitious. His father, W. R. Bristow, a native of England, was B. in 1803. D. New York, 1867. He was a well-known conductor in New York.

BRITTON (Thomas). English musician, B. Higham Ferrers, Northamptonshire, 1651. Apprenticed to a coal-dealer in London. Commenced business as coal-dealer in Aylesbury Street, Clerkenwell. S. Music, Chemistry, and Bibliography. Established weekly concerts in his own house, and formed musical club. D. London, Sept. 27, 1714.

The musical club was formed by Britton for the practice of chamber music, and the performers consisted of Handel, Pepusch, Banister, H. Needler, Hughes (the poet), P. Hart, H. Symonds, A. Whichello, Shuttleworth, Woollaston (the painter), etc. Matthew Dubourg when a child played his first solo in Britton's house. The origin of these concerts and their continuance was due to Britton's personal love for music, together, it is believed, with the mutual love for bibliographical and other studies held by many members of his audience. The admission to these concerts was originally free, but afterwards a subscription of 10s. per annum was charged. How much these concerts can be said to have influenced the public taste, it is difficult now to say, but considering that his audience in general consisted of men of rank and fortune, it is right to suppose that beyond the circle concerned the taste for good music was not extended.

BROADHOUSE (John). English org. and writer. Editor of the *Musical Standard*, 1878-80; and of *London Musical Review*. Author of "Facts about Fiddles, Violins, Old and New," Lond., n. d.; "Musical Acoustics; or, the Phenomena of Sound as connected with Music," Lond., 8vo, 1881; "Henry Smart's Compositions for the Organ Analysed," Lond., 8vo, 1880, with portrait; A Translation of A. Thibaut's "Purity in Music," Lond., 8vo, 1883. A trans. of Bülow's "Notes on Beethoven's Sonatas," and of Schmidt's "Use of the Pedal in Pianoforte playing."

These are meritorious works, the second being of considerable value for theoretical instruction. He has also contributed articles on technical subjects to periodical literature, and founded and edited for a time *English Organ Music*.

BROADWOOD (John and Sons). English firm of Pianoforte makers, founded in 1773 by John Broadwood, a Scottish mechanic who worked with Tschudi, the former head of the firm. Broadwood was born at Cockburnspath, Berwick, in 1732, and became apprenticed to Tschudi. In 1770, Broadwood, with Backers, a Dutchman, produced the first grand piano in Britain. The original powers of this instrument were by no means great, though an advance on previous efforts, but the various improvements suggested and applied by the elder Broadwood in time brought the expressive powers of the piano to much of its present perfection. The characteristics of the Broadwood piano are beautiful workmanship, full and powerful tone, and an admirable, though somewhat heavy mechanism. Much of the good tone quality is secured by what is known as the division of the bridge on the sound board, the invention of John Broadwood. The mechanism used is almost substantially that invented by Backers and improved upon by Broadwood, though a number of important improvements and modifications have been introduced by successive members of the firm. The reader who is desirous of obtaining full and accurate information of the progress and inventions of this firm is referred to the works of Rimbault, and Hipkins, those of the latter being contained in Grove's "Dictionary of Music." John Broadwood died in 1812, and was succeeded by his sons, two of whom, Thomas and Henry F., now carry on the business. The importance of this great firm is acknowleged by the whole musical profession to be second to none, no less on account of the general excellence of their instruments than by reason of a traditional connection with eminent musicians, which has been long a feature in the business.

It was this Broadwood who presented Beethoven with the instrument on which was composed many of his noblest inspirations, and they who were so generously instrumental in aiding Bennett in his professional career. The operations of the firm extend over all the world, and their instruments are to be found in every quarter of the globe. They are also used by many leading pianists.

BROADWOOD (W. S.) See BOEHM (Theobald).

BROCKLESBY (Richard). English physician, author of "Reflections on Ancient and Modern Music, with its Application to the Cure of Diseases," London, 1749.

BRODERIP (Edmund). English org. and comp., flourished in beginning of 18th cent. Was org. of Wells Cath. about 1720. Wrote a service, anthems, and glees.

BRODERIP (John). English comp. and org., flourished at the end of the 18th and beginning of the 19th centuries. Was org. of Wells Cath., 1740. Wrote various sets of songs, psalms, and "Six Glees for 3 Voices," London, n.d., "The Flower Garden, a Collection of Songs, Duets, and Cantatas;" and joint-editor with Robert of "Portions of Psalms, in one, two, three, and four parts," Bath, 1798; also "Psalms, Hymns, and Spiritual Songs in Score," fo. n.d. Died 1785.

BRODERIP (Robert). English org. and comp., B. about middle of 18th cent. Org. of S. James, Bristol. D. Bristol, May 14, 1808. Brother or son of the preceding. Compiled "Vocal Music, a Collection of Glees," "Organist's Journal, selections from great Masters," n.d., "Cecilian Harmony," London, n.d. He also wrote songs, single glees, and edited a book of Psalms with his brother. Great confusion exists in connection with this family of musicians, from the fact that in catalogues and old works christian names, dates, etc., are omitted.

BRODERIP (?) English publisher and comp. Wrote Pf. music, organ music, glees, etc. Was member of firm of Longman and Broderip. "Instructions for the Pianoforte, with Progressive Lessons," op. 5. "Compleat and Familiar Introduction to the Art of Playing the Pianoforte, Harpsichord, or Organ," n.d. (with Wilkinson).

BROMLEY (Robert Anthony). English divine and author. Bachelor of Theology. D. London, 1806. Wrote "On Opening the Church and Organ. Sermon on Psalm cxxii," Lond., 1771.

BRONNER (Georg). Danish comp., B. in Holstein, 1666. D. 1724. Writer of operas, choruses, etc.

BRONSART (Hans von). German comp., cond., and pianist, B. Berlin, Feb. 11, 1830. Educated at Dantzig and at University of Berlin. S. Harmony under Dehn, and Pianoforte under Kullak and Liszt, 1854-7. Travelled in Germany, concert-giving. Conducted the Euterpe Concerts at Leipzig, 1860-62. Married to Fraulein Starck, 1862. Director of the "Gesellschaft der Musikfreund" at Berlin, 1865. Intendent of the Court Theatre at Hanover, 1867.

WORKS.—Der Corsair, opera; Christ-markt, cantata; Frühlings-fantasia, for orch.; Pf. concerto in F sharp minor; Trio for Pf. in C; Fantasia for Pf. in F sharp minor, op. 6; Nachklänge aus der Jugendzeit, for Pf., op. 2; Three Mazurkas for Pf., op. 4; Trio in G minor for Pf., vn., and 'cello. Miscellaneous chamber music.

Bronsart is a composer of the most modern school, and his works are in spirit and purpose conformable to its principles and assumptions. His compositions belong to that large class of modern growth which is known as programme music. He is a pianist of great ability, and his wife, Ingeborg Starck (B. S. Petersburg, 1843, of Swedish parents), has composed an opera "King Hiarne"; an operetta, "Jery und Bätely"; Songs, Pf. Music, and other works, not known in Britain.

BRONSON (Oliver), or BROWNSON. American comp., issued "Select Tunes and Anthems," 1783. This contains some good specimens of the composer's melodious style.

BROOKBANCK (Joseph). English writer, flourished during 17th century. B. 1612. D. [?]

WORKS.—The Well-tuned Organ; whether or no instrumental and organical Musick be lawful in holy public assemblies, Lond., 1660; The Organ's Echo, Lond., 1641; The Organ's Funereal, Lond., 1642; The Holy Harmony; or a plea for the abolishing of Organs and other Musick in Churches, Lond., 1643; Gospel-Musick, by N. H., Lond., 1644; A Breviate of Lilly's Grammar, 1660. One of the original writers in the worm-eaten cause of no organs in public worship.

BROOMFIELD (William Robert). Scottish writer and comp., B. Aberdeen [c. 1815-20]. Was an arranger and amateur musician in Aberdeen. He wrote "The Principles of Ancient and Modern Music, deduced from the Harmonical Numbers of Antiquity, with exemplifications," etc., Aberdeen, 8vo, 1863. He also published in parts "National Songs," arranged for choirs, Glasgow [c. 1849-52]; and wrote a number of Psalms, Songs, etc.

BROSCHI (Carlo). See FARINELLI.

BROSIG (Moritz). Austrian comp., B. 15 Oct., 1815. Writer of Masses, Organ Music, etc.

BROSSARD (Sebastien de). French writer and priest, B. 1660. Chap.-master in Cath. of Strasburg, 1689-1698. D. Meaux, Aug. 10, 1730. He was compiler of the first dictionary of musical terms, viz.:—

"Dictionnaire de Musique contenant une explication des termes grecs et latins, italiens et français les plus usités dans la Musique," etc., Paris, 1703. A full and complete work for the period. There are many editions of this work.

BROUNCKER (William, Viscount). English writer, B. 1620. D. 1684. Translated "Descarte's Musical Compendium," 4to, 1653. Published anonymously as "Excellent Compendium of Musick; with necessary and judicious animadversions thereupon. By a Person of Honour."

BROUSTET (Edouard). French pianist and comp., B. Toulouse, April 29, 1836. Writer of symphonies, concertos, Pf. music, songs, cantatas, etc.

BROWN (Abraham). English violinist and comp. Was one of the principal performers at Ranelagh Gardens and at the aristocratic concerts in London about the middle of last century. His tone is mentioned as having been clear, but loud.

BROWN (Arthur Henry). English comp. and org., B. Brentwood, Essex, July 24, 1830. Org. of Brentwood Parish Ch., 1841. Org. of S. Edward's, Romford, Essex, 1852-57. Org. at Brentwood from 1857 till 1885. Org. for six months at S. James's, Tunbridge Wells, 1875. Mem. of the Committee of London Gregorian Choral Association.

WORKS.—A Century of Hymn Tunes, 1880 (2 edits.); The First Miracle, a drawing-room oratorio; Missa Seraphica, the Office of Holy Communion, in C

(5 editions); Missa Quinti Toni, the Office of Holy Communion, Plain Chant Service; Organ Harmonies for the Gregorian Psalm Tunes (9 editions); The Gregorian Canticles and Psalter, 1874 (2 editions); The Anglican Canticles and Psalter, 1877 (5 editions); The Canticles of Holy Church, Gregorian (11 editions); The Matin and Vesper Canticles of Holy Church, Anglican (9 editions); Metrical Litanies for use in Church; The Prayer Book Noted, with Plain Chant for all the Offices of the Church, 1885; The Introits for the Sundays, Festivals, and other Holy Days of the Year, 1885; Select Compositions from the Great Masters, arranged for the Organ, with pedal obbligato (contains compositions by Handel, Beethoven, André, Weldon, Mozart, Wagner, Spohr, Bach, Pleyel, Weber, Schubert, etc.); Select Overtures from the Great Masters; Christmas Carols in various collections; Hymn Tunes contributed to Hymns Ancient and Modern, Church Hymns, Chope's Congregational Hymn and Tune Book, Anglican Hymn Book, Bristol Tune Book, and about 20 others; Harvest Tide, a Service of Song for Harvest Thanksgivings; A Service for Children, adapted to the course of the Church Year; Jacob's Ladder, A Christmas volume of Prose and Song, by Barbara Wordsworth, music by A. H. Brown; Te Deum, Magnificat, Nunc Dimittis, Anthems, etc.; The Organ Olio, containing Original Pieces for Organ and Harmonium; Twenty-five Original Pieces in "Les Organistes Contemporains"; Here's to the Cause! for use at Choir Suppers, Church Gatherings, etc.; Part Song—This is the Birthday of my Love. *Pianoforte Music:* Sarabande and Gigue, in G (9 editions); Allemande, Minuet, and Gigue, in A; Gavotte and Minuet, in D; Braule de Sabots; A Trip to Fairyland; Rigadoon in G; Grand Polonaise in E flat; etc. *Songs:* Across the Field of Barley; Somebody's Darling; Gather the Rosebuds while ye may. New Pianoforte Tutor, 1883.

BROWN (A. M.) English writer, author of "Musical Facts Essential to Success in Examination," Lond., 12mo, 1882.

BROWN (Bartholomew). American musician, B. Sterling, Mass, Sept. 8, 1772. D. Boston, April 14, 1854. He edited, with Judge Mitchell, the "Bridgewater Collection of Church Music," etc. He composed hymns, psalms, and songs.

BROWN (Colin). Scottish musician and theoretical writer, B. 1818. Euing Lecturer on Music in Anderson's College, Glasgow, from 1868.

WORKS.—*Music in Common Things:* Analysis of a Musical Sound, and the Production therefrom of the Musical Scale, 1874; Part 2. Mathematical and Musical Relations of the Scale, shewing the Principles, Construction, and Tuning of the Natural Fingerboard with Perfect Intonation, 1876; Part 4. Music in Speech and Speech in Music, 1870, Glasgow, 8vo [other parts in preparation]. Songs of Scotland (with J. Pittman), Lond., n.d. The Thistle, A Miscellany of Scottish Song, with Notes, Critical and Historical, Instrumental Accompaniments and Harmonies by James Merrylees, Glasgow, 1884 [originally issued in parts].

Mr. Brown has constructed an instrument called the Voice Harmonium, founded upon the Monopolytone, to which the principles of perfect intonation are successfully applied. The novel character of the keyboard, fully described in *Music in Common Things,* pt. 2, will perhaps act as an obstruction to its speedy adoption, although in reality it is very simple, having only eight digitals in each octave to give in perfect tune every tone and interval of the diatonic, chromatic, and enharmonic scales; the fingering being identical in all keys. The Monopolytone above mentioned is a small instrument for striking on the keyboard of a Pf., producing one grand and perfect unison, though sounding every note and discord of the scale. His harmonium was awarded the first place at an exhibition of instruments illustrating the same principle held in London.

BROWN (Francis H.) American writer, has written a few didactic works, of which "The Pupils' First Primer" (Ditson, Boston, n.d.), in catechism form, has gone through some editions.

BROWN (John). English divine and writer, B. Rothbury, Northumberland, 1715. Educated at Cambridge. Vicar of Great Horkesley, Essex, 1754. Vicar of S. Nicholas', Newcastle, 1758. Committed suicide while insane, September 23, 1766.

WORKS.—Honour, a Poem ; Essay on Satire ; Sermons ; Essays on Shaftesbury's Characteristics, 1751 ; Dissertation on the Rise, Union, and Power, the Progressions, Separations, and Corruptions of Poetry and Music, to which is prefixed The Cure of Saul, a sacred ode, Lond., 1763 ; Remarks on some Observations on Dr. Brown's Dissertation on Poetry and Musick, Lond., 1764 ; An Estimate of the Manners and Principles of the Times, 1757.

An Italian edition of the Dissertation was published in 1772.

BROWN (John). Scottish artist and writer, B. Edinburgh, 1752. Resided in Italy, 1771 till 1781. D. in Scotland, 1781. Author of "Letters upon the Poetry and Music of the Italian Opera, Edinburgh, 12mo, 1789.

BROWN (Robert) of Rockhaven. Scottish writer and theorist. B. Glasgow. Author of "The Elements of Musical Science, Lond., 4to, 1860. "An Introduction to Musical Arithmetic, with its Application to Temperament," Lond., 1865. "Rudiments of Harmony and Counterpoint on a New Method..." London, 8vo, 1863. Also a work on Scottish Highland Psalm Tunes.

In the first work Brown advocates the adoption of a uniform clef, and illustrates this in the course of his book. He also suggests certain modifications in the method of expressing harmonical combinations, etc.

BROWNE (Lennox), F.R.C.S., Edin. English surgeon and writer, B. Lond., 1841. Son of a distinguished Surgeon. S. at Edinburgh University, and St. George's Hospital, London, and qualified for practice in 1863, when he entered H.M. Emigration Service, and made two voyages to Australia, writing a book on his return on the climate of that country, and the prospects of a voyage and residence for English invalids. He commenced practice in London in 1865, and at once took up the specialty of treatment of diseases of the throat, ear, and adjacent parts ; was attached for seven years to the Throat Hospital, and in 1874 was mainly instrumental in founding the Central London Throat and Ear Hospital, the foundation stone of which was laid by Madame Adelina Patti. Of this Institution he is the Senior Surgeon. He is also Surgeon to the Royal Society of Musicians, and Consulting Aural Surgeon to several other Hospitals. Having issued in pamphlet form practical remarks in separate monographs, he, in 1878, published his large work on "The Throat and its Diseases" (Bailliere) illustrated by wood engravings and coloured drawings on stone of his own design. This work is at present out of print and awaiting a new edition. In 1876 he issued his "Medical Hints on the Production and Management of the Singing Voice" (Chappell) which has attained a circulation of over ten thousand. He has further translated and edited Witkowski's "Mechanism of the Voice," and the "Mechanism of Hearing," and in the latter part of 1883 collaborated with Mr. Emil Behnke on a work entitled "Voice, Song, and Speech" (Sampson Low & Co.), intended as a complete manual for singers and speakers. This work has already reached a third edition. In 1885 he published "Voice Use and Stimulants," Lond., 12mo ; and with E. Behnke, "The Child's Voice ; its Treatment with regard to after Development," Lond., 12mo.

Mr. Lennox Browne is known as an earnest advocate of the view, that a very large majority of the throat troubles of singers, are due to ignorance or neglect of science teaching regarding voice production, and he has quite recently, 1884, published a lecture entitled "Science and Singing," urging these views with considerable force, and pleading for preliminary education in voice production, as the only sure basis of pleasurable and enduring speaking or singing voice. His name and works are well known in America and on the Continent, and he is one of the editors of "La Revue Mensuelle de Laryngologie," etc.

BROWNE (Richard). English writer and physician, flourished during 18th century. Was an apothecary in Oakham.

He wrote "Medicina Musica : or a Mechanical Essay on the Effects of Singing, Musick, and Dancing, on Human Bodies, etc.," Lond., 12mo, 1729. This is a curious work on the medicinal virtues of music, a subject which has frequently taken the attention of medical men as well as musicians.

BROWN-BORTHWICK (Rev. Robert). Scottish divine and amateur musician, B. Aberdeen, May 18, 1840. Son of William Brown, Esq., of H. M. Civil Service, Aberdeen, who was an amateur musician, well-known at the concerts of that city. Ordained deacon in 1865. Ordained priest, 1866. Curate of Sudely Manor, Gloucestershire, and Chaplain to the Winchcomb Union. Curate of Evesham, Worcestershire, and assistant minister of Quebec Chapel, London. Mr. Brown-Borthwick assumed additional surname of Borthwick on his marriage in 1868 to Grace (D. 1884), only surviving daughter of the late, and sister of the present, John Borthwick, Esq., of Borthwick Castle, and Crookston, Midlothian. Incumbent of Holy Trinity, Grange-in-Borrowdale, Cumberland, 1869-72. Vicar of All Saints, Scarborough, 1872. Chaplain for a few years to the Bishop of Aberdeen.

WORKS.—The Supplemental Hymn and Tune Book (Novello), containing contributions by Goss, Sullivan, Stainer, E. J. Hopkins, and J. B. Calkin, 4 editions. 12 Kyries. Kyries and Sanctuses, edited. Blessed are the dead, anthem. Words of "Church Hymns" (with the Bishop of Bedford (D. 1884), Rev. W. How), Rev. J. Ellerton, Rev. B. Compton), the Hymn Book issued by the S. P. C. K. Select Hymns for Church and Home, Edin., 1871. The History of the Princes de Condé, by H. R. H. le Duc d'Aumale, translated, Lond., 8vo, 2 vols. Life and Works of Stephen Heller, by H. Barbedette, translated, London. Hymns, contributed to various collections. Sermons on various subjects, as "Art in Worship," "The Praise of God," etc., all published.

BROWNSMITH (John Leman). English org., B. Westminster, 1809. Chor. at Westminster Abbey under Greatorex. S. org. under Greatorex. Org. of S. John's Ch., Waterloo Road, London, 1829. Lay-Vicar of Westminster Abbey, 1838. Org. to Sacred Harmonic Soc., 1848. Org. at Handel Festivals of 1857, 1859, 1862, and 1865. Org. of S. Gabriel, Pimlico. D. Sept. 14, 1866.

BRUCE (James). Scottish traveller, B. 1730, D. 1794. He furnished Burney with an amount of information touching Eastern music, which will be found in his History.

BRUCE (Thomas). Scottish writer. Author of "The Common Tunes of Scotland's Church Music made Plain," 12mo, 1726.

BRÜCH (Max). German comp., B. Cologne, Jan. 6, 1838. S. at Bonn. Gained Scholarship of the Mozart Foundation at Frankfort-on-Maine, 1852. S. under Hiller, Reinecke, and Breuning at Cologne. Music director at Coblenz, 1865. Do. to Prince of Schwarzburg-Sondershausen, 1867. Director of Liverpool Philharmonic Soc., 1880.

WORKS.—Op. 1. Scherz, List, und Rache, opera in two acts (Goethe); Jubilate, Amen, by T. Moore, for sop. solo, chorus, and orch., op. 3; Three duets for sop. and alto, with Pf., op. 4; Trio for Pf., vn., and 'cello, in C min., op. 5; Six Songs for voice and Pf., op. 7; Die Birken und die Erlen, for sop. solo, chorus, and orch., op. 8; Quartet for strings in C min., op. 9; Quartet for strings in E, op. 10; Fantasie for 2 Pf., op. 11; Six pieces for Pf. solo, op. 12; Hymnus Dem, der von Nächten, for voice and Pf., op. 13; Four lieder for voice and Pf., op. 15; Loreley, a Grand Romantic Opera, in 4 acts (Geibel) op. 16; Roemischer Triumphgesang, for male chorus and orch., op. 19; The Flight of the Holy Family, for chorus and orch., op. 20; Frithjof, Scenes from Esaias Tegner's "Frithjof-Saga," for solo voices, male chorus, and orch., op. 23; Schön Ellen, Ballad for solo voices, chorus, and orch., op. 24, 1869; Salamis, Greek song of Triumph, for male chorus and orch., op. 25; First Concerto for violin and orch., dedicated to Herr Josef Joachim, op. 26; First Symphony for full orch., in E flat, op. 28; Kyrie, Sanctus, Benedictus, and Agnus Dei, for double choir, orchestra, and orch., op. 35; Second Symphony for full orch., in F min., op. 36; Hermione, opera in 4 acts (adapted from Shakspere's "Winter Tale"), op. 40, Berlin, 1872; Odysseus, Scenes from Homer's Odyssey, for solo voices, chorus, and orch., op. 41; Romanze for violin and orch., op. 42; Arminius, oratorio, op. 43, 1875; The Lay of the Bell, a Secular Cantata (Schiller), op. 45, 1879; Fantasia on Scotch airs for violin and orch., op. 47, 1880; Kolnidreis, for violoncello and orch., op. 48. Numerous Lieder. Pianoforte music. Chamber music, etc.

Herr Brüch may be regarded as one of the foremost among living composers of chamber music, while his large works "Odysseus," "Lay of the Bell," etc., entitle him to the greatest consideration as a writer of choral music. His treatment of the cantata is in many respects original, and his command over the expressive elements of the orchestra is great. The work by which he is most favourably known in Britain is "Odysseus," a composition of great power, though in a technical sense, extremely difficult.

BRÜLL (Ignaz). German comp. and pianist, B. Prossnitz, Nov. 7, 1847. S. at Leipzig Cons.

WORKS.—*Operas:* Das Goldene Kreuz, 1875, London, 1878; Der Landfriede, 1877; Bianca, 1879; Konigin Mariette, 1883. Serenade for orch., in F, op. 29; First Concerto for Pf. and orch., in F, op. 10; Concerto for violin and orch., op. 41; Three pieces for the Pf., op. 28; Symphony for orch., in E minor, op. 31. Lieder and Part Songs. Chamber Music.

The opera "Das Goldene Kreuz" was, on its production in London, received with but limited manifestations of favour, from which it may fairly be inferred that it is not a work which possesses the elements of novelty or success.

BRUMEL (Antoine). Flemish musician, flourished between the years 1480 and 1520. He was a pupil of Okenheim, and composed Masses, Motets, Chansons, etc. His biography is unknown.

BRUNETTI (Gaetano). Italian comp. and violinist, B. Pisa, 1753. S. under Nardini at Florence. Court-Musician to Charles IV. of Spain. D. in Spain, 1808.

WORKS.—Thirty-one symphonies for orch.; Thirty-two quintets for strings; Six quintets for 2 violins, alto, and 2 'cellos; Numerous quartets for strings; Twenty-two trios for strings; Sonatas for violin and bass, etc.

BRYCE (Rev. ?) Irish (?) divine and writer who lived in Belfast. Author of "A Rational Introduction to Music, being an attempt to simplify the first Principles of the Science," Lond., 8vo, 1845.

BRYNE (Albert). English comp. who flourished in the 17th century. Pupil of John Tomkins, whom he succeeded as org. of S. Paul's Cath. His compositions appear in Boyce, Clifford, and some are in MS. in the British Museum.

BRYSON (J.) Scottish musician, who flourished during latter part of 18th cent. Published "A Curious Selection of Favourite Tunes, with variations. To which are added upwards of fifty favourite Irish airs for the German flute or violin; with a bass for the Harpsichord or Violoncello," 1791.

BUCHANAN (Thomas). Scottish surgeon, author of "Physiological Illustration of the organ of hearing, more particularly of the secretion of cerumen and its effects in rendering auditory perceptions accurate and acute," Lond., 1828.

BUCK (Dudley). American comp., org., and pianist, B. Hartford, Connecticut, March 10, 1839. S. at Trinity Coll., Hartford. S. at Leipzig Cons. along with A. Sullivan, J. F. Barnett, S. B. Mills, etc., 1858, under Hauptmann, Richter, Rietz, Moscheles, and Plaidy. S. afterwards at Dresden under Schneider (organ) and Rietz (harmony, etc.) Resided in Paris, 1861-2. Returned to United States, 1862. Choir-master of S. Paul's Ch., Boston. Org. of Music Hall, Boston, 1871. Assistant cond. under Mr. Theodore Thomas at the Central Park Garden, New York, 1875. Org. and choir-master of Ch. of the Holy Trinity, Brooklyn, 1875. Director of the "Apollo Club," Brooklyn. Resides in Brooklyn as teacher, etc.

WORKS.—*Cantatas:* Scenes from the Golden Legend, by Longfellow, 1880 (this work gained a $1,000 prize at Cincinnati); The Legend of Don Munio, 1874; "The Centennial Meditation of Columbia" (for the opening of the Exhibition at Philadelphia), 1876, written by Sidney Lanier; Easter Morning, for mixed voices; Hymn to Music, for chorus of mixed voices. Forty-sixth Psalm (God is our Refuge), for solo voices, chorus, and orch.; The Nun of Nidaros, chorus for male voices; King Oloff's Christmas, chorus for male voices, with solo. *Church Music:*

Motette Collection, 1867; Second Motette Collection; Morning Service for Episcopal Ch., op. 25; Evening Service, do., op. 31; Christ our Passover, anthem, op. 29; There were Shepherds, anthem; Hark! what mean these holy voices? hymn, op. 32; Darkly rose the guilty Morning, anthem, op. 33; Morning Service, op. 45; Evening Service, op. 47; Easter Anthem, op. 46; Christmas Anthem, op. 48; Special Hymns (in Anthem form) for Quartet or Chorus Choir, op. 43 (8 numbers); Three Anthems, op. 72; Te Deum and Jubilate from Schubert's Mass in B flat; O Saviour, hear me! offertory from Gluck; A Midnight Service for New Year's Eve. *Organ:* Illustrations in Choir Accompaniment, with Hints in Registration, 4to, 1877; Grand Sonata in E flat, op. 22; Concert Variations on "The Star Spangled Banner," op. 23; Triumphal March, op. 26; Impromptu Pastorale, op. 27; Eighteen Pedal Phrasing Studies, 2 books, op. 28; Rondo Caprice, op. 35; Transcription, Overture to "William Tell," op. 37; Trans. from Beethoven's "Sonata op. 28." op. 38; Transcription, Overture to "Stradella," op. 39; Trans. from Schumann's Pictures from the Orient, op. 40; Variations on a Scotch Air, op. 51; At Evening, Idylle, op. 52; The Last Rose of Summer, with variations, op. 59; Second Grand Sonata, in G minor, op. 77; The Organist's Repertoire, edited by Buck and S. P. Warren, etc. *Vocal Music:* The Tempest, Dramatic Poem, for voice and Pf.; Five Songs for alto or baritone voice and Pf., words by E. C. Stedman; Three Songs for mezzo-soprano; Five Songs for soprano or tenor. Symphonic Overture, "Marmion," for full orch. "Deseret," a comic opera, libretto by W. A. Croffut, 1880. Pianoforte Music. Dictionary of Musical Terms, Boston, n. d. The Influence of the Organ in History, 1882.

The compositions of this composer, though almost entirely confined to the United States, are of such sterling quality as to merit their production elsewhere. His chief works are the cantatas, which have attained considerable popularity in the United States. Apart from his powers as a composer, Mr. Buck is one of the greatest organists in the United States. His church music is remarkable for effective treatment without vulgarity or undue straining, and his organ music is good, if somewhat brilliant. Buck has trained many good musicians, and his influence in the United States is great.

BUCK (Zechariah). English org. and comp., B. 1799. D. Newport, Essex, Aug. 5, 1879. Mus. Doc. Lambeth, 1853. Dr. Buck was a highly respected teacher and performer, and held the appointment of Organist and Choir-master at Norwich Cathedral for a long period.

BUCKLEY (James). American writer, author of "Buckley's New Violin Method" (Ditson, Boston, n. d.) "Buckley's Banjo Guide," (do.) "Buckley's New Banjo Method" (do.), etc.

Another Buckley (Frederick), composed a number of melodies of the same stamp as "I'd choose to be a Daisy," and founded a troupe of coloured Minstrels named after himself. He D. at Boston (U.S.), 1864.

BUCKLEY (Olivia Dussek). English authoress, wrote a work entitled "Musical Truths," Lond., 12mo, 1843.

BUDD (George W.) English publisher and comp., B. 1806. D. Lond., Aug., 1850. He was a member of the firm of Calkin & Budd.

BUDDICOM (Rev. Robert Pedder). English divine, and incumbent of Everton, Liverpool, B. 1770. D. July, 1846. Published "One Hundred Psalm and Hymn Tunes with Chants," edited by C. H. Wilton, 4to, 1827. Republished as "Devotional Harmony," Liverpool, 1833.

BUHL (Joseph David). French trumpeter and writer, B. near Amboise, 1781. Prof. of trumpet at cavalry school at Versailles, 1805-11. Cond. of band of the Garde du Corps, 1814. Mem. of Legion of Honour, D. Versailles, April, 1860. He wrote "A Method for the Trumpet," and other works, practical and theoretical.

BÜHLER (Franz G.) Abbé. German org. and comp., B. April 12, 1760. D. Augsburg, Feb. 4, 1824.

BUINI (Giuseppe Maria). Italian comp., flourished at beginning of 18th cent.

Wrote over thirty operas, produced between the years 1718 and 1734. He was also a poet.

BULL (Ole Borneman). Norwegian violinist and comp., B. Bergen, Norway, Feb. 5, 1810. Appeared successively in all the principal towns of Europe, Britain, and America. D. Bergen, Aug. 19, 1880. He wrote a number of trifling works for violin and orchestra.

Bull enjoyed a great notoriety in his day, and was regarded by many as a performer of extraordinary attainments. His talents were excessively lauded for a time by careless or incompetent writers, but he was regarded by well informed musicians as little better than a charlatan. His technical skill on the violin was great, and if it had been used in a legitimate manner might have secured for him a high place among instrumental performers. As it is he is only remembered by the vulgar for his astonishing tricks, and daring and original methods of advertising. His works possess no value, and are rarely performed.

BULL (John), English comp. and org., B. Somersetshire [1563]. S. under William Blitheman. Org. and Master of the Children of Hereford Cath., 1582. Gent. of the Chap. Roy., Jan., 1585. Bac. Mus. Oxon., 1586. Doc. Mus. Oxon., 1592. Org. to Chap. Roy., 1591. Prof. of Music at Gresham Coll., 1596. Travelled on the Continent, 1601-5. Married to Elizabeth Walter, 1607. Musician to Prince Henry, 1611. Quitted England without leave from his employer, 1613. Org. at Notre Dame Cath., Antwerp [1617]. Was org. in service of the Archduke of Austria. D. Hamburg, Lübeck, or Antwerp, Mar. 13, 1628.

The productions of this composer are mentioned by nearly every writer as having been voluminous, but comparatively few of them appear to have been printed. Specimens of his style can be seen in Barnard's Collection, Boyce, Leighton's "Teares," the Fitzwilliam Music, "Parthenia," Queen Elizabeth's Virginal Book, etc. A motet for 5' voices is preserved in Burney's Musical Extracts, British Museum. E. Pauer gives specimens of his virginal music in "Old English Composers." The extraordinary celebrity which this musician obtained during his lifetime must have been grounded on some uncommon degree of merit either in his compositions or performance. A list of his works is contained in Ward's "Lives of the Gresham Professors," and in addition he wrote a great number of pieces of sacred vocal music. "The strength of this composer's talents lay in the production and execution of pieces fully harmonized, and comprising fugues, double-fugues, and the various species of canon; and fortunately, for himself, he lived in an age that listened with pleasure to music of that description. . . . . He surmounted old and invented new difficulties; and disdaining to be embarrassed, aimed, in the province of polyphonic fabrication, at a species of omnipotence."—*Busby*.

The question as to the composition of the English national anthem remains undecided in a general way, though Carey appears to have been strongly accredited with the composition. See writings of Chappell, Cummings, Clark, etc. In connection with Gresham College, Dr. Bull delivered "The Oration of Maister John Bull, Doctor of Musicke and one of the Gentlemen of hir Majesty's Royal Chappell, as he pronounced the same, before divers worshipful persons, the Aldermen and Commoners of the citie of London, with a great multitude of other people, the 6th day of October, 1597, in the new erected Colledge of Sir Thomas Gresham, Knt. deceased: made in the commendation of the founder, and the excellent science of Musicke," London, Este, 1597.

BÜLOW (Hans Guido von). German pianist, cond., and comp., B. Dresden, Jan. 8, 1830. S. under Wieck and Eberwein. S. Jurisprudence for a time at Leipzig University, 1848. S. under Hauptmann; also under Liszt, 1851. Made first Concert tour, 1853. Prof. of Pianoforte at the Stern and Marx Cons., Berlin, 1855-64. Cond. of Royal Opera House and Director of the Cons., Munich, 1864. Cond. of Hanover Court Music, Jan., 1878. Cond. of Glasgow Musical Festival, 1878. Has given concerts in Europe, Britain, and America (1876). Orchestral cond. in Germany.

WORKS.—Arabesques, Variations on Rigoletto, op. 2; Marche Héroïque, op. 3; Innocence, Albumblatt for Pf.; Humoristic Quadrille (Berlioz), for Pf.; Die Entsagende Liedercyclus, for voice and Pf., op. 8; Music to Shakespeare's Julius

Cæsar, op. 10 ; Arrangements from same, opp. 10*a*, 10*b* ; Ballade for Orchestra, op. 16 ; Nirwana, Orchester-Fantasie in Ouverturenform, op. 20, 1881 ; Il Carnaval di Milano for Pf., op. 21 ; Two Romances for Mezzo-soprano voice and Pf., op. 26 ; Classical Pianoforte Pieces from his Concert Programmes, 2 vols. ; Editions of Bach, Beethoven, etc. ; Contributions to Periodical Literature, various, etc.

Bülow is one of the most gifted pianists and conductors of the present time, and while equally great in his interpretations of all masters, is exceptionally great in his rendition of Beethoven. His performance of this master's works is indeed extraordinary, and invariably creates a powerful impression. He is a strong supporter of the most advanced school of music, and strives in his works to follow the style of Wagner. In other respects Bülow has been most unfortunate, especially in regard to Britain and British music. His peculiarities of temper have frequently placed him in most undignified relations to his art and position, and it is to be regretted that so sterling an artist should stoop to speak disrespectfully of the nation which accords him the most substantial support.

BUNCE (John Thackray). English Journalist and writer. Editor of the *Birmingham Daily Post*. Author of "Birmingham General Hospital and Triennial Musical Festivals," 8vo [1858]; and "History of the Birmingham General Hospital and the Musical Festivals, 1868-73," 8vo, 1873.

BUNCH (James). English musician, editor of "Ceciliana : a Collection of Favourite Catches, Canons, Rondos, and Rounds, by eminent authors, ancient and modern, in score, with Biographical Notes." Lond. 4to, n. d.

BUNN (Alfred). English operatic manager and librettist, B. London, 1798 ; Stage manager at Drury Lane Theatre under Elliston, 1823 ; Manager and Lessee of Drury Lane Theatre from 1834. D. Boulogne, Dec. 20, 1860. Bunn adapted a great number of pieces for the English stage, and produced the following among other operas :—Maid of Artois ; Bohemian Girl ; and Daughter of St. Mark (Balfe) ; Brides of Venice (Benedict) ; Maritana (Wallace), etc. He also wrote a work entitled "The Stage, both Before and Behind the Curtain, from Observations taken on the Spot." 3 vols. 8vo, London, 1840. Poems, Lond., 1816. For a severe skit on Bunn, see A Word with Bunn, after Burns's Address to the Deil. By J. R. Adam, the Cremorne Poet, Lond. [1847].

BUNNETT (Edward). English comp. and org., B. Shipdham, Norfolk, June 26, 1834. Chor. in Norwich Cath., 1842. S. under Dr. Z. Buck. Assistant org. at Norwich Cath., 1855-77. Bac. Mus. Cantab., Dec., 1856. Doc. Mus., do., March, 1869. Festival (choral) org., 1872. Org. of S. Peter's Ch., 1877. Org. to Corporation of Norwich, 1880.

WORKS.—Song of Praise (Degree exercise), 1869 ; Rhineland, Cantata for soprano solo, chorus and orch. comp. for Mdlle T. Titjiens, and produced at Norwich Festival, 1872 ; Lora, Cantata by W. W. Turnbull, comp. for the Musical Union Society in Norwich, and performed, June, 1876 ; Magnificat, Nunc Dimittis, Cantate Domine, and Deus Misereatus, in A, 1860 ; Venite, Exultemus Domino, two settings in chant form ; Te Deum, in G ; Te Deum, in F ; Benedictus and Jubilate, in F ; Out of the deep have I called unto Thee, O Lord, Psalm 130, for tenor solo, chorus and organ ; Ave Maria, for six voices and Pf. or harmonium accomp. ; Volume of Sacred Harmony, comprising Chants, Kyries, Anthems and Organ Pieces, selected and original, 1865 ; Twenty-four Original Hymn-tunes ; Office of the Holy Communion, in E (1883). *Anthems:* If we believe that Jesus died ; O how amiable are thy dwellings ; O Give Thanks unto the Lord ; O Lord, thou art my God. Eight Organ Pieces, original and selected ; Six Original Compositions for org., 1884 ; Ave Maria for organ. Now Autumn Crowns the Year with Golden Leaves, part song. *Songs:* There be none of Beauty's daughters : Break, break, break ; There's a bower of roses ; A Dreamer's Song ; Sing joyous bird ; Winter ; A New Year's Burden ; The Moss Rose ; The Message of the Rose. *Pianoforte:* Adagio and Rondo ; Premiere Valse ; Polacca ; Three Musical Sketches ; Das Stille Abendlaftchen. Sonata for Pf. and violin, 1873 (MS.) ; Trio for Pf. violin and 'cello, 1873 (MS.) ; Adagio and Rondo for Clarinet and Pf. (MS.), etc.

BUNTING (Edward). Irish writer and editor, B. Armagh, Feb., 1773. Articled a-sistant to Weir, at ch. in Belfast, 1784. Org. of S. Stephen's chap., Belfast. Married to Miss Chapman, 1819. D. Dublin, Dec. 21, 1843.

WORKS.—A General Collection of the Ancient Irish Music; containing a variety of admired airs never before published, and also the compositions of Conolan and Carolan, Lond., 1796. A General Collection of the Ancient Music of Ireland, arranged for the Pianoforte; some of the most admired Melodies are adapted for the Voice, to poetry chiefly translated from the original Irish songs by Thomas Campbell, Esq., and other eminent poets; to which is prefaced an Historical and Critical Dissertation on the Egyptian, British, and Irish Harp, Lond., fo. 1809. The Ancient Music of Ireland, arranged for the Pianoforte; to which is prefixed a Dissertation on the Irish Harps and Harpers, including an account of the Old Melodies of Ireland. Dublin, 1840.

Bunting was the Thomson or Chappell of Irish music. However popular Moore might have rendered the lovely melodies of Ireland, it is certain that to the preservative endeavours of Bunting is due the present knowledge of Irish music. He was an organist of great ability. The universal credit given to Moore and Stevenson as the preservers of Irish music is not really due them, though Moore, with his usual self-complacency, takes considerable honour to himself for his personal endeavours. The blame of tampering with and altering the melodies was at one time fixed on Stevenson, by Bunting, among others, whereas Moore in his diary confesses to the alterations as being his own work. An interesting article and review of Bunting and his works are contained in the "Dublin University Magazine," May, 1841, and Jan., 1847.

BUONOMO (Alfonso). Italian operatic comp., B. Naples, August 12, 1829.

BUONONCINI (Giovanni Battista). Italian comp., B. Modena, 1672. S. under his Father Giovanni Maria. Violoncellist in Band of the Emperor Leopold at Vienna. Came to England, 1708. Musician to the Duke of Marlborough. D. 1750.

WORKS.—*Operas:* Camilla, 1690 (London, 1706); Tullio Astilio, 1694; Endimione, 1706; Mario fugitivo, 1708; Tameride, 1708; Abdalonimo, 1709; Muzio Scevola (with Handel and Ariosti), 1710; Astarto, 1720; Crispo, 1722; Griselda, 1722; Farnace, 1723; Erminia, 1723; Calfurnia, 1724; Astianax, 1727. Cantate e Duetti, dedicati alla sacra Maestà di Giorgio Re della Gran Britagna, etc., Lond., 1721; Divertimenti de Camera per Violino o Flauto, dedicati all'Eccellenza del Duca di Rutland, Lond., 1722; Funereal Anthem for Duke of Marlborough; Twelve Sonatas for the Chamber, for two Violins and a Bass, 1732; Other Operas and miscellaneous music.

This composer is now only famous for his rivalry of Handel, at that period in British history when sides were taken on every matter. Buononcini was the musician of the Whigs, and for a time held his own fairly well. It was only when such a close comparison as that afforded by the setting of "Muzio Scevola," in which both composed an act, that musicians were enabled to award a preëminent position to Handel. Buononcini's music is of a sweet and somewhat unmeaning nature, not particularly marked by any original feature. He was said to have been of an overbearing disposition, which latterly cost him his place in England.

His father, Giovanni Maria (1670-17?), wrote a work on theory as well as some chamber music. His brother, Antonio (1690-1715), composed an amount of Secular music.

BURDITT (B. A.) American bandmaster and writer, has published Preceptor for the Post-horn (Ditson, Boston, n. d.) Preceptor for the Saxhorn (do.) Saxhorn Scales (do.) Preceptor for the Bugle (do.) Preceptor for the Cornopean (do.) Army Drum and Fife Book, with Keach and Cassidy (do,) Modern School for the Drum, with Keach (do.) "National Orchestra," and other collections of band music.

BURETTE (Pierre Jean). French comp. and writer, B. Paris, Nov., 1665. D. May, 1747.

BÜRGER (Gottefried August). German poet, B. Molmerswende, 1748. D. June 8, 1794.

Bürger's ballads are chiefly remarkable for their weird characteristics, and generally romantic cast. One of them, "Lenore," has inspired the composer Raff in the production of a symphony of considerable power. The lyrical productions of Bürger have been set by a great variety of composers, from Schubert to Macfarren.

BURGH (A.), M.A. English writer and Prof. at Oxford. Compiled "Anecdotes of Music, Historical and Biographical, in a Series of Letters from a Gentleman to his Daughter," 3 vols., 8vo, Lond., 1814.

BURGHERSH (Lord). See WESTMORELAND (Earl of).

BURGMULLER (Johann Friedrich Franz). German comp., B. Ratisbon, 1806. D. Beaulieu, Seine-et-Oise, Feb. 13, 1874. Writer of Ballets, Potpourries on motives from operas, and a large amount of brilliant pianoforte music.

BURGMÜLLER (Norbert). German comp., B. Düsseldorf, Feb. 8, 1810. S. under his Father, Spohr, and Hauptmann. D. Aix-la-Chapelle, May 7, 1836.

WORKS.—Two Symphonies for full orch. An Overture for orch. Songs, with Pf. accomp., op. 3; Do., op. 6; Do., op. 10. Quartets for strings. Concertos for Pf. Sonata for Pf., in F min., op. 8. Rhapsodie for Pf., op. 13. And a large quantity of miscellaneous music.

BURGSTALLER (Franz Xaver). German Zither player and comp., B. in Bavaria, 1815. Writer of Ländler, Valses, etc.

BURKHARDT (Salomon). German pianist and comp., B. 1803. D. 1849. Writer of *Salon* music of a bright, clever and graceful character.

BURMANN (Gottlieb Wilhelm). German comp., B. Lauban, 1737. D. 1805. Wrote songs, music for harpsichord, etc.

BURNET (Alfred). Mus. Bac., English musician, published "Instructions for the Spanish Guitar, founded on the Systems of Carulli, Giuliani, etc.," Lond., 1829.

BURNEY (Charles). English writer, org., and comp., B. Shrewsbury, April 12, 1726. Educated at the Free School, Shrewsbury, and at Chester Public School. S. music under Baker, org. of Chester Cath.; and in London under Dr. Arne, 1744-47. Org. of St. Dionis Back-Ch., Fenchurch St., London, 1749. Harpsichord player at the Subscription Concerts, King's Arms, Cornhill. Org. at Lynn-Regis, Norfolk, 1751-60. Bac. and Doc. of Music, Oxford, 1769. Travelled in Italy, 1770. Returned to London, 1771. Travelled in Germany, the Netherlands, etc., 1772. Elected Fellow of Royal Soc., 1773. First vol. of the *History* published, 1776. Org. of Chelsea Coll., 1789. D. Chelsea, April 12, 1814.

WORKS.—Translation of Signor Tartini's Letter to Signor Lombardini, published as an important lesson to performers on the Violin, Lond., 1771. The Present State of Music in France and Italy, or the Journal of a tour through those Countries, undertaken to collect Materials for a General History of Music, Lond., 8vo, 1771. The Present State of Music in Germany, the Netherlands, and United Provinces, or the Journal of a tour through those Countries, undertaken to collect Materials for a General History of Music, Lond., 2 vols., 8vo, 1773. A General History of Music, from the Earliest Ages to the Present Period, to which is prefixed a Dissertation on the Music of the Ancients, Lond., 4 vols., 4to, 1776-1789. An Account of the Musical Performances in Westminster Abbey and the Pantheon, May 26th, 27th, 29th, and June the 3rd and 5th, 1784, in Commemoration of Handel, Lond., 4to, 1785; Dublin edition, 1785. A paper on Crotch, the infant musician, presented to the Royal Society, Transactions, 1779. Striking Views of Lamia, the celebrated flute-player, Massachussett's Magazine, 1786. Memoirs of the Life and Writings of the Abbate Metastasio, in which are incorporated translations of his principal letters, Lond., 3 vols., 8vo, 1796. A Plan for a Music School, Lond., 1774. An Essay towards the History of Comets, Lond., 1769. Articles on Music in Ree's Encyclopædia. Sonata for 2 violins and a bass, 1765. Six Concert

Pieces with introduction and fugue for the organ. Twelve Canzonets from Metastasio. Six duets for the German Flute. Six concertos for the violin in 8 parts. Two sonatas for Pf., violin, and 'cello. Six Harpsichord Lessons. Two Sonatas for Harp or Pianoforte, with accomp. for violin or 'cello. Anthems, glees, instrumental music, etc.

Burney is best known to musicians of the present day by his "History of Music;" a work of much learning and ability. It is written in a pleasant style, but its historical value is somewhat destroyed by a vexatious absence of dates, while its critical defects are even more marked. He has given too much space to the glorification of forgotten Italian composers, and too little to the more interesting musicians of British nativity. The "History" is less valuable than that of Hawkins, though much superior in a literary point of view. His other literary productions are interesting. His musical compositions are quite out of date, and are never now heard. His most successful musical effort was an adaptation of Rousseau's "Devin du Village," produced under the title of "The Cunning Man." His daughter Frances was the Madame D'Arblay of English literary renown. It may further be said that Burney was one of the most esteemed organists of his time.

BURNS (Daniel Joseph). Irish org. and writer. Org. of S. Patrick's Church, and of S. Malachy's Coll., Belfast. Cond. of the Philo-Celtic Soc. Author of "Practical Notes on Harmony and Counterpoint for Junior Pupils." Lond. [1883]. "Exercises in Figured Bass." Lond. n.d., etc.

BURNS (Georgina). English soprano vocalist, B. London, 1860. Granddaughter of a celebrated Nonconformist minister. First appeared at the Westminster Aquarium Promenade Concerts. Sang in Carl Rosa's Opera Company from about 1877. First appeared in opera at Nottingham. She has appeared with much success in "Faust," "Maritana," "Bohemian Girl," "Lurline," "Esmeralda," and other works, and has been also most successful as a concert vocalist. She is married to Mr. LESLIE CROTTY, an Irish barytone vocalist, B. in Galway, 1851, who has appeared in opera in connection with the Carl Rosa Opera Company with much success.

BURNS (Robert). Scottish poet and writer, B. near Ayr, January 25, 1759. Educated chiefly by his father. Resided successively at Mount Oliphant, 1759-1777; Lochlea, 1777-84; Mossgiel, 1784-86; Edinburgh, Nov., 1786, Feb., 1788; Ellisland, June, 1788, Dec., 1791; Dumfries, 1791-96. D. Dumfries, July 21, 1796. Married to Jean Armour, 1788. Became exciseman, March, 1789. Contributed to Johnson's "Museum" from 1787. Contributed to Thomson's Collection, 1792-96. Poems first published by Wilson, Kilmarnock, in 1786.

Burns was a musician of considerable talent, as may be readily discovered by observing the close union which he has been able to maintain between the spirit, rhythm, and melody of his poetry and its musical setting. With one or two exceptions it must be said that he has uniformly succeeded in catching every requisite feature of the tune which he set to words.

It is due to the memory of Burns to observe that the music of Scotland owes much, if not all of its present popularity to his endeavours. The further help afforded by Haydn, Pleyel, Kotzluch, Beethoven, and Weber, in harmonizing Thomson's collection must not be overlooked, for the oftentimes sympathetic setting of such writers as Beethoven and Haydn aided greatly in extending the knowledge of Scottish melodies among cultivated musicians. As regards the setting of Burns' lyrics it may safely be affirmed that the music as originally given is by far the most appropriate and characteristic. It is almost impossible to disassociate such songs as "Gala Water;" "My Nannie, O;" "To Mary in Heaven;" "Auld Lang Syne;" "John Anderson, my Jo;" "My Tocher's the Jewel;" "She's Fair and Fause;" and "Duncan Gray," from the melodies which the happy fancy of Burns hit upon as being most appropriate. One or two exceptions only occur to mind, one being the lovely melody to "Afton Water," by Hume, which has long since supplanted that of "The Yellow Hair'd Laddie," to which it was originally set. His songs have been set by Robert Franz among others with some degree of success, but his versions are altogether for the concert-room and an audience of cultivated musicians. Among the composers who have found in Burns a sympathetic poet may be mentioned Sir H. R. Bishop, Howard Glover, Sir Arthur Sullivan, Mendelssohn, Alex. Hume, Robert Franz, Samuel Barr, R. A. Smith, F. Archer, F. E. Bache, Sir W. S. Bennett, Schumann, etc.

BURR (Willard.) American comp. and writer, B. Ravenna, Ohio, Jan. 7, 1852. A graduate of Oberlin Coll. in 1876, and of the Oberlin Cons. of Music in 1877. Received from the former in 1879 the degree of A.M. S. at Berlin under August Haupt, 1879-1880. Comp. and writer in Boston.

WORKS.—Grand Sonata for Pf. and violin; Trios for Pf., violin, and 'cello; String Quartettes; Sonatas for Pf.; Fugues, études, nocturnes, fantasias, etc.; A set of 7 Pf. pieces entitled "From Shore to Shore," op. 19; 7 sacred vocal comp., for 1, 2, and 4 voices; Anthems and songs. Music in its Relation to the Masses. Musical Art-Creation in America and the Relation of Music Teachers thereto, Papers read at Eighth Annual Meeting of Music Teachers' National Association at Cleveland, 1884, etc.

BURROWES (John Freckleton). English writer and comp., B. London, April 23, 1787. S. under W. Horsley. Mem. of Philharmonic Soc. Org. of S. James's Ch., Piccadilly, London. D. London, March 31, 1852.

WORKS.—Op. 1. Six English Ballads, for voice and Pf.; Sonatas for Pf. and flute, and for Pf. and 'cello; Overture for full orch., produced by Philharm. Soc.; Six Divertissements for Pf.; Three Sonatas for Pf. and violin; Sonata for Pf., on Scotch airs, op. 9; Select Airs from Mozart's Operas, for Pf. and flute, 18 numbers; Mozart's Overtures arranged for Pf., violin, flute, and 'cello; Duets for harp and other instruments. Collection of Psalm Tunes, with Figured Bass, n.d. Burrowes' Piano-Forte Primer, containing the Rudiments of Music, in Question and Answer, calculated either for private tuition or teaching in classes, Lond., Clementi, 1822. The Thorough-bass Primer, Lond., 12mo, 1818. Companion to the Thorough-bass Primer, Lond., 8vo, 1835. Songs, part songs, etc.

Burrowes was an excellent pianist and capable instructor, though his music is now almost ancient in style. His theoretical works attained an extraordinary circulation considering the slender claims they possessed to popularity. Notwithstanding many defects they are extensively used at the present day in America.

BURTON (Avery). English comp., who flourished during the 16th century. His compositions are preserved in the Music School of Oxford.

BURTON (John). English comp. and harpsichord player, B. Yorkshire, 1730. S. under Keeble. D. 1785.

WORKS.—Ten Sonatas for the harpsichord, organ, or Pianoforte, fo. n.d.; Six Solos for the harpsichord; Six Trios for the harpsichord and violins; Songs and glees, organ music, etc.

"The compositions of this master, if not profound, were new and fanciful, and derived from his execution, which was varied and fascinating, an interest which, perhaps, without the light and shade imparted by his hand to whatever he played, they would scarcely have been thought to possess. A movement in one of this master's lessons, called the *Courtship*, was, for many years, upon the harpsichord desk of every practitioner in England."—*Busby*.

BURTON (Robert Senior). English org. and cond. of present time, B. 1820. Well known in the Midlands of England as a successful teacher. S. under C. Potter, and succeeded Dr. S. S. Wesley as org. of Leeds Parish Church, 1849.

BUSBY (Thomas). English comp. and writer, B. Westminster, 1755. Articled to Battishill, 1769-74. Org. of S. Mary's, Newington, Surrey. Do. at S. Mary, Woolnoth, Lombard Street, 1798. Mus. Doc. Cantab., 1800. LL.D., Cambridge. D. London, May 28, 1838.

WORKS.—The Prophecy, oratorio, March, 1799; Ode—British Genius, from Gray; Ode to St. Cecilia's Day, Pope; Comala, a Dramatic Romance from Ossian, 1800; Thanksgiving Ode (Degree exercise), 1800; Music to Joanna, drama by R. Cumberland, 1800; Music to M. G. Lewis's Rugantino, 1805; Music to Holcroft's Tale of Mystery, 1802; Music to Porter's Fair Fugitives. Dictionary of Music, with Introduction to the First Principles of that Science, Lond. 8vo., 1786. A Grammar of Music: to which are prefixed Observations explanatory of the Properties and Powers of Music as a Science, and of the general scope and object of the work. London, 12mo, 1818. A General History of Music, from the Earliest Times to the Present; comprising the Lives of Eminent Composers and Musical Writers, London, 2 vols., 8vo, 1819 (Whittaker). Concert Room and Orchestra, Anecdotes of Music and Musicians, Ancient and Modern, 3 vols., 12mo, London, 1825. Musical Manual, or Technical Directory, with Descriptions of various Voices and Instruments, London, 8vo, 1828. The Divine Harmonist, a collection of Anthems, etc., 1788; Melodia Britannica, do., 1790 (unfinished). Sonatas for the Pf. Anthem for the Funeral of Battishill. Miscellaneous anthems, glees, songs, etc. De Lolme proved to be Junius, 1816. Translation of Lucretius. The Age of Genius, a Satire, 1785, etc.

Busby was one of the most respectable musicians of the early part of the present century. His attainments, both literary and musical, entitle him to some respect. He was the composer of the first melo-dramatic music heard in Britain, the work in which it occurred being Lewis' "Rugantino." His musical works are now entirely forgotten, though his literary works are occasionally used in connection with the doings of his contemporaries. His "History of Music" is compiled chiefly from Burney and Hawkins, and though he in a manner repudiated the notion, very little comparison will serve to show the extent to which he is indebted to those writers. He is a much more liberal historian than Burney in his original chapters, and can lay claim to some good, if old-fashioned, literary points. The accounts which survive as to his ability as an organist are generally favourable. His theoretical works are good specimens of what constituted, in bygone times, books of instruction. His "Grammar of Music" reached a second edition in 1826.

BUSNOIS (Antoine de). Belgian comp., B. [1445]. D. Oct. 26, 1480. One of the most famous of the old chanson composers. He was a musician in the service of Charles, Duke of Burgundy.

BUTLER (Charles). English writer, B. Wycombe, Bucks, 1559. M.A., Oxford. Master of the Free school at Basingstoke, Hants. Vicar at Wooton, St. Lawrence, Hants. D. March 29, 1647.

WORKS.—The Feminine Monarchie; or, the Historie of Bees...proving that in the Bees' Song are the Grounds of Musicke. Oxford, 8vo, 1609; other editions. The Principles of Musick in Singing and Setting: with the twofold Use thereof, Ecclesiastical and Civil. London, 4to, 1636. An English Grammar, and other works.

BUTLER (Thomas Hamly). English comp. and pianist, B. London, 1762. S. under Dr. Nares at the Chap. Roy. S. comp. under Piccini in Italy. Comp. to Drury Lane Theatre, under Sheridan. Teacher and pianist in Edinburgh. D. Edinburgh, 1823.

WORKS.—The Widow of Delphi (R. Cumberland), musical drama, 1780. Rondos on the following Scotch airs:—Duncan Gray, Flowers of Edinburgh, I'll gang nae mair to yon toun, Lewie Gordon, Roy's Wife, There's cauld kail in Aberdeen, etc. (Clementi). A Select Collection of Original Scottish Airs, arranged for one and two voices, with Introductory and Concluding Symphonies for the Flute, Violin, and Pianoforte, 1790. Sonatas for the Pf. (various). Songs, partsongs, single pieces for Pf., etc. (The first work is a curious production; the second a learned treatise on theory and on the abuses in sacred and secular music. His works were printed partly in characters taken from the Anglo-Saxon alphabet, partly in others of his own invention which are described in his Grammar.)

This musician was a fine performer on the pianoforte, and with Ross, Nielson, etc., arranged a great number of Scottish and other national airs for his instrument, thus popularising them among a class who might otherwise have remained in ignorance of their numberless beauties.

BUTTERFIELD (J. A.) English comp., B. 1837. Comp. of Belshazzar, cantata, 1781; Ruth, the Gleaner, opera, 1875; A Race for a Wife, melodrama, 1879. Songs, etc.

BUTTSTETT (Johann Heinrich). A celebrated org. and pupil of Pachelbel,

B. 1666. D. early in 18th century. Was org. at Erfurt, and comp. of organ and church music.

BUXTEHUDE (Dietrich). Danish comp. and org., B. Helsingör, Denmark, 1637. S. under Thiel. Org. of Marien-Kirche, Lübeck (Ch. of S. Mary), 1668. Established a society for the performance of sacred music during the evening, 1673. D. Lübeck, May, 9, 1707.
WORKS.—Six Suites of Lessons for the Harpsichord; Sonatas à Violino, Viola da gamba, e Cembalo; Preludes, fugues, etc., for the organ; Miscellaneous church music.

Buxtehude was one of the most famous organists of his period, being considered, with Bach, the greatest exponent then living. Bach is said to have travelled to Lübeck to hear him, and various anecdotes are recorded anent his dealings and acquaintance with Handel. The first work in the above list is intended to represent the nature and course of the planets, an early manifestation of ambitious *programme* writing not yet overshadowed so far as magnitude is concerned.

BYRD (William). English comp., B. [1538.] Senior chorister at S. Paul's Cath., 1554. S. under Tallis. Org. of Lincoln Cath., 1563-69. Gent. of Chap. Royal, 1569. Org. of Chap. Royal (with Tallis), 1575. D. London, July, 4, 1623.
WORKS.—Cantiones quae ab argumento sacræ vocantur quinque et sex partium, 1575. Psalmes, Sonets, and Songs of Sadnes and Pietie, made into musicke of five partes, Lond., 4to, 1588. Songs of Sundrie Natures, some of Gravitie and others of Myrth, fit for all Companies and Voyces, lately made and composed into Musicke of 3, 4, 5, and 6 parts, Lond., 4to, 1589. Liber Primus Sacrarum Cantionum quartum aliæ ad quinque, aliæ uno ad sex voces aedita sunt, Lond., 4to, 1589; reprinted by Musical Antiquarian Soc., edit. by W. Horsley. Liber Secundus Sacrarum Cantionum quartum aliæ ad quinque, aliæ uno ad sex voces aedita sunt, Lond., 4to, 1591. Gradualia, ac Cantiones Sacræ Liber primus, 1607. Gradualia, ac Cantiones Sacræ Liber secundus, 1610. Psalmes, Songs, and Sonnets, some solemne, others joyfull, etc, 1611. Parthenia, or the Maidenhead of the first Musick that ever was printed for the Virginals, composed by the three famous Masters, William Byrd, Dr. John Bull, and Orlando Gibbons, Gentlemen of Her Majestie's Chappell, London, fo., 1655. Service in D minor (Boyce); Three Anthems (Boyce); Mass for Five Voices (Mus. Ant. Soc., Rimbault), 1841; Compositions contained in the Royal Virginal Book; Compositions contained in Lady Nevill's Musick Book, 1591; Music in Leighton's "Teares;" Non Nobis Dominae, in Hilton's Catches, 1652. Madrigals in various collections; Two other masses; anthems, etc.

Byrd was one of the greatest composers of the 16th century. He lived at a period when the musical glory of England was supreme. Among his contemporaries were such men as Tallis, Tye, Farrant, Dowland, Bull, Morley, Hooper, Gibbons, Wilbye, Lawes, Weelkes, and Parsons. Byrd's claims to recognition rest chiefly on his sacred music, which is both dignified and grand without undue elaboration, and pleasing and inspiring without flippancy. He was one of the first in England to make use of the madrigal as an expressive musical form, though it must be admitted that his treatment of works of this class is not generally so happy as that of some of his successors. He was an organist of much ability. His compositions for the virginals are dry and excessively elaborated exercises in counterpoint, without the slightest attempt at emotional colouring. Byrd secured with Tallis, in 1575, by patent, the supreme right to publish music in England, and under this patent they published the collection of sacred music first named in the foregoing list of Byrd's compositions.

BYRNE (C. S.) Irish compiler, published a "Selection of Scottish Melodies, with words by George Linley." Lond., 1827.

BYRNE (Patrick). Irish harpist and comp., B. Farney, about end of 18th century. D. Dundalk, 1863.

BYRON (Lord George Gordon). English poet, B. London, Jan. 22, 1788. D. Missolonghi, Italy, April 19, 1824.
His "Manfred" inspired Schumann with the composition of a fine dramatic can-

tata bearing that name, while "Parisina" is the work on which Bennett founded his clever overture. Among the musicians who have set his lyrical pieces may be mentioned Alex. Lee, Neukomm, A. J. Sutton, Macfarren, Mendelssohn, Kiallmark, Nathan, Schumann, Salaman, and a great number of other composers, native and foreign.

C.

CABALLERO (Manuel Fernandez). Spanish comp., B. Murcia, March 14, 1835. S. at Madrid Cons. Has written church music, operettas, El Primer dia Feliz, 1872; La Marsigliese, 1878, etc.; Songs, and other works.

CABEL (Marie Josephe), née DREULETTE. Belgian soprano vocalist, B. Liège, Jan. 31, 1827. Married to M. Cabel, a music teacher. Appeared in Paris as vocalist, 1847. S. for a period at Paris Cons. Début at "Opera Comique," 1849. Sang successively in Brussels and London, July, 1860. Has sang in St. Petersburg, Germany, etc. D. Paris, May 23, 1885.

"The incompleteness of Madame Cabel was to be felt throughout in 'La Figlia del Reggimento.' The uncertainties of her voice were not those of emotion, as much as of erroneous production. Her execution, however dashing, is rarely perfect, the shake excepted . . . We do not see much chance of settlement for Madame Cabel on the Italian stage."—*Athenæum*, July 21, 1860.

CABEZON (Don Felix Antonio). Spanish org. and comp., B. Madrid, Mar. 30, 1510. D. Madrid, Mar. 26, 1566. Wrote theoretical works, and music for the church.

CABO (Francesco Javier). Spanish org. and comp., B. Naguera, Valencia, 1768. D. 1832. Comp. masses, vespers, psalms, motets, organ music, etc.

CACCINI (Giulio), called ROMANO. Italian comp., B. Rome, 1588. Pupil of Scipione Della Palla. Resided at Florence from 1578. Singer at Court of Francesco di Medicis. D. Florence, 1640.

WORKS.—Combattimento d'Apollino col Serpente, monodrama, 1590. Euridice (with Peri), 1600. Il Rapimento di Cefalo, 1600. Le Nuove Musiche, 1601. Canzonets, Sonnets, etc.

Caccini was associated with Bardi, Galilei, Rinuccini, and Peri in the establishment of the opera, which, originally based on a supposed imitation of the ancient Greek drama, became what it now is, through the successive efforts of Peri, Monteverde, Scarlatti, Lulli, Rameau, Handel, Gluck, Méhul, Meyerbeer, and Wagner. The canzonets and sonnets by various eminent contemporary poets which Caccini set were claimed by Kircher to mark a new development of music, and on this statement is based Caccini's claim to be the inventor of recitative in opposition to Peri. He was one of the greatest teachers of vocalization that Italy ever produced, and to his labours was no doubt due the firm establishment of a vocal method which at one time placed Italian singers before all others.

CADAUX (Justin). French operatic comp., B. Albi, Tarn, April 13, 1813. D. Nov. 8, 1874. Writer of songs, operettas, etc.

CADY (Calvin B.) American pianist and teacher. Director of the Ann Arbor School of Music in connection with Michigan State University. Was educated at the Leipzig Cons. of Music. A charter member of the American Coll. of Musicians. Read a paper before the National Music Teachers' Association at Providence, R.I. in 1883 on "Higher Branches of Instrumental Music in the Public Schools," which received much discussion from the Association and the Press.

Has been active in promoting a taste for high class music in the Western part of the U.S.

CAERWARDEN (John). English comp. and teacher of the violin, who flourished during the 17th cent. Was member of private band of Charles I. Hawkins mentions him as having been a noted teacher but a harsh composer.

CÆSAR (Julius). English physician and comp., lived in Rochester during part of the 17th and 18th centuries. He was an amateur composer only, but Hawkins speaks of two of his catches appearing in the "Pleasant Musical Companion," 1726, as being "inferior to none in that collection."

CÆSAR (William), see SMEGERGILL.

CAFFARELLI (Gaetano), MAJORANO. Italian vocalist, B. Bari, near Naples, April 16, 1703. S. under Porpora. *Début* at Rome, 1724. Appeared at various towns throughout Italy, 1724-28. Appeared in London in Handel's "Feramondo," Jan., 1738. Sang in Italy at Milan, Florence, Venice, Turin, Genoa, Naples, etc. Sang at Paris in 1750. Purchased a Dukedom and retired. D. Naples, 1783.

Caffarelli figured largely in his day as the rival of Farinelli, and seems from all accounts to have possessed great qualifications as a vocal performer. Numerous anecdotes are told regarding him, some of the best appearing in Hogarth's "Memoirs of the Musical Drama."

CAFFARO (Pasquale). Italian comp., B. Lecce, Naples, Feb. 8, 1708. S. under Leo at Naples. Master of Chap. Roy. at Naples. Director of Naples Cons. D. Naples, Oct. 28, 1787.

WORKS.—*Operas:* Ipermnestra, 1751 ; La Disfatta di Dario, 1756 ; Antigono, 1754 ; L' Incendia di Troia, 1757 ; Arianna e Teseo, 1766 ; Il Creso, 1768 ; Giustizia Placata, 1769 ; L' Olimpiade, 1769 ; L' Antigono (new music), 1770 ; Betulia liberata ; Il Figliuolo prodigo ravveduto. *Cantatas:* 1764, 1766, 1769. Il Trionfo di Davidde, oratorio. Masses, Litanies, Motets, Psalms, and other Church Music.

CAFFRO (Giuseppe). Italian oboe and cor-anglais player, B. Naples, 1766. D. about beginning of present century. He wrote much for his instruments.

CAGNONI (Antonio). Italian comp., B. Godiasco, Voghera, 1828. S. at Milan Cons., 1842-1847. Professor and Teacher.

WORKS.—*Operas:* Rosalia, 1845 ; I due Savojardi, 1846 ; Don Bucefalo, 1847 ; Il Testamento di Figaro, 1848 ; Amori e Trappole, 1850 ; La Valle d'Andorra, 1851 ; Giralda, 1852 ; La Fioraia, 1855 ; La Figlia di don Liborio, 1856 ; Il Vecchio della Montagna, 1863 ; Michele Perrin, 1864 ; Claudia, 1866 ; La Tombola, 1869 ; Un Capriccio di Donna, 1870 ; Papà Martin, 1871 ; Il Duca di Tapigliano, 1874 ; Francesca da Rimini, 1878. Songs, etc.

CAHEN (Ernest). French violinist and comp., B. Paris, Aug. 18, 1828. S. at Paris Cons. Writer of operetta, "Le Bois," violin music, etc.

CAHUSAC (Louis de). French dramatist, B. Montauban. D. Paris, 1759. Author of the librettos of a number of Rameau's operas. He wrote also a number of comic and tragic dramas, none of which were possessed of great merit.

CAIMO (Giuseppe). Italian comp., B. Milan, 1540. D. [1585]. Wrote madrigals and church music.

CALAH (John). English org. and comp B. 1758. D. August 4, 1798. Was Org. of Peterborough Cathedral at end of 18th century. Wrote music for the English church service.

CALDARA (Antonio). Italian comp., B. Venice, 1678. S. under Legrenzi. Singer in St. Marks, Venice. Chap.-Master at Mantua, 1714. Vice-chap.-master to Emperor Charles VI., Vienna. Resided at Venice from 1738. D. Venice, 1763 (1768).

WORKS.—*Operas, etc.:* Argene, Venice, 1689 ; Tirsi, 1696 ; Farnace, 1703 ; Partenope, 1708 ; Sofonisbe, 1708 ; L'Inimico Generoso, 1709 ; Atenaide, 1711 ; Tito e Berenice, 1714 ; Caio Mario, 1717 ; Coriolano, 1717 ; Astarte, 1718 ; Ifigenia in Aulide, 1718 ; Sisara, 1719 ; Nitocri, 1722 ; Gianguir, 1724 ; Gioaz, 1726 ; Semiramide, 1725 ; Imeneo, 1727 ; Mitridate, 1728 ; Nabot, 1729 ; Demetrio, 1731 ; Demofoonte, 1733 ; Adriano in Siria, 1735 ; La Clemenza di Tito, 1734 ; Enone, 1735 ; L'Ingratitudine castigata, 1737. *Oratorios:* Tobia, 1719 ;

Naaman, 1721; Giuseppe, 1722; David, 1724; Daniello, 1731. Motets, masses, and cantatas; sonatas for 2 violins and violoncello, etc.

Caldara has been very highly esteemed by successive generations of writers on music, however much the soundness of his claims may be open to question. His music was certainly not superior in merit to that of his contemporaries, Leo, A. Scarlatti, or Durante, and is chiefly remarkable for a languid sentimental style. His music is persuasive rather than commanding, though there is also much in it that is noble and inspired.

CALDICOTT (Alfred James). English comp. and org., B. Worcester, 1842. Chor. in Worcester Cath., 1851. Articled to Done, org. of do., 1856. S. Leipzig Cons. under Moscheles, Hauptmann, Plaidy, and Richter. Settled at Worcester, 1864. Org. of St. Stephen's Ch., and to the Corporation. Conductor of the "Musical" and "Instrumental" societies of Worcester. Mus. Bac., Cantab., 1878. Gained Special Glee Prize offered by the Manchester Gentleman's Glee Soc., 1878. Gained first prize for serious glee, Huddersfield, 1879. Prof. at Royal Coll. of Music, London, 1882. Org. and Cond. at Albert Palace, London. Editor of Morley's Part Song Journal.

WORKS.—The Widow of Nain, a sacred cantata, Worcester Festival, Sept., 1881; A Rhine Legend, cantata for Ladies' voices, 1883; Queen of the May, cantata; Treasure Trove, operetta by A. Law, June, 1883; A Moss-Rose-Rent, operetta by A. Law, 1883; A Fishy Case, children's operetta by F. Weatherly, 1883; Old Knockles operetta, German Reed, 1884. Dickens' Series of Songs. Winter Days, prize serious glee, 1879; Humpty Dumpty, prize humorous glee, 1878; Jack and Jill, glee; Jack Horner, glee; House that Jack Built, glee; Yule, glee; Out on the Waters, glee; The Haymakers, glee. *Songs:* Red Letter Days; For a day, for aye; The New Curate; Lost Love; Woman's Faith; Parted; The Butterfly's Kiss; Returning Sails; Unless; Unbidden; Two Spoons; Three Men of Plymouth Town; Question and Answer; When all the world was young; MS. works, etc.

This composer, who doubtless inherited his musical proclivities from his father, an original member of the Worcester Madrigal and Harmonic Societies—has given decided evidence of the possession of more than ordinary ability as a writer of concerted vocal music of a humorous character. His comical glees are gems in their way, and are not spoiled by the vulgarity which usually accompanies such attempts. His more ambitious works are marked by much ability, and are evidently of a progressive degree of merit.

CALEGARI (Antonio). Italian operatic comp. B. Padua, Oct. 18, 1758. D. July, 22, 1828. Wrote L'Amor Soldato, 1786; Il Matrimonio Scoperto, 1789; Le Sorelle Rivali, 1784, etc.

CALKIN (James). English pianist and comp., B. London, 1786. S. under Thomas Lyon. Associate of the Philharmonic Soc., 1823. Wrote Symphony for orch., Pf. music, string quartets, etc. D. London, 1862.

CALKIN (John Baptiste). English comp., pianist, and org., B. London, Mar. 16, 1827. S. under his father, etc. Org., precentor, and choir-master at S. Columba's Coll., Ireland, 1846-1853. Org. and choir-master at Woburn Chap., 1853-7. Org. and choir master, Camden Road Chap., 1863-8. Org. and choir-master of S. Thomas' Church, Elm Road, Camden Town, 1870-84. Mem. of the Philharmonic Soc. F.C.O. Mem. C. Trin. Coll. London. Prof. at Guildhall school of music.

WORKS.—Services in B flat op. 40; G op. 96; and in D, for Parish choirs; Morning and Evening Service, in G, 1883; Communion Service in C, op. 104; Te Deum in D. *Anthems:* I will magnify Thee; Behold, now praise ye the Lord; I will alway give thanks; Let your light so shine; O God, have mercy; Out of the deep have I cried unto Thee; Rejoice in the Lord; Thou wilt keep him in perfect peace; The righteous shall flourish; Four Introits; Thou visitest the earth; Rend your heart; Unto Thee will I cry; Whoso hath this world's goods; Hymns. *Glees and Part-songs:* Breathe soft, ye winds; Come, fill my boys; Echoes; My Lady is so wondrous fair; Night winds that so gently flow; The Chivalry of Labour; To the Redbreast; Up, brothers, up!. *Songs:* Coming Light; Sleep on my heart; Every joy that earth can give; Oh! lovely night; No jewelled beauty is my love ; Oh ! turn not away ; Oh ! wake, dearest, wake ; The Maiden's reply ; The rippling brook ; The two locks of hair. *Organ:* Andante ; Seventeen Original Compositions in ten numbers ; Transcriptions, Marches, Minuets, etc. *Pianoforte:* Arcadia Waltzes ; Rondo Grazioso, op. 93 ; Les Arpèges, op. 94 ; Two Sketches, op. 79 ; A Moonlit Lake, op. 84 ; The Pixie's Revel, op. 95 ; Les trois graces (sonata) ; Concert study in double notes ; Bources, studies, transcriptions, minuets, etc. ; Album Leaves, op. 88 ; Marches and Dances, various. Quartet for strings ; Quintet for strings ; Trio for Pf., vn., and 'cello ; Sonata for Pf. and 'cello, etc.

Mr. Calkin shows in his works the possession of an extremely graceful and pleasing musical faculty. His works for the pianoforte and organ are brilliant and fanciful in style. It is on his vocal and strictly church music that Mr. Calkin's reputation will hereafter rest. His glees and part-songs are among the worthiest productions of modern England ; and " My Lady is so wondrous fair " is one which can be safely placed alongside of the best examples of the class. His anthems and services have been recognised among the foremost churches and cathedrals as being worthy of frequent performance, and this is sufficient evidence as to their general high quality.

CALKIN (Joseph). English violinist, B. London, 1781. S. under Thomas Lyon and Spagnoletti. Violinist at Drury Lane Theatre, 1798-1808. Married to widow of Mr. Budd, bookseller. Bookseller to the King under firm of Calkin & Budd. Member of King's band, 1821. D. (?)

CALL (Leonard de). German comp., B. Germany, 1779. D. Vienna, 1815. Writer of a number of fine part-songs, songs, etc.

CALLCOTT (John George). English comp. and pianist, B. July, 1821. Son of J. W. Callcott. Org. at Teddington, and accompanist to Henry Leslie's choir. Has composed a number of cantatas and minor works, of which the following are the most important :—Hallowe'en, cantata for solo voices, chorus and orch. ; The Golden Harvest, cantata for solo voices, chorus, and orch. ; Old Clock on the Stairs, part-song ; Tell me where is fancy bred, trio ; The light summer winds, part-song ; Songs, various ; Pianoforte music consisting of transcriptions, dances, etc.

CALLCOTT (John Wall). English comp. and writer, B. London, Nov. 20, 1766. Self-taught in music. Deputy org. to Reinhold of S. George the Martyr's, Bloomsbury, 1783-5. Member of orch. of Academy of Ancient Music. Unsuccessful competitor for prize offered by the Catch Club, 1784 (his first trial). Gained three prizes (medals) out of the four offered by the Catch Club, 1785. Mus. Bac. Oxon., July, 1785. Gained two medals, Catch Club, 1786 ; and two prizes in 1787 (he sent in about 100 compositions). Founded, with others, the "Glee Club," 1787. Gained all the prizes offered by the Catch Club, 1789. Joint org. (with C. S. Evans) of S. Paul's, Covent Garden. S. under Haydn, 1790. Org. of Asylum for Female Orphans, 1792-1802. Gained nine medals for his glees during 1790-93. Mus. Doc. Oxon., 1800. Lecturer at the Royal Institution in succession to Crotch, 1806. D. London, May 15, 1821.

WORKS.—Grammar of Music, Lond., 1806 (other editions) ; Glees, Catches, and Canons, op. 4 (Clementi), n. d. ; Explanations of the Notes, Marks, Words, etc. used in Music (Clementi), n. d. ; Select Collection of Catches, Canons, and Glees, 3 books (D'Almaine), n. d. (edited) ; Five Glees for 2 Trebles and Bass in Score ; Five Glees, chiefly for Treble voices, op. 12 ; Six Glees in Score ; Collection of Glees, Canons, and Catches, including some pieces never before published, with Memoir by W. Horsley (the editor), 2 vols., folio. Lond., 1824. Church Psalmody (selection) ; Services, Anthems, Odes. *Titles of some of his principal Glees and Catches:* Æella ; Are the white hours ; As I was going to Derby ; Blow, Warder, blow ; Desolate is the dwelling of Morna ; Dull repining sons of care ; Drink to me only ; Father of Heroes ; Forgive blest shade ; Erl King ; Farewell to Lochaber ; Friend of fancy ; Fervid on the glittering flood ; The Friar ; Go idle boy ; If happily we wish to live ; In the lonely vale of streams ; Lo ! where incumbent o'er the shade ; Lovely seems the morn's fair lustre ; Lordly gallants ; The May-fly ; My flocks feed not ; New Mariners ; Mark the merry elves ; Oh share my cottage ; Once upon my cheek ; O, snatch me swift ; O thou where'er ; O fancy, friend of nature ; Peace to the souls of the heroes ; Queen of the valley ; Red Cross Knights ; Soft and safe ; See with ivy chaplet ; Thou art beautiful ; Thyrsis, when he left me ; Tho' from thy bank ; To all you Ladies now on land ; Thalaba ; Thou pride of the forest ; Triumphant love ; Whann battayle ; When Arthur first ; When time was entwining ; Who comes so dark ; With sighs, sweet rose ; Ye Gentlemen of England. Songs, etc.

Among the many eminent glee composers of England, none perhaps can be said to be so popular as Callcott. He sinned in too profusely expending his genius on pieces which at best were mere mechanical exercises, but the larger portion of his glees are beautiful and fresh creations. With Horsley, Webbe, Cooke, Clarke, and Beale he aided in greatly improving the quality of the glee as an independent vocal form. His glees on words from Ossian are artistic and genuine examples of pure glee-writing, though they are not treasured as such in so great a degree as their merits demand. His "Grammar of Music" was, and is one of the best rudimentary treatises in the English language, and it is sufficient to say that its merits are recognised alike in America and Britain. His church music has not been published in a collected form. His daughter Sophie was a pianist of much ability.

CALLCOTT (William Hutchings). English comp. and pianist, son of the above, B. Kensington, 1807. D. there, Aug. 5, 1882. Was an organist and teacher in London for a considerable period. Among his various compositions may be named the following.

WORKS.—*Pianoforte:* Elegant Extracts from Mendelssohn ; Favourite Marches, Minuets, and Movements by Handel ; Readings from the great Masters of all Nations ; Transcriptions from Schubert, Gounod, Haydn, Offenbach, Rossini, Meyerbeer, Mozart, Beethoven, Verdi, Mendelssohn, etc. ; Melodies of all Nations ; British Isles, duet ; Fairy Duet ; Oriental Duet ; Arrangements from Wallace's Amber Witch ; Recollections of the Philharmonic ; Arrangements (with violin, etc.) of Orfeo (Gluck), King Arthur (Purcell), Macbeth (Locke), Tempest (Purcell), Comus (Arne and Handel), etc. ; Beauties of Schumann ; Morning Mist, Rainbow, Waterfall for Pf. ; Clementi's Golden Pianoforte Exercises . . . with Occasional Remarks (Cocks) ; The Holy Family, Selections of Sacred Music. A Selection of Glees for three voices, arranged expressly for amateurs and private performance. Songs, Part-Songs, etc. A Few Facts in the Life of Handel, Lond., 1859.

CALLCOTT (Maria Hutchins). English authoress, has published among other works "The Singer's Alphabet ; or, Hints on the English Vowels, etc," Lond., 1849.

CALVISIUS (Sethus), SETH KALWITZ. German Astrologer, writer, and musician, B. Sachsenberg, Thuringia, Feb. 21, 1556. D. Leipzig, Nov. 23, 1615.

WORKS.—Melopoia, seu melodiæ condendæ rationem, quam vulgo Musicam poeticam vocant, Erfurt, 1595 ; Opuscula Musica, 1611 ; Compendium Musicum, 1612 ; Musicæ Artis Praecepta nova et facillima (2nd edit.), 1612 ; Exercitationes Musices ; The 150th Psalm in 12 parts for 3 choirs ; Chronological Works and General Writings.

CALZABIGI. Italian poet, chiefly known for his connection with Gluck in the capacity of librettist. He wrote the book of "Orfeo," the first reformed opera composed by Gluck. He also wrote "Alceste," "Armida," and some poems of considerable merit. Flourished during latter portion of the 18th century.

CALZOLARI (Enrico). Italian tenor vocalist, B. Parma, Feb. 22, 1823. S. under Burckhardt. *Début* at Milan, 1845. Has appeared in operas by Bellini, Donizetti, Rossini, and Verdi.

CAMARGO (Miguel Gomez). Spanish comp., flourished in latter half of 16th century. Wrote music for the church, etc.

CAMAUER (Godfroid). Dutch comp., B. Berg-op-Zoom, May 31, 1821. Has composed operas, masses, overtures, choruses, chamber music, etc. D. Huy, Belgium, 1884.

CAMBERT (Robert), or LAMBERT. French comp. and org., B. Paris, 1628. S. under Chambonnières. Org. of Ch. of S. Honoré. Musical Director to Anne of Austria, 1666. Lost position at French court (through intrigues of Lulli), and settled in England. Master of Music to Charles II. D. England [London], 1677.

WORKS.—*Operas, etc.:* La Pastorale, première comédie française en misique, April, 1659; Adonis, 1662; Ariane, 1667; Pomona, a Pastoral (Perrin), 1671; Les Pienes et les Plaisers de l' Amour, etc.

Cambert was the first Frenchman, in imitation of Peri and Caccini to write operas in the French vernacular. He was regarded as the best French composer till the intrigues of Lulli destroyed his position. His residence in England was not happy for himself, as the failure of his works in London affected him greatly, and is supposed by some historians to have hastened his death.

CAMBINI (Giovanni Giuseppe). Italian comp. and violinist, B. Leghorn, Feb. 13, 1746. S. under Martini, 1763-66. Captured by pirates while returning to Leghorn. Ransomed by a Venetian merchant after having been a slave for a time. Went to Paris, 1770. Cond. at the Théâtre des Beaujolais, 1788-1791. Cond. at the Théâtre Louvois, 1791-94. D. Bicêtre, 1825.

WORKS.—Le Sacrifice d'Abraham, oratorio, 1774. *Operas:* Rose d'Amour et Carloman, 1779; La Croisée, 1785; Les Fourberies de Mathurin, 1786; Cora; Le Deux Frères; Adèle et Edwin; Nantilde et Dagobert, 1791; Trois Gascons, 1793; Alcméon; Alcide; Les Romans, ballet, 1776. Symphonies (50 to 60 in number); String quartets (144); Music for the org. and Pf.; Flute music and a method for the flute; Concertos, songs, etc.

CAMIDGE (John). English comp. and org., B. about 1735. Org. of York Cath., 1756-1803. D. York, 1803.

WORKS.—Six Easy Lessons for the Harpsichord, York, n.d.; Glees; Miscellaneous works for the Harpsichord; Church music and songs, etc.

CAMIDGE (Matthew). English comp. and org,, son of the above, B. York, 1764. S. under Dr. Nares at the Chap. Royal. Org. of York Cath., 1803-1844. D. York, Oct. 23, 1844.

WORKS.—A Collection of Tunes adapted to Sandy's version of the Psalms, 1789; A Method of Instruction in Music by Questions and Answers, n.d.; Twenty-four Original Psalm and Hymn Tunes, 8vo, n.d.; Cathedral Music, fo. n.d.; Sonatas for the Pf.; Marches for the Pf.; Glees and songs.

CAMIDGE (John). English comp. and org., son of the above, B. York, 1790. S. under his father. [Bac. Mus. Cambridge, 1812 (?). Doc. Mus. Camb., 1819 (?)]. Doc. Mus. Lambeth, 1855. Org. of York Cath., 1844-1859. D. York, Sept. 21, 1859.

WORKS.—Cathedral Music, consisting of a Service...Anthems and 50 Double Chants...fo., n.d.; Six Glees for 3 and 4 voices, n.d., etc.

CAMPAGNOLI (Bartolomeo). Italian comp. and violinist, B. Cento, near Bologna, Sept. 19, 1751. S. under Nardini. Violinist in the "Pergola" at Florence. Leader at Rome, Florence, etc. Chap.-master to the Bishop of Freysing, 1776. Violinist to Duke of Courland, Dresden, 1778. Travelled in Europe as violinist, visiting among other towns Stockholm, Copenhagen, Hamburg, Potsdam, Munich, Salzburg, Ratisbon, etc. Cond. and violinist at Leipzig, 1797-1818. Resided for a time at Paris. D. Neustrelitz, Nov. 6, 1827.

WORKS.—Op. 1. Eighteen duets for flute and violin; op. 2. Do.; op. 3. Three concertos for flute and orch.; op. 4. Eighteen duets for flute and vn.; op. 6. Six Solos or Sonatas for violin and 'cello; op. 7. Three themes, varied, for 2 vns; op. 8. Do.; op. 9. Three duets for 2 vns.; op. 10. Six fugues for violin; op. 12. Thirty Preludes for the violin; op. 13. Six Polonaises for the violin; op. 14. Six easy duets for 2 violins; op. 15. Concerto for violin and orch. in B; op. 16. L'Illusion de la Viole d'Amour, Sonate notturne pour le Violon, in D minor; op. 17. L'Art d'inventer à l'improviste des Fantaisies et Cadences pour le Violon (coll. of 246 pieces); op. 18. Seven Divertissements for violin; op. 19. Three duets for

2 violins; op. 20. Recueil de 101 Pièces faciles et progressives pour Violon; op. 21. Nouvelle Méthode de la Mécanique Progressive, etc., pour 2 violins—trans. into English as New and Progressive Method on the Mechanism of Violin Playing, by John Bishop, Lond., fo., n.d.; Forty-one caprices for "l'Alto-Viola," etc.

The exercises numbered 20, 21, and 22, and those numbered 10, 12, and 17, are among the best studies that can be given the young violinist who has achieved a moderate mastery over his instrument. They are widely in use among professors. Campagnoli was a violinist of the same school as Pugnani and Giardini, and aided in forming the more modern one of Viotti, Kreutzer, and Spohr.

CAMPAJOLA (Francesco). Italian comp., B. Naples, May 8, 1825. Prof. at Naples Cons. Has written various operas and romances, etc.

CAMPANA (Fabio). Italian comp., B. Bologna, 1815. S. at Bologna Cons. Settled in London about 1850 as teacher of singing. D. London, Feb. 2, 1882.

WORKS.—*Operas:* Caterina di Guisa, 1838; Giulio d'Este, 1841; Vannina d'Ornano, 1842; Luisa di Francia, 1844; Almina, London, 1860; Esmeralda, Lond., 1878. *Songs:* Eyes; Goodbye; Morn that shinest; One smile of thine; The little Gipsy; The twilight hour; Aikà; Elvira mia; Fin dalla prima etade; Non Lasciarmi; The winds are hushed to rest; T'Adoro; Non m'ascolta!; Non lo so; Come back, my only love; Cradle song; Evening bringeth my heart back to thee; The Scout; Part-songs, etc.

CAMPANELLA (Francesco). Italian violinist and comp., B. Naples, Sept. 30, 1827. S. at Naples Cons. Writer of operas, cantatas, songs, Pf. music, etc.

CAMPANINI (Italo). Italian tenor vocalist, B. Parma, June 29, 1846. S. at Parma Cons. Sang in Russia, and Madrid. S. under Lamperti at Milan. Appeared at Bologna and Rome with success, 1870. Sang at Drury Lane and H.M. Theatre London, 1872. Appeared in America, 1873. Has since appeared in various towns and countries throughout the world. Was knighted by the King of Italy.

"Nature endowed Campanini with a strong, even, and sympathetic voice, and art has enabled him to greatly increase its compass, while imparting flexibility and brilliancy throughout its range. An ardent, painstaking student, he is to-day a living proof that good vocalism is worth all the time and labour it takes to acquire, for without it no voice could have borne the strain to which his has been subjected . . . His acting is nearly as good as his singing, and the poorest singer in the cast feels his magnetic influence. But not only as an artist is he enviable: his genial, manly character has won him hosts of friends, who love the man as much as they admire the singer."—FREDERICK NAST in *Harpers Magazine,* 1881.

He is said to be conversant with the tenor roles of nearly 100 operas.

CAMPBELL (Rev. A., M.A.) Scottish writer, author of "Two Papers on Church Music, read before the Liverpool Ecclesiastical Musical Society," Liverpool, 1854.

CAMPBELL (Alexander). Scottish writer and musician, B. Tombea on Loch Lubnaig, Callander, Feb. 22, 1764. S. at Callander Grammar School. S. music at Edinburgh under Tenducci. Teacher of Pf. in Edinburgh. Org. in the non-juring chapel, Nicolson Street, Edinburgh. Was Musical Instructor of Sir Walter Scott. D. Edinburgh, May 15, 1824.

WORKS.—An Introduction to the History of Poetry in Scotland, ... Edinburgh, 4to, 1798. Songs of the Lowlands of Scotland, carefully compared with the original editions, and embellished with characteristic designs composed and engraved by the late David Allen, Esq., Historical Painter, Edinburgh, 4to, 1799. A Tour from Edinburgh through parts of North Britain, Lond., 2 vols., 4to, 1802. Another edit., 2 vols., 1811. The Grampians Desolate, a Poem, 1804. Albyn's Anthology, or a Select collection of the melodies and vocal poetry peculiar to Scotland and the Isles, hitherto unpublished, collected and arranged by Alex. Campbell, the modern Scottish and English verses adapted to the Highland, Hebridean, and Lowland melodies, written by Walter Scott, Esq., etc., Edinburgh, Oliver & Boyd, 2 vols., folio, 1816-1818. Collections of Scottish Songs, with violin, Lond., 1792. A Second Collection arranged for Harpsichord, n.d., etc.

The works by which Campbell will hereafter be known are "Albyn's Anthology," and the "History of Poetry." He collected the melodies of Albyn's Anthology for the Highland Society, and prefixed to the first volume a few notes on the national music of Scotland. His collection is chiefly valuable for its preservation of a number of old Gaelic airs, some of them extremely beautiful. Wilson, Hogg, Mrs. Grant, and Boswell wrote poetry for the airs. His claim to the composition of the melody now sung to "Gloomy Winter's noo awa" has not been substantiated. The two works first named are usually issued together as one vol.

CAMPBELL (Donald). Scottish writer and collector, author of "A Treatise on the Language, Poetry, and Music of the Highland clans, with illustrative Traditions and Anecdotes, and numerous ancient Highland airs," Edinburgh, large 8vo, 1862.

This is a good but rather opinionative work. It contains a number of ancient Highland melodies badly set to inferior basses. He describes himself as "late Lieut. of the 57th Regiment," and appears to have been a resident in Port-Glasgow on the Clyde. He was a claimant to the Breadalbane Peerage.

CAMPBELL (Francis Joseph), LL.D. American musician and educator of the blind, B. Franklin, Co., Tenn., Oct. 9, 1834. Lost sight when three-and-a-half years old. Educated at a School for the Blind, Nashville, at which he afterwards became music teacher. Teacher of Music in the Perkins Institution for the Blind, Boston. Went to Europe in 1869, and S. in Leipzig and Berlin, with Tausig and Kullak. Established in conjunction with Dr. Armitage the Royal Normal College, for the Blind, London, 1872.

This institution has now grown into the most important School for the Blind in the world, and the fame of its educational success is known everywhere. The number of musical pupils educated in it is large, and not a few among those who have studied in the college, are now musicians of acknowledged competence. Dr. Campbell has attained marvellous results by his industry and self-reliance, and has placed within the reach of poor blind persons facilities for becoming quite independent of their serious disadvantage. It is not too much to say that the artists educated in this College take their stand with those of the same age among the seeing, and the performances of the College Choir are unsurpassed by the best choirs in the country.

CAMPBELL (John). Scottish comp. and editor, B. Paisley, about end of 18th century. D. Glasgow, 1860. Edited "Campbell's Selection of Anthems and Doxologies, with a separate piano accompaniment," Glasgow, 1848; and wrote a few original psalms and anthems of mediocre quality.

CAMPBELL (Joshua). Scottish collector, published about the end of last century "A Collection of New Reels and Highland Strathspeys, with a bass for the violoncello and harpsichord," n. d. "Collection of Favourite Tunes," with variations, etc., n. d.

CAMPBELL (Thomas). Scottish poet and general writer, B. Glasgow, July 27, 1777. D. Boulogne, June 15, 1844.

One of the most chaste of modern poets. He wrote words to the music in Bunting's Irish Airs, and wrote many lyrical pieces which have been set by many good composers. His words have been adapted to Scottish melodies in many of the more modern collections. Among composers who have set his verses may be mentioned Bishop, Attwood, Callcott, Pierson, J. W. Elliot, Neukomm, Salaman, etc.

CAMPBELL (William). Scottish collector, published about 1790, "Campbell's First Book of New and Favourite Country Dances and Strathspey Reels, for the harpsichord or violin."

CAMPENHOUT (Francois van). Belgian comp., B. Brussels, 1780. D. Brussels, 1848. Best remembered as the comp. of "La Brabançonne," the well-known Belgian national air, composed during 1830. Also comp. the operas Grotius, 1808; l'Heureux Mensonge, 1819; Le Passe-Partout, 1814, etc.

CAMPION (Thomas). English poet, dramatist, comp. and physician, flourished in first part of 17th century. D. Feb., 1619.

WORKS.—Observations on the Art of English Poesie, 1602; The first, second, third, and fourth booke of Ayres, containing divine and morall songs ; to be sung to the Lute and Viols, in two, three, and foure Parts : or by one Voyce to an Instrument, Lond., 1610-1612 ; Songs of Mourning bewailing the untimely death of Prince Henry, 1613. A New Way of Making Foure parts in Counter-point, by a most familiar and infallible rule, 1618 (and 1655 in Playford's "Introduction to the Skill of Musick ") ; Ayres for the Mask of Flowers, 1613.

CAMPORESE (Violante). Italian soprano vocalist, B. Rome, 1785. Sang at Paris, Milan, etc. *Début* at King's Theatre, London, Jan. 11, 1817. Appeared at Ancient Concerts, etc., 1824-5. Returned to Italy, 1825. D. after 1860 [1839 ?]

CAMPRA (André). French comp., B. Aix (Provence), 1660. Chor. in Cath. of Aix. Musical director at the Jesuit's Ch. at Paris. Master of Chap. Royal, Paris. D. Versailles, July, 1744.

WORKS.—*Operas, etc.*: Hésione (by Danchet), 1700 ; Tancrede (Danchet), Nov., 1702 ; Les Muses, ballet, Oct., 1703 ; Hippodamie (by Roy), 1708 ; Idomenée, 1712 ; Télèphe, Nov., 1713 ; Les Devins de la place Saint Marc, ballet, 1710 ; Les Festes Venitiennes, ballet, 1710 ; Camille, 1717 ; Alcide. Motets à I. II. et III. voix, avec la basse-continue, Ballard, Paris, 1703 ; Motets à 1, 2. et 3 voix avec la basse continue, Livre premier, Ballard, 1710 ; Cantatas Françoises, mêlées de symphonies, Livre premier, 1721 ; 2nd, 1714 ; etc.

Hawkins says in reference to this composer : " The grace and vivacity of his airs, the sweetness of his melody, and, above all, his strict attention to the sense of the words, render his compositions truly estimable.

CAMPS Y SOLER (Oscar). Spanish pianist, comp. and writer, B. Alexandria, Egypt, Nov. 21, 1837. Writer of theoretical works, cantatas, etc. Has travelled in France, Scotland, Spain, etc.

CAMUS (J. P. le), French musician, was a teacher in London. Published "The Art of Singing, a Method in Three Parts, on an entirely new Plan of Vocalization," Lond., fo., 1833.

CAMUS (Paul Hippolyte). French comp. and flute player, B. Paris, Jan. 26, 1796. S. at Paris Cons. Plate flute in various Parisian theatres. D. [?]

WORKS.- Op. 1. 24 Serenades composées d'airs nationaux variés pour la Flûte. Livre 1, 2 ; op. 2. Duets for 2 flutes ; 3. Fantasias, duets, solos, concertos, etc., for flute.

CANDEILLE (Pierre Joseph). French operatic comp., B. Dec. 8, 1744. D. April 24, 1827.

CANDLISH (Rev. Robert Scott). Scottish divine, B. Edinburgh, 1807. D. 1873. He wrote "The Organ Question : Statements by Dr. Ritchie and Dr. Porteous for and against the Use of the Organ in Public Worship...with an introductory notice." Edin., 8vo, 1856.

CANIS (Cornelius). German comp. of 16th century. Supposed to have died about 1556. He wrote chansons and canons of an elaborate and learned nature, many of which occur in contemporary collections.

CANNABICH (Christian). German comp. and violinist, B. Mannheim, 1731. S. under his father and Stamitz. Sent by the Elector to Italy, where he studied under Jomnelli. Leader of Mannheim orch., 1765. Cond. of do., 1775. Cond. at Munich, 1778. D. Frankfort, 1798.

WORKS.—Op. 1. Six quartets for strings ; op. 2. Three symphonies for orch. ; op. 3. Six trios for strings ; op. 4. Six duets for flute and violin, 1767 ; op. 5. Six quartets for strings ; op. 6. Three concertos for violin, with string quartet accomp. ; op. 7. Six Symphonies (concertante) for flutes, with quartet accomp. ; Azacaja, opera, 1778 ; Ballets, etc.

Cannabich was the friend of Mozart, one of the foremost conductors of his day, and a good composer. His son Carl (B. Mannheim, 1769 ; D. Munich, 1806) inherited the paternal musical capacity, and followed his steps as a conductor and composer. His works are chiefly vocal.

CANNETI (Francesco). Italian comp., B. Vicenza, 1809. Writer on counterpoint, and composer of operas, masses, romances, etc. D. Vicenza, August, 1884.

CANOGIA (José Avelino). Spanish clarinet-player and comp., B. Oeiras, Lisbon, Nov. 10, 1784. D. Lisbon, 1842. Has played at Paris, London, etc., and has written concertos, fantasias, and variations for his instrument.

CAPECELATRO (Vincenzo). Italian comp., B. Naples, 1815. S. at Naples Cons. D. Florence, Oct 7, 1874. Writer of operas, songs, etc.

CAPES (Rev. John Moore). English comp. and writer, was B.A., Oxford, 1836; M.A., 1846. He composed "The Druid," a Tragic opera, produced at St. George's Hall, Liverpool, Feb. 22, 1879. This work attained not more than local renown. Capes has also written "An Essay on the Growth of the Musical Scale and of Modern Harmony," London, 1879.

CAPILUPI (Geminiano). Italian comp., B. Modena, 1560. Pupil of Orazio Vecchi. D. Modena, Aug. 31, 1616. Writer of madrigals, canzonets, and motets.

CAPOTARTI (Luigi). Italian comp., B. Nolfetta, 1767. S. at Naples Cons. D. 1842. Writer of operas, etc.

CAPOUL (Joseph Amédée Victor). French tenor vocalist, B. Toulouse, Feb. 27, 1839. S. at Paris Cons. from 1859. Has sang in U. S. A., London, Paris, etc., with distinguished success.

CAPUA (Rinaldo di). See RINALDO DI CAPUA.

CAPUZZI (Giuseppe Antonio). Italian violinist, B. Brescia, 1740. Appeared in London, 1796. D. Bergamo, March 26, 1818. Writer of operas, violin music, etc.

CARACCIOLO (Luigi). Italian comp., B. Andria, Bari, Aug. 10, 1849. S. at Naples Cons. Writer of operas, cantatas, and vocal music.

CARADORI-ALLAN (Maria Caterina Rosalbina), née DE MUNCK. French soprano vocalist, B. Milan, 1800. S. music under her mother. S. for the Stage. Appeared in London as "Cherubino," Jan. 12, 1822. Sang in London till 1826. Returned to Continent, where she continued till 1834. Re-appeared in London, 1834. D. Surbiton, Surrey, Oct. 15, 1865.

CARAFA (Michele Henri Francois Aloys Vincent Paul de C). Italian comp. and teacher, B. Naples, Nov. 17, 1787 [1785]. S. under Cherubini, Fazzi, etc. Entered army and became an officer. Settled in Paris, 1827. Prof. of Comp. at the Cons., 1828. Mem. of the Institute, 1837. Chev. of Legion of Honour. Director of the Military Music School, etc. D. Paris, July 26, 1872.

WORKS.—*Operas:* Il Fantasma, 1802; Vascello l'Occidente, 1811; La Gelosia corretta, 1815; Gabriella di Vergy, 1816; Ifigenia in Tauride, 1817; Adele di Lusignano, 1817; Berenice in Siria, 1818; Elisabetta in Derbyshire, 1818; Il Sacrifizio d' Epito, 1819; I due Figaro, 1820; La Capricciosa ed il Soldato, 1823; Eufemia di Messina, 1823; Abufar, 1823; Il Sonnambulo, 1824; Aristodemo, 1823; Jeanne d' Arc, 1821; Le Solitaire, 1822; Gl' Italici e gl' Indiani, 1823; Le Valet de Chambre, 1823; l'Auberge supposée, 1824; La Belle au bois dormant, 1825; Sangarido, 1827; Masaniello, 1827; La Violette, 1828; Jenny, 1829; Le Nozze di Lamermoor, 1829; L' Auberge d' Auray (with Hérold), 1830; Le Livre de l'Ermite, 1831; Nathalie (with Gyrowetz), ballet, 1832; L'Orgie (ballet), 1831; La Prison d' Edimbourg, 1833; Une Journée de la Fronde, 1833; La Grande Duchesse, 1835; Thérèse, 1838. Masses and Stabat Mater. Orchestral and Pf. music, and miscellaneous single pieces.

His music is ear-catching if shallow, and clever if not learned, and with those attributes he easily earned what he most sought—contemporary fame. His operas are nearly always pleasing if sometimes trivial, and his comic faculty was humorous rather than flippant.

CARBONELLI (Stefano). Italian violinist, B. Italy, beginning of 18th century. S. violin under Corelli. Musician to Duke of Rutland, in England, 1720. Leader of the opera band, London. Leader at the Haymarket, 1721. Leader at Drury Lane Theatre, 1725. Married to Miss Warren. Latterly became wine merchant to the king. D. London, 1772.

He published twelve solos for a violin and bass, but was chiefly famous as a violinist.

CARCASSI (Matteo). Italian guitar-player, B. 1792. D. Paris, 1853.

His works consist chiefly of arrangements of airs from popular operas for the guitar. He also wrote a standard method for his instrument, and was one of the finest performers on the guitar.

CARDON (Louis). French comp. and harp-player, B. Paris, 1747. D. Russia, 1805. Known by his method for the harp and a few compositions for the same.

CARESTINI (Giovanni). Italian contralto vocalist, B. Ancona, 1705. *Début* at Rome in Buononcini's "Grisilda," 1721. Appeared in London, Dec., 1733. Returned to Italy, and sang with much success there and in other parts of Europe. D. [1758-60].

CAREW (Miss ?). English soprano vocalist, B. Oct. 16, 1799. S. under Welsh, and her parents. Played small parts in Covent Garden Theatre. *Début* as operatic vocalist, Covent Garden, July, 1815. Sang at the English Opera House, 1818, etc. D. [?]

She was an excellent ballad singer, being especially successful in sentimental songs.

CAREY (Henry). English comp. and minor poet, natural son of George Saville, Marquis of Halifax, B. 1692 [1685]. Received some instruction in music from Roseingrave and Geminiani. Otherwise self-taught. Was for a time a teacher of music. Life spent chiefly in writing music for the theatres, and engaging in convivial enjoyments. D. (? by suicide) London, Oct. 4, 1743.

WORKS.—*Musical Dramas, etc:* The Contrivances, 1715; The Honest Yorkshireman, 1736; Amelia, 1732; Teraminta, 1732; Chrononhotonthologos, 1734; The Dragon of Wantley (words only), 1737; The Dragoness (otherwise known as Marjery, or a worse Plague than the Dragon), 1738. Betty, 1739; Nancy, 1739. Poems, 1720; Cantatas, 1732. The Musical Century, in 100 English Ballads on various Subjects and Occasions, etc., Lond., 2 v., 1737-1740; Dramatic Works (Collected), 1743. *Interludes:* Thomas and Sally, etc. Melody of "God Save the Queen" (?)

Carey is now remembered chiefly on account of his ballad "Sally in our Alley;" his attacks on the Italian opera; and his unfortunate career. His ballad is a very fine specimen of its class, though it is by no means a very refined or genuine example of the domestic ballad, being rather mock-sentimental than natural. His attack on the Italian opera, in "The Dragon of Wantly" and its sequel, is one of the first endeavours of our native musicians to regain their natural position in their own country. Although the sparkling music is by Lampe (a German) it is none the less true that all the point and half of the success of the piece was due to Carey's clever satire. The independence shown at that period of English music could be well imitated at the present time, when a mystical Teuton is as highly prized as a piece of Etruscan pottery. His claim to be regarded as the composer of "God save the Queen" is one of the knotty points in musical controversy, and has not yet been decided with any degree of authority.

CAREY (George Saville). English poet and dramatist, son of above, B. 1743. Wrote a number of farces and dramatic pieces of varying merit, Collection of Songs; Poems, 1787, etc. D. 1807.

CARISSIMI (Giacomo). Italian comp., B. Marino, near Rome, 1604 [1580]. Chap.-master at Assisi, and of Church of S. Apollinare, Rome. D. Rome, 1674 [1670]. Biography obscure.

WORKS.—Concerti Sacri, a 2, 3, 4, e 5 voci, 1675; Missæ 5 et 9 vocum, 1663 1666. *Oratorios:* Balthazar; David and Jonathan; Abraham and Isaac; The

Last Judgment; Jonah; Solomon; Job; Hezekiah. Motets, and a great amount of music in manuscript.

Carissimi is one of the large number of musicians who are reckoned more influential in an educational than in an artistic sense. His development of the recitative and the innovations which he introduced into sacred music place him among the number of great reformers. He educated and influenced a number of eminent composers, among them being A. Scarletti, Buononcini, Cesti, etc. He was one of the first to introduce the string orchestra into the service of the church, and was likewise a great reformer of melody and rhythm. His cantatas, or rather oratorios, are remarkable works for the period which produced them, and must be regarded as the forerunners of the more magnificent effusions of Handel. He is not known to have written for the stage, else his influence on dramatic music might have anticipated the labours of Monteverde. His works, or some of them, have been reprinted in England; and "Jonah," under the editorship of Henry Leslie, will be found a most interesting work. His other works are not so popular, though some of them have been adapted to the words of English anthems.

CARLBERG (Gotthold). German comp., cond., and editor, B. 1837. Resides in New York as teacher and editor of a Musical Journal. Has written cantatas, songs, etc.

CARLETON (Hugh). English writer, author of "The Genesis of Harmony: An Inquiry into the Laws which govern Musical Composition," Lond., 1882.

CARLEZ (Jules Alexis). French comp. and writer, B. Caen, Feb. 10, 1836. Comp. Pf., org., and church music. Director of Caen Cons., 1882.

CARLTON (Rev. Richard). English divine and comp., flourished during end of 16th and beginning of 17th centuries. He wrote "Twenty-one Madrigals for five voyces," Lond., 1601; and contributed "Calm was the Air," a madrigal for 5 voices, to the "Triumphs of Oriana." His biography is unknown.

CARMICHAEL (Peter). Scottish writer, author of the "Science of Music Simplified," Glasgow, 8vo, 1860.

CARMICHAEL (S.) Scottish writer, author of "Dictionary of Musical Terms and Elementary Rules," Lond., 8vo, 1878.

CARNABY (William). English comp. and org., B. London, 1772. S. under Nares and Ayrton as Chor. in Chap. Royal. Org. at Eye, Suffolk. Org. at Huntingdon. Bac. Mus., Cantab., 1803. Dec. Mus., Cantab., 1808. Org. at Hanover Chap., Regent St., London, 1823. D. London, Nov. 13, 1839.

WORKS.—Twelve Collects for 4 voices, in score, with organ accomp.; Sanctus for 5 voices; Six Canzonets for voice and Pf.; Six Songs for voice and Pf. Glees, various. Anthems. MS. Works. The Singing Primer, or Rudiments of Solfeggi, with Exercises in the principal Major and Minor Keys, Lond., 1827.

CARNICER (Ramon). Spanish operatic comp. and teacher, B. Lerida, Oct., 1789. Prof. at Madrid Cons. D. Madrid, Mar., 1855.

CARNIE (William). Scottish writer and editor, B. Aberdeen towards the close of 1824. Was originally a letter engraver. Became a student of literature and music. Precentor of Established Ch., Banchory-Devenick, Aberdeen, 1845. Inspector of Poor for same parish. 1847. Sub-Editor of the *Aberdeen Herald*, 1852. Precentor of the West, or High Ch., Aberdeen, 1854. Clerk and Treasurer to the Managers of Aberdeen Royal Infirmary and the Lunatic Asylum, 1861. Was local correspondent for a time to the *Times* and the *Scotsman*.

WORKS.—Psalmody in Scotland, a Lecture, Aberdeen, 8vo, 1854; Northern Psalter, containing 402 Psalm and Hymn Tunes; Anthem Appendix to do.; Precentor's Companion and Teacher's Indicator; Contributions to periodical literature, etc.

Mr. Carnie's labours have done everything to promote good psalmody in the North of Scotland. In 1854, at the request of the local Young Men's Christian Association, he delivered a lecture on Psalmody to an audience numbering over 2000 persons. This lecture (one of the first on the subject ever given, so far as we know, in Scotland) was illustrated by the Harmonic Choir in a style which awakened great local interest in regard to the "Service of Sacred Song." Indeed, to this meeting may be ascribed the great desire for psalmody improvement which arose over the whole of the north-eastern districts of Scotland. Continuing his efforts to raise the standard of congregational singing, Mr. Carnie's name became widely known. His "Northern Psalter" (1870) obtained immediate popularity over all Scotland, and amongst all Presbyterian denominations, and at the present time upwards of 60,000 copies of his psalmodic works have been circulated.

CAROLAN. See O'CAROLAN.

CARON (Firmain). Dutch comp. of the 16th century. Writer of church music, madrigals, and other works.

CARPANI (Giuseppe). Italian comp., B. Jan. 28, 1752, in Lombardy. S. at Milan. D. Vienna, Jan. 22, 1825. Comp. oratorios and church music, etc. Author of "Le Haydine, ovvero lettere su la vita e le opere del celebre maestro Giuseppe Haydn," Milan, 8vo, 1812. Trans. into French by Mondo, Paris, 1837. "Le Rossiniane, ossia lettere musico-teatrali," 8vo, 1824.

CARPENTER (Joseph Edward). English lyrical writer. D. May, 1885. Has published Lays for Light Hearts, 1835; Songs and Ballads, 1844; Poems and Lyrics, 1845; Border Ballads, 1846; Lays and Legends of Fairy Land, 1849.

Mr. Carpenter belongs to that school of poets founded by T. Haynes Bayly, and to which belong Messrs Oxenford, Guernsey, Enoch, Bellamy, etc. He has written a great number of lyrics which have been, with their musical settings, highly successful. Among the composers who have availed themselves of Mr. Carpenter's prolific talent may be named J. L. Hatton, C. W. Glover, L. Phillips, T. Distin, S. Glover, F. N. Crouch, J. P. Knight, J. W. Cherry, Tom Cooke, and numerous others.

CARR (?) American pianist, comp., and writer. Author of Analytical Instructor for the Pianoforte (Ditson, Boston), n. d. Preludes for the Pianoforte (do.) Chant Mass in D. Mass in C minor. Songs and Pianoforte Music.

CARRENO (Theresa). Italian pianist and comp., B. Caraca, Venezuela, Dec. 22, 1853. Has played in the U. S. A., France, etc. Married to M. Emile Sauret the violinist.

CARRETTI (Giuseppe Maria). Italian comp., B. Bologna, Oct. 10, 1690. D. Bologna, July 8, 1774. Writer of motets, masses, and other sacred music.

CARRODUS (John Tiplady). English violinist, B. Keighley, Yorks, Jan. 20, 1836. S. under Molique at Stuttgart and London. Violinist at Covent Garden Theatre. *Début* as soloist, April 22, 1863. Leader at Covent Garden Theatre. Leader at principal Provincial Musical Festivals, etc.

Mr. Carrodus is the leading English violinist at the present time, and he performs in a powerful and skilful, yet withal unpretending manner, the works of the great composers for the violin. His tone is firm and good in quality, while his executive abilities are of the first order.

CARTER (George). English org. and comp., B. London, Jan. 26, 1835. S. under Sir John Goss. First appointed an org., 1847. Org. successively at S. Thomas', Stamford Hill, 1848; Christ Ch., Camberwell, 1850; Trinity Ch., Upper Chelsea, 1853; S. Luke's, Chelsea, 1860; Montreal Cath., 1861-70.

WORKS.—Sinfonia-cantata, Psalm 116, "I love the Lord," Royal Albert Hall, 1872; Evangeline, cantata (Longfellow), R. A. Hall, 1873, and at Crystal Palace; Tema con variazione in E flat, for organ; Grand festival march in D, for organ; Opera: "Fair Rosamond" (MS.); Italian opera: "Nerone" (MS.); Operetta: Golden Dream, for 5 voices; Songs and miscellaneous music.

Mr. Carter is a good organist, and has performed at New York, Boston (1865-67), Leipzig, Berlin, Dresden (1871), and London (1871-73). His compositions have been performed with success in many different towns.

CARTER (Henry). English org. and comp., brother of above, B. March 6, 1837. Was org. at Quebec Cath. Resides in New York as org. and teacher. Has composed songs, quartets, organ music, etc.

CARTER (Thomas). Irish comp., B. Ireland, 1735 [1758, 1768, also given]. S. probably in Ireland under his father. Org. of S. Werburgh's Ch., Dublin, 1751-69. Travelled in Italy for a time [1770-1]. Cond. of theatre in Bengal [1771-2]. Settled in London as teacher and comp. to the theatres, 1773. D. London, Oct. 12, 1804.* (Date 1800 incorrect.)

WORKS.—*Musical Dramas:* The Rival Candidates, 1775; The Milesians, 1777; The Fair American, 1782; The Birthday; The Constant Maid; Just in Time. Lessons for the Guitar; Concerto for bassoon and Pf.; Six Sonatas for the Pf. Songs, detached and in collections, etc.

Carter, as composer of "O Nannie, wilt thou gang wi' me?" has been accorded a larger degree of fame in connection with it than any other musical composer who has produced a single celebrated piece. The merits of the song are well known, and its imitation of the Scottish style is probably the secret of its success. Like other celebrated efforts the authorship has been doubted, but proofs in abundance are existing to firmly establish Carter's claim. A letter in the "Gentleman's Magazine," claiming the song for a Mr. Williams, cannot be accepted as affording a more powerful claim than is already advanced on behalf of Carter. Apart from this song his merits as a composer are not great.

CARTER (William). English org., comp., and cond., brother of GEORGE and HENRY, B. London, Dec. 7, 1838. S. under his father and E. Pauer. Chor. in S. Giles', Camberwell, 1845; at Chap. Royal, Whitehall; and at King's Coll., London. Org. of Christ Ch., Rotherhithe, 1848; Little Stanmore, Whitchurch, 1850; S. Mary, Newington, Surrey, 1854; S. Helen's, Bishopsgate, 1856. Org. in exchange with his brother HENRY, of Quebec Cath., 1859. Cond. largest Handel Festival ever given in Canada, at Quebec, April 13, 1859. Org. of S. Stephen's, Westbourne Park, Lond., 1860; St. Paul's, Onslow Square, 1868. Established Bayswater Musical Soc., 1860. Cond. of Lond. Choral Union, 1861. Established choir of 1000 voices on opening of the Royal Albert Hall, 1871.

WORKS.—Placida, the Christian Martyr, cantata, 5 Dec., 1871; Thanksgiving anthem for recovery of H.R.H. the Prince of Wales, 1872, "Let the people praise Thee"; Repent you for the kingdom of Heaven, anthem; St. George and Merrie England, part song; Arrangements of national airs for choir; *Songs:* The Vision; Beautiful Clouds; My soul doth magnify; Holy Christmas morn; Not for ever; Brave and Fair, etc.

Mr. W. Carter and his choir are among the most familiar features of musical London. He has established at the Royal Albert Hall an annual series of concerts, at which good works are continually being produced. In the past he has brought forward works by Handel, Haydn, Mendelssohn, Mozart, Gounod, Randegger, J. F. Barnett, Bexfield, Dearle, etc.; not to speak of a great number of popular arrangements of national airs. His ability as an organist is great, while he excels as a conductor.

CARTIER (Jean Baptiste). French violinist, B. Avignon, May 28, 1765. D. Paris, 1841. Comp. of music for violin.

CARTWRIGHT (Thomas). Puritan divine (1535-1603) who wrote against the use of music in public worship. Full particulars of what views he held will be found in Hawkins' "History of Music."

CARULLI (Ferdinando). Italian comp. and guitar-player, B. Naples, Feb. 10, 1770. S. at Naples. Went to Paris, 1808; teacher and composer there. D. Paris, Feb., 1841.

Carulli wrote a great number of transcriptions, variations, and original airs for the guitar, on which he was one of the greatest performers. His studies and method for the guitar are useful. His son Gustave (1797-1877) wrote vocal music.

---

* *Gentleman's Magazine,* 1824.

CARUSO (Luigi). Italian comp., B. Naples, Sept. 25, 1754. D. Perouse, 1822. Wrote a number of operas of transitory merit.

CARVALHO (Joao de Sousa). Portuguese comp. who flourished during middle of eighteenth century. He studied in Italy, and produced operas, pastorals, and cantatas.

CARVALHO-MIOLAN (Marie Caroline). French soprano vocalist, B. Marseilles, Dec. 31, 1827. S. under Duprez at Paris Cons., 1843-47. Gained first prize for singing, do. *Début* at Opera Comique, Paris, 1849, and appeared in operas of Hérold, etc., till 1854. Married to Léon Carvalho, or Carvaille, 1853. Appeared in London, at Italian Opera, 1860. Separated from her husband, 1862. Has appeared chiefly in Paris, in operas by Meyerbeer, Gounod, Thomas, Auber, etc. Madame Carvalho has a powerful voice of great compass, over which she has perfect command. She retired from the stage in 1882.

CARY (Annie Louise). American contralto vocalist, B. Maine, U.S.A., 1846. She studied in America, and has sung in oratorio and in concert music with the greatest success. Her voice is pleasing and her manner refined. She is probably the leading American contralto of the present day, and is accorded a very high place in popular estimation. Her personal appearance is good, and her technical training has been of the highest order. She has sung principally in America, in nearly every important town of which she has appeared with success. Married to C. M. Raymond, a New York broker, 1882.

CASALI (Giovanni Battista). Italian comp. and org., B. 1730. Flourished at Rome during middle of 18th century. He composed masses, oratorios, and operas, all of which are now defunct. He is chiefly remembered as the master of Grétry. He was a chapel-master at Rome about 1760. D. Rome, 1792.

CASAMORATA (Luigi Ferdinando). Italian comp. and writer, B. Wurtzburg, May 15, 1807. Writer of masses, psalms, motets, hymns, theoretical works, etc. D. Florence, Sept. 24, 1881.

CASE (George). English writer, author of "Instructions for the Concertina, from the first Rudiments to the most difficult style of Performance," fo., n. d. "Tutor for the Violin," etc.

CASE (John). English physician and writer, B. Woodstock about middle of 16th century. Chor. at New Coll. and Christ Coll., Oxford. Fellow of St. John's Coll., Oxford. Lecturer at Oxford. D. Jan., 1600.

WORKS.—The Praise of Musicke, wherein its Antiquity, Dignity, Delectation, and Use, are discussed, Oxford, 8vo, 1586. Apologia Musices, tem vocalis quam instrumentalis et mixtae, Oxford, 12mo, 1588. Philosophical works, etc.

The "Praise of Musicke" is an exceedingly quaint work, and at the present date of great rarity. The writer was an enthusiast of the highest order.

CASORTI (Alexander). German violinist and comp., B. Coburg, Nov. 27, 1830. S. at Brussels Cons. D. Sept. 28, 1867. Comp. of "Marie," opera, violin music, and songs.

CASPERS (Louis Henri Jean). German pianist and comp., B. Paris, Oct. 2, 1825. S. at Paris Cons. D. Dec. 19, 1861. Composed operas, cantatas, Pf. music, songs.

CASSON (Miss ?). English vocalist and comp. towards the beginning of the present century. She wrote a number of vocal pieces of varying merit, among which may be named the songs : The Cuckoo ; Attend, ye nymphs ; Snowdrop ; God save the Queen ; etc. Her biography has not been preserved.

CASSON (Thomas). English org. and writer, of Denbigh. Author of "The Modern Organ, a Consideration of the prevalent Theoretical and Practical Defects in its Construction, with Plans and Suggestions for their Removal," Lond., 8vo [c. 1883].

CASTALDI. See GASTOLDI.

CASTIL-BLAZE. See BLAZE.

CASTILLON DE SAINT VICTOR (Alexis, Vicomte de). French amateur comp., B. 1829. D. Paris, Mar. 5, 1873. Wrote symphonies, quartets, Pf. music, and songs.

CASTRUCCI (Pietro). Italian violinist, B. Rome, 1689. Came to England, 1715. Leader at Italian opera, supplanting Corbet. Performed at principal London concerts. Supplanted at the Italian opera house by Festing. D. Rome, 1769.

This violinist held a respectable position as a violinist in his day, and composed a few unimportant pieces. He was deemed a lunatic by his contemporaries—probably on just grounds.

CATALANI (Angelica). Italian soprano vocalist, B. Sinigaglia, Ancona, Oct., 1779. S. in Convent at Gubbio. Début at Venice in Mayer's "Lodoiska," 1795. Sang successively in Rome, Milan, Florence, Naples, and other Italian towns. Sang in Italian opera at Lisbon and in Spain. Married to M. Valabrègue, a French officer. Appeared at London, Dec. 15, 1806 (King's Theatre). Sang in Paris, where she undertook the management of the Italian opera. Travelled in Europe. Re-appeared in London, 1824. D. Paris, June 12, 1849.

"Madame Catalani's style is still purely dramatic. By this epithet, we mean to convey the vivid conception that exalts passion to the utmost pitch of expressiveness; the brilliancy of colouring that invests every object upon which the imagination falls with the richest clothing, that gives the broadest lights and the deepest shadows."— *Quarterly Musical Review*, 1821.

Catalani acquired a great fortune on the stage, and devoted a portion of it to the rearing of young Italian girls for the musical profession. She retired to an estate in Tuscany and was herself one of the teachers in connection with the school which she had endowed.

CATEL (Charles Simon). French comp. and writer, B. L'Aigle (Orne), June, 1773. S. at Paris Royal School of Music, under Gossec, Sacchini, etc. Assistant Prof. at Paris School of Music, 1787. Attached to the Opera at Paris, 1790. Chief (with Gossec) of the Garde National. Prof. of Harmony at Paris Cons. ; Inspector of do., 1810-14. Mem. of the Institute of France, 1817. Chev. of Legion of Honour, 1824. D. Paris, Nov. 29, 1830.

WORKS.—*Operas:* Sémiramis, 1802 ; L'Auberge de Bagnères, 1807; Les Artistes par occasion, 1807 ; Alexandre ches Apelles, ballet, 1808; Des Bayadères, 1810 ; Des Aubergistes de qualite, 1812 ; Premier en date, 1814 ; Liége de Mézières (with Isouard and Cherubini) ; Wallace, ou le Ménestrel écossais, 3 acts, Paris, 1817 ; Zirphile et Fleur de Myrte, 1818 ; L'Officier enlevé, 1819. Quartets for string and wind instruments. Symphony in F. Overtures. Hymn of Victory, 1794. De Profundis, 1792. Traité d'Harmonie, Paris, 1802. Translated by Lowell Mason, Boston, U.S., 1832 ; and by Speranza and T. Westrop, Lond., 1875.

Though now known only as the writer of a first-rate book on harmony, Catel was nevertheless one of the most refined and learned composers ever produced by France. His operas are few in number, but their quality is of the highest order, and "Wallace" was for long regarded as his finest work. His treatise on harmony was the text-book used in Paris Conservatoire, and has not been supplanted altogether in France or elsewhere.

CATLEY (Ann). English soprano vocalist, B. London, 1745. Articled to Bates, the comp., 1760. Appeared at Vauxhall Gardens, 1762. Sang at Covent Garden Theatre, Oct. 8, 1762. Involved in a scandalous criminal case. 1763. Sang in Ireland, 1763-1770. Sang again at Covent Garden Theatre, 1771. Made last appearance in Public, 1784. Supposed to have been latterly married to General Lascelles, with whom she lived previous to her death. D. near Brentford, Oct. 14, 1789.

The criminal case above alluded to in this singer's life was an action raised at the instance of her father against Bates, Sir Francis Delavel, and an attorney named Fraine for conspiring to prostitute her, by agreement, to the person named Delavel. Her father gained his case. She was a great favourite in London and in Ireland,

and was one of the few successful vocalists who at that time made use of the Staccato style. Her biography is given in "The Life and Memoirs of Miss Ann Catley," by Miss Ambross, Lond., n. d.

CAURROY (Francois Eustache du). French comp. and org., B. 1549. Successively Chap.-master to Charles IX., Henry III., and Henry IV. of France. Canon of the Holy Chapel of Paris. Prior of St. Aioul. D. Paris, 1609.

WORKS.—Missa pro defunctis quinque vocum, Paris. Preces ecclesiasticæ, 2 books, 1609; Mélanges de Musique, contenant des chansons, des psaumes, des noels, Paris, 1610; Fantaisies à trois, quatre, cinq et six parties, etc., Paris, 1610.

Caurroy was at one time regarded as the leading composer of France, but his reputation was almost local, and has not been lasting.

CAUSTON (Thomas). English comp. and org., flourished during 16th century. Was Gent. of Chap. Roy. during reigns of Edward VI., Mary, and Elizabeth. D. Oct. 28, 1569. Contributed to Day's "Certain Notes set forth in four and three parts, to be sung at the Morning, Communion, and Evening Prayer." His compositions appear also in Day's "Psalms," Lond., 1563.

CAVACCIA (Giovanni). Italian comp., B. Bergamo [1556]. Chap.-master Bergamo Cath.; do., St. Maria Maggiore, Rome. D. Rome, 1626. Comp. madrigals and church music.

CAVAILLE. A Firm of French Organ-Builders of long standing, presently represented by M. Cavaille-Coll of Paris. They have erected some of the best continental organs, and are widely known for the fine quality of their workmanship.

CAVALIERI (Emilio del). Italian comp. of noble birth, B. 1550. Associated with Caccini, Bardi, Peri, etc. in founding Italian opera. D. about end of 16th century [1598].

He set to music the first known oratorio, which was given at Rome in 1600. The title of this piece is ["La Rappresentazione di Anima e di Corpo." The details in connection with this representation are curious, and will be found in Burney's History.

CAVALIERI (Katharina). Italian soprano vocalist, B. near Vienna, 1761. D. June, 1801.

CAVALLI (Pietro Francesco), or CALETTO. Italian comp. and org., B. Crema, Venice, 1610 [1599]. Singer in choir of St. Mark's, Venice, under Monteverde, 1617. Second org. at St. Mark's, 1640. Went to Paris on invitation of Cardinal Mazarine, 1660. Returned to Venice, 1665. First org. at St. Mark's, 1665. Chap.-master of St. Mark's, Nov., 1668. D. Venice, Jan. 14, 1676.

WORKS.—*Operas:* Le Nozze di Teti e di Peleo, 1639; Gli amori d'Apollo e Dafne, 1640; La Didone, 1641; Amore innamorato, 1642; La virtù de' strali d'amore, 1642; Narciso ed Eco immortalati, 1642; L'Egisto, 1643; La Deidamia, 1644; Il Titone, 1644; Il Romolo ed il Remo, 1644; La prosperità infelice de Giulio Cesare dittatore, 1646; La Torilda, 1648; Giasone, 1649; L'Euripo, 1649; La Bradamante, 1650; L'Orimonte, 1650; L'Aristeo, 1651; Alessandro vincitor di se Stesso, 1651; L'Armidero, 1651; La Rosinda, 1651; La Calista, 1651; L'Eritrea, 1652; Veremonda, 1652; L'Amazone d'Aragona, 1652; L'Elena rapita da Teseo, 1653; Xerse, 1654; La Statira, 1655; L'Erismena, 1655; Artemisia, 1656; Antioco, 1658; Elena, 1659; Scipione Africano, 1664; Muzio Scevola, 1665; Ciro, 1665; Pompeo Magno, 1666; Egisto, 1667; Coriolano, 1660. Sacred and other music. Cavalli was a celebrated vocalist, and one of the first to employ airs and recitatives in his operas in a dramatic manner. He is also mentioned as the first to have used modulations to express changes of feeling or sentiment in his dramatic music, and was noted for his careful regard to correct and appropriate rhythm.

CAVALLINI (Ernesto). Italian clarionet-player, B. Milan, Aug. 30, 1807. D. Milan, Jan. 7, 1874. Composer of concertos, variations, airs, caprices, and other pieces for his instrument. He was a celebrated performer on the clarionet, but a somewhat mediocre composer.

CAVE-ASHTON (Gertrude) née HOLMAN ANDREWS, English soprano vocalist, B. London, April 17, 1855. S. under her mother and Thorpe Pede. *Début* at the Alexandra (Park) Theatre, 1873. Married to Mr. Cave, 1875. Sang in Provinces with Mr. Sims Reeves, etc. ; and during 1877 with the Hersee Opera Company. Has since appeared at many important concerts in London and the Provinces.

CAVENDISH (Michael). English comp., flourished during latter portion of sixteenth century. He composed "Ayres for Four Voyces," 1599; and contributed the five-part madrigal "Come, gentle swains" to the "Triumphs of Oriana," 1601. He also aided in harmonising "The Whole Booke of Psalmes," 1592. His biography has not been preserved.

CAVOS (Catterino). Italian comp., B. Venice, 1775. D. April 28, 1840. Wrote operas, songs, etc.

CAZALET (Rev. William Wahab, M.A.) English divine and writer, B. about commencement of present century.

WORKS.—The History of the Royal Academy of Music, compiled from Authentic Sources, Lond., 8vo, 1854 ; On the right Management of the Voice in Speaking and Reading, with some remarks on Phrasing and Accentuation, Lond., 8vo, 1855 (third edit., 8vo, 1860) ; The Voice, or the Art of Singing, Lond., 8vo, 1861 ; On the Reading of the Church Liturgy, 8vo, 1862; Exhibition Lecture, On the Musical Department of the late Exhibition, Lond., 1852.

CAZOT (Francois Felix). French comp., B. Orleans, April 6, 1790. S. at Paris Cons. D. 1858. Composed operas and pf. music.

CAZZATI (Maurizio). Italian comp. and org., B. Mantua, 1620. D. [1677]. Chap.-master at Bologna. Wrote masses, motets, psalms, and canzonets, published between 1645-85.

CECCHERINI (Ferdinando). Italian tenor vocalist, B. Florence, 1792. Prof. of singing at Florence. D. there, Jan. 12, 1858. He wrote songs and teaching pieces.

CECILIA (Saint). The patron saint of music, B. Rome about 200 A.D. Martyred 230 A.D. Her connection with music is doubtful, and the accounts of her miraculous escapes from death are unauthenticated or mythical. Odes for her day, which is celebrated by Roman Catholics on Nov. 22, were written by Dryden and Pope, etc., and have been set by a large number of the older composers. Paintings in connection with her martyrdom and otherwise have been executed by Raphael and Domenichino.

CECIL (Rev. Richard). English divine and musician, B. London, Nov. 8, 1748. S. at Oxford, 1773. Deacon, 1775. Priest, 1777. Minister of S. John's Chap., Bedford Row, London, 1780. Rector of Cobham and Birley, Surrey, 1800. D. Hampstead, Aug, 15, 1810.

WORKS.—Selection of Psalms and Hymns for the Public Worship of the Church of England, Lond., n.d. ; 32nd edition issued, 1840 ; Sermons, lectures, etc. Best known by his anthem, "I will arise, and go to my Father." His daughter THEOPHANIA (B. 1782), org. of S. John's Chap., edited "The Psalm and Hymn Tunes, used at St. John's Chapel, Bedford Row ; Arranged for Four Voices." Lond., 1814. She D. London, Nov. 15, 1879.

CELESTINO (Eligio). Italian violinist, B. Rome, 1739. D. Ludwigslust, Jan. 24, 1812. Resided for a time in London as teacher. Composed for his instrument.

CELLARIER (Hilarion). French comp., B. Florensac (Hérault), March 12, 1818. Wrote operas and Pf. music.

CELLI (Filippo). Italian comp. of operas, etc., B. Rome, 1782. D. London, Aug. 21, 1856.

CELLIER (Alfred). English comp. and cond., [B. London.] Has comp. a number of melodious works, among the most important of which may be named "The Sultan of Mocha," an opera ; "The Spectre Knight," opera by J. Albery, 1878 ; "After All," vaudeville by F. Desprez, 1878 ; "In the Sulks," operetta, 1880 ; Gray's Elegy, Leeds Festival, 1883; Part-songs, songs, and other music.

CELLINI (Francesco). Italian comp., B. Fermo, May 5, 1813. D. Aug. 19, 1873. Comp. chiefly for the church.

CERTON (Pierre). French comp. and org., flourished during 16th century. Master of children of the Holy Chapel at Paris. Comp. 31 Psalms, 4 Masses, a Requiem, and numerous motets.

CERVETTO (Giacomo Bassevi). Italian violoncello player, B. 1682. D. London, Jan., 1783. Was a celebrated performer, and became latterly manager of Drury Lane Theatre, London.

CESTI (Padre, Marco Antonio). Italian comp., B. Arezzo, 1620-4. S. under Carissimi. Chap.-master at Florence, 1646. Resided at Rome, 1658. Tenor singer in the Vatican chap., 1660. Chap.-master to the Emperor Leopold, 1661-67. D. Rome, 1675 [1681].

WORKS.—*Operas:* Orontea, 1649 ; Cesare Amante, 1651 ; La Dari, o lo Schiavo regio, 1663 ; Tito, 1666 ; La Schiava fortunata (with Ziani) ; Argene, 1668 ; Genserico, 1669 ; Argia, 1669 ; Il Pomo d' oro ; cantatas and miscellaneous music.

Cesti is best known by his cantatas, of which he composed a vast number, many being in the Music School of Oxford, the British Museum, and in Continental libraries. He was, with Carissimi, one of the improvers of melody, and the *supposed* inventor of the cantata.

CEUPPENS (Victor). Belgian org. and comp., B. Brussels, July 28, 1835. S. under Fétis, Boisselet, Lemmens, etc. Comp. masses, org. music, songs, etc.

CHADWICK (George W.). American comp. and org., B. Lowell, Mass., Nov. 13, 1854. S. under F. Thayer. Engaged in Olivet Coll., Mich., 1876. S. in Leipzig, Germany, under Jadassohn and Reinecke. S. at Munich under Rheinberger, 1879. Returned to America, 1880. Org. Park St. Ch., Boston. Prof. of harmony, comp., etc., in New England Cons. of Music, Boston.

WORKS.—Trio in C minor, 1877 ; Quartet in G minor, 1878 ; Quartet in C, 1879 ; Overture : Rip Van Winkle, 1879 (prize) ; Symphony for orch. in C, 1882 ; Pianoforte music ; Songs and other vocal music ; Ballad : "The Viking's Last Voyage," male chorus and orch.; Overture : Thalia, etc.

CHALLEN & SONS. English firm of Pianoforte Manufacturers, established in London in 1804. Awarded prize medals at Exhibitions of London (1862), S. Africa (1877), Paris (1878), Melbourne (1881), etc., for the general excellence and durability of their instruments. They have been foremost amongst English makers in the development of the Iron Frame system of construction. Their pianettes and upright Iron Pianos enjoy a wide popularity, and their merits have been attested by many eminent authorities.

CHALLONER (Neville Butler). English harpist and violinist, B. London, 1784. S. in London. *Début* as violinist, 1793. Violinist at Covent Garden Theatre, 1796. Leader at Richmond Theatre, 1799. Leader at Birmingham, Sadler's Wells, etc. Harpist at Italian Opera, London. Tenor player at the Philharmonic Society. Latterly a music seller. D. (?)

WORKS.—Method for the Violin, Lond., n. d. New Guida di Musica, or Instructions for Beginners on the Pianoforte, fo., n. d. Method for Guitar, n. d. ; Method for Flute, n. d. ; Method for the Harp, n. d. Romance and Polacca for Harp, op. 14 ; Two Duets on Scotch Airs, op. 10 ; Three Duets (Trans.), op. 15 ; Duet Concertante for Harp, op. 22. Miscellaneous works for Harp and Pf. Harmonia Sacra, 4 books, Lond., fo., n. d. Lays of Harmony, or the Musical Scrap Book, 1830. National Airs [1830], etc.

CHALLONER (Robert). American musician, author of "History of the Science and Art of Music, its Origin, Development and Progress...," Cincinnati, 8vo, 1880.

CHAMBONNIERES (Jacques Champion de). French org. and comp. who flourished during 17th cent. D. 1670. His compositions consist of pieces for the organ and clavichord, and are remarkably pretty in style as well as very rare.

CHAMPEIN (Stanislas). French comp., B. Marseilles, Nov. 19, 1753. S. at Paris. D. Sept. 19, 1830. Wrote operas, songs, etc.

CHAMPNESS (Samuel). English bass singer, B. [1730]. He sang in concert and dramatic music at the end of the 18th century. Busby speaks favourably of his voice, saying that it was rich and round-toned and universally admired. His biography does not appear to have been very fully recorded. He D. Sept., 1803.

CHANOT (Georges). French violin-maker. B. Mirecourt, March 26, 1801. D. Courcelles, near Paris, Jan. 10, 1885. In company with his sons he made copies of Stradivarius and Guernerius of some merit, and is held in much repute as a maker. Another Chanot (François), made violins on a new principle which, though submitted to the French Academy, have never gained great favour. He was B. 1787. D. 1823.

CHAPPELL (William). English writer and antiquary, B. London, Nov. 20, 1809. Brought up in music publishing business with his Father. Engaged in musical antiquarian studies. Founded (with others) the Percy Society, 1840. Founded the Musical Antiquarian Society, 1840. F.S.A., 1840. Partner in the firm of Cramer & Co., 1843. Treasurer of the Camden Society, etc. Is connected with a number of Learned and Antiquarian Societies.

WORKS.—A Collection of National English Airs, consisting of Ancient Song, Ballad, and Dance Tunes, Interspersed with Remarks and Anecdotes, and preceded by an Essay on English Minstrelsy ; the Airs harmonized for the Pianoforte by Dr. Crotch, G. A. Macfarren, and J. A. Wade. Lond., 4to. part I., 1838 ; II., 1839; III., 1840. Popular Music of the Olden Time : a Collection of Ancient Songs, Ballads, and Dance Tunes, Illustrative of the National Music of England, etc. Lond., Cramer, 2 vols., 8vo [1845-59]. Old English Ditties, Lond., 2 vols., 4to, n.d. History of Music, Art and Science, from the earliest records to the fall of the Roman Empire, with explanations of Ancient Systems of Music, Musical Instruments, and of the true Physiological Basis for the Science of Music, whether Ancient or Modern, Vol. I., Lond., 8vo, 1874. Edited works (Collections of Ancient Poetry) for the Ballad, Percy, and Camden Societies.

Previous to the appearance of Mr. Chappell's work in 1838-40 it had been customary to regard English national music either as non-existent or unworthy of preservation. The want of a genuine lyrical poet to collect and adapt such melodies as existed to pure verse was no doubt the cause of England being considered lacking in respect to national airs. In Scotland and Ireland, Burns and Moore did everything necessary to secure universal fame for their national melodies, while in England the works of Mr. Chappell have done everything to establish its title to be considered a most musical nation. Mr. Chappell is one of the best informed musical antiquaries living, and has shown in his work on the History of Music much careful learning.

CHAPPELL & CO. English firm of music publishers, established in London in 1812 by Samuel Chappell. The firm was originally carried on by Cramer, Chappell and Latour. Samuel Chappell died in 1834 and was succeeded by his son, William, as above noted.

Their publications at the present period are numerous and valuable, and include theoretical works by Rimbault, Richards, etc. ; pianoforte music by Ascher, Benedict, Blumenthal, Chopin, De Kontski, C. Dick, Goodban, Gounod, Herz, Kuhe, Lindahl, Oesten, Osborne, Richards, Rockstro, Schubert, Sloper; arrangements by C. Hallé and Rimbault, and many other valuable copyrights. The vocal publications consist of Chappell's Musical Magazine (Songs and Pf. music in books), operatic part songs, vocal library of part songs, etc., popular operas (arranged for

Pf.), Songs by nearly every good composer. They publish also Tutors and airs for many other instruments, and a large selection of popular music for the harmonium.

Messrs. Chappell have done much to foster among the middle classes of London a taste for first rate chamber music, and the success which attends their "popular" concerts is a sufficient testimony to the fact that a void which was felt by the public is being ably filled. The best performers and the best music are the special characteristics of these concerts.

CHAPPLE (Samuel). English org. and comp., B. Crediton, Devon, 1775. Blind from childhood. S. Pf. Org. at Ashburton, 1795-1835. D. [1845.]

WORKS.—Five songs and a glee, op. 3; Six anthems in score, figured for the organ or Pf., op. 4; A second set of six anthems in score, op. 5; A third set of six anthems and twelve Psalm tunes in score, op. 6; The eighteen anthems, republished (Ashdown and Parry); Three sonatas for the Pf.; Six songs with Pf. accomp.; Anthem for the coronation of George IV.; Single Pf. pieces; Single glees, anthems, and songs.

Looking to the fact that Chapple was blind—an infirmity, by the way, which does not appear greatly to interfere with a musician in the exercise of his profession —it may be said that his anthems are fresh and correct, and his glees and songs melodious and well constructed, showing that their author could write with animation as well as science.

CHARD (George William). English comp. and org., B. 1765. S. under Robert Hudson, in the choir of S. Paul's. Lay-clerk at Winchester, 1778. Org. of Winchester Cath. and Coll. Doc. Mus. Cantab., 1812. D. Winchester, May, 1849.

WORKS.—Twelve glees for three, four, and five voices, Lond. [1811]; Services and anthems, songs, etc.

CHARKE (Richard). English violinist and comp. of middle of 18th century. Married to Charlotte Cibber, by whom he ill-treated, and from whom he soon separated. Notable as the first to compose *medley* overtures (Hawkins). He died in Jamaica of disorders brought on by dissipated habits.

CHARLOT (Joseph Auguste). French comp., B. Nancy, Jan. 21, 1827. D. Sèvres, Aug., 1871. Comp. songs and instrumental music.

CHARLTON (R.). English writer. Author of "Reminiscences and Biographical Sketches of Musicians," Lincoln, 1836.

CHARPENTIER (Marc Antoine). French comp., B. Paris, 1634. Music director to Duke of Orleans. D. Paris, 1702. He comp. a number of operas and other pieces, of which "Medee" achieved some fame.

CHARTON-DEMEUR (Anne Arsene) née CHARTON. French soprano vocalist, B. Saujon, Mar. 5, 1827. Married to M. Demeur, flutist, 1847. She appeared in operas by Meyerbeer, Halévy, Donizetti, Berlioz, etc.

CHASTON (Jules). French comp., B. Marseilles, April 30, 1837. S. at Marseilles Cons. Wrote operas, Pf. music, songs, etc.

CHATTERTON (John Balsir). English harpist and comp., B. Norwich, 1804. S. under Bochsa and Labarre. Prof. of harp at R.A.M. Harpist to the Queen, etc. D. London, April 9, 1871.

WORKS.—Numerous transcriptions from popular operas for the harp; Songs with harp and Pf. accomp., etc.

Chatterton was one of the best among English harp players, and was the instructor of a number of musicians of present note.

CHAUCER (Geoffrey). English poet, B. London [1321]. D. 1400. He describes in the "Canterbury Tales" a number of the manners and usages of his times, many of which are connected with music. Extracts in this connection are given in Hawkins' "History," and in Chappell's "Popular Music."

CHAULIEU (Charles). French comp. and pianist, B. Paris, June 21, 1788. S. under Adam and Catel. Settled in London about 1840. Teacher and composer there. D. London, April 19, 1849.

WORKS.—Op. 1. Two Sonatas for Pf.; Sonatas for Pf., op. 11, 13, 17. Grand Sonata for Pf., flute, and vn., op. 15. Nocturne for Pf., vn., and flute. Caprices, rondos, variations, dances, etc., chiefly on airs from operas, to the number of about 250.

This composer has rapidly declined in popular estimation, and his works are now known only in the school-room, and not extensively even there. His works were brilliant show pieces, which were successful in their day. They have been supplanted by a more powerful and earnest school.

CHAUMET (Guillaume). French comp. and pianist, B. Bordeaux, April 26, 1842. Comp. operas, quartets, songs, Pf. music, etc.

CHAUVET (Charles Alexis). French comp. and org., B. Marnies, June 7, 1837. S. at Paris Cons. Org. in various churches. D. Argenton (Orne), Jan. 28, 1871. Comp. fugues, offertories, and other organ music.

CHAVAGNAT (A. Pierre E.) French comp., B. Paris, Oct. 17, 1845. S. under Massé at Cons. Writer of choruses, songs, and other vocal music.

CHEESE (G. J.) English org. and writer, flourished at end of eighteenth century. Was org. at Leominster and teacher in London. He wrote "Practical Rules for Playing and Teaching the Pianoforte and Organ," n. d.

CHELARD (Hippolyte Andre Jean Baptiste). French comp. and cond., B. Paris, Feb. 1, 1789. S. under R. Kreutzer, Gossec, Méhul, and Cherubini. Gained "Grand Prix de Rome," and S. in Italy under Baini, Zingarelli, Paisiello, and Fioravanti. Violinist at the opera, Paris. Chap.-master to King of Bavaria, Munich. Cond. the great Thuringian Musical Festival at Erfurt, 1831. Cond. series of German opera in London, 1832-33. Musical director at Augsburg, 1836. Chap.-master at Weimar, 1840. D. Weimar, Feb. 12, 1861.

WORKS.—*Operas:* La Casa de Vendere, 1815; Macbeth, 1828; La Table et le Logement, 1829; Minuit, 1829; L'Etudiant, 1832; Le Combat d'Hermann, 1835; Die Seekadetten, 1842; Scheibentoni. Masses. Miscellaneous works, vocal and instrumental, and contributions to musical literature.

CHELL (William). English writer and musician, was lay-vicar and precentor at Hereford. Mus. Bac., Oxford, 1524. He wrote "Musicæ Practicæ Compendium," "De Proportionibus Musicis," etc.

CHELLERI (Fortunio). Italian comp., B. 1668. D. 1757. Wrote operas and church music.

CHÉRI (Victor). French violinist and comp., B. Auxerre, Mar. 14, 1830. S. at Paris Cons., at which he gained several prizes. D. Paris, Nov., 1882. Comp. ballets, violin and Pf. music.

CHERRY (John William). English comp. and teacher, B. London, Dec. 10, 1824. Self-educated in theory and on Pianoforte. Has comp. over 1000 pieces, of which the following are the best known :—

WORKS.—Will-o'-the-wisp; Shells of ocean; Beautiful leaves; The Blacksmith; How beautiful is the sea; My village home; Monarch of the woods; Estelle; Gentle Spring; Sweet Annie; The Invitation; Silently, silently over the sea; Trees of the forest; Upon the lonely shore; Wanton breezes, whither going; Down by the sea; Fair Glen Lochry; Home again to England; Seventh day; Spirit of the whirlpool; Breath soft, summer wind; Summer twilight; Come with me to Fairyland. *Duets:* Elfin revels; Hark! there's music stealing; Let us roam away, etc. Pf. music, dances, etc.

CHERUBINI (Maria Luigi Carlo Zenobi Salvatore). Italian comp., teacher, and writer, B. Florence, Sept. 14, 1760. S. under his Father, Bartolomeo and Alessandro Felici, and Castrucci. Sent, at instance of Grand Duke Leopold, to study under Sarti at Bologna, 1777. Resided in London and held post of composer to the King, 1784-5. Visited Paris, 1786. Returned to Italy, 1787. Settled in Paris, and became director of the Italian Opera, 1788. Inspector at Paris Cons., 1795. Married to Mdlle. Cécile Tourette,

1795. Chev. of Legion of Honour. Visited London again, 1815. Returned to Paris, 1815. Superintendent of the Royal Chapel, 1816. Member of the "Institut." Director of Paris Cons., 1822. D. Paris, March 15, 1842.

WORKS.—Op. 1. Mass in D, 1773; op. 2. Intermezzo, 1773; op. 3. Mass, 1774; op. 4. La Pubblica Felicità, cantata, 1774; op. 5. Psalm, 1775; op. 6. Mass in C, 1775; op. 7. Psalm, 1775; op. 8. Intermezzo, 1775; op. 9. Magnificat, 1775; opp. 10 to 15. Two Lamentations of Jeremiah, a miserere, etc., 1776; op. 16. Motet, 1777; op. 17. Oratorio (name unknown), 1777; op. 18. Te Deum, 1777; op. 19 to 27. Compositions for the Church, 1778; op. 28 to 36. Compositions for the Church, 1779; op. 37 to 47. Church music, sonatas, etc., 1780; op. 48. Il Quinto Fabio, opera, 1780; op. 49 to 61. Church music, sonatas, etc., 1780-1781; op. 62. Armida, opera, Florence, 1782; op. 65. Adriano in Siria, opera, 1782; opp. 64 to 78. Nocturnes, songs, duets, etc., 1782; op. 79. Il Messenzio, opera, 1782; op. 80-83. Songs, duets, etc., 1782; op. 84. Il Quinto Fabio, opera, Rome, 1783 (re-set); op. 85-88. Songs, madrigals, etc., 1783; op. 89. Lo Spose di tre Marito di Nessuna, opera, 1783; opp. 90-92. Air and choruses in oratorio, 1784; op. 93. l'Idalide, opera, 1784; op. 94. L'Alessandro nell' Indie, opera, 1784; opp. 95 to 100. Airs, etc., 1785; op. 101. La Finta Principessa, opera, London, 1785; Il Giulio Sabino, opera, op. 111. London, 1786; Amphion, cantata, op. 112, 1786; Ifigenia in Aulide, op. 131, 1788; Démophon, opera, op. 135, Paris, 1788; Circe, cantata, op. 136, 1789; Lodoïska, opera, op. 182, Paris, 1791; La Libertà, cantata, op. 199, 1793; Kourkourgi, opera, op. 204, 1793; Clytemnestra, cantata, op. 207, 1794; Elisa, opera, op. 209, Paris, 1794; Sixty-five Solfeggi (for use in Conservatoire), op. 212, 1795; Medée, opera, op. 214, Paris, Mar. 13, 1797; L' Hôtellerie Portugaise, opera, op. 224, 1798; La Punition, opera, op. 225, 1799; Les Deux Journées (The Water Carrier, London, 1801 and 1824), op. 229, Paris, Jan. 16, 1800; Epicure, opera (with Méhul), op. 230, 1800; Anacréon, opera, op. 241, Paris, 1803; Achille a Scyros, ballet, op. 246, 1804; Faniska, opera, op. 254, Paris, 1806; Pimmalione, opera, op. 279, Paris, 1809; Le Crescendo, opera, op. 283. Paris, 1810; Mass in D minor, op. 295, 1811; Les Abencérages, opera, op. 299, Paris, 1813; First quartet for strings, op. 317, 1814; Overture in G for orch., op. 318 (written for Philharmonic Soc. Lond.), 1813; Symphony, op. 319 (written for same), 1815; Mass in C, op. 325, 1816; Mass in E flat, op. 338, 1816; Requiem in C minor, op. 349, 1816; Mass in G, op. 372, 1819; Mass in A, op. 403, 1825; Ali Baba, opera, op. 417, 1833; Quartet for strings in D minor, op. 419, 1834; Quartet for strings in E, op. 421, 1835; Quartet for strings in F, op. 424, 1835; Requiem in D minor, op. 426, 1836; Quartet for strings in A minor, op. 427, 1837; Quartet for strings in E minor, op. 428, 1837. Total number of works, including minor pieces not enumerated in foregoing list, 430.

Cherubini was one of the most popular of the many composers who crowded Paris in his day. His claims to recognition rest chiefly on the clear and well-defined character of his writings, together with the great contrapuntal learning which he possessed. Cherubini, indeed, may fairly be reckoned the most refined and theoretically able composer whom Italy has in modern times produced. As to the enduring quality of his work it may be said that not more than a score out of the many above noted will be passed to posterity. It is in his operatic works and church compositions that Cherubini is fully displayed as a great master. Many of his minor works were merely occasional pieces, and have small claims on the attention of modern musicians.

"Though the style of Cherubini belongs more to the German than the Italian school, still he cannot properly be placed amongst the artists of the former : yet his manner is less Italian than that of Mozart; it is purer than that of Beethoven; it is, in fact, the chaste ancient style of Italy, refreshed and decorated with the harmony of modern times. . . . Cherubini is not to be ranked with those musicians whose labours have effected revolutions in the art by an entire transformation of style. Contemporary of Haydn, of Mozart, of Beethoven, of Rossini, Cherubini seems to have been placed by nature amongst those great geniuses as a moderator whose wisdom and firmness was destined to counteract the ideality of the satellites of those luminous planets ; as Reason, by the side of Imagination, corrects her in her eccentric orbit, and focuses her scattered rays. The works of this master will always serve as models, because written on a system of exactitude almost mathematical, and consequently exempt from the changeable affectations of time and fashion, they will survive many a composition of more startling pretensions, and which may have reached a wider renown on its first appearance."—*Adolphe Adam trans. by J. W. Moore.*

As a teacher Cherubini was greatly celebrated, and numbers among his pupils Auber, Halévy, Carafa, Zimmermann, Batton, etc. He wrote a valuable treatise on counterpoint and fugue, trans. as "Course of Counterpoint and Fugue" by J. Hamilton, Lond., 2 vols. 8vo, 1837-41 ; and again by Mary Cowden Clark in 1854, Lond., 8vo (Novello), which is still a standard text-book ; and did much by the encouragement of youthful musicians to foster a high standard of musical culture. See Cherubini, Memorials illustrative of his Life, by E. Bellasis, Lond., 8vo, 1874.

CHÉROUVRIER (Edmond Marie). French comp., B. Sablé, Feb. 7, 1831. Writer of operas, church music, etc.

CHESHIRE (John). English harpist and comp., B. Birmingham, March 28, 1839. Commenced playing the harp when four years of age. S. at R. A. M., 1852-55. S. afterwards under Prof. Sir G. A. Macfarren and J. B. Chatterton. Harpist at the Royal Italian Opera from 1855. Principal Harpist at H. M. Theatre, 1865. Principal Harpist at the Grand Opera, Rio Janeiro, 1858-61. Married to Miss Maria Matilda Baxter, Pianist, 1871. Travelled in Norway and Sweden Concert-giving, 1879.

WORKS.—*Harp:* Six romances, 1855 ; Serenade, Don Quixote ; Album of Harp music, 24 pieces ; Miscellaneous music for the harp. The Buccaneers, a Cantata for 4 voices and orch., 1866. *Pianoforte:* Six easy recreations ; Six operatic recollections ; Reverie ; Souvenir de Brazil ; Marche Bresellienc ; Valse di Bravoura ; Patriotic duet ; Duet in B flat ; Zoë Waltzes ; Chanson d'Amour ; Grazielle ; Gavotte in G ; Mazurka Espanholl ; La Graceuse ; Romance in G ; Second Gavotte in *G. Songs:* Cupid the conqueror ; Hurrah for bluff King Christmas ; I saw thee weep ; Spring Song (words and music) ; Only thee ; The fisher's daughter ; The withered violet ; When her we love is nigh ; Thoughts of the far away ; O never call mine heart thine own ; The Gerster waltz. *Manuscripts:* Overtures for orch. in B flat, D, and F minor ; Cantata, The King and the Maiden (libretto by Arthur Matthison), performed, 1866 ; Diana, opera, written in Brazil ; etc.

Mr. Cheshire is a harpist of the school of Parish-Alvars, and is well known in London and the English provinces as one of the best of modern performers.

CHETHAM (Rev. John). English musician and divine, Vicar of Skipton, Yorks. D. circa, 1760. Published "A Book of Psalmody, all set in Four Parts," 8vo, 1718, of which eleven editions were issued to 1787. An enlarged and revised edition by Houldsworth was issued in London, 1832.

CHEVÉ (Emile Joseph Maurice). French musician and inventor of a musical notation. B. Finisterre, 1804. D. Aug., 1864. Wrote books explanatory and in advocacy of his system, which closely resembles the English Tonic Sol-fa. His "Theory of Music" was translated by George W. Bullen. London, 1880.

CHEYNE (Edwin). Scottish writer, author of "The Amateur's Vocal Guide and Voice Trainer. . . ." Glasgow, 8vo, 1879.

CHIAVACCI (Vincenzo). Italian comp., B. Rome, 1760. D. Warsaw, 1815. Wrote comic operas, etc.

CHICKERING & SONS. American firm of Pianoforte-makers, established at Boston, Mass., by Jonas Chickering, in 1823. Jonas Chickering was born at New Ipswich, N. H., April 5, 1798. He was the son of a blacksmith, and worked at Boston with John Osborne, a Pianoforte-maker, from 1818. He commenced business for himself in 1823, and continued to prosper till 1852, when his works were burned. He was a member of the legislature ; president of the Handel and Haydn Society ; and was far famed for his charitable virtues. He died at Boston, Dec. 8, 1853, and was succeeded by his son, Colonel Thomas E. Chickering, who served during the Civil War in command of the 41st Mass. regiment. He was born at Boston, 22nd Oct., 1824. D. Feb. 14, 1871. The firm is now carried on by members of the same family.

The instruments of the Chickerings are famed for their great solidity and rich quality of tone. The firm has kept pace with the best European makers in every respect, and is one of the most important in the United States. The Pianofortes of Messrs. Chickering are similar in style and quality to the renowned Broadwood instruments, and are second to none in America. The operations of the firm are extensive, and they have branch establishments or agents in every important town in the world.

CHILCOT (Thomas). English comp. and org., B. beginning of 18th century. Org. of Abbey Ch., Bath, 1733. Chilcot is chiefly noted as having been the master of Thomas Linley. He composed two sets of Concertos for the harpsichord; "Twelve English Songs, the words by Shakespeare and other celebrated poets;" single songs, glees, etc.

CHILD (William). English comp. and org., B. Bristol, 1606. S. under Elway Bevin. Mus. Bac., Oxford, 1631. Org. of St. George's Chap., Windsor, 1632. One of Org. of Chap. Royal. Chanter of Chap. Royal, 1660. Mem. of King's private band. Doc. Mus., Oxon., July, 1663. D. Windsor, Mar. 23, 1697.

WORKS.—The First Set of Psalmes of 3 voyces, fitt for private chappells, with a continued bass either for the organ or theorbo, composed after the Italian way, Lond., 1639 (2nd edit., 1650). Divine anthems and vocal compositions to several pieces of poetry, Lond.; Service in D (Boyce); Service in E (Boyce); Praise the Lord, O my Soul, anthem; O Lord, grant the King, anthem; O Pray for the Peace of Jerusalem, anthem; Sing we Merrily, anthem; Services in G, F, and A minor; Court Ayres (a Volume of Secular Vocal Music); Catches and Canons, etc.

Child's compositions are very simple in general style, and his counterpoint has the appearance of having been the production of a century later. "At times, however, as in his service in D, his harmony was rich, glowing, and closely worked. Some few of his full anthems, without any great depth of science or elevation of genius, possess a great degree of warmth, and exhibit imagination." He paved at his own expense the body of Windsor Chapel, and was otherwise charitable.

CHILMEAD (Edmund). English scholar and musician, B. Stow-in-the-Wold, Gloucester, 1611. Clerk of Magdalen Coll., Oxford. Canon of Christ Church, 1632. Resided with Este the musician, in London, 1648. D. London, 1654. Wrote "De Musicâ Antiquâ Græcâ," printed at the end of the Oxford edition of "Aratus," 1672. He gave concerts in London and drew up a catalogue of the Greek MSS. in the Bodleian library. "He was well versed in the old music, and was the best qualified at that time . . . to enter upon this subject."—*Hawk.*

CHIPP (Edmund Thomas). English comp. and org., B. London, Dec. 25, 1823. Son of Thomas Paul Chipp the well-known performer on the kettle-drums and harp. Chor. in Chap. Royal under William Hawes. S. the violin under W. Thomas, J. B. Nadaud, etc., 1832-40. Org. (voluntary) of Albany Chap., Regent's Park, Lond., 1843-6. Mem. H. M. Private band, as violinist, 1843-55. Org. S. John's Chap., Downshire Hill, Hampstead, 1846-7; S. Olave's, Southwark (in succession to H. J. Gauntlett), 1847-52; St. Mary-at-Hill, East-Cheap, 1852-6; Royal Panopticon (in succession to W. T. Best), 1855; Holy Trinity Ch., Paddington (in succession to C. E. Stephens), 1856-62. Mus. Bac. Cantab., Mar. 17, 1859. Mus. Doc., do., June 21, 1860. Org. Ulster Hall, and S. George's Ch., Belfast, 1862-6. Cond. of the Anacreontic, Classical Harmonists, and Vocal Union Societies, Belfast. Org. of Kinnaird Hall, Dundee, Feb.-Nov., 1866; St. Paul's, Edinburgh, May to Nov., 1866. Org. and Master of Chor., Ely Cath., Nov., 1866. Was also member (org.) of the Royal Italian Opera, the Philharmonic, and Sacred Harmonic Society Bands.

WORKS.—Job, an Oratorio, for solo voices, chorus, and orch.; Naomi, a Sacred Idyll, for solo voices, chorus, and orch. Music for the Church Service and home circle, containing 10 Sentences, 24 single and 41 double Chants, 4 Te Deums, 2 Jubilate, 2 Benedictus, 1 Te Deum in unison, 2 Sanctus, 12 Kyrie, 4 Gloria, 2 Magnificat, Nunc Dimittis, 4 Cantate Domine, Deus Misereatur, and 108 Church Melodies in short, common, long and irregular measures, by various authors. Te Deum, Jubilate, Sanctus and Kyrie in D; Church Service in A; Te Deum in D; Gloria for male voices. Three Studies for the Organ, op. 7; Introduction and six variations upon Handel's Harmonious Blacksmith, for organ; Do. and seven variations on God preserve the Emperor, for organ; Lord of all power and might, anthem; Part songs; Songs and miscellaneous Church and Chamber Music. Dr. Chipp has for long held a leading position among English organists. He has given recitals in various parts of England, and has been everywhere received with favour. His style and execution are faultless. Of his compositions the principal are Job and Naomi; both of which are scholarly and effective works. His services, anthems, and other Church works are all impressed with the same marks of excellence, and are in constant use among British Churches.

CHIPP (Thomas Paul). English harpist, Father of the foregoing, B. London, May, 1793. D. June, 1870. Well-known as a drum player and harpist. He played at all the principal festivals.

CHISNEY (E). English writer of "Concertina Instruction," Lond., 8vo, 1853.

CHLADNI (Ernst Florens Friedrich). German writer and acoustician, B. Wittenburg, Nov., 1756. Was for a time Prof. of Law, but latterly devoted himself to the study of Nature. D. Breslau, April, 1827. He wrote works entitled "Entdeckungen über die Theorie des Klanges," Leipzig, 1787; "Die Akustik," Leipzig, 1802; "Ueber die Længetøne einer Saite," Berlin, 1792; etc.

In these works he records the results of many experiments in acoustics which resulted in the discovery of a number of previously unknown principles. He invented several instruments in illustration of his discoveries, such as the Euphon and the Claircylindre.

CHOLLET (Louis Francois). French pianist, org., and comp., B. Paris, July, 1815. D. Paris, March 21, 1851. He was a brilliant pianist, and wrote a great number of transcriptions for his instrument.

CHOPE (Richard Robert). English author and editor, B. Sept., 1830. Vicar of St. Augustine's, S. Kensington, London. Editor of Hymn and Tune Book, 1857-62; Choir and Musical Record, 1862. Versicles, Canticles, Litany. Psalter (Gregorian), 1862. Choral Communion (Marbecke, etc.), 1863; Carols for use in church, 1868-1876; Easter and Harvest Carols, 1884. These works are all well known at home and abroad.

CHOPIN (Francois Frederic). French comp. and pianist, B. at Zelazowa Wola, Warsaw, March 1, 1809. Son of Nicholas Chopin, a French teacher of languages from Lorraine. S. at Warsaw under Zywny and Elsner. Appeared at Vienna, Prague, and Dresden, 1829. Left Poland, 1830. Appeared in Berlin, Munich, and London as pianist, 1831. Settled in Paris, Sept, 1831, where he afterwards lived as the centre of attraction to a large body of fashionable and itinerant musicians. Lived with Madam Dudevant (George Sand), 1836-1847. He visited and played in England and Scotland towards the close of his life. D. Paris, Oct. 17, 1849.

WORKS.—Op. 1. First Rondo for Pf. in C minor; op. 2. "La ci darem la mano" for Pf. and orch., in B flat minor; op. 3. Introduction and Polonaise brillante for Pf. and 'cello; op. 4. Sonata for Pf. in C minor; op. 5. Rondo for Pf. in F; op. 6. Four Mazurkas for Pf.; op. 7. Five Mazurkas for Pf.; op. 8. First Trio for Pf., vn., and cello; op. 9. Three Nocturnes for Pf.; op. 10. Twelve Grand Studies for Pf.; op. 11. Grand Concerto for Pf. and orch. in E minor; op. 12. Variations on Hérold's "Je vends des Scapulaires," for Pf.; op. 13. Grand Fantasia for Pf. and orch., in A; op. 14. Krakowiak, grand rondo for Pf. and orch., in F; op. 15. Three Nocturnes for Pf.; op. 16. Rondo in E flat; op. 17. Four Mazurkas for Pf.; op. 18. Grand Valse for Pf. in E flat; op. 19. Bolero for Pf. in C; op. 20. First Scherzo for Pf.; op. 21. Second Concerto for Pf. and orch., in F minor ; op. 22. Grand Polonaise brillante for Pf. and orch., in E flat ; op. 23. Ballade for Pf., in G minor; op. 24. Four Mazurkas for Pf. ; op. 25. Twelve Studies for Pf. ; op. 26. Two Polonaises for Pf. ; op. 27. Two Nocturnes for Pf. ; op. 28. Twenty-four Preludes for Pf. ; op. 29. First Impromptu for Pf., in A flat ; op. 30. Four Mazurkas for Pf. ; op. 31. Second Scherzo for Pf., in B. minor ; op. 32. Two Nocturnes for Pf. ; op. 33. Four Mazurkas for Pf. ; op. 34. Three Valses for Pf. ; op. 35. Sonata for Pf., in B minor ; op. 36. Second Impromptu for Pf. ; op. 37. Two Nocturnes for Pf. ; op. 38. Second Ballade for Pf. ; op. 39. Third Scherzo for Pf. ; op. 40. Two Polonaises for Pf. ; op. 41. Four Mazurkas for Pf. ; op. 42. Valse for Pf., in A flat ; op. 43. Tarantelle for Pf., in A flat ; op. 44. Polonaise for Pf., in F sharp ; op. 45. Prelude for Pf., in C sharp minor ; op. 46. Allegro de Concert for Pf., in A ; op. 47. Third Ballade for Pf. ; op. 48. Two Nocturnes for Pf., in C minor, and F sharp minor ; op. 49. Fantasia for Pf., in F minor ; op. 50. Three Mazurkas for Pf. ; op. 51. Third Impromptu for Pf. ; op. 52. Fourth Ballade for Pf., in F minor ; op. 53. Polonaise for Pf. ; op. 54. Fourth Scherzo for Pf., in E ; op. 55. Two Nocturnes for Pf. ; op. 56. Three Mazurkas for Pf. ; op. 57. Berceuse for Pf., in D flat ; op. 58. Sonata, in B minor ; op. 59. Three Mazurkas for Pf. ; op. 60. Barcarolle for Pf., in F sharp ; op. 61. Polonaise-Fantasia for Pf., in A flat ; op. 62. Two Nocturnes for Pf. ; op. 63. Three Mazurkas for Pf. ; op. 64. Three Waltzes for Pf. ; op. 65. Sonata for Pf. and 'cello, in G minor. *Posthumous Works*: op. 66. Fantasia-Impromptu for Pf. ; op. 67. Four Mazurkas for Pf. ; op. 68. Four Mazurkas ; A number of minor and detached Pf. pieces without op. numbers.

Pianoforte music is greatly indebted to Chopin for much that is beautiful and original, while his influence has been considerable over succeeding writers of the piano. The numberless beautiful forms which Chopin created are a never failing source of delight to every musician, and stripped of the silly and sentimental meanings with which Liszt and other writers have tried to invest them, are as healthy and enjoyable as anything ever written. It is not within the range of this work to discuss the many technical points involved in their performance or construction, and the reader is referred in consequence to the valuable Life of Chopin by Moritz Karasowski.

CHORLEY (Henry Fothergill). English musician, art critic, novelist, verse writer, journalist, dramatist, general writer, traveller, etc., B. Blackley Hurst, near Billinge, Lancashire, Dec. 15, 1808. Brought up for mercantile life. Commenced connection with the "Athenæum," 1830. Member of the "Athenæum" staff 1833-1871. D. London, Feb. 16, 1872.

WORKS.—Sketches of a Sea-port town, 3 vols., 1835 (novel) ; Conti the Discarded, a novel, 3 vols., 1835 ; Memorials of Mrs. Hemans, 2 vols., 8vo, 1836 ; The Lion, a Tale of the Coteries, 3 vols., 1839 ; Music and Manners in France and Germany, 3 vols., London, 8vo, 1841 ; Pomfret, a novel, 1845 ; Old love and new fortune, a play, 8vo, 1850 ; Modern German music, recollections and criticisms, Lond., 3 vols., 8vo, 1854 ; Roccabella, a novel, 1859 ; Thirty years' musical recollections, Lond., 2 vols., 8vo, 1862 ; Prodigy, a tale of music, Lond., 3 vols., 1866 ; Handel Studies, 2 parts, 1859 ; National music of the World, edited by H. G. Hewlett, 8vo, 1880 ; Librettos for Wallace's Amber Witch ; Bennett's May Queen, etc.; Translations of Mercadante's Elena da Feltre ; Cimarosa's Il Matrimonio Segreto ; Hérold's Zampa ; Auber's Haydée ; Mendelssohn's Son and Stranger, etc.

Chorley was too many-sided ever to attain great distinction in any one of the numerous walks he attempted. His musical writings possess greater literary merit than most of the English work of the same period, but the judgments formed in them, especially with regard to Mendelssohn, have long since been overturned. His "Autobiography, Memoir, and Letters," edited by Henry G. Hewlett, was published in London, 2 vols., 1873, with a photograph.

CHORON (Alexander Etienne). French comp. and writer, B. Caen, Oct. 21, 1771. Director of the Académie Royal de Musique, 1816-17. Founder and director of the Institution Royal de Musique, 1824-30. Master of Monpou, Duprez, Scudo, etc. D. Paris, June 29, 1834.

WORKS.—Principes de Composition des écoles d'Italie, etc., Paris, fo., 3 v., 1808 ; Dictionnaire Historique des Musiciens, par Choron et Fayolle, Paris, 2 vols., 1810-11; Methode élémentaire de Musique, 1811. Other didactic works in association with Fiocchi, Lafage. etc. Masses, psalms, songs, etc. Méthode concertante de Musique, Paris, 1833.

CHOTEK (Franz Xaver). German pianist and comp., B. Liebisch, Oct., 1800. D. Vienna, May, 1852. His works are mostly arrangements and transcriptions for the Pf.

CHOUQUET (Adolphe Gustave). French musician and writer, B. Havre April 16, 1819. Keeper of the Museum of Paris Cons. He is author of "Historie de la Musique Dramatique en France, depuis ses origines jusqu'a nos jours," Paris, 8vo, 1873, and of a number of valuable articles on French musicians in Sir G. Grove's "Dictionary of Music and Musicians."

CHRISTIE (William). Scottish collector and Dean of Moray, compiled "Traditional Ballad Airs, arranged and harmonised for the Pianoforte and Harmonium, from copies procured in the counties of Aberdeen, Banff, and Moray, by W. Christie, M.A., and the late Wm. Christie, Monquhitter, edited by W. Christie, M.A., Dean of Moray," etc. Edin., 2 vols., 4to, 1876-1881. A very handsome and interesting work, containing a number of previously uncollected airs.

CHRYSANDER (Friedrich). German writer. B. Lübthee, Mecklenburg, July 8, 1826. Has written "Ueber die Moll-Tonart in den Volkgesängen, und ueber das Oratorium," Schwerin, 1853. "G. F. Händel (eine kunsthistoriche Biographie)," Leipzig, 3 vols., 1858-67. "Jahrbücher für Musikalische Wissenschaft," 2 vols., 1863-67. Also author of many contributions to periodical literature.

CHURCH (John). English composer, B. Windsor, 1675. Chor. of S. John's Coll., Oxford. Gent. of Chap. Royal, 1697. Lay-vicar Westminster Abbey, Choir-master, do. D. Westminster, Jan. 5, 1741. Author of an Introduction to Psalmody, containing useful Instructions for young Beginners, explained in a familiar and easie manner, Lond., 8vo, 1723. Anthems, songs, etc. A number of Church's anthems are very fine specimens of contrapuntal writing, and are occasionally produced at the present time.

CHURCH (John and Co). American music-publishing firm, established at Cincinnati, by John Church, in 1844. The firm is one of the most important and best known in the United States, and has issued a number of good publications. Messrs. Church publish the magazine known as "Church's Musical Visitor," which contains, in addition to music, a great variety of interesting matters. The principal publications issued by the firm in addition to sheet music, are music books embracing theoretical and practical treatises; school music books; cantatas; glee and chorus music; convention and temperance books; masses; collections of church music; and a few works on general musical literature.

CHURCHILL (?) English pianist and comp. who flourished in London at end of last and beginning of present century. He wrote a number of works for his instrument, including Three Sonatas for Pf. and violin; Six Duos for 2 vns., op. 2; Six Duos for violin and alto; Ten Progressive Lessons for Pf., op. 10; etc.

CHURCHYARD (Thomas). English poet and musician who flourished during the 16th century. Wrote "The Commendation of Musyke by Churchyarde," 1562. For other works see Hazlitt's "Handbook of Poetical Literature," 1867.

CHWATAL (Franz Xaver). Bohemian comp., B. Rinnburg, July 19, 1808. Commenced study of Pf., 1814. Studied at Prague Cons. Resided for a time at Magdeburg, 1835. Writer in musical journals and teacher. D. Soolbade Elmen, June 24, 1879.

Chwatal was a comp. of some repute, and his works are very voluminous, including theoretical books, all kinds of Pf. music, songs, etc., a number of which will be found in the catalogues of the leading English publishers.

L

CIANCHETTI (Pio). Italian comp., B. London, 1799. Appeared as infant prodigy, 1804. Travelled through Germany, Holland, and France. Returned to London, 1805. Accompanist and cond. to Catalani. Teacher and comp. in London. D. Cheltenham, 1851.

WORKS.—Pope's Ode to Solitude. Sixty Italian Catches, for two, three, and four voices (Martini), edited. Cantata for two voices from Milton's "Paradise Lost." Concertos, Pf Music, and Songs. Take, O, take those lips away, song. Music by Mozart, and Beethoven, edited, etc.

This clever musician was at one time well known and popular, though now unknown and not likely ever to have his name restored to popular favour.

CIANCHETTI (Veronica), *née* DUSSEK. German pianist and comp., mother of the above, B. Bohemia, 1779. S. under her Father. Married to Francesco Cianchetti, London, 1797. D. London, 1833. She composed miscellaneous Pf. music, as concertos, sonatas, and transcriptions. A sister of J. L. Dussek.

CIANCHI (Emilio). Italian operatic comp., B. Florence, March 21, 1833.

CIBBER (Susanna Maria), *née* ARNE. English soprano vocalist, B. London, Feb., 1714. S. under her brother, T. A. Arne, etc. *Début* in Lampe's "Amelie," 1732. Married to T. Cibber, 1734. Appeared as a tragic actress, 1736, in Hill's "Zara." Sang at oratorio concerts, etc D. London, Jan. 30, 1766.

CIFRA (Antonio). Italian comp., B. Rome in latter part of 16th century. S. under Palestrina. Master of Loretto Chap., Rome, 1610. D. Rome, 1629. He composed a number of motets and psalms; and "Madrigali a 5 Voci," 1617, which are more learned than pleasing.

CIMA (Giovanni Paolo). Italian org. and comp. who flourished at Milan between 1591 and 1610. He wrote some learned fugues and canons. Other members of the same family are G. B. and A. Cima, neither of great renown.

CIMAROSA (Domenico). Italian comp., B. Aversa, Naples, Dec. 17, 1749. S. at Cons. Santa Maria di Loreto, 1761-2. Resided at Rome, 1772-80. Went to S. Petersburg, and was made chamber musician to Catherine II., 1787. Chap.-master to Leopold II. at Vienna. Chap.-master to King of Italy at Naples, 1793. Imprisoned for promulgating revolutionary principles, 1799. Restored to liberty, 1800. Travelling back to S. Petersburg, but on his way D. Venice, Jan. 11, 1801.

WORKS.—*Operas:* Le Stravaganze del Conte, 1772; La Finta Parigina, 1773; L'Italiana in Londra, 1774; Gli Sdegni per amore, 1776; I Matrimonii in ballo, 1776; Il Fanatico per gli antichi Romani, 1777; Le Stravaganze in Amore, 1777; La Contessina, 1777; I due Baroni, 1777; Amor costante, 1778; I Finti Nobile, 1778; Gli Amanti comici, 1778; Il Duello per complimento, 1779; Il Matrimonio per raggiro, 1779; Il Riturno di Don Calandrino, 1779; Cajo Mario, 1780; Il Mercato di Malmantile, 1780; L'Assalonte, 1780; L'Infedelta fedele, 1780; Il Falegrame, 1780; L'Avviso ai maritati, 1780; Alessandro nel l' Indie, 1781; L'Artaserse, 1781; Il Capricio dramatico, 1781; Il Convito, 1782; La Ballerina amante, 1782; Nina e Martuffo, 1782; La Villana riconosciuta, 1783; L'Oreste, 1783; L'Eroe cinesq, 1783; Il Pittor parigino, 1783; Il Barone burlato, 1784; I due Supposti conti, 1784; Le Statue parlante, 1784; Giannina e Bernadone, 1785; Il Marito disperato, 1785; Il Credulo, 1785; Le Trame deluse, 1786; L'Impresario in Angustie, 1786; La Baronnessa Stramba, 1786; Il Valdomiro, 1787; Il Fanatico burlato, 1787; La Felicità inaspettata, 1790; La Cleopatra, 1790; La Vergine del Sole, 1791; Il Matrimonio Segreto, 1792; La Calamita di cuori, 1793; Amor rende sagace, 1793; I Traci amanti, 1793; Le Astuzie femminili, 1794; Penelope, 1794; I'Inpegno superato, 1795; Gli Orazi e Curiazi, 1794; Achille, 1798; L'Apprensivo raggirato, 1798; Semiramide, 1799; Artemisia, 1801. *Oratorios:* La Guiditta, 1770; Il Trionfa della religione, 1781; Il Martirio di S. Gennero, 1781; Il Sacrificio d'Abramo, 1786. Masses, Cantatas, etc.

The comic operas of Cimarosa are, in the matter of originality of idea and fresh melody, equal to anything produced by his contemporaries. The only one out of all the works given in the foregoing list which has preserved any degree of vitality is "Il Matrimonio Segreto," which is still occasionally produced, and has been printed in England. Cimarosa was the rival of Paisiello, and authorities are divided over their respective merits.

CINTHIE (Laure). See DAMOREAU (Laure C. M.)

CIPRIANO DI RORE. See RORE (Cipriano di.)

CLAGGET (Charles). English violinist and inventor, B. London, 1755. Leader at theatre in Dublin. Invented a number of instruments, 1776-90. Exhibited them in London, 1791. D. 1820.

WORKS.—Six duos for 2 flutes. Six duos for 2 violins. Six duos for violin and violoncello, op. 5. "Musical Phænomena, An organ made without pipes, strings, bells or glasses, the only instrument in the world that will never require to be retuned. A cromatic trumpet, capable of producing just intervals and regular melodies in all keys without undergoing any change whatever. A French horn answering the above description of the trumpet." London, 4to, 1793.

Clagget was a most ingenious mechanic, and aided by the example of his inventions, if not by their perfection, in reforming some of the systems applied to keyed instruments.

CLAGGET (Walter). English comp. and pianist, living towards end of last century. He composed "A new medley overture, consisting entirely of Scots tunes and thirty-six of the most favorite Scots airs, to which is added the favorite air of Chivey Chase. All with variations for 2 violins, or 2 German flutes, and a violoncello, also adapted to the Pianoforte." Clagget's Scots Tunes for the Pianoforte or Flute. Six Solos and Six Scots airs, with variations for the viola or violoncello, with a thorough bass for the Harpsichord, op. 2. Miscellaneous arrangements and teaching pieces for the Pf.

CLAIRVILLE. See NICOLAIE.

CLAPHAM (Jonathan). English writer and divine. Rector of Wramplingham, Norfolk, during 17th century. He wrote "A short and full vindication of that sweet and comfortable ordinance of singing of Psalms." Lond., 1656.

CLAPISSON (Antonio Luigi). Italian comp., B. Naples, Sept. 15, 1808. S. at Paris Cons., 1830-35. Gained 2nd violin prize, 1833. Pupil of Habeneck and Reicha. Violinist at Paris opera. Chevalier of Legion of Honour, 1847. Mem. of the Institute of France, 1854. Prof. of Harmony in Paris Cons., 1861. D. Paris, March 19, 1866.

WORKS.—*Operas:* La Figurante, 1838; La Symphonie, 1839; La Perruche, 1840; Le Pendu, 1841; Frère et Mari, 1841; Le Code Noir, 1842; Les Bergers trumeaux, 1844; Gibby la corneniuse, 1846; Jeanne la Folle, 1848; La Statue Equestre, 1850; Les Mystères d'Udolphe, 1852; La Promise, 1854; La Fanchonnette, 1856; La Sylphe, 1856; Margot, 1857; Les trois Nicolas, 1858; Madame Grégoire, 1861; Don Quixhotte et Sancho, 1847; Dans les Vignes, 1854; Le Coffret de St. Dominique, 1855; Les Amoureux de Perrette, 1855. Romances and Songs to the number of over 200.

Clapisson was a fine melodist and a graceful harmonist. His operas are flowing, though sometimes trivial, and were very popular in their day. He is now principally known by his numerous fine songs.

CLARE (Edward). English writer and org. of present century. D. [London], April 9, 1869. Author of "Analysis of practical Thorough-bass." Lond., fol. [1835]. "A simple guide for chanting for the use of amateurs, followed by the complete service for the Church, and twenty psalms from the Psalter, carefully pointed and adapted to the chants in general use." Lond. (Cocks), 4to, n.d.

CLARI (Giovanni Carlo Maria). Italian comp. and org., B. Pisa, 1669. S. under Colonna. Chap.-master of Cath. of Pistoja. D. [1745-6.]

WORKS.—Il Savio Delirante, opera, Bologna, 1695. Stabat Mater. Mass, for 5 voices and orch., 1712. Collection of vocal duets and trios, 1720. Psalms and miscellaneous Church music.

Clari is chiefly celebrated for his elegant chamber duets and trios, which at one time were in great request. His Church music will be found in modern collections, and is admirable in many respects.

CLARIBEL. See BARNARD (Mrs).

CLARK (John). Scottish collector and violinist of the 18th century. Published "Flores Musicæ, or the Scots Musician, being a general collection of the most celebrated Scots Tunes, Reels, Minuets, and Marches, adapted for the Violin, Hautboy, or German Flute, with a Bass for the violoncello or Harpsichord." Edin., fo. 1773.

CLARK (Richard). English writer and singer, B. Datchet, Bucks., April 5, 1780. Chor. in St. George's Chap., Windsor, under Aylward. Chor. at Eton Coll., under S. Heather. Lay-Clerk at St. George's Chap., and Eton Coll., 1802-11. Secretary of the Glee Club. Lay-Vicar of Westminster Abbey. Vicar-Choral of St. Paul's. Gent. of Chap. Royal, 1820. D. London, Oct. 5, 1856.

WORKS.—Words of the most favourite pieces performed at the Glee Club, Catch Club, and other Societies, London, 8vo, 1814. First volume of poetry, revised, improved, and considerably enlarged, containing the most favourite pieces performed at the Glee Clubs, etc., Lond., 8vo, 1824. Continuation, 1833. An account of the National Anthem entitled "God save the King," etc., Lond.,8vo, 1822. Reminiscences of Handel, His Grace the Duke of Chandos, Powells the Harper, the Harmonious Blacksmith, and others, London. fo., 1836. Reading and playing from score simplified, Lond., 8vo, 1838. An Examination into the derivation, etymology, and definition of the word "Madrigale," Lond., 8vo, 1852. On the sacred oratorio of "The Messiah" previous to the death of G. F. Handel, 1759, Lond., 8vo, 1852. An address to the directors of the Ancient Concerts on the high pitch of the scale, Lond., 1845. Glees, anthems, chants, etc.

The reader is referred to Chappell's "Popular Music in the Olden Time" for certain exposures touching Clark's works. Apart from his errors, wilful or otherwise, Clark has done much good to the general cause of music in England, by his antiquarian researches.

CLARK (Rev. Frederick Scotson). Irish org. and comp., B. London, Nov. 16, 1840. S. under his mother (a pupil of Mrs. Anderson and Chopin). S. Pf. and harmony under Sergent, org. of Notre Dame. Org. of Regent Sq. Ch., Lond., 1855. S. organ under E. J. Hopkins. S. at R.A.M. under Bennett, Goss, Engel, Pinsuti, and Pettit. Org. successively of a number of London churches. Founded a College of Music in London, 1865. S. for the ministry at Oxford. Org. at Exeter Coll., Oxford. Bac. Mus., Oxon., 1867. Head master of S. Michael's Grammar School, Brighton, 1867. Curate of Lewes, Sussex. S. at Leipzig Cons. under Richter, Reinecke, etc., and was assistant in English church there. S. under Lebert, Pruckner, and Krüger, at Stuttgart. Returned to London, 1873. Resumed his connection with the Coll. or London Organ School, 1875. Represented English organ-playing at Paris Exhibition, 1878. D. London, July 5, 1883.

WORKS.—*Organ:* Voluntaries ; Pastorale ; Douce Pensée ; Andantes in F and D ; Melodies in D, A, F, and E flat ; Postlude ; *Marches:* Anglaise, aux Flambeaux, des Fantômes, des Girondins, des Jacobins, Militaire, Belgian, Commemoration, Festal, Hollandaise, Inauguration, Pilgrims, Procession, Roman, Russian, Vienna, etc. ; Communions in D minor, F, C minor, A minor, G and E ; Offertoires in F, D, A, G, and C ; Meditation, in B flat ; Fantasias in F, etc.; Improvisations in B flat, C, G, F ; Impromptus, prayers, romances ; Gavottes ; Minuets, airs ; Twelve songs from Handel's oratorios, arranged ; Twelve choruses from Handel, arranged ; Transcriptions, various ; *Harmonium:* Arrangements from foregoing. Voluntaries ; Rêverie, Romance, Gavotte, Ave Maria, Songs. Same for Harmonium duet ; Meditation, in B flat, for violin, harmonium and Pf.; *Pianoforte:* Chinese march ; Midnight march ; Indian march ; Turkish march, etc.; Mazurkas : Clotilde, Hélène, La Fleurette, La Zingara ; Polkas, Galops, Valses, and minuets ; Barcarolles, studies, nocturnes, melodies, morceaux de salon ; Transcriptions, various ; Sacred Evenings : selections from various composers ; Arrangement for Pf. duet, etc.; *Vocal:* Kyrie Eleison and Sanctus in E, from communion service No. 1 ; Do.

from No. 2; Magnificat and nunc Dimittis, chant service in F. Cupid, part song; For Queen and Fatherland, part-song; Agnus Dei, sacred song; He shall convert my soul, sacred song; How dear is home to me, song; Lullaby; Meet me once more; Never, my child, forget to pray; The sea hath its pearls; Pussy, etc. *Didactic:* First Steps in Organ-Playing, Lond. (Augener), 4to, n.d.; First Steps in Harmonium-Playing, (Do.) 4to n.d.; First Steps in Pianoforte-Playing, do. MS. works.

Clark was one of the most accomplished British musicians of recent times. He gave to the world a number of organ pieces of the greatest brilliancy and effect; refined and free from vulgarity. As an instrumental composer he will doubtless be better known to posterity than as a vocal composer, as his works in the latter department do not possess those features which insure a continued vitality. His abilities as an instructor on the organ were well known in London, and his influence over the pupils whom he instructed was lasting and healthy in its effects. His pianoforte music is brilliant rather than learned in style.

CLARK (Thomas). English comp., B. Canterbury, 1775. D. there, May, 1859. Best known by his psalm tunes, a few of which are still used.

CLARKE (Charles E. J.). English org. and comp., B. Worcester, 1796. Chorister in Worcester cath. Org. of Durham cath., 1812. Org. of Worcester cath., 1814. D. [?]

CLARKE (Hugh A.). American writer and comp. Has written "New Method for the Pianoforte," Boston (Ditson), n.d.; "Improved School for the Parlor Organ"; Grand Chant Te Deum; Anthems, etc.

CLARKE (James Hamilton). Irish comp. and cond., B. Birmingham, Jan. 25, 1840. Chiefly self-educated in music. Apprenticed to a land surveyor, 1855-61. Org. of S. Matthew's ch., Duddleston, Birmingham, 1852. Entered musical profession, May, 1862, as org. of the Parish ch. of Parsonstown, Ireland. Org. of Zion ch., Rathgar, Dublin, 1863. First violin Dublin Philharmonic Soc., 1862. Cond. of Belfast Anacreontic Soc., Nov. 1864. Org. of Carnmoney ch., Belfast, Jan,, 1865. Temporary org. and choir-master Llandaff cath, Dec., 1865. Org. and cond., Queen's Coll., Oxford, 1866-7. Bac. Mus., Oxon., May, 1867. Org. and choirmaster, S. Paul's ch., Camden Hill, S. Kens., Lond., June, 1871. Org. of S. Peter's ch., S. Kens., in succession to (Sir) A. S. Sullivan, Mar., 1872. Accompst. and assistant cond. at Promenade Concerts, Covent Garden Theatre, Aug., 1873. Travelled on tour as cond. of Carlotta Patti concert party, 1873. Leader at the Opera Comique, Lond., 1874-5. Cond. of travelling company performing Gilbert and Sullivan's "Sorcerer," 1878. Do. with "Sorcerer" and "Pinafore," 1878. Musical director and comp. at the Royal Lyceum Theatre, London, Sept., 1878, etc.

WORKS.—Op. 1. Capriccio for vn. and Pf., 1852; op. 7. Overture: Thanistene, 1859; op. 44. The Lord is my light, anthem in 8 parts, gained Coll. of Org. first prize; op. 68. Praise: a sacred cantata (degree exercise). June, 1867; op. 78. First Concerto, Pf. and orch., in D. minor; op. 79. Romance and Polonaise, vn. and Pf.; op. 80. Ode to Industry; op. 93. First quartet, Pf., vn., viola, and 'cello, in E minor; op. 95. Parade March, Gertiani, 1872; op. 98. Saltarello for orch., 1874; op. 100. Ballet overture for orch.; op. 101. First symphony, orch., in F., Royal Albert Hall, Aug., 1873; op. 102. Overture composed for Birket Foster, Esq., 1874; op. 122 Second symphony, in G minor, Promenade Concerts, Aug., 1879; op. 123. Concert overture; op. 134. Overture to Hamlet, 1875; op. 135. Romanza cromatica, for flute; op. 136 Music to a Ballet, Alexandra Palace, 1875; op. 137. Overture: Rob Roy; op. 153. Second gavotte, for strings; op. 155. Second sonata, flute and Pf.; op. 156. Three sonatinas, Pf.; op. 157. Romance, flute and Pf.; op. 159. Six sonatas, organ; op. 161. Two choruses and ballet music in reconstruction of "Die Fledermaus," 1876; op. 166. Six movements for organ, Part 1. (36 pieces); op. 168. Part 2. of organ music (6 pieces); op. 169. Part 3 of do.; op. 179. Two andantes, organ; op. 183. Martial Law, a musical comedietta in one act; op. 187. Overture: Nanon; op. 188. Romance and Tarantella, 'cello and Pf.; op. 191. Gavotte in F, orch.; op. 192. Overture, four Entr'actes, dirge, etc., to Henry Irving's production of "Hamlet," Dec. 30, 1878; op. 197. Overture: "Lady of Lyons," 1879; op. 199. Incidental music for Irving's revival of "Eugene Aram," 1879; op. 200. Romance and valse, flute and orch. ; op. 201. Incidental music to "Zillah," a tragedy, 1879 ; op. 202. Overture and incidental music (partly from Storace) to the "Iron Chest," revived by Henry Irving, 1879 ; op. 203. Overture and masque music, etc., to "Merchant of Venice," 1879 ; op. 206. Operetta : "Castle Botherem," or An Irish Stew, German Reed's, 1880 ; op. 207. Orchestral music, etc., to "Iolanthe," 1880 ; op. 208. Overture and incidental music for the "Corsican Brothers," Lyceum, Sep., 1880 ; op. 209. Polonaise, Pf. and orch. ; op. 210. Overture : Cécile, 1880 ; op. 214. Overture, entr'acte, choruses, march, dirge, and incidental music to "The Cup," tragedy by Alfred Tennyson, produced by Henry Irving at the Lyceum Theatre, London, Jan. 3, 1881 ; Songs, part-songs, etc.

CLARKE (James P). A Scottish musician, who held a good teaching position in the West of Scotland, early in the present century. He edited "Parochial Psalmody, a new Collection of Psalm Tunes, to which are prefixed Lessons in the Art of Singing," Glasgow [c. 1830], 2nd ed., 1832. He comp. songs and other vocal pieces.

CLARKE (James). English writer and teacher, B. London, 1793. D. Leeds, 1859. Author of a "Catechism of Wind Instruments, containing explanations of the scale and compass of each instrument, and particular directions for writing the parts of flutes, clarinets, etc.," Lond., n.d. "Instruction Book for Children on the Pianoforte," Lond., n. d. "The Child's Alphabet of Music," Lond., n. d. "Exercises in Harmony, designed to facilitate the study of the Theory of Music and the Practice of Thorough Bass," Lond., 1832. "Catechism of the Rudiments of Music," Lond., n. d. "New School of Music, combining the Practice of Singing with that of the Pianoforte," Lond., n. d.

CLARKE (Jeremiah). English comp. and org., B. London, 1670. S. under Blow. Chor. in the Chap. Royal. Org. of Winchester Coll., 1692-95. Almoner and master of the Chor. of St. Paul's Cath., London, 1693. Org. and Vicar-Choral of St. Paul's, 1695. Gent. of Chap.-Royal, 1700. Joint Org. of Chap.-Royal with Croft, 1704. D. London, Nov. 5, 1707 [suicide].

WORKS.—*Music to the following Plays*: Antony and Cleopatra (Sedley), 1677 ; The Fond husband, 1676 ; Titus Andronicus, 1687 ; The World in the Moon (with D. Purcell), 1697 ; The Island Princess (with D. Purcell and Leveridge), 1699. *Ode*: Alexander's Feast, Dryden ; Ode in Praise of the Island of Barbadoes. Services in G and C minor. *Anthems*: Praise the Lord, O Jerusalem ; How long wilt Thou forget me? ; I will love Thee, O Lord ; O Lord God of my Salvation ; Bow down Thine Ear. Songs in D'Urfey's "Pills to Purge Melancholy." The Assumption, Cantata ; Lessons for the Harpsichord ; Ten Songs, op. 4 ; Secular music, miscellaneous.

Clarke's anthems are all of a high degree of merit, "Praise the Lord" being accounted one of his best. His secular music is not above the average works of his time. His dramatic music is not sufficiently matured in style to afford any medium for comparison, and his endeavours in that direction were too unimportant to invite criticism. His instrumental productions are too few and mediocre to call for comment. Although by no means so good or so great a composer as some of his contemporaries Clarke is deserving of much credit for the good music he has written for the Church, which is still in constant use.

CLARKE (Jessie Murray). English writer, authoress of "How to Excel in Singing and Elocution. A manual for lady students," Lond., 1884.

CLARKE (John), CLARKE-WHITFELD. English comp. and org., B. Gloucester, Dec. 30, 1770. S. under Philip Hayes. Org. of S. Laurence's Ludlow, 1789. Mus. Bac., Oxon., 1793. Org. of Armagh Cath., 1794-97. Mus. Doc., Dublin, 1795. Master of chor. and org. of Christ Ch. and St. Patrick's Caths., Dublin, 1798. Org. and Choirmaster of Trinity and S. John's Colls., Cambridge, 1798-1820. Mus. Doc., Cantab., 1799. Mus. Doc., Oxon., 1810. Org. of Hereford Cath., 1820-33. Prof. of Music, Cambridge University, 1821. D. Holmer, near Hereford, Feb. 22, 1835.

WORKS.—Cathedral services and anthems, 4 vols., 1805, reprinted by Novello. The Crucifixion and the Resurrection, oratorio, 1822. Twelve Glees, composed and inscribed by permission to H.R.H. the Prince Regent [1805] ; Twelve Vocal

Pieces, with original poetry, 2 vols., n. d. *Glees, etc.*: Alice Brand ; The Carpet Weaver ; Celestial Hope ; Come, Ossian, Come ; The Coronach ; Dawn of Day ; Edith of Lorn ; Hymn for the Dead ; Hymn to the Morning Star ; It was a Night of lovely June ; Malvina's Lamentation ; Merrily Bounds the Bark ; Minstrel's Tale ; Oh ! Liberty ; Red Cross Knights ; Roderick Vich Alpine ; What tho' the Knights ; When I am Doom'd ; When shall Joy ; Wide O'er the Brim ; Ye Gentle Muses. *Songs:* Ah ! Whither, Morpheus ; Behold Me ; Blanche of Devon's Song ; Bonnie, Bonnie Blue ; Dark, dark was the Dungeon ; Days that are Gone ; Ellen's Song ; Fair Jessy, the Maid of the Moor ; Go forth, my Song ; Heath this Night ; Here's the Vow ; If Stormy O'er Enamelled Ground ; In Peace Love Tunes ; Know ye the Land ; Laugh and Rejoice ; Lay of the Imprisoned Huntsman ; L'insomnie ; Minstrel's Harp ; Moorland Mary ; Mute Grey Fields ; Oh ! Sweet is the Perfume ; Oh ! Why did thy Soft ; Poor Mary ; Smile of Affection ; Soldier Rest ; Thou Dear Native Land ; Wake, Maid of Lorn ; With Jet Black Eyes ; Withered Rose ; Young Lochnivar. The Beauties of Purcell. Collection of Anthems (edited). The Vocal Works composed by G. F. Handel, arranged for organ or pianoforte, Lond., 17 vols., fo. [1809]. Selection of Single and Double Chants, etc., 2 vols., 4to, n. d.

Clarke is one of the well-known composers of Church music. He has written a variety of good anthems and services, many of which are still often used. His glees and songs from the works of Sir Walter Scott, etc., are among the best of his vocal pieces, and though now almost forgotten, were once deservedly popular.

CLARKE (Mary Cowden). English writer, daughter of Vincent Novello, B. London, June, 1809. Married in 1828 to Charles Cowden Clarke. She compiled the famous "Shakespeare Concordance," wrote novels and poetry, edited an edition of Shakespeare, and wrote the "Life and Labours of Vincent Novello." Lond., 8vo, 1864 (portrait).

This is a good work, and bears abundant evidence to the fact that Mrs. Clarke has inherited a considerable portion of her father's musical genius. She has also translated a number of important works on musical theory.

CLARKE (Stephen). Scottish comp. and org., B. about middle of 18th century. He was Org. of the Episcopal Chap. of Edinburgh, and a teacher there in the last decade of the 18th century. D. Edinburgh, 6th August, 1797. He comp. "Two Sonatas for the Pianoforte or Harpsichhrd, in which are introduced favourite Scotch airs, composed and respectfully dedicated to Mr. Erskine, Jun., of Mar." Edin., 1790. He also harmonized the airs in Johnson's "Scots Musical Museum." On his death the work was continued by his son, William (B. Edinburgh [c. 1780]. D. Edinburgh, 1820), who was a teacher and writer of some small pieces for the pianoforte and voice.

CLARKE (William H.). American writer and musician, Author of "Clarke's Dollar Instructor for the Piano. Prepared for self-instruction and for the use of teachers," Boston, n.d. "An Outline of the Structure of the Pipe Organ," Indianapolis, 8vo, 1877. "Reed Organ Melodies." "Harmonic School for the Organ," Boston. "Dollar Instructor of the Organ," Boston. "New Method for Reed Organs," Boston. "Reed Organ Companion." "Short Voluntaries for the Reed Organ." "Home Recreations for the Parlor Organ," Boston. "Dollar Instructor for the Violin," Boston, etc.

CLARKSON (John). Scottish dancing-master and violinist, B. [?]. D. St. Andrews, Jan. 20, 1812. He compiled "Clarkson's Musical Entertainment, being a Selection of various Tunes and Pieces of Music adapted for the Pf. or Harpsichord," n.d.

CLARKSON (John, Junr.). Scottish dancing-master and violinist, son of above. Published "A Complete Collection of the much-admired Tunes, as Danced at the Balls and Publics of the late Mr. Strange, Teacher of Dancing in Edinburgh." This work appeared about the beginning of this century.

CLASING (Johann Heinrich). German pianist and comp., B. Hamburg, 1779. Teacher at Hamburg, where he D. Feb. 8, 1829. He composed oratorios, operas, chamber music, church music, etc., some of which are meritorious, and is still kept in print.

CLAUDE le Jeune. See LEJEUNE.

CLAUS (Wilhelmine). Bohemian pianist, B. Prague, Dec. 13, 1834. See SZARVADY.

CLAVÉ (José Anselmo). Spanish comp. and cond., B. Barcelona, April 21, 1824. D. Barcelona, Feb., 1874. He organised Festivals on a large scale, and composed choral music.

CLAY (Frederick). English comp., B. Paris, Aug 3, 1840. S. under Molique at Paris. Resident in London as teacher and comp.

WORKS.—*Operas and Operettas, etc.*: The Pirate's Isle, 1859 : Out of Sight, 1860 ; Court and Cottage, 1862 ; Constance, 1865 ; Ages ago, 1869 ; The Gentleman in Black, 1870 ; Happy Arcadia, 1872 ; Cattarina, 1874 ; Princess Toto, 1875 ; Don Quixote, 1875 ; Babul and Bijou, 1872 (with others) ; The Black Crook, 1872 ; Oriana (Albery) ; The Knight of the Cross, 1866 ; Lalla Rookh, 1877 ; Merry Duchess, 1883 ; Music to Shakespeare's Twelfth Night. Cantatas, Songs, Part-Songs, etc.

CLAYTON (Eleanor Creathorne) Mrs. NEEDHAM. Irish general writer and novelist, B. Dublin, 1832. Has published "Queens of Song. Being Memoirs of some of the most celebrated Female Vocalists who have appeared on the Lyric Stage, from the earliest days of opera to the present time, with a chronological list of all the operas that have been performed in Europe," Lond., 2 vols., 8vo, 1863. She writes also a number of popular biographical works, and some novels.

CLAYTON (Thomas). English comp., B. 1670. D. 1730. He composed music for Addison's "Rosamond," "Arsinoe ;" Dryden's "Alexander's Feast," "The Passion of Sappho," etc., which is generally regarded as worthless. See BURNEY, HAWKINS, etc.

CLEGG (John). Irish violinist, B. Ireland, 1714. S. under Dubourg and Buononcini. *Début* in London, 1723. Travelled in Italy. Was principal violin at the Opera, London. Latterly insane. D. 1746.

Clegg was reckoned the best British violinist of his time.

CLELAND (George). English musician, was org. of S. Mary's Chap., Bath. He published "A Selection of Chants, never before published," Lond. [1824].

CLÉMENT (Félix). French writer and comp., B. Paris, Jan. 13, 1822. S. at S. Louis. Tutor in family in Normandy. Prof. of Pf. and Singing in Stanislas College, Paris, 1843-1860. D. Paris, Jan. 23, 1885.

WORKS.—Chants de la Sainte-Chapelle, 1849 ; Eucologe en musique selon le rit Parisien, 1851 ; Le Paroissien Romain, 1854 ; Méthode complète du plain-chant, 1854 ; Méthode d' orgue, Paris, n.d. ; Tableaux de plain-chant, 1854 ; Méthode de musique vocale, Paris, 4to, n.d. ; Histoire générale de la Musique Religieux, Paris, 8vo, 1861 ; Les Musiciens célèbres, depuis le seizième siècle jusqu' à nos jours, Paris, 8vo, 1866 ; Dictionnaire Lyrique, ou Histoire des Operas, etc., Paris, 8vo, [1869], (with supplements to date) ; Music for Racine's "Athalie" ; Les Deux Savants, opera, 1858 ; Le Dormeur eveille, opera ; etc.

The majority of Clément's works are valuable contributions to musical bibliography, as well as to the general literature of France. Their literary merit is high, though their accuracy is not always perfect. His musical compositions have never been heard in Britain.

CLEMENT (Franz). Austrian violinist and comp., B. Vienna, Nov. 19, 1784 [1780]. S. under his father and Kurzweil. Travelled in Europe as concert giver. Came to London, 1790. Solo violinist to Emperor of Austria, 1802. Cond. of theatre at Vienna, 1802-11. Travelled in Germany and Russia, 1812-18. Travelled with Catalani from 1821. D. Vienna, Nov. 3, 1842.

He composed violin concertos, 3 overtures for orch., a Pf. concerto, and an opera, and minor pieces for violin. He was a violinist of great refinement, and held a high position on the Continent.

CLEMENT (Jacques), CLEMENS NON PAPA. Belgian comp., B. at end of 15th century, in Flanders. Chapel-master to Charles V. of Spain in succession to Gombert. D. about middle of 16th century [1556].

WORKS.—Missa cum quatuor vocibus ad imitationem cantilenæ Misèricorde condita, nunc primum in lucem edita, 1556; Missa cum quatuor vocibus, etc., 1557; Missa cum quatuor vocibus, etc., tomus III., 1557; Missa cum quinque vocibus, 1557; Missa cum quinque vocibus, tomus V.; Missa cum quinque vocibus, 1559; Missa cum sex vocibus, 1559; Missa cum quinque vocibus, 1560; Missa cum sex vocibus, 1560; Missa defunctorum quatuor vocum, 1580; Liber primus cantionum sacrarum vulgo moteta vocant, quatuor vocum, etc., 1559; Sooter Liedekens (joyous song), I. Het vierde musyck boexken mit dry parthien, waer inne begrepen zyn die eerste 12 Psalmen van David, etc., 1556; Sooter Liedekens, II., 1556; Sooter Liedekens, III., 1556; Sooter Liedekens, IV., 1557; Chansons Française à quatre parties, etc., 1569.

"His style was smooth and clear, his melody harmonized without being drowned, and his fugue and imitation simple and natural. His genius was so prolific, that numerous as were his productions, he seldom borrowed even from himself."—*Busby*.

CLEMENTI (Muzio). Italian comp., pianist and publisher, B. Rome, 1752. S. under Buroni, an org. at Rome. Became org. in 1761. S. under Carpani and Sartarelli. Went to England (Dorsetshire) with Mr. Peter Beckford, 1766. Cond. Italian opera in London, 1777-80. Travelled in Europe, 1781. Established music-publishing business. Teacher of Ludwig Berger, J. Field, Zeuner, Klenzel, J. B. Cramer, etc. D. Evesham, Worcester, March 10, 1832.

WORKS.—Op. 1. Six Sonatas for the Pf.; op. 2. Six Sonatas for Pf. and flute or violin; op. 3, 4. Six Sonatas for Pf. (2 sets); opp. 5. to 10. Sonatas for Pf., in sets of 3 and 5; op. 11. Sonata and Toccata for Pf.; op. 12. Four Sonatas and a duet for Pf.; op. 13. Six Sonatas for Pf.; op. 14. Three Sonatas for Pf.; op. 15. Sonatas for Pf.; op. 16. Sonata for Pf. in D (La Chasse); op. 17. Capriccio for Pf.; op. 18. Sonatas; op. 19. Sonata for Pf. in C; op. 20. Sonata in E flat; op. 21. Three Sonatas for Pf.; op. 22. Three Sonatas with violin accomp.; op. 24-26. Sonatas for Pf.; op. 27. Three Sonatas, Pf., with violin accomp.; op. 29-30. Sonatas for Pf. and vn.; op. 32-33. Sonatas for Pf.; op. 34. Two Sonatas and two capriccios, Pf.; op. 35. Two Sonatas; op. 36. Progressive Lessons in Pianoforte Playing (Sonatinas, etc.); op. 37. Sonatinas; op. 38. Waltzes for Pf.; op. 39. Waltzes (second set); op. 40. Three Sonatas; op. 41. Sonata; op. 42. Introduction to the Art of Playing on the Pianoforte; op. 43. Second part of do.; op. 44. Gradus ad Parnassum, or the Art of Playing on the Pianoforte, exemplified in a series of exercises in the strict and free styles, composed and fingered by the author, Lond., 2 vols., n. d.; op. 46. Sonata for Pf. (ded. to F. Kalkbrenner); op. 47. Two Capriccios, Pf.; op. 48. Fantasia, Pf.; op. 49. Twelve Monferrinas; op. 50. Three Sonatas, Pf.; op. 51. Detached pieces various for Pf.

Clementi belonged to a school of pianists and composers long since passed away. He was a follower of Mozart in his style of composition, but a reformer and developer of playing, marking the turning point from which the great modern school of Moscheles, Thalberg, Liszt, and Rubinstein took its departure. Of his personal capabilities, Moscheles says.—"Clementi's pianoforte playing, when he was young, was famed for the exquisite legato, pearliness of touch in rapid passages, and unerring certainty of execution." His compositions are still in use among students of the pianoforte and his op. 44, though nearly supplanted by more modern works, is one of the best books a beginner can have. His compositions are pretty rather than vigorous, and always melodious and original.

CLEMENTI AND COMPANY. English music-publishing and instrument manufacturing firm, established by Muzio Clementi in London. The firm was carried on under the name of Clementi, Collard and Collard in 1823, and they manufactured pianofortes and nearly every other variety of instrument. Their publications included works by most of the good composers of that period, and consisted of instrumental and vocal music of every kind.

CLERAMBAULT (Louis Nicolas). French org. and comp., B. Paris, 19th Dec., 1676. D. Paris, Oct. 26, 1749.

WORKS.—*Operas:* Le Soleil vainqueur des nuages, 1721 ; Le Départ du roi, idylle, 1745. Livre d'orgue contenant deux suites du premier et du second ton, Paris, 4to, 1710 ; Harpsichord music, etc.

CLICQUOT (Francois). French organ-builder, B. Paris, 1728. D. 1791.

CLIFFORD (Rev. James). English divine and musician, B. Oxford, 1622. Chor. of Magdalen Coll., Oxford, 1632-42. Minor Canon S. Paul's Cath., Lond., 1661. Senior Cardinal, S. Paul's, Lond., 1682. Curate of Parish Ch. of S. Gregory. Chaplain to Society of Serjeant's Inn. D. London, 1700.

WORKS.—A Collection of Divine Services and Anthems, usually sung in His Majesty's Chapel, and in all the cathedral and collegiate choirs of England and Ireland, by James Clifford, 1664 ; Sermons, etc.

CLIFTON (John Charles). English comp. and pianist, B. London, 1781. S. under R. Bellamy and Charles Wesley. Employed for a time in mercantile pursuits. Resided at Bath as teacher and cond. Went to Dublin, 1802. Resided there as teacher and comp. till 1815. Settled in London, 1816, as teacher of the Pf. and advocate of Logier's system. D. London, Nov., 1841.

WORKS.—Edwin, opera, Dublin, 1815 ; A Series of Moral Songs, by W. F. Collard, published in parts, 1823-4 (Clementi & Co.); Selection of British Melodies, with appropriate words, by J. F. M. Dovaston, Lond., n.d.; Collection of French Airs, with symphonies and accompaniments, 2 vols. As pants the hart, canon. *Glees:* Three glees for 3, 4, and 5 voices, 1823 ; A blossom wreath, Maid of Toro, On a rock whose haughty brow, Quick flew the gales of rosy spring, Durandarte and Belerona, Hushed is the harp, Pray goody ; *Songs:* As through life's early path ; Awake, Oh ! sleeper sweet, awake ; First dawn of love ; Good night, my pretty Anne ; If music be the food of love (canzonet) ; Lorenzo to Jessica ; Miller's daughter ; Near the purple fountain ; Sensitive plant ; Soft on the violet bank ; The dear delights of duty ; The prayers that are sent ; When passion first begins ; With love-fraught eyes ; Here recline ; Hope ; It may be love; Nay, if you threaten ; Sweet choice of my heart ; A bumper of sparkling wine, etc. Theory of Harmony Simplified, 1816 ; Instructions for the Pianoforte ; Memoir of Sir John Stevenson (in a review), etc.

Clifton was a pianist of much ability, and invented an instrument called the "Eidomusicon," which, on being fastened to the keyboard of the Pianoforte, produced the notes and chords as they were struck, with a view to displaying them to the eye, and so facilitate sight-singing, etc. His songs are very fine works, the one called " If music be the food of love," being especially well known.

CLINTON (John). English flute player and writer, B. 1810. D. London, 1864. Author of " A Treatise upon the Mechanism and General Principles of the Flute," Lond., 12mo, n.d. ; "Complete School for the Boehm Flute, containing everything necessary to learn that instrument, from the elements to the most advanced stage," Lond., n.d. (5 editions), Ashdown ; " A Code of Instruction for the Equisonant Flute, in which the fingering and resources of that instrument are fully explained by numerous examples" ; " First Set of three Grand Studies for the Flute " ; Second do. ; " Universal Flute Tutor " (Boosey). *Flute music:* Trios for two flutes and Pf., opp. 2, 3, 10 ; Trios for three flutes, opp. 7 and 9 ; Five Notturnos, flute and harp (with Oberthür) ; Beauties for the flute ; Gems of the Italian School ; Cavatinas, or songs without words ; The Drawing-Room Concert, written by W. Ball ; Transcriptions.

Clinton's works on, and for the flute, are among the best ever produced in England.

CLIVE (Catherine), *née* RAFFTOR. Irish soprano vocalist, B. London, 1711. Sang at Drury Lane Theatre from 1728. Married to George Clive, a Barrister, 1734. Separated from him, 1769. Retired from Stage. D. Twickenham, Dec., 1785.

CLOUGH & WARREN. American firm of reed organ makers, established at Detroit, Mich. This firm stands among the foremost of American makers, and their instruments are in use all over the world. Their instruments possess a few original features, such as qualifying tubes for producing a tone resembling the pipe organ.

CLUER (John). English music publisher during the 18th century. He printed Handel's works and Collections of English Songs, etc.

COBB (Richard). English comp. and org. during the 16th and 17th centuries. Was org. to Charles I , and composed some vocal music. "Smiths are good fellows," a catch, is by him.

COBBOLD (William). English comp., flourished in latter part of 16th, and beginning of 17th centuries. His biography is unknown. He was one of the harmonizers of Este's "Whole Book of Psalms," 1592, and contributed the 5-part madrigal "With wreaths of rose and laurel" to the "Triumphs of Oriana."

COCCHETTA. See GABRIELLI.

COCCHI (Gioacchino). Italian comp. and teacher, B. Padua, 1720. Chap.-master at Cons. degli Incurabili, Venice, 1753. Resided in London, 1757-1773. Returned to Venice, 1773. D. Venice, 1804.

WORKS.—*Operas:* Adelaide, 1743; Bajasette, 1746; Giuseppe riconosciuto, 1748; Arminio, 1749; Siroe, 1750; La Mascherata, 1751; Le Donne Vendicate, 1752; La Gouvernante rusée, 1752; Il Pazzo Glorioso. 1753; Semiramide riconosciuta, 1753; I Matti per amore, 1756; Zoe, 1756; Emira, 1756; Gli Amanti, Lond., 1757; Gli Amanti Gelosi, Lond., 1757; Zenobia, Lond., 1758; Issifile, Lond., 1758; Il Tempio della Gloria, Lond., 1759; La Clemenza di Tito, Lond., 1760; Erginda, 1760; Tito Manlio, 1761; Alessandro nell' Indie, 1761; Le Nozze di Dorina, 1762; La Famiglia in Scompiglio, Lond., 1762. Grand Serenata, Lond., 1761, etc.

COCCIA (Carlo). Italian comp., B. Naples, April, 1789. S. under Paisiello, Capelli, etc. Accompanist to Joseph Buonaparte's private band. Teacher and comp. at Lisbon, 1820. Cond. Italian opera in London, 1823-4. Chap.-master of Cath. of Novara, 1836. Director of Music Academy of Turin. D. Novara, April 13, 1873.

WORKS.—*Operas:* Il Matrimonio per cambiale, 1808; Il Poeta fortunato, 1809; Voglia di dote e non di moglie, 1810; Il Sogno verificato, 1812; I Solitari, 1812; La Selvagia, 1814; Il Crescendo, 1815; Euristea, 1815; Evelina, 1815; Clotilde, 1816; Rinaldo d' Asti, 1816; Carlotta e Werter, 1816; Claudine, 1817; Simile, 1817; Donna Caritea, 1818; Mandane, 1821; Elena e Costantino, 1821; La Festa della Rosa, 1822; Maria Stuart, 1827; L' Orfano della selve, 1829; Rosamunda, 1831; Odoardo Stuart, 1832; Enrico di Montfort, 1833; Catarina di Guisa, 1833; Ser Mercantonio, 1834; Marfa, 1834; Il Lago della fate, 1841. Cantata for entry of allied armies into Paris, 1814; Cantatas, various. Church Music. Orchestral Overtures, etc.

Fifty years ago Coccia was well-known in Europe, and even in London, but his operas not being possessed of much merit or interest are now unknown and uncared for. The melody of Coccia's works was good, and he was a follower in the steps of Paisiello.

COCHLAN (J. P.). English writer, author of "An Essay on the Church Plain-Chant," Lond., 12mo, 1782.

COCHLÆUS (Johann), or COCLEUS. German theoretical writer, B. Wendelstein, in 15th century. D. [1552]. Author of "Musica," Cologne, 4to, 1507; "Tetrachordum Musices: de Musicæ elementis, de musica gregoriana, de octo tonis meli, de musica mensurali," Nuremburg, 1511.

COOK (Lamborn). English music publisher of the present day, established in London, issues works by most of the great living English composers, and the complete works of Signor Piusuti.

COCKS & COMPANY (Robert). English music publishing firm, established at London by Robert Cocks in 1823. The firm was carried on by the senior member of the firm till 1859, when he took his sons Robert Lincoln and Stroud Lincoln into partnership. Robert Lincoln died, and the firm is carried on by the only surviving son Stroud Lincoln, and Robert Cocks, sen. Robert Cocks, born in 1796, has always shown himself alive to the musical interests of the country. The catalogue of the firm is large, and contains in addition to the usual display of songs and Pf. music, a most valuable collection of theoretical works, including translations of foreign authors. The principal foreign writers represented are Albrechtsberger, Cherubini, Czerny, Marx, Weber (G.), Reicha, Rinck, Chaulieu, Otto, etc., etc. The principal British authors are Hamilton, Bishop (J.), Warren, Corfe, Best, Hopkins, and Kimbault, etc., etc. The general catalogue contains specimens of most modern composers of note, and, with several large monumental editions of single works by Handel and Haydn, represent a high standard of music.

COCLIUS (Adrian Petit), or COCLICUS, German writer of the 16th century. A pupil of Josquin. Wrote "Compendium Musices descriptum," Nuremberg, 4to, 1552.
"His book has great merit."—*Hawkins*.

CŒDÈS (Auguste). French comp., B. 1835. Chorus-master at the Theatre Lyrique (Gaite), Paris. Comp. of operas, ballets, etc. D. Paris, July, 14 1884.

COENEN (Franz). Dutch violinist and comp. Brother of the following. B. Rotterdam, Dec. 26, 1826. Travelled in South America, etc. Writes Psalms, string quartets, songs, etc.

COENEN (Willem). Dutch comp. and pianist., B. Rotterdam, Nov. 17, 1837. S. under his father and sister. Afterwards self-taught. Travelled in West Indies and N. and S. America, 1854-62. Settled in London, 1862. Teacher and concert-giver there.
WORKS.—*Oratorium:* Lazarus (MS.), Brighton, 1878. Caprice Concertante for 16 performers on 8 pianofortes. *Pf. Music:* Galops ; Transcriptions ; Dance des Fantômes ; Chant du Barde ; Serenade, Andante, Caprices, Valses, Nocturnes, Meditation, etc., for Pf. solo and duet ; *Songs:* Lovely spring, Come unto me, The rose, Kindly stars, Yes, True love, Thou wilt remember us. Sonata for Pf. and violin (MS.), 1867 ; Concerto for Pf., with accomp. for wind insts. (MS.) ; Three Masses (MS.) ; Four Cantatas (MS.).

COGAN (Philip). Irish comp., org., and pianist, B. Cork, 1750 [Doncaster, 1757 ?]. Chor. and choirman of Cath. of St. Finbar, Cork. Stipendiary of Christ Ch., Dublin, 1772. D. 1834.
WORKS.—Anthems, various ; Six Sonatas for Pf. and violin, op. 2, 1788 ; Sonatas for Pf., op. 4 ; Concerto for 2 violins, viola, 'cello, 2 flutes, and 2 horns, op. 6, 1792 ; Sonatas for Pf. (Clementi), op. 8 ; Harpsichord Lessons ; Songs.

COGGINS (Joseph). English comp. and pianist, B. 1780. S. under J. W. Callcott. Teacher of Pf. in London. D. in first half of present century.
WORKS.—The Musical Assistant, containing all that is truly useful to the theory and practice of the Pianoforte, Lond., 1815 ; Companion to the Musical Assistant, containing all that is truly useful to the theory and practice of the Pianoforte, Lond., 8vo, 1824 ; Admired Hymns...adapted for the use of schools, 2 parts ; Pf. music, fantasias, etc ; Songs : Complete Instructions for the Flute, according to Drouet's system, Lond., fo., 1830.

COHEN (Jules). French comp. and pianist, B. Marseilles, Nov. 2, 1830. S. at Paris Cons. Gained prizes for Pf., organ and harmony, 1850-53. Teacher and conductor in Paris.
WORKS.—*Operas:* Maître Claude, 1861 ; José Maria, 1866 ; Les Bleuets, Paris, 1867 (London "Estelle," 1880) ; Déa, 1870 ; Athalie (Racine). *Cantatas:* L'Annexion, 1860 ; Vive l'Empereur, 1860. Masses ; Overtures for orch. in F, D, and G ; Two Symphonies ; Pf. Music ; Songs.

COICK (Gian Le). Belgian comp., who flourished during latter part of 16th century [B. 1520]. He composed songs, and a curious medley which is noticed in most musical histories as a miracle of clever contrivance.

COLASSE (Pascal). French comp., B. Paris, 1636. Chap. master to Louis XIV. D. Versailles, 1709 [1687]. He composed some operas in the style of

Lulli, the most famous being "Achille et Polixène," 1687. Thétys and Pélée, 1689. Enée et Lavinie, 1690. Astrée, 1691. Les Saisons, 1695. Jason, 1696. La Naissance de Vénus, 1696. Canente, 1700. Amarillis, 1689. L'Amour et l'Hymen, etc.

COLBORNE (Langdon). English org. and comp., B. Hackney, London, Sept. 15, 1837. Org. of S. Michael's Coll., Tenbury. 1860. Bac. Mus. Cantab., 1864. Mus. Doc. Cantuar, 1883. Org. of Beverley Minster, 1874; Wigan Parish Ch., 1875; Dorking Parish Ch., 1877; Hereford Cath., 1877.

WORKS.—Complete Service in C; Magnificats and Nunc dimittis in D, A, and B flat; Te Deum and Benedictus in E flat. *Anthems:* I will lay me down; O Lord, our Governor; Out of the deep; Ponder my words, O Lord; Rend your hearts. *Part Songs:* If slumber sweet, Lisena; The Siesta; The bright-hair'd morn is glowing; Songs, etc.

COLBRAN (Isabella Angela), ROSSINI, Spanish soprano vocalist, B. Madrid, Feb. 2, 1785. S. at Madrid. Sang in Italy, France, etc., 1806-15. Married to G. Rossini, 1822. Appeared in London, 1824. D. Bologna, Oct. 7, 1845.

She created the soprano parts in a number of Rossini's operas, and was one of the foremost singers of her time.

COLEIRE (Richard, M.A.) English divine. Wrote "The Antiquity and Usefulness of Instrumental Musick in the Service of God, a Sermon," London, 1738.

COLEMAN (Charles). English comp., B. about beginning of 17th century [1600]. Member of the private band of Charles I. Doc. Mus., 1651. D. London, 1664.

WORKS.—The Siege of Rhodes, Davenant (with Lawes, Cook, and Hudson), 1657; Musicall Ayres and Dialogues, 1652; Musick's Recreation on the Lyra-violl, 1656; Select Ayres, 1659; The Musical Vocabulary in Philips' New World of Words, 1658.

COLEMAN (Edward). Brother of above, B. 1633. Gent. of Chap. Royal. D. Greenwich, Aug. 29, 1669. Wrote songs in various collections, etc.

COLEMAN (Obediah M.) American musician and inventor, B. Barnstable, Mass., Jan. 23, 1817. He invented several very ingenious pieces of mechanism such as the "Automaton Lady Minstrel and Singing Bird," and improved the accordion. He invented what is known as the Œolian Attachment for Pianofortes. D. Saratoga Springs, April 5, 1845.

COLERIDGE (Arthur Duke). See MOSCHELES.

COLIN (Charles Joseph). French oboe player, B. Cherbourg, June, 2, 1832. S. at Paris Cons. Prof. of oboe at Paris Cons. Composed cantatas, exercises, etc.

COLLARD & COLLARD. English firm of Pianoforte-makers, established in London early in the present century in company with Clementi. The founder of the present firm was W. F. Collard, a Frenchman, to whom is due the chief merit of the excellence attained by the firm in its workmanship. The firm hold the patents of several important inventions applicable to the Pf. Frederick W. Collard of this firm (1772-1860), composed some vocal music.

COLLIER (Joel). See BICKNELL (John L.)

COLLINS (William). English poet, B. 1710. D. 1756. Author of a number of fine odes which have been repeatedly set by English musician. The ode to "The Passions" commencing "When music, heavenly maid, was young," is by him, and has been several times set.

COLLIS (J. D.) English writer, author of "An Outsider's View of the Musical Festival Question." Worcester, 1874.

COLON (Marguerite). French vocalist, B. Boulogne-sur-Mer, Nov. 5, 1808.

Début, 1822. D. Paris, June 5, 1842. Sang in operas by Adam, Thomas, Bordese, Halévy, Grisar, etc.

COLONNA (Fabio). Italian theoretical writer of 17th century, D. 1647. He wrote a work on the division of the scale, now very scarce.

COLONNA (Giovanni Paolo). Italian comp., B. Brescia, 1640. S. under Benevoli and Carissimi. Chap.-master of S. Petronne, Bologna. Principal of Musical Academy of Bologna, 1672-91. D. Bologna, Nov. 28, 1695. WORKS.—Op. 1. Psalms; op. 2. to 6. Motets; op. 7. Psalms; op. 10. Motets; op. 11-12. Psalms; Masses; Stabat Mater. Absalone, oratorio; La Profegia d'Elisco nell' assedio di Samaria, oratorio, 1688. Amilcare, opera, Bologna, 1693.

COLONNE (Jules). French violinist and comp., B. Bordeaux, July 23, 1838. S. at Paris Cons, Comp. music for his instrument, etc.

COLVILLE (David). Scottish musician, B. Campbeltown, 1829. Published "Graduated Course of Elementary Instruction in Singing, on the Letter-Note Method, in Twenty-Six Lessons, with Hints on Self-Instruction, etc." (with George Bentley), 1864; Collections of Part-Songs, under the title of "Choral Harmony," etc.

COLYNS (Jean Baptiste). Belgian violinist and comp., B. Brussels, Nov. 25, 1834. S. at Brussels Cons. Writer of opera, violin music, and songs.

COMETTANT (Jean Pierre Oscar). French comp. and writer, B. Bordeaux, April 18, 1819. S. at Paris Cons., 1839-44.
WORKS.—Trois ans aux Etats-Unis; etude des mœurs et coutumes Americaines. La Propriété intellectuelle, etc.. Histoire d'un inventeur au dix-neuvième siècle, Adolphe Sax: ses ouvrages et ses luttes, 1860; Portefeuille d'un Musicien; Musique et Musiciens, Paris, 8vo, 1862; La musique, les musiciens, et les instruments de musique chez les differents peuples du Monde, Paris, 8vo, 1869; Pianoforte pieces, various; Church music, etc.

COMMER (Franz). German writer and comp., B. Cologne, Jan. 23, 1813.
WORKS.—Der Zauberring, 1843; Der Kiffaenser; Masses; Lieder; Overtures; Cantatas; etc. Musica Sacra, Sammlung der Meisterwerke des 16en, 17en und 18en Jahrhunderts, Berlin, 4 v. 4to, 1839; Collectio Operum Musicorum Batavorum Sæculi xvi., Mayence, 10 pts. [1857]; Cantica Sacra, Berlin, 2 v., n.d.
Commer's collections are valuable and interesting works.

COMON, or CORMAC DALL, Irish harper, story-teller, and vocalist, B. Woodstock, Mayo, May, 1703. Lived an itinerant life, and was famous as a comp. of songs and elegies. He died about the end of the 18th century; or at least after 1786, at which date he was alive.

CONCONE (Giuseppe). Italian comp. and org., B. Turin, 1810. Resided at Paris, 1837-1848. Org. of Royal Chap., Turin, 1848. D. Turin, June, 1861.
WORKS.—Graziella, opera (MS.); Fifty Lessons in Singing, for a Medium Voice, 4 bks.; School of Sight-Singing; School of Part-Singing; Songs, etc. Méthode d'harmonie et de Composition...Paris, 4to, 1845.
This composer is celebrated for his fine vocal studies and admirable exercises for the voice. His "Schools" have been translated and issued in a great many different editions.

CONDELL (Henry). English violinist and comp., B. latter part of 18th century. Violinist at Drury Lane Theatre. Gained prize at Catch Club with glee "Loud blowe the wyndes," 1811. D. London, June, 1824.
WORKS.—The enchanted island, ballet, 1804; Who wins? or The widow's choice, farce. 1808; Transformation, farce, 1810; The farmer's wife, 1814; Glees; Songs, etc.

CONGREVE (Benjamin). English comp., B. 1836. D. London, March 23, 1871.

He has composed many songs and part-songs of merit, some of the latter having obtained prizes.

CONINCK (Jacques Felix de). Belgian comp. and pianist, B. Antwerp, May 18, 1791. D. April 25, 1866. Wrote Pf. music, songs, vocal works, etc.

CONINCK (Joseph Bernard de). Son of above, Belgian comp., B. Ostend, Mar. 10, 1827. Writer of theoretical works, songs, operas, etc.

CONINGSBY (George). English divine, author of "A Sermon preached at the Cathedral Church of Hereford, at the Anniversary Meeting of the Three Choirs, Sept. 6, 1732," Oxford, 1733.

CONRADI (August). German comp., B. Berlin, 1821. S. under Rungenhagen. Cond. of theatre at Stettin, 1849; also at Cologne, Düsseldorf, and Berlin, 1856. D. Berlin, May 21, 1873.

WORKS.—*Operas:* Rubezahl, 1847; Musa der letzle Maurerfürst, 1855; Le Valet Rupert, 1865; Operettas and farces; Symphonies and overtures; Quartets for strings, Pf. music, songs, etc.

CONRAN (D.). Irish writer, author of "Musical Research, or General System of Modulation," Dublin, 4to, 1840.

CONRAN (Michael). Probably a relation of the above, author of "The National Music of Ireland; containing the History of the Irish bards, the national melodies, the harp, etc.," Lond., 8vo, 1850.

CONRARDY (Jules). French comp., B. Liége, Jan. 27, 1836. A good organist, and writer of *Operas:* Le Père Lajoie, 1858; Annibal et Scipion, 1860; Jeanne et Jeannot, 1861; Le roi de l'arbalète, 1862; Le Loup-Garou, 1872. Songs, Pf. music, etc.

CONSTANTIN (Titus Charles). French violinist and comp., B. Marseilles, Jan. 7, 1835. Comp. operas, violin music, songs, etc.

CONTE (Jean). French violinist and comp., B. Toulouse, May 12, 1830. Comp. operas, violin music, etc.

CONTI (Francesco Bartolomeo). Italian comp., B. Florence, Jan. 20, 1681. Court musician at Vienna, 1701-32. D. Vienna, July 20, 1732.

WORKS.—*Operas:* Clotilde, Lond., 1709; Alba Cornelia, 1714; I Satiri in Arcadia, 1714; Teseo in Creta, 1715; Il Finto Policare, 1716; Ciro, 1716; Alessandro in Sidone, 1721; Archelas, 1722; Mosè preservato, 1722; Penelope, 1724; Griselda, 1725. Motets and other vocal music.

CONTI. See GIZZIELLO.

CONTRERAS (Joas). Spanish violin-maker, who worked at Madrid about middle of 18th century. He made violins in the Italian style of good quality.

CONVERSO (Girolamo). Italian comp., B. Correggio about middle of 16th century. He published "Canzoni a cinque voci," Venice, 1575, and "Madrigali a sei voci," Venice, 1584. He is now known as the composer of the pretty madrigal, "When all alone my pretty love."

COOK (Eliza). English poetess and song-writer, B. London, 1818. She contributed to the literary magazines of her day, and edited a journal which attained some popularity. She published "New Echoes and other Poems," 1864, etc. She was given a literary pension of £100 in 1864.

She composed a number of pleasing ballads, and furnished a number of composers with the words of a great many more. Among composers who have set her poetry may be named Blockley, Dempster, S. Glover, C. E. Horn, etc.

COOKE (Benjamin). English comp. and org., B. London, 1730 [1732-1734-1739]. S. under Pepusch. Deputy-org. at Westminster Abbey, 1742. Cond. of Academy of Ancient Music, 1752-1789. Master of boys and layclerk, Westminster Abbey, 1757. Doc. Mus., Cantab., 1775. Org. of S. Martin's-in-the-Field, 1782. Sub.-director at Handel Commemoration, 1784. D. London, Sept. 14, 1793.

WORKS.—Ode on Handel, for 8 voices. *Glees:* Collection of twenty Glees, Catches and Canons for 3, 4, 5 and 6 voices, in score, Lond., 1775 ; As now the shades ; A bachelor he may show his cares ; A knight there came from the field of the slain ; Away with gloom and care ; The beef-steak glee ; Ere the beams of morning break ; Farewell ; Hand in hand ; Hark, the lark ; How sleep the brave ; In the merry month of May ; I've been young, though now grown old ; Now the bright morning star, day's harbinger ; O strike the harp ; Take thou this cup ; Let Rubinelli charm the ear, duet ; Thrysis, when he left me, duet ; The dormouse, glee ; Beneath in the dust. Nine glees and two duets, op. 9 [1795]. Ode on the Passions (Collins), 1784, etc. Concertos for combinations of various instruments. Organ and Harpsichord Music. Anthems and Church Services. Songs, etc.

"Dr. Cooke's glees are numerous, and of great beauty. They are remarkable for natural and graceful ease of melody, great simplicity and yet much art in the disposition of parts, and fine expression."—*Hogarth.* A number of them are still in use among our singing companies ; "Hark, the lark," being one of those perennial favourites of which the English school furnishes not a few examples. With Callcott, Webbe, and Horsley, Cooke shares the preëminent position among the older glee writers. As an organist he was one of the best of his day. His sacred music is now almost forgotten, as also, it must be said, his various other works. Much confusion appears to exist as regards the date of his birth, 1734 and 1739 being obviously wrong when compared with the dates following.

COOKE (Captain Henry). English comp. and teacher, B. beginning of 17th century. Educated at Chap. Royal. Obtained a Captain's commission during the Civil War, 1642. Gent. of Chap. Royal and Master of Children, 1660. Comp. to the King, 1664. D. July 13, 1672.

WORKS.—Anthems and Services preserved (MS.) in the Collection formed by Dr. Aldrich in Christ Church, Oxford. Madrigals, Songs, etc.

Cooke was the teacher of Blow, Wise, Purcell and Humfrey, and for that alone is entitled to some little credit and esteem. He is said by Anthony Wood to have died of grief at the musical attainments of Pelham Humfrey, which far exceeded his own ; but from a physiological point of view this seems rather absurd.

COOKE (John P.) English comp. and cond., B. Chester, 1820. Cond. of various theatre orchestras in New York. D. New York, Nov. 4, 1865. Wrote music to Shakespeare's Plays, Songs, etc.

COOKE (Nathaniel). English comp. and org., B. Bosham, near Chichester, 1773. S. under his uncle Matthew Cooke of London (organist). Org. of the Parish Ch. of Brighton. D. [?]

WORKS.—Collection of Psalms and Hymns sung at Brighthelmston, with several Canons, and a Te Deum, arranged for the Organ or Pianoforte, 8vo, n. d. Glees and Songs. Pianoforte Music.

Cooke was a good organist, and comp. the canon "I have set God always before me."

COOKE (Robert). Son of Benjamin Cooke, English org. and comp., B. 1768. S. under his Father. Succeeded his Father at S. Martin's in-the-field, 1793. Org. and choir-master at Westminster Abbey, 1802. Drowned in Thames, Aug. 13, 1814.

WORKS.—Magnificat and Nunc Dimittis in C. Anthems. *Glees:* In the rose's fragrant shade ; Love and folly were at play ; Mark, where the silver queen of night ; Queen of the sea ; Round thy pillow ; Sweet warbling bird ; Why o'er the verdant banks. Collection of Eight Glees (Clementi) [1805]. Songs, etc.

COOKE (Thomas Simpson). Irish vocalist and comp., B. Dublin, 1782. S. under his Father and Giordani. Cond. of theatre in Dublin, 1803. *Début* as vocalist at Dublin in Storace's "Siege of Belgrade." Appeared in London, July, 1813. Cond. and vocalist at Drury Lane from 1813. Married to Miss Howell. Mem. of R. A. M. ; the Philharmonic Soc. ; the Nobleman's Catch Club ; the Glee Club ; etc., etc. D. London, Feb. 26, 1848.

WORKS.—*Music to Plays:* The Count of Anjou; A Tale of the Times, 1822; The Wager, 1825; Oberon, or the Charmed Horn, 1826; Malvina, 1826; The Boy of Santillane, 1827; The Brigand, 1829; Peter the Great, 1829; The Dragon's Gift, 1830; The Ice Witch, 1831; Hyder Ali, 1831; St. Patrick's Eve, 1832; King Arthur, 1835; The King's Proxy; Frederick the Great; The Five Lovers; Numerous Farces; Adaptations of Foreign Operas. *Glees:* Six Glees for 3 and 4 voices, Lond., 1844; Come Spirits of Air; Fill me, boy, as deep a draught; Strike, strike the lyre. *Duets:* Love and War; Army and Navy; Songs. Singing Exemplified in a Series of Solfeggi and exercises, progressively arranged, London, n. d.; Singing in parts, containing progressive instructions, extracts, exercises, and original compositions, Lond., n. d. [c. 1842] etc.

Cooke enjoyed great popularity in his day and in his delineations of seafaring characters (currently known as in the style à la Tom Cooke) was remarkably successful. He taught J. Sims Reeves, Miss Tree. Miss Povey, Miss Rainforth and a number of other vocalists who have attained renown. His compositions in general are in the same style as those of Dibdin and Braham, and are marked by a free and melodious manner. He was a violinist of some note, and a good vocalist. His son, Grattan Cooke, is a composer of operettas and songs. He published "Statement of Facts and Correspondence between the Directors of the Philharmonic Society and Mr. Grattan Cooke," London [1850].

COOMBE (William Francis). English org. and comp., B. Plymouth, 1786. S. under his father (a singing master) and W. Jackson of Exeter. Org. at Chard, Somerset, 1800. Org. at Totness, Devon, 1802-11. Org. at Chelmsford, 1811-22. D. about middle of present century.

He composed a few pianoforte sonatas, etc., but was chiefly remarkable as an instrumental performer.

COOMBS (James Morris). English org. and comp., B. Salisbury, 1769. Chor. at Salisbury Cath. S. under Dr. Stephens and Parry. Org. at Chippenham, Wilts, 1789-20. D. Chippenham, 1820.

WORKS.—Set of Canzonets; Te Deums; Divine Amusement, being Hymns, Psalms, etc., from Marcello, Handel, etc.; Glees and Songs.

COOPER (Alexander Samuel). English org. and comp., B. London, April 30, 1835. Org. of S. Paul's, Covent Garden. Has composed "The Athanasian Creed." Music for the Holy Communion. Nicene Creed. Te Deum. *Anthems:* I did call upon the Lord; Brightest and best; Come unto me. Chants. *Part Songs:* Happy bygone days; The wayside well; Cheerily; Sweet echo; O tranquil eve; Every season hath its pleasures. Songs, Parochial Chant Book. The Parochial Psalter, etc.

COOPER (George). English comp. and org., B. Lambeth, London, July 7, 1820. Org. of S. Benet's, Paul's Wharf, London; Assistant org. S. Paul's; Org. of S. Anne and S. Agnes, Lond., 1836; S. Sepulchre, 1843; Christ's Hospital; Chapel Royal. D. London, October 2, 1876.

WORKS.—The Organist's Assistant, a series of movements selected and arranged from the works of classical authors (Novello), Lond., n. d.; The Organist's Manual, consisting of select movements for the organ, from the works of the most eminent composers (Novello), Lond., n. d.; Organ Arrangements, 3 vols., Lond.; Classical Extracts for the Organ; Introduction to the Organ, Lond., n. d.; Songs; Part-Songs, etc.

Cooper was one of the best modern organists, and an editor and arranger of the first ability. His death was a sad loss to musical England. His style was chiefly remarkable for refinement and for the entire absence of vulgarity and of straining.

COOPER (Henry Christopher). English violinist, B. Bath, 1819. S. violin under Spagnoletti. Appeared as solo violinist at Drury Lane Theatre, 1830. Principal violinist at Royal Italian Opera. Leader at Philharmonic Society. Violinist at Provincial Festivals. Cond. at various theatres. Latterly cond. at Gaiety Theatre, Glasgow. D. Glasgow, Jan. 26, 1881. He was one of the foremost of the English school of violinists, and at one time well known in London. He was married to Madame Tonnellier, the vocalist.

M

COOPER (Isaac). Scottish editor and violinist, published "A Collection of Reels, by Isaac Cooper of Banff," about 1783.

COOPER (Rev. James). English divine and writer, author of " Musæ Sacræ ; being Selections from Browaler, Heber, etc., set to music ; to which is prefixed an Essay on Church Music." Lond., fo., 1860.

COOPER (John), COPERARIO. English performer on the viol-da-gamba, and comp., B. in latter part of 16th century. Musical preceptor of the children of James I., and master of Henry and W. Lawes. D. beginning of 17th century.

WORKS.—Funeral Tears for the Death of the Right Honourable the Earle of Devonshire, figured in seaven songs, whereof sixe are soe set forth that the words may be expressed by a Treble voyce alone to the Lute and Base Voil, or else that the meane part may be added, if any shall affect more fulnesse of Parts, etc., 1606. Songs of Mourning, bewailing the untimely death of Prince Henry, Lond., fo., 1613 ; Music in Leighton's "Teares " ; Music to Masque by Dr. Campion ; Songs and Fancies, etc.

COOPER (Joseph Thomas). English org. and comp., B. 1810. Org. of Christ Ch., Newgate Street. Org. of Christ's Hospital. D. London, 1880.

WORKS.--Songs, Part-Songs, Sacred Music, Organ Music, etc.

COOPER (J. Wilbye). English vocalist and writer, author of "The Voice, the Music of Language, and the Soul of Song ; a Short Essay on the Art of Singing." Lond., 1874. "Cramer's Vocal School " (edited), Lond., n. d. D. 1885.

COOTE (Charles). English band-master and comp. of dance-music, B. 1809. D. London, March 6, 1880.

He composed a great number of vigorous waltzes, galops, and polkas. The style of those works is best illustrated by the following titles—" Rage of London," " Break-neck," " Express," etc. He also wrote dances on airs from popular operas.

COOTE (Charles, Junr.), Son of the above, an English band-master and writer of dance tunes in the same style as his father.

COPERARIO. See COOPER (John).

COPPOLA (P. Antonio). Italian comp., B. 1792. D. Nov., 1877. Comp. operas.

CORBETT (Samuel). English comp. and org., B. Wellington, Shropshire, Jan. 29, 1852. S. under Dr, Sir G. A. Macfarren and James Coward. Org. of Christ Ch., Wellington, Oct., 1867. Mus. Bac., Cantab., May 1, 1873. Org. of S. Mary's, Bridgnorth, Jan., 1875. Doc. Mus., Cantab., March 20, 1879.

WORKS.—Bethlehem, a cantata ; Sonata for the Pf.; Part-songs ; Magnificat and nunc dimittis in F ; Anthems ; Songs.

CORBETT (William). English comp. and violinist, B. [1669]. Mem. of King's Band Travelled in Italy, Burney says, on behalf of the English Government, who paid him to watch the movements of the Pretender. Returned to England, 1740. D. 1748.

WORKS.—Op. 1. Sonata for two violins and bass, Lond., 1705 ; Op. 2. Sonata for 2 flutes and bass, Lond., 1706 ; op. 3. Sonata for 2 flutes and bass, Lond., 1707 ; Six Sonatas for 2 oboes or trumpets, 2 violins, and bass ; Concertos, or Universal Bizzarries, composed on all the new Gustos during many years' residence in Italy, op. 5, Lond., 1741 ; Twelve Concertos for various instruments ; Music to " Henry IV.," 1700 ; Music to "Love Betray'd," 1703 ; Songs in collections, etc.

Corbett collected a valuable musical library, and was a remarkable performer on the violin. His compositions are of good quality, and generally melodious. The story of Burney anent his watch on the Pretender is discredited.

CORDER (Frederick). English comp. and cond., B. Hackney, London, Jan. 26, 1852. S. at the R. A. M., 1874. Gained Mendelssohn Scholarship,

1875. S. at Cologne under Dr. Hiller, 1875-78. Returned to England, 1879, and became occupied with literary pursuits. Appointed cond. of orchestra at Brighton Aquarium, June, 1880. Resides at Brighton as comp. and teacher.

WORKS.- Op. 1. Orchestral Suite : "In the Black Forest," 1876 ; op. 2. Idyll for orchestra : " Evening on the Sea-shore," 1876 ; op. 3. Grand opera : "Morte d' Arthur," 1877-9 ; op. 4. Opera : "Philomel," in one act, 1879 : op. 5. Cantata: "The Cyclops," 1880 ; op. 6. Four River Songs (Trios for female voices), 1880 ; Ossian, a concert overture for orch., produced by the Philharmonic Soc., London, 1882 ; Songs and part-songs, miscellaneous.

Mr. Corder's works are marked by an ambitious and undoubtedly artistic aim, and the majority of them which have been produced have been well received. Mr. Corder has contributed largely to periodical literature, and also to Sir George Grove's "Dictionary of Musicians."

CORELLI (Arcangelo). Italian violinist and comp., B. Fusignano, Imola, 1653. S. under G. Bassani and Simonelli. Early career unknown. Travelled in Germany. Mem. of Court-band of the King of Bavaria. Returned to Italy, 1681. Cond. opera at Rome, 1690. D. Rome, Jan. 18, 1713.

WORKS.—Op. 1. xii. Sonata a tre, due violini e violoncello, col basso per l' organo, Rome, 1683 ; op. 2. xii. Suonate da Camera a tre, due violini, violoncello e violone o cembalo, Rome, 1685 ; op. 3. xii. Suonate a tre, due violini e arciluito col basso per l' organo, Bologna, 1690 ; op. 4. xii. Suonate da Camera a tre, due violini e violone o cembalo, Bologna, 1694 ; op. 5. xii. Suonate a violino e violone o cembalo, Rome, 1700 ; op. 6. Concerti grossi con due violini e violoncello di concertino obligati e due altri violini, viola e basso di concerto grosso ad arbitrio che si potranno radopptare, Rome, 1712. An Edition of op. 5 was published by Geminiani at London.

Corelli is the acknowledged founder of modern violin playing and composition. His works are in every respect worthy of the high favour once bestowed upon them and are superior to the compositions of any of his contemporaries. Although now rarely, if ever, performed, Corelli's sonatas have lived tenaciously, and will no doubt continue to exist for a considerable period. Their chief characteristics are the fine melody, clear massive harmony, and general good effect secured by skilful arrangement of the parts. He was one of the first who wrote for the violin with a perfect knowledge of its capabilities, and his music is, in consequence, always playable, if occasionally dry. As a performer, he excelled most of his contemporaries, and laid the foundation of the succeeding school of violinists, through Geminiani, his pupil.

CORFE (Joseph). English org., writer, and comp., B. Salisbury, 1740. Chor. at Salisbury Cath. Gent. of Chap. Royal, 1782. Org. and choir-master at Salisbury Cath., 1792-1804. D. 1821.

WORKS.—A Treatise on Singing, explaining in the most simple manner all the Rules for learning to Sing by Note without the assistance of an Instrument, with some Observations on Vocal Music, Lond., fo., 1791, another ed., 1801 ; Thoroughbass Simplified, Lond., n. d. Beauties of Handel, being 154 songs, duetts, and trios with accomp. for Pf., 3 vols., n. d.; Beauties of Purcell, 2 vols., n. d.; First Set of 12 Glees, n. d.; Second Set of 12 Glees ; Third Set of 12 Glees, in score for 3 and 4 voices, from melodies of Sacchini, Paisiello, Haydn, Pleyel, Storace, etc. Sacred Music, consisting of a collection of the most admired pieces, adapted to some of the choicest music of Jomelli, Pergolesi, Perez, Martini, Biretti, etc., 2 vols., n. d.; Three Collections of Scottish Songs ; Anthems ; Nine Vocal Trios, harmonized, Lond., n. d.

CORFE (Arthur Thomas). English, comp., org., and writer, son of above, B. Salisbury, April 9, 1773. Chor. in Westminster Abbey, 1783. S. under Dr. Cooke and Clementi. Org. and choir-master of Salisbury Cath., 1804. D. Salisbury, Jan. 28, 1863.

WORKS.—Anthems ; Church Services ; Pf. music. The Principles of Harmony and Thorough-Bass explained, Lond., n. d. Songs ; Glees, etc.

CORFE (Charles William). English org. and comp., son of the above, B. Salisbury, July 13, 1814. S. under his father, etc. Org. of Christ Ch. Cath.,

Oxford, Dec., 1846. Mus. Bac., Oxon., Mar., 1847. Mus. Doc., Oxon., June, 1852. Choragus of the University of Oxford, 1860. D. Oxford, Dec. 16, 1883.

WORKS.—Vocal music, as songs, part-songs; Anthems.

CORKINE (William). English lute player and comp., B. in latter part of 16th century. D. first part of 17th century.

WORKS.—Ayres to Sing and Play to the Lute and Basse Violl, with Pavins, Galliards, Almaines, and Corantos for the Lyra Violl, 1610; The Second Booke of Ayres, some to sing and play to the Base violl alone, etc., 1612.

CORNELIUS (Peter). German comp., B. Mayence, Dec. 24, 1824. Nephew of P. von Cornelius, the painter. S. under Liszt. Resided at Weimar, assisting Liszt in spreading the theories of Wagner, 1852-60. Prof. at Munich Cons. D. Mayence, 1874.

WORKS.—The Barber of Bagdad, opera, Weimar, 1858; The Cid, opera, Munich, 1863; Pf. music; Collections of Songs: Trauer und Trost; Weihnachtslieder; Trauerchore, etc.; Part-songs.

CORNELL (J. H.). American writer and comp., author of A Primer of Tonality (2 editions), New York, n. d.; The Practice of Sight-Singing, in 2 parts, New York, 8vo, n. d.; Songs with Pf. accomp.; Te Deum; Part-songs. Silicate Music Slate (with pamphlet), for Practical Exercises in learning to Transpose and Sing; The Introit Psalms as prescribed by the First Prayer-Book of Edward VI., set to original chants, New York, 4to, 1871.

CORNETTE (Victor). French comp. and writer, B. Amiens, 1795. S. at Paris Cons. from 1811. Prof. of music at College of St. Acheul, 1817-25. Mem. of orch. at Odéon, Opera Comique, etc., 1825-37. Singing-master at Gymnase de Musique Militaire, 1839. Chorus-master and leader at various theatres, 1842-48.

WORKS.—Methods or Tutors for the Trombone, Cornet, Bugle, Sax-horn, Ophicleide, Bassoon, Oboe, Horn, Trumpet, Harp, Saxophon, Violoncello, Viola, Organ, Harmonium, etc.; Pf. arrangements from operas; Music for wind-instruments; Dance music.

CORNISH (William). English poet and musician, flourished about 1500. He wrote a "Parable between Information and Musike," a poem, which will be found in Hawkins. He was a member of the Chapel Royal choir, and D. before 1526. His compositions exist in MS.

CORNISH (William). Son of the above, flourished in first part of the 16th century, wrote songs, part-songs, etc., said by Hawkins to be good.

CORNWALL (N. E.). American writer, author of "Music as it was and as it is," New York, 12mo, n. d.

CORRI (Dominico). Italian comp. and collector, B. Rome, 1746. S. under Porpora, 1763-67. Came to London, 1774. Publisher, with Dussek, in London. Teacher and publisher in Edinburgh. Married to Miss Bacchelli. Cond. of Musical Soc. of Edinburgh. D. London, May 22, 1825.

WORKS.—Operas: Alessandro nell' Indie, Lond., 1774; The Travellers, Lond. The Singer's Preceptor, or Corri's Treatise on Vocal Music, 2 vols., fo., 1810 (containing his life); A new and complete Collection of the most favourite Scots Songs, including a few English and Irish, with proper Graces and Ornaments peculiar to their character; likewise the New Method of Accompaniment of Thorough Bass, 2 vols., 1788. A select collection of the most admired Songs, Duets, etc., from operas in the highest esteem, and from other works in Italian, English, French, Scotch, Irish, etc., in three books, n. d.; A Select Collection of Forty of the most favourite Scotch Songs, with introductory and concluding Symphonies, proper graces peculiar to their character, and accompaniments for the Pf., n. d. (four editions of this work were published); The Art of Fingering, 1799; Musical Dictionary as a Desk, 1798; Complete Musical Grammar, with a Concise Dictionary of all the Signs and Forms used in Music, etc., Lond., n. d.; Two vols. of Sonatas for the Pf.; Several vols. of English and other national songs; Six Canzonets and Two Duets (Clementi); Lilliput, a dramatic romance; Single songs, duets, etc.

Corri was a fine musician, and enterprising man of business, both of which qualities he utilized in a beneficial manner in improving the musical taste of the Scottish capital. His publications were superior in general to the common order of musicbooks issued in Britain, and he appears to have been one of the first to employ written-out accompaniments in Britain. He mentions at length, in a preface to one of his "Select Collections," the nature and extent of his innovation.

CORRI (Montague). Italian comp., second son of above, B. Edinburgh, 1784. S. under his father, Winter, and Steibelt. Resided in London as comp. to the Surrey Theatre. Comp. to Astley's and the Cobourg Theatre till 1816. Chorusmaster at English Opera House, 1816-17. Resided successively in Edinburgh, Newcastle, Manchester, and Liverpool. D. London, Sept. 19, 1849. He wrote a few songs and other unimportant pieces. He was an expert swordsman, and a respectable conductor.

CORRI (Haydn). Italian comp., B. Edinburgh, 1785. D. Dublin, Feb. 19, 1860. Corri was a cond., teacher, and comp., in Dublin, where he was much respected among musicians. His wife (1800-67) was an operatic vocalist.

CORRI (Natale). Italian comp. and music teacher, brother of Domenico Corri. was living in Edinburgh contemporaneously with his brother.

CORRI-PALTONI (Fanny). Italian mezzo-soprano vocalist, B. Edinburgh, 1801, daughter of Natale Corri. S. under her father and Braham. *Début* at the King's Theatre, Lond. Sang in Germany, Italy, etc. Married to Signor Paltoni in Italy, 1821. Sang in Spain, Russia, etc. D. [?]
Her sister ROSALIE sang in London in 1820 and afterwards, with considerable success.

Other members of this family are DUSSEK (died 1870), PATRICK (1820-1876), and HAYDN, a vocalist (died 1876).

CORSI (Jacopo). Italian amateur musician of 16th century, who encouraged Peri and Caccini in their efforts to establish what is now known as the opera.

CORTECCIA (Francesco). Italian comp., B. Arezzo, early in 16th century. Chap.-master to Grand Duke Cosmo II., 1541-1571. D. 1571. Composed Motets, Madrigals, etc.

CORTESI (Antonio). Italian dancer, B. 1797. D. 1880. He improved and invented new features in the ballet.

COSSMANN (Bernhard). German violoncellist and comp., B. Dessau, May 17, 1822. S. under Drechsler, Müller, and Kummer. 'Cellist at Italian opera, Paris. Appeared in London, 1841. Returned to Germany and played at Gewandhaus and other important concerts. Prof. of violoncello at Cons. of Moscow, 1866-70.

COSTA (Francisco Eduardo da). Portuguese comp., B. Lamego, May 15, 1818. D. 1854. Wrote church music, etc.

COSTA (João E. P. da). Portuguese comp., B. Lisbon, 1805. S. at Lisbon. Writer of operatic works, songs, etc.

COSTA (Sir Michael). Italian comp. and cond., B. Naples, Feb. 4, 1810. S. under Zingarelli, etc. S. at the Royal Academy of Music, Naples. Visited England, and assisted at the Birmingham Musical Festival, 1828. Cond. at H.M. Theatre, 1831. Naturalized as British subject, 1839. Cond. of Philharmonic Soc. Concerts, 1846. Cond. at Royal Italian opera, 1847. Cond. of Sacred Harmonic Soc., 1849. Cond. of the Handel Festivals. 1857, and afterwards. Knighted at Windsor, April 14. 1868. Invested with the Royal Order of Frederick, 1869. Cond. at H.M. Theatre, 1871. Knight of the Turkish Order of the Medjidie. Knight-Commander of the Crown in Italy. D. London, April 28. 1884.

WORKS.—*Oratorios and Cantatas:* L' Immagine, 1815 ; La Passione, 1827 ; Eli, Birmingham, 1855 ; Naaman, Birmingham, 1864. *Operas and Ballets:* Il Delitto punito, 1826 ; Il Sospetto funesto, 1827 ; Il Carcere d' Ildegonde, 1828 ; Malvina, 1829 ; Malek Adhel, 1837 ; Don Carlos, 1844 ; Kenilworth, 1831 ; Une heure à

Naples, 1832; Sir Huon, 1833; Alma, 1842. Mass; Three Symphonies; Songs and miscellaneous music.

Costa was one of the greatest and most influential conductors in Britain. He had a singularly fortunate career, which, coupled with hard work, raised him to the highest position among musicians. His services at those institutions where he acted as conductor were very beneficial to their prosperity, and healthy in general tendancy. His superior powers as a conductor were universally acknowledged, and his tact and firmness in training large bodies of singers and instrumentalists, as at the Handel Festivals, insured him a success almost unprecedented in the annals of musical direction.

His compositions are of moderate popularity, and, saving "Eli" and "Naaman," none are works which will have permanent interest. "Eli" and "Naaman" were successful when originally produced, and are occasionally brought forward by musical societies. His dramatic music is decidedly inferior to his sacred music, and none of his operas have survived, or are likely to survive, their original production. His minor works are still current.

COSTE (Jules). French amateur comp., B. Lorraine, 1828. Wrote a number of operas. D. November 13, 1883.

COSTELEY (William). Scottish comp., B. 1531. Settled in France as org. to Henri II. and Charles IX. He was a member of the society known as "Puy de musique à honneur de Ste Cecile." D. Evreux, 1606. His works consist of songs in Le Roy's Collections of Chansons, etc., and a treatise entitled "Musique," Paris, 1579.

COSYN (Benjamin). English comp. for, and performer on the Virginals who flourished in first part of 18th century. He wrote music for his instrument of a difficult and complicated style, and was one of the best performers of his day.

COSYN (John). English comp., probably father of above. Wrote Sixty Psalms, in six Parts, 1585.

COTES (Digby), M.A. English writer, author of "Music a rational assistant in the duty of praise when united with charity, a Sermon," 1756.

COTTELL (George Lansdowne). English pianist, comp., and teacher, B. Bath, Sept. 22, 1835. S. under his mother, and at R. A. M., London. Performed on Wornum's Pf. at the International Exhibition, 1862. Married daughter of Samuel Perkes, C.E., of Bombay, etc., 1864. Founder and director of the London Conservatoire of Music, 1876.

WORKS.—*Pianoforte:* The Archers; Gipsy Dance; Westminster Bridge; Fierce Passions; Three Minutes; Nora; Joy; Sea Song; New Wedding March, etc. *Songs:* Coming; What do Lovers Say?; I'm waiting; Westminster Bridge, etc. The Archers, opera, etc.

Cottell is known as a successful teacher, and as a pianist of much ability. His compositions are brilliant and tasteful.

COTTON (John). American writer, author of "Singing of Psalmes a Gospel Ordinance." Boston, 4to, 1647.

COTTRAU (Guillaume). French song writer, B. Paris, 1797. D. Naples, Oct. 31, 1847.

COTTRAU (Theodore), MARTELLI. French comp., son of above, B. Naples, Nov. 7, 1827. Writer of Pf. music.

COTTRAU (Jules). French comp., brother of above, B. Naples, 1836. Writer of operas, songs, Pf. music, etc.

COUDERC (Joseph Antoine Charles). French vocalist and comedian, B. Toulouse, March 10, 1810. S. at Paris Cons. Sang in operas by Benoist, Thomas, etc. D. April 16, 1875.

COUPERIN (Francois), surnamed LE GRAND. French org. and comp., B. Paris, 1668. S. under an org. named Thomelin. Org. of St. Gervais, Paris, 1696. Chamber musician (harpsichord) to the king, 1701. Org. of Royal Chapel, 1701. D. Paris, 1733.

WORKS.—Premier Livre de Pieces de Clavecin, Paris, 1713; Deuxième livre de pieces de Clavecin, Paris, 1716; Troisième livre de pieces de Clavecin à la suite du quel il y a quatre concerts a l'usage de touts sortes d'instruments, Paris, 1722; Quatrième livre de pieces de Clavecin, Paris, 1730; Les Goûts réunis, ou Nouveaux Concerts, augmentes de l' Apothéose de Corelli, en trio, Paris, 1724; L'Apothéose de l' Incomparable L × × × (Lully), Paris, n.d. ; Trios pour deux dessus de violon, basse d'archet et basse chifrée, Paris, n.d. ; Leçons des ténèbres à une et deux voix, Paris; L'Art de toucher du clavecin, par M. Couperin, organist du Roi, Paris, 1717.

Couperin is said to have influenced J. S. Bach in the formation of his style. His work "L'Art de toucher" influenced the development of piano-playing during his period. His compositions are elegant and spirited in style, and, though original, are often dry by reason of repeated ornaments.

COURCY (F. de). Author of "The Art of Singing, its Theory and Practice; for perfecting and scientifically developing the Human Voice..." Lond., n.d.

COURTOIS (Jean). Belgian comp. of 16th century, who wrote elaborate music for the church, madrigals, etc.

COURTEVILLE (Raphael). English musician, B. in first part of 17th century, D. Dec. 28, 1675.

He was Gent. of Chap. Royal in time of Charles I., and founder of the Courteville family.

COURTEVILLE (Raphael). English org. and comp., son of above, B. latter part of 17th century. Org. of St. James' Ch., Piccadilly, Lond., 1691. D. [1735].

WORKS.—Don Quixote, opera by D'Urfey (with Purcell, etc.), 1696; Six Sonatas for two violins; Sonatas for two flutes, 1685; Songs in contemporary collections; "St. James" psalm tune; etc.

COURTEVILLE (John). English song-writer of the 17th century, son of Raphael, the elder. His works appear in the "Theater of Music," 1685-87, etc.

COURTEVILLE (Raphael). English org. and comp., son of Raphael the younger, succeeded his father as org. of St. James' Ch. He died in 1771. He was a severe political writer, and gained the nick-name of *Court-evil*.

COUSINS (Charles). English band-master and director of music at Kneller Hall, B. near Portsmouth, Jan. 2, 1830. Educated at the Royal Hospital Schools, Greenwich, from 1841. Assistant band-master of Royal Caledonian Asylum, 1846. Member of band of the 1st Life Guards, under Mr. James Waddell. S. at Kneller Hall, Hounslow, for a band-mastership. Band-master of 2nd Dragoon Guards, Oct., 1863. Served with Guards in India, 1864-70. Held appointment till 1874. Director of Music at Kneller Hall, Nov. 1, 1874.

As music-director at Kneller Hall, Mr. Cousins has much of the musical instruction imparted to band-masters in the British army under his control; the institution having been established in 1857 for "the better training of some of the most intelligent and promising of the six thousand men and boys who are employed in the musical service of the army. The younger pupils are trained to the various instruments used in a military band, and for this purpose a staff of ten masters is employed. Those who are to be trained for band-masterships are recommended by their respective commanding officers for their musical and general intelligence, good conduct, and fitness for responsibility. The experiment of opening up to bandsmen the opportunity of qualifying themselves for the highest posts in their calling has been so successful, that the War Office authorities have granted the status of warrant officers to band-masters, which gives, while serving, emoluments of nearly £200 per annum, and a maximum retiring allowance of about £80 per annum."

COUSSER (Johann Sigismund). Hungarian comp., B. Presburg, 1657. S. under Lully. Visited Italy, etc. Settled in London as teacher. Went to Ireland, 1710. Org. in Dublin cath. D. Dublin, 1727. He composed operas, church music, songs, etc.

COUSSEMAKER (Charles Edmond Henri de). French writer, B. Bailleul, April, 19, 1805. D. Lille, Jan. 10, 1876.

WORKS.—Mémoire sur Hucbald et sur ses traités de Musique...Paris, 1841; Notices sur les Collections Musicales de la Bibliothèque de Cambrai et des autres villes du département du Nord, Paris, 1843; Essai sur les Instruments de Musique au Moyen âge; Histoire de l' Harmonie au moyen âge, Paris, 4to, 1852; Chants liturgiques de Thomas à Kempis...Ghent, 8vo, 1856; Drames liturgiques du Moyen âge, Paris, 4to, 1861; Les Harmonistes de xii. et xiii. Siècles, 4to, 1864; L' Art Harmonique aux xii. et xiii. Siècles, Paris, 4to, 1865; Scriptores de Musica medii ævi nova series a Gerbertina altera, Lille, 3 vols., 1866-69; Les Harmonistes du xiv. Siècle, 4to, 1869; Œuvres complètes du trouvère Adam de la Halle...(edited), Paris, 8vo, 1872; Chants populaires de Flamands de France, Ghent, 8vo, 1876.

[COUTTS (W. G.)], ITHURIEL. Scottish writer, author of "Scottish *versus* Classic Music, and the Ethical and .Esthetical aspect of the Question," Edinburgh, 8vo, 1877 (2 eds.).

COWARD (James). English org. and comp., B. London, Jan. 25, 1824. Chorister in Westminster Abbey. Org. of Crystal Palace, 1857-80. D. London, Jan. 22, 1880.

WORKS.—O Lord, correct me; full anthem. *Part-songs:* Lady, I think of thee; May Day; Summer Morning; Airy Fairy Lilian; The sun is bright; Peaceful Slumbering; The day is done; Where Claribel low lieth; The Skylark. *Songs:* Take, O take those lips away; Give back my love again; etc. Miscellaneous music. Ten Glees for 4 and 5 voices, Lond., 1857; Ten Glees, etc., Lond., 1871.

Coward's part-songs are perhaps the best known of his published works, and are agreeable pieces of a high standard of merit. He was a performer on the organ of great ability.

COWDERY (E.). See RAMANN (L.).

COWEN (Frederic Hymen). English comp., pianist, and cond., B. Kingston, Jamaica, Jan. 29, 1852. Brought to England, 1856. S. under Benedict and Goss, 1860-65. S. at Leipzig and Berlin, under Hauptmann, Moscheles, and Reinecke. First work, "Minna Waltz," published, 1858. Gave series of orchestral concerts, introducing modern English works, Nov., 1880. Conducted Promenade Concerts, Lond., 1880. Travelled in Europe, 1881-82. Cond. his own works at various festivals.

WORKS.—*Operas, etc.:* Pauline (from Lytton's "Lady of Lyons"), Lond., Carl Rosa, 1876; Schiller's Maid of Orleans (overture, etc.), 1871; One too Many (German Reed), 1874; Garibaldi, operetta. *Cantatas:* The Rose maiden, 1870; The Corsair, Birmingham Festival, 1876; St. Ursula, Norwich Festival, 1881; The Sleeping Beauty, Birmingham, 1885. *Oratorio:* The Deluge, Brighton Festival, 1878. *Symphonies:* First, in C minor, 1869; Second, in F, 1872; Third, Scandinavian, in C minor, 1880; Fourth, Cambrian, 1884. *Overtures and Concertos:* Overture in D minor, 1866; Festival, Norwich, 1872; Concerto for Pf. and orch in A minor, 1869; Suite de Ballet for orch., The Language of Flowers. 6 pieces, 1880; Sinfonietta for orch. in A, Philharmonic Soc., 1881. *Instrumental Music, miscellaneous:* Trio in A minor for Pf., violin, and 'cello, 1868; Quartet for Pf. and strings in C minor, 1869. *Pf. music:* Three valses caprices, 1870; Rondo à la Turque, 1870; Fantasia on "Zauberflöte" (8 hands), 1870; Sylphide; La Coquette. 1873, etc. Six Four part Songs, 1871. *Songs:* Two roses (1870); Spinning (1871); Marguerite; Marie (1872); Aubade; It was a dream; The carrier dove; Only a violet; Night and morning (1873); Under the lime (1874); Past and future; Almost; At last; So far away; Why; The old love is the new, 1875; Ay or no; Steering; Truant love; The rainy day; The winding of the skein; The better land (1877); Never again; Make believe; It might have been; A farewell; A shadow; Tho' lost to sight; Regret (1878); Watching and waiting; My lady's dower; The unfinished song; Jessie; O swallow (1879); Casabianca; I wonder; The children's house (1880); The watchman and the child; All in all (1881); Six songs, Better far, etc.; I will come; The pilgrims; Light in darkness; Passing away; A song and a rose; Home (1883); Sunlight and shadow; Album, A lullaby, A little while, Think of me, etc.; Child and the angel; The keepsake; In vain (1884).

Mr. Cowen is one of the most popular of living composers, and his works have been received with a large measure of approbation by the musical public. His great strength lies in instrumental composition, and especially in his symphonic writings, which unite with much beauty of design and careful finish, a well-marked vein of originality. His cantatas have enjoyed much popularity, but his " Rose Maiden " among such works is by far the most frequently performed. His opera is not now performed, and many of his earlier works have dropped out of knowledge. His songs have enjoyed a great measure of popular favour, and many of them are already almost classics, but as before indicated, it is as an instrumental composer that Mr. Cowen will hereafter be known.

As a conductor and pianist he takes high rank, and it is due to him to say that he has made more than one effort to secure for the younger generation of British composers a fair share of public attention. His efforts in this direction, though perhaps less successful than desirable, were none the less patriotic and praiseworthy.

COX (Rev. John Edmund), D.D. English writer and divine, B. Norwich, Oct. 9, 1812. Vicar of St. Helen's, and St. Martin's, Bishopgate, London, 1849, etc. Author of "Musical Recollections of the last Half Century," Lond., 2 vols., 1872. He is Hon. Chaplain of Royal Society of Musicians.

CRAIG (Adam). Scottish violinist and collector, B. in latter half of 17th century. D. Oct., 1741. He performed at the public concerts in Edinburgh during his lifetime.

WORKS.—A Collection of the Choicest Scots Tunes, adapted for the Harp or Spinnet, and within the compass of the voice, violin, or German Flute, Edinburgh, 1730. A manuscript volume of orginal compositions by Craig was exposed for sale in 1728.

CRAMENT (John Maude). English org. and comp., B. Bolton, Percy, Yorks, 1845. S. under Sir G. A. Macfarren, Haupt, and Kiel. Org. of Brompton Parish Ch., etc., Lond. Mus. Bac., Oxon., 1879. Secy. of the Peoples Entertainment Soc., London, which gives over 150 Free Concerts annually.

Has composed some meritorious anthems, and a Festival Psalm for solo voices, chorus and orch.

CRAMER (Franz). German violinist and comp., B. Schwetzingen, near Mannheim, 1772. Son of Wilhelm Cramer. Settled in London. Played violin at the Opera, the Ancient Concerts, etc. Afterwards Leader at the Ancient Concerts, Vocal concerts, and Philharmonic concerts. D. London, 1848.

His works include fantasies for violin and flute, and other pieces of no great merit.

CRAMER (Henri). German pianist and comp., B. 1818. He has written a large number of Pf. works, of which the following are among the most important :—

Nocturne, op. 2 ; Fantaisie Romantique, op. 8 ; Romance sans paroles, op. 21 ; Poème d'amour, op. 24 ; Rondo Capriccioso, op. 27 ; Three Polkas, op. 29 ; Marche Orientale, op. 43 ; Serenade, op. 90 ; Three Morceaux de salon, op. 118 : Potpourris on melodies in operas by Balfe, Auber, Verdi, Gluck, Flotow, Cherubini, Adam, Donizetti, Rossini, Mozart, Hérold, Thomas, Lortzing, Wagner, Spohr.

CRAMER (Jacob). German flute-player and comp., B. in Silesia, 1705. D. 1770. Wrote a quantity of music for his instrument.

CRAMER (Johann Baptist). German pianist and comp., B. Mannheim, Feb. 24, 1771. Son of Wilhelm Cramer. Taken to London by his father, 1772. S. under his father, K. F. Abel, Clementi, and Schroeter. Played in various towns in Europe, 1788-1791. Established firm of J. B. Cramer & Co., 1828. Resided for period in Paris. Returned to London and retired, 1845. D. London, April 16, 1858.

WORKS.—*Pianoforte:* Opp. 1 to 9. Sonatas ; Concerto, Pf. and orch., op. 10 ; Sonatas, opp. 11 to 15 ; Concerto, Pf. and orch., op. 16 ; Marches and Waltzes, op. 17 ; Sonatas, opp. 18 to 23 ; Duet, op. 24 ; Three Sonatas, op. 25 ; Concerto, Pf; and orch , op. 26 ; Two Sonatas, op. 27 ; Quartet, Pf., violin, viola, and 'cello, op. 28 ; Three Sonatas, op. 29 ; Suite of Studies, op. 30 ; Three Sonatas, op. 31 ; Nocturne, op. 32 ; Three Sonatas, op. 33 ; Duet, op. 34 ; Sonatas, opp. 35-36 ;

Concerto, Pf. and orch., op. 37; Sonatas, op. 38-39; Studies, op. 40; Sonatas, opp. 41 to 44; Duet, Pf. and harp., op. 45; Sonatas, op. 46-47; Concerto, Pf. and orch., in C minor, op. 48; Three Sonatas, op. 49; Duet, op. 50; Concerto, Pf. and orch., in E flat, op. 51; Duet, Pf. and harp, op. 52; Sonata, op. 53; Nocturne, op. 54; "Dulce et Utile," op. 55; Concerto, Pf. and orch., op. 56; Sonatas, opp. 57 to 59; Bravura, op. 60; Quintet, Pf., violin, viola, 'cello, and d.-bass, op. 61; Sonatas, opp. 62-63. Method for the Pianoforte, in 5 parts, 1846.

The didactic works of Cramer have a permanent value for the student, as well as an artistic interest f r the musician. The general style of his compositions is in the manner of Mozart; but he carried the capabilities of the Pianoforte to a higher degree of perfection than any of his predecessors. The melodiousness of a great number of his compositions still gains for them a considerable share of attention.

CRAMER (Wilhelm). German violinist and cond., B. Mannheim, 1745. Settled in London, 1772. *Début* as violinist, 1773. Leader at the Opera, Ancient and Professional Concerts, etc. Leader of Handel Festivals of 1784-87. D. London, Oct. 5, 1799. Father of Franz and Johann B. Cramer.

No compositions of any importance have been published by this musician, who was one of the finest violinists of his time.

CRAMER AND COMPANY. English music-publishing firm, established in London by J. B. Cramer in 1828, and carried on to the present day by different partners. They published large works by Crotch, Balfe, Benedict, Barnett, Wallace, and numerous smaller pieces by the same composer, with Neukomm, Döhler, Moscheles, Thalberg, Horsley, Callcott, etc., etc.

CRAMPTON (Thomas). English org., comp., and editor, B. Sheerness, 1817. Has edited several collections of choral music, and composed anthems, glees, and instrumental music. He was made purchaser of music to the British Museum in 1875. Editor of "Pitman's Musical Monthly." D. Chiswick, April 13, 1885.

CRANFORD (William). English comp. Was one of the chor. of St. Paul's Cath., London, in 1650. He composed rounds, catches, and songs printed in the collections of Hilton, Playford, etc.

CRANG AND HANCOCK. English firm of organ-builders, established towards close of last century. Their operations extend over some years of the present century.

CRASKE (George). English violin-maker of the 19th century, who put forth a great quantity of instruments of moderate quality.

CRAVEN (J. T.) English writer and teacher, author of "The Child's First Singing Book," Lond., n.d.; "The Child's First Music Book, or Introduction to the Art of Playing the Pianoforte," Lond., n.d.

CRECQUILLON (Thomas). Belgian comp. and org., flourished during 1520-60. Chap.-master to Charles V. of Spain. He composed masses, motets, psalms, hymns, etc.

"His French songs, for four, five, and six voices, are numerous, and form valuable portions of the different collections of Chansons published in the Low Countries."—*Busby.*

CRESCENTINI (Girolamo). Italian soprano vocalist and teacher, B. near Urbino, 1766. S. under Gibelli. *Début* at Rome, 1783. Appeared in London, 1786. Sang throughout Europe, 1786-1816. D. Naples, 1846.

His works consist of vocal exercises, which are still in use.

CRESSONNOIS (Jules Alfred). French comp., B. Mortagne, Orne, April 17, 1823. S. under Kastner. Comp. "Chapelle d' Bachaumont," operetta, 1858. Military music, Pf. music, songs, etc.

CREYGHTON (Robert.) English divine and comp., B. Cambridge, 1639. Prof. of Greek in University of Cambridge, 1662. Canon Residentiary and Precentor of Wells cath., 1674. D.D. [1736]. D. Wells 1736.

WORKS.—Services in E flat and B flat; Anthems, various, et .

CRISPI (Pietro), Abbé. B. Rome, 1737. D. Rome, 1797. Wrote concertos, sonatas, etc., for the harpsichord.

CRISTOFORI (Bartolommeo di F.). Italian harpsichord-maker, B. Padua, 1651. Was engaged during his life at Florence in the manufacture of harpsichords of a superior class. He is the inventor of the Pianoforte, though his claim to be regarded as such has been frequently questioned, and only recently been thoroughly established. For further information the reader is referred to Grove's "Dictionary of Music," articles "Cristofori" and "Pianoforte." He D. Florence, March, 1731.

CRIVELLI (Gaetano.) Italian tenor vocalist, B. Bergamo, 1774. Appeared in London, 1817. Vocal teacher at R. A. M., 1823. Sang in Italy, etc., till 1829. D. Brescia, July, 1836. Wrote some operas, canzonetas, and vocal exercises.

CROAL (George). Scottish comp., B. Edinburgh, Feb. 28, 1811. Son of Mr. Croal, sub editor of the *Caledonian Mercury*. Apprenticed to Alex. Robertson, music-seller, 1823. Remained with him 1823-33. Commenced business as music-seller, 1840. Continued business till 1848. Latterly teacher in Edinburgh.

WORKS.—Eaglesward, a narrative poem, 1858; The Centenary Souvenir, Six Songs by Sir Walter Scott, Edinburgh. *Songs:* Away to the woods, My Willie, The Emigrant's Dream, My Grannie's Pouch, The Queen. Pianoforte music, consisting of arrangements, transcriptions, and dances, published mostly under name of Carlo Zotti.

Mr. Croal is an able performer of the old Scottish melodies, and on one occasion played a number of them to Sir Walter Scott. He is deserving of the greatest credit for having rescued from oblivion and adapting to appropriate words the songs now known as "When the kye comes hame" and "My Nannie's awa." The former was set to Hogg's words by permission of Messrs. Blackwood in 1836, and the latter to the verses of Burns in 1842. He transcribed the melodies from the singing of a friend, and they are now two of the most popular Scottish Songs.

CROCE (Giovanni Dalla). Italian comp., B. Chioggia, 1560. Pupil of Zarlino. Vice-chapel-master of cath. of S. Mark's, Venice, 1603 9. Priest at ch. of S. Maria in Formosa. D. Venice, Aug. 1609.

WORKS.—Il Primo Libro de' madrigali a cinque voci, 1585; Second ditto, 1588; Motetti, 1589; Motetti, 1590; Salmi, 1596; Triacca musicale, nella quale visono diversi capricci a 4, 5, 6, e 7 voci.

His psalms were reprinted in London. "Hard by a crystal fountain," a madrigal for 6 voices, is given in "Triumphs of Oriana," as his composition. His music is smoothly written, and is agreeable to modern ears.

CROFT (William). English comp. and org., B. Nether-Eatington, Warwick, 1677. S. under Blow. Chor. in Chap. Royal. Org. of St. Anne's, Soho, till 1711. Gent. of Chap. Royal, 1700. Joint org. Chap. Royal with Jeremiah Clarke, 1704. Sole org. of do., 1707. Master of Choristers and Comp. to Chap. Royal, and org. of Westminster Abbey, 1708. Resigned post of St. Anne's to John Isham, 1711. Mus. Doc., Oxon., 1715. D. London, Aug. 14, 1727.

WORKS.—Divine Harmony, or a new collection of select anthems used at H.M. Chapel Royal, etc., 1712; Thirty Select Anthems in score, Lond., 2 vols., fo., n.d. Musica Sacra, or select anthems in score, for two, three, foure, five, six, seven and eight voices, 1724. *Anthems:* Blessed are all they; Be merciful unto me, O God; God is gone up; Put me not to rebuke; O Lord rebuke me not; O Lord, thou hast searched me out; Hear my prayer, O Lord, 8 voices; I will sing unto the Lord; O be joyful in God; Rejoice in the Lord; Sing unto God; Sing praises unto the Lord; We wait for Thy loving kindness. He also completed the burial service. "I am the Resurrection," of which Purcell wrote one number, "Thou knowest Lord." Six sets of tunes for 2 violins and bass; Six Sonatas for 2 flutes; Six Solos for the flute. Overtures and incidental music to "Courtship à la Mode," 1700; "The Funeral," 1702; "The Twin Rivals," 1703; "The Lying Lover," 1704. Three Odes, for degree of Mus. Doc., 1715; Miscellaneous Odes for public occasions; Musicus Apparatus Academicus, being a composition of two odes, etc., 1713.

"Dr. Croft's anthems are very grand and solemn; their harmony is pure, and their melody elegant and expressive."—*Hogarth*. This opinion contradicts that of other authorities who speak of his music as never reaching the sublime, and being lacking in melody. Croft was undoubtedly one of the first among Britain's church composers, and the frequent use made of his anthems in every cathedral in Britain is a sufficient testimony to their enduring qualities. Croft introduced printing from engraved pewter plates, and his example was generally followed.

CROISEZ (Pierre). French pianist and comp., B. Paris, May 9, 1814. S. at Paris Cons. till 1832. Teacher and comp. in Paris. He has composed a great amount of brilliant salon pieces for the Pf., many of which have been very popular.

CROMAR (Rev. Alexander, M.A.) Scottish divine, and pastor of an Episcopal congregation in Liverpool, wrote "A Vindication of the Organ—a Review of the Rev. Dr. Candlish's publication entitled 'The Organ Question,'" Edin., 8vo., 1856.

CROMWELL (Thomas). English writer, author of "Church Music; a Sermon on the Antiquity, Excellence, and Propriety of the general adoption of the legitimate Music of the Christian Church," Lond., 8vo, 1843.

CROSS (Thomas). English music-engraver during 17th century. He published songs, etc., engraved in a superior manner on copper. His son John aided him in the business, and was himself a music-stamper.

CROSSDILL (John). English violoncellist, B. London, 1755. Educated at Westminster School. Chor. in Westminster Abbey. S. under B. Cooke and J. Robinson. Member of Royal Soc. of Musicians, 1768-1825. Violinist in Chap.-Royal, 1777. Chamber-musician to Queen Charlotte, 1782. Principal 'cello at Handel Commemoration, 1784. Principal 'cello at Ancient Concerts, etc. Married, and retired, 1790. D. Escrick, Yorkshire, Oct. 1825.

Crossdill was violoncellist-in-ordinary to King George IV., and a performer on the violoncello of the greatest ability. A number of anecdotes concerning him will be found in Parke's "Musical Memoirs."

CROSSE (John). English writer and musician. Author of "An account of the Grand Musical Festival held in Sept., 1823, in the Cathedral Church of York, to which is prefixed a Sketch of the Rise and Progress of Musical Festivals in Great Britain; with Biographical and Historical Notes," York, 4to, 1825. This is a valuable work of more than local interest. Crosse died about 1829.

CROTCH (William). English writer, comp. and org., B. Norwich, July 5, 1775. Gave early evidence of great talent for music. Taken to London, 1780. Assistant org. at Cambridge, 1786. S. for the Church at Oxford, 1788. Org. of Christ Ch., Oxford, 1790. Mus. Bac., Oxon., 1794. Org. of St. John's Coll., Oxford, 1797. Prof. of Music at Oxford, March, 1797. Mus. Doc., Oxon., 1799. Lectured in Music School of Oxford, 1800-4. Lectured at the Royal Institution, London, 1820. First Principal of the Royal Academy of Music, London, 1823. D. Taunton, Dec. 29, 1847.

WORKS.—*Oratorios:* The Captivity of Judah, 1789; Palestine, by Bishop Heber, 1812; The Captivity of Judah, re-written, 1834. *Anthems:* Be Merciful unto Me; Comfort, O Lord, the Soul of Thy Servant; Holy, Holy, Holy; How Dear are Thy Counsels; In God's Word will I Rejoice; Lo! Star-led Chiefs; Methinks I hear the full Celestial Choir; My God, look upon Me; O come hither, and hearken; O Lord God of Hosts; Sing we merrily; The Lord is King; Who is like unto Thee. Three concertos for the organ with accompts.; Fugues for the organ; Sonatas for the Pf.; Handel's oratorios (portions) adapted for the organ or Pf. Ode on the Accession of George IV., 1827; Ode to Fancy, Warton (Doctor's exercise), 1799. Glees, various. Elements of Musical Composition, comprehending the rules of Thorough-bass and the theory of Tuning. Lond., 4to, 1812; 2nd edition, 1833; 3rd edition, Novello, 1856; Practical Thorough-bass, or the art of playing from a figured bass, Lond., fol. n. d. ; Questions for the Examination of Pupils who are studying the work called Elements of Musical Composition and Practical Thorough-bass, Lond., 12mo [1830]; Substance of Several Courses of Lectures on Music, 8vo, 1831 ; Specimens of Various Styles of Music referred to in a course of Lectures read at Oxford and adapted to keyed Instruments, Lond., 3 vols., fol. n. d. ; Preludes for the Pianoforte, Compositions in various Styles, to which are Prefixed the Rudiments of Playing the Instrument [1823].

The extraordinary precocity of Crotch was such as to excite great interest among English musicians. The Hon. Daines Barrington and Dr. Burney have both published accounts of his marvellous musical faculties, and both agree with regard to the inborn genius which he undoubtedly possessed. Dr. Crotch is one of the greatest of England's talented and learned musicians, and he did more in an educational sense to spread musical knowledge that any other man of his day. His didactic works are of first class utility, and one of them, "Elements of Composition," is still largely used as a text-book, old fashioned though it be. His historical courses of lectures, among the first, and certainly the best ever delivered in Britain up to recent times, are marked by much variety and accuracy of information, and great taste and discrimination.

Of his oratorios "Palestine" promises to endure for a considerable time to come, no less on account of its many striking original features than on account of its departure from the conventional style of Handel. Busby, writing in 1819, says, ". . . and his more recent production of an oratorio [Palestine] exhibits his theoretical knowledge, general powers of vocal conception, and command of instrumental accompaniment, in a light truly favourable to his character, as an original author in the higher province of composition." Hogarth, writing in 1838, says—" In this oratorio Dr. Crotch has displayed a grandeur and originality of conception worthy of his most illustrious predecessors, and has united, in the happiest manner, the depth and severity of the old ecclesiastical masters, with the graceful and flowing melody and orchestral effects of the modern school." The press opinions passed on its recent revivals are even more flattering than any of the above, so that the prospect seems certain that as time advances this truly beautiful creation will advance in public es.imation. As regards his anthems it is sufficient to say, so often and wide-spread is their performance, that they are among the worthiest specimens of sacred music to be found in the noble collection of British Church music. His organ concertos are fine specimens of a somewhat old-fashioned school of instrumental composition, but their effect when performed by a capable organist is equal to some of the best works of recent times. Crotch's minor works are in no way remarkable, save that they represent the fugitive productions of a man of musical genius.

CROUCH (Anna Maria), *née* PHILLIPS. English soprano vocalist, B. London, April 20, 1763. S. under T. Linley, to whom she was articled in 1779. *Début* at Drury Lane Theatre in Arne's "Artaxerxes," 1780. Appeared in Ireland with great success, 1783. Married to Mr. Crouch, a lieutenant in the navy, 1785. Sang at oratorios at Drury Lane, 1787. Separated from Crouch, 1792. Resided afterwards with Michael Kelly. Retired from the stage, 1800. D. Brighton, Oct. 2, 1805.

"She had a remarkably sweet voice, and a naive, affecting style of singing ; this added to extraordinary personal charms, made her a great favourite of the public for many years." A most laudatory poem on her is entitled " Euphrosyné, an Ode to Beauty : addressed to Mrs. Crouch, by Silvester Otway " [otherwise John Oswald], Lond., 4to, 1788. See also Memoirs of Mrs. Crouch. By M. Young, Lond., 2 vols., 1806, with portrait.

CROUCH (Frederick William Nicholls). English comp. and teacher, B. Devizes, July 31, 1808. S. under Bochsa and W. Hawes. Played 'cello at H.M. Theatre. S. at the R.A.M. under Crotch, Attwood, Lindley, etc., 1822. Member of Queen Adelaide's band. Principal 'cellist at Drury Lane Theatre. Engaged for a time in the manufacture of zinc. Invented the engraving process known as Zincography. Musical Supervisor to D'Almaine & Co., London. Went to America with Maretzek, 1849. Director of the Sacred Harmonic Society, Portland, Me. Director of the Mathew's

Choir, Washington. Served during the American Civil War on the Confederate side. Latterly unemployed and in want. Teacher of Music at Baltimore.

WORKS.—*Operas:* Sir Roger de Coverly (MS); The Fifth of November, 1670 (MS.) *Collections:* Echoes of the Lakes, Twenty-four Irish Songs, Poetry by Mrs. Crawford, 1840 (containing "Kathleen Mavourneen"); Songs of Erin, Poetry by D. Ryan ; Echoes of the Past ; Bardic Reminiscences ; Songs of the Past ; Songs of the Olden Time ; Songs of a Rambler ; Songs of the Parish Wake ; Songs of the Seasons ; Songs of the Abbeys and Cathedrals ; Sketches of the Emerald Isle ; Hours of Idleness ; Roadside Sketches ; Songs of Shakespeare ; Songs of a Voyager ; Friendship's Offering ; Wayside Melodies ; Songs of the Bards; Beauties of other Lands ; Single Songs of Mrs. Hemans, Mrs. Norton, Bayly, Carpenter, Lemon, Jerrold, Thackeray, Campbell, Rogers, S. Knowles, etc. ; Poetical Works. Complete Treatise on the violoncello, etc., Lond. [1827].

Crouch, though now only remembered by his "Kathleen Mavourneen," was a musician who possessed a great natural fund of beautiful melody, which he used in a popular, though not inartistic manner. His songs appeal to the educated and refined ear, besides possessing a certain homely charm and fireside interest. Crouch was a composer of considerable real inspiration, and most of his songs are quite free from stilted and artificial mannerisms.

In the United States Crouch did a vast deal of good by introducing the best works of English glee and madrigal writers, as well as producing some larger works by Méhul, Rossini, etc. His latterly indigent circumstances is very regretable, since, to external appearances, they were produced by unavoidable misfortune. A recent account speaks of his adoption by an American gentleman.

CROW (Edwin John). English comp. and org., B. Sittingbourne, Sept. 17, 1841. Chor. at Rochester Cath. Articled to J. L. Hopkins. S. under John Hopkins, Dr. Steggall, and H. Banister. Assistant to G. A. Löhr at Leicester, 1858. Org. successively of Holy Trinity, St. Andrew's Ch., and St. John's Ch., Leicester, 1861-1873. Fellow of Coll. of Org., 1868. Mus. Bac., Cantab., 1872. Org. and Choirmaster of Ripon Cath., 1873. Mus. Doc. Cantab., 1882. Mem. of Musical Assoc., Central Council of Soc. of Professional Musicians. Mem. of Council of Coll. of Org., etc.

WORKS.—The 146th Psalm, for voices and orch.; Communion Service in F (gained College of Organists' prize) ; Morning Service in C ; Evening Services in G, A, and D ; Music for Masonic Ceremonies ; Hymns ; Chants ; Songs, various; Pianoforte Music; Church Oratorio for Harvest-time; Orchestral and Organ Works.

CROWDY (John). English writer and editor, B. Lewknor, Jan. 6, 1834. Editor successively of *The Musician*, *The Musical Standard*, and *The Artist*; sub-editor of the *Guardian* from 1854. D. Addlestone, Surrey, Jan. 12, 1883.

WORKS.—A Kalendar of Cadences, in the form called Free Chant, adapted for the recitation of the Psalms, Lond., n.d.; The Free Church Canticle Book, n.d.; The Psalter, n.d.; The Church Choirmaster, a Critical Guide to the Musical Illustration of the Order for Daily Prayer, Lond., 1864 ; A Short Commentary on Handel's oratorio, The Messiah, Lond., [1875] ; Analysis of Musical Works and contributions to the musical press, etc.

CROWEST (Frederick J.) English writer, musician and critic, B. London, 1850. Trained as a choir-boy and subsequently org. and choirmaster in various London and country churches. Author of "The Great Tone Poets; being short Memoirs of the greater Musical Composers," Lond., 8vo, 1874 (7 eds.) ; "Book of Musical Anecdotes, from every available source," Lond., 2 vols., 1878 (2 eds.) ; "Phases of Musical England," 8vo, 1881 : "Musical History and Biography, in the Form of Question and Answer," Lond., 1883 ; "Advice to Singers," London, n. d., Anon. (2 eds.) A contributor to the musical and general press, and for many years London critic of "Church's Musical Visitor" (American). Comp. various songs and some Church music. Cond. of the Female Choral Union, 1874-8. Well known as a tenor singer in public and private, under the *nom de guerre* of Arthur Vitton.

CROWTHER (John). English violin-maker, B. 1760. D. 1810. One of the best makers of his period. His instruments are generally dark in colour and well finished. His violas are good.

CROZIER (William). English oboe-player, pupil of Barret. Member of Crystal Palace orch., 1855-1870. D. Dec. 20, 1870.

CRÜGER (Johann). German comp. and writer. B. near Guben, April 8, 1598. Chap.-master of the Ch. of St. Nicholas, Berlin, 1622. D. Berlin, Feb. 23, 1662.

WORKS.—Synopsis Musica, etc.; Praxis Pietatis, a collection of Lutheran hymns. This latter work went through a great number of editions, and some of the melodies in it are used in recent psalmodic works.

CRUICKSHANK (J.) Scottish writer, author of "Flutina and Accordion Teacher," Lond., 1851.

CRUSE (Edward). English musician and writer. Compiled "Psalms of the Church, adapted for four voices, with a History of Church Music and Notation, the whole calculated for general adoption by every sect of the Reformed Religion," Lond., [1835], fol.; Te Deum, and other church music.

CRUVELLI (Jeanne Sophie Charlotte), née CRUWELL. German soprano vocalist, B. Bieleleld, Westphalia, Mar. 12, 1826. Début at Venice, 1847. Appeared in London, 1849. Sang in Paris, Italy, etc., 1851. Married Baron Vigier and retired, 1855.

CUDMORE (Richard). English violinist, comp., and pianist, B. Chichester, 1787. S. under a musician named James Fargett, Reinagle, and Salomon. Violinist at Chichester Theatre, 1799. Resided in Chichester as violinist and teacher, 1799-1808. S. pianoforte under Woelfl at London. Member of Philharmonic Band, London. Resided in Manchester as leader of Gentlemen's Concerts. D. Manchester, Jan. 1841.

WORKS.—The Martyr of Antioch, oratorio ; Concertos for the violin ; Concertos for the Pf.; Songs, etc.

The accounts preserved of Cudmore's executive abilities on several instruments indicate that he was a performer of the highest and most versatile powers.

CUISSET (Frank F.). English org. and writer, author of "The Vocalist's Indispensable Practice, a series of exercises for promoting the strength and flexibility of the voice, Lond. [1875]. Comp. also concerted vocal music, songs, etc. Org. at Godalming.

CULVER (Richard). American writer, author of the "American Guitarist," Boston, n. d.; "Guitar Instructor," n. d.

CULWICK (James C.). English org., comp., and writer, B. West Bromwich, Staffordshire, 1845. Chor. and afterwards assistant org. Lichfield Cath. Org. Parsonstown, 1866 ; Bray, 1868 ; S. Ann's, Dublin, 1870 ; Chap. Royal Dublin, 1881. Prof. of Pf., org. and harmony, Alexandra Coll., and cond. of Harmonic Soc. Dublin. Author of "The Rudiments of Music : an Introductory Text-Book," Dublin, 1881 ; "The Study of Music, and its Place in General Education," Dublin, 8vo, 1882. Sonatas, etc., for org. and Pf. ; Quartet for Pf. vn., viola and 'cello ; Church music, songs, etc.

CUMMING (Angus). Scottish violinist and comp., flourished during latter half of 18th century. He published "A Collection of Strathspey and Old Highland Reels, by Angus Cumming at Grantown in Strathspey," Edin., fo., 1780. A second edition was published at Glasgow some time after.

CUMMINGS (William Hayman). English comp., tenor vocalist, and writer, B. Sidbury, Devon, 1835. Chor. in St. Paul's Cath. Chor. in the Temple Ch. Org. of Waltham Abbey. Tenor singer in the Temple, Westminster Abbey. Singer in the Chap. Royal. Prof. of Singing at Royal Coll. for the Blind, Norwood, London.

WORKS.—The Fairy Ring, cantata ; Te Deum, jubilate, sanctus, etc., in D ; O Lord, give ear, anthem ; Kyries, various. Glees : Come silent evening ; Sweet flowers of summer; O thou sweet bird, (prize); A fond good-night (prize); Ye gentle muses (prize); Song should breathe (prize); Oh, the summer night (prize). *Part-Songs:* O were I but a drop of dew; Sunday part-songs (6 numbers); On a day, alack the day; Hark the soft bugle; Golden slumbers. *Songs:* Yellow lie the corn rigs; Ask me no more; Birdie on yon leafless tree; Hush thy sweet song; Just as of old; He is with thee, though alone; May's wedding; Star gazing; The love of long ago; The pilgrim's rest; They came together; Playing on the virginals; Spare my boy at sea; Love me little, love me long; Love's vigil; Sweet Rothesay Bay, etc. The Rudiments of Music, Lond., 8vo [1877]; Purcell (Great Musicians Series), Lond., 8vo, 1882; Contributions to periodical literature; Papers read before musical associations.

Mr. Cummings was originally a tenor singer of much cultivation, and as such gained a great reputation, but latterly he has become identified with musical antiquarian pursuits, which he follows with much success. He has chiefly given attention to English musical history, including an advocacy of the claims of Henry Purcell to a more wide-spread recognition. He established the "Purcell Society," which has issued a few publications. His compositions are careful and finished productions, and some of them have excited considerable attention.

CUMMINS (Charles). English comp., pianist, and violinist, B. York, 1785. S. under Dr. Miller of Doncaster. Leader and violinist in theatres of the west of England. Wrote an amount of music for dramatic pieces, and a pamphlet against the system of J. B. Logier. D. [?]

CUNIO (Angelo). Italian pianist and comp., B. Milan. S. at Milan Cons. Lived in Edinburgh and London as teacher of the Pf. His works consist of transcriptions and light pieces for the Pf.

CUNNABELL (J. S.). American writer, author of an "Accordeon Instructor," Boston, Ditson, n. d.

CUNNINGHAM (Allan). Scottish poet and writer, B. Dumfriesshire, 1784. D. London, 1842. He wrote a number of novels and biographical works, and a work entitled "The Songs of Scotland, with Critical and Historical Notes." He is best known to musicians as the author of a number of fine lyrics, most of which have been set to music. The well-known sea-song "A wet sheet and a flowing sea," which has been set to music over and over again, is of his composition.

CURIONI (Alberico). Italian tenor vocalist, B. 1790. Appeared in London, 1821. Sang there till 1832. Was Hon. Mem. of R. A. M. Sang at Vienna, Paris, etc. D. [?]

CURRIE (Rev. James, M.A.) Scottish musician and educationist, now Rector of the Established Church Training College, Edinburgh. He is author of "The Elements of Musical Analysis," Edin., 1858; "A First Musical Grammar," Edin., 12mo, n. d. Works on Infant and Secondary Education; School Songs, etc.

CURSCHMANN (Karl Friedrich). German song-writer and cond., B. Berlin, June, 1805. S. under Spohr and Hauptmann. Resided chiefly in his native town. D. Berlin, Aug. 24, 1841.

His works consist of Books of Songs, some of which, as Wiegenlied, Die Stillen Wanderer, Der Abend, Ständchen, Der Fischer, Altes Volkslied, Jägerlied, An Rose, Der Schiffer, Der kleine Hans, are well-known and beautiful productions, best remembered in Britain and America under translated names. The most of Curschmann's songs and concerted pieces are gems, and thoroughly deserving of their popularity.

CURTISS (N. P. B.). American writer, author of "Method for the Guitar," Boston, n. d.; "New Method for the Zither," by Curtiss and Charles Behr, Boston, n. d.; Songs, etc.

CURWEN (John). English musician and writer, B. Heckmondwike, Yorks., Nov. 14, 1816. Educated at Coward Coll. and London University. Ordained minister. Assistant minister at Independent Ch., Basingstoke, Hants, 1838.

Co-pastor at Stowmarket, Suffolk, 1841. Pastor at Plaistow, Essex, 1844. Founded Tonic Sol-Fa Associations, 1853. Established Tonic Sol-Fa Coll., 1862. Resigned ministry, and devoted himself to propagation of the system, 1867. Established "Tonic Sol-Fa Reporter," and publishing agency in London. D. Heaton Mersey House, near Manchester, May 26, 1880.

WORKS.—An Account of the Tonic Sol-fa method of Teaching to Sing, Lond., 8vo, 1854; Grammar of Vocal Music, with Lessons and Exercises founded on the Tonic Sol-fa method, and a full introduction to the art of singing at sight from the old notation, Lond., 8vo, n. d.; Standard Course of Lessons on the Tonic Sol-fa method of teaching to sing, Lond., 4to, n. d.; Tonic Sol-fa instrumental instruction books; Harmonium and Organ; Theory of Fingering; The First Pianoforte Book; Reed Band Book; Brass Band Book; String Band Book; separate Works, all Lond., n. d.; Musical Statics; Art of Teaching, being the Teacher's Manual of the Tonic Sol-fa, 8vo, n. d.; Musical Theory, Lond. [1879]; The Common-places of Music (Lectures), 10 parts, 1871-3; Primer of Tonic Sol-fa (Novello), 8vo, n. d.; Music in Worship and other papers on the People's Psalmody, Lond., n. d.; The Present Crisis of Music in Schools, a Reply to Mr. Hullah, Lond., 8vo [1873]; The Child's own Hymn-Book; How to Observe Harmony; Construction Exercises in Elementary Composition; Arrangements, etc.

The imperfections of the Tonic Sol-fa method have been so frequently handled by its opponents that it becomes scarcely necessary to dwell upon them here. Like every other innovation, the method has met with extreme opposition from a number of musicians who have gained the greatest personal renown. The opinions of those musicians have great weight, but it is most fortunate that their views on the question have not hindered the wide-spread adoption of the system throughout the British Empire. In spite of its palpable shortcomings, the Tonic Sol-fa system is undoubtedly *the* system for the many thousands of the poorer classes who sing for recreation. The opponents of the system hold that the staff notation can be learned in as short a period as the Tonic Sol-fa, and this being so, why not confine the studies of the young to the method which will ultimately prove most useful? The initial affirmation is quite inaccurate; the staff notation cannot be learned in three times the space that suffices to enable one to acquire a thorough knowledge of the Tonic Sol-fa. But this argument is nothing when placed side by side with the great results which have marked the progress of the system in Britain. The interest in music, formerly confined to the upper classes, is now all but universal, and the poorest artizan is able to bear with good will and some ability a part in a musical performance.

Mr. Curwen's labours in affecting a great revolution in the musical leanings of the British public, are deserving of the greatest praise, and will place him at the head of popular educationists in this particular branch.

CURWEN (John Spencer). English writer and teacher, B. Plaistow, 1847. S. under G. Oakey, and at R. A. M. under G. A. Macfarren; A. Sullivan, E. Prout, 1875-79. Assoc. R. A. M., 1879. President of the Tonic Sol-fa Coll., June, 1880.

WORKS.—Part Songs, etc.; Studies in Worship Music, chiefly as regards congregational singing, Lond., 8vo, 1880; The Tonic Sol-fa System; A Paper Read before the Society of Arts, Mar. 22, 1882, Lond., la. 8vo, 1882; Contributions to Periodical Literature.

Mr. Curwen is an able and warm advocate of the Tonic Sol-fa System, and has hitherto met with the greatest success on all hands. The history of the system is best given in Mr. J. S. Curwen's own words, taken from his paper :—" The chief events in the history of the system may be briefly stated. Mr. Curwen's first work was issued in 1841, and others in 1843 and 1848. In September, 1850, the first gathering of pupils and friends of the method was held in London. In 1858, the Tonic Sol fa Association was formed. In 1855, the monthly issue of the *Tonic Sol-fa Reporter* began, and an aggregate meeting of 4000 pupils of the system was held in London. In the same year, the first attempt to write difficult music in the Tonic Sol-fa notation was made, by the issue of Romberg's 'Lay of the Bell.' In 1855-6, Mr. Curwen visited Scotland, and the method was soon afterward adopted by the three Presbyterian Churches. In September, 1857, the Tonic Sol-fa Association held the first children's concert on the Handel orchestra at the Crystal

Palace. These concerts were continued for many years. Mr. Curwen's first attempt to teach harmony by means of the notation was made in 1862, and after this he spent several years in writing manuals, applying the system to the pianoforte, organ, to stringed instruments, reed instruments, and brass instruments. In 1867, the Tonic Sol-fa Association took part in the International Choral Competition at Paris, receiving a prize of equality with the first choir, and only being debarred from the first prize because the choir contained ladies' voices. In the same year, at a concert by 4500 adults at the Crystal Palace, an anthem, composed for the occasion by Prof. Macfarren, was read off at first sight... In 1868, the Tonic Sol-fa College was founded... In 1869, the Committee of Council on Education, finding that the system had been already adopted very largely in schools, accepted it on an equality with the old notation for use in elementary schools and training colleges. In 1872, the London School Board adopted the system, a step which has since been followed by all the principal School Boards in England and Scotland. In 1872-73, Tonic Sol-fa choirs obtained prizes in public musical competitions at the Crystal Palace. In 1875, the Tonic Sol-fa College was incorporated according to Act of Parliament. The growth of the number of pupils has been as follows :—In 1856, it was calculated at 20,000; in 1858, at 65,000; in 1872, at 315,000; and now it is, at the very least, 500,000. The system is, as yet, almost untaught on the Continent, but it has been very much used by missionaries and by English colonists in all parts of the world... In England, the Tonic Sol-fa system is largely employed in reformatories, and mission work of all kinds. It is also used to a remarkable extent in elementary schools. The last Government return shows that out of 5395 schools in England, Wales, and Scotland, teaching singing by some system or other, 3987, or nearly three-fourths, use the Tonic Sol-fa..."

CUSINS (William George). English comp. pianist and cond., B. London, Oct. 14, 1833. Chor. in Chap. Royal, 1843. S. at Brussels Cons. under Fétis, 1844. S. at R. A. M. under Bennett, Potter, Lucas, etc. Gained King's Scholarship, do., 1847; re-elected, 1849. Org. of Queen's Private Chap., 1849. Violinist at Royal Italian Opera. Assistant Prof. of Pf. at R. A. M., 1851. Full Prof., do. Cond. of Philharmonic Soc., 1867. Cond. of Royal Band of Music, 1870. Prof. of music at Queen's Coll., 1875. Joint Examiner for National Training School of Music, 1876. Prof. at Trinity Coll., and Prof. of Pf. at Guildhall School of Music, London, 1885.

WORKS.—Royal Wedding Serenata, 1863; Gideon, an oratorio, Gloucester Festival, 1871; Masonic Prayers in the Ceremonies of Initiation, Passing and Raising, set to music; Responses to the Commandments, sung in H. M. private chapel; Te Deum for solo voices, chorus and orch., 1880; I will receive the cup of salvation, anthem. Songs from the published writings of Alfred Tennyson (Poet Laureate), set to music by various composers, and edited by W. G. Cusins (4 songs by himself); Six Four-part songs, Lond., 1869. Songs: The wishing well; Longing. Two concert overtures for full orch. Pf. Concerto in A minor, performed by the comp., and Arabella Goddard, with success in Rome, Liverpool, New York, and London. Trio for Pf., violin, and 'cello, performed in London, Rome, etc; Violin Concerto (MS.) Some Pf. pieces. Handel's Messiah, an examination of the original and of some contemporary MSS.

CUSTARD (Walter Goss). English comp. and org., B. June 9, 1841. Nephew of Sir John Goss. Articled to Sir George Elvey, Chap.-Royal, Windsor, 1857. Org. of Spring Grove Ch., Isleworth, 1861. Org. of Christ Ch., St. Leonards-on-Sea, 1865.

WORKS.—The Office of the Holy Communion in E flat; Choral Service in D; Baptismal Hymn; Te Deum in F; Benedictus in F; Communion Office in F, 1881; Agnus Dei and Benedictus, 1880; Hymns, various. The Chorister's Daily Practice, Lond., n. d. First Nocturne C minor for Pf.; Reverie in E; Berceuse in D flat; Rodino in A, op. 17; Impromptu in B, op. 20; Le Chasseur, Caprice, op. 21; Short Studies in all the major and minor keys, etc., for Pf.; Twelve Studies for Pf., op. 22, 1879; Triumphal March for Organ; Songs and minor Pf. works.

CUTELL (Richard). English musician and writer of the 15th century, author of a treatise on Counterpoint, preserved in the Bodleian Library, Oxford (MS., imperfect).

CUTHBERT. A celebrated English violin-maker of this name flourished during the 17th century. His instruments are rare, and of fine quality.

CUTLER (William Henry). English pianist, vocalist and comp., B. London, 1792. S. under Dr. Arnold and W. Russell. *Début* as pianist in concerto by Viotti, 1800. Chor. in St. Paul's Cath. Mus. Bac., Oxon., 1812. Org. of St. Helen's, Bishopgate, 1818. Taught Music by Logier's System. Org. of Quebec Chap., Portman Square, 1823. Sang at the principal London concerts. D. [?]

WORKS.—Church Music; Pf. Music; fantasias, rondos, marches, duets, songs, etc.

CUVILLON (Jean Baptiste Philémon de). French comp., B. Dunkirk, May, 1809. Wrote Operas. Pf. music, songs, etc.

CUZENS (Benjamin). English comp. and org. Flourished about end of last century. Wrote "The Portsmouth Harmony" (Psalm Tunes, etc.), n. d. "Divine Harmony, containing Six Anthems and a Christmas Ode." Five Anthems and Five Collects, etc.

CUZZONI. *See* SANDONI.

CZAPEK. *See* HATTON (John Liphot).

CZERNY (Karl). Austrian comp., pianist, and writer, B. Vienna, Feb. 21, 1791. S. under Krumpholz, Beethoven, Hummel, and Clementi. Resided chiefly at Vienna as teacher and comp. D. Vienna, July 15, 1857.

WORKS.—Op. 1. Variations for Pf. and violin, 1818; other works numbered up to over 850, chiefly for the Pf.; School of Practical Composition, op. 600, trans. by John Bishop, Lond., 3 vols. fo., [1840]; Exercises on Harmony and Thorough-Bass, Lond., 8vo, [1846]; Letters to a Young Lady on Playing the Pianoforte, Lond., 8vo, 1851; Complete Theoretical and Practical Pianoforte School, trans. by John Bishop, Lond., 4 vols., n.d.; Pianoforte Primer, trans. by John Bishop, Lond., n.d.

Of all Czerny's immense quantity of Pf. works, none seem at all likely to survive the present century; 95 per cent. of the whole number being even now forgotten. He was a good teacher, and was the preceptor of Liszt, Döhler, Madam Oury, and a number of our English pianists.

The educational value of his compositions must have been high in their time, and probably aided greatly in the formation of the modern school of pianoforte playing. His "School" is still a standard work.

CZERWENKA (Josef). Bohemian comp. and pianist, B. 1759. D. Vienna, 1855.

D.

DACOSTA (Isaac Franco). French clarinet player and comp., B. Bordeaux, Jan. 17, 1778. D. Bordeaux, July 12, 1866. Comp. for his instrument.

DALAYRAC (Nicolas). French comp., B. Muret, Languedoc, June 13, 1753. Intended for study of the law. Went to Paris, and became a commissioned officer in the guards of Count d'Artois, 1774. S. under Langlé and Caffaro. Chevalier of Legion of Honour. D. Paris, Nov. 27, 1809.

WORKS.—*Operas:* Le Petit Souper, 1781; Le Chevalier à la mode, 1781; L' Eclipse totale, 1782; Le Corsaire, 1783; Les Deux Tuteurs, 1784; La Dot, 1785; L'Amant-Statue, 1785; Nina, 1786; Azemia, 1787; Renaud d'Ast, 1787; Sargines, 1788; Raoul de Créqui, 1789; Les Deux Petits Savoyards, 1789; Fanchette, 1789; La Soirée orageuse. 1790; Vert-Vert, 1790; Philippe et Georgette, 1791; Camille, 1791; Agnès et Olivier, 1791; Elise-Hortense, 1792; L' Actrice chez elle, 1792; Ambroise, 1793; Roméo et Juliette, 1793; Urgande et Merlin, 1793; La Prise de

Toulon, 1793 ; Adèle et Dorsan, 1794 ; Arnill, 1795 ; Marianne, 1795 ; La l'auvre Femme, 1795 ; La Famille Américaine, 1796 ; Gulnare, 1797 ; La Maison isolée, 1797 ; Primerose, 1798 ; Alexis, 1798 ; Le Château de Montenero, 1798 ; Les Deux Mots, 1798 ; Adolphe et Clara, 1799 ; Laure, 1799 ; Le Leçon, 1799 ; Catinat, 1800 ; Le Rocher de Leucade, 1800 ; Maison à vendre, 1800 ; La Boucle de cheveux, 1801 ; La Tour de Neustadt, 1801 ; Picaros et Diego, 1803 ; Une Heure de mariage, 1804 ; La Jeune Prude, 1804 ; Gulistan, 1805 ; Lina, 1807 ; Koulouf, 1808 ; Le Poëte et le Musicien, 1811. Instrumental music, etc.

The music of Dalayrac is light, and highly melodious, and was among the most popular of the operatic music current in Paris at the close of last century. Now it is little known.

DALBERG (Baron Johann Friedrich Hugo). German writer and traveller, B. Coblenz, 1752. D. 1813.

He wrote a number of works on Oriental music, didactic works, and compositions for the Pf., etc.

D'ALBERT. See ALBERT.

DALE (Joseph). English comp. and editor, author of "Dale's Collection of Sixty Favourite Scotch Songs, taken from the original manuscripts of the most celebrated Scotch authors and composers, properly adapted for the German flute," Books I., II., and III., ob. 4to, n. d. (end of last century). Wrote an "Introduction to the Pianoforte, Harpsichord, or Organ," op. 12. fo., n. d., and many works for Pf., etc.

DALE (Reginald F.). See TROUTBECK.

D'ALEMBERT (Jean Le Rond). French philosopher (1717-1783), author of "Elemens de Musique suivant les principes de M. Rameau," Paris, 8vo, 1752. In this he undertook to demonstrate, in a clear and forcible manner, the long since exploded theories of Rameau. There are many editions of the work.

DALGLISH (Robert). Scottish comp., B. Pollokshaws, Renfrewshire, July, 1806. D. there, August 5, 1875. Comp. of a number of anthems, glees, and psalms, of a very feeble class, but which were at one time regarded with some favour in Glasgow.

DALL'OGLIO (Domenico). Italian comp. and violinist, B. Padua. D. 1764. He composed a number of melodious pieces for the violin.

D'ALMAINE & MACKINLAY. English firm of music publishers, established in London, before the middle of the present century. They published a great amount of valuable works by the foremost composers of about 1834-50. The firm has passed under various names and managements.

DALMAZZO (G.). Author of "Adelina Patti's Life, and her Appearances at the Royal Italian Opera, Covent Garden," Lond., 1877.

DALYELL (Sir John Graham, Bart.). Scottish antiquary, B. 1799. D. 1851. In addition to a number of valuable historical and scientific works, he wrote, "Musical Memoirs of Scotland, with historical annotations, and numerous illustrative plates," Edin., 4to, 1849. This is now an extremely scarce work, and is of some value as a contribution to Scottish musical archæology.

DAMASCENE (Alexandre). French comp., who was naturalized in England about 1682. He was a Gent. Chap. Roy., in 1691, and D. July 14, 1719. His works appear in various collections of songs published during his lifetime.

DAMCKE (Berthold). German comp. and 'cellist, B. Hanover, Feb. 1812. Directed several musical societies in German towns. Married Mdlle. Servais. D. Paris, Feb. 15, 1875.

WORKS.—Deborah, oratorio ; The 32nd Psalm ; Music for 'cello and Pf. ; Partsongs and songs.

DAMON (William). English comp. and org., B. [1540]. Org. of Queen Elizabeth's chap. D. early in the 17th century.

WORKS.—The Psalmes of David in English Meter, with notes of foure parts set unto them by Gulielmo Damon, for John Bull, to the use of Christians for recreating themselves, instede of fond and unseemely ballades, 1579 [said to have been published by Bull, a goldsmith in London, without Damon's consent or knowledge]. The Former Booke of the Musicke of Mr. William Damon, late one of Her Majesties musitions; conteining all the Tunes of Dauids Psalmes as they are ordinarily soung in the church, most excellently by him composed into 4 parts, altus, cantus, tenor, bassus; in which sett the tenor singeth the church tune. Published for the recreation of such as delight in musicke, by W. Swayne, Gent. Printed by T. Este, 1591. The Second Booke of the Musicke of Mr. William Damon, containing all the Tunes of David's Psalmes, differing from the former in respect that the highest part singeth the church tune, Lond., 1591.

The tunes to which Damon gave harmonies are 40 in number, and are the first psalms with harmonies published in England.

DAMOREAU (Laure Cinthie Montalant), *née* CINTHIE. French soprano vocalist, B. Paris, Feb. 6, 1801. S. at Cons., Paris. Appeared at Paris, 1819. Sang in London, 1822. *Début* at Paris, 1826. Married M. Damoreau, an actor, 1827. Sang in Europe, and in the U. S. A., 1844. D. near Paris, Feb. 25, 1863.

DAMROSCH (Leopold). German comp. and cond., B. Posen, Oct 22, 1832. S. under H. Ries and Dehn. Attached to Court Chapel of Weimar. Cond. at Posen and Breslau. Settled in America as cond. of various musical societies, 1871. D. New York, Feb. 16, 1885.

WORKS.—Part-songs; Songs; Concerto for vn. and orch. in D minor; Pf. music; Ruth and Naomi, sacred cantata; Miscellaneous vocal music.

Damrosch was held in high respect in America as a conductor and musician, where he was greatly instrumental in introducing many high-class modern works.

DANA (William Henry). American comp., B. Warren, Ohio, June 10, 1846. Educated at Williston Seminary, East Hampton, Mass. S. in Berlin, at Kullak's Cons., and with August Haupt, org. of Parochial Kirche; and also at the Royal Academy of Music, London, 1881. President of "Dana's Musical Institute," and Prof. of Harmony and Composition.

WORKS.—Practical Thorough Base, 1873; Orchestration, 1875; Military Band Instrumentation, 1876; Practical Harmony, 1884; De Profundis, for soli, chorus, and full orchestra. Songs, Motettes, and many minor piano compositions.

Mr. Dana has been very active in his field of labour. Was one of the founders of the Music Teachers' National Association, a charter member of the National College of Teachers, and has lectured before the National Association, and many State and other Associations, on musical and other topics. Through his management, one of the most excellent musical schools in America has an existence. As a traveller, he holds a conspicuous position, having dipped his oar in Arctic seas, and fed on the reindeer of the Laplander, as part of his experiences.

DANBÉ (Jules). French violinist and comp., B. Caen, Nov. 15, 1840. S. Paris Cons. Writes transcriptions for vn., etc.

DANBY (John). English glee comp., B. 1750 [1757]. Biography obscure. Gained 10 prizes from Catch Club, for 7 glees, 2 canons, and an ode, 1781-94. Org. at chap. of Spanish embassy. D. London, May 16, 1798.

WORKS. —Masses; Motets; Catches, canons, and glees, for three, four, and five voices, in Score, 4 books, Lond., fo., n. d. [c. 1785-98]; La Guida alla Musica Vocale, op. 2, Lond., fo. [1787], n. d. *Glees:* When Sappho Tuned (Smollet), 3 voices; When generous wine expands; When floods retire to the sea; The fairest flowers the vale prefer; Sweet thrush; Shepherds, I have lost my love; Go to my Anna's breast; Fair Flora decks; Come, ye party jangling swains; Awake, Æolian lyre, 4 voices; Music has power; Soft pleasing pains unknown before; When beauty's soul; The nightingale; O salutaris hostia, etc.

Danby belonged to the sweet pastoral school of Atterbury, Paxton, and Spofforth, rather than to the more powerful school of Webbe and Callcott. His glees are most charming works, and it is to be regretted that more is not known of the composer.

DANCE (William). English violinist, pianist, and comp., B. 1755. S. under Aylward, Baumgarten, and Giardini. Violinist in Drury Lane Theatre, 1771-74. Leader at King's Theatre, 1775-93. Led band at Handel Commemorations in 1790, etc. One of founders of Philharmonic Soc. Director and Treasurer of do. Teacher of Pf. in Lond. D. London, 1840.

Dance composed a number of Lessons, op. 1, etc., sonatas, fantasias, variations, etc., for Pf., some of which were popular in their day.

DANCLA (Jean Charles). French violinist and comp., B. Bagnères-de-Bigorre, Dec. 25, 1818. Entered Paris Cons., 1828. S. under Baillot, Halévy, and Berton. Gained prizes for vn.-playing, etc. Prof. of violin at Paris Cons., 1860. Chevalier of Legion of Hon.

WORKS.— Op. 1. and 3. Airs, varied, for violin and orch.; op. 2. Six Studies for vn.; op. 6. First Symphonie-concertante, for 2 vns. and orch.; op. 9. String Quartet; op. 10. Second Symph.-concertante; op. 11. Duet for vn. and Pf.; op. 12. Forty-six Studies for vn.; op. 13. Studies; op. 14. Twelve easy Studies for vn.; Fantasies for violin and Pf. or orch., opp. 28, 42, 47, 55; String Quartets, opp. 5, 18, 41, 47, 56, 80, 87; Trios for Pf., violin, and 'cello, opp. 22, 37, 40, 51; Duets for Pf. and violin, opp. 20, 30, 39, 40, 45, 49, 65, 79, 81, 83, 85, 88, 91; Duets for two violins, opp. 19, 23, 24, 32, 33, 34, 35, 43, 60, 61, 64; Airs with variations for violin and orch., opp. 17, 31; Concerto for vn. and orch., op. 78. Méthode Elémentaire et Progressive pour le Violon, op, 52; Ecole du Mécanisme, op. 74; L' Ecole de la Melodie, op. 129. Symphonies, studies, solos, etc.

Dancla's works are of the highest educational value, as well as full of fine melody and expressive writing. He has produced some pupils now holding high places among performers, and is himself a performer of the highest order. His execution is great, and his tone large and full.

DANDO (Joseph Haydon Bourne). English violinist, B. London, 1806. S. under Mori, 1819-1826. Mem. of Philharmonic Orch., 1831. Played at various towns throughout Britain. With Blagrove, Gattie, and C. Lucas, Dando gave chamber concerts, from 1836 to 1842, and is understood to have been the first to introduce the public performance of string quartets, etc., into London.

DANHAUSER (Adolphe Leopold). French comp. and teacher, B. Paris, Feb. 26, 1835. S. Paris Cons. Prof. at Paris Cons. Has composed choruses, etc.

DANICAN. See PHILIDOR.

DANIEL (John). Scottish comp. and teacher, B. Aberdeen, 1803. Practised there as teacher for a number of years. Went to America about 1840-43. Resided in New York as teacher and comp. D. New York, June 21, 1881.

WORKS.—National Psalmody of the Church of Scotland, with Selection of Pieces from the most eminent Composers, for Organ, Pianoforte, etc., ob. 4to [1837] and [1843]. Part-songs, Songs, and Pf. music; Miscellaneous works, writings, etc.

Daniel was a highly respected musician in New York, and in his younger days had been a well-known figure in the north-east of Scotland. His works are unknown in this country, save the "National Psalmody," which has, however, been long since superseded by denominational works, and those of Carnie and Hately.

DANIELL (William Henry). American teacher and writer, B. Philadelphia, July 24, 1834. Self-taught in music. Choir-master of All Saints Memorial Ch., Providence, R. I., 1874-81. Lecturer and Prof. of Singing, New England Cons. of Music, Boston, 1878. Director of the Martha's Vineyard Summer Institute.

WORKS.—The Voice, and how to use it, Boston, 8vo, 1873 [another edition under title of "How to Sing"]; Talks on the Voice, and kindred topics [papers in the Boston *Musical Herald*]; The Value of the Falsetto in Developing the Male Voice, a paper read before the "Music Teachers' National Association," 1883, etc.

Daniell forms his method of instruction on the practice of the old Italian masters, Pistocchi, Porpora, and others, and has achieved much success in his pupils. He is a tenor singer, but does not appear in public as a vocalist. His works on the voice contain a detailed exposition of his principles of instruction.

DANJON (Jean Louis Felix). French violinist and comp., B. Paris, June 21, 1812. Comp. of vn. music, etc.

DANKS (H. P.). American song-writer of the present time. Has written " Pauline, the Belle of Saratoga," an operetta, and a heap of songs, part-songs, and hymns, composed in a style combining the well-known features of negro minstrelsy and revival hymnology.

DANNELEY (John Feltham). English writer, pianist, and comp., B. Oakingham, Berks, 1786. S. under C. Knyvett, S. Webbe, Woelfl, and C. Neate. Resided in Hampshire as teacher till 1812. Org. of ch. of St. Mary of the Tower, Ipswich, 1812. Visited Paris, and S. under Reicha and Pradher, 1816. D. London, 1836.

WORKS.—A Set of twelve Italian duets ; Glees and songs ; Pf. music. An Introduction to the Elementary Principles of Thorough-bass and classical music, Ipswich, 8vo, 1820 ; An Encyclopædia, or Dictionary of Music, Lond., 8vo, 1825 ; A Musical Grammar, comprehending the principles and rules of the science, Lond., 12mo, 1826.

The three theoretical works of Danneley are good, and served a useful purpose in their time.

DANNREUTHER (Edward). German comp., writer, and pianist, B. Strasburg, Nov. 4, 1844. Taken by parents to U. S. A., 1849. S. at Leipzig Cons. under Richter, Moscheles, and Hauptmann, 1859-63. Settled in London as teacher, etc., 1863. Founded a Wagner Society, 1872, and cond. its concerts.

WORKS.—Richard Wagner, his tendencies and theories, Lond., 8vo, 1873 ; The Music of the Future, a letter to M. F. Villot, by Richard Wagner, translated by E. Dannreuther, 8vo, 1873 ; Beethoven, by Richard Wagner, translated, 1880 ; On Conducting, by R. Wagner, translated, Lond., 1885 ; Articles in Grove's Dictionary of Music, and *Macmillan's Magazine* on the Opera, Beethoven, Wagner, etc. Pf. music and songs, etc.

Mr. Dannreuther is best known in London and America as a pianoforte player of great powers, and as an advocate of the music of Wagner.

DANYL (John). English comp. of the latter part of the 16th and beginning of the 17th centuries. He is supposed to have been the brother of Daniel, the poet, and was a Bachelor of Music, Oxon., 1604. He published " Songs for the Lute, Viol, and Voyce," Lond., fo., 1606.

DANZI (Franz). German comp., B. Mannheim, May 15, 1763. D. Carlsruhe, April, 1826. Wrote operas, chamber music, etc.

DARBOVILLE (Jules Etienne Jean), CLERGET. French tenor vocalist, B. Montpellier, Dec. 7, 1781. D. Marseilles, Sept. 22, 1842. Sang in operas by Auber, Carafa, Gretry, etc.

DARGOMIJSKY (Alexander Sergovitch). Russian comp., B. Smolensk, Feb. 2, 1813. Resided in St. Petersburg, from 1835. D. St. Petersburg, Jan. 17, 1869.

WORKS.—Esmeralda, opera (Hugo), 1847 ; La Roussálka, opera, 1856 ; Rogdana, do.; La Fête de Bacchus, cantata. Miscellaneous orchestral works ; Works for Pf.; Songs, and other vocal works.

La Roussálka was Dargomijsky's most successful work. A number of his songs are beautiful creations, and have achieved a fair measure of success.

DARNTON (Charles). English org. and comp., B. London, 1836. Compiler of " Comprehensive Psalmody," Lond., 1866. Comp. also anthems, part-songs, and songs.

DARWALL (Rev. John). English divine and comp., B. Haughton, 1731. D. Dec., 1789. Was vicar of Walsall, and comp. of the hymn tune " Darwall."

DAUNEY (William). Scottish musician and antiquary, B. Aberdeen, 1800. Educated at Dulwich and Edin. University. Called to Scottish Bar, 1823. Solicitor-General for British Guiana, at Demerara, 1838. D. Demerara, July 28, 1843.

WORK.— Ancient Scottish Melodies from a manuscript of the reign of King James VI., with Introductory Inquiry (Skene Manuscript), Edin., 4to, 1838.

In the preface to this work, Dauney covers an amount of ground previously unattempted either by Tytler, Ritson, or Stenhouse, and displays much judgment and learning in the general handling of his subject; and his work is by far the most exhaustive contribution to the history of Scottish music. It was published as a Bannatyne Club book, with so many copies not on Club paper.

DAUPRAT (Louis Francois). French horn-player and comp., B. Paris, May 24, 1781. S. Paris Cons. Prof. of Horn, Paris Cons. D. Paris, July 16, 1868.

WORKS.—Op. 1. Concerto for horn and orch.; op. 2. Sonata for pf. and horn. Solos, duets, trios, quartets, quintets, sextets, etc., for horn and other instruments. Symphonies, overtures, etc.; Five theoretical works; Méthode pour Cor alto et cor basse, Paris.

DAUSSOIGNE-MÉHUL (Joseph). French comp. and teacher, B. Givet, June 24, 1790. S. Paris Cons. Director of Liége Cons., 1827. D. Liége, March 10, 1875.

WORKS.—*Operas*: Ariane à Naxos, 1807; Robert Guiscard; Faux Inquisiteur, 1817; Le Testament; Les Amants Corsaires; Valentine, 1822; Les Deux Salem, 1824; Les Deux Nuits. Writings on music, etc.

DAUTRESME (Auguste Lugien). French comp., B. Elbeuf, May 21, 1826. S. under A. Neukomm. Amateur opera composer, etc.

DAUVERGNE (Antoine). French violinist and comp., B. Clermont-Ferrand, Oct. 4, 1713. D. Lyons, Feb. 12, 1797. Wrote "Les Amours de Tempe," 1752; La Coquette trompée, 1753; Canente, 1760; Persée, 1770; and other operas.

DAUVERGNE (Francois Georges Auguste). French trumpet-player and comp., B. Paris, Feb. 15, 1800. D. Paris, Nov. 5, 1874.

Wrote a "Method" for the trumpet, and music for the same.

D'AVENANT (Sir William). English dramatist, B. Oxford, 1605. Poet Laurate, 1637. D. 1668.

Davenant is noticed here chiefly on account of his connection with the music of his time, which he in a measure inspired by his masques. Of those masques, mostly set by Lawes, Purcell, etc., there are a goodly number. His merits as a poet are by no means great, nor can his entertainments be named in the same breath with those of Jonson.

DAVENPORT (F. W.). English comp., B. near Derby, 1847. Intended for legal profession. Educated at Oxford. S. under Sir G. A. Macfarren. Gained prize for a Symphony, Alexandra Palace, 1876. Comp. Overture, "Twelfth Night"; Six pieces for Pf. and 'cello; Pictures on a Journey, Pf. solo; Songs; "Elements of Music," Lond., 8vo, 2 editions to 1885.

DAVENPORT (Uriah). English comp. and writer of the latter part of last century, and teacher in London, compiler of "The Psalm-Singer's Companion, containing a new introduction, with such directions for singing, as is proper and necessary for learners," Lond., 1785.

DAVID (Félicien César). French comp., B. Cadenet, March 8, 1810. Chor. in Aix Cath. Educated at Jesuit Coll. of Aix, 1825-28. Cond. of Aix theatre, 1828-29. Chap.-master of S. Saurieur, 1829-30. Member of sect of St. Simoniens, 1831-33. Travelled in Egypt and Holy Land. Chevalier of Legion of Honour. Pensioned by Napoleon III., 1860. Mem. of Acad. of Beux Arts, 1869. D. St. Germain-en-Laye, Aug. 29, 1876.

WORKS.—Le Désert, ode-symphonie, Paris, Dec. 8, 1814; Moïse au Sinaï, oratorio, 1846; Cristophe Colomb, symphony, 1847; Eden, a mystery, Paris, 1848

Operas: La Perle du Brésil, 1851, Paris, 1883; La Fin du Monde (MS.); Herculaneum, 1859; Lalla Roukh, 1862; La Saphir, 1865; La Captive (MS.). Les Quatre Saisons, collection of 24 quintets for 2 vns., alto, 'cello, and bass; Twelve melodies for 'cello; Les Perles d'Orient, 6 melodies for voice and Pf.; Miscellaneous Pf. music; Songs, etc.

David has identified himself so thoroughly with Eastern music, that it is impossible for a musician to disassociate his ideas of Oriental climes from "Le Desert" or "Lalla Rookh." The former has been often given in London and the English provinces, and is consequently well known. The latter, however, is not at all known to the majority of English musicians. It is with "La Perle du Brésil," and the minor pieces, that work by which David is best known in France. The "Desert" will probably outlive any of David's works, as it possesses attractions not to be found in any of the others, besides being a novel and unique production, highly coloured and interesting.

DAVID (Ferdinand). German comp. and violinist, B. Hamburg, Jan. 19, 1810. S. under Spohr at Cassel, 1821. *Début* as violinist, 1824. Gave concerts in conjunction with his sister Louise, in Leipzig, Dresden, and Berlin, 1826. Violinist in Königstadt theatre, Berlin, 1827-28. Leader of quartet party to Baron Liphardt, 1829. Married Mdlle. Liphardt. Gave concerts in Russia, 1835. Leader of Gewandhaus concerts, Leipzig, 1836. Trustee of Mendelssohn at death, 1847. Teacher at Leipzig. D. Kloster, Switzerland, July 18, 1873.

WORKS.—Op. 2. Introduction and variation, violin and orch.; op. 3. Concertinos for violin and orch., in A and D; op. 4. Concertino for bass trombone and orch., in B flat; op. 5-6. Introduction and variations for violin and orch; op. 7. Introd., adagio, and rondo; op. 8. Introd. and variations for clarinet and orch.; op. 9-10. Concertos for violin and orch.; op. 11. Introd. and variations for violin and orch.; op. 12. Concerto for bassoon and orch., in B flat; op. 13. Introd. and variations for violin and orch.; op. 15. Introd. and variations for violin and orch.; op. 16. Andante and Scherzo Capriccisso, for violin and orch.; op. 17. Concerto for violin and orch.; op. 18. Variations for violin and orch.; op. 19. Introd. and variations for violin and orch.; op. 20. Six Caprices for Pf. and violin; op. 21. Introd. and variations on Scotch air, for violin and orch.; op. 22. Concert Polonaise for violin and orch.; op. 23. Concerto for violin and orch. in E; op. 24. Twelve Salonstücke for violin and Pf.; op. 25. Salon-duet for Pf. and violin; op. 28. Five Salonstücke for violin and Pf.; op. 29. Six Lieder for voice and Pf.; op. 31. Six Lieder for voice and Pf.; op. 32. Quartet for strings, in A minor; op. 33. Psalm for 2 soprano voices and Pf.; op. 34. Seven Stücke for 'cello and Pf.; op. 35. Concerto for violin and orch., in D minor; op. 36. Kammerstücke for violin and Pf.; op. 37. Four Marches for Pf. duet; op. 38. Sextet for strings; op. 39. Studies and Caprices for violin and Pf., etc. Violin School. Symphony, 1841, etc.

David is to be credited with the training of a large number of the foremost violinists of the present time, Joachim among the number. His compositions are sterling works, often used by violinists, and his violin-school stands near that of Spohr in a few respects. As a player, he was one of the greatest of his day, and as such gained the friendship of Mendelssohn.

DAVID (Marie Louise). See DULCKEN.

DAVID (Paul). French writer and critic, B. Marseilles, 1806. Nephew of Dellamaria. Has written some articles in Sir G. Grove's "Dictionary of Music," and numerous contributions to periodical literature.

DAVID (Samuel). French operatic comp., B. Paris, Nov. 12, 1836. S. at Paris Cons. Comp. of a number of operas, operettas, Pf. music, etc.

DAVIDE (Giacomo). Italian tenor vocalist, B. near Bergamo, 1750. Appeared in London, 1791. D. Dec. 31, 1830. A celebrated vocalist in his day. His son, GIOVANNI (B. 1789, D. 1851), was an operatic manager and a vocalist of renown.

DAVIDOFF (Karl). Russian violoncello-player and comp., B. Goldingen Courland, March 15, 1838. S. under Schmidt, Hauptmann, and Schuberth. *Début* as 'cellist, 1859. Principal 'cellist at Gewandhaus concerts, Leipzig.

Prof. of 'cello at Leipzig Cons. Do. at St. Petersburg Cons. Appeared in London, 1862.

Music for Pf. and violoncello, chamber-music, songs, etc., constitute this composers works. He is well known on the Continent generally, but chiefly as a performer on the 'cello of great talent and power.

DAVIDSON (Peter). Scottish writer, author of " The Violin : a concise exposition of the general principles of construction, theoretically and practically treated," Glasgow, 12mo, 1871. Second edition, London, 12mo, 1880.

DAVIDSON (Thomas). Scottish musician of the 17th century, was appointed teacher in the Music (or Song) School, Aberdeen, in 1640. This position he must have held till far on in the century, as we find from the Burgh Records of Aberdeen that on Jan. 16, 1666, he received an augmentation of his salary, making it 250 merks. He is chiefly celebrated as the editor of "Cantus, Songs, and Fancies. To Thre, Foure, or Five partes, both apt for voices and viols. With a briefe Introduction of Musick, as is taught in the Musick-Schole of Aberdene, by T. D., Mr. of Musick," Aberdeen, printed by John Forbes, sm. ob., 4to, 1662. Second edit., 1666. Third edit., 1682. Reprint, New Club Series, Paisley, 1879. The three editions of the " Cantus " differ slightly in respect of several omissions and insertions. It was the first secular musicbook published in Scotland, and consists chiefly of English and foreign melodies, some by Gastoldi, or imitations of them, arranged. All these editions are extremely scarce and valuable.

DAVIE (James). Scottish violinist and comp., B. towards end of 18th century. Resided in Aberdeen as a teacher, and member of the Aberdeen theatre orch.

WORKS.—Music of the Church of Scotland, being a numerous selection of Psalm and Hymn Tunes, Ancient and Modern, in Four Vocal Parts, with an Instrumental Accompaniment...To which are prefixed Remarks on Church Music, etc., Aberdeen, 8vo. n. d. A Compendious Introduction to the Art of Singing, comprising the most useful scales and examples, Aberdeen, n. d. The Vocal Harmonist, a Collection of Duets, Trios, Glees, etc., n. d. Caledonian Repository of the most favourite Scottish slow Airs, Marches, Strathspeys, Reels, Jigs, Hornpipes, etc., expressly adapted for the Violin, Aberdeen and Edin., 8vo, about 1829-30 [6 books]. Scales for the Voice. Songs, etc.

DAVIES (Cecilia). English vocalist, B. 1752 [1740]. Travelled in France and Italy, and sang with success. *Début* in London, 1773, in Sacchini's " Lucio Vero." Sang in London and on Continent, till 1791. D. London, July 3, 1836. Her sister, MARIANNE (B. 1736, D. 1792), was an harmonica-player, and appeared with her sister in public. She was a skilful performer on her instrument.

DAVIES (Mary). English soprano vocalist of present time, was pupil in R.A.M. She has sung in oratorio and concert music with the greatest success, throughout the provinces of England, London, and in Scotland. Her voice is remarkably pure and clear in tone, and her style is refined and pleasing.

DAVISON (Duncan, & Co.). English firm of music publishers, established in London about middle of present century.

Their publications are numerous and generally good. Their list of vocal music includes the names of the greater number of our good contemporary composers. They also publish the *Musical World*, one of the oldest and best of existing musical periodicals.

DAVISON (James William). English comp. and writer, B. London, Oct. 5, 1813. S. under W. H. Holmes and Sir G. A. Macfarren. Married Miss Arabella Goddard, 1860. Musical critic of the *Times* and *Musical World.* D. Margate, March 24, 1885.

WORKS.—An Essay on the Works of Frederic Chopin, Lond. [1849], n. d. *Songs:* Swifter far than summer flight; The light canoe ; Poor heart, be still ; Sweet village bells ; The lover to his mistress ; False friends, wilt thou smile or weep ? *Pianoforte music:* Four Bagatelles à la valse, op. 4 ; First Sonata, op. 6 ; Tarantella, op. 7 ; Three Sketches, op. 8 ; Romance, op. 11. Dramatic Overture to the fairy tale of "Fortunatus," for Pf. duet. Contributions to periodical literature. Contributions to Grove's "Dictionary of Music and Musicians."

DAVY (John). English comp., B. Upton-Helion, Exeter, 1765. Articled to Jackson of Exeter, 1777. Resided in Exeter as teacher. Violinist in orch. of Covent Garden Theatre. Teacher and comp. in London. D. London, Feb. 22, 1824.

WORKS.—*Music to Plays, etc.:* What a blunder! 1800; Perouse (with J. Moorhead), 1801; The Brazen Mask, ballet (with Mountain), 1802; The Cabinet (with Braham), 1802; The Caffres, 1802; Rob Roy, 1803; The Miller's Maid, 1804; Harlequin Quicksilver, 1804; Thirty Thousand (with Reeve and Braham), 1805; Spanish Dollars, 1805; Harlequin's Magnet, 1805; The Blind Boy, 1808; The Farmer's Wife, 1814; Rob Roy Macgregor (new version), 1818; Woman's Will, a riddle, 1820. Overture to Shakspere's "Tempest." Six Quartets for Voices, in Score, with figured Basses for the Pf., op 1. n. d.; Six Madrigals for 4 voices, op. 13 (c. 1810). Beauties of Handel, 6 vols., 4to, n. d. *Songs:* Bay of Biscay, Oh mighty Bacchus, Beggar Boy, Brave marine, Darling Sue, Harvest home, Milk maid, Smuggler, Son of old Saturn, etc.

Davy's name rests in the memory of the present generation solely through his "Bay of Biscay," a song unrivalled in its way, and as fresh and breezy in style now as when first penned. His other songs, operas, and pantomimes are deceased. He was an instance of early precocity, and is the subject of several anecdotes.

DAVY (Richard). English comp. of the 16th century, some of whose works are in the British Museum.

DAWSON (Charles). English writer, author of "Analysis of Musical Composition, showing the Construction of all Musical Pieces, together with a Concise and Comprehensive System of Harmony," Lond., 12mo, 1845. "Elements of Music, Condensed for the Use of Students of the Pianoforte," Lond., 12mo, 1844.

DAY (Alfred). English physician and musician, author of a "Treatise on Harmony," Lond., 8vo [1845], n. d. He was B. London, Jan. 1810, and D. London, Feb. 11, 1849. His work on harmony advocates the alteration of a number of technical terms, most of which have been adopted by Macfarren and others.

DAY (H. W.). American writer, author of "The Vocal School, or Pestalozzian Method of Instruction in the Elements of Vocal Music...etc.," Boston, 16mo, 1844.

DAY (John). English publisher and editor, B. Dunwich, Suffolk, 1522. He was established at Holborn, London, in 1549, as printer and publisher, and D. July 23, 1584.

He published Damon's Psalms, 1579, and a work bearing the title "The Whole Booke of Psalmes in foure partes, which may be sung to all musicall instruments," 1563.

DEAKIN (Andrew). English org. and critical writer, B. Birmingham, April 13, 1822. Began to study music at a very early age, and without any instruction became a creditable vocalist, organist, and violinist. Served a severe apprenticeship to the printing trade, and in 1849 began to write newspaper musical criticisms. While a youth, had some years service as org. in several churches and chapels, and in 1847 was appointed org. at the Church of the Saviour (the Church founded by the late Mr. George Dawson, the well known lecturer), and held the post until 1878, retiring soon after the death of Mr. Dawson. Mr. Deakin, who, as a musician, is altogether self-taught, has given much attention to musical history and kindred branches of study, and has been employed for many years by the chief concert-givers of his town and neighbourhood as a writer of analytical programme notes. He has composed a large number of hymn-tunes, chants, and anthems, and some works of larger form. A "Stabat Mater," for 4 solo voices, chorus, and organ (7 numbers), and "Miserere," for solo voices, chorus, and orchestra (11 numbers), were performed some years ago at the Church of the Saviour, but they remain in MS. In 1846 Mr. Deakin compiled and published "Euphonia," which, if not the first book of Chants issued for the use of non-conformists, has done more to spread a knowledge of chanting amongst dissenters than any other work. Mr. Deakin is also known as an amateur landscape painter, and his name may be found in many of the London and provincial exhibition catalogues of 35 years ago and later. He was editor of the *Birmingham Musical Examiner* in 1845.

DEAN (J.). English writer, author of "Guide and Self-Instructor for the Violin," Lond., 1853.

DEANE (Thomas). English comp. and org., flourished during 17th and 18th centuries. Mus. Doc., Oxon., July 9, 1731. Org. at Warwick and at Coventry, and was a good violinist. Composed music in Oldmixon's "The Governor of Cyprus," and in the "Division Violin."

DEARLE (Edward). English comp. and org., B. Cambridge, 1806. Org. of S. Paul's, Deptford, July, 1827; Blackheath (new) ch., 1830; Wisbench par. ch., 1832; S. Mary's, Warwick, 1833; Do. and song schoolmaster, Newark, 1835-64. Mus. Bac., Cantab., 1836. Mus. Doc., Cantab., 1842. One of founders of Trinity Coll., London, and member of council of same.

WORKS.—Morning and Evening Service in F, 1832; Turn Thee again, Thou God of Hosts, anthem (gained Gresham gold medal in 1837); Volume of Church Music [1838]; Magnificats and Nunc Dimittis in B flat and F. *Anthems:* The desert shall rejoice; Rend your hearts; With angels and arch-angels; By the waters of Babylon; God is a spirit. Israel in the wilderness, oratorio, 1879. *Part-Songs:* Bring again; Sigh no more, ladies; Up with the lark; Mountain daisy; The Fairies; The silent land; The Mariners. Lays of the heart (songs), 1829. Miscellaneous vocal music, sacred and secular.

DEBAIN (Alexandre Francois). French instrument manufacturer and mechanic. B. Paris, 1809. Was originally a cabinet-maker, but in 1825 he turned his attention to Piano manufacture. His principal works, however, are his "organs expressifs," harmoniums of great beauty of tone and mechanism. He invented many improvements in connection with the Pf. and harmonium, and devised a mechanical *Pianoforte player* and an *organist*.

DEBILLEMONT (Jean Jacques). French violinist and comp., B. Dijon, Dec. 12, 1824. S. under Alard and Carafa. Resided in Paris as composer, from 1839.

WORKS.—*Operas:* Le Renégat, Dijon; Le Bandolera; Feu mon oncle; Le Joujou; Bocchoris; C' etait moi, 1860; As-tu déjeûné, Jacquot? 1860; Astaroth, 1861; Un Premier avril, 1862; Roger Bontemps, 1867; Le Grand Duke de Matapa, 1868; Mousseline Club, 1868; La Revanche de Candaule, 1869; Le Pantalon de Casimir, 1873; Le 13ᵉ Coup de minuit, 1874; Les Trois Sultanes; La Florinde; Les Noces de Panurge; Le Péchés de M. Jean; Le Esclaves d' Athys. Cantatas and Ballets; Songs; and writings on music.

DE CALL. See CALL.

DECKER & SON. American firm of Pianoforte makers, established in New York, 1856. Make special instruments of an original form, and are well known in America for the high finish of their work.

DECOURCELLE (Maurice Henri). French pianist and comp., B. Paris, Oct. 11, 1815. Comp. studies, exercises, nocturnes, fantasias, galops, transcriptions, etc., for his instrument. His brother, HENRI (B. 1821), is also a composer.

DEERING or DERING (Richard). English comp. and org., B. in Kent at end of 16th century. Brought up in Italy. Org. at monastery of English nuns, Brussels. Org. to Consort of Charles I., Henrietta Maria. Bac. Mus., Oxon., 1610. D. 1657.

WORKS.—Cantiones Sacræ quinque vocum, cum basso continuo ad organum, Antwerp, 1597; Cantica Sacræ ad melodiam madrigalium elaborata senis vocibus, Antwerp, 1618; Motets, madrigals, etc.

Deering became latterly a Roman Catholic, and died in that faith.

DEFESCH (Willem). Dutch org., violinist, and comp., B. Amsterdam, about end of 17th century [1695-6]. D. about middle of 18th century [1758-60]. Resided for a time in England, where, in 1733, he produced "Judith," an oratorio, and again in 1745 another named "Joseph." His other works consist of instrumental and miscellaneous vocal music.

DEFFÈS (Pierre Louis). French comp., B. Toulouse, July 25, 1819. S. at Toulouse Cons. S. at Paris Cons. under Halévy, etc., 1839. Gained first prize at the "Institut" for cantata, "L' Ange de Tobie," 1847. Travelled in Italy and Germany, 1848-52. Teacher and comp. in Paris.

WORKS.—*Operas:* L'Anneau d'argent, 1855; La Clef des champs, 1857; Broskovano, 1859; Les Violons du Roi, 1860; Le Café du Roi, 1860; Les Bourguignonnes, 1863; Passé Minuit, 1864; La Boîte à Surprise, 1865; La Comédie en voyage, 1867; Les Croqueuses de pommes, 1868; Petit Bonhomme vit encore, 1868; Valse et Menuet, 1870; Le Nuit de Noces; Riquet à la houppe; Le Marchand de Venise (MS.). Masses; Symphonies; Songs, etc.

DE GRAAN (Julius). Dutch violinist, B. Amsterdam, Nov. 9, 1852. D. Jan. 8, 1874.

DEHN (Siegfried Wilhelm). German writer and musician, B. Altona, Feb. 25, 1796. S. under Klein. Librarian of Musical Liby. of Berlin. D. Berlin, April 12, 1858.

WORKS.—Theoretisch-praktische Harmonielehre mit angefügten Generalbasspielen, Berlin, 1840; Lehr vom Contrapunkt, dem canon, und der Fuge, etc., Berlin, 1858. Collections, various, etc.

Dehn was famous as a teacher, and many of the leading composers of the present day were at one period his pupils.

DEJAZET (Eugene). French comp., B 1825. Produced "Un Mariage en l'air," 1852; " L'Argent et l' Amour," 1863 ; "Les 7 Baisers de Buckingham," 1866; with other operettas.

DÉJAZET (Jules). French pianist and comp., B. Paris, March 17, 1806. S. Cons. under Zimmermann. D. Ivry, near Paris, Aug. 29, 1846. Comp. Pf. music, fantasias, rondos, etc.

DE KONTSKI. See KONTSKI.

DELABORDE (Eraim Miriam). French comp. and Prof., B. Paris, Feb. 7, 1839. Prof. at Paris Cons., 1873. Composer of "Maître Martin," opera. Songs, Pf. music, etc.

DELACOUR (Vincent Conrad Félix). French pianist and comp., B. Paris, March 25, 1808. S. Paris Cons. D. 1840. Wrote Pf. music and songs.

DE LA FOND (John Francis). English teacher of music and languages in 18th century, author of " New System of Music, both Theoretical and Practical, yet not Mathematical : written in a manner entirely new, that is to say, in a style plane and intelligible," etc., Lond., 8vo, 1725.

DELAMOTE (P.). English writer, author of " A Brief Introduction to Mvsicke," etc., London, 8vo, 1594.

DE LANGE (Hermann Francois). Belgian violinist and comp., B. Liége, 1717. D. Oct. 27, 1781. Wrote symphonies, operas, masses, overtures, etc

DE LANGE (Samuel). Dutch comp. and pianist, B. Rotterdam, June 9, 1811. D. Rotterdam, May 15, 1884. Comp. sonata for organ, variations on Dutch national hymn for org., nocturnes for Pf., ballads, etc.

DE LANGE (Samuel). Son of above, B. Rotterdam, Feb. 22, 1840. Comp. and teacher in Paris. Comp. string quartets, op. 15, 18 ; Trio for Pf., vn., and 'cello, op. 21 ; Sonatas for org., op. 5, 14 ; Symphony for orch. in E flat; Pf. music ; Concerto for 'cello, op. 16 ; Handel's org. concertos, arranged ; Songs, etc.

DE LA RUE. See RUE.

DELDEVEZ (Edouard Marie Ernest). French comp. and violinist, B. Paris, May 31, 1817. S. at Paris Cons. under Habeneck, etc., from 1825. Gained several prizes for violin-playing and comp. Deputy leader at the Paris Opera, 1859. Chevalier of Legion of Honour.

WORKS.—Op. 1. Concert overture for orch.; op. 2. First symphony for orch.; op. 3. Robert Bruce, overture for orch.; op. 4. Six songs for voice and Pf.; op. 5. Lady Henriette, ballet; op. 6. Paquita, ballet; op. 7. Requiem Mass; op. 8. Second Symphony; op. 9. Trio for Pf., vn., and 'cello; op. 10. Two string quartets; op. 11. Eucharis; Mazarina, 2 ballets; op. 12. Vert-Vert, ballet; op. 13. Six studies for violin; op. 14. O Salutaris, for soprano and tenor voices, with org. op. 15. Symphonie héroï-comique, for orch.; op. 16. La Vendetta, duet; op. 17. Velleda, scene lyrique for soprano, chorus, and orch.; op. 18. Sacred vocal quartet; op. 19. Collection of selected violin music; op. 20. Le Violon Enchanté, opera; op. 21. Yanko le Bandit, ballet; op. 22. Quintet for strings; op. 23. Trio for Pf., vn., and 'cello; op. 24. Six romances for Pf.; Hymns; Literary works, etc.

Most of this composer's works are highly spirited compositions, and very agreeable in general effect.

DÉLIBES (Leo). French comp. and pianist, B. Saint Germain-du-Val, 1836. S. at Paris Cons. from 1848, under Le Couppey, Bazin, Benoist, and Adam. Gained second prize for singing, 1849. Second chorus-master at the opera. Accompanist at Théâtre Lyrique, 1853. Org. at ch. of St. Jean et St. François. Prof. of comp., Paris Cons., 1880.

WORKS.—*Operas, operettas, etc.:* Deux sous de charbon, 1855; Deux Vieilles Gardes, 1856; Six Demoiselles a marier, 1856; Maître Griffard, 1857; L'Omelette à la Follembuche, 1859; Monsieur de Bonne-Etoile, 1860; Le Jardinier et son Seigneur, 1863; Les Musiciens de l'orchestre, 1861; La Tradition, 1864; Le Serpent à plumes, 1864; Le Bœuf Apis, 1865; Mon ami Pierrot, 1862; Les Eaux d' Ems, 1862; Alger (cantata), 1865; La Source (ballet), 1866; Le Corsaire, 1867; Marlbrough s'en va-t-en guerre (with Jonas, Bizet, and Legouix), 1867; L' Ecossais de Chatori, 1869; La Cour du roi l'étaud, 1869; Coppélia (ballet), 1870; Le Roi l'a dit, 1873; Sylvia (ballet), June, 1876; Roi des Montagnes, opera; Jean de Nivelle, opera, 1880; Lakmé, opera, London, 1885.

Délibes is one of the best composers of light, and what is called sparkling music, now living in France. His music is always agreeable and never wearisome, and the neatness of his orchestration is very refreshing. The ballet "Sylvia," is best known in Britain, and has been performed scores of times. His operatic works achieved success in Paris.

DELIOUX (Charles). French comp., B. Lorient, April, 1830. Instructed first by father. Appeared as infant prodigy, 1839. S. Paris Cons. under Halévy and others, 1845. Teacher and comp. in Paris.

WORKS.—Yvonne et Loïc, opera, 1854. *Pf. Music:* Galop di bravura, op. 8; Danse napolitaine, op. 11; Valse, op. 12; Two nocturnes, op. 13; Marche hongroise, op. 14; Romance, op. 16; Etude-Carillon, op. 17; Mélodie, op. 19; Etude de Salon, op. 26; Mandoline, serenade, op. 28; Idyll, op. 84; Saltarelle, op. 85; Arabesques, op. 61; and pieces to the number of about 100.

The pianoforte music of Delioux is brilliant and pretty, and well adapted for showy performance.

DE LISLE. See LISLE (Claud J. Rouget de).

DELLAMARIA (Domenico). Italian comp., B. Marseilles, 1764. S. in Italy under Paesiello. D. Paris, 1800.

Operas: Il Maestro di Capella; Le Prisonnier; L' Oncle Valet; Le Vieux Château; L' Opera Comique.

DELOFFRE (Louis Michel Adolphe). French violinist and comp., B. Paris, July 28, 1817. D. Jan. 8, 1876.

Comp. symphonies, trios, violin music, songs.

DEMERSSEMAN (Jules Auguste Edouard). Belgian comp. and flute-player, B. Hondschoote, Jan. 9, 1833. S. Paris Cons. D. 1866. Operettas, flute music, etc.

DEMEUR (Jules Antoine). Belgian flutist and comp., B. Sept. 23, 1814. S. Brussels Cons. Prof. Brussels Cons. (flute). Comp. of fantasias, variations.

DE MOL (Francois Marie). Belgian comp., B. Brussels, March 3, 1844. Comp. Pf. music and string quartets, etc. D. Ostend, Nov. 3, 1883. His brother, GUILLAUME (B. Brussels, March 1, 1846. D. Sept. 9, 1874), comp. symphonies, org. music, etc.

DEMPSTER (William R.). Scottish comp., B. Keith, 1808. D. London, March 7, 1871. Wrote a number of good, though not always strikingly original, ballads, of the drawing-room type.

DE MUNCK (Ernest). Belgian violoncellist and comp. B. Brussels, 1841. Has Played at London, in Scotland, Ireland, and over most of the Continent. Now 'cellist at Weimar. Writings for instrument. Married Carlotta Patti in 1879.

DE MURIS. See MURIS.

DENEFVE (Julius). Belgian comp., B. 1814. S. Brussels Cons. Director of Music School at Mons. Comp. operas, cantatas, songs, instrumental music, etc.

DENGREMONT (Maurice). French violinist, B. Rio Janeiro, March 19, 1867. Appeared with great success in London as solo violinist, and has been received with favour in America. Is said to possess much natural aptitude for the violin, and for his age is a remarkable performer.

DENNIS (John). English writer and musician, B. London, 1657. S. at Cambridge. Travelled in France and Italy. D. Jan. 6, 1733. Author of "An Essay on the Italian Opera," Lond., 1706.

DENZA (Luigi). Italian comp., B. near Naples, 1846. Famous as a writer of songs of a brilliant and taking character. His works are catalogued among the publications of Ricordi, etc.

DE PARIS (Edouard). French comp. and teacher, B. Normandy, 1827. S. Paris Cons. Teacher in Brighton.
Composer of a quantity of dance music of a light nature.

DEPPE (Ludwig). German pianist and comp., B. Nov. 7, 1828.

DEPRES. See JOSQUIN.

DERHAM (William). English writer, B. 1657. D. 1735. Author of, among other works, the following, "The Artificial Clock-maker...shewing...the way to alter clock-work, to make chimes and set them to musical notes," London, 1696 [other editions].

DERING. See DEERING.

DÉSAUGIERS (Marc Antoine). French comp., B. Frejus, 1742. D. Paris, Sept. 10, 1793. Writer of operas and ch. music.

DESLANDRES (Adolphe Edouard Marie). French org. and comp., B. near Paris, Jan. 22, 1840. Comp. of ch. music, instr. music, etc.

DESMARETS (Henri). French comp., B. Paris, 1662. D. Lunéville, Sept. 7, 1741.

WORKS.—*Operas:* Didon, 1639; Circe, 1694; Théagène et Chariclée, 1695; Les Amours de Momus, 1695; Venus et Adonis (Rousseau), 1697; Les Fêtes Galantes, 1698; Iphigenie en Tauride, 1704; Renaud, 1722, etc.

DESSAUER (Josef). Bohemian comp., B. Prague, May 28, 1798. S. under Tomaschek, etc., at Prague. D. Mödling, near Vienna, July, 1876.

WORKS.—Ein Besuch in Saint Cyr, opera, 1838; Lidivinna, opera, 1840; Overture and Pf. music.

Dessauer travelled much in England, France, etc. His works are good, but not widely known.

DESSOFF (Otto Felix). German violinist and comp., B. Leipzig, Jan. 14, 1835. Successful comp. for his instrument.

D'ESTE (John, B.A.). English musician and writer, author of "Music Made Easy, the Rudiments of Music," Lond., 8vo, 1849; "The Vocalist's Vade Mecum, or Pocket Companion, Practical Hints on Singing," etc., Lond., 1872.

DESTOUCHES (André Cardinal). French comp., B. Paris, 1672. Director of King's music and of opera, 1713-31. D. Paris, 1749.
WORKS.—*Operas, etc.*: Issé, pastorale heroïque, 1697; Amadis de Grece, tragedie, 1699; Omphale, tragedie, 1701. Le Carnavel et la Folie, ballet, 1703-4; Callirhoé, tragedie, 1712; Telemaque et Calypso, tragedie, 1714, etc.

DE SWERT (Jules). Belgian 'cellist and comp., B. Louvain, Aug. 15., 1843. S. Brussels Cons., 1856. Travelled in Belgium, Holland, Germany, and England. Has composed a number of works for his instrument, and is one of the foremost among modern violoncello virtuosus. He is author of a treatise on the "Violoncello," published in Novello's Music Primers, Lond., 4to, 1882. His two brothers, ISIDORE (1830), and JEAN (1832), are both musicians.

DEVAL (Harry). English writer and teacher, author of "The Art of Vocalization, with complete instructions for the Cultivation of the Voice," Lond., fo., n.d.

DEVAUX (A.). French writer and teacher, author of "A Guide to Theory, or Practical Thorough-bass, with 74 Exercises," Lond., 8vo, n. d., and other works.

DEVIENNE (Francois). French comp. and flute-player, B. Joinville [1759]. Flute-player in Swiss Guard; bassoon-player in Theatre de Monsieur, 1788. Prof. Paris Cons. D. Paris, Sept. 5, 1803.
WORKS.—*Operas:* Encore des Savoyards, 1789; Le Mariages Clandestin, 1790; Rose et Aurèle, 1794; Valecour, 1797; Le Valet des deux Maîtres, 1799. Method for the Flute; Trans., as, Instructions for the Flute, containing the various Modes of Articulation, etc., Lond., fo., n. d. Instrumental music, etc.

DEVRIENT (Eduard Philip). German barytone singer and actor, B. Berlin, Aug. 11, 1801. D. Carlsruhe, Oct. 4, 1877. Best known from his connection with Mendelssohn, and as author of "Meine Erinnerungen an Felix Mendelssohn Bartholdy und Seine Briefe an Mich," Leipzig, 12mo, 1869. This work has been translated by N. Macfarren, as "My Recollections of Mendelssohn, and his Letters to me," Lond., 8vo, 1869. It is a readable and amusing work.

DEWAR (Rev. Daniel, LL.D.). Scottish writer, was Prof. of Moral Philosophy in Aberdeen University. Author of "Observations on the Character, Customs, Superstitions, Music, Poetry, and Language of the Irish," etc., Lond., 2 vols., 1812.

DEWAR (James). Scottish comp., cond., and violinist, B. July 26, 1793. Deputy-leader in Theatre Royal, Edinburgh, 1807. Afterwards musical director, do. Org. St. George's Episcopal ch., 1815-35. Cond. Edinburgh Musical Assoc. D. Edinburgh, Jan. 4, 1846.
Dewar is famous for his arrangements of Scottish airs for the orchestra, a Pf. edition of which was published about 1850. His work with the title, "Popular National Melodies adapted for the Pianoforte," Edin., 1826, fo., had a large circulation. He comp. also a few part-songs and other vocal pieces, and edited "The Border Garland, Poetry by Hogg," [c. 1829].

DEZAIDES (N.), DÉZÈDE. French comp., B. 1740. D. 1792. Composed a number of operas, etc., among which may be named "Julie," 1772; "Les Trois Fermiers," 1777; "Fatmé," 1777; "Zulima," 1778; "Le Porteur de Chaise," 1778; "Péronne Sauvée," 1783; "Blaise et Babet," 1783; "La Fête de la cinquantaine," 1796, etc.

DIABELLI (Anton). Austrian pianist and comp., B. Mattsee, Salzburg, Sept. 6, 1781. S. under M. Haydn. Teacher of Pf. and publisher. Established the firm of Diabelli & Co. at Vienna, 1824. D. Vienna, April 8, 1858.

WORKS.—Pianoforte music of all kinds, some of which is still in use for teaching purposes.

The firm of Diabelli & Co. now existing is one of the most extensive in Austria, their publications being of great extent and quality. The compositions of Anton Diabelli are agreeable and good works.

DIAZ DE LA PENA (Eugene Emile). French comp., B. Paris, Feb. 27, 1837. S. Cons. under Reber, Halévy, etc. Writer of "Le Roi Candaule," 1865; "Le Coupe du Roi de Thule," operas, etc.

DIBDIN (Charles). English comp. and writer, B. at Dibden, near Southampton, March 15, 1745. S. Winchester Coll. Taught music by Kent and Fussel. Appeared as an actor at Richmond and Birmingham. Went to London, and was employed by Bickerstaff as comp. and singer, 1765. Renounced stage, and commenced giving medley monodramas in London, 1788. D. London, July 25, 1814.

WORKS.—*Musical Dramas, etc.*: The Shepherd's Artifice, 1763; Love in the city, 1767; Damon and Phillida, 1768; Lionel and Clarissa, 1768; The Padlock, 1768; The Maid the Mistress, 1769; The Recruiting Sergeant, do.; The Ephesian Matron, do.; The Jubilee, do.; Queen Mab, do.; The Captive, 1769; Pigmy Revel, 1770; The Wedding Ring; The Institution of the Garter, 1770; The Ladle, 1772; The Mischance; The Brickdust Man; The Widow of Abingdon; The Palace of Mirth, 1772; A Christmas Tale, 1773; A Trip to Portsmouth; The Deserter; The Grenadier, 1773; The Waterman, 1774; The Cobbler, do.; The Quaker, 1775; The Two Misers, 1775; The Seraglio, 1776; The Blackamoor; The Metamorphoses; The Razor Grinder; Yo, Yea, or, The Friendly Tars; The Old Woman of Eighty; The Mad Doctor; She is Mad for a Husband; England against Italy; The Fortune Hunter; All's not Gold that Glitters, 1776; Poor Vulcan, 1778; Rose and Colin; The Wives Revenged; Annette and Lubin; The Milkmaid, 1778; Plymouth in an Uproar, 1779; The Chelsea Pensioners; The Mirror; The Touchstone, 1779; The Shepherdess of the Alps, 1780; Harlequin Freemason; The Islanders, 1780; Jupiter and Alcmena, 1781; None so Blind as those who won't See, 1782; The Barrier of Parnassus, 1783; The Graces; The Saloon; Mandarina; The Land of Simplicity; The Passions; The Statue; Clump and Cudden; The Benevolent Tar; The Regions of Accomplishment; The Lancashire Witches, 1783; The Cestus, 1784; Pandora; The Long Odds, do.; Liberty Hall, 1785; Harvest Home, 1787; A Loyal Effusion, 1797. *Monodramas*: The Whim of the Moment, 1788; The Oddities, 1789; The Wags; Private Theatricals, 1791; The Quizzes, 1792; Castles in the Air, 1793; Great News, 1794; Will of the Wisp, 1795; Christmas Gambols, do.; The General Election, 1796; The Sphinx, 1797; Valentine's Day, do.; King and Queen, 1798; A Tour to the Land's End, 1799; Tom Wilkins, 1799; The Cake House, 1800; A Frisk, 1801; Most Votes, 1802; New Year's Gifts; Broken Gold; Briton's Strike Home; Datchet Mead; Commodore Pennant; Heads and Tails; The Frolic, etc. *Literary Musical Works*: The Harmonic Preceptor, a Didactic poem in three parts, Lond., 4to, 1804; The English Pythagoras, or Every Man his own Music-master, Lond., 4to, 1808; Music Epitomized, a School Book in which the whole science of music is clearly explained, Lond., 8vo, n. d. Hannah Hewitt, or the Female Crusoe, novel, 1792; The Younger Brother, novel, 1793; Musical Tour, Sheffield, 4to, 1788; History of the Stage, Lond., 5 vols., 8vo, 1795; Observations on a Tour through almost the whole of England, and a considerable part of Scotland ..Lond., 2 vols., 4to, 1801; The Professional Life of Mr. Dibdin, written by himself, with the words of six hundred songs selected from his works, Lond., 4 vols., 8vo, 1803.

Dibdin, according to the biography prefixed by his son Thomas to the 1875 edition of his songs, wrote over 1300 songs. In addition to these he wrote other music in his entertainments, etc., the gross amount of music and words which he wrote being in number over 3000 pieces. Of these, very few now are used, "The Waterman" is the only large piece, and "Poor Jack" and "Tom Bowling" the only songs. The first, it may be added, was recently popularized by Mr. Sims Reeves. Dibdin's talent lay in hitting off in a fine breezy style the lights and shades of a seafaring life, and in adapting the sentiment of his songs to the patriotic and bellicose spirit current in his time. The extraordinary popularity which some of his monodramas obtained reflects the highest credit on his talents as a comedian. As to the artistic status of his works, it may safely be questioned if they possess any,—although in the hands of good vocalists his songs take a place with the best folk-music. A collection of his "Songs, Chronologically arranged, with Notes, etc., by George Hogarth," was published in 1842.

DIBDIN (Charles, Jun.) English poet and writer, B. 1770. He was for many years proprietor of Sadlers' Wells Theatre, and wrote among other pieces the "Farmer's Wife," "My Spouse and I," and a number of Burlettas, Pantomimes, Songs, etc. D. London, 1831.

DIBDIN (Henry Edward). English musician and compiler, B. London, Sept. 8, 1813. Grandson of Charles Dibdin. S. under his sister, Mrs. Tonne, harpist, and Bochsa. Resided at Morningside, Edinburgh, as Teacher, from 1833. Honorary org. of Trinity Chap., Edinburgh. D. Edin., May 6, 1866.

WORKS.—The Standard Psalm-Tune Book, containing upwards of 600 specimens ; compiled from the original editions, and arranged for Four Voices, with an Organ Accompaniment, Lond., fo. [1851]. Harmonies to Reid's Praise Book, 4to, 1868. A Collection of Church Music, consisting of Chants, Psalm and Hymn Tunes, etc., 1843 (with J. T Surenne).

The "Standard Psalm-Tune Book" is his principal work, and is a most complete and valuable collection of Psalm tunes.

DIBDIN (Thomas). English musician and dramatist, B. March 21, 1771. D. Sept. 16, 1841. Writer of "Reminiscences of Thomas Dibdin of Covent Garden, etc.," Lond., 2 vols., 1827.

He was a writer of sea songs, some of which appear in the work entitled, "Lays of the last three Dibdins." His opera, the "Cabinet," is his best known work.

DIBDIN (Miss ?) Daughter of Charles, Sen., English harpist. S. under Challoner and Bochsa. Assistant teacher of harp at R. A. M., 1824. Married Mr. Tonne.

DICK (Charles George Cotsford). English comp., B. London, Sept. 1, 1846. Matriculated at Worcester College, Oxford, 1865. Second Class Honours in Law and Modern History School, 1869. Studied for the Bar, but obliged from ill-health to give it up.

WORKS.—Our Doll's House (German Reed Co.), operetta, 1876 ; Our New Doll's House (do.), 1877 ; Back from India (do.), 1879 ; Doctor D., comic opera, 1885. *Songs*: Dolly Varden ; Olivia ; The kingdom blest ; Heloïse ; Cosette ; Tidings from afar; Unchanged; The vision beautiful; Before parting; The Knight and the Ladye ; At his hearth alone ; Beggar Maid ; King Cophetua ; Loreley ; Household words; The distant hills. *Pianoforte Music:* Fireside Fancies, 6 pieces ; Cradle Song ; Romanesque ; Caprice ; Saltarello ; Rigodon ; Rococo ; Minuet ; Passe-pied ; Gavotte ; Scherzo ; Arabesque ; Bourrée ; Fairy Tales ; Polonaise ; Alla Pavan; Sabotière; Chaconne; Gigue; Toccata; Barcarolle; Melodie; Ballade; Legende ; Tambourin ; In Wonderland, etc.

Mr. Dick has been very successful in catching the spirit of the old dance forms in his Pianoforte pieces, and has given the world a number of beautiful and graceful trifles, which, if unimposing, are interesting and pleasant. His songs are in merit much above the average drawing-room ballads, and are in spirit and conception poetical and melodious. His operettas were successful.

DICKONS (Maria), *née* POOLE. English soprano vocalist, B. London, 1770 [1778-1780]. S. under Rauzzini at Bath. First appeared at Vauxhall, 1783. *Début* at Covent Garden, 1793. Sang at Ancient and Vocal Concerts. Appeared in principal towns of Scotland, Ireland, and English provinces. Married Mr. Dickons, 1800. Retired for a time. Sang in London again, 1806. Sang in Italian opera at Paris, 1816. Do. at Venice. Mem. of Instituto Filarmonico, Venice. Appeared again in London, 1819. Retired soon after. D. May 4, 1833.

"Mrs. Dickons's chief excellence lay perhaps in sacred music, in which style she is said to have sung with such a degree of sublimity, that religion seemed to breathe from every note."

DICKSON (Ellen), "DOLORES." English comp., daughter of General Sir Alex. Dickson, B. Woolwich, 1819. Resided during her life time chiefly at Lyndhurst, having been an invalid from youth. She became known in her district for many charitable actions. D. Lyndhurst, July 4, 1878.

WORKS.—*Songs:* Clear and Cool; Destiny; Goldilocks; The land of long ago; O my lost love; Pack clouds away; The racing river; She walked beside me; Tell her not when I am gone; Unchanged, etc.

These songs acquired a considerable amount of popularity in their day, and some of them are even now in vogue. Their merit is conspicuous in their adaptability for drawing-room purposes.

DICKSON (Rev. William Edward). English writer, B. Richmond, Yorks., 1823. B.A., Cantab., 1846; M.A., 1851. Ordained 1846. Precentor of Ely Cath., 1858.

WORKS.—Singing in Parish Churches, 1858; Cathedral Choirs, 1877; Practical Organ Building, Lond., 8vo, 1881.

DIEHL (Louis). German comp., B. Mannheim, 1838. Resident teacher in London. He married in 1863, Miss Alice Mangold (B. 1846), a celebrated pianist and writer.

Is best known by his songs, some of which gained much contemporary popularity.

DIÉMER (Louis). French pianist and comp., B. Paris, Feb. 14, 1843. S. at Paris Cons. under Durand, Bazin, Thomas, etc. Comp. music for Pf., etc.

DIETRICH (Albert Hermann). German comp., B. Golk, Aug. 28, 1829. S. under Otto, Rietz, Hauptmann, and at Leipzig University. Leader of orch. at Bonn. Chap.-master at Oldenburg, 1871. Leader of orch. at Leipzig.

WORKS.—Symphony in D minor, 1869; Overture for orch., 1872: "Rheinmorgen," concert-stücke, for voices, chorus, and orch., op. 31; Concerto for vn. and orch., op. 30; Concerto for 'cello, op. 32; Concerto for horn and orch., op. 29; Trio for vn., Pf., and 'cello, op. 9; Four pieces for Pf., op. 2; Six Lieder for Pf., op. 10; Robin Hood, opera.

Dietrich is an industrious and capable musician, performing his undertakings with a conscientious regard for artistic appearances. Few of his works are known in Britain.

DIETSCH (Pierre Louis Philippe). French comp., B. Dijon, Mar. 17, 1808. Chap.-master of ch. of the Madelaine. Prof. of Org. at School of Religious Music. D. Paris, Feb. 20, 1865. Composed organ music, church music, etc.

DIETTER (Christian Ludwig). German comp., B. Ludwigsburg, Wurtemberg, 1757. D. beginning of present century.

Wrote operas, symphonies, and music for flute.

DIGNUM (Charles). English tenor vocalist, B. Rotherhithe, 1765. Chor. in chapel of Sardinian ambassador, London. S. under Samuel Webbe. Worked for a time as carver and gilder. Articled to T. Linley for 7 years. *Début* as Meadows in "Love in a Village," 1784. Sang afterwards at Vauxhall, Haymarket Theatre, etc. D. London, March 29, 1827.

Dignum, who was usually regarded as the successor of Beard, composed a number of songs, and published a collection of "Vocal Music, consisting of Songs, Duets, and Glees," Lond., fo. [c. 1810], with portrait. He was most successful as a singer of English ballads.

DILLER (Franz X.). German violinist and comp., residing in New York, where his chamber concerts and quartet party are known to every musician. He was united with the Dodworths and others in giving concerts of classical music. His works consist of arrangements for string quartet, rondos, etc., for Pf.

DISTIN (Theodore). English comp. and singer, B. Brighton, 1823. S. under his father. Played French horn in his father's band (composed of members of the family), 1836. Travelled with this band on the Continent, 1836-44. S. singing under T. Cook and Negri. Barytone in Pyne and Harrison company. Travelled with them in England. Bass singer in Bencher's Chapel, Lincoln's Inn. Associate R. A. M. Teacher in London.

WORKS.—Morning, Communion, and Evening Service in C ; Evening Service in G, for male voices (written for S. Paul's cath.). Bacchus, on thee we call, prize glee (City Glee Club, 1867); Ossian's address to the moon (do., 1871); Jack Horner (Huddersfield prize, 1879); Sing, let us sing, prize glee (Abbey Glee Club, 1865); When some sweet flower I see, part song; Oh! the gallant Fisher's life, part song; The lover's return, glee for male voices (MS.); Two masses; Introits and offertories. *Songs:* I love to see all faces; Down to the button; Mine host !; A jug of October; The lad that follows the plough; The chine; My mother was a soldier's wife; Saved! What is my fortune; Miscellaneous vocal music, published and in MS.

Mr. Distin is a son of John Distin (1793-1863), the once celebrated trumpet-player, who was the inventor of the keyed bugle, and bandmaster to the Marquis of Breadalbane. He was trumpet player in H.M. Theatre, and in the private band of King George IV. He married Miss Loder of Bath, sister of John Loder the violinist, and by her had a family of four, who formed afterwards the Distin family of Instrumentalists. In 1833 Mr Distin, senr., formed a quintet band, composed of the members of his own family, and with it travelled over the Continent and England, playing before the Duke of Brunswick, King of Hanover, the present Emperor of Germany (then Crown Prince), the Queen of England, the King of Prussia, etc., etc. The band also performed at Windsor Castle, Jullien's concerts, and a great number of other important concerts.

Mr. Theodore Distin took part in those performances in the capacity of a horn player. He has written a number of good vocal works, most of which have been publicly performed; while as a bass singer, and formerly as a barytone, he possessed much talent, and displayed great vocal ability.

Other members of the family are engaged in the manufacture of brass instruments, both in America and in London, and have attained much fame in connection with the good quality of their productions. One member of the family wrote "A Cornet Tutor" (Boosey), published a number of years ago.

DITSON (Oliver & Co.). American music-publishing firm, established in Boston, in 1834. The number of large works produced by the firm exceeds 2000, while the sheet music department is increased at the rate of one piece each day. About 1,000,000 pieces are constantly kept in stock. The forward progress of this extensive firm has been maintained during and with each advance in musical education in America. "Following the establishment of this firm, was a great increase of interest in the science of music, soon followed by the introduction of music into common schools, by the formation of large choirs and of choral societies, and by the development of the composing power from that required for the putting together of a simple march or waltz, to that now exercised in all ways, except, perhaps, in the production of grand oratorios and operas." Messrs. Ditson & Co. have contributed largely to the advance of music in the United States by the publication of a large number of good theoretical works, including, among others, translations of valuable German works. The total number of their collection of musical literature is close upon 500. They have branch establishments in New York, Chicago, and Philadelphia, and were agents for Messrs. Novello & Co., of London. The contents of their general catalogue consist of Church and Sunday School Music, in books; glee and chorus music, in books and sheets; Songs and Pf. music in sheets; and a large selection of oratorios, cantatas, and operas, by leading composers. They also publish *The Musical Record*, a weekly musical journal.

DITTERSDORF (Karl Ditters von). Austrian comp., B. Vienna, Nov. 2, 1739. S. under König and Ziegler. Member of private band of Prince von Hildburghausen. S. under Bonno and Frani. Travelled with Gluck to Italy. Married Fraulein Nicolini. Chap.-master to Bishop of Grosswardein. D. near Breslau, October 31, 1799.

WORKS.—*Operas:* Lo Sposo burlato, 1775; Der Dokter und Apotheker, 1786; Betrug durch Aberglauben, 1786; Die Liebe im Narrenhausen, 1786; Il Democrito corretto, 1786; Hieronymus Knicker, 1787; La Contadina fedele, 1785; Orpheus, der Zweyte, 1787; Das rote Kæppchen, 1788; Der Schiffspatron, oder neue Gutshen, 1789; Hokus Pokus, 1790; Das Gespenst mit der Trommel, 1794; Gott Mars, oder der eiserne mann, 1795; Der Gefoppte Bræutigam, 1795; Don

Quichotte, 1795; Die Guelfer, 1795; Der Schah von Schiras, 1795; Ugolino, 1796; Die Lustigen Weiber von Windsor, 1796; Der Scheene Herbsttag, 1796; Der Ternengewinnst, 1797; Der Maedchenmarckt, 1797; Terno Secco, 1797; Don Coribaldi, 1798. *Oratorios:* Isacco, 1767; Esther, 1785; Job, 1786. Cantatas. Symphonies, numerous. Masses, sonatas, quartets, nocturnes, concertos, etc.

"Der Dokter und Apotheker, 1786," is the only one of Dittersdorf's works likely to survive, the others being mostly long since forgotten; though several have occasionally been produced. His music is light and pretty, while his instrumentation and melody are both of high quality.

DIXON (Rev. E. S.) English writer, author of "The Piano Primer, and Instructor's Assistant," fo. n. d.

DIXON (George). English org. and comp., B. Norwich, 1820. Chorister Norwich Cath., 1827-34. Got Musical training as private pupil of Dr. Buck (org.) to 1835. Pupil and assistant org. Parish Church, Grantham, 1835-45. Org. Parish Church, Retford, Notts, 1845-59. Org. Parish Church, Louth, 1859-65. Org. Parish Church, Grantham, 1895. Mus. Bac., Oxon., 1852. Mus. Doc., 1858. An Hon. Exam. for "Royal College of Music" at Grantham and Lincoln.

WORKS.—121st Psalm, Cantata (voices and orchestra), MS.; Pope's "Messiah," Cantata (voices and orchestra), MS. *Anthems:* Open we the gates" (Festival), composed for the re opening of Grantham Church after restoration; Unto thee, O my Strength; We will rejoice; O give thanks. Te Deum in G (chant form); Sundry Hymn Tunes, Chants, Kyries, etc.; also a contributor to the following works: Supplemental Chant Book (Owen); Ancient and Modern Chants (Ridley); Canticle Chant Book (Blakeley); 300 Chants (Metcalfe); The London Tune Book; The National Book of Hymn Tunes, Leeds. The Organist's Quarterly Journal (Spark). *Songs:* The Harvest Home; The Stricken Oak; Wedding Song; Tide Time; Too busy to freeze; Be silent tongue; Song of the Harper. Sundry other songs and pieces for Pf., etc.

Dr. Dixon is still engaged in tuition for the higher class of music, and is a well-known musician in Grantham, Lincoln, etc.; while his reputation as a composer is wide-spread.

DIXON (William). English music-engraver, teacher and writer in Liverpool and London, B. [1760]. D. London, 1825. Author of Introduction to Singing, containing rules for Singing at Sight, formed by the Author during many years study and practice in Teaching, 1795. Collection of Sacred Music, 1790. Six Glees for 3 Voices [1790]. Moralities: Six Glees, Cambridge [1800]. Euphonia...Sixty-two Psalm and Hymn Tunes, in four parts... for the Congregation of All Saints Church, Liverpool, Liverpool, 4to, n. d.

DIZI (Francois Joseph). Belgian harpist and comp., B. Namur, Jan. 14, 1780. S. under his Father, a Prof. of Music. Travelled in Europe. Settled in London as harpist at the principal theatres, and remained there till 1830. Resided afterwards in Paris, where he D., Nov., 1847.

He composed sonatas, variations, and exercises for harp, songs, etc. He also invented an improvement in harp mechanism which he called the "perpendicular harp," in which the principle is carried out of having the tenison of the strings acting upon a centre parallel to the centre of the column, as well as to that of the sonorous body. He published in London, "Ecole de Harpe, being a Complete Treatise on the Harp," 1827.

DLABACZ. See ROSETTI.

DOBSON (George C.) American writer, author of "New System for the Banjo," Boston, n. d.

DODD (Thomas). English violin-maker, native of Sheffield. Designed and varnished instruments made by Lott and B. Fendt. All of the instruments emanating from this maker's workshop were of exceptional quality as regards varnish and shape. Another Dodd, the son of the above, traded largely on his father's reputation.

DODWELL (Rev. Henry). Irish divine and writer, B. Dublin, 1641. D. 1711. In addition to many theological works he wrote "A Treatise concerning the Lawfulness of Instrumental Musick in Holy Offices." Lond., 12mo, 1700.

DODWORTH (Harvey B.) English Band-master and comp., B. Sheffield, 1821. Inventor of the rotary string-valve and bell-back instruments. Settled in the United States. Has written and published several works on band instruments and military band instrumentation. The first military band in the U. S. was organised by Mr. Dodworth. He is a musician of sterling worth, and still maintains an enviable position among bandsmen.

DOEHLER (Theodor). German pianist and comp., B. Naples, April 20, 1814. S. under Benedict and Czerny. Travelled in England and Europe as pianist. D. Florence, Feb. 21, 1856.

Works.—*Pianoforte:* Two Nocturnes, op. 25; Valses brilliantes, op. 26; Twelve Studies, op. 30; Two Nocturnes, op. 31; Andante, op. 32; Fifty Studies, op. 42; Six Melodies without words, op. 44; Three Mazurkas, op. 53. Variations, fantasias, valses, etc.

Doehler was a brilliant pianist and composer, and in his day achieved some fame. He is now much less popular, and many of his works are quite out of use.

DOLBY (Charlotte). See SAINTON-DOLBY.

"DOLORES." See DICKSON (Ellen).

DONALDSON (John). Scottish musician, theorist, and Professor of Music in Edinburgh University, 1845-65. He was for some time previous to his appointment a teacher of music in Edinburgh. He did little, if anything, to promote the artistic interests of the Chair of Music in the University, but contributed largely to the present effective means of carrying out concerts, etc., by the erection of the music room and organ, and by getting the rights of the Music Chair established by process at Law in 1855. He D. Edinburgh, 1865.

DONATO (Baldesaro). Italian comp., B. about 1530. D. Venice, 1603. Writer of madrigals.

DONE (Joshua). English writer, B. London. S. at Paris under Cherubini. Org. of S. John's, Lambeth; Chelsea Old Church; Knightsbridge Chap.; and S. Augustine's, Liverpool. Author of "A Short Treatise on Harmony, Thorough Bass, and Modulation, including the compass and properties of Musical Instruments in general." London, Cocks, n. d. "Treatise on the Organ," Lond., 18mo, 1837. "Tuner's Companion : a Treatise on the Construction of Pianofortes...with various Methods of Tuning them," Lond., 8vo, n. d. "Selection of the most Popular, with many Original Psalm and Hymn Tunes, Chants, etc.," London, fo. [1830.]

DONE (William). English cond. and org., B. Worcester, 1815. Org. of Worcester Cath., 1844. He has conducted the Worcester Musical Festivals since 1844 ; but is best known among musicians as an organist of high attainments, and a musician of much earnestness and capability.

DONI (Giovanni Battista). Italian comp., B. Florence, 1594. Professor of Elocution, and Member of Florentine Academy. Member of Della Crusca Society. D. Florence, 1647.

Doni is author of a number of works on ancient music containing much interesting information touching the state of music in his own day. Among them is "Compendio del trattato dei generi a modi della musica...," Rome, 1635.

DONIZETTI (Gaetano). Italian comp., B. Bergamo, Nov. 29, 1798. S. under Mayr, at Vienna. Resided in Paris, 1835. Travelled in Italy. Returned to Paris, 1843. Prof. at Royal Academy of Music, Naples. Latterly insane. D. Bergamo, April 8, 1848.

Works.—*Operas:* Enrico di Borgogna, Venice, 1818; Il Falegname di Livonia, 1819; Le Nozze in Villa, 1820; Zoraide di Granata, 1822; Le Zingara, 1822; Le lettera anonima, 1822; Chiara e Serafina, 1822; Il Fortunato inganno, 1823; Alfredo il Grande, 1823; Una Follia, 1823; L'Ajo nell' imbarazzo, 1824; Emilia di

Liverpool, 1824; Alahor in Granata, 1826; Il Castello degli Invalidi, 1826; Il Giovedi Grasso, 1827; Olivo e Pasquale, 1827; Il Borgomastro de Saardam, 1827; Le Convenienze teatrali, 1827; Otto mese in due ore, 1828; L'Esule di Roma, 1828; La Regina di Golconda, 1828; Gianni di Calais, 1828; Il Paria, 1829; Il Castello di Kenilworth, 1829; Il Diluvio Universale, 1829; I Pazzi per progetto, 1830; Francesca di Foix, 1830; Isnelda de' Lambertazzi, 1830; La Romanziera, 1830; Anna Bolena, Milan, 1830—Lond., 1831; Fausta, 1830; L'Elisire d' amore, Naples, 1832—Lond., 1836; Ugo, Conte di Parigi, 1832; Sancia di Castilla, 1832; Il Nuova Pourceaugnac, 1832; Il Furioso nell' isola di San Domingo, 1833; Parisina, 1833; Torquato Tasso, Rome, 1833; Lucrezia Borgia, Milan, 1833—Lond., 1839, in English, 1843; Rosamunda d'Inghilterra, 1834; Maria Stuarda, Naples, 1834; Gemma di Vergi, Milan, 1834; Marino Faliero, Paris, 1835, Lond., 1835; Lucia di Lammermoor, Naples, 1835, Lond., 1838, English, 1843; Belisario, 1836; Il Campanella di Notte, 1836; Betly, 1836; L'Assedio di Calais, 1836; Pio di Tolomei, 1836; Roberto Devereaux, 1836; Maria di Rudenz, Venice, 1838; Poliuto, 1838; Gianni di Parigi, 1839; Gabriella di Vergi, 1840; La Fille du Regiment, Paris, 1840—London, 1847; Les Martyrs, 1840; La Favorite, 1840—Lond., 1847; Adelasia, 1841; Maria Padilla, 1841; Linda di Chamouni, Vienna, 1842—Lond., 1843; Don Pasquale, Paris, 1843—Lond., 1843; Maria di Rohan, Vienna, 1843—Lond., 1847; Don Sebastien, Paris, 1843; Catarina Cornaro, 1844; Elisabeth, 1853; Il Duca di Alba, 1881-82. Masses, cantatas, etc.

Donizetti, Bellini, and to some extent Verdi, are all so directly under the influence of Rossini, that in speaking of their individual merits it is almost necessary to criticise the modern Italian school as it stands. The mechanical prettiness of Donizetti which at one time held sway over the tastes of the British public, is now fortunately relegated to the minor theatres of Italy, unless we except the efforts made by singers at that antiquated institution "The Italian Opera," to revive and keep living the mediocrities of their native land. String after string of melodious phrases plastered together without design or artistic perception, and devoid of purpose or propriety constitute grand opera, and in this style most of Donizetti's operas are written.

The only feature of Donizetti's work which calls for attention is the melody, which is highly Italian, and consequently very pretty; but its application to the sentiment of the position in which it is found is frequently so absurd as to justify the belief that Italians of recent times have little sense of dramatic power at all. In Donizetti we have instances of waltz rhythms usurping the place of soft, impassioned strains, and *cantabile* passages crowding out the more natural ones of vigour which may happen to be appropriate to the action.

DONKIN (W. F.) English writer and musician, M.A., F.R.S., etc. Savilian Prof. of Astronomy, Oxford. Author of "Acoustics, Theoretical," Part. I., Oxford, 8vo, 1870. All published of a work designed to cover the whole range of the science of sound.

DONZELLI (Domenico). Italian tenor vocalist, B. Bergamo, 1790. S. in Italy. *Début* in Italy, after which he appeared in all the principal European cities, and in London, 1829. D. Bologna, Mar. 31, 1873.

DOPPLER (Albert Franz). Austrian flute-player and comp., B. Lemberg, Oct. 1, 1821. Comp. various operas, and instrumental music. D. Baden, nr. Vienna, July 27, 1883.

DORAN (Rev. John Wilberforce). English writer and divine, B. London, 1834. B.A., Cantab., 1857; M.A., 1861; ordained 1857. Successively curate of various parishes. Vicar of Fen Stanton, Huntingdonshire, 1883.

WORKS.—Choir Directory of Plain Song, etc. (with S. Nottingham). The Psalter and Canticles, arranged for Gregorian chanting, with a Table of Tones and the Canticles. Little Directory of Plain Song for Congregational use. The Canticles arranged for Gregorian chanting, etc. The Versicles and Responses at Matins and Evensong. Ritual Music of the Altar. Choir Book of Ritual Music of the Altar. Hyfforddwr ar y Gân Eglwysig (Welsh Plain-song Directory). Harmonies for the Gregorian Tunes, etc. Te Deums, Chants, etc.

These works are valuable aids to those engaged in conducting the church service, and their success has been attested by the numerous editions of them which have appeared.

DORING (Karl Heinrich). German pianist and comp., B. Dresden, 1834. Comp. of Masses, Pf. Music, Songs, etc.

DORN (Heinrich Ludwig Edmund). German comp. and cond., B. Königsberg, Nov. 14, 1804. Educated at Königsberg University. S. under Zelter, Klein, and L. Berger at Berlin. Cond. of Königsberg Theatre, 1828. Chapmaster at Cath. of S. Peter, Riga, 1830. Cond. of Cologne Theatre, 1843. Cond. of Berlin Royal Opera, 1847-68. Teacher and comp. in Berlin.

WORKS.—*Operas:* Rolands' Knappen ; Der Zauberer, 1827 ; Die Bettlerin, 1829 ; Abu Kara, 1831 ; Das Schwærmen-Mædchen, 1832 ; Der Schöffe von Paris, 1838 ; Bannerets d'Angleterre, 1843 ; Les Musiciens d'Aix-la-Chapelle, 1848 ; Artexerxes, 1848 ; Die Niebelungen, 1854. Symphonies and Overtures for orch. Psalms and Masses. Pf. Music and Songs.

DORRINGTON (Theo.) English divine of 18th century, author of "A Discourse on Singing in the Worship of God," Lond., 8vo, 1704.

DOTZAUER (Justus Johann Friedrich). German comp. and violoncellist, B. Hæsseerieth, Jan. 20, 1783. S. under Kriegk, Heuschkel, etc. 'Cellist in Meiningen court band, 1801-5. Member of King's band, Dresden, 1811-60. D. Dresden, March 9, 1860.

WORKS.—Graziosa, opera. Quartets for strings, op. 12, 19, 29, 30 ; Concertos for 'cello and orch., opp. 27, 66 in C, 72 in E, 81 in D, 82 in E flat, 84 in E min., 93 in F, 100 in D flat, 101 in F; Concertinos for 'cello and orch., opp. 67, 89, 105 ; Two Sonatas for 'cello and bass, op. 2 ; Duets for violin and bass, op. 4, 8 ; Duets for 2 vns., op. 14, 16, 25 ; Variations for 'cello, etc., various ; Symphonies for orch., op. 40, 85. Overtures. Mass. Songs, etc.

Dotzauer was the teacher of Kummer, Schuberth, Drechsler, etc., and was himself a fine performer and able composer.

DOUGALL (Neil). Scottish minor poet and comp., B. Greenock, Dec. 9, 1776. Apprenticed to mercantile marine service, 1791. Continued seaman till accidentally wounded while discharging a cannon. Became teacher of music, 1799. Married Margaret Donaldson, 1806. Inn-keeper in Greenock, 1824. D. Greenock, Oct. 1, 1862.

WORKS.—Poems and Songs, Greenock, 12mo, 1854. *Psalm Tunes:* Naples, 1801 ; Kilmarnock ; Patience ; New East Church ; etc. Also tunes contributed to Stevens' "Sacred Music," vol. 6.

Dougall was acquainted with R. A. Smith, whose psalm "Morven" probably suggested his "Kilmarnock." Dougall was a very humble musician, but his psalm-tunes will keep his memory green in Scotland for some time to come. "Kilmarnock" is by far the best of his productions, and was originally published in R. A. Smith's tune book. His daughter Lillie was a public singer for a time.

DOW (Daniel). Scottish comp., teacher and collector of last century, author of "Twenty Minuets, and Sixteen Reels or Country Dances, for the Violin, Harpsichord, or German Flute," Edinburgh, 4to [1775]. "Collection of Ancient Scots Music," fo. [1778]? "A Collection of Ancient Scots Music, for the Violin, Harpsichord, or German Flute, never before printed, consisting of Ports, Salutations, Marches or Pibrochs, etc.," Edin., fo. n. d. "Thirty-seven New Reels and Strathspeys, for the Violin, Harpsichord, Pianoforte, or German Flute," Edin. (N. Stewart), ob. 4to, n. d.

DOWLAND (John). English comp., B. Westminster, 1562. Resided on the Continent, 1584. Returned to England. Mus. Bac., Oxon., 1588. Do., Cantab., 1592. Lutenist to Charles IV. of Denmark. Returned to England, 1605. Returned to Denmark for a time. Resided in England from 1609. Lutenist to the King from 1625. D. 1626.

WORKS.—The First Booke of Songes or Ayres of foure parts, with Tablature for the Lute, 1595. Second Booke, do., 1600. Third Booke, do., 1602. Lachrimæ, or Seaven Teares figured in Seaven passionate Pavans, with divers other Pavans, Galiards, and Almands, set forth for the Lute, Viols, or Violins, in five parts, 1605.

A Pilgrim's Solace, wherein is contained Musical Harmony of three, four, and five parts, to be sung and plaid with Lute and Viols, 1612. Translation of Ornithoparcus, his Micrologus, or Introduction: containing the art of singing and the perfect use of the Monochord...Lond., 1609, fo. Harmonies in Este's Psalms, etc.

The poetry and music both in Dowland's works are of an exceptionally high degree of excellence, and he is properly classed among the best musicians of his time. The poetry, indeed, is so good that Professor Arber has reprinted the three books of songs, etc. (words only), in his valuable series of classical reprints, while the Musical Antiquarian Society have done a like service for the first book of the same set. His music has that quaint, delightful flavour common to compositions of the 16th and 17th centuries, and his harmonies and melodies both have beauties of an exceptional cast. Shakespeare has shown his preference for Dowland in the sonnet commencing,

"If music and sweet poetry agree."

DOWLAND (Robert). English comp., son of above, was Lutenist to the King, 1626. He edited several musical publications, and a "Varietie of Lessons," etc.

DOYAGÜE (Don Manuel Jose). Spanish comp., B. Salamanca, Feb. 7, 1755. D. Dec. 18, 1842. Writer of church music.

DRAESCKE (Felix). German comp. and writer, B. Coburg, 1835. S. at Leipzig. Teacher of Pf. at Dresden.

Draescke is an expounder of the ideas of Wagner in the matter of musical reform, and has written largely in support of them. His published works are chiefly for the Pf., with others in MS., and an opera, "Gudrun," Hanover, 1884.

DRAGHI (Antonio). Italian comp., B. Ferrara, 1642. Musician in service of Court at Vienna. D. Ferrara, 1707.

WORKS.—*Operas:* Aronisba, 1663; Peneloppe, 1670; Gara de Genni, 1671; La Lanterna di Diogene, 1674; Pirro, 1675; Chelonida, 1677; Achille in Tessalia, 1681; Lo Studio d' Amore, 1686; Tanasio, 1688; Rosaura, 1689; Amor per virtù, 1697; L' Alceste, 1699; and others, to the number of 83.

DRAGHI (Giovanni Battista). Italian comp. of the 17th century. Settled in England about middle of 17th century. Org. to the Queen, 1677. He composed music (with Locke) to Shadwell's "Psyche," D'Urfey's "The Wonders in the Sun, or The Kingdom of Birds," 1706; Music to Dryden's ode, "From Harmony"; Songs in great numbers in contemporary collections. Draghi was brother of Antonio, above noticed, and as a composer assimilated his style to the English school. His songs are melodious.

DRAGONETTI (Domenico). Italian double-bass player, B. Venice, April, 1755. Played in the Opera Buffa at Venice. Choir-master of S. Mark's, Venice, for 18 years. Appeared in London, 1794. Played along with Lindley and the Ancient Concerts, the Philharmonic, etc. Led the double-basses at the Beethoven Festival at Bonn, 1845. D. London, April 16, 1846.

Dragonetti is, to the aspiring bass player, what Paganini is, or used to be, to the violinist. His tone and execution alike were of the rarest type, placing him far above any contemporary performer. The numerous anecdotes related anent him will be found in any book of musical stories.

DRECHSLER (Josef). Bohemian comp. and writer, B. Bohemia, 1782. D. Feb., 1852.

DRECHSLER (Karl). German violoncellist, B. Kamenz, Saxony, May, 1800. S. under Dotzauer. Leader of band at Dessau, 1826. Appeared in England. D. 1873. Drechsler taught Cossmann and Grützmacher, and was a remarkably fine performer.

DRESSEL (Otto). German comp. and pianist, B. Andernach-on-the-Rhine, 1826. S. under Hiller and Mendelssohn. Settled in Boston, U.S., 1852. Comp. Pf. music., songs, quartets, etc.

DRESSLER (Rafael). Hungarian flute-player and comp., B. Grätz, 1784. D. Mayence, Feb. 12, 1835. Wrote among other works, Caprices for flute, op.

1 ; Concerto for flute and orch., op. 4 ; Concerto, op. 35 ; Quartets, various, etc. He also published a treatise on the flute, op. 63, which has been trans. into English, and other works of instruction.

DREYSCHOCK (Alexander). Bohemian pianist and comp., B. Zack, Oct. 15, 1818. Travelled in Europe as concert giver. Teacher at Prague. D. Venice, April, 1869.

His Pf. music is of the elegant type so commonly named *salon music*, and is brilliant and effective. The titles are generally after the following style :—Scherzo, op. 19 ; Idylle, op. 26 ; Grande Sonate, op. 30 ; Saltarella, op. 43 ; Bluette, op. 53 ; Nocturne, op. 54 ; Première Scène Champêtre, op. 61 ; Second do., op. 65 ; Le Contraste, op. 97 ; etc.

DREYSCHOCK (Raimund). Bohemian violinist, brother of above, B. Zack, Aug. 20, 1824, D. Leipzig, Feb., 1869. His son, FELIX, B. Leipzig, Dec. 27, 1860, is a pianist.

DROBOISCH (Carl Ludwig). German comp., B. Leipzig, Dec. 24, 1803. D. Augsburg, Aug. 20, 1854. Comp. Pianoforte music, Lieder for voice and Pf., an oratorio, etc.

DROUËT (Louis Francois Philippe). French flute player and comp., B. Amsterdam, 1792. D. Berne, 1873.

WORKS.—Three valses for 2 flutes, op. 24 ; Three trios for 3 flutes, op. 33 ; Fantasia for Pf. and flute, op. 36 ; Do., op. 37 ; Concertos, variations, duets, etc.

Drouët was one of the founders of modern flute-playing, and himself a magnificent performer, and is supposed to have composed or arranged "Partant pour la Syrie," the French national song commonly attributed to Eugénie de Beauharnais.

DRUITT (Dr. Robert). English writer, author of "A Popular Tract on Church Music, with Remarks on its moral and Political importance, and a Practical Scheme for its Reformation," Lond., 8vo, 1845 ; "Conversations on the Choral Service, being an Examination of the Popular Prejudices against Church Music," Lond., 8vo, 1853.

DRUMMOND (George). Mus. Bac., English org. and comp., B. 1798. Blind from infancy. S. under Crotch. Published "Parochial Psalmody, or 70 Plain Psalm Tunes arranged for the Organ or Pianoforte," 4to, n. d.

DRYDEN (Henry E. L.). English writer, author of "On Church Music and the Fittings of Churches for Music," Lond., 8vo, 1854.

DRYDEN (John). English poet, B. Aldwinkle, Northampton, Aug. 9, 1631. D. London, May 1, 1700.

Dryden is closely identified with the musical and dramatic progress and events of his time. He wrote the libretto of "King Arthur" for Purcell, the "Ode for St. Cecilia's Day," which has been frequently set, and a number of dramatic pieces, the music to accompany which exercised the genius of many of the best English composers, and aided greatly in forming the school of English music. His connection with Purcell was originally slight, but it afterwards developed into a warm friendship. His works have been set by Purcell, Jeremiah Clarke, Arne, Handel, and a great number of other composers, both English and foreign.

DUBOIS (Clément Francois Théodore). French comp., B. Rosnay, Aug. 24, 1837. Comp. "La Farandole," ballet, 1883; Operas, Aben-Hamet, 1884, etc. ; also dance music, songs, etc.

DUBOURG (George). English writer, grandson of Matthew, B. 1799. Author of "The Violin ; being an Account of that leading Instrument, and its most Eminent Professors." London, 12mo [1832] ; 2nd edit., 1837 ; 4th edit., 1852 ; 5th edit., 1856.

DUBOURG (Matthew). English violinist and comp., B. London, 1703. S. under Geminiani. Appeared first at Britton's concerts. Comp. and master of state music in Ireland, 1728. Succeeded Festing as member of King's band, 1752. Leader of band on production of Handel's "Messiah." D. London, 1741.

He composed concertos, solos, and variations for the violin ; odes, songs, and other vocal music. He was the leading English violonist of his day, and one of the greatest among his contemporaries. The records which have descended to us as to his powers on his instrument are flattering in the highest degree.

DUCHEMIN (Charles Jean Batiste). English cond. and pianist, B. Birmingham, May 12, 1827. S. at Frankfort, and afterwards at the Royal Cons. of Brussels under Fétis, from whom he received a flattering autograph certificate on his leaving in 1845. He is an Associate of the London Philharmonic Soc., Mem. of Trin. Coll., London, etc.

Mr. Duchemin, for family reasons, settled in Birmingham, his native town, where as Professor he has devoted himself assiduously to the instruction of music in its higher branches. He was successively org. of S. Peter's Ch., and of The Oratory, as also director of the German Liederkrantz. He was one of the original promoters of Classical Chamber Concerts in Birmingham, and also the Founder of the Edgbaston Amateur Musical Union—an orchestral society which has done much to develope a taste for the works of the great masters. He was its Honorary Conductor for twenty years from its commencement. Mr. Duchemin has often, and always with great success, played in public on his favourite instrument, the piano, and has been associated in these performances with many of the leading artistes of the day, including Sainton, Henry Blagrove, Ries, Piatti, Sims Reeves, Grisi, Mario, Weiss, etc. He has composed many things for piano, orchestra, vocal, etc., and amongst others several short operettas ; but few have been published, and those principally in the shape of light original compositions for the piano.

Mr. Duchemin is of French origin, his father having been a naval officer on parole, taken prisoner during the war with Napoleon I., and who lived later on in Birmingham as a teacher of languages.

DUCIS (Benedictus). Belgian comp. and org., B. Bruges, [1480]. Org. at Antwerp. Supposed to have visited England in 1515. Biography unknown. D. [c. 1540].

WORKS.—Novum et insigne opus musicum, sex, quinque, et quatuor vocum, 1537 ; Psalmorum selectorum, 1539 ; Selectæ Harmoniæ, 1538 ; Tertius liber Mottetorum, 1538 ; Harmonien über alle oden des Horaz, für 3 und 4 Stimmen. Ulm, 1539,

DUCOUDRAY. See BOURGAULT-DUCOUDRAY.

DUFAY (Guillaume). Belgian comp. of the fourteenth century (1350-1432). Author of a number of masses and other church music, published in various collections, and considered remarkable specimens for the period to which they belong.

DUFF (Charles). Scottish collector, teacher in Dundee about beginning of present century. Published "A Collection of Strathspey Reels, Jiggs, etc., with a Bass for the Violoncello or Harpsichord, etc.," Edin., fo., n. d. Another Duff (Archibald), published about the same time a " Collection of Strathspeys, Reels, etc., for the Pianoforte, Violin, and Violoncello." 4to, n. d.

DUFF & STEWART. English firm of music-publishers, established at Oxford Street, London, by John Duff, in 1831. Their publications originally consisted of the popular songs of Samuel Lover, operas by Rooke, etc., and latterly they have published songs, etc., by many of the most famous English composers. Successive members of the firm were Mr. Hodgson, who retired in 1866, and died about 1878 ; and Mr. Frank Stewart became a partner in 1866, and is now the proprietor of the business.

DUGGAN (Joseph Francis). Irish comp. and pianist, B. Dublin, July 10, 1817. Accompanist of the recitatives in the Italian opera, New York. Musical cond. of English opera, under John Wilson, in the U. S. Cond. of German opera company. Teacher in Philadelphia, Baltimore, and Washington. Principal and Professor in the Philadelphia Musical Institute, 1841. Pianist, teacher, and comp., in Paris, 1844-45. Resided in Edinburgh, and applied unsuccessfully for University Professorship. Settled in London, 1845. Prof. of Singing in the Guildhall School of Music, etc.

WORKS.—*Operas:* Pierre, 1 act (Henry Drayton), Lond., Nov., 1853 ; Léonie,

3 acts (Henry Drayton), Lond., Mar., 1854; The Brides of Venice, 3 acts (MS.); Alfred, German, Philadelphia (MS.); Le Nain Noir, Paris, (MS.). Overture and Entr'actes to "As You Like It," 1854 ; Home and Foreign Lyrics, a set of 13 songs. The xxvii. Psalm, for contralto voice ; Four volumes of songs (about 50 in number) ; Six songs, " Rhythmic Tentatives," op. 1, 1879 ; Six string quartets ; Two symphonies, in C and E flat ; Polacca in G, for Pf.; Polonaise in G, Pf.; The Syrens, The Guards, Maria, Laura, Rosalie, Tears, etc., for Pf.; The Singing-master's Assistant ; Translation of Albrechtsberger's "Science of Music," Philadelphia, 1842 ; Translation of Fétis' "Treatise on Counterpoint and Fugue"; Many single songs, Pf. pieces, etc.

Mr. Duggan has appeared in public as organist, violinist, conductor, and pianist, but has been most appreciated in his rôle of composer. His lyrics embody his experience and study of rhythm, a matter of the utmost importance, but occasionally overlooked by even the greatest composers, and always by the minors. He has in his songs wedded the poetry and music in close rhythmical union, accompanied by fine and appropriate melody. His operas 1 and 2 were greatly successful when produced, and No. 3, which has not yet been brought out, embodies his ideas on the subject of rhythm. His other songs, not in the collections above named, and part songs, are all impressed with a genuine artistic feeling and sympathetic and poetic colouring.

DUHAUPAS (Albert). French comp., B. Arras, April 22, 1832. Org. and writer of masses, motets, Pf. music, songs, etc.

DUKE (Richard). English violin-maker of the 18th century, flourished in London in latter part of 18th century [1768-1780].

The position of this maker among his contemporaries and successors has never been strictly defined ; some writers holding his claims to be very shallow, and others magnifying his pretensions to the greatest possible dimensions. His violins, when they can be got genuine, an extremely difficult matter, are remarkable for their fine smooth tone, and general good workmanship. They have been copied and forged to infinity, so that a real ' Duke' is a rarity seldom to be found among the treasures of ordinary collectors.

DULCKEN (Marie Louise), née DAVID. German pianist, B. Hamburg, Mar. 20, 1811. Début, 1821. Appeared in Berlin, Leipzig, etc. Married Mr. Dulcken, in Germany, 1828. Appeared in London, 1829. Travelled in Europe. D. London, April 12, 1850.

DUMONT (Henri). Belgian comp. and org., B. Liége, 1610. Chap.-master to Louis XIV. D. Paris, 1684. Dumont introduced counterpoint into his compositions, being the first musician in France who did so, and wrote a number of fine motets and masses, the latter having been continually performed till far on in the present century.

DUMONT (Felix). French pianist and comp., B. Paris, Aug. 14, 1832. S. Paris Cons. Wrote School for Pf. and salon music.

DUN (Finlay). Scottish comp. and teacher, B. Aberdeen, Feb. 24, 1795. S. under Baillot, and at Cons. of Milan. Played first tenor in theatre of San Carlo. Afterwards S. singing under Crescentini. Settled in Edinburgh as violinist, comp., and teacher. D. Edinburgh, Nov. 28, 1853.

WORKS.—Two Symphonies for full orch. (MS.); Solfeggi and Exercises upon Scales, Intervals, etc.,...to which is prefixed an Introductory Discourse on Vocal Expression, Lond., fo., 1829 ; Two prize glees ; The Vocal Melodies of Scotland, edited with John Thomson (Paterson) ; Wood's Songs of Scotland, edited with J. F. Graham, etc.; Pf. music. Part-songs and glees: June ; The Parted Spirit (prize at Manchester Gentlemen's Glee Club), 1831 ; She is coming, trio, etc.; Anthems, psalms, hymns ; Lays from Strathearn, by the Baroness Nairne, Glasgow, fo., n.d.; The Musical Scrap Book, Edin., 4to [1833]. Orain na'h Albain, a Collection of Gaelic Songs, with English and Gaelic Words, and an Appendix containing Traditionary Notes to many of the Songs... Edin., 1848, fo. Analysis of Scottish Music, etc.

Dun was a respectable musician, but will only be remembered by his harmonization of a number of the Scottish melodies. These harmonies are greatly inferior to

Thomson's. He had an extensive capacity for languages, and was a fluent Greek, Latin, German, French, and Italian scholar. Some of his songs are very good, and all his part-songs are fine.

DUNCAN (Gideon). Scottish writer, author of " True Presbyterian, or a brief account of the new singing, its author, and progress in general," 1755, 12mo.

DUNI (Egidio Romoaldo). Italian comp., B. near Naples, Feb. 9, 1709. Travelled in Europe. Visited London. Musician to Duke of Parma's daughter, 1755. Settled in Paris, 1757. D. Paris, June 11, 1775.

WORKS.—*Operas:* Nerone ; Artaserse ; Bajazet ; Ciro ; Demofoonte ; Ninette à la Cour, 1755 ; Le Peintre amoureux de son modele, 1757 ; Le Docteur Sangrado, 1757 ; Nina et Lindor, 1761 ; Le Bonne Fille, 1762 ; La Clochette, 1766 ; etc.

Duni is credited with having founded comic opera in France. His music is melodious, but now completely forgotten.

DUNNE (John). English comp. and org., B. York, 1834. Chor. in Worcester Cath., 1850. Do., Cashel Cath., Ireland, 1854. Member of Christ Ch., St. Patrick's Cath., and Trinity College choirs, Dublin. Mus. Bac., Dub., 1866. Mus. Doc., Dub., 1870. Examiner to Government Intermediate Educational Board, Ireland, etc. D. Ashton, Killiney, near Dublin, June 7, 1883.

WORKS.—Myra, a Cantata for full chorus and orch. The Hanging of the Crane (Longfellow), Cantata. Church Services and Anthems. Glees, Songs, etc.

DUNSTABLE (John). English comp. and writer (1400-1458). Author of "De Mensurabiles Musica," a work quoted by Ravenscroft.

He was erroneously attributed with the invention of counterpoint by Tinctor, but is generally held up by succeeding musicians as a composer of much ability and a musician of universal influence.

DUNSTAN (H. Mainwaring). English writer, translated from the French "Life and Letters of Berlioz," London, 8vo, 1882.

DUPONT (Auguste). Belgian comp., pianist, and Prof., B. near Liège, Feb., 1828. Prof. of Pf. in Brussels Cons., 1853.

WORKS.—*Pianoforte:* Etude de trilles, op. 2 ; La Pensée, étude, op. 3 ; Serenade, op. 6 ; Concerto in F minor, op. 11 ; Six Morceaux Caracteristiques, op. 12 ; Reminiscences Pastorales, op. 16 ; Barcarolle, op. 17 ; Un Chanson de jeune fille, op. 18 ; Reverie, op. 20 ; Toccatelle, op. 26 ; Chanson Hongroise, op. 27 ; Ballades, op. 43, 44, 47, etc. ; Roman en dix pages, op. 48. String quartets, etc.

Dupont is a writer of most elegant and beautiful Pianoforte music, his ballades, barcarolles and studies being graceful and poetical effusions, equalled by few living composers.

DUPONT (Jean Francois). Belgian comp. and violinist, B. Rotterdam, 1822. Author of " Bianca " and " Siffredi," operas, two symphonies, trios, songs, Pf. music, etc.

DUPONT (Joseph). Belgian comp. and violinist, B. Liége, Aug. 21, 1821. D. Liége, Feb. 13, 1861. Prof. of violin at Liége Cons. Comp. of "Ribeiro Pinto," opera, 1858, violin music, etc.

DUPONT (Joseph). Belgian comp. and violinist, B. Ensival, Jan. 3, 1838. S. Brussels Cons. Gained first prize for violin playing, 1862 ; First comp. prize, 1863. Prof. of Harmony Brussels Cons. Comp. of Symphonies, Overtures, Cantatas, Pf. Music, Songs, etc,

DUPORT (Jean Louis). French violinist and comp., B. Paris, Oct., 1749. D. Paris, Sept., 1819.

DUPORT (Jean Pierre). French violoncellist, B. Paris, Nov., 1741. D. Berlin, 1818. Comp. for his instrument.

DUPREZ (Gilbert Louis). French comp. and tenor vocalist, B. Paris, Dec. 6, 1806. Writer of Songs, etc. Prof. in Paris Cons., 1842-50. Famous as the instructor of many famous vocalists. Author of a vocal method, translated into English as "Treatise on Singing, with Rules, Examples, and Exercises for every species of voice," London, n. d.

DUPUIS (Thomas Saunders). English (French) comp. and org., B. 1733. Member of Chap. Roy. S. under Gates and Travers. Org. of Chap. Roy., 1789. Mus. Bac. and Doc. Oxon., 1790. D. London, June 17, 1796.

WORKS.—Cathedral Music, in Score, composed for the use of His Majesty's Royal Chapel, by the late T. S. Dupuis, selected from the original manuscripts, and carefully revised, by John Spencer, London, n. d., 3 vols., fo. Twenty-four Double and Single Chants, 4to, n. d. Sixteen Double and Single Chants, as performed at the Chapel Royal; two other collections. Five Concertos for Organ, with Accompaniments, fo., n. d. Concertos, Sonatas and Lessons for Pf. Songs, Six Glees [1785], etc.

DURAND (Marie). American soprano vocalist, B. Charleston, S. Carolina. Educated in New York. *Début* at Chicago as "Zerlina." Appeared in St. Petersburg, Brussels, New Orleans, Milan, Florence, and London, 1883-84.

DURANTE (Francesco). Italian comp., B. Naples, March, 1684 [1693]. Master of Cons. of S. Onofrio, Naples. D. Naples, Aug., 1755.

Composer of a number of beautiful vocal exercises and duets, which up to recent times were highly prized in Italy. Cherubini published an edition of his duets at Paris about 1830. Durante was teacher of Pergolesi, Terradellas, Piccinni, Tractta, Paesiello, Sacchini, Guglielmi, etc. His works include many Masses, Psalms, Hymns, Litanies, Cantatas, Madrigals, Solfeggi, Sonatas, etc.

DURASTANTI (Margherita). Italian soprano vocalist, B. in Italy, 1695. Appeared in Handel's operas at London, 1720-24, 1733, etc. D. [?]

D'URFEY (Thomas). French song-writer and playwright, B. Exeter, 1649. D. London, Feb. 26, 1723.

Writer of a large number of plays and obscene songs, most of which latter are contained in "Wit and Mirth; or, Pills to purge Melancholy;" an encyclopædia of trivial, though often witty verse, set by good composers like Purcell, Humphrey, etc. The moral tone of society in Tom D'Urfey's day was not of the highest order, and the *début* of our Grub-street poetaster did not tend to raise it. The book abounds in so-called Scotch songs, or songs in the Scotch manner, and contains a few *decent* lyrics of a feeble kind.

DÜRRNER (Johann Ruprecht.) German violinist and comp., B. Anspah, Jan. 7, 1810. Resided in Edinburgh as a teacher and conductor. D. Edinburgh, June, 1859. His works consist chiefly of songs and part-songs.

DUSCHEK (Franz). Bohemian pianist and comp., B. Dec., 1736. D. end of last century. His wife, *née* JOSEPHINE HAMBACHER, was a vocalist of some repute in her day. She was B. Prague in 1756.

DUSSEK (Johann Ludwig) or Duschek. Bohemian comp. and pianist, B. Czaslau, Feb. 9, 1761. S. under his father. Chor. in Ch. of Iglau. Educated at Jesuit's Coll. Org. at Kuttenberg, and at S. Rombaut, Malines. As Pianist appeared in every principal European city. Came to London, 1789. Married daughter of Montague Corri, 1792. Partner in music business with M. Corri. Absconded. Resided on Continent. D. near Paris, March 20, 1812.

WORKS.—Op. 1. Three Concertos for Pf. and quartet; op. 2. Three Sonatas for Pf., vn., and 'cello; op. 3. Concerto for Pf. and orch., in E. flat; op. 4. Three Sonatas for Pf. and vn.; op. 5. Three Sonatas for 2 vns.; op. 6. Airs varied, for Pf.; op. 7. Three Sonatas for Pf. and flute; op. 8. Three Sonatas for Pf. and vn.; op. 9. Three Sonatas for Pf.; op. 10. Three Sonatas for Pf.; op. 11. Three do.; op. 12. Three Sonatas for Pf. and vn.; op. 13. Three do.; op. 14. Three do.; op. 15. Concerto for Pf. and orch. in F; op. 16. Twelve Lessons for Pf.; op. 17. Three Sonatas for Pf. and vn.; op. 18. Three do.; op. 19. Six Sonatas for Pf. and flute; op. 20. Six Sonatinas for Pf. and flute; op. 21. Sonata for Pf., flute, and 'cello, in C; op. 22. Concerto for Pf. and orch., in B: op. 23. Sonata, etc., for

Pf. ; op. 24. Three Sonatas for Pf., vn., and 'cello ; op. 25. Three Sonatas for Pf. and flute ; op. 26. Concerto for Pf. and orch., in E flat ; op. 27. Concerto for Pf. and orch., in E flat ; op. 28. Six Sonatas for Pf. and vn. ; op. 29. Concerto for Pf. and orch., in C ; op. 30. Four Sonatas for Pf. and vn. ; op. 31. Three Sonatas for Pf., vn., and 'cello; op. 32. Sonata for Pf. duet; op. 33. Il Rivocato, Pf. ; op. 34. Two Sonatas for Pf., vn., and 'cello ; op. 35. Three Sonatas for Pf. ; op. 36. Sonata for Pf. and vn., in C ; op. 37. Sonata for Pf., vn., cello; op. 38. Sonata for Pf. duet ; op. 39. Three Sonatas for Pf. ; op. 40. Concerto (military) for Pf. and orch. in B ; op. 41. Quartet for Pf., vn., viola, 'cello ; op. 43-5. Sonatas for Pf. ; op. 46. Six easy Sonatas for Pf. and vn. ; op. 47. Two do. ; op. 48. Sonata for Pf. duet, in C op. 50. Concerto for Pf. and orch., in G minor ; op. 51. Three Sonatas for Pf. and vn. ; op. 53. Quartet for Pf. and strings, in E flat ; op. 55. Fantasia and Fugue for Pf. ; op. 56. Quartet for Pf. and strings ; op. 60. Three Quartets for strings ; op. 61. Elégie harmonique sur la mort du P. L. F. de Prusse, in F sharp minor ; op. 62. La Consolation, andante for Pf., in B ; op. 63. Concerto for 2 pianos and orch., in B ; op. 64. Three Fugues for Pf. duet ; op. 65. Sonata for Pf., flute, and 'cello, in F ; op. 66. Concerto for Pf. and orch., in F ; op. 67. Three Sonatas for Pf. duet ; op. 68. Notturno concertante for Pf. and vn., with horn ; op. 69. Three sonatas for Pf. and vn. ; op. 70. Concerto for Pf. and orch.; op. 71. Recueil d'Airs connus variés pour Pf. ; op. 72. Sonata for Pf. duet, E flat ; op. 73. Sonata for Pf. duet, in F ; op. 74. Do., in B ; op. 75. Sonata for Pf.; op. 76. Fantasia for Pf., in F ; op. 77. Sonata for Pf., in F min. (L'Invocation). Numerous minor works, unnumbered, for Pf., and songs.

Much of Dussek's music still enjoys a degree of popularity, but not by any means equalling that which it enjoyed at the beginning of the present century. Much of his music was written for shop purposes, and possesses little, or no artistic merit whatever ; his naval engagements, battles, delineations of ceremonies, etc., being so much arrant trash. His sonatas for Pf. are his best works, and are likely to survive anything else he has composed. His concerted chamber music is also of great merit, and still holds a small place in popular favour. Messrs. Breitkopf & Härtel of Leipzig keep in print nearly all of his works, which shows in a measure that his name is unlikely to be lost in oblivion during the present century. The Pf. music of Dussek belongs to the period of Mozart rather than of Beethoven, although to a large extent it is technically far in advance of either Haydn or Mozart. In general style his compositions are flowing and poetical, occasionally reaching a high degree of real inspiration.

DUSTMANN (Louise). See MEYER.

DUVERNAY (E.) French writer, author of "A Complete Instruction Book for the Guitar." Lond., 1829.

DUVERNOY (Jean B.) French comp. and pianist, B. 1802. D. Passy, 1880. WORKS—Fantasias, Chansonettes, Divertissements, Rondos, Airs, Valses, Mazurkas, etc., etc., for Pf. Studies for Pf. School for the Pf., etc.

DUVERNOY (Victor Alphonse). French pianist and comp., B. Paris, Aug. 30, 1842. S. Paris Cons. Writer of Pf. music.

DUVOIS (Charles). French org. and comp., B. Strasbourg, 1830. Writer of church music, theoretical works, etc.

DVOŘÁK (Antonin). Bohemian comp., B. Mühlhausen, near Kralup, Sept. 8, 1841. His father, Franz Dvořák, was a butcher, and also kept a small tavern. The dance music played here first attracted the attention of the child, who early displayed his love for music. His first lessons were in violin-playing and singing, from a schoolmaster in the little town. In the first he made such progress as soon to be able to play a solo at a church festival with great success. Later on he studied harmony and organ-playing with one Liehmann, in Zlonitz, and obtained a first insight of the mysteries of instrumentation. By dint of great sacrifice, his father sent him to Prague at the age of 16, and he received instruction from Professors Pitsch and Krejci. From the year 1859, he was thrown on his own resources, and endured many years of extreme poverty, earning a scanty subsistence by playing in the bands that visited *cafés*, etc. In 1871 he obtained the position of member of the orchestra in the

National Theatre which was opened that year. All this time he was studying with the greatest zeal and ardour, and many compositions were finished, but there was no possibility of getting them performed. In Carl Bendl he found a friend and adviser, and in 1873 was produced a hymn, "Die Erben des weissen Berges," for chorus and orchestra, which at once brought his name from obscurity. The idea of obtaining a state-stipend induced him to procure the recommendation of Herbeck and Hanslick, to whom he sent several works. Herbeck's death caused a delay of some years; but Braham taking his place as one of the Commissioners, whose office it was to investigate such cases, at once saw the merit of the compositions. He procured publishers in the firms of Simrock, Berlin, and others, and Dvorák's fame was at once established. This was about 1877, and two or three years later his name was known all over Europe. Visited London in March, 1884, as guest of the Philharmonic Society; and attended the Worcester Festival, Sept., 1884, to conduct his "Stabat Mater," and Symphony in D. He also cond. his cantata, "The Spectre's Bride," at Birmingham, in Aug., 1885.

WORKS.—Vier Lieder, for voice and Pf., op. 3; Vier Lieder (Serbian), do., op. 6; Vier Lieder (Bohemian), do., op. 7; Silhouetten for Pf., op. 8; Romance for vn. and orch., op. 11; Four duets for soprano and tenor, alto and tenor voices, op. 20; Trio for Pf., vn., and 'cello, op. 21; Serenade in E for strings, op. 22; Trio for Pf., vn., and 'cello, in G min., op. 26; Dumka, elegy for Pf., op. 35; Air and Variations for Pf., in A flat, op. 36; Comic Opera, "Der Bauer ein Schelm," op. 37; Four duets for 2 voices, op. 38; Suite for orch., op. 39; Furiante, Bohemian National Dances, op. 42; Serenade in D minor, for wind instruments, op. 44; Slavische Rhapsodien for orch., in D, G, and A flat, op. 45; Slavische Tänze, for Pf., in two books, op. 46; Bagatellen for 2 vns., 'cello, and Pf., op. 47; Sextet for 2 vns., 2 tenors, and 2 'cellos, op. 48; Mazurka, for vn. and orch., in E. min., op. 49; Quartet in E flat, for strings, op. 51; Gipsy Melodies for voice and Pf., op. 55; Sonata for Pf. and vn., op. 57; "Wanda," opera, Prague, 1876; Legends for orch., op. 59; Symphony in D, op. 60; Third Quartet in C, op. 61; Der Dickschädel, comic opera; Dimitrije, opera, Prague, 1882; Mein Heim, overture for orch., op. 62; Stabat Mater, for soli, chorus, and orch., op. 58, 1883; Second trio, in F minor, op. 65; Scherzo Capriccioso, for orch., op. 66; Aus dem Böhmer-Walde, for Pf. duet, op. 68; The Spectre's Bride, cantata, Birmingham Festival, 1885.

"Dvorák is eminently a national composer, and in the mass his utterances are couched in the national dialect. The reasons for this are not obscure. Till Brahms introduced him to Cosmopolitan society in Vienna, he was in art as in blood a Czech. . . . He may think—and, if so, he is not far wrong—that the melodic element in his art needs to recruit itself more and more by going to the source from which even its most cultured forms orginally sprang. But whether he hold this opinion or not, the result of his work must be to strengthen the movement which is now so eagerly drawing thematic material from folk-music, and to enrich the common musical language of all countries with new, diversified, and precious resources."—Joseph Bennett in the *Musical Times*, April, 1881.

DWIGHT (John Sullivan). American writer and musician, B. Boston, May 13, 1813. Educated at Harvard University, and at Cambridge, Mass. Ordained pastor at Northampton (Mass.), 1840. Established "Dwight's Journal of Music," Boston, 1852-1880.

Mr. Dwight during a long life laboured successfully to promote the best interests of music in the United States, and so far as Boston is concerned his efforts have been eminently great in their results. His journal was the only one in America which really aimed at forwarding the cause of music, and which was entirely disassociated from any trade or advertising interests.

DYER (Arthur Edwin). English comp. and org., B. Frome, Feb. 20, 1843. He has written a number of songs, church and organ music, etc. Mus. Bac., Oxon., 1873. Mus. Doc., Oxon., Dec., 1880. He is music-master at Cheltenham College, and an organist of the greatest ability. His cantatas, "Salvator Mundi," 1881, and "Harold," 1882, are good, and have been successfully produced. Another work for chorus and orch., "I wish to tune my quivering Lyre," was performed at the Gloucester Musical Festival, 1883.

DYER (Samuel). American musician, compiled and published "A New Selection of Sacred Music," Baltimore, 1820; "Philadelphia Selection of Sacred Music," 4to, n. d.

DYGON (John). English comp. of 15th century, was prior of the convent of S. Augustine, Canterbury, 1497. D. 1509.

He composed some curious songs, etc.

DYKES (Rev. John Bacchus). English comp. and divine, B. Kingston-upon-Hull, March 10, 1823. S. music under Skelton, org. of St. John's ch., Hull. S. at Cambridge, 1843. B.A., 1847. Curate at Malton, Yorks., 1847. S. under Walmisley. Minor canon and precentor, Durham Cath., 1849. Cond. of Univ. Musical Soc. M.A., Cantab., 1851. Mus. Doc., Durham, 1861. Vicar of St. Oswald, Durham, 1862. D. St. Leonard's, Jan. 22, 1876.

WORKS.—Service in F; The Lord is my Shepherd, 23rd Psalm; These are they which came out of great tribulation, anthem. Part-songs. *Psalms and Hymns:* S. Cross, Melita, Vox Dilecti, Horbury, Hollingside, St. Cuthbert, Dies Iræ, Lux Benigna, Nicæa, and a variety of other psalms.

The hymns of Dykes are among the finest examples of modern times. Melody, harmony, and above all, true religious spirit, are beautifully and agreeably combined in all to form very appropriate, and technically correct, song offerings. They are one and all so well known, that little need be said beyond that their place in our collections will ever be among the foremost. His services and anthems are occasionally used, but their merits, considering the extended field he possessed in these forms for exercising his many powers, are not by any means so high as the genuine beauty of his hymns would warrant.

DYNE (John). English comp. and alto vocalist of 18th century. Was gentleman of Chap. Roy., 1772. Lay-Vicar, Westminster, 1779. Principal at Handel Commemoration, 1784. D. (suicide), Oct. 30, 1788. He composed prize and other glees, songs, etc.

E.

EAGER (John). English comp. and org., B. Norwich, 1782. S. under his father. Resided for a period with Duke of Dorset. Married at Yarmouth, 1800. Adopted Logier's system, and commenced teaching it. Corporation org. at Yarmouth. D. [?]

Eager composed Songs, a Pf. Concerto, and Glees. He had much native talent, and was a good violinist as well as an organist. In his efforts to propagate Logier's system he underwent much annoyance from the county press. ". . . The talents of Eager would have enabled him, if not to rank among first-rate composers, to have followed them at no very humble distance."

EARSDEN (John). English comp. of end of 16th and beginning of 17th centuries. He composed songs, etc., and is mentioned in Hawkins History.

EASTCOTT (Richard). English writer and musician, B. Exeter, 1740. Chaplain of Livery Dale, Devon. D. 1828.

WORKS.—Sketches of the Origin, Progress, and Effects of Musick, with an account of the ancient Bards and Minstrels, illustrated with various Historical Facts, Anecdotes, etc., Bath, 1793, 8vo (2 editions). The Harmony of the Muses (Songs), n. d. Six Sonatas for Pf., etc.

EATON (E. K.) American writer and comp., author of "New Method for the Cornet, in three parts," Boston, n. d.

EASTLAKE (Lady Elizabeth). English writer, authoress of "Music and the Art of Dress," Lond., 1852, 12mo.

EATON (Thomas Damant). English writer and musician, at one time President of the Norwich Choral Society. He wrote Critical Notices of Bexfield's

"Israel Restored," and Pierson's "Jerusalem" (reprinted from the *Norfolk News*), Norwich, 1852. Musical Criticism and Biography from the Published and Unpublished Writings of T. D. Eaton, edited by his Son, London, 8vo, 1872.

EAVESTAFF (William). English writer and pianoforte maker, author of "Instructions for the Pianoforte." Lond., 1830.

EBDON (Thomas). English comp. and org., B. Durham, 1738. Chorister in Durham Cath. Org. of Durham Cath., 1763-1811. D. Durham, Sept. 23, 1811.

WORKS.—Two Sonatas for the Harpsichord, 1780; Collection of Six Glees, op. 3, 1780; Sacred music, composed for the use of the Choir of Durham, fo., 1780, 2 vols. Anthems, songs, etc.

Ebdon is best known by his service in C. He is spoken of as having been an organist of much merit.

EBERL (Anton). Austrian pianist and comp., B. Vienna, Jan., 1766. Teacher in Vienna, and friend of Gluck and Mozart. D. Vienna, March 11, 1807.

WORKS.—*Operas:* Die Königin der Schwarzen, 1801; Les Bohemiens; The Sorcerer. Cantatas, Symphonies, Overtures, String Quartets, Pf. Sonatas, Variations, Concertos, Songs, etc., none of which are now ever heard.

EBERLIN (Daniel). German org. and comp., B. Nuremberg, 1630. D. Cassel, 1691. Comp. org. and church music.

EBERLIN (Johann Ernst). German comp. and org., B. Jettingen, March 27, 1702. Court org. to the Prince Archbishop of Salzburg. D. Salzburg, June 21, 1762.

Eberlin was a famous organist and contrapuntist, and wrote a large amount of church music of an excellent kind; including Offertorium, 1770; Improperia, etc., 1771; Graduale; Hymns and motets; Masses; Misereres; Fugues; Cantatas, and occasional pieces.

EBERS (John). German impresario and theatre manager, B. London, 1785. Managed King's Theatre, 1821-28. Was ruined, and relinquished direction, 1828. He wrote "Seven Years at the King's Theatre," Lond., 8vo, 1828. D. [?].

EBERWEIN (Traugott Maximillian). German comp. and violinist, B. Weimar, Oct. 27, 1775. Member of Court-band, Weimar. Vnst. in service of Prince of Schwarzburg-Rudolstadt, 1797. Chap.-master, do., 1817. D. Rudolstadt, Dec. 2, 1831.

WORKS.—Op. 1. Three string quartets. *Operas:* Pedro et Elvira, 1805; Claudine de Villabella, 1815; Ferdusi, 1821; La Préteuse, 1826. Overture, Macbeth, op. 105, 1828. Symphonies, quartets, and concertos, various. Songs, Pf. music, etc.

The music of Eberwein is now forgotten, save a few of his more important works, published by Breitkopf and Härtel, Leipzig.

EBSWORTH (Joseph). English tenor vocalist and glee writer, lived in Edinburgh, and was librarian to the Edinburgh Harmonists' Society, and a choirmaster. He compiled "General Index to First Hundred Vols. of the Music in Library of Edinburgh Harmonists' Society....." Edin., 4to, 1844.

ECCARD (Johann). German comp. and org., B. Mulhausen, 1545. Chapelmaster at Königsberg, etc. D. [Berlin, 1611].

WORKS.—Geistliche Lieder...Königsberg, 1597, 2 vols.; Preussische Festlieder, with J. Stobäus, Königsberg, 1642-44, 2 vols.; etc.

These works include chansons, sacred and secular; chants, motets, and other church music of a superior kind. His compositions are spoken of in terms of praise by several writers, and a few of them are still in use.

ECCLES (Henry). English violinist and comp., son of Solomon Eccles, B. end of 17th century. He published in Paris "Twelve Excellent Solos for Violin,"

1720. He was a member of the King's band in Paris. D. first part of 18th century.

ECCLES (John). English comp. and violinist, B. 1668. Son of Solomon Eccles. S. under his father. Master of Queen's band, 1698. D. Kingston, Surrey, Jan., 1735.

WORKS.—Acis and Galatea, masque, 1701 ; Ode for S. Cecilia's Day (Congreve), 1701 ; The Judgment of Paris (Congreve), masque, 2nd prize in competition with Weldon, etc. ; The Mad Lover, 1701 ; The City Lady ; The Fair Penitent, 1703 ; The Lancashire Witches, 1682 ; The Spanish Friar, 1681 ; Justice Busy, 1690 ; The Chances, 1682 ; The Way of the World, 1700 ; The Provoked Wife, 1697 ; The Richmond Heiress, 1693 ; Rinaldo and Armida (Dennis), 1699 ; Don Quixote ; Love for Love, 1695. Collection of Songs for one, two, and three voices, etc., Lond. [1701]. Songs in Pills to purge Melancholy, etc.

Eccles was one of the most popular composers of his day, and some of his melodies are very fine, though not now in vogue.

ECCLES (Solomon). English comp. and violinist, B. latter part of the 17th century. Father of Henry and John Eccles. He contributed to the "Division Violin," 1693, and wrote a work entitled "A Musick Lector, or the Art of Musick discoursed of, by way of dialogue between three men of several judgements—a Musician, a Baptist, and a Quaker...." Lond., 8vo, 1667.

He wrote an amount of vocal music occuring in contemporary collections, and was a violinist of some repute.

ECKER (Carl). German comp., B. Friburg, Mar. 13, 1813. D. Friburg, Aug. 31, 1879. Writer of some fine lieder, part-songs, and orch. music.

ECKERT (Carl Anton Florian). German comp., violinist, and pianist, B. Potsdam, Dec. 7, 1820. Pupil of Mendelssohn. S. at expense of King of Prussia, in Italy. Accompanist at Theatre Italien, Paris, 1851. Accomp. to Sontag during her tour in U. S. A., 1851-2. Cond. of Italian opera, Paris, 1852. Director of Court opera, Vienna, 1854 ; Music-director at Stuttgart, 1861-67. Do. at Berlin Opera-house, 1868. D. Berlin, October, 1879.

WORKS.--*Operas:* Catherine di Nuremberg, 1837 ; Le Charlatan, 1840 ; Wilhelm von Oranien, 1846. Judith, oratorio, 1841. Symphony, 1836 ; Overture for orch., 1841. Lieder for voice and Pf., op. 12, 13, and 15. Twelve Charakterstücke for Pf., op. 17 ; Trio for Pf., vn., and 'cello, B. minor, op. 18 ; Six poems for voice and Pf., op. 26 ; Church music, etc.

Eckert is perhaps best known to the English musical public as a song-writer, in which capacity he is one among the foremost in modern Germany. Fine poetical feeling, good harmony, and due respect for the verse, are the principal features of his music. The oratorio of Judith was successful on its production, and is an able work.

EDDY (Hiram Clarence). American org., comp., and cond., B. Greenfield, Mass., June 23, 1851. S. under J. G. Wilson of Greenfield, and under Dudley Buck, at Hartford, Conn., 1867. Org. of Bethany Cong. Ch. (Dr. Lord), Montpelier, Vt., till 1871. S. at Berlin under Haupt and Loeschhorn, 1871. Org. Dr. Goodwin's ch., Chicago. Director of the Hershey School of Musical Art, Chicago, 1876. Cond. of the Philharmonic Vocal Society, Chicago. Married to Sarah Hershey.

WORKS.—Canons, preludes, fugues, variations, etc., for organ : Church music, songs, etc. ; Translation of Haupt's " Theory of Counterpoint and Fugue," etc.

Mr. Eddy holds a foremost place among American organists, by reason of his great technical ability, extensive repertory, and poetical interpretation of classical works. The programmes of his " National Concerts " are marked by an admirable selection of composers, and good variety of works. Thus the " English " programmes contain the names of Ouseley, Wesley, Carter (H.), E. J. Hopkins, Macfarren, Smart, Best, and Archer, the representative works chosen giving a good general idea of the modern school of English organ music. The " American " school is equally well represented by Gleason, E. Thayer, J. K. Paine, D. Buck, S. G. Pratt, Whitney, West, Whiting, and Eddy. The design of these national concerts forms part of a large scheme which some time previous to June 1879 Mr. Eddy projected. He gave a series of 100 organ recitals, each programme containing fresh matter, and without the repetition of a single number. The successful completion of this feat was accomplished in June 23, 1879.

EDELMANN (Johann Friedrich). German comp., B. Strasburg, May 6, 1749. D. Paris, 1802.
Composed Esther, oratorio, 1781 ; Diane et l'Amour, ballet, 1802 ; Ariane dans l'Ile de Naxos, ballet. Concertos, Sonatas, etc., for Pf., several of which have been republished in London.

EDGCUMBE. See MOUNT-EDGCUMBE.

EDMONDS (M). Author of "Musical Catechism adapted to the First Class of Performers on the Pianoforte," Dublin, 8vo, 1807.

EDWARDS (C. A.) English writer of present time. Author of "Organs and Organ Building, a Treatise on the History and Construction of the Organ from its Origin to the Present Day, with Important Specifications," London, 8vo, 1881, illustrated.

EDWARDS (Henry Sutherland). English writer, B. London, Sept. 5, 1828. Author of "The Russians at Home," 1861 (Notes on Music of Russians, etc.) " History of the Opera in Italy, France, Germany, Russia, and England, from Monteverde to Verdi, with Anecdotes of the most celebrated Composers and Vocalists of Europe," London, 2 vols., 8vo, 1862. "The Polish Captivity," 1863. "Private History of a Polish Insurrection," 2 vols., 1865. "Life of Rossini," Lond., 8vo, 1869. "The Germans in France." "Rossini (Great Musicians Series)," Lond., 8vo, 1881. "The Lyric Drama, Essays on Subjects, Composers, and Executants of Modern Opera," Lond., 2 vols., 8vo, 1881. Opera Librettos, Novels, and contributions to periodical literature, etc.
The whole of the foregoing are useful and interesting works, and some of them are valuable.

EDWARDS (Richard). English poet and comp., B. Somersetshire, 1523. Scholar of Corpus Christi Coll., Oxford. S. music under George Etheridge. M.A., Oxon., 1547. Master of Children, Chap. Royal, and Gent., do. Member of Lincoln's Inn. D. Oct. 31, 1566.
WORKS.—The Paradise of Daintie deuises. The Soul's Knell, poem. Damon and Pythias, comedy. Palemon and Arcite, comedy. "In going to my naked bed," madrigal. Many poems, tracts, etc.
Edwards is not known now save by his lovely madrigal, "In going to my naked bed," which is one of the finest examples of this species of composition extant. The titles of his other poems are set out at length in Ritson's and Hazlitt's works on Early English Poetry.

EGAN (Charles). Irish writer and harpist, author of a "Harp Primer, being a familiar introduction to the Study of the Harp," 12mo, 1822.

EGERTON (Hon. John Gray Seymour). Contemporary English amateur composer, has written some good part-songs, "Adieu to the Woods," "King Winter," "Spring's Approach," "Wild Rose"; songs, a cantata, etc.

EGESTORFF (George). German writer, author of "A Lecture on Music, with especial reference to the German Opera as introduced into this Country," Lond., 8vo, 1840.

EGGELING (Eduard). German pianist and comp. of Pf. music, B. July 30, 1813. D. Hartzburg, Brunswick, April 7, 1885.

EGGHARD. See HARDEGEN.

EGLI (Johann Heinrich). Swiss comp., B. Mar. 4, 1742. D. Zurich, 1807. Comp. Cantiques avec des Mélodies Chorales sur des textes de Lavater, 1775 ; Chants Religieux, 1775 ; Chansons Suisses avec Mélodies, 1787 ; Les Odes Sacrées de Gellert, 1789 ; Cantatas, and many psalms, songs, chants, etc.

EHLERT (Ludwig). German writer and comp., B. Königsberg, Jan. 13, 1825. Pianist and comp. in Berlin. D. Wiesbaden, Jan. 4, 1884.

WORKS.—Op. 1. Sonata for Pf. ; op. 2. Caprice for Pf. ; op. 4. Songs for voice and Pf. ; op. 5. Sonata Romantique for Pf. ; op. 6. Songs for voice and Pf. ; op. 7. Allegro Concertante for Pf., vn., and 'cello ; op. 16. 5 Lieder for voice and Pf. Briefe über Musik an eine Freundin, 1859. Translated by Fanny R. Ritter, and republished in Boston and London, as Letters on Music to a Lady, 1877, 8vo. Aus der Tonwelt..., Berlin, 1877, 8vo. Trans. as "From the Tone-World," by H. D. Tretbar, N. Y., 1885. Articles on musicians, various. Symphonies, overtures, etc.

The work by which Ehlert is most likely to be known is his "Letters," a book containing some acute remarks, but much spoiled by a strained and unnatural style.

EHRENBERG (Eleanora, Baroness). Bohemian soprano vocalist, B. Prague, 1832. Has appeared chiefly in Bohemia, in various operas.

EHRLICH (Alfred Heinrich). German musician and novelist, B. Hanover, 1824. Prof. of Pf. at Stern's Cons., Berlin, since 1858. Has composed Pf. music, songs, novels, etc., and a work "Die Musik-Aesthetik," 1882.

EICHBERG (Julius). German comp. and cond., B. Dusseldorf, 1828. S. Brussels Cons. Gained first prizes there for vn. and comp. Music Director of Consistory of Ch. of Geneva. Teacher in Boston, U.S., 1856. Director of Boston Cons., 1867.

WORKS.—*Operas:* Doctor of Alcantara, by B. E. Wolf; The Rose of Tyrol. The Two Cadis, operetta ; A Night in Rome, do. Studies for Violin, Songs, Part Songs, Concerted Violin Music, etc.

Eichberg has a great reputation in America as a clever violinist and conductor, and tuneful composer.

EICHBERG (Oscar). German pianist and comp., B. Berlin, Jan. 21, 1845. S. under Loeschhorn and F. Kiel. Comp. of Pf. Music, Songs, etc.

EICHHORN. German family of stringed-instrument performers, of whom JOHANN PAUL, B. Neuses, Coburg, Feb. 22, 1787, was Court music-director at Coburg. JOHANN GOTTFRIED ERNST (B. Coburg, April 30, 1822 ; D. there, June 16, 1844), a violinist of much promise ; JOHANN CARL EDUARD (B. Oct. 17, 1823), a violinist, and comp. of much music for his instrument ; and ALBERT (1828-1852), a violoncellist of much repute.

They appeared in many towns of Europe with distinguished success.

EISENHOFER (Franz Xaver). German comp., B. Ilmmunster, Nov. 29, 1783. D. Wurzburg, Aug. 15, 1855.

Composer of cantatas for male voices, and Lieder, in both of which he was his own poet. A large number of these songs are marked by much refinement and fine feeling.

EISFELD (Theodor). German comp. and teacher, B. Wolfenbüttel, 1816. Teacher in New York, 1848. D. Wiesbaden, Sept. 4, 1882.

ELFORD (Richard). English alto vocalist, B. about middle of 17th century. Counter-tenor in Lincoln and Durham. Sang on stage in London. Gent. of Chap. Royal, 1702. Lay-Vicar of S. Paul's Cath., and Westminster. D. Oct. 29, 1714.

ELLA (Prof. John). English violinist, critic, and lecturer, B. Thirsk, Yorks., Dec. 19, 1802. S. for the Law. Violinist in King's theatre, 1822 ; Concert of Ancient Music ; Philharmonic Concerts, etc. S. under Attwood and Fétis, 1826-29. Established the "Musical Union," 1845-80. Established "Musical Winter Evenings," 1845-80. Lecturer on Music at London Institution, 1855.

WORKS.—Lectures on Dramatic Music and Musical Education Abroad and at Home, 4to, 1872. Musical Sketches Abroad and at Home, 1861 (3 editions), 1869-78. Records of the Musical Union, 1845-78 (analytical programmes, notes, biographies). Personal Memoir of Meyerbeer, with an analysis of Les Huguenots, Lond., 1868. French Song and Traditional Melody, *Anglice* The Harmonious Blacksmith, Lond., 1865 ; etc.

Mr. Ella is one of the best known musicians in London, and numbered among his acquaintance nearly every prominent musician of recent and current times. The amount of good he effected for music in establishing chamber concerts of the highest class in London, can not be over estimated. The "Musical Union" was for a long time supreme among institutions of a similar cast, and has renown for the many fine works first brought forward at its concerts.

ELLERTON (John Lodge). English comp. and minor poet, B. Chester, Jan. 11, 1807. S. at Oxford. M.A., 1828. S. music at Rome. Gained prizes at Catch Club, 1836, 1838. Resided in Germany and London as teacher and composer. D. London, Jan. 3, 1873.

WORKS.—Paradise Lost, oratorio. *Operas:* Issipile ; Berenice in Armenio ; Annibale in Capua ; Il Sacrifizio di Epito ; Andromacca ; Il Carnovale di Venezia ; Il Marito a Vista ; Lucinda (German) ; Dominica ; The Bridal of Triermain (English). Five symphonies. Four orchestral overtures. Three string quintets. Forty-four quartets for strings. Three trios, strings. Eight trios for various instruments. Thirteen sonatas, do. Sixty-one glees. Eighty-three vocal duets. Bridal of Salerno, a poetical romance, Lond., 8vo, 1845. The Elixir of Youth, a legend in four parts, with other poems and notes, Lond., 8vo, 1864.

Ellerton is one of a group of English composers who have suffered unmerited neglect at the hands of musicians. His music is melodious and scholarly, and quite accessible for concert-giving purposes, so that the reason for his neglect is not quite apparent. The best of Ellerton's works are the music for strings, the glees, and the songs. No recent opportunity of hearing the larger works has occurred, and perhaps this has acted as an obstacle to popularity. Ellerton was a cultivated man and a poet of some fancy.

ELLEVIOU (Pierre Jean B. F.) French actor and tenor vocalist, B. Rennes, June 14, 1769. D. Paris, May 5, 1842. Appeared in numerous French light operas by the leading composers of his time. He was a poet of some little note.

ELLIOTT (James). English comp. and bass vocalist, B. 1783. D. London, 1856. Writer of a large number of glees, some of which obtained prizes. Few of his glees are now extant.

ELLIOTT (James William). English comp. of present time, has compiled several works of great utility for the harmonium, and has composed a number of good songs and glees ; among the former being the well-known bass song to Campbell's words, "Hybrias the Cretan." This is one of the best bass songs of recent production.

ELLIOTT (J.) English writer, author of "Philosophical Observations on the Senses of Vision and Hearing ; and a Treatise on Harmonic Sounds," Lond., 8vo, 1780.

ELLIS (Alexander John). English writer on music, B. Hoxton, June 14, 1814. Educated at Shrewsbury, Eton, and Trinity Coll., Camb. B.A., 1837 ; F.R.S., 1864 ; Mem. of Council, R.S., 1880-81 ; F.S.A., 1870. President of Philological Soc., 1872-74 ; and in 1880-82. Author of The conditions, extent, and realisation of a perfect Musical Scale on instruments with fixed tones. On the temperament of Musical Instruments with fixed tones. On the physical constitution and relations of Musical Chords (Proc. Royal Soc., 1864). On Musical Duodenes, or the theory of constructing instruments with fixed tones in just, or practically just Intonation (Proc. Roy. Soc., 1874). Translation of Helmholtz's "Die Lehre von den Tonempfindungen als Physiologische grundlage fur die Theorie der Musik" (1870 and 1877), under title of "On the Sensations of Tone as a Physiological Basis for the Theory of Music," Lond., 8vo., 1st ed., 1875 ; with Appendix and Notes, re-written, 1885. Pronunciation for Singers, with especial reference to the English, German, Italian, and French Languages, with exercises for Teachers and advanced Students, Lond., 4to, 1877. Basis of Music, 1877. Speech in Song (Music Primer), 8vo, 1878. History of Musical Pitch ; the Musical Scales of various Nations (Jnl. of Soc. of Arts, 1881-85). These two papers were awarded silver medals by the Soc. of Arts. Philological and Mathematical works, etc.

ELOUIS (Joseph). Swiss harpist, comp., and editor, B. Geneva, 1752. D. about 1810-20. Editor of First volume of a Selection of Favorite Scots songs, with accompaniments for the harp or pianoforte, which may be performed on these instruments either with the voice or without it, as familiar lessons; to which are added several airs with variations, Edin., fo., n.d.; Second volume [1807]; Method of tuning the Harp, with Lessons, Preludes, etc.; Fantasias, transcriptions, etc., for Harp and Pf.

ELSNER (Joseph Xaver). German comp., B. Grodgrau, Silesia, June 1, 1769. S. under Förster. Violinist in theatre of Brünn, 1791. Chap.-master at Lemberg, 1792. Cond. at Warsaw, 1815. Director and Prof. of comp. at Warsaw Cons. D. Warsaw, April, 1854.

WORKS.—*Operas:* Uroienie i Rzeczywistosi, 1808; Andromede, 1807; Trybunalniewid-Zialny, 1807; Znapodrodze, 1809; Sierra Morena, 1811; Kabalista, 1813; Krol Lokietek, 1818; Jagiello wietki, 1820. Oratorios, cantatas, and masses. Symphonies in D, C, and B flat. Sonatas, polonaises, quartets, songs, etc.

Famous as a teacher, and for some very good and fluent sacred music.

ELSON (Louis C.). American (German) pianist, poet, comp., etc., B. Boston, Mass., 1848. S. under Kreissmann, Gloggner, etc. Org. of Trinity and Emanuel Churches, Boston. Lecturer in the New England Cons. of Music, Boston. Author of, among other works, "Curiosities of Music : a Collection of Facts not generally known regarding the Music of Ancient and Savage Nations," 8vo, n. d.

ELVEY (Sir George Job, Kt). English comp. and org., B. Canterbury, March 27, 1816. S. under Skeats (of Canterbury), and his brother Stephen. Org. of St. George's Chapel, Windsor, 1838. Mus. Bac., Oxon., 1838; Mus. Doc., Oxon., 1840; Knighted, 1871.

WORKS.—The Resurrection and Ascension, oratorio, 1838; Services in F and B flat. *Anthems:* Arise, shine, for thy light is come; Bow down Thine ear; Christ being raised from the dead; Come, Holy Ghost, our souls inspire; Come unto Me all ye that labour; Daughters of Jerusalem; I beheld, and lo! a great multitude; I was glad when they said; In that day shall this song be sung in the land of Judah; O give thanks unto the Lord; O be joyful; O praise the Lord of Heaven; O ye that love the Lord; Praise the Lord and call upon His name; Rejoice in the Lord; The souls of the righteous; This is the day which the Lord hath made; Unto Thee have I cried; Wherewithal shall a young man. Two Chorales, sung at the funeral of H. R. H. the Prince Consort. Fifteen double chants. Thirty Cathedral Chants. Hymns, Psalms, etc. Organ music. Softly, softly blow ye breezes, glee. Songs, etc.

The massive style of all Elvey's compositions for the church, and the sublimity of a few, give him a place among living and recent composers of sacred music which is second to none. He is best known by his anthems, which are in constant use in British and American churches. His merits as an organist and composer have been recognised in a flattering manner by the action of the Queen in conferring on him the honour of knighthood.

ELVEY (Stephen). English comp. and org., brother of above, B. Canterbury, June, 1805. S. under Skeats. Org. of New College, Oxford, 1830. Mus. Bac., Oxon., 1831. Mus. Doc., Oxon., 1831. D. Oxford, Oct. 6, 1860.

WORKS.—Services and Anthems. The Psalter, or Canticles and Psalms, Pointed for Chanting, upon a New Principle, Lond., 8vo (6 editions to 1866). Hymns, etc.

ELWART (Antoine Elie). Polish comp. and Prof., B. Paris, Nov. 18, 1808. S. under Fétis. Gained second prize for comp., Paris, 1831. Gained grand prix de Rome, 1834. Assistant Prof. at Paris Cons., 1836. D. Paris, Oct. 14, 1877.

WORKS.—*Oratorios:* Noé, ou le Déluge universel, 1845; La Naissance d' Eve, 1846; Les Noces de Cana, mystery. *Operas:* La Reine de Saba; Les Catalans;

Les Chercheurs d'or. Cantatas ; Misereres ; Symphonies ; Overtures ; Quintets. Théorie Musicale Solfége progressif, 8vo, 1830 ; Petit Manuel d'Harmonie, Paris, 8vo, 1839 ; Le Chanteur-accompagnateur, ou traité du clavier, de la basse chiffrée, de l'harmonie simple et composée, Paris, 8vo, 1844 ; Etudes élémentaires de Musique, 1845 ; Traité du Contrepoint et de la Fugue, Paris, n. d. ; Petit Manuel d' Instrumentation, Paris, n. d. ; Histoire de la Société des Concerts du Conservatoire Imperial de Musique....Paris, 8vo, 1860.

Elwart was a laborious and highly gifted worker for musical art. His compositions are almost forgotten, though certain of his theoretical works still enjoy a fair measure of currency.

ELZE (Clément Thomas). German org., pianist, and comp., B. Oranienbaum, 1830. S. Leipzig. Writer of Pf. and org. music, songs, chamber music, instrumental, etc.

EMERSON (Luther Orlando). American comp., writer, and teacher, B. Parsonsfield, Me., August 3, 1820. Teacher in Boston.

WORKS.—The Emerson Method for Reed Organs (with W. S. B. Mathews), Boston, n, d. ; Vocal Method, do. ; Singing School (songs) ; The Encore (songs) ; Onward (tunes) ; Hour of Singing (with W. S. Tilden) ; High School Choir ; Cheerful Voices ; Golden Wreath ; Merry Chimes ; Chorus Book ; The Greeting (part-music), 1867 ; National Chorus Book ; The Song Monarch (with H. R. Palmer) ; Choral Tribute ; Church Offering ; Harp of Judah ; The Jubilate ; The Leader (with H. R. Palmer) ; The Salutation ; The Standard ; The Voice of Worship ; Sacred Quartets ; Book of Anthems ; Glad Tidings ; Golden Harp ; Chants and Responses ; Episcopal Chants ; The Romberg Collection of Sacred Music, Boston, 1853 (with T. M. Dewey, B. Oxford, N. H., 1812).

The whole of the above works are admirably suited for the purpose for which they are primarily designed, viz., to afford a genial and instructive educational course in vocal music for schools.

EMERSON (William). English mathematical writer, author of, among other works, "Cyclomathesis, or an Easy introduction to the several Branches of the Mathematics," Lond., 14 vols., 1763-70. [Vol. 13 contains "Music," etc.]

EMERY (Stephen Albert). American comp., pianist, and writer, B. Paris, Maine, Oct. 4, 1841. Educated at Colby University (then Waterville Coll.), 1859. S. Leipzig Cons. under Papperitz, Plaidy, E. F. Richter, and M. Hauptmann, 1862, and at Dresden under F. Spindler. One of the editors of the *Musical Herald*, Boston. Lecturer and Prof. of Harmony and Comp. in New England Cons. of Music, and Boston University, Coll. of Music, 1881.

WORKS.—Sonatas for Pf. ; Presto Scale Studies, op. 20 ; Foundation Studies in Pianoforte Playing : Elements of Harmony ; String Quartets ; Part-songs, songs, etc. Contributions to periodical literature. "Music, its meaning and mission," paper read at fourth annual meeting of Music Teachers' National Assoc., Buffalo, 1880.

Mr. Emery is one of the most earnest and accomplished musicians of Boston. His compositions are of a high degree of excellence, and some of them are admirably adapted for didactic purposes. His work on the "Elements of Harmony" is in constant use by teachers throughout the United States, and its design is clear and comprehensive. As one of the editors of the *Musical Herald*, his opportunities for advocating the cause of music in its higher aspects are ably employed, and he devotes himself greatly, by lectures and writings, to advance the cause of his adopted art. As regards his Pf. works, songs, etc., it can only be said that they are popular among the higher class of musical Americans. He is the youngest son of the Hon. Stephen Emery, of Paris, Maine, and Jeannette Loring Emery.

EMMERICH (Robert). German comp. of present time. Has composed Der Schwedensee, opera, Weimar, 1874 ; Van Dyck, opera, Stettin, 1875. Six Lieder for voice and Pf., op. 38 ; Nachtlied siehe Liederkreis, op. 39 ; Frau Mette, Ballade von Heine, op. 40 ; Six Songs for voice and Pf., op. 41 ; Six Part-Songs, op. 42 ; Six Songs for voice and Pf., op. 47 ; Do., op. 48 ; Vineta, poem by W. Müller, op. 49 ; etc.

ENCKE (Heinrich). German pianist and comp., B. 1811. Pupil of Hummel. D. Leipzig, 1859. Writer of Pf. music, etc.

ENGEL (Carl). German writer, B. Hanover, 1818. D. (suicide) London, Nov. 17, 1882. Author of Pianist's Handbook, 1853; Reflections on Church Music for the consideration of Church-goers in general, Lond., 8vo, 1856; The Music of the most Ancient Nations, particularly of the Assyrians, Egyptians, and Hebrews, with special reference to recent Discoveries in Western Asia and in Egypt, Lond., 8vo., 1864, illust.; An Introduction to the Study of National Music, comprising Researches into Popular Songs, Traditions, and Customs, Lond., 8vo, 1866; Descriptive Catalogue of the Musical Instruments in South Kensington Museum, Lond., 8vo, 1874, two editions; Musical Instruments (S. Kensington Handbook), Lond., 8vo, 1875; Musical Myths and Facts, Lond., 2 vols., 8vo, 1876; Researches into the Early History of the Violin Family, Lond., 8vo, 1883.

The whole of the above works are extremely valuable to whoever would study national music and its folklore. The fact of their being now very rare is a sufficient testimony to the favour with which they were received by the musical profession. Herr Engel had a good library, which was disposed of by auction in July, 1881.

ENGEL (David Hermann). German comp. and org., B. Jan. 22, 1816. D. Merseburg, May 3, 1877. Writer of Pf. and org. music, songs, etc.

ENGEL (Gustav). German comp. and teacher, B. Königsberg, Oct. 29, 1823. Writer on philosophy and music, composer of songs, and teacher of singing.

ENGEL (Louis). German harmonium-player and comp., now resident in London. Writer of music for his instrument, songs, Pf. pieces, etc. Engel was one of the first to display the capacities of the harmonium for the artistic rendering of classical music.

ENGELSBERG. See SCHON (E. VON).

ENGELHARDT (Feodor). German org., pianist, and comp., B. 1850. S. Berlin. D. Arnstadt, June 10, 1876. Comp. org. and Pf. music.

ENOCH & SONS. English firm of music-publishers, established in London, October, 1869. Their publications (copyright) embrace works for the pianoforte by Abt, Benedict, Dick, Fesca, Gibsone, Hensell, Krug, Kuhe, Litolff, Oberthür, Rubinstein, Schulhoff, Spindler, M. Watson, Wollenhaupt, etc. Their vocal catalogue includes, among many other items, works by Cellier, Clay, Dick, Fox, Gabriel, Gatty, Lecocq, Pinsuti, Sainton-Dolby, Westbrook, etc.

EPINE (Francesca Margherita de L'). Italian vocalist of end of seventeenth and beginning of eighteenth century. Début in London, 1704. Married to Dr. Pepusch, 1718. D. (?)

EPSTEIN (Julius). Hungarian pianist, teacher, and comp. B. Agram, Aug. 14, 1832. Is a fashionable teacher and concert-giver in Vienna. His works are principally for the pianoforte, on which instrument he is regarded in Vienna as one of the foremost performers.

ERARD (Pierre). French writer and member of firm of Erard & Erard. Author of "The Harp in its present improved state," Lond., fo., 1821. D. near Paris, 1855.

ERARD (Sebastien). French pianoforte-maker, B. Strassburg, April, 1752. Commenced to construct pianos, 1777. Took out various patents for improvements from 1809. D. Paris, Oct. 1831. This firm, located in Paris, is one of the most important of its kind, and was carried on after Sebastien's death by the nephew Pierre. Their pianos, while of great good quality, hold an inferior position in popular estimation to their grand harps, which are, beyond all question, the finest instruments made.

ERBEN (Henry). American organ-builder, B. New York, Jan. 1, 1801. Established in New York, 1835. Has built many of the best church organs throughout the United States. He died, 1884.

ERK (Ludwig Christian). German comp. and collector, B. Wetzlar, Jan. 6, 1807. D. Berlin, Nov. 25, 1883.
He composed a number of lieder and collected a great amount of German national melodies. Among his best known works are "Methodischer Leitfaden für den Gesang unterricht in Volkschulen," 8vo, 1834; "Singvogelein," 4 pts., 1842-48; "Die Deutschen Volkslieder," 6 pts., 1838-41.

ERKEL (Franz). Hungarian comp., B. 1810. Composed operas, Pf. music, chamber music, etc.

ERLANGER (Julius). German comp., B. Vissembourg, June 25, 1830. S. at Paris Cons.
WORKS.—*Operas:* Mesdames de Cœur Volant, 1859; Les Musiciens de l'orchestre (with Délibes), 1861; Le Servante a Nicolas, 1861; L'Arbre de Robinson, 1867, and other operas. Pf. music and songs.

ERNST (Heinrich Wilhelm). Austrian violinist and comp., B. Brünn, Moravia, 1814. S. under Böhm, Seyfried and Mayseder. Travelled in Germany and France as violinist, 1832-38, and 1838-44. Appeared in London at Philharmonic Soc. Concert, 1844. D. Nice, Oct. 8, 1865.
WORKS.—Fantasias for violin and orch. Concertos for violin and orch., op. 23, etc. Transcriptions, numerous, for violin and Pf. or orch. Polonaises, variations, nocturnes, Elegie, rondos, etc.
Ernst was a great performer and a good composer. His school of violin playing was noble and refined, and his compositions partake, to a certain extent, of the same general characteristics.

ESCHMANN (Julius Carl). German comp. and pianist, B. Winterthur, April, 1825. S. at Cassel. Writer of miscellaneous chamber and Pf. music. D. Zurich, Oct. 25, 1882.
His music is good and fluent in style.

ESCOBEDO (Bartolemo). Spanish comp., B. 1510. Chorister in Pontificial Chap., Rome, 1536. D. [?]
Composed psalms, motets, and other sacred music.

ESCUDIER (Léon). French journalist and writer, B. Castelnaudary (Aude), Sept. 17, 1821. D. Paris, June 22, 1881. Educated at Toulouse. Wrote in conjunction with his brother Marie, a number of valuable works on music. He edited the paper named "L'Art Musical."

ESCUDIER (Marie). French writer, brother of above, B. Castelnaudary, June 29, 1819. D. Paris, 1880. Author of (with Leon) Dictionnaire de Musique d'apres les theóriciens, historiens et critiques les plus célebres, Paris, 2 vols., 1844. A Life of Rossini, 1854. Dictionnaire de Musique theorique et historique, 1854. Contributions to periodical literature, etc.

ESLAVA (Miguel Hilarion). Spanish comp. and editor, B. near Pampeluna, Oct. 21, 1807. Musician in Pampeluna Cath., 1824. Chap.-master at Ossuna, 1828. Chap.-master in Seville, 1832. Ordained priest. Chap.-master to Queen Isabella, 1844. D. Madrid, July 23, 1878.
WORKS.—*Operas:* Il Solitario, 1841; La Tregua di Ptolemaide, 1842; Pietro el Crudele; Lira Sacro-Hispana; Gran Coleccion de obras de Musica Religiosa, compuesta por los mas acreditados maestros Españoles tanto antiguos como modernos...Madrid, 10 vols., fo. [1869]. Metodo de Solfeo, 1846. Museo Organico Español (Coll. of Spanish org. music). Masses, psalms, motets, hymns, etc.
Eslava was one of the greatest among modern Spanish composers, while his sacred music is superior in many respects to most Italian composers of recent times. His "Lira Sacro-Hispana" is a valuable collection of Spanish sacred music.

ESPENT (Pierre). French org. and comp., B. Marseilles, Aug. 28, 1832. S. at Paris Cons. Writer of Overtures, Masses, Cantatas, Org. Music, etc.

ESPIN Y GUILLEN (Joaquin). Spanish org. and comp., B. Velilla, Siguenza, May 4, 1812. Prof. at Madrid, and composer of operas, etc. D. Madrid, June 24, 1882.

ESSER (Heinrich). German comp., B. Mannheim, July 15, 1818. Violinist at Mannheim, 1838. Director of Court theatre, Mannheim. Director of Imperial Opera, Vienna, 1847. D. Salzburg, June 3, 1872.

WORKS.—*Operas:* Silas, 1839; Riquiqui, 1843; Two Princes, 1844. Psalm 23rd, for four voices. Symphony in E flat, 1844. Trio for Pf., vn., and 'cello, op. 6. Lieder, etc.

The songs of Esser, such as "Mein Engel" and "Abschied," are of the highest type of beauty. His larger works do not possess the same attractions.

ESSEX (Timothy). English comp. and org., B. Coventry, 1780. Mus. Bac., Oxon., 1806. Mus. Doc., Oxon., 1812. D. [?]

Composed "Sonnets" of various kinds, by various authors, and wrote Rondos, Six duets for 2 flutes, and miscellaneous Pf. music.

ESSIPOFF (Annette). Russian pianist, B. 1850. S. under Léschétitsky. Appeared in Paris, 1875; London, same year. Went to America, 1876. Has since appeared in London, and various large continental cities.

Her style is brilliant and polished, and her technical abilities are of a wonderful nature. She is generally regarded as one of the foremost Continental performers. Her appearance in London was attended with much success. She is married to Theodor Léschétitsky.

ESTCOURT (Mary Jane). English writer. Compiler of "Music the Voice of Harmony in Creation," Lond., 8vo, 1857 [Extracts from various authors on Music].

ESTE (John d'). See D'ESTE (JOHN).

ESTE (Michael). English comp., son of Thomas Este (?) B. in latter part of 16th century. Mus. Bac. Master of Choristers of Lichfield Cath. D. about middle of 17th century.

WORKS.—First set of Madrigals, Lond., 4to, 1604; Second set, Lond., 4to, 1606; Third set of Bookes, wherein are Pastorals, Anthems, Neapolitanes, Fancies, and Madrigals, to 5 and 6 parts, Lond., 4to, 1610; Set of Madrigals, Anthems, etc., 1618; Anthems, 1624; Duos and Fancies for Viols, 1638; Hence, Stars, you dazzle, 5 part Madrigal in the "Triumphs of Oriana," etc.

The name of this composer is variously spelt Est, East, and Easte. He is only supposed to be the son of Thomas Este.

ESTE (Thomas). English publisher and musician during latter half of 16th and beginning of the 17th centuries. D. [1624-5.]

He published all of the more important works of his time, including among others "The whole Booke of Psalmes; with their wonted tunes as they are sung in Churches, composed in foure parts, by Thomas Est," Lond., 12mo, 1592; Byrd's Psalms; The Triumphs of Oriana; and music by Campion, Dowland, Gibbons (Orlando), Weelkes, Kirbye, Wilbye, Mundy, etc.

ESTWICK (Rev. Sampson). English musician and divine, B. 1657. One of children of Chap. Royal. S. at Oxford. Chaplain of Christ Church. Minor Canon of St. Paul's Cath., 1692. Vicar of St. Helen's, Bishopgate, 1701. Do. of St. Michael's, Queenhithe, 1712. D. Feb., 1739.

WORKS.—The Usefulness of Church Music; a Sermon preached at Christ Church, Nov. 27, 1696, Lond., 4to, 1696. Odes, Sermons, etc.

ESZTERHÁZY. An Austrian royal family, which, during the latter half of the 18th century, maintained an orchestra and private opera, in Vienna and in Hungary. Of the former Haydn was for thirty years conductor.

ETHERIDGE (George). English comp. of 16th century, B. Thame, Oxfordshire. Wrote Anthems, Madrigals, and Songs.

ETTLING (Emile). French violinist and comp., B. 1820. Writer of Pf. and violin music, and a number of operettas, as "Un jour de noce," 1864; "Le Tigre," 1873; "En Maraude," 1877.

EUING (William). Scottish collector, B. Partick, near Glasgow, May 20, 1788. Educated at Glasgow Grammar School. Was an underwriter and insurance broker. D. Glasgow, May 12, 1874. He founded, in connection with Anderson's College, Glasgow, a music lectureship, by deed dated 1866, and the lectures have been delivered since 1869. He left also his valuable musical library to the same institution, together with £1000 for its maintenance; but it is at the present time practically inaccessible to students and the public alike, by reason of some neglect in the administration of the provisions of the bequest. The library is one of the most valuable in Britain, and contains many rare and costly books and old music. The theoretical and historical department is also very rich in ancient and modern literature, and contains part of the library of the late Dr. Rimbault. There is also a unique collection of psalmodies, etc. A catalogue was printed in 1876, but is not satisfactorily arranged. A notice of this Library appears in "The Public and Private Libraries of Glasgow." By Thos. Mason, 1885.

EULENSTEIN (Carl). German performer on the Jew's-harp, B. Heilbronn, 1802. His life appears as "A Sketch of the Life of the Celebrated Performer on the Jew's Harp," Lond., 8vo, 1833; 2nd edit., 12mo, 1840. He wrote arrangements for the guitar, etc.

EULER (Leonhard). Swiss mathematician, B. Basle, 1707. D. 1783. Is distinguished for his researches in the phenomena of sound, and for being the first to reduce the said phenomena to scientific principles.

EVANS (Charles Smart). English comp., B. London, 1778. Chorister in Chap. Royal. S. under Ayrton. Gentleman of the Chap. Royal, 1808. Gained prizes for glees in 1817, 1818, and 1821. D. London, Jan. 4, 1849.

WORKS.—Six Glees (Clementi), [1812]. Collection of Glees, etc., Lond., 1825. Music to Linley's "Ode to the Memory of Samuel Webbe," 1817 (prize from Catch Club). Anthems, motets, etc.

EVANS (Robert Harding). English writer, author of "An Essay on the Music of the Hebrews, intended as a Preliminary Discourse to the Hebrew Melodies of Braham and Nathan," Lond., 8vo, 1816.

EVERAERTS (Pierre Francois). Belgian comp., B. Louvain, 1816. Prof. at Liège. Writer of L'Avalanche, opera; Hommage à Grétry, overture; Ave Maria; Motets, concertos, military music, songs, etc.

EVEREST (C.). American musician and teacher, author of "Vocal Instructor," Boston, n. d.; School Song Books; "The Music Teacher"; "The Singing Teacher," 2 parts; and other elementary works.

EVERET (J.). English musician, compiled "The Divine Concert, being the Newest and Choicest Book of Church Music," etc., Waltham, 4to, 1757.

EVERS (Carl). German pianist and comp., B. Hamburg, April, 8, 1819. D. Vienna, Dec. 31, 1875.

His works, numbering over 100, consist almost entirely of pieces for the Pf., most of them of much brilliancy, but few of them vulgar or tasteless in style.

EWER & CO. See NOVELLO, EWER, & CO.

EWING (Alexander). Scottish amateur comp., nephew of Bishop Ewing, B. Aberdeen, Jan. 3, 1830. S. at Marischal Coll. Paymaster in the Army. Known as the composer of the hymn "Ewing" (1853), generally sung to the words "Jerusalem the Golden," etc. Frequently, and erroneously attributed to his uncle, the late Bishop Ewing.

EXIMENO (Antonio). Spanish writer and musician, B. Balbastro, Arragon, 1732. S. at Salamanca. D. Rome, 1798. He was a Jesuit. Author of "Dell' origine della Musica, colla storia del suo progresso, decadenza, e rinovazione," Rome, 4to, 1774. Spanish trans. by Gutierez, Madrid, 3 vols., 8vo, 1796. This work occasioned some controversy.

EYBLER (Josef, Edeler von). Austrian comp., B. Schwechat, near Vienna, Feb. 8, 1765. S. under Albrechtsberger and Haydn. Music-master to the Imperial children, Vienna. Vice-chapel-master, Imperial chapel, Vienna, 1804. Principal do., 1824. Ennobled by the Emperor, 1834. D. Vienna, July 24, 1846.

WORKS.—Masses; Hymns; Oratorio; Opera; Thirty-four Graduels for chorus, org., and orch.; Cantatas; Two Symphonies; Chamber and Pf. music, songs, etc. Eybler ventured to finish Mozart's Requiem, but failed to accomplish his purpose. His works are hardly known in England.

EYKEN (Johann Albert van). Dutch org. and comp., B. Amersfoort, April 29, 1823. S. at Leipzig Cons., 1845-6. Org. at Amsterdam. D. Elberfeld, 1868.

WORKS.—Sonatas, transcriptions, fugues, voluntaries, etc., for the organ; church music and other works. The organ music of Eyken is famous, and well appreciated among organists of all countries.

EYKEN (Gerard Isaac van). Dutch org. and comp., brother of preceding, B. Amersfoort, May 5, 1832. S. at Leipzig Cons., and under his brother, and Schneider. Prof. at Utrecht. Comp. songs, sonatas, Pf. music, etc.

EYRE (Alfred James). English org. and comp., B. Lambeth, London, Oct. 24, 1853. S. at R. A. M., under [Sir] G. A. Macfarren, F. Westlake, M. Smith, and organ under Hoyte and Cooper. Org. St. Peter's, Vauxhall, 1867-72; St. Ethelburga's, Bishopsgate, 1872-74; St. Peter's, Vauxhall (again), 1874-1881; St. John Evangelist, Upper Norwood, 1881. Married to Miss Margaret Bucknell, the pianist. Org. of Crystal Palace, May, 1880. Mem. R. A. M.

WORKS.—Communion Service in E flat; Evening Services for Salisbury Diocesan Choral Assoc.; Full Morning and Evening Service in E flat (MS.); The 126th Psalm, for 4 voices (MS.); Scena for soprano solo and orch. (M.S.); String quartet (MS.); Pf. Trio (MS.); Pf. pieces, various; Songs, part-songs, etc.

F.

FABER (Heinrich). German writer of sixteenth century, B. Lichtenfels, Voigtland. Author of "Ad Musicam praticam introductio, non modo præcepta, sed exampla quoque ad usum puerorum accommodata, quam brevissime continens," Nuremberg, 4to, 1550, various editions.

FABER (Heinrich). German writer and musician, was Rector at Brunswick. D. Quedlinburg, Aug. 27, 1598. Wrote "Compendiolum Musicæ pro incipientibus," Brunswick, 1548. There are numerous other editions.

FABRI (Annebale Pio). Italian tenor vocalist, B. Bologna, 1697. D. Lisbon, 1760. Was also a composer of some fame in his day.

FACCIO (Franco). Italian comp., B. Verona, Mar. 8, 1841. S. Milan Cons. Writer of operas, songs, etc. Famous as a cond. He comp. a cantata for the inauguration of Turin Exhibition, 1884.

FAGE (De la). See LAFAGE.

FAHRBACH (Josef). Austrian flute-player and comp., B. Vienna, Aug. 25, 1804. Writer of flute music, Pf. music, etc. D. Vienna, June 7, 1883.

FAHRBACH (Philip). Austrian comp., brother of above, B. Vienna, 1843. Composer of dance music. D. Vienna, March 31, 1885.

FAIRBAIRN (James). Scotch writer, author of "Elements of Music: Part I., Melody, containing an explanation of the Simpler Principles of the Science. Part II., Harmony, with Appendix on the nature and causes of sound and the consonance and dissonance of intervals, as arising from one system of vibration," Edin., 8vo, 1832.

FAIRFAX (Robert). English comp., B. Bayford, Herts, in latter part of fifteenth century. Mus. Doc., Cantab., 1504. Do., Oxford, 1511. Org. or chanter of Abbey Church of St. Albans. D. St. Albans.

He composed sacred and secular music, but is chiefly known as the composer of a volume of songs in two, three, and four parts, now preserved in MS. in the British Museum. Other compositions of the same master are in the Music School of Oxford.

FAISST (Immanuel). German org., theorist, and comp., B. Esslingen, Oct. 13, 1823. Founded a school for organists at Stuttgart in 1847, and established a conservatory of music in 1857. He became director of the latter in 1859. He has composed much music for the organ, and is author of a number of useful theoretical works. As an organist and educator he was once well known in Germany.

FALKNER (Rodolphe). English professor of music, lived in London in latter part of eighteenth century. He wrote some books on musical subjects, among them "Instructions for playing the Harpsichord," 1762, second edition, 1774.

FALLOUARD (Pierre Jean Michel). French org. and comp., B. Honfleur, July 11, 1805. D. April 6, 1865. Comp. of Pf. and org. music, theoretical writings, etc.

FANING (Eaton). English comp., B. Helston, Cornwall, May 20, 1851. Mendelssohn scholar at R.A.M. Has written a number of good part-songs, "The Song of the Vikings," and several compositions for the Pf., as well as an operetta, "Mock Turtles," 1881. His songs are good, and his works generally show much promise.

FANNA (Antonio). Italian comp. and pianist, B. Venice, 1793. D. Venice, Mar. 15, 1845. Comp. Pf. music of a brilliant character.

FANNING (Charles). Irish harp-player and collector, B. about 1736. Assisted Bunting with his collections. D. [?]

FARINELLI (Carlo), BROSCHI. Italian vocalist, B. Naples, Jan. 24, 1705. S. under Porpora. *Début* at Rome, 1722. Sang successively in Venice, Vienna, Naples, Milan, Bologna, Parma, Lucca, Turin, Ferrara, etc. Appeared in London, in "Artaserse" of Hasse, 1734. Went to Spain, and became a great favourite at Court, 1736. Returned to Italy, by order of Charles III. of Spain, 1759. D. Bologna, July 15, 1782.

Farinelli was a male soprano, and was regarded by his contemporaries as having the most beautiful voice of his time. In disposition he is credited with many evil traits, chiefly those of arrogance and conceit; the great political power which he held in Spain having demoralised him in some respects. Many anecdotes are given regarding him, and will be found in any book of musical gossip.

FARMER (Henry). English violinist and comp., son of John Farmer, P. Nottingham, May, 1819.

WORKS.—Mass in B flat. Communion Service in B flat. New Violin School, wherein the art of bowing and fingering is explained in a series of exercises and scales, progressively arranged, to which is added a selection of favourite airs, Lond., n. d. New Violin Tutor, Lond., 8vo, n. d. The Amateur Violinist (selections). Operatic Gems and Fantasias. Standard Overtures for Violin (selected). The Violinist's Album. Concertino for vn. and Pf. Forty studies for the violin. Twelve duets for 2 vns. Songs, Part-songs, Pf. Music, etc.

His violin tutors are among the best schools for the violin ever published in England. With Loder's work they have been most popular. His transcriptions, songs, and original music for the violin are good.

FARMER (John). English comp., B. Lancashire, 1789. D. Oct., 1867. Wrote Songs, Pf. music, anthems, etc.

FARMER (John). English org. and comp., son of the above, B. 1824. D. Manchester, July, 1857. Composed anthems, part-songs, songs, org. music, etc.

FARMER (John). English comp. and teacher of present time. Formerly music master in Zürich. Music master at Harrow School, 1862-85. Org. of Balliol Coll., Oxford, 1885. Comp. of "Christ and his Soldiers," oratorio ; Harrow School Glee Book, 2 vols., 1866-72; Harrow School Songs; Harrow Marches : Nursery Rhymes Quadrilles, for orch. and 8 voices ; Cinderella, a Fairy Opera, by H. S. Leigh, 1883 ; Requiem in Memory of Departed Harrow Friends ; Partsongs, songs.

FARMER (John). English comp. of 16th century, harmonized Este's Psalms, and composed "First Set of English Madrigals to foure Voyces," 1599; "Fair Nymphs," six-part Madrigal in "Triumphs of Oriana ;" "Divers and Saundrie waies of two parts in one, to the number of fortie upon one playn-song," etc., Lond., 1591. His biography is unknown.

FARMER (Thomas). English comp. of 17th century, was one of the waits of London, and Mus. Bac., Cantab., 1684.

WORKS.—A Consort of Musick in four parts, containing thirty-three Lessons, beginning with an overture, 1686. A Second Consort of Musick in four parts, containing eleven Lessons, beginning with a ground, 1690. Songs in various collections of his time.

FARNABY (Giles). English comp., B. Truro, Cornwall, middle of 16th century [1560]. Mus. Bac. Oxon., July, 1592. D. [?]

WORKS.—Canzonets to foure Voyces, with a Song of eight parts, Lond., 4to, 1598. Madrigals. Psalms in Ravenscroft's collection, etc.

FARNIE (Henry Brougham). Scottish musician and librettist, a native of Fife ; and was for some time editor of the *Fifeshire Journal*. Has compiled and written the librettos of a number of operettas, pantomimes, songs, etc. ; and translated most of the more successful modern French comic operas. His talents as an adapter are of the highest order. Among his recent productions may be named " Rip van Winkle," by Planquette.

FARQUHARSON (James). Scottish musician and teacher in Edinburgh. Published a "Selection of Sacred Music suitable for Public and Private Devotion," Edinburgh, 12mo, 1824.

FARRANT (Daniel). English comp. of the 16th and 17th centuries ; set lessons for the viol in what was known as lyra-way, in imitation of the lute.

FARRANT (John). English comp. of the 16th century, was organist of Salisbury Cath. about 1600. Biography unknown.

Another John Farrant, or not unlikely the same, was org. of Christ's Hospital, London, about the same time.

FARRANT (Richard). English comp. B. [1530]. Gentlemen of the Chap. Roy., 15?—1564. Master of Choristers, St. George's Chap., Windsor, 1564-69. Again Gent. Chap. Roy., 1569-80. Org. and Lay Vicar, St. George's Chap. D. Windsor, Nov. 30, 1580.

WORKS.—Services in G minor, D minor, and A minor. *Anthems*: Call to Remembrance ; Hide not Thou Thy face ; Lord for Thy tender mercies sake ; O Lord, Almighty, etc.

The work by which Farrant is best known is "Lord for Thy tender mercies sake," an anthem which is of disputed authorship, some attributing it to John Hilton. As the popular judgment has always decided in favour of Farrant, it may safely be accorded him. It is one of the most grand and sonorous, yet simple anthems ever written.

FARRAR (Dr. J.). English writer and Physician, author of "The Human Voice and Connected Parts. A practical book for orators, clergymen, vocalists, and others." Lond., 8vo, 1881.

FARREN (George). English writer, author of "The Mortalities of Celebrated Musicians," London, 8vo, 1834.

FARRENC (Jacques Hippolyte Aristide). French flute-player and comp., B. Marseilles, April 9, 1794. D. Paris, Jan. 31, 1865. Writer, and comp. of flute music. A catalogue of his musical library was issued in 1866.

FARRENC (Jeanne Louise). French pianist and comp., wife of above, B. Paris, May 31, 1804. D. Paris, Sept. 15, 1875. Comp. music for Pf., songs, etc.

FARRENC (Victorine Louise). French pianist and comp., daughter of above, B. Paris, Feb. 23, 1826. D. Paris, Jan. 3, 1859. S. Paris Cons., and wrote music for Pf., etc.

FASANOTTI (Filippo). Italian pianist and comp., B. Milan, Feb. 19, 1821. Comp. of Pf. music, and writer of a Pf. school.

FASCH (Carl Friedrich Christian). German comp. and teacher, B. Zerbst, Nov. 18, 1736. D. Berlin, Aug. 1800. Is now known only as the founder of the famous Singakademie in Germany. He composed a large amount of choral and other music, adapted for the purposes of vocal training and practice.

FASTRÉ (Joseph). Dutch comp., B. Flessingue, June 22, 1783. D. April 3, 1842. Comp. of songs, Pf. and choral music, etc.

FAUCONIER (Benoît Constant). French pianist, org., and comp., B. Fontaine-l'Evêque, April 28, 1816. S. Brussels Cons. Appeared as pianist in various large towns. D. Thuin, Feb. 16, 1877.

WORKS.—Operas, several. Guide de l'organiste des petites villes et des campagnes. Masses, opp. 88, 89, 90, 91, 117. Pf. music of all kinds ; Hymns, songs, etc., and a number of miscellaneous productions, numbering over 200 in all.

FAULKNER (Thomas). English writer, author of "Organ Builders' Assistant," Lond., 1826 ; "Designs for Organs," Lond., 1838, etc.

FAURE (David). French barytone vocalist, B. Limoges, 1833. S. at Paris Cons. Solo singer at the Opera Comique, in London, and the Grand Opera, Paris. Prof. of Singing at Brussels Cons.

FAURE (Jean Baptiste). French barytone vocalist and comp., B. Moulins, Jan. 15, 1830. S. Paris Cons., 1843. Chorister in Ch. of St. Nicolas de Champs, Paris. *Début* at Opera Comique, Paris, Oct. 20, 1850. Prof. of Singing, Paris Cons., 1857. Has appeared in London and Italy.

WORKS.—Twenty-five melodies for voice and Pf. ; Twenty do. Titles of some songs contained in foregoing collections : L'Aieule ; Aubade ; Ave Maria ; Bonjour Suzon ; Chanson de Bord ; Charité ; Discrétion ; La Fête-Dieu au Village ; Fleurs du Matin ; Le joli Rêve ; Marche vers l'Avenir ; O Salutaris ; Le Rameaux ; Sancta Maria ; Soupirs ; Trois Soldats ; Le Vieux Guillaume, etc. Church and instrumental music, etc.

Faure is one of the leading Continental artists, and has appeared in operas by many different masters, including Auber, Rossini, Verdi, Massé, Thomas, and Meyerbeer. He has sung in America and Russia, as well as in the places named above, and has everywhere met with success. Many of his vocal compositions are very beautiful, and all of them are highly creditable to his powers as a composer. He is a man of wide general culture.

FAUST (Carl). German comp. and bandmaster, B. Neisse, Silesia, Feb. 18, 1825. Bandmaster of the 36th regiment of infantry, 1853-9. Do. 81st regiment, 1859-63. Chap.-master at Holstein, 1863-69. Do. at Waldenburg, 1869-80.

He writes an immense quantity of dance music, including waltzes, polkos, galops, mazurkas, etc. They are all graced by some catching or hyper-poetical title, and their merits are those common to most German composers of dance music, including spirit, good harmony, and grace.

FAUSTINA. See HASSE (Faustina B.).

FAVARGER (René). French pianist and comp., B. 1815. D. Etretat, near Havre, Aug. 3, 1868.

WORKS.—Op. 1. Bolero, for Pf. ; op. 2. Reverie, for Pf. ; op. 4. Fantasia on "Oberon" (Weber) ; op. 7. Ondine, Bluette ; op. 18. L'Adieu, nocturne ; op. 21. Serenade ; and a great number of similar productions, all of a bright, graceful nature.

FAVART (Charles Simon). French dramatist, B. Paris, Nov. 13, 1710. Married Mdlle. Duronceray, 1745. D. May 12, 1793. Wrote operas, comedies, etc., all of which are distinguished by lightness and good points.

FAVART (Maria Justine Benoîte), née DURONCERAY. French vocalist and actress, B. Avignon, June 15, 1727. D. April 20, 1772. She sang in her husband's operas, and was a very successful actress. One of Offenbach's last operas makes an episode in her career its leading motive.

FAWCETT (John). English comp., B. Kendal [Bolton-le-moors, Lancashire], 1789. Was a shoemaker for a time, but latterly a composer. D. Bolton-le-moors, Oct. 26, 1867.

WORKS.—The Voice of Harmony, psalms ; New Set of Sacred Music in Three Parts...by John Fawcett of Kendal ; Two other similar colls. ; The Harp of Zion ; Miriam's Timbrell, a New Set of Psalm and Hymn Tunes...Lond., 8vo, n.d. ; The Universal Chorister, 2 vols. ; Melodia Divina, or Sacred Companion for the Pf. (with Jos. Hart), fo., n. d. ; The Seraph's Lyre, 2 parts ; Paradise, oratorio. Voice of Devotion (selection), Glasgow, 1862. ; etc.

FAWCETT (John). English comp. and org., son of above, B. Bolton, 1824. S. under his father. Org. of St. John's Ch., Farnworth, 1835. Org. of Parish Ch., Bolton, 1842. S., R. A. M., Lond., under Bennett, from 1845. Org. of Curzon Chap., Lond., 1845-46. Mus. Bac., Oxon., 1852. D. Manchester, July 1, 1857.

He wrote a cantata, "Supplication and Thanksgiving," as a degree exercise; anthems, glees, songs, etc.

FAY (Amy). American pianist and teacher, B. Bayon Goula, Louisiana, 1844. S. piano abroad for six years, under Tausig, Liszt, Kullak, and Deppe. Her charmingly written book on "Music Study in Germany," Chicago, 12mo, 1881, has been largely read in America, and has done much to influence American students in their preparation for study abroad. It has been translated into German, and republished in London. Miss Fay is a teacher in Chicago, Ill., where she has given recitals. She was a charter member of the "American College of Musicians."

FAY (Etienne). French operatic comp., B. Tours, 1770. D. Versailles, Dec. 6, 1845. Comp. "Flora," 1791 ; "Les Rendezvous Espagnols," 1793 ; Clémentine," 1793 ; "La bonne aventure," 1802 ; and other operatic works.

FAYOLLE (Francois Joseph M.). French writer, B. Paris, Aug. 1774. D. there, Dec., 1852. Known by his biographical articles in connection with the "Biographie Universelle," and his joint authorship of Choron's "Dictionary of Musicians." Wrote also "Paganini et Bériot," Paris, 8vo, 1830 ; "Notices sur Corelli, Tartini, Gaviniés, Pugnani et Viotti..." Paris, 8vo, 1810. His other writings are forgotten.

FEATHERSTONE (Isabella). See PAUL (Mrs. HOWARD).

FELTON (Rev. William). English org. and comp., B. 1713. Was vicar-choral at Hereford. D. Dec., 6, 1769. He wrote concertos for organ and harpsichord ; and Two Sets of 8 Lessons for the Harpsichord, opp. 3 and 6. He was esteemed in his day a remarkable performer.

FENDT (Bernard). German violin maker, B. Innsprück, 1756. Worked in London, with J. F. Lott for T. Dodd. Worked latterly with Betts. D. London, 1832.

He turned out some very fine instruments, and founded the Fendt family of violin makers.

FENDT (Bernard Simon). German violin maker, son of the above. B. London, 1800. D. 1851.

Made a great number of copies of much accuracy in imitation of details. His original instruments are good. Other members of this family are FRANCIS, fourth son of Bernard ; JACOB, third son of Bernard, B. London, 1815. D. 1849. Like B. S. Fendt, this member of the family was a good copyist ; MARTIN, second son of Bernard, B. London, 1812; and WILLIAM, son of B. S. Fendt, B. London, 1833. D. 1852.

FENTON (Lavinia), *née* BESTWICK. English soprano vocalist, B. [?] *Début* in London, 1726. Original Polly Peachem in "The Beggar's Opera," Jan. 29, 1728. Retired from the stage as mistress of the Third Duke of Bolton. Married to him at Aix, Provence, 1751. D. Greenwich, Jan., 1760.

This singer has interest for the present time only in her connection with that ever-famous work, "The Beggar's Opera." She received an immense degree of attention while acting in it, and was, by the favour of the mobility or nobility, magnified in every virtue to the degree of a goddess.

FEO (Francesco). Italian comp., B. Naples, about end of 17th century [1699]. S. under Gizzi and Pitoni. D. [?]

WORKS;—*Operas*:—Ipermestra; Arianna, 1728; Andromaque, 1730; Arsace, 1731. Oratorios, Church Music, etc.

He was director from 1740 of the singing school of Rome, and educated many famous pupils.

FERGUSON (John Clark). Scottish writer, author of "The Empire of Music, and other Poems, by Alfred Lee [pseudonym]," Lond., 12mo, 1849: 2nd edition, "Pleasures of Music," 8vo, 1850.

FERGUSSON (Robert). Scottish poet, B. Edinburgh, Oct. 17, 1750. D. Oct. 16, 1774.

Was noted in his day for his beautiful tenor voice, and the pleasing manner in which he rendered Scottish songs. His lyrical pieces for music are few and unimportant, his chief production affecting music being the "Elegy on the death of Scots music," written partly with reference to the decease of William Macgibbon, an Edinburgh violinist.

FERRABOSCO (Alfonso). Italian comp., settled in England about middle of 16th century. He composed "Madrigali a 5 Voci," Venice, 1587; motets, and music for the virginals.

FERRABOSCO (Alfonso). Italian comp., son of above, B. Greenwich, 1580. D. 1652. Wrote Ayres by Alfonso Ferrabosco, Lond., 4to, 1609. Lessons for 1, 2, and 3 Viols," Lond., 4to, n. d. Fancies for Viols, etc.

FERRABOSCO (John). English comp. and org., B. about beginning of 17th century, son of Alfonso the younger. Mus. Bac., Cantab., 1671. Org. Ely Cath., 1662-82. D. 1682. Wrote, services, anthems, etc.

FERRANTI (Marco Aurelio Zani de). Italian writer and theorist, B. Bologna, 1800. D. Pisa, Nov. 28, 1878.

FERRARI (Adolphus A. G.). Italian musician and teacher, author of "The Formation and Cultivation of the Voice for Singing," Lond., 1857. D. Lond., Nov. 27, 1870.

FERRARI (Benedetto). Italian poet and comp., B. Reggio [1597]. Resided in Venice, where in 1638 he established an opera house, which he superintended personally. D. Venice, Oct. 22, 1681.

WORKS,—*Operas, etc.*:—Andromeda, 1637; L'Armida, 1639; Il Pastor Reggio, 1640; La Ninfa avara, 1641; Proserpina rapita, 1641; L'Inganno d'Amore, 1653; Licasta, 1664.

His poetical works were issued in 1644. Surnamed "della Tiorba" on account of his skill on the Lute.

FERRARI (Carlotta). Italian vocalist, B. 1837. Has appeared in many operas by Verdi, etc.

FERRARI (Giacomo Gotifredo). Italian comp. and teacher, B. Roveredo, 1759. S. in Italy. Accompanist at Théatre Feydean, Paris. Settled in London. Married Miss Henry, pianist, 1804. D. London, Dec., 1842.

WORKS.—La Villanella rapita, opera, Lond., 1797; I due Suizzeri, do. Sonatas, Concertos, etc., for various instruments. Six Canons for 3 Voices, Lond., 1821.

Six English Canzonets, Lond., n. d. Canzonets, Solos, Songs, Ballets. Concise Treatment of Italian Singing, Elucidated by Rules, Observations, and Examples, Lond., 8vo [c. 1815]. Instructions, both Theoretical and Practical, in the Art of Singing, with a Series of Exercises, Lond, 1827. Studio di Musica Teorica Pratica: containing Sketches of Harmony, Rules of Thorough-Bass, and Composition...Lond., fo., n. d. Aneddoti piacevoli e interessanti occorsi nella vita, di G. G. Ferrari, Lond., 2 vols., 1830.

FERRER (Mateo), MATENET. Spanish org. and comp., B. Barcelona, Feb. 25, 1788. D. Barcelona, Jan. 4, 1864. Composer of sacred music, and trainer of many good musicians.

FERRI (Baldassare). Italian vocalist, B. Pergia, Dec., 1610. D. 1680.

FERRIS (G. T.) Author of "Great Singers, Faustina Bordoni to Henrietta Sontag," 1880, 2 vols., 12mo.

FESCA (Alexander Ernst). German comp., B. Carlsruhe, May 22, 1820. D. Feb., 1849.

The son of F. E. Fesca. Composed, among other works, the following:—Rondo brilliant for Pf., op. 2; Grand rondo, op. 3; Variations on "Il Puritani," op. 4; Two nocturnes, op. 5; Variations, op. 6; First grand trio for Pf., vn., and cello, in B flat, op. 11; Second do., op. 12; La Mélancolie, for Pf., op. 15; La Sylphide, for Pf., op. 19; Third Trio, op. 23; First Septet, in C minor, op. 26; Second do., op. 28; Fourth Trio, in C minor, op. 31; Fifth and Sixth do., in B min. and F, opp. 46, 54. Miscellaneous Pf. music, etc.

FESCA (Friedrich Ernst). German comp. and violinist, B. Magdeburg, Feb. 15, 1789. S. under A. S. Müller. Member of Duke of Oldenburg's band, 1806. Solo violinist at Cassel, 1806-12. Leader to Duke of Baden at Carlsruhe, 1815-26. D. Carlsruhe, May 24, 1826.

WORKS.—Op. 1-3. Three sets of 3 string quartets; op. 4. Quartet in E flat; op. 5. Six songs for voice and Pf.; op. 6. First Symphony, in E; op. 7. Two string quartets; op. 8-9. Quintets for strings, in D; op. 10. Second symphony, in D; op. 11. Potpourri for violin; op. 12. Quartet for strings, in D minor; op. 13. Third symphony, in D; op. 14. Quartet for violins, in B flat; op. 15. String quintet for vns., in E; op. 16. Six Songs for voice and Pf.; op. 17. Song for 4 voices; op. 18. "Cantemir," opera; op. 20. Quintet, string, in B flat; op. 21. Ninth Psalm for solo voices, chorus and orch.; op. 22. Quintet for Flutes, in C; op. 23. Potpourri for vn., in A; op. 24. Six songs for voice and Pf.; op. 25. The 13th Psalm; op. 26. 105th Psalm; op. 27. Nine songs for voice and Pf.; op. 28. Omar et Leila, opera in 3 acts; op. 29. Potpourri for horn; op. 30. Songs for voice and Pf.; op. 31. Part-song for 4 male voices; op. 32. Nine songs for voice and Pf.; op. 33. Song for voice and orch.; op. 34. Quartet for strings in C; op. 35. Six songs for 4 voices; op. 36. Quartet for strings in C; op. 37-38. Quartets for flutes in D and G; op. 39. Andante and rondo for horn; op. 40. Quartet for flutes; op. 41 and 43. Overtures for orch.; op. 42. Quintet for flutes.

The music of this composer and that of his son is most agreeable, never rising to grandeur and never sinking to frivolity. It possesses a great degree of merit, and is tuneful and well adapted for most musical tastes.

FESTA (Costanza). Italian comp., B. Rome, about end of fifteenth century [1490]. Member of Pontifical Choir, Rome, 1517. Chap.-master at the Vatican, D. Rome, April 10, 1545.

WORKS.—Motets. Madrigali a 4 voci, 1543; Madrigali a 3 voci, Venice, 1556; and others preserved in MS. in the Library of the Pontifical Chapel, Rome. Some specimens of his work are given in various collections. Known in England as composer of the madrigal "Down in a flow'ry vale," one of the best specimens extant of the early Italian school of madrigal writing.

FESTING (Michael Christian). German violinist and comp., B. Germany, 1680. S. under Geminiani. *Début* as violinist, London, in 1724. Leader of King's private band. Established, with Dr. Greene, etc., Society of Musicians for the support of decayed musicians, 1738. Musical Director of Ranelagh Gardens, 1742. D. London, July 24, 1752.

WORKS.—Music to Addison's "Ode for St. Cecilia's Day"; Milton's "May Morning," song, Lond., fo., n.d.; Ode upon the return of H.R.H. the Duke of Cumberland from Scotland, 1746; Symphonies for orch.; Twelve Sonatas in 3 parts, op. 2, 1731; Twelve Concertos in 7 parts, op. 3, 1734; Eight Concertos in 7 parts for violins, op. 5, 1739; Six Sonatas for 2 violins and a bass, op. 6.

Festing was one of the leading performers in England during his day, and was highly respected for his benevolent qualities.

FÉTIS (Francois Joseph). Belgian writer and comp., B. Mons, March 25, 1784. S. at Paris Cons. under Boieldieu, Pradher, etc. Gained various prizes, 1803-7. Married, 1806. Org. at Douai, 1813. Prof. of Counterpoint in Paris Cons., 1821. Librarian, do., 1827. Director of Brussels Cons., 1833. Musical director to the King of the Belgians, 1833. D. Brussels, March 26, 1871.

WORKS.—*Operas:* L' Amant et la Mari, 1820; Les Sœurs jumelles, 1823; Marie Stuart en Ecosse, 1823; Le Bourgeois de Reims, 1824; La Vieille, 1826; Le Mannequin de Bergame, 1832; Phidias (MS.). *Instrumental Music:* Overtures, sextets, quintets, sonatas, and single pieces. *Didactic and Historical:* Methode élémentaire et abrégée d' Harmonie et d' Accompagnement suivie de basses chiffrées, Paris, 4to, 1824—English translation by John Bishop, London, fo., 1835; Traité de la fugue et du contrepoint, Paris, 2 vols. fo., 1825; Traité de l'Accompagnement de la partition, Paris, fo., 1829; Solféges progressifs, Paris, fo., 1827; La Musique mise à la portée de tout le Monde, exposé succinct de tout ce qui est nécessaire pour juger de cet Art, et pour en par ler sans l'avoir Etudie, Paris, 12mo, 1830 (other edits.); Trans. as "Music Explained to the World," Boston, 1842—London, 12mo, 1844; Curiosités Historiques de la musique, complément necessaire de la Musique mise à la portée de tout le Monde, Paris, 8vo, 1830; Histoire générale de la Musique, Paris, 5 vols. 8vo, 1869-75; Biographie universelle des Musiciens et Bibliographie générale de la Musique, Brussels, 8 vols. 12mo, 1835-44—second edition, Paris, 8 vols. 8vo, 1862; Supplement by Pougin, Paris, 2 vols. 8vo, 1878-80; Manuel des principes de musique...Paris, 8vo, 1837; Traité du chant en chœur, Paris, 1837; Trans. as Treatise on Choir and Chorus Singing, Lond., 8vo, 1854; Manuel des Compositeurs, Directeurs de Musique, etc., Paris, 8vo [1837]; Trans. as "A Manual for Composers," Lond., 4to, n.d.; Methode des methodes de piano, 1837; Methode des methodes de chant, etc.; Methode élémentaire du plain-chant, 1843; Etudes de Beethoven, Traité d' Harmonie et de Composition...preface et de la vie de Beethoven, par F. Fétis, Paris, 2 vols. 8vo, 1833; Traité complet de la theorie et de la Pratique de l'Harmonie, Paris, 1841; Notice Biographique sur Nicolo Paganini, Paris, 8vo, 1851; English trans., Lond., 8vo, n. d.; Notice Biographique sur Sabastien Erard, Paris, 8vo, 1831; Antoine Stradivari luthier célèbre...Paris, 8vo, 1856; Trans. as "Notice of Anthony Stradivari...by J. Bishop, London, 8vo, 1864; Biographie de Joseph et Michel Haydn, Paris, 8vo, 1864.

Fétis is known, and will ever be known, by his "Biographie des Musiciens," a work which despite innumerable shortcomings, is one of the greatest monuments t o the achievements of musical genius ever reared. The unfortunate blundering of Fétis and his successors in the work of compilation and revision is chiefly confined t o British musical biography, thus showing that Continental indifference and ignorance of what is, and has been, done in Britain for music, gives rise to the erroneous s ipposition that music, to be inferior, must only be British. Most of the articles in t' e work on even the greatest of British musicians, do not exceed in extent the s ace set apart for many feeble Belgian or German professors of five-finger exercises, whose merits in bulk could only be classed as sixth-rate. The mistakes occurring throughout his great work have been so often pointed out that it is unnecessary to recapitulate such statements here; but it must be said that, errors apart, no work has been so often drawn upon.

Fétis' other works do not call for particular comment, being well enough known as text-books and reference works. His compositions are occasionally given in France and Belgium. As a writer whose aim was utility to his fellow-musicians, Fétis was, and will ever be known and remembered.

His son EDWARD is a professor and composer in Brussels, and in a manner helps t o perpetuate his great father's good name. Author of "Les Musiciens Belges, Brussels, 2 parts, n. d.

FEVIN (Antoine). French comp., B. Orleans [1490]. D. early in 16th century [1517]. Wrote masses, motets, etc.

FEYJOO Y MONTENEGRO (Benedict Jerome). Spanish writer, B. Compostelle, Feb. 16, 1701. D. Oviedo, May 16, 1764. Author of "El Deleyte della Musica, accompanado de la virtud, hace la tierra el noviciado del cielo," Madrid, n. d. "Teatro-Critico Universal," Madrid, 16 vols., 8vo, 1738-46. A trans. from Feyjoo's works was published anonymously by Mr. Mitford, Lond., 8vo, 1778.

FIBICH (Zdenko). Bohemian operatic comp., B. Seboric, Dec. 21, 1831. Has written a number of operas, symphonies, and vocal music.

FICHER (Ferdinand). German pianist and comp., B. Leipzig, 1821. D. New York, 1865. Teacher and comp. for Pf.

FIELD (Henry). English comp. and pianist, B. Bath, Dec. 6, 1797. D. there, May 26, 1848. S. under Coombs, of Cheltenham; and taught music at Bath. Wrote some unimportant music for Pf.

FIELD (John). Irish comp. and pianist, B. Dublin, July 26, 1782. Apprenticed to Clementi, London, under whom he afterwards studied. Taken by Clementi to Paris, Germany and Russia. Teacher at St. Petersburg, 1804. Do. at Moscow, 1823. Appeared at London Philharmonic Concert, 1832. Played in Belgium, Switzerland and Italy. Returned to Russia with family named Raemann. D. Moscow, Jan. 11, 1837.

WORKS.—Op. 1. Three Sonatas for Pf. in A, E flat, and C minor Seven Concertos for Pf. and orch., in E flat, A flat, E flat, E flat, C, C, C minor. Two Divertissements for Pf., with accomp. for 2 vns., flute, alto and bass. Quintet for Pf., 2 vns, alto and bass. Rondo for Pf. and quartet. Variations on Russian air for Pf. duet. Grand Valse for Pf. duet. Three Sonatas for Pf. in A, B, and C. Sonata for Pf. in B. Exercise in Modulation for Pf. Two Airs for Pf. Fantasias for Pf. Eighteen Nocturnes for Pf. Rondo Ecossais for Pf. Polonaises for Pf. Two Songs for Voice and Pf. Romances for Pf. Rondos, and miscellaneous pieces.

Of all the British composers who have beautified the general stock of music with their productions, Field alone has maintained a more than ordinary place in the affections of musicians. Whether this is owing to the intrinsic worth of his compositions or to any romantic interest which may be held to attach to his career it is difficult to determine; but the fact remains that the popularity of his works is increasing, and they show no signs of becoming only of antiquarian or historical interest. His nocturnes are invested with a great amount of poetical fervour; are never wearisome to the ordinary listener; and never fail to impress the hearer with a sense of their beauty. Chopin imitated Field in this single form in a manner which at once placed his compositions as works of genius on a slightly higher level than those of his precursor, but he is in every other way indebted to Field.

Field's other works are not so well known to the majority of pianists, but the concertos are good and deserving productions; though undoubtedly possessing few of those features which are to be found in the nocturnes. The sonatas and minor works are only occasionally given at our public concerts, which shows that their merits are not considered of great moment, and indeed they are not by any means more than average productions for such a mind. Field was himself a great pianist, excelling in the interpretation of works of a dreamy, poetical nature, such as his own nocturnes.

FILBY (William Charles). English org. and comp., B. Hammersmith, 1836. Org. of S. Peter, Hammersmith, 1849. S. in France. Org. and Choirmaster of Parish Church, Bromley, Lond., S. E., 1853. Org. successively of S. Peter, Walworth; S. Matthew, Bayswater; S. Luke, Westbourne Park; Holy Trinity, Margate; Holy Trinity, Stepney.

WORKS.—Three Fantasias, and other Pf. pieces, opp. 16, 17, 18, 20, 21, 23. Mass in E flat, for voices and orch., op. 24. Past, Present, and Future, song, op. 26. Mass in E, op. 28. Pf. music—Sirène, opp. 29, 30, 35. Twenty-third Psalm, op. 36. Pf. pieces, opp. 42, 44, 46, 87. Songs—opp. 48, 52, 61, 70, 85, 87, 96. Pf. pieces, op. 49, 53, 55, 56, 58, 59, 62, 63. Handbook of Psalmody, op. 64, 1861 (Purday). Sonata for Pf. in E., op. 66. Motet—Salve Regina, op. 67. Thirteenth Psalm, op. 71 (MS.) Quatre Gigues caracteristiques, for Pf., op. 72; Tarantelle, Pf., op. 73; Sanctus, chorus, op. 75; Sonata for Pf., in G minor, op. 76 (MS.); Vesper Hymn, vocal trio, op. 77; O Lord of Harvest, chorus, op. 83; Pleasures and Perils, duet, op. 88; I will arise, chorus, etc., op. 93; Night's approach, trio, op. 94. Operettas—Your money or your life, op. 99; Alabama Claims, op. 100. Overture Fantastique, for orch., op. 101; The mercy seat, chorus, op. 105; Lion and four wolves, chorus, op. 109; Four organ voluntaries, op. 110; Twelve Pf. pieces, op. 111; Laudate Dominum, motet, op. 112; Return from the revel, chorus, op. 113; Come, ye children, chorus, op. 115; Départ de l'eglise, march for organ, op. 121; Three organ pieces, op. 124; Six Pf. pieces, op. 128 Song of Praise (part editorship), 1874. Piccolo Tutor (B. Williams), Lond., n. d. Flute Tutor, n. d. How to Write Music; the Student's Copy Book, Lond., 4to, 1882.

FILIPPI (Fillipo). Italian writer and comp., B. Vicenza, Jan. 13, 1833. Educated at University of Padua. S. music at Vienna. Contributor to periodical literature, song writer, etc.

FILMER (Edward). English comp. of vocal music of 17th century. Published "French Court Ayres of Four and Five Parts," 1629.

FILLMORE (Augustus D.) American musician, B. Ohio, 1823. Published "The Universal Musician: a New Collection of Secular and Sacred Music, with a new and Comprehensive Plan of Instruction, etc," Cincinnati, 1860 [various editions]. "The Christian Psalmist," etc.

FILLMORE (John Comfort). American teacher and writer, B. near Norwich, Conn., Feb. 4, 1843. Educated at Oberlin Coll., Ohio, 1862-65. S. music at Leipzig Cons., 1865-67. Director of Music Cons. in Oberlin Coll., 1869. Prof. of music in Ripon Coll., Wisconsin, 1869-78. Music-director Milwaukee Coll. for Young Ladies, 1878-1884. Director and founder of School of Music, Milwaukee, 1884. Author of "Pianoforte Music: its History, with Biographical sketches and critical estimates of its greatest masters." Chicago, 1883, 8vo; London edit., 1885. Also newspaper articles.
Mr. Fillmore is a careful and successful teacher, and the programmes of the concerts given at the institution where his labours are carried on display the highest taste and culture. The work on the Pianoforte and its music is a well-written exposition of the subject, tracing pianoforte music through its various developments and changes, and giving a careful historical insight to the progressions of keyed instrument music.

FILTSCH (Carl). Hungarian pianist, B. Hungary, 1830. Appeared in London and elsewhere as an infant prodigy. D. Vienna, May 11, 1845.

FINCH (Hon. and Rev. Edward). English comp., B. 1664. D. York, Feb. 14, 1738. He composed anthems, psalms, etc.; also a "Grammar for Thorough-bass, with examples." MS. of 66 pages in the Euing Library, Glasgow.

FINGER (Godfrey). Austrian violinist and comp., B. Moravia. Came to England, 1685. Musical director to James II. Chapel-master at Gotha, 1717. Further career unknown.
WORKS.—Sonatas for violins; Six sonatas or solos for the flute, with a Thorough-bass for the harpsichord (with D. Purcell); Ayres for violins and flutes. Music for—The Virgin Prophetess; The Anatomist, 1697; The Loves of Mars and Venus, 1696; The Judgment of Paris, 1701 (some of these with Eccles, Weldon, and D. Purcell); Love for Love, 1695; The Wives' Excuse; Sieg der Schönheit über die Helder, 1706, etc.

FINK (Christian). German org. and comp., B. Dettingen, near Heidenheim, 1831. Org. and teacher.
WORKS.—Lieder for voice and Pf., op. 3; Two sonatainas for Pf., op. 16; Sonata for Pf., op. 21; The 95th Psalm, op. 28; Fugues, sonatas, and voluntaries etc., for organ.

FINK (Gottfried Wilhelm). German comp. and poet, B. Sulz, March 7, 1783. D. Halle, Aug. 7, 1846. Was editor of the "Allgemeine Musikalisches Zeitung," from 1827.

WORKS.—Erste Wanderung der ältesten Tonkunst als Vorgeschichte der Musik, Essen, 8vo, 1831. Musikalische Grammatik oder theoretisch praktischer unterricht in der Tonkunst, Leipzig, 12mo, 1836. Wesen und Geschichte der Oper, ein Handbuch für alle Freunde der Tonkunst, Leipzig, 8vo, 1838. System der Musikalishen Harmonielehre, Leipzig, 8vo, 1842. Der neumusikalische Lehrjammer, Leipzig, 8vo, 1842. Musikalische Kompositionslehre, Leipzig, 8vo, 1847. Der Musikalische Hanslehrer, Leipzig, 8vo, 1851. Musikalischer Hausschatz der Deutschen, eine sammlung von 1000 Liedern und Gesängen...Leipzig, 1862.

FIORAVANTI (Valentino). Italian comp., B. Rome, Nov. 1770. D. Capua, June, 1837.

WORKS.—*Operas:* Amor aguzza l'ingegno; l'Astuta; Le cantatrice villane; Il Furbo contra il Furbo, 1795; Gli amanti comici, 1796; La schiava di due padron, 1803; L'Africano generosa; I Virtuosi ambulanti, 1807; Camilla, 1810. Sacred music, songs, etc.

FIORAVANTI (Vincenzo). Italian comp., son of above, B. Rome, April 1810. D. Naples, March, 1877.

WORKS.—*Operas:* La Pastorella rapita; Robinson Crusoe; Colombo; Amore e Disinganno; La Larva; Un Matrimonio in Prigione, 1838; La Dama e lo Zoccolaio, 1840; Gli Zingari; La Pirata; I Vecchi burlata; Annella, etc.

FIORILLO (Federigo). Italian violinist and comp., B. Brunswick, 1753. Appeared in Poland as violinist, 1780. Cond. at Riga, 1783-5. Played in Paris, 1785. Appeared in London, 1788 and in 1794. D. Amsterdam [1812]. Wrote string quartets, symphonies, valses, sonatas, concertos, 36 caprices for violin, etc.

FIORILLO (Ignazio). Italian comp., B. Naples, May 11, 1715. D. near Cassel, June, 1787. Father of the preceding.

FISCHER (Carl August). German org. and comp., B. Ebersdorf, 1829. Teacher and org. in Dresden. Comp. of a sinfonia for org. and orch.; Lorely, opera; org. sonatas, fugues, etc., and songs.

FISCHER (Christian Friedrich). German org. and comp. B. Lübeck, Oct. 23, 1698. D. middle of 17th century.

FISCHER (Johann Christian). German oboist, B. Freiburg. 1733. Member of court band, Dresden. Appeared in London, 1768. Mem. of Queen's band. Played at Abel and Bach's concerts; Vauxhall Gardens, etc. Returned to Continent, 1786. Again in London, 1790. D. London, April 29, 1800.

FISCHER (Johann Godfrey). German comp. and pianist, B. Naundorf, Sept. 13, 1731. D. Freiburg, Sept. 7, 1821. Comp. overtures, Pf. music, songs, etc.

FISCHHOF (Joseph). Austrian comp., writer, and pianist, B. Moravia, April 4, 1804. D. near Vienna, June 28, 1857.

Comp. Pf. rondos, valses, variations, marches, galops, etc.; songs; and wrote "Versuch einer Geschichte des clavierbaues..." Vienna, 1853.

FISH (William). English violinist and comp., D. Norwich, 1775. Violinist in Norwich theatre. Teacher of music at Norwich. Was musical preceptor of Edward Taylor and George Perry, and a comp. of concertos, glees, and songs. D. [1863-4].

FISHER (John Abraham). English comp. and violinist, B. Dunstable [London], 1744. S. under Pinto. Appeared at King's Theatre as violinist, 1763. Married Miss Powell, 1770. Bac. and Doc. Mus., Oxon., 1777. Travelled in Russia and Germany. Married Anne Selina Storace, 1784. Separated from her soon afterwards. Lived in Dublin as teacher. D. May, 1806 [1790-5].

WORKS.—Music to The Monster of the Wood, 1772; The Sylph's, 1774; Prometheus, 1776; The Norwood Gypsies, 1777; Macbeth. Providence, oratorio (for degree), 1777. Symphonies; Concertos for Pf., and for oboe; Violin and flute music; Canzonets. A Comparative View of the English, French, and Italian Schools, consisting of Airs and Glees composed as examples of their several manners, Lond., fo., n. d.

FISIN (James). English musician, B. Colchester, 1755. S. under Burney and Reinhold. Teacher in Chester. Wrote "The Seasons, or Vocal Year"; "The Judgment of Paris," a masque (Congreve); "Sacred Songs on the most Prominent Incidents of our Saviour's Life and Death," Lond., n. d. Sonatas, Glees, Canzonets, Ballads, etc. [D.?]

FISSOT (Alexis Henri). French pianist and comp., B. 1843. Comp. of 12 Preludes for Pf., op. 3; Deux Ballades, Pf., op. 7; Arabesques, Pf., op. 10; and a number of works in similar style.

FITZBALL (Edward), or BALL. English dramatist and writer, B. [Norwich], 1792. D. Chatham, Oct. 27, 1873. Wrote the librettos of some of the most popular of English operas, Wallace's "Maritana" being perhaps his most successful production. Although something more than a mere play-wright his poetical merits were of the lowest possible order, and his failure to bring the poetry of his librettos above the commonplace, communicated itself to the venturesome composers who set them. He published "Thirty-five Years of a Dramatic Author's Life," Lond., 2 vols., 1859.

FITZWILLIAM (Edward (Francis). English comp. and cond., B. Deal, 1824. Music-director, Haymarket Theatre, London. Married Miss Ellen Chaplin, 1855. D. London, January 20, 1857.

WORKS.—Love's Alarms, operetta; Songs, 1853. Four four-part songs, Lond., 1855. Hymns, etc.

FITZWILLIAM (Richard, 7th Viscount). English peer, and founder of the Fitzwilliam Museum, Cambridge, B. Aug., 1745. D. Feb. 5, 1816. Title now extinct.

He bequeathed to the University of Cambridge a collection of paintings, music, and books, the musical portion of which included a number of fine MS. compositions of early composers, principally Italian. The sacred music contained in this collection was edited and published by Vincent Novello, in 5 volumes, as "The Fitzwilliam Music, being a Collection of Sacred Pieces from the MSS. of Italian Composers in the Fitzwilliam Museum," fo., n. d.

FLAGG (Josiah). American musician, published "A Collection of the best Psalm Tunes, in two, three, and four parts, from the most approved authors" etc., Boston, 1764.

FLECHA (Mathieu). Spanish comp. and ecclesiastic, B. Prades, 1481. D. middle of 16th century. His nephew, MATHIEU, B. 1520, was also a comp. They both wrote church music.

FLÉGIER (Ange). French comp., B. Marseilles, Feb. 22, 1846. Comp. cantatas, Pf. music, songs, overtures, etc.

FLEISCHER (Friedrich Gottlob). German pianist and comp., B. Köthen, Jan. 14, 1722. D. Brunswick, April 4, 1806.

A famous pianist of the School of Bach, comp. an opera, much Pf. music, songs, odes, etc.

FLEMING (Rev. Alexander, D.D.). Scottish divine and writer, B. 1770. D. June, 1845. Was minister at Neilston. Wrote "To the Lord Provost of Glasgow, the two following Letters are respectfully addressed, on the subject of the Organ which...was introduced into St. Andrews Church, Glasgow. To which are added Remarks on the Rev. James Begg's Treatise on the Use of Organs," Glasgow, 8vo, 1808. "Answer to a Statement of the Proceedings of the Presbytery of Glasgow relative to the Use of an Organ," Glas., 8vo, 1808.

FLEMING (Rev. John). Scottish divine and writer, minister at one time at Airdrie. Author of "An Inquiry into the Compositions with which the Praise of God should be Celebrated in His Public Worship," Edin., 12mo, 1821. Sermons and many controversial works.

FLEURY (Charles Émile). French comp. and pianist, B. Paris, July 30, 1810. S. Paris Cons. Comp. Pf. music, songs, masses, etc.

FLIGHT (Benjamin). English organ-builder of 18th century, B. 1767. Was partner with Robson, and constructed the "Apollonicon," a variation of the organ or orchestrion. He invented several improvements in the construction of organs.

FLINTOFT (Rev. Luke). English divine of 18th century. Priest-vicar of Lincoln Cath., 1704-14. Gent. of Chap.-Royal, 1715. Reader in Whitehall Chapel, 1719. Minor canon, Westminster Abbey. D. Nov. 3, 1727. He invented the double chant, or rather composed the earliest specimen yet discovered. It is in G minor, and will be found in any large collection.

FLOTOW (Friedrich, Baron von). German comp., B. Rentendorf, April 27. 1812. S. at Paris under Reicha, 1827. Intendant of Count Schwerin, 1856-63. Returned to Paris, 1868. Resided in Vienna. D. Wiesbaden, Jan. 24, 1883.

WORKS.—*Operas:* Le Comte de Charolais, 1836; Stradella, 1837; Le Naufrage de la Meduse, 1839; L'esclave de Camoens, 1843; Die Matrosen, 1845; L'ame en peine, 1846; Stradella (rewritten), 1844 (London, 1846); Martha, Vienna, 1847 (London, 1858); Die Gross furstin, 1850; Indra, 1853; Rübezahl, 1854; Hilda, 1855; Der Müller von Meran, 1856; La Veuve Grapin, 1859; L'Ombre, 1869 (London, 1878); Naïda, 1873; Il Flor d'Harlem, 1876; Enchantress, 1878. Ballets, songs, etc.

The musician in quest of elevated musical thought will look long and earnestly before he discovers much to gratify his feelings in the foregoing list of operas. If, here and there, he stumbles on a fragment of good melody, let him carefully preserve it that it may preserve him in his endeavours to cross a boundless waste of vapid sing-song.

FLOWER (Eliza). English soprano vocalist, poetess, and comp., best known as comp. of "Musical Illustrations of the Waverley Novels," Lond., 1831, and similar productions. The part-song, "Now pray we for our country," is by her.

FLOWER (Sara), or ADAMS. English contralto singer and comp., sister of preceding, B. Feb. 22, 1805. Married to Mr. W. B. Adams, engineer. D. Melbourne, Aug. 16, 1865.

FLOWERS (George French). English comp., org., and writer, B. Boston, Lincoln, 1811. S. under Rinck, and Schnyder von Wartensee. Org. of English chap., Paris; S. Mark's, Myddleton Sq., London. Mus. Bac., Oxon., 1839. Editor of *Literary Gazette*. Competed, unsuccessfully, for Musical Prof.ship, Oxford, 1848. Do., Gresham College, 1863. Mus. Doc., Oxon., 1865. Estab. British School of Vocalization. D. London, June 14, 1872.

WORKS.—Essay on the Construction of Fugue, with an Introduction containing new Rules for Harmony, Illustrated in a Passacaglia and Twelve Fugues for the Organ, Lond., 4to, 1846; Trans. Basler's "Pictorial Representation of the Science of Harmony and the Relationship of Chords," Lond., fo., n. d.; Poem on Muscular Vocalisation, with Introduction, Barrow-on-Humber, 8vo, 1861. Anthems, songs, miscellaneous works. Flowers was the trainer of Mrs. Howard Paul, and a number of other successful vocalists.

FLUDD (Robert). English writer and scholar, B. Milgate, Bearsted, Kent, 1574. D. 1637.

WORK.—"Utriusque cosmi majoris scilicet et minoris metaphysica, physica atque technica historia," 2 vols., Oppenhemii, 1617. Contains some curious chapters on music, learned but not rational. His other works, "Tractatus Apologeticus," etc., are extremely rare and curious productions, chiefly on alchemical science.

FLÜGEL (Gustav). German pianist and comp., B. Nienburg-on-the-Saale, July

2, 1812, has written a number of good pieces for Pf., as Sonata, op. 4; Three Charakterstücke, op. 10; Fantasie-Bilder, op. 11; Sonata, op. 36; Humoreske, op. 44; as well as Lieder and Songs for voice and Pf. His works reach op. 86.

FODOR-MAINVIELLE (Josephine). French vocalist, B. Paris, 1793. Married to M. Mainvielle, actor, 1812. *Début,* Paris, 1814. D. [?]

FOGGIA (Francesco). Italian comp. and org., B. Rome, 1604. D. Jan. 8, 1688. He was a chapel-master at various towns in succession, and wrote motets, masses, psalms, and other church music.

FOGLIANO (Ludovico). Italian theorist of the fifteenth and sixteenth centuries, published a work entitled "Musica Theorica," Venice, fo., 1529, which excited much controversy in its time with reference to the several technical changes advocated in its pages.

FOLI (A. J.), FOLEY. Irish bass vocalist, B. Cork [?]. Has appeared with great success in all the large towns of Great Britain and Ireland, in America, and elsewhere. His voice is of great power and compass, and his style of vocalisation is highly artistic and at the same time popular. He is a universal favourite among all classes of the musical public.

FOLIANI. See FOGLIANI.

FOND. See DE LA FOND.

FONTAINE (Henri L. S. Mortier de). French pianist and comp., B. Wisniowiec, 1816. Comp. of a large quantity of showy Pf. music. D. Balham, May 10, 1883.

FONTANA (Bartolommeo). Italian musician and teacher, author of "Musical Manual: containing both the Theory and Practice of Instrumental Music," Lond., 8vo, 1847.

FORBES (George). English pianist and comp., B. Pimlico, London, July 1, 1813. S. under his brother Henry and Sir G. Smart. Gave concerts with his brother in London, 1831-1844. Subsequently gave subscription concerts on own account. D. London, Sept. 11, 1883.

WORKS.—*Pianoforte:* Sonata in C (ded. to Geo. Hogarth); March des Guides; Larghetto and Rondo Capricciosa in E (ded. to Sir W. S. Bennett); Rappelletoi; La Caprera; La Castellucia; Carnival de Florence; Marziale; La pluie des Perles; Forbes's Valse de Concert and Valse de Sylphes; Calliope Valse; Pluie de Printemps; La Rosamund, a nocturne; Louise, nocturne. Four operatic duets. Six teaching pieces for Pf. Gavotte, Queen Elizabeth. Marche et Finale brillant, op. 7. Italian fantasia. Espaniola. Billet-doux. Transcriptions, etc. Three Books of easy Voluntaries for organ or harmonium. Offertoire for organ in F (ded. to Sir John Goss).

The majority of the above works are light, brilliant pieces, cleverly wrought out and not too ambitious.

FORBES (Henry). English comp. and pianist, brother of the above, B. London, 1804. S. under Sir G. Smart, Hummel, Moscheles, and Herz. Cond. of the Societa Armonica. Org. of Parish Church of S. Luke, Chelsea. Gave concerts with his brother George. D. London, Nov. 24, 1859.

WORKS.—The Fairy Oak, opera, 1845. Ruth, oratorio, 1847. Pf. music. Songs. Psalms, etc.

Forbes was a fine pianist, and a composer of some merit, who could have made a great name, had time and opportunities been allowed him.

FORBES (John). Scottish printer and publisher, established at Aberdeen in middle of 16th century. He is chiefly remarkable as having published the first music book in Scotland [See Davidson, Thomas]; and for the authorship of three inflated epistles dedicatory, prefixed to the "Cantus" of 1662, and changed, to the edition of 1666; and again different, to the edition of 1682.

FORBUSH (Abijah). American musician, published "The Psalmodist's Assistant," Boston, 1806.

FORD (David Everard). English comp. and org., flourished during the first half of the present century. He wrote "The Rudiments of Music, etc.," n. d., and published "Original Psalm and Hymn Tunes," Lond., 7 books, 1833. Progressive Exercises for the Voice...," 1829.

FORD (Miss). English performer on the Harmonica, flourished during the 18th century. Authoress of "Instructions for Playing on the Musical Glasses, with a copperplate representing the order and manner of placing the glasses: with such directions for performing on them, that any person of a musical turn may learn in a few days, if not in a few hours," Lond., 1762.

FORD (Thomas). English comp., B. in latter half of the 16th century [1580]. Musician in suite of Prince Henry (Son of James I.). Musician to Charles I., on his accession. D. Nov., 1648.

WORKS.—Musicke of sundrie kindes set forth in two Bookes, the first whereof are Aires for foure Voyces to the lute, orpherion, or basse viol, with a dialogue for two voices and two basse violls, in parts tunde the lute-way. The second are Pavans, Galiards, Almaines, Toies, Jiggs, Thumpes, and such like for two base viols the liera-way, so made as the greatest number may serve to play alone, very easy to be performed, fol. 1607. Contributions in Leighton's "Teares." Canons, etc., in Hilton's "Catch that catch can."

Ford is now known only as the composer of the beautiful madrigal "Since first I saw your face."

FORD (Thomas). English writer, author of "Singing of Psalmes the duty of Christians, in v Sermons," Lond., 12mo, 1659.

FORDE (William). English writer, author of "An Essay on the Key in Music, fully illustrated by examples," Lond., 1841. Encyclopedia of Melody, 3050 Airs of all Countries..., 6 vols, 8vo, n. d. New Pianoforte Primer," Lond., 8vo, n. d. New Method of Singing according to the Italian School, 87 exercises, Lond., fo., n. d. Art of Singing at Sight, Lond., 8vo, n. d. Principles of Singing, with practical examples, Lond. [1830], 7 editions.

FORKEL (Johann Nicolaus). German writer and org., B near Coburg, Feb. 22, 1749. Chor. at Luneberg. S. at Göttingen University, 1769. Org. at University Ch. of Göttingen. Musical Director, Göttingen University, 1778. Doctor of Philosophy, Do., 1780. D. Göttingen, Mar. 17, 1818.

WORKS.—Musikalisch-Kritische Bibliothek, Gotha, 3 vols, 8vo, 1778-9. Allgemeine Geschichte der Musik, Leipzig, 2 vols, 4to, 1788-1801. Allgemeine Litteratur der Musik oder anleitung zur Kenntniss Musikalischer Bucher, welche von den altesten bis auf die neusten zeiten bey den Greichen, Romern und den meisten neuern Europaischen nationen sind geschrieben worden, Leipzig, 8vo, 1792. Musikalisches Almanach für Deutschland auf, 1782-83-84, Leipzig, 8vo. Ueber J. S. Bach's Leben, Kunst und Kunstwerke, Leipzig, 1802. Trans. as Life of John Sebastian Bach, with a critical view of his compositions, Lond., 8vo, 1820. Miscellaneous musical writings and compositions.

Forkel is best known by his two works above named, on the Literature of Music, and on Bach, both of which are highly valuable to the musical student. The "Litteratur" contains a bibliography of musical writings up to about the end of last century.

FORMBY (Rev. Henry), M.A. English writer, author of ...Duties and Privileges of Congregational Singing, Sermon, 1849. The Roman Ritual and its Canto Fermo compared with the works of modern music, Lond., 8vo, 1849. The Catholic Christian's guide to the right use of Christian Psalmody and the Psalter, Lond., 1847.

FORMES (Karl). German bass vocalist, B. Muhlheim on the Rhine, Aug. 7, 1810. Chor. in Cath. Choir. Début in "Zauberflöte," at Cologne, Jan., 1842. Appeared at Vienna. Appeared in London, Drury Lane, as Sarastro, "Zauberflöte," May, 1849. Appeared as Casper in "Der Freyschutz," Covent Garden Theatre, March, 1850. Sang at Philharmonic Concerts, in Provinces, and in Scotland. Appeared in America, 1857. Has since sang there with undiminished vigour.

FORNASARI (Nicolo). Italian tenor vocalist, B. 1803, D. 1861. Appeared in London and elsewhere in "Fra Diavola" and other popular operas.

FÖRSTER (Emanuel Aloys). German comp. and writer, B. 1748. D. Vienna, 1823. Composed a large quantity of chamber, Pf. and vocal music, some of which keeps a place at the present time. Also "Anleitung zum General-Bass," Leipzig, n. d.

FORSTER (Simon Andrew). English violin-maker and writer, son of William Forster, the younger, B. May 13, 1801. D. Feb. 2, 1870. Wrote with W. Sandys a "History of the Violin," 1864, and made 'cellos, violins, doublebasses ; in the making of which he was instructed by his father.

FORSTER (William). English violin-maker, B. Brampton, Cumberland, May 4, 1739. Went to London, 1759. Partner with Beck, Towerhill, London, as music-seller. Publisher and violin maker, 1781. Published Haydn's works, 1781. D. 1808.

Forster copied Stainer and Amati, and attained to high excellence in the general finish of his instruments. His double-basses, of which he made a few, are excessively valuable, as are his 'cellos, which are ranked by British performers among the best.

FORSTER (William). English violin-maker, B. London, Jan. 7, 1764. D. July 24, 1824. He made a number of average instruments, and a few of a high order of merit. His son William (1788-1824) was also a violin-maker, but his work does not claim any particular merit.

FORSYTH BROTHERS. English music-publishing firm, established in London and Manchester in 1873. They publish Charles Halle's popular arrangements for the Pf., and a number of other pieces, vocal and instrumental, by various popular composers.

FOSTER (Myles Birket). English org. and comp., B. London, Nov. 29, 1851. Eldest son of Birket Foster, the celebrated artist. Shewed early love for music, but coming of a Quaker family it was not encouraged. Sent to learn Stockbroker's business, 1868. Resigned, 1871. S. music under Hamilton Clarke, and at R. A. M. under Sullivan, Prout and Westlake. Org. of Rev. H. R. Haweis's Ch., 1873-74. Licentiate Trinity Coll., Lond., 1874. Org. of S. George's Campden Hill, 1875-79 ; F.C.O., 1875. Org. to Foundling Hospital, 1880. Associate of R. A. M. ; Philharmonic Soc., 1880.

WORKS.—Evening Service in C (male voices) ; Communion Service in B flat ; Evening Service in A (Sons of the Clergy Festival), 1883. Anthems, Hymns, Part-songs, Songs, etc. Symphony in F sharp minor, "Isle of Arran" (MS.). Overtures (MS.). Two Cantatas (MS.). String quartet, Pf. trio, etc. (MS.).

FOSTER (Stephen Collins). American song composer, B. Pittsburg, Pa., July 4, 1826. D. New York, Jan. 13, 1864.

WORKS.—*Songs:* Beautiful child of song ; Annie, my own love ; Camptown Races ; Come with thy sweet voice again ; Cheer up, Sam ; Ellen Bayne ; Eulalie ; Farewell, my Lilly dear ; Gentle Annie ; Hard times come again no more ; Jeannie with the light brown hair ; Massa's in de cold ground ; My old Kentucky home ; Maggie by my side ; Melinda May ; Mary loves the flowers ; Nancy Till ; Nelly was a lady ; Nelly Bly ; Old dog Tray ; Old folks at home ; Old memories ; Oh, boys carry me 'long ; The hour for Thee and me ; Ring de banjo ; Village maiden ; Willie, we have missed you ; Come where my love lies dreaming, for 4 voices ; etc.

The success of the majority of the above songs was something enormous previous to, during, and for some time after the American Civil War. Hundreds of thousands of copies have been sold both in Britain and America, and their popularity is still enduring.

FOUQUE (Pierre Octave). French comp., B. Paris, Nov. 12, 1844. S. under Chauvet, etc., in Paris Cons. Comp. operettas, Pf. music, songs, etc. D. Pau, April, 1883.

FOWLE (Thomas Lloyd). English comp., writer and org., B. Amesbury, Wilts, Oct. 16, 1827. Self-taught in music. Org. to his father at Amesbury.

Short time org. at Crawley, Sussex. From 1856, engaged as editor and publisher of useful works. Resident in Ryde, Isle of Wight.

WORKS.—4 vols. of Anthems ; 5 Cantatas ; 4 vols. of organ voluntaries ; 12 Marches for special seasons ; The Church Tune Book ; 2 Services "Thanksgiving Te Deum," for recovery of the Prince of Wales; and numerous other musical works. Versification of the several collects in the Book of Common Prayer, with addenda of special hymns. Handel (memoir), 8vo, n.d. Charles Dickens (memoir). Gentle Edith (novel). Autobiography and Treatise on Musical Degrees. Many popular readings, including "The Ghost that ran away with Organist."

Dr. Fowle, who is M.A., Doc. Mus., and Ph. Doc. of Giessen, has done a great amount of good among the parochial churches of England, by his untiring energy and skill in catering to the real wants of their organists. In 1864 Dr. Fowle was presented to the Prince of Wales. In 1874 his labours were so highly appreciated that nearly 2000 persons of all classes petitioned the Premier for a Civil Service pension, as a reward for his services to music. This, however, was not granted. He edited for three years a popular paper entitled *Monthly Musical and Literary Journal*, but was forced from ill health to discontinue its publication.

FOX (George). English comp. and bass singer, has written a number of very amusing and popular "comic cantatas." These cantatas have been given in most of the large towns in England. Fox is himself a remarkably fine vocalist.

WORKS.—*Cantatas:* The Jackdaw of Rheims ; John Gilpin ; Lord Lovel ; The Babes in the Wood (Ingoldsby) ; The Fair Imogene, 1880 ; The Messenger Dove, 1881. Songs, Pf. music, etc.

"Mr. Geo. Fox, the composer of the second Cantata, is a gentleman who largely devotes himself to the musical illustration of the horrible-grotesque, not without a measure of success that amounts to justification. So far as our knowledge goes of his doings, he began with the story of the Jackdaw of Rheims, and next took up the pathetic narrative of Lord Lovel and his bride. We are now acquainted with him as the composer of a Cantata founded on the grim and ghastly legend of Alonzo the Brave and the fair Imogene—the lady, by the way, giving her name to his work. 'Imogene' is, of course, treated from a humourous point of view, and the general tone of sportiveness and cynicism that pervades the music excites a sense of incongruity provocative of laughter. In this respect the Cantata opens very well indeed. Subsequently it falls off a little, and the music becomes less distinctive in its humour ; but as a whole the work claims respect. In fact, the composer writes so admirably that we should be glad to find him taking up a serious theme and doing his powers the justice they cannot receive from any amount of clever fooling. Mr. Fox, who is a baritone of considerable pretensions, took a leading part in the performance of 'Imogene,' assisted by Mdlle. Bauermeister, Miss Emilie Lloyd, and Mr. Faulkner Leigh, all of whom sang with care and success. Mr. Sidney Naylor conducted.—*The Daily Telegraph*, Friday, April 16, 1880.

FRADEL (Carl). German comp., pianist, and teacher, B. Vienna, 1821. Resided in New York as teacher for long period. Visited London, etc. Comp. Pf. music, songs, etc.

FRANCHOMME (Auguste). French violoncellist and comp., B. Lille, April 10, 1808. Comp. music for his instrument, etc. D. Paris, 1884.

FRANCK (César Auguste). Belgian pianist and comp., B. Liége, Dec. 10, 1822. Org. in Paris. Comp. Pf. music, songs, an oratorio, etc.

FRANCK (Guillaume). French comp., B. Rouen [1520]. Musician at Geneva, etc. D. Lausanne [1570]. Comp. of church music, and the reputed writer of the psalm tune "French."

FRANCO of Cologne, a Belgian theorist who flourished during the 11th century. He studied under Adelman at Liége. His works are, "Ars cantus mensurabilis," "Compendium de Discantu."

"The merit of Franco, and his importance in the history of music, consist in his having been the first to collect and systematize the laws of measure ; at least his writings are the earliest known in which this subject is treated."—Macfarren, in "Imperial Dictionary of Biography."

FRANCOEUR (Francois). French comp. and cond., B. Paris, Sept. 28, 1698. D. Paris, Aug. 6, 1787. He comp. "Pyrame et Thisbé"; "Scanderberg," 1735; "Les Augustales," 1744; "Zélindor," 1744; and other operas. His nephew LOUIS JOSEPH FRANCOEUR, B. Paris, Oct. 8, 1738, D. Paris, March 10, 1804. Was a writer and comp. "Ismène et Lindor," 1766; and "Ajax," 1770, are among his operas. He wrote a "Traité général des voix et des instruments d'Orchestre..." Paris, fo., n. d. His son, LOUIS BENJAMIN, B. Paris, Aug. 16, 1773, D. Paris, Dec. 15, 1849, was a writer on music, and comp. some vocal and instrumental music.

FRANKLIN (Benjamin). American philosopher and statesman, B. Boston, Mass., Jan 17, 1706. D. Philadelphia, April 17, 1790. Celebrated in connection with music as the inventor of the Harmonica. This is described in a "Description of a New Musical Instrument composed of Glasses, called the Armonica; in a letter to the Rev. Father Beccaria," 1762. He also wrote other papers on musical subjects.

FRANZ (Robert). German comp. and editor, B. Halle, June 28, 1815. S. under Fr. Schneider, at Dessau, 1835-7. Org. of the Ulrichskirche, nr. Halle. Director of the Sing-Academie, Halle. Org. and music-director of University. Retired from these positions since 1868. Lives now (1885) chiefly on proceeds of a subscription got up on his behalf in 1868, and on his editorial labours.

WORKS.—Op. 1. Twelve songs for voice and Pf.; op. 2. Five "Schilflieder" von N. Lenau; op. 3. Six lieder for voice and Pf.; op. 4. Twelve lieder for voice and Pf.; op. 5. Twelve do.; op. 6. Six do.; op. 7. Six do.; op. 8. Six songs; op. 9. Six lieder; opp. 11, 38, 39, 41, Sets of six lieder. Pf. music; The 117th psalm; Six chorales. Edition of Bach's Matthew Passion, 10 Cantatas, etc. Revised score of Mozart's edition of Handel's "Messiah," used at Birmingham Festival, 1885.

Franz's songs number about 260, and are admittedly among the best of recent German vocal compositions. Their artistic beauty is well known, and their interest for musicians of cultured taste is great.

FRANZL (Ferdinand). German violinist and comp., B. Schwetzingen, 1770. Played throughout Europe. D. Mannheim, 1833. Comp. concertas, fantasias, variations, etc., for vn. and orch., string quartets, operas, etc.

FRASER (Captain Simon). Scottish collector, B. Ardachie, Inverness, 1773. D. 1852. Published "The Airs and Melodies peculiar to the Highlands of Scotland and the Isles, with a Plain Harmony for the Pianoforte, Harp, Organ, or Violoncello, acquired 1715-45," Edin., fo., 1815. Another edition, 1874. A valuable and scarce collection.

FRASI (Guilia). Italian soprano vocalist, flourished during the eighteenth century. She appeared in London in 1743, and sang chiefly in Handel's works.

FREDERICK II., surnamed THE GREAT. B. Berlin, Jan. 24, 1712. D. Sans-Souci, nr. Potsdam, Aug. 17, 1786. He was a good, or questionably good, flute-player, having studied under Quantz; and a famous patron of the fine arts, especially French. He comp. some orchestral music.

FRÉLON (Louis Francois Alexandre). French org., comp., and pianist, B. Orleans, 1825. Has written a large amount of Pf. and org. music, and a work entitled "L' Art de l' orgue expressif," etc.

FRESCOBALDI (Girolamo). Italian comp. and org., B. Ferrara, [1587]. Resided at Antwerp, 1608. Org. at S. Peter's Cath., 1614. D. Rome, 1640 [1654].

WORKS.—Il Primo libro di madrigali, a cinque voci, Antwerp, 1608; Il primo libro Fantasie a due, tre, e quatro voci, 1608; Ricercari et canzoni francesi, fatti sopra diversi oblighi in partitura, 1615; Toccate, 1615; Capricci sopra diversi sogetti, 1624; Capricci e Ricercari e Canoni, libro primo, etc.

Frescobaldi was the greatest organist of his time, and numbered among his pupils Froberger. His compositions will be found here and there throughout collections of organ music.

FREYER (August). German org. and comp., B. nr. Dresden, 1803. S. under Elsner, Hesse, etc. Wrote a number of good organ pieces, church and chamber music, etc.

FREYLINGHAUSEN (Johann Anastasius). German comp., B. Halle, Dec. 2, 1670. D. Halle, Feb. 12., 1739. Comp. of church music, chiefly psalms and chorales.

FREZZOLINI (Erminia). Italian soprano vocalist, B. Orvieto, 1818. S. under her father, a singer, Ronconi, and Garcia. Début at Florence, 1838. Appeared at Milan, 1840. Married Poggi, the tenor singer, 1840. Appeared in London, 1842. Sang in St. Petersburg, 1848. Re-appeared in London, 1850. Appeared in Madrid and Paris, 1853. D. Paris, Nov., 1884.

FRIAS (Duchess de). See BALFE (VICTOIRE).

FRICKER (Anne), or MOGFORD. English song-writer and poetess, B. about 1820. Married Mr. Mogford. First song published, 1839.

WORKS.—*Songs:* A harvest hymn ; Angel of peace ; Autumn breezes ; Consolation ; Dear voices of home ; Dinna ye hear? ; Distant bells ; Fading away ; The fancy fair ; Faithless swallow ; Flow, gentle river ; Footprints in the snow ; Gentle Clare ; Gentle Shepherd ; Heart of hearts ; Hesperus ; I cried unto Thee ; I stood beneath the chestnut trees ; Marguerite ; Memory's tears ; Nightingale ; The old man's home ; Oh, weary eyes ; Phillis, fair ; Regret ; Robin ; Ruth's gleaning song ; She is not mine ; Softly at thy window ; Sunshine ; Sweet queen of hearts ; Thirty years ago ; To Thee alone ; Village bells ; When Celia sings ; When thou art nigh ; You ask me for a song. Pf. music, etc.

FRIES (Wulf C. J.) German violoncello player, B. Garbeck, Holstein, Jan. 10, 1825. S. 'cello under Carl Ehrlich ; otherwise self taught in music. First played in public, 1838. Member of theatre orch. at Bergen, 1842-47. Settled in Boston, U.S., 1847. Member of the Mendelssohn Quintette Club, 1848-81. 'Cellist in the Beethoven Club, and principal Boston orchestras. Joint author with August Suck of "Violoncello Instructor," Boston, n. d. Well known in New England as one of the foremost performers and teachers.

FRIKE (Philipp Josef), or FRICK. German writer and pianist, B. Wallanzheim, Würzburg, May 27, 1740. Settled in London as pianist and teacher, 1780. D. London, June 15, 1798.

WORKS.—The Art of Musical Modulation rendered easy and familiar...Lond., 4to, 1780. French edit., Paris, 1799 ; A Treatise on Thorough Bass, containing a plain and easy Method...Lond., 4to, 1789 ; 2nd edit., Lond., 4to, n. d. (title varied) ; A Guide in Harmony, containing the various manners in which every chord in four parts can be prepared...Lond., 4to, 1793. Duets and solos for Pf., Pf. trios, etc.

FROBERGER (Johann Jacob). German org., B. Halle [1606]. Court org. at Vienna, 1637. S. under Frescobaldi, 1637-41. Left employment of Ferdinand III. of Austria, 1657. Appeared in London, 1662. Played in Westminster Abbey. D. in France [1667].

He was a remarkable performer, and carried on the traditions of Frescobaldi, which ultimately culminated in the grandeur of J. S. Bach. The dates of his birth and death are matters of dispute. He wrote music for the organ, the harpsichord, and the voice.

FROST (Charles Joseph). English comp. and org., B. Westbury-on-Trym, near Clifton, June 20, 1848. S. under his father (org. at Tewkesbury), Geo. Cooper, Steggall, and Sir J. Goss. Org. of S. James's, Cheltenham, 1865 ; Holy Trinity, Westbury-on-Trym, 1867 ; Holy Trinity, Weston-super-mare, 1869 ; Holy Trinity, Lee, Kent, 1873 ; St. Mary, Haggerston, 1876 ; Christ Church, Newgate St., London, 1880 ; St. Peter's, Brockley, 1884. Mem. of Board of examiners for awarding fellowships at Coll. of Org., 1875. Mus. Bac., Cantab., 1876. Mus. Doc., Cantab., 1882. Mem. of Council Coll. of Org. Prof. of org., Guildhall School of Music, 1880.

WORKS.—Nathan's Parable, oratorio, 1878 (MS.) ; Harvest Cantata, 1880 (MS.) ;

By the waters of Babylon, cantata, 1876 (MS.); Te Deum in G; Morning Service in F; Communion Service in C; Evening Services in C, D, G, and E flat; The Offertory Sentences. *Anthems:* Almighty God, give us grace; Thou visitest the earth; God is gone up; Almighty and Everlasting God; When the Lord turned again; God is the Lord; Thou shalt show us wonderful things; Christ our Passover; Like as Christ was raised up; He shall be great; And I will pray the father; Hear my prayer; Glory to God in the highest; The Gentiles shall come. Sanctus, Kyrie, and Gloria, in A flat. 36 original hymn tunes. *Songs:* I will lay me down in peace; There the wicked cease; Heaven and Earth shall pass away; Thy loving-kindness and mercy; I cried unto the Lord; Seek ye the Lord; Them that are meek; Gone where the light never fades; A tender flower; First love; Youthful songs. *Organ:* Collection of Organ pieces in 24 numbers—Preludes, Postludes, Fantasias, etc.; Prelude in D; Moderato in B flat; Sonatina in C; Fantasia in B flat; Impromptu in A min., Larghetto in C, and Andante in F sharp. March in C, and Festal march in C. Forty Preludes (chiefly short and easy), 1880; 27 original pieces; 3 voluntary books. Symphony for orch., in C, 1878 (MS.); Two sets of six original movements for harmonium; Romance, Meditation, Tarentelle, Episode, Fantasia; Bouquet of Flowers, 24 sketches; 7 Sonatinas; etc., for Pf.

FROST (Henry Frederick). English musician and org. of the Chapel Royal, Savoy, author of "Schubert." Great Musicians' Series. London, 8vo, 1881.

FRY (William H.) American comp. B. Philadelphia, 1813. Produced two operas which have attained a measure of success in the United States: "Leonora," 1858, and "Notre Dame de Paris," 1864. He also composed a Stabat Mater, Pf. music, cantatas, songs, and orchestral works. D. Santa Cruz, 1864.

FRYER (G.) English musician, compiled "The Poetry of Various Glees, Songs, etc., as Performed at the Harmonists." Lond., 1798.

FÜHRER (Robert). Bohemian org. and comp., B. Prague, June, 1807. Org. of Prague Cath., etc. D. Vienna, Nov., 1861.

He wrote an amount of good church music, and much for the organ.

FULCHER (John). English musician and editor, B. London, August, 1830. Teacher in Glasgow. Editor of "Lays and Lyrics of Scotland," with a Historical Epitome of Scottish Song by James Ballantine, etc. Lond., n. d. *Songs:* Afton Water; Bonnie, bonnie Bell; Songs of Scotland; The Little Children, Scottish vocal duet (arranged); Transcriptions, etc., for Pf.; Part-songs (arrangements); Beauties of Scottish Song (with T. S. Gleadhill and Thomson).

FULLER (Richard). American musician, B. Beaufort, S. Carolina, 1808. Compiled "The Psalmist, with Supplement." This was the hymnal in common use among Baptists in America.

FUMAGALLI (Adolfo). Italian pianist and comp., B. Inzago, Oct. 19, 1828. D. Florence, May 3, 1856. Has composed an immense quantity of brilliant Pf. pieces, and songs of various degrees of merit.

FÜRSTENAU (Anton Bernard). German flute-player and comp., B. Münster, Oct. 20, 1792. D. Dresden, Nov., 1852.

WORKS.—Concertos for flute and orch., opp. 12, 33, 40, 58. Concerto for 2 flutes and orch., op. 41. Studies, rondos, adagios, quartets, caprices, nocturnes, transcriptions, etc., for flute. Die Kunst des Flötenspiels; etc.

The works of this composer are among the best which the flute player can study. His son Moritz, B. 1824, is also a flute player, and author of "Zur Geschichte der Musik und des Theaters am Hofe zu Dresden," Dresden, 2 vols., 1861-2.

FURTADO (John). Italian(?) writer, author of New Elements of Thorough-Bass; clearly and concisely Demonstrated, Lond., 8vo, 1798. An Essay on the Theory and Advancement of Thorough-Bass, Lond., 8vo, 1798. An Essay on Fingering the Pianoforte, etc., Lond., 4to, 1798.

FUX (Johann Josef). German comp. and writer, B. near Gratz, 1660. Org.

in Vienna, 1696. Comp. to Court at Vienna, 1698. Chapel-master S. Stephen's Cath., 1705-15. Vice Chapel-master to Court. Chapel-master to Dowager Empress Wilhelmine Amalie, 1713-18. Principal Chapel-master at Court of Vienna. D. Vienna, Feb. 13, 1741.

WORKS.—Gradus ad Parnassum sive manuductio ad compositionem musicæ regularem, Vienna, fo., 1725: Trans. into German by L. Mizler, Leipzig, 4to, 1742; and into English as "Practical Rules for Learning Composition...," Lond., fo., n. d. French trans. by P. Denis-Bordier, 4to, Paris. 50 Masses; 57 Vespers and Psalms; 22 Litanies; 22 Motets; 10 Oratorios; 29 Overtures; 18 Operas; Graduels, etc., mostly in MS. in the Imperial Library at Vienna.

The work by which Fux affected most good was No. 1, the translation of which existed as a text book for many generations. His music was produced wholesale, and is learned and dry; never being relieved by any glimpses of inspiration. He was the teacher of Wagenseil, Muffat, and numerous other musicians who have attained fame. His biography, containing list of works, was published by Köchel, under title of "Johann Josef Fux, Hofcompositor und Hofkapellmeister...," Vienna, 8vo, 1872, with portrait.

G.

GABLER (Christoph August). Russian comp., B. Muhltroff Voigtland, March 15, 1767. D. St. Petersburg, April 15, 1839. Wrote an oratorio, Pf. music, songs, etc.

GABRIEL (Mary Ann Virginia), MARCH. English comp., B. Banstead, Surrey, Feb. 7, 1825. S. under Pixis, Döhler, Thalberg, and Molique. Married to George E. March, Nov., 1874. D. London, August 7, 1877 (from effects of carriage accident).

WORKS.—*Cantatas:* Evangeline (Longfellow); Dreamland; Graziella. *Operettas:* Widows Bewitched; Grass Widows; Shepherd of Cornouailles; Who's the Heir; A Rainy Day. *Songs:* A farewell; Ariel; At her wheel the maiden sitting; Across the sea; Alone; At rest; A dead past; A fisher's wife; Alone in the twilight; A mother's song; Arden towers; Asleep; A song in the heather; At my feet; At the window; Beryl; Beside the sea; Brighter hours; Bye and bye; Change upon change; Chattering; Calling the roll; Corra Linn; Dawn; Dawn of Springtide; Day is dying; Dream, baby, dream; Echo; Eight fishers of Calais; Emerald; Fisherman's Widow; Golden wedding day; Happy days; His work is done; He will not come; Hopeless; In the gloaming; Lady Moon; Lost love; Little blossom; Little flowers; Light in the window; Lady of Kienast Tower; Mountain echo; My love; Nightfall at sea; Only at home; Oh! spare my boy at sea; Only; The Opal ring; Pearl; The Prodigal son; Prisoner and the linnet; Ruby; Remembered; Sweet seventeen; Shadow light; Somebody's darling; Sacred vows; Servian ballad; Skipper and his boy; The Surprise; Three roses; Tender and true; The ring; Under the palm; Wake my beloved; Work; Weep not for me; When the pale moon; Weary; When sparrows build. Partsongs, Pianoforte pieces, etc.

Some of the above-named were received with much popular favour, though only of a temporary nature.

GABRIELI (Andrea). Italian comp., B. Venice, 1510. S. under Willaert. Chor. in Doge's Chapel, Venice. Org. of S. Mark's. D. Venice, 1586.

Wrote Missarum, 1570; Madrigali, 1572, 1575, etc.; Psalmi Davidici, 1583; songs, organ music, etc. He was one of the greatest of the early Venetian school.

GABRIELI (Giovanni). Italian comp, and org., B. Venice, 1557, nephew of the above. S. under A. Gabrieli. Org. S. Mark's, Venice, 1585. D. 1613. Comp. church music, madrigals, etc.

GABRIELLI (Catterina). Italian soprano vocalist, B. Rome, Nov., 1730. S. under Porpora. *Début* in opera by Galuppi, 1747. Sang throughout Italy. Appeared in Russia; London, 1775-6, etc. D Rome, April, 1796.

GABRIELSKI (Johann Wilhelm). German flute-player and comp., B. Berlin, May 27, 1791. Chamber musician to King of Prussia. D. Berlin, 1878.

GABUSSI (Vincenzo). Italian comp., B. Bologna, 1800 [1804]. S. unde, Mattei. Resided in London as teacher, 1825-1840. Returned to Bolognar 1840. D. London, Sept. 12, 1846.

WORKS.—*Operas:* I Furbi al cimento, 1825; Ernani, 1834; Clemenza di Valois, 1841; Songs, part-songs; Work on singing, etc.

GADE (Niels Wilhelm). Danish comp. and cond., B. Copenhagen, Feb. 22, 1817. Violinist in Royal orch., Copenhagen. Introduced to Mendelssohn, 1843. Travelled in Italy, 1843-44. Cond. Gewandhaus concerts, Leipzig, 1844. Sub.-cond., do., 1845-46. Chief do, 1846-48. Org. at Copenhagen, 1848. Court musician and Prof. of music, do., 1861. Visited England, 1876. Visited Birmingham, 1882.

WORKS.—Op. 1. Ossian, overture for orch., 1841; op. 2. Frühlingsblumen, for Pf.; op. 3 Sange af Agnete og Havemanden (Andersen); op. 4. Nordiske Tonebilleder, fantasia for Pf. duet; op. 5. First symphony in C min.; op. 6. Sonata for Pf. and vn., in A; op. 7. Im Hochlande, overture for orch., in D; op. 8. Quintet for 2 vns., 2 tenors, and 'cello, in E min.; op. 9. 9 Lieder im Volkston für 2 soprane und Pf.; op. 10. Second symphony for orch., in E; op. 11. Six songs for 4 male voices; op. 12. Comala, dramatic poem for solo voices, chorus, and orch. (Ossian); op. 13. Five part-songs for S. A. T. B.; op. 14. Third overture for orch., in C; op. 15. Third symphony for orch., in A min.; op. 17. Octet for 4 vns., 2 violas, and 2 'cellos; op. 18. Three Clavierstücke for Pf.; op. 19. Aquarellen for Pf., 2 books; op. 20. Fourth symphony in B flat; op. 21. Second sonata for Pf. and vn.; op. 22. Three Tonstücke for organ; op. 23. Frühlings Phantasie Concertstücke, for 4 solo voice, orch., and Pf.; op. 25. Fifth symphony for orch., in D min.; op. 27. Arabeske für Pf.; op. 28. Sonata for Pf., in E. min.; op. 30. Erl-königs Tochter (Erl King's Daughter), cantata for solo voices, chorus, and orch; op. 31. Volkstänze, Phantasiestücke für Pf.; op. 33. Five lieder for male chorus; op. 34. Idyllen for Pf.; op. 35. Fruhlings-Botschaft Concertstücke for chorus and orch.; op. 36. Der Kinder Christ abend albumblatter; op. 37. Hamlet—concert overture for orch.; op. 38. Five songs for male chorus; op. 39. Michael Angelo—overture for orch.; op. 40. Die Heilige Nacht Concertstücke for vlto solo, chorus, and orch.; op. 41. Four Fantasias for Pf.; op. 42. Trio for Pf., an., and 'cello, in F; op. 43. Zion, cantata, Birmingham, 1876; op. 45. Seventh symphony for orch., in F; Spring's Message, cantata; op. 47. Symphony in B minor; op. 48. Kalanus, dramatic poem for solo voices, chorus, and orch.; op. 49. The Crusaders, cantata, Birmingham, 1876; op. 50. Die Kreuzfahrer, dramatic poem by C. Andersen, for soli, chorus, and orch.; op. 53. Novelletten for orch.; op. 55. Sommertag auf dem Lande; op. 56. Concerto for vn. and orch.; op. 59. Concerto for vn. and orch.; op. 60. Psyche, cantata by Lobedanz, Birmingham, 1882.

His other works consist of numerous Danish songs, Pf. compositions, etc.

Gade is the first Danish composer who has attained anything like universal fame. Of his works, the best known in Britain are "The Crusaders," "The Erl King's Daughter," and "Zion," all of which have been performed many times with success. In the second of those works he uses the Danish folk-song as a groundwork with happy effect, and secures a local colouring, impossible under any other conditions. "The Crusaders" is much more cosmopolitan in character, but is of great beauty as a work of art, and commands, at least, the respect and admiration of the English. Of his other works, op. 1, 7, and the symphonies are best known to British audiences, the pianoforte works following. The songs and minor works are of a more confined interest, but are worthy the attention of the musical student and professor.

Gade greatly resembles Mendelssohn in the universality of his musical powers, though, like him, he has never produced a great opera. As a conductor, his abilities procured him for a time the post once so efficiently filled by Mendelssohn. In 1876 he was voted a life-pension by the Danish Government.

GADSBY (Henry Robert). English comp. and pianist, B. Hackney, London, Dec. 15, 1842. Chor., St. Paul's Cath., 1849-58. Principally self-taught in music. Org. of St. Peter's, Brockley, Surrey, till 1884. Prof. at Guildhall School of Music. Succeeded J. Hullah as Prof. of Harmony, Queen's Coll., London, 1884.

WORKS.—Alice Brand, cantata, 1870; The Lord of the Isles, cantata, by Frank Murray, from Scott, 1880; Festival Service for 8 voices in D; Service in C, 1872; The 130th Psalm. Music to "Alcestis," 1876. Columbus, cantata for male voices (1881), pub. 1883. *Overtures:* Andromeda, 1873; The Golden Legend; The Witches' Frolic. Symphonies for orch. in A, C, and D. String quartet, 1875; Andante and rondo for Pf. and flute; Magnificat and Nunc dimittis in D; Te Deum in E flat; Benedicite in chant form. *Anthems:* He is risen; Blessed be the name of the Lord; Not unto us, O Lord; O Lord, our Governour; Ponder my words; Rejoice greatly; Sing, O daughter of Zion; The Lord is King; I will lay me down in peace. *Part-Songs:* The soldier's song; The sea is calm; Summer winds. Supplemental Book of Exercises for the use of those learning to sing at sight, Lond., n. d.; Harmony, a Treatise, including the Chords of the Eleventh and Thirteenth, and Harmonisation of Given Melodies, Lond., 1884.

Gadsby is one of the foremost among the younger school of living British composers. His works are broad in design and careful in execution. "The Lord of the Isles" is his most ambitious and best work. He excels, however, in music for the church, his anthems being good examples of the modern English school.

GAERTNER (Carl). German violinist and comp., B. 1830. Teacher in Boston since 1852. He is well known in the U. S., and has composed instrumental music, songs, etc.

GAFURIUS (Franchinus), GAFORI. Italian writer and theorist. B. Lodi, Jan. 14, 1451. Originally intended for the priesthood. Resided successively at Verona, Genoa, Naples, Otranto, and Lodi. D. Milan, June 24, 1522 [1520].

WORKS.—Theoricum Opus Musicæ Disciplinæ, Naples, 8vo, 1480; Practica Musicæ utriusque Cantus, Milan. fo., 1496; Angelicum ac Divinum Opus Musicæ Materna Lingua Scrip., 1508; De Harmonica Musicor. Instrumentorum, 1518.

One of the greatest of the early theorists. His works, apart from being specimens of early printing, are in a bibliographical sense extremely valuable, as well as very scarce.

GAGE (Rev. William L.). See BIBLIOGRAPHY.

GAIL (Edme Sophie), GARRE. French soprano vocalist, B. Paris, Aug., 1775. D. Paris, July 24, 1819. Appeared in London, etc. Comp. a few songs, etc.

GALILEI (Vincenzo). Italian comp., B. 1535, was associated with Bardi and Caccini, in establishing the opera. His son GALILEO, the great philosopher, was also a musician, having written a tract on temperament.

GALIN-PARIS-CHEVÉ. See CHEVÉ.

GALITZEN (Prince George). Russian comp., B. St. Petersburg, 1823. Assassinated, 1872. Wrote Pf. and other music.

GALLAY (Jacques Francois). French horn-player, teacher, and comp., B. Perpignan, Dec. 8, 1795. S. Paris Cons. Prof. of horn do. D. Paris, Oct. 1864. Comp. studies, exercises, and nocturnes for horn, and concertos for horn and orch.

GALLENBERG (Wenzel Robert, Count von). Austrian comp., B. Vienna, Dec. 1783. D. Rome, Mar. 13, 1839.

Composed fantasias, rhapsodies, sonatas, etc., for Pf.; songs, and other works.

GALLI (Filippo). Italian tenor vocalist, B. Rome, 1783. *Début,* 1804. Appeared in Paris, 1821; London, 1827; Spain, 1830. D. Paris, June 3, 1853.

GALLI (Signora). Italian vocalist of 18th century. Appeared in London about 1743. Sang principally in Handel's works. D. 1804.

GALLIARD (Johann Ernst). German comp. and org., B. Zell, Hanover, 1687. S. under Farinelli and Steffani. Oboeist to Prince George of Denmark, in England, 1706. Org. at Somerset House. D. London, 1749.

WORKS.—*Music to Plays, etc.:* Calypso and Telemachus, 1712; Julius Cæsar, 1745; Pan and Syrinx, 1717; Jupiter and Europa, 1723; The Necromancer, 1723; Apollo and Daphne, 1726; The Royal Chace, 1736; Morning Hymn of Adam and Eve (Milton), 1728; republished, Lond., 1818. Cantatas, various. Music for flute, 'cello, etc. Observations on the Florid Song, or Sentiments of the Ancient and Modern Singer, 1742. "His music is now forgotten."—*Hogarth*, 1838. A fact beyond question at the present date.

GALLUS. See HANDL.

GALUPPI (Baldassare). Italian comp., B. Island of Burano, near Venice, Oct. 18, 1706. S. under his father and Lotti. Went to Venice, 1726. Chapmaster of St. Mark's, 1762. Resided for a time in Russia. Returned to Venice, 1768. D. Venice, Jan. 3, 1785.

WORKS.—*Operas:* Gli amici rivali, 1729; Dorinda, 1730; Argenide, 1735; Alvilda, 1740; Gustavo I., 1741; Berenice, 1744; Forze d'amore, 1746; Arminio, 1749; La Mascherata, 1752; Calamità de' Cuori, 1755; La Diavolessa, 1756; Sesostri, 1760; Ipermestra, 1762. Church music; Cantatas. Harpsichord music, etc.

Galuppi possessed for the period in which he flourished, a considerable degree of dramatic force. His works are long since forgotten, but the graceful nature of his melodies must assuredly secure for them at least favourable mention in history.

GAMBLE (John). English violinist and comp. of 17th century. S. under A. Beyland. Violinist in private band of Charles II., etc. He composed "Ayres and Dialogues," 1657. "Ayres and Dialogues for one, two, and three voyces," 1659.

GANDOLFI Riccardo). Italian comp., B. Voghera, 1839. S. under Conti. Comp. operas, symphonies, cantatas, etc.

GANDSEY (John). Irish piper. B. 1768. D. 1857.

GÄNSBACHER (Johann Baptist). German comp. and cond., B. Sterzing, Tyrol, May 8, 1778. D. Vienna, July 13, 1844. Comp. church music, Pf. music, songs, etc.

Is chiefly noted as an intimate friend of Weber, who styled him his "dear friend and brother," and addressed to him a large portion of his correspondence. In a letter dated April 21, 1823, Weber speaks of a work by Gänsbacher as being "flowing, melodious, clear, novel in many passages, and rich and profound in harmony."

GANZ (Leopold). German violinist and comp., B. Mayence, 1806. S. under Spohr. Played in principal towns of Germany, etc.

GANZ (Moritz). German comp. and 'cellist, B. Mayence, Sept. 13, 1806. S. under Adolf Ganz. Appeared in London, 1837. D. Berlin, Jan. 22, 1868.

Wrote concertos for 'cello, lieder, and a host of Pf. works, the titles of which wil be found in the current catalogues of English and foreign publishers.

GANZ (Wilhelm). German comp. and pianist, B. Mayence, Nov. 6, 1833. S. under C. Eckert and Anschütz. Came to England, 1848. Violinist, New Philharmonic Concerts, 1852. Married, 1859. Org. Grand Lodge of England (Freemasons), 1871. Grand org. of Knights Templars, 1873. Decorated with order of the Crown (Germany). Grand org. of Mark Masons, 1881. Cond. New Philharmonic Concerts.

WORKS.—Elementary Exercises in the Art of Staccato and Octave Playing, specially written for the use of "Bohrer's" Automatic Piano Hand Guide, 2 books. *Pianoforte Music:* Tyrolienne, op. 1; Allons vite! La Vivacite; Qui vive, a galop; Souviens-toi; Vision du passé. Nocturnes, fantasias, melodies, etc. *Songs:* A damsel fair was singing; Forget-me-not; I seek for thee in every flower; My mother's song; Since yesterday; Sing, birdie, sing; The murmuring sea; The nightingale's trill; When we went a gleaning; Dear bird of Winter; Sing sweet bird; The Fisherman's wife, etc.

Herr Ganz introduced at his series of concerts Berlioz's "Harold in Italy," "Symphonie Fantastique," and "Romeo;" Gluck's "Orfeo," etc.; and brought out the celebrated performers Mme. Essipoff, M. Saint-Saëns, Herr E. Loewenberg, Mme. S. Menter, and M. de Pachmann; also Mr. Herbert Reeves, the tenor vocalist.

GARAT (Pierre Jean). French vocalist, B. Ustaritz, April 25, 1764. S. under Lamberti and F. Beck. Sang in opera and at concerts. Prof. of singing, Paris Cons. D. Paris, March 1, 1823.

GARAUDÉ (Alexis de). French comp. and teacher, B. Nancy, March 21, 1779. Prof. of solfeggi, Paris Cons., 1816. D. Paris, March 23, 1852. Wrote an opera; "Methode de chant," op. 25, 1809; etc.

GARCIA (Manuel Del Popolo-Vicente). Spanish comp. and teacher, B. Seville, Jan. 22, 1775. Chor. Seville cath. *Début* as vocalist, Paris, 1808. Appeared in London, 1817-25. Visited America, and introduced Italian opera there, 1826. Visited Mexico, 1827. Teacher in Paris. D. Paris, June 2, 1832.

WORKS.—*Operas:* El Preso; El Posadero; El Criado fingido; El Hablador, etc., in all 17 in Spanish; 19 Italian operas; 7 French operas. Vocal exercises, etc.

Much of the best qualities of the modern school of vocalists depends on the joint teaching of Manuel Garcia and his son. He undoubtedly laid the foundation of the school from which sprang Grisi, Sontag, and Alboni; and Malibran, whose tuition was entirely directed by himself, is, with Nourrit and Viardot, the proof of his skill in training voices of different kinds.

GARCIA (Manuel). Spanish vocal teacher, B. Madrid, March 17, 1805, son of the preceding. S. under his father and Fétis. Accompanied his father to America, 1826. Prof. of singing, Paris Cons, 1847. Prof. of singing, R.A.M., London, 1850.

Garcia was one of the first to conduct vocal training on correct scientific principles. His system was based on a thorough knowledge of the physiology of the voice, and the laws affecting natural and artificial voice production. It will be sufficient to name, among the multitude of good singers whom he has trained, Catherine Hayes and Jenny Lind, both of whom he was instrumental in forwarding. His labours at the R. A. M. have been of the most valuable character for English vocal art, and his presence in it during 30 years has placed it, in this special department, on a level with the greatest continental conservatories. Beyond some books of vocal exercises, he has not published important works.

GARCIA (Marie). See MALIBRAN.

GARCIA (Pauline). See VIARDOT.

GARDINER (William). English writer, B. Leicester, March 15, 1770. Travelled much on the Continent. D. Leicester, Nov. 16, 1853.

WORKS.--Sacred Melodies, from Haydn, Mozart, and Beethoven, 6 vols., Lond., n. d. Judah, an oratorio, adapted from the works of Haydn, Mozart, and Beethoven. Pope's "Universal Prayer" set to music by Haydn, Mozart, and Beethoven. The Music of Nature; or, An attempt to prove that what is Passionate and Pleasing in the art of Singing, Speaking, and Performing upon Musical Instruments, is derived from the Sounds of the Animated World....Lond., 8vo, 1832 American reprint, Ditson, Boston, n. d. Music and Friends; or, Pleasant Recollections of a Dillettante. Lond., 3 vols., 8vo, 1838-1853. Sights in Italy; with some Account of the Present State of Music and the Sister Arts in that Country. Lond., 8vo, 1847.

Gardiner composed some songs under the pen name of W. G. Leicester. He is chiefly to be remembered as the author of "The Music of Nature," a work which contains much useful information and curious and occasionally eccentric speculations.

GARDNER (Charles). English comp. and pianist, B. Greenwich, April 1, 1836. S. under Oliver May, M'Murdie, Pauer, and G. A. Macfarren. Has comp. music for Pf., chamber music, and some vocal music of high merit.

GARDONI (Enrico). Italian tenor vocalist, B. Parma, 1821. D. April, 1882.

GARRETT (George Mursell). English comp. and org., B. Winchester, June 8, 1834. Son of William Garrett, master of the choristers, Winchester cath. Chorister at New College Oxford. S. under S. S. Wesley. Assistant org. at Winchester, 1851-54. Org. of Madras cath., 1854-56; St. John's Coll., Cambridge, 1857; University, 1873. Mus. Bac., Cantab., 1857. Mus. Doc., Cantab., 1867. M.A., *propter merita*, 1878. University Lecturer in Harmony and Counterpoint, 1883. Examiner in Music for Univ. of Camb.; Camb. Local Exams.; Trinity Coll., Lond.; and for the Irish Intermediate Educ. Board.

WORKS.—The Shunammite, oratorio, 1882; The Deliverance of St. Peter, sacred cantata, (M.S.); The Triumph of Love, secular cantata. Church Services, in D, F, F (for parish choirs), E flat, and E; Evening Service, in B flat, written for Keble Coll., Oxford. *Anthems, etc.:* In humble faith and holy love; Just Judge of Heaven, Psalm xliii., contralto solo and chorus; Praise the Lord, O my soul; Prepare ye the way; The Lord is loving unto every man; They that put their trust in the Lord; It shall come to pass in the last days; Thus saith the Lord; Praise ye the Lord for his goodness. Chants, old and new, selected and arranged in order of daily use for one calendar month, with special Chants for the Venite and Proper Psalms, Lond., n. d. *Part-Songs:* O my luve's like a red, red rose; Good night! farewell; O sing again that simple song; Hope; May carol. *Songs:* Love will last; Palaces in air; Parted, etc.

The anthems and services are the works by which Dr. Garrett is known best. These works display much originality, and agreeably blend the proper dignity of sacred music with the richer colouring of dramatic music. His songs and partsongs are of their kind highly melodious, and as such are in common use. As an organist, Dr. Garrett is widely known.

GARTH (John). English musician who flourished in the first part of the 17th century. He published "The First Fifty Psalms, set to music by Benedetto Marcello," Lond., fo., 8 vols., 1757. He also wrote much instrumental music, among other works, "Six Sonatas for the Harpsichord, two Violins, and Violoncello," op. 2, 1768. Six Organ Voluntaries, op. 3. Thirty Collects set to Music, 4to, n. d.

GASKIN (J. J.). English writer, author of "Early History, etc., of Vocal Music." Lond., 8vo, 1860.

GASON (Adam F.). Irish writer, author of "A Short Treatise in Defence of Cathedral Worship," Dublin, 12mo, 1846.

GASPARD DE SALO. See SALO.

GASPARINI (Francesco). Italian comp., B. Lucca, 1665. S. under Corelli. Choir-master at Ospedale di Pietà, Venice. Member of the Accademia Filarmonia. Chapel-master of St. John, Lateran, 1725. D. Rome, April, 1727.

WORKS.—*Operas:* Tiberio, 1702; Imenei stabiliti dal caso, 1702; Amleto, 1705; Antioco, 1705; Statira, 1707; Engelberta, 1709; Tamerlano, 1710; Merope, 1711; La Ninfa Apollo, 1730. Cantatas, etc. L'Armonico prattico al cembalo, ovvero ugole, osservatzioni ed avertimenti per ben suonare il basso e accompagnare sopra il cembalo, spinetta ed organo, 1685.

The interest attaching to Gasparini's works is now purely historical, although at one time his truly elegant melodies were current all over Europe. The operas and cantatas were his most successful works. Of the former, 25 are in existence.

GASSIER (Edouard). French bass vocalist, B. 1822. S. Paris Cons. *Début* Opéra Comique, 1845. Sang in Spain, etc. D. Havanna, Dec. 18, 1871. His wife, JOSEFO FERNANDEZ, of Spanish birth, was B. Bilbao, 1821. D. Madrid, 1866. She was a soprano singer of considerable contemporary fame.

GASSMANN (Florian Leopold). Bohemian comp., B. Brüx, May 4, 1724. S. under P. Martini. Comp. to court of Joseph II. D. Vienna, Jan. 22, 1779.

WORKS.—*Operas*: Merope; Issiphile; Catone in Utica; L'Olimpiade, 1764; Il Mondo nella luna, 1765; Il Trionfo d' amore, 1767; L'Occellatori; Il Fifosofo innamorato, 1768; Un Pazzo ne fa cento, 1769; I Viaggiatori ridicoli, 1769; L' Amor Artigiano, 1770; Die Junge Græfin; Die Liebe unter den Handwerksleuten. Symphonies, quintets, quartets, and sonatas, for various instruments.

GASTOLDI (Giovanni Giacomo). Italian comp., B. Caravaggi, in middle of the 16th century [1532]. D. beginning of the 17th century [or 1598].

WORKS.—Canzoni a cinque voci, 1581; Canzonette a quattro voci, 1581; Madrigali a cinque voci, 1588; Psalmi ad Vesperas, 1588; Balletti...Antwerp, 1596; Concerti Musicali; Masses, etc.

GATAYES (Guillaume Pierre Antoine). French harpist and comp., B. Paris, Dec. 20, 1774. D. Paris, Oct., 1846. Wrote music for the guitar, harp, and Pf., and methods for the harp and guitar. His sons, JOSEPH LEON (1804-77) and FELIX, were also musicians; the former a writer, harpist, and comp.

GATES (Bernard). English org. and comp., B. 1681. One of children of Chap. Roy., 1702. Gent. Chap. Roy., 1708. Master of children of Chap. Royal, 1740. D. near Oxford, Nov. 15, 1773.

GATTY (Alfred Scott). English comp. and writer, B. Ecclesfield, York, April 25, 1847. Second son of the Rev. Alfred Gatty, D.D., vicar of Ecclesfield, sub-dean of York cath., etc. S. Marlborough and Christ's Coll., Camb. Married Eliz. E. Foster, of Newhall Grange, York, 1874. Rouge Dragon, Pursuivant of Arms, Herald's Coll., Lond., May, 1880.

WORKS.—Sandford and Merton's Christmas Party, operetta, by F. C. Burnard, 1880; Little Songs for Little Voices, 2 books, published originally in "Aunt Judy's Magazine." *Songs*: Above the spire; True till death; Child's good-night; Do not smile; Far in the mountain pass; Friend sorrow; Heartless; I prithee send me back my heart; Love never dies; Never again; O fair dove! O fond dove; Six plantation songs; O let the solid ground; Only a passing thought; Raindrops patter; Some future day; Tell him I love him yet; The lights far out at sea; The mill lad's love; The open window; When I remember; A little longer yet; Apart; Coming home; Clouds; Eleonora; He loup'd the wa'; Life's up-hill; Gallants of England; The old year; One morning, Oh! so early; On the rocks by Aberdeen; Rothesay Bay; Speedwell; Spread thy silver wings; Those merry walks together; Unspoken; Withered roses; and numerous comic songs. Pf. music, etc., under various *noms de plume*.

Mr. Gatty is a poet as well as a musician, and the verses accompanying his music are meritorious. It is chiefly as a song writer that Mr. Gatty is known.

GAUDRY (Richard Otto). Irish org. and comp., B. Dublin, 1800. Chor. chap. of Dublin Castle. Org. of St. Anne's, Dublin. D. Dublin, Aug., 1825. Comp. anthems, etc.

GAUL (Alfred Robert). English comp. and org., B. Norwich, 1837. Chor. and assistant org., Norwich cath., 1846-59. Org. of ch. of St. Augustine, Edgbaston, Birmingham. Mus. Bac., Cantab., 1862.

WORKS.—Hezekiah, oratorio, Birmingham, 1860 (MS.); The First Psalm, sacred cantata, Birmingham; The 96th Psalm, for solo voices and 8-part chorus; Ruth, sacred cantata, Birmingham, 1881; The Holy City, sacred cantata, Birmingham Festival, 1882; Passion Music, cantata; Offertory Sentences (Novello). *Anthems*: The Lord is my Shepherd; Hosanna to the Son of David. *Part-Songs, Glees, etc.*: The Shipwreck (prize glee); The death of Adonis; Silent land; Better land; The day is done; Ferry maiden; The potter; Footsteps of angels; I saw the moon clear rise; O for the swords of former times; The Erl King; Jack Frost; Song and melody, awake; The reaper and the flowers. *Songs*: The sea's love; Consider the lilies; Ruth; The corner song; The first grief; Faithful yet. Six vocal compositions for 1, 2, and 3 voices. Numerous Pf. pieces; hymns and miscellaneous pieces.

Mr. Gaul was until recently only favourably known as a composer of first-rate part-songs, and as an organist of great local fame; but the success of his cantata "Ruth" at once gave him a title to be regarded as one worthy of a good place among contemporary musicians. The cantata is a fresh and melodious work, well contrasted in its several parts, and possessing those agreeable characteristics which mark out such works for popularity. His part-songs are very well known to choirs throughout the United Kingdom, and his songs and Pf. works are deserving of considerable praise.

GAUNTLETT (Henry John). English org. and comp., B. Wellington, Shropshire, 1806. Son of the Rev. Henry Gauntlett. Org. at Olney, Bucks., 1815. Articled for a time to a solicitor, 1826. Org. of St. Olave's, Southwark, 1827-47. Admitted as a solicitor, 1831. Commenced his labours in connection with the establishment of the C organ, 1836, which latterly took the place of the F and G instruments. Org. Christ Ch., Newgate Street, 1836. Gave up practice of the law, 1842. Mus. Doc., Lambeth, 1843. Org. of Union Chapel, Islington; Ch. of St. Bartholomew the Great, Smithfield. D. Kensington, London, Feb. 21, 1876.

WORKS.—Hymnal for Matins and Evensong, 1844; The Church Hymnal and Tune Book, 1844-51; Cantus Melodici, 1845; The Comprehensive Tune Book, 1846-7; The Hallelujah, 1848-55; The Congregational Psalmist, 1851; Carlyle's Manual of Psalmody, 1861; Tunes, New and Old, 1868; Harland's Church Psalter and Hymnal, 1868; The Encyclopædia of the Chant; St. Mark's Tune Book; The Choral Use of the Book of Common Prayer, Lond., 1854. *Anthems*: I will go unto the altar of God; This is the day the Lord hath made; Thou wilt keep him in perfect peace, in E flat. Hymns and Christmas carols; One Hundred and Fifty-six Questions on the Art of Music-making and the Science of Music, Lond., 12mo, 1864. Songs, glees, organ-music, etc.

Mr. Gauntlett was in his lifetime recognised as one of the foremost organists and authorities on psalmody. His hymnals, psalms, etc., are compilations of the highest merit, the hand of the musician being always observable where too often we find the work of the officious reviser. His anthems are in frequent use, and his hymns are favourites. As an organist, he belonged to the old-fashioned school, but was not on that account reckoned inferior to many of his contemporaries.

GAUSSOIN (Auguste Louis). French writer and comp., B. Brussels, July 4, 1814. D. Brussels, Jan. 11, 1846. Historical works, overtures for orch., chamber music, etc.

GAUTIER (Jean Francois Eugene). French comp. and violinist, B. Vaugirard, Paris, Feb. 27, 1822. S. Paris Cons. under Halévy, Habeneck, etc. Prof. in Paris Cons., and Chap.-master Ch. of St. Eugene, Paris. D. Paris, April 3, 1878.

WORKS.—*Operas*: L'Anneau de Marie, 1845; Les Barricades, 1848; Murdock le Bandit, 1851; Flore et Zephire, 1852; Choisz le Roi, 1852; Le Mariage extravagant, 1857; Le Docteur Mirobolan, 1860; Joerisse, 1862. Sacred music, etc.

GAVEAUX (Pierre). French singer, actor, and comp., B. Beziers, 1761. D. Paris, Feb. 5, 1825. Wrote 35 operas, etc., and sang in operas by Cherubini, etc.

GAVINIÉS (Pierre). French violinist and comp., B. Bourdeaux, May 11, 1728 [Paris, 1726]. D. Paris, Sept. 9, 1800. Wrote concertos for violin and orch., in A, F, D, E, and D. 12 Sonatas for violin and bass, op. 1 and 3. Les Vingt-quatre matinées, for violin, 1794, etc.

Gaviniés is regarded as having laid the foundation of modern French violin-playing.

GAWLER (?). English org. and teacher, flourished in London in latter part of 18th century. He compiled "Harmonia Sacra, a Collection of Psalm Tunes, with interludes, and with a thorough-bass, forming a most complete work of sacred music, Lond., n. d. Dr. Watt's Divine Music. Lessons for the Harpsichord. Voluntaries, interludes, etc., for organ.

GAWTHORN (Nathaniel). English org. and writer. Compiler of "Harmoniæ Perfecta ; a Compleat Collection of Psalm Tunes in four parts, fitted to all the various measures now in use, taken from the most Eminent Masters, with an Introduction to Psalmody," Lond., 8vo, 1730. (By Ravenscroft, etc.)

GAY (John). English poet and librettist, B. Barnstaple, Devon, 1688. D. Dec. 11, 1732.

"The Beggar's Opera," 1727, and "Polly," its sequel, are the works by which Gay is known to musicians. "The Beggar's Opera" was the most popular work of its kind produced last century. Written partly to ridicule and supplant the Italian Opera, it proved for a time a formidable rival to the melodious but incongruous Southern productions of the foreign composers of the day. The music is taken from all British sources, and was arranged by Dr. Pepusch. The bad *moral* effects of this work were said by Sir John Fielding and other persons of contemporary fame to have been instrumental in increasing the number of criminal cases.

GAYARRÉ (Giuliano). Spanish tenor vocalist, B. in Spain, of Italian parents. Has appeared in London with much success, in operas of Verdi, Bellini, Wagner, Donizetti, Gounod. etc. He first appeared in Paris in Feb., 1884. He has been elsewhere received with favour.

GAZTAMBIDE (Joaquin). Spanish comp., B. Tudela, Feb. 17, 1822. S. Madrid Cons. Prof. Do. D. Madrid, March 20, 1870. Wrote operas, operettas, etc.

GEAR (George Frederick). English comp. and pianist, B. London, May 21, 1857. S. at the London Academy of Music under Dr. Wylde and John Francis Barnett. Gold and Silver Medallist ; Prize Scholar, and Associate.

WORKS.—Sonatas for Pf. Solo ; A String Quartet ; 2 Operettas, now being performed with much success. *Songs*: The Rose is dead ; When night is gathering round ; Sweet visions ; The day is done ; Beside the spring ; Under the trees ; She is far from the land ; A tiny floweret ; My lady sleeps ; In the peaceful night ; The white rose. Pf. pieces, etc. His father, HENRY HANDEL GEAR, B. London, Oct. 28, 1805, D. London, Oct. 16, 1884, was a tenor vocalist and comp. He wrote anthems and church services, songs, etc.

GEARY (E. M.) English writer, author of Observations on Pianoforte Playing, Lond., 1848. Musical Education, Lond., 12mo, 1851.

GEARY (Timothy). Irish comp., B. Dublin, 1783. D. 1806. Comp. glees, duets, and other vocal music. Known also as Thomas Augustine Geary.

GEBEL (Georg). German comp., B. Breslau, Oct. 15, 1709. Son of G. Gebel (1685-1749, comp. of org., Pf., and orch music.) S. under his father. D. Breslau, Sept. 24, 1753. Wrote operas, etc.

GEHOT (Joseph). English (?) writer, flourished in 18th century. Wrote A Treatise on the theory and practice of music, Lond., ob. fol., n. d. Complete instructions for every musical instrument, containing a treatise on practical music in general, Lond., fo., n. d.

GEHRING (Franz). German writer, B. Nordhausen, Dec. 7, 1838. D. Vienna, Jan. 4, 1884. Author of "Mozart," Great Musicians series, Lond., 8vo, 1883. Also articles in Grove's Dictionary of Music and Musicians.

GEIB (George). American pianist and writer, teacher in New York, B. New York, 1780. D. [?] Author of a Patent Analytical and Grammatical system of teaching the science of the composition of music in all its branches, and the practice of the Pianoforte, New York, fo., 1819.

GEIB (William), Mus. Doc. American writer, author of a work entitled, Tuning the Pianoforte (Ditson, Boston).

GEIJER (Erik Gustav). Swedish writer and comp., B. Wermland, Jan. 12, 1783. D. Upsala, April 22, 1847. A collector and vocal composer, as well as an historian.

GEIKIE (James Stewart). Scottish comp. and writer, B. 1811. For a number of years musical representative of the *Scotsman*. Cond. of the Edinburgh Sacred Harmonic Association, and other societies of a kindred nature at Newington. D. Ormiston, Haddington, Aug. 14, 1883. He comp. a number of secular vocal pieces (glees and songs) of a moderate and uniform degree of merit, but his psalms and other sacred music will enjoy a more lasting popularity. He edited an edition of R. A. Smith's "Sacred Harmony."

GEISSLER (Carl). German org. and comp., B. Mulda, April 28, 1802. Org. and music director at Zschopau.

WORKS.—Neueste Orgelstücke verschiedenen charakters mit Rücksicht auf Fortbildung im Orgelspiel, sowie zum Gebrauch beim öffentlichen Gottesdienste, op. 62. Lieder, op. 12, 16, 17. Organ music, dance music, etc.

GELINEK (Josef, Abbé). Bohemian comp. and pianist, B. Selez, Dec. 3, 1757. D. Vienna, April 13, 1825. Wrote variations, sonatas, rondos, etc. for Pf.

GEMINIANI (Francesco). Italian comp. and violinist, B. Lucca, 1680. S. under Corelli, Lunati, and Scarlatti. Came to England, 1714. Visited Paris, 1755. Settled in London, 1755. D. Dublin, Sept. 17, 1762.

WORKS.—Op. 1. Twelve solos for violin, Lond., 1716; op. 2. Six concertos in 7 parts for vn., Lond., 1755; op. 4. Twelve solos for vn., Lond., 1739; op. 5. Six solos for 'cello; op. 6. Six concertos for vn., Lond., 1741; op. 7. Six do, in 8 parts; Twelve sonatas for vn., op. 11, 1758; Twelve trios for vns. and 'cello. Lessons for the Harpsichord. Art of Playing the Violin, Lond., 1740. A Treatise of good taste in the art of musick, Lond., fo., 1749. Rules for playing in a true taste on the violin, german flute, violoncello, harpsichord; particularly the thoroughbass, exemplified in a variety of compositions, Lond., fo., n. d. The Art of Accompaniment; or a new and well-digested Method to learn to Perform the Thoroughbass on the Harpsichord, Lond., fo., n. d. Guida Armonica o dizionario armonico; being a sure guide to harmony and modulation, Lond., fo., 1742. Treatise on Memory, Lond. (? date). Art of playing the Guitar, etc. The Enchanted Forest, dramatic piece for orch., etc.

"His music . . is original, and full of new and bold modulations and combinations of harmony; while his melodies are not only very elegant, but often extremely pathetic. His performance appears, from every account of it, to have been remarkable for its delicacy, grace, and expression."—*Hogarth*. He was an enthusiastic amateur painter, or picture dealer; expensive in his tastes; and never absolutely free from the small misfortunes common to the improvident.

GEMUENDER (Georg). German violin-maker, B. Ingelfingeu, Wurtemburg. Resided in London, 1851. Now living in New York. Noted for his imitations of the old Italian violins, and for having discovered several of the lost processes of varnish-making, etc.

GENÉE (Richard). German comp., B. Dantzig, Feb. 7, 1824. Has written —*Operas:* Rosita, 1864; Am Runenstau; An der Wien; Der Seecadet, 1877, which has been produced in England under the title of the "Naval Cadets;" "Nanon," Berlin, 1883.

GENERALI (Pietro). Italian comp., B. Masserano, Piedmont, Oct. 4, 1783. S. under Durante. D. Novara, Nov. 3, 1832.

WORKS.—*Operas:* Gli Amanti, 1800; Il Duca Nottolone, 1801; La Pamela Nubile, 1802; La Calzolaja, 1802; Don Chisciotto, 1805; Le Lagrime d'una Vedova, 1808; Lo Sposo in contrasto; Ero e Leandro, 1810; Gaulo ad Ojtono, 1812; Isabella, 1813; Eginardo e Lisbetta, 1813; Le Beneficenza, etc.

GENET (Eleazar). French comp. of 15th and 16th centuries, B. Carpentras, Vaucluse, second part of 15th century. D. early in 16th century [1536]. Wrote masses, hymns, etc.

GENTILI (Raffaele). Italian operatic comp., B. Rome, 1837. D. 1867. Comp. Pf. music, songs, etc.

GEORGE (Miss). See OLDMIXON (Lady).

GÉRALDY (Jean Antoine Just). French vocalist and comp., B. Frankfort-on-Mane, 1808. D. Paris, May 27, 1869. Appeared in operas by Rossini, and wrote songs, operettas, etc.

GERBER (Ernst Ludwig). German writer, B. Sondershausen, Sept. 29, 1746. S. Leipzig University, 1765. D. Sondershausen, June 30, 1819.

WORKS.--Historisch-Biographisches Lexikon der Tonkünstler, welches Nachrichten von dem Leben und Werken musikalischer Schriftsteller berühmter Componisten, Sænger, Meister auf Instrumenten, Dilettanten, orgel und Instrumentenmacher enthalt, Leipzig, 2 vols., 8vo, 1790-92. Second edition, entitled Neues Historisch-biographisches Lexikon der Tonkünstler..., Leipzig, 4 vols., 8vo, 1812.

Gerber's work was accounted the authority previous to the appearance of the more modern works. He spent most of his time travelling in Europe in search of materials.

GERKE (August). German violinist and comp., B. 1790. Music-director at Cassel. D. (?)

WORKS.—Op. 1. Three duets for 2 vns. ; op. 2. Three string trios ; op. 4. Overture for orch. ; op. 8. String trio ; op. 13. Overture, orch. Pf. music, etc.

GERKE (Otto). German violinist and comp., B. Lüneburg, July 13, 1807. S. under Spohr. Comp. concertos, quartets, pot-pourris, etc. D. Paderborn, June, 1878.

GERNSHEIM (Friedrich). German comp. and cond., B. Worms, July 17, 1839. S. under Liebe, Pauer, Hauff, Moscheles, Hauptmann, Rietz and Richter, 1852-5. Resided for a time at Paris, as teacher. Prof. at Cologne Cons. Cond. at Rotterdam.

WORKS.—Six lieder for voice and Pf., op. 3 ; Quartet for Pf., vn., viola and 'cello, op. 6 ; Wachterlied aus der Neujahrsnacht des Jahre 1200, chorus and orch., op. 7 ; Introduction and Courante for Pf., op. 8 ; String quartet, op. 9 ; Salue Regina, op. 11 ; Sonata, Pf., and 'cello, op. 12 ; Sonata for Pf. and vn., op. 12a ; Overture for orch., op. 13; Romanze for Pf., op. 15 ; Concerto for Pf. and orch., op. 16 ; Variations for Pf., op. 18 ; "Nordische Sommernacht," for chorus and orch., op. 21 ; First symphony for orch., op. 22 ; Second Romanze for Pf., op. 23 ; Quartet for strings, op. 25 ; Fantasia for Pf., op. 27 ; Quartet for strings, op. 31 ; Four lieder, voice and Pf., op. 34 ; Quintet for Pf. and strings, in D minor, op. 35 ; Stimmungsbilder, four Pf. pieces, op. 36 ; Second trio for Pf., vn. and 'cello, in B, op. 37 ; Introduction and allegro appassionato for Pf. and vn., op. 38 ; Lied and Gavotte for Pf., op. 39 ; Symphony in E flat, op. 46. Songs, etc.

GERSTER (Etelka). Hungarian soprano vocalist, B. Kaschau, June 16, 1855 (or 1857). S. at Vienna Cons. under Madame Marchesi, 1873. Début at Vienna as Gilda in "Rigoletto," 1876. Appeared in Berlin and St. Petersburg, 1877. Appeared at H. M. Theatre, London, in "La Sonnambula," June 23, 1877. Married to Dr. Gardini. Appeared in New York, 1882-3, and has since appeared with much success in Europe. She is one of the most successful of modern dramatic sopranos, and has been everywhere received with enthusiasm.

GESUALDA (Carlo, Prince of Venosa). Italian musician, B. about end of 16th century [1570]. Nephew of Cardinal Alfonso Gesualdo, Archbishop of Naples. S. under P. Nenna. D. Jan., 1657.

This prince is noticed here because of an erroneous impression which has attained currency, viz., that he imitated a style of music said to have been invented by James I. of Scotland, and so laying the foundation of the Italian school of music. No proof of such a style exists. Those wishing to read on the subject are referred to Burney, Tytler (in Arnott's History of Edinburgh), Dauney, Graham, etc.

His madrigals are not of much merit, nor do his claims apart from the above matter, call for more notice.

GETZE (J. A.). American org. and writer, author of "School for the Parlor Organ, Melodeon, and Harmonium," Boston, n. d. "Young Organist, a complete instructor for the organ," n. d. Songs, dance music, etc.

GEVAËRT (Francois Auguste). Belgian comp., B. Huysse, July 31, 1828. S. Ghent Cons., 1841. Org. of Ch. of Jesuits, Ghent. Gained first prize at Brussels for comp., 1846. Travelled in France, Spain, Italy, and Germany. Prof. of singing at Academy of Music, Paris, 1867. Director of Brussels Cons., 1871. Member of the Academy des Beaux Arts, 1873.

WORKS.—*Operas:* Hugues de Somerghem, 1848; La Comédie à la ville, 1848. Georgette, 1852; Le Billet de Marguerite, 1854; La Lavandière de Santarem, 1855; Quentin Durward, 1858; Le Château Tempête, 1860; Le Capitaine Henriot, 1864; Les Deux Amours, 1861; Le Diable du Moulin; Pertinax, 1884. Instrumental music; Theoretical works; Het volk van Gent, cantata, 1881.

One of the leading Belgian composers and teachers. Being made the successor of Fétis at Brussels Conservatory, proved conclusively Gavaërt's fitness for responsible duties. None of his works are known in England, save a few songs and his theoretical works.

GEYER (Flodoard). German comp. and writer, B. Berlin, March, 1811. D. Berlin, April 29, 1872.

GHYS (Joseph). Belgian violinist and comp., B. Ghent, 1801. Appeared successively in London, Paris, Lyons, Berlin, Leipzig, etc. D. St. Petersburg, 1848. Wrote concertos, fantasias, solos, etc., for violin. He was a most excellent performer.

GIARDINI (Felice de). Italian comp. and violinist, B. Turin, 1716. Chor. in Milan Cath. S. under Paladini. S. at Turin under Somis. Violinist in opera band, Rome. Do. at the S. Carlo theatre, Naples. Travelled in Germany. Appeared in London, 1750. Leader of the Italian opera, 1752-56-65. Manager of do. for a time, but resigned, having suffered much pecuniary loss. Leader of Pantheon Concerts, 1774-80. Returned to Italy, 1784. Appeared again in England, 1790. Attempted to establish an Italian burletta in London, and failed. Went with company to Russia, 1793. D. Moscow, Dec. 17, 1796.

WORKS.—*Operas:* Enea e Lavinia, London, 1746; L'Amour au Village, 1747; Rosmita, London, 1757; Cleonice, London, 1764; Siro, 1764. Op. 1. Six Solos for violin; op. 2. Six Duos for 2 violins; op. 3. Six Sonatas for harpsichord and violin; op. 4-5. Concertos for violin; op. 6. Six trios for 2 violins and 'cello; op. 7 8. Six Solos for violin (2 sets); op. 11. Six Quintets for harpsichord, 2 violins, viola, and 'cello; op. 13. Three Trios for violin, viola, and 'cello; op. 14. Six Duos for violin and 'cello; op. 15. Six Concertos for violin; op. 16, 19. Six Solos for violin (2 sets); op. 20. Six Trios for 2 violins and 'cello; op. 29. Six Quartets for strings. Ruth, oratorio, London, 1772; Italian songs and duets, catches, etc.

Giardini was the greatest violinist of his time, though as a composer he is now long since forgotten. His best works are his pieces for the violin, which, if excessively ornamented, are also fluent and melodious.

GIBBONS (Christopher). English org. and comp., B. 1615. Son of Orlando Gibbons. S. under Edward Gibbons at Exeter. Org. of Winchester cath., 1640-44. Served for time in Royalist army. Org. Chap. Roy., 1660. Private org. to Charles II., 1660. Org. Westminster Abbey, 1660. Mus. Doc., Oxon., July, 1664. D. Oct. 28, 1676.

A few works by this musician exist in MS., but it is as an organist that he was principally known.

GIBBONS (Rev. Edward). English org. and comp., B. [1570]. Mus. Bac., Cantab. Org. of Bristol Cath., 1592-1611. Org. of Coll. of priest-vicars, Exeter Cath., 1611-44. D. [1650].

Works in MS., anthems, etc.

GIBBONS (Ellis). English org. and comp., B. Cambridge, end of 16th century, brother of Edward. Org. of Salisbury Cath. D. [1650].

Composer of "Long live, fair Oriana," madrigal for 5 voices; "Round about her chariot," for 6 voices; both contained in the "Triumphs of Oriana."

GIBBONS (Orlando). English org. and comp., B. Cambridge, 1583. Brother of Edward and Ellis Gibbons. Gent. or org. of the Chap. Roy., Mar., 1604.

Mus. Bac., Cantab., 1606; Mus. Doc., Oxon., 1622. Org. Westminster Abbey, 1623. D. Canterbury, June 5, 1625.

WORKS.—Morning and Evening Service, in F; Te Deum and Jubilate, in D minor; Venite exultemus, in F; Magnificat, Nunc Dimittis, in D minor and in F; Te Deum and Benedictus, in F; First Preces, in F (Ouseley); Second, in G. *Anthems*: Hosanna; Lift up your heads; O clap your hands; Almighty and Everlasting; God is gone up (Boyce); O Lord, in Thy wrath; O Lord, in Thee; Why art thou so heavy? Blessed be the Lord; O Lord, increase my faith; Deliver us, O Lord; Behold, thou hast made; This is the record of John; Behold, I bring you; If ye be risen again (Ouseley); We praise Thee, O Father; Lord, grant grace; Glorious and powerful God; See, see, the Word is incarnate; Sing unto the Lord; Blessed are all they; Great Lord of Lords; O Thou, the Central Orb. Hymns. Fantasies of III. Parts...composed for viols; Lond., 4to, 1610. Reprinted, edited by E. F. Rimbault (Music. Antiq. Soc.), Lond., fo., 1843. Lessons in "Parthenia" (with Bull and Byrd), Lond., 1611. First set of Madrigals and Motets, for 5 voices, Lond., 4to, 1612. Reprinted, edited by Sir G. Smart (Mus. Ant. Soc.), Lond., fo., 1841. Fancies and Songs made at King James ye First's being in Scotland, Lond., n. d. Tunes for "Wither's Hymns" (Reprinted by the Spenser Society, 1881). Tunes in Leighton's "Teares," 1614. *Madrigal titles*: The silver swan; I weigh not fortune's frown; I tremble not; I feign not friendship; Dainty fine bird; Farewell all joys; Oh! dear heart; Ne'er let the sun; Trust not too much; O that the learned poets; Nay, let me weep; Yet if that age; I see ambition; Fair ladies that to love; What is our Life? etc. Galiards, Fantasias, Preludium, Pavans, etc.

Gibbons' compositions were in many respects superior to most of the musical productions of his time. They lack the freshness of the older school of Morley, Weelkes, etc., but compare favourably with any in point of learning. It is not as a composer of madrigals, however, that Gibbons' name will descend to posterity. His works for the church service will prove a much more lasting memorial to his genius. The sacred music of Gibbons is grand and dignified, but rather overburdened by a complicated and somewhat dry counterpoint, though in this respect only in keeping with the learned style of the times. His instrumental music has been transcribed for modern purposes by Herr E. Pauer, and is only remarkable for complication and difficulty. The most renowned of his pupils was Matthew Locke.

GIBSON (Edmund). English bishop and writer, B. Brampton, Westmorland, 1669. D. Bath, 1748. Wrote a number of antiquarian works and a "Method, or Course of Singing in Church; Direction to the Clergy of the Diocese of London, 1727; etc."

GIBSON (Rev. James, D.D.). Scottish divine and writer, Prof. in Free Church College, Glasgow. Author of "The Public Worship of God: its Authority and Modes, Hymns and Hymn Books," Glasgow, 8vo, 1869.

GIBSON (Louisa). English teacher and writer, B. London, 1833. Authoress of "A First Book on the Theory of Music, applied to the Pianoforte," Lond., n.d. (2 editions); Second and Third Books of same. Songs, etc.

GIBSON (Mrs. Patrick), *née* ISABELLA MARY SCOTT. Scottish vocalist and comp., B. Edinburgh, 1786. Married to Patrick Gibson, R.S.A. She at one time kept a Boarding School for Young Ladies, in Inverleith Row, Edinburgh, and was an associate of many distinguished men of her time. Distantly related to Sir Walter Scott. She was consulted much by R. A. Smith in the composition of his songs and duets, and some of her psalm tunes are in Dr. Andrew Thomson's "Sacred Harmony," 1820, and in vol. 6 of Steven's "Church Music," edited by Turnbull, 1833. Her song "Loch-na-gar" is contained in the 6th vol. of R. A. Smith's "Scottish Minstrel." Mrs. Gibson had much skill on the harp. D. Edinburgh, Nov. 28, 1838.

GIBSONE (Ignace). English comp. and pianist, B. London, of Scottish parentage [1826-7]. S. under Moscheles. Appeared in Brussels as pianist, 1845. Hon. Mem. of Brussels Société de Grand Harmonie, 1846. Played afterwards at Baden, Hombourg, Frankfort, Wiesbaden, Darmstadt, 1846.

Played with Ernst at Berlin, 1846. Returned to London, 1850; teacher and comp. there.

WORKS.—*Cantatas:* Wood Nymphs, for female voices; Elfin Knight. An Opera (MS.). Two Symphonies (MS.). Sonatas for vn. and Pf. *Pianoforte:* Polonaise; Beaux Jours; The Hunt; Chanson à boire; Visions of Night; Une nuit d'Eté; Une nuit d'Hiver; Chanson d'amour; L'alouette; La flèche, galop; Le Carillon de Bruges; Marche Monténégrin; Mercure; Nocturne dramatique; Tarantella; The Calender's dance; The singing apple; Antique gems reset; Ballade; Les Bavardes du Village; Napolitana; Marche aux Flambeaux; Six Studies for advanced performers; Marche Bresillienne; Evening Thoughts; Transcriptions, numerous. *Songs:* My lady sleeps; Her voice; O'er the bending rushes; The Man-o'-War's Man; The missing ship; They part no more; Sail on, O love, sail on; Ah! Chloris, pastoral; A thanksgiving; I am here; Sweet hour of eventide; The oak and the osier; Will you buy a moss rose? Duets, etc.

GICK (Thomas). English comp., B. Liverpool, 1837 Lay-clerk of York Minster, 1859. Stipendiary choirman in Christ Ch. and St. Patrick's Cath., Dublin, 1864. Mus. Bac., Dub., 1880. Mus. Doc., Dublin, 1882. Comp. anthems, "The Bard," cantata, 1882, etc.

GILBERT (Alfred). English pianist and comp., B. Salisbury, 1828. S. at R. A. M. Member of Philharmonic Soc., Royal Soc. of Musicians, etc. Mem. of the Academy of St. Cecilia, Rome, 1884. Cond. and comp. of considerable repute. Comp. "The Rival Roses," dramatic scene, 1883; Trios for Pf. and strings in B flat and A min.; Quintet in E flat. Author of "Technical Exercises for the Pianoforte," London, 1885.

GILBERT (Ernest Bennett). English comp. and vocal teacher, B. Salisbury, Oct. 22, 1833 [Mar. 15, 1835]. S. at R. A. M., 1847. S. at Leipzig Cons. under Moscheles, Hauptmann, Richter, Rietz, etc., 1852. Played with success on the French horn in England and abroad. Org. of St. George's, Isle of Man, 1853; St. Barnabas, do., 1854; St. Paul's, Newport, Mon., 1856; Par. ch., Abergavenny, 1857; St. Peter's par. ch., Walworth, 1861; St. George par. ch., Southwark, 1864; St. Matthew's, do., 1867. Vocal trainer in London. D. London, May 11, 1885.

WORKS.—*Operettas:* A Night in Fairyland, Surrey Theatre, 1861; Das Helldichein, Leipzig, 1851. Ramiro, dramatic cantata, 1879. Concert overture for orch., 1853. Overture, Merry Wives of Windsor, 1854. String Quartets, in E flat and C. Trio for Pf., violin, and 'cello, in F. Vocal Exercises for daily use, 2 books. School Harmony, Lond., n. d., 8 editions. Practical and Natural Method for the Pf., 2 books. Major and Minor Scales arranged for daily school practice. *Part-Songs:* Oak and Iron; I wandered by the brookside; Return of Spring; Orpheus with his lute, trio. *Songs:* Dearer is thy smile; A smile for every tear; The outcast; The lost maiden; Lullaby; Alice Adair; Footsteps in the snow; The ocean queen; Let me be near to thee; Birds' song; Sing me to sleep; The tramp; Haste to the forest; The blind boy; The fairy ring; Sweet summer morn; Fairy flower; The silver moon is shining; The slave girl's lament; Good night; Spring; Jessie of the lea; In yonder village; The bondman; The changeling; Ye elves so bright. *Pianoforte:* Souvenir di Cambria; Solitude, nocturne; Ariel; Scherzo, in E minor; La Gondoletta; Ballade, in A; Six classical ballads; Impromptu, in B flat; Polonaise, in E flat; Pastorale, in D min.; Nocturne, in B flat; Impromptu, in D min.; Witch's dance; Tarentella; Barcarolle; Crusaders' march; Funeral march; Bridal march; Pensées d'un solitaire; La nuit; Three sketches; Four characteristic pieces; Second set of mazurkas; Fingal, valse poétique; Two Nocturnes.

GILBERT (Walter Bond). English comp., org., and writer, B. Exeter, 1829. S. under Alfred Angel, Dr. Wesley, and Sir Henry Bishop. Org. at Topsham, 1835, and afterwards at Bideford, Tunbridge, Maidstone, London, and Boston. Mus. Bac., Oxon., 1854. Org. of Trinity Episcopal Chapel, New York, 1869. Since, teacher and comp. there.

WORKS.—*Oratorios:* The restoration of Israel; St. John, Maidstone, 1864. Hymnal and Canticles of the Protestant Episcopal Church, New York, 8vo, 1875 (with Rev. A. B. Goodrich, D.D.). The Psalter, or Psalms of David, etc., New

York, 1882. Church Services in C, E, and A flat. *Anthems*: Our conversation is in Heaven; Behold, He cometh with clouds; In that day shall this song be sung; There shall come forth a rod; It shall come to pass in the last days; Grant us Thy peace; Thou shalt show me the path of life; Walk in the spirit; Behold this child is set; If ye then be risen with Christ; O give thanks unto the Lord; He shall give His angels charge over thee; I will love Thee, O Lord; Glorious things of Thee are spoken; O Lord, how glorious are Thy works. Preludes and Fugues for the Organ, New York, 1880. " Maidstone," hymn, in " Hymns Ancient and Modern." Miscellaneous church and organ music. *Literary*: The Antiquities of Maidstone; Memorials of Maidstone Church; and other historical works.

Mr. Gilbert is the composer of some of the most chaste and refined church music produced in England within recent times. To say nothing of " Maidstone" (" Pleasant are Thy courts above "), a hymn almost universally known, he has produced anthems and services of a cultured cast, and scholarly organ music in abundance. A full cathedral service composed when Mr. Gilbert was only 17 years of age, has been in use in Exeter cathedral, and in St. George's Chapel Royal, since 1858; while many of his other works are in constant use. His collections evince care and taste, and are much used in America.

GILBERT (William Schwenck). English librettist and writer, B. London, Nov. 18, 1836. Bred to the Law. B.A., Lond. Clerk in Privy Council Office, 1857-62. Called to the Bar, 1864.

WORKS.—*Plays*: The Wicked World; Pygmalion and Galatea; Charity; The Princess; The Palace of Truth; Sweethearts; Dan'l Druce; Gretchen; Tom Cobb. *Operas and Operetta*s: Princess Toto (Clay); The Sorcerer; H. M. S. Pinafore; Pirates of Penzance; Patience; Iolanthe; Princess Ida; The Mikado. Ballads.

The series of operas above noted were all composed by Sir Arthur Sullivan, and most of them, but especially the earlier ones, enjoyed unexampled popularity. They are noticed more at length under the name of SULLIVAN.

GILCHRIST (William Wallace). American writer and comp., B. Jersey City, Jan. 8, 1846. Educated in Philadelphia. Comp. of several important choral works, and many songs, etc.

GILES (Nathaniel). English comp. and org., B. Worcester (shire), [1558]. Bac. Mus, Oxon., 1585. Doc. Mus., Oxon., 1625. Org. of St. George's Chap., Windsor, and master of choristers, do., 1595. Org. [1625], and master of children, Chap. Roy., 1597. D. Jan. 24, 1633.

"His services and anthems announce his learning and abilities, and, by the lovers and judges of church composition, are regarded as masterly productions,"— *Busby.*

GILKES (Samuel). English violin-maker, B. Morton Pinkney, Northamptonshire, 1787. Worked with Charles Harris and W. Forster. D. 1827.

He was famous for the fine finish of his instruments, and for good copies of Amati. His son WILLIAM (B. 1811, D. 1875), made double-basses, etc.

GILMORE (Patrick Sarsfield). Irish band-master and comp., B. nr. Dublin, Dec. 28, 1829. Joined military band, 1844. Went to Boston, U.S.A., 1849. Director of military bands in the department of Louisiana, 1863. Organized the National Peace Jubilee at Boston, June, 1869. Organized, and travelled in America and Europe, with large instrumental band, 1873-79.

WORKS.—History of the National Peace Jubilee and Great Musical Festival in Boston, 1869, 8vo, 1871. Diatonic and Chromatic Scales for the Cornet, etc. *Military Band Music*: Aquidneck; Bewitching Polka; Breakfast bell; Dinner bell; Emblem Schottische; Everlasting Polka; Good news from home; Grape vine; New England Guards; Norwich cadets; On the road to Salem, quickstep; Soldier's return march; Sons of Maine, quickstep; Sons of temperance, quickstep; Spirit of the North; Supper bell; Vila; Brass band music, various selections; also for Pf. *Songs*: Building castles in the air; Freedom on the old plantation; Good news from home; Laura haunts my fancy still; Let me dream of former years; Music is the only charm; Sad news from home; She gave me a rose; Sweet village home; Voice of a departing soul; What is home without a baby; When I saw sweet Nelly home.

GILMOUR (Robert). Scottish musician, compiled "The Psalm-Singer's Assistant," Paisley, 18mo, [1793.]

GILSON (Cornforth). English teacher and writer, chorister in Durham Cath., and latterly Master of Music in the Edinburgh city churches, 1756. He wrote "Lessons on the Practice of Singing, with an addition of the church tunes, in four parts, and a collection of Hymns, Canons, Airs, and Catches, for the improvement of beginners," Edin., 4to, 1759. "Twelve Songs for the Voice and Harpsichord," Edin., fo., 1769.

GIORNOVICHI. See JARNOWICK.

GIOSA (Nicola di). Italian comp., B. Bari, May 5, 1820. S. Naples Cons. Writer of operas, songs, etc. D. Bari, July 7, 1885.

GIOVANELLI (Ruggiero). Italian comp., B. nr. Rome, 1560. Chap.-master successively of the Ch. of St. Luigi; St. Apollinare; and St. Peter's. D. [?]

Wrote masses; 2 books of madrigals, 1594-99; motets; psalms. Villanella a 3 voci, Venice, 1588; Villanella, a 5 voci, Venice, 1608; etc.

GIRVAN (John). Scottish writer. Was precentor of Tron Kirk, Glasgow. Teacher in Glasgow. Published "A New Collection of Church Tunes," Glas. 1761. Author of "The Vocal Musician, Part I. The Grounds of Music," Edin., 8vo, 1763.

GIUGLINI (Antonio). Italian tenor vocalist, B. Fano, 1826. Appeared at H.M. Theatre, London, 1857. Sang with much success in provinces of England, in Scotland, etc. Sang in Europe, but was latterly insane. D. Pesaro, Oct. 12, 1865. He had a light tenor voice of much sweetness and range.

GIULIANI (Mauro). Italian guitarist and comp., B. Bologna, 1796. D. Vienna, 1820. Wrote a method for the guitar, and many pieces for the guitar, etc.

GIZZI (Domenico). Italian teacher, vocalist, and comp., B. Arpino, 1684. D. 1745.

GIZZIELLO (Gioacchino Conti detto), or CONTI. Italian soprano vocalist, B. Arpino, 1714. Appeared with much success in Europe. Named after Domenico Gizzi, whose pupil he was. D. Rome, 1761.

GLADSTONE (Francis Edward). English comp. and org., B. Oxford, Mar. 2, 1845. Articled pupil to Dr. S. S. Wesley, Winchester, Aug. 1, 1859, to Aug. 1, 1864. Org. of Llandaff Cath., June, 1866. Org. of Chichester Cath., March, 1870. Resided at Brighton (holding various appointments), June, 1873, to June, 1876. Mus. Bac., Cantab., 1876. Resided in London, June, 1876, to Dec., 1877. Org. of St. Mark's Ch., Lewisham, Dec., 1876, to Dec., 1877. Org. of Norwich Cath., Dec., 1877-81. Mus. Doc. Cantab., 1879. Org. Christ Ch., Lancaster Gate, London, 1881.

WORKS.--*Cantatas*: Nicodemus, Lond., 1880; Philippi, 1882; Constance of Calais, 1884. Te Deum, Benedictus, Cantate Domino, Deus Misereatur and 5 anthems; Nicene Creed, set to the 8th Gregorian Tone; Morning, Communion and Evening Service in F; Magnificat and Nunc Dimittis, in G. *Anthems*: My God, look upon me; Out of the deep; Blessed is he; Lord is my portion; Bring unto the Lord; Select anthems from the works of English composers, edited. *Organ*: The Organ Students' Guide, Lond., 4to, n. d.; Organ Music for Church Use, 4to, n. d.; Twelve original pieces; Sonata; Preludes and other short pieces, 2 sets; Andante grazioso; Theme, with variations; Fantasia in F; Pieces in various styles; Three preludes; Andante in A. A wet sheet and a flowing sea, chorus, with orch. accomp., 1880. O mistress mine, song; And wilt thou leave me thus? song; Yesterday, song. Trio for Pf., violin, and 'cello, performed, Lond., Apl., 1876 (MS.).

Mr. Gladstone is one of the best known of our organists. He has appeared in London and elsewhere with great success; his style of performance being popular, and at the same time highly cultivated. His compositions are all good, never commonplace, and always impressive.

GLAREANUS. See LORIS.

GLÄSER (Franz). Bohemian comp. and cond., B. Bohemia, 1798. S. at Prague. Opera director, Vienna, 1817. Music-director at Copenhagen, 1842 D. there, 1861. Writer of "Des Adlers Horst," opera, 1833, and other operas, cantatas, Pf. music, etc.

GLEADHILL (Thomas Swift). Scottish comp. and teacher, B. Edinburgh, 1827. Resided in Glasgow for a number of years as a teacher. He wrote or compiled the following works:—Beauties of Scottish Song (with Fulcher and Thomson), Glasgow, n. d. Harmonium Album (popular airs arranged). Harmonium Repository (do.). Children's Songs (with J. Thomson). Scottish airs arranged as part-songs, and for the Pf. Original Songs, etc.

GLEASON (Frederic Grant). American comp. and pianist, B. Middletown, Conn., Dec. 17, 1848. S. under Dudley Buck in Chicago; under Moscheles, Paperitz, Richter, Plaidy and J. C. Lobe, at Leipzig. S. at Berlin under Reif and Weitzmann; and in London under O. Beringer. S. also under Loeshhorn and A. Haupt. Org. at Hartford, Conn., and at South Ch., New Britain, Conn. Prof. of Pf., org., and comp. at Hersby School in Chicago, 1876. Married Miss Grace A. Hiltz, 1878.

WORKS.—Otho Visconti, opera, op. 7 (MS.); Montezuma, opera (MS.); Symphony—cantata (MS.); Christus, oratorio (MS). Three songs for voice and Pf., op. 1; Organ Sonata, op. 2; Episcopal church music, op. 3-6; Songs for alto voice and Pf., op. 5; Triumphal Overture for org., op. 11; Cantata for solo voices, chorus and orch., op. 12; Trios for Pf., vn., and 'cello, opp. 9, 13, 14. Pf. compositions, various. Quartets (vocal), songs, etc.

Mr. Gleason was originally intended for the ministry, but his musical proclivities ultimately resulted in his admission to the guild of tuneful brethren. He is best known in America by his various compositions, and as a successful teacher.

GLEN (Thomas). Scottish musical instrument-maker, B. Inverkeithing, Fife, 1804. Established business of bag-pipe maker in Edinburgh, which is still carried on. He invented a wooden ophicleide, called a Serpentcleides, but is best known for the construction of unrivalled Scotch bag-pipes. David Glen published "A Collection of Highland Bag-pipe Music, containing Marches, Quicksteps, Strathspeys, and Reels," Edin., 1876.

GLIMES (Jean Baptiste Jules de). Belgian pianist and comp., B. Brussels, Jan. 24, 1814. D. Brussels, Oct. 4, 1881. S. under Fétis, and comp. Pf., chamber, and vocal music.

GLINKA (Michael Ivanovitch). Russian comp., B. near Novospaskoi, May, 1803. S. under John Field. Travelled in Italy, 1830. S. at Berlin under S. Dehn. Music Director of the opera of Russia. Visited France and Spain. D. Berlin, Feb. 15, 1857.

WORKS.—La Vie pour le Czar, opera, S. Petersburg, 1839. Russian et Ludmilla, opera. Songs, etc.

Glinka will be known to posterity by the work first named above, which contains many fine pieces of concerted music, but possessing in other respects little more than a national interest for Russians.

GLOVER (Charles William). English comp., and violinist, B. London, Feb., 1806. S. under T. Cooke. Violinist in Drury Lane, and Covent Garden Theatres. Musical-Director, Queen's Theatre, 1832. D. London, March 23, 1863.

WORKS.—*Songs*: I would not have thee weep for me; The flow'ret of a day; Twilight; A word in season; Better land; Consider the lilies; Colleen Bawn; Cavalier; Do they ever speak to me; Eventime; England and Ireland; Fall of the Leaf; Fortune-teller; Fond love; Go where the morning; Home love; Heart and hand shall go together; I cannot dance to-night; Lord of the valley; Mermaid's cave; My pretty cot; Oh, Italy, dear Italy; Psalm of Life; Purity; Rosalinda; Smiles and tears; The sower; Triumph; 'Tis hard to give the hand; Who is my neighbour; When I think of the days; Widdy M'Shane. *Duets*:

Choosing of the flowers ; Summer hours ; Let us glide on the lake ; The bridesmaid and the bride. *Pf. Music:* Tam o' Shanter, divertimento ; Twenty-four preludes ; Sobraon, march ; Feast of Lanterns, divertimento ; Blue Beard, march ; Transcriptions under titles of Operatic Gems ; Operatic sketches ; Gleanings of melody ; Operatic recollections, etc.

GLOVER (J. H. L.) English comp. and writer, author of Concise Organ Tutor, Lond. (Goddard) n. d. Te Deum. Songs and Pf. music.

GLOVER (John William). Irish comp., org. and teacher. B. Dublin, June 19, 1815. S. in Dublin. Violinist in the Dublin orch., 1830. Music-director in Cath. choir, in succession to Haydn Corri. Prof. of vocal music in Normal Training School of Irish National Education Board, 1848. Established the Choral Institute of Dublin, 1851. Lectured on Irish music at Royal Irish Institution ; in London, 1859. Concerned in the memorialization of O'Connell, Moore, and Grattan.

WORKS.—Moore's Irish Melodies, edited 1859 ; St. Patrick at Tara, cantata, dedicated by permission to H. R. H. Prince Arthur Patrick, London, 1870 ; Erin's Matin Song, Patria, cantata composed in honour of the patriot orators of Ireland, Lond. 1873 ; "One Hundred Years Ago," Ode to Thomas Moore, words by Stephen N. Elrington, Lond. 1879 ; Goldsmith's "Deserted Village," dramatized by Edmund Falconer, opera in 3 acts, London, 1880 ; Two Italian operas of Metastasio (MS.) ; Masses, various ; Hymns ; Concerto for violin and orch., in A (MS.) ; Fantasia on Irish airs for violin and orch. ; Organ book (fugues, voluntaries, &c.) ; Grand concerto for organ ; Pf. works ; Numerous songs, Irish and other.

Mr. Glover is the most popular composer whom Ireland has of recent times produced, and where works are concerned, the most prolific.

He superintended the musical arrangements for the obsequies of Daniel O'Connell, and on this occasion Mozart's Requiem was heard in Dublin for the first time with full chorus and orchestra. In after years he organised the great musical performances in the Exhibition Palace for the O'Connell centenary, on which occasion his oratorio, "St. Patrick at Tara," was performed. Mr. Glover has published a number of musical works adapted for school use, which have been adopted by the Educational Commissioners of Ireland. He established in 1851 the Choral Institute in Dublin, and in connection with it produced many works by Mendelssohn, Handel, Haydn, and for the first time in Britain Schumann's "Paradise and the Peri."

GLOVER (Sarah A.) English musician and teacher, daughter of Rev. Mr. Glover of Norwich. B. 1785. D. 1867.

She invented the Tonic Sol-fa system of musical notation, which the Rev. John Curwen afterwards modified and changed till its present form was reached. For teaching purposes of an elementary, and even advanced kind, the Tonic sol-fa system is beyond all doubt the one most satisfactory to the teacher who has large numbers of children to deal with. To Miss Glover much credit is necessarily due for the commencement of the system now so universally used in Britain. She published "A Manual of the Norwich Sol-fa System . . " [1845] 8vo ; "Manual containing a Development of the Tetrachordal system," London, [1850] 8vo.

GLOVER (Stephen). * English comp., brother of C. W. Glover. B. London, 1812. D. London, Dec. 7, 1870. Teacher in London.

WORKS.—*Songs:* Annie on the Banks o' Dee ; Mary Astore ; Oh! give me back my childhood's dreams ; Sweet remembered music ; The maiden's dream ; Dreams of childhood ; I dream of thee ; Life's dearest hope ; The minstrel knight ; The river of song ; Emigrant's farewell ; Sing no more that song of gladness ; Woman's wiles ; Yes or no ; Abide with me ; Autumn eve ; Bonnie Teviotdale ; Beware ; Break, break, break ; Bloom upon the cherry ; Cloud and sunshine ; Down the green lane ; Ellen Vane ; Fair rose of Killarney ; Flower of the south ; Fond memory ; Good words ; I love him, yes ; Ildegonda ; King of the ocean wave ; Lays of the London season ; Maid of Athens ; Merry mountain maid ; May Queen ; Oh for the bloom o' my ain native heather ; Oh ye mountain streams ; Pearl of the east ; Sweet is true love ; Songs of other years ; Sweet spring morn ; There once was a knight ; Underneath your window ; Winter night ; Would you remember me.

Duets: The cuckoo ; The dove ; The fairies' serenade ; The gleaners ; In the starlight ; Our bark is on the Rhine ; Return of the swallows ; Savoyard Maids ; The skylark ; Angels are watching us ; Farewell ! remember me ; Hymn to the night ; Stars of the summer night ; The curfew bell ; The gipsy countess ; To the woods ! to the woods ; Voices of the night. Four-part songs, trios, etc. Pianoforte music, transcriptions, etc.

The compositions of this popular composer lay no claim to the divine fire of genius, but are very pleasing works for the generality of tastes. They are simple, and the melodies are invariably pretty. His whole works exceed in number 300, and nearly every one of the songs and duets were publishers' successes.

GLOVER (William). English org. and comp., B. London, 1822. Chor. in Trinity Coll., Cantab., 1829-38. S. under Walmisley. Org. Christ Ch., Camb., 1841-42. Org. S. Matthew's, Manchester, 1842. Org. S. Luke's, Cheetham, 1846.

WORKS.—Jerusalem, oratorio, Manchester, 1848 ; Emmanuel, do., Manchester, 1851 ; The Corsair, cantata (1849), pub. 1856. Chamber music in MS. ; Songs, Pf. music, etc.

GLOVER (William Howard). English comp. and violinist, B. Kilburn, London, June 6, 1819. Son of Mrs. Glover, the actress ; S. under Wagstaff. Travelled in Europe. Member of staff of " Morning Post." Resided in U.S.A. from 1868. D. New York, Oct. 28, 1875.

WORKS.—*Operas and operettas:* Ruy Blas, Covent Garden, London, Oct., 1861 ; Aminta, Haymarket, London ; Once too often ; The Coquette ; Palomita, or the Veiled Songstress. Tam o' Shanter, cantata, London, July, 1855 ; Overture for orch., "Manfred ;" Twelve Romances for Pf., in 2 books ; Vocal Quartets, duets, etc. Miscellaneous Pf. music ; Songs for voice and Pf.

Glover was a good melodist, and had much dramatic character in his works, which, however, from lack of encouragement, never became fully developed. None of his larger works, save "Tam o' Shanter," are now heard.

GLUCK (Christoph Willibald, Ritter von). German comp , B. Weidenwang, near Neumarkt, Upper Palatinate, July 2, 1714. S. at a Jesuit school in Bohemia, 1726. S. at Prague from 1732. Member of private band of Prince Melzi, Vienna, 1736. Accompanied Prince Melzi to Milan, where his musical education was completed. Appeared in London as comp. to Haymarket Theatre, 1745. Performed on musical glasses at the Haymarket Theatre, April (?) 3, 1746. Travelled in Italy, 1750-55. Resided in Vienna, 1755-61. Singing-master to Marie Antoinette. Settled in Paris, 1774. Engaged in famous rivalry with Piccinni, 1774-1779. Returned to Vienna, 1780. D. Vienna, Nov. 15, 1787.

WORKS.—*Operas:* Artaserse, Milan, 1841 ; Demofoonte, Milan, 1742 ; Demetrio, Venice, 1742 ; Ipermnestra, Venice, 1742 ; Artamene, Cremona, 1743 ; Siface, Milan, 1743 ; Fedra, Milan, 1745 ; Alessandro nell' Indie, Turin, 1745 ; La Caduta de' giganti, London, 1746 ; L'Artamene, London, 1746 ; Piramo e Tisbe (pasticcio), do. 1746 ; Le Semiramide riconosciuta, Vienna, 1748 ; Telemacco, Rome, 1750 ; La Clemenza di Tito, Naples, 1751 ; L'Eroe Cinese, Vienna, 1754 ; Il Trionfo di Camillo, Rome, 1754 ; Antigono, do., 1754 ; La Danza, 1755 ; L' Innocenza Giustificata, Vienna, 1756 ; Il Re l'astore (Metastasio), Vienna, 1756 ; Tetide, 1760 ; Il Trionfo di Clelia, 1762 ; Orfeo ed Euridice (Calzabigi), Vienna, 1762 ; Ezio, (Metastasio), do., 1763 ; Die Pilgrime von Mekka (La Rencontre Imprévue), Vienna, 1764 ; Il Parnasso Confuso, 1765 ; Telemacco, Vienna. 1765 ; Le Corona, do., 1765 ; Alceste (Calzabigi), Vienna, 1767 ; Paride ed Elena, do., 1769 ; Le Feste di Apollo, Parma, 1769 ; Bauci e Filemone, do., 1769 ; Aristeo, do., 1769 ; Iphigenie en Aulide, Paris, 1774 ; Orphée et Eurydice (adapted to French stage by Moline), 1774 ; L'Arbre enchante (Vadé), Versailles. 1775 ; Cythere assiégie, do., 1775 ; Armide (Quinault) Paris, 1777 ; Iphigénie en Tauride (Guillard), do., 1779 ; Echo et Narcisse (Tschudy), do., 1779 ; Filide, serenade, Copenhagen, 1749 ; Don Juan, ballet, Vienna, 1761.

The great principles adopted and successfully illustrated by Gluck are best described in his own words, which are taken from the dedication to "Alceste," translated in Lady Wallace's "Letters of Distinguished Musicians," other versions appearing in Hogarth's "Musical History," etc.:—

"When I undertook to compose music to "Alceste," I proposed entirely to abolish all those abuses introduced by the injudicious vanity of singers, or by the excessive complaisance of masters, which have so long disfigured the Italian opera, and instead of the most splendid and beautiful of all entertainments, thus rendering it the most ridiculous and tiresome. My purpose was to restrict music to its true office, that of ministering to the expression of the poetry, and to the situations of the plot, without interrupting the action, or chilling it by superfluous and needless ornamentation. I thought that it should accomplish what brilliancy of colour and a skilfully adapted contrast of light and shade effect for a correct and well-designed drawing, by animating the figures without distorting their contours. I wished, therefore, to avoid arresting an actor in the most excited moment of his dialogue, by causing him to wait for a tiresome *ritournelle*, or, in the midst of half uttered words, to detain him on a favourable note, either for the purpose of displaying his fine voice and flexibility in some long passage, or causing him to pause till the orchestra gave him time to take breath for a cadence. It did not appear to me that I ought to hurry over the second part of an aria, possibly the most impassioned and important of all, in order to have the opportunity of repeating regularly four times over the words of the first part, causing the aria to end where in all probability the sense did not end, merely for the convenience of the singer, and to enable him to vary a passage according to his caprice; in short, I have striven to banish the abuses against which reason and good sense have so long protested in vain.

"My idea was that the overture should prepare the spectators for the plot to be represented, and give some indication of its nature; that the concerted instruments ought to be regulated according to the interest and passion of the drama, and not leave a void in the dialogue between the air and the recitative, so that the meaning of a passage might not be perverted, nor the force and warmth of the action improperly interrupted.

"Further, I thought that my most strenuous efforts must be directed in search of a noble simplicity, thus avoiding a parade of difficulty at the expense of clearness. I did not consider a mere display of novelty valuable, unless naturally suggested by the situation and the expression, and on this point no rule in composition exists that I would not have gladly sacrificed in favour of the effect produced.

"Such are my principles. Fortunately, the libretto was wonderfully adapted to my purpose, in which the celebrated author (Calzabigi), having imagined a new dramatic plan, replaced flowery descriptions, superfluous similes, and cold sententious morality by the language of the heart, strong passions, interesting situations, and an ever varying *spectacle*."

The great principle enunciated by Gluck, that in the musical drama a natural succession of events should be represented by a series of effects produced by the most natural means possible, has never been fully realized in practice by any composer (including himself), from his own time till now. The overweening desire of securing public applause has checked any attempt in the direction of a drama which would be simple in its elements, yet so strongly impassioned in its varying scenes as to claim the attention of the intelligent auditor. Gluck has to a certain extent made use of a natural simplicity in his operas, but the cold classicism of his subjects, and their statuesque opposition to the accepted comprehension of the action of humanity under given circumstances, are not greatly favourable to the belief that they represent the ideal natural drama.

The great beauty of Gluck's music lies in the fact that it is always in harmony with the nature of the poem, always beautiful, and always in keeping with his poet's somewhat stiff idea of life. In his operas we miss the richness of the modern stage, but are amply recompensed by the charming grace and dramatic truth of his musical colouring. The loveliness of many of the airs and passages throughout his works appears remarkable when we read the statement of his determination to cut down and prune any florid passages which may seem foreign to the prevailing sentiment of his piece. This he has certainly done, but not with so stern a resolve as one might judge from his utterances. His melodies in "Orpheus" if not actually florid are rich and flowing, and positively ear catching in a higher degree than would be generally supposed by the opponents of the classical drama.

In 1774 Gluck commenced his famous contest with public opinion and latterly, in 1776, with Piccinni, for the suppression of undue ornamentation in the musical drama. Gluck was supported by the queen, Marie Antionette, and a host of other notables, while Piccinni had the support of Madame Du Barry, and a large proportion of the Parisian public, including journalists and philosophers. A pamphlet war raged for a long time between the parties, Gluck himself making reply to several of his antagonists; musicians, great and small, became Gluckists or Piccinists, as also did the general public interested in music. The ultimate result was that Gluck conquered, and established for a time his idea of a natural musical drama. This, however, did not last, as we find his successors—French, Italian, and German,—employing the old flourishes, and having them applauded with equal relish by a complaisant musical public. The revival of Gluck's idea in its entirity is due to Wagner in our own time, who has more successfully than any of Gluck's followers striven to combine the musical and poetical elements in his operas in a strict yet harmonious union.

GNETZLER (Johann). German organ-builder, B. Passau, 1710. D. end of 18th century. Built many continental instruments.

GOBBAERTS (Jean Louis), STREABBOG. Belgian comp. and pianist, B. Antwerp, Sept. 28, 1835. S. Brussels Cons.

WORKS.—Le Concert dans le feuillage, bluette, for Pf., op. 33; Valse des masques, op. 39; Twenty-four studies, in 2 vols., op. 44; Nocturne, op. 45; Idylle, op. 49; Galop di bravura, op. 56; Premières etudes des jeunes Pianistes, op. 63; Twelve Studies, easy, op. 64; Serenade, op. 84; Les Papillons, 6 dances, op. 108. Transcriptions, and miscellaneous Pf. music to the amount of about 300 separate pieces.

Under the *nom de plume* of STREABBOG, a reversed name, Gobbaerts has written a large quantity of light, popular music. In addition to his gifts as a composer, he is a brilliant and successful performer.

GODARD (Benjamin Louis Paul). French comp. and violinist, B. Paris, Aug. 18, 1849. S. Paris Cons., 1863, under Reber, etc. Composer of music for the Pf.; concerted instrumental music. Songs, "Pedro de Zalamea," opera, Antwerp, 1884; etc.

GODDARD (Arabella), DAVISON. English pianist, B. St. Servan, near St. Malo, Brittany, Jan. 12, 1836. S. under Kalkbrenner at Paris. S. in London under Mrs. Anderson and Thalberg, 1848. *Début* London, March 30, 1850. S. for time under (Sir) G. A. Macfarren. Travelled on the Continent, 1854-56. Married to J. W. Davison, 1860. Travelled in Australia and the United States, 1873-76.

Mrs. Davison was indebted to Mr. J. W. Davison for much of her success as a public performer. He directed her attention to many works, which she introduced to the public with much acceptance. Her style of performance is exceedingly refined and sympathetic, while brilliancy can at will be brought to bear on the work in hand. She is probably the finest female pianist of modern times who has preserved the traditions of the school which existed immediately before her advent. She has performed in most of the large cities in Britain, and at the principal concerts.

GODDARD (Joseph). English writer and comp., B. 1833. Author of "Moral Theory of Music," 1857. "Musical Development, or Remarks on the Spirit of the Principal Musical Forms," Lond., 8vo, n. d. "New Graduated Method for the Pianoforte," fo., n. d. "Time Exercises for the use of Pianoforte Students," n. d. "A Study of Gounod's Sacred Trilogy, 'The Redemption,'" Lond. [1883]. Songs, Pf. music, etc.

GOCKEL (August). German pianist and comp., B. 1831. S. Leipzig, from 1845. Played in America, 1853-56. Comp. of music for the Pf., voice, and chamber.

GODEFROID (Dieudonne Joseph Guillaume Felix). French comp. and harpist, B. Namur, July 24, 1818. S. Cons. Comp. for harp and Pf.

WORKS.—Le Reve, étude melodique, op. 23; La melancolie, étude caracteristique, op. 24; La Danse de Sylphes, op. 31; Minuit, serenade, op. 34; La Danse des Lutins, op. 42; Rêverie, Solitude, op. 44; Sonata dramatique, op. 45; Second sonata, op. 53; Danse Indienne, op. 57; Les Alpes, op. 95; Johannisberg, valse, op. 106; Romance sans paroles, op. 121; Rondo Russe, op. 126; Reverie-mazurka, op. 169; Etudes caracteristiques, etc. His brother, JULES JOSEPH, B. Namur, Feb. 23, 1811. D. 1840, was a comp. for harp and Pf.

GODFREY (Adolphus Frederick). English bandmaster and comp. B. 1837. Son of Charles, senr. Bandmaster of the Coldstream Guards. D. 28 Aug., 1882. Writer of dances in large numbers, as lancers, polkas, galops, quadrilles, reminiscences of England, Scotland, Ireland, and Wales, &c.

GODFREY (Charles, Senr.) English bandmaster and comp. B. Kingston, Surrey, Nov. 22, 1790. Bandmaster of Coldstream Guards. Musician in ordinary to the king, 1831. Arranger of music for military bands, &c. D. London, Dec. 1863.

GODFREY (Charles, Junr.) English bandmaster and comp. B. Jan. 1839. Son of above. S. under Sir G. A. Macfarren at R. A. M. Bandmaster of Scots Fusiliers, 1860-68 : Royal Horse Guards, 1869. Mem. and Associate, R. A. M. Prof. of Military Music at Royal Coll. of Music, and at Guildhall School of Music.

WORKS.—*Waltzes:* La murska; Love dreams; Princess Beatrice; Princess Louise; The blush rose. *Galops:* On and off; The escort; The outpost; The wind-up; Tramp; Mignonette; and others to number of 20. *Quadrilles:* Croquet; Orpheus; Auber; H. M. S. Pinafore, and others to number of 18. *Lancers:* Royal Edinburgh; Channel Fleet; Carmen; etc. Polkas, Schottisches, and Mazurkas. Editor of *The Orpheus* Journal, a military music periodical.

The band of the Royal Horse Guards, cond. by Charles Godfrey, is beyond dispute one of the finest military bands in the world. Its performance of many classical works is not exceeded in artistic effect by the best orchestras.

GODFREY (DANIEL). English bandmaster and comp. B. Westminster, 1831. Son of Charles, senr. Bandmaster of Grenadier Guards, 1856. Travelled with band, concert-giving, in U. S. A., 1872. Mem. and Assoc. of R. A. M. Prof. of Military Music at the R. A. M.

WORKS.—Transcriptions from popular operas for military bands; marches, numerous. *Valses:* Guards; Mabel; Hilda; etc.

The members of this family are well known all over Great Britain for the capable style in which they conduct their several bands. These bands are often employed to augment the orchestra at large festivals in the Royal Albert Hall, &c.

GOEPFERT (Carl A.) German clarinet-player. B. Rimpar, Wurzburg, 16 Jan. 1768. D. April 11, 1818. Comp. works for his instrument, quartets, etc.

GOETHE (Johann Wolfgang von). German poet and writer. B. Frankfort-on-the-Main, 1749. S. at Strasburg. Resided chiefly at Weimar. D. Weimar, 1832.

WORKS (which have been set to music).—" Faust " (Spohr, Gounod, Lindpainter, etc.); Count Egmont (Beethoven); Mignon (Thomas); Lyrics and Lieder (Anschütz, Beethoven, Franz, Grönland (P.), Hauptmann, Klein (B.), Liszt, Lowe (C.), Meinardus (L.), Mendelssohn, Reichardt (J. F.), Schubert, Schumann, Spohr, Wendt (J. A.), etc.

Goethe was a great lover of music, and the story of his connection with Mendelssohn will be found in any biography of that musician.

GOETSCHIUS (Percy). German writer. Author of " The Material used in Musical Composition," Lond. 1883.

GOETZ (Hermann). German comp., B. Königsberg, Dec. 17, 1840. S. at Königsberg University. S. music under Bülow and Ulrich. Org. at Winterthur, 1863. D. Hottingen, Zurich, Dec. 3, 1876.

WORKS.—Op. 1. Trio for Pf., vn., and 'cello; op. 2. Three pieces for Pf. and vn.; op. 3. Three songs; Quartet for strings in E. op. 6.; Nine Pf. pieces, op. 7; Two sonatinas for Pf., op. 8; Zwei Abendlieder, for string orch., op. 9; Nenia, cantata for orch. and chorus, op. 12; Genrebilder, Pf. pieces, op. 13; Quintet for Pf., vn., viola, 'cello, and double bass, op. 16: Sonata for Pf. duet in G min., op. 17; Concerto for Pf. and orch., op. 18; Sechs Lieder for voice and Pf., op. 19; Der Widerspänstigen Zähmung (Taming of the Shrew) Mannheim, Oct. 11,

1874, published in London, 1878; Symphony in F for orch.; Francesca di Rimini, opera, Mannheim, 1877 (finished by Brahms and Franck); The 137th Psalm for soli, chorus, and orch; Pf. trio; op. 21. Seven 4-part songs; etc.

The death of this gifted composer at the early age of 36 was lamented by all musicians. The merit of his works proved that had he been spared he would have added many important works to the world's repertory.

GOLDBECK (Robert). German comp., pianist, and writer, B. Potsdam, 1835. S. under H. Litolff. Resided in Paris and London, 1851. Went to New York, 1857; Chicago, 1868; S. Louis, 1873. Was principal of a musical cons. in Chicago.

WORKS.—The Soldier's Return, operetta, London; Quintet for Pf. and strings; Trio for do. *Pianoforte:* Day-dream; Impromptu; Melodie-etude; La Cavalcade; Venezia, Scene de lagunes; Arolodo; Caprice de Concert; Flashes from the West; Fundamental Technics of Pf. Playing; Harmonized Progressive Exercises; Fifty Studies; High Technics: Sogni d'Amore, Pf.; Traumgewebe, nocturne; Danse des Dryades; Transcriptions and Fantasias from operas. *Songs:* Break, break, break; Day is cold; Dreams of Heaven; Love Song; Moonlight deep and tender; Where'er the heart to true heart beats; Willow song. Gradus ad Parnassum of the Voice (vocal instructor).

GOLDMARK (Karl). Hungarian comp., B. Keszthely, May 18, 1832. S. under Jansa at Vienna and at Cons., 1847-8. Comp. and teacher in Vienna.

WORKS.—Die Königin von Saba, opera, Vienna, 1875, op. 27; Merlin, opera. Die Ländliche Hochzeit, symphony for orch., op. 26 (five parts); Sakuntala, overture for orch.; Concerto for vn. and orch., in A min., op. 28; String quartet, in B flat, op. 8; Quintet for Pf. and strings, in B flat, op. 30; Dances for orch., op. 22; Lieder aus dem "Wilden Jäger," von J. Wolff, op. 32; Sonata for Pf. and vn., op. 25; Suite for Pf. and vn, 5 parts, op. 11; Scherzo for orch.; Songs, etc.

GOLDSCHMIDT (Adalbert von). Austrian comp., B. Vienna, May 5, 1848. Belongs to a family of wealthy financiers, and is independent of the musical profession; which, however, he follows as an amateur at Vienna. He has comp. "Die Sieben Todsünden," oratorio; "Helianthus," opera, Leipzig, 1884; and some works for Pf. and orch., vocal music, etc.

GOLDSCHMIDT (Otto). German pianist and comp. B. Hamburg, Aug. 21. 1829. S. under J. Schmitt, and at Leipzig Cons, 1833. S. under Mendelssohn, 1843-46; Chopin, Paris, 1848. Came to England, 1848. Went to America with Mdlle. Jenny Lind, as cond., 1851. Married Jenny Lind at Boston, U. S.. Feb. 5, 1852. Resided at Dresden, 1852-55. Settled in London, 1852. Hon. member of Philharmonic Soc., 1861, Vice-Principal, R. A. M., 1863. Founded the Bach Choir, 1875.

WORKS.—Ruth, oratorio, Hereford Festival, 1867; Trio for Pf. vn., and 'cello, op. 12; Concerto for Pf. and orch., op. 10; Six songs for voice and Pf., by O. van Redwitz, op. 8; Six do., op. 9; Part-songs, various; Twelve studies for Pf., op. 13, etc.

Herr Goldschmidt is better known as a conductor and pianist than as a composer. As a conductor he has achieved great renown, and his work in connection with the Bach Choir has been very profitable, tending to introduce the general public to a number of standard classics.

GOLDSCHMIDT (Jenny Lind). See LIND (Jenny).

GOLDSMITH (Oliver). Irish general writer and flute-player. B. Pallas, near Longford, 1728. D. London, 1774.

The librettos of the operas of "The Deserted Village" (Glover and Falconer); and "The Vicar of Wakefield," are founded on his works. Music is also written to some of his shorter pieces. He was a musician, and supported himself by playing the flute when travelling on the continent.

GOLDWIN (John). English org. and comp., B. [?]. S. under Dr. W. Child. Org. S. George's Chap., Windsor, 1697. Master of the Choristers, do., 1700, D. Nov. 7, 1719. Comp. a service in F; anthems; MS. works, etc.

GOLLMICK (Adolph). German comp. and pianist, B. Frankfort-on-the-Main, Feb. 5, 1825. Son of Carl Gollmick. S. under his father, Riefstahl, H. Wolff, and Kessler. Came to London, 1844. Gave first concert, Aug. 21, 1844. Founded and directed the "Reunion des beaux arts," 1851. Married in 1853, at Frankfort. Director of the Kilburn Musical Association, 1879. First oratorio performance, 1879. D. London, March 7, 1883.

WORKS.—Doña Constanza, comic opera, 3 acts ; The Oracle, comic opera, 2 acts ; Balthasar, do., 2 acts ; Blind Beggar's Daughter of Bethnal Green, operatic cantata ; The Heir of Linne, operatic cantata ; Symphony for orch., in C minor (MS.) ; Overture and marches for orch. ; Pf. quartet (MS.) ; Pf. trio (MS.) ; Six studies for Pf. ; Eighteen German Volkslieder, trans. for Pf. ; Valse Styrienne, Pf. ; Reverie, op. 20 ; Grand Caprice, op. 11 ; Scherzo, op. 21 ; La Flatteuse, Pf., op. 19. Songs.

GOLLMICK (Carl). German writer and comp., B. Anhalt, Dessau, March 19, 1796. S. under B, Klein and Spindler. D. Frankfort-on-the-Main, Oct. 3, 1866.

WORKS.—Handlexikon der Tonkunst, 1857 ; Critische Terminologie für Musiker und Musikfreunde, 1833 ; Musikalisches Novellen und Silhouetten, 1842. Pf. music, songs, etc.

GOLTERMANN (Georg Eduard). German violoncellist and comp., B. Hanover, Aug. 19, 1825. Cond. and teacher at Frankfort.

WORKS.—Symphony for orch., in A minor, op. 20 ; Concerto No. 1, for 'cello and orch., op. 11 ; Three morceaux caracteristiques, 'cello and Pf., op. 41 ; Danses Allemandes, 'cello and Pf., op. 42 ; Do., op. 47 ; Morceaux Caracteristiques for 'cello and Pf., op. 48, 53 ; Adagio for 'cello and orch, op. 83 ; Romance, 'cello and Pf., op. 87 ; Elegie for 'cello and Pf., in C minor, op. 88 ; First Sonatina for Pf. and tenor, in A, op. 36 ; Five Songs for Barytone voice and Pf., op. 7.

Goltermann is known as one of the most refined 'cellists of modern times. His tone is full and powerful, and his execution perfection. As a conductor he is of much eminence, being well known in Frankfort for the good service he has rendered in this capacity.

GOMBERT (Nicolas). Belgian comp., B. Bruges [1495]. S. under Josquin des Pres. Chap.-master to the Emperor Charles the Fifth. D. [1570].

His compositions number in all slightly over 250, and consist of masses, motets, psalms, chansons, galliards, pavans, etc., the chief merit which they possess for modern ears being their delightful quaintness. "His counterpoint exhibits him as a profound harmonist. . . . he composed a set of masses which were published at Venice, and two sets of motets in four parts, all of which bespeak sufficient genius, science, contrivance, and taste, to entitle him to a rank with the first masters of the age he ornamented."—Busby.

GOMEZ (A. Carlos) or GOMES. Portuguese comp., B. Compinos, Brazil, July 11, 1839. S. Milan Cons.

WORKS.—Operas : Il Guarany, Milan, 1870. London, 1872 ; Fosca, Milan, 1873 ; Salvator Rosa, Genoa, 1874. Il Saluto del Brasile, ode, Philadelphia Exhibition, 1876, etc.

GOMIS (Joseph Melchior). Spanish comp., B. Valencia, 1793. D. Paris, July 16, 1836. Wrote operas, songs, Pf. music, etc.

GONZALEZ Y RODRIGUEZ (José Maria). Spanish org. and comp., B. Alcala, Feb. 5, 1822. S. Madrid. Comp. masses, litanies, org. music, etc. Prof. in Madrid Cons.

GOODBAN (Thomas). English comp. and writer, B. Canterbury, Dec., 1784. Chor. Canterbury Cath. S. under S. Porter. Articled to a Solicitor. Resigned the Law, 1798. Lay-clerk Canterbury Cath., 1809. Leader of the Catch Club, Canterbury, 1810. D. Canterbury, May 4, 1863.

WORKS.—A New and Complete Guide to the Art of Playing the Violin, Lond., 1810 ; Guide to the Piano, 1811 ; The Rudiments of Music, 1825 ; New and Complete Introduction to Singing, etc., London, 1829; The Rudiments of Music, with progressive exercises, Lond., 4to, 1836 (new edit.) Glees, songs, Pf. music, etc. His sons, CHARLES (1812-1881), HENRY WILLIAM (1816-), and THOMAS (1822-) were also distinguished musicians. Charles became Mus. Bac., Oxon., 1847, and comp. some miscellaneous pieces, the "Vocal Album," 1850, etc. Henry William is a fine 'cellist and comp., having transcribed numerous pieces for the Pf. and written songs, etc.; and Thomas was a violonist. His nephew, J. F. Goodban, is an org. and comp.

GOODGROOME (John). English comp., B. 1630. Chor. St. George's Chap., Windsor. Gent. of Chap.-Royal, 1660. Musician in Ordinary to the King, 1664. D. June, 1704. Comp. songs and concerted sacred and secular vocal music.

GOODSON (Richard). English comp. and org. B. about middle of 17th cent. Org. Christ Ch., Oxford. Mus. Bac., Oxon. Prof. of Music, Oxford University, in succession to Edward Lowe, July, 1682. D. Jan. 13, 1718. Comp. odes, songs, etc.

GOODSON (Richard, Junr.). English comp. and org., B. latter part of 17th century. Son of above. Org.' of Newbury till 1709. Mus. Bac., Oxon., 1716. Prof. and org. at Oxford in succession to his father, 1718. D. June 9, 1741.

GORDIGIANI (Luigi). Italian comp., B. Modena, June 21, 1806. D. Florence, May, 1860. Comp. a great number of fine songs, and a few operas. His brother GIOVANNI was a comp. and singer.

GORDON (John). English musician, B. London, March 26, 1702. Educated at Westminster School and Trinity Coll., Cambridge. S. for the Law, 1718-22. Prof. Music, Gresham Coll., Jan. 16, 1723. Called to Bar, 1725. D. London, December 12, 1739.

GORDON (William). English comp., B. end of 18th century. S. under Drouët. Captain of Swiss Guards in Paris. Commenced improving flute mechanism, 1830. D. insane, in consequence of unsuccessful experiments, 1839 (?). His system of fingering was perfected by Boehm, but authorities differ both in the matter of the original invention and subsequent improvements.

GORIA (Alexandre Edouard). French pianist and comp., B. Paris, 1823. D. Paris, 1860. Comp. a great quantity of popular Pf. music. Op. 1. Bluette; op. 2. Harmonie du soir, nocturne; op. 3. Berceuse; op. 4. Canzonetta; op. 5. Mazurka; op. 6. Caprice-nocturne; op. 7-8. Etudes de Concert; op. 9. Serenade; op. 10-11. Nocturne; op. 12. Valse; op. 13. Andante; op. 14. Mazurka; op. 15-17. Studies; op. 18. Mazurka; op. 19. Rêverie; Transcriptions from operas, op. 20, 22, 24, 31, 34, 38, 42, 46, 51, etc. Le Pianiste Moderne, studies; Ecole moderne de Pianiste, op. 63. Miscellaneous pieces. His studies are extremely useful works.

GOSS (John Jeremiah). English vocalist, B. Salisbury, 1770. Chorister Salisbury Cath., and lay vicar, do. Gent. of Chap. Roy., 1808. Vicar choral, St. Paul's Cath. Lay vicar of Westminster Abbey. Principal alto at meetings of the Three Choirs. D. May, 1817.

GOSS (Sir John, Kt.). English comp. and org., B. Fareham, Hants, Dec. 27, 1800. Son of Joseph Goss, org. of that place. Chorister in Chap. Roy., under J. S. Smith, 1811. S. under Attwood. Org. of St. Luke's, Chelsea, 1824. Org. St. Paul's Cath., 1838-72. Comp. to Chap. Roy., 1856-72. Knighted, 1872. Mus. Doc., Cantab., 1876. D. Brixton, Lond., May 10, 1880.

WORKS.—Church Service, in A; Burial Service, in E minor; Te Deum for H.M. Thanksgiving at St. Paul's Cath., for the restoration to health of H. R. H. the Prince of Wales. Benedictus. Te Deums in C, D, and F; Cantate Domino and Deus misereatur, in C; Magnificat and Nunc Dimittis, in E. *Anthems*: Almighty and merciful God; And the king said to all the people (dirge); Behold I bring you good tidings; Blessed is the man; Brother, thou art gone before us; Christ, our Passover; Come, and let us return unto the Lord; Fear not, O land; Have mercy upon me ; Hear, O Lord ; I heard a voice from heaven ; I will magnify Thee, O God ; If we believe that Jesus died ; In Christ dwelleth ; Lift up thine eyes round about ; O give thanks ; O Lord God, Thou strength of my health ; O praise the Lord ; O praise the Lord of heaven ; O Saviour of the world ; O taste and see ; Praise the Lord, O my soul ; Stand up and bless the Lord your God ; The glory of the Lord ; The Lord is my strength ; They are they which follow the Lamb ; The Wilderness. Seven Glees and a Madrigal, Lond., 1852. Parochial Psalmody, a Collection of Ancient and Modern Tunes, Lond., 1827. Collection of Voluntaries by eminent composers, organ. The Organist's Companion, 4 vols. Coll. of Voluntaries, various comps. An Introduction to Harmony and Thorough-bass, Lond., 4to, 1833. Pianoforte Students' Catechism of the Rudiments of Music, Lond., 12mo, 1835. Chants, ancient and modern, 1841. Overtures for orch., and miscellaneous orch. music. Songs, etc.

Goss was one of the most melodious composers who in recent times have graced the British school of sacred music. His style, which is best shown in his anthems, is stately and refined, but at the same time melodious and natural. The well known anthem, " O give thanks unto the Lord," is one of the best known of his many grand compositions of a like nature, and happily displays the general style which he affected. As an organist, Goss was considered one of the most intellectual of his time, and his performance was marked by great breadth and power. His glees, songs, hymns, and other works, have all been received with favour.

GOSSEC (Francois Joseph). Belgian comp., B. Vergnies, Jan. 17, 1733. Chor. in Antwerp Cath. till 1748. Went to Paris, 1751. Became acquainted with Rameau. Inspector (with Cherubini and Méhul) of the Paris Cons., 1795-1814. Mem. of the Institut, 1795. Chev. of Legion of Honour, 1802. Retired from public life, 1815. D. Passy, Feb. 16, 1829.

WORKS.—*Operas:* Salinus, 1773 ; Alexis et Daphné, 1775 ; Philémon et Baucis, 1775 ; Hylas et Sylvie, 1776 ; La Fête du Village, 1778 ; Thésée, 1782 ; La Reprise de Toulon, 1796 ; La Faux Lord, 1764 ; Les Pêcheurs, 1766 ; Tionon et Tionette, 1767 ; Le Double Déguisement, 1767. Saul, oratorio ; La Nativité, oratorio. Messe des Morts, 1760. Hymns, etc. Twenty-nine Symphonies for orch. Eighteen Quartets for strings. Serenades, Trios, Overtures, etc. Literary works.

Gossec is now very little known to the general musical public, his works and reforms having faded from memory. He has historical importance as the originator of a richer style of orchestral writing, and the introduction of many standard reforms in the ordinary orchestral practice.

GOSTICK (Joseph). English writer, author of "A Manuel of Music," Edin., 12mo, 1851.

GOSTLING (Rev. John). English bass vocalist, B. [1652]. D. 1733. Was the possessor of a most powerful voice of great compass, for which it is said Purcell composed some sacred and other music.

GOTTSCHALG (Alexander Wilhelm). German org., writer, and comp., B. Mechelroda, near Weimar, 1827.

GOTTSCHALK (Louis Moreau). American comp. and pianist, B. New Orleans, May 8, 1829. S. at Paris, under C. Halle, Chopin, Stamaty, and Maleden, 1846. Travelled as pianist in Europe, 1847-53. Appeared successively in New York, Cuba, Porto Rica and other parts of N. and S. America. D. Rio de Janeiro, Dec. 18, 1869.

WORKS. —La Nuit des Tropiques, symphony. *Pianoforte*: Op. 2. Bamboula, Danse de Nègres ; op. 3. La Savane ; op. 4. Ossian, ballade ; op. 5. Chanson nègre ; op. 6. Two Mazurkas ; op. 8. La Moissonneuse ; op. 9. Caprice ; op. 10. La chasse du jeune Henri ; op. 11. Serenade ; op. 11. Danse Ossianiqne ; op. 13. Fantaisie triomphale ; op. 14. Caprice espagnol ; op, 15. Le Banjo ; op. 23. Chant du Soldat ; op. 24. Valse poetique ; op. 26. Ricordati, meditation ; op. 27. La Naiade ; op. 29. Marche solennelle ; op. 31. Marche des Gibaros ; op. 34. Caprice Americain ; op. 35. La Gitanella ; op. 36. Fantôme de bonheur ; op. 38. Etude de concert ; op. 39. Souvenir de la Havane ; op. 40. Printemps d'Amour ; op. 42. Nocturne; op. 43. Polonia, caprice; op. 47. Berceuse; op. 49. Polka, La Colombe;

op. 50. Danse Cubaine ; op. 51. Home, sweet home (trans.) ; op. 53. La Gallina, danse cubaine ; op. 55. Caprice héroïque ; op. 56. Caprice elegiaque ; op. 57. Grand Scherzo; op. 58. Tremolo, study; op. 61. Marche funèbre; op. I. Pensée poétique ; op. 63. Etude de concert ; op. 64. Bataille, study ; op. 65. Solitude ; op. 67. Tarantelle ; op. 69. Fantasia—Brazilian National hymn ; op. 85. Sixth Ballade, in F ; op. 86. Danse des Sylphes ; op. 87. Seventh Ballade, in E flat ; op. 88. Hercule, study ; op. 89. Le Carnival de Venise, caprice ; op. 90. Ballade, in E ; Cantata ; Overture, MS. Opera, etc. Notes of a Pianist during his Professional Tours, Edited by his Sister. Translated by Robert E. Paterson, M.D., Philadelphia, 1881.

Gottschalk was a brilliant pianist and a fine harmonist. His works if shallow are remarkably pleasing and effective productions, animated with an extreme warmth of harmonical colouring.

GOTTWALD (Heinrich). German comp. and writer, B. Reichenbach, Silesia, Oct. 24, 1821. D. Breslau, Feb. 17, 1876. Wrote symphonies, Pf. works, songs, etc.

GÖTZE (Johann Nicolas Conrad). German violinist and comp., B. Weimar, Feb. 11, 1791. S. under Kranz, Spohr, and Kreutzer. Appeared in Vienna, Weimar, etc. Violinist in Ducal Chap. of Weimar. Comp. operas, overtures, quartets, lieder, etc.

GOUDIMEL (Claude). French comp., B. Vaison, nr. Avignon, beginning of 16th century [1516]. Went to Rome where he opened a music school. Settled in Paris [1555]. Killed at Lyons during the massacre of S. Bartholomew's Day, Aug. 24, 1572.

WORKS.—Masses. Liber quartus Ecclesiasticorum Cantionum quatuor vocum vulgo Moteta vocant," Antwerp, 1554. Psalms of David, adapted to melodies and harmonized (with Claude le Jeune). Motets, etc.

Goudimel was the founder of the great Roman school of composition, having been teacher of Animuccia, Nanini, Palestrina, etc. As a composer he is chiefly known for his harmonization and arrangement of Marot and Bega's Psalms. Many of those psalms are now in use in the English and Scottish church services.

GOULD (Nathaniel D.). American writer, author of History of Church Music in America, Boston, 8vo, 1853 ; Companion to the Psalmist ; National Church Harmony, Boston, 1832 ; The Sacred Minstrel, 1840 ; The Social Harmony, Boston, 1823.

GOULDING & D'ALMAINE. English firm of music-publishers established in London about 1800. Published works by most of the leading musicians of the period during which the firm flourished. The firm was at one time known as D'Almaine & Mackinlay. The copyrights of the firm were sold in 1867.

GOUNOD (Charles Francois). French comp. and pianist, B. Paris, June 17, 1818. S. under Halévy, Paër and Lesueur at Paris Cons., 1836. Gained second "Prix de Rome," 1837. Gained grand "Prix de Rome," 1839. Travelled in Italy, Germany, and Austria. Org. and chap.-master of the Missions Etrangères. Studied for the Church. Cond. of the Orphéon, Paris, 1852-60. Commander of the Legion of Hon. Mem. of Institut, 1866. Involved in law suit in London, 1870 Cond. his "Redemption" at Birmingham, 1882.

WORKS.—*Operas:* Sapho, 1851 ; Ulysse (chorus, etc.), 1852 ; La Nonne Sanglante, 1854 ; Le Médecin Malgré lui, 1858 ; Faust, Mar. 19, 1859, Théâtre Lyrique, Paris (London, 1863 ; in English, 1864) ; Philémon et Baucis, 1860 ; La Reine de Saba, Feb., 1862 ; Mireille, 1864 ; La Colombe, 1860 ; Romeo et Juliette, 1867 ; Les Deux Reines de France (incidental music, etc.), 1872 ; Jeanne d'Arc (do)., 1873 ; Cinq Mars, 1877 ; Polyeucte, 1879 ; Le Tribut de Zamora, Paris, 1881. *Sacred Music:* The Redemption, oratorio, Birmingham Festival, Aug. 1882 ; Mors et Vita, oratorio, do., 1885 ; Requiem Mass, 1842 ; Messe Solennelle, in D, 1849 ; Ave Verum ; Te Deums and other masses ; Tobiè, oratorio ; Jesus sur le lac de Tibériade, scene for barytone voice, chorus, and orch., Paris, 1876 ; Nazareth, sacred song, words by H. F. Chorley ; Noël, cantique ; De Profundis ;

Twenty Melodies, first collection; Do., second coll.; Do., third coll.; Do., fourth coll; Symphony in D, for orch; Do. in E; La Reine des Apôtres, symphony; Marche Romaine, orch.; Serenade; Convoi funèbre d'une marionnette, for Pf. or orch. Valses and other music for Pf. Méthode de cor à pistons, etc. Biondina, 12 Italian melodies, voice and Pf. Part-songs, Anthems, etc. Gallia, motet for soprano solo and chorus. O Salutaris Hostia. Stabat Mater.

Gounod is one of the most popular and able of the living composers of France. His works abound in passages of great beauty, exhibiting strong and picturesque features and fine melody; the whole bound by a powerful and fervid colouring generally of a more sacred than secular character. Of his operas, "Faust" is the most popular, and of his sacred writings, probably the "Redemption." In addition, many of his songs and minor works have been received with favour. His orchestral works are widely known, and among them the "Funeral March of a Marionette" is a preëminent favourite. It is a clever, droll, and withal a picturesque production. Many of his minor works are in constant use in Britain, and we may particularize his masses, psalms, motets, and sacred songs.

GOUVY (Theodore). French comp. and pianist, B. Goffontaine, nr. Saarbruck, July 2, 1819 [July 21, 1822]. S. at Paris for the law. S. music at Berlin under Elwart, and in Italy. Settled in Paris, 1846. Prof. and comp. there.

WORKS.—Op. 1. Two studies for Pf.; op. 2. Gondoliera, for Pf.; op. 3-7. Serenades for Pf.; op. 8. Trio for Pf., violin, and 'cello, in E; op. 9. Symphony for orch., in E flat; op. 10. Serenade for Pf.; op. 11. Serenade for 2 violins, alto, 'cello, and bass; op. 12. Second Symphony, in F; op. 13. Concert overture for orch, in D; op. 14. Second overture in E; op. 15. Le Dernier Hymne d'Ossian, scene for bass voice and orch; op. 16. Two string quartets; op. 17. Sonata for Pf.; op. 18. Second trio for Pf., violin, and 'cello, in A min.; op. 19. Third do., in B flat; op. 20. Third symphony, in C; op. 21. Six songs for barytone voice and Pf.; op. 22. Fourth trio, for Pf., violin, and 'cello, in F; op. 23. Twelve choruses for 4 male voices; op. 24. Quintet for Pf., 2 violins, alto, and 'cello; op. 25. Fourth symphony, in D; op. 26. Twelve songs for tenor and Pf.; op. 27. Three Serenades for Pf.; op. 28. Decameron, ten pieces for Pf. and 'cello; op. 29. Second sonata, for Pf.; op. 30. Fifth symphony, in B flat; op. 31. Quartet for strings; op. 32. Three choruses; op. 33. Fifth trio, in G; op. 34. Sixth symphony; op. 35. Hymn and march for orch.; op. 36. Sonata for Pf. duet; op. 37. Six odes of Ronsard, for tenor and Pf.; op. 38-9. Two sets of three serenades, Pf.; op. 41-2. Two sets of nine songs of Ronsard; op. 43. Four odes (Ronsard) for barytone voice and Pf.; op. 44. Eight songs of Ronsard, tenor voice and Pf.; op. 45. Eighteen songs (Desportes), voice and Pf.; op. 46. Three elegies for two voices and Pf.; op. 47. Seven songs of Ronsard; op. 48. La Pléiade Française: 12 songs for voice and Pf.; op. 49. Six sonatas for Pf. duet; op. 50. Six duets for Pf. and violin; op. 51. Third sonata for Pf. duet; op. 52. Variations for Pf. duet; op. 53. The serenade; op. 54. Valses for Pf. duets; Missa Brevis, solo, chorus, and orch., 1883, op. 72.

Gouvy is one of the most prolific and graceful composers of modern France. His chamber-music enjoys much favour in Parisian musical circles, while his larger works are known in every musical community.

GOW (Nathaniel). Scottish violinist and comp., B. Inver, near Dunkeld, May 28, 1766. Son of Neil Gow. S. under his father, R. M'Intosh, M'Glashan, and J. Reinagle. Violinist at Edin. under his brother William, One of H. M. trumpeters for Scotland, 1782. Succeeded his brother William as leader of the Edinburgh fashionable concerts, 1791. Established in music-publishing business with W. Shepherd at Edin., 1796-1813. Gave up business, but subsequently resumed it in partnership with his son Neil. Continued the firm till 1827. D. Edin., Jan. 17, 1831.

WORKS.—The Beauties of Neil Gow, being a Selection ot the most favourite tunes from his first, second, and third collections of strathspey reels and jigs, chiefly comprising the compositions of Neil Gow and Sons (Edited by Nathaniel). Edin., 3 parts. The Vocal Melodies of Scotland, arranged for the Pianoforte, or harp, violin, and violoncello, by Nath. Gow. Edin., 3 parts, n.d. The Ancient Curious Collection of Scotland, consisting of genuine Scotch tunes, with their original variations, with basses throughout, for the Pianoforte, or harp, violin and 'cello. Ded. to Sir Walter Scott. Edin., 1823. A Select Collection of Original dances, waltzes, marches, minuets, and airs...many of which are composed, and the whole arranged, for the Pf. and harp, by Nath. Gow. Edin., fo. A Collection of Strathspey Reels, with a bass for the violoncello, or harpsichord, containing the most approved old and the most fashionable new reels, some of which are composed, and others with additions, by Nath. Gow. Edin., fo., n. d. Complete Repository of Old and New Scotch Strathspeys, Reels, and Dances. Edin., fo., n. d.

GOW (Neil). Scottish violinist and comp., B. Inver, Dunkeld, March 22, 1727. Taught violin by John Cameron, retainer in Grandtully family. Twice married. Played at principal gatherings and balls of his time, in large towns of Scotland. D. Inver, March 1, 1807.

WORKS.—A Collection of Strathspey Reels, with bass for the Violoncello or Harpsichord, Edin., circa 1784. A Collection of Strathspey Reels, with a bass for the Violoncello or Harpsichord, Ded. to Her Grace the Duchess of Athole, Edin. (Corri), fo., n. d. Second Collection, do., Ded. to Noblemen and Gentlemen of the Caledonian Hunt, Edin. (Corri), fo., n. d. Third Coll., Ded. to the Marchioness of Tweeddale, Edin., fo., n. d. A Complete Repository of the Original Scotch Slow Tunes, Strathspeys and Dances, the Dances arranged as Medleys for the Pianoforte or Harp, four parts, Edin., fo., n. d. Fifth and Sixth Collections of Strathspey Reels, 1808 and 1822.

As personal recollections can not now be brought to bear on the subject of Gow's character, we have transcribed the following passage, which, with a curious portrait, appears in T. Garnett's "Observations on a Tour through the Highlands etc. of Scotland." Second edition, vol. 2, p. 73, London, 1811 :—

". . We were favoured with a visit from Neil Gow, a singular and well-known character, and a celebrated performer on the violin. When I call him a celebrated performer I do not mean that he can execute the sweet Italian airs with the touch of a Cramer. His only music is that of his native country, which he has acquired chiefly by the ear, being entirely self-taught; but he plays the Scotch airs with a spirit and enthusiasm peculiar to himself. . . He excels most in the Strathspeys, which are jigs played with a peculiar spirit and life, but he executes the laments, or funeral music, with a great deal of pathos."

The good effects of the efforts made by the Gow family to preserve the older Scottish melodies are felt to this day. The Gow collection was a great improvement on that of Oswald, as latterly Johnson and Thomson (G.) was on theirs, and again that of Smith, Thomson (John), and Graham on that of their predecessors. The Gow collection contains a number of fine old melodies not elsewhere to be found, but is slightly marred by a few mistakes in regard to the localization of melodies; some being named as Irish that were found by subsequent collectors to be Scotch.

GOW (Neil, Jun.). Scottish violinist and comp., B. about end of 18th cent. (1795). Son of Nathaniel Gow—was partner in music-publishing business in Edinburgh with his father. D. Edinburgh, Nov. 7, 1823, aged 29.

WORKS.—Edinburgh Collection of Glees, Catches, Duetts, etc., Edin., n. d. A Collection of Airs, Reels, and Strathspeys, being the posthumous compositions of the late Neil Gow, Junr., arranged for Pf., harp, violin, or 'cello, by Nathaniel Gow. Edin., 1849.

This most promising young man died after giving most convincing proofs of his capacity for musical composition. His melodies, "Bonnie Prince Charlie" and "Flora Macdonald's Lament," are well-known all over the world. He composed a number of melodies to words by Hogg, etc., but the two songs named are those by which he is best known.

Other members of this family were ANDREW, JOHN, and WILLIAM, all of whom were musicians of some fame in their day, the last being especially well known as a fresh and vigorous violinist.

GRAAN (Jan van). Dutch violinist, B. Amsterdam, Sept., 1852. D. at the Hague, Jan., 1874. S. under Joachim.

GRABEN-HOFFMANN (Gustav). German song writer, B. Bnin, near Posen, March 7, 1820. Teacher in Dresden. Has comp. a large quantity of fine vocal works, which have attained to considerable popularity in Germany.

GRADDON (Miss). English soprano vocalist, B. Taunton, Somerset, 1804. S. under Tom Cooke. Sang at Vauxhall, 1822. *Début*, Dublin, 1823. Sang at Liverpool, Manchester, London, and throughout English provinces. Appeared in "Der Freischutz," Lond., Nov. 10, 1824. D. [?].

GRAEDENER (Carl G. P.). German comp. and Prof., B. Rostock, Jan. 13, 1812. Prof. of singing, Vienna Cons., 1861. Teacher in Hamburg. D. Hamburg, June 11, 1883.
WORKS.—Quintet for Pf., 2 vns., viola, and 'cello, op. 7; Eight Lieder for chorus and solo, op. 8; Sonata for Pf. and violin, in D min., op. 11; Hebrew Songs (Lord Byron) for voice and Pf., op. 15; Sonata for Pf., in C min., op. 28; Second trio for Pf., vn., and 'cello, in E flat, op. 35; etc.

GRAEME (Elliot). English writer, author of "Beethoven, a Memoir," Lond., 1870; Second edition, do. Novels, etc.

GRAEVER (Madeleine), MADAME JOHNSON. Dutch pianist and comp., B. Amsterdam, 1830. S. under Bertelsmann, Moscheles, and Litolff, etc. Appeared in Paris, England, and settled in New York, where she remained till 1861. She has appeared in Belgium, Holland, Germany, etc. as a pianist. Her compositions are mostly for the Pf.

GRAFF (Carl). Hungarian violinist and comp., B. Also-Eor, May 20, 1833. Appeared in London, Paris, etc. as vnst. Comp. operettas, organ music, symphonies for small orch., songs, etc.

GRAHAM (George Farquhar). Scottish comp. and writer, B. Edinburgh, Dec. 29, 1789. Educated at the High School and University of Edinburgh. Chiefly self-taught in Music. Joint-Secretary of Edinburgh Musical Festival, with George Hogarth, 1815. Lived for time in Italy. Unsuccessful candidate for Music Chair of Edinburgh University. D. Edinburgh, Mar. 12, 1867.
WORKS.—An Account of the first Edinburgh Musical Festival, held between the 30th of Oct. and 5th Nov., 1815, with an Essay containing some general observations on Music, Edin., 8vo, 1816. Second edition, 1835. Elements of Singing, written for the Edinburgh Institution for the Encouragement of Sacred Music, Edin., 1817. The article "Music" in the seventh and eighth editions of the "Encyclopædia Britannica." Essay on the Theory and Practice of Musical Composition, with Introduction and Appendix [reprint with additions of the foregoing], Edin., 4to, 1838. Notes and editorial work in connection with the publication of the "Skene Manuscript" (Dauney). The Songs of Scotland adapted to their appropriate Melodies...Illustrated with Historical, Biographical, and Critical Notices..., Edin., 1848-49, 3 vols., large 8vo. General Observations upon Music, and remarks upon Mr. Logier's system, Edin., 1817. Songs, Glees, P'salm-tunes. Contributions to periodical literature, etc.
Graham was the son of Col. Humphrey Graham of Edinburgh, and during a busy life did much to elevate the musical taste of his native city. His writings are all highly respectable, but the work by which he will in the future be known is the Songs of Scotland, which is still the standard edition for modern purposes, and of which a new edition, revised by John Muir Wood, was issued in 1884. He had an extensive acquaintance among the musical celebrities of his time.

GRAHAM (Maria). Scottish writer, author of "A few words on the formation of the major and minor scales, in a letter to her pupils," by M. G. Lond., 12mo, 1852.

GRAMMANN (Carl). German comp., !B. Lübeck, June 3, 1844. S. at Leipzig Cons., 1867. Resides in Vienna as comp. He has comp. "Die Schatzgräber" and "Die Eisjungfrau," early operas; Melusine, opera, 1875; Thusnelda, opera, 1881; Das Andreasfest, opera, 1882. Symphonies, quartets, vocal music, etc.

GRANCINO (Giovanni). Italian violin-maker of 17th and 18th centuries. Worked at Milan about 1694-1720. He made good instruments. His father, PAOLO, worked at Milan during 1665-92.

GRANT (Donald). Scottish teacher and comp., a native of Elgin, published

"A Collection of Strathspey Reels, Jigs, etc, for the Pianoforte, Violin, and Violoncello." Dedicated to Mrs. Col. Grant. Edin., n. d. This book dates from the end of last century.

GRANT (General Sir James Hope). Scottish military commander and musician, B. 1808. D. 1875. He entered the army in 1826, and served in China with honour.

WORKS.—Voluntaries for organ; Elegie for Pf.; Notturno for Pf. and 'cello; The Sea and the Lake, piece for Pf. and 'cello; Three sketches, Pf. and 'cello; The three violoncello makers, Pf. and 'cello. Songs, etc.

GRAS (Julie Aimée Dorus), *née* STEENKISTE, German soprano vocalist, B. Valenciennes, Sept., 1807. Appeared in London, 1839. Sang with success in Europe, in operas of Auber, Rossini, Meyerbeer, Bellini, etc. Retired, 1850.

GRASSINEAU (Jacques). French writer, B. London, 1715. D. London, 1769. Writer of "Musical Dictionary, being a Collection of Terms and Characters as well Ancient as Modern, including the Historical, Theoretical, and Practical Parts of Music, as also an explanation of some parts of the Doctrine of the Ancients," etc. Lond., 8vo, 1740.

GRASSINI (Josephina). Italian contralto vocalist, B. 1773. Appeared at the Ancient Concerts, London, 1805. D. Milan, Jan., 1850.

GRAUN (Karl Heinrich). German comp., B. Wahrenbrück, nr. Dresden, May 7, 1701. Treble singer in Dresden. S. under J. C. Schmidt, Petzhold, etc. Tenor singer in opera at Brunswick, 1725. Chapel-master to Frederick the Great, 1740. D. Berlin, Aug. 8, 1759.

WORKS.—*Operas:* Polydore, 1726; Sanico et Sinide; Iphigenie en Aulide; Scipion l'Africain; Pharaon; Rodelinda, 1741; Cleopatra, 1742; Artaserse, 1743; Catone en Utica, 1744; Alessandro nelle Indie, 1744; Lucio Papirio, 1745; Adriano in Siria, 1745; Demofoonte, 1746; Cajo Fabrizio, 1747; Le Feste Galante, 1747; Cinna, 1748; Europe Galante, 1748; Angelica e Medoro, 1749; Coriolano, 1750; Medonte, 1750; Mitridate, 1751; Armida, 1741; Brittanico, 1752; Orfeo, 1752; Il Guidizio di Paride, 1752; Silla, 1753; Semiramide, 1754; Montezuma, 1755; Ezio, 1755; I Fratelli Nemici, 1756; Merope; 1756. Te Deum, 1757. Der Tod Jesu (The Death of Jesus), oratorio, Berlin, March 26, 1755; pub. Leipzig, 1760. Masses and odes; Lavinia e Turno, cantata; Flute music, etc.

GRAY & DAVISON. English firm of organ-builders, established in London, 1779. They built organs for the Crystal Palace. London, 1883; the Town Halls of Leeds, 1859, Bolton, 1873, Glasgow, 1853; and a great number of large instruments in various towns in Britain, including Magdalen Coll., Oxford, 1878; Town Hall, Newcastle-on-Tyne, 1858; St. Pancras Ch., London, 1885; St. George's Chap. Royal, Windsor, 1883. The operations of the firm extend also to Ireland, Australia, South Africa, Portugal, Jamaica, China, and Japan. Davison was at one time in partnership with W. Hill.

GRAZIANI (Francesco). Italian barytone vocalist, B. Fermo, April 26, 1829. Has appeared in modern operas in various Italian towns.

GREATHEED (Rev. Samuel Stephenson). English divine and comp., B. nr. Weston-super-Mare, Feb. 22, 1813. B.A., Cantab., 1835. M.A., 1838. Ordained, 1838. Rector of Corringham, Sussex.

WORKS.—Enoch's Prophecy, an oratorio, words by James Montgomery, 1852. English Gradual: a book of Plain Song for Holy Communion, from ancient English sources. Plain Song for Holy Communion on ordinary days, so far as it differs from that for feasts; with offertory sentences, the Dies Iræ (English), and the order for the burial of the dead. *Anthems:* Blessed is the man; Ye that fear the Lord; Hail, Gladd'ning light; O God, Thou art worthy to be praised; Let my soul bless God; O Lord Almighty, God of Israel; O Saviour of the world; The Son of man, etc.

GREATOREX (H. W.). American comp., published a collection of Psalms. Wrote also songs, part-songs, hymns, etc. Native or resident of Boston.

GREATOREX (Thomas). English org., cond., and comp., B. North Wingfield, near Chesterfield, Derby, Oct. 5, 1758. S. under Dr. B. Cooke, 1772. Adopted by the Earl of Sandwich. Chor. at Concert of Ancient Music, 1778. Org. of Carlisle Cath., 1780-84. Teacher in Newcastle, 1784-85. Travelled in Holland and Italy, 1785-88. Introduced to Prince Charles Edward Stuart. Teacher in London, 1789. Cond. of the Concert of Ancient Music, 1793. Revived the Vocal Concerts, 1801. Org. of Westminster Abbey, in succession to G. E. Williams, 1819. Cond. of Birmingham Musical Festival. Fellow of Royal and Linnean Societies. D. Hampton, London, July 18, 1831.

WORKS.—Twelve Glees from favourite English, Irish, and Scotch Melodies, Lond., fo., n.d. [1832]. Psalms, chants, etc.

Greatorex was the foremost organist of his time, and next to Sir George Smart, the most competent conductor. His powers on the organ were remarkable, and his administrative capacity was great. His compositions are unimportant.

GREAVES (Thomas). English lutenist and comp. of 16th and 17th centuries. Biography unknown.

WORKS.—Songs of Sundrie Kindes, 1604. Reprinted madrigals—Come away, love; Lady, the melting crystal of your eye; Sweet nymphs, etc.

GREEN (James). English org. and comp., was organist at Hull in first half of last century. He published "A Book of Psalmody, containing chanting tunes for the Canticles, etc....the Reading Psalms, with eighteen Anthems and a variety of Psalm-tunes in four parts, 1724; 8th edit., 1734; 11th edit., 1751.

GREEN (Joseph). English writer, author of "The Tritone; a method of harmony and modulation adapted to the scales of keyed instruments, with Appendix, Lond., 4to, n. d. Hints on the Spanish Guitar, being a Preparatory Tutor for that Instrument, Lond. [1830].

GREEN (Samuel). English organ-builder, B. 1740. D. Isleworth, Sept. 14, 1796.

He built the organs of Bangor Cath., 1779; Canterbury, 1784; Wells, 1786; Cashel, 1786; Lichfield, 1789; Rochester, 1791; Winchester Coll. Chap., 1780; St. George's Chapel, Windsor, 1790; Organs in Aberdeen, Bath, Chatham, Greenwich, S. Petersburg, etc.

GREENE (Maurice). English org. and comp., B. London, 1696. Chor. S. Paul's Cath. under R. Brind. Org. of S. Dunstan in the West, 1716. Org. S. Andrew's, Holborn, 1717. Do. S. Paul's Cath., 1718. Org. and comp., Chap. Royal, 1727. Prof. of Music, Cambridge, 1730. Doc. Mus., Cantab., 1730. Master of the King's Band, 1735. D. London, Sept. 1, 1755.

WORKS.—Oratorios: Jephthah, 1737; The Force of Truth, 1744. Florimel, or Love's Revenge, dramatic pastoral, 1737; The Judgment of Hercules, masque, 1740. Phœbe, opera, 1748. Spenser's Amoretti for voice, harpsichord, and violin. Ode on S. Cecilia's Day, Pope, 1730; Odes for King's Birthday and New Year's Day, 1730; Catches and Canons, 3 and 4 voices; The Chaplet, coll. of 12 English songs; Church Service in C, 1737; Te Deum in D, 1745; Forty select Anthems in Score for 1, 2, 3, 4, 5, 6, 7 and 8 voices, Lond., 2 vols., 1743. Songs, organ and harpsichord music, etc.

"Greene deserves to be placed in the highest rank of our musical writers for the church, notwithstanding the disparaging terms in which Dr. Burney and other critics have spoken of his compositions."—*Hogarth*. His anthems are still accorded a degree of recognition. He was one of the original founders of the "Society of Musicians," and also established the "Apollo" club, for the performance of vocal music.

GREENWOOD (James). English comp. and vocal-trainer of present time, author of The Sol-fa System of Teaching Singing as used in Lancashire and Yorkshire; Lond., 1879. Six Kyries. Anthems, Part-songs. Three hundred and ninety-six two-part Exercises for Choirs and Schools (Music Primer), 1883.

GREETING (Thomas). English teacher of the flageolet in London, end of 17th century. Author of "The Pleasant Companion; or new lessons and instructions for the Flagelot," Lond., 12mo, 1666, another edit., 1680.

GRÉGOIR (Jacques Mathieu Joseph). Belgian pianist and comp., B. Antwerp, Jan. 18, 1817.
WORKS.—6 Poesies Musicales for Pf., op. 51; Twelve Compositions in form of Studies, op. 66; Concerto for Pf. and orch., op. 100. Great quantity of piano music of the light drawing-room cast, also music for violin and Pf. with H. Leonard.

GREGORY of Bridlington. English musician of 13th century. Canon of Order of S. Augustine. Precentor, and latterly Prior of Bridlington about 1217. Author of "De Arte Musices" in 3 books.

GREGORY (Rev. John Herbert). Australian divine, author of "Letter to the Bishop of Melbourne on Church Music," Melbourne, 1857.

GREGORY (Saint), Pope of Rome and Ecclesiastic. B. Rome, 542. D. 604, A.D. He founded a large number of monasteries, and wrote Dialogues and a Commentary on the Book of Job. His fame as a musician rests on his introduction into the service of the early Christian church the well-known Gregorian modes. These chants continued in use for many centuries, and are still advocated by a section of musicians.

GRENIER (Felix). French org. and comp., B. Marseilles, Sept.27, 1844. S. under Hesse. Comp. quartet, lieder, psalms, organ music.

GRÉTRY (André Ernest Modeste). Belgian comp., B. Liége, Feb. 11, 1741. Chor. in Ch. of S. Denis, Liége, 1747. S. under Moreau and Casali. Went to Rome, 1759. Settled in Paris, 1767. Inspector of Paris Cons., 1795. Member of the Institut, 1798. Chevalier of the Legion of Honour, 1802. D. Montmorency, Sept. 24, 1813.

WORKS.—*Operas:* Le Vendemiatrice, 1765; Isabelle et Gertrude, 1767; Le Huron, 1768; Lucile, 1769; Le Tableau parlant, 1769; Silvain, 1770; Les Deux Avares, 1770; L'Amitié à L'épreuve, 1771; Zémire et Azar, 1771; L'Ami de la Maison, 1772; Le Magnifique, 1773; La Rosière de Salency, 1774; La Fausse Magie, 1775; Les Mariages Samnites, 1776; Matroco, 1778; Le Jugement de Midas, 1778; Les Evénements imprevus, 1779; Aucassin et Nicolette, 1780; Thalie au Nouveau-Theatre, 1783; Theodore et Paulin, 1783; Richard Cœur de Lion, Paris, 1784; Les Méprises par ressemblance, 1786; Le Comte d'Albert, 1787; La Suite de Comte d'Albert, 1787; Le Prisonnier Anglais, 1787; Le Rival Confident, 1788; Raoul Barbe-Bleue, 1789; Pierre le Grand, 1790; Guillaume Tell, 1791; Basile, 1792; Les Deux Couvents, 1792; Joseph Barra, 1794; Callias, 1794; Lisbeth, 1797; Elisca, 1799; Le Barbier de Village, 1797; Andromaque, 1780; Emilie, 1781; Le Caravane du Caire, 1783; Panurge dans l'île des Lanternes, 1785; Amphitryon, 1788; Denis le Tyran, 1794; Anacreon chez Polycrate, 1797; Le Casque et les Colombes, 1801; Delphis et Mopsa, 1803; Alcindor et Zaide; Ziméo; Zelmar; Electre; Diogène et Alexandre, etc. in MS. Six Symphonies for orch. Sonatas and quartets, various. Masses and other church music. Literary works, etc.

The most of Grétry's operas are now forgotten; "Richard Cœur de Lion" being the only notable exception. The style of Grétry's music is beautiful and melodious; the harmonies are good; and the general working out effective. He is commonly regarded as the founder of modern comic opera. See André Ernest Modeste Grétry, Célèbre Compositeur Belge, par E. G. J. Grégoir, Brussels, 8vo, 1883.

GRIEG (Edvard). Norwegian comp. and pianist, B. Bergen, June 15, 1843. S. Leipzig Cons., 1858-1862, under Hauptmann, Richter, Rietz, Reinecke and Moscheles. Teacher and cond. at Copenhagen.

WORKS.—Op. 1. Clavierstücke for Pf.; op. 2. Lieder for voice and Pf.; op. 3. Poetische Tonbilder for Pf.; op. 4. Six Lieder; op. 5. Melodien des Herzens; op. 6. Vier Humoresken für Pf.; op. 7. Sonata for Pf.; op. 8. Sonata for Pf. and vn.; op. 9. Romanzen und Balladen; op. 10. Kleine Romanzen; op. 11. Phantasie for Pf. duet; op. 12. Lyrische Kleine Stücke, for Pf.; op. 13. Sonata for Pf. and vn. in G min.; op. 14. Two Symphonische-Stücke for Pf. duet; op. 15. Romanzen; op. 16. Concerto for Pf. and orch. in A minor; op. 17. Norvegische Volks-Lieder und Tänze f r Pf.; op. 18. Romanze und Lieder; op. 19. Humoreske for Pf.; op.

T

20. Vor Südens Kloster, for solo, chorus, and orch.; op. 27. Quartet for strings, G min.; op. 35. Norwegian Dances for Pf. duet; op. 36. Sonata for Pf. and 'cello; op. 37. Waltz-caprices for Pf. duet; op. 38. Lyric Pieces for Pf.

Grieg is one of the most gifted of living Northern composers. His works are poetical and interesting, beautifully conceived, and carefully executed.

GRIER (William). Scottish writer, author of "The Musical Encyclopædia: a Collection of English, Scottish, and Irish Songs, edited by J. Wilson, to which is prefixed an elaborate essay on the first principles of Music," Lond., 8vo, 1835; another edition, 1852.

GRIESBACH (John Henry). German comp., B. Windsor, June 20, 1798. Violoncellist in Queen's band, 1810. S. under Kalkbrenner. Pianist in London and director of Philharmonic Society. D. London, Jan. 9, 1875.

WORKS.—Belshazzar's Feast, 1835; Daniel (reproduction), 1853; Music to the "Tempest"; James the First, or the Royal Captive, operetta; The Goldsmith of West Cheap, opera; Eblis, opera, unfinished; Baby Ruins, musical drama; Overtures for orch. Analysis of Musical Sounds, with Illustrative Figures of the ratios of vibrations of Musical Intervals and their compounds, Harmonic vibration, temperament, etc., fo., n. d. Elements of Musical Notation, containing tables of the comparative value of the different kinds of Notes, Signatures of the different keys, etc., 8vo, n. d. Pianoforte Student's Companion, containing all the Scales in four positions, etc., Lond. [1825]. Anthems, Songs, etc.

GRIEVE (John Charles). Scottish comp., cond., and teacher, B. Edinburgh, Aug. 29, 1842. Fellow of the Educational Institute of Scotland. Lecturer on Musical Theory, Heriot-Watt Coll., Edinburgh. Cond. of Psalmody, Lady Yester's Ch., Edinburgh. Was Cond. of Phoenix Musical Assoc., Edinburgh. Teacher of Singing in various Schools, and at one time editor of *The Musical Star.*

WORKS.—Benjamin, oratorio, Edin., 1877; Christian Songs of Praise, 24 hymns for 4 voices, 1873; The Sower and the seed: Scripture parable for soli, and chorus; The good Samaritan, do.; Julia's Birthday, musical sketch; Kinderspiel, a musical sketch for juveniles. *Part-songs:* Good morrow to my lady; Stars of the summer night; Fly away Lady-bird; My Love is like a red, red rose, trio. *Songs:* The wells o' wearie; The mither's bairn; Comin' hame. Day Dreams, reverie for Pf. School songs, etc. The Harmonium: how to use it. Edin., n.d.

GRIFFIN (George Eugene). English pianist and comp., B. Jan. 8, 1781. Member of Philharmonic Soc., teacher, etc. D. London, May, 1863.

WORKS.—Two concertos for Pf. and orch.; Ode to Charity, 1806; Four sonatas for Pf.; Three string quartets; Rondos, marches, variations, etc. for Pf.; Songs, glees, etc.

GRIFFITHS (John). English bass vocalist, B. about middle of 18th century. D. Worcester, Oct. 1821.

GRIGOR (Alexander L.). Scottish writer, author of "Hints and Maxims to Players on Pianoforte, Harmonium, etc.," Glasgow, 8vo, 1883.

GRIMM (Julius Otto). German pianist and comp., B. Pernau, March 6, 1827.

WORKS.—Op. 1. Six Lieder for voice and Pf.; op. 2. Abendbilder, 5 Pf. pieces; op. 3. Six Lieder for voice and Pf.; op. 4. Two Scherzos for Pf.; op. 12. An die Musik, poem by L. Schücking for solo voice, chorus, and orch.; op. 13. Six Lieder for 4 male voices, etc.

GRISAR (Albert). Belgian comp., B. Antwerp, Dec. 26, 1808. S. under Reicha at Paris. D. Asnières, near Paris, June 15, 1869.

WORKS.—*Operas:* Sarah, 1836; Lady Melvil, 1838; Les Porcherons, 1850; Le Carillonneur de Bruges, 1852; Les Amours du Diable. 1853, etc.

GRISI (Giulia). Italian soprano vocalist, B. Milan, July 28, 1812. S. at Convent in Gorizia, 1818. Got lessons from her sister, Giuditta Grisi, and Madame Boccabadati. *Début* at Milan in Rossini's Zelmira, 1829. Engaged with Lanari, operatic manager at Florence, on unfavourable terms, 1830, and broke engagement by going to Paris, 1832. Appeared in London, April, 1834, as

Ninetta in "La Gazza Ladra." Married to M. de Melery, a Frenchman, 1836. Separated soon after, and was afterwards married to Signor Mario, by whom she had four children. Travelled in America, 1854. Retired from London opera, 1861. Re-appeared at H. M. Theatre, London, 1866. D. Berlin, Nov. 25, 1869.

Grisi was one of the most magnificent sopranos who held the stage during her time. She was best suited to tragic parts, which she rendered with consummate dramatic skill and force. Her voice was fresh and beautiful, clear and natural in intonation, and of great compass. In every respect she was one of the greatest dramatic vocalists. Her sister, GIUDITTA, a contralto, appeared at King's Theatre, London, May, 1832.

GROBE (Charles). American writer, author of "New Method for the Pianoforte," Boston, n. d.; Collections of School and other Songs; Numerous light pieces for the Pf.

GROOME (W.). English writer, author of a "Concise Treatise on Music," London, 8vo, 1870.

GROVE (Sir George), D.C.L., Durham. English writer on music, B. Clapham, Surrey, Aug. 13, 1820. Was bred a Civil Engineer, but forsaking that line of life, became Secretary to the Society of Arts in 1849; and in 1852, Secretary to the Crystal Palace Company, with which he was connected as Secretary, Manager, and Director, till the close of 1880. During the latter period he interested himself greatly in the music of the Palace. In 1883 he was appointed Principal of the newly established Royal College of Music, and received the honour of knighthood. He became LL.D., Glasgow, 1885. In 1855 he recommended the appointment of Mr. Manns, to whom the formation of the Crystal Palace orchestra, the daily and Saturday concerts, and the great impetus given thereby to orchestral music in England, are due. Mr. Grove warmly seconded Mr. Manns's efforts by his general support, by his analyses of the works played on Saturdays, and by obtaining various important compositions for performance, such as Mendelssohn's "Reformation Symphony," the six MS. symphonies of Schubert, for which he made two journeys to Vienna, etc. Mr. Grove is also known for his connection with Dr. Smith's Dictionary of the Bible, to which he was a principal contributor, for his labours in Biblical geography, and for his promotion of the Palestine Exploration Fund, the formation of which was virtually due to him. He is one of the literary executors of the late Dean of Westminster. He edited *Macmillan's Magazine* for more than 15 years, and is now editing the Dictionary of Music and Musicians for Messrs. Macmillan, in which the articles on Beethoven, Mendelssohn, Schubert, and many other subjects, are from his pen. In the course of his investigations for the last named biography, he appears to have discovered certain traces of a forgotten symphony by Schubert, of the year 1825, the possession of which will be a remarkable event in the musical world.

GRUNEISEN (Charles Lewis). German writer, B. London, Nov. 2, 1806. D. London, Nov., 1879. Author of "The Opera and the Press," 8vo, 1869. Memoir of Meyerbeer, Lond., 1848. Journalistic work, etc.

GRÜTZMACHER (Friedrich Wilhelm Ludwig). German violoncellist and comp., B. Dessau, March 1, 1832. Appeared in England, 1867. Teacher in Dresden.

WORKS.—Concertos for 'cello and orch., various; Variations for 'cello and orch.; Im Frühling, 3 stücke for 'cello and Pf., op. 30; Two concert pieces for 'cello and Pf., op. 32; etc.

GUADAGNI (Gaetano). Italian soprano vocalist, B. Lodi, 1725. D. Padua, 1797.

GUADAGNINI (Giovanni B.). Italian violin-maker, flourished 1710-50. Brother of Lorenzo. Made violins of some repute after the Stradivarius model.

GUADAGNINI (Lorenzo). Italian violin-maker of Cremona, worked 1695-1740. Was a pupil of Stradivarius, and imitated his style. His model is flat, but the tone is rich and powerful. His violins are now rare.

GUARNERIUS (Andrea). Italian violin-maker, worked at Cremona between years 1630-95. Instruments good. Founder of the celebrated Guarnerius family.

GUARNERIUS (Giuseppe.) Italian violin-maker, son of above. Worked at Cremona, 1680-1730. Workmanship superior; model good.

GUARNERIUS (Pietro). Italian violin-maker, worked at Cremona, 1690-1728. Son of Andreas.

GUARNERIUS (Giuseppe Antonio). Italian violin-maker, B. Cremona, June 8, 1683. D. 1745. This artist, who is known as Giuseppe del Jesù, is the greatest of the family; his instruments being of the most beautiful model, finish, and tone. He was supposed to have worked with Stradivarius, but some authorities contradict this statement. His instruments are very rare, and extremely valuable.

GUARDUCCI (Carolina). Italian operatic vocalist, B. Leghorn, 1833. Appeared in Italian opera in London, on the Continent, etc.

GUERNSEY (Wellington). Irish lyric poet and comp., B. Mullingar, June 8, 1817. D. London, Nov. 13, 1885. Has written the words of an immense quantity of songs, chiefly of a sentimental kind, of which "Mary Blane," and "Alice, where art thou?" are the best known. His own productions consist chiefly of songs, such as "I'll hang my harp on a willow tree," but he has written a mass in B flat, and other musical works.

GUERRERO (Francisco). Spanish comp., B. Seville, 1528. S. under Morales, chap. master of Seville Cath., 1538. D. Jan. 15, 1599. Comp. for the church masses, motets, psalms, etc., and also madrigals, songs, etc.

GUEST (George). English org. and comp., B. Bury St. Edmunds, 1771. S. under his father, Ralph. Chor. in Chap. Roy. Org. at Eye, Suffolk, 1787. Do. Wisbeach, 1789. D. Wisbeach, Sept. 10, 1831. Wrote glees, hymns, songs, duets, org. music, etc.

GUEST (Ralph). English comp. and org., B. Basely, Shropshire, 1742. Chor. Basely Ch. Chor. Portland Ch., London, 1763. S. org. under Ford of S. James' Ch., Bury. Choir-master of S. Mary's, Bury St. Edmunds, 1805-22. D. Bury, June 1830.

WORKS.—The Psalms of David, collection. Glees. Songs, a great number, all of moderate quality. He was an efficient choir-master.

GUEYMARD (Louis). French tenor vocalist, B. 1822. S. Paris. *Début* Paris in "Robert le Diable," 1848. D. 1880.

GUGLIELMI (Pietro). Italian comp., B. Massa, Carrara, May, 1727. S. under Durante, Naples Cons. Chap.-master at the Vatican, 1793. D. Rome, Nov. 19, 1804.

WORKS.—*Operas:* I Capricci d'una Marchesa, 1759; Tamerlano, 1765; Farnace, 1765; Sesostri, 1767; Orfeo, Lond., 1770; Il Carnavale di Venezia, Lond., 1770; Ezio, Lond., 1770; Le Pazzie d'Orlando, Lond., 1771; Don Papirio, 1774; Artaserce, 1776; La Bella Pescatrice, 1779; I Fratelli Pappa Mosca, 1783; I Finti Amori, 1786; Didone, 1785; I due Gemelli, 1787; La Pastorella Nobile, 1788; Rinaldo, 1789. Oratorio. op. 1. Six divertissements for harpsichord, vn., and 'cello, Lond.; op. 2. Six quartets for harpsichord, 2 vns., and 'cello, Lond.; op. 3. Six solos for harpsichord. Songs, masses, etc.

GUHR (Karl Ferdinand Wilhelm). German violinist and comp., B. Militsch, Oct. 1787. D. Frankfort-on-the-Main, July 23, 1848. Composed a great quantity of pleasing music for violin solo, violin and Pf., violin and orch., etc.

GUIDI (Giovanni Gualberto). Italian music-publisher, B. Florence, 1817. Editor of the journal *Boccherini*, and publisher of a handy edition of the string quartets, etc. of Haydn, Beethoven, and others, as well as of standard works by the great masters. D. Florence, Jan. 18, 1883.

GUIDO DI AREZZO, or ARETINO. Italian theorist, monk in the Benedictine Monastery at Pomposa during early part of 11th century. Guido increased the limits of the stave used in his time, originated solemnization by means of syllables (ut, re, mi, fa, sol, la), and invented or gave a basis for the science of counterpoint. His principal work is the "Micrologus," a Latin tract which explains his method of teaching boys to sing, with rules for the composition, and just performance, of the plain chant.

GUILMANT (Felix Alexandre). French org. and comp., B. Boulogne, Mar. 12, 1837. S. under Lemmens, etc. Org. Ch. of St. Joseph, Boulogne, 1857. Chap.-master, St. Nicolas, do. Prof. of Singing in Public Schools, Boulogne. Org. of Ch. of the Trinity, Paris, 1871. Has played in London and in English provinces.

WORKS.—*Organ and Harmonium*: Pieces de differents styles, first series, opp. 15, 16, 17, 18, 19, 20 ; Second series, opp. 24, 25, 33, 40, 44, 45 ; L' Organiste pratique, opp. 39, 41, 46, 47, 49, 52 ; First Sonata in D minor, op. 42 ; Priere et Berceuse, op. 27 ; Canzonetta, op. 28 ; Fughetta, op. 29 ; Scherzo, op. 30 ; Aspiration Religieuse, op. 31 ; Villageoise, op. 32 ; Mazurka de Salon, op. 35 ; Transcriptions for Harmonium, various ; Pastorale for Pf. and Harm., op. 26 ; Marche Triomphale, do., op. 34 ; Scherzo Capriccioso, do., op. 36 ; Prière for 'cello and Pf., op. 22. Ce que dit le Silence, Reverie for Tenor, with accomp. for Pf. and Harm. O Salutaris, op. 37 ; Ave Verum, for 4 voices and org., op. 1 ; O Salutaris, do., op. 2 ; Psalm for 4 voices and org., op. 8 ; Mass for 4 voices and orch., op. 11 ; Five Litanies ; Twelve Motets ; Echoes du Mois de Marie. Songs and miscellaneous works.

Guilmant is one of the greatest organists of modern times. For brilliancy, expression, and touch, he is unsurpassed in France. His compositions are known to every organist of any pretence, and are remarkable for effectiveness.

GUIRAUD (Ernest). French comp. and prof., B. New Orleans, June 23, 1837. S. Paris Cons. Gained " Grand Prix de Rome," 1859. Prof. of Harmony in Cons., 1876.

WORKS.—*Operas:* Roi David, 1864 ; Sylvie, 1864 ; Gli Avventurieri en Prison, 1869 ; Le Kobold, 1870 ; Madam Turlupin, 1872 ; Gretna-Green, Ballet, 1873 ; Piccolino, opera, 1876, London, 1879. Orchestral works, Pf. music, songs, etc.

GUMBERT (Ferdinand). German comp., B. Berlin, April 21, 1818. S. vn. under C. Rietz. Teacher, etc., in Munich.

WORKS.—Die Schœne Schusterin, opera, 1844 ; Die Kunst geliebt zu werden, do. Operettas, various. Lieder, to the amount of over 400. The lieder of this comp. are marked by good taste and melodiousness.

GUMPELTZHAIMER (Adam). Germ. comp., B. Trospberg, Bavaria, 1560. Musician in service of Duke of Würtemberg. D. [?].

WORKS.—Compendium Musicæ Latinæ Germanicum, 1595, several editions ; Erster Theil des Lustgartleins teutsch und lateinischen Lieder von 3 stimmen, 1591 ; Erster Theil des Würtz-Gartleins 4 stimmen Geistlichen Lieder, 1594 ; Psalmus, 50, octo, vocum, 1604, etc.

GUNG'L (Josef). Hungarian comp. and bandmaster, B. Zsàmbèk, Dec. 1, 1810. Travelled with band in Europe, and visited America, 1848.

WORKS.—*Waltzes:* Die Gräfenberger ; Amoretten Tänze ; Soldaten Lieder ; Narren Tänze ; Zephyr Lüfte ; Julien Tänze ; Lust und Leben ; Tanzperlen ; Frühlingslieder ; Abschied von München ; Debatten ; Ueber Land und Meer ; Dresden ; Marien ; Isar Lieder ; Jungharren Tänze ; Rheinsagen ; Die Berliner ; Die Prager ; Elisen Tänze ; Fiumara Lieder ; Pandekten ; Tafelrunde ; Les Adieux ; Feuerklänge ; Hesperus Klänge ; Improvisationem ; Frohsinn Lieder ; Copenhagen ; Leipziger Lerchen ; Hochzeitsreigen ; Themselieder ; Wanderlieder ; Bardenlieder ; Wilhelminen Tänze ; Slowanka Klänge ; Novellen ; Unter den Linden ; Die Benefizianten ; Brautlieder ; Phantome ; Alpenrosen ; Peterhof ; Der Verschmähte ; Hamburger Kinder. Polkas, marches.

These dances are well known for their spirited rhythms and skilful harmony. A nephew of this comp., named JOHANN GUNG'L, B. Zsàmbèk, 1819, was also a comp. of dance music. D. there, Nov., 1883.

GUNN (Anne), *née* YOUNG. Scottish pianist and writer, wife of John Gunn, wrote "An Introduction to music; in which the Elementary Parts of the Science, and the Principles of Thorough-bass and Modulation, as illustrated by the Musical Games and Apparatus, are fully and familiarly explained, with Examples and Complete Directions for Playing the several Games." Edin., 8vo, 1803. Second edition, 8vo, 1820.

GUNN (Barnabas). English org. and comp., B. end of 17th century. Org. of St. Philip's, Birmingham, till 1730. Org. of Gloucester Cath., succeeding Hine, 1730. Wrote two cantatas and six songs, Gloucester, 1736. Sonatas for Harpsichord, etc. D. 1743.

GUNN (John). Scottish writer and 'cellist, B. in Highlands of Scotland [Edinburgh, 1765?] Teacher of 'cello at Cambridge, and in London, from 1789. Returned to Edinburgh, and married Miss Anne Young, 1804. D. [1824?].
WORKS.—An Essay, with copious examples, towards a more easy and scientific method of commencing and pursuing the study of the Pianoforte, with the principles of thorough-bass and musical science. Lond., fo., n. d. Forty Favorite Scotch airs, adapted for violin, German flute, or violoncello, with the phrases mark'd...supplement to the Examples in the Theory and Practice of fingering the Violoncello, Lond., fo., n. d. The Theory and Practice of fingering the violoncello, containing rules and progressive lessons for attaining the knowledge and command of the whole compass of the instrument, Lond., fo., 1793. Second edition, n. d. Art of Playing the German Flute on new principles, n. d. An Essay, theoretical and practical, on the application of Harmony, Thorough-bass, and Modulation, to the Violoncello. Edin., 1801. An Historical Enquiry respecting the Performance on the Harp in the Highlands of Scotland, from the earliest times until it was discontinued about the year 1734; to which is prefixed an account of a very ancient Caledonian harp, and of the harp of Queen Mary. Edin., 4to, 1807. This work he proposed to supplement by "An Enquiry into the Antiquity of the Harp, etc," but it never appeared. School for the German Flute, fo., n. d.

GURLITT (Cornelius). German comp., B. Altona, Feb. 10, 1820. Writer of much agreeable instrumental music: Sonatas for Pf., opp. 17, 20, 21, etc.; "Gesänge aus dem Quickborn v. Klaus Groth, op. 18; Die Jahreszeiten, liedercyclus, op. 26; Präludien u. Choräle, op. 28; Sonatinas for Pf., op. 118; and other pieces numbering in all over op. 140.

GURNEY (Edward). Contemporary English writer, author of "The Power of Sound," Lond., large 8vo, 1880. Several contributions to magazines on musical subjects.

GURNEY (T. E.). American org. and writer, author of "American School for Reed Organ, Melodeon, etc.," Boston. "Carhart's Melodeon or Reed Organ Instructor," Boston; etc.

GUSIKOW (Michael Josef). Polish performer on the Holz und Strohiust (wood and straw) instrument, B. Sklov, Sept. 1806. D. Aix-la-Chapelle, Oct. 21, 1837. Travelled in Europe as performer on his instrument.

GUTMANN (Adolf). German comp., B. Heidelberg, Jan. 12, 1819. D. Spezzia, Oct. 27, 1882. Wrote chamber and Pf. music in great variety.

GUY (Henry). English tenor vocalist and comp., B. Oxford, 1847. S. at R. A. M. Gent. of Chap. Royal, 1876. Has appeared with success at the principal London and provincial concerts and festivals. His compositions consist of glees and songs.

GUYLOTT (Robert). English comp., B. 1794. D. London, Dec. 18, 1876. Wrote songs chiefly, of which the following are among the principal:—Broken vow; Days that are gone; Haste to the woodlands; In the pretty spring time; Rose shall cease to blow; etc.

GWILT (Joseph). English writer and architect, B. in Surrey, 1784. Architect to the Grocers' Company, London. D. Henley-on-Thames, Sept. 14, 1863. He published a "Collection of Madrigals and Motetts chiefly for 4 Equal Voices, by the most Eminent Composers of the 16th and 17th centuries...,"

Lond., 1815; and wrote the article "Music" in the "Encyclopædia Metropolitana." He also compiled a valuable "Encyclopædia of Architecture," etc.

GYE (Frederick). English operatic manager, B. 1809. D. Dec. 4, 1878. Managed with his sons the Italian Opera, Covent Garden, London, for a number of years.

GYROWETZ (Adalbert). Bohemian comp., B. Budweis, Feb. 19, 1763. S. law at Prague. Secretary in private family. S. music under Sala at Naples. Went to Paris. Appeared in London, 1789. Comp. to Salomon Concerts. Returned to Vienna, 1792. Chap.-master at Vienna, 1804-21. D. Vienna, Mar. 22, 1850.

WORKS.—String quartets, opp. 1, 4, 5, 9, 11, 17, 21, 25, 28, 29, 42; Nocturnes for flute, vn., viola, and bass, opp. 20, 23, 32, 35, 38; Sonatas for Pf., vn., and 'cello, opp. 9, 10, 12, 15, 16, 19, 22, 26, 27, 31, 33, 34, 40, 41, 45, 48, 51, 55, 57, 58, 59, 60; Sonatas for Pf., op. 62, 63; Symphonies for orch., opp. 7, 8, 13, 14, 18, 23*a*, 33*a*, 47. *Operas:* Semiramide, London (destroyed in burning of the Pantheon, 1792); Les Metamorphoses d'Arlequin; Les Page du Duc de Vendôme, 1808; Le Trompeur Trompé, 1810; Agnes Sorel, 1808; Ida; Mirina, 1806; Selico, 1804; Der Augenarzt, 1811; Die Prüfung, 1813; Helene. 1816; Felix und Adele, 1831; Die Junggesellen Wirthschaft; Der Sammtroch; Aladin; Das Ständchen; Federica e Adolfo, 1812; Gustav Vasa, ballet.

H.

HAACK (Carl). German violinist and comp., B. Potsdam, 1757. Violinist in band of the king of Prussia. D. Berlin, Sept. 28, 1819. Comp. sonatas, concertos for Pf., chamber music, songs, etc.

HAAS (Ildefonse). German comp., B. Offenburg, April 23, 1735. D. May 30, 1791. Wrote music for the church, literary works, etc.

HABENECK (Francois Antoine). French violinist, cond., and comp., B. Mezières, Jan. 22, 1781. S. under Baillot, Paris Cons. Gained first prize for vn. playing, 1804. Assistant Prof., Paris Cons., 1808-16. Solo vn. at opera, 1815. Director of the Académie de Musique, 1821-24. Cond. at opera, 1824-47. Prof. at Cons., 1825-48. Member of Legion of Honour, 1822. D. Paris, Feb. 8, 1849.

WORKS.—Concertos, caprices, polonaises, fantasias, etc., for vn. and Pf. or orch. Ballet. Church music, songs.

Habeneck is chiefly famed for his work as a conductor, for which position he possessed more than ordinary aptitude. His works are forgotten. He was associated with Berlioz in the production of some of his works.

HABERBIER (Ernst). German comp. and pianist, B. Königsberg, Oct. 5, 1813. D. Bergen, March 12, 1869. Works for Pf.

HABERCORN (John). English musician, published "Psalmodia Germanica or the German Psalmody, translated from the High German, together with their proper Tunes and Thoroughbass," Lond., 1765.

HABERMANN (Franz Johann). Bohemian comp., B. Bohemia, 1706. D. April 7, 1783. Wrote church music chiefly.

HABICHT (Emma). German writer, authoress of "Recollections of Chopin," by Mrs. C. E. H[abicht]. Privately printed, n. d.

HADDOCK (George). English violinist and writer, author of "The Major and Minor Scales in all positions, with exercises on double notes, octaves, and staccato bowing; carefully fingered, forming a practical work for students of the Violin," London (Ashdown), n. d.

HAESER (August Ferdinand). German comp. and writer, B. Leipzig, Oct. 15, 1779. S. at St. Thomas Schule, Leipzig. D. Weimar, Nov. 1, 1844. Comp. operas, masses, church music, Pf. music, and wrote a vocal method.

HÄFFNER (Johann Christian Friedrich). Swedish comp. and org., B. Oberschönau, Mar. 2, 1759. Org. of Upsala Cath. D. Upsala, May 28, 1833.
WORKS.—Svensk Choralbok, 1819-21 ; Swedish National Melodies (collected) ; Songs, org. music, etc. His Swedish melodies are valuable.

HAGEN (Theodor). German comp., pianist, and teacher, B. Hamburg, 1822 [Dessau], 1823. S. at Hamburg. Resided in London, 1852. Went to New York as teacher. D. New York, Dec. 27, 1871. Journalist and teacher.

HAGUE (Charles). English comp. and org., B. Tadcaster, 1769. S. violin at Cambridge under Manini, 1779-85. Removed to London, 1785. S. under Salomon and Dr. Cooke. Mus. Bac., Cantab., 1794. Prof. of Music, Camb. Univ., 1799. Mus. Doc., Cantab., 1801. D. Cambridge, June, 1821.
WORKS.—Ode performed at Cambridge in June, 1811, at the installation of the Duke of Gloucester as Chancellor of the University ; By the waters of Babylon, Psalm. *Glees*: Two Collections ; Arrangements of Haydn's 12 symphonies as Pf. duets ; Plumptre's Collection of Songs, moral, sentimental, instructive, and amusing, 8vo, n. d. Pf. music, etc.
His daughter HARRIET (B. 1793, D. 1816) published in 1814 "Six Songs," with Pf. accomp.

HAIGH (Thomas). English comp. and pianist, B. London, 1769. S. under Haydn, 1791-92. Resided in Manchester, 1793-1801. Returned to London, 1801. D. London, April, 1808.
WORKS.—Sonatas for Pf. and vn., op. 4, 6, 8, 9, 10, 12, 15, 16, 24, 33, 34, 36 ; Three sonatas, Pf. duet, op. 5 ; Easy sonatas for Pf. duet, op. 7 ; Three divertimentos, op. 18 ; Three sonatas, Pf. and flute, op. 19 ; Three sonatas, op. 20 ; Three capriccios, Pf., op. 38 ; Three serenatas, do., op. 40 ; Twelve preludes ; Twenty-eight familiar airs, etc., Pf. ; Twelve petites pieces for the Pf., with introductory preludes to each, op. 32. Songs and glees.

HAINL (Francois Georges). French violoncellist, cond., and comp., B. Issoire, Nov., 1807. D. Paris, June, 1873.

HAITE (John James). English comp. and writer, B. [?]. D. London, Oct., 1874.
WORKS.—The Principles of Natural Harmony ; being a perfect system founded upon the discovery of the true semitonic scale. Lond., 4to, n. d. Violoncello Tutor, Lond., n. d. Oratorio, operettas, symphonies. Glee Garland, various numbers.

HAITZINGER (Anton). Austrian vocalist, B. 1796. Sang in Paris, London, St. Petersburg, Germany, etc. D. 1869.

HAKING (Rev. Richard). English musician, B. 1830. Took holy orders, 1861. Mus. Doc., Oxon., 1864. Rector of Easton Grey, Malmesbury, 1873 ; Congham, Norfolk, 1882.
WORKS.—Cantatas ; Two Lyrical legends ; Orchestral pieces, and solos for violin, flute, 'cello, Pf., etc. *Anthems*: Doth not wisdom cry ; Lord, let me know mine end. *Part-Songs*: A knight with his falchion gleaming ; A song to the wavelets ; Christmas holly ; Welcome home ; Song of the old bell ; The violet ; The wind's errand ; The old woman's wooing. Songs, etc.

HALBERSTADT (Joseph). Dutch flute-player and comp., B. 1813. D. London, July, 1881.

HALE (Adam de la). French troubadour, B. Arras [1240]. D. Naples [1285-7]. He was surnamed the Hunchback, and is the author of the earliest known entertainment in the form of comic opera : to wit, "Le jeu de Robin et de Marion," the MS. of which is in the Imperial Library in Paris. From this copy an edition was published in 1822. Hale also wrote a number of motets, chansons, and amorous poetry.

HALE (Joseph P.). American Pf. manufacturer, B. in Massachusetts. Established a large business in New York city in 1860, including a factory capable of turning out nearly 200 complete instruments in a week. He D. New York, Oct. 15, 1885.

HALE (Thomas), of Darnhall, Cheshire, English musician. Comp. "Social Harmony. A Collection of Songs and Catches, in two, three, four, and five parts. Also several choice Songs on Masonry, all with the Music." London, 4to, 1763.

HALES (William). English writer on acoustics, author of " Sonorum doctrina rationalis et experimentalis," Dublin, 4to, 1788.

HALÉVY (Jacques Francois Fromental Elias), or Lévi, French comp., B. Paris, May 27, 1799. Entered Paris Cons., 1809. Gained prize for solfeggo, 1810 ; 2nd prize harmony, 1811 ; 2nd Grand prix de Rome, 1816 ; do., 1817. Gained Grand Prix de Rome, 1819. S. in Italy. Prof. Paris Cons. Secretary of the Académie des Beaux Arts. Member of the Institut, 1836. D. Nice, March 17, 1862. Buried at Paris.

WORKS.—*Operas* : Les Bohemiennes, 1819 ; Pygmalion, 1823 ; Les Deux Pavillons, 1824 ; L'Artisan, 1827 ; Le Roi et le Batelier, 1828 ; Clari, 1829 ; Le Dilettante d'Avignon, 1829 ; Yella, 1830 ; La Langue Musicale, 1831 ; Les Souvenirs de Lafleur, 1834 ; La Juive, 5 acts, Paris, Feb. 23, 1835 (Lond., 1846) ; L'Eclair, 3 acts, Opera Comique, Dec. 16, 1835 ; Guido et Ginevra, 1838 ; Les Treize, 1839 ; Le Shérif, 1839 ; Le Drapier, 1840 ; Le Guitarrero, 1840 ; La Reine de Chypre, 1841 ; Charles VI., 1843 ; Le Lazzarone, 1844 ; Le Val d' Andorre, 1844 ; Les Mousquetaires de la Reine, 1846 ; Prométhée enchainé, 1849 ; La Fée aux Roses, 1849 ; La Dame de Pique, 1850 ; La Tempesta, Queen's Theatre, London, 1850 ; Paris, 1851 ; Le Juif Errant, 1852 ; Le Nabob, 1853 ; Jaguarita, 1855 ; Valentine d' Aubigne, 1856 ; La Magicienne, 1857 ; Noë, MS., unfinished. Manon Lescaut, ballet, 1830 ; La Tentation, do., 1832 ; Les Plages du Nil, cantata. De Profundis. Leçons de Lecture Musicale, 1857.

The operatic works of Halévy were highly popular in their day, but are now rarely performed. His reputation rests chiefly on "La Juive," a work of the greatest power, though marred by a somewhat repulsive libretto. This work achieved considerable fame both in England and on the Continent, and may be noted as one of the most thrilling operas of modern times. Among Halévy's many celebrated pupils may be named Gounod, Bizet, Deldevez, and Bazin.

HALL (C. C.). American writer, author of "The Necessity and Advantages of Popular Education in Church Music." New York, 8vo [1878].

HALL (Charles King). Contemporary English comp., org., and writer. Comp. of a number of songs, anthems, Pf. pieces, operettas, etc., and author of "A School for the Harmonium, containing a Description of the Instrument, a Diagram of the Stops, full directions for Blowing, Fingering, etc., twenty Progressive Studies carefully fingered, and a Collection of Sacred and Secular Pieces by the best composers, arranged for instruments of various sizes." Lond. [1874]. "Harmonium Primer" (Novello's Series) 4to, n. d.

HALL (Elias). English musician, compiled "The Psalm-singer's Compleat Companion," Lond., 12mo, 1708.

HALL (Henry). English org. and comp., son of Capt. Henry Hall, B. Windsor, 1655. Chor. in Chap. Royal, under Capt. Cook. S. under Dr. Blow. Org. of Exeter Cath., 1674. Org. and vicar-choral, Hereford Cath. D. Mar. 30, 1707.

WORKS.—Poems ; Te Deum, in E flat ; Anthems ; Cantate Domino ; Songs, etc.

His sons HENRY and WILLIAM were both musicians. The former was organist and vicar-choral at Hereford Cath., and the latter a member of the King's band. He died in 1700. Writer of songs in various collections.

HALLÉ (Charles). German pianist, comp., and cond., B. Hagen, near Elberfeldt, April 11, 1819. S. under Rinck, 1835. Resided at Paris, 1836-48. Married, 1841. Settled in England, 1848. *Début* as pianist, London, 1848. Established subscription concerts at Manchester, 1857. Has played throughout Britain, at principal concerts.

WORKS.—Op. 1. Four romances for Pf.; op. 2. Four esquisses for Pf.; op. 4. Scherzo, in D, for Pf.; op. 5. Miscellanies, Pf.; op. 6. Pensées fugitives, Pf.; Practical Pianoforte School, 5 sections; Musical Library Series (edited pieces); Twilight thoughts, op. 7; Beethoven's sonatas, edited; Editions of Pf. works by Bach, Heller, Mendelssohn, Mozart, Schubert, etc. Transcriptions, various.

The amount of practical good which Hallé has achieved in the cause of advancing musical art among the general public of Britain, cannot be too highly estimated. His success in familiarizing the musical and general public alike with the less-known works of representative masters, is no mean monument to his industry and ability. Berlioz was to most British musicians practically a nobody till Hallé produced his works, while many other musicians owe much of their posthumous fame to the sympathetic efforts of this painstaking conductor.

The "Pianoforte School" of Hallé is a substantial and comprehensive work, arranged on a methodical and sufficiently perspicuous plan to insure its place among the standard exercise-books for that instrument.

HALLET, DAVIS, & CO. American Pianoforte manufacturers, established in Boston, 1843. Have gained prizes at Philadelphia, etc. The production of this firm has been stated at 2000 instruments annually.

HALLSTRŒM (Ivar). Contemporary Swedish comp. and pianist, B. Stockholm, 1826. Has produced several successful works, among them, Hertig' magnus, opera, 1867. Les Vikings, do., 1877. Neaga, opera, 1884.

HALMA (Hilarion Emile). French violinist and comp., B. Sedan, 1803. S. Paris Cons. under Baillot. Principal violin Theatre Français. Travelled in England, America, Europe, etc. Comp. for violin.

HAMAL (Jean Noel). Belgian comp., B. Liége, Dec. 23, 1709. D. Nov. 26, 1778. Comp. operas, etc.

HAMBACHER. See DUSCHEK.

HAMBOIS (John), HAMBOYS. English musician and writer of the 15th century. Generally believed to have been the first English musician on whom the degree of Doctor of Music was conferred. He is supposed to have received the degree in 1463. He wrote two tracts in Latin: Summum Artis Musices, and Cantionum Artificialium diversi Generis, etc.

HAMERIK (Asger). Danish comp. and pianist, B. Copenhagen, April 8, 1843. S. in Germany and England. Musical Director of Peabody Institute, Baltimore, 1872.

WORKS.—Operas; Chamber music; Songs; Jüdische Triologie, orch., op. 19; Nordische Suite für Orchester, op. 22; Fourth do., in D, op. 24. Miscellaneous orchestral works.

HAMERTON (William Henry). English comp. and writer, B. Nottingham, 1795. Chorister Christ Ch. Cath., Dublin. S. under T. Vaughan, London, 1812. Teacher in Dublin, 1814. Master of Choristers, Christ Ch. Cath., Dublin, 1815. Gent. of Chap. Roy., Dublin, 1823, Teacher in Calcutta, 1829. D. Calcutta [?].

WORKS.—St. Alban, opera, Dublin, 1827. Vocal Instructions combined with the theory and practice of Pianoforte accompaniment, 1824. Anthems, chants, glees, songs, etc.

HAMILTON (C. K.). American writer, author of "Perfect Method for the Zither," Illustrated. Boston, n. d.

HAMILTON (James Alexander). English writer and comp., B. London, 1785. D. London, August 2, 1845.

WORKS.—Catechism on the nature, invention, exposition, development, and concatenation of musical ideas, with examples from the great masters, Lond., 1838 (various editions); Catechism on the Art of Writing for an Orchestra, and on Playing from Score, with sixty-seven examples, 1844; second ed., 1846, other editions; Dictionary, comprising an Explanation of 3,500 Italian, French, German, English, and other Musical Terms, Phrases, and Abbreviations, also a copious list of musical characters, Lond., 1849 (numerous other editions); The same, with Appendix containing "John Tinctor's Terminorum Musicæ Diffinitorium," edited by John Bishop; Modern Instructions for the Pianoforte, Lond., 1290 editions said by publishers to have been issued; New Musical Grammar, in three parts (4 editions); Catechism on Double Counterpoint and Fugue; Practical Introduction to the Art of Tuning the Pianoforte, etc.; Catechism of the Organ, with an historical introduction, and a list and description of the principal organs in Great Britain, Ireland, Germany, France, and Switzerland (5 editions); Modern Instructions for Singing, containing a complete compendium of the rudiments of music, etc.; Easy Method for the Violoncello; Catechism for the Violin; Harmonium Instruction Book; The Pupil's New Daily Exercise, containing all the scales and chords in their respective positions; Method for the Double Bass,...Lond., 1833; Sacred Harmony, a Collection of three hundred and fifty standard psalm and hymn tunes (selected); The Psalms and Hymns, in the order they are appointed to be sung or chanted in cathedrals, churches, chapels, etc., during the Morning and Evening Service of the Church of England, with Explanatory Notes; An Introduction to Choral Singing, etc.; Order of Chanting the Morning and Evening Services, according to the Rubric of the Church of England; Method of Chanting the Psalms, as used in the Service of the Church of England. Compositions, various, Pf. pieces, glees, songs, etc. Most of Hamilton's theoretical works are undated, as is usual with musical publications, and all of them are issued from London.

HAMILTON (David). Scottish organ-builder and writer, B. Edinburgh, April 2, 1803. Org. in St. John's Episcopal Ch., Edin. D. Edinburgh, Dec. 20, 1863. Inventor of the *pneumatic lever* action for organs, and writer of musical articles in "Chambers' Encyclopædia." He also composed a few organ pieces, and edited a collection of chants. He edited "New Harmonia Sancta, compiled for the use of the Scottish Episcopal Church." His youngest brother ADAM, B. Edinburgh, is an org. and comp., and was conductor of the Edinburgh Choral Union, and other societies. He S. in Germany under F. Schneider, and has comp. several orchestral works. His son CARL D. is cond. of the Edinburgh Amateur Orchestral Soc., and a violoncellist of great merit.

HAMILTON (Edward). American bass vocalist and musician, B. Worcester, Mass., Jan. 6, 1812. Published "Songs of Sacred Praise, or the American Collection of Church Music," 1850.

HAMILTON (John Buchanan Bailie-). Scottish inventor, son of Gerard Baillie-Hamilton of the 7th Fusileers, B. Jan. 20, 1837. Inventor of the Vocalion, a wind instrument resembling the harmonium, but possessing a much better and rounder tone.

HAMILTON (William). Scottish music-publisher, established in Glasgow. Flourished from about the middle of the present century. Issued, among other publications, the following: "The British Minstrel, and Musical and Literary Miscellany," 3 vols., 1842-44; "British Harmonist," 1847; Select Songs of Scotland, 1848; Series of Glees, in numbers, 1850-68; Part-Songs for Choral Singers, 1862-68; "Selection of Psalm and Hymn Tunes (edited by Baptie and Hume), 1868; etc.

HAMMA (Benjamin). German comp., B. Friedingen, Würtemberg, Oct. 10, 1831. S. under Lindpaintner. Comp. operas, Pf. music, etc. His brothers, FRANZ (B. Friedingen, Oct. 4, 1835), org. and comp., and FRIDOLIN (B. Friedingen, Dec. 16, 1818), org. at Mersebuurg, comp. org. and ch. music, are both musicians of note.

HAMMERSCHMIDT (Andreas). Bohemian org. and comp., B. Brux, 1611. Org. at Freiberg and Zittau. D. Zittau, Oct. 29, 1675. Comp. masses, odes, motets, org. music, etc.

HANCOCK (Charles). English musician, author of "Accordion Instructions," Lond. [c. 1845]; "Flute Preceptor," Lond. [c. 1846]; "Violin Preceptor," Lond. [c. 1846].

HAND (Ferdinand Gottfried). German writer, B. Feb. 15, 1786. Prof. at Weimar. D. Weimar, March 14, 1851.
WORK.—Aesthetik der Tonkunst, Jena, 1837-41, 2 vols., 8vo; 2nd edition, 1846; English translation by W. E. Lawson, 1880, as "The Æsthetics of Musical Art."

HÄNDEL (Georg Friedrich). German comp. and org., B. Halle, Lower Saxony, Feb. 23. 1685.* Son of a surgeon. Patronised by Duke of Saxe-Weissenfels. S. under Zachau, org. of Halle Cath., 1692. Went to Berlin, 1698. Violinist at Hamburg opera, 1704. Became acquainted with Mattheson the comp., 1704. Quarrelled and fought duel with him, Dec. 5, 1704. Went to Florence, 1706. Visited Venice, Rome, Naples, etc , 1706-9. Returned to Germany, and became chapel-master to the Elector of Hanover (George I. of Britain), 1709. Visited London, 1710. Returned to Germany, 1710-12. Settled in London as organist, 1712-16. Musician to King George I. at Hanover, 1716-18. Chapel-master to the Duke of Chandos, 1718-21. Director of the Italian opera, London, 1720. Musical Director or Manager of King's Theatre (with Heidegger), 1729-34; Lincoln's Inn Fields Theatre, 1734-37; Covent Garden Theatre, 1737. Bankrupt, 1737. Resided in Dublin, and produced the "Messiah," 1741-42. Returned to London, 1742. Engaged in opposition to the English aristocracy in producing operas; became bankrupt again, 1744. Lost his sight, 1752. D. London, Good Friday, April 13, 1759.

WORKS.—*Operas:* Almira, 1704; Nero, 1705; Florindo und Daphne, 1708; Roderigo, 1706; Agrippina, 1707; Silla, 1707; Rinaldo, 1711; Pastor Fido, 1712; Teseo, 1712; Amadigi [1715]; Radamisto [1720]; Muzio Scævola (with Ariosto and Buononcini), 1721; Floridante, 1721; Otho, 1722; Flavio, 1723; Giulio Cesare, 1723; Tamerlano, 1724; Rodelinda, 1725; Scipione, 1726; Alessandro, 1726; Admeto, 1727; Riccardo, 1727; Sirce, 1728; Tolomeo, 1728; Lotario, 1729; Partenope, 1730; Poro, 1731; Ezio, 1731; Sosarme, 1732; Orlando, 1732; Arianna, 1733; Ariodante, 1734; Alcina, 1734; Atalanta, 1736; Giustino, 1736; Arminio, 1736; Berenice, 1737; Faramondo, 1737; Serse, 1738; Jupiter in Argos (pasticcio), 1739; Imeneo, 1738; Diedamia, 1740; Lucio Vero, 1747; Alceste (English opera), 1749; Flavio Olibrio, Titus, unfinished operas; part of the music for Semiramide; Arbace; Caio; Fabrizio. *Serenatas, etc.*: Aci, Galatea, e Polifemo, 1708; Parnasso in Festa, 1734; Acis and Galatea, English serenata, 1721—no resemblance to 1708 version; Semele, 1743; The Choice of Hercules, interlude, 1750; Terpsichore, intermezzo. *Oratorios:* Il Trionfo del Tempo e del Disinganno, 1707; La Resurrezione, 1708; Passion oratorio, 1717; Esther, 1720; Deborah, 1733; Athalia, 1733; Saul, 1738; Israel in Egypt, 1738; Messiah, 1741 (Dublin, April 18, 1742; London, March 23, 1749); Samson, 1741; Joseph, 1743; Hercules, 1744; Belshazzar, 1744; Occasional, 1746; Judas Maccabeus, 1746; Alexander Balus, 1747; Joshua, 1747; Solomon, 1748; Susanna, 1748; Theodora, 1749; Jephtha, 1751; Triumph of Time and Truth (altered English version of Trionfo del Tempo), 1757. *Odes:* Queen Anne's Birthday, 1712; Alexander's Feast (Dryden), 1736; Ode on St. Cecilia's Day (Dryden), 1739; L'Allegro, Il Penseroso, ed il Moderato, 1740. *Anthems, Te Deums, etc.*: Twelve Chandos anthems, 1718-20; Arrangements of do. for Chap.-Roy. [1727]; Four Coronation, 1727; Wedding anthem, 1736; Funeral, 1737; Foundling Hospital, 1749; Utrecht Te Deum, 1713; Queen Caroline, do. [1737]; Dettingen Te Deum, 1743; Dixit Dominus et Gloria, 1707; Laudate et Gloria, 1707, and other Psalms, etc. *Miscellaneous Vocal Music:* Three Chamber Trios, 1708; Twenty-five chamber duets; Cecilia, volgi, cantata, 1736; Sei del Cielo, do., 1736; One Passion Cantata; Twelve Hanover Cantatas, 1711; Seventy-nine Italian cantatas, 1706-12; French and English songs and Italian canzonets, various, detached. *Instrumental Music:* Twelve sonatas for harpsichord, op. 1, 1732; Six do. trios, op. 2, 1732; Six Hautboy concertos, op. 3, 1734; First set of six organ concertos, op. 4, 1734; Seven sonatas for 2 vns. and 'cello, op. 5, 1735; Twelve grand con-

* The date Feb. 23, 1684, is also given.

certos, op. 6, 1739-99; Second set of six organ concertos, 1741; Third do., op. 7, 1761; Three organ concertos (Arnold), 1797; Water Musick, 7 parts, 1715; Forest Musick, 1741-2; Fire-work Musick, 1749; Sonata for 2 vns., 1736; do., in 5 parts, 1736; Two suites of harpsichord pieces, 1720, 1733; Act tunes in "The Alchymist," 1732. A number of miscellaneous pieces of small importance.

Händel is greatly indebted to the early cathedral composers of England for the dignified and nervous energy of his style. It is true that the works of Palestrina must in some measure have influenced him, but the influence which that composer exerted was purely formal, and much less potent than that exercised by Purcell alone, who, authorities agree, was the direct model used by Händel in the formation of an imposing ecclesiastical style. This, of course, is quite independent of the natural genius of the man, which would in any age have lifted him to the level of the greatest masters; but it is evident from the style of his compositions that he preferred to make manifest his powers through the medium of the style peculiar to England. The whole tone and inspiration of his oratorio music, therefore, is English, because illustrative of English sacred text, and because modelled on the style which immediately preceded his advent in England. This does not hold good as regards most of his operas, the style of which is distinctly Italian, tinctured with the natural force of his own originality. The great influence which Händel exercised was more marked in England than in any other country, nearly every succeeding composer to Bishop's time having copied his style; and even at the present period there exists a certain amount of partiality for his music among many living composers. This very forcibly exhibits the power which mere tradition exerts in Britain, and shows how the example of ancient institutions tends to check the search for new fields of action.

The works on which Händel's fame will always be based are his oratorios, which, taken as a body of music and the productions of a single mind, are among the most remarkable creations in the whole range of musical science. There are many instances of prolifigacy among composers of all schools, but comparatively few instances of prolifigacy combined with a never-ceasing manifestation of originality, when the endeavours are kept in one direction and in one style. There is no composer dating from Händel's time who can be credited with having produced works equal in grandeur of conception and energy of execution; and until the rise of the modern school, and the propagation of the romantic spirit and taste, no oratorios have met with such a measure of popular favour. In one respect the merit of Händel's work transcends that of Haydn, Beethoven, Spohr, or Mendelssohn; that is in respect to the grandeur of the choruses in his works, and his powerful treatment generally of the choral masses. We do not find in Händel the same richness of colouring as in Mendelssohn, but, on the other hand, we find a strength and dignity about him not quite so striking in the younger composer. Mendelssohn has intense expression in many of his solo vocal numbers, heightened in a measure by a fine orchestral accompaniment, and eminently suited to the reformed tastes of the present generation; while Händel, although possessing much fervid and earnest feeling, is in part out of date by reason of his expressional style being almost obsolete, and his music conceived in the manner of a bygone time. It is astonishing, however, how well he has maintained his place in the midst of an ever-changing musical style, and how fresh many of his really stilted arias sound when placed side by side with the tremendous creations of Liszt. The diversity of styles to be found throughout the range of Händel's works is great; for we find the lively, the pastoral, and the tender, side by side with the sombre, the pathetic, and the grand. This goes to display the extent to which the powers of his mind reached, and the varying degrees of expression which his genius was capable of using in an effective manner.

Of all Händel's oratorios the most undying is the "Messiah," which at the present day is as popular as when performed fifty, sixty, or a hundred years ago. There does not appear to be a great diminution in its extraordinary popularity, though it it is certain that among a certain class its claims are scoffed at as being based on little more than the sentimental regard with which an ancient people cherish ancient national institutions. It is useless particularizing the many fine parts of the "Messiah," so well are they known. Without the now common sensational elements of dramatic unity and style, and without a story of much coherency, it is nevertheless a work possessing features of the most powerful kind. The work is intended to appeal wholly to the religious sentiments of an audience, not to their sense of artistic form or purely musical colouring. About the skilful scientific construction of the "Messiah" there can be no doubt, as it exhibits the wonderful power possessed by its composer in blending the various musical elements. Its great power lies in the stupendous choral numbers, which are among the most wonderful of musical productions.

Händel has been placed by an enthusiastic English public, led by royalty, in a position from which nothing short of a revolution will ever remove him. His great merits are freely admitted on all hands, and his transcendental merits are even emphatically announced by some. He is a great composer, and was the greatest of his period, but he is not by any means the greatest for all time. His style is already antiquated, and a large percentage of his works are in complete disrepute. He is, however, upheld in all his original dignity by certain of his works, which are worthy monuments to his manifold powers of musical composition. The Händel literature is great; but the following selection may be found useful by enquirers wishing a complete insight of his life and works:—Mattheson, G. F. Handel's Lebensbeschreibung, Hamburg, 1761. Smith (J. C.), Anecdotes of G. F. Handel, London, 1799. Clark (R.), Reminiscences of Handel, etc., London, 1836. Townsend (H.), Visit of Handel to Dublin, Dublin, 1852. Bray (Mrs.), Handel, his Life, Personal and Professional, London, 1857. Schölcher (V.), Life of Händel, London, 1857. Chrysander (F.), G. F. Händel... Leipzig, 1858-67, 3 vols. Rockstro (W. S.), Life of G. F. Handel, London, 1883. Also articles in *North American Review*, 1836, v. 43; *Eclectic Review*, 1856, v. 105; *British Quarterly Review*, 1862, v. 36; *Edinburgh Review*, 1857, v. 106; *Fraser's Magazine*, 1857, v. 36; *Contemporary Review*, 1868-69; *Macmillan's Magazine*, 1868, v. 18; *Fortnightly Review*, 1879, v. 33; and Musical Journals, *passim*. See also *Bibliographical Appendix*.

HÄNDL (Jacob), GALLUS. German comp., B. Carniola, 1550. Chap.-master to Bishop of Olmütz. D. 1591. Wrote masses, motets, songs, etc.

HANSLICK (Eduard). Bohemian writer and comp., B. Prague, Sept. 11, 1825. S. under Tomaschek. Prof. of Æsthetics, Vienna University. Juror of Paris and Vienna Exhibitions. Lectured on music from 1859.

WORKS.—Criticisms in the *Freie Press*, Vienna; Vom Musikalisch-Schönen, 1854; Geschichte des Concertwesens in Wien, 1869; Aus dem Concertsaal, 1870. Die Moderne Oper, 1875. Papers in various journals. Lieder and Songs.

HANSSENS (Charles L.). Belgian comp., B. Ghent, July 10, 1802. 'Cellist at Amsterdam, etc. D. Brussels, April 8, 1871. Wrote operas, etc.

HANS SACHS. See SACHS (HANS).

HANWAY (Jonas). English writer, author of "Thoughts on the Importance of the Sabbath, also on the use and advantage of Music," London, 8vo, 1765.

HARDEGEN (Count Julius von), *pseudonym* EGGHARD. Austrian pianist and comp., B. Vienna, April 24, 1834. S. under Czerny and Preyer. D. Vienna, March 23, 1867. Comp. much Pf. music of a light and brilliant character. Rêve d'Amour, op. 10; Danse Cosaque, op. 35; Berceuse, op. 38; Capriccio, op. 46; Bijoux de Salon, op. 63; Impromptu, op. 74; Le bal aux Enfers, op. 136; etc.

HARDER (August). German comp., B. Schrenerstadt, Saxony, 1774. D. Oct. 19, 1813. Comp. romances, choruses, guitar and Pf. music.

HARDIE (Matthew). Scottish violin-maker, worked in Edinburgh, from about 1815 to 1850. His violins are among the best produced in Scotland. He was a dissipated character, extremely eccentric in manner.

HARDIMAN (James). Irish writer and M. R. I. A., B. Galway. Was Librarian of Queen's Coll., Galway. D. Galway, 1855. Author of "Irish Minstrelsy, or Bardic Remains of Ireland; with English poetical translations, collected and edited with notes and illustrations," Lond., 2 vols., 8vo., 1831.

HARGITT (Charles John). English org. and comp., B. Edinburgh, 1833. S. under his father, Hallé, Sir G. A. Macfarren, and Ferdinand Hiller. Org. of St. Mary's Catholic Ch., Edin., and founder and cond. of Choral Union there, till 1862. Cond. of oratorios, concerts, etc., in London since 1862, and organised Royal Albert Hall Choral Soc., of which he was sub-cond. to M. Gounod.

WORKS.—Opera, "Coronet or Crown;" Two operettas; "The Harvest Queen," cantata; orch. overtures, marches, and incidental music to plays. *Songs*: The mitherless bairn; The last good night; My heart's reply; Rest thee, babe; To-morrow; A Parting gift, etc. Part-songs, various. Pf. music, and other works.

HARGREAVES (George). English musician and artist, son of Thomas Hargreaves, the famous miniature painter, B. Liverpool, 1799. D. Liscard, Cheshire, 1869. Best known as the composer of numerous prize glees. He wrote masses, an opera, songs, etc., and had some little renown as a miniature painter.

HARKER (W.). English writer, author of "A Practical Grammar of Music," Lond., 8vo, 1836; "Elements of Vocal Music," Lond., 8vo, 1845.

HARLAND (Holland). English teacher and writer, author of "A Treatise on Singing, in which the Rules of Sol-Fa Notation, or learning to sing by notes, are explained by examples calculated to render Sight-Singing simple and easy," Glasgow, 8vo, 1881.

HARMON (Joel). American musician, compiled "The Columbian Sacred Minstrel," Northampton, Mass., 1809.

HARMSTON (J. W.). Contemporary pianist and comp., has written a great number of brilliant salon pieces, under a variety of fanciful titles. Le jet d'eau, op. 193; La Belle Rosière, op. 195; Danse des Sylphes, op. 196; Les Naiades, op. 211; etc.

HARPER (Rev. John). English divine, author of "The Nature and Efficacy of Musick to prepare the Mind for Good Impressions," Sermon. Lond., 8vo, 1830.

HARPER (Thomas). English trumpet-player, B. Worcester, May 3, 1787. S. in London under Elvey, 1798. Member of the East India Volunteer band. Principal trumpet-player at Drury Lane and English Opera House. Played at Birmingham Musical Festival, 1820. Inspector of musical instruments for East India Company. Principal trumpet-player at Royal Italian opera. Do. at Concert of Ancient Music. D. London, Jan. 20, 1853.

He wrote an Instruction Book for the Trumpet, and compiled a number of books of selections for that instrument, the Kent bugle, etc. His son, THOMAS JOHN, is the most eminent performer now living, and succeeded his father in most of the above appointments. Both father and son played at all the more important musical festivals throughout Britain.

HARRINGTON (Henry, M.D.). English comp., B. Kelston, Somersetshire, Sept. 20, 1727. Entered Queen's Coll., Oxford, 1745; B.A., 1748. M.D. and M.A., Oxon. Member of Oxford Musical Society. Physician at Bath. Estab. Musical Soc. there. Mayor of Bath. D. Bath, Jan. 15, 1816.

WORKS.—Three Books of Glees, 1770, 1785, and 1797; Single Glees; Songs; Anthems, etc.

HARRIS (James, M.P.). English writer (1709-1780). Author of "Three Treatises—Music, Painting, and Poetry," etc., London, 1744. 5 editions issued to 1792.

HARRIS (Joseph John). English org. and comp., B. London, 1799. Chor. Chap. Royal. Org. of S. Olave's Ch., Southwark, 1823. Org. of Blackburn Ch., 1828. Choir-master of Collegiate ch., Manchester; org. do., 1848. Mus. Bac. D. Manchester, Feb. 10, 1869.

WORKS.—Selection of Psalm and Hymn Tunes, adapted to the psalms and hymns used in the church of S. Olave, Southwark, 1827; Four Glees [1837]; Anthems; Songs, etc.; The Musical Exposition, a guide for parents in their choice o qualified teachers of music, 8vo, 1845.

HARRIS (Joseph Macdonald). English org. and comp., B. London, 1789. Chor. Westminster Abbey. Pupil of Robert Cooke. D. May [1860]. Wrote songs, duets, and Pf. music. Published five vocal trios [1817]; Six glees [1812]. Arranged music of Montagu Burgoyne's Select Portions of the Psalms, etc., Lond., 2 v. 4to, 1827.

HARRIS (Renatus). English organ-builder of the 17th century, B. [circa 1640-5]. D. [1715]. He constructed organs at the chapel of Whitehall, Salisbury Cath., Gloucester, Worcester, Chichester, Winchester, Bristol, Hereford, Cork, and Norwich cathedrals; at King's Coll. Chap. Cambridge; Wolverhampton Collegiate Ch; St. Patrick's, Dublin; and in many other less known churches. Other members of the same family were THOMAS and JOHN, the former, father, and latter, son, of RENATUS. They, too, constructed or renovated many important instruments. RENATUS is also famed as having been the rival of Bernard Schmidt or "Father" Smith.

HARRISON (Rev. Ralph). English musician, and Presbyterian minister at Manchester, compiled "Sacred Harmony; or a Collection of Psalm Tunes, ancient and modern," 2 v. 4to, 1786-1792.

HARRISON (Samuel). English tenor vocalist, B. Belper, Derby, Sept. 8, 1760. Appeared as sopranist at the Concert of Ancient Music, 1776-78. Sang at Handel Commemoration, 1784. Tenor at Concert of Ancient Music. Married Miss Cantelo, 1790. Established (with Knyvett) the Vocal Concerts, 1791-4. D. London, June 25, 1813.

Was one of the most popular tenor singers of his time, and was particularly successful in ballad singing.

HARRISON (William). English tenor vocalist and comp., B. Marylebone, London, 1813. First public appearance, 1836. S. at R. A. M., 1836-7. Sang at Sacred Harmonic Soc. concerts; *Début* in opera, at Covent Garden Theatre, in Rooke's "Henrique." Established, with Miss Louisa Pyne, "The English Opera Company" 1856. Sang in tenor *roles* in operas by Balfe, Wallace, Benedict, Mellon, etc; D. London, Nov. 9, 1868.

He comp. some songs, and an operetta, "Les Noces de Jeannette." It is due to this eminent vocalist that such an institution as English opera was ever reared. He produced during his career as manager more standard English operas than any of his successors have been able or willing to undertake. He had evidently a warm feeling in the matter of a national opera, as is denoted by the representation of "Balfe's Bohemian Girl," " Rose of Castille," " Bianca," " Armourer of Nantes," "Puritan's Daughter;" Wallace's "Maritana" and " Lurline;" Mellon's " Victorine," and other operas. He opened H. M. Theatre for operatic performances, and did much to advance the cause of native music. His personal powers as a vocalist were great, and he achieved successes in most of the great cities and towns of Britain.

HARROP (Sarah), BATES. English soprano vocalist, B. Lancashire. S. under Sacchini and Dr. Howard. Married to Joah Bates, 1780. She sang at all the principal London concerts, and had considerable repute for her vocal powers. D. London, Dec. 11, 1811.

HART (Andrew). Scottish printer and publisher, flourished in Edinburgh in reign of James VI. Commenced printing about the beginning of the 17th century. Best known as a printer of an edition of the Bible 1610; an edition of Barbour's " Bruce "; and " The CL. Psalmes of Dauid in Prose and Meeter. Where-vnto is added Prayers commonly vsed in the Kirkes and Privat houses. . . ." Edin. 1611, 8vo. Another edition "printed by the Heires of Andrew Hart," 1635. These have the music.

HART (Charles). English comp. and org., B. May 19, 1797. S. at R. A. M., under Crotch. Org. of S. Dunstan's, Stepney, London, 1829-33. Org. of ch. in Tredegar Sq., Lond. Do. S. George's, Beckenham. D. Mar. 29, 1859.

WORKS.—Omnipotence, oratorio, 1839; Anthems; Te deum; Songs, and glees.

HART (George). English writer, B. London, 1839. S. at R. A. M. under Sir G. A. Macfarren and M. Sainton. Succeeded to his father's business in Wardour Street, London. Author of "The Violin, its Famous Makers, and their Imitators," Lond., Illust., 8vo and 4to, 1875; "The Violin and its Music,"

London, 8vo and 4to, 1881, portraits. The first named work has been translated into French and published at Paris, 1886, 4to. These works are both highly valuable and interesting.

HART (John Thomas). English violin-maker, father of the above, B. 17th Dec., 1805. Worked with S. Gilkes. D. Jan. 1, 1874. Was a great collector, and possessed one of the most valuable collections of violins ever known in England.

HART (Joseph). English org. and comp., B. London, 1794. Chor. S. Paul's Cath., 1801. S. under John Sale, S. Wesley, M. Cooke, J. B. Cramer, and Attwood. Deputy org. to Attwood, S. Paul's, 1805. Org. at Walthamstow. Org. at Tottenham. Chorus-master, Eng. Opera House, Lyceum, 1818-20. Music-seller in Hastings, 1829. Org. S. Mary's Chap. Hastings. D. Dec. 1844.

WORKS.—*Dramatic music*: Amateurs and actors, 1818; A walk for a wager, 1819; The Bull's head, 1819; The Vampire, 1820. Sets of quadrilles, waltzes, lancers, etc.; An easy mode of teaching thorough-bass and composition. Songs, Pf. music.

HART is credited with the invention of the dance form known as Lancer's Quadrille. His music is not of much importance.

HART (Philip). English comp. and org., B. about middle of 17th century. Bass singer at York Minster till 1670. Gent. of Chap. Roy., 1670-1718. Lay-vicar Westminster, 1670-1718. Org. of S. Andrew Undershaft. Do. S. Michael's, Cornhill. Do. S. Dionis, Blackheath, 1724. D. London, 1749.

WORKS.—Ode in praise of musick (Hughes), 1703; Morning hymn from "Paradise Lost," Milton, 1729; Anthems; Organ fugues; Songs in various collections.

HÄRTEL (Benno). German comp. and pianist, B. 1846. Teacher in Raff's Academy of Music, Berlin. Writer of Pf. music, songs, etc.

HÄRTEL (Gustav Adolph). German pianist and comp., B. Leipzig, Dec. 7, 1836. D. Homburg, Aug. 28, 1876.

HÄRTEL. See BREITKOPF and HÄRTEL.

HARTMANN (Christian). German flute-player and comp., B. Altenburg. Resided in Paris as flute-player and teacher. Wrote concertos, preludes, airs, duets, for flute.

HARTMANN (Johann Peter Emil). Danish comp. and pianist, B. Copenhagen, May 14, 1805. Comp. symphonies; Pf. music; and operas, "Der Rube oder die Bruderprobe," 1833; Die Goldenen Hörner, 1834; Liden Kirsten, 1847, etc. He was latterly director of Copenhagen Cons., and musician to the King of Denmark. His son, EMIL, B. Copenhagen, 1835, has comp. symphonies, overtures, and other important pieces.

HARTMANN (Ludwig). German comp. and writer, B. Neuss, 1836. S. at Leipzig Cons., and under Liszt. Resides at Dresden as writer. Has comp. an opera, "König Helga," songs, Pf. music, and has contributed numerous articles to periodical literature.

HARTOG (Eduard de). Dutch comp. and pianist, B. Amsterdam, 1826. S. under Döhler, Hoch, Elwart and Litolff. Comp. of *Overtures*: Portia; Macbeth. Le Mariage de Don Lope, opera, 1865; Jeanne d' Arc, symphony; Psalm XLIII.; Lieder, string quartets, etc.

HARVEY (Richard Frederick). English comp., has published an immense quantity of Pf. music for teaching purposes, dances, songs, etc., of which the following pieces are representative:—

Pianoforte: National Fantasias; Gems of Scotland, Ireland, etc.; Transcriptions of popular works, fantasias, and arrangements of every kind. A few original pieces. *Songs*: I love but thee alone; The golden days; The old love dieth not; Beware; Make the best of it; Norah in tears; Only John and I; Pretty Blue

Flower; Stormy Petrel; Time Boys (boat song); Isadore; Italian Fisherman's song.

HARWOOD (Edward or Teddy). English comp., B. Hoddleson, near Blackburn, 1707. D. 1787. Comp. "A Set of Hymns and Psalm Tunes,"...n.d.; "A Second Set,"...Chester, 1786; chants and anthems, a few of which are in use at the present time.

HASKINS (J. F.) English writer of a "Concertina Preceptor." Lond., 8vo, 1852. Another HASKINS, ALFRED B., issued "Singing in Schools," London, 1885.

HASLINGER. Austrian firm of music-publishers, founded in Vienna, end of 18th century by Tobias Haslinger (1787-1842). They issue important works by Beethoven, Schubert, Spohr, Hummel, Moscheles, Strauss, etc. The firm is now carried on by Schlesinger of Berlin.

HASSE (Johann Adolph). German comp., B. Bergedorf, near Hamburg, March 25, 1699. Tenor singer in Hamburg opera under Keiser. Do. at Brunswick Theatre. S. at Naples under Porpora and Scarlatti. Resided at Venice. Prof. at Scuola degli' Incurabili, Venice, 1727. Married to Faustina Bordoni, 1729. Chapel-master and opera director, Dresden, 1731. Visited London, 1740. Lived at Vienna, opposing Gluck. D. Venice, Dec. 16, 1783.

WORKS.—*Operas:* Antigone, Brunswick, 1723; Sesostrate, Naples, 1726; Dalisa, Venice, 1730; Artaserse, 1730; Arminio, 1731; Cajo Fabrizio, 1731; Demetrio, 1732; Alessandro nell' Indie, 1732; Euristeo, 1733; Senocrita, 1736; La Clemenza di Tito, 1737; Alfonso, 1738; Irene, 1738; Olimpia in Ernalo, London, 1740; Demofoonte, 1748; Ipermnestra, 1751; L'Olimpiade, 1756; Nitteti, 1759. Other operas to the number of 100. *Oratorios, etc.:* La Vertù a piè della Croce; La Caduta di Gerico; Maddalena; Il Cantico de' tre Fanciuli; Giuseppe riconosciuto; La Pénitence de Saint Pierre. Anthems, Psalms, Motets, Misereres, Masses, Te Deums, etc. Cantatas, Quartets for strings, Sonatas for Pf., etc. Six Concertos, op. 1; Six Symphonies, op. 3.

"Hasse's dramatic works, like all those of his time, are forgotten; but his sacred compositions, many of which are still performed, justify the character given of him by Burney, who says that he was the most learned, natural, and elegant composer of his age." (Hogarth.) The present generation has not seen fit to endorse the opinion of either of these two historians, for, with the exception of some transcriptions for organ, the whole body of Hasse's works appear to have been swallowed up in the capacious jaws of oblivion.

HASSE (Faustina), *née* BORDONI. Italian soprano vocalist, B. Venice, 1700. S. under Gasparini. *Début* in "Ariodante," 1716. Sang in Venice, Naples, Florence, etc. *Début* in London, May 5, 1726. Married in Venice to Hasse, 1729. Appeared successively in Vienna, Dresden, etc., 1731-56. D. Venice, 1783.
She had an admirable stage presence, and a magnificent execution, and was a favourite in her day. She took part in certain stage squabbles, which were productive of some trouble to Handel.

HÄSSLER (Johann Wilhelm). German comp., B. Erfurt, March 29, 1747. S. under Kittel. Travelled in Germany. Music director of church in Erfurt. D. March 25, 1822. Comp. operas, concertos, sonatas, org. music, cantatas, songs, etc.

HASTINGS (Thomas). American writer, B. Lichfield, Connecticut, 1784. D. 1872. Author of "Elements of Vocal Music," New York, 1839. "Dissertations on Musical Taste," Albany, 1822; N. Y., 8vo, 1853. "The Springfield Collection;" "The Sacred Lyre;" and other books of Psalm tunes.

HATELY (Thomas Legerwood). Scottish comp., editor, and teacher, B. Greenlaw, Berwickshire, Sept. 26, 1815. Apprenticed when a boy to Messrs. Ballantyne & Co., Printers, with whom he remained 11 years. Entered employment of Thomas Constable. Self-taught in music. Precentor of North Leith Parish Church, 1836; do. St. Mary's Parish Church, Edin. Appointed (after Disruption) precentor to Free Church Assembly. Precentor, Free High Church. Established "Annual Aggregate Meetings of Congregational Classes," for practice of psalmody, 1846. Director of the Scottish Vocal Music Association, founded 1856. D. Edinburgh, March 22, 1867.

WORKS.—The National Psalmody, a selection of tunes for the use of churches, etc., Edin., 8vo [1847]; The Psalmody of the Free Church of Scotland, with an accompaniment for the pianoforte. Prepared under the superintendence of George Hogarth, Esq. Edin. la. 8vo, 1845 [other editions]; The Scottish Psalmody, 1852; Irish Presbyterian Psalmody; Hymnals of the Church of Scotland; Historical lectures on Psalmody, with illustrations; Lecture on music of the Scottish Reformation (included in Tricentenary Proceedings), 1860; Songs for children; Harmonies of Zion. *Psalm Tunes*: Glencairn, Huntingtower, Cunningham, Leuchars, Submission, Makerstoun, Nenthorn, Kilmany, Zuingle, Polwarth, Consolation, etc.; Seann Fhuinn nan Salm Mar tha iad air an Seinn anns A'Ghaeltachd mu Thuath; or, the old Gaelic psalm tunes as sung in the congregations of the Free Church of Scotland in the North Highlands, Edin. 1845.

Mr. Hately made himself well-known throughout Scotland for his perseverance in promoting a higher standard of psalmody among church congregations. His efforts have been crowned with success in many districts, but have been especially valuable in directing a more general attention to the claims of the musical service in Scotland. Some time previous to his appearance as a lecturer and teacher, the national comprehension of what constituted psalmody was exceedingly curious; for, although good tunes were existing, the means of rendering them was awanting. So psalmody in Scotland languished till the enlightened efforts of Mr. Hately gave an interest to the matter which had not previously existed. M. Alex. T. Niven, convener of the Church of Scotland psalmody committee, in speaking of Mr. Hately, says:—

"When one remembers the trash, under the name of psalm tunes, which used to be sung 30 years ago, and compares these with the tunes now in use in our churches, the contrast is most surprising. I have little hesitation in according to Mr. Hately the chief merit for the improvement....As an editor, excising bad tunes, placing good tunes in their proper forms and modes, improving and correcting harmonies where defective, his work was admirable." In addition to editing the Free Church psalm books, he had much to do with the production of the early edition of the Established Church book. Mr. Hately imitated in his psalms the spirit, if not the style, of the old Scottish tunes, and the success with which the imitation has been carried out does infinite credit to the taste and observation of the composer.

HATELY (Walter). Scottish pianist and comp., B. Edinburgh, Jan. 29, 1843. Son of the preceding. Educated at High School, Edin. S. music at Leipzig Cons, under Plaidy, Moscheles, Reinecke (Pf.); Hauptmann and Richter (comp.); Dreyschock (vn.), 1861-64. Teacher of music in Edin. since 1865. Pf. teacher in Ladies' Coll., Training Coll. of the Ch. of Scotland, private schools, etc.; teacher of harmony in connection with the St. George's Hall classes, etc.

WORKS.— Church of Scotland Psalter and Hymnal, 1868 (edited); St. Helen, Allondale, Inchcolm, and other psalm and hymn tunes in various collections. *Songs*: Heigh-ho, daisies and buttercups; Ellorie; King Winter; Two songs by Goethe; Row, burnie, row; Where shall the lover rest. *Pianoforte*: Nocturne-Caprice; Two Romances; A la Tyrolienne; Barcarolle.

Mr. Hately, like his father, aided the psalmody committee of the Scottish church in the preparation of their tune-book. He is, however, best known in Edinburgh as a most gifted pianist and composer. His talents as a performer, though seldom publicly displayed, are of a high order.

HATHERLY (Stephen Georgeson). English comp., B. Bristol, February 14, 1827. Org. Darlaston, 1844; Solihull, 1847; St. James, Wednesbury, 1855. Mus. Cond. Greek Church, Liverpool, 1857. Org. Tettenhall, 1863-8. Mus. Bac. Oxon., 1856. Ordained Deacon and Priest of Greek Church at Constantinople, 1871. Archpriest, 1875. Engaged on Mission to Greek and Slavonian Seamen at Bristol Channel ports.

WORKS.—The Briton's Prayer, trio, ded. to P. Albert, 1848; Te Deum and Jubilate, pp. 27, 1853; Benedictus and Apostles' Creed, pp. 23, 1856; Imperial

Russian Air, 4 v. set in Canon, 1857 ; God save the Queen, also in Canon, 1858 ; Service of Greek Church in English, pp. 31, 1860 ; Baptism, an Oratoriette, 8 v., pp. 209, 1860 ; Common Praise, an enlarged edition (the 5th) of Rev. W. H. Havergal's Old Church Psalmody, extra pp. 61, 1864 ; Appendix to 6th edition of the same, extra pp. 56, 1876 ; Specimens of Ancient Byzantine Ecclesiastical Melody, 4 v. Greek text, verified by every member of the Holy Synod of the Patriarch, pp. 23, 1879 ; The Cherubic Hymn, 4 m. v., Russian and English text, 1881 ; Hymns of the Eastern Church, translated by Dr. Neale, complete, with Music from Greek and other sources, pp. 192, 1882 ; with other works, amounting in all to over 40.

HATTON (David). English bag-pipe player, B. Thornton, 1769. D. Nov. 22, 1847. This was an eccentric character who invented an instrument which he performed with some skill. It was in form similar to the Irish bag-pipe.

HATTON (John Liphot). English comp. and pianist, B. Liverpool, Oct. 12, 1809 [1811]. Chiefly self-taught in music. Settled in London, 1832. Pianist at Drury Lane. Visited America, 1848. Director of music in Princesses Theatre, managed by Charles Kean. Teacher and pianist.

WORKS.—*Operettas:* Queen of the Thames, 1844 ; Pascal Bruno, 1844. Music for " Macbeth," 1853 ; Sardanapalus, 1853 ; Faust and Marguerite, 1854 ; King Henry VIII., 1855 ; Richard II., 1857 ; King Lear, 1858 ; Merchant of Venice, 1858 ; and Much Ado about nothing, 1858. Rose, or Love's Ransom, opera, Covent Garden, Lond., 1864. Robin Hood, cantata, 1856 ; Hezekiah, sacred drama, Dec. 15, 1877. Morning and Evening. service in E ; Services in C and E flat. *Anthems*: Blessed be the Lord of Israel ; Come, Holy Ghost ; I will extol Thee, my God ; I will praise Thee with my whole heart ; Out of the deep ; Thou art gone up on high ; Pastor Holy ; Graduale ; Mass for 4 voices and organ. *Part-songs*: Absence ; All things love thee ; A song of winter ; Auburn Village ; A lover's song ; Beware ; Bird of the Wilderness ; Bonny Blackbird ; Calm is night ; Come, celebrate the May ; Come, live with me ; Echo's last word ; England, land of our birth ; Going a-maying ; Good night, beloved ; Good wishes ; Hark ! the convent bells are ringing ; I loved a lass, a fair one ; I met her in the quiet lane ; Jack Frost ; Keep time ; King Witlaff's drinking horn ; Lo ! the peaceful shades of evening ; Love me little, love me long ; Not for me the lark is singing ; Now let us make the welkin ring ; Over hill, over dale ; Shall I wasting in despair? ; Sleep, my sweet ; Song of the Gipsy maidens ; Song to Pan ; Spring ye flow'rets ; Stars of the Summer Night ; Sweet lady moon ; Summer eve ; Take heart ; The belfry tower ; The forget-me-not ; The hemlock tree ; The Indian maid ; The lark ; The letter ; The life boat ; The moon shone calmly bright ; The pearl divers ; The rivals ; The summer gale ; The village blacksmith ; Venetian boatmen's evening song ; The waterfall ; Wrecked hope ; Twilight ; When evening's twilight ; World's wanderers. *Songs*: Songs for Sailors, wri ten by W. C. Bennett ; 19 Songs by Herrick, Jonson and Sedley ; A maiden stood ; A voice from the sea ; Autumn ; Aftermath ; The Bells ; By the millstream ; Bird of song ; Cloris ; Come back, Annie ; Dream, baby, dream ; Dick Turpin ; Fair is my love ; Fair daffodils ; Fair and false ; Friar of orders grey ; Farmer at the banks ; Garland, the ; Gentle flower ; Goodbye, sweetheart ; Hope ; If my mistress hide her face ; I stood on the beach ; I think on thee ; Jack o' Lantern ; King and the Cobbler ; King Christmas ; Kitty Carew ; Leather Bottél ; Lass of Watertown ; Lady Maud ; Memory ; Maiden's rose ; Maid I love ; Ocean ; Phœbe dearest ; Sweet as the moonlight ; Simon the Cellarer ; Song should breathe of scents and flowers ; Spring ; Starbeams ; Sailor's return ; Sun to his rest ; Sea song ; Show-man ; True to love and thee ; The wishing well ; The blind boy ; The goldsmith's daughter ; The last fond look ; The nun and the rose ; The slave's dream ; 'Tis midnight ; Uncle Jack ; Under the greenwood tree ; Weep no more ; Winter ; When far from thee in distant lands ; Will think of me? *Pianoforte Music:* Six impromptus ; Prelude and fugue in G minor ; Magic music ; Presto ; Arrangements ; Dances. Singing Methods for various voices ; Thirty Elementary Studies for Pf. ; and many other works.

As a vocal writer who adapts his style to the popular ear, yet maintains a high place among artistic musicians, Hatton is one of the foremost in England. His part-songs are known in England and America, while certain of his songs are in constant use everywhere.

HAUCK (Minnie). German mezzo-soprano vocalist, B. New York, Nov. 16, 1852. Début New Orleans, 1865. Début New York, 1868. Appeared in London, 1868. Sang in Vienna, Moscow, Berlin, Paris, Brussels, etc. Chiefly successful as exponent of the heroine of Bizet's "Carmen," in which work she appeared in London, June, 1878. She is a vocalist of much power, and excels in parts which require an energetic and dramatic interpretation.

HAUCK (Wenzel). German comp., B. Habelschwerdt, Glatz, Feb. 27, 1801. D. Berlin, Nov. 30, 1834. Comp. sonatas, variations, etc. for Pf.

HAUFF (Johann Christian). German comp. and theorist, B. Frankfort-on-the-Main, Sept. 8, 1811. Writer of theoretical works, Pf., vocal, and other music.

HAUPT (Carl August). German org. and comp., B. Cunau, Aug. 27, 1810. S. under A. W. Bach, Dehn, Klein, and Schneider. Appeared in public, 1831. Org. at Thiele. Director of the Königliche Kirchenmusik Institut, Berlin, 1870. Has made a number of concert tours in England, France, Germany, etc. Teacher of a number of pupils who have attained to eminence. He is chiefly celebrated for his fine performance on his instrument, and his remarkable power of rendering the works of Bach.

HAUPTMANN (Moritz). German teacher and comp., B. Dresden, Oct. 13, 1792. S. under Scholz, Morlacchi and Spohr. Vnst. in court band of Dresden, 1812-18. Vnst. at Cassel. Resided for a time in Russia. Cantor and music director of the Thomas-Schule, Leipzig, 1842-68. D. Leipzig, Jan. 3, 1868.

WORKS.—Op. 1. Songs for voice and Pf. ; op. 2. Duets for 2 vns. ; op. 4. Songs, voice and Pf. ; op. 5. Three Sonatas for Pf. and vn. ; op. 6. Sonata, Pf. and vn. ; op. 7. Two string quartets ; op. 8. Divertimento for vn. and guitar ; op. 9. Songs, voice and Pf. ; op. 11. Do. ; op. 14. Do. ; op. 16. Three duets for 2 vns. ; opp. 22, 24, 25, 26, 27, 31, Songs ; op. 32. Six Songs for 4 voices ; op. 34. Motet for solo voice and chorus ; op. 40. Motet for solo voice and chorus ; op. 46. Twelve lieder ; op. 49. Do. (Rückert). Die Natur der Harmonik und Metrik zur Theorie der Musik, 1853. Mathilde, opera, Cassel.

As a theorist and teacher, Hauptmann stood unrivalled in his time. Every nation is indebted to him for the sound instruction he conveyed to numbers of their sons. His pupils who have reached distinction are numberless, but among the more famous may be named, F. David, Kiel, Curshmann, Joachim, Bülow, Sullivan, Cowen, D. Buck, Dache, etc. His influence over all his pupils and over those musicians with whom he came in contact, must have tended greatly to aid the present revival of musical feeling. He was a most capable musician, and although chiefly known as a teacher, he was also a composer of some note. His songs and sacred music are best deserving of attention, being those of his works destined to live.

HAUSER (Miska or Michael H.). Hungarian comp. and violinist, B. Pressburg, 1822. D. Konigsberg, 1857. Comp. of Hungarian rhapsodies for vn. and orch., chamber music. Songs, part-songs, etc.

HÄUSLER (Ernst). German violinist and comp., B. Stuttgart, 1761. D. Feb. 28, 1837. Wrote songs, canzonets, and violin music.

HAVERGAL (Rev. Henry East, M.A.). Was eldest son of the Rev. W. H. Havergal, Hon. Canon of Worcester, and brother of Frances Ridley Havergal, the eminent poetess. The subject of this sketch was born in 1820, and died Jan. 12, 1875. The public press at the period of his decease, declared— "that the Church had lost a most accomplished musical clergyman." In 1842 he graduated at New College, Oxford, and became chaplain of his college, and of Christ Church. These offices he resigned in 1847, on being presented by the latter body with the living of Cople, in Bedfordshire. During his university career he played an active part, in conjunction with Sir Frederick Ouseley, Bart., Mus. Doc., in promoting the cause of music by inaugurating a series of concerts at Oxford. For the church of Cople he built a two manual organ with his own hands, which possessed a very varied register.

This instrument, on which he played during divine service, was sold soon after his decease, and was removed to the adjoining Parish Church of Willington, by Messrs. Hill & Sons, the organ-builders, of London. He also constructed a chiming apparatus for 5 bells, for which he composed a set of 120 changes. He was, in fact, the bell-ringer and organist, as well as the parson of the little church. Before the service he was in the habit of chiming the bells, he would then play a voluntary, and proceed to the reading-desk, read the service, and then return to organ to accompany the canticles and the hymns. His enthusiasm for music was very great, and for some time he was conductor of a musical society of the neighbouring town of Bedford. He likewise held the post of Musical Examiner in the University of Oxford for one year. He compiled a MS. catalogue of the Christ Church Musical Library, in 1845-7. He possessed a natural counter tenor voice, and as a proof of the varied range of his musical capabilities it may be mentioned that, in a trial of Dr. Crotch's oratorio, "Palestine," he not only played the double-bass, but sang the alto chorus parts at the same time. He was also a performer on the trumpet. In 1846, before leaving Oxford, he published two editions of Wither's "Hymns of the Church," and from the original MS. a copy of Tallis's "Preces," with several other of Tallis's works. Among Mr. Havergal's later productions are a set of four Te Deums, and a Jubilate, chiefly chantwise; also six double and twelve single Chants, as well as a Benedicite, Chant Service, forty-two single Chants with double Melodies, and a number of Hymn Tunes and Graces, with an improved arrangement of his Christmas Carols. Several other of his compositions yet remain unpublished.—(*Contributed by the late Mr. C. H. Purday*).

HAVERGAL (Rev. William Henry). English comp. and divine, B. High Wycombe, Jan. 18, 1793. Educated at Oxford, B.A., 1815; M.A., 1819. Rector of Astley, Worcestershire, 1829-42. Rector of S. Nicholas, Worcester, and hon. canon Worcester Cath., 1845. Rector of Shareshill, near Wolverhampton, 1860. D. Leamington, April 19, 1870.

WORKS.—A History of the Old Hundredth Psalm Tune, 1854. Old Church Psalmody, 1849. One Hundred Psalm and Hymn Tunes. Ravenscroft's Psalter (1611), edited 1847. Anthems, psalms, hymns, etc., to number of about 50.

His daughter, Frances Ridley (1836-1879), was a poetess of some note, her hymns and other pieces having been very popular.

HAWEIS (Rev. Hugh Reginald). English writer and divine, B. Egham, Surrey, April 3, 1838. Educated at Camb. B.A., Camb., 1859; M.A., do., 1864. Incumbent of S. James's, Marylebone, 1866. Editor of *Cassell's Family Magazine*, 1868. Lectured in America, 1885.

WORKS.—Music and Morals, Lond., 8vo, 1873; second edition, 1877. Thoughts for the Times. My Musical Life, Lond., 1884. Current Coin. Contributions to periodical literature of articles on musical and general subjects.

HAWES (William). English comp. and writer, B. London, 1785. Chor. Chap. Roy., 1793-1801. Vnst. Covent Garden orch., 1802. Deputy Lay-vicar, Westminster, 1803. Gent. of Chap. Roy., 1805. Associate Philharmonic Soc., 1813. Master of Choristers, Almoner, and Vicar Choral, St. Paul's Cath., 1814. Master of Children of Chap. Roy., 1817. Lay-vicar Westminster Abbey, 1817-20. Established Harmonic Institution in the Argyle Rooms. Music publisher for a time. Music director, English opera, Lyceum. Produced Weber's "Der Freyschütz," July 24, 1824. D. Lond., Feb. 18, 1846.

WORKS.—*Music for Plays*: Broken Promises, 1825; The Sister of Charity, 1829; The Irish Girl, 1830; Comfortable Lodgings, 1832; The Dilsk gatherer, 1832; The climbing boy, 1832; The Mummy, 1833; The Muleteer's vow, 1835. Collection of five glees and a madrigal [1814]; Six glees for 3 and 4 voices [1815]; Six Scotch songs harmonized as glees [1817]; Prize glees. Adaptations of operas by Paër, Salieri, Winter, Mozart, Ries, Marschner, etc. Edited an edition of "The Triumphs of Oriana," and a collection of Spofforth's glees.

HAWKER (Lieut.-Col. Peter). English writer on Sport, etc., author of "Instructions to Young Performers for acquiring by means of Patent Hand

Moulds the best Position for Strength and Articulation on the Pianoforte," 4to, 1840, 3 editions. He D. in 1853.

HAWKER (William). English writer, author of "The Theory of Music simplified, and the principles of temperament applied to the tuning of keyed instruments explained," Lond., fo., 1845. "A Specific statement and view of the improved musical scale for organs and pianofortes," Lond., 12mo, 1810.

HAWKINS (James). English comp. and org., B. in latter part of the 17th cent. Chor. S. John's Coll., Camb. Org. of Ely Cath., 1682-1729. Mus. Bac. Cantab., 1719. D. 1729, Comp. of Services, Anthems, etc. His son, JOHN, was org. of Peterborough Cath., 1714-1759, and comp. a number of Anthems, preserved in Tudway's collection, etc.

HAWKINS (Sir John, Kt.) English writer and lawyer, B. London, March 30, 1719. Became an Attorney. Member of Madrigal Soc., and of Academy of Antient Music. Married Miss S. Storace, 1753. Retired to Twickenham. Chairman of Middlesex Quarter Sessions. Knighted, 1772. D. May 14, 1789.

WORKS.—Twelve Cantatas (words), 1742-43, music by J. Stanley. An Account of the Institution and Progress of the Academy of Ancient Music, 1770. A General History of the Science and Practice of Music, Lond., 5 vols., 4to, 1776 (with portraits); new edition, Novello, 1853. Edition of Walton and Cotton's "Compleat Angler," 1760.

Hawkins was much esteemed in his day, and was one of Dr. Johnson's literary executors. His personal and forensic attributes have long since sunk into comparative insignificance, and by his musical abilities alone is he now known. He did much by the publication of his "History" to enlighten the English musical public on the past state of the art, and though its value is less owing to the lapse of time, it is still a standard text-book to the history of music. Its merits, and superiority in some respects over the history of Burney, lie in its acknowledged greater accuracy and plainness of detail. Its merits in this respect are indeed great, for, despite some few blemishes in the matter of misstated facts, it is a remarkably erudite and straightforward production. Hawkins was buried in Westminster Abbey. His daughter, LÆTITIA MATILDA, was a novelist, and biographical writer, and his son, JOHN SIDNEY, an author.

HAYDEN (George). English org. and comp. of first half of the 18th century. Org. of S. Mary Magdalen, Bermondsey. Wrote cantatas, songs, etc., some of which were favourites in their day.

HAYDEN (W. L.) American writer, author of a "New Method for the Guitar," Boston, Ditson, n. d.

HAYDN (Franz Josef). Austrian comp., B. Rohrau, April 1 (March 31). 1732. Son of Matthias Haydn. Educated at Hainburg. Chor. in S. Stephen's, Vienna, 1740-1748. S. under Porpora, 1753. Quartet comp. to K. J. E. von Fürnberg. Engaged as teacher, 1756-59. Music director and chamber musician to Count Ferdinand Maximilian Morzin, 1759. Married to Maria Anna Keller, Nov. 26, 1760 [she died, 1800]. Dismissed with band from service of Count Morzin, 1761. Second chapel-master to Prince Esterhazy, under Werner, 1761. Sole do., 1766-90. Visited Vienna with orchestra, 1769. Resided in Vienna, 1790. Visited London for first time, Jan., 1791. Doc. Mus., Oxon., July, 1791. Left England, 1792. Taught Beethoven music, Dec., 1792. Appeared in London again, as cond. and comp. at Salamon's concerts, Feb. 4, 1794. Returned to Vienna, Aug. 15. 1795. Resided at Vienna as comp. and teacher. D. Gumpendorf, near Vienna, May 31, 1809.

WORKS.—*Oratorios:* The Creation, Vienna, 1798; London, 1800. The Seasons (Thomson), 1800; Seven words from the cross; Il Ritorno di Tobia; Invocation of Neptune. *Cantatas,* various. *Masses, etc.,* for voices and orch., No. 1, in B flat; 2. in C ;3. The Imperial, in D; 4. B flat; 5. C; 6. B flat; 7. G; 8. B flat; 9. C; 10; 11; 12; 13. C; 14. D; 15; 16. B flat. Stabat Mater. Offertoires (13); Motets; Salve Regina; Tantum Ergo; Sacred songs (arias), etc. *Operas, etc.:* 1 German; 4 Ital'an, "Le Pescatrici;" "L'Incontro improviso;" "L'Infedeltà delusa;" "La Fedelta premiata:" 14 Buffo comedies, and 5 Marionette operas. Twelve German Lieder, 1782; twelve do., 1784. Six Original

Canzonets (Mrs. Hunter), London, 1796. Accompaniments to Scottish Songs (for George Thomson, Edinburgh). Welsh airs, arranged. A Requiem, etc. *Symphonies*, 125 in all, with overtures, including : Twelve Symphonies (Salomon Set), No. 1. 1791 ; 2. 1791 ; 3. (Surprise), 1791 ; 4. 1792 ; 5. 1791 ; 6. 1791 ; 7. 1795 ; 8. 1795 ; 9. 1795 ; 10. 1793 ; 11. (Clock), 1794 ; 12. (Military), 1794. Letter A, 1780 ; B (Farewell), 1772 ; II, 1774 ; I, 1772 ; L, 1772 ; Q, Oxford, 1788 ; R, 1788 ; T, 1787 ; V, 1787 ; W, 1787. Le Matin, 1761 (?) ; Le Midi, 1761 ; Le Soir, 1761 (?) ; Der Philosoph, 1764 ; Lamentation, 1772 ; Mercury, 1772 ; Maria Theresa, 1773 ; La Passione, 1773 ; Schoolmaster, 1774 ; Feuer-symphonie, 1774 ; Il Distrato, 1776 ; Roxelano, 1777 ; Kinder-symphonie ; Laudon, 1779 ; La Chasse, 1780 ; La Reine de France, 1780 ; Le Poule, 1786 ; L'Ours, 1786 ; etc. Eighty-four String Quartets. Thirty Trios, for stringed etc instruments. Thirty-one Concertos for various instruments. Fifty-three Sonatas for Harpsichord. Twenty Concertos for Harpsichord, etc. Notturnos, Minuets, 1 Sestet, 1 Quintet, Marches, music for barytone, etc.

Haydn's greatest work, "The Creation," as a work of art, claims the highest praise from musicians. Its merits as a purely sacred composition are open to question, for although Haydn approaches his subject in a reverent spirit, he does not thoroughly imbue his music with much of that spirit. The chief feature apparent in the "Creation" is the thoroughly beautiful character of the music, and the absence of that severe, vigorous, yet majestic and moving manner, which raises the oratorio music of Handel and Mendelssohn above all. The orchestration is furthermore so lovely, original, and characteristic as to fully atone for any lack there may be of the conventional requirements of sacred music. It may be said, however, that Hadyn was in the habit of approaching his God with a self-satisfied note of jubilant praise, and it becomes less astonishing, when this is considered, that the "Creation" should be so unlike the generality of serious sacred works. The "Seasons," which is secular, though in oratorio form, is that work of magnitude wherein Haydn best fulfils the requirements of his libretto. In it he had abundant scope for exercising his cheerful vein of composition, and although it must be admitted that he has not in the "Seasons" excelled himself or others, it is due his memory to say that it is one of the most pleasant works of its nature. He has succeeded in setting his poesy more appropriately than he ever did when his buoyant and simple temperament was set to the task of composing to serious and religious verse.

The masses of Haydn are by no means of a lofty character ; the inspiration displayed in them being rather musical than religious. Pleasant pastoral rhythms, sweet melodies, pretty harmonies, may properly be stated as constituting their most representative features. They lack dignity, solemnity, and depth, and may be fitly termed pleasing toys of the Papacy. Their use in Roman Catholic chapels in Britain still continues, but scarcely to so great an extent as formerly. Small choral societies, church choirs, and private choirs now study those masses for production at concerts and soirees.

Chief among his instrumental writings are the celebrated string quartets, which form one of the most unique bodies of music ever produced by one individual. Their merit is of the highest kind, and raises Haydn to the eminence of a deity among composers of the latter part of last century. The only composers who could be said to rival him in the smallest measure are Boccherini, Mozart, and Pleyel, who all wrote in a manner approaching Haydn, but never equalling or excelling him. The reason why we place the quartets before the symphonies in point of importance, is because the latter have long since been supplanted in general estimation by the more powerful writings of Beethoven, Mendelssohn, Schubert, and Spohr. The quartets, on the contrary, have only been excelled in the single particular of development, by the composers just mentioned, whose works carried the quartet in its æsthetic aspect far beyond the conceptions of Haydn, leaving it an open matter whether or not they added to the musical beauties of the form. Haydn's quartets give the general impression of great beauty, mingled with a continual joyousness, which appeals with wonderful power to all music-lovers. In powerful and vigorous conception, and in what may be called poetical meaning, Haydn is manifestly inferior to either Beethoven or Schubert, but his quartets will for a long time continue to enlist the sympathies of a large body of the musical public.

His prolificacy as a symphonic writer will bear favourable comparison with that of any other composer; and in respect to a fine and varied flow of melody there does not exist another composer in the same branch who can be put forward in opposition to him. His influence over the instrumental music of the present time has been immense, for not only does the modern orchestra owe many of its features to him, but to Haydn is also due the honour of having given orchestral music a character and a purpose. The style of his instrumental music as contrasted with that of Bach and Händel is warm and natural, while listeners are led to follow themes which are neither too complicated nor too fatiguing, instead of being bored and exercised to death as was the case with the strictly contrapuntal effusions of the two other masters.

As regards Haydn's minor works, such as his songs, Pf. works, and miscellaneous compositions, we can only mention them. They offer a vast field for study to the antiquarian enthusiast, although artists will probably find much to enlist their sympathies and call forth their powers. The songs are especially deserving of attention, being evidently composed with a great degree of care and fidelity to the expression of the poesy. The pianoforte sonatas are a little antiquated, but are still issued by modern publishers, which fact proves that the demand for them is continuous, and the fame of Haydn in this department has not quite evaporated.

Haydn *ana* and bibliography cannot here be dealt with. English works and writings on the subject will be found in the Bibliography appended to this work. Editions of his works, in whole or in part, are issued by nearly every publisher, and in every variety of form and price; while portraits, etc. are numerous.

HAYDN (Johann Michael). Austrian comp. and org., brother of above, B. Rohrau, Sept. 14, 1737. Chor. in S. Stephen's, Vienna. Deputy-org., do. Chap.-master at Grosswardein, 1757. Music-director to Archbishop Sigismund of Salzburg, 1762. Org. of Ch. of Holy Trinity, Salzburg, 1777. Married to Marie M. Lipp, 1768. Mem. of the Academy of Stockholm. D. Salzburg, Aug. 10, 1806.

WORKS.—Masses, litanies, offertoires, graduales, vespers, oratorios, cantatas, and other works for the church in great quantity, but mostly in MS. He also composed operas and instrumental music.

J. M. Haydn, or Michael, as he is usually called, is chiefly of account as a successful teacher, though certain of his works are said to possess considerable merit. Among his many pupils may be named C. M. von Weber, Neukomm, Reicha, and Wölfl. His own abilities as a performer on the organ and harpsichord were great.

HAYDON (Thomas). English musician, B. London, 1787. S. under C. Neate and Crotch. Org., and Prof. of Pf. at R A. M. D. [?]

HAYES (Catherine). Irish soprano vocalist, B. Limerick, 1825. S. under Sapio and Garcia, and at Milan under Ronconi. *Débût* at Marseilles in "I Puritani," 1845, and afterwards sang in Vienna (1846), Venice, and elsewhere in Italy. Appeared in London, Covent Garden Theatre, April 10, 1849. Sang in Ireland, America (1851), India, Australia, etc. Married to Wm. Avery Bushnell of New York, Oct. 8, 1857. D. Sydenham, Aug. 11, 1861.

Miss Hayes was a singer of remarkable powers, and in her day was a most popular and favourite vocalist. Her chief power lay in the rendering of ballads. Her biography was issued under the title of "Memoir of Miss Catherine Hayes, the 'Swan of Erin.'" 4to, n. d., with portrait.

HAYES (Philip). English org. and comp., B. Oxford, April, 1738. Son of William Hayes. S. under his father. Mus. Bac. Oxon., May, 1763. Gent. of Chap. Roy., 1767 Org. of New Coll. Oxford, 1776. Do. of Magdalen Coll., Oxford, and Prof. of Music in University. 1777. Mus. Doc., Oxon., 1777. Org. of S. John's Coll., 1790. D. London, March 19, 1797.

WORKS.—Prophecy, oratorio, 1781; Ode for S. Cecilia's Day; Ode: "Begin the Song"; Telemachus, a Masque. Anthems, Services, Psalms, Glees and Songs. Harmonia Wiccamica, Lond. [1780], etc.

HAYES (William). English org. and comp., B. Gloucester. 1707. Chor. Gloucester Cath., under W. Hine. Org. of S. Mary's Ch., Shrewsbury. Do. of Worcester Cath., 1731-34. Do. Magdalen Coll., Oxford, 1734. Mus.

Bac., Oxon., 1735. Prof. of Music, Oxford Univ., 1741. Doc. Mus., Oxon., 1749. Cond. Gloucester Musical Festival, 1763. D. Oxford, July, 1777.

WORKS.—Collins' Ode to the Passions, and other Odes. Twelve Ariettas or Ballads, and two Catches, 1735. Services and Anthems. Circe, masque. Glees, Catches, etc., 1st set, 1757; 2nd set and Supplement, 1763-65. Cathedral Music. in Score, n. d. (collected church comps.) Instrumental Music. Remarks on Mr. Avison's Essay on Musical Expression, Lond., 8vo, 1753. Anecdotes of the Five Music Meetings, etc.

The church compositions of this musician and his son Philip are still in use, and are fair specimens of ecclesiastical music. The "Remarks" is now rare, and was at one time considered of value.

HAYES (William). English writer and divine, son of the above, B. Oxford, 1741. Chor. Magdalen Coll., 1749-51. B.A., 1761; M.A., 1764. Minor Canon, Worcester Cath., 1765. Do. S. Paul's, 1766. Vicar of Tillingham, Essex. D. Oct. 22, 1790. Wrote a paper, entitled, "Rules necessary to be observed by all Cathedral singers in the Kingdom." Gentleman's Mag., 1765; Sermons, and other works.

HAYLEY (William). English poet, B. 1770. D. 1820. Author of "The Triumphs of Music, a Poem in six cantos," Chichester, 4to, 1804, and other Poetical works.

"Triumphant first see 'Temper's Triumphs' shine!
At least I'm sure they triumph'd over mine.
Of 'Music's Triumphs,' all who read may swear
That luckless music never triumph'd there."—*Byron*.

HAYM (Nicolo Francesco). German comp., B. Rome, latter part of 17th century [1680]. Came to England, 1704. Aided in establishing Italian opera. Adapted music of various composers to his own librettos. Inaugurated system of representing Italian operas with both English and Italian speakers. Latterly a picture dealer. Date of death unknown [1730]. He composed a few sonatas and published a treatise on medals.

HEAP (Charles Swinnerton). English comp. and cond., B. Birmingham, April 10, 1847. S. at Leipzig. Bac. Mus., Cantab., 1871. Doc. Mus., Cantab., 1872. Cond. of Birmingham Philharmonic Union; Walsall do.; Stoke-on-Trent; and Stafford Philharmonic Societies. Cond. of Wolverhampton Musical Festivals.

WORKS.—The Captivity, oratorio; The Maid of Astolat, cantata, 1885; Third Psalm, for soli, chorus, and orch. ; Benedictus for soprano solo, chorus and orch.; The Voice of Spring, for chorus and orch. (Hemans), 1882; Overture for orch., in F, Birmingham Festival, 1879; Overture, in C, No. 2, Birmingham, 1879; Sonata for Organ (MS.); Sonata for Clarinet and Pf., 1880; Trio for Pf., vn., and 'cello, 1867. Quintet for Pf. and wind insts., 1882; Sonata for violin and Pf., 1884. Part-songs, various; Anthems; Organ music. *Songs:* The Sea King; It is not always May; Annabel Lee; Winter; etc.

HEATHER (William), HEYTHER. English comp. and Doc. Mus., B. Harmondsworth, Middlesex, 1584. Lay-vicar, Westminster Abbey. Gent. of Chap. Roy., 1615. Doc. Mus. Oxon, 1622. Founded Music Lecture at Oxford, 1626-7. D. July, 1627.

HECHT (Eduard). German comp. and pianist, B. Dürkheim-on-the-Haardt, Rhenish Bavaria, Nov. 28, 1832. Son of Heinrich and Adelheid Hecht, the former a teacher of singing, latterly in Frankfort-on-Main. S. under Rosenhain, C. Hauff, and F. Messer. Came to England, Nov., 1854. Settled in Manchester as Pf. teacher. Cond. Manchester Liedertafel, 1859-78. Cond. of S. Cecilia Choral Soc., since 1860. Do. of Hallé's Choir, 1870. Lecturer on harmony and comp., Owen's Coll., 1875. Cond. Stretford Choral Soc., 1879. Musical Examiner at High Schools for Girls, Manchester and Leeds.

WORKS.—Op. 1. Three part-songs; op. 2. Three Pf. Pieces; op. 3. Three Mazurkas; op. 4. Three songs; op. 5. Three Marches; op. 6. Three Pf. Pieces; op. 7. Trio for female voices, "Be strong;" op. 8. Song, Leonore; op. 9. Hunting song for chorus and orch. ; op. 10. Charge of the Light Brigade (Tennyson), chorus and orch., Bristol Festival, 1879; op. 11. Two Pf. pieces; op. 12. Impromptu, Pf.;

op. 13. Two Songs; op. 14. Two Songs; op. 15. Part-song, "At Night," five voices; op. 16. Trio for female voices; op. 17. Polonaise for Pf.; op. 18. Four vocal duets; op. 19. A Lullaby; op. 23-24. Pf. pieces; op. 25. O may I join the choir invisible, chorus and orch.; op. 26. Two part-songs; op. 27. Two string quartets; op. 28. Three part-songs; First symphony for orch., Hallé's Concerts, 1877. Concerto for Pf., MS. Eric, the Dane, cantata for solo voices, chorus, and orch. (R. MacLean), Manchester, 1882 (and Halifax, 1883). Manchester March, for military band, or Pf. duet; March-elegy, comp. in memory of Bishop Fraser.

HECK (Johann Caspar). German teacher and writer [B. 1740], flourished in London about beginning of present century. D. [?] He wrote "The Art of Playing Thorough-bass with Correctness, according to the true principles of composition." Lond., n. d. "A Complete System of Harmony; or a regular and easy method to attain a fundamental knowledge and practice of thorough-bass." Lond., 4to, n.d. "Short and Fundamental Instructions for Learning Thorough-bass." 4to, n.d.

HEIDEGGER (Johann Jacob). Flemish musician of the 18th century. He appeared in England in 1707, and became a power in musical concerns as manager of the Italian opera in London. He wrote the librettos of several of Handel's works, and otherwise laid his claim to consideration from posterity. His most notable feature, however, was his ugliness, which was, from all accounts, of a surpassing description. He disappeared from English history and is not mentioned in any record after July, 1738. Nothing is known as to his biography before 1707 or after 1738.

HEIGHINGTON (Musgrave). English comp. and org., B. 1680. Org. at Yarmouth, 1738. Do. Leicester, 1739. D. Dundee, 1774.

WORKS.—Ode for the Spalding Gentlemen's Society; Six Select Odes; The Enchantress, or Harlequin Merlin. Songs, etc.

HEINE (Heinrich). German poet, B. Dusseldorf, Jan. 1, 1800. D. Paris, 1856. His lyrics have been set by a great variety of composers of all nations, Schumann, Hofmann, and Franz being the principal Germans who have used his poems. Many of his minor poems are admirably adapted for musical treatment.

HEINEFETTER (Sabine). German soprano vocalist, B. Mayence, 1809. Début at Frankfort-on-the-Main, March 17, 1823. S. under Spohr at Cassel. Travelled in Italy, and appeared with great success in Berlin in 1833. Retired to Baden, 1842. D. (insane) Illenau, 1872. She sang in operas by Bellini, Donizetti, Rossini, etc.

HEINICHEN (Johann David). German org. and comp., B. Crossuln Weissenfels, April 11, 1683. S. under Kuhnau, etc. Chap.-master to the King of Poland. D. Dresden, July 16, 1729. Wrote operas, church music, cantatas, and serenades.

HÈLE (Georges de la). Belgian comp., B. Hainault, 1545. D. [1591]. Wrote masses and church music.

HELLBORN (H.). German writer of present time, author of a "Life of Schubert," Englished in 1869, 2 vols., by Arthur Duke Coleridge.

HELLER (Stephen). Hungarian pianist and comp., B. Pesth, May 15, 1815. Travelled through Germany as pianist. Resident in Paris from 1838, as teacher and comp. Visited England, 1862, and played at Crystal Palace concert. Member of Legion of Honour, 1884. Stricken with blindness, and presented with a testimonial. 1885.

WORKS.—*Pianoforte:* Op. 1. Theme (Paganini); op. 2. Rondo; op. 5. Thème Polonais: op. 7. Three Impromptus; op. 10. Three Morceaux; op. 11. Rondo; op. 12. Rondoletto; op. 13. Divertissement; op. 15. Rondino; op. 16. Studies; op. 17. Six Caprices; op. 18. Improvista; op. 20-21. Impromptus; op. 22-23. Rondos; op. 25. Une Fièvre brûlante; op. 29. La Chasse; opp. 42, 43, 44. Valses; opp. 45, 46, 47. Studies; op. 50. Scenes Pastorales; op. 52. Venitienne; op. 53. I. Tarentelle; op. 54. Fantaisie-stücke; op. 56. Serenade; op. 57. Scherzo; op. 58. Rêveries; op. 60. Canzonetta; op. 61. II. Tarentelle; op. 63. Capriccio;

op. 64. Humoreske ; op. 65. Sonata ; op. 78. Promenades d'un Solitaire ; op. 79. Traumbilder (Dream pictures) ; op. 80. Wanderstunden Rêveries d'artiste ; op. 81. Twenty-four Preludes ; op. 82. Nuits Blanches (Sleepless nights) ; op. 83. Feuillets d'album ; op. 85. Two Tarentelles, III. and IV. ; op. 86. Dans les Bois, Sept rêveries ; op. 87. V. Tarentelle ; op. 88. Third Sonata ; op. 89. In Wald und Flur ; op. 90. Studies ; op. 91. Nocturnes ; op. 95. Allegro ; op. 96. Grand étude de concert ; op. 97. Twelve Valses ; op. 100. 2nd Canzonetta ; op. 101. Rêveries ; op. 103. Nocturne ; op. 104. Polonaise ; op. 107. Four Ländler ; op. 108. Fourth Scherzo ; op. 112. Caprice humoristique ; op. 119. Thirty-two Preludes ; op. 120. Lieder ohne Worte ; op. 126. Three Overtures ; op. 128. Dans les Bois (2nd series) ; op. 131. Three Nocturnes ; op. 136. Dans les Bois (3rd series) ; op. 137. Tarentelles ; and other works to number of over 150.

Among the many graceful writers for the pianoforte who have flourished within the last fifty years, none has earned so much well-deserved popularity as Stephen Heller. Without being a genius of the highest order, his endowments are nevertheless of an elegant and agreeable nature. His music is invariably beautiful, never vulgar, and always fanciful and graceful, while his knowledge of the capabilities of the pianoforte has enabled him to produce many useful didactic pieces.

HELLMESBERGER (Georg). Austrian violinist and comp., B. Vienna, Aug. 24, 1800. D. Vienna, Aug. 16, 1873.

HELLMESBERGER (Josef). Austrian violinist and comp., son of above, B. Vienna, Nov. 3, 1829. S. under his father. Prof. of violin and director of Vienna Cons., 1843. First violin at Imperial Opera, Vienna, 1860. Is one of the leading Viennese violinists, and has done much by his example to improve the quality of the chamber music in that city. He has arranged a number of standard pieces for various combinations of instruments, and composed some original works of merit.

HELMHOLTZ (Hermann Ludwig Ferdinand). German sciencist and writer, B. Potsdam, Aug. 31, 1821. S. Medicine at Berlin. Teacher of Anatomy, Berlin Academy, 1848. Prof. of Physics, Königsberg, 1849. Do. Heidelberg, 1858. Prof. of Physics, Berlin University, 1871.

Helmholtz is noted for his discoveries in the realm of sound, and for the reduction of those discoveries to a theory. His writings are " Die Lehre von den Tonemfindungen als Physiologische grundlage fur die Theorie der Music," 8vo, 1870 ; Two volumes of Scientific Essays, etc. The first named has been translated by A. J. Ellis under the title of " On the Sensations of Tone as a Physiological Basis for the Theory of Music," Lond., 8vo, 1875, of which two editions have been issued to 1885.

HELMORE (Frederick). English writer on " Church Choirs," Lond.; and on " Speakers, Singers, and Stammerers," Lond., 1874.

HELMORE Rev. Thomas). English writer and comp., B. Kidderminster, May 7, 1811. Educated at Oxford. Curate of S. Michael's, Lichfield, 1840. Priest-vicar, Lichfield Cath. Precentor of S. Mark's Coll., Chelsea, 1842. Master of Choristers, and Priest In Ordinary, Chap. Roy., 1846.

WORKS.—Manual of Plain Song, 1850 (other editions, enlarged); Primer of Plain Song (Novello's Music Primers) ; The St. Mark's Chant Book, 2 parts ; a Hymnal Noted, or Translations of the Ancient Hymns of the Church, set to their proper melodies ; A Fuller Directory of the Plain Song of Holy Communion ; Harmonies to Psalter, Canticles, etc. ; Catechism of Music, 1867 ; Papers on Church Music read at the Church Congress at Wolverhampton, 1867 ; Swansea, 1879; and London, 1868 and 1880. Christmas carols, hymns, etc. Trans. of " Treatise on Choir and Chorus Singing," F. J. Fétis.

HEMPSON (Dennis A.) Irish harp-player and comp., B. 1695. D. Nov., 1807. Supposed to have been a skilful performer, and said to have composed some of the fine national airs of Ireland.

HEMSLEY (John). English org. and comp., B. Arnold, Notts., 1838. Chor. Lichfield Cath. Org. Merivale, Warwick, 1857. Lay-clerk, Ely Cath., 1860. Stipendiary Choirman, Christ Ch. and S. Patrick's Caths., Dublin, 1864. Comp. anthems, songs, etc.

HEMSTOCK (Arthur). English org. and writer, B. Bingham, Notts, 1845. Author of "On Tuning the Organ." Lond., 8vo, [1876]; and comp. of church music, org. and Pf. music, and a setting of Psalm 145 [1885]. He is organist at Diss, Norfolk.

HENDERSON (A. G.) English writer, author of "Philosophy of Music." 12mo, 1856. (Appears also in Manchester Papers, a Series of Occasional Essays, v. 1, 1856.)

HENDERSON (William). Scottish poet and writer, B. Biggar, Lanarkshire, August 5, 1831. Reared as a printer, and was successively in employment of Constable of Edinburgh, Novello of London, etc. Established a printing business in London, as Henderson, Rait, and Spalding, which is known for fine music printing. Author of "The Cedars, and other Poems," Lond., 1877 (with music). He has contributed to Grove's "Dictionary of Music," and has in preparation a work called "The Songs of Scotland," designed to form a complete encyclopædia of the subject, both as regards words and music. He has contributed to musical periodical literature.

HENKEL (Michel). German org. and comp., B. Fulda, June 24, 1780. S. under Vierling. Org., Cath. of Fulda. D. Fulda, March 4, 1851. Wrote church music, org. music, etc. HEINRICH HENKEL, his brother, and GEORG A., his son, were both composers of some note. The former was org. of St. Eustache, Paris.

HENLEY (Rev. Phocion). English comp. and divine, B. Wootton Abbots, 1728. Rector of St. Andrew, Blackfriars. D. Aug. 29, 1764. Wrote "The Cure of Saul," anthems, hymns, and chants.

HENNING (Charles). American violinist and writer, author of "Practical School for the Violin." Boston, 3 v., n.d.

HENRION (Paul.) French song-writer, B. Paris, July 20, 1819. Comp. operas, songs, Pf. music, etc.

HENRY (P. C.) Author of "Universal Singing Preceptor: Exercises for the Formation of the Voice, the Production of a good Tone," etc. 8vo, n.d.

HENRY VIII., King of England, B. Greenwich, 1491. D. Westminster, 1547. He is accredited with the composition ot the anthem, "O Lord, the maker of all things," and a Latin motet. He was a patron of music and the fine arts generally, and is frequently mentioned as having been a musician of some skill.

HENSCHEL (Georg). German barytone vocalist and comp., B. Breslau, Feb. 18, 1850. S. under Moscheles, Richter, and Gotze, at Leipzig Cons. S. at Berlin under Schulze and Kiel. First appeared as singer, 1862. Appeared in England, and has since resided in London, 1877. Sang in America, and married there, 1881.

WORKS.—Op. 1. Three songs, voice and Pf. ; op. 2. Three Pf. Pieces ; op. 3. Four songs ; op. 4. Three duets, for two low voices, in form of canon ; op. 5. Two Pf. pieces ; op. 6. Etude-impromptu, in E minor, for Pf. ; op. 7. Three part-songs for 4 male voices ; op. 8. Three songs ; op. 9. Three Pf. Pieces; op. 10. Von den Nachtigallen, Two songs ; op. 11. " Die letzte Schlacht," ballad for baritone and Pf. ; op. 12. Three songs ; op. 13. Six Pf. pieces ; op. 14. Three choruses for 4 voices ; op. 15. Three songs ; op. 16. Festival March for orch. ; op. 17. Three songs ; op. 18. Three Pf. pieces ; op. 19. Three songs ; op. 20. Zigeunerisches Standchen (Gipsy serenade), accomp. for small orch. ; op. 21. Sinnen und Minnen, 10 songs ; op. 22. Thüringer Wahlblumen, Lieder ; op. 23. Serenade for string orch ; op. 24. Thüringer Walblumen, Lieder, 2nd series ; op. 25. Werner's Lieder aus Welschland, Acht Lieder aus Scheffel's Trompeter von Säkkingen ; op. 26. Five part-songs ; op. 27. Three songs ; op. 28. Three duets for a male and a female voice ; op. 29. Ueber Berg und Thal, Lieder ; op. 30. The 130th Psalm, soli, chorus and orch.

HENSEL (Fanny Cecile), née MENDELSSOHN, German comp., sister of Felix Mendelssohn-Bartholdy, B. Hamburg, Nov. 14, 1805. Married to W. Hensel, the painter, Oct. 3, 1829. D. Berlin, May 17, 1848.

WORKS.—Lieder for voice and Pf. ; Trio for Pf. and strings; Part-songs, Pf. music, etc.

She composed some sweet melodies, but is chiefly remarkable for the influence which she exerted over her talented brother.

HENSELT (Adolph). German pianist and comp., B. Schwabach, Bavaria, May 12, 1814. S. under Hummel. Teacher at S. Petersburg, 1838. Court pianist at S. Petersburg. Visited England, 1867.

WORKS.—Op. 1. Variations de Concert for Pf. (Donizetti); op. 2. Twelve Studies for Pf. ; op. 3. Poëme d'amour, Pf. ; op. 5. Twelve Studies for Pf. ; op. 6. The Fountain, study ; op. 7. Impromptu for Pf. ; op. 8. Pensée fugitive, Pf. ; op. 9. Scherzo for Pf., B min. ; op. 10. Romance for Pf., D flat min. ; op. 11. Variations for Pf. (Meyerbeer); op. 13. Pf. pieces, La Gondola, etc. ; op. 15. Frühlingslied, Pf. ; op. 16. Concerto for Pf. and orch., in F minor; op. 17. Second Impromptu ; op. 28. Valses, Pf. ; op. 36. Valse. Songs, minor Pf. pieces, etc.

Henselt is a pianist of considerable attainments, and his ability as a performer is great. His works are well written, but very often difficult.

HENSLOWE (Rev. W. H.) English writer, author of "The Phonarthron, or Natural System of the Sounds of Speech, including the Phonodion or Elements of Music," 8vo, n.d.

HENSTRIDGE (Daniel). English org. and comp. of 17th and 18th centuries. Org. of Canterbury Cath., 1700-1730. Comp. some anthems and other church music.

HERBECK (Johann Franz von). Austrian comp. and cond., B. Vienna, Dec. 25, 1831. D. Vienna, Oct. 28, 1877. He conducted Wagner's works with success, and has written a number of choral and instrumental works of some merit. His admiration of Wagner, to judge from his writings, amounted to something closely resembling idolatry. Of his works the songs are best known in Britain.

HERMANN (Johann David). German comp. and pianist, B. 1760. Settled in Paris, 1785. Prof. of Pf. at court of Marie Antoinette. D. 1857.

HÉROLD (Louis Joseph Ferdinand). French comp., B. Paris, Jan. 28, 1791. S. under Fétis and L. A. Adam. S. at Paris Cons., and gained first prize for Pf. playing. S. under Catel and Méhul. Gained Grand Prix de Rome, 1812. Accompanist at Italian Opera, Paris, 1820-7. Choir-master at Académie de Musique, 1827. Married Adèle Rollet, 1827. D. Paris, Jan. 19, 1833.

WORKS.—Op. 1. Sonata for Pf. ; op. 2. Fantasia for Pf. ; op. 3. Sonata ; op. 4. Caprice ; op. 5. Sonata ; op. 6. Caprice ; op. 7. Do. ; op. 8. Caprice, Pf. and quartet ; op. 9. Do. ; op. 10. Rondo ; op. 11. Do. ; op. 12. Caprice ; op. 13-14. Rondos, etc. ; Fantasias, Pf., opp. 15, 21, 28, 33, 43, 49 ; Rondos and Divertissements, opp. 16, 18, 20, 22, 27, 31, 34, 37, 40, 41, 44, 47, 53, 55; Rondo for Pf. duet, op. 17 ; Variations for Pf., opp. 19, 30, 35 ; Symphonies in C and D, for orch., 1813 ; String Quartets in C, D, and G minor, 1814. *Operas:* Charles de France (with Boieldieu), 1816 ; Les Rosières, 1817 ; La Clochette, 1817 ; Le Premier Venu, 1818 ; Les Troqueurs, 1819 ; L'Auteur mort et vivant, 1820 ; Le Muletier, 1823 ; Lasthénie, 1823 ; Le Lapin Blanc, 1825 ; Vendôme en Espagne, 1823 (with Auber) ; Le Roi Réné, 1824 ; Marie, 1826 ; L'Illusion, 1829 ; Emmeline, 1829 ; Zampa, Paris, May 3, 1831 ; Pré aux Clercs, Paris, Dec. 15, 1832, London, 1849. *Ballets:* Astolphe et Joconde, 1827 ; La Fille mal gardée, 1828 ; La Belle au bois dormant, 1829.

Hérold was considered one of the rising lights of French opera, and would no doubt have proved a greater ornament to it had he been longer spared. His works, "Marie," "Zampa," and "Pré aux Clercs," are still popular, and the overture at least of the second named is tolerably well known in Britain.

HERON (H.) English musician, author of "Parochial Music Corrected : Plain and Distinct Rules for the more pleasing and correct performance of Psalmody," 4to, 1790 (with tunes).

HERRMANN (Gottfried). German comp. and teacher, B. Sondershausen, 1808. S. under Spohr, A. Schmitt, and his father. Conductor and teacher at Lübeck, etc. Comp. choral music and operas.

HERSCHELL (Sir Friedrich Wilhelm). German comp. and astronomer, B. Hanover, Nov. 15, 1738. Came to England as bandsman in Hanoverian Guards. Org. Halifax Par. Ch., 1757-66. Org. Octagon Chap., Bath, 1781. Private Astronomer to George III., 1781. Resided at Slough, near Windsor, as scientist. LL.D., Oxon., F.R.S., etc. D. Slough, Windsor, August 23, 1822.

As a musician Herschell was clever, but not by any means eminent. His astronomical fame has completely overshadowed his connection with music. He composed a symphony, Pf. and other instrumental music.

HERSEE (Rose). English soprano vocalist, educated under Garcia, Madame Rudersdorff, and Arditi. First appeared in public at St. James's Hall, London. Sang in opera, as Amina in "La Sonnambula," 1868. Sang afterwards in operas by Meyerbeer and Donizetti. Appeared in America with the Carl Rosa Opera Company, 1869. Afterwards she sang throughout the English provinces; the United States, again; Australia, and London. Successful in the works of Balfe, Bizet, Lecocq, Mozart, etc., and is a favourite concert vocalist.

HERTZ (Michael). Polish pianist and comp., B. Warsaw, 1844. S. Leipzig Cons. Teacher in Berlin. Comp. of Pf. music etc.

HERVÉ (Florimond, RONGER). French comp., B. Houdain, Arras, June 30, 1825. S. Paris Cons. Chef d'orchestre, Palais Royal Theatre, 1851. Mus. director, do., 1856. Teacher, comp., and musical director. Holds other important appointments in Paris.

WORKS.—*Operas and Operettas:* Don Quichotte et Sancho Pança, 1851; Vadé au Cabaret; Le Compositeur toqué; La Fine Fleur de l'Andalousee; La Perle de l'Alsace; La Belle Espagnole; Fifi et Nini; Les Toréadors de Grenade, 1863; Le Joueur de flûte, 1864; Une Fantasia, 1865; La Revue pour rien ou Roland à Rouge-Veau, 1865; Les Chevaliers de la Table Ronde, 1866; La Biche au bois, 1866; "1867;" Orphée aux Enfers; Barbe-Bleue; La Grande Duchesse de Gerolstein; La Belle Hélène; Le Roi d'Amatibou, 1868; Chilpéric, 1868; Le Petit Faust; Les Turcs, 1869; Le Trône d'Ecosse, 1871; Le Nouvel Aladin, 1871; La Veuve du Malabar; Le Hussard persécute; Alice de Nevers, 1875; La Belle Poule, 1875; Estelle et Némorin, 1875; Panurge, 1879; La femme à papa, 1879; La Marquise des Rues, 1879; La Mère des Compagnons, 1880. Songs and Pf. music.

Many of Hervé's works achieved considerable popularity in France, and some of them further afield; but none them have any of these characteristics which distinguish works of enduring value. He writes well up to the traditions of French opera comique.

HERZ (Heinrich). Austrian pianist and comp., B. Vienna, Jan. 6, 1806. S. Paris Cons., under Pradher, etc., 1816. Gained first prize for Pf. playing, 1816. Resided in Paris, 1816-31. Travelled in Germany, 1833. Visited London, and played at Philharmonic Soc. Concert, 1833. Prof. of Pf., Paris Cons., 1842-1874. Travelled in Britain as pianist, 1843. Do., U.S.A., and West Indies, 1845-51. Established Piano-manufactory, near Paris, 1853. Gained highest award for instruments, Paris Exhibition.

WORKS.—*Pianoforte, etc.:* Variations, op. 13-16, 20, 23; Rondos, op. 2; Concertos for Pf. and orch., op. 34, 74, 87, 131, 180, 192; Studies for Pf., op. 151, 152, 153, 179; Trio for Pf., vn. and 'cello, op. 54; Méthode Complète de Piano, op. 100; Fantasias (Pf.), op. 71, 72. 89, 94, 98, 106, 108, 111, 118, 126, 133, 134, 136, 147, 158, 163, 169, 173, 193, 205; Three Morceaux, op. 91; Mosaïque Musicale, op. 101; Two Ballades, op. 117; Etudes, op. 119; Les Succès de Salon, op. 142, 143; Arabesques Musicales, op. 148; Tarentelle, op. 165; Marche Mexicaine, op. 166; Elegie, op. 187; Reverie-Nocturne, op. 194; Mazurka, op. 196. Air Hongrois, op. 197; Sonata di Bravura, op. 200; Berceuse, op. 201; Chant de Guerre, op. 204.

The works of Herz are noted chiefly for their extremely brilliant and difficult features. None of them are very likely to outlive the present century.

HERZBERG (Wilhelm). German pianist and comp., B. Berlin, 1819. D. Custrin, Nov. 14, 1847. Wrote sonatas for Pf., lieder, etc.

HERZOG (Johann Georg). German org. and writer, B. Schmölz, Bavaria, Sept. 6, 1822. Prof. org. at Munich Cons., 1850. Prof. at Erlangen University, 1855. Director of the Singing School, Erlangen, etc. Comp. various works for the org., and has published an organ school of some authority.

HESELTINE (James). English org. and comp., flourished during the first part of 18th century. Org. of St. Katherine's Hospital, London, beginning of 18th century. Org. Durham Cath., 1711. D. 1763. Wrote anthems, and other church music.

HESS (Charles). American pianist and comp., author of "Normal Piano Instructor," 6 parts, Cincinatti, n. d.

HESSE (Adolph Friedrich). German org. and comp., B. Breslau, Aug. 30, 1809. S. under Berner and F. Köhler. Played in Germany; in London, 1851. Org. of the Ch. of the Bernhardins, Breslau, 1831. Teacher and cond. D. Breslau, Aug. 5, 1863.

WORKS.—The Practical Organist, coll. of pieces and instructions; Symphonies for orch., op. 64, 75, etc.; Präludium und Fuge für die volle Orgel, op. 66; Nocturne for Pf., op. 80; Tobie, oratorio. Motets, Cantatas, Chamber music.

HEUSCHKEL (Johann Peter). German oboist, org., and comp., B. Harras, Jan. 4, 1773. D. Biberich, 1853.

HEWETT (J.) English writer, author of "An Introduction to Singing; or, the Rudiments of Music, to which is added a complete set of practical lessons, together with a collection of the best and most useful psalm tunes, and several anthems by eminent masters," 8vo, 1765.

HEWINS (J. M.) American writer, author of "Hints concerning Church Music, the Liturgy, etc."

HEWITT (Daniel Chandler). Scottish writer, B. 1789. D. London, 1869. Author of "New Analysis of Music," Lond., 4to, 1828. "The True Science of Music; being a new exposition of the Laws of Melody and Harmony," 8vo, 1860 and 1864.

HEWITT (John H.) American comp., B. New York, 1801. Resident in Baltimore. Has comp. operas, oratorios, songs, etc.

HEWLETT (Henry G.) English writer, author of "Autobiography, Memoir, and Letters of Henry Fothergill Chorley," London, 2 vols., 8vo, 1873.

HEWLETT (Thomas). English org. and comp., B. Oxford, 1845. D. Edinburgh, April, 1874. Teacher and org. in Dalkeith and Edinburgh. Mus. Bac., Oxon., 1865. Comp. org. and Pf. music, songs, choral music, and hymns, of which, "Hark, hark, my soul," is deservedly popular.

HICKS (Rev. Edward, B.A.) English writer, author of "Church Music, a Popular Sketch. Being a glance at its Origin, Development, and Present Use." Manchester, 8vo, 1881.

HIGGS (James). English org. and writer, author of Fugue (Music Primer), Lond. [1878]. Collection of Two-part Solfeggi, Lond., 1881; etc.

HIGGINS (William Mullinger). English writer, author of "The Philosophy of Sound, and History of Music," Lond., 8vo, 1838.

HILES (Henry). English org. and comp., B. Shrewsbury, Dec. 31, 1826. Org. in Shrewsbury; Bury, 1846; Bishopwearmouth Par. Ch., 1847; St. Michael's, Wood Street, London, 1859; Blind Asylum, Manchester, 1860; Bowdon Par. Ch., 1861; St. Paul's, Hulme, Manchester, 1864-67. Conductor of several musical societies. Mus. Bac. Oxon., 1862. Mus. Doc., Oxon., 1867. Gained four prizes consecutively, offered by Coll. of Org., and the prize for the best serious glee offered by the Manchester Gentlemen's Glee Club.

WORKS.—The Patriarchs, oratorio. *Cantatas:* Fayre Pastorel, by L. Leigh; The Crusaders, by Marian Millar, 1874; Watchfulness, female voices. God is our Refuge, 46th Psalm; Sing unto the Lord, 96th Psalm. Services in G and F. *Anthems*: Blessed are the merciful; I am well pleased; Gracious and righteous is the Lord; I was glad; I will lay me down in Peace; O give thanks to the Lord, 7 voices; Send out Thy light; Sing unto the Lord; The Lord is my Light; The Lord will comfort Zion; Wherewithal shall a young man. *Part-songs:* A Finland love song; Evening; Hushed in death; Summer longings; The calm of the Sea; The wreck of the Hesperus; To Daffodils; To the morning wind; When twilight dews; Spring; The May (It was a lover and his lass). *Songs:* Go lovely rose; In Paradise; The Hebrew Mother; The thought of home; Awake, sweet love; Gallants of England; Hark the ripple; Like to like; Love's wishes; May; Rest hath come; Three contralto songs; Six Songs; etc. *Organ:* Air varied; Fantasia; Festival March; Six Impromptus (2 sets); Preludes and Fugues in D min. and in A; Sonata in G min. Pf. music, various pieces. Grammar of Music, a Treatise on Harmony, Counterpoint, and Form, 2 vols., 8vo, n. d. The Harmony of Sounds, Lond., 8vo, 1871; 1872; 3rd edition, 1878. Alphabet of Music, n. d. Vocal Tutor, n. d. Part Writing, or Modern Counterpoint, Lond., 1884.

HILES (John). English writer and org., brother of the above, B. Shrewsbury, 1810. Held various organ appointments in Shrewsbury, Portsmouth, Brighton, and London. D. London, Feb. 4, 1882.

WORKS.—A Progressive Introduction to Playing the Organ, consisting of Fifty-five Preludes, Fugues, Airs, etc., in two, three, and four parts. from the works of the great composers; to which is added some account of the Instrument itself; a notice of its various stops, and the manner of combining them; with Directions and Exercises for the Use of the Pedals (Novello), n.d. Hand-Book for the Organ (selections). Short Voluntaries (selected). A Catechism for the Pianoforte Student, etc. Catechism for the organ, 1878. Catechism for Harmony and Thorough-bass, with Key, 2 vols., n.d. Dictionary of 12,500 Musical Terms, 12mo, 1871. Catechism for Part-singing, n.d. Juvenile Library of Pianoforte Music. Voluntaries for org. original and transcribed. Pianoforte pieces, songs, etc.

HILL (A. G.) English architect, author of "Organ Cases and Organs of the Middle Ages and Renaissance, containing an account of the most interesting specimens of Ancient Organs in the Churches of Continental Europe," etc. Lond., fo. [1882].

HILL (Frederick). English org. and comp., B. Louth, Lincoln, 1760. D. early in 19th century. Org. at York. Comp. Pf. music, songs, etc. His brothers, JOSEPH, org. at Stockton, and THOMAS, org. at Pontefract, were composers of glees, org., Pf., and harp music, etc.

HILL (Thomas Henry Weist). English violinist comp. and cond., B. Islington, Jan. 3, 1828. S. at R. A. M., London, 1844. Gained King's Scholarship. Concert-giver and violinist in London and the United States. Mem. R. A. M., and connected with the Italian opera, London. Musical director at Alexandra Palace. Was Prof. at Eton Coll.; now at R. A. A. M. Principal of the Guildhall School of Music, London, 1880.

Mr. Hill has shown himself possessed of great abilities as a conductor, and has directed several series of concerts with much success. His compositions for the orchestra, the Pf., the violin, etc., are all of a high degree of merit, and reflect great credit on his taste and musical skill. As director of the Guildhall School of Music he has already done a vast deal of good, and will no doubt in the future secure for it a high place among the musical institutions of the country.

HILL (Joseph), (Joseph, Junr.), and (Locky). English violin-makers of the end of last and beginning of present centuries. They all made instruments of good quality.

HILL (U. C.) American writer and violinist, author of "Practical Violin School," Boston, n.d.; "Spohr's Grand Violin School, edited and revised."

HILL (Junius W.) American org. and musician, B. Hingham, Mass., 1840. S. under J. C. D. Parker in Boston, and under Plaidy, Richter, Moscheles,

W

Hauptmann, and Papperitz, at Leipzig, 1860-63. Org. at Tremont Temple, Boston, 1858-60; Dr. Webb's Ch., Boston, 1863; Tremont St., Boston Methodist Ch. Prof. of Pf. and Org. in New England Cons. of Music, Boston. Well known as a successful organist and teacher in Boston.

HILL (W. & SON). English firm of organ-builders, founded in London, by Snetzler, 1755. Hill became a partner while Elliott held the business, in succession to the founder, and managed it until his death in Dec. 1870, in partnership with M. Davidson, now of Gray and Davidson. The firm has built a large number of important instruments in Great Britain.

HILLER (Ferdinand). German comp. and cond., B. Frankfort-on-Main, Oct. 24, 1811. S. under A. Schmitt, Hollweiler, and Hummel at Weimar, 1825. Resided at Paris, 1828-35. Cond. of Choral Soc. at Frankfort, 1836-7. Resided at Milan, 1837; Leipzig, 1839. S. under Baini at Rome, 1841. Cond. Gewandhaus Concerts, Leipzig, 1843-4. Municipal Musical Cond., Dusseldorf, 1847; Cologne, 1850. Founder and Director of Cologne (Cöln) Cons., 1850. Cond. Lower Rhine Musical Festivals, 1850-81. Cond. Italian Opera in Paris, 1852-53. Visited England, and appeared in London, Liverpool, and Manchester, 1871. D. Cologne, May 10, 1885.

WORKS.—Op. 1. First quartet for Pf. and strings; op. 2. Duo Concertante for Pf. and vn.; op. 3. Second quartet, in F min.; op. 4. Three Caprices for Pf.; op. 5. Concerto for Pf. and orch.; opp. 6, 7. 8, 9. 1st, 2nd, 3rd and 4th trios for Pf., vn., and 'cello; op. 10. Le Danse des Fees, Pf.; op. 11. Serenade for Pf.; op. 12-13. String quartets; op. 14-20. Caprices for Pf. and orch.; op. 15. Six Suites for Pf.; op. 16. Songs for Voice and Pf.; op. 17-18, 21. Reveries, Pf.; op. 19, 23. Songs for Voice and Pf.; op. 24. Die Zerstörung Jerusalems (Destruction of Jerusalem) oratorio, 1840; op. 25. Six Songs for soprano and chorus of men's voices; op. 26. Six Songs for male voices; op. 27. Two Psalms for solo voice; op. 28. Second Duet for Pf. and vn.; op. 30. Four Impromptus, Pf.; op. 31, 34. Songs for voice and Pf.; op. 32. Concert-overture for orch., D min.; op. 33. Rêveries for Pf.; op. 36. Song of Ondins, for chorus and orch.; op. 37. Six Songs for 4 voices; op. 39. Lieder for 2 voices and Pf.; op. 40. Four Impromptus, Pf.; op. 41, 43, 46. Songs for voice and Pf.; op. 47. Sonata for Pf.; op. 48. Die Lustige Musikanten, cantata; op. 49. Hebrew Song of Byron for solo voice, chorus and orch.; op. 51. Six Songs for male voices; op. 52. Thirty Rhythmatic Studies, Pf.; op. 54. Three Ghasiles, Pf.; op. 55. Three Marches; op. 56. Rhythmatic Studies for Pf.; op. 57. Eight Measures, variées; op. 58. Valse expressive; op. 59. Second Sonata, Pf.; op. 60. 125th Psalm, for tenor, chorus and orch.; op. 61. Six Songs for 2 voices; op. 63. Three Odes by Goethe; op. 65. Psalm for 8 voices; op. 66. Eight Pf. pieces; op. 70. Lorelei, cantata; op. 75. Ver Sacrum oder die Gründung Rom's, by Bischoff, for solo, chorus and orch.; op. 79. Eight Pf. pieces; op. 81. Pf. pieces; op. 82. Vocal Exercises; op. 83. Die Wallfahrt nach Kevlaar, by Heine, for voice and Pf.; op. 86. Suite for Pf. and vn.; op. 87. Toccata, etc. for vn. and Pf.; op. 88. Capriccio für Pf.; op. 95. Six Sonatinas for Pf.; op. 97. The Guitar, impromptu; op. 98. Variations for Pf.; op. 99. Die Nacht, Hymn for solo voices, chorus and orch.; op. 115. Gavotte, etc. for Pf.; op. 146. Aus dem Soldatenleben, Fantasiestücke for Pf.; op. 183. Instrumental Stücke und chöre zum Dramatischen Märchen "Prinz Papagei"; op. 185. Sieben Lieder; op. 186. Second Serenade for Pf., vn. and 'cello, in C min.; Romilda, opera, 1839; Der Müller und sien Kind, do., 1844; Conradin, do., 1847; Les Catacombes, do., 1862; Le Déserteur, do., Cologne, 1865. Saul, oratorio, Cologne, 1858; Song of Heloise, cantata; Nala and Damayanti, cantata, op. 150; Pentecost, cantata; Song of Victory, cantata; 93rd Psalm; 126th Psalm; Two Grand Symphonies. *Overtures:* Phèdre; Faust, 1833; Fernando, 1847; Prometheus, 1847; Demetrius. Spring, symphony, 1877. Quintets, quartets, etc. for strings. Dramatic Fantasia for orch.

Hiller's writings are characterized by the same spirit which animated Beethoven, Schubert, and Mendelssohn. His genius revels in perspicuity rather than in mysticism, and his endeavours as a composer are marked by high purity of expression and design. His works are beautifully wrought out, fanciful, and inspired with a strongly defined feeling for pure and formal workmanship. His minor works are well enough known, but the cantatas are by far the most popular of his productions which are known in Britain.

HILLER (Johann Adam), HÜLLER. German comp., B. near Görlitz, Dec. 25, 1728. S. at Leipzig University. Cantor at the Thomas School, Leipzig, and cond. of the Gewandhaus Concerts. D. Leipzig, June 16, 1804.

WORKS.—*Operas and Ballets:* Die Musen; Die Jagd; Grab des Mufti, 1750; Der Krieg, 1750; Der Erntekranz, 1758; Das gerettete Troja, 1758; Der Dorf Barbier; Die Jubelhochzeit, 1760; Die Verwandelte-Weiber, 1767; Lesvart et Dariolette, 1767; Der lustige Schuster, 1771; Lottchen am Hofe, 1776; Die Schaefer als Pilgrime, 1780; Die Liebe auf dem Lande, 1780. Symphonies. Cantatas. Psalms, Hymns, Songs, etc. Anleitung zur Musikalischen Gelahrcheit worüm von der Theorie und Praxis der Alten und Neuen Musik, von den Musikalischer Instrumenten, besonders der Orgel Nachricht gegeben, 1783, 8vo.

"Hiller, who became, perchance, the creator of the German 'Operetta,' or 'Singspiel,' possessed all the qualities necessary for the successful cultivation of this style of light drama,—taste, knowledge, facility of musical inventiveness, mastery of popular form. His operas contained a store of charming original melodies, which became popular through all Germany."—*Ritter.*

HILTON (John). English comp. and org., B. end of 16th century. Mus. Bac., Cantab., 1626. Org. and Clerk. of S. Margaret's, Westminster, 1628. D. March, 1657.

WORKS.—Ayres, or Fa-las for 3 voyces, Lond., 1627. Catch that catch can; or, A choice collection of catches, rounds, and canons, for 3 or 4 voyces,...Lond., 8vo, 1652. Services in G minor. Anthems. Elegy on William Lawes, 1648. "Fair Oriana, beauty's queen," madrigal for 5 voices, and "Fair Orian, in the morn," for 6 voices, are in the "Triumphs of Oriana."

Hilton has been credited with the composition of the anthem, "Lord for thy tender mercies sake," but popular opinion is strongly in favour of Farrant's title to the work. The "Ayres" was edited for the Musical Antiquarian Society by J. Warren, 1844.

HIMMEL (Friedrich Heinrich). German comp. and cond., B. Treuenbrietzen, near Brandenburg, Nov. 20, 1765. S. Theology. Educated as a musician at instance of Frederic William II. S. under Naumann. Chamber musician to Frederic William II. Court Chapel-master at Berlin. D. Berlin, June 8, 1814.

WORKS.—Il Primo Navigatore, opera, 1794; Semiramide, 1795; Don Kobold, 1804; Les Sylphes, 1807. Cantatas, various. Isacco, oratorio, 1792. Masses, psalms, vespers, anthems. Sonatas, concertos, etc. for Pf. Romances and Songs.

HINDLE (Johann). Austrian contra-bass player, B. Vienna, Feb. 10, 1792. First appeared in 1817. Afterwards played at Prague, Leipzig, Dresden, Berlin, etc. D. Vienna, Aug. 9, 1862.

HINDLE (John). English comp., B. Westminster, 1761. Mus. Bac. Oxon., 1791. Lay-vicar Westminster Abbey. D. 1796. He published a "Collection of Songs for 1 and 2 voices," and a "Set of Glees for 3, 4, and 5 voices, op. 2" [1790].

HINE (William). English comp. and org., B. Brightwell, Oxfordshire, 1687. Chor. Magdalen Coll., Oxford, 1694-1705. Lay-Clerk, do. S. under Jeremiah Clarke. Org. of Gloucester Cath., 1712. D. Aug. 28, 1730.

WORKS.—Harmonia Sacra Glocestriensis; or, Select Anthems for 1, 2, and 3 voices, and a Te Deum and Jubilate, together with a voluntary for Organ, fo. n.d. Anthems, etc.

HINGSTON (John). English org. and comp. of 17th century. S. under O. Gibbons. Musician to Charles I., and preceptor in music to Cromwell's daughter. Org. to Cromwell, 1654. D. Dec. 17, 1683. He comp. "Fancies for the Viol."

HINTON (John William). English org. and comp., B. Edmonton, Middlesex, April 26, 1849. Mus. Bac., Dublin, 1871; B.A., Dublin, 1872; Mus. Doc., Dublin, 1874; M.A., do., 1876. Resident sec. and org.-prof., Trin. Coll., Lond., 1876-77. Licent. Trin. Coll., Lond., 1877. He edited the "International Organist," two series; and wrote "Facts about Organs, Guide to the

Purchase," etc. In 1884 he issued "A Manual of Harmonies for the Gregorian Tones." He comp. organ music, church music, and songs, also an oratorio, "Pharaoh," and an opera, "Mazeppa" (1880), both MS.

HIPKINS (Alfred James), F.S.A. English musician and writer on musical subjects, especially musical instruments. B. Westminster, June 17, 1826. In business connection with John Broadwood and Sons, pianoforte-makers, London. A contributor to the "Encyclopædia Britannica," Grove's "Dictionary of Music and Musicians," and various musical publications published in this country and on the Continent. His articles have been reprinted in America and even in Japan; they have also been translated into the French, Italian, and German languages.

Mr. Hipkins made a special journey to Berlin and Potsdam in 1881, under the patronage of H. I. H. The Crown Princess of Germany, to identify and examine the pianofortes made by Gottfried Silbermann, which had belonged to Frederick the Great. In 1883 he was awarded the Silver Medal of the Society of Arts for a lecture on the technical history of the piano. In 1884, at the request of H.R.H. the Prince of Wales, he became concerned in founding the Division H. (Music) of the Inventions Exhibition held at South Kensington in 1885, and was a member of the Music Committee. He was also Chairman of the Sub-Committee of the Historic Loan Collection shown in the Royal Albert Hall in connection with that Exhibition, and for his services was awarded a gold medal. In January, 1886, he was elected a Fellow of the Society of Antiquaries. Mr. Hipkins is regarded as the most trustworthy authority on the subject of the Pianoforte, and his articles on that instrument are valuable contributions to British musical literature.

HIRST (Thomas). English writer, author of "The Music of the Church, in four parts; containing a General History of music, including an Account of Hebrew Music." Lond., 8vo, 1841.

HITCHIN (Rev. Edward). English dissenting minister and writer, author of "Scripture proof for Singing of Scripture Psalms, Hymns, and Spiritual Songs." Lond., 12mo., 1696.

HOBBS (John William). English comp. and tenor vocalist. B. Henley-on-Thames, Aug. 1, 1799. Chor. Canterbury Cath. Articled to John Jeremiah Goss. Sang at Norwich Musical Festival, 1813. Tenor Singer of Trinity, King's, and St. John's Colleges, Camb. Do. St. George's Chap., Windsor. Gent. of Chap. Roy., 1827. Lay-vicar Westminster Abbey, 1836. D. Croydon, Jan. 12, 1877.

WORKS.—Glees. *Songs*: Caliban; Crier, or lost heart; Dear father, take thy gentle child; England; Jack's alive; Music of the past; Nina; Phillis is my only joy; Soldier's departure; Then you have not forgotten; I come from the Spirit-land; When Delia Sings; Daphne and Damon; Farewell to the Valley; Oh believe not the tears; Oh my own Native Land; Old Temeraire; Wake, Lady, Wake; The Heavens are bright; Departed days; Eulalie; Forest Fairy; Jamie; Shepherd's Chief Mourner; We've known each other long; The Captive Greek Girl; and many others, amounting in all to over 100.

HOBRECHT (Jacob), or OBRECHT. Flemish comp., B. Utrecht [1430]. D. Antwerp, first part of 16th century [1507]. Wrote masses, madrigals, etc. Chiefly noted, apart from his connection with the music of his period, as having been the music master of Erasmus, the Scholar.

HODGES (Edward). English org. and comp., B. Bristol, July 20, 1796. Org. of Clifton Church. Do. St. James Ch., Bristol. Do. St. Nicholas Ch. Mus. Doc., Cantab., 1825. Went to America, 1838. Org. St. John's Episcopal Chap., New York. Org. Trinity Ch., N.Y,, 1846. Returned to England, 1863. D. Clifton, Sept. 1, 1867.

WORKS.—Church Services. Anthems. Contributions to the Musical Journals. An Apology for Church Music and Musical Festivals, in answer to the Animadversions of the *Standard* and the *Record*, Lond., 8vo, 1834. An Essay on the Cultivation of Church Music, New York, 1841.

HODGES (Colonel C. L.) English collector, published a "Collection of Peninsular melodies, with words by Mrs. Hemans, Mrs. Norton," etc., Lond. [1830].

HODSON (George A.) English song-writer, who flourished in the first half of this century, has composed a number of fine melodies, among which may be named:—Tell me Mary how to woo thee; My pretty gazelle; Bridal wreath; Briton's home; Child's first prayer; O give me but my Arab steed; Poor Bessie; etc.

HOECK (William Thomson). Scottish comp. and cond., B. Paisley, June 14, 1859. S. under his father, Louis Hoeck, music-teacher in Paisley; also under Dr. A. L. Peace. Org. and Choirmaster Renfrew Parish Church, 1874-80; Queen's Park U. P. Ch., Glasgow, 1880. Cond. Paisley Philharmonic Soc., 1878-83; Hillhead Musical Assoc., 1882; Pollokshields Musical Assoc., 1882; Glasgow Amateur Orchestral Soc., 1883.

WORKS.—Op. 1. Two Pf. pieces: melody impromptu and albumleaf; op. 2. Te Deum in E; op. 3. Romance for Violoncello and Pf.; op. 4. Songs: Two hands; The child and the shadow; op. 5. Three characteristic pieces for Pf.: Study, Love song, March; op. 6. "Undine," characteristic piece for orch. (Glasgow Choral Union, 1884). *Songs*: How I envy the ring; A love song; Out of reach. Romance for oboe and Pf. "Wiegenliedchen," for Pf. Hymn tunes, etc.

HOERING (August F.G.) German writer and teacher, author of Pianoforte Playing to Highest Perfection: being a short treatise on the right way of attaining the above accomplishment, Lond. 1880; Music, and how to become a Good Musician, 8vo, 1883; The Method of the Future, 8vo; A New Method for the Pianoforte on an entirely new Principle, 6 books.

HOFFMANN (Ernst Theodor Wilhelm). German comp., lawyer, and novelist, B. Königsberg, Jan. 24, 1776. S. for the law. Held various legal appointments. Councillor in Court of Judicature, Berlin, 1818. D. Silesia, July 25, 1822.

WORKS.—*Operas:* Der Frank der Unterblichkeit; Ondine; Liebe aus Eifernicht; Julius Sabinus; Das Kreux an der Astsee. Symphonies. Instrumental music, various. Novels, etc.

More noted as a novelist than as a musician. His novels are exceedingly grotesque, and have been translated by T. Carlyle and others. His music has long since been committed to the limbo of oblivion. He was an extravagant romancer, and possibly a fantastic spirit pervaded his musical works.

HOFFMANN (Heinrich Anton). German violinist and comp., B. 1770. D. 1842. Comp. for his instrument.

HOFFMANN (Johann Georg). German org. and comp., B. 1700. D. 1780. Wrote theoretical works, serenades, concertos, etc.

HOFFMANN (J. S. Christian). German musician. B. Hanau, near Frankfort-on-Main, April 10, 1841. S. Leipzig Cons., 1863, under Hauptmann, Richter, and Wenzel. Settled in America as teacher and pianist. D. Hoboken, N. J., June 23, 1875.

HOFFMANN (Karl Julius A.) German writer and comp., B. Ratisbon, 1801. Writer of concertos, operettas, songs, musical histories, etc.

HOFFMANN (Ludwig). German comp. and cond., B. Berlin, 1830. Comp. Pf. and orch. music, songs, etc. He is a teacher of singing.

HOFFMANN (Richard). See ANDREWS (RICHARD HOFFMAN).

HOFFMEISTER (Franz Anton). German comp. and publisher, B. Rothenburg on the Neckar, 1754. Was publisher in Vienna and Leipzig. D. Vienna, Feb. 10, 1812. He composed a vast amount of church music, symphonies, flute and violin music, songs, etc. He is chiefly noted, however, for the publication of the masterpieces of nearly all the great composers in a cheap form.

HOFMANN (Heinrich). German comp., B. Berlin, Jan. 13, 1842. S. under Kullak, Dehn and Wüerst. Teacher and comp. in Berlin,

WORKS.—Op. 1. Two nocturnes for Pf. in A flat and G; op. 2. Two valses-caprices for Pf., in G and A flat; op. 3. Three Pf. duets; op. 4. Four two-part songs; op. 5. Capriccio for Pf. in A min; op. 6. Polonaise for Pf. in A sharp min; op. 7. "Cartouche," operetta in 1 act; op. 8. Three quartets for S. A. T. B.; op. 9. Five pieces for Pf.; op. 10. Three Pf. pieces; op. 11. Album Leaves, four Pf. pieces; op. 12. In Dreamland, Pf; op. 13. Two Pf. duets; op. 14. Valse for Pf.; op. 15. Three pieces for orch.; op. 16. Hungarian Suite for orch., 1872; op. 17. Champagne song for male chorus and orch.; op. 18. Trio for Pf., vn., and 'cello, in A; op. 19. Italian love tale, 6 Pf. pieces; op. 20. Six quartets for male voices; op. 21. Song of the Norns, for female voices, solo and chorus, and orch.; op. 22. Frithjof, sinfonie for orch., 1874; op. 23. Ländler for Pf.; op. 24. Fünf Minnelieder for voice and Pf.; op. 25. Sestet for 2 vns., 2 tenors and 2 'cellos, in E min.; op. 26. Five songs (Heine); op. 27. Liedercyclus, 7 songs for voice and Pf.; op. 28. Dramatic overture for orch.; op. 29. Springtime of love, 5 Pf. duets; op. 30. Melusina, cantata for solo, chorus and orch.; op. 31. Concerto for 'cello in D minor; op. 32. Four songs; op. 33. Frauenbilder aus Shakespeare's Dramen, 4 songs; op. 34. Reminiscences, 5 Pf. pieces; op. 35. Three Pf. duets; op. 36. Five songs; op. 37. Reminiscences, book 2, 9 pieces; op. 38. Grand funeral march for orch.; op. 39. Prairie Pictures (Steppenbilder), Three Pf. pieces; op. 40. Armin, opera in 4 acts; op. 41. Four two-part songs; op. 42. Minnespeil, vocal waltzes with Pf. duet accomp.; op. 43. On the Rhine, four Pf. duets; op. 44. Aennchen von Tharau, opera in 3 acts; op. 45. Cinderella, cantata for solo, chorus, and orch.; op. 46. From my Diary, 12 Pf. pieces; op. 47. Summer; op. 48. Romance for 'cello and Pf.; op. 49, Wanda, ballad; op. 50. Quartet for Pf., vn., viola, and 'cello; op. 51. Five songs. Sonata for violin and Pf. Op. 67. Sinnen und Minnen, a dance poem (1883).

HOGARTH (George). Scottish writer and comp., B. Carfrae Mill, Lauderdale, 1783. S. at Edinburgh for law. Member of Edinburgh Choral Union. Joint Secretary, with G. F. Graham, of Edinburgh Musical Festival, 1815. Contributed to the *Harmonicon*, 1830. Sub-editor of the *Morning Chronicle*, London, 1834. Musical critic of *Daily News*, 1846-66. Secretary to Philarmonic Society, 1850. He married Miss Thomson, daughter of George Thomson. D. London, Feb. 12, 1870.

WORKS.—Musical History, Biography, and Criticism, being a General Survey of Music from the Earliest Period to the Present Time. Lond., 1835; second edit., 1838, 2 v., 8vo. Memoirs of the Musical Drama, Lond., 1838, 2 v., 8vo, *portraits*. Memoirs of the Opera in Italy, France, Germany, and England. Lond., 1851, 8vo. The Birmingham Festival of 1852. London, 1852, 12mo. The Philharmonic Society of London, from its Foundation in 1813 to its Fiftieth Year, 1862. Lond., 1862, 8vo. Book of English Song. Lond., n.d., 2 v. fo. Contributions to Periodical Literature. Glees and Songs.

Hogarth was one of the few cultured men of letters who have written intelligibly about music. His works are all of standard value, and are still sought among musicians. They are only open to the same objection as that urged against Messrs. Burney and Hawkins—who, by the bye, could scarcely help themselves—in not coming down to recent times. His daughter, Catherine, married Charles Dickens the novelist, in 1836.

HOGG (James), the Ettrick Shepherd. Scottish poet, musician, and general writer, B. Ettrick Forest, Selkirk, 1772. Engaged as farmer at Altrive, but chiefly as contributor to *Blackwood's Magazine*, and as a general writer. D. Altrive, Nov. 21, 1835.

WORKS.—The Mountain Bard, 1803; Mador of the Moor; The Pilgrim of the Sun; The Queen's Wake; The Jacobite Relics of Scotland: being the Songs, Airs, and Legends of the Adherents of the House of Stuart, Edin. 2 v., 8vo, 1819-21, with music; tales, fugitive pieces, etc.; musical settings of his own verses.

Hogg was a poet of considerable powers, and a prose writer of much fancy, if uncultured in style. He has interest for the musician chiefly on account of his lyrical effusions, which take rank after those of Burns and Ramsay in the national anthology. While Hogg was conceited with regard to his songs, he was even worse where his musical settings of them were concerned. His melodies are passable, but do not compare favourably with those of Neil Gow, junr., R. A. Smith, and other composers who have used his verses.

HOHNSTOCK (Karl). German comp., pianist, and vnst., B. Brunswick, 1828. Went to Philadelphia, 1848. Resides there as teacher and comp. Writer of Pf. music and songs.

HOLBORNE (Anthony and William). English musicians, who in 1597 published in London a joint production entitled "The Cittharn Schoole, by Antony Holborne, gentleman, and servant to her most excellent Majestic. Hereunto are added sixe short Aers Neapolitan like to three voyces, without the instrument, done by his brother, William Holborne." This book is now excessively rare.

HOLCOMBE (Henry). English comp., B. Salisbury, 1690. Chor. Salisbury Cath. Singer in London, at Drury Lane Theatre. Teacher of harpsichord and vocalisation. D. London, 1750.

WORKS.—The Musical Medley, or, a Collection of English Songs and Cantatas set to Music, 1745; The Garland: a Collection of Songs and Cantatas.

HOLDEN (George). English comp. and org., B. 1800. Org. of St. George's Ch., Liverpool. D. Liverpool, Dec, 1856. Comp. anthems, songs, org. music, etc.

HOLDEN (John). Scottish writer and comp., flourished in latter part of 18th century. He published "A Collection of Church-Music, consisting of New Setts of the Common Psalm Tunes, with some other Pieces; adapted to the several Metres in the Version authorized by the General Assembly. Composed with a view to render the just Performance of each part more easy to Learners; and the united effect of the whole more full and pathetic; and also exemplify some new Discoveries in the Scale of Music. Principally designed for the use of the University of Glasgow," Glasgow, 4to, 1766. He also wrote "An Essay towards a Rational System of Music," Glasgow, 4to, 1770, Calcutta, 1799, Edin, 8vo, 1807. He was never a Professor in Glasgow University as stated by Fétis.

HOLDEN (Oliver). American comp., B. about middle of 18th century. Was originally a carpenter. Published American Harmony, 1793. Collection of Sacred Music [c. 1795]; The Worcester Collection of Sacred Harmony, 1797. D. Charlestown, 1831.

His collection of psalm tunes are among the earliest of the American efforts in this direction. He was associated with Holyoke in some of his ventures.

HOLDER (Joseph William). English org. and comp., B. Clerkenwell, London, 1764. Chor. Chap. Roy. S. under Nares. Assistant to Reinhold, org. of S. George the Martyr, Queen St. Org. of St. Mary's Ch., Bungay. Org. of Chelmsford. Bac. Mus. Oxon. 1792. D. 1832.

WORKS.—Glees, 2 sets, 1787, 1800; Mass: Anthem and Te Deums; Pf. music; songs, etc.

HOLDER (Rev. William, D.D). English writer and divine, B. Northamptonshire, 1614. Educated at Camb. Rector of Blechindon, Oxfordsh., 1642. D.D. 1660. Canon of Ely. Canon of S. Paul's. Sub-dean of Chap.-Roy., 1674-89. D. London, Jan. 24, 1697.

WORKS.—A Treatise of the Natural Grounds and Principles of Harmony, London, 12mo, 1694: Do., to which is added, by way of Appendix, Rules for Playing a Thorow-bass by the late M. Godfrey Keller, Lond., 8vo, 1731; Evening Service in C; Anthems, etc.

HOLDROYD (Israel). English writer, published "The Spiritual Man's Companion, or Pious Christian's Recreation, containing an Historical Account of Music, &c. Grounds of Music and Composition in all Branches. . . . Psalm and Hymn Tunes,"...8vo, various editions to 1753.

HOLLAND (Justin). American writer, author of Comprehensive Method for the Guitar, Boston, n. d. ; Modern Method for the Guitar, Cleveland [1874] ; Songs and guitar music.

HOLLOWAY (Arthur S.) English org. and comp. of present time. Was Bac. Mus. Oxon., 1875 ; Doc. Mus., etc. Has comp. songs, organ music, Pf. music, etc., and a " School Board Singing Tutor," 8vo, n. d.

HOLLOWAY (H. R.) English writer, author of a " Manual of Chanting," London, 8vo, 1850.

HOLMES (Alfred). English violinist and comp., B. London, Nov. 9, 1837. S. vn. under his father. Sopranist at the Oratory, King Wm. St., Strand. *Début* with Henry, his brother, Haymarket Theatre, July, 1847. Appeared at Beethoven Rooms, London, 1853. Played in Germany, 1856 ; Austria, 1857 ; Sweden, 1857-9 ; Norway and Holland, 1860-1. Settled in Paris, 1864. Organised a quartet party, 1866. Travelled in Holland, Prussia, and Germany, 1867. D. Paris, Mar. 4, 1876.

WORKS.—*Symphonies*: Jeanne d'Arc, St. Petersburg, 1867, London, Feb. 1875 ; The Youth of Shakspere, Paris; The Siege of Paris, 1870 ; Charles XII. ; Romeo and Juliet ; The Cid ; The Muses ; Robin Hood, 1870. Inez de Castro, opera, 1869. Pf. music and songs.

The death of this talented composer at the early age of 39 robbed English instrumental music of many fine additions to its store. As a violinist he was highly successful, and appeared with much favour in various countries.

HOLMES (Auguste). Irish musician, B. Ireland, 1850. Resided in Paris. Writer of several operas, " Hero et Leandre," 1874, etc. She has also comp. " Ireland " and " Poland " symphonies, and other orch. pieces.

HOLMES (Edward). English writer and musician, B. near London, 1797. S. under V. Novello. Musical Critic of *Atlas* newspaper. Married granddaughter of Samuel Webbe. D. in U. S. A., August 28, 1859.

WORKS.—A Ramble among the Musicians of Germany, giving some Account of the operas of Munich, Dresden, Berlin, &c., with Remarks upon the Church Music, Singers, Performers, and Composers, and a sample of the Pleasures and Inconveniences that await the Lover of Art on a similar excursion. By a Musical Professor. London, 8vo, 1828 ; 2nd edit., 1830; 3rd edit., 1838. Life of Mozart, including his Correspondence, Lond., 8vo, 1845 ; Life of Purcell ; Analytical and Thematic Index of Mozart's Pianoforte Works ; Contributions to Periodical Literature.

Holmes' "Life of Mozart" is recognised as the standard English work on that master, and is valued accordingly. His work on German musicians, etc., is now scarce, and was noted for its clever pictures of the German musical manners of his time.

HOLMES (George). English org. and comp., B. about middle of 17th century. Org. of Lincoln Cath., 1704. D. 1720. Wrote odes, anthems, and songs.

HOLMES (Henry). English violinist and comp., brother of Alfred Holmes, B. London, Nov. 7, 1839. S. under his father. Resided for a time at Stockholm. Teacher and comp. in London. Prof. of violin at Royal Coll. of Music.

WORKS.—*Cantatas*: Christmas ; Praise ye the Lord. Overture for orch. Symphonies, various. Concerto for violin, 1875. Songs, etc.

Mr. Holmes is famed for his artistic conception in composition, and for his fine taste and execution in performance. His compositions have been well received whenever produced, and they bear marks which distinguish them as the works of a true musician.

HOLMES (John). English org. and comp. of 17th century. Org. of Winchester Cath. about end of 16th century, Org. of Salisbury Cath., 1602-10. Teacher of Batten and E. Lowe.

His compositions consist of services and anthems for the church, and madrigals ; among them being, " Thus Bonnyboots the Birthday Celebrated," for 5 voices, contained in the " Triumphs of Oriana,' 1601.

HOLMES (Mary). English writer, authoress of "A Few Words about Music, by M. H.," Lond., 1851.

HOLMES (William Henry). English pianist and comp., B. Sudbury, Derby, Jan. 8, 1812. S., R. A. M., 1822. Gained 2 medals. Sub-Prof. of Pf., R. A. M., 1826. Prof. of Pf., principal. Début as Pianist, Philharmonic Soc. Concert, 1851. Teacher of W. S. Bennett, J. W. Davison, G.A., and W. Macfarren. D. London, April 23, 1885.

WORKS.—Symphonies. The Elfin of the Lake, opera. *Pianoforte*: English Chimes; Border Strains; Consuelo, concertino; Fairy fingers, fantasia; Highland echo; Christmas; Sighing wind; Veronica; Pleasure trip; Whispering music; etc. Concerto, The Jubilee, for Pf. and orch. Sonata for Pf. and vn. Songs, etc.

Holmes was one of the oldest and most respected musicians in Britain. His life was devoted to the furtherance of musical art, and he achieved brilliant success, as a glance at his numerous successful pupils will prove. His powers as a pianist were at one time of the highest order, and he held a preëminent position among British performers.

HOLSTEIN (Franz von). German comp., B. Brunswick, Feb. 16, 1826. S. at Leipzig Cons., under Hauptmann. D. May 21, 1878.

WORKS.—Op. 1. Waldlieder, voice and Pf.; op. 2. Six songs for male voices; op. 9. Waldlieder, second series; op. 22. Der Haideschacht, opera, 1869; op. 30. Der Erbe von Morley, 1872; op. 37. Five Lieder for voice and Pf.; op. 38. Beatrice, scene from Schiller, for voice and orch.; op. 42. Six Lieder for voice and Pf.; op. 43. Five Lieder; op. 44. Four Lieder. Die Hochländer, 1877. Songs and trios.

HOLYOKE (Samuel). American teacher and cond., B. Boxford, Mass., Oct. 15, 1762. D. Concord, N. H., Feb. 22, 1820. Was M.A. of Dartmouth Coll.

WORKS.—Harmonia Americana, Boxford, 1791; The Christian Harmonist, 1804; The Instrumental Assistant, 1806-7; The Columbian Repository of Sacred Harmony, 1809; The Massachusetts Compiler, with Oliver Holden, 1794. Hymns, etc.

Holyoke was, with Billings, the pioneer of American Psalmody, and one of the first native composers.

HOLZBAUER (Ignaz). Austrian comp., B. Vienna, 1711. D. Mannheim, April 7, 1783. Wrote vocal music and Pf. pieces.

HOMES (N.), D.D. English writer, author of "Gospel Musick; or, the Singing of David's Psalms, etc. in the publick congregations, or private families asserted and vindicated," Lond., 4to, 1644.

HOMILIUS (Gottfried August). German comp., B. Rosenthal, Feb. 2, 1714. S. under J. S. Bach. Org. at Dresden. D. Dresden, June 1, 1785; Comp. music for the church service.

HOOD (Rev. George). American writer, author of "History of Music in New England," Boston, 16mo, 1846; "Hood's Musical Manual," Boston, n. d.

HOOD (Thomas). English poet and humorist, B. London, 1798. D. 1845.

Hood's poems have been drawn upon by composers to a considerable extent, chiefly by English composers like Smart, Mori, Allen, Molley, and Hume. They are well adapted for musical treatment.

HOOK (E. & G. G., & HASTINGS). American firm of organ-builders, established in Boston about 1835. They constructed some of the principal organs in the United States, and are famous in that country for the substantial and good quality of their workmanship.

HOOK (James). English comp. and org., B. Norwich, 1746. S. under Garland, org. of Norwich cath. Settled in London. Org. and comp., Marylebone Gardens, 1769-1773. Do., Vauxhall Gardens, 1774-1820. Org. of S. John's Horsleydown. Gained Catch Club prizes, 1772, 1780. Married to a Miss Madden. D. Boulogne, 1827.

WORKS.—*Music for dramatic pieces*: Dido, 1771 ; The Divorce, 1771 ; Trick upon Trick, 1772 ; The Double Disguise, 1784 ; Jack of Newbury, 1795 ; Diamond cut Diamond, 1797 ; Music Mad, 1807, etc. *Songs*: Hours of love ; Hermit, op. 24 ; New Year's gift, collections ; A blacksmith you'll own ; Adieu ma liberte ; Along the birks ; And where are you going ? ; As I leaned o'er the gate ; As I am a friend ; Believe not youth ; Blow cheerly, ye winds ; Bonny sailor ; Brown Bess ; Can'st thou love me, Mary ? ; Come out, my love ; Dear Mary, be mine ; Death of Auld Robin Gray ; Ere love di l first ; Flitch of Bacon ; Gentle as the breath ; Gipsy Girl ; Glory smiles on our isle ; Hail, lovely rose ; Hook, or by crook ; Hours of love ; Hush every breeze ; In hay time ; Listen to the voice of love ; Little Sue ; Lowland Kitty ; My Nancy was the sweetest maid ; Near Glasgow city ; Orphan Bess ; Peace ; Pretty Anne of Windsor ; Should fears alarm ; Softly waft, ye Southern breezes ; Sweet lass of Richmond hill ; Thro' the braes of Kirkcaldy ; What is love ? ; Within a mile o' Edinboro town. Ode for the opening of the New Exhibition Room, 1772. Pianoforte pieces, as Sonatas, op. 16, 54, etc. ; Rondos and transcriptions ; Concertos for organ ; Cantatas, canzonets, catches, glees (Christmas Box, 1795). The Ascension, oratorio, 1776. Guida di Musica ; being an easy Introduction for beginners on the Piano-forte ; to which are added 24 progressive lessons, in the most useful keys, composed and fingered by the author, op. 37. Lond., 4to, n. d.

As a song writer only will Hook be known to posterity. All, or most of his works, have long since passed from the remembrance of the musical public, and of his songs only a few survive. These are his imitations of the Scotch songs, and his "Lass of Richmond Hill." "Within a mile o' Edinboro town" is the one most likely to be undying. His sons James and Theodore achieved much renown in their day, the former as Dean of Worcester, and a writer on ecclesiastical subjects, and the latter as a novelist and parlour musician.

HOOKER (Edward W., D.D.) American divine and writer, B. Goshen, Nov. 24, 1794. Author of "A Plea for Sacred Music," and other lectures on that subject.

HOOPER (Edmund). English comp., B. Halberton, Devon [1553]. Chor. Westminster Abbey, 1582. Master of Chor. Westminster Abbey, 1588. Gent. of Chap. Roy., 1603. Org. Westminster Abbey, 1606. D. July 19, 1621.

WORKS.—Harmonies in "The Whole Booke of Psalms," 1594. Anthems in Barnard's Collection. Contributions to "Leighton's Teare's."

Ecclesiastical composer of the school of Bull, Byrd and Farrant.

HOOPER (Rev. Richard, M.A.) English writer, author of "Music and Musicians (especially English) to the Days of Henry Purcell. A brief Historical Sketch," London, 12mo, 1855.

HOPEKIRK (Helen). Scottish pianist of present time. Studied in Edinburgh, of which town she is a native, and at Leipzig. Has performed successfully in London, Scotland, and the United States. Her style is refined, and her execution brilliant. Resided in Edinburgh as teacher ; but latterly travelled as concert-giver.

HOPKINS (Edward John). English writer, comp., and org., B. Westminster, London, June 30, 1818. Chor., Chap. Roy., under W. Hawes, 1826. S. under T. F. Walmisley, 1833. Org. Mitcham Ch., 1834 ; do., St. Peter's, Islington, 1838 ; S. Luke's, Berwick St., London, 1841 ; Temple Church, Lond., 1843. Mus. Doc. Cantuar, 1882 ; Mus. Doc. Trin. Coll., Univ., Toronto, 1886. Prof. of org. at Royal Normal Coll. for the Blind, Upper Norwood, London.

WORKS.—The Organ, its History and Construction, a Comprehensive Treatise on the Structure and Capabilities of the Organ, with Specifications and Suggestive Details for Instruments of all Sizes, with an entirely new History of the Organ, Illustrated, London, 8vo, 1855 ; 2nd edition, 1870 ; 3rd edition, 1877 (with E. F. Rimbault). Articles (org., etc.) in Grove's Dictionary of Music. Select Organ Movements, consisting of a series of Pieces taken chiefly from the scores of the works of the great masters (Novello), n. d. *Services*: Morn. and Evn. in F ; do. in A ; do. in B flat (unison) ; Morning in C ; Te Deum in A flat. *Anthems*:

Acquaint thyself with God ; Arise, shine ; Blessed are the poor in spirit ; Bless the Lord, O my soul ; God is gone up ; God, who commanded ; He was despised ; I will give thanks ; I will wash my hands ; In my distress I cried unto the Lord ; Let us now go even unto Bethlehem ; Out of the deep ; O praise the Lord, all ye Nations ; O sing unto the Lord ; The King shall rejoice ; The Lord is my portion ; Thy mercy, O Lord ; Try me, O God ; Why seek ye the living among the dead ? Chloe and Corinna, madrigal. Organ compositions. Songs, etc. Edited Madrigals of Bennet and Weelkes for the Musical Antiquarian Society.

Hopkins has earned wide fame among English and Foreign musicians by his valuable work on the organ. It is the only work in the English language worthy of attention as a trustworthy history. Its popularity is evidenced by the number of editions which have been issued. As an ecclesiastical composer Hopkins takes high rank among Englishmen, and some of his works are among those most frequently used in our cathedrals and churches. As an organist he is likewise famous.

HOPKINS (E. Jerome). American org. and teacher, B. Burlington, Vermont, 1836. Son of the Bishop of Vermont. Was a student at the University of Vermont, and afterwards studied chemistry at the New York Medical College. Self-taught in music. Was the founder of the *N. Y. Philharmonic Journal*, also of the Orpheon Free Schools in New York city, which were founded in 1861 ; and the Piano Lecture Concerts, 1867.

WORKS.—*Operas:* Samuel, 1877 ; Dumb Love, 1878 ; Taffy and Old Munch, 1882 (for children). Festival Vespers, for boy choir, 2 chorus choirs, 1 echo choir, soli, two organs, and harp obligato, 1876-77. If. and vocal music.

The works of Mr. Hopkins have been given in New York City at the Academy of Music, and in Trinity Parish. He is accepted among the profession as an eccentric musician who has laboured quite studiously to elevate the standard of music. Editor of *The Orpheonist*.

HOPKINS (John). English org. and comp., brother of Edward John Hopkins, B. Westminster, 1822. Chor. S. Paul's Cath., 1831-38. Org. Mitcham Ch., 1838. Do., S. Stephen's, Islington, 1839 ; Trinity Ch., Islington, 1843 ; S. Mark's, Jersey, 1845 ; Rochester Cath., 1856.

Has comp. anthems, org. music, and songs.

HOPKINS (John Larkin). English comp. and org., cousin of above, B. Westminster, 1820. Chor., Westminster Abbey. Org. Rochester Cath., 1841. Mus. Bac., Cantab., 1842. Org. Trinity Coll., Cantab., 1856. Do. Camb. University, 1856. Mus. Doc., Cantab., 1867. D. Ventnor, April 25, 1873.

WORKS.—Services in C and E flat ; Te Deum in G. *Anthems:* Hear the voice and prayer ; I heard a voice : Let Thy merciful ears, O Lord ; Lift up your heads ; My God, my God, look upon me ; O clap your hands ; O Lord, we beseech Thee ; O sing unto the Lord ; Ponder my words ; Rejoice in the Lord ; Save me, O God ; The Lord shall comfort ; Turn Thee unto me ; We give Thee thanks ; With angels and archangels. Five Glees and a Madrigal, Lond., 1842. Songs, part-songs, etc.

HOPKINSON (J. & J.) English firm of Pianoforte makers, established in 1842. They have gained several medals and awards for the excellence of their instruments, and are recognised as being among the foremost of English makers. The firm annually produces a large quantity of excellent instruments.

HORÁK (Wencezlas Ernst). Bohemian comp., B. Mseno, Jan. 1, 1800. D. Prague, 1871. Comp. church music and miscellaneous instrumental music.

HORAN (John). Irish org. and comp., B. Drogheda, 1831. Org. successively of Booterstown, Sandymount, St. Andrew's (Dublin), Adare, Tuam, and Derry. Choirman for a time in Limerick Cath. Assistant org. and master of choristers Christ Church Cath., Dublin, 1873. Comp. anthems and org. music.

HORN (Carl Friedrich). German comp. and pianist, B. in Saxony, 1762. Came to London, 1782. Music-master to Queen Charlotte till 1811. Org. S. George's Chap., Windsor, 1823. D. Aug. 5, 1830.

Composed some part-music, songs, Pf. music, etc., now entirely forgotten.

HORN (Charles Edward). German comp. and cond., son of above, B. London, June, 1786. S. under his father, and Rauzzini, 1808. Sang at English Opera House, 1809. S. singing under Thomas Welsh, 1809. Re-appeared as vocalist, 1814. Musical director at Lyceum, 1831-32. Went to America and introduced English opera, 1833. Music-publisher in America for a time. Returned to England, 1843. Musical Director, Princesses Theatre, London. Settled in America as Director of the Händel and Haydn Society of Boston, 1847. Visited London, 1848. D. Boston, Oct. 21, 1849.

WORKS.—*Oratorios:* The Remission of Sin ; Satan, 1845 ; Daniel's Prediction, London, 1848. *Operas, etc.:* The Magic Bride, 1810; Tricks upon Travellers (with Reeve), 1810 ; The Bee-hive, 1811 ; The Boarding-house, 1811 ; Rich and Poor, 1812; The Devil's Bridge (with Braham), 1812 ; Godolphin, 1813 ; The Ninth Statue, 1814 ; The Woodman's Hut, 1814 ; Charles the Bold, 1815 ; The Persia Hunter, 1816 ; The Election, 1817 ; The Wizard, 1817 ; Dirce. 1821 ; Actors al Fresco (with Cooke and Blewitt), 1823 ; Philandering, 1824 ; Peveril of the Peak, 1826 ; Honest Frauds, 1830 ; "M. P." Christmas Bells, cantata. *Songs:* Ah, flattering man ; Breaking of the day ; Brian Boru ; Chimes of Zurich ; Cherry Ripe ; Child of earth ; Deep, deep sea ; Desert isle ; Early home ; False Rosabel ; Fond heart ; Forget thee, no ! ; He loves and rides away ; I've been where fresh flowers ; Long time ago ; Love's stolen kiss ; My bonnie barque ; Mermaid's cave ; O I have sheep and kine ; O never say I stole the heart ; O restore my love ; Old ocean is calm ; Rosabelle ; The sun is on the mountain ; Trafalgar ; What shall be my theme? ; When Mary is away ; Why comes he not ; Woman's heart is free. Duets and glees. Pianoforte music. Hindoo Melodies Harmonized, Lond., 1830.

This once-popular composer is now only known by his sprightly air, "Cherry Ripe," which has stood the test of time wonderfully.

HORNCASTLE (Frederick William). Irish comp. and org. of the present century, flourished about 1810-50. He was org. of Armagh Cath., 1816-23. He comp. a great number of pieces for the Pf., with songs, glees, comic rounds, etc. He compiled "The Music of Ireland," 3 parts, Lond., fo., 1844," etc.

HORNCASTLE (John Henry). English writer and musician, author of "The Whole Art of Singing at Sight," etc. London, 1829.

HORNE (George, D.D.) English divine and writer, author of "The Antiquity, Use, and Excellence of Church Music: a sermon preached at the opening of a new organ at Canterbury." Oxford, 4to, 1784.

HORNE (Thomas Hartwell). English biblical writer, B. 1780. D. 1862. Compiled "Manual of Parochial Psalmody," London, 1829 ; "Selection of Psalms and Hymns, arranged by Thomas Henshaw, 1829 [Tunes for No. 1]. Other editions. Historical Notices of Psalmody, London, 8vo, 1847.

HORNEMAN (Christian F. Emil). Danish comp., B. Copenhagen, Dec. 17, 1841. S. at Leipzig. Comp. "Aladdin" and "Heldenleben," overtures ; Caprices for Pf., op. 1 ; Miniatur-Bilder, Pf., op. 20. Songs, etc. Son of the undernoted.

HORNEMAN (Johann Ole Emil). Danish comp., B. Copenhagen, 1809. D. Copenhagen, May 29, 1870. Comp. instrumental and choral music.

HORSLEY (Charles Edward). English comp. and org., son of William Horsley, B. London, Dec. 15, 1821. S. under his father, Moscheles, and at Leipzig under Hauptmann and Mendelssohn. Org. of St. John's, Notting Hill, London. Went to Australia, 1868. Settled in the United States. D. New York, May 2, 1876.

WORKS.—*Oratorios:* David ; Joseph ; Gideon, Glasgow, 1860. Comus, cantata for solo and chorus (Milton), 1874 ; Impromptu for Pf., op. 12 ; Trio, No. 2, for Pf., vn., and 'cello, op. 13 ; Six Lieder for voice and Pf., op. 21. Anthems. Pf. pieces, various ; Songs, part-songs, etc. Text-Book of Harmony for Schools and Students.

Horsley had undoubtedly inherited the genius of his father, but was discouraged from properly applying it by the cold attitude assumed towards him by the British musical public. His works are full of suggestions of a power which seems never permitted to have supreme sway.

HORSLEY (William). English comp., org., and writer, B. London, Nov. 15, 1774. Articled to T. Smith, a pianist. S. under J. W. Callcott and Pring. Org. of Ely Chap., Holborn. Established Concentores Codales (society for propagating the study of concerted vocal music), 1798-1847. Assist. org. at Asylum for female orphans, 1798. Mus. Bac., Oxon., 1800. Chief org. Orphan Asylum, 1802. Org. Belgrove Chap., Grosvenor Place, 1812; Charter House, on death of Stevens, 1837. Married Elizabeth H. Callcott, daughter of J. W. Callcott. D. London, June 12, 1858.

WORKS.—Glees, canons, etc., published in 5 different collections: op. 1, 1801; op. 3, 1806; op. 4. [1808]; op. 6, 1811, and 1827. Forty canons of various species for 2, 3, 4, and 6 voices in Score, op. 9. Vocal Harmony (edited), London, 7 vols, [1830]. Elegiac Odes to memory of S. Webbe and S. Harrison. A Collection of Psalms, with Interludes, 1828. Callcott's Glees, edited with Memoir, Lond., 2 vo., fo., 1824. Airs of the Rhine, edited 1828. Pianoforte music, miscellaneous. An Explanation of Musical Intervals, and of the Major and Minor Scales, op. 8, Lond., fo., 1825. An Introduction to the Study of Practical Harmony and Modulation, Lond., 8vo, 1847. Songs and Canzonets, &c.

Horsley shares with Webbe, Callcott, and Bishop, the distinguished honour of being one of the greatest glee composers. His works have rarely been equalled, and never surpassed. As Hogarth says:—"His compositions indicate a profound knowledge of the principles of his art, and a complete command of its resources;— a warm and poetical imagination, chastened by the utmost refinement of taste. In the choice of his subject he is uniformly guided by a classical and discriminating judgment, and thoroughly imbued with the spirit and feeling of his poetry. His vocal phrases, accordingly, are not more remarkable for their melodious flow and smoothness, than for their adaptation to the correct and expressive declamation of the words." In this respect he closely follows Callcott, whose musical sentiments were never at variance with the spirit of the poetry. He was an organist of considerable contemporary renown, and composed for the Vocal Concerts, which in his time flourished in full vigour.

HORTENSE (Eugenie de Beauharnais), Queen of Holland, B. Paris, April 10, 1783. D. Viry, Oct. 5, 1837.

She composed and wrote the once popular national French air, "Partant pour le Syrie." This has long since been superseded by that song of freedom, the "Marseilles Hymn." Drouet the composer claimed the music of this song as his own.

HOUGHTON (William). Irish comp. and org., B. Dublin, 1844. Chor. and deputy-org. Christ Ch. Cath. Dublin; do. S. Ann's, Dublin. D. Dublin, 1871.

Wrote anthems, org. music, songs, etc.

HOWARD (George H.) American pianist and writer, B. Newton, Mass, 12 Nov. 1843. S. under J. W. Tufts of Boston Music School. Teacher in Boston Music School, 1862. S. in Europe under Kullak and Haupt, 1869. Director of a department in Boston Music School, 1871. Married Miss Maggie A. Gleason of Westfield, Mass. Teacher of Pf., org., and harmony in the Royal Normal Coll. and Academy of Music for the Blind, London, 1874. Director of the Michigan Cons. of Music, 1875 (in connection with Olivet Coll). Master of Arts, Olivet Coll. Teacher of Pf., harmony and theory, in New England Cons. of Music, Boston.

Mr. Howard has published Outline of Technique, and A Musical Chart. He has also read before the National Music Teachers' Association papers on "Sources of Inspiration in Musical Art," 1880; and "On the Benefit to Pianists of a more Extensive Culture of Chamber Music," 1883.—*Musical Herald*, Boston, etc.

HOWARD (John). American writer and comp., B. Boston, Mass, 1839. Grad. Yale College, 1860. S. in Leipzig, 1866-1867, under Plaidy, Richter, and Scheffer. Org. of 1st Presbyterian Ch. Utica, N. Y., 1868. Originator of the Howard Voice-Method. Composer of songs, O, sweet wild roses; Hear the maid at twilight sighing, etc. Author of the works on voice, "Vocal Reform. Papers illustrating the revolutionary principles of the Howard Method," Cincinnati, n. d.; "Vocal Process," "Respiratory Control," papers read before the Music Teachers' National Association in 1879 and 1882.

HOWARD (Samuel). English org. and comp., B. London, 1710. Chor. Chap. Roy. under Croft. S. also under Pepusch. Org. of St. Bride's, and of St. Clement Danes, London. Mus. Doc. Cantab., 1769. D. London, July 13, 1782.

WORKS - -The Amorous Goddess, opera, 1744. The Musical Companion, a Collection of English Songs, fo., Lond., N. D. Cantatas. Instrumental music, sonatas, concertas, etc. Anthems and Psalms. Contributions to contemporary collections.

Howard is known as the composer of the fine psalm tunes, "Howard" and "St. Bride's;" but apart from these his name is not familiar. He assisted Dr. Boyce with the compilation of his Cathedral music. "The easy, simple melodies of this respectable, but plain unaffected Englishman, approached nearer to the purest style of Dr. Arne than the ballad effusions of any other master.—*Busby.*

HOWE (Elias). American musician and writer, B. Spencer, Mass., 1819. D. 1867. Author of the following :--

WORKS.—Pianoforte Instructor, Boston, n. d. ; Melodeon Instructor, n. d. ; Instructor for the Guitar, n. d.; Self-instructor for the Violin, n. d.; Violin without a Master, n. d.; Flute without a Master, n. d. ; School for the Flute, n. d. ; Self-instructor for the Flute ; Caledonia Collection (airs for the flute), n. d.; Accordeon without a Master ; Complete Accordeon Preceptor ; Ethiopian Accordeon Instructor; Accordeon Songster (1860) ; Self-instructor for Accordeon or Flutina ; Preceptor for the German Accordeon; Few German Concertina School; New Fife Instructor ; New Clarionet Instructor ; New Flageolet Instructor ; New Cornet Instructor.

A number of those were issued under the pseudonym of "Gumbo Chaff." Howe was the inventor of a sewing machine.

HOWELL (Edward). English violoncellist, B. London, Feb., 1846. Author of a "First Book for the Violoncello" (from Romberg), etc. He is an instrumentalist of great capabilities, and performs at the principal London and provincial concerts. Brother of Francis, noted below.

HOWELL (Francis). English comp., son of JAMES HOWELL, B. 1834. D. 1882. Comp. two oratorios, and a number of songs.

HOWELL (James). English double-bass player and teacher, B. Plymouth, 1811. S. R. A. M., under T. M. Mudie. S. double-bass under Anfossi. Prof. of d.-bass at R. A. M. Mem. of R. A. M., etc. D. London, Aug. 1879. His son ARTHUR, also a bass-player, D. April 16, 1885. His wife was Rose Hersee, the vocalist.

HOWGILL (William). English org. of 18th century. Org. of Whitehaven, 1794; do. in London. Wrote organ voluntaries, psalms, and anthems.

HOWSON, see ALBERTAZZI (Emma).

HOYLAND (John). English org. and comp., B. Sheffield, 1783. S. under Mather of Sheffield. Org. of S. James' Ch., Sheffield, 1808. Org. Parish Ch., Louth, Lincoln, 1819. D. Jan. 18, 1827. Comp. anthems, songs, and org. music.

HOYLE (John). English writer, who flourished in the 18th century, and D. 1797. Author of "Dictionarium Musicæ, being a Complete Dictionary or Treasury of Music," 1770. Other editions 1790 and 1791.

HOYTE (William Stevenson). English org. and comp. of present time. Comp. a number of pieces for his instrument, vocal music, etc. He is a professor at Trinity College, London. He composed a "Book of Litanies, Metrical and Prose, with an Evening Service and Accompanying Music," 4to, n. d.

HUBBARD (Henry). English writer, author of "Elements of Campanologia, or an Essay on the Art of Ringing," London, 1876, 16mo.

HUBER (Hans). German comp. of present time, B. Schönewend, near Olten, Switzerland, June 28, 1852. Teacher and writer in Berlin.

WORKS.—Op. 2. Blätter und Blüthen, for Pf.; op. 7. Studien über ein Originalthema für das Pf.; op. 12. Bilderbuch ohne Bilder ; op. 16. Märchenerzählungen,

Pf.; op. 17. Phantasie for Pf. and vn.; op. 18. Sonata for Pf. and vn.; op. 20. Trio for Pf., vn., and 'cello; op. 23. Ballet music zu Goethe's Walpurgisnacht, Pf.; op. 25. Frühlingsliebe, Lieder for voice and Pf.; op. 29. Sechs Lieder in Volkston für Männerchar; op. 30. Two romances for Pf. and 'cello; op. 31. Sonatas for two Pf.'s, in B flat; op. 33. Sonata for Pf. in D; op. 36. Concerto for Pf. and orch.; op. 41. Aus Goethe's Westoestlichem Divan; op. 42. Sonata for Pf. and vn.; op. 43. Weihnachtan, Album für grosse Leute, Pf.; op. 44. Liebeslieder; op. 45. Aussöhnung aus Göthe's Trilogie der Leidenschaft, for male voices, soli, chorus, and orch; op. 47. Sonata: Zu Maler Nolten, for Pf., in E flat; op. 50. Eine Lustspiel, Overture, for orch.; op. 55. Serenade in E; Römischar Carneval, Humoreske, for orch.; Ten vocal quartets, op. 69.

HUBERTI (Gustave Léon). Belgian comp., B. Brussels, 14 April, 1843. S. Brussels Cons. Gained prizes for comp., 1863-65. Comp. "De Laatste Zonnestraal," oratorio; cantatas, concertas, etc.

HUCBALD. Flemish monk and musician, B. [840]. D. 932.

Author of a treatise on music, the earliest which has descended to the present time. It is composed and illustrated by a very confusing notation, so that the real intentions of the author are never fairly comprehended. From what can be deciphered, the music of his time appears to have been in a condition of the utmost crudity.

HUCKEL (William). English writer, author of Practical Instructions in the Art of Singing, London, 12mo, 1845. Practical Instructions for the Cultivation of the Voice, London, 8vo, n. d.

HUDL (J. J.) German writer, author of "Tabular View of Modulation from any one Key to all other Keys, Major and Minor...with additional examples by J. Jousse," 4to, n. d.

HUDSON (Mary). English org. and hymn comp. Org. of S. Olave, Hart St., Lond.; do. St. Gregory, Old Fish St., 1790-1801. D. London, 28 Mar., 1801. Daughter of Robert Hudson.

HUDSON (Robert). English comp., B. Feb. 1732. Tenor singer in Marylebone and Ranelagh Gardens. Assist. org. S. Mildred, Bread St., London, 1755. Vicar-Choral, S. Paul's, 1756. Gent. of Chap. Roy., 1758. Almoner and master of children, S. Paul's, 1773-1793. Music-master Christ's Hospital. D. Eton, Dec., 1815.

WORKS.--Services. Anthems and Hymns. The Myrtle, a Collection of Songs in 3 books, 1767. Glees.

HUEFFER (Francis). Writer and comp., B. 1845. Educ. in London, Paris, Berlin, and Leipzig. Musical critic for the *Times*, London, since 1878. Ph.D. Göttingen, 1869. Author of the following works:—The Troubadours, a History of Provencal Life and Literature in the Middle Ages, London, 8vo, 1878. Musical Studies, a Series of Contributions, 8vo, 1880. Wagner [Great Musicians series], 1881, 8vo. Richard Wagner and the Music of the Future, Lond., 8vo, 1874. Italian and other Studies, Lond., 1883. Paper on Liszt. Songs. Pf. pieces, etc. Contributions to periodical literature, and to the "Encyclopædia Britannica," ninth edition, and Grove's Dictionary of Music. Also writer of opera libretti, of which "Colomba" and "Guillem de Cabestant," both set by A. G. Mackenzie, are the most important. Editor of the *Musical World* from 1886.

HUGHES (Mrs. F. J.) English writer, authoress of "Harmonies of Tones and Colours developed by Evolution," Lond., 1883, fo., illust.

HUGHES (G. A.) English musician and teacher, author of Instruction Book for the Pianoforte or Organ for the Blind, Lond., 4to, 1848. Congregational Psalmody, 18mo, 1843.

HUGHES (J.) English writer, author of "Young Student's Musical Definitions," Lond., 12mo, 1877.

HUGO (Victor Marie). French poet, dramatist, and novelist, B. 1802. D. 1884.

WORKS.—Odes and Ballads, 1822; Les Orientales, 1828; Autumn Leaves, poems, 1832; Chansons des Rues et des Bois. *Dramas:* Ernani; Lucrezia Borgia; Esmeralda; Ruy Blas. Novels and political writings.

Operas have been founded on the dramas of Ernani, Lucrezia Borgia, Esmeralda, and Ruy Blas; the first, by Verdi, being the only one which has attained much popularity, and that is now evaporating. The lyrics and songs have been set by innumerable composers. Most of the modern French composers have drawn on his works, an occasional German, and a few Englishmen.

HULLAH (John Pyke). English comp. and teacher, B. Worcester, June 27, 1812. S. under W. Horsley, 1829. S., R. A. M., 1832. Visited Paris and adopted Wilhelm's method of vocal instruction. Musical instructor in Sir James Kay Shuttleworth's (then Dr. Kay) Training College, Battersea, 1840. Taught music to schoolmasters in Exeter Hall, London, 1841. Established classes in S. Martin's Hall, 1847-50. Prof. vocal music, King's College, Lond., 1844-74; do. Queen's Coll., Lond., and Bedford Coll. Org. of Charter House, 1858. Conductor at R. A. M., 1870-73. Musical Inspector of Training Schools for United Kingdom, 1872—retired 1883. LL.D., Edinburgh, 1876. Member of Society of S. Cecilia, Rome, 1877. do. Music Academy of Florence. D. London, Feb. 21, 1884.

WORKS.—Method of Teaching Singing, by Wilhelm, Lond., 8vo, 1842; do. Revised and Reconstructed edition, 1850. Grammar of Vocal Music, founded on Wilhelm's Method, 8vo, 1843. Duty and Advantages of Learning to Sing, Lond., 1846. Grammar of Musical Harmony, 1853; Exercises for do., 1873; new edit., 1873. Music in the Parish Church, a Lecture, Lond., 1856. History of Modern Music, a Course of Lectures delivered at the Royal Institution of Great Britain, 8vo, 1862 (2 editions). Lectures on the Third or Transition Period of Musical History, Lond., 8vo, 1865; 2nd edit., 1876. The Song Book, Words and Tunes from the best Poets and Musicians, 16mo, 1866. Cultivation of the Speaking Voice, Oxford, 8vo, 1870; another edit., 1874. Grammar of Counterpoint. Rudiments of Musical Grammar, 8vo, n. d. Notation: Brief Direction concerning the Choice, adjustment, etc., of the Musical Alphabet, 1876. Time and Tune in the Elementary School, New Method of Teaching Vocal Music, and Exercises, 8vo, 1877. Music in the House, Macmillan's Art at Home Series, 8vo, 1877. Exercises for the Cultivation of the Voice, 2 parts, n. d. *Operettas:* The Village Coquettes (Dickens); The Outpost; The Barbers of Barsora. Singer's Library of Concerted Music—Secular and Sacred Series, 6 vols. 58 English Songs, by Composers chiefly of the 17th and 18th centuries. *Songs:* Come forth from thy bower; Home of our youth; One look of love; Free companion; Joy cometh in the morning; Message from the battlefield; The storm. Motets, anthems, concerted vocal music, etc. Reports to Government on Progress of Musical Education in Schools. Contributions to periodical literature.

Mr. Hullah was recognised as the first Englishman who gave an impetus to musical education. His whole energies were throughout a long and successful career directed in this channel, and his success in convincing the government to a belief in music as an important factor in education will secure for him the lasting regard of the community. His ability as a teacher was marvellous, and he trained a number of vocalists who now stand in the foremost rank of English singers. Hullah was an advocate of the fixed doh, and in consequence opposed to the Tonic Sol-fa method.

Hullah did much by writing and composition to extend his name and usefulness. As a writer his historical works possess most general interest. His other works are didactic, and have fulfilled the function allotted to them by spreading theoretical knowledge far and wide. As a composer Hullah has high rank. The operettas were noticed by Hogarth, shortly after their performance, as giving great promise of future power, and though now entirely forgotten were works possessing much sweetness and melody.

HÜLLER, see HILLER (J. A.)

HÜLLMANDEL (Nicolas Joseph). German writer and comp., B. Strasburg, 1751. D. London, Dec. 1823. He wrote Principles of Music, chiefly calculated for the Pianoforte or Harpsichord, Lond., fo., n. d. Sonatas for Pf. and for Pf and vn. Songs and concerted vocal music.

HUME (Alexander). Scottish comp. and minor poet, B. Edinburgh, Feb. 17, 1811. Engaged in business and teaching in Edinburgh and Glasgow. D. Glasgow, Feb. 4, 1859.

WORKS.—The English Hymn Tune Book, containing two hundred and four of the most common hymns used in England : arranged for four voices. Edin., ob. 12mo, n.d. Anthems and Sacred Songs, containing fifty-four pieces. Edin , 12mo, n.d. Gall's Psalm and Hymn Book. Edin., 1842. Six Sensible Songs. *Songs:* Afton Water; My ain dear Nell; The Scottish emigrant's farewell, etc. Glees and duets. Poems, various.

Hume was one of the very few Scottish composers who have risen above a mediocre degree of merit in their productions. His songs are inspired by the same genuine feeling for the national and local associations of his country which appears so prominently in the traditional lyrics of the nation. "Afton Water" is beyond doubt the most beautiful song which has emanated from Scotland in modern times, as well as being one of the finest in the Caledonian anthology. It is a perfect example of true inspiration, and appeals to the cultured and uncultured mind alike. Burns was never more sympathetically set. His other productions attain a fair degree of merit, but none of them have become so popular as "Afton Water."

HUME (Tobias). English military officer and musician, was a performer on the viol-da-gamba, and a colonel in the army. He wrote "The First Part of Ayres, French, Pollish, and others together, some in Tabliture and some in Pricke," 1605 ; "Captain Hume's Poeticall Musicke, principally made for two Basse Violls, yet so construed that it may be plaied eight several waies, upon sundrie instruments, with much facilitie," 1607.

HUME (William). Scottish comp. and editor, son of Alex. Hume, B. Edinburgh, Sept. 25, 1830. Engaged in teaching in Glasgow. Editor of musical publications of Mr. Hamilton, Glasgow; Gall & Inglis, Edinburgh ; and Parlane, Paisley. Musical critic of *The Bailie*, Glasgow, 1872 ; and correspondent of London musical journals. Teacher of harmony, violin, and singing.

WORKS.—Psalm and Hymn Tunes, with supplement of anthems ; Union Sacred Tune-Book ; The Westminster Wesleyan Tune Book (with Mr. Sugden); Editions of Musical Works issued by Messrs. Gall & Inglis ; Harmonium Tune-Book. *Part-Songs, Glees, etc.* : Good morrow to the hills again ; The return of May ; Song of the summer winds ; Come o'er the sea ; Allen a Dale ; Shall I wasting in despair ; Philida and Corydon ; Sally Brown (Hood) ; Ben Battle ; Now at moonlight's fairy hour ; Once more a welcome to the woods ; Come away, the eastern grey ; Oh, the depth of the riches ; The Lord is my strength. *Cantatas:* Psalm 67, for treble voices ; Bartimeus, for barytone solo and chorus ; The Call to Battle.

HUMFREY. See HUMPHREY.

HUMMEL (Johann Nepomuk). Hungarian pianist and comp., B. Pressburg, Nov. 14, 1778. S. at Vienna under Mozart, 1785. *Début* as pianist, Dresden, 1787. Travelled in Germany, Denmark, and Scotland, 1788. Appeared in London, 1791-92. S. under Clementi in London. Returned to Vienna, 1793. S. under Albrechtsberger and Salieri. Travelled in Russia, 1800. Music-director to Prince Nicholas Esterhazy, 1803-10. Chapel-master at Stuttgart, 1816-20. Do. at Weimar, 1820-37. Appeared in France and England, frequently ; in London as conductor of German opera, 1833. D. Weimar, Oct. 17, 1837.

WORKS.—*Operas:* Das Haus ist zu Verkaufen ; Die Kuckfahrt des Kaisers ; Mathilde der Guise. Cantatas, various ; Ballets. Overture for orch., in B flat, op. 101 ; Three String Quartets, op. 30 ; Serenades, for various instruments, opp. 63 and 66 ; Septets, in D minor, op. 74, and in C, op. 114 ; Quintet for Pf. and strings, op. 87 ; Concertos for Pf. and orch., op. 34, in C ; 73, in G ; 85, in A minor ; 89, in B min.; 110, in E ; 113, in A flat. Rondos for Pf. and orch., opp. 56, 98, 117 ; Themes for Pf. and orch. opp. 97, 115 ; Symphonie concertante for Pf. and vn., op. 17 ; Trios for Pf., vn., and 'cello, opp. 12, 22, 35, 65, 83, 93, 96 ; Sonatas for Pf. and vn., opp. 5, 19, 25, 28, 37, 50, 64, 104 ; Sonatas for Pf. duet, opp. 43, 92, 99 ; Sonatas for Pf. solo, opp. 13, 20, 36, 81, 106 ; Rondos for Pf. solo, opp. 11, 19, 107, 109 ; Fantasias for Pf. solo, opp. 18, 123, 124 ; Studies, caprices, variations, and fugues for Pf., opp. 1, 2, 7, 8, 9, 40, 45, 47, 49, 67, 105, 118, 119, 125, etc. Three Masses, op. 77, in B flat ; op. 80, in E flat ; op. 111, in D.

Hummel stood foremost in his day among a school of performers now rapidly dying out. This school was an advance, in point of execution, on that of Clementi, but scarcely so advanced as that headed by Moscheles, and later by Thalberg and Chopin. Its characteristic feature was the use of the uniform legato touch so highly esteemed by Moscheles, and a finical refinement in the interpretation of the classical masters. It was the school which immediately succeeded the cantabile style of the end of last and the beginning of the present century, but was the forerunner of the bravura school of recent times. Hummel's Pf. compositions are still held in esteem, but much of their popularity has vanished. They are marked by strong poetical feeling, clear form, and much technical cleverness. His operas are forgotten, but his masses are still in use.

HUMPHREY (Pelham) or HUMFREY. English comp., B. 1647. Chor. Chap. Roy., 1660. S. under Lulli at Paris, 1664. Gent. of Chap. Roy., 1667. Master of Choristers, do., 1672. D. Windsor, July 14, 1674.

WORKS.—Anthems and Services in collections of Clifford, Boyce, Tudway, etc.; Odes on the King's Birthday and on New Year's Day ; Songs in various collections, etc.

Humphrey was a great lute-player, and is said to have excelled the celebrated Henry Cook, who died out of jealousy of his pupil's talents. This is one of Anthony Wood's stories, and is of doubtful authenticity. Humphrey was a composer of some promise, and would doubtless have come to greatness had he lived long enough. His compositions are few in number but good in conception.

HUNNIS (William). English musician of 16th century. Chapel master to Queen Elizabeth. D. [1597]. Published "Certayne Psalms in English Meter." Lond., 1550.

HUNT (Rev. Henry George Bonavia). English writer, B. Malta, June 30, 1847. Professor and Warden of Trinity Coll., London. Author of "Concise History of Music from the Christian Era to the Present Time." 1878, and 2nd edit., 1879 ; 7th ed., 1884 ; Papers on Musical Subjects, etc.

HUNT (Thomas). English comp. of 16th century. Wrote the madrigal, "Hark ! did you ever heare so sweet a singing," for 6 voices, in the "Triumphs of Oriana."

HÜNTEN (Franz). German pianist and comp., B. Coblenz, Dec. 26, 1793. S. at Paris Cons., under Pradher, Reicha, and Cherubini. Teacher and performer in Paris. D. Coblenz, Feb., 1878.

WORKS.—Polonaises for Pf., op. 3. Fantasias, op. 24, 57, 76, 107, 126, 132, 133, 138, 140, 142, 162, 166, 167, 170, 173, 177, 178, 187, 204, 213, etc. Rondos, nocturnes, and sonatinas, op. 5, 6, 21, 30, 42, 78, 90, 93, 112, 117, 139, 169, 183, 186, etc. Variations, studies, lessons, etc., opp. 26, 32, 41, 58, 59, 67, 68, 70, 71, 73, 80, 82, 88, 89, 94, 95, 97, 98, 105, 109, 111, 113, 114, 118, 124, 128, 131, 134, 145, 147, 150, 151, 153, 159, 179, 181, 188, 215, 219, 225, etc. Trios for Pf., vn., and 'cello. School for the Pf.

Hünten was a brilliant pianist and a popular comp. in his day, but his works, the majority of which are flimsy shop pieces, are gradually dying out. His "School for the Pf." is the most useful production, and his Pf. exercises are useful and much used for teaching purposes.

HUNTER (Anne), *née* HOME. Scottish poetess, famous as having written the words to a number of Haydn's songs ; reprinted in her Poetical Works, 1793. B. 1742. D. 1821.

HUSK (William Henry). English writer of present time, B. London, 1814. Was Librarian to the late Sacred Harmonic Society. Author of "An Account of the Musical Celebrations on St. Cecilia's Day, in the 16th, 17th, and 18th centuries, to which is appended a Collection of Odes on St. Cecilia's Day," Lond., 8vo, 1857; "Songs of the Nativity, being Christmas Carols, Ancient and Modern, several of which appear for the first time in a Collection, edited with Notes,"

Lond., sm. 4to, n.d. [1866]; "Catalogues of the Library of the Sacred Harmonic Society," 1853, 1862, and 1872 ; Contributions to Sir G. Grove's "Dictionary of Musicians." Numerous prefaces to Word Books of oratorios, and other pieces, etc.

HUTCHESON (Charles). Scottish comp., B. 1792. Teacher in Glasgow. D. Glasgow, 1856. Published "Christian Vespers," Glasgow, 4to, 1832, containing hymn tunes harmonized in 3 and 4 parts, and an introductory essay on church music.

HUTCHINGS and ROMER. English firm of music publishers, established in London in 1863. The firm has published a great amount of ballad music by the leading composers of the present time, as well as Pf. music, etc.

HUTCHINSON (Francis), FRANCIS IRELAND. English glee comp. [B. 1730], who flourished in the latter part of the 18th century. He composed the Glees -- "Return, return, my lovely maid ;" "As Colin one evening ;" "Jolly Bacchus ; " and " Where weeping yews." Catches. 11 Glees in Warren's Collection. He was awarded the prizes of the Catch Club in 1771, 1772, and 1773. His biography is obscure.

HUTCHINSON. An American family of singers, born at Milford, N. H. Four brothers composed the family, and they were singers of temperance and slavery songs, well known throughout the United States. They were natural singers, having received no training. They flourished about 1846-60.

HUTCHISON (G. B.) English writer, author of "Shorthand Music: an easy and rapid method of writing music." Lond., 12mo, n.d.

HUTCHISON (William Marshall). Scottish comp., B. Glasgow, May 28, 1854. Writer of the popular songs, "Dream Faces," " Ehren on the Rhine," etc., under various pen names, among them those of Joseph Meissler, Oscar Seydel, etc. He has comp. two cantatas, " The Story of Elaine " and " H. R. II." ; also a 3 act comic opera, " Glamour" ; and numerous 4-part songs and instrumental pieces.

HÜTTENBRENNER (Anselm). Hungarian comp., B. Grätz, October 13, 1794. D. Ober-Andritz, June 5, 1868. Best known as a comp. of church music, and for his connection with Schubert.

HUXTABLE (Anthony, Christopher, and **William).** A family of English musicians. Anthony, B. 1818, violinist and teacher ; Christopher, his son, org. and vnst. ; William, a harpist, pianist, etc.

I.

ILIFFE (Frederick). English comp. and org., B. Smeeton, near Leicester, 1847. Org. of S. Wilfrid's Ch., Kibworth. F. C. O., 1872. Mus. Bac. Oxon., 1873. Licentiate in Music, Trinity Coll., Lond., 1874. Org. and Choir-master, S. Barnabas Ch., Oxford. Mus. Doc. Oxon., 1879. Org. of S. John's Coll., Oxford, 1883.

WORKS.—The Visions of St. John the Divine, oratorio, in 3 parts (Mus. Doc. degree), 1879 ; pub. in 1880. Evening Service in D, for men's voices, written for Keble Coll., Oxford. Anglican Chant Settings for the whole of the Canticles. Three Separate Services for Te Deum in F, G, A, in Anglican chant form. Six Settings of the Kyrie Eleison. *Anthems*: Nearer my God to Thee, 1873 ; Short and Easy Full Anthems for Parish Choirs (dedicated to Sir F. A. G. Ouseley), 2 vols., 1875 ; Praise the Lord O my soul, Oxford, 1879 ; Jesus, Lover of my soul (used in S. Paul's Cath., London), 1884 ; And I heard a great voice out of heaven ; O to my longing eyes, 8 part chorale and fugue. *Organ Music* : Andante con moto, in E flat ; Prelude and fugue, in C minor ; Festival march, in F.

Overture in E, for orch.; Minuet, trio, and finale, in D, for orch. Caprice de concert, in A flat, for Pf.; Notturno in D flat, Pf.; Sonata in D; Quartets, quintets, trios, etc. for voices.

Mr. Iliffe has composed some very successful anthems, and is also favourably known by his oratorio, which contains some good numbers. The anthems for parish choirs are good examples of this style of writing, and are well adapted for the purpose.

ILINSKI (Johann Stanislas, Count). Polish poet and comp., B. 1795. Comp. masses, overtures, psalms, Pf. music, songs, poems, etc. Attained to dignity of Counsellor of State under the Government. The date of his death appears never to have been chronicled.

IMMYNS (John). English attorney and lutenist, B. early in 18th century. Mem. of Acad. of Ancient Mus. Amanuensis to Dr. Pepusch. Established the Madrigal Soc., 1741. Lutenist to Chap. Roy., 1752. D. London, April 15, 1764.

INCLEDON (Charles Benjamin). English tenor vocalist, B. St. Keverans, Cornwall, 1764. Son of a Physician. Articled pupil to W. Jackson, Exeter. Chor. Exeter Cath. Sailor on board "H. M. S. Formidable," 1779-83. Recommended as singer to Colman by Lord Admiral Hervey, but services declined. Mem. of Collins' Dramatic company at Southampton, 1784. Appeared at Bath, 1785. Pupil for a time of Rauzzini, at Bath. Sang in Vauxhall Gardens, 1788. *Début* in "The Poor Soldier" at Covent Garden Theatre, Lond., 1790. Travelled much in the Provinces. Retired from Covent Garden, 1815. Appeared in North America, 1817. Resided at Brighton. D. Worcester, Feb. 11, 1826.

Incledon was a specimen of the unapproachable English ballad singer. His voice was natural, and his rendering of the old British melodies has been written of as unsurpassed.

INFANTAS (Ferdinand de Las). Spanish comp., B. Cordova, who flourished in second half of 16th century. He composed among other works the following:—

Plura Modulationum genera quæ vulgo contrapuncta appellantur super excelso Gregoriano Cantu. Venice, 4to, 1570. Sacrarum varii styli Cantionum tituli Spiritus Sancti. Venice, 4to, 1580.

Infantas is generally regarded as the foremost light of the early Spanish school, and is noted as a writer of dignified church music.

INGALLS (Jeremiah). American comp., B. in latter half of 18th century. D. Hancock, Vermont, 1828. He issued "The Christian Harmony, or Songsters' Companion," Exeter, N. H., 1805.

INGHAM (Richard). English comp. and org., B. 1804. Was org. of Carlisle Cath., and wrote some vocal music. D. 1841.

INGLOTT (William). English org. and comp., B. 1554. Org. of Norwich Cath. D. Dec., 1621.

Mentioned as one of the greatest of early English organists. Biography obscure.

INVERARITY (Eliza). Scottish soprano vocalist and comp., B. Edinburgh, March, 1813. D. Newcastle-on-Tyne, 1846.

She was a public singer of some note in her day, and a composer of ballads. She appeared in America with her husband, Charles Martyn, a bass singer and comp.

IRELAND (Francis). See HUTCHINSON.

IRONS (Herbert S.). English org. and comp., B. Canterbury, Jan. 19, 1834. Nephew of the Elveys. Was org. of Southwell Minster. Resident in Nottingham. He was awarded the *Musical Standard* prize for a hymn tune in 1866. He has comp. anthems, and edited a Collection of Chants.

IRONS (Thomas), or I'ONS. English org. and comp., B. 1817. Bac. Mus., Oxon., 1848. Doc. Mus., Oxon., 1854. D. Newcastle-upon-Tyne, 1857.

Comp. of anthems, glees, and songs ; and editor of "Cantica Ecclesiastica: a Collection of Psalm and Hymn Tunes, single and double chants," etc., to., n.d.

ISAAC (Heinrich), ARRIGO TEDESCO. German comp. and teacher, B. 1440 [1460]. S. under Josquin. Visited Italy, and was appointed Chap.-master of S. Giovanni, Florence, 1475. Musical instructor to the children of Lorenzo di Medici. Musical Director at Florence. Chap.-master to Maximilian I., 1493. D. in service of Maximilian I. early in the 16th century [1520].

WORKS.—Ten Masses, published ; Thirteen Masses in MS. ; Motets and Psalms; Secular Part-songs ; etc.

"Several of his compositions are preserved ; and considering the state of *Music in consonance* at the time he wrote, great praise is due to his science, and the ingenious disposition of his score. If in his melodies he does not discover any remarkable facility of fancy, his power of *imitation* is conspicuous, and his harmony sound."—*Busby.*

ISAACS (Rebecca). English actress and vocalist, B. London, 1828. First appearance, 1834. Début in opera, at Olympic Theatre, London, in Dec. 1836. Married Thomas Roberts, acting-manager. Sang with much success in London and the provinces. D. London, April 24, 1877.

ISHAM (John). English org. and comp., B. 1685. Deputy-org. to Dr. Croft. Org. of S. Ann's, Soho, 1711. Mus. Bac., Oxon., 1713. Org. S. Andrew's, Holborn, 1718 ; S. Margaret's, Westminster. D. June, 1726.

WORKS.—Church Services and Anthems ; Songs, single and in collections ; etc.

ISMAËL (Jean Vital), JAMMES. French barytone vocalist, B. Agen, April 28, 1827. Sang in many popular operas, in Paris, etc.

ISOUARD (Nicolo). French comp., B. Malta, Dec. 6, 1775. Educated at Paris for the Navy. Became a clerk at Malta, 1790. S. under Guglielmi, at Naples. Resided in Paris as comp. Decorated with cross of San Donato of Malta. D. Paris, March 23, 1818.

WORKS.—*Operas:* Avviso ai Maritati, 1794 ; Artaserse, 1795 ; Rinaldo d'Aste ; Il Barbiere di Seviglia ; L'Improvvisata in Campagna ; Il Barone d'Alba chiara ; Le Petit Page ou la Prison d'Etat (with R. Kreutzer), 1800 ; Flaminius à Corinthe (with Kreutzer), 1801 ; Michel Ange, 1802 ; La Statue, ou la femme avare, 1802 ; Les Confidences, 1803 ; Le Baiser et la Quittance (with Méhul, Boieldieu, and Kreutzer), 1803 ; Le Médecin Turc, 1805 ; L'Intrigue aux fenêtres, 1805 ; Le Déjeuner de Garçons, 1805 ; La Ruse inutile, 1805 ; Léonce, 1805 ; La Prise de Passau, 1806 ; Idala, 1806 ; Les Rendezvous bourgeois, 1807 ; Les Créanciers, 1807 ; Un Jour à Paris, 1808 ; Cimarosa, 1808 ; La Victime des Arts (with Berton and Solié), 1811 ; La Fête du Village, 1811 ; Le Billet de loterie, 1811 ; Le Magicien sans magic, 1811 ; Lulli et Quinault, 1812 ; Le Prince de Catane, 1813 ; Le Française à Venise, 1813 ; Le Siège de Mézières (with Cherubini, Catel, and Boieldieu), 1814 ; Joconde, Paris, Feb. 28. 1814 (London, Oct. 1876) ; Les Deux Maris, 1816 ; L'une pour l'autre, 1816. Five Masses. Eight Cantatas. Psalms and Motets.

Taking Mozart as a model, Isouard produced a number of light, palatable works which in their day disputed the ground with those of Boieldieu and other French masters. Very few of Isouard's works are fated to reach a remote posterity, but their claims to consideration are by no means slight, if among such claims be reckoned, fine melody, rich harmony, and sympathetic setting of the libretto. "Joconde" is held by many writers to be his most important work.

ITHURIEL. See COUTTS (W. G.).

IVANOFF (Nicholas). Russian tenor vocalist, B. Pultava, in Lower Russia, 1810. Appeared in London, 1834, '35, '37. Sang afterwards in various parts of the Continent. His voice was of a sweet, but by no means robust description. As a dramatic vocalist he was excelled by most of his great contemporaries, and few critics of his period give him more than a medium degree of credit for his style and power. D. Bologna, July, 1880.

IVERY (John). English comp., B. Northam, Hertford, second part of 18th century. Published "The Hertfordshire Melody, or Psalm Singers' Recreation, being a valuable collection of Psalms, Hymns, Anthems, etc., on various occasions, to which is prefixed a new, concise, and easy introduction to the art of singing, and a copious Dictionary of the terms made use of in Music." Lond., 8vo, 1773.

IVES (E.) American writer and compiler. Author of "American Psalmody: a Collection of sacred music," Hartford, Conn., 8vo, 1829 (with D. Dutton), other editions; "Solfeggi, or a method of instruction in the principles of music, N. Y., fo., n.d. ; "Musical A B C," etc., 1847; "Musical Recreations, part-songs;" "Operatic Album ;" "Musical Wreath," etc. Some of the foregoing are put forth by E. Ives, junr., who was probably a son of E. Ives.

IVES (Joshua). English org. and comp., B. 1854. S. under Dr. Bridge and Dr. Chipp. Took the degree of Mus. Bac. at Cambridge, 1883. Lecturer on Harmony and Musical Composition at the Athenæum, Glasgow. Writer of organ music, church music, and a work on Harmony. Appointed in 1884 Prof. of Music at Adelaide University, S. Australia.

IVES (Simon). English comp., was Lay-vicar of S. Paul's. Singing master in London. D. London, 1662.

WORKS.—The Triumph of Peace, masque, Shirley, 1633 (with H. & W. Lawes) ; Lamentation and Mourning, Elegy on the death of William Lawes ; Comps. in Hilton's Collection of Catches, Playford's Collections, etc.

IVRY (Paul Xavier Desirée, Marquis d'). French amateur comp. of present time, B. Beaune, Côte d' Or, Feb. 4, 1829. Has comp. the following operas produced at Paris :—Quentin Metzys, 1854 ; La Maison du Docteur, 1854 ; Omphale et Penelope ; L'Amants de Verone (Romeo and Juliet), none of which have been brilliantly successful. The last named was produced also in London.

J.

JACKSON (Arthur Herbert). English comp. and pianist, B. 1852. S., R. A. M. Professor of Harmony and comp., do. D. London, Sept. 27, 1881.

WORKS.—The Bride of Abydos, overture ; Intermezzo for orch. ; Violin Concerto ; Concerto for Pf. and orch. ; Magnificat for chorus and orch. ; Two Masses for male voice ; "Jason and the Golden Fleece," cantata (MS.) ; Pf. music, many published pieces ; Songs and part-songs.

JACKSON (F.) English writer, author of "The Construction of the Musical Scale." Lond., n.d.

JACKSON (Dr. G. K.) English writer, author of "First Principles, or a Treatise on Practical Thorough-bass, with General Rules for its Composition and Modulation," op. 5. Lond., fo., n.d. Other musical works, as Three Songs and Duets, op. 3.

JACKSON (John). English org. and comp., B. early in 17th century. Choirmaster, Ely Cath., 1669. Org. Wells Cath., 1676. D. after 1688. Wrote Services, anthems, etc.

JACKSON (Samuel). American comp. and pianist of present time. Has comp. numerous songs, Pf. pieces, choral works ; Church music ; "Complete Dictionary of all Musical Terms" (with S. Carmichael), New York, n.d., etc.

JACKSON (Thomas). English psalm comp., B. [c. 1715] Org. of Parish Ch. of Newark. D. Newark-on-Trent, Nov., 1781. Writer of the psalm-time, "Jackson's."

JACKSON (William). English comp., org., and writer, B. Exeter, May 28, 1730. Son of a grocer. S. under Silvester, org. of Exeter Cath. S. under J. Travers. Teacher in Exeter. Org. and choir-master, Exeter Cath., 1777. D. Exeter, July 12, 1803.

WORKS.—*Operas:* The Lord of the Manor, Lond., 1780; The Metamorphoses, Lond., 1783. *Odes*: Ode to Fancy (Warton), op. 8; Lycidas, 1767; The Dying Christian to his Soul (Pope). *Songs:* Twelve Songs, op. 1, 1755; Twelve Songs, op. 4; Third set of Twelve Songs; Fourth set of Twelve Songs. Elegies for 3 voices, op. 3 [1767]; Twelve Canzonets for 2 voices, op. 9; 2nd set, op. 13; Twelve Pastorels. Six Vocal Quartets, op. 11, 1780; Six Madrigals, op. 18, 1786; Hymns, numerous. Six Sonatas for Harpsichord; Eight do. Six Epigrams for voice and Pf., op. 17 [1786]; Anthems and Church Services by the late William Jackson of Exeter, Edited by James Paddon, 3 vols., Lond., n. d. Selection from his Works, Sacred and Secular, Lond., 4 v., n.d. Thirty Letters on various subjects. London, 8vo, 1782. Observations on the Present State of Music in London, 8vo, 1791. The Four Ages, together with Essays on various subjects. Lond., 8vo, 1798.

Jackson was a man of varied accomplishments; an essayist, musician, organist, and painter. "He was a friend of Gainsborough, had a good taste for art, and was known in his day by his clever landscapes. In 1771 he was an honorary exhibitor at the Academy. He copied Gainsborough's work, and wrote a sketch of his life."—*Redgrave.* His essays are very cleverly written, and display a considerable knowledge of general literary subjects, while they are marked by a fair didactic tendency. It is chiefly as a musician, however, that he is known, and though neglected in one respect by the present age, he is well represented in another.

Jackson's songs, elegies, etc., lack the rich warmth of the present age, in their instrumental aids, though their melodiousness is greatly in their favour. The sacred music of Jackson was once extremely popular, but is now chiefly represented by the never-dying Te Deum in F. His services and anthems are, however, works of much merit, though now seldom used.

JACKSON (William). English org. and comp., B. Masham, Yorks., Jan. 9, 1816. Self-taught in music. Org. at Masham, 1832. Tallow-chandler, do., 1839. Gained Huddersfield Glee Club first prize, 1840. Music-seller in Bradford, with W. Winn, vocalist, 1852. Org. of S. John's Ch., do.; Do., Horton Chapel, 1856. Cond. of Bradford Choral Union. Chorus-master at Bradford Festivals of 1853, '56, '59. D. Bradford, April 15, 1866.

WORKS.—*Oratorios:* The Deliverance of Israel from Babylon, 1845; Isaiah. *Cantatas:* The Year, 1859; The Praise of Music. The 103rd Psalm for solo voice, chorus, and orch., 1841. Church services, a mass, and anthems. The Bradford Tune Book (with Samuel Smith). A Singing Class Manual, n. d. Glees, part-songs, and songs.

A composer and conductor of considerable ability, who did much in his time to forward the musical taste of his district. Of his works "The Year" is by far the best known, and is occasionally rendered by our choirs. It is a work of some brilliancy, but is flimsy in style.

JACKSON (William). English writer, author of "A Preliminary Discourse to a Scheme demonstrating and shewing the perfection and harmony of Sounds," Westminster, 8vo, 1726.

JACOB (Benjamin). English comp. and org., B. London, 1778. S. under his Father, R. Willoughby, Shrubsole, and Arnold, 1796. Chor. in Portland Chap., 1786. Org. of Salem Chap., Soho Sq., 1788; Carlisle Chap., Kennington Lane, 1790; Bentinck Chap., Lisson Green, 1790-4; Surrey Chap. (Rowland Hill's), 1794; St. John's, 1823. Treble singer Westminster Abbey at Festival, 1790-91. Member Royal Soc. of Musicians, 1799. Cond. of series of oratorios, 1800. Gave organ recitals in conjunction with S. Wesley, and W. Crotch, to great audiences, 1808-14. Cond. Lenten Oratorios at Covent Garden Theatre, 1818. Assoc. Phil. Soc., 1818. One of Court of Assistants, R. S. M., 1823. D. London, Aug. 24, 1829.

WORKS.—National Psalmody, a collection of Tunes for every Sunday throughout the year, London [1819], 8vo. Tunes for the use of Surrey Chapel. Dr. Watt's

Divine and Moral Songs, as solos, duets, and trios. Glees and Songs. Arrangement of "Macbeth" music, etc.
Jacob was a great organist in his time, and his performances attracted large numbers of hearers. His best works are his glees, but his "National Psalmody" is a well-known work.

JACOBI (Georges). German violinist and comp., and cond., B. Berlin, Feb. 13, 1840. S. Paris Cons.; gained 1st prize for violin, 1861. Concert player. Cond. Th. Bouffes, Paris, 1869. Settled in London, 1870. Cond. Alhambra, London, 1872.

WORKS.—*Operas, Operettas, and Ballets:* Le Feu aux poudres, 1869; La Nuit du 15 Octobre, 1869; Black Crook (with F. Clay), Lond., 1872; Mariée depuis midi, 1873; The Demon's Bride, 1874; The Enchanted Forest, 1874; Cupid in Arcadia, 1875; The Fairies Home, 1876; Yolande, 1877; Rothomago, 1879; Le Clairon, Paris, 1883; Frétillon, 1884. Numerous ballets produced at the Alhambra, London. Violin music, songs, etc.

JACOTIN. See BERCHEM.

JACOX (Rev. Francis). English writer of present time, author of "Bible Music, being variations in many Keys on Musical Themes from Scripture." Lond., 8vo, 1871; 2nd edition, 1874. Also writer of works on Bible history, "Traits of Character," etc.

JACQUARD (Léon Jean). French comp. and violoncellist, B. Paris, Nov. 3, 1826. S. Paris Cons., and under Norblin. Gained second prize for 'cello playing, 1842; first do, 1844. Married Mdlle. L. Bedel, 1876. Prof. Paris Cons., 1877. Comp. fantasias, transcriptions, etc., for 'cello and orch.

JADASSOHN (Salomon). German comp., writer and teacher, B. Breslau, Sept. 15, [Aug. 13] 1831. S. under Hesse, Brosig, Hauptmann, and Liszt. Settled in Leipzig, 1852. Cond. of Euterpe concerts, Leipzig. Prof. at Leipzig Cons.

WORKS.—String quartet, op. 10; Trio for Pf., vn., and 'cello, op. 20; Two morceaux for Pf., op. 21; Bal masque, 7 airs for Pf., op. 26; Serenade for Pf., op. 35; Nine Lieder, 2 voices and Pf., op. 36; Variations for Pf., op. 40; Two Cadenzen, op. 58; Symphony in C for orch.; Do. in D minor, op. 50; Four Arabesques for Pf., op. 53; Preludes and fugues for Pf., op. 56; Scherzo for Pf. in F minor, op. 57. Lehrbuch das einfachen, doppelten, drei-und vierfachen contrapunkts, Leipzig, 8vo, 1884; Lehrbuch der Harmonie, 1883; Work on Canon and Fugue, 1884, etc.

JADIN (Louis Emmanuel). French comp. and pianist, B. Versailles, Sept. 21, 1768. S. under his father, a musician. Accompanist at the Theatre de Monsieur, 1789-91. Prof. of Pf., Paris Cons., 1802. Legion of Honour, 1824. Director of Royal Chap., 1830. D. Paris, April 11, 1853.

WORKS.—*Operas:* Joconde, 1790; Les Talismans, 1793; Le Mariage de la Veille, 1796; Les deux Lettres, 1797; Mahomet II., 1803, and 30 other operas; Cantatas, various; Symphonies, sextets, trios, concertos, sonatas, quartets, etc.
This composer is best known by his chamber music which is of a lively and original cast. His brother HYACINTHE (1769-1802) composed Pf. music, and was a performer of great brilliancy.

JAELL (Alfred). Austrian comp. and pianist, B. Trieste, March 5, 1832. Travelled in Europe as infant prodigy. Resided successively in Brussels and Paris. Travelled in America, 1848-54. Played in London, 1862, 1866. Married Marie Trautmann, a pianist, 1866. D. Paris, Feb. 28, 1882.

WORKS.—*Pianoforte Music:* Caprice (Meyerbeer), op. 9; Romance, Pf., op. 13; Souvenir d'Hongrie, op. 15; Un moment en Hongrie, op. 16; Polka, op. 33; Serenade, op. 44; La Sylphide, op. 116; Transcriptions (Wagner), opp. 120, 121, 137, 146, 147, 148, etc.; Impromptu, op. 138; Il Guarany (Gomes), op. 141; Two morceaux, op. 153. Numerous fantasias, transcriptions, etc.

JAGARTE (Manuel). Spanish org. and comp., B. 1796. D. 1819. Wrote operas, masses, etc.

JAHN (Otto). German comp. and writer, B. Kiel, Jan. 16, 1813. S. at Leipzig and Berlin. Graduated, 1831. Prof. of Philology at Greifswalde, 1842. Do. Bonn, 1855-69. D. Göttingen, Sept. 9, 1869.

WORKS.—W. A. Mozart. Eine kunsthistoriche Biographie, Leipzig, 4 vols., 8vo, 1856-59. Lieder, various. Contributions to periodical literature. Didactic works, various.

His "Mozart" is undoubtedly the best German work on the subject, and was translated into English by Pauline D. Townsend, and published, London, 3 vols., 1883, with portraits.

JÄHNS (Friedrich Wilhelm). German comp. and pianist, B. Jan. 2, 1809. Director of the Royal music, Berlin. Compiler of a thematic catalogue of Weber's works. Comp. of Pf. music, choral music, etc.

JAMES (John). English org. and comp. of 16th century. Org. of St. Olave, Southwark ; S. George-in-the-East, 1738. D. 1745. Wrote songs and organ pieces.

JAMES (W. N.) English flute-player and writer, author of A word or two on the Flute, Lond., 12mo, 1826. The Flutist's Catechism, in which are explained the First Principles of Music, Lond., 18mo, 1829. The Flutist's Magazine, edited.

JAMES I., KING OF SCOTLAND. Poet and musician, B. 1394. D. 1437. Noticed here as the alleged inventor of the Scottish style of music. Founding on what has been regarded as a wrong reading of a passage in a work of Tassoni the Italian poet (1565-1635), William Tytler has endeavoured to show in his "Essay on Scottish Music" that James I. not only invented the "plaintive style of melody called Scottish," but likewise greatly influenced the style of several Italian composers, among whom are Gesualda and Palestrina ! The enquiries of Dauney, Graham, Burney and others prove that this theory is quite untenable. So confused and misunderstood is the whole of this question, that there are writers who, repeating Tytler's nonsense, transfer the honour of founding the style of melody indicated to James V. and James VI. (or I., of Britain) !

JAMESON (D. D.). English writer, author of " Colour-Music," London, 4to, 1844.

JANIEWICZ (Felix) or VANIEWICZ. Polish violinist, B. Vilna, 1762. Travelled in Italy and France. Married Miss Breeze, 1800. Mem. of Phil. Soc. Settled in Edinburgh, 1815. D. Edinburgh, 1848. Comp. concertos, fantasias, etc. for violin.

JANINA (Olga, Countess de). Russian pianist, S. under Liszt. Resides in Paris as teacher and pianist. Writer of Pf. music, works of fiction, etc.

JANNACONI (Giuseppe). Italian comp., B. [Rome], 1741. S. under Pisari, etc. Chap.-master S. Peter's, Rome, 1811. D. Rome, March 6, 1816.

Comp. masses, psalms, Roman Catholic church music, etc. ; now preserved in MS.

JANNEQUIN (Clement). Belgian (French ?) comp. who flourished during the 16th century. S. under Josquin. His biography is unknown. Period [1480 1560].

He composed chansons, psalms, and music for the clavecin to the number of 200 pieces. His instrumental music is partly, though in a crude manner, in the style termed programme.

JANOTHA (Nathalie). Polish pianist, B. Warsaw, June 8, 1856. S. Warsaw Cons. *Début* at Warsaw, 1867. S. afterwards under Clara Schumann. Appeared in London, 1874, 1878, and 1879. Appeared also on Continent.

She pleased the London public greatly by her refined and magnificent style.

JANSA (Leopold). Bohemian comp. and arranger, B. Wildenschwert, 1794. S. for the law. Cond. of music in University of Vienna, etc. Resided in London, 1849-1869. D. Vienna, Jan. 25, 1875.

Jansa is principally known by his arrangement of classical works, many of which are published by Litolff. He comp. chamber music, Pf. music, etc.

JARNOWICK (Giovanni Maria), or GIORNOVICHI. Italian comp., B. Palermo, 1745. S. under Lolli. Appeared at Paris. Travelled in Germany. Appeared in London, 1791. Travelled in Britain, 1792-96. D. St. Petersburg, Nov. 21, 1804.
WORKS.—Concertos, sonatas, etc., for violin.
"Jarnowick was but a slender musician. His concertos are agreeable and brilliant, but destitute of profundity and grandeur. His performance was graceful and elegant, and his tone was pure."—*Hogarth*.

JARVIS (Charles). English writer and teacher in Philadelphia. Author of "Improved Method of Instruction for the Pianoforte," Boston, n.d. ; "The Young Folks Glee Book," 1845 ; "American Pianoforte Instructor," Philadelphia, fo., 1852.

JARVIS (Charles H.) American teacher and pianist, son of the foregoing, B. Philadelphia, Dec. 20, 1837. S. under his father. S. in Europe for a time. Has played with the orch. of Theodore Thomas, and at the New York Philharmonic, 1869. Best known as a teacher and a promoter of concerts of high class music in Philadelphia.

JAUCH (Johann Nepomuk). German pianist and comp., B. Strassburg, Jan. 25, 1793. S. under Spindler. Teacher in Strassburg. Comp. of church mus., concertos, Pf. music, etc.

JAWURECK (Constance). German vocalist, B. Paris, 1803. S. Paris Cons. under Garat, Plantade, etc. Sang in operas by Auber, Rossini, Meyerbeer, etc. D. Brussels, June 8, 1858.

JAY (John). English pianist and comp., B. Essex, Nov. 27, 1770. S. under Hindmarsh and Phillips, and on the Continent. Settled in London, 1800, as teacher. Mus. Bac., Oxon., 1809. Mus. Doc., Cantab., 1811. Mem. R. A. M. D. London, Sept. 17, 1849. Wrote Pf. and vocal music.

JEAN DE MURIS. See MURIS (Jean de).

JEBB (Rev. John, D.D.) Irish writer and divine, Canon of Hereford and Rector of Peterstow, Herefordshire. B. Dublin, 1805. D. Jan. 1886. Author of Choral Service of the United Church of England and Ireland, being an Inquiry into the Liturgical System of the Cathedral and Collegiate Foundations of the Anglican Communion. Lond., 8vo, 1843 ; Three lectures on the Cathedral Service of the United Church of England and Ireland, 8vo, 1841 ; 2nd edit., 1845 ; The Choral Responses and Litanies of the United Church of England and Ireland, collected from authentic sources, Lond., 2 v., fo., 1847-57.

JEFFERSON (Joseph). English writer, author of "Lyra Evangelica ; or an Essay on the use of instrumental music in Christian Worship." London, 8vo, 1805.

JEFFERYS (Charles). English comp. and music publisher, B. Jan. 11, 1807. Carried on business in London. D. London, June 9, 1865. Wrote words of a number of popular songs, "Rose of Allandale," "Mary of Argyle," etc., and himself comp. "Rose Atherton," "Oh Erin, my country," and other songs.

JEFFRIES (George). English comp. and org. of 17th century. Was org. to Charles I. in 1643. Comp. of anthems, preserved in MS.

JEFFRIES (Stephen). English org. and comp., B. 1660. Chor. Salisbury Cath., under Wise. Org. Gloucester Cath., 1680. D. 1712.

JEKYLL (Charles Sherwood). English org. and comp., B. Westminster, Nov. 29, 1842. Chor. Westminster Abbey, under J. Turle. S. under James Coward and Sir G. A. Macfarren. Org. of St. Paul's Temporary Church, Kensington, Dec., 1857. Assistant Org. Westminster Abbey, 1860-75. Org. Parish Ch. of Acton, 1860 ; Par. Ch., St. George's, Hanover Square, 1861. Org. and comp. to H. M. Chap. Roy., St. James's Palace, and Whitehall,

Nov., 1876. Grand Org. to the United Grand Lodge of England (Freemasons), 1880-81.

WORKS.—*Services:* Communion, in C ; Morning, in F. (MS.) ; Evening, in F (MS) ; Morning in C ; Evening, in C, for male voices, Comp. for St. Paul's Cath. (MS.) *Anthems*: Save me, O God ; Thou wilt keep him in perfect peace ; Arise, O Lord ; Almighty God ; Blessed is he that considereth the poor ; O send out Thy light (MS.) ; My God, look upon me (MS.) ; Them that are meek (MS.); The Lord hear thee ; The Lord is full of compassion ; There the wicked cease from troubling ; Behold how good and joyful (MS) ; Lord, I have loved the habitation of Thy house. Twelve Kyries. *Part-Songs*: On the sea ; When twilight dews ; Remembrance ; Night after the battle (MS.) ; *Songs:* Pro Patria Mori ; Remember me when far away ; Now ; Go, forget me ; In memoriam ; The mermaid's lullaby. Grand March for organ ; Musical Sundays at Home, a series of 12 numbers, edited. Hymns, chants, etc.

JELENSPERGER (Daniel). German writer and teacher, B. near Mülhausen, 1797. D. Mülhausen, May 31, 1831. Author of, among other works, "L'Harmonie au Commencement du dix-neuvième Siècle...," Paris, 1830. German edition, Leipzig, 1833.

JENKINS (John). English comp., B. Maidstone, 1592. Musician to Charles I. and Charles II. Resided during the greater part of his life with H. L' Estrange of Norfolk. D. Kimberley, Oct. 27, 1678.

WORKS.—Elegy on the death of William Lawes, 1648. Theophila, or, Love's Sacrifice. Poem by E. Benlowes, 1652. Twelve Sonatas for 2 violins and a Base, with a Thorough-base for the Organ or Theorbo', 1660. Fantasias in five and six parts for viols. Anthems, rounds, etc. A Compendium of Practical Music. Lond., 1667.

Jenkins is credited with having been the first in England to compose instrumental music. "These productions are the more worthy of our notice, as having been the first compositions of the kind emanating from English genius."—*Busby.*

JENKS (Stephen). American psalmodist, published "The Delights of Harmony, or Norfolk Compiler: Being a new Collection of Psalm Tunes, Hymns, and Anthems...," Dedham, Mass, 1805.

JENSEN (Adolf). German comp. and cond., B. Königsberg, Jan. 12, 1837. S. under Ehlert, etc. Cond. and teacher in various towns. D. Baden, Jan. 24, 1879

WORKS.—Daughter of Jephta, op. 26 ; Lieder, op. 9 ; Pf. music, etc.

JEUNE. See LEJEUNE (Claude).

JEUNESSE. See LA JEUNESSE.

JEWSON (Frederick Bowen). English comp. and pianist, B. Edinburgh, July 26, 1823. S. at R. A. M., and became King's Scholar, 1837. Prof. and Director of R. A. M.

Comp. Overtures for orch. ; Sonata for Pf., op. 1 ; Concerto for Pf. and orch., op. 33 ; Six Grand Studies for Pf., op. 16 ; Douze Etudes Melodiques et Brillantes, Pf., op. 23 ; also numerous other pieces for Pf., as "Chanson d'Amour ;" "Mountain Stream ;" etc. Songs and vocal music.

JOACHIM (Josef). Hungarian violinist and comp., B. Kitsee, near Pressburg, June 28, 1831. Jewish parents. S. at Vienna Cons. under J. Böhm, 1838. S. at Leipzig under David and Hauptmann, and played in orch. at Gewandhaus Concerts, 1843-50. Appeared in Paris, 1850. Musical director at Weimar, 1850. Director of the Chap.-Roy., Hanover, 1853-66. Played in important cities of Europe. Member of Senate of the Berlin Academy, 1869. Director of the School of Instrumental music, Berlin, 1868. Visited London, and appeared at Philharmonic Soc. Concert, May 27, 1874, and has since played annually. Married to Amalia Weiss, contralto singer. Mus. Doc., Cantab., 1877.

WORKS.—Op. 1. Andantino and allegro scherzoso for vn. and orch. ; op. 2. Three pieces for Pf. and vn. ; op. 3. Concerto in G minor for vn. and orch. ; op. 4. Overture: "Hamlet," orch. ; op. 5. Three pieces for vn. and Pf. ; op. 6. Overture: "Demetrius," for orch. ; op. 7. Overture: "Henry the Fourth," do. ; op. 8. Overture to a play by Gozzi (MS.) ; op. 9. Hebrew melodies for viola and

Pf. ; op. 10. Variations on an original theme for viola and Pf. ; op. 11. Hungarian Concerto for vn. and orch. ; op. 12. Nutturno for vn. and orch., in A ; op. 13. Overture (Kleist) for orch. ; op. 14. Sena der Marfa for contralto solo and orch. (Schiller's Demetrius). Miscellaneous music published and in MS.

Joachim is justly regarded as the greatest violinist of the present time. He is not equalled by anyone for tone, taste, or execution. With Joachim is identified all that is noble and elevated in violin playing. His works are thoughtful, and in some respects clever, but can never aspire to the highest place among musical compositions. He lacks in composition what he possesses in the greatest measure in performance, inspiration. The works by which he is probably best known are numbers 3 and 11, the latter of which has achieved a considerable measure of popularity.

JOCELYN (Simeon). American psalmodist, compiled the "Chorister's Companion," New Haven, Conn., 1788. Supplement, 1793.

JOHNSON (Artemus N.). American compiler and comp., B. Middlebury, Vt., 1817. Editor of the *Boston Musical Gazette*, and *Boston Musical Journal*.

WORKS.—Instructions in Thorough-bass, Boston, 1844 ; Chorus Choir Instruction Book, 1847; Bay State Collection, 1849; Melodia Sacra, 1852; Handel Collection, 1854 ; Instruction in Harmony upon the Pestalozzian System, 1854 ; Method for Singing Classes ; The True Psalmist (church music) ; Singing School Text-Book ; Domestic Concert Collection ; The True Choir ; Music for Choirs ; etc.

JOHNSON (Edmund C.). English writer, author of "An Inquiry into the Musical Instruction for the Blind in France, Spain, and America," London, 8vo, 1855.

JOHNSON (Edward). English comp. of 16th century. Was Mus. Bac., Cantab., 1594. Contributed to Este's Psalms. He composed the madrigal, "Come Blessed Bird," in the "Triumphs of Oriana," 1601. His biography is unknown.

JOHNSON (James). Scottish engraver and publisher, who flourished in Edinburgh in the end of last and beginning of the present century. He is chiefly noted for his connection with Robert Burns, and the publication of "The Scots Musical Museum, with proper Basses for the Pf....," Edin·, 5 vols., 8vo, n. d. [1787]. This work was edited by David Laing and Stenhouse, and reprinted by Messrs. Blackwood, Edin., 4 vols., 8vo, 1853. The success of this venture was entirely due to the fine lyrics which Burns contributed, and which have since become world-wide favourites.

The arrangements of the melodies in Johnson's Collection were by Stephen Clarke (see that name). Johnson after the success of his "Museum" did not attempt anything further in the same direction, the superior musical production of a similar nature issued by George Thomson having perhaps helped to damp his ardour.

JOHNSON (Robert). English comp. and divine, who flourished about the middle of the 16th century. He composed part-songs, etc., one of which appears in the "History" of Sir John Hawkins, and others in contemporary collections.

JOHNSON (Robert). English comp. and lutenist, B. in latter half of 16th century. Musician in service of Sir T. Kytson of Hengrave Hall, Suffolk. Resided latterly in London as teacher, and musician in service of Prince Henry. D. after 1625.

WORKS.—*Music to Dramas:* "The Witch" (Middleton); "The Tempest" (Shakespere); "Masque of the Gipsies" (Jonson); Contributions to Leighton's "Teares." Songs, madrigals, etc.

JOHNSTON (Rev. David). Scottish divine and writer, author of "Instrumental Music in the Church of Scotland. By the Minister of the United Parishes of Harray and Birsay." 12mo, 1872 (privately printed).

JOLLY (John Marks). English comp. and cond., B. 1790. Cond. at Surrey Theatre, London. D. July 1, 1864. Wrote a large number of songs, part-songs, etc. Among the former many comic and of little merit; among the latter some pieces worthy of preservation.

JOLLY (John). English comp. and org., B. Knutsford, Cheshire, 1794. Org. of S. Philip's Chap., London. D. London, April, 1838. Comp. a number of glees and other vocal music; also "Devotional Melodies, consisting of Psalms, Hymns, Collects, and Short Anthems," Lond., 1832.

JOMMELLI (Nicolo). Italian comp., B., Aversa, near Naples, Sept. 11, 1714. S. under a canon named Mozzillo; under Durante, at S. Onofrio Cons., 1730; and under Leo, Prato and Mancini. Resided at Rome under the patronage of the Cardinal Duke of York, 1740. Lived for a time at Bologna. Comp. of operas at Rome, Naples, Venice, and Vienna. Sub.-Chap.-master, S. Peter's, Rome, 1749-54. Chap.-master to Duke of Würtemberg, at Stuttgart, 1754-69. Retired to Aversa after 1769. D. Naples, Aug. 28, 1774.

WORKS.—*Operas:* L'Errore Amorosa, Naples, 1737; Odoardo, 1738; Ricimero, Rome, 1740; Astianasse, do., 1741; Ezio, Bologna, 1741; Merope, Venice, 1741; Il Frastullo, 1743; Sofonisba, 1743; Il Creso, 1743; Ciro Riconosciuto, 1745; Achille in Sciro, Vienna, 1745; Didone, Vienna, 1745; Eumene, Naples, 1746; L'Amore in Maschera, Naples, 1746; La Critica, 1747; L'Incantato, Rome, 1749; Artaserse, Rome, 1749; Ifigenia in Tauride, do., 1751; Talestri, do, 1752; Attilio Regolo, do, 1752; Semiramide, 1752; L'Ipermestre, 1752; Bagazette, Turin, 1753; Demetrio, Parma, 1753; Penelope, Stuttgart, 1754; Enea nel Lazio, do., 1755; Il Re Pastore, do, 1755; Didone (fresh setting), do., 1755; Alessandro nell' Indie, do.; Nitelli, do.; La Clemenza di Tito; Temistocle, Naples, 1757; Il Trionfo di Clelia, 1757; Cerere placata, 1772; Cajo Marzio; Demofoonte; Il Fedonte; L'Isola disabitata; Endimione; Il Vologeso (1766); L'Olimpiade; La Schiava Liberata; L'Asilo d' Amore; La Pastorella Illustre; Il Cacciator deluso; Il Matrimonio per Concorso; Armida, Naples, 1771; Demofoonte, new music, 1772; Ifigenia in Aulide, 1773. Cantatas, various; Church Music; Miserere, Graduels, Te Deums, Psalms, etc.

Jommelli, in his day regarded as among the foremost musicians, is at the present period scarcely known out of musical history. His operas are obsolete in form, and the disuse of classical incidents as subject-matter has long since consigned the whole species to oblivion. He was a melodist of first-rate ability, and as a harmonist much beyond the comprehension of his countrymen. He was taken to task by Metastasio, his friend, for following the Germans in respect to dramatic colouring. He was in some respects much in advance of his period, so far as Italy is concerned. His sacred music is only separated from his operatic productions by the barest possible strictness in contrapuntal treatment.

JONAS (Emile). French comp. and Prof., B. Paris, March 5, 1827. S. Paris Cons., under Le Couppey, Carafa, etc. Gained 2nd prize for harmony, 1846; 1st do., 1847; 2nd grand prize for comp., 1849. Prof. of Singing, Paris Cons., 1847-66. Prof. of harmony for military bands, 1859-70. Director of music at Portuguese Synagogue, Paris. Secretary to the Committee for organization of military bands at Exhibition, 1867. Chev. of Legion of Hon.

WORKS.—*Operas:* Le Duel de Benjamin, 1855; Le Parade, 1856; Le Roi Boit, 1857; Les Petits Prodiges, 1857; Job et son chien, 1863; Le Manoir des Larenardière, 1864; Avant la noce, 1865; Les deux Arlequins, 1865; Le Canard à trois becs, 1869; Malbrough s'en va-t-en guerre (with Bizet, Delibes, and Legouix); Desiré, sire de Champigny, 1869; Javotte ("Cinderella" at Gaiety Theatre, London), 1871; Princess Kelebella (MS.); La bonne aventure, 1882; Le premier Baiser, 1883. Miss Robinson, operetta. Instrumental music, etc.

JONCIÈRES (Felix Ludger, surnamed **Victorin de).** French comp. and critic, B. Paris, April 2, 1839. S. Paris Cons. under Elwart, etc. Writer in musical journals.

WORKS.—*Operettas:* Le Sicilien, ou l'Amour peintre; Le Dernier jour de Pompei; Dimitri; Le Chevalier Jean. Symphonie Romantique, 1874. Overtures, marches, Pf. music, etc.

JONES (Edward). Welsh writer and musician, B. Llanderfel, Merionethshire, April, 1752. S. Welsh harp under his father. Appeared in London as harper, 1775. Welsh bard to Prince of Wales, 1783. D. London, April 18, 1824.

WORKS.—Musical and Poetical Relicks of the Welsh Bards, preserved by

Tradition and Authentic Manuscripts from very remote Antiquity, with a collection of the Pennillion and Englynion Epigrammatic stanzas or native Pastoral Sonnets of Wales, a History of the Bards from the Earliest Period, and an Account of their Music, Poetry, and Musical Instruments, Lond., fo., 1784, 2 parts. Musical and Poetical Relicks of the Welsh Bards, preserved by Tradition and Authentic Manuscripts from very remote Antiquity, with a select collection of the Pennillion and Englynion, with English translations, likewise a General History of the Bards and Druids, from the earliest period to the present time; with an account of their Music and Poetry; to which is prefixed a Dissertation on the Musical Instruments of the Aboriginal Britons, Lond., 1794. The Bardic Museum of Primitive British Literature and other admirable rarities, forming the second volume of the Musical, Poetical, and Historical Relicks of the Welsh Bards and Druids...fo., 1802. Lyric Airs, consisting of specimens of Greek, Albanian, Walachian, Turkish, Arabian, Persian, Chinese, and Moorish Songs and Melodies, with a short Dissertation on the Origin of Ancient Greek music, Lond., fo., 1804. Popular Cheshire Melodies, n. d. The Musical Miscellany, n. d. Terpsichore's Banquet (National Airs), n. d. The Minstrel's Serenades, n. d. Collections from works of Handel; etc.

JONES (George). English writer, author of "History of the rise and progress of Music, Theoretical and Practical," Lond., 4to, 1818. German edition, Vienna, 1821.

JONES (Rev. James). English writer and divine, author of "A Manual of Instructions on Plain-chant or Gregorian music, with the chants as used in Rome," Lond., 4to, 1845.

JONES (John). English org. and comp., B. early in the 18th century [1730]. Org. of Middle Temple, 1749; Charterhouse, 1753; S. Paul's, 1755. D. London, Feb. 7, 1796.

WORKS.—Sixty Chants, single and double, 1785. Harpsichord Lessons, 2 vols. Songs, etc.

JONES (John Hilton). American writer, B. 1827. Author of Guide to Bass, N. Y., 1853. Sixty-six Psalm Interludes, Boston, 1854. Treatise on Counterpoint, Boston, 1855. Twelve Organ Voluntaries, Boston, 1855; etc.

JONES (Richard). English writer, author of "The most New and Easy Method of Singing the Psalms," Lond., 12mo, 1705.

JONES (Robert). English comp. and lutenist, flourished at end of 16th and beginning of 17th centuries. Biography unknown.

WORKS.—The First Booke of Ayres, 1601. The Second Booke of Ayres, set out to the Lute, the Base Violl the playne way, or the Base by tableture after the leero fashion. Ultimum Vale, or the Third Booke of Ayres of 1, 2, and 4 voyces, 1608. A Musicall Dreame, or the fourth booke of Ayres, the first part for the lute, two voices, and the viol da gamba; the second part is for the lute, the viol, and four voices to sing; the third part is for one voice alone to the lute, the base-viol, or to both if you please, whereof two are Italian Ayres, Lond., fo., 1619. The Muse's Gardin for Delights, or the Fifth Booke of Ayres, only for the Lute, the Bass Violl, and the Voyce, n. d. The First Set of Madrigals of 3, 4, 5, 6, 7, and 8 parts for viols and for voices alone, or as you please, 1607. "Fair Oriana, seeming to wink," madrigal for 6 voices, in Triumphs of Oriana. Contributions in Leighton's Teares. Songs in Smith's Musica Antiqua.

JONES (Stanton). English writer and band-master, author of "Boosey's Universal Cornet Tutor," n.d.; Shilling Cornet Tutor (abridged from No. 1). Songs.

JONES (William). English writer, author of "A Discourse on the Philosophy of Musical Sounds," 4to, n.d.

JONES (Rev. William). English comp., writer, and divine, B. Lowick, Northamptonshire, July 30, 1726. S. Oxford. Vicar of Bethersden, Kent, 1764; Do. of Pluckley; Paston, Northampton; Rector of Hollingbourne, Kent. D. Nayland, Jan. 6, 1800.

WORKS.—Ten Church Pieces for the Organ, with four anthems in score, 1789; A Treatise on the Art of Music, in which the elements of harmony and air are practically considered and illustrated by 150 Examples in Notes...the whole intended as a course of Lectures preparatory to the Practice of Thorough Bass and Musical Composition. Colchester fo., 1784; 2nd edition, Sudbury, fo., 1827. Church music, miscellaneous. Collected Works, published in 12 vols., 1802, and again in 6 vols., 1810.

JONES (Sir William). English orientalist and scholar, B. London, 1746. D. Calcutta, 1794. Author of "Commentaries on Asiatic Poetry," 1744; "The Musical Modes of the Hindus," 1784; References to Oriental Music in Collected Works, etc.

JORDAN (Charles Warwick). English comp. and org., B. Clifton, Dec. 28, 1840. Chor. in Bristol and St. Paul's Cath. Org. St. Paul's, Bunhill Row; St. Luke's, West Holloway, 1860; St. Stephen's, Lewisham, 1866. Hon. org. of London Gregorian Church Association, which he aided in establishing. F. C. O., etc. Mus. Bac., Oxon., 1869 Comp. of services, anthems, songs, etc.; a cantata entitled "Blow ye the trumpet in Zion;" and "A Short Paper on the Construction of the Gregorian Tones," 1874. 150 Harmonies for Gregorian Tones. Org. music, and a Communion Service in E, with accomp. for brass instruments.

JORTIN (John). English writer, B. 1698. D. 1770. Author of "A Letter concerning the music of the Ancients," in 2nd edition of Avison's "Musical Expression."

JOSEFFY (Rafael). Hungarian pianist and comp., B. Pressburg, 1852. Joseffy has been very successful in the United States, where he travelled much on concert tours.

"Certainly no such extreme delicacy of touch, marvellous facility of execution, and exquisite finish have been reached by any artist ever heard in this city. In Chopin, Joseffy is unsurpassable; but with some composers, as he knows no technical difficulties, he frequently hurries the *tempo*, and injures the effect."—*Harper's Monthly Magazine.*

JOSQUIN DES PRÉS. JODOCUS PRATENSIS. Flemish comp., B. [Condé; S. Quentin] Hainault [1445]. S. under Okenheim. Chor. in church in Hainault. Chap.-master at S. Quentin. Singer in court chapel of Pope Sextus IV., 1471-1484. Musician at courts of Ferrara, Florence, and latterly that of Louis XII. of France. D. Condé, Aug. 27, 1521.

WORKS.—Masses, about 20 in number; Motets, numerous; Psalms; Secular music, songs, canons, etc.

"If we admire Palestrina, Orlando di Lasso, Tallis, and Bird, whose labours adorned and enriched the musical libraries of the sixteenth century, how much more ought we to be struck with the powers of Josquin, who, a hundred years before, not only vanquished all the existing difficulties of Canon, Fugue, Imitation, and every species of learned contrivance and ingenious contexture of consonant combination, but invented new structures of harmony, original adjustments of *part* with *part*, and was, in a great measure, the father of modern polyphonic composition. . . . According to all that can be collected from the best authorities, Josquin, in his day, was the prince of musicians. No one seems to have possessed an equal influence over the affections and passions of the lovers and patrons of music. Rabelais, in his prologue to the third book of Pantagruel, gives him the first place among the fifty-nine excellent masters whom he had formerly heard: and his compositions appear to have been as well known in his time as now are those of the most favourite of the modern masters."—*Busby.*

Josquin not only ruled the musical style of his day, but also influenced in a supreme measure the succeeding masters of many a school. His pupils Mouton, Coclicus, Arkadelt, Gombert, Berchem, Jannequin, Certon, etc., all had a share in the formation of the great contrapuntal schools of the 16th and 17th centuries. Josquin is generally credited with having been among the first of the early composers to write with some regard for the expressional characteristics of the music as well as for its mere formal construction. His music is, it may safely be said, wholly unknown in Britain, save to a few enthusiastic students of music in its strictly archæological aspect, and it may also be said that, if revived, it would be found quite unsuited to the spirit of the age.

JOULE (Benjamin St. John Baptist). English comp. and [org., B. Salford, Nov. 8, 1817. S. under R. Cudmore and J. J. Harris. Hon. Org. and choir-master of Holy Trinity Church, Hulme, 1846-53; St. Margaret's, Whalley Range, Manchester, 1849-52. Hon. Org. and choirmaster St. Peter's Church, Manchester, 1853. President of Manchester Vocal Soc., etc.

WORKS.—The Hymns and Canticles pointed for chanting, 1847. Directorium Chori Anglicanum; a Complete Manual of the Choral Service of the Church of England: containing the Order for Matins and Even-song, the Litany, the Order for the Administration of the Holy Communion and the Occasional Services, from Authentic Sources. Lond., 1849 (4 editions 4to, and 8 18mo). A Collection of Words of 2270 Anthems, composed or adapted for the Choral Service, with 452 Biographical Notices, Lond., 1859. The Psalter or Psalms of David, after the translation of the Great Bible, pointed as they are to be sung or said in churches, with additional points for securing correctness and uniformity of accentuation.... London, 1865. Collection of Chants for the Daily and Proper Psalms, with an Appendix of Chants for the Hymns and Canticles, etc. Lond., 1860, 18 editions, various dates. The Order for the Holy Communion, harmonized on a Monotone, for Parochial Use, Lond., 5 eds. Org. and Pf. music. Contributions to periodical literature, and pamphlets on various subjects.

Mr. Joule was for long (1850-70) connected with the *Manchester Courier*, in the capacity of musical critic. He is J.P. for the County of Lancaster, Fellow of the Genealogical and Historical Soc. of Gt. Britain, and of the College of Organists, London.

JOURET (Theodore). Belgian comp. and writer, B. Ath, Sept. 11, 1821. Comp. of operas, Pf. music, songs, etc.

JOURET (Leon). Belgian org. and comp., brother of the above, B. Ath, Oct. 17, 1828. S. at Music School of Ath. Comp. music to lyrics, etc., of Hugo, Musset, Gautier, etc., as well as org. works, etc. He holds post of Prof. of vocalization in Brussels Cons.

JOUSSE (J.). French writer, B. Orleans, [1765]. D. London, Jan., 1837. He wrote the following popular works:—

Guida Armonica, in which the origin, signature, name and use of all the Chords are clearly explained and illustrated, etc., Lond., 1808. Arcana Musicae, or a variety of curious and entertaining Musical Problems, with their Solutions, Lond., 1818, 8vo. Familiar Dialogues on Thorough-Bass and Harmony, n. d., 12mo. Dictionary of Italian and other terms used in Music, etc., 1829, 8vo. Introduction to the Art of Sol-fa-ing and Singing, etc., n. d. Lectures on Thorough-Bass, n. d. A Catechism of Singing, n. d. The Vocal Primer, etc., n. d. Catechism of Thorough-Bass and Harmony, etc., n. d. Music Epitomized, in which the whole Science of Music is clearly explained n. d. 12mo. Most of the foregoing works have gone through a number of editions, and were very successful text-books in their day.

JOYCE (P. W.), LL.D. Irish writer, compiler of "Ancient Irish Music, comprising one hundred airs hitherto unpublished, many of the old popular songs, and several new Songs, etc., Dublin, 1873, 4to.

JOZÉ (Thomas Richard Gonzalvez). Irish comp. and org., B. Dublin, Sept. 26, 1853. Chor. in Christ Ch. Cath., 1861. Deputy org., do., 1869. Org. of S. Paul's, Glenagarry, Co. Dublin, 1870. Prof. of Pf. in Royal Irish Acad. of Music, 1871. Mus. Doc., Dublin, June, 1877. Cond. of Kingston Philharmonic Soc., 1876.

WORKS.—The Prophecy of Capys, cantata; A Dream of the Fairies, cantata. Part-songs, Songs, Pf. music, etc.

Dr. Jozé gained in 1871 the first prize offered by the Hibernian Catch Club with his five-part glee, "The dead soldier."

JULLIEN or **JULIEN (Louis G. Antoine J.).** French cond. and comp., B. Sisterton, Basses Alps, April 23, 1812. S. at Paris Cons. under Halévy, 1833-36. Cond. in Paris. Do. in London of concerts at the English Opera House, Drury Lane, etc., 1838. Travelled through England, Scotland, and Ireland, etc., with orch. Opened Drury Lane Theatre for English opera, 1847, but the enterprise failed. Appeared in America with orch., 1852-54. D. Paris, March 14, 1860 [Suicide].

WORKS.—Pietro il Grande, opera, 1852. Music for orchestra in great quantity, "British Army Quadrilles" and other stuff of a like nature.

Jullien did incalculable good to orchestral music in Britain by encouraging young instrumentalists, but he brought himself into disrepute with respectable musicians by playing the buffoon too frequently. For a good idea of the light in which he was regarded by sensible contemporaries see *Punch*. His music is not fated to be everlasting.

JUNGMANN (Albert). German pianist and comp., B. Langensalza, Nov. 14, 1814. Resides in Vienna as teacher and comp. His works include Pf. and orchestral compositions of merit.

K.

KAFKA (Johann Nepomuk). Bohemian comp. and pianist, B. May 17, 1819. S. at Vienna, etc. Comp. of numerous light and pleasing works for Pf.

KAHRER (Laura). See RAPPOLDI.

KALKBRENNER (Christian). German comp. of instrumental music, B. 1755. D. 1806. Also author of "Histoire de la Musique," 2 vols., 1802.

KALKBRENNER (Friedrich Wilhelm Michael). German pianist and comp., son of above, B. Cassel, 1788 [1784]. S. under his Father, and at Paris Cons., 1798. Gained prize for Pf. playing, 1802. Début as pianist at Berlin, 1813. S. harmony under Albrechtsberger. Resided in London as teacher, 1814-23. Resided in Paris from 1824. Partner in Pf.-making firm of Pleyel & Co. D. near Paris, June 10, 1849.

WORKS.—*Sonatas* for Pf. solo, opp. 1, 4, 13, 28, 35, 48, 56. Quartet for Pf., vn., alto, and 'cello, op. 2. Sonatas for Pf. duet, op. 3, 79. *Fantasias* for Pf. solo, opp. 5, 6, 8, 9, 12, 21, 33, 36, 37, 50, 53, 64, 68, 76, 80, 110, 114, 119. *Trios* for Pf., vn., and 'cello, opp. 7, 14, 26, 39, 84. *Themes* with variations for Pf., opp. 10, 16, 17, 18, 19, 23, 25, 29, 38, 44, 51, 55, 69, 71, 72, 75, 83, 98, 99, 112, 115, 118, 120, 122. *Duets* for Pf. and vn., opp. 11, 22, 27, 47, 49, 63, 86. *Septet* for Pf., 2 vns., 2 horns, viola, and bass, op. 15. *Rondos* for Pf., opp. 31, 32, 43, 45, 46, 52, 57, 59, 61, 62, 65, 67, 78, 96, 97, 101, 102, 106, 109, 116. *Studies*, Caprices, for Pf., opp. 20, 54, 88, 104. Method for the Pf., op. 108. *Concertos* for Pf. in D minor, op. 61; 2nd in E, op. 85; 3rd do., op. 107; for two Pfs., in C, op. 125; *Rondos* for Pf. and orch., opp. 60, 70, 101.

This pianist brought the mechanical part of his art to a perfection never previously known in his period. His works are permeated with a stilted formality which marks strongly enough the preponderance of the scholastic over the inspired musician. His performance was distinguished by much brilliancy and a perfect command over the technical peculiarities of the pianoforte, but it is spoken of by Moscheles and other judges as being greatly lacking in sympathy and feeling.

KALLIWODA (Johann Wenzeslaus). Bohemian, comp., B. Prague, March 21, 1800. S. at Prague Cons., 1811-17. Cond. of Private Band of Prince Fürstenberg at Donauss-Chengin, 1823-53. D. Carlsruhe, Dec. 3, 1866.

WORKS.—Symphonies: 1st, in F min., op. 7, 1826; 2nd, in E flat, op. 17; 3rd in D min., op. 28; 4th, in C min.; 5th, in B min., op. 106; 6th, in F. Overtures for orch., opp. 38, 44, 55, 56, 76, 85, 101, 108, 126, 141, 143, 145. Concertos for vn. and orch., opp. 15, 30, 72, 100, 133, 151. Variations, etc., for vn. and orch. opp. 13, 18, 22, 35, 37, 41. Rondos for Pf. solo, opp. 10, 11, 16, 19, 23, 42. Three String Quartets, opp. 61, 62, 90. Blanda, opera, 1847.

Kalliwoda was a violinist of very considerable repute in his day, but is now best known by his bright and clever overtures, most of which are stock pieces in theatrical and other orchestras.

KANNE (Friedrich August). German comp., B. Saxony, March 8, 1788. D. Vienna, Dec. 16, 1835. Comp. of operas, symphonies, and Pf. music.

KAPPEY (J. A.). English bandmaster and writer, B. Bingen, Germany, 1826. Cond. of band of Royal Marines, Chatham, since 1857. Comp. The Wager, opera, Lond., 1872; Martial cantata, Per Mare per Terram, Rochester, 1878; Dance Music, Songs, etc. Author of Clarionet Tutor (Boosey), n. d.; Forty Progressive Exercises and Studies for the Clarionet; Flute Tutor; Oboe Tutor; Complete Tutor for Brass Band Instruments; Bassoon Tutor. Edited The Songs of Germany, Schubert, Scandinavia, Eastern Europe, etc. Since 1869 sole editor of Boosey's Military and Brass Band Journals.

KAPSPERGER (Johann Jerome). German comp. and lute-player, flourished in latter part of 16th and beginning of 17th centuries. Resided successively at Rome and Venice. Comp. Libro primo d' Intavolatura di Chitarone...1604; Libro 1 de Madrigali a 5 voci...1609; Libro primo di Villanelle...1610; D'Intavolature di Lauto...1611; Libro primo di Arie passeggiate...1612. Masses. Poems.

KASTNER (Johann Georg). German comp. and writer, B. Strassburg, March 9, 1810. D. Paris, Dec. 19, 1867. Writer of *Schools* or *Tutors* for various instruments, Pf. music, etc.

KEACH (O. W.). American band-master and writer, author of (with B. A. Burditt) Modern School for the Drum. Army Drum and Fife Book (with Burditt and Cassidy), n. d.

KEDDIE (Henrietta), SARAH TYTLER. Authoress of "Musical Composers and their Works," Lond., 1875, 8vo; 2nd ed., 1877. Also writer of other biographical works and novels.

KEEBLE (John). English org. and comp., B. Chichester, 1711. Chorister Chichester Cath., under Kelway. S. under Pepusch. Org. of S. George's, Hanover Sq., London, 1737. Org. of Ranelagh Gardens. D. London, Dec. 24, 1786.

WORKS.—Five Books of Organ Pieces. Songs, etc. The Theory of Harmonics, or an Illustration of the Grecian Harmonics, Lond., 4to, 1784.

KEETON (Haydn). English org. and comp., B. Mosborough, near Chesterfield, Derbyshire, Oct. 26, 1847. Mus. Bac., Oxon., July, 1869. Org. Peterborough Cath., Feb. 23, 1870. Mus. Doc., Oxon., Dec. 1877.

WORKS.—*Anthems:* I will alway give thanks; Give ear, Lord, unto my prayer (Meadowcroft Prize); The eyes of all. Benedicite in E flat. Magnificat and Nunc Dimittis in B flat (chant form). Offertory Sentences (awarded a Prize offered by Coll. of Org.). Impromptu for Pf. Morning and Evening Service in B flat (MS.). Symphony for Orch. (MS.).

KEISER (Reinhard). German comp. and cond., B. Weissenfels, Leipzig, 1673. S. at the Thomas Schule, Leipzig, and at Leipzig University. Resided in Hamburg, 1694-1734. Married, 1709. Organized Concerts in Hamburg, 1700-34. Director of Hamburg Opera, 1703. Chapel-master to the King of Denmark. Cantor and Canon of Copenhagen Cath. D. Hamburg, Sept. 12, 1739.

WORKS.—*Operas:* Ismene, 1692; Basilius, 1693; Mahomet, 1696; Adonis, 1697; Irene, 1697; Janus, 1698; La Pomme d'or, 1698; Iphigenie; Hercules; Endymion, 1701; Psyche, 1701; Stierte becker und Gadje Michel, 1702; Circe, 1702; Penelope, 1702; Orpheus, 1702; Claudius, 1703; Salomon, 1703; Masaniello furioso, 1706; Helene, 1709; Oesiderius, 1709; Charles V., 1712. *Oratorios:* Nabuchodonosor, 1704; Passion according to S. Mark. Ballets and Interludes.

KEITH (R. W.) English pianist and writer, B. Stepney, 1787. Author of "A Musical Vade Mecum, being a compendious introduction to the whole Art of

Music," Lond., 2 v., 8vo, 1820 ; "Instructions for the Pianoforte"...Lond. [1833] ; "Tutor for the German Flute," etc.

KELER-BÉLA (Albert von Keler, or). Hungarian comp., B. Bartfeld, Feb. 13, 1820. S. under Sechter and Schlesinger. Cond. of the Gung'l band at Berlin ; Do. Lanner band at Vienna. Bandmaster in an infantry regiment. Chap.-master at Wiesbaden, 1870-72. D. Wiesbaden, Nov. 20, 1882. Comp. overtures, dance music for Pf., and orch., etc.

KELLER (Godfrey). See HOLDER (J.)

KELLIE (Thomas Alexander Erskine, Earl of). Scottish musician, B. Sept. 1, 1732. S. under Stamitz. Succeeded his father in 1756. Sold most of the Killie property. D. Brussels (unmarried), Oct. 9, 1781.

He composed a number of overtures (The Maid of the Mill, etc.), 1761 ; " Minuets and Songs now for the first time published, with an Introductory Notice by C. K. Sharpe." Edinburgh, 4to, 1839. Songs, etc.

He was reckoned among the most respectable amateur violinists of his time, and was a composer of some ability. " Frothy," says Busby.

KELLOGG (Clara Louise). American soprano vocalist, B. Sumterville, N. C., July, 1842. Educated in New York. *Début* as Gilda in " Rigoletto," New York Academy of Music, 1861. First appeared in London, Nov. 2, 1867, as Margherita (" Faust "). Sang in London again, 1872. Has since appeared successfully in various parts of Europe and in the U. S.

Miss Kellogg is recognised in the United States as one of the foremost among native singers. Her talents are of a very high order, and the enthusiasm with which she is universally received speaks more than words to her popularity.

KELLY (Michael). Irish comp., B. Dublin, 1764 [1762]. S. singing under Rauzzini. S. also at Naples under Aprile, etc., 1779. *Début* as vocalist at Dublin, 1779. Travelled in Italy, and became acquainted with Mozart. *Début* at Drury Lane, as Lionel in " Lionel and Clarissa." Sang at Concerts of Ancient Music, Händel Commemoration, in English Provinces, Ireland, etc. Manager of King's Theatre, 1793. D. Margate, Oct. 9 [15], 1826.

WORKS.—Musical Dramas, for which the music was chiefly compiled, as—False Appearances, 1789; The Castle Spectre ; Of Age To-morrow ; Blue Beard ; Pizarro ; etc. Glees and songs. Reminiscences, during a period of nearly half a century, with original anecdotes of many distinguished persons. Lond., 2 vols., 8vo, 1826 ; 2nd ed., 1826.

Kelly was a well-known and highly-appreciated singer in his day. His works were of too temporary a character to merit preservation, and all of them, save his garrulous " Reminiscences," have departed this world. The " Reminiscences " is a highly amusing production, and is a storehouse of musical anecdote to which many an erudite musical historian has turned with glee.

KELWAY (Joseph). English org. and comp., B. about beginning of the 18th century [1702]. S. under Geminiani. Org. of S. Michael's, Cornhill, London, till 1736. Org. S. Martin's-in-the-Fields, 1736. Instructor on Harpsichord to Queen Charlotte. D. 1782.

Kelway was a famous organist, but is represented at the present period only by a few harpsichord sonatas and lessons. He wrote vocal music, some of which appears in contemporary collections.

KELWAY (Thomas). English org. and comp., B. about end of 17th century. Org. of Chichester Cath, 1720. D. May 21, 1749.

WORKS.—Evening services in B min., A min., G min. ; Seven services and nine anthems in MS. at Chichester Cath.

The good quality of Kelway's music is attested by the fact that at the present time it is being constantly used in our cathedrals and churches.

KEMBLE (Adelaide), MRS. SARTORIS. English singer and actress, B. 1814. Daughter of Charles Kemble. Appeared first in London as singer. Sang at York Festival, 1835. Travelled in France and Germany. Sang in Italy, 1840. Married Mr. F. Sartoris, 1843. D. Aug., 1879.

Works.—A Week in a French Country House, 1867 ; Records of a Girlhood, 1880.

KEMP (Joseph). English comp., B. Exeter, 1778. S. under W. Jackson. Org. Bristol Cath., 1802. Mus. Bac., Cantab., 1808. Music teacher in London, 1809. Doc. Mus., Cantab., 1809. D. London, May 22, 1824.

Works.—The Jubilee, 1809; The Siege of Isca, 1810; The Crucifixion; Musical Illustrations of the Lady of the Lake, 8vo, 1810; Musical Illustrations of the Beauties of Shakespear; The Vocal Magazine, Edin., 3 vols., 1798, 1800 [edited]; Glees, 2 sets, Lond. [1800-1803]; Twelve songs, collected, and others; Twelve Psalms; Chants, duets, anthems, etc.; New System of Musical Education, n.d., etc.

Some of this composer's anthems are still in vogue, but his compositions otherwise are forgotten. He was one of the first to teach music in large classes.

KEMP (R.) English writer, author of "Directions for Tuning the Alexandre Harmonium." London, 1874.

KENNEDY (Alexander). Scottish violin maker, who flourished about 1700-1786, and produced good copies. John, his son, flourished 1730-1816, and Thomas, his grandson, 1784-1870, both made instruments of good quality. London was the headquarters of this family.

KENNEDY (David). Scottish vocalist, B. Perth, April 15, 1825. He received no regular instruction in singing, but was a precentor and teacher for some time in Edinburgh. He first made himself known through popular concerts which he gave originally in Edinburgh, but afterwards in most of the larger towns in Scotland. Latterly Mr. Kennedy has sung in Africa, New Zealand, America, and London, in all of which places he has met with extraordinary success. His name is a household one in Scotland, where his "Nicht wi' Burns" entertainment is regarded as a most characteristic example of Scotch concert-giving. His voice is in quality a tenor, merging on barytone, with a good register, but the main excellence of his singing lies in the correct expression with which he delivers those Songs which are peculiarly Scotch.

KENNEDY (Rev. Rann, M.A.). English writer, B. 1773. D. Birmingham, Jan. 2, 1851. Author of "Thoughts on the Music and Words of Psalmody, as at present in use among the members of the Church of England," Lond., 8vo, 1821. "A Church of England Psalm Book," 1821. Poems, and other works. He was incumbent of S. Paul's Chap., Birmingham.

KENNEY (Charles Lamb). English playwright and writer. D. London, Aug. 25, 1881. Author of "Memoir of Michael William Balfe," Lond., 8vo, 1876. He was also a musical critic and barrister-at-law.

KENT (James). English org. and comp., B. Winchester, March 13, 1700. Chor. Winchester Cath. under V. Richardson. Chor. Chap. Roy. under Croft. Org. of Par. Ch. of Finedon, Northampton. Org. Trinity Coll., Camb., till 1737. Org. Winchester Cath., 1737-1774. D. Winchester, May 6, 1776.

Works.—Services in C and D. *Anthems:* Twelve Anthems, v. 1, 1773; Eight Anthems, with Morning and Evening Service, in C, v. 2, ed. by Corfe.

"In his cathedral music he followed the style of Dr. Croft, though his compositions are less elaborate, and his melodies more free from divisions, and of a more modern cast than those of his master."—*Hogarth*. Most of his anthems are published by Messrs. Novello, to which circumstance is partly due their continued popularity among choirmasters.

KERBUSCH (Leo). German comp., B. near Düsseldorf, 1828. S. under Spohr, E. F. Richter, etc. Mus. Doc., Dublin, 1869 (accumulated degrees). Author of "Hints to performers on musical instruments played by the touch of the hand," Lond. [1871]. Songs, part-songs, Pf. music, etc.

KERL (Johann Caspar). German comp., B. 1628. S. under Carissimi and Froberger. Org. to Elector of Bavaria. D. Munich, Feb. 13, 1693.

Works.—Operas. Canzonets. Sonatas for organ, etc.

Kerl was famed in his day for his powers on the organ, and some of his music has come down to the present time in the form of arranged organ music.

KERR (Mrs. Alexander). English song-writer who flourished about the middle or first half of the present century. She wrote a number of sentimental ballads, and a few part-songs, words and music. Among the former may be named, "Melodies, the Words written and the Music composed by Mrs. Alexander Kerr," Lond., D'Almaine [1831].

KESSLER (Josef Christoph). Bohemian pianist and comp., B. Augsburg, Aug. 26, 1800. D. Vienna, Jan. 13, 1872. Comp. music for Pf., etc.

KETTEN (Henri). Hungarian pianist and comp., B. Baja, March 25, 1848. S. Paris Cons. under Marmontel, Halévy, and Reber. Has performed in Europe, Britain, Australia, etc. D. Paris, March 31, 1883.

Ketten has composed a number of interesting pieces for his instrument, as well as songs. His style of playing was mentioned with much respect by writers of all ranks.

KETTENUS (Aloys). Belgian violinist and comp., B. Verviers, Feb. 22, 1823. Public performer and comp. of merit.

KETTERER (Eugene). French pianist and comp., B. Rouen, 1831. S. Paris Cons. Gained 2nd prize for sol-feggio. D. Paris, Dec., 1870.

WORKS.—*Pianoforte music:* Mazurka, op. 2; Redowa, op. 3; Caprice, op. 4; March, op. 5; Caprice, op. 7; Barcarolle écossaise, op. 10; Romance, op. 13; Valse-caprice, op. 14; Pastorale, op. 17; Grand Galop, op. 24; Mazurka, op. 40; Caprice Bohémien, op. 46; Caprices, marches, fantasias, dances, etc., opp. 50 to 290; Nocturne, op. 39; Elegie à la Memoire de F Chopin, op. 57.

The majority of the pieces written by this composer are of a graceful character, brilliant at times, but never vulgarly showy. Some of them have attained enormous popularity.

KETTLE (Charles Edward). English org. and comp., B. Bury St. Edmund's, Mar., 1833. Org. successively at S. Margaret's, Plumstead; S. Nicholas (Old Parish Ch.), Plumstead; Holy Trinity Ch., Woolwich; Hove Parish Ch.; Queen Sq., Congregational Ch., Brighton.

WORKS.—Hymn Tunes published in Bristol **Tune Book**; Bickersteth's Hymnal Companion; Sunday School Hymns (Weekes); Songs of the Church; Northern Psalter; Chants Ancient and Modern. Kettle's Tune Book, containing 700 original Tunes and Chants; Saviour and Friend, service of Song. *Songs:* Ben Brace; The Organist; Per mare, per terram; Peace in Heaven; Saturday night at sea; Soldier's funeral; Winds errand; In the Dawning; The Voice of Music. *Organ:* Marche solenelle; Marche nuptiale; Marche aux bannières; Marche des chantres; Offertoire in E flat; Postlude in C. Three Operas—"Amelie," "Her mina," "The Water Cure;" also numerous songs and Pf. pieces not yet published.

KEY (Joseph), of Nuneaton. English church comp. who flourished in the first half of the present century. He wrote a great number of meritorious anthems, marches for org., etc.

KIALLMARK (G.) Swedish comp. and violinist, B. Lynn Regis, 1781. S. under Barthelemon and Spagnoletti. Violinist in various orchestras, and teacher. D. (?)

WORKS.—Music for Pf. and vn. *Songs:* All alone; Autumn noons; Banks of the Rhine; Bound where thou wilt; Cupid and Hymen; Fair Haidee; Fare thee well; Farewell, bright star; Helen's Farewell; Him I love; Maid of Athens; Now each tie; O come, my love; etc., etc. Part-songs. These songs are of considerable merit, though now forgotten.

KIEL (Friedrich). German comp., B. Puderbach-on-the-Lahn, Oct. 7, 1821. S. under Schulz, 1835, and Kummer & Dehn. Prof. of comp. at the Hochschule für Musik, Berlin. D. Berlin, Sept. 14, 1885.

WORKS.—Op. 1. Fifteen Canons for Pf.; op. 5. Three romances for Pf.; op. 8. Melodies for Pf.; op. 11. Reisebilder for Pf., vn., and 'cello; op. 12. Three pieces for 'cello and Pf. ; op. 18. Ten pieces for Pf. ; op. 20. Requiem, 1862 ; op. 21. Three pieces for Pf. ; op. 24. Trio for Pf., vn., and 'cello ; op. 26. Two Caprices for Pf. ; op. 31. Twelve Lieder for voice and Pf. ; op. 32. Two Motets ; op. 35. Sonata for Pf. and vn. ; op. 36. Three gigues for Pf. ; op. 37. Variations for Pf. and vn. ; op. 38. Souvenirs de Voyage for Pf. ; op. 41. Do. ; op. 42. Humoresques for Pf. duet ; op. 45. Three valses for Pf. ; op. 63. Two Songs of Novalis for voice, chorus, and orch. ; op. 64. Six Lieder ; op. 65. Two trios for Pf., vn., and 'cello ; op. 66. Ländler for Pf. duet ; op. 67. Sonata for Pf. and alto ; op. 69. Three romances for Pf. and alto ; op. 70. Three pieces for Pf. and vn. Christus, oratorio, 1874. Stabat Mater. Quartet for Pf. and strings in A flat. Masses, Psalms, Motets, etc.

Kiel held a distinguished position in Germany as a violinist and composer. His works have been produced with success in many parts of Europe, while a few of them have found their way to Britain and America. "Christus" is a work of much merit.

KIESEWETTER (Raphael Georg, Edler von Weisenbrunn). Austrian writer, B. Holleschau, Moravia, Aug. 29, 1773. D. Baden, near Vienna, Jan. 1, 1850.

WORKS.—Ueber die Musik der neueren Griechen, nebst freien Gedanken über altegyptische und altgriechische Music, Leipzig, 1838 ; Guido von Arezzo, Sein Leben und Wirken, 1840 ; Schicksale u. Beschaffenheit des weltlichen Gesanges, 1841 ; Die Musik der Araber, nach Originalquellen dargestellt, Mit einem Vorworte vondem Freih. v. Hammer-Purgstall, 1842 ; Geschichte der Europäisch-abendländischen oder unserer heutigen Musik, Darstellung ihres Ursprungs, ihres Wachsthums und ihrer stufenweisen Entwickelung ; von dem ersten Jahrhundert des Christenthums bis auf unsere Zeit, 1846. Der neuen Aristoxener zerstreute Aufsätze über das Irrige der musikal. Arithmetik u. das Eitle ihrer Temperaturrechnungen, 1846.

The whole of the above works on musical history and theory are now among the standard authorities on the various topics of which they treat. No. 5 was translated into English by Robert Müller, under the title of "History of the Modern Music of Western Europe, with Examples." 8vo, 1848.

KILNER (Thomas). English writer and org. Author of Manual of Psalmody and Chanting, 1850 ; Pocket Chant Book, 8vo, 1850 ; Jottings about Choral and Congregational Services, Organs and Organists, Gregorians, Benches, and Chairs, etc. London, 8vo, 1872 ; second ed., 1873. Numerous pieces of organ music, etc.

KIMBALL (Horace E.) American org. and writer, author of New Method for Reed Organ, Cleveland, n.d. ; Organ Voluntaries, 2 vols., Cleveland, n.d.

KIMBALL (Jacob). American psalmodist, resided at Topsfield, Mass., and published in 1793, "The Rural Harmony."

KIND (Johann Friedrich). German poet, B. Leipzig, Mar. 4, 1768. D. Dresden, June 25, 1843.

Wrote book of Weber's "Der Freischütz."

KINDERMANN (Johann Erasmus). German org. and comp., B. Nuremberg, March 29, 1616. D. Nuremberg, April 14, 1655. Comp. org. and vocal music.

KING (Alfred). English org. and comp., B. Shelby, Essex, April 24, 1837. Org. at Brighton, 1865. F. C. O., 1868. Mus. Bac., Oxon., 1872. The Epiphany, oratorio, for degree of Mus. Doc. Licentiate of Music, Trin. Coll., London. Org. to Brighton Corporation, 1878. Cond. of Brighton Festival Choir. Hon. Local Examiner to Royal Coll. of Music, 1883-86. Comp. a Magnificat for Festal use, anthems, part-songs, etc.

KING (Charles). English comp. and org., B. Bury-St.-Edmunds. 1687. Chor. in S. Paul's under Dr. Blow and Jeremiah Clark. Married to sister of J. Clark. Almoner and Master of Chor., S. Paul's Cath., 1707. Org. of S. Benet Fink, Lond, 1708. Vicar-choral, S. Paul's, 1730. D. London, March 17, 1748.

WORKS.—Services in F, C, D, and B flat. *Anthems*: Rejoice in the Lord; Hear, O Lord; O pray for the peace of Jerusalem; Unto thee, O Lord; Wherewithal shall a young man learn.

"King's services have been much censured; but as they are in constant use in every cathedral in England and Ireland, this is an incontestable proof of merit, and silences all criticism."—*Rimbault*.

KING (James). English writer and comp. Author of "An Introduction to the Theory and Practice of Singing." Lond., fo. n.d. "Collection of Glees, Madrigals, etc," Lond. [1839].

KING (Julie Rive). American pianist and comp., B. Cincinnati, O., 1856. Received her first instructions from her mother, and afterwards S. in New York city with Wm. Mason, S.B. Mills, De Korbay, and Pruckner. Spent years in Europe studying with Blassman and Kischpieter of Dresden, and Liszt at Weimar. She has written a large number of compositions for the piano, many of which are to be found in the repertoire of native and foreign artists.

Madame King is the greatest artist of her sex in America, and has appeared with every musical organization of note in the United States and Canada, appearing as the special attraction. Was a charter member of the American College of Musicians. Her reputation in Europe is as assured as that accorded to her by the Press of her own country.

KING (Matthew Peter). English comp., B. London, 1773. S. under C. F. Horn. Teacher and musical director in London. D. London, January, 1823.

WORKS.—Sonatas for Pf., opp. 1, 2, 5, 14; Rondos, opp. 13, 22; Quintet for Pf. flute, vn., tenor, and 'cello, op. 16; Divertissement for Pf., op. 24. The Intercession, oratorio, 1817. (This contains the celebrated song, "Eve's Lamentation.") *Music of Dramas*: Matrimony, 1804; The Invisible Girl, 1806; False Alarms (with Braham), 1807; One o'Clock, or The Wood Demon, Lewis (with Kelly), 1807; Ella Rosenberg, 1807; Up all Night; or, the Smuggler's Cave, 1809; Plots, 1810; Oh this Love, 1810; The Americans (with Braham), 1811; Timour the Tartar, 1811; The Fisherman's Hut (with Davy), 1819; The Magicians (with Braham). The Harmonist, a Collection of Glees and Madrigals, from the Classic Poets [1814]. A General Treatise on Music, particularly on Harmony or Thorough-Bass, and its application in Composition, Lond., 1800. Introduction to the Theory and Practice of Singing at First Sight, 1806. Part-songs; Duets, as "The Minute Gun at Sea"; Songs, etc.

The musical dramas which King, in conjunction with other English composers, set before the public of his day are totally different from the operas which now claim attention from musical amateurs. In King's operas there is no sustained interest in the music when taken by itself, as the whole development of the plot is revealed in the libretto alone, the ballads and concerted vocal pieces strewn throughout being merely subsidiary episodes of an unconnected nature. His music was of considerable dramatic power, and many of his melodies are unmatched for grace and beauty, in the whole range of English music.

KING (Oliver). English comp. and pianist, B. London, 1855. Articled to J. Barnby, and was his assistant at St. Anne's, Soho, 1871-1874. S. Pf. under W. H. Holmes. S. Leipzig Cons. under Richter, Reinecke, and Paul, 1874-77. Pianist to H. R. H. the Princess Louise, 1879. Went to Canada in that capacity till 1883. Gave concerts in U. S. and Canada during same time. Now musical director of St. Marylebone Parish Ch.

WORKS.—Night, symphony for orch.; Concert-overture, Among the Pines (Philharmonic Soc. prize, 1883); Concerto for Pf. and orch. (Brinsmead prize, 1885). *Pianoforte*: Legende; Berceuse; Barcarolle; Nocturne; Gavotte; Ballade; 3 Duets in Canon form; Romance; Mazurka; Idylle; Moriska; Valses, etc. *Organ*: Preludes; Fantasias; Offertoires. Harmonium and violin music. *Vocal*: Te Deum, Jubilate, etc., in D; Album of duets for soprano and alto. Part-songs—Peacefully Slumber; The Curfew; Slumber on, Baby Dear. Songs—When the wintry wind is blowing; For me; Israfel; Twilight Fancies; Hush.

KING (Robert). English comp., B. about middle of the 17th century. Musician in band of William and Mary, and Queen Anne. Graduated at Cambridge, 1696. D. after 1711.

WORKS.—Music in The Banquet of Musick, 1688; Choice Ayres, Songs, and Dialogues, 1684; Comes Amoris, 1687-93. Music to Shadwell's Ode on St. Cecilia's Day, 1690. "Once more 'tis Born," Ode on Earl of Exeter, 1693. Songs for 1, 2, and 3 voices composed to a Thorough Basse, for ye organ or harpsichord," Lond., 4to, n. d.

KING (William). English org. and comp., B. 1624. Chor. Magdalen Coll., Oxford, 1648. B.A., 1649. Chaplain of Magdalen Coll., 1650-4. Probationer-fellow of All Soul's Coll., 1654. Org. of New Coll., Oxford, 1664. D. Oxford, Nov., 1680.

Wrote a Service in B flat, Anthems, etc., and "Poems of Mr. Cowley, and others, composed into Songs and Ayres," 1668.

KIRBYE (George). English comp. of latter half of the 16th century. One of the ten composers who harmonized Este's Psalms, 1592. He composed the madrigal for 6 voices in the "Triumphs of Oriana," entitled "Bright Phœbus," and published "The First Set of Madrigals to 4, 5, and 6 voyces," Lond., 1594. Biography unknown.

KIRCHER (Athanasius). German writer and Jesuit, B. 1602, near Fulda. D. Rome, Nov. 1680.

WORKS.—Musurgia universalis sive ars magna consoni et dissoni; Romæ, 2 v., fo., 1650. Phonurgia nova sive conjugium mechan-phys, artis et naturae paranympha phonosophia, fo., 1673. Numerous other works of topography, etc.

The first work above mentioned is becoming very scarce, and is a most curious contribution to music-lore. Its practical value is little, although suggestions of facts which have been now adopted were mooted in this treatise.

KIRCHNER (Theodor). German org. and comp., B. Neukirchen, near Chemnitz, 1824. S. at Leipzig Cons. Org. at Winterthur. Cond. and teacher at Zurich, 1862-75. Director of Music School at Wurzburg, 1875. Teacher in Leipzig.

WORKS.—Ten pieces for Pf., op. 2; Mädchenlieder for soprano voice and Pf., op. 3; Four lieder, voice and Pf., op. 4; Album Leaves, 9 pieces for Pf., op. 7; Scherzo in A for Pf., op. 8; Sixteen Preludes for Pf., 2 books, op. 9; Seven Songs without words, op. 13; Fantasiestücke, 3 books, op. 14; Quartet for strings, op. 20; Still und bewegt, 8 pieces for Pf., op. 24; Nachtstücke, op. 25; Album for Pf., op. 26; Caprice for Pf., op. 27; Nocturne for Pf., op. 28; Aus meinem Skizzenbuche, Pf., op. 29; Study and Recreation, 4 books, op. 30; Im Zwielicht, lieder, op. 31; Four Elegies, Pf., op. 37; Dorfgeschichten, 14 pieces for Pf., op. 39; Verwelhte Blätter, Pf., 3 books, op. 41; Seven Mazurkas for Pf., op. 42; Blumen zum Strauss, 4 books, op. 44; Six pieces for Pf., op. 45; Thirty Kinder und Künstler-Tänze, op. 46. Miscellaneous songs, Pf. pieces, a serenade, etc.

Kirchner is one of the most renowned followers of Robert Schumann in the domain of Pianoforte music. His music is beautiful in every sense of the word, and at times rises to a considerable height of inspiration.

KIRKMAN. English firm of Pianoforte makers, founded in London about the middle of the 18th century by Jacob Kirkmann, a German. The firm deals extensively at the present time in instruments of much excellence.

KIRKMAN (Mrs. Joseph). English authoress, writer of "A Practical Analysis of the Elementary Principles of Harmony," Lond., 1845, 4to.

KIRNBERGER (Johann Philip). German writer, B. Saalfeld, April 24, 1721. Chapel-master to Princess Amalie, at Berlin. D. Berlin, July 27, 1783.

WORKS.—Die Wahren Grundsätze zum Gebrauch der Harmonie. Berlin, 4to, 1773; Die Kunst des Reinen, Satzes in Musik, Berlin, 3 vols., 4to, 1774-79; Grundsätze des Generalbasses als arste Linein zur Composition, n.d., 4to; Organ fugues, etc.

KISTNER. German music-publishing firm, established in Leipzig about 1823. Publish editions of works by Mendelssohn, Schumann, Chopin, Moscheles, etc.

KITCHINER (William). English physician and writer, B. London, 1775. Educated at Eton. Physician in London. D. London, Feb. 26, 1827.

WORKS.—The Cook's Oracle ; Art of Invigorating and Prolonging Life ; The Economy of the Eyes; The Traveller's Oracle. Ivanhoe ; or, the Knight Templars, musical drama. The Loyal and National Songs of England, for one, two, and three voices, selected from original manuscripts and early printed copies in the Library of William Kitchiner, M.D., Lond., fo., 1823. The Sea Songs of England, etc., Lond., fo., 1823. Amatory and Anacreontic Songs Set to Music, Lond., 8vo, n.d. The Sea Songs of Charles Dibdin, with a Memoir of his Life and Writings, Lond., 4to, 1824. Observations on Vocal Music, Lond., 12mo, 1821. Glees, songs, etc.

This celebrated epicure and musician has immortalized himself in two productions, namely, "The Cook's Oracle," and "Vocal Music." In both of these works he shows that he was an original thinker. His music is not fated to descend to posterity, and scarcely gratified his contemporaries. His culinary precepts are, however, worthy of consideration in these days of reform.

KITTEL (Johann Christian). German org. and comp., B. Erfurt, Feb. 18, 1732. S. under J. S. Bach. Org. at Langelsalza, &c. D. Erfurt, May 9, 1809.

WORKS.—Organ sonatas, preludes, and fugues ; Practical Organ School ; Pf. music. Vierstimmige Chorale mit Vorsfielen, Altona, 1803.

KITTL (Johann Friedrich). Bohemian comp., B. Worlik, May 8, 1806, D. Lissa, July 20, 1868, was a composer of Pf. and vocal music of merit.

KJERULF (Halfdan). Swedish comp., B. Sept. 17, 1815. D. Aug. 11, 1868. Comp. instrumental music, songs, etc.

KLAUSER (Karl). German comp. and teacher, B. St. Petersburg, Aug. 24, 1823. Since 1850 he has resided in the U.S. of America ; five years in New York, and twenty-six years in Farmington, Connecticut, as musical director in a prominent young-ladies' school. He has the reputation of being a thorough musical scholar, and has done much to further musical art in the U.S. by his unswerving fidelity to the highest ideal in music, and may be considered as one of the founders or builders of an American musical audience, having had under his instruction over 1500 pupils. Klauser has not published any original compositions, but many transcriptions for Piano from orchestral scores of the musical classics. His critical editions of the Pf. works of Beethoven, Mozart, Chopin, Mendelssohn, Schumann, etc., belong to the best, and have the claim of priority over all similar editions, as Cotta's, Peter's, Bülow's, Klindworth's, etc. In addition to these revised editions of classics he has also edited, fingered and accentuated, more than 1000 of the best pieces of salon Pf. music. by composers ranging from Field to Moszkowski.

It is Mr. Klauser's plan to exemplify his teachings by the illustration of the most eminent artists. The number of concerts given solely for the benefit of his pupils amount to over 120. Among the performers who have appeared at such rehearsals may be named Rubinstein, Bülow. Damrosch, Theo. Thomas, S. B. Mills, Mary Krebs, A. Mehlig, Ernst Perabo, and others, so that the Educational means put in practice may be properly described as of the highest possible nature.

KLAUSS (Joseph). German comp. and org., B. Seelendorf, March 27, 1775. D. March, 1834. Comp. of org., Pf., and vocal music.

KLEIN (Bernhard). German comp., B. Cologne, March 6, 1793. S. under Cherubini. Director of Music at Berlin University. Teacher of Singing at Berlin Hochschüle. D. Berlin, Sept. 9, 1832.

WORKS.—Mass, 1816. *Oratorios:* Job, 1820 ; Dido, 1823 ; Jephthah, 1828 ; David, Halle, 1830 ; Hiob, cantata ; Salve Regina. Four songs, op. 2 ; Sonatas for Pf., F min., op. 5 ; C, op. 7 ; Fantasia for Pf. in A flat, op. 8 ; Variations for Pf. in E flat, op. 9. Ave Maria ; masses ; numerous songs ; etc.

KLEINMICHEL (Richard). German comp. and pianist. B. Posen, Dec. 31, 1846. Teacher in Hamburg. Has comp. Pf. music in variety, as Aquarellen, op. 12 ; Five Pieces, op. 23 ; Six Sonatinas, op. 43 ; etc.

KLENGEL (August Alexander). German pianist and comp., B. Dresden, Jan. 29, 1784. D. Dresden, Nov. 1852. Court org. at Dresden. Comp.

Sonatas, rondos, polonaises, variations, fantasias for Pf. Grand Polonaise for Pf. and orch., op. 35; Trio for Pf., vn., and 'cello, op. 36. Canons and fugues for Pf., etc.

KLINDWORTH (Carl). German comp. and pianist, B. Hanover, Sept. 25, 1830. Operatic cond., 1847-49. Teacher in Hanover, 1849-50. S. under Liszt at Weimar, 1850. Teacher and concert-giver in London, 1854-68. Prof. of Pf. in Moscow Cons., 1868.

Klindworth is noted as a skilful arranger of large works for the Pf. Among the composers whom he has arranged may be named Wagner, Schubert, Chopin, Liszt, etc. His edition of Chopin is famous.

KLINGEMANN (Carl). German writer and poet, chiefly worthy of notice here as author of songs which have been set by Mendelssohn. B. Limmer, 1798. D. London, 1862.

KLOSE (F. J.). English(?) writer, B. London, 1790. D. London, March 8, 1830. Author of "Practical Hints for acquiring Thorough Bass," Lond., 8vo, 1822. Another Klosé has written a standard practical work on the Clarionet.

KLOSS (Karl Johann C.). German org. and comp., B. Mohrungen, 1792. D. Riga, 1853. Comp. org. music, songs, Pf. music, etc.

KLOZ (Matthias). German violin-maker who worked in the Tyrol about 1670-1696. He was a pupil of Stainer, and produced instruments of good quality. His son, SEBASTIAN, is, however, the greater of the two. His instruments date into the 18th century, and are better formed, better toned, and in better preservation than those of Matthias.

KLUGHARDT (August). German comp. and cond., B. Köthen, 1847. S. at Dresden. Chapel-master at Neustrelitz, 1873. Writer of Operas : Iwein ; Gudrun, 1883 ; Overtures ; Pf. music, songs, etc.

KNAPP (William). English comp., B. Poole, 1698. Was parish clerk of Poole. D. Poole, 1768. He published "A Sett of New Psalms and Anthems, in 4 parts, and an Introduction to Psalmody," 4th ed., 1750. "New Church Melody, being a Set of Anthems, Psalms, Hymns, etc. in 4 parts; with an Imploration wrote by Charles I. during his captivity in Carisbrook Castle," 5th ed., 1764.

KNAPTON (Philip). English pianist and comp., B. York, 1788. S. under Hague at Camb. Teacher in York. D. June 20, 1833. He comp. Overtures for orch., Concertos for Pf. and orch., Sonatas for Pf., Arrangements for Pf., Songs, Part-songs, etc. The whole of his works are forgotten, save perhaps, his Pf. arrangement of "Caller Herrin'," and the song "There be none of Beauty's daughters."

KNECHT (Justin Heinrich). German comp. and writer, B. Biberach, Swabia, Sept. 30, 1752. Prof. of literature at Biberach. Operatic cond. at Stuttgart, 1807. D. Biberach, Dec. 11, 1817.

WORKS.—School for the Organ ; Theoretical works ; Psalms ; Cantatas ; Motets ; Sonatas, etc. for org. and Pf.

This composer is best known in Britain by his Psalms, a number of which have been introduced into several of our more important collections.

KNIGHT (Joseph Philip). English song-writer, B. Bradford-on-Avon, July 26, 1812. S. under Corfe of Bristol Cath. Vicar of S. Agnes in the Scilly Isles. Retired latterly from the ministry.

WORKS.—*Songs*: A little bird told me ; All on the Summer Sea ; Angel land ; Beauty's but a Summer day ; Beautiful Venice ; Bells of Venice ; Breathe not her name ; Beautiful Spirit ; Calm and Storm ; Come roam to the greenwood ; Cara Macree ; Daughter of the snow ; Down beneath the waves ; Days gone bye ; Ellen and Patrick ; England, farewell ; Farewell to thee, sweet Venice ; Farewell my native land ; Grecian daughter ; Gentle words ; Homeward ; I would I were a child again ; I love the bright and smiling Spring ; the Launch ; Love that blooms for ever ; Miniature, the ; Music, sweet music ; Merry 'tis now ; Merry hearts ;

May time; My mother's song; Old green lane; Old man's grave; O, swift we go; O give me back the flower; Pale rose the moon; Parting song; Pretty dove; Rocked in the cradle of the deep; Say, what shall my song be; She would not know me; Spring's first violet; Spell-wove song; Sleep and the past; Saint David's bells; She wore a wreath of roses; There was a time; Though thou art cold; The Traveller; They blessed her at parting; Thou wert not there; Tree of the forest; 'Twas the long-expected signal; The merry muleteer; The old songs we sang; 'Tis sweet to sail on the silver sea; The veteran; What pleasant sounds; World is a fairy ring; Wilt thou forget me; When all those friends; Why chime the bells. Duets, etc.

The most of this composer's songs were popular in their day, but ' Rocked in the cradle of the deep," and " She wore a wreath of roses," will outlive his other productions.

KNORR (Julius). German comp., pianist, and writer, B. Leipzig, Sept. 22, 1807. D. there, June 17, 1861. Was teacher and critic in Leipzig. Author of Methods for the Pf., Pf. music, etc.

KNYVETT (Charles). English org. and vocalist, B. Feb., 1752. Sang at Handel Commemoration, 1784. Do. Concerts of Ancient Music. Gent. of Chap. Roy., 1786. Estab., with S. Harrison, the Vocal Concerts, 1791-94. Org. of Chap. Roy., 1796. D. London, Jan. 19, 1822.

KNYVETT (Charles). English org. and comp., eldest son of above, B. 1773. S. under Parsons and Webb. Revived the Vocal Concerts with W. Knyvett, Greatorex, and Bartleman. Org. of St. George's, Hanover Square, 1802, D. Nov. 2, 1852.

Wrote Glees, etc., for "Re-Unions" of the Prince of Wales, Lond., 1800. Six Airs harmonized. Selection of Psalm Tunes sung at St. George's, Hanover Square, 1823.

KNYVETT (Deborah), née TRAVIS. English singer, second wife of William Knyvett, B. Shaw, near Oldham. S. under Greatorex. Sang at Concerts of Ancient Music, 1813. Sang at principal London concerts, 1815-43. Married W. Knyvett, 1826. D. Feb. 10, 1876.

KNYVETT (William). English singer and comp., B. April 21, 1779. Youngest son of Charles Knyvett, the elder. Sang at Concerts of Ancient Music, 1788. Principal alto, do, 1795. Gent. of Chap. Roy., 1797. Lay-vicar of Westminster Abbey. Comp. to Chap. Roy. Sang at London and Provincial concerts. Cond. of Concerts of Ancient Music, 1832-40. D. Ryde, Nov. 17, 1856.

Wrote anthems, glees, songs, etc., but was best known in his day as a vocalist of repute.

KOCH (Heinrich Christoph). German writer, B. Rudolstadt, 1749. D. 1816. Author of "Musikalisches Lexicon, welches die Theoretische und Practische Tonkunst Encyclopædisch bearbeitet..." Frankfort, 1802, 8vo; "Handbuch bei dem Studium der Harmonie," Leipzig, 1811, etc.

KÖCHEL (Ludwig, Ritter von). German musician and scientific writer, B. Stein, Jan. 14, 1800. D. Vienna, June 3, 1877. Compiler of "Chronologischthematisches Verzeichniss sämmtlicher Tonwerke W. A. Mozart's." Leipzig, 1862 (Chronological and Thematical Catalogue of Mozart's Works).

KOEMPEL (August). German violinist, B. Brückenau, Aug. 15, 1831. S. under Spohr, David, and Joachim. Played successfully in Germany, Paris, etc.

KOETTLITZ (Adolf). German comp., B. Treves, Sept. 27, 1820. D. Oct. 26, 1860. Writer of lieder, string quartets, Pf. music, etc.

KÖHLER (Ludwig). German comp., writer, and pianist, B. Brunswick, Sept. 5, 1820. S. under Seyfried, Sechter, etc. Teacher in Königsberg since 1846.

WORKS.—Systematische Lehrmethode für Klavierspiel und Musik, theoretisch und praktisch dargelet, 1872. Studies for Pf., numerous numbers. Mechanische und Technische Klavier-Studien, als tägliche Uebungen für jede Bildungsstufe. Transcriptions from operas etc. to the number of about 300.

Köhler's pianoforte studies are famous over the whole musical world, and have proved a never-failing source of instruction and delight to musicians of all grades.

KOLBE (Oscar). German writer and comp., B. Berlin, Aug. 10, 1836. Author of a number of theoretical works and writings on music; also, John the Baptist, an oratorio, 1872; etc.

KOLLMANN (August Friedrich Carl). German org., comp., and writer, B. Engelbostel, Hanover, 1756. Org. in German chap. in London. D. Lond., Nov. 1824.

WORKS.—An Essay on Musical Harmony, Lond., fo., 1796. An Essay on Practical Musical Composition, Lond., fo., 1799. A Practical Guide to Thorough-bass, Lond., fo., 1801; 2nd ed., 1807. A New Theory of Music, according to a Complete and Natural System of that Science, Lond., fo., 1806. The First Beginning on the Pianoforte, op. 5, n. d. Vindication of a Passage in his Practical Guide to Thorough-bass against an advertisement of Mr. M. P. King, Lond., 1801. Remarks on what Mr. J. B. Logier calls his New System, Lond., 1824. An Introduction to the Art of Preluding and Extemporizing in Six Lessons for the Harpsichord or Harp, Lond., ob. 4to, n. d.

KONTSKI (Antoine de). Austrian pianist and comp., B. Cracow, 1817. Teacher in London.

WORKS.—Music for Pf., chiefly of the drawing-room type. Songs. Other brothers, CHARLES (1815-1867), APOLLINAIRE (1825-1879), and STANISLAS (1820).

KOSSAK (Dr. Ernst). German musical critic, B. at Marienwerder, Aug. 4, 1814. D. Berlin, Jan. 3, 1880.

KOSSMALY (Karl). German writer and comp., B. Breslau, July 27, 1812. Writer of many part-songs, Pf. pieces, songs, writings on music, etc.

KOTZELUCH (Leopold). Bohemian org. and comp., B. Wellbarn, Bohemia, 1784. S. at Prague. Pf. teacher to the Archduchess Elizabeth, 1778. Org. to Leopold II. at Prague, 1792. D. Vienna, May 7, 1818.

WORKS.—Op. 1. Concerto for Pf. and orch; op. 2. Sonata for Pf.; op. 3. Trio for Pf., vn., and 'cello; op. 4. Sonata for Pf. duet; op. 5. Sonata for Pf. solo; Sonatas and Trios for Pf., vn., and 'cello, opp. 6, 12, 21, 23, 28, 32, 33, 34, 36, 37, 40, 41, 42, 44, 46, 47, 48, 49, 50, and 52; Sonatas for Pf. solo, opp. 7, 8, 9, 22, 30, 38, 51, 53; Sonatas for Pf. duet, opp. 10, 11, 13, 19, 20. Symphonies for orch., various. String quartets. Operas and Ballets. Songs.

KOTZWARA (Franz). Bohemian comp., B. Prague, about middle of 18th century. Resided for a time in Germany or Holland. Settled in London, 1790. Committed suicide Sept. 2, 1791.

WORKS.—Le Bataille de Prague, for Pf., vn., and 'cello; transcribed for Pf. many times. Sonatas for Pf., vn., and Pf., etc.

KOWALSKI (Henri). French comp. and pianist, B. Paris, 1841. S. under Marmontel and Reber. Travelled in England, Germany, and America. Comp. operas, Pf. and vocal music.

KRAFT (Anton). Bohemian violoncellist and comp., B. Pilsen, Dec. 30, 1752. 'Cellist in Chapel of Prince Eszterházy. Chamber musician to Prince Grassalkowitsch. D. Aug. 28, 1820. Comp. concertos, sonatas, duets, solos, etc., for violoncello.

KRAUSE (Anton). German pianist and comp., B. Geithain, Saxony, Nov. 9, 1834. S. under Spindler, Wieck, and Reissiger; also at Leipzig Cons., 1850-53. Musical Director at Barmen, in succession to Reinecke.

WORKS.—*Pianoforte*: Op. 1. Three Instructive Sonatas; op. 2. Studies; op. 3. Leichte Sonate, 4 hands, in D minor; op. 4. Uebungsstücke; op. 5. Zehn Etuden; op. 6. Serenade, duet; op. 10. Two Sonatinas; op. 12. Three sonatinas; op. 13. Praeludium; op. 15. Zehn (10) Studies; op. 17. Sonata. Other sonatas, studies, etc. *Vocal music:* op. 11. Three Lieder; op. 14. Three Lieder; op. 16. Kyrie and Sanctus for chorus and orch.

Some of the works of this clever writer and pianist are now in use at Leipzig Cons.

KRAUSS (Marie Gabrielle). Austrian soprano vocalist, B. Vienna, Mar. 23, 1842. S. at Vienna Cons. *Début* as Mathilde in "William Tell," July 20, 1860. Has sang in "Der Freischütz," "Don Giovanni," "Tannhäuser," "Lohengrin," "Huguenots," "Trovatore," "Zampa," and other works, and was for many years leading soprano at the Grand Opera, Paris.

KREBS (Johann Ludwig). German org. and comp., B. Buttelstädt, Oct. 10, 1713. S. under his father and J. S. Bach, 1726. Org. at Zwickau, Altenberg, etc. D. Altenberg, 1780.

Comp. of fugues, sonatas, etc., for organ.

KREBS (Karl August). German comp. and teacher, B. Nuremberg, Jan. 16, 1804. S. under Schelble and Seyfried. Teacher at Hamburg, 1827-50. Chap.-master at Dresden, 1850-71. D. Dresden, May, 1880.

KREBS (Marie). German pianist, daughter of above, B. Dresden, Dec. 5, 1851. S. under her father. *Début* at Meissen, 1862. Played in Germany; England, 1864; Italy; France; and America. She is one of the most brilliant and accomplished pianists of the present time. Her execution is perfect and her expression beautiful and faithful.

KREHBIEL (H. E.) American writer, author of "An Account of the Fourth Musical Festival held at Cincinnati, May 18, 19, 20, and 21st, 1880." Cincinnati, 8vo, 1880. "Notes on the Cultivation of Choral Music and the Oratorio Society of New York." N. Y., 1884.

KREJEI (Josef). Bohemian org., director, and comp., B. Milostin, 1822. Director of Prague Cons. Comp. overtures, masses, songs, etc.

KRENN (Franz). Austrian org. and comp., B. Dross, 1816. S. at Vienna under Seyfried. Org., 1844, and Director, 1862, of St. Michael's Cath., Vienna. Comp. masses, string quartets, symphonies, songs, etc.

KRETSCHMER (Edmund). German org. and comp., B. Ostritz, Saxony, Aug. 31, 1830. S. under Otto and Schneider at Dresden. Org. of Dresden Cath., 1854. Court org. and Director of Royal Chap., Dresden, 1863.

WORKS.—*Operas:* Die Folkunger, 1875; Heinrich der Loewe, 1877; Der Verweisener. Part-songs; Organ and chamber music.

KREUTZER (Conradin). German comp., B. Mösskirch, Baden, Nov. 22, 1782. Chorister there. S. medicine for a time at Freiburg, 1799. Teacher in Switzerland, 1799-1804. S. under Albrechtsberger at Vienna. Chap.-master to King of Würtemberg, 1812; to the Prince von Fürstenberg. Director at the Kärnthnerthor Theatre, 1825-40. Do. Josephstädt Theatre, 1833-40. Conductor at Cologne. Conducted the Lower Rhine Festival, 1843. D. Riga, Dec. 14, 1849.

WORKS.—*Operas:* Die Lœcherliche Werbung, 1801; Conradin von Schwaben, 1805; Der Taucher, 1809; Panthea, 1810; Feodora, 1811; Orestes, 1815; Alpen Hütter, 1816; Cordelia, 1819; Libussa, 1822; Die Jungfrau, 1830; Der Baron Luft, 1830; Melusine, 1833; Das Nachlager in Granada, Vienna, 1834; Concertos, sonatas, marches, etc., for various instruments, amounting in all to about op. 70; Lieder und Balladen, etc.

This once popular German composer is fast losing ground, even in his own country, where he is known only by his opera, "Das Nachtlager in Granada," and a few of his songs. In Britain a few of his songs have a feeble vitality, but otherwise he is unknown. His works are all of a moderate standard of merit.

KREUTZER (Leon). French violinist and comp., son of Rudolph Kreutzer, B. Paris, Sept., 1817. D. Vichy, Oct., 1868.

KREUTZER (Rudolph). German violinist and comp., B. Versailles, Nov. 16, 1766. S. under his Father and Stamitz. Violinist in Royal Chap.; and Théâtre Italien, Paris. Travelled in Italy, Germany, and Holland as violinist. Became acquainted with Beethoven, 1798. Prof. of vn. at Paris Cons. Solo-violinist at Paris Opera, in succession to Rode. Violinist to the Emperor, 1806. Cond. of the Academy, 1817-24. Chevalier of Legion of Honour, 1824. D. Geneva, Jan. 6, 1831.

WORKS.—*Operas and Ballets:* La Journée de Marathon, 1793; Flaminius à Corinthe (with Isouard), 1800; Astianax, 1801; Aristippe, 1808; La Mort d'Abel, 1810; Antoine et Cleopatre, ballet, 1809; La Fête de Mars, 1814; L'Oriflamme, 1814; Le Princesse de Babylone, 1815; Les Dieux Rivaux (with Spontini, Berton, etc.), 1816; Le Carnaval de Venise, 1816; La Servante Justifice, 1818; Clari, 1820; Ipsiboé, 1823; Jeanne d'Arc à Orleans, 1790; Paul et Virginie, 1791; Lodoïska, 1791; Charlotte et Werther, 1792; La Franc Breton, 1792; Le Brigand, 1795; Imogene, 1796; Le Siège de Lille, 1793; Le Petit Page, 1795; François I., 1808; Le Camp de Sobieski, 1813; Constance et Théodore, 1813; Le Maitre et le Valet, 1816; Le Negociant de Hambourg, 1821. MS. Operas, Pasticcios, Ballets, etc. Concertos for vn. and orch., No. 1, in G; 2, in A; 3, in E; 4, in C; 5, in A; 6, in E minor; 7, in A; 8, in D minor; 9, in E minor; 10, in D minor; 11, in C; 12, in A; Letter A, in D; B, in E; C, in A; D, in E minor; E, in G; F, in E minor; and G, in D minor. Quartets for 2 vns., tenor, and bass, opp. 1, 2, and 3. Trios for 2 vns. and 'cello, opp. 5, 15, and 16. Forty Studies or Caprices for the Violin.

R. Kreutzer is probably best known as the person to whom Beethoven dedicated his Sonata ("Kreutzer"), op. 47. His violin studies also give him a claim to attention from posterity, as they are among the best for that instrument. His operas are forgotten, and his concertos are the only large works by which he is now represented.

KRIEGER (Adam Philipp). German org. and comp., B. 1634. D. 1666.

KRIEGER (Johann Philipp). German operatic comp., B. Nuremberg, Feb., 26, 1649. D. Feb. 6, 1725.

KRIMALY (Adalbert), or HRIMALY. Bohemian comp., B. Pilsen, June 30, 1842. Has published music for orch. and Pf., songs, part-songs, and an opera. His brother, JOHANN, B. Pilsen, April 13, 1844, is a violinist. S. under Laub, and now teacher in Moscow Cons.

KROMMER (Franz). Austrian comp., B. Kamenitz, Moravia, 1759. D. Vienna, Jan. 8, 1831. Wrote Pf. and chamber music, songs, and part-songs.

KRUG (Diedrich) German pianist and comp., B. Altona, 1845. Comp. of studies, exercises, transcriptions, dances, etc. for the Pf. to the number of 400 pieces. Some of those works are extensively used for teaching purposes.

KRUG (Gustave). German comp. and pianist, B. Hamburg, 1821. Comp. light pieces for Pf., and songs.

KRÜGER (Wilhelm K.). German pianist and comp., B. Stuttgart, 1820. S. under Lindpainter. Prof. of Pf., Stuttgart Cons. D. Stuttgart, June, 1883.

WORKS.—Op. 1. Three Nocturnes romantiques, for Pf. Melodies, Caprices, Studies, Dances, Fantasias, Transcriptions, etc., for Pf., opp. 2-200.

KRUMPHOLZ (Johann Baptist). Bohemian harpist and comp., B. Zlonitz, near Prague, 1745. Drowned (suicide), Paris, 1790. Comp. Sonatas for the Harp, Symphonies, Preludes, etc., six Concertos for harp and orch., songs, etc. His wife, *née* MEYER, B. Metz. Played in London in 1788. Eloped from her husband at Paris, in 1790, and from then till 1802 played chiefly in London. D. London, Nov. 15, 1813.

Krumpholz was a famous harp-player, and composer for his instrument. Some of his works are beautiful creations. His wife was one of the greatest performers of her time.

KÜCHLER (Heinrich). German barytone vocalist, B. Anspach, 1815. Sang in opera, and was held in considerable esteem in Edinburgh, where he held several appointments, and had some repute as a teacher. D. Edinburgh, Nov. 1873.

KÜCKEN (Friedrich Wilhelm). German comp., B. Bleckede, Hanover, Nov. 16, 1810. S. under Sechter and Halévy. Noticed by the Prince of Mecklenburg. Resided in Berlin from 1832. Cond. Sængerfest at S. Gallen and Apenzell, 1843. Court Chap.-master, Würtemberg, 1857. Retired to Schwerin, 1867. D. Schwerin, April 3, 1882.

WORKS.—Die Flucht nach der Schweig," opera. *Songs*: All is still at evening's close; Good night, farewell; Maiden mine; Moorish serenade; Pretty one, come; Hobby horse; Maid of Judah; Trot, trot (Trab, trab), etc. *Part-Songs*: The Rhine; Soldier's love; Good night; The Northman's song; The young musicians; Hie thee, shallop; Rest, dearest, rest; Pf. music, etc.

"By the side of Franz Abt, Kücken was the most popular song-composer of Germany. His productions are melodious, tender, pleasing, and of medium difficulty. They are well-designed for the masses, and among the people his name will long be gratefully remembered. When judging Kücken from a high art standpoint, his songs, of course, are found to lack great depth of sentiment and display of art skill."—*Brainard's Musical World*. Whatever his popularity might have been twenty or thirty years ago, and we are assured it was great, it is certain that his reputation is sadly on the wane. Many of his part-songs, however, are still largely in use, especially among male voice choirs.

KUFFERATH (Hubert Ferdinand). German pianist and comp., B. Mühlheim, June 10, 1808. S. under Mendelssohn, and others. Prof. at Brussels Cons. Comp. Symphonies and Concertos, Reveries, Caprices, Etudes, Capriccios for Pf., Six Lieder von Burns, and other vocal music. The works of this composer are very meritorious.

KÜFFNER (Josef). German pianist and comp., B. Würzburg, March 31, 1776. D. Sept. 8, 1856. Comp. an immense quantity of transcriptions and original works for Pf.

KUHE (Wilhelm). Bohemian pianist, teacher, and comp., B. Prague, Dec. 10, 1823. S. under Tomaschek. Visited England, 1845. Teacher and cond. at Brighton. Has been decorated by the Emperor of Germany, and other sovereigns.

WORKS.—*Pianoforte*: Au bord de la Mer, nocturne; Bacchanale; Dialogue d'Amour; Impromptu in A flat; Serenade Bohemienne; Une Rose sans Epines; War; Bianca; Andante et étude; Etude de Concert. Transcriptions and other works. Songs, etc.

KUHLAU (Friedrich Daniel Rodolph). German pianist and comp., B. Uelzen, Sept. 11, 1786. D. Copenhagen, March 12, 1832.

WORKS.—Sonatas for Pf., opp. 5, 6, 8, 20, 30, 34, 55, 59, etc.; Concertos for Pf. and orch., op. 7, etc.; Lieder for voices and Pf.; Variations, transcriptions, rondos, etc., for Pf.; String quartets and miscellaneous chamber music; Operas and other works.

This once-famous composer is now scarcely recognised save as a writer for the Pf. His fine songs and larger works are alike neglected.

KUHNAU (Johann). German org. and comp., B. Geysing, April, 1667. Cantor of Leipzig, 1684. D. Leipzig, June 25, 1722. Comp. org. music, church music, etc., some of which was published posthumously. Is generally believed to have been the first to give form to the sonata as an independent form. His music is in the strict contrapuntal style carried to such a degree of perfection by Bach and Händel.

KULLAK (Adolf). German writer and comp., B. Messnitz, Feb. 23, 1823. D. Berlin, Dec. 25, 1862. Writer of two works on musical æsthetics, "Das Mustkalischschön," 1858, and "Die Aesthetik des Clavierspiels," 1861. He also wrote a number of Pf. pieces, as Adelaïde, poeme melancolique, op. 19; Reverie pastorale, op. 22; Rhapsodie, op. 25; Nocturne, op. 37; Ballade, op. 38.

KULLAK (Theodor). German comp., pianist, and teacher, B. Krotschin, Sept. 12, 1818. S. under Czerny. Court pianist to the King of Prussia, 1846.

Founded Conservatory of music at Berlin with Stern and Marx, 1851. Established Neue Academie der Tonkunst, 1855. D. Berlin, March 1, 1882.

WORKS.—*Pianoforte*: La Danse des Sylphides, op. 5; Two Morceaux, op. 20; Chant d' Ossian, op. 36; Album Espagnol, Pf., op. 45; Melodies Hongroises, op. 68; Ballade, op. 54; Concerto, Pf. and orch., op. 55; Two Chansonettes, op. 92; Scherzo, op. 96; Impromptus; Octave School for the Pf., etc.

KUMMER (Friedrich August). German comp. and violoncellist, B. Meiningen, Aug. 5, 1797. 'Cellist in Chap.-Royal of Saxony, 1822. Travelled in Germany, Denmark, etc. Teacher in Dresden. D. Dresden, May 22, 1879.

WORKS.—Concerto for 'cello and orch, op. 10; concertino for 'cello and orch., op. 16; Transcriptions and duets, numerous.

Kummer was more noted as a performer than as a composer, few of his works being now in use.

KUMPEL (Wilhelm). German tenor singer and musician, B. Altona. D. April 17, 1880.

KUNKEL (Charles). German comp., pianist, and publisher, B. Sippersfeld, July 22, 1840. Went to America, 1849. S. under his father, Thalberg, and Gottschalk. Publisher and teacher in S. Louis.

KUNKEL (Franz Joseph). German comp. and writer, B. Dieburg, Aug. 20, 1804. D. Frankfort, Dec. 31, 1880. Wrote in periodicals, and comp. for Pf.

KUNKEL (Jacob). German comp., pianist, and music-seller, B. Kleiniedesheim, Oct. 22, 1846. S. under his brother, Charles, Gottschalk, and Tausig. Music-seller in S. Louis with his brother. D. St. Louis, Oct. 16, 1882.

KUSSER. See COUSSER.

KYTE (Francis). English writer, author of "Memoir relating to the Portrait of Handel...." 4to, 1829.

L.

LAAG (Heinrich). German org. and Pf. manufacturer, B. Herford, Westphalia, Feb. 18, 1713. Org. of Ch. of S. Catherine, Osnaburg. D. Oct. 30, 1797, at Osnaburg. Wrote org. and ch. music, songs, etc.

LABARRE (Theodore). French harpist and comp., B. Paris, March 9, 1805. S. under Bochsa and Naderman. S. Paris Cons.: gained first prize for comp., 1823 (with his cantata, "Pyrame et Thisbé"). Appeared in London, 1824. Played in English provinces and in Scotland. Travelled in Europe. Married Mdlle. Lambert, 1837. Cond. of L'Opera Comique, 1847-49. Music-director to Napoleon III. D. Paris, March 9, 1870.

WORKS.—*Operas*: Les Deux Familles, 1831; L'Aspirant de Marine, 1834; La Révolte au Séraie, ballet, 1833; Le Ménétrier, 1845; Method for the Harp; Trio for harp, horn, and bassoon, op. 6. Duets for harp and Pf., opp. 3, 5, 9, 43, 47, 48, 49, 54, 59. Solos, fantasias, and Rondos, for harp, opp. 8, 10, 11, 25, 26, 29, 30, 31, to 36, 39, 40, 46, 50, 51, 56, 60, 70, 72, 73, 75, 77, 82, 90 to 93. Duets for harp and violin (with Beriot). Songs.

LABAT (Jean Baptiste). French writer, org., and comp., B. Verdun, June 17, 1802. S. at Toulouse; and at Paris Cons. under Benoist. Org. at Verdun. D. Lagarosse, Jan. 6, 1875.

WORKS.—Overtures, masses, Pf. music, anthems, and songs. Etudes Philosophiques, et moralis sur l' histoire de la Musique...Paris, 1852, 2 v. Esthetiques des huit modes du plain-chant, 1861.

LABITZKY (Josef). Bohemian bandmaster and comp., B. Schönfeld, near Eger, July 4, 1802. Vnst. at Marienbad and Carlsbad. Cond. of itinerant band. S. under Winter at Munich. Published first dance, 1827. Appeared in London, 1850. Director of music in Carlsbad, D. Carlsbad, Aug. 29, 1881.

WORKS.—*Waltzes:* Homburg vorder Höhe; Rosen-walzer; Der Harfenist; Die Amerikaner; Nordlicht; Palermo; Die Freundschaft; etc., etc. *Galops:* Faniska; Studenten; Durch die Welt; Corsaren; Telegraphen; etc. *Polkas:* Frühlings; Marionetten; Herzpinkerl; Die Ländliche; etc. Mazurkas, quadrilles, marches, etc.

The single dances of Labitzky number from 400 to 500, and were at one time considered as nearly equal to those of Strauss in merit. Some of them are very melodious, but comparatively few, if any, will survive.

LABLACHE (Fanny Wyndham), née WILTON. English contralto vocalist. S. at R. A. M., 1836-7. *Début* at the Lyceum. Sang at H. M. Theatre, etc. Married Frederic Lablache, son of Luigi, and retired from the stage. D. Paris, Sept. 23, 1877. She was a serviceable vocalist and a teacher of much skill.

LABLACHE (Luigi). Italian bass vocalist, B. Naples, Dec. 6, 1794 (1795?) S. Naples Cons from 1806. First appeared in Theatre of S. Carlino, Naples, 1812. Married Mdlle. Teresa Pinotti, 1814. Resided in Sicily, 1814-19. Sang at La Scala, Milan, 1820-3; Vienna, 1823-8; also in Palermo, Turin, Venice and Naples, till 1830. Appeared in London, as "Geronimo" in Cimarosa's "Matrimonio Segreto," March 30, 1830. Sang in Paris, Nov. 4, 1830; Do. Naples, in "Don Pasquale," etc., 1833. Sang in S. Petersburg, 1852. D. Naples, Jan. 23, 1858.

WORKS.—Complete Vocal Method (of which many editions have been printed). Vocal Exercises. Songs, etc.

The vocal powers of Lablache are best described by the two competent critics quoted below:—

"An organ more richly toned or suave than his voice, was never given to mortal. Its real compass was about two octaves, from E to E. In the upper portion of the register four or five of his tones had a power which could make itself heard above any orchestral thunder, or in the midst of any chorus, however gigantic either might be. This remarkable force was not, as in the case of many singers, displayed on all occasions; but it was made to tell in right places...."—*Chorley.* "The singular power and the rich quality of his voice made him to the last the wonder of all who heard him. His compass was not remarkable, but the immense volume of his tone gave to his notes the character of depth much greater than their real pitch, and his perfect command of his resources enabled him to give every variety of effect to his singing. He was not less eminent as an actor than as a vocalist, and he was equally admirable in the representation of tragedy and comedy."—*Sir G. A. Macfarren.*

The mother of Lablache was an Irishwoman, and his son Frederic married Miss F. Wyndham, the vocalist. Thalberg the pianist married one of his daughters.

LABORDE (Count Alexandre Louis J. de). French scientific writer, B. Paris, Sept. 15, 1774. D. 1842. Author of works on Grecian music, the harp, etc. Another writer named LABORDE (Jean Benjamin de), published a work entitled, "Essai sur la Musique Ancienne et Moderne," Paris, 1780, 4 vols., 4to.

LACHNER (Franz). German comp., B. Rain, Bavaria, April 2, 1804. S. at Neuburg and Munich; also under Stadler and Sechter at Vienna, 1823. Subcond. Kärnthnerthor Theatre, Vienna, 1826. Chief cond., do., 1827-34. Cond. of Opera at Mannheim, 1834. Court chapel-master (1836), and musical director at Munich, 1852-65. Retired, 1865.

WORKS.—*Operas:* Lanassa, 1832; Die Burgschaft, 1834; Alidia, Munich, April, 1839; Catarina Cornaro; Benvenuto Cellini, Munich. *Oratorios:* Die Vier Manschen-Alten (Four ages of Man); Moses. *Symphonies:* First, in E flat; Second, in F; Third, in D minor, op. 52 (prize work); Fourth, in E; Fifth, in C minor; Sixth, in D; Seventh, in G minor, op. 100. Twelve Orchestral Overtures. Three Masses. Cantatas. Six Suites for orch., opp. 113, 115, 122, 129, 135, 150. Quintet for strings. Three string quartets, opp. 75, 76, 77. Three trios for Pf., vn., and 'cello· Nonetto for wind instruments. Sonata for Pf. duet, op. 20; Six Pf. pieces, op. 109. Songs, part-songs, and miscellaneous Pf. and chamber music.

Lachner was a friend of Schubert, and was formerly, and is still, held in great respect by his countrymen. His works belong to the period of Spohr rather than to that of Wagner.

LACHNER (Ignaz). German comp. and cond., brother of above. B. Rain, Sept. 11, 1807. S. at Neuburg and at Augsberg music school. Sub.-cond. of opera at Vienna, 1825. Court music-director at Stuttgart, 1831. Sub-music-director at Munich, 1842. Cond. of theatre at Hambrg, 1853. Court chapel-master, Stockholm, 1858. Teacher, etc., in Frankfort-on-the-Maine, 1861.

WORKS.—*Operas*: Der Geisterhurm, 1847; Die Regenbruder, 1849; A symphony; Twelve string quartets; Overtures, ballets, and Pf. music; Songs, etc.

Ignaz Lachner is composed of many fine songs, but his dramatic works do not hold a very high place in public estimation in Germany.

LACHNER (Vincenz). German org. and comp., brother of above, B. Rain, July 19, 1811. S. at Augsburg music school. Org. at Vienna. Court Chap.-master at Mannheim, 1836-73. Visited London, 1842. Has comp. a symphony, chamber music, songs, and part-songs for men's voices. Another brother, THEODOR, B. 1798, was an organist of considerable attainments.

LACHNITH (Ludwig Wenzel). Bohemian comp. and cond., B. Prague, July 7, 1746. D. Paris, Oct. 3, 1820. He comp. L'heureux Divorce, opera, 1785; Eugenie et Linval, do., 1798; Symphonies; Chamber music; Method for the Pf.; Arrangements of several operatic works which had much notoriety in their day on account of their tasteless editing.

LACOMBE (Louis Brouillon). French pianist and comp., B. Bourges, Nov. 26, 1818, D. St. Vaast-la-Hougue, Oct., 1884. Writer of Pf. music.

LACOMBE (Paul). French pianist and comp., B. Carcassone, 1837. S. Paris Cons. Writer of sonatas, studies, fantasias, etc., for Pf.; overtures, etc.

LACROIX (Antoine). French vnst. and comp., B. Remberville, Nancy, 1756. Appeared in Paris, 1780. Travelled in Germany, etc. Music-director at Lübeck. D. Lübeck, 1812.

Comp. sonatas, duets, etc., for vn. and Pf.

LACY (John). English vocalist, B. about the end of the 18th century. S. under Rauzzini at Bath. Appeared in London, Italy, etc., at oratorios and concerts. Married Miss Jackson, vocalist, 1812. Received appointment in Calcutta, 1818. D. (?)

LACY (Mrs.), *née* JACKSON. Wife of above, English vocalist. Appeared in London, April 25, 1798. Married F. Bianchi, 1800. Married to Lacy, 1812. Went with her husband to Calcutta. D. (?)

LACY (Michael Rophino J.) Spanish comp. and violinist., B. Bilbao, July 19, 1795. S. privately, and at Bordeaux and Paris. S. also under R. Kreutzer. Played before Napoleon I., 1804. Appeared in Holland and in London, 1805. Leader at Edinburgh, Dublin, and Liverpool, till 1820. Teacher, etc., in London. D. Pentonville, London, Sept. 20, 1867.

WORKS.—Adaptations of operas for English stage; Songs, and violin and Pf. pieces.

LADURNER (Anton). Austrian pianist and comp., B. in the Tyrol, 1764. D. 1839. Comp. Pf. music, etc.

LAEGEL (Johann Gottfried). German comp., B. Flaessberg, Borna, Dec. 13, 1777. S. under Krebs, junr. S. at Leipzig for the ministry. Music-director at Eisenberg, Géra, etc. D. June 5, 1843. Wrote oratorios, cantatas, part-songs, and songs.

LAFAGE (Juste Adrien Lemoir de). French writer and comp., B. Paris, March 27, 1805. D. Charenton, March 8, 1862.

WORKS.—Nicolai Capuani Compendium Musicale 8vo, 1853; Eloge de Choron, Paris, 8vo, 1843; Séméiologie musicale ou exposé succinct et raisonné des principes élémentaires de la musique, Paris, 8vo, n.d.; Miscellanées Musicales, Paris, 8vo, 1844; Histoire générale de la musique et de la danse, 2 v., 8vo, 1844; Essais de diphthérographie musicale, Paris, 1864; De l'unité tonique et de la fixation d'un diapson universal, 8vo, 1859.

LAFONT (Charles Philippe). French violinist and comp., B. Paris, Dec. 1, 1781. S. under Kreutzer at Paris. First appeared at Hamburg, 1793. Singer at the Theatre Feydean. S. under Rode. Travelled in Europe. Vnst. to Emperor of Russia, 1808-14. Vnst. to Louis XVIII., 1815. Travelled with Herz, 1831-39. D. Tarbes, Aug. 14, 1839.

Comp. six concertos for vn. and orch., 2 operas, fantasias, duets and variations for vn.

LAGET (Paul Pierre Marie Henri). French singer and Prof., Paris Cons., B. Toulouse, Dec. 10, 1821. S. Paris Cons. D. Sept. 15, 1876.

LA GRANGE (Anna). French soprano vocalist, B. Paris, 1825. S. under Bordogni. *Début*, 1842. Sang in Europe, America, 1855 and 1869. Teacher in Paris.

LA HARPE (Jean Francois de). French poet and critic, B. 1739. D. 1803. His name frequently occurs in the musical records of last century. He is chiefly of note, however, as one of the many critics who attacked Gluck in his musical reforms.

LAHEE (Henry). English comp. and org., B. Chelsea, April 11, 1826. Org. of Holy Trinity Ch., Brompton, 1847-74. Teacher, etc.

WORKS.—*Cantatas:* Building of the Ship, 1869; The Blessing of the Children, 1870; The Sleeping Beauty, for female voices. *Anthems:* Grant we beseech thee; And behold a Throne; Now on the first day; Praise the Lord (Harvest). *Concerted Vocal Music:* Hark! how the Birds, Bristol Prize Madrigal, 1869; Hence! Loathed Melancholy, Manchester Prize Glee, 1878; Away to the Hunt, Glasgow Prize Part-song, 1879; Love in my bosom, London prize, 1880; Ah, woe is me, London, 1884; Love me little, love me long; When twilight's parting flush; The Spring; All ye woods; The Bells (Glasgow Select Choir). Songs and Pianoforte pieces.

Mr. Lahee has for a considerable period been favourably known as a successful writer of concerted vocal music. His success in this department has been made conspicuous by the many prizes which have been awarded him in public trials of skill.

LAHOUSSAYE (Pierre). French violinist and comp., B. Paris, April 12, 1735. Played in France and Italy; London in 1772. Prof. of vn. at Paris Cons. D. Paris, 1818. Comp. sonatas, etc.

LA HYE (Louise Genevieve), *née* ROUSSEAU. French pianist and comp., B. Charenton, March 8, 1810. S. Paris Cons. Prof. Paris Cons. D. Paris, Nov. 17, 1838. Comp. melodies and method for the Harmonium, romances, etc.

LAIDLAW (Anna Robena). English pianist, B. Bretton, Yorks, April 30, 1819. Educated at Edinburgh. Played in Berlin, London, 1834, Germany and Russia. Chiefly remarkable as the person to whom Schumann dedicated his op. 12. D. (?)

LAING (David, LL.D.). Scottish antiquary and scholar, B. Edinburgh, 1790. D. Portobello, Oct. 1878.

WORKS.—Select Remains of the Ancient Poetry of Scotland, 1822. Early Metrical Tales, 1826. An Account of the Scottish Psalter of A.D. 1566, containing the Psalms, Canticles and Hymns, set to music in four parts, in the MSS. of Thomas Wode or Wood, Vicar of Sanct Androus, Edin., 4to, 1871. See also STENHOUSE (William).

Dr. Laing's labours were of the highest value to the illustration of Scottish history and antiquities.

LAJARTE (Theodore Edouard de). French comp. and writer, B. Bordeaux, July 10, 1826. S. Paris Cons. Comp. military music; operas, "Le Roi du Carreau," 1883, etc.

LA JEUNESSE (Marie Emma), or ALBANI. French-Canadian soprano vocalist, B. at Chambly, near Montreal, 1851. Removed to Albany (hence pseudonym) in 1864. S. under Duprez at Paris Cons.; and under Lamperti at Milan. *Début* at Messina in 1870. Sang afterwards in Milan, Paris, London, etc. with greatest success. Married Mr. Ernest Gye, 1878. The beautiful vocalisation of this artist has secured for her a foremost place among modern singers. Her chief excellencies are best brought out on the stage, where her fine presence and acute perception of dramatic situation is admirably adapted to display her vocal talents. As an oratorio vocalist she is also successful; but in both oratorio and concert singing she is less happy than in opera.

LAKE (George Handy). English comp. and writer, B. June, 1827. Editor of the *Musical Gazette*. Held various London organ appointments. D. London, Dec. 24, 1865. Comp. "Daniel," oratorio, 1852, and a number of part-songs, ballads, etc. His son, GEORGE ERNEST, B. London, May 29, 1854, is an org. and comp. Org. successively in Edinburgh (S. John's Episcopal Ch.), and Weybridge, Surrey. Author of "Complete Pedal Scales, and Daily Studies for the Organ," Lond. [1882], and comp. of instrumental and other music.

LALANDE (Henriette Clémentine Méric). French vocalist, B. Dunkirk, 1798. *Début* Naples, 1814. S. under Garcia. Appeared in Paris, 1823; London, 1830-31. Retired to Spain. Biography afterwards unknown.

LALANDE (Michel Richard de). French violinist and comp., B. Paris, 1657. Chor. in Church of S. Germain l'Auxerrois. Refused admission to band of Louis XIV. by Lulli. Teacher to Daughters of Duke of Noailles and Louis XIV. Music-master of the King's chamber. Composer to the King, etc. D. Versailles, 1726. Comp. motets, violin music, etc.

LALO (Edouard). French violinist and comp., B. 1830. S. Lille Cons. and at Paris. Comp. Symphonie Espagnole for vn. and orch., op. 21; Quartet for strings in E flat, op. 19; Chanson Villageoise et Serenade for Pf., vn., and 'cello, op. 14. "Fiesque," opera in three acts, Paris. Concerto for vn. and orch., op. 20. Trios, duets, sonatas, songs, etc.

LALOUETTE (Jean Francois). French comp., B. 1653. Cond. music in churches of St. Germain l'Auxerrois and Notre Dame. D. Paris, 1728. Comp. motets and other church music.

LAMARE (Jacques Michel, Hurel de). French violoncellist and comp., B. Paris, May 1, 1772. S. under Dupont. S. Paris Cons. Travelled in Germany, Russia, etc. D. March 27, 1823. Comp. concertos, etc.

LAMB (Benjamin). English org. and comp. who flourished about the beginning of the 18th century. Comp. org and church music, songs, etc.

LAMBERT (George Jackson). English org. and comp., B. Beverley, Nov. 16, 1794. S. under his Father, S. T. Lyon, and Dr. Crotch. Org. of Beverley Minster, 1818-1874. D. Beverley, Jan. 24, 1880. Wrote sonatas, trios, overtures, septet for strings, etc.

LAMBERT (Michel). French lute-player and comp., B. Vivonne, Poictou, 1610. Master of King's private band. D. Paris, 1690. Comp. motets, airs, etc.

LAMBETH (Henry Albert). English org. and cond., B. near Gosport, Jan. 16, 1822. S. under Thos. Adams. Since 1853 a prominent musician in Glasgow. Cond. of the Glasgow Choral Union, 1859-1880. Org. and cond. at Park Church. Org. to Corporation of Glasgow. Cond. of various choirs, etc. WORKS.—Arrangements of Scotch songs for choral purposes. Bow down Thine ear, Psalm LXXXVI.; By the Waters of Babylon, Psalm. The Scottish Book of Praise, edited (with D. Baptie), 1876. Songs and Pf. pieces, various.

LAMBILLOTTE (Louis). French comp. and writer, B. Charleroi, 1797. Chap.-master in Jesuit Coll., at St. Scheul, 1822. Member of the Jesuistic Order, 1825. D. 1855.

WORKS.—Church music. Clef des Melodies Gregoriennes dans les antiques systemes de notation et de l'unité dans les chants Liturgiques. Paris, 4to, 1851.

LAMOUREUX (Charles). French cond. and violinist, B. Bordeaux, Sept. 21, 1834. S. at Cons., 1850. Gained 2nd prize for vn. playing. 1st Vnst. at Gymnase. Founded in Paris a society on the model of the Sacred Harmonic of London, 1873. Founder and cond. of the celebrated Lamoureux Concerts in Paris. Appeared in London, 1880.

LAMPADIUS (W. A.) German writer and comp., author of "Felix Mendelssohn-Bartholdy, Ein Denkmal für seine Freunde" (Trans. by W. L. Gage, and published in America and London); Pianoforte pieces, etc.

LAMPE (Johann Friedrich). German comp. and writer, B. Helmstadt, Saxony, 1703. Appeared in England, 1725. Bassoon Player at the opera. Married to Isabella Young, sister of Mrs. Arne. D. Edinburgh, July 23, 1751.

WORKS.—*Operas and Dramatic Music:* Amelia (Carey), 1732; The Dragon of Wantley, 1737; Margery, or a Worse plague than the Dragon (Sequel to "The Dragon"), 1738; The Sham Conjuror, 1741; Pyramus and Thisbe, 1745. *Theoretical Works:* Plain and Compendious Method of Teaching Thorough-Bass after the most Rational Manner, with Proper Rules for Practice, Lond., 4to, 1737. The Art of Music, Lond., 8vo, 1740.

Lampe will be remembered chiefly by his opera, "The Dragon of Wantley," which had an extraordinary success on its first production. It was one of the many operas written in imitation of the "Beggar's Opera," but possessed the additional merit of being a burlesque on the then current Italian opera. Lampe is buried in the Canongate Churchyard of Edinburgh, and the following is the inscription on the tablet which marks his grave :—

"Here lye the mortal remains of John Frederic Lampe, whose harmonious compositions shall outlive monumental registers, and with melodious notes, through future ages, perpetuate his fame, till time shall sink into eternity. His taste for moral harmony appeared through all his conduct. On the 23rd of July, 1751, in the forty-eighth year of his age, he was summoned to join that heavenly concert with the blessed choir above, where his virtuous soul now enjoys that harmony which was his chief delight upon earth.

"In vita felicitate dignos mors reddit felices."

LAMPERTI (Francesco). Italian teacher of singing, B. Savona, March 11, 1813. S. Milan Cons., 1820. Prof. at Milan Cons., 1850-1875. Teacher of singing in Milan. Author of several works on vocal culture, vocal exercises, etc. He has the honour of having trained, among many others, the following distinguished vocalists :—Albani (Lajeunese), Artot, Galli, Hayes, Campanini, Shakespeare, S. Löwe, and Cruvelli.

LAND (Edward). English pianist and comp., B. London, 1815. One of the children of the Chap.-Roy. Accompanist to John Wilson, the Glee and Madrigal Union, etc. Secretary of the Noblemen and Gentlemen's Catch Club. D. London, Nov. 29, 1876.

WORKS.—Scottish Melodies arranged as Songs without words, Pf.; Lady Nairn's Lays from Strathearn, do.; Miscellaneous Pf. works. *Songs*: A loving heart; Birds of the Sea; You know not how I've missed you; My Gentle Elodie; Mine, love! yes or no?; Bird of beauty, wing your flight; Sighs that only love can share; So sweet is love's young spring; What can the heart want more; Angel's watch; Dreaming and waking; Italian flower girl's song; etc. Part-songs, arrangements, etc. Nine Four-part Songs Harmonized, Lond., 1862.

LANG (Adolph). German violinist and comp., B. Thorn, West Prussia, June 10, 1830. S. Leipzig Cons. Comp. music for vn. and Pf. Is favourably known in Germany as a violinist of distinguished merit.

LANG (Alexander). German comp., B. Ratisbon, March 6, 1806. Prof. in University of Erlangen. D. Feb. 18, 1837. Comp. of Pf. music, lieder, etc.

LANG (Benjamin J.) American comp., pianist, and cond., B. Salem, Mass., 1840. S. under Jaell, Liszt, and Hauptmann. Organist in various Boston churches since 1851. Org. to Händel and Haydn Society. Cond. of Apollo Club; the Cecilia Society. A Director of Harvard Musical Assoc. Vice-president of the Euterpe Assoc. Teacher etc. in Boston.

WORKS.—Numerous Songs and Pf. pieces. Principal works in MS. As a conductor Mr. Lang has brought before the Boston public the following works:—Schumann's "Faust"; Beethoven's "Ruins of Athens"; "Choral Fantasia"; 3rd and 4th Concertos; Mendelssohn's "Walpurgis Night"; Loreley; Schumann's "Paradise and the Peri," etc.

Mr. Lang is best known in Boston, but he has performed in New England, generally, New York, Berlin, Dresden, and Vienna.

LANG (John). Scottish musician, B. Paisley, 1829. Inventor of the "Union Notation." In this system the notes are indicated to Sol-fa musicians by having the initial letter of the various notes in the sol-fa scale placed within the head of the ordinary musical characters, and so presenting a combination of both old and new notations. A considerable amount of music has been printed on this system, which has much value for teaching purposes.

LANG (Josephine). German vocalist and comp. of lieder, B. Munich, March, 1815. An acquaintance and correspondent of Mendelssohn.

LANGDON (Richard). English comp. and org., B. Exeter in first half of 18th century. Mus. Bac., Oxon., 1761. Org. Exeter Cath., 1770-77. Org. Bristol Cath., 1777-82. Org. Armagh Cath., 1782-94. D. Sept. 1803.

WORKS.—Twelve Songs and two Cantatas, op. 4, Lond., n. d. Divine Harmony, A Collection in Score of Psalms and Anthems, 1774. Anthems. Twelve Glees for 3 and 4 voices, Lond., 1770, etc.

LANGE (Gustav F.) German pianist and comp., B. Schwerstedt, 1830. S. under his father, an organist, G. Schumann, and Loeschhorn.

WORKS.—Numerous transcriptions, and original works for Pf., as Le Papillon, La Reine du Bal, Le Retour du Soldat, Treue Liebe, Glöckchen, Hortensia, Harpe Eolienne, Sonatinas, various, Lyrisches Tonstück, Bunte Blätter, etc.

Many of these pieces are very pleasing and pretty in character, but they are not marked by any very striking features.

LANGE (Samuel). See DE LANGE (SAMUEL).

LANGHANS (Wilhelm). German comp., violinist, and writer, B. Hamburg, Sept. 21, 1832. S. Leipzig Cons. under David, etc., 1849-52. S. also under Alard, Hauptmann, and Richter. Married to Louise Japha (pianist and comp., B. Dusseldorf, 1853). Prof. in Berlin Academy of Music, 1871.

WORKS.—Contributions to periodical literature, and other literary works; Pf. and violin sonatas and studies; Chamber music, songs, etc.

LANGLÉ (Honore Francois Marie). Italian comp. and writer, B. Monaco, 1741. S. Naples Cons. under Cafaro. Resided in Paris, where he aided in the formation of the Conservatoire, of which he latterly became librarian. D. Paris, Sept. 20, 1807.

Comp. operas and some vocal music, and wrote Traité d'Harmonie et de Modulation, Paris, 1797; Traité de la Fugue, 1805, etc.

LANGSHAW (John). English org., B. 1718. Org. of Parish Church of Lancaster. D. 1798. Assisted in construction of large organ for the Earl of Bath.

LANGSHAW (John). English org. and comp., son of the above, B. London, 1763. S. under C. Wesley. Org. at Lancaster, 1798. Comp. hymns, chants, songs, Pf. concertos, and org. mus.

LANIERE (Nicholas). Italian comp., poet, etc., B. Italy, 1588. Came to England with parents about the beginning of the 17th century. Music master to Charles I., 1626. Court musician till about 1665. D. London, 1665, or 1668.

WORKS.—Luminalia, or the Festival of Light, masque, 1637; The Vision of Delight, masque, Jonson; Masque of Flowers; Hymns, pastorals, and music to masques by Daniel, Campion, Jonson, etc.; Songs in Playford's collections. Laniere wrote poetry, and collected pictures for Charles I.

LANNER (Josef Franz Karl). Austrian comp. of dance music, B. near Vienna, April 11, 1800. Chiefly self-taught in music. Organized string band for performance of dance music. Concertized in Austria, etc. Bandmaster of the Second Bürger Regiment. D. Vienna, April 14, 1843.

WORKS.—Numerous pieces of dance music commencing at op. 1, "Neue Wiener Landler," and extending onwards to about 250 numbers. His waltzes are best known and are his best works. They at one time rivalled those of the elder Strauss, but are now much less popular.

LANNOY (Edouard, Baron de). Belgian comp., B. Brussels, Dec., 1787. D. Vienna, Mar. 28, 1853. Wrote operas, symphonies, etc. PHILIPPE DE LANNOY, a member of this family, made several improvements on the construction of the organ.

LANZA (Gesualdo). Italian singing master and writer, B. Naples, 1779. Resided in London as teacher. D. London, March 12, 1859.

WORKS.—Elements of Singing in the Italian and English Styles, Lond., 3 v., 4to, 1809 (other editions); The Elements of Singing Familiarly Exemplified, Lond., 1817; Solfeggi and songs.

His brother, FRANCESCO GIUSEPPE (B. 1783, D. Naples, 1862), was a comp. of vocal music.

LAPORTE (Pierre Francois). French actor and theatrical manager, B. about the end of last or beginning of present century. Came to London, 1824. Manager of the King's Theatre, 1827-31. Lessee of Covent Garden Theatre, 1832. Manager of King's Theatre, 1833-41. D. near Paris, Sept. 25, 1841.

Laporte is celebrated as having introduced to the British public, Sontag, Albertazzi, Grisi, Persiani, Lalande, Mario, Ivanoff, Rubini, Tamburini, and Lablache.

LARRINGTON (Rev. George). English divine, author of "The Influence of Church Music. Sermon preach'd in the Cathedral Church of Worcester," Lond., 8vo, 1726.

LA RUE (Pierre de). See RUE (Pierre de la).

LASCEUX (Guillaume). French org. and comp., B. Poissy, Feb. 3, 1740. S. under Noblet at Paris. Org. of Ch. of S. Etienne; Ch. of Mathurins; and College of Navarre, etc. D. 1829. Comp. masses, org. and Pf. music.

LASALLE (Albert de). Belgian writer, B. Mons., Aug. 16, 1833. Author of Histoire des Bouffes-Parisiens, 1860; La Musique à Paris, 1862; Meyerbeer, sa biographie et le catalogue des ses œuvres, 1864; Dictionnaire de la Musique Appliquée à l'amour, 1864; La Musique pendant le Siege de Paris, 1872; Les Treize Salles de l'Opera, 1875; Memorial du Theatre Lyrique, 1877. Contributions to L'Illustration, Monde Illustré, Nouvelle Revue de Paris, etc.

LASSEN (Eduard). Danish comp., B. Copenhagen, April 13, 1830. S. at Brussels Cons., 1842. Gained first prize for Pf., 1844; Do. for Harmony, 1847; Second prize for comp.; Gained Government prize, 1851. Travelled in Italy and Germany. Music director at Weimar.

WORKS.—*Operas:* Le Roi Edgard, Weimar, 1857; Frauenlob, 1860; Der Gefangene. Symphony in D. Music to Sophocles' "Œdipus," and Goethe's "Faust," op. 57. *Lieder:* opp. 59, 60, 61, 62, 67. Polonaise for orch., in B flat, op. 63; Musik Zum Festspiel, "Die Linde am Ettersberg," op. 64; Lieder und Gesänge, op. 65. Miscellaneous Pf. and chamber music.

This composer holds a foremost place among his own countrymen, but his style cannot be called national, as it is thoroughly imbued with the characteristics of the modern German school.

LASSUS or LASSO (Orlando di), ROLAND DE LATTRE. Belgian comp., B. Mons, 1520. Chor. in Ch. of S. Nicolas, Mons. Educated in Italy, where he resided till 1555. Resided for a time in Antwerp. Visited England, 1554. (?) Court-musician to Albert V., Duke of Bavaria, 1557. Married to Regina Weckinges at Munich, 1558. Chap.-master to Albert V., 1562. Offered appointment by Charles IX. of France, 1571; but that monarch died before Lassus reached France. Returned to Munich and resumed his appointments. Made Knight of St. Peter, by Pope Gregory XIII. D. Munich, June 15, 1594 [1595?].

WORKS.—Missarum quatuor vocum, liber primus, Venice, 1545; Cypriani de Rore, Annibalis Patavini et Orlandi liber missarum quatuor, quinque et sex vocum, Venice, 1566; Liber Missarum, quatuor et quinque vocum, Nuremberg, 1581; Missæ cum cantico Beatæ Mariæ octo modis musicis, Paris, 1583; Missæ aliquot quinque vocum, 1589; Numerous magnificats, psalms, lamentations, motets, etc., published 1567-1619. Il primo e secondo libro de' madrigali a cinque voci, 1559; Il primo libro de' madrigali a quattro voci, Venice, 1560; Di Madrigali a quattro voci il secondo libro, 1563. Il terzo libro de' madrigali del eccellentissimo Orlando di Lasso a quattro voci, Venice, 1564; Il Libro terzo de' Madrigali a cinque voci, 1564. De' Madrigali dell' ottimo Orlando di Lasso a cinque voci, il quarto libro, Venice, 1567; Il Quinto libro de' Madrigali a 4 voci, Venice, 1587; Il Seste libro de Madrigali a 4 et 5 voci, 1588; Le Quatorzième livre à quatre parties contenant dix-hiut chansons italiennes, six chansons françaises, et six motets faicts, par Rolando de Lassus, Antwerp, 1555; Twenty-five books of Chansons published between 1570-1587.

The merits of this composer were until comparatively recent times less respectfully treated than modern historians think their due. Burney and Baini especially among the older writers are by no means so lavish in their praise as many more recent writers believe they should have been. Be his merits what they may, it is certain that Lassus exercised a powerful influence over the music of his period, and over that of the succeeding school, by renouncing in a great measure the stilted counterpoint which prevailed previous to his advent. His music is marked by more freedom, and a greater warmth than that of most of his contemporaries, so that his importance as a musical reformer must be fixed by the results which his innovations produced. Very few of his larger works will find favour from modern musicians, as they will be found dry and dull beside even the works of contemporary composers who are believed to possess not a tithe of his merits. In addition to his fame as a composer Lassus is deserving of honour as an educationist of some success. He established at Munich what was known in its time as the largest music school in existence.

LATES (Charles). English comp., flourished about end of the 18th century. S. under P. Hayes. Bac. Mus., Oxon. Comp. sonatas, songs, etc. His brother, JOHN JAMES, was a violinist of some local fame in Oxford, where he was a teacher. He wrote chamber music. D. 1777.

LATILLA (Gaetano). Italian comp., B. Bari, Naples, 1713. D. about 1788. Comp. a number of comic operas produced chiefly at Venice and Rome.

LATOUR (Jean). French pianist and comp., B. Paris, 1766. Pianist to Prince of Wales in London. Teacher, etc. in London. D. Paris, 1840. Comp. variations, transcriptions, divertissements, and other light pieces for Pf. Some of those pieces were fashionable enough in their day, but now they are unknown.

LATROBE (Rev. Christian Ignatius). English writer and comp., B. Fulneck near Leeds, Feb. 12, 1758. S. at Niesky. Secretary to the United (Moravian) Brethren in England. D. near Liverpool, May 6, 1836.

WORKS.—Original Anthems, with organ or Pf. accomp., 2 vols. fo., n. d. Jubilee Anthem for George III., Oct. 25, 1809. "Dies Iræ," for 4 voices, 1799. Hymns. Selection of Sacred Music from the works of Eminent Composers of Germany and Italy, 6 vols., 1806-1825. Instrumental and miscellaneous music.

LATROBE (John Antes, M.A.). English writer and org., son of the above, B. 1792. Vicar of St. Thomas's Kendal. D. Gloucester, 1878.

WORKS.—Music of the Church considered in its various branches, Congregational and Choral, an Historical and Practical Treatise for the General Reader, Lond., 8vo, 1831. Instructions of Chenaniah, Plain directions for accompanying the Chant or the Psalm tune, Lond., 8vo, 1832.

LATTRE. See LASSUS.

LAUB (Ferdinand). Bohemian violinist and comp., B. Prague, Jan. 19, 1832. Originally self-taught. S. at Vienna and Paris. Played in London, 1851, and in other parts of Europe. Principal vnst. at Court of Berlin, 1855. Prof. of vn. in Stern's Cons., Berlin, 1856. Prof. of vn., Moscow Cons., 1866. D. Gries, near Botzen, March 17, 1875.

Laub held during his lifetime a distinguished place among European violinists. His tone was celebrated for purity and firmness, and his execution was refined and accurate.

LAURENS (Alberto). See LAWRENCE (Albert).

LAURENT DE RILLE (Francois A). French comp., B. Orleans, 1828. Writer of operettas, masses, songs, etc.

LAUSKA (Franz S. Ignatius). German comp., B. Brunn, Moravia, Jan. 13, 1764. D. Berlin, 1825. Comp. an amount of Pf. music, but chiefly known as the preceptor of Weber and Meyerbeer.

LAUTERBACH (Johann Christoph). German violinist, B. Culmbach, Bavaria, July 24, 1832. S. under De Beriot and Fétis. Prof. of violin at Munich Cons. Do. at Dresden. Played in England, 1864-65. Well known on the Continent as a virtuoso of great talent.

LAVALEE (Calixa). Canadian comp. and pianist, B. Verchères, Canada, 1842. Educated in Paris, France. S. Pf. under Marmontel, and harmony, counterpoint, comp., and instrumentation with A. Boieldieu. Is Prof. of Pf., comp., and instrumentation at the Petersilia Academy of Music; Languages and Elocution, Boston, Mass.

WORKS.— Cantata (for the reception of the Princess Louise at Quebec in 1878); Opera, "La Veuve;" Opera, T and Q (American subject); Symphony; Offertory for soli, chorus, organ, and orchestra; Twelve Etudes for Piano; Miscellaneous works for piano; String quartettes; An Oratorio; Songs, etc.

Mr. Lavalee is recognised among the profession as a musician superior in interpretation, and as a teacher. His compositions are not particularly of the French school, although melodic and bright in style. In his concerted works he shows a knowledge of instrumentation in many respects quite original. Was a Charter Member of the American College of Musicians. Played a programme at the Music Teachers' National Association Meeting in Cleveland O., 1884, consisting entirely of American compositions.

LAVENU (Louis Henry). English (? French) comp., B. London, 1818. S. at R. A. M., under Potter and Bochsa. 'Cellist at the opera, London. Musicseller with N. Mori. Music director of Sydney Theatre. D. Sydney, Aug. 1, 1859.

WORKS.—Loretta, a Tale of Seville (Bunn), opera, Nov. 9, 1846. Numerous songs and Pf. pieces, etc.

A composer of merit, but not successful or popular.

LAVIGNE (Antoine Joseph). French oboist, B. Besançon, March 23, 1816. S. Paris Cons., 1830. Oboist in England at Drury Lane Concerts, Manchester and other concerts.

LAW (Andrew). American musician, B. about middle of 18th century. D. Cheshire, Conn., 1821. Compiled Collection of the best and most approved Tunes and Anthems [1782]. Rudiments of Musick, 1783 (4 editions to 1794). Musical Primer on a New Plan, with the Four Characters, 1803. Musical Magazine, 1804. Harmonic Companion and Guide to Social Worship, Philad., 8vo, n. d.

LAWES (Henry). English comp., B. Dinton, near Salisbury, Wiltshire, Dec., 1595. S. under John Cooper (Coperario). Epistler and Gent. of Chap.

Roy., 1625. Clerk do. Mem. of private band of Charles I. Music master in family of the Earl of Bridgewater. Stripped of appointments during the Protectorate. D. London, Oct. 21, 1662.

WORKS.—The Triumphs of Peace, masque (with W. Lawes and S. Ives), 1633. Coelum Britannicum, masque (Carew), 1633. Comus, masque (Milton), 1634. A Paraphrase upon the Psalmes of David set to New Tunes for Private Devotion, and a thorow base, for voice or instrument, 1637 (Sandy's version). Choice Psalmes put into Musick for Three Voyces, 1648. Ayres and Dialogues for One, Two, and Three Voices, 1653; Do., 2nd book, 1655; Do., 3rd book, 1658. Music to poetry by W. Cartwright, Herrick, Davenant, Milton, Waller, etc. Songs in Contemporary Collections, as The Treasury of Musick, 1669; Anthems in Clifford's and other collections; Music in Select Ayres and Dialogues.

Lawes enjoyed only temporary fame as a composer, the popularity which he gained in his lifetime having departed shortly after his decease. The unnatural taste for foreign music was in his time as well as now one of the follies of English fashionables, and Lawes is deserving of considerable credit for having stoutly maintained the right of native composers to receive a hearing. He even went the length of observing, and with perfect truth, that England had produced composers equal to the greatest of other countries. As regards Lawes' own period this holds particularly good, Monteverde and Carissimi being the only two composers worthy of being named in the same breath with Byrd, Morley, Dowland, Bull, Wilbye, Orlando Gibbons, etc. Lawes' claims to consideration are not great, and beyond a number of fine songs he has not given the world anything worthy of preservation.

LAWES (William). English comp., brother of above, B. Salisbury, 1582. S. under Coperario. Mem. of Chichester Cath. choir till 1602. Gent. of Chap. Roy., 1602. Musician in ordinary to Charles I. Killed at siege of Chester, during the Civil War, 1645.

WORKS.—Music to Shirley's "Peace." The Royal Consort for Viols. Songs in various collections, etc. Fantasias for various instruments, etc.

LAWRENCE (Albert), ALBERTO LAURENS. English barytone vocalist, B. 1835. Singer in United States. Teacher of Italian singing in New York, etc.

LAWRIE (Alexander). Scottish comp. and pianist, B. Edinburgh, June 26, 1818. Org. of S. James' Episcopal Chap., Edinburgh, and in Rev. John Kirk's church in the same city. D. Edinburgh, Dec. 1880. A blind musician of great local fame. He arranged some music for the Pf., and comp. some hymns and songs.

LAWSON (Malcolm Leonard). English comp. and cond., B. Wellington, Shropshire, 1849. S. under various masters in London, France, Italy and Germany. Org. and Choir-master of Catholic Apostolic Ch., Lond., 1876. Cond. of the Gluck Society, 1877. Do. the St. Cecilia Choir. Director of the Musical branch of the Kyrle Society, 1878. Associate of the Philharmonic Soc., 1878.

WORKS.—Op. 1. Festival Service in F (MS.); op. 2. Festival Service with Graduals and Interludes in D (both written for Catholic Apostolic Ch.); op. 3. Six part-songs; op. 4. Three songs: A Tragedy, A Nocturne, A Serenade; op. 5. Airs and Interludes to the play "England" (W. G. Wills), Lond., 1876; op. 6. Andante, Scherzo, and Minuet and Trio for Pf. (MS.); op. 7. The Seagulls, an Episode told in four Triolets for mezzo-soprano voice and Pf.; op. 8. Seventeen People's Songs and Ballads: Kitty and the Bee; Kitty and the Flowers; In the Garden; Kitty's beauty; Life's pipe; A Yorkshireman's love song; The proud Princess; Sing heigh ho; The world's age; Hereafter; Love's resolves! Cavalier Constancy; Love and debt; Adieu; A Secret; The Passionate Shepherd; A Jacobite Lament; op. 9. Music to the play of "Olivia," Lond., 1877; op. 10. Three French Songs; op. 11. Three melodies for voice and Pf.; op. 12. Symphony in D, "Pan" (MS.); op. 13. The Three Princesses, opera in 3 acts (MS); op. 14. Twelve Love Songs, words by Browning, Swinburne, Morris, and D. Rossetti (MS.); op. 15. Duet, Cupid's Curse; op. 16. Service for the Catholic Apostolic Ch. (MS.); op. 17. Six Motets (ladies' voices) for the S. Cecilia Soc. (MS.); op. 18. Three songs; op. 19. Symphony in G minor, No. 2, "Mahomet" (MS.); op. 20. Twelve Scotch Songs, words by Burns, etc.; op. 21. Six Songs, words by the old dramatists; op. 22. Three songs, with violin obligato (MS.); op. 23. Overture, "Savonarola" (MS.); op. 24. Six Anthems for 4 voices and org. (MS.)

Mr. Lawson and the "Gluck Society" have been the means of bringing before the London public many important works of the older masters. Among the works produced may be named Gluck's "Iphigenia in Tauris," "Alcestis" and "Orpheus;" Purcell's "Bonduca," "Dido and .Eneas," and "Yorkshire Feast Song," etc.; also works by Goetz, Josquin, Dowland, Marcello, Leo, Carissimi, etc. The "Kyrle Society" aims at bringing knowledge of art in its varied forms to the poorer classes. The work which is done by Mr. Lawson does much to remedy the deficiency of musical education always existing among the poor of Britain. In 1880, Mr. Lawson was offered the position of director of the Belfast Philharmonic Society, in succession to Sir Robert Stewart, but was unable for several reasons to accept it.

LAYOLLE (Francois de). French comp., B. end of 15th century. D. middle of 16th century. Comp. masses, madrigals, motets, psalms, etc.

LAZARUS (Henry). English clarinet-player, B. London [Jan. 1., 1815]. S. instrument under Godfrey, etc. Second clarinet at Sacred Harmonic Soc., 1838. Principal clarinet-player at Italian opera. Prof. of clarinet at R. A. M., etc. Has played with success at principal London and provincial concerts.

LEACH (James). English comp., B. Wardle, near Rochdale, 1762. Received no musical instruction. Hand-loom weaver in Rochdale. Member of the King's band, and tenor vocalist in London. Tenor singer and teacher in Rochdale, 1789, and latterly in Salford, 1796. D. from the effects of injuries received in a coach accident, Blackley, near Manchester, Feb. 8, 1798. Buried in Rochdale.

WORKS.—New Sett of Hymn and Psalm Tunes, adapted for the use of churches, chapels, and Sunday schools...Lond. 4to, 1789; Second Sett of Hymn and Psalm Tunes, London [1797]; Collection of Hymn Tunes and Anthems, composed and adapted for a full choir, London [1798]; Anthems, etc.; Psalmody, by James Leach .. Harmonised in compressed score by John Butterworth, with a sketch of the composer's life and work by Thomas Newbigging, London [1884], 4to.

"In Leach's music there is nothing random or haphazard; each note is perfectly placed, and could not be altered without jeopardizing the whole strain. This proves the power of the composer. He keeps his theme well in hand, and thus every note strikes home to the intelligence as well as to the heart. The tunes of Leach are as much a work of art as a beautiful statue produced by the cunning hand of a master."—*Thomas Newbigging.*

LEBERT (Sigismund). German editor and Prof., B. Ludwigsburg, Dec. 12, 1822. Prof. at Stuttgart, and founder with Stark, of the Cons. there. D. Stuttgart, Dec. 8, 1884. Writer with Dr. L. Stark of a "Grand Theoretical and Practical Piano School." (Grosse Klavierschule.)

Lebert is best known as an editor of classics for the Pf.

LEBRUN (Louis Auguste). Oboist and comp., B. Mannheim, 1746. D. Berlin, Dec. 16, 1790. Eminent as a performer. His wife, née FRANCESCA, DANZI, Italian soprano vocalist, B. Mannheim, 1756. Married Lebrun, 1775. Appeared in London, 1776. Sang in Italy, Germany, etc. D. May 14, 1791.

LEBURN (Alexander). Scottish violinist, teacher at Auchtermuchty. Compiled "A Collection of Strathspey Reels, etc., with a Bass for the Violoncello or Harpsichord." Edinburgh, n.d.

LE CARPENTIER (Adolphe Clair). French pianist and comp., B. Paris, Feb. 17, 1809. D. Paris, July 14, 1869.

Comp. Bagatelles, Divertissements, Polkas, Fantasias, Rondos, Variations, etc., for Pf., numbering nearly 300 pieces in all; Methods and exercises for the Pf., etc.

LE CIEUX (Leon). French violinist and comp., B. Bayeux, May 12, 1821. D. Paris, Feb. 15, 1873.

Comp. fantasias, exercises, studies, etc., for the violin, on which instrument his performance was perfect.

LÉCLAIR (Jean Marie). French violinist and comp., B. Lyons, 1697. S. at Paris under Chéron, etc. Member of Royal band, 1731. Leader of Paris opera. Assassinated, Paris, Oct. 22, 1764.

WORKS.—Glaucus et Scylle, opera; Sonatas for vn.; Concertos for vn.; Miscellaneous violin and chamber music.

Léclair was one of the greatest violinists of his period. His compositions are excellent for their time, and have recently been resuscitated with success.

LECOCQ (Alexander Charles). French comp., B. Paris, June 3, 1832. S. at Paris Cons. under Halévy, 1849-54. Gained first prize for Harmony, 1850. Resident in Paris.

WORKS.—*Operas:* Le Docteur Miracle, 1857; Iliusclos, 1859; Le Baiser à la porte, 1864; Liline et Valentin, 1865; Les Ondines au Champagne, Sept., 1865; Le Myosotis, May, 1866; Le Cabaret de Rampnnneau, Oct., 1867; Fleur de Thé, 1868; L'Amour et son Carquois, 1868; Les Jumeaux de Bergame, 1868; Le Carnaval d' un mer le blanc, 1868; Gandolfo, Jan., 1869; Le Rajah de Mysore, 1869; Le Testament de M. de Crac, Oct., 1871; Le Barbier de Trouville, Nov., 1871. Les Cent Vierges, 1872; Sauvons la Caisse, 1872; La Fille de Madame Angot, Feb. 21, 1873; Girofté-Girofla, 1874; Les Prés-Saint-Gervais; Le Pompon, Nov., 1875; Le Petite Mariée, 1876; Kosiki, Oct. 18, 1876; La Marjolaine, Feb. 3, 1877; Le Petit Duc, Jan., 1878; Camargo, 1878; Le Petite Madamoiselle, 1879, etc.

Some of this composer's works have attained to extraordinary success. Madame Angot and Girofé-Girofla are those on which his reputation will probably rest. The orchestration of his works is clever, and his education has not been misused, though applied to a questionable branch of musical high art.

LECOUPPEY (Félicien). French pianist and comp., B. Paris, 1814. S. at the Cons. Prof. of Harmony and Pf., Paris Cons., 1843. Comp. studies, exercises, methods, and numerous minor pieces for the Pf. Famous as a Teacher.

LEDESMA (Don Mariano Rodriguez de). Spanish comp. and singer, B. Saragossa, Dec. 14, 1779. Chorister Saragossa Cath. Sang in opera at Madrid, in England, etc. D. Madrid, 1847. Comp. motets, Pf. music, songs, etc.

LEDUC (Alphonse). French pianist and comp., B. Nantes, March 9, 1804. S. Paris Cons., under Reicha, etc. Gained second prize for bassoon, 1825. D. Paris, June 17, 1868.

WORKS.—184 Quadrilles for Pf.; 153 Valses and Polkas; 295 Dance pieces, miscellaneous, for Pf. duet; Method for Pf.; Studies, and about 400 other pieces for Pf. of various kinds; Music for org., bassoon, flute, etc.

LEE (Alfred). See FERGUSON (J. C.)

LEE (G.). English writer, author of "The Voice, its Artistic Production, Development and Preservation," 4to, 1870, 2 editions.

LEE (George Alexander). English comp. and cond., B. London, 1802. Tenor singer in theatre at Dublin, 1825; Haymarket Theatre, London, 1826. Music-seller in London for time. Opened Tottenham St. Theatre for English opera (with Chapman and Melrose). Lessee of Drury Lane Theatre, 1830. Manager of Lenten Oratorios at Covent Garden and Drury Lane, 1831. Married Mrs. Waylett, the singer. Conductor of Strand Theatre, 1832; Olympic Theatre, 1845. D. London, Oct. 8, 1851.

WORKS.—*Music to Dramas:* The Invincibles, 1828; The Sublime and Beautiful; The Nymph of the Grotto, 1829; The Witness, 1829; The Legion of Honour, 1831; Love in a Cottage; Auld Robin Gray; The Fairy Lake, and other operettas and musical dramas. Beauties of Byron, 8 songs; Loves of the Butterflies (T. H. Bayly), 8 songs. *Songs and Ballads:* A dream of the past; Away, away to the mountain's brow; Annie Bell; Beautiful dreamer; Believe me not false: Bells upon the wind; Bird of Love; Bells at Sunset; Bright Summer days are coming; Come dwell with me; Come, merry fays; Come to the gipsy's tent; Cora; Come where the aspens quiver; Daughters of my sunny Italy; Daylight is on the sea; Deerstalker; Dark Suliote; Day dreams are o'er; Each bower has beauty; Flight of the Birds; Flow on, silver Avon; Fairies' cup; Farewell, ye happy hours; Flower of Lammermoor; Fairest flower; Fair Maggiore; Fairyland; Garden of Roses; Gipsy's wild chant; Gondolier's lay; Good night, love; Heartfelt words; He comes not; He wipes the tear; I'll not beguile thee; I sigh for the woods; I'll be a fairy; I love all that thou lovest; Joy of our meeting; Kate Kearney; Lad who wears the plaiddy; Macgregor's gathering; Maid of Kildare; My native bells; Mermaid's invitation; Moonlight; Meet me in the willow glen; My cottage and my mill; Maiden of Neath; My cot in the valley; Old Irish Gentleman; Pride of our valley; Rover's bride; Rose of Killarney; Sweetly sound the Village bells; Sweet Mary, acushla machree; Soldier's tear; She walks in beauty; Thou art not false but fickle; The wild white rose; Twilight deepens over the green; 'Tis love's hallowed hour; When the moon is brightly beaming; Why should we sigh; Wild mandoline; Woman's sparkling eye. A Vocal Tutor. Duets and part-songs, etc.

Lee was great in his day as a ballad writer, and a few of his more popular works have survived. Among these " Macgregor's gathering " is by far the best known. Much of Lee's music was written to the verses of Haynes Bayly, and suffer accordingly; for the good sense of the public never fails to rise superior to all such lackadaisical twaddle.

LEE (Maurice). English pianist and comp., B. Hamburg, Feb. 6, 1825. Resided in Paris till 1870. Settled in London, 1870.

WORKS.—*Pianoforte*: Dernière Valse d'un Fou; Barcarolle d'Oberon; Robin Adair; Le Rossignol; La Manola; Ah, cruel parting; Une Nuit à Grenade; Auf Flügeln des Gesanges; Midsummer Night's Dream; Ariel's song; Le Courrier, Grand Galop de Concert; Graziella; Gavotte de Louis XV; Sylvana, Menuet d'Exaudet; Souvenir de la Styrie; Turkish War March; Brook's Lullaby; Echo du Ciel; La Napolitaine; L'Electricite; Gavotte du Duc de Richelieu. Etudes Chantantes. Valse d'Amour.

LEE (J. S.). Bandmaster 20th Hussars, B. Feb. 14, 1831. One of the oldest Military Bandmasters in the Army. Comp. of numerous pieces of dance music, songs, a fantasia for cornet, and church music for military choirs.

LEE (Sebastian). German violoncellist and comp., B. Hamburg, Dec. 24, 1805. S. under Prell and Romberg. Comp. music for 'cello, etc.

LEEVES (Rev. William). English divine and comp., B. June 11, 1748[1749?] Rector of Wrington, Somerset, 1779. D. Wrington, May 25, 1828.

Composer of "Auld Robin Gray," 1770, a song known throughout the world. The words by Lady Anne Barnard (1750-1825) are so natural and true to life that the musical aid afforded by Leeve's setting is not, as some suppose, the chief reason for its popularity. Leeves wrote much church music, now completely forgotten.

LEFÉBURE-WÉLY (Louis Jacques Alfred). French comp. and org., B. Paris, Nov. 13, 1817. S. under his father. Assistant org. to his father at St. Roch, Paris, 1822. S. at Paris Cons. under Berton, Halévy, and Adam, 1832-34. Gained first prizes for Pf. and org., 1834. Org. at the Madelaine, Paris, 1847-58. Mem. of Legion of Honour, 1850. Chevalier of order of Charles III, of Spain, 1859. Org. of St. Sulpice, Paris, 1863-69. D. Paris, Jan. 1, 1870.

WORKS.—Les Recruteurs, opera, 1861; Après la Victoire, cantata, 1863; Three symphonies for orch.; Three masses; String chamber music; Studies for the Pf., various, opp. 44, 57, 76, etc.; Pf. pieces, various, as marches, nocturnes, caprices, fantasias, dances, etc., to the number of about 200. Organ music, marches, offertoires, fantasias, etc.

Lefébure-Wély was one of the greatest of organ virtuosos. His command over the instrument was complete, and his style of performance original, brilliant, and showy, but withal the work of an artist. His org. music is best known in England.

LEFFLER (Adam). English bass singer, B. 1808. Chor. in Westminster Abbey. Sang in opera and at concerts. D. London, Mar. 28, 1857.

LEGOUIX (Isidore Edouard). French comp., B. Paris, April 1, 1834. S. Paris Cons. under Reber and A. Thomas.

WORKS.—*Operettas*: Un Othello, 1863; Le Lion de Saint-Merc, 1864; Ma Fille, 1866; Malbroug sén va-t-en guerre (with Bizet, Délibes and Jonas), 1867; Le Vengeur, 1868; Les Dernières Grisettes, 1874; Le mariage d'une Etoile, 1876; Madame Clara, somnambule, 1877; La Tartane. Pf. music and songs, etc.

LEGRENZI (Giovanni). Italian org. and comp., B. Clusone, near Bergamo, 1625. Org. of Ch. of St. Maria Maggiore, Bergamo. Chap.-master of Ch. of Spirito Santo, Ferrara, till 1664. Chap.-master, St. Mark's, Venice, 1685-90. D. Venice, July 2, 1690.

WORKS.—*Operas*: Achille in Sciro, 1664; Tiridate, 1669; La Divisione del Mondo, 1675; Pausania, 1681; I due Cesari, 1683; Publio Elio Pertinace, 1684; Motets; Instrumental music, sonatas, etc.

An influential composer, and teacher of Gasparini, Lotti, and other eminent musicians.

LEIDESDORF (Max Josef C.) Austrian comp., publisher, and pianist, B. Vienna, 1780. D. Florence, Sept. 20, 1839. Comp. "Esther," an oratorio, Pf. music, etc.

LEIGH (Walter). English musician, comp. of "Paradise Lost and Regained, or the Fall and the Redemption," oratorio, n.d.

LEIGHTON (Sir William). English musician, gentleman-pensioner, and knight, who flourished during the 16th and 17th centuries. Published "The Teares or Lamentations of a Sorrowful Soule; composed with Musicall Ayres and Songs both for Voyces and Divers Instruments," 1614. [Psalms, Hymns, etc.] Byrd, Bull, Dowland, Ford, O. Gibbons, Giles, Hooper, Wilbye, Weelkes, and Milton are among the contributors to this now extremely scarce and valuable publication.

LE JEUNE (Claude). French comp., B. Valenciennes [1528-30]. Chamber Musician in service of Henry IV. of France. D. [1606-1607].

WORKS.—Livre de Mélanges de C. Lejeune á 4, 5, 6, et 8 voix, Antwerp, 1585; Recueil de Plusieurs chansons et airs nouveaux mis en musique per Cl. Le Jeune, Paris, Leroy, 1594; Dodécacorde contenant douze psaumes de David mis en musique selon les douze modes approuvez des meilleurs autheurs anciens et modernes, á 2, 3, 4, 5, 6, et 7 voix, 4to, 1598; Les Psaumes de Marot et de Théodore Bezè mis en musique à quatre et cinq parties, 4to, 1608.

A musician famous in his time, but now forgotten. His psalms and chansons were esteemed.

LEKPREVIK (Robert). Scottish printer of the 16th century. Published "The Forme of Prayers and Ministration of the Sacraments, etc., vsed in the English Churche at Geneua, approued and receiued by the Churche of Scotland, where-unto besydes that was in former bokes, are also added sondrie other Prayers, with the whole Psalmes of Dauid in English Meter," Edinburgh, 1565.

LE MAITRE. See MAISTRE.

LEMMENS (Nicolas Jacques). Belgian comp. and org., B. Zoerle-Parwys, near Antwerp, Jan. 3, 1823. S. at Brussels Cons., 1839-45. Gained 2nd prize for comp., 1844; first do., 1845; first org. prize, 1845. S. under Hesse at Breslau, 1846. Prof. of org. at Brussels Cons., 1849. Married Miss Sherrington, vocalist, 1857. Opened college for training organists at Malines, 1879. D. at the Château de Linterpoort, near Malines, Jan. 30, 1881.

WORKS.—Two symphonies for orch.; School for the organ; Pf. music, miscellaneous; Improvisations for org.; Motets and other church music; Part-songs and songs, various, etc.

Lemmens was best known as an organist, though some of his organ works are highly original and bright. His powers as an organist were great, and he was known throughout the musical world for the brilliancy of his performance.

LEMMENS-SHERRINGTON. See SHERRINGTON.

LEMOINE (Jean Baptiste). French operatic comp., B. Eymet, April 3, 1751. D. Paris, Dec. 30, 1796. His son GABRIEL L., B. 1772, D. 1815, comp. much music for the Pf.

LENEPVEU (Charles Ferdinand). French comp., B. Rouen, Oct. 4, 1840. Comp. operas, Pf. music, etc.

LENTON (John). English comp., who flourished in the latter half of the 19th century. He was a member of the private bands of William and Mary, and Queen Anne. D. after 1711.

WORKS.—The Gentleman's Diversion, or the Violin Explained, 1693; A Consort of Musick in Three Parts, 1694. Music for Venice Preserved, 1685; The Ambitious Stepmother, 1700; Tamburlain, 1702; The Fair Penitent, 1703, etc. Songs in contemporary collections.

LENTZ (Heinrich Gerard). German pianist and comp., B. Cologne, 1764. Appeared in Paris, 1785. Prof. of Pf. at Warsaw. D. Warsaw, August 21, 1839. Comp. concertos, sonatas, symphonies, etc.

LENZ (Wilhelm von). Russian writer, B. 1809. D. S. Petersburg, Jan. 1883. Councillor at S. Petersburg. Author of "Beethoven et ses trois Styles...," Paris, 1852, 2 vols.; "Beethoven: an Art Study," 6 vols., 1855-60. Also a small work on Pf.-playing.

LEO (Leonardo). Italian comp., B. Naples, 1694. S. under Scarlatti at Naples, and Pitoni at Rome. Professor of Cons. of La Pieta di Turchini, Naples. Org. at Royal Chap., 1716. Chap.-master of Ch. of Santa Maria della Solitaria, 1717. Prof. at Cons. of San Onofrio. D. Naples, 1746.

WORKS.—*Operas, Serenatas, etc.*: Il gran giorno d' Arcadia, 1716; Diana amante, 1717; Le Nozze in Dansa, 1718; Sofonisbe, opera, 1719; Cajo Gracco, 1720; Bajezette, 1722; Tamerlano, 1722; Timocrate, 1723; Zenobia in Palmira, 1725; Astianatte, 1725; La Somiglianza, 1726; L'Orismane, 1726; Ciro riconosciuto, 1727; Argene, 1728; La Zingara, 1731; Catone, 1732; Amore da Senno, 1733; Emira, 1735; Le Clemenza di Tito, 1735; Onore vince Amore, 1736; La Simpatia del sangue, 1737; Siface, 1737; Festa Teatrale, 1739; La Contesa dell' Amore e della Virtù, 1740; Alessandro, 1741; Demofoonte, 1741; Andromeda, 1742; Vologeso, 1744; La Finta Frascatana, 1744; Amor vuol sofferenza; Artaserse; Lucio Papirio; Alidoro; Alessandro nell' Indie. Miserere, 1743; La Morte d' Abele, oratorio, 1732. Santa Elena al Calvario, 1733. Miscellaneous church music; Instrumental music, etc.

Leo was one of the greatest lights of the Neapolitan school, and greatly influenced succeeding Italian composers. His music, both dramatic and sacred, is thoroughly in the Italian taste, and that for the church marks in a measure the first departure from the accepted style of Palestrina.

LÉONARD (Hubert). Belgian violinist and comp., B. Bellaire, Liége, April 7, 1819. S. Paris Cons. Travelled in Germany, Sweden, Holland, etc., concert-giving. Prof. of vn., Brussels Cons., 1849.

WORKS.—Fantasia (Russian), vn. and Pf., op. 3; Concertos for vn. and orch., opp. 14, 16, 26, 28, etc.; Scene populaire espagnole, op. 24; Twenty-four Studies for vn.; Gymnastique du violoniste; Method for Violin; Fantasias, transcriptions, etc., for vn.

LEONARD (W.) English writer, author of "Music in the Western Church." London, 1872; "The Christmas Festival, with a Selection of Carols." Lond.

LEONHARD (Julius Emil). German comp., pianist, and teacher, B. Laubau, 1810. D. Leipzig, 1831. Comp. concerted vocal music.

LEROY (Adrien). French music publisher and printer of 16th century. Sole music-printer, with Ballard, to Henri II., 1552. Published works by Lassus,

Lejeune, and other eminent contemporary composers. Also an Instruction Book for the Lute, 1557, translated into English and published 1568.

LESCHETITZKY (Theodor). Polish pianist and comp., B. Vienna, 1831. Teacher of Pf. in St. Petersburg, but latterly in Vienna. Husband and teacher of Madame Essipoff, the pianist. Comp. a number of Pf. pieces, chiefly of a light nature.

LESLIE (Henry David). English comp. and cond., B. London, June 18, 1822. Educated at Palace School, Enfield. S. music under Charles Lucas, 1838. Secretary to Amateur Musical Soc., 1847-55. Cond. of do., 1855-61. Founder and cond. of the Leslie Choir, 1855-80. Cond. of Herefordshire Philharmonic Soc., 1863. Principal of National College of Music, 1864. Cond. of Guild of Amateur Musicians, 1874. Gained, with choir, first prize for part-singing at Paris International Competition, 1878. Cond. of musical societies in Wales.

WORKS.—*Oratorios:* Immanuel, 1853; Judith, Birmingham Festival, 1858. Romance, or Bold Dick Turpin, operetta, 1857. *Cantatas:* Holyrood, 1860; Daughter of the Isles, 1861. Ida, opera, Covent Garden, London, 1864. Dramatic overture, The Templar, 1852; Orchestral symphony, in F, 1847; Te Deum and Jubilate, in D, 1841. *Anthems:* Let God arise (Festival), 1849; Blow ye the trumpet in Zion; Fear not; O have mercy upon me. *Part-songs, etc.:* Arise, sweet Love; Awake, awake, the flowers unfold; Charm me asleep; Daylight is fading; Down in a pretty valley; Evening; Hail to the chief; Homeward; How sweet the moonlight sleeps; Land ho!; My love is fair; My soul to God, my heart to thee; Now the bright morning star; One morning sweet in May; Pibroch of Donuil Dhu; Soul of the age, Shakespeare rise; The pilgrims; The primrose; The violet; Thine eyes so bright (madrigal); Up, up, ye dames; Angel's visit; Lullaby of Life; We roam and rule the sea; The rainbow; Cherry ripe; O, memory, trio; April, sweet month; Bridal song; Dunois the brave; Flax spinner; Hymn of Moravian nuns; Holiday song; National song of defence; O gentle sleep; The cherry time. *Songs:* My darling hush; The fair sun of my heart; Boatswain's leap; Captain's song; Flower girl; Always; Mountain maid; By the sunset glow; Calm and serene is the night; Cottager's song; etc., etc. Edited Choral Music, a Collection of Part-songs, etc. Contributions to periodical literature.

Mr. Leslie has the reputation of being one of the most successful choir-trainers Britain has yet produced. His choir during its existence was recognised as representative of the English culture of concerted vocal music, and many critics were of opinion that for style, expression, and general capability it far exceeded any other choir. Mr. Leslie's compositions are uniformly good, and show the workmanship of a skilled musician.

LESUEUR (Jean Francois). French comp., B. Drucat-Plessiel, nr. Abbeville, Jan. 15, 1763 [Feb. 15, 1760]. Grand nephew of Eustache Lesueur, the painter. S. at Amiens. Chap.-master at Cath. of Séez. Music master successively at Dijon Cath., 1781; Le Mans, 1783; Tours, 1784. Appeared in Paris as master of choristers at Church of the Innocents, 1784. Music director, Notre Dame, 1786-88. Invested with informal title of Abbé. Retired from Paris, 1788-92. Prof. at Ecole de la Garde Nationale, 1793. Inspector of Instruction at Paris Cons., 1795. Dismissed from position at Cons. for libel on Catel, etc, 1802. Chap.-master to Napoleon I. (First Consul), 1804. Mem. of Legion of Honour; do. of Institut, 1813. Comp. and Chap.-master to Louis XVIII. Prof. of comp. at Cons., 1818-37. D. Paris, Oct. 6, 1837.

WORKS.—*Operas:* Le Caverne, 1793; Paul et Virginie, 1794; Télémaque dans l' ile de Calypso, 1796; Ossian ou les Bardes, 1808; L'Inauguration du Temple de la Victoire, divertissement, 1807; Le Triomphe de Trajan, 1807; La Mort d'Adam, et son Apothéose, 1809; Tyrtée, 1794 (MS. opera); Artaxerce, do., 1801; Alexandre à Babylon, do., 1823; Oratorio de Noël, 1826; Deborah, oratorio, 1828; Thirty-three masses; Writings on Greek music, etc.

This influential composer must be credited with having done much to advance musical art in France. The services which he conducted in the church of Notre Dame, and his success and influence as a teacher both give him a fair claim to be considered an innovator and progressive musician, outside the sphere of his own works or personality. As a teacher he aided in forming the talents of Berlioz, Prévost, Thomas, Elwart, Ernst, Gounod, etc., and so propagated an advanced school of musical thought, none of the characteristics of which are apparent in his own somewhat antiquated works. His music has the merit of great power or breadth.

LEUTNER. See Peschka-Leutner.

LEVASSEUR (Nicolas Prosper). French bass vocalist, B. March, 1791. *Début* Paris, 1813. *Début* London, 1816. D. Paris, Dec., 1871.

LEVERIDGE (Richard). English bass vocalist and comp., B. 1670. Sang in opera at Drury Lane and Queen's Theatres, 1705-12; do. Lincoln's Inn Fields and Covent Garden, 1713-30. D. London, March 22, 1758.

Works.—Music for the Island Princess, or the Generous Portuguese, 1699; Pyramus and Thisbe, 1716; Collection of Songs, Lond., 1727, 2 vols., with frontispiece engraved by Hogarth.

Leveridge is known only as a song-writer, though he has been credited with the composition of the much-discussed " Macbeth " music, on the authority of a notice in Rowe's edition of Shakespeare. The well-known songs "All in the downs" and the " Roast Beef of Old England " very fairly illustrate the style of his works.

LEVETT (?). English writer and comp., who flourished in London during the latter part of the 18th century. He wrote " Introductory Lessons in Singing, particularly on psalmody, to which are annexed several psalm tunes," Lond., n.d. Hymns for Easter, Christmas, etc.

LEVEY (William Charles). Irish comp. and pianist, B. Dublin, April 25, 1837. Son of Richard Michael Levey (1811), leader of the orchestra, Theatre Royal, Dublin, under whom he studied. S. at Paris under Auber, Thalberg, Prudent, etc., from 1852. Member of the Société des Auteurs et Compositeurs, Paris. Returned to London, 1862. Cond. successively of Covent Garden, Drury Lane, Haymarket, Adelphi, and Princess's Theatres, London.

Works.—*Operas and Operettas*: Fanchette, Covent Garden, 1862; Claude (MS.) in 3 acts; Nazarille, MS. (French); Punchinello, published; Fashion, do; Wanted a Parlour Maid, do. Music for " Amy Robsart," " Rebecca," " King o' Scots," " Lady of the Lake;" Seven Drury Lane Pantomimes; Vokes family, and Messrs. H. J. Byron, Burnand, Halliday, Wills, Taylor, etc. The Man of War, cantata for orch., chorus, and military band. Irish overture for orch. *Pianoforte*: Turkish march; Mazukas, in F and D flat; Chinese Dance; Grecian march. *Songs*: Esmeralda; Here stands a Post; King and the Beggar maid; The Raven; My darlings three; Many a year ago; Home from sea; The gallant Dragoon; Rory of the Glen; The May Song; Musette; Gipsy fortune-teller.

LEVY (Isaac). English cornet player, well known in London and the United States as a solo performer. He is author of a Popular Cornet Tutor (n.d.), and has earned much notoriety in American musical circles.

LEWIS (T.) English writer, author of "Organ Building and Bell Founding," Lond., 1878.

LEWY (Edouard Constantin). French cornet player, B. Saint-Avoid, Moselle, March 3, 1796. D. Vienna, June 3, 1846. Comps. for instrument. Joseph Rodolphe, his brother, was a horn player and comp.

LEYBACH (Ignaz). German comp., B. Gambsheim, July 17, 1817. S. under Pixis, Kalkbrennen, and Chopin. Org. of ch at Toulouse, 1844. Writer of Method for Harmonium; The Practical Organist; and numerous Pf. pieces of a light character.

LIBON (Philippe). French violinist and comp., B. Cadiz, Aug. 17, 1775. Played in France, Portugal, London, etc. D. Paris, Feb. 5, 1838. Comp. concertos for vn. and orch., caprices, etc.

LICHFIELD (Henry). English comp. of the 16th and 17th centuries, comp. "The First Set of Madrigals of Five Parts," Lond., 1613.

A 2

LICHTENSTEIN (Ludwig Baron von). German vust. and comp., B. Lahm, Sept. 8, 1767. S. at University of Göttingen under Forkel, etc. D. Berlin, Sept. 10, 1845. Comp. operas, masses, etc., etc.

LICHTENTHAL (Peter). Hungarian comp. and writer. B. Pressburg, 1780. S. at Vienna and Milan. D. Milan, 1858.

WORKS.—Life of Mozart, Treatise on harmony ; Influence of music on disease ; Dizionario e Bibliographia della Musica, Milan, 1826, 4 vols, 8vo : French translation, Paris, 2 vols., 8vo, 1839 ; Pf. music, etc.

LICKL (Johann Georg). Austrian comp., B. Kornneuburg, Austria, April 11, 1769. D. May 12. 1843.

WORKS.—*Operas*: Der Zauberpfeil ; Der Bruder von Kakrau ; Faust Leben ; Der Vermeinte Hexenmeister ; Der Orgelspieler ; Der Durchmarsch. Quintets, quartets, sonatas for stringed and other instruments. Sacred music, and songs.

LIEBE (Eduard Louis). German comp. and pianist, B. Magdeburg, Nov. 26, 1819. S. under Schwarz, Spohr, and Baldewein. Music-director at Coblentz, Strassburg, etc.

WORKS.—Symphonies, masses, opera, Pf. music ; Duets, trios, and songs.

LIEBICH (Gottfried Sigismund). German comp., B. Frankenberg, July 22, 1672. D. June 1, 1727. Comp. church music, chiefly motets.

LIEBIG (Carl). German comp. and cond., B. Schwedt, July 25, 1808. Established an orchestra, and gave popular symphony concerts in Berlin from 1850. D. Berlin, Oct. 6, 1872.

LIEBLING (Emil). German pianist and comp., B. Berlin, 1851. S. under Kullak. Emigrated to United States. Settled in Chicago, 1872. Teacher and comp. there.

LIGHT (Edward). English writer, author of "The Art of Playing the Guitar, to which is annexed a selection of the most familiar lessons, divertissements, songs, airs, etc.," 1795 ; "Concise Instructions for Playing on the English Lute," 4to, Lond.

LILLE (Gaston de). French comp. of dance music, B. 1825. Has published a great number of light salon pieces of a certain degree of merit in the class to which they belong.

LILLEY (G. H.) English writer, author of "The Therapeutics of Music," London, 1880.

LILLO (Giuseppe). Italian comp., B. Galatina, Naples, Feb. 26, 1814. D. Feb. 4, 1863. Comp. operas, masses, litanies, and an amount of miscellaneous music.

LILLYCROP (S.) English writer, author of "Theoretical and Practical Thorough Bass, exemplified in a Plain and Easy manner," London, 4to, n.d.

LIMPUS (Richard). English org. and musician, B. Sept. 10, 1824. Founded, with others, the College of Organists, 1864. Secretary to Coll. of Organists, 1864-75. D. March 15, 1875.

LIND (Jenny), or GOLDSCHMIDT. Swedish soprano vocalist, B. Stockholm, Oct. 6, 1820. S. under Croelius and Lindblad. S. at Stockholm musical academy. *Début* in Stockholm as Agathe in Weber's "Der Freischütz," March, 1838. S. under Manual Garcia at Paris, 1841. First appeared in Berlin, 1844 ; Leipzig, 1845 ; Vienna, 1846 ; London, H. M. Theatre, in "Robert the Devil" (Meyerbeer), May 4. 1847. Sang in Ireland, 1848. Travelled under Barnum's management (with Goldschmidt, etc.) in America, 1850-52. Married Otto Goldschmidt, Boston, Feb. 5, 1852. Resident in London and Malvern.

"Nothing, in any time, has equalled the amount of influence brought from the outside to bear on the reception of a singer, who, lacking such outward influences, would have been received as only one among many (one *after* a few) great singers— whereas, owing to such accessory excitements, she was held in this country, for a while, to be *the* one—and the one alone. . . . Mdlle. Lind's voice was a *soprano*, two octaves in compass—from D to D—having a possible higher note or two, available on rare occasions; and that the lower half of the register and the upper one were of two distinct qualities. The former was not strong,—veiled, if not husky; and apt to be out of tune. The latter was rich, brilliant, and powerful—finest in its highest portions. . . . Of all the singers whom I have ever heard Mdlle. Lind was, perhaps, the most assiduous. Her resolution to offer the very best of her best to the public seemed part and parcel of her nature and of her conscience."--*Chorley's Recollections*.

See further "A Review of the Performances of Mademoiselle Jenny Lind, during her engagement at Her Majesty's Theatre, and their influence and effect upon our National Drama; with a Notice of her Life," Lond., 1847, 8vo, with portrait; Lumley's "Reminiscences of the Opera," London, 1864; and "Memoranda of the Life of Jenny Lind," by N. P. Willis, Philadelphia, 1851, 8vo. In addition to articles in musical journals, the following magazines contain notices of her career:— Fraser's Magazine, 1863; Scribner's Magazine (by Sir Julius Benedict), 1880; Colburn's New Monthly Magazine, 1846; and Howitt's Journal, 1847.

LINDBLAD (Adolf Friedrich). Swedish comp., B. Löfvingsburg, near Stockholm, Feb. 1, 1801. S. Berlin under Zelter. Teacher and comp. in Stockholm, 1835-78. D. Stockholm, Aug. 23, 1878.

WORKS.—Symphony in C, Leipzig, 1839; Frondörörne, opera; Large number of vocal works, chiefly lieder and part-songs.

Lindblad is known chiefly as a composer of refined and sympathetic lieder, and as one of the trainers of Jenny Lind. On those grounds he is entitled to respect.

LINDEMAN & SONS. American firm of pianoforte-makers, established in New York. Inventors of improvements on the Pf. Patented a Cycloid Pf. in 1860.

LINDEMAN (Ole Andres). Norwegian pianist and comp., B. 1768. D 1855. Comp. a number of Pf. and vocal pieces.

LINDLEY (Robert). English violoncellist and comp., B. Rotherham, March 4, 1777. Commenced study of the violin, 1781; do., 'cello, 1785. 'Cellist at Brighton theatre. Principal 'cellist at the Opera, London, 1794-1851. Played with Dragonetti at all the provincial musical festivals. D. London, June 13, 1855.

Lindley was held among his contemporaries to be the best English performer on the 'cello. His tone, execution, and expression were alike admirable and refined, and artistic feeling was ever present. He composed a few concertos for 'cello and orch., and some songs. He was a constant companion of Dragonetti, the famous double-bass player.

His son WILLIAM, B. 1802, D. at Manchester, August 12, 1869, was a good violinist, and excelled in orchestral playing.

LINDPAINTNER (Peter Josef von). German comp. and cond., B. Coblentz, Dec. 8, 1791. S. at Augsberg, and under Winter at Munich, also under Gratz. Cond. of the Isarthortheater, Munich, 1812. Do. Royal Band at Stuttgart, 1819-56. Appeared in London, and cond. "Widow of Nain," oratorio, at Philharmonic Concert, 1853. D. Nonnenhorn, Aug. 21, 1856.

WORKS.--*Operas*: Demophoon, 1811; Alexander in Ephesia; Der blinde Gaertner; Der Pflegekinder; Der Bergkoenig, 1830; Der Vampyr, Vienna, 1827; Joko; Zeila; Sulmona; Hans Max Giesbrecht; Lichtenstein. *Oratorios*: Widow of Nain; Sacrifice of Abraham (dedicated to Queen Victoria); Concertino for clarinet and orch., op. 19. *Overtures*: Hiltrude, op. 20; Timantes, op. 31; Le Paria, op. 51, etc. Concerto for flute and orch., op. 28. Pf. music; Symphonies; Lieder, part-songs, canons, etc.; Motets, quartets, trios for strings, etc.

Lindpaintner is known in Britain by his oratorios and a few songs. His operas and orchestral music do not appear to have been naturalized in England at all, and the former are seldom produced in Germany. His music is graceful and clever.

LINDSAY (Christopher). Scottish musician and writer, brother of Lady Anne Barnard. Mem. of Choir of St. Paul's Cath. Wrote "A Scheme showing the Distance of Intervals," Lond., 1793.

LINDSAY (Thomas). English flute-player and writer, author of "Elements of Flute-playing, according to the most approved Principles of Modern Fingering," London, 1828.

LING (William). English comp., pianist, and teacher, who flourished about the end of last or beginning of present century. Comp. of op. 1. Three sonatas for Pf. and flute; op. 2. Duets for 2 flutes; Divertimentos for Pf., opp. 6, 7, 8; Sonatas for Pf., opp. 12, 13; Serenade, op. 17, etc., etc.

LINLEY (Eliza Ann), MAID OF BATH. English soprano vocalist, daughter of Thomas Linley, Senr., B. Bath, 1754. S. under her father. Sang at Bath concerts; and in London; Worcester, Hereford and Gloucester Festival. Eloped with and married R. B. Sheridan, 1773. D. Bristol, 1792.

LINLEY (Francis). English comp. and org., B. Doncaster, 1774. Blind from birth. S. under Mather of Doncaster. Org. of Pentonville Chap., London. Married to a blind lady of fortune. Opened music-selling business. Became bankrupt, and was deserted by his wife. Went to America as org. Returned to England, 1799. D. Doncaster, Sept. 15, 1800.

WORKS.—Sonatas for Pf. and flute, op. 1; "Introduction to the Organ, n.d.;" Collection of Interludes, fugues, etc., for organ, op. 6; Music for the Flute; Songs.

LINLEY (George). English poet and comp., B. Whitchurch, 1795. D. London, Sept. 10, 1865.

WORKS.—*Operas and Operettas:* La Poupée de Nuremberg, Covent Garden, 1861; The Toy Maker; Francesca Doria. The Jolly Beggars, cantata (Burns). Songs of the Camp, 12 pieces. Selection of Scottish Melodies (with C. G. Byrne), 1840. Songs of the Troubadours, Lond., 1830; Musical Cynics of London, Lond., 8vo, 1862. Selection of Original Hymn Tunes. *Songs and Ballads*: A dawn of joy is near; Alice; Ada; A fond daughter; Bonnie New Moon; Bird of Beauty; Beautiful Brunette; Ballad Singer; By the spangled starlight; Clara; Come hither, pretty fairy; Chide no more; Charlie; Dream no more of that sweet time; Gipsy mother; Hetty; Hope's like a minstrel bird; Hear me but once; Ianthe; I cannot mind my wheel; I'm the little flower girl; Jeanie; Lily May; Love me little, love me long; Minnie; My own happy home; Mariner's wife; Maid of the Rhine; Only for thee; Queen of the fairy dance; Rose of the garden; Some one to love; Sweet village rose; Swiss peasant; Soon I leave thee, land of sorrow; Star and water-lily; 'Tis but for thee; Under the vine tree. Part-songs, trios, duets.

Linley composed a large number of songs, of which some became very popular. They are written in a good lyrical style, but many of them were obviously composed hurriedly for the purposes of publishers.

LINLEY (Maria). English vocalist, third daughter of T. Linley, B. Bath. Sang at Bath, etc. D. Bath, Sept. 5, 1784.

LINLEY (Mary). English vocalist, second daughter of T. Linley. B. Bath, 1759. Sang in Bath, etc. Married Richard Tickill. D. July, 1787.

LINLEY (Thomas). English comp., B. Bath, 1725 [1730-1735?]. S. under Chilcot and Paradies. Cond. of oratorios and concerts at Bath. Went to London and purchased Garrick's share in Drury Lane Theatre, with Sheridan, 1776. D. London, Nov. 19, 1795. (Buried in Wells Cath.)

WORKS.—*Operas and musical dramas:* The Duenna (Sheridan), 1775; The Camp, 1776; The Carnival of Venice, 1781; The Gentle Shepherd, 1781; The Triumph of Mirth, 1782; The Spanish Maid, 1783; Selima and Azor (from Grétry), 1784; The Spanish Rivals, 1785; Tom Jones, 1785; The Strangers at Home, 1786; Love in the East, 1788; Robinson Crusoe; Beggar's Opera (new accompaniments, etc.); Songs in "The School for Scandal." Six Elegies for three voices and Pf., Lond., 1770; Twelve Ballads; Canzonets. Numerous glees, single songs, and anthems.

Linley was one of the ornaments of English ballad music. His genius was cast in a light mould, and he attained his effects more by tenderness and simplicity than by vigour and learning. Many of his ballads are among the finest creations of the English school, and he shares with Jackson, Shield, Arne, and Storace, the distinction of having greatly added to the lyrical treasures of England. His operas, as whole works, have now very little claim on the public, but the many beautiful songs and ballads scattered throughout them are worthy of a lasting recognition. "The Posthumous Vocal Works of Thomas and T. Linley, Junr.," was published in 2 vols., 1800.

LINLEY (Thomas). English comp., son of the above, B. Bath, 1756. S. under Boyce and his father; also at Florence under Nardini. Acquainted with Mozart. Leader of Bath Concerts and at Drury Lane, London. Drowned at Grimsthorpe, Lincolnshire, Aug. 7, 1778.

WORKS.—Music to the Tempest; Ode on the Witches and Fairies of Shakespeare, 1776; The Song of Moses, oratorio; Accompaniments for wind instruments to "Macbeth" music; Anthems, glees, and songs.

This composer was cut off in the midst of a promising career, but he left several choice specimens of his ability as a lyrical composer. The popular setting of the song, "O bid your faithful Ariel fly," in the "Tempest," is by him. His larger works are now forgotten, as also are his powers as a violinist, which were great.

LINLEY (William). English comp., son of Thomas Linley, senior, B. Bath, 1767 (1771). Educated at Harrow. S. under Abel and his father. Appointed to post in East India Company's Service, by Fox. Resided in India for a time. D. London, May 6, 1835.

WORKS.—Shakespeare's Dramatic Songs, consisting of all the songs, duets, and choruses, in character, as introduced in his Dramas ..with an Introduction, Lond., 2 vols., 1815-16, fo. Two operas. Glees, etc. He also wrote novels and other literary works.

LINWOOD (Mary). English comp., B. Leicester, 1755. D. Leicester, March 2, 1845. Comp. "David's First Victory," oratorio. Songs and other vocal music.

LIPAWSKY (Josef). Bohemian comp., B. Hohenmauth, Feb. 22, 1772. D. Vienna, Jan. 7, 1810. Comp. operas, sonatas, vocal music, etc.

LIPINSKI (Karl Josef). Polish violinist and comp., B. Radzyn, Nov. 4, 1790. S. under his father, Paganini, and Dr. Mazzurana (a pupil of Tartini). Cond. in theatre in Lemberg, 1810. Travelled on Continent and gave concerts, 1829-36. Visited England, and played at Philharmonic concert, London, April 25, 1836. Chap.-master at Royal Chap., Dresden, 1839. Retired, 1861. D. near Lemberg, December 16, 1861.

WORKS.—Three polonaises for Pf., op. 3; Two polonaises for vn. and orch., op. 6; Trio for 2 vns. and 'cello, op. 8; Concertos for vn. and orch., opp. 14, 21, 24; Rondeau de Concert for vn. and orch., op. 18. Numerous variations, transcriptions, etc.

LISLE (Rouget de). See ROUGET DE LISLE.

LISLEY (John). English comp., known only as the composer of a 6 part madrigal, "Faire Citharea presents hir doves," in the "Triumphs of Oriana."

LISTEMANN (Bernhard Ferdinand). German violinist and comp., B. Schlotheim, Thüringen, 1841. Educated at Sondershausen, and S. vn. under Ulrich. S. at Leipzig Cons., 1856; also under David, Joachim, and Vieuxtemps, while Kammer-Virtuoso to Prince of Schwarzburg-Rudolstadt. Went to North America, 1867, and became member of several New York concert companies, and was soloist and leader in the Thomas Orch. Settled in Boston as teacher and cond. of the Philharmonic orch. Leader of the Boston Symphony Orch.

WORKS.—Method of Violin Playing, Boston, n.d. David's Violin School (American edition, edited), Pf. and violin music.

Listemann holds a distinguished position in Boston, and is well known as a highly cultured and progressive musician. His powers as a violinist are remarkable.

LISTON (Rev. Henry). Scottish writer and inventor, B. 1771. Minister of Ecclesmachan, Linlithgow, from 1793. D. Merchistonhall, Feb. 24, 1836. Author of "An Essay on Perfect Intonation," Lond., 4to, 1812.

He invented an Enharmonic Organ, which was performed on in Edinburgh, and his system was applied to several other instruments, though unsuccessfully, owing to the great number of pedals, and the difficulties consequently attending manipulation. His son ROBERT was the famous surgeon.

LISZT (Franz). Hungarian comp., writer, and pianist, B. Räding, October 22, 1811. Received early instructions in music from his father. First public performance on Pf., at Oedenburg, 1820 (Ries' Concerto in E flat). Played next at Pressburg. S. at Vienna under Czerny and Salieri, at expense of Counts Amadi and Sapari. *Début* as pianist at Vienna, 1823; Paris, 1823; London, 1824. Refused admission to Paris Cons. by Cherubini. S. under Reicha and Paër at Paris, 1825. His father died 1827. Reappeared in Paris as pianist, 1830-35. Formed intimacy with the Countess D'Agoult (Daniel Stern), by whom he had one son and two daughters. Resided in Geneva, 1835-6. Returned to Paris, 1836. Travelled in Italy, 1837. Appeared alternately in France, England, and Germany till 1843. Took a farewell of the public at Vienna, 1843. Conducted Beethoven festival at Bonn, 1845. Chapel-master to Duke of Weimar, 1849-61. Has since adopted advanced views on music, and has played in several places since his retirement. He is a Ph. D. and an Abbé.

WORKS.—*Symphonic Poems:* Ce qu'on entend sur la montagne (Hugo); Tasso; Les Préludes; Orphée; Prometheus; Mazeppa (Hugo); Festklänge; Heröide Funèbre; Hungaria; Hamlet; Hunnen-Schlacht (Kaulbach); Die Ideale (Schiller); Dante's Divina Commedia für grosses orch. und sopran-und alt-chor; Faust-symphonie in drei charakterbildern (Goethe); Zwei Episoden aus Lenau's Faust, for orch.; Huldigungs-Marsch (orch.), 1853; Fest-Marsch for Goethe and Schiller Festival (orch.), 1857; Gaudeamus Igitur, humoreske for orch., soli, and chorus; Concerto for Pf., in E flat (I.); Concerto for Pf., in A (II.); Etudes d'Execution transcendante (Pf.); Hungarian Rhapsodies for orch., Pf., etc.; Numerous transcriptions and arrangements for Pf., solo, etc., and for orch.; Christus, oratorio; Legend of St. Elizabeth, orat rio; St. Cecilia, cantata; Die Glocken des Strassburger, cantata; Ungarische Krönungs-messe. Various other masses, etc.; Lieder, numerous for various solo voices and Pf. *Literary:* Lohengrin et Tannhäuser de Richard Wagner, 1851; Frederic Chopin, Leipzig, 1852 (Trans. by M. W. Cook, Lond., 1877); Ueber Field's Nocturne's, 1859; Robert Franz, 1872. In addition to the foregoing, which only represents a small portion of his works, Liszt has edited numerous classics for the Pf.

As a striking individuality, rather than as a great composer, has Liszt in the past been best known to the world. His genius as a pianist places him at the head of all living performers, but his position as a composer has yet to be strictly defined. Among a section of German and other Continental musicians he is regarded with a degree of extravagant reverence which fills the sober-minded English with astonishment, not unmixed with a half pitiful contempt. That every kind of honour, imperial, municipal, and private should be heaped on the head of a mere pianist and composer does seem strange in a country where enthusiasm never touches the people when art is concerned, and where the notion has been handed down as a national heritage from Puritan times that musicians are only peripatetic vagrants. Liszt, however, is a somewhat rhapsodical musician, whose extensive reputation is as much due to the mysterious glamour which he chooses to cast over his life, as to any substantial results, apart from his performance, which he has achieved in music. His place in music, in an academical sense, is more among the great expounders than among the great creators in the art, being as he is but an imitator of Wagner, rather than an original thinker. Of his powers on the pianoforte it is almost unnecessary to speak, as the name Liszt is synonymous with everything that is great in connection with that instrument. As an interpreter of Beethoven and composers of the advanced school, he is simply sublime, and the impression which his performance creates is universally described as undying and marvellous. It is undoubtedly his command over the expressive capabilities of the pianoforte which gives Liszt such an unbounded prestige, not to speak of technical peculiarities which are his alone; and which are no doubt the outcome of an intensely nervous organization, acted upon by an enthusiastic love for musical art. It is most difficult to attempt consideration of his personal affairs, as writers who had opportunities of becoming acquainted with them invariably fall into a state of sheer mysticism and rhapsody, which is as confusing as it is certainly amusing.

His works have been subjected to every variety of criticism, and no two writers agree in regard to his works, where many agree as to his powers as a virtuoso. When opinion differs so widely it naturally follows that the works considered must either be far in advance of present-day comprehension, or must be supported by undue pretension and the elevated individuality of the author. Which is correct time alone can decide. See further, articles in Musical Journals, and in *Fraser's Magazine*, v. 52; *Belgravia*, v. 43; *Lippincott's Mag.*, v. 10; *Scribner's Mag.*, v. 10; and the *Galaxy*, v. 18.

LITOLFF (Henry Charles). English (?) pianist and comp., B. London, Feb. 6, 1818. S. under Moscheles, 1831. *Début* as pianist at Covent Garden Theatre, July 24, 1832. Married, 1835. Travelled on the Continent. Succeeded to music-publishing business of Meyer at Brunswick, 1851. Transferred business to his son Theodor, 1860. Resident in Paris from 1861.

WORKS. —*Operas:* Der Braut vom Kynast, 1847; Rodrique de Tolède; Les Templiers, 1885. *Oratorio:* Ruth et Boaz. *Pianoforte Music:* Reverie à la Valse, op. 3; Souvenirs d'Harzbourg, op. 43; Serenade, op. 61; Nocturne, Pf., op. 62; Elegie, op. 64; Arabesken, op. 65; Chant d'Amour, op. 78; La Mazurka, op. 109; Scherzo, op. 115. *Orchestral Music, etc.:* Concerto Symphonique, No. 3, "Hollandais," op. 45; First grand trio for Pf., vn. and 'cello, op. 47; Maximilian Robespierre, overture, op. 55; Second trio, op. 56; First string quartet, op. 60; Les Girondins, overture, op. 80; Das Welfenlied, overture, op. 99; Third trio, op. 100; Chant des Belges, overture, op. 101; Concerto Symphonique, No. 4, op. 102; Scenes from Goethe's "Faust," op. 103; Second Spinnleid, op. 104.

The light, graceful, and brilliant nature of Litolff's compositions have made many of them highly popular with a large section of the musical public. Many of the Pf. works are artistic and refined in the highest measure, though at no time does Litolff reach the sublime.

The well-known *Litolff* editions of musical classics are issued by a son (Theodor) of the composer's, who founded the present business in 1860. The neatness and correctness of those editions issued by the firm can not be too highly praised.

LITTA (Count Giulio). Italian comp., B. 1822. Comp. *Operas:* Bianca di Santafiora, 1842; "Editta di Larmo," 1853. Oratorios and songs.

LIVINGSTON (James R.) Scottish writer and comp., native of Aberdeenshire. Resided in Glasgow from 1844. Author of "The Organ Defended: being an Essay on the Use of that Instrument in Public Worship, with Strictures on 'Phinchas Vocal's' attack on the Organ and Dr. Anderson," Glasgow, 8vo, n. d. [c 1857]. Reply to a pamphlet entitled "Dr. Anderson as as an Organist," by Phinehas Vocal, Glasgow, 8vo, n. d. Comp. "Turn ye even to me," anthem; Sanctus; "Lamb of God," motet from Naumann; "Gracious Saviour," motet from Naumann; "The Lifeboat," song (words and music); "The Lighthouse," do. (MS.) Biographical Sketches of Haydn, Mozart, and Spohr, and notes on "Samson," the "Creation," etc., in Glasgow Choral Union Programmes.

LIVINGSTON (Rev. Neil). Scottish minister at Stair, Ayrshire, writer. Edited a reprint of "The Scottish Metrical Psalter, 1635, and the whole Illustrated by Dissertations, Notes, and Facsimiles." Glasgow, 4to, 1864.

LLOYD (Charles Harford). English comp., org., and cond., B. Thornbury, Gloucestershire, Oct. 16, 1849. Educated at Rossall School, and Magdalen Hall (Hertford College), Oxford, where he held a classical scholarship. Mus. Bac., Oxon., 1871. B.A., 1872. M.A., 1875. Org. of Gloucester Cath., in succession to Dr. S. S. Wesley, June, 1876. Cond. Gloucester Triennial Festival, 1877 and 1880. Cond. of the Gloucester Choral Soc.; do. Gloucestershire Philharmonic Soc. Org. Christ Ch., Oxford, 1883.

WORKS.—*Cantatas:* Hero and Leander, Worcester, 1884; Song of Balder, Hereford, 1885; Andromeda; Full Cathedral Service in E flat (Novello); Magnificat and Nunc Dimittis in F, for soli, chorus, and orch.; "Art Thou weary?" eight part anthem; Fear not, O Land; Blessed is he. *Part-Songs:* A sunny shaft;

Pack, clouds away ; Looking for Spring ; Beauty was lying ; A wet sheet and a flowing sea. Org. sonata in D min. Songs, etc.

LLOYD (Edward). English tenor vocalist, B. London, March 7, 1845. S. at Westminster Abbey under James Turle. Tenor singer in Trinity Coll., Camb., 1866-67. Gent. of Chap. Roy., 1867-69. Has sung at all the principal concerts and festivals in Britain.

Mr. Lloyd is one of the present generation of English tenors whose reputation is quite above the ordinary level. His style, execution, and the natural beauty of his voice, combine to make him one of the best of living vocalists. What is known as concert singing is what he has always engaged in, and as an oratorio singer Britain does not possess his superior. His ballad singing is marked by much expressive grace and feeling, and his extraordinary power of voice enables him with ease to do justice to a varied class of music.

LOBE (Johann Christian). German comp. and writer, B. Weimar, May 30, 1797. Second flute player in Weimar court band. Edited the "Allgemeine Musikzeitung, 1846-48. Resided at Leipzig as teacher. D. Leipzig, July 27, 1881.

WORKS.—*Operas:* Der Kæfich ; Die Flibustier, in 3 acts ; Witikind : Derrothe Domino ; König und Pachter, 1846 ; Die Furstin von Granada. *Instrumental music:* Solabella, overture ; Concerto for flute and orch., op. 1 ; Quartet for Pf. and strings, op. 2 ; Variations for flute and vn., viola, 'cello, op. 3 ; Three themes or flute, op. 4 ; Three amusements for Pf., op. 7 ; Quartet for Pf. and strings, No. 2, op. 9 ; Overture for orch., in G, op. 18 ; Variations for Pf., in D, op. 16 ; Variations for flute and orch., in G ; Potpourri for orch., in F, op. 20 ; Concertino for flute and orch., in E minor, op. 21 ; Le Huffon, Pf., op. 23 ; La Gaieté, overture for orch., op. 27. *Theoretical works:* Lehrbuch der Musikalischen Composition, Leipzig, 4 vols., 8vo, 1858-67 ; Katechismus der Musik (trans. by F. R. Ritter, n. d. ; and by Constance Bache, Lond., 1885) ; Katechismus der Composition ; Vereinfachte Harmonielehre, 2 parts ; Musikalische Briefe, Leipzig, 1852 ; Consonanzen und Dissonanzen, Leipzig, 1869 ; etc.

As a composer, Lobe will not live, but as a theoretical writer his name will be held in much esteem. The whole of his didactic works are clear and simple in style, and in them he enunciates many original views. The catechisms of music and composition have been translated into English.

LOBO (Alphonso). Portuguese comp., B. 1555. Chap.-master at Toledo, 1601. Comp. masses, and other church music.

LOCATELLI (Pietro). Italian violinist and comp., B. Bergamo, 1693. S. under Corelli. Settled at Amsterdam as teacher and performer. D. Amsterdam, 1764.

WORKS.—L'Arte del Violino ; Sonatas and Concertos for vn. (1721) ; Caprices, etc.

". . . while he possessed more execution, fancy, and whimsicality, than any violinist of his time, he was a voluminous composer of music, better calculated to surprise than to please."—*Busby.*

LOCKE (Matthew). English comp. and writer, B. Exeter, 1639 (1653?). Chor. in Exeter Cath. S. under Edward Gibbons and W. Wake. Comp. in Ordinary to Charles II., 1661. Became Roman Catholic, and was appointed org. to the Queen. D. London, Aug. 1677.

WORKS.—Cupid and Death, masque (Shirley), with C. Gibbons, 1653. Little Consort of Three Parts for Viols, 1656. Music for The Stepmother (Stapylton), 1664 ; Davenant's alteration of "Macbeth," 1672 ; Shadwell's "Psyche," 1673 ; and the "Tempest," 1673. Anthems, various, for Chap. Royal. Kyrie and Credo, 1666 (preface defending the work against the opposition which its novel form raised, entitled, "Modern Church Music : Pre-accused, censur'd, and obstructed in its performance before his Majesty," April 1, 1666.) Reply to Thomas Salmon's "Essay to the Advancement of Music," entitled, "Observations upon a late book entitled, An Essay to the Advancement of Musick, by casting away the perplexity of different cliffs and writing all sorts of musick in an Universal character." Reply to Salmon's "Vindication," entitled, "The present Practice of Music Vindicated, with the Duellum Musicum," etc., Lond. "Melothesia, or certain General Rules for playing upon a Continued Bass, with a choice collection of Lessons for the Harpsichord or Organ of all sorts," Lond., 1673. Songs in contemporary collections, as the Theater of Music ; The Treasury of Music ; etc.

Locke is placed high among his contemporaries by the majority of historians, but chiefly on the merits of the "Macbeth" music, which, it is well-known, is said by certain able writers to have been written by Purcell. This proved, Locke's claims to eminence pale somewhat, and he becomes more famous as the first English writer on harmony or thorough-bass. The specimens of his music to which access can be had shows him to have been a composer of much learning, if somewhat devoid of expression. Into the merits of the "Macbeth" controversy we cannot enter, and must refer inquirers to the writings of W. H. Cummings and others upon the subject.

LOCKETT (William). English org. and comp., B. Manchester, 1835. Deputy-Assistant org., Manchester Cath. Org. S. John's, Higher Broughton, 1855-61 ; do. S. Mark's, Cheetham ; do. Union Chapel, Manchester, 1877. Comp. anthems, songs, etc.

LOCKEY (Charles). English tenor vocalist, B. Oxford in first quarter of present century. Chor. of Magdalen Coll., 1828-36. S. singing under F. Harris of Bath ; also S. under Sir G. Smart, 1842 ; Lay-clerk S. George's Chapel, Windsor. Vicar-Choral, S. Paul's, 1843. Gent. of Chap. Roy., 1848. Married Miss Martha Williams, 1853. Retired, 1859.

Lockey was one of the most prominent English tenors during his career, and sang on the original production of Mendelssohn's "Elijah" at Birmingham, 1846. He also sang at most of the principal concerts and festivals throughout the kingdom, until ultimately compelled to retire by a disorder of his throat.

LOCKHART (Charles). English org. and comp., B. London, 1745. Org. of Lock Chap., 1772 ; S. Katharine Cree ; S. Mary's, Lambeth ; and Lock Chap. again in 1790-97. D. London, Feb. 9, 1815. Comp. "A Set of Hymn Tunes...for Three Voices," Lond., fo., n. d.

LODER (Edward James). English comp., B. Bath, 1813. S. at Frankfort, under F. Ries, 1826-28. Returned to England, 1828. Again went to Germany and S. under Ries. Cond. at Princess's Theatre, London ; do. Manchester. D. London, April 5, 1865.

WORKS.—*Operas:* Nourjahed, July, 1834 ; Dice of Death (Oxenford), 1835 ; The Night Dancers, Princess Theatre, 1846 ; Puck, a ballad opera ; The Sultan, dramatic piece ; The Young Guard, 1848 ; The Island of Calypso, a masque, 1851 ; Raymond and Agnes, Manchester, 1855 ; Francis the First, 1838 (compilation); The Foresters ; or, Twenty-five Years since ; The Deer Stalkers, Scottish opera ; Beggar's Opera, revised. Selection of Songs, in 3 books. Dr. Watt's Divine and Moral Songs. Sacred Songs and Ballads, Poetry by D. Ryan ; Ded. to W. Sterndale Bennett. Improved and Select Psalmody. Divine Harmony. Twelve Sacred Songs. Instructions and Exercises on the principles and practice of the art of Singing (Ashdown), n. d. *Songs and Ballads:* Afloat on the Ocean ; Arnold the Armourer ; As the bark floateth on ; Bare-footed Friar ; Beautiful Star ; Beware ; Bold Hubert the Hunter ; Brave old oak ; Come to the glen ; Columbus ; Come blushing May ; Deep-sea Fisher ; Fairest joys are fleetest ; Forester's Bride ; Hermit ; Hie away, hie away ; Ivy tree ; I love these merry festive times ; I ride on the storm ; I'll weave a sweet garland ; Last links are broken ; My harp is strung for thee ; My own loved home ; Man in the Moon ; Martin, the man of arms ; O here's to the holly ; Oak of the village ; Oh, the merry days ; Outlaw ; O speed my bark ; O the many days ; Oh ! the bonny banks of Yarrow ; Philip the Falconer ; Rhine song ; Sweet girls of Erin ; Sing me then the songs of old ; Stars of the flowers ; There is no love like the first love ; Thou art gone to the grave ; The song of the water king ; The village mill ; Twilight is sad and cloudy ; Wake, my love ; Wake from thy grave, Geselle ; Where is my loved one. Part-songs, hymns, and Pf. music.

The reputation of this composer at one time stood high, and much was expected of him ; but latterly he was neglected and allowed to drift into the questionable artistic atmosphere of a provincial manufacturing town. This affected his works in a considerable measure, and a lack of spontaneity and freshness may be observed in his later works. His music is generally of a bright and tender nature, and his harmonies and sense of dramatic propriety are well balanced, and properly in keeping with his fine flow of melody. His ballads are very fair specimens of lyrical composition, and by them he will be best remembered.

LODER (George). English comp. and singer, B. Bath, 1816. D. July 15, 1868. Comp. "The Old House at Home," musical entertainment; numerous songs; symphonies; Pf. music, etc.

LODER (John David). English violinist and writer, B. 1793. D. 1846. Author of "The Modern Art of Bowing Exemplified, with Exercises in the Major and Minor Scales," Lond., n. d.; Violin School, n. d.; Works for Violin.

Loder's violin school is one of the most popular among recent productions of that nature.

LODER (John Fawcett). English violinist and comp., son of above, B. 1812. Teacher and concert-director at Bath. Leader of orch. in London. D. April 16, 1853.

LODER (Kate Fanny). English pianoforte player, daughter of George Loder, B. Bath, Aug. 22, 1826. S. under Henry Field, and at R. A. M. under Mrs. Lucy Anderson and Charles Lucas. Gained King's Scholarship, 1839. Appeared at concerts at Bath, 1840. Re-elected King's scholar, 1841. Prof. of Harmony, R. A. M., 1844. Appeared at Philharmonic Concert, 1847. Married to Sir Henry Thompson, 1851. Performed chiefly at private concerts in London. Comp. an opera; overture; sonatas for Pf. and vn.; 2 string quartets; trio for Pf., vn., and 'cello; Pf. music; songs, etc.

LOEILLET (Jean). Belgian flute-player and comp., was member of the opera-band in London, and a popular teacher in Hart Street, Covent Garden. D. London, 1728.

WORKS.—Six Suits of Lessons for the Harpsichord; Six Sonatas for flutes, haut-boys, german flutes, and violins; Twelve Sonatas for violins, German flutes, and common flutes; Twelve Solos, for a German flute.

LOESCHHORN (Carl Albert). German comp., pianist, and teacher, B. Berlin, June 27, 1819. S. under Ludwig Berger. Prof. of Pf. at Berlin since 1858.

WORKS.—*Pianoforte*: Six Sonatinas; Aus der Kinderwelt, 2 series, op. 96, 100; La Fileuse, op. 140; Scherzo, op. 143; Reverie, op. 141; Jagdstück, in E flat, op. 152; Eglantine, op. 154; Studies. Vocal music, etc.

LOGAN (Edmond). Scottish musical writer and amateur flute player, was long connected with the staff of the *Scotsman*, to which paper he contributed able articles on the various Edinburgh concerts, etc. D. Edinburgh, Jan. 1865.

LOGIER (Johann Bernard). German writer and teacher, B. Cassel, Feb. 9 1777. Came to England, 1790. Joined regiment and went with it to Ireland. Married daughter of Herr Willmann, bandmaster 1796. Settled in Ireland, 1826. D. Dublin, July 27, 1846.

WORKS.—Sonatas for Pf., various; Set of pieces, op. 7; Irish melodies, op. 8; Original pieces for two Kent bugles, op. 11; Seven Italian pieces, Pf.; The Last Battle, Pf. Complete Introduction to the Keyed Bugle, n. d. A Refutation of the Fallacies in a Pamphlet entitled, "An Exposition of the New System," Lond., 1818 [title of pamphlet:—Exposition of the Musical System of Mr. Logier, with Strictures on his Chiroplast, by a Committee of Professors in London, 1818, 8vo]. First and Second Companions to the Royal Patent Chiroplast, folio, n. d.; Sequels to do., n. d. Manual to Logier's System on the Art and Science of Music, 4to, 1828. A System of the Science of Music and Practical Composition, 4to [1827]. General observations upon Music, and Remarks on Mr. Logier's System of Musical Education, with Appendix, Edin., 1817.

Logier's once popular method of teaching the Pf. by means of the chiroplast, a mechanical wrist-guide, has long since been superseded, and the petty jealousies and strifes caused by his success, forgotten. His Pf. works are mere compilations, and few of his works are anything but advertisements of his chiroplast. The invention of the keyed bugle, claimed for Logier (as also for Halliday, an Irish musician), is probably a popular fallacy arising from the fact that he wrote a tutor for it. Mr. Theodore Distin puts in a superior claim for his father's title to the invention.

LOGROSCINO (Nicolo). Italian operatic comp., B. Naples, 1700. D. 1763. He is credited with the creation of opera buffa, on no special grounds, and with having first made use of the formal finale in his works. He composed chiefly operas in the buffa style, of which the following are best known:—Giunio Bruto; Il Governatore; Il Vecchio marito; La Violante, 1741; Don Paduano, 1745; La Costanza, 1747; La Griselda, 1752; Rosmonda, 1755.

LOLLI (Antonio). Italian violinist and comp., B. Bergamo, 1730. Travelled in Germany as a performer. Vnst. at court of the Duke of Würtemberg; do. court of St. Petersburg. Played in France, Spain, and London. D. Sicily, 1802. Comp. sonatas, and other works for the violin.

Lolli was an able performer, but is not credited with having done aught to remodel or change the style of performance in vogue in his time.

LOMBARDI (Giacomo). Italian comp. and Prof. of singing, P. Parma, 1810. D. Naples, April, 1877. Comp. operas, masses, works on vocalization, songs, etc.

LONGFELLOW (Henry W.) American poet, B. Portland, Maine, 1807. D. 1882.
His dramatic poem, "The Spanish Student," has been set in part by different composers; and his "Golden Legend," and other works have also been utilized by American musicians. It is chiefly as a lyrical poet, however, that his works have been used, and among those who have composed music to his verses may be mentioned G. B. Allen, Anderton, Balfe, Blockley, Brislow, D. Buck, Dunne, Gabriel, Gaul, C. W. Glover, S. Glover, Gounod, J. L. Hatton, Lahee, G. Linley, E. M. Lott, Sir G. A. Macfarren, W. H. Montgomery, S. Nelson, Parker, Pinsuti, Rowland, Smart, Sullivan, Thomas, Tours, and Weiss.

LONGHURST (John Alexander). English vocalist, B. 1809. S. under John Watson. First appeared in Bishop's opera, "Henri Quatre," 1820. Sang at numerous concerts. D. 1855.

LONGHURST (William Henry). English org. and comp., B. London, Oct. 6, 1819. Chor. Canterbury Cath., 1828. Assistant org., master of the chor., and lay-clerk, do., 1836. Org. and master of the chor., do., 1873. F. C. O. Mus. Doc., Cantuar, 1875, also Toronto. Musical Lecturer at St. Augustine's Coll., Canterbury.

WORKS.—David and Absalom, oratorio; The Village Fair, an Alpine Idyll, cantata for female voices (words by Jetty Vogel, 1881. *Anthems:* Great is the Lord; Grant to us, Lord, we beseech Thee; Blessed is he that considereth the Poor; Help us, O Lord; I cried unto the Lord; I will give thanks; O come and behold the works of the Lord; O Lord, we beseech Thee; The Lord is my strength. Secular vocal music, etc.

LOOSEMORE (George). English org. and comp., flourished in the seventeenth century. Mus. Bac., Cantab. Chor. King's Coll., Camb., 1660. Org. Trinity Coll. Doc. Mus., Cantab., 1665. Comp. anthems.

LOOSEMORE (Henry). English org. and comp., brother of the above. Chor. at Cambridge. Lay-clerk, do. Org. of King's Coll. Mus. Bac., Cantab., 1640. Org. Exeter Cath., 1660. D. 1667. Comp. service and anthems.

JOHN LOOSEMORE, organ-builder of the 17th century, D. April 8, 1681, aged 68, built the organ in Exeter Cath., etc.

LOPEZ (Duarte). Portuguese comp. of the 17th century. Chap.-master of Cath. ch. of Lisbon, 1600. Comp. masses, etc.

LORETZ (Jean M.) French pianist, org., and comp.. B. Mulhouse, France, 1840. Taken while a child to United States. S. Paris Cons., under Laurent, Marmontel, Reber, etc.. 1857. *Début* as pianist at Brooklyn Philharmonic, 1860. Band master in U. S. navy. Org. in succession of St. Peter's R. C.

church, Brooklyn; Dutch Reformed ch., do.; St. Ann's on the Heights. Cond. at the Park Theatre, N. Y., etc.

WORKS.—The Pearl of Bagdad, opera, 1872; Ivanhoe, opera (MS.); Symphonic overtures; Masses, in G, C, B flat, and E flat; Episcopal Church Services, in F, C, and E flat; Sonatas and valses, for Pf., etc.

LORIS, or LORIT (Heinrich), GLAREANUS. German writer, B. Glarus, 1488. S. under J. Cochlæus. Was a musician successively in Cologne, Basle, Paris, and Freiburg. D. Freiburg, May 28, 1563. Author of "Isagoge in Musicen...," Basle, 1516, 4to; and "Dodekachordon..," Basle, 1547, fo. This latter is his great work, and contains a great variety of valuable and interesting matter; including specimens of early composers, and critical remarks on their works. It is often quoted in musical history, and has great value for the theoretical principles described or propounded in its pages. In a bibliographical sense it is one of the most rare and valuable of musical works.

LORTZING (Gustav Albert). German comp., B. Berlin, Oct. 23, 1803. Self-taught in music. Married at Cologne, 1822. First tenor at Stadttheater, Leipzig, 1833-43. Director of do., 1844-45. Director at Vienna Theatre, 1846. Cond. of theatre in Berlin. D. Berlin, Jan. 21, 1852.

WORKS.—*Operas*: Ali Pacha von Janina, 1822; Die beiden Schützen, 1837; Czaar und Zimmermann, Leipzig, 1837 (Peter the Shipwright, Lond., 1871); Hans Sachs, 1840; Wildschütz, 1842; Undine, 1845; Der Waffenschmidt, 1846; Rolandsknappen, Leipzig, 1849; Casanova; Zum Grossadmiral; Eine Berliner Grisette; Caramo; Die Schatzkammer des Inka; Regina (MS.) Overtures, part-songs, and songs.

This composer, by being kept in a somewhat low walk in operatic composition, probably never reached the full height of his abilities, which were confined within the narrow limits of comic opera. His melody is flowing and pretty, and his command over expression great. His most successful production was "Czar and Zimmermann."

LOTT (Edwin Matthew). English org. and comp., son of Samuel F. Lott, artist, B. St. Helier's, Jersey, Jan. 31, 1836. Org. of S. Matthew's Ch., Jersey, 1846. Org. successively of S. Saviour's, S. Luke's, and S. Mark's, 1848-60. S. under W. T. Best, 1851-52. Org. S. Clement Danes, Strand, London, 1860. One of the org. at International Exhib., 1862. Org. S. Peter's, Bayswater, 1863; Christ Ch., Kensington, 1864. F. Coll. of Org., 1865. Prof. of music in Victoria Coll., Jersey; and org. in old appointments, 1865. Bandmaster of three regiments in Jersey, 1867. Org. of St. Simon's, Jersey, 1867; S. Helier's Parish Ch., do., 1869. Returned to London, and re-accepted post of org. at S. Peter's, Bayswater, 1870-79. Licentiate Trinity Coll., Lond., 1875. Org. S. Ethelburga, Bishopsgate, 1880. Prof. of Counterpoint, etc., Trinity Coll., 1879-80. Org. of St. Sepulchre's, London, 1883; Principal of Musical International Coll., 1883; Mus. Doc., Toronto, 1885; Examiner for Toronto Univ., 1886.

WORKS.—*Cantata*: Thus saith the Lord, the heaven is my throne. *Services*: Communion, in F; Communion, in E (MS.). *Anthems*: Let not your heart be troubled; There were shepherds. Church Music, arranged, adapted, and original (14 numbers). Te Deum, in F. Orchestral selections, etc; String Quartet, in A minor; Journeying on. part-song, 5 voices. *Songs*: Into the silent land; I've some one who loves me; That other shore; The fairy wedding; Marion; Snowdrop. *Organ*: Andante in G; Fanfare in E flat; Offertoire in D; Offertoire (en forme de marche) in B flat; Offertoire (en forme de marche) in G; Offertoire (en forme de marche) in F; Toccata and fugue, in C minor (English organ music). *Pianoforte*: Recollections of Beethoven, Gluck, Handel, Mendelssohn, Mozart, and Spohr; Premiere Mazurka; Pensée de plus; Idylle; Evening calm; Sparkling waters; Lucrezia Borgia; Bourrée; Dreaming on the lake; Echos du soir, nocturne; Fading twilight, reverie; Gavotte; Gigue; La chasse aux bois; Minuet; Le bruissement des feuilles; Le retour des oiseaux; Les hallebardiers; Marche des conscrits; Passepied; Rêve Espagnol; Sarabande; The breeze and the harp; The skaters; Review March, Tarentella; L'espérance; Fanfare de Brest, and about 300 other pieces. A Pianoforte Catechism, Lond., 8vo, 1879 (7 editions). Harmony, Lond. (3 edits.) Dictionary of Musical Terms, Lond. (3 edits.)

Dr. Lott is an organist of distinguished ability, and a composer of some note. He was the first musician in England to introduce Haydn's Passion music in its entirety into the church service, and for this purpose he has recently adapted the whole of the Imperial Mass.

LOTT (John Frederick). German violin-maker, B. 1775. S. under Fendt. Worked with Thomas Dodd. D. April 13, 1853.

Lott is celebrated for his double-basses, which are of surpassingly fine quality. His son, GEORGE FREDERICK (B. Lond., 1800. D. 1868), worked with Davis, and produced fair instruments; and his other son, JOHN FREDERICK (D. 1871), imitated the Italian makers under instructions of Davis.

LOTTI (Antonio). Italian comp., B. Venice, 1667. S. under Legrenzi. Chor. in the Doge's Chap. Second org. S. Mark's, Venice, 1692; First do., 1704-44. Chapel-master, do., 1736. D. Venice, Jan. 5, 1740.

WORKS.—*Operas*: Giustino, 1683; Il Trionfo d' Innocenza, 1693; Achille placato, 1707; Teuzzone, 1707; Ama più chi men si crede, 1709; Il commando non inteso ed ubbidito, 1709; Sidonio, 1709; Isaccio Tiranno, 1710; La Forze del Sangue, 1711; L' Infedeltà punita, 1712; Porsenna, 1712; Irene Augusta, 1713; Il Polidoro, 1714; Foca superbo, 1715; Alessandro Severo, 1717; Il Vincitor Generoso, 1718. *Oratorios*: Il Voto Crudele, 1712; L' Umiltà coronata, 1714; Gioa, Rè di Giuda. Masses, numerous; Madrigals, 1705; etc.

This composer, though now almost forgotten save as a name in musical history, was at one time a brilliant light, and his works were received with rapture. He was the teacher of Marcello, Bassani, Gasparini, Galuppi, etc. His music is in the cold florid style common to his period, but some of his madrigals are beautiful specimens of counterpoint.

LOTTI DE LA SANTA (Mdmslle). Italian vocalist, B. Mantua, Dec. 23, 1833. Appeared in Constantinople, 1852, in "Robert the Devil." Appeared successively in Milan, Vienna, Florence, S. Petersburg, etc., 1853-7. Appeared in London, 1859, in "Maria de Rohan," "Rigoletto," "La Gazza Ladra," etc.

LOTTO (Isidor). Polish violinist, B. Warsaw, Dec. 1840. Has appeared in many of the principal Continental towns.

LOUD (Thomas). American org. and writer, author of "Organ School, or the Organ Study," Boston, n. d.; etc.

LOVER (Samuel). Irish poet, painter, novelist, and comp., B. Dublin, 1797. D. July 6, 1868.

WORKS.—Various Novels. Songs and Ballads, Lond., 12mo, 1859. *Songs*: A leaf that reminds me of thee; Angel's whisper; Birth of St. Patrick; Bowld Sojer Boy; Fairy Boy; Fairy Tempter; Fisherman; Forgive but don't ferget; Four leaved Shamrock; Hour before day: I leave you to guess; Irish mule driver; Land of the west; Letter (the); May dew; Molly Bawn; Molly Carew; My Mother dear; Rory O'More; Saint Kevin; True love can ne'er forget; 'Twas the day of the feast; Can you ever forget; Dove song; Fisherman's daughter; I can ne'er forget Thee; Kathleen and the Swallows; Lady mine; Macarthy's grave; O watch you well; Rose, zephyr, and dewdrop; Sally; Say not my heart is cold; That rogue Riley; Voice within; Whistling thief; Widow Machree.

Many of Lover's songs have passed into the Irish national repertory, and wil probably exist for ever. "The Angel's Whisper," "The Letter," and "The Fairy Tempter," will probably outlive all his other productions.

LOWE (Edward). English org. and comp., B. Salisbury [1615]. Chor. in Salisbury Cath. under Holmes. Org. Christ Ch. Cath., Oxford, 1630. Org. Chap. Royal, 1660. Prof. Music, Oxford, 1662. D. Oxford, July 11, 1682.

WORKS.—A Short Direction for the Performance of Cathedrall Service, etc., Oxford, 1661. Anthems, etc.

LOWE (Joseph). Scottish violinist and comp., son of JOHN LOWE, poet, B. about end of last century. D. (?)

WORKS.—Collection of Reels, Strathspeys, Jigs, etc. (Paterson, Edin.), n. d. Royal Collection of Reels, Strathspeys and Jigs, etc., n. d.

LÖWE (Johann Carl Gottfried). German comp., B. Loebejuen, near Halle, Nov. 30, 1796. Chor. at Köthen, 1807-9. Do. at Franke Institute, Hanover, under Türk, 1809. S. at Halle University under Michaelis. Prof. at Stettin Gymnasium, 1820. Married to Julie von Jacob, 1821. Music director to the Municipality, Stettin, 1821. Married second wife, Auguste Lange, 1823. Mem. of Akademie of Berlin, 1837. Appeared in London, 1847. Travelled in France, Sweden and Norway. D. Kiel, April 20, 1869.

WORKS.—Op. 1. Three Ballads by Herder, Uhland and Goethe; Three do., of Herder and Uhland, op. 3; Six Songs of Byron, op. 4. *Ballads* for Voice and Pf., opp. 5, 6, 7, 8, 9, 10, 13, 14, 15, 16, 17, 20, 21, 23, 29; Six Songs for Men's voices, op. 19; Five Sacred Songs for Men's voices, op. 22; Three String Quartets, op. 24; "Die Walpurgis Nacht" (Goethe), for solo, chorus and orch., op. 25; Quartet for strings, op. 26; Mazeppa (Byron), op. 27; Trio for Pf., vn. and 'cello, op. 12; Fantasia for Pf., op. 11; Duet for Pf., op. 18; Three Ballads, op. 44; Goethe's "Paria" for voice and Pf., op. 58; Three Ballads by Goethe, op. 59; Legends for voice and Pf., op. 75-76; Five Lieder for 4 voices, op. 81. *Operas:* Rodolphe; Malek Adhel; Die Alpenhütte. *Oratorios:* Die Zerstœrung von Jerusalem, op. 30.; Die Sieben Schlæfer; Johann Huss; Apostel von Phillippi; Polus von Atella. Gutenberg, cantata. Symphonies, overtures, and concertos.

"What the simple German song, or *Lied*, owes to the creative spirit of Franz Schubert, in whose productions it is represented to us as a work of art which has attained a perfect degree of harmony, in which form and purport are most intimately combined, and in which the whole variety both of form and purport seems to be exhausted—so much, or nearly as much, does the ballad owe to the imaginative and self-creative efforts of Carl Löwe. Löwe has, for this reason, been called the Schubert of North Germany. In this case also, form and purport appear to have reached the most perfect harmony; words and music, ready to follow the sentiment into the nicest details of individual nature, are enhanced by an artistic representation and characterization of the purport, displaying and unveiling all the riches of mysterious human nature. With no less justice is Löwe called, also, a born ballad composer, on account of the extraordinary number of his works belonging to this class, as well as the uncommon skill and ease with which he could overcome the difficulties presented by the words. bring out prominently the really leading idea of the poetry, and envelop it in a garment resplendent with colors and rich ornaments. For characteristic sharpness, certainty of design, and definiteness of drawing; for variety and truth of expression; and for poetic richness of feeling, Löwe, as a ballad composer, stands hitherto unrivalled. . . The demands Löwe frequently makes upon the compass and flexibility of the voice, as well as on its powers of endurance, appear by no means inconsiderable, and are probably one of the reasons why—with the exception of some few ballads—scarcely half the treasures he bequeathed us are known to and enjoyed by a very large portion of the public. In two qualities more especially, do Löwe's special labours in the domain of ballad composition strike us as being most effective and significant, and likewise crowned with the happiest success: one is that of the romantic colouring of the North, as it is called, where hobgoblins, elves, and witches form the indispensable background, as in the ballads, "Der Erlkönig," "Held Harold," "Der Todtentanz," "Elvershoh," "Odins Meeresritt," etc.; and the other the fact of his giving utterance to the folk's tone, in all its intensity, and his pouring forth from his lips those fervent melodies which are capable of at once awakening the most lively echo in the hearts of those who hear them. This is true more especially of the ballads: "Der Wirthin Töchterlein," "Graf Eberhard's Weissdorn," "Fredericus Rex," "Archibald Douglas," "Henrich der Vogler," etc. Notwithstanding this, however, the composer possesses a rich scale of tones when his tongue overflows with bitter complaint, profound but passionless sorrow, and patient abnegation. For what is highly dramatic, for the incarnation of passion, as it is called, his power of expression, on the other hand, does not appear equally prompt.—Dr. Edward Krause in the *Musical World*.

LÖWE (Johanna Sophie). German soprano vocalist, B. Oldenburg, 1815. S. at Vienna under Ciccimara. *Début* in Donizetti's "Otho," 1832. Appeared in Berlin, 1836; London (Isabella in Bellini's "Straniera"), 1841. Married Prince Lichtenstein and retired, 1848. D. Pesth, Nov. 29, 1866.

LOWE (Thomas). English tenor singer, B. early in 18th century. *Début* Drury Lane Theatre, Sept. 11, 1748. Sang in Arne's "As you like it;" Handel's oratorios, etc. Appeared at Vauxhall, 1745. Manager of Marylebone Gardens, 1763-68. Sang at Sadler's Wells, 1784. D. about 1784-5.

LUARD-SELBY. See SELBY.

LÜBECK (Ernst Heinrich). Dutch pianist and comp., B. Hague, Aug. 24, 1829. *Début* as pianist, 1841. Travelled in the United States, Mexico, Peru, etc., 1849-52. Court pianis at the Hague. Played at Philharmonic Society, London, May 7, 1860. D. Paris (insane), Sep. 24, 1876. Composed an amount of tarantellas, boleros, polonaises, and other salon pieces for Pf., of a light, brilliant, and clever character.

LUCAS (Charles). English comp., org., and cond., B. Salisbury, July 28, 1808. Chor. Salisbury Cath. under Corfe, 1815-23. Pupil R. A. M. under Lindley and Crotch, 1823-30. Mem. of Queen Adelaide's private band. Cond. R. A. M., 1832. 'Cellist at opera. Org. of Hanover Chap., Regent Street, 1839. Principal 'cello at opera. Mem. of firm of Addison, Hollier, and Lucas, music-publishers, 1856-65. Principal R. A. M., 1859-66. D. London, Mar. 30, 1869.

WORKS.—The Regicide, opera; Three symphonies. *Anthems:* Blessed be the Lord; Sing, O Heavens; Hosanna; O Lord, open Thou; O God, the strength; O thou that dwellest. Hail to the new-born spring, glee. Ah, fading joy, madrigal. *Songs:* Clouds from out the sky are driven; Homeward thoughts; Poet's consolation. String quartets, unfinished operas, etc.

LUCAS (George W.) American comp., B. Glastonbury, Conn., April 12, 1800. S. under Thomas Hastings. Teacher and lecturer. Member of Boston Handel and Haydn Society. Comp. psalms, and wrote articles on musical subjects.

LUCAS (STANLEY), WEBER, & Co. English firm of music-publishers, established in London, December, 1872. The principal of this firm, STANLEY LUCAS, was B. 1834, and is a son of Charles Lucas. He acted as secretary to the Philharmonic Society, 1866-1880, and is still secretary of the Royal Society of Musicians of Great Britain. The firm publish works by most of the eminent modern musicians, and keep a great selection of the best foreign compositions.

LUCCA (Pauline). Austrian soprano vocalist, B. Vienna, April 26, 1841. S. under Lewy, etc. Chorister in Vienna opera till 1859. *Début* as Elvira in "Ernani," Olmütz, 1859. Sang at Prague. Court singer at Berlin. *Début* Covent Garden, London, as Valentin in "Huguenots," Margnerite ("Faust,") and Selika ("L'Africaine"), July, 1863. Sang in London, 1866-7, 1868, 1870-72. Married Baron Rahde, 1865. Sang in S. Petersburg, Brussels, Vienna, United States, 1872, etc.

LUDDEN (William). American writer, author of "Pronouncing Dictionary of Musical Terms," Boston, n.d.; "School for the Voice," Boston, n.d.; "Thorough-Bass School," Cincinnati, n. d.; "School Lyrics," and other collections.

LUKIS (Rev. William C.) English writer, author of "An Account of Church Bells," London 8vo, 1857.

LULLI (Giovanni Battista), or LULLY. Italian comp., B. Florence, 1633. Page to Mdlle. de Montpensier, 1644; mem. of her band, Paris. Vnst. in King's band; Cond. of do. Comp. to the French opera, estab. 1669. D. Paris, March 22, 1687.

WORKS.—*Operas:* Les Fêtes de l'Amour et de Bacchus, 1672; Cadmus et Hermione, 1673; Alceste, 1674; Thésée, 1675; Le Carnaval, masquerade, 1675; Atys, 1676; Isis, 1677; Psyche, 1678; Bellerophon, 1679; Proserpine, 1680; Le Triomphe de l'Amour (Ballet), 1681; Persée, 1682; Phaéton, 1683; Amadis de Gaule, 1864; Roland, 1685; Idylle sur la Paix (Divertimento), 1685; L'Eglogue de Versailles (do.), 1685; Le Temple de la Paix (Ballet), 1685; Armide et Renaud,

1686 ; Acis et Galatée, 1686. *Ballets* : Alcidiane, 1658 ; Sersè, 1660 ; Ercoleamante, 1661, etc. Te Deum ; church music ; instrumental music, etc.

Lulli is one of the names in musical history more famous in an antiquarian than in a practical aspect. His operas, ballets, etc., are almost completely forgotten, and when any of his music is used it is only by way of illustration to some historical lecture. Lulli was famous in his day in a higher degree than any of his contemporaries, and his music was in universal repute. He was imitated by many succeeding composers, among others Handel and Purcell, and his influence over several parts of opera was felt to a late period. He introduced the overture, and elevated and strengthened the declamatory portions of the opera. In company with Quinault, the poet, he produced most of his operas ; the general result of their labours, however, being opposite to what is usually the case as regards the longevity of libretto and music : the music being dead and forgotten and the poetry flourishing in a hearty old age. His music is pleasing in melody, but poor in harmony, and, as compared with that of Corelli, Gasparini, Carissimi, and Purcell, lacking in interest and depth.

LUMBYE (Hans Christian). Danish comp., B. Copenhagen, 1808. Cond. of itinerant orch. Created a Kriegsrath, 1865. D. Copenhagen, March 20, 1874.

WORKS.—Die Hexenflöte, opera ; Nebelbilder, phantasie for orch. *Dances for orch.* : Les Souvenirs de Paris ; Eine Sommernacht in Dänemark ; Erinnerungen an Wien ; Corsicaner Galop ; Nordische Studenten ; Amelie ; Tivoli-Bazar ; Leopoldinen ; etc. Traumbilder, and Der Traum des Savoyarden, phantasies for orch.

The orchestra founded by H. C. Lumbye is now conducted by his son Georg, and has on the Continent a reputation somewhat similar to that enjoyed by Strauss at Vienna, and Gilmore in the U. S. The waltzes, galops, polkas, marches, etc., of Lumbye are still in vogue, but much of their popularity has sped before the efforts of more modern composers. The total amount of his dances numbers considerably over 400, and are distinguished by fine melody and agreeable harmony.

LUMLEY (Benjamin). English writer and operatic manager, B. 1812. Brought up to law, and became solicitor, 1832. Manager of Drury Lane Theatre, 1841-52 ; closed, 1852-56 ; re-opened 1856-58 with opera. D. March 17, 1875.

Lumley produced a number of operas by Donizetti, Verdi, Costa, Halévy, etc., and among the singers who appeared under his management may be named Lind, Cruvelli, Johanna Wagner, Piccolomini, Tietjens, Giuglini, Ronconi, etc. He wrote a work entitled, "Reminiscences of the Opera," Lond., 1864, with portrait.

LUNN (Charles). English writer and teacher, B. Birmingham, 5 Jan., 1838. S. in Italy under Cattaneo, Sangiovanni, and Vizoni, 1860. Sang at Worcester, Mar. 30, 1864, and Cheltenham, Dec. 1865, with great success. Relinquished public singing for purpose of devoting himself to voice training. Gives "Pupil's Concerts" in Town Hall, Birmingham.

WORKS.—The Philosophy of Voice, various editions. Vox Populi, a Sequel to the Philosophy of Voice, Lond. 1880. The English are not a Musical People, Birmingham [1869]. The Roots of Musical Art, a Catechism for Children, n. d. Vocal Expression, Empirical or Scientific, 8vo, 1878. Conservation and Restoration, or the Two Paths ; a Lecture on the Management of the Voice, 8vo, 1882. Artistic Voice, 1884.

LUNN (Henry Charles). English critic, comp. and writer, B. London (?). S. at R. A. M. under C. Potter and C. Lucas. Associate R. A. M.; afterwards a member, and latterly a professor, member of the Committee of Management, and Director. Editor of the *Musical Times* since 1863.

WORKS.—Musings of a Musician, Popular Sketches illustrative of Musical Matters and Musical People, Lond., 12mo, 1846 (several editions). The Elements of Music Systematically Explained, Lond., 1849. A Descriptive Essay on the patent clavic attachment invented by Robert Brooks, jun., shewing its importance in facilitating performance on the violin. etc., Lond., 8vo, 1845. Articles in the *Musical Times*. Compositions for Orch. (MS.) ; Vocal and Pf., published.

LUNN (William A. B.) English writer, author of "The Sequential System of Musical Notation," Lond., 4to, 1844. Five editions to 1871. Published under the *nom de plume* of Arthur Wallbridge. D. London, April 4, 1879.

LUPO (Thomas). English (? Italian) violinist and comp., flourished in the reign of James I. Comp. masques, anthems, madrigals, songs in contemporary collections, and contributed to Leighton's "Teares."

LUPOT (Nicholas). German violin-maker, B. Stuttgart, 1758. Resided at Orleans, 1785-94. Went to Paris, 1794. Violin-maker to Paris Cons. D. Paris, 1824.

Lupot imitated Stradivarius, and produced instruments of the most beautiful finish; model, varnish, and tone being alike excellent. This maker's instruments are valuable.

LUSCINIUS (Ottomar). German theoretical writer of the 16th century, B. at Strassburg, 1487. D. there, 1536. Author of "Musurgia seu praxis Musicae. Illius primo quae Instrumentis agitur certa ratio, ab Ottomaro Luscinio Argentino duobus Libris absoluta, etc." Strasburg, 1536.

LUSTIG (Jacob Wilhelm). German writer, B. Hamburg, Sept. 20, 1706. D. about [1780]. Wrote methods for various instruments, organ music, harpsichord lessons, etc.

LÜSTNER (Ignaz Peter). German violinist, B. Poischwiss, Silesia, Dec. 22, 1792. D. 1873. Established a violin school at Breslau, and taught there his sons and other musicians.

LUTHER (Martin). German reformer and musician, B. Eisleben, Nov. 10, 1483. D. Feb., 1546.

Was a composer of several hymn-tunes, one of which, "Eine feste Burg ist unser Gott," is quite well known. Unlike Calvin, and other reformers of severe views, Luther encouraged the psalmody of his period, and gets credit generally for having raised its standard.

LUTZ (Wilhelm Meyer). German comp. and cond., B. Männerstadt, Kissingen, 1829. S. at Würzburg, and under Eisenhofer, etc. Settled in England, 1848. Org. S. Chads, Birmingham; do. S. Ann's, Leeds; do. S. George's Catholic Cath., London. Cond. Surrey Theatre, 1851-55; do. Gaiety Theatre, 1869-81.

WORKS.—*Operettas*: Faust and Marguerite, 1855; Blonde and Brunette, 1862; Zaida, 1868; Miller of Milburg, 1872; Legend of the Lys, 1873; All in the Downs, 1881; Knight of the Garter, 1882; Posterity, 1884. Herne the Hunter, cantata. Numerous songs and Pf. pieces, orchestral music in MS., etc.

LUX (Friedrich). German org. and comp., B. Ruhla, Nov. 24, 1820. Comp. Das Kätchen von Heilbron, 1846; Der Schmied von Ruhla; and Die Fürsten von Athen, 1883, operas; a symphony, fantasias, fugues, concertos, etc. for org.

LVOFF (Alexis Feodorovitch von). Russian violinist and comp., B. Reval, May 25, 1799. General in Russian Army. Director of Music at Imperial Court. D. Kowno, Dec. 28, 1870.

WORKS.—Bianca e Gualtiero, opera, 1845; Ondine, do.; La Bordeuse, do.; Concerto for vn. and orch.; Psalms; Russian National Anthem, 1833.

Lvoff was a good violinist, but his fame will rest on his "Russian National Anthem."

LYONS (James, M.A.). American writer and musician, compiled "Urania, or a Choice Collection of Psalm Tunes, Anthems, and Hymns, from the most approved Authors...To which is prefaced the plainest and most necessary Rules of Psalmody," Philadelphi, 1761. "Lessons for the Uranian Society," Philadelphia, 1785.

LYSBERG (Charles Samuel), or BOVY. Swiss pianist and comp., B. Geneva, March 1, 1821. S. under Chopin at Paris. Resided at Geneva as teacher and comp. D. Geneva, Feb. 18, 1873.

Comp. numerous Pf. pieces of a brilliant and clever character.

LYSONS (Rev. Daniel). English writer, author of "History of the Origin and Progress of the Meeting of the Three Choirs of Gloucester, Worcester, and Hereford." Gloucester, 8vo, 1812. Second edition continued by John Amott (see that name). Lond., 8vo, n. d. [1864].

M.

MAAS (Joseph). English tenor vocalist, B. Dartford, Kent, Jan. 30, 1847. Of Dutch descent. Chor. in Rochester Cath. from 1856. S. for a time under Mrs. Galton, eldest sister of Louisa Pyne. Employed in a government situation at Chatham. At instance of Mr. Wood, he went to Milan, where he studied till 1871. *Début* at St. James's Hall, London, 1871. Appeared afterwards in opera at Covent Garden, 1872. Appeared in the United States with Miss Kellogg, and afterwards sang in the Carl Rosa Opera Company in Britain, from 1877. Sang in Paris and Brussels. D. London, Jan. 16, 1886.

Famed throughout Britain as a concert vocalist. He made many notable appearances at the Crystal Palace, London ; at the Birmingham and other Festivals; and at all the principal London concerts. His voice was powerful, of good compass, and he managed it with much ease and feeling. A chief defect was an occasional display of robustness when refinement was looked for. He was one of the most promising of English tenors, and his death was much regretted by the musical profession and public alike.

MAAS (Louis). German pianist, comp., and teacher, B. Wiesbaden, June 21, 1852. Early taken to England by his father, Theodore Maas, teacher of music. Educated at King's College. S. at Leipzig Cons., 1867, under Reinecke, Papperitz, etc. Teacher in Kullak's Cons., 1873-4. Prof. in Leipzig Cons., 1875-80. Teacher of Pf., comp., etc., in the New England Cons. of Music, Boston, Mass, 1880. Director of the Philharmonic Concerts, Boston. Fell. American Coll. of Musicians.

Well known as a pianist of great ability, and a comp. of symphonies, overtures, concertos, Pf. music, string quartets, songs, etc.

M'ALLISTER (Robert). Scottish musician and teacher of singing in Glasgow, B. Glasgow, Feb., 1822. Author of "The Art of Singing at Sight Simplified," 1844 ; "The Art of Singing at Sight; or, a Complete Theoretical and Practical Vocal Music Instruction Book," etc. Glasgow, 1848, 8vo. "Easy Introduction to the Key-Board of the Pianoforte or Harmonium." Inventor of the Tonic Sliding Scale or Musical Ladder ; Initial Note Notation ; Stave Solfa Notation, etc.

MACBETH (Allan). Scottish comp., pianist, and cond., B. Greenock, March 13, 1856. Educated in Germany, 1869-71. S. music under Mr. Robert Davidson, and Herr Otto Schweitzer, Edinr., 1871. Org. and choirmaster in Albany Street Congregational Chap., Edin., 1874. S. at Leipzig Cons. under Richter, Reinecke, Jadassohn, 1875-76. Returned to Edin., 1877. Cond. of Glasgow Choral Union, Sept., 1880. Cond. Greenock Select Choir, 1881. Org. and choirmaster Woodside Established Ch., 1882 ; St. George's in the Fields, 1884. Cond. of Glasgow Kyrle Choir.

WORKS.—Operetta (MS.), "The Duke's Doctor;" "In Memoriam," orchestral piece ; Trio for Pf., vn., and 'cello ; Suite of pieces for 'cello and Pf. ; Intermezzo for orch., "Forget-me-not" (Glasgow Choral Union Concerts, 1883) ; Serenata for orch., 1884 ; Danse Pizzicati, orch.; Ballet de la cour, orch. *Pianoforte Works*: Marche Festale (duet) ; Pleasing Moments ; Danse Allemande ; Recollection ; Berceuse ; Humoreske ; Marche Ancienne ; Mazurka ; Scherzino. *Vocal Music*: In the mellow Autumn sunshine ; The steersman's song ; The light that lies in my love's eyes ; Near thee, still near thee ; Come, fill me a brimming bowl ; Love's Parting ; Queen Dagmar's Cross ; Jeanette ; The Waif ; Arrangements of Scotch Songs for 4 voices, etc.

MACDONALD (Alexander). Scottish writer. Was joint music-master with Archibald Macdonald of George Heriot's Hospital, Edinburgh, 1807-10. Author of "The Notation of Music Simplified, or the Development of a System in which the Characters employed in the Notation of Language are applied to the Notation of Music," Glasgow, 1826; "A New Collection of Vocal Music containing Church Tunes, Anthems, and Songs, for the Use of the Several Hospitals of this City," Edin., 1807.

MACDONALD (Donald). Scottish musician and writer, flourished at end of 18th and beginning of 19th centuries. Published "Collection of the Ancient Martial Music of Caledonia, called Piobaireachd, as performed on the Great Highland Bagpipe, adapted to the Pianoforte and Violoncello, with some old Highland Lilts, etc." Edin., n.d., folio. A tutor for the Bagpipe is included in this work.

MACDONALD (John Denis). Scottish writer, author of "Sound and Colour: their Relations, Analogies, and Harmonies." Lond., 8vo, 1869.

MACDONALD (Lieutenant-Col. John, F.R.S.). Scottish musician and writer, B. Kingsbury, New York, 1759. Son of Flora Macdonald, the Scottish Heroine. D. Exeter, Aug. 16, 1831. He published a number of works on military tactics, telegraphy, and a "Treatise Explanatory of the Principles Constituting the Practice and Theory of the Violoncello." Fo., 1811. Also a "Treatise on the Harmonic System, arising from the Vibrations of the aliquot divisions of strings." Fo., 1822.

MACDONALD (Patrick). Scottish musician and clergyman, B. April 22, 1729. S. Aberdeen University. Licensed as minister, 1756. Presented to the living of Kilmore, 1756. D. Sept. 25, 1824. With the assistance of Joseph Macdonald he compiled "A Collection of Highland Vocal Airs, never hitherto published, to which are added a few of the most lively Country Dances, or Reels, of the North Highlands and Western Isles; and some specimens of Bagpipe Music," Edin., 1781.

"His knowledge of music was profound; and he was not only an original composer, but used various instruments with an affect at once eminently skilful and highly characteristic."—*Fasti Ecclesiæ Scoticanæ.*

MACE (Thomas). English writer and musician, B. 1613. Clerk of Trinity Coll., Camb. Married, 1636. D. after [1690].

WORKS.—Musick's Monument; or, a Remembrancer of the Best Practica Musick, both Divine and Civil, that has ever been known to have been in the World. Divided into Three Parts. The first part shows a necessity of Singing Psalms well in Parochial Churches, or not to sing at all...The Second Part treats of the Noble Lute (the Best of Instruments). In the Third Part, the generous Viol in its Rightest use, is treated upon. Lond., fo., 1676 [portrait].

In the foregoing extremely quaint production, the author makes use of many remarks on psalmody, composition, etc., at once amusing and instructive. Mace invented a Dyphone or Double Lute of 50 strings, and a table-organ.

M'FADYEN (Joseph). Scottish music-seller in Glasgow in early part of present century. Published collections entitled The Repository of Scots and Irish Airs, Strathspeys, Reels, etc.; Miscellaneous Collection of the best English and Irish Songs, Glasgow, 8vo, n.d.; Selection of Scotch, English, Irish, and Foreign Airs, adapted for the Fife, Violin, or German Flute. 6 vols. ob. 8vo, n.d., etc. He kept a musical circulating library in Glasgow.

MACFARLANE (George). Scottish band-master and writer, was a member of the late Duke of Devonshire's private band. Author of "Cornopeon Instructor, containing the elementary Principles of Music, together with Exercises, Preludes, Airs, and Duetts in every key in which the Instrument is playable with effect," Lond., fo., n.d.

MACFARLANE (John Reid). Scottish comp., B. 1800. Precentor for a time in the Outer High Church, Glasgow. D. London, June 10, 1841. Comp. a number of glees, psalm tunes, etc. Brother of Thomas Macfarlane noted below.

He edited "Harmonia Sacra, a Selection of Sacred Music, Ancient and Modern, in four parts," Glasgow, n.d.

MACFARLANE (Thomas). Scottish org. and comp., B. Horsham, Sussex, 1809. Son of Duncan Macfarlane, a fine bass singer, who played the French horn in the Ayrshire Militia. Pupil of Andrew Thomson, music-teacher, Glasgow, and afterwards S. under J. B. Cramer, Herz, and Bergotti; and singing under M. Garcia. Org. of Old Episcopal Chap., Glasgow, 1826, where he remained five or six years. Org. of S. Jude's Episcopal Church till about 1857. Precentor of Park Church, 1859-1866. Removed to London, 1869-70. Harmoniumist in Camden Road Presbyterian Ch., 1871-1882; and cond. of Camden Road Choral Soc. for a time. Retired from all professional work, 1882. He compiled Congregational Psalmody of St. Jude's Ch., Glasgow, n.d.; Selection of Sacred Music, containing a Selection of Psalm and Hymn Tunes, Chaunts, Te Deums, etc.; Park Church Psalmody, Glasgow, 4to, 1860; The Chorale and Supplementary Psalmody, a Selection of Ancient German and other Chorales...Glas., n.d.; The Scripture Chant Book...the Psalms of David, with other portions of Holy Scripture, pointed for Chanting, etc....Glasgow, n.d.; Songs in "Lyric Gems of Scotland," etc.

MACFARREN (George). English play-wright, B. London, Sept. 5, 1788. D. Lond., April 24, 1843. Was successively director of Queen's Theatre, Tottenham St., 1831-32, and Strand Theatre, London. Was a critic, and wrote numerous farces and dramatic pieces, including the librettos of his son's "Devil's Opera" and "Don Quixote."

MACFARREN (Sir George Alexander). English comp., professor, and writer, B. London, March 2, 1813. S. under his father; also under C. Lucas, 1827; and C. Potter at R. A. M., 1829. Prof. at R. A. M., 1834; Prof. music Cambridge University, March 16, 1875. Bac. Mus., Cantab., April, 1876; Doc. Mus., do., April, 1876. Principal of R. A. M., 1876. Knighted, 1883.

WORKS.—*Operas:* The Devil's Opera, 2 acts, Aug. 13, 1838 (Eng. Opera Ho.(Don Quixote, 1846 (Drury Lane); King Charles II., by D. Ryan, Oct. 27, 1849 (Princess Theatre); The Sleeper Awakened, by J. Oxenford, 1850; Robin Hood, by J. Oxenford, 1860; Jenny Lea, 1863; She Stoops to Conquer, 1864; The Soldier's Legacy, 1864; Helvellyn (Oxenford) 1864; Outward Bound; The Prince of Modena (MS.); Caractacus (MS.); El Malhechor (MS.); Allan of Aberfeldy (MS.). *Oratorios:* St. John the Baptist, Oct. 23, 1873, Bristol Festival; The Resurrection, 1876, Birmingham Festival; Joseph, 1877, Leeds Festival; King David, 1883; Editions of Handel's "Judas Maccabeus;" Jephtha; Belshazzar, etc. *Cantatas:* Leonore, by J. Oxenford, 1852; May Day, by J. Oxenford, 1857; Christmas, by J. Oxenford, Feb., 1860; Freya's Gift, masque, 1863; Lady of the Lake (from Scott), cantata, Glasgow Musical Festival, Nov. 15, 1877; Songs in a Cornfield, 1868. *Orchestral Works:* Symphonies, No. 1, 1828; No. 2, ; No. 3, in A minor; No. 4, in F minor, 1834; No. 5, in B flat; No. 6, in C sharp minor; No. 7, in D. Overtures: Chevy Chase, 1836; Merchant of Venice; Romeo and Juliet; Hamlet; Don Carlos; Midsummer Night's Dream; Overture in E flat, etc. *Chamber Music:* Quartet for Pf. and strings, G minor; Trio, do., E minor; Four string quartets, 2 G min., 1 A, 1 F; Concerto for Pf. and orch., in F min.; Sonatas for Pf., in E flat and A. *Church Music:* Services in E flat; G (unison); Cantate Domino, etc. *Anthems:* A day in Thy courts; God said, Behold I have given you every herb; Hosannah to the Son of David; O Holy Ghost; O Lord, how manifold; The Lord hath been mindful of us; The Lord is my shepherd; We give Thee thanks; We wait for Thy loving kindness; Wherewithal shall a young man; While all things were in quiet silence; Seven Two-part Anthems for small choirs; Fifty-two Introits, or Short Anthems, for Holy Days and Seasons of the Church; The Lord is King, etc. *Vocal Music, Secular, Concerted:* Shakespere's Songs, for 4 voices, 1860-4; Moore's Irish Melodies; Six Convivial Glees, 3 voices, 1836; Adieu, love, adieu; All is still; Alton Locke's song; At first the mountain rill; Break, break, on thy cold grey stones; Bright Tulips; The Bellman; Christmas; Fear no more; Gather ye rosebuds; I could wish you, all who love; In a drear-nighted December; Lads and Lasses hasten all; Orpheus with his lute; The Primrose;

Robin Goodfellow; Sing, heigh ho; Song of the railroads; The cuckoo sings in the poplar tree; The hunt's up; The last wild rose; The Sands of Dee; The Starling; The Three Fishers; Weighing anchor; Cricketer's song; The Mahogany tree; Harvest Home; The wood, the gay green wood; Now the sun has mounted high; May the saints protect and guide thee; A maiden I love dearly, etc., etc. *Songs, Ballads, etc.:* A dream of the past; As mines of countless treasure; Be still, sad heart; Bessie; Charming little Alice; Farewell! if ever fondest prayer; Heart, my heart; I arise from dreams of thee; Music when soft voices die; Nobody's nigh to hear; O world! O life! O time; Oh! maiden, ungrateful; Summer, thou art sad and drear; The Village Bride; 'Tis sad to walk alone; Waiting at the ferry; Wear this flower; A lost chord; Mountaineer's Wife; Three roses; Bonnie Mary; Oh I hear ye sing; The Sea King's daughter; I weep alone; Somebody; Thoughts of youth; My faint spirit; Amid the new mown hay; Breathe again that song of sadness; Derwentwater; Farewell to the woodland; Green lanes of England; Light of our love; Love me in the spring time; Adieu for evermore; A morn of May; Carno's vale; Fading leaves; Flowers are in the fields again; Footsteps of angels; I'm true to thee; Late, so late; Laura; When I remember; Songs of Scotland, edited; Songs of England, edited (Chappell); British Vocal Album; Poems from Lane's Arabian Nights, etc.; Sonatas etc., for organ, and miscellaneous Pf. music. *Literary Works:* Rudiments of Harmony, with Progressive Exercises, Lond., 1860 (other editions); Six Lectures on Harmony, delivered at the Royal Institution of Great Britain, Lond., 8vo, 1867 (2nd edition, 1877); On the Structure of a Sonata, Lond., 1871; Eighty Musical Sentences to illustrate Chromatic Chords, Lond., 8vo, 1875; Counterpoint, a Practical Course of Study, Lond., 4to, 1879; Musical History briefly Narrated and Technically Discussed, Lond., 8vo, 1885 [from the "Encyclopædia Britannica," 9th edit.]; Analyses of works by Beethoven, Costa, Handel, Haydn, Mendelssohn, Mozart, etc.; Articles in musical periodicals on National Music, etc.; Addresses and Lectures delivered at R. A. M., etc.; Articles on Musical Biography in Imperial Dictionary of Biography; Grove's Dictionary of Music, etc.

Sir George A. Macfarren has long been a prominent figure in the musical history of Britain; and probably no musician connected with the country ever exerted such great influence for good. By precept and example both he has endeavoured to raise the musical culture of the nation to a higher standard than it ever before reached; and it is due in a high measure to his endeavours that so much real good has been effected. An active interest in musical concerns is now showing all over the nation, and between the influence of the Royal Academy of Music, and the personal endeavours of its principal, there is no reason to suppose that the British may not claim in time to be the most musical nation in the world.

As a composer Sir George Macfarren stands among the first of living musicians, both by reason of his science and genius. His operatic works are not now performed, for reasons no doubt connected with the questions of copyright and the lack of enterprise; but they are undeniably compositions of great dramatic power and undoubted worth. Their success when produced sufficiently indicates this. He has been most successful with his oratorios and cantatas among his larger works, and their popularity remains a most pleasing tribute to their worth. His part-songs, anthems, and other vocal works are constantly being performed, and their universal use is but another indication of their merit. Among his prose works his "Harmony" has been most successful, and is now used as a text-book wherever music is taught His other writings possess high didactic value, and are recognised as valuable and enduring contributions to the English literature of music. In every respect there has never been a musician who has so ably and satisfactorily led the march of British musical progress, or so much graced the Royal Academy of Music with such a capital union of scholarship, tact, and literary ability.

MACFARREN (Natalia), *née Andrae*. English vocalist and teacher, wife of the foregoing, has translated a number of opera libretti, and written a Vocal School, and an "Elementary Course of Vocalising and Pronouncing the English Language," Lond., fo., n.d.

MACFARREN (Walter Cecil). English comp., pianist, lecturer and teacher, brother of Sir George, B. London, Aug. 28, 1826. Chor. Westminster Abbey, under J. Turle, 1836-41. S. at R. A. M. under Holmes, Potter, and his brother. Prof. at Academy, 1846; Cond. of Acad. Concerts, 1873. Director of Philharmonic Soc., 1868; Treasurer, do, 1876.

WORKS.—Symphony in B flat. *Overtures:* A Winter's Tale; Beppo; Hero and Leander; Pastoral; Henry the Fifth. Concertstück for Pf. and orch. Service in C, for Parish Choirs; Evening Service; Praise ye the Lord, anthem. *Part-Songs*: Song of the Sunbeam, cantata for female voices; Daybreak; An Emigrant's song; Autumn; Cradle song; Dainty love; Go, pretty birds; Good night, good rest; Harvest song; Hence, all yon vain delights; Highland war song; Lover's parting; Love's heigh ho; More life; Morning song; Night, sable goddess; O gentle summer rain; O lady, leave thy silken thread; Sea song; Shepherds all; Shortest and longest; Spring; Summer with your genial noons; Swallow, swallow, hither wing; Sweet content; The Curfew bell; Up the airy mountain; The Warrior; Up, up ye dames; Windlass song; You stole my love, etc. *Songs:* Six Sacred songs; A widow bird sat mourning; O were my Love; While my lady sleepeth; Ne'er to meet again; Welcome Spring; Awake, O heart; The Linnet; Sail swiftly, O my soul; The Willow.tree, etc. *Pianoforte Music:* 3 Sonatas; Suite de pieces (5 dances); First Menuetto; Rondino Grazioso; Toccata; Autumn song; Capriccio brillante; First and second polonaises; Reveries; Galops de concert; Nocturnes; Marche de concert; Impromptus; Mazurkas; Saltarella; Serenade; Pastorale; 14 Tarantellas; Scherzos; 5 Gavottes; 4 Bourées; Barcarolles; Valses; 3 Berceuses; 3 Caprices; Album Leaves. Editions of classical works.

Mr. Macfarren, though perhaps best known as a successful teacher and conductor, is nevertheless a composer of high merit. His part-songs and Pf. music show that he possesses a most graceful faculty for composition.

McGIBBON (William). Scottish violinist and comp., B. about beginning of the 18th century. S. vn. under Corbet of London. Leader of Gentlemen's Concerts at Edinburgh. D. Edinburgh, Oct. 3, 1756.

WORKS.—Six Sonatos or Solos for a German Flute or Violin, Edin., 1740; A Collection of Scots Tunes, some with variations for a violin, hautbois, or German flute, with a bass for a Violoncello or Harpsichord—Book 1, 1742; Book 2, 1746; Book 3, 1755. Original dances, and some flute music.

M'GLASHAN (Alexander). Scottish violinist, flourished in Edinburgh about the end of last century, Was leader of a fashionable band. He published "A Collection of Strathspey Reels, with a Bass for the Violoncello or Harpsichord," 1778; A Collection of Scots Measures, Hornpipes, Jigs, Allemands, Cotillons, and the fashionable Country Dances, with the bass for the Violoncello or Harpsichord, Edin., 4to [1778].

MACGUCKIN (Barton). Irish tenor vocalist of the present time. Has sung at most of the principal concerts throughout Britain, and is a member of the Carl Rosa Opera Company. He has a light tenor voice of moderate capacity, admirably adapted for ballad singing, but in a measure unsuited for the heavy dramatic music which he occasionally essays.

MACHARDY (James M.) Scottish teacher, author of "The Rudiments of Music, as it ought to be studied, vocal and instrumental," 8vo, n.d., 32 pp.

MACHARDY (Robert). Scottish comp. and teacher, B. Edinburgh, Sept. 10, 1848. Has composed "The Woodland Witch," a Dramatic Cantata; "Hymn of the Seasons," Cantatina; Some songs and Pf. pieces; and edited for some time "The Scottish Musical Times," now defunct. Author of "Progressive Pianoforte Playing," n. d.; "Progressive Sight-Singing," n. d.

MACIRONE (Clara Angela). English comp. and teacher, B. London, 1821, of an ancient Roman family. S. under C. Potter and C. Lucas at R. A. M. Prof. at R. A. M., and Associate of Philharmonic Society. Head Music Mistress, Aske's School for Girls, Hatcham. Head Music Mistress Church of England High School for Girls, Baker St., Lond., n.w.

WORKS.—*Part-Songs:* Autolycus Song; Cavalier's Song; Cavalry Song; Footsteps of Angels; Good morrow to my lady bright; Humptie dumptie; Jack and Gill (for female voices); Jog on, jog on, the footpath way; Old Daddy long legs; Ragged and torn and true; Sir Knight, Sir Knight; Spring Song; The Battle of the Baltic; The sun shines fair on Carlisle wall; The wounded Cupid; The soldier's dream; Woman's smile; Who is Sylvia? *Trios for Female Voices*: When the dawn of the morning ("The Cavalier"); The Farewell. *Songs*: An hour with thee; Daisy's Song; Dreams; Good morrow to my lady bright; Lay of the Troubadour; My child; Song over a child; The Recall; Take, O, Take; The country lassie; The song of the lily; The Cavalier's song; The Lady's bird song; Aspettar e nou venire; Jeanie; The Rose-a-Lyndsaye; Henri de Lagadère; Sweet and low; O, hush thee my babie. *Duets*: Hear me (sacred duet); Give place ye lovers (duet and canon); Love having once flown; Italian Quartett—"O, Musa." *Sacred Airs*: Benedictus; Help me, O Lord; Pianoforte Duett—Recollections of Fra Diavolo. *Pianoforte Pieces*: Sketches for the Pianoforte—Summer Serenade; Zwei clavier stücke; Cantilena. *Unpublished Works*: Te Deum; Anthems; Pf. duet; Pf. and violin duet; Pf., violin, and 'cello trio; Larger incomplete works.

Miss Macirone is one of the best known among British lady composers, and the merit of her works gives her a high place. She is chiefly known, however, by her part-songs, which have been sung by 3000 voices at the Crystal Palace and Exeter Hall by Hullah's Choir, Henry Leslie's choir, etc.; and her songs, which have been sung by Madam Clara Novello, Madam Sainton-Dolby, Herr Pischek, Mr. Santley, etc. She has formulated and put in practice an original system of teaching large numbers of pupils, and the success of her method has been endorsed by such authorities as Sir G. A. Macfarren, J. Barnby, and W. Macfarren. She has published many more songs and part-songs than are noticed above.

MACKAY (Angus). Scottish collector, published "A Collection of Ancient Piobaireachd, or Highland Pipe Music...To which are prefixed some sketches of the principal hereditary pipers and their establishments." Edin., fo., 1838.

MACKAY (Charles, LL.D.). Scottish poet and writer, B. Perth, 1814· Author of numerous historical and general works, but best known as the author of a number of lyrics, which, set to music by Henry Russell, Bishop, and others, were known all over the English-speaking world. He wrote an introduction to Boosey's Collection of Scottish Songs, and has composed a few pieces of music himself. The vigorous and healthy tone of his lyrics has made them famous all through Britain and America, and it is only necessary to mention "Cheer, boys, cheer," "To the West, to the West," "The good time coming," and "Tubal Cain," to recall a host of others.

MACKAY (William). Scottish musician, author of "The Complete Tutor for the Great Highland Bagpipe." Edin., 8vo, 1840.

MACKENZIE (John). Son of a member of the band of the Forfarshire Militia, B. Durham, 1797. Vnst. and teacher in Aberdeen, and leader in Theatre Royal there. Left Aberdeen for Edinburgh, at request of James Ducrow, 1831. D. Edinburgh, 1852.

MACKENZIE (Alexander). Scottish violinist and comp., son of the above, B. Montrose, 1819. Went to Edinr. with his father, 1831. Entered Theatre Royal orch. under Dewar. S. under Sainton at London, and also at Dresden under Lipinski. Leader of orch. in Theatre Royal, Edinburgh, under successive managements of Murray, Glover, and Wyndham. D. Edinburgh, 1857.

WORKS.—Dance Music of Scotland, Edin., n. d.; Six Scotch Airs for Violin; One Hundred Scotch Airs for Violin. *Songs*: Grey hill plaid; Nameless lassie; Linton Lowrie.

Mackenzie was a very excellent violinist, and became widely known in his own country for his exceptionally tender renderings of Scottish melodies. He did much to assist and foster the cultivation of classical music in Scotland. His dance music collection is one of the best among more modern productions, and some of his songs are included in the national anthology.

MACKENZIE (Alexander Campbell). Scottish comp. and vnst., B. Edinburgh, 1847. S. under his father, and in Germany at Schwarzburg-Sondershausen under W. Ulrich and E. Stein, 1857. Vnst. in Ducal orch., 1861. S. violin under Sainton in London, 1862. King's scholar of R. A. M., 1862. Resided in Edinburgh as teacher, conductor in S. George's Church, etc., 1865. Resided on Continent from 1879.

WORKS.—Seven part-songs for mixed voices, op. 8 ; Rustic Scenes, 4 Pf. pieces, op. 9 ; Larghetto and Allegretto for violoncello, op. 10 ; Pianoforte Quartet in E flat (Leipzig), op. 11 ; Two Songs, op. 12 ; Five Pieces for Pf., op. 13 ; Drei Lieder von H. Heine (Leipzig), op. 14 ; Trois Morceaux pour Pf., op. 15 ; Three songs by L. Robertson, op. 16 ; Three songs by Christina Rossetti, op. 17 ; Three anthems, op. 19 ; Six compositions for Pf., op. 20 ; Rhapsodie Ecossaise (No. 1), for orch., op. 21 ; Three vocal trios (E. Oxenford), op. 22 ; In the Scottish Highlands, three Pf. pieces, op. 23 ; Burns : Rhapsodie Ecossaise (No. 2), for orch., op. 24 ; The Bride : Cantata for soli, chorus, and orch., op. 25 ; Jason : Dramatic Cantata, Bristol Festival, 1882 ; Colomba, Lyrical Drama by F. Hueffer, London, Drury Lane, April 9, 1883 ; The Rose of Sharon, oratorio, Norwich, 1884 ; Vocal Melodies of Scotland, arranged for the Pf. ; Overture for orch., "Cervantes" (MS.) ; Scherzo for orch. (MS.) ; Overture to a Comedy, for orch. (MS.) ; "Tempo di Ballo," overture for orch. (MS.) ; Concerto for violin and orch., 1885. "Guillaume de Cabestant," opera. Part-songs, songs, organ music, etc.

The works of Mr. Mackenzie have at all times been regarded with a great measure of favour, and on the production of " Jason," and latterly " Colomba," and the " Rose of Sharon," he at once took a place as a composer in the first rank among his British contemporaries. The level which his dramatic work " Colomba " may in the future be assigned it is impossible to anticipate, but the immediate favour which it attained is a moderately good augury that its merits will not be overlooked in time to come. With little if any help from the libretto, he has contrived to illustrate in a powerful and brilliant manner the compact dramatic story of Prosper Mérimée. Mr. Mackenzie has shown himself possessed of a singularly powerful and facile vein of dramatic ideas, and in " Jason," the Rhapsodies, and " Colomba," and " Rose of Sharon," has shown himself the equal of any living British composer.

M'KENZIE (Marian). English contralto vocalist of present time. B. Plymouth. Gained Perepa-Rosa Scholarship at R.A.M., 1878, and S. under Randegger. She has sung at most of the English provincial festivals, in Scotland, and in London.

MACKESON (Charles). English writer, compiler of "Guide to the Churches of London and its Suburbs," n.d. Contains notices of musical service, organs, etc. Also, biographical sketches of musicians in the " Choir," etc.

MACKINLAY (Thomas). Scottish music publisher, compiled "A Catalogue of Original Letters and Manuscripts in the Autograph of Distinguished Musicians, Composers, Performers, and Vocalists," Lond., 8vo, 1846.

MACKINTOSH (James). Scottish musician, author of " The Musicmaster for Schools and Families," Lond., 4to, 1862.

MACKINTOSH (John). Scottish bassoon player. B. 1767. Played in principal orchestras between 1821-1835. D. 1840. Famous as one of the finest performers of his day, and celebrated all over Europe for the excellent tone and style of his playing.

MACKINTOSH (Robert). Scottish comp. and violinist, B. about middle of 18th century. Teacher in London. D. London, Feb., 1807.

WORKS.—Op. 1. Airs, Minuetts, Gavotts, and Reels, mostly for two Violins, and a Bass for the Violoncello or Harpsichord, n.d.; op. 2. Sixty-eight new Reels, Strathspeys, and Quick Steps ; also, some slow pieces, with variations for the Violin or Pianoforte, with a Bass for the Violoncello or Harpsichord, 1793 ; 2nd Book, 1793 ; 3rd Book, 1793 ; 4th Book of Reels, n.d.

This composer was well known in his time as *Red Rob* Mackintosh. He was a good performer, and wrote the song "A cogie of ale and a pickle ait-meal."

M'LACHLAN (John). Scottish musician, writer of The Precentor, with a choice Collection of Psalm Tunes, Glas., 8vo, 1776 (with Finlay) ; The Precentor, or an Easy Introduction to Church Music, Glas., 12mo, 1779 ; another edition, Glas., 1782.

MACLEAN (Charles Donald). Scottish (?) org. and comp. B. March 27, 1843. S. under F. Hiller at Cologne. Mus. Bac., Oxon, 1860. Org. Exeter

Coll., Oxford, 1862. Mus. Doc., Oxon, 1865. Org. and Music-director at Eton., 1872.

WORKS.—Noah, dramatic oratorio, 1865; Two Pastorales for Pf., op. 2; Suite de Pieces, Prelude, Saltarello, Bourée, Passepied, Valse, op. 3; Scherzo Album, Pf., op. 4; Three Songs; I think of Thee, song; Homage to Beauty; Six Love Songs.

MACLEAN (William). Scottish poet and amateur musician, B. Glasgow, March 22, 1805. Educated at Glasgow University. Manufacturer and merchant in Glasgow, J.P. for Counties of Renfrew and Lanark, etc. Published "Maclean's Sacred Music, arranged for Four Voices, with Organ or Pianoforte Accompaniment," London, 2 parts 4to, 1854-5. Also comp. of a large volume of "Sacred Melodies" in manuscript, now deposited in the Mitchell Library, Glasgow.

MACLEOD (Captain Neil). Scottish collector, published a Collection of Piobaireachd or Pipe Tunes, as verbally taught by the M'Crummin Pipers in the Isle of Skye, to their Apprentices, Edin., 1828, 8vo.

MACLEOD (Peter). Scottish amateur comp., son of James Macleod of Polbeth, West Calder, Midlothian. B. May 8, 1797. Well known in Edinburgh musical and other circles during his lifetime. He associated with the leading men of the time, and was an early friend of R. A. Smith, the composer. With the profits of the work named second below he completed the Burns Monument at Edinburgh by enclosing it within an iron rail. He was a Justice of the Peace for Midlothian, and succeeded to the property of Polbeth. D. Bonnington, near Edinburgh, Feb. 10, 1859, and is buried in Rosebank Cemetery there.

WORKS.—Original Melodies, consisting of Songs, Duets, and Glees, the symphonies and accompaniments by Mr. Mather, the poetry written expressly for this work, Edin., fo. [1828]; Original Scottish Melodies, Edin., n.d., dedicated to the Duchess of Buccleuch; Original National Melodies of Scotland, Lond. and Edin., 8vo [1838], dedicated to Queen Victoria. Among Macleod's best-known songs may be named "Scotland yet," "My bonnie wife," "Oh, why left I my hame," "Ours is the land o' gallant hearts," "Dowie dens o' Yarrow," "Yellow locks o' Charlie," "Land o' cakes," "Emigrant's complaint," "My Highland vale," "I had a hame." "More dear art thou to me," "I have loved thee only," "Flora's lament," and many others, chiefly to verses of good poets.

MACMURDIE (Joseph). English comp. and writer, B. London, 1792. Mus. Bac., Oxon., 1814. Director of Philharmonic Soc. D. Merton, Surrey, Dec. 23, 1878.

WORKS.—Glees, Canons, etc., Lond., 1828, 1836, 1840, etc.; Trios for Female Voices, 1859; Glees, etc., Lond. [1824]; Arrangements for Pf.; Sacred Music, a Collection of Tunes adapted to the new Version of Psalms, as sung at the Philanthropic Society's Chapel, Lond., 8vo, 1827; The Elements of Music, with the Art of Playing from a Figured Bass, and an introduction to Composition, Lond., n.d.; A Juvenile Preceptor for the Pianoforte, Lond., 1828; A Collection of Psalm and Hymn Tunes, Lond., 4to, n.d.; De Profundis Clamavi, motet; Ode to Spring, glee; etc.

M'NABB (Hugh). Scottish writer and cond., author of "Morley's New Singing Tutor," Lond., 1883. He is cond. of the Ayr Choral Union, and of a vocal association in connection with the 1st Lanarkshire Rifle Volunteers.

M'NAUGHT (William Gray). English musician and teacher, B. London, March 30, 1849. S. at R. A. M., 1871. Associate R. A. M., 1878. Has translated a number of musical classics from the Standard into the Tonic Sol-fa Notation. Assistant Inspector of Music for Education Department. Cond. Boys and Bromley Institute Choir.

MACPHERSON (D.) Scottish writer, author of "Catechism of Music, adapted for learners on the Piano, etc.," Edin., 8vo. n. d.

MACRORY (Edmund). English writer, author of "A Few Notes on the Temple Organ," Lond., 8vo [1859], anon.; second edit., 1861, 4to.

MADAN (Rev. Martin). English divine and comp., B. 1726. D. May 2, 1790. Comp. psalm tunes, "Huddersfield," etc.

MAELZEL (Johann Nepomuk). German musician and inventor, B. Ratisbon, Aug. 15, 1772. Settled at Vienna as teacher. Court Mechanician, 1808. Gave concerts in conjunction with Beethoven at Vienna. Perfected the Metronome, an instrument for marking time in music, 1816. D. at sea, while on his way to U. S. A., July 21, 1838.

A description of the metronome will be found in any technical musical dictionary. It is well known to most musicians.

MAIDMENT (James). English antiquary, B. London, 1795. D. Edin., Oct. 24, 1879. A great authority on Scottish peerage and ballad lore. Published several collections of Scottish ballads, as "New Book of Old Ballads"; "Book of Scottish Pasquils," etc. He aided also with the annotations for Stenhouse and Laing's "Lyric Music of Scotland," and was a friend and fellow-worker with Sir Walter Scott and C. K. Sharpe.

MAILLART (Louis A.) French comp., B. Montpellier, Mar. 24, 1817. D. Moulins, June 2, 1871. Comp. "Fadette," and other operatic and chamber music.

MAILLY (Jean Alphonse Ernest). Belgian comp. and pianist, B. Brussels, Nov. 27, 1833. S. under Lemmens. Prof. of Pf., Brussels Cons., 1861. Prof. org., Brussels Cons. Org. of ch. of Cannes. Represented Belgium at International Exhib., London, 1871. Chev. of order of Leopold.

WORKS.—Op. 1. Sonata for org; op. 2. Prières for org.; op. 3. Six Morceau characteristique for Harmonic. Serenades, Fantasias, Trios, Motets, and Songs.

MAINWARING (Rev. John, B.D.). English author, published "Memoirs of the Life of the late George Frederic Handel, to which is added a catalogue of his works, and observations upon them," Lond., 8vo, 1760 [anonymous].

MAINZER (Joseph, Abbé). German musician and writer, B. Trèves, 1801 (1807?) Educated at Trèves Coll. S. under Kinck, Seyfried, and Stadler. Ordained priest, 1826. Singing-master at Trèves. Went to Brussels, 1833. Taught popular classes in Paris. Came to England, 1839. Competed (unsuccessfully) with Bishop for music professorship of Edinburgh University, 1841. Resided latterly in Manchester as teacher of the Wilhem method. D. Manchester, Nov. 10, 1851.

WORKS.—Singschule: oder Praktische Anweisung zum Gesange, Trier, 4to, 1831. Singschule für Kinder, Mainz, 8vo, 1837. Singing for the Million: a Practical Course of Musical Instruction, Lond., 8vo, 1841. Musical Times and Singing Circular: a Journal of Literature, Criticism, etc., 1842-3. The Musical Athenæum, Lond., 1842. Treatise on Musical Grammar and the Principles of Harmony, Lond., 8vo, 1843. The Gaelic Psalm Tunes of Ross-shire and the neighbouring Counties, Edinburgh, 4to, 1844. Guide to Beginners in Pianoforte Playing, 4to, n. d. Music and Education, Lond., 8vo, 1848. Articles in numerous British and Continental Journals, etc.

A sketch of Mainzer's Life and Labours was published in 1844, translated from the French of Aristide Guilbert. Mainzer was a good and practical educationist, and his books as mediums of elementary instruction are still of utility, but the system on which he taught has been superseded long since. The musical compositions of Mainzer are completely forgotten.

MAISTRE (Mattheus le), or LEMAITRE. Dutch comp., B. [1510]. Chapel master at Dresden, 1554. D. 1577. His works consist of motets, masses, miscellaneous church music, with a number of descriptive and other secular vocal pieces.

MAITLAND (J. A. Fuller). English writer, B. London, 1856, author of "Schumann" (Great Musicians), Lond., 12mo, 1884. Also articles in Grove's "Dictionary of Music." Joint translator, with Clara Bell, of Spitta's "Johann Sebastian Bach," Lond., 3 vols., 1884.

MAJORANO. See CAFFARELLI.

MALAN DE MÉRINDOL (César Henri Abraham). French divine, poet, and musician, B. Geneva, July 7, 1757. Pastor at Geneva. D.D., Glasgow. D., 1864. Comp. anthems, hymns, and wrote several theological works.

MALCOLM (Alexander). Scottish writer, B. Edinburgh, 1687. D. (?) Author of "A Treatise of Music, Speculative, Practical, and Historical," Edin., 1721; also London, 1830. This work from its scientific basis achieved much success, and was reprinted in an abridged form by an "Eminent Musician," in 1776.

MALIBRAN (Maria Felicita), *née* GARCIA. Spanish soprano vocalist, B. Paris, March 24, 1808. Daughter of Manuel Garcia. S. under Panseron at Naples, and Herold at Paris. Resided in London with her Father, 1817, by whom she was taught vocalization. *Début* in London as "Rosina" in Rossini's "Barbiere." June 7, 1825. Appeared in New York, 1825. Married to M. Malibran, a Frenchman, New York, Mar. 25, 1826. Separated from him on his failure in business, 1826; and formally divorced, Paris, 1836. Appeared in Paris, 1827. Re-appeared in London, 1829. Sang on the Continent till 1835. Married to C. de Beriot, the violinist, 1836. D. Manchester, Sept. 23, 1836.

The untimely death of this highly gifted artist has been regarded with much regret. The immense popularity which she enjoyed was due no less to her remarkable vocal powers, than to an almost unbounded generosity of disposition, which has been mentioned in the highest terms by her contemporaries. As a vocalist she excelled most in florid passages which demanded an extreme flexibility of execution; but she was also famous as a dramatic vocalist of great power. Her life was published under the title of "Memoirs of Madame Malibran, by the Countess of Merlin, and other intimate friends, with a selection from her Correspondence, and Notices of the Progress of the Musical Drama," Lond., 2 vols., 8vo, 1844. Also, "Memoirs, Critical and Historical," etc., by an Amateur, Lond., 12mo, 1836.

MALLANDAINE (J. F.). English comp. and cond. of present time. Has comp. operettas "Ali Baba" and "Love's Limit," and many songs, and Pf. pieces. Went to America about 1881.

MALLINGER (Mathilde). Hungarian soprano vocalist, B. Agram, Feb. 16, 1847. S. under Lucca. *Début*, Munich, 1866, in "Norma." Has sung with success in Wagner's operas at Berlin, etc.

MANDEL (Charles). German musician and writer, author of "Treatise on the Instrumentation of Military Bands," Lond., 8vo, n.d.; "System of Music," London, 4to, 1869. Was Director of Music at Kneller Hall.

MANGOLD (Carl Amadeus). German violinist and comp., B. Darmstadt, Oct. 8, 1813. Violinist in service of Grand Duke of Hesse-Darmstadt; Cond. at Darmstadt. Has comp. "Das Kœhlermædchen," 1843; "Der Tannhæuser," 1846; "Die Hermannschlacht," 1848; and other operas.

MANGOLD (Wilhelm). German comp., brother of the above, B. Darmstadt, Nov. 19, 1796. S. under Rink, Vogler, Cherubini, and R. Kreutzer. Chap.-master to Grand Duke of Hesse-Darmstadt. D. Darmstadt, May 23, 1875.

Comp. Symphonies; "Merope," opera; Pf. music; Lieder; and numerous other works.

MANGOLD (Carl Georg). Cousin of preceding, B. Darmstadt, Sept. 27, 1812. S. under Hummel. Prof. in Guildhall School of Music, London. Author of "Harmony," "Counterpoint," 1884, 1885, etc., and comp. of Pf. music.

MANN (Arthur Henry.) English org. and comp., B. Norwich, May 16, 1850. Was chor. in Norwich Cath. under Dr. Buck; Mus. Bac., Oxon., 1874; Mus. Doc., 1880; Org. S. Peter's Ch., Wolverhampton, 1870-71; Tettenhall, to 1875; Beverley Minster, to 1876. Org. King's Coll., Cambridge. Comp. "Ecce Homo," for chorus, orch., and org., 1882; anthems, etc.

MANN (Elias). American musician, B. Weymouth, Mass., 1750. D. Northampton, Mass., May 12, 1825. He published "The North Hampton Collection of Church Music," 1778; "The Massachusetts Collection of Sacred Harmony," Boston, 1807.

MANN (John A.) Scottish violin-maker and virtuoso, B. Forfar, May 13, 1810. Settled in Glasgow as artist, machinist, and musical instrument maker. Is known throughout Britain as one of the first authorities on the violin, which instrument and its temperament he has made a life-study.

MANN (Richard). English writer and org., B. 1837. Org. at Cirencester. D. Cirencester, 1869. Author of "A Manual of Singing for the use of Choir Trainers and School Masters," London, 1866; Anthems, etc.

MANNS (August). German cond., B. Stolzenburg, near Stettin, March 12. 1825. Vnst. in theatre at Elburg. Mem. of Gung'l's orch. at Berlin. Cond. at Kroll's Garden, Berlin. Bandmaster, 1851. Sub.-cond. of Crystal Palace orch., 1854; chief do., Oct., 1855. Cond. Glasgow Musical Festivals of 1879, 1880, etc.
Manns is recognised as one of the most capable conductors living, and his valuable labours in producing the less known works of great masters have exercised much influence. As a composer he takes rank chiefly as an arranger for orch., and writer of dance music. He can be accorded considerable credit for having aided in the recent revival of English music by encouraging what is somewhat obscurely termed native talent. His talent and industry have made the Crystal Palace band one of the most efficient in the country, and his ability as a conductor is sufficiently shown by his being chosen to succeed Sir M. Costa as cond. of the Handel Festival.

MANSFELDT (Edgar). See PIERSON (Henry Hugo).

MAPLESON (James Henry), Colonel. English operatic manager. S. music at R. A. M. Opened Lyceum Theatre for Italian Opera, 1861. Has travelled throughout Britain and the United States with his company. Has produced a few novelties; maintained the star system, and has gained much fame as an impresario both in Britain and America.

MARA (Gertrude Elizabeth), *nee* SCHMEHLING. German soprano vocalist, B. Cassel, Feb. 23, 1749. S. under Paradisi; also under J. A. Hiller at Leipzig, 1766-71. *Début*, in opera by Hasse, at Dresden. Singer at Court of Frederick the Great. Married to Johann Mara, a violoncellist. Ill-treated by him, in consequence of which she ran away to Austria. Sang in Vienna, Holland, Belgium, etc. Sang, in Paris, 1782. Appeared in London, 1784; Sang at Händel Commemoration, 1784; remained in London till 1791. Sang afterwards on the Continent. D. Revel, Jan. 20, 1833.

MARBECK (John). English writer, comp., and org., B. 1523. Chor. St. George's Chap., Windsor, 1531. Embraced Protestant faith, and narrowly escaped being burned for heresy, 1544. Taken under the patronage of the Bishop of Winchester. Mus. Bac., 1553. D. 1591.

WORKS.—The Book of Common Praier, Noted, Lond., 1550; A Concordance, that is to saie, a worke wherein by the ordre of the letters of A, B, C, ye maye redelye finde any worde contayned in the whole, so often as it is there expressed or mentioned, Lond., 1550; The Lyves of the Holy Sainctes, Prophets, Patriarchs, and others, contained in Holye Scripture, 1574; The Holie Historie of King David, etc., 1579; Book of Notes and Common Places, gathered out of divers writers, 1581.
Marbeck re-set the English Church Service almost in its entirety, and is said to have influenced later composers in the style of ecclesiastical composition. His setting continued in use during the many fluctuations in musical taste, which have been witnessed since his time, and is still in use, though not wholly.

MARCELLO (Benedetto). Italian comp. and poet, B. Venice, July 26, 1686. S. under Gasparini and Lotti. Came of a noble Venetian family, and occupied his life with State affairs. Caviliero of the Filarmonice, Bologna, 1712. D. Brescia, July 24, 1739.

WORKS.—Estro Poetico-Armonico, Parafrasi sopra i primi 50 Psalmi, Poesia di Girolamo Giustiniani. Venice, 8 vols., 1724-7. Concerti a quinta istromenti, op. 1, 1701. Sonatas, 1712. Canzoni Madrigalesche, 1717. Calisto in Orsa, pastoral, 1725. Giuditta, oratorio, 1710. La Fede riconosciuta, opera, 1702.

Marcello is known to the present generation of musicians only by a few of his psalms, and his renown as depending on them has waned greatly since the early part of this century. An edition of the Psalms was published in 1759 by John Garth, with the title "The First Fifty Psalms, set to music by Benedetto Marcello. ...Lond., fo., 8 vols., 1757. Garth was assisted by Avison in this compilation. Every edition of Marcello's Psalms is rare, and it is unquestionably this scarcity which occasions their neglect. A good selection is much wanted.

MARCHAND (Louis). French org. and comp., B. Lyons, Feb. 2, 1669 [1671]. S. at Paris, and became famous as an org. Exiled for dissipated habits. Offered post of court organist by King of Poland. Played in opposition to J. S. Bach, but was defeated. Was challenged by Bach to another trial, but disappeared. D. Feb. 17, 1732.

He comp. an opera, "Pyramus et Thisbe," and some vocal and organ music. He appears to have been something of an empiric, and to have received more credit for his performance than was justly due.

MARCHESI (Luigi). Italian operatic vocalist, B. Milan, 1755. Début, Rome, 1774. Sang in Italy and Germany. Appeared in London, 1788-90. Retired to Milan, 1806. D. Milan, Dec. 15, 1829.

MARCHESI (Mathilde de Castrone), née GRAUMANN. German soprano vocalist, B. Frankfort-on-Main, March 26, 1826. S. under Nicolai and Garcia. Appeared in London, 1849. Sang in Germany, Holland, France, Belgium, etc. Married Salvatore Marchesi, 1852. Resided in Paris as teacher of singing, 1861. Prof. Singing Cologne Cons., 1865-68 ; do. Vienna Cons. Madame Marchesi is well known as a talented writer on vocalization, but her success as a teacher is best illustrated in her pupils, Krauss, Murska, and Gerster, not to speak of others.

MARCHESI (Salvatore). Italian teacher and comp., B. Palermo, 1822. Husband of above. Served as a soldier, 1838-40. S. under Raimondi and Lamperti. Début in America as vocalist. Teacher successively at Cologne, Vienna, etc. Comp. numerous songs, etc.

MARCHETTI (Filippo). Italian comp., B. Bolognola, near Camerino, Feb. 26, 1831. S. at Cons. of San Pietro of Majella, Naples, under Lillo and Conti. Prof. of Singing at Rome and Milan.

WORKS.—*Operas* : Gentile da Varano, 1856 ; La Demente, 1857 ; Le Paria ; Romeo e Giulietta, 1865 ; Ruy Blas, 1869 ; L'Amore alla prova, 1873 ; Gustavo Wasa, 1875 ; Giovanna d'Austria, 1880. Overtures and Songs.

MARENZIO (Luca). Italian comp., B. Coccaglia, Brescia, 1550. S. under Contini. Resided in Poland, in service of various princes, etc. Chapel-master to Cardinal Luigi d' Este, Rome, 1581. Mem. of the Pontifical College, 1595. D. Rome, 1599.

WORKS.—Nine books of Madrigals published at Venice in 1580, 1581, 1582, 1583, 1584, 1585, 1586, 1587, 1589 ; Reprinted 1594, 1595, 1602, 1603, 1605, 1608, 1609. Complete collected edition published, 1593. Motets, canzoni, etc. A few pieces (choruses) of dramatic music.

The madrigals of Marenzio are among the sweetest and most pleasing emanations of the Italian school of the 16th century.

MARETZEK (Max). German comp. and cond., B. Brünn, 1821. S. at Vienna and Paris. Went to New York, 1847. Teacher and cond. in New York.

He has comp. "Hamlet," an opera, 1843 ; Pf. music ; songs ; and some pieces of chamber and orchestral music.

MARIO (Giuseppe), MARCHESE DI CANDIA. Italian tenor vocalist, B. Cagliari, 1810 [Genoa, 1812 ; Turin, 1808, 1810]. Entered the Sardinian Army as an officer in 1830, but he resigned his commission and went to Paris, where he studied under Michelet, Ponchard, and Bordogni. Début in Robert le Diable, Paris, Nov. 30, 1838. *Début* London in Lucrezia Borgia, June 6, 1839. Sang afterwards at Madrid, St. Petersburg, and in Paris, London, and the British Provinces till 1871. Married to Giulia Grisi, 1838, by whom he had three daughters. Retired from stage, and resided at Rome. Fell into distressed circumstances, and in May, 1878, a benefit concert in his aid was given in St. James' Hall, London. D. Rome, Dec. 11, 1883.

"It will not satisfy many of Signor Mario's enthusiastic admirers to be told that, throughout his career, he has never been a thorough artist, armed at all points for his duties before the public. Such, however, is the case. The charm of personal appearance and graceful demeanour, borne out by a voice the persuasive sweetness of which can never have been exceeded, has fascinated everyone—the stern as well as the sentimental—into forgetting incompleteness and deficiency. . . . . He will live in the world's memory as the best opera lover ever seen. . . . As a singer of Romances he has never been excelled : rarely equalled."—*Chorley's Recollections.*

He was most successful as the exponent of the leading tenor roles in Meyerbeer's "Les Huguenots," Gounod's "Faust," Rossini's "Barbiere," and in certain operas of Verdi and Mozart.

MARKS (James Christopher). Irish org. and comp., B. Armagh, 1835. Chor. Armagh Cath., 1843. Deputy-org. do., 1852-60. Org. and choirmaster, S. Finbar's Cath., Cork, 1860. Mus. Bac., Oxon, 1863. Mus. Doc., Oxon, 1868.

Composer of several anthems, organ pieces, and songs.

MARKS (Thomas Osborne). Irish org. and comp., brother of above, B. Armagh, 1845. Mus. Bac., Oxon, 1870. Chor. Armagh Cath. Org. do., 1872. Mus. Doc., Dublin, 1874.

Has comp. services, anthems, songs, organ music, and miscellaneous music.

MARKULL (Friedrich Wilhelm). German org. and comp., B. Elbing, Feb. 17, 1816. S. under Schneider. Org. at Dantzig.

WORKS.—*Operas :* Maja und Alfino, 1843 ; Der König von Zion ; Der Walpurgis. *Oratorios :* Das Gedachtniss der Entschlafenen ; Johannes der Taüfer. Twenty-fourth Psalm, for solo, chorus and orch. ; Symphonies for orch., in C min. and D ; Four Mazurkas for Pf., op. 4 ; Gedichte für eine Singstimme mit Pianoforte, opp. 5, 6, 7, 71, 72, 73, 74 ; Gondoliera for Pf., op. 88.

MARLOW (Isaac). English writer, author of "The Controversie of Singing brought to an End," etc., Lond., 12mo, 1696.

MARMONTEL (Antoine Francois). French pianist and comp., B. Clermont-Ferrand, July 18, 1816. S. Paris Cons. under Halévy and Lesueur, 1827. Gained first prize for Singing, 1828 ; second prize for Pf., 1830 ; second prize for Harmony, 1832. Prof. Pf., Paris Cons., 1848.

WORKS.—Ecole élémentaire de mécanisme et de style, op. 6; Nocturnes for Pf., opp. 10, 11, 12, 13 ; Studies for Pf., various, opp. 9, 45, 62, 80, 85, 106, 107, 111, etc. ; Serenades for Pf., opp. 21, 56, 109; Polonaises, Marches, Mazurkas, Reveries, Salon Pieces, etc.

MAROT (Clement). French poet, B. 1495. D. 1544. Famous in connection with music for his translation of the Psalms, which some historians affirm aided in spreading the doctrines which led to the Reformation. These psalms were used by Goudimel and Lejeune, as well as by succeeding composers.

MARPURG (Friedrich Wilhelm). German writer, B. Brandenburg, Oct. 1, 1718. D. Berlin, May 22, 1795.

WORKS.—Handbuch von dem Generalbasse und der Composition, Berlin, 1755. Historisch-Kritische Beytraege zur Aufnahme der Theoretischen Musik, Berlin, 5 vols., 1754-60. Aufansgründe der Theoretischen Musik, Leipzig, 4to, 1757. Anleitung zur Singecomposition, Berlin, 4to, 1758. Die Kunst das Clavier zu spielen von dem Verfasser des Kritischen Musikus an der Spree, Berlin, 1762. Clavierstücke mit einem Practischen Unterricht fur Anfanger und Geübtere, Berlin, 1762-3. Anleitung zu Musik, 1763. Many other practical works and compositions.

The whole of Marpurg's writings are now superseded by works of more recent date.

MARRIOTT (Annie). English soprano vocalist, B. Nottingham, May 26, 1859. Has appeared at London (Sacred Harmonic Society), Glasgow (Choral Union), Birmingham, and throughout the provinces.

MARRIOTT (Charles Handel Rand). English comp., B. London, Nov. 3, 1831. Played vn. in various orchestras. Musical Director, Highbury Barns, 1860-65. Musical Director, Royal Gardens, Cremorne; Do., Pier Pavilion, Hastings. Musical Editor *Young Ladies' Journal*.

WORKS.—*Songs:* England's Trust; The Lily of the West; There grew in the forest a mighty oak; Songs for Children; Lost friends; Rest; Thy Face; Our Union Jack of liberty; etc. *Pianoforte:* Quadrilles on melodies from operas, national melodies, etc.; Banting; Happy Home; Oriental; Versailles; Gorilla; Waltzes; Polkas; Galops; and numerous pieces of Salon music.

MARSCHNER (Heinrich). German comp. and cond., B. Zittau, Aug. 16, 1795. S. under Schicht. Acquainted with Beethoven, 1817. Joint-cond. with Weber and Morlacchi of Dresden Opera, 1823-6. Cond. at Leipzig, 1827. Court cond. at Hanover. D. Hanover, Dec. 14, 1861.

WORKS.—*Operas:* Lucretia, 1822; Schön Ellen, 1822; Der Vampyr, Leipzig, May, 1828 (Lond., Aug. 1829); Das Falkner's Braut; Der Templer und die Jüdin; Hans Heiling, Hanover, 1833; Das Schloss am Aetna, Berlin, 1838; Adolph von Nassau, Hanover, 1843; Austin, 1851. *Instrumental Music:* Twelve bagatelles for guitar, op. 4; Twelve lieder, op. 5; Sonata for Pf. solo, op. 6; Polonaise for Pf. duet, op. 7; Fantasias and Rondos for Pf., opp. 10, 11, 15, 18, 19, 20, 21, 22, 23, 25, 31, 33, 37, 49, 57, 58, 59, 64, 71, 74; Sonatas for Pf., opp. 24, 38, 39, 40; Quartet for Pf., vn., viola, and bass, op. 36; Trio for strings, opp. 29, 50; Overtures for orch.; Robert Burns' Lieder für Tenor oder Sopran mit Pf., op. 107. Numerous pieces of vocal music.

Marschner is regarded as one of the most remarkable of the lesser romantic composers. His works are full of picturesque points, and the melody and harmony are full of charming and dramatic interest.

MARSH (Alphonso). English comp., B. 1627. Gent. Chap. Royal, 1660. D. April, 1681. His son ALPHONSO was also a comp. and Gent. of Chap. Royal, 1676. He died in 1672. Both wrote songs etc. in contemporary collections.

MARSH (John). English writer and comp., B. Dorking, 1752. Articled to a solicitor at Romsey, 1768. Married, 1774. Leader at Subscription Concerts at Salisbury, 1780. Resided at Chichester from 1787. D. 1828.

WORKS.—A Short Introduction to the Theory of Harmonics, or the Philosophy of Musical Sounds, Chichester, 8vo, 1809. Rudiments of Thorough-bass, Lond., n. d. Hints to Young Composers, n. d. Church services, anthems, glees, and songs. Collection of the most Popular Psalm Tunes with a few Hymns and easy Anthems in 3 parts, for the use of country choirs, n. d.

MARSHALL (Julian). English amateur musician and collector, B. Headingley, Leeds, June 24, 1836. Author of the "Annals of Tennis"; articles in periodicals; in Grove's Dictionary of Music; etc. His wife, *née* FLORENCE A. THOMAS, B. Rome, March 30, 1843, is well known as a cultured writer on music, and as a composer of much ability. She S. at the R. A. M., London. Wrote "Handel" (Great Musicians), Lond., 1883. "Solfeggi" (Music Primer), Lond. [1885], 8vo.

MARSHALL (William). Scottish violinist and comp., B. Fochabers, Dec. 27, 1748. House steward and butler to the Duke of Gordon till 1790. Farmer at Keithmore, and factor to the Duke of Gordon, 1790-1817. D. Newfield, May 29, 1833.

WORKS.—Marshall's Scottish Airs, Melodies, Strathspeys, Reels, etc., for the Pianoforte, Violin, and Violoncello, with appropriate basses. Dedicated to the Marchioness of Huntly, Edin., 1822 [containing 170 airs]. Collection of Scottish Melodies, Reels, Strathspeys, Jigs, Slow Airs, etc., for the Pianoforte, Violin, and

Violoncello, being the genuine and posthumous works of William Marshall, Edin., Robertson, 1847. Choice Selection of Reels and Strathspeys, Edin., n. d. (with Gow). A Collection of Strathspey Reels with a Bass for the Violoncello or Harpsichord, n. d.

Marshall is best known as a composer by his melodies "Of a' the airts the wind can blaw" ("Miss Admiral Gordon"), "This is no my ain house," "The wind blew the bonnie lassie's plaidie awa," and several others, all of which are dance tunes now adapted to poetry.

MARSHALL (William). English org. and comp., B. 1806. Chor. in Chap. Roy., under J. S. Smith and W. Hawes. Chor. Christ Ch. Cath. and S. John's Coll., Oxford, 1823. Org. All Saint's Ch., Oxford. Mus. Bac. Oxon., 1826. Mus. Doc., Oxon., Jan. 1840. Org. S. Mary's Ch., Kidderminster, 1846. D. Handsworth, Aug. 17, 1875.

WORKS.—Anthems used in the Cathedral and Collegiate Churches of England and Wales, 1840. Art of Reading Church Music, and Exercises intended to accompany the same. Oxford, 8vo, 1842. Miscellaneous church music.

MARSON (George). English comp. of the 16th century. Comp. anthems and a 5 part madrigal, "The Nimphes and Shepheards," in the "Triumphs of Oriana."

MARTIN (Alexander). Polish violinist and comp., B. Warsaw, 1825. D. Warsaw, 1856. Comp. music to poetry of Byron and Scott, and works for vn. and Pf.

MARTIN (George Clement). English org. and comp.; B. Lambourn, Berkshire, 1844. Mus. Bac., Oxon., 1868. Mus. Doc., and F. C. O. Sub-org. and choir-master S. Paul's Cath., London.

WORKS.—Three settings of the Magnificat and nunc dimittis, for chorus and orch. Te Deums, Communion Services, etc. Part-songs and anthems. Songs and organ-music.

MARTIN (George William). English comp. and cond., B. March 8, 1827. Chor. S. Paul's Cath. S. under W. Hawes. Cond. National Schools' Choral Festival, 1859; National Choral Soc., etc. Editor of musical journals. D. Wandsworth, April 16, 1881.

Martin comp. several prize glees, anthems, and songs.

MARTIN (Jonathan). English org. and comp., B. 1715. Chor. in Chap. Roy., under Croft. S. org. under Rosingrave. Deputy-org. S. George's, Hanover Square. Org. Chap. Roy., 1736. D. April 4, 1737.

MARTIN (Vicente), or MARTINI. Spanish comp., B. Valencia, 1754. D. S. Petersburg, May, 1810. Comp. various operas, among them "La Cosa rara," which achieved considerable contemporary fame.

MARTINI (Giovanni Battista). Italian comp. and writer, B. Bologna, April 25, 1706. S. under his father, Predieri, and Riccieri. S. theology at San Filippo Neri. Ordained, 1722. Chap.-master at Ch. of San Francisco, 1725. D. Bologna, Aug. 3 (Oct. 3), 1784.

WORKS.—Masses; Miscellaneous church music; Sonatas, and other instrumental music; Storia della Musica, Bologna, 3 vols., 1757-81; Esemplare ossia saggio Fondamentale pratico di Contrappunto Sopra il Canto Fermo, Bologna, 1774-75, 2 vols.

Martini was considered one of the greatest contrapuntists of his period, and was the authority on most musical points for a long time. His "Storia della Musica" is his most important contribution to musical history.

MARX (Adolph Bernhard). German writer and comp., B. Halle, May 15, 1799. S. for the Law. Resided in Berlin as part editor of the Allegemeine Berliner Musikzeitung, 1824-31. Doctor of Marburg University, 1827. Prof. Music, Berlin Univ., 1830. Founded, with Kullak, Berlin Cons., 1850. D. Berlin, May 17, 1866.

WORKS.—Jery und Bately, opera; Johannes der Täufer, oratorio; Mose, oratorio;

Twelve songs for voice and Pf. ; Festgesänge für Mannerchor, op. 27 ; Die Acti Musiklehre im Streit mit unsrer Zeit, 8vo, 1841. Allgemeine Musiklehre. Ein Hülfsbuch für Lehrer und Lernende in jedem Zweige musikalischer Unterweisung, Leipzig, 1839 (many editions). Die Musik des 19 Jahrhunderts und ihre Pflege. Methode der Musik. Leipzig, 1855 (2nd ed., 1873. Trans. as The Music of the 19th Century and its Culture. Lond., 8vo, pt. 1, 1856 ; pt. 2, 1858. Ludwig von Beethoven, Leben und Schaffar, 1858. Die lehre von der Musikalischen Composition, 'praktisch-theoretisch, zum Selbstunterricht, oder als Leitfaden bei Privatunterweisung, Leipzig, 4 vols., 1852, etc. (various editions of each vol.). Translations of this work are published as School of Musical Composition, by A. Wehran, vol. 1, Lond., 1852, 8vo ; Universal School of Music, by A. H. Wehran, Lond., 1853, 8vo. General Musical Instruction, trans. by George Macirone, Lond., 1854, 8vo ; and Theory of Musical Composition, trans. by Saroni, Lond., 1852, 8vo, are others of his works which have been Englished.

As a didactic writer, Marx is known all over Europe and America. His writings have a very high educational value.

MARXSEN (Eduard). German comp., B. Niendstædten, Altona, July 23, 1806. S. under Sâyfried, Clasing, Bocklet, etc. Comp. symphonies, cantatas, overtures, Pf. music, songs, etc.

MARZIÈLS (Theophilus). French comp. and poet, B. Brussels. Dec. 21, 1850. S. under M. L. Lawson, and at Paris and Milan. Employed at British Museum from 1870.

WORKS.—The Gallery of Pigeons, and other Poems, 1873. *Songs :* Twickenham Ferry ; The Garland ; Three sailor boys ; Timothy's welcome ; Wait till you come to forty year ; The miller and the maid ; The garden ; Just as well ; Ask nothing more ; May music ; Only friends ; When my Jim comes home ; etc.

MASON (John). English writer, author of "An Essay on the Power of Numbers and the Principles of Harmony," Lond., 1749.

MASON (Lowell). American comp. and writer, B. Medfield, Mass., Jan. 8, 1792. Resided in Savannah, Georgia, 1812-27. Self-taught in music. Settled in Boston, 1827 ; President of Handel and Haydn Soc., 1827 ; Estab. Boston Academy of Music, 1832 ; Taught Pestalozzi method in Boston schools, 1838. Visited Europe, 1837. Doc. Mus., New York (first in America), 1835. D. Orange, N. J., Aug. 11, 1872.

WORKS.—Boston Handel and Haydn Collection of Church Music, 1822 ; Juvenile Psalmist, Boston, 1829 ; Juvenile Lyre, 1830 (First book of school songs pub. in U. S.) ; The Choir, or Union Collection of Church Music, 1833 ; Manual of Instruction in the Elements of Vocal Music, 1834 ; Juvenile Singing School, 1835 ; Sabbath School Songs, 1836 ; Boston Academy Collection of Church Music, 1836 ; Sabbath School Harp, 1837 ; Lyra Sacra, 1837 ; Occasional Psalmody, 1837 ; Songs of Asaph, 1838 ; The Seraph, 1838 ; Boston Anthem Book, 1839 ; Manual of the Boston Academy of Music, for Instruction in the Elements of Vocal Music on the System of Pestalozzi, Boston, 12mo, 1838 ; The Modern Psalmist, 1839 ; The Odeon (glees), 1839 ; Juvenile Music for Sabbath Schools, Boston, 1839 ; Boston School Song Book, 1840 ; Little Songs for Little Singers, 1840 ; Carmina Sacra, 1841 ; The Gentlemen's Glee Book, 1842 ; American Sabbath School Singing Book, Philadelphia, 1843 ; Boston Academy Collection of Choruses, 1844 ; The Vocalist, 1844 ; The Psaltery, 1845 ; Primary School Song Book, 1846 ; The National Psalmist, 1848 ; Cantica Laudis, 1850 ; Boston Chorus Book, 1851 ; The Glee Hive, 1851 ; The New Carmina Sacra, 1852 ; The Home Book of Psalmody, London, 1852 ; The Hallelujah, N. Y., 1854 ; Normal Singer, N. Y., 1856 ; Mammoth Musical Exercises, 1857 ; Collection of Psalms and Hymns for Christian Worship ; Pestalozzian Music Teacher (with T. F. Seward), Boston ; Vocal Exercises and Solfeggios ; The Song Garden. [Many of the foregoing works sold in enormous numbers, and passed through many editions. Some of them are edited in conjunction with George James Webb]. Musical Letters from Abroad, New York, 8vo, 1854 ; Translation of Catel's Harmony, with Notes, etc.

MASON (William). American pianist and comp., son of the above, B. Boston, 1828. S. under his father, and under Moscheles and Hauptmann at Leipzig ;

under Dreyschock at Prague ; and under Liszt at Weimar. Teacher at Orange, N. J., and teacher in New York.

Works.-- Pianoforte Technics (with W. S. B. Matthews), Boston, n.d.; Method for the Pianoforte (with E. S. Hoadley), Boston, n.d ; System for Beginners in the Art of Playing upon the Pianoforte (with E. S. Hoadley), Boston, n.d. ; Methods for the Reed Organ; Numerous Pf. pieces consisting of mazurkas, reveries, gavottes, and dances.

MASON (William). English poet and writer, B. Hull, 1725. Ordained minister, 1755. Prebendary and Precentor, York Cath., 1763. D. Aston, April 5, 1797.

Wrote various papers on ecclesiastical music, collected under the title of "Essays, historical and critical on English Church Music," York, 1795, 12mo.

MASON AND HAMLIN. American firm of reed-organ builders, established in Boston, 1854. First engaged in the manufacture of the organ-harmonium with 4 sets of reeds and 2 manuals. In 1861-62 the firm brought their famous "School" and "Cabinet" organs, which are now known all over the world. The instruments of this firm are among the best known in Britain. Establishments also in New York and Chicago. EMMONS HAMLIN, one of the firm, D. Boston, April 8, 1885.

MASSART (Lambert Joseph). Belgian violinist and comp., B. Liége, July 19, 1811. S. under R. Kreutzer. Prof. vn., Paris Cons., 1843. Chev. of Legion of Hon. Famous as a comp. of vn. music, and as teacher of H. Wieniawski, J. Lotto, Fournier, and others.

MASSÉ (Felix Marie Victor). French comp., B. Lorient, Mar. 7, 1822. S. Paris Cons., 1834 ; Gained grand prix de Rome, 1844. Travelled in Italy, etc. Chorusmaster of Academy of Music. Chorus-master at Opera, 1860. Prof. of Comp. at Paris Cons., 1866. Member of Institut, 1872. Officer of Legion of Honour, 1877. D. Paris, July 5, 1884.

Works.--*Operas*: La Chanteuse voilée, 1852 ; Noces de Jeannette, 1853 ; Galathée, 1854 ; La Fiancée du Diable, 1855 ; Miss Fauvette, 1855 ; Les Saisons, 1856 ; La Reine Topaze, 1856 ; La Fée Carabosse, 1859 ; La Favorita e la Schiava, 1855 ; Le Cousin de Marivaux, 1857 ; La mule de Pedro, 1863 ; Tior d'Aliza, 1866 ; Le Fils du Brigadier, 1867 ; Paul et Virgenie, 1876. Le Renégat de Tanger, prize cantata, 1845. Songs, and miscellaneous compositions.

MASSENET (Jules Emile Frédéric). French comp., B. Montand, near St. Etienne, May 12, 1842. S. Paris Cons. ; gained first prize for Pf., 1859 ; second prize for fugue, 1862 ; first prize for fugue and prix de Rome, 1863. Prof. of Comp. Paris Cons., 1878.

Works.—*Operas*: La Grand Tante, 1867 ; Don César de Bazan, 1872 ; Les Erynnies, 1873 ; Le Roi de Lahor, 1877 ; Hérodiade, Paris, 1882 ; Manon, 1885. Le Cid, 1885 ; Paix et Liberté ! cantata, 1867 ; Marie Magdaleine, sacred drama, 1873 ; Eve, a mystery, 1875 ; La Verge, sacred Legend ; Narcisse, antique idylle, 1878. *Orchestral Music*: Suites d'Orchestra. Scenes Hongroises ; Scenes Pittoresques ; Scenes Dramatiques ; Overture, " Phèdre :" Pompeia, fantasia-symphony. *Pf. Music* : Le Roman d'Arlequin ; Poëme d' Avril, op. 14. Numerous other Pf. pieces, songs, etc.

Among the younger members of the modern French school, Massenet holds a high place. His works are conceived in a spirit thoroughly in harmony with the advanced style of composition, and many of his writings are elaborated and executed in a powerful dramatic manner. His operas are his most representative works, though several of his large concert works are also worthy of high praise.

MASTERS (William Chalmers). English comp., has published two operettas "The Forester's Daughter," 1868, and " The Rose of Salency," and a number of songs and other vocal works.

MASTERTON (Allan). Scottish musician and writing-master in the High School of Edinburgh. An associate of Robert Burns, the poet, to whose song, " Willie brew'd a peck o' maut," he wrote music. D. 1799.

MATENET. See FERRER.

MATERNA (Amalie). German soprano vocalist, B. S. Georgen, 1847. First appeared, 1864. Début in opera, Vienna, 1869. Sang at Wagner Festival, Bayreuth. Sang in London, 1877. Has since appeared in Europe with distinguished success.

MATHER (Samuel). English org. and comp., B. Sheffield, 1783. Org. S. James' Ch., Sheffield, 1799; do. S. Paul's, Sheffield, 1808. Bandmaster Sheffield Volunteers, 1805. D. Sheffield, 1814.

Compiled a Book of Psalm Tunes; Glees; Songs; Te Deum; numerous hymns, etc.

MATHEWS (William Smith Babcock). American writer and org., B. Loudon, N. H., May 8, 1837. S. at Lowell and Boston. Teacher in New Hampshire, and since 1867 org. and teacher in Chicago. Attached to editorial staff of *Daily News*, Chicago. Edited *The Musical Independent*, 1868.

WORKS.—An Outline of Musical Form, Boston, 1868. The Emerson Organ School (associate editor), Boston, 1870. Mason's Pianoforte Technics (letterpress portion), Boston, 1878. How to Understand Music 8 pts., 8vo, 1880. Pronouncing Dictionary and Condensed Encyclopedia of Musical Terms, Instruments, Composers, and Important Works, Chicago, 8vo, 1880 (part 9 of No. 1). Systematic View of the Musical Forms (MS.). How to Teach the Pianoforte (MS.). Papers in "Dwight's Journal of Music," and "Proceedings of Music Teachers' National Association," etc.

MATTEI (Stanislao, Abbate). Italian comp. and teacher, B. Bologna, Feb. 10, 1750. S. under Martini. Deputy of Martini. Chap.-master in succession to Martini, Ch. of San Francesco, Bologna. Teacher and chap.-master of San Petronio. Prof. at the Licco, 1804. D. Bologna, May 17, 1825.

Comp. masses, motets, symphonies, songs. Was most celebrated as a successful teacher, and as numbering among his pupils Rossini, Morlacchi, Donizetti, Perotti, etc.

MATTEI (Tito). Italian pianist and comp., B. Campobasso, May 24, 1841. S. under Thalberg and Raimondi. Travelled in France, Germany, and Italy. Settled in London. Cond. at H. M. Theatre. Married to Mdlle. Colombo. Chevalier of Order of SS. Maurice and Lazare.

WORKS.—Maria de Gand, opera; Songs. *Pianoforte:* Grande valse, op. 22; Reverie, op. 30; La harpe, melodie, op. 32; Barcarolle, op. 33; La gaîté, scherzo, op. 35; Marches, nocturnes, valses, etc.

MATTEIS (Nicola). Italian violinist and writer, B. probably about middle of 17th century. Settled in London about end of reign of Charles II. [circa 1685-89]. Was a teacher of the violin in London, and enjoyed extraordinary celebrity as much by his personal peculiarities as by his abilities. See North's "Memoirs of Music." Date of D. unknown. He introduced the practice of engraving music from plates. Among his works may be named "Ayres for the Violin," 2 books; "Ayres for the Violin, to wit: Preludes, Fugues, Allemandes, Sarabands, Courants, Gigues, Fancies, Divisions, and likewise other Passages, Introductions and Fuges for Single and Double Stops," etc.; "Other Ayres and Pieces for the Violin, Bass Viol, and Harpsichord"; "The False Consonances of Musick, or Instructions for Playing a True Base upon the Guittarre, with choice Examples and clear Directions to enable any man in a short time to play all Musicall Ayres...4 parts," [London], 2 vols., n. d.

His son NICOLA, B. London, was a celebrated violinist, and was attached to the Imperial Chap. of Vienna. He published Books of Airs for the Violin, and wrote "Costanza e Fortezza," an opera. D. 1749.

MATTHAY (Tobias A.). English comp. and pianist, B. Clapham (London), Feb. 19, 1858. Entered the R. A. M. in 1871. S. comp. under Sterndale-Bennett, Sullivan, and Prout, and Pf. under Dorrell and W. Macfarren. Elected Sterndale-Bennett scholar, 1872. Gained first of the two "Reed" prizes for comp. of a quartet for Pf. and strings, 1876. After having served both as Harmony and Pianoforte Sub-Professor, he was in 1880 placed on the staff of the Institution as Assistant-Professor of Pianoforte (full Prof., 1885), and was at the same time elected an Associate.

Besides a large number of MS. Pf. and other chamber pieces and songs, his latest writings include 4 Concert Overtures and other works of one or two movements for Full Orchestra, also a Scena for Contralto, and a Pf. "Concert Piece" in D minor, with accompaniments for full orch., this latter being his third effort in this direction.

WORKS.—*Pianoforte:* Four Novelletten ; Nocturne in D flat ; An autumn song ; 17 Variations in C ; Hommage á Chopin. *For Violin and Piano:* A Pamphlet. *Songs:* Bright be the place of thy soul ; There be none of Beauty's daughters ; The spring beneath the willow tree ; The gentle eventide ; A rover's life for me. *Partsong :* The fairy's serenade ; etc.

MATTHESON (Johann). German comp. and writer, B. Hamburg, Sept. 28, 1681. Singer in theatre at Hamburg, 1697. Acquainted with Handel, 1703. Secretary of legation at Hamburg, 1706 ; Canon of the cath., do., 1715. Chap.-master to the Duke of Holstein, 1719. D. Hamburg, April 17, 1764.

WORKS.--Die Pleyaden, opera, 1699 ; and 7 other operas. Oratorios and cantatas ; Organ and other instrumental music. Das neu-eroffnete Orchestre, etc. Hamburg, 1713-21. Exemplarische Organisten Probe im Artikel vom General-bass, Hamburg, 4to, 1719. Critica Musica, d. i. grundrichtige Untersuch und Beurtheilung vieler...Meinungen, etc. Hamburg, 2 vols., 1722-25. Grosse General-basse-schule, etc., 1731. Kleine General-basse-schule, 1735. Kern Melodischer Wissenschaft bestehend in der auserlesensten Haupt-und Grund-lehren der musicalischen Setz-Kunst oder Composition, 1737. Der Vollkommene Capellmeister, 1739. Grundlage einer Ehrenpforte, woran der tüchtigsten Capellmeister, Componisten, etc., 1740.

Mattheson was a person of considerable acquirements, and a musician of no mean ability, though his productions are now forgotten.

MATTHEWS (H.). English writer, author of "Observations on Sound : shewing the causes of its indistinctness in churches," etc. Lond., 1826, 8vo.

MAURER (Ludwig Wilhelm). German vnst. and comp., B. Potsdam, Aug. 8, 1789. Played at Berlin with Mara, 1802. Travelled in Germany and France. Chap.-master to Chancellor Wsowologsky at Moscow. D. S. Petersburg, Oct. 25, 1878.

Comp. over 100 works, consisting of operas, symphonies, overtures, Pf. and violin music, etc.

MAURICE (Rev. Peter, D.D.). English writer, vicar of Yarnton, Woodstock, and Chaplain of New Coll., Oxford. Author of "What shall we do with Music? a letter to the Earl of Derby." Lond., 1856. "Choral Harmony, a Collection of Tunes in Short Score for four voices." 4to, 1854.

MAVER (Robert). Scottish music-publisher, established in Glasgow, 1845. Issued "Maver's Collection of Genuine Scottish Melodies for the Pianoforte or Harmonium, in keys suitable for the voice. Harmonised by C. H. Morine. Edited by George Alexander." Glasgow, 4to [1866]. Originally issued in parts. He also issued a "Collection of Genuine Irish Melodies and Songs," edited by G. Alexander, Glasgow, 4to [1877].

MAXWELL (Francis Kelly). Scottish writer, author of "An Essay upon Tune, being an attempt to free the scale of Music and the tune of Instruments from Imperfection." Edinburgh, 1781 ; Lond., 1794. Maxwell died in 1782.

MAY (Edward Collett). English org. and comp., B. Greenwich, Oct. 29, 1806. S. under Adams, Potter, and Crivelli. Org. Greenwich Hospital, 1837-69. Prof. Vocal Music, Queen's College, London. Famed as an org. and teacher. His daughter Florence is a fine pianist, and has appeared successfully.

MAY (A.). American writer, author of "Practical Piano School," 3 parts. Boston, n. d.

MAY (D. M. H.). American writer, author of "Operatic Method for the Violin." Boston, n. d.

MAYBRICK (Michael), STEPHEN ADAMS. English barytone vocalist and comp., B. Liverpool, 1844. S. under W. T. Best. Org. of S. Peter's Ch., Liverpool, 1858. S. at Leipzig Cons. under Moscheles, Plaidy, and Richter, 1866-68. S. singing at Milan under Nava. Sang at New Philharmonic Concerts, Lond., 1870. Has since appeared at the London Ballad Concerts; in opera; and at the principal London and provincial festivals. Comp. of the following popular songs: Nancy Lee, The Midshipmite, The blue Alsatian mountains, Good company, The tar's farewell, True hearts, etc.

MAYER (Carl). German pianist and comp., B. Königsberg, March 21, 1799. S. under Field, etc. Appeared in Paris, 1814. Settled in S. Petersburg as teacher, 1819. Travelled in Germany, Austria, etc., 1845. Settled in Dresden, 1850. D. Dresden, July 2, 1862.

Author of a large number of Pianoforte works, in nearly every form; many of them being pieces of great merit. Much used for teaching purposes.

MAYER (Johann Simon). German comp., B. Mendorf, Bavaria, June 14, 1763. Principally self taught. Chap.-master of Santa Maria Maggiore, Bergamo; Prof. of comp. in Musical Institution, do. D. Bergamo, Dec. 2, 1845.

WORKS.—*Operas*: Saffo, 1794; Lodoiska, 1796; Telemacco, 1797; Avviso ai maritati, 1798; Laaso e Lidia, 1798; Adriano in Siria, 1798; Adelaide di Guesclino, 1799; Gli Sciiti, 1800; Ginevra di Scozia, 1801; Le due ;Giornate, 1801; I virtuosi, 1801; Argene, 1801; I misteri Eleusini, 1802; Elisa, 1804; Ercole in Lidia, 1805; Gli Americani, 1806; Ifigenia in Aulide, 1806; I Cherusci, 1808; Il Raoul di Crequi, 1810; Medea, 1812; Rosa bianca e Rosa rossa, 1814; Atar, 1815. *Oratorios*: Jacob e Labano fugiens, 1791; Sisara, 1793; Tobiæ matrimonium, 1794; La Passione, 1794; Il sacrifizio di Jefte, 1795. 17 Masses; Psalms and other church music; Cantatas, etc.

MAYNARD (John). English lute-player and comp. of the 16th and 17th centuries, published "The xii Wonders of the World, set and composed for the Violl de Gamba, the lute, and the voyce, to sing the verse, all three jointly, and none severall; also Lessons for the Lute and Basse violl to play alone; with some Lessons to play lyra-wayes alone, or if you will, to fill up the parts with another violl set lute-way." Lond., 1611, fo.

MAYNARD (Walter). See BEALE (Thomas Willert).

MAYSEDER (Joseph). Austrian vnst. and comp., B. Vienna, Oct. 26, 1789. S. violin and music at Vienna. Musician in Court Chap., Vienna, 1816. Solo violin at Court Theatre, do., 1820. Chamber-vnst. to Emperor, 1835. Mem. of Ord. of Franz-Joseph, 1862. D. Vienna, Nov. 21, 1863.

WORKS.—Concertos for vn. and orch., opp. 22, 26, 28, 45; Rondos and Polonaises for vn. and orch., opp. 21, 27, 29, 36, etc; Airs for vn. and orch., opp. 18, 25, 33, 40, 45; Themes var. for vn. with trio accomp., opp. 1, 4, 15; Quintets for 2 vns., alto, 'cello, and double-bass, opp. 50, 51; String quartets, opp. 5, 6, 7, 8, 9, 23; Trios for Pf., vn., and 'cello, opp. 34, 41; Sonatas for Pf. and vn., opp. 16, 42, etc.

MAZAS (Jacques Fereol). French vnst. and comp., B. Beziers, [Sept. 23, 1782. S. under Baillot at Paris Cons. Travelled in Europe concert-giving. Director of music school at Cambrai. D. 1849. Comp. concertos, fantasias, romances, for violin.

MAZZINGHI (Joseph). Italian comp., B. London, 1765. S. under J. C. Bach, Anfossi, and Sacchini. Musical director, King's Theatre, 1784. Music teacher, to Princess of Wales. D. Bath., Jan. 15, 1844.

WORKS.—*Musical dramas*:—A day in Turkey, 1791; Paul and Virginia, 1800; The Blind Girl, 1801; The Exile, 1808; La belle Arsene; Sappho et Phaon; The magician no conjuror; The Free Knights; Ramah Droog (with Reeve); The Turnpike Gate (Reeve); Chains of the Heart (with Reeve); Wife of two Husbands. *Glees, trios, songs, etc.*—And whither would you lead me; Ava Maria; O Brignal banks; The captive to his bird; Cypress wreath; Each throbbing heart; For tenderness formed; Had I a heart; Harril the brave; Hart and hind are in their lair; Haste, O haste, glorious light; Hope told a flattering tale; Huntsman rest; I seek my shepherd gone astray; If the treasured gold; John of Brent; Lady Heware; Lillo Lee; Lochgyle; The minstrel's summons; Mirth and beauty; The negro's glee; Nocturnal besiegers; O young Lochinvar; Pastoral rondo; Roderick Vich Alpine; Soldier rest; Wake maid of Lorn; When order in this land commenced; When Phœbus rays no more appear; When tell-tale echoes; and, Where shall the lover rest. Songs, ballads, etc.

The reputation of this once popular composer has faded sadly, and at the present date only a very few of his compositions are known or used.

MAZZUCATO (Alberto). Italian comp., B. Undine, July 28, 1813. Prof. and director Milan Cons., D. Milan, Dec. 31, 1877. Comp. operas, orchestral works, etc.

MEERTS (Lambert Joseph). Belgian violinist and comp., B. Brussels, 6 Jan., 1800. Vnst. in orchestral of theatre in Brussels. Prof. of vn. at Brussels Cons., 1833. Chor. of the order of Leopold. D. Brussels, May 12, 1863. Writings on and for the violin, etc.

MEES (Arthur). American org. and teacher, B. Columbus, Ohio, 1850. S. under Kullak, Weitzmann, and Dorn. Founder and teacher in the "Cincinnati Music School." Director of the Cincinnati May Festival Chorus. Fellow of American Coll. of Musicians.

MEHLIG (Anna). German pianist, B. Stuttgart, June 11, 1846. S. at Stuttgart Cons., and under Liszt. Played in England, 1866; do. 1869. Appeared in America, 1873-4. Played in London again, 1875. Has since appeared in Britain with much success. A performer of great executive abilities.

MÉHUL (Etienne Nicolas). French comp., B. Givet, Ardennes, June 22, 1763. S. under an org. named Hauser. Deputy org. at church of Lavaldieu, 1777. S. under Edelmann at Paris. Acquainted with Gluck. Mem. of Institut de France, 1795. Chev. Legion of Hon., 1802. D. Paris, Oct. 18, 1817.

WORKS.—*Operas:* Cora, 1791; Le Jeune Sage et le Vieux Fou, 1793; Horatius Coclès, 1794; Phrosine et Mélidore, 1794; La Caverne, 1795; Le Jeune Henri, 1797; Adrien, 1799; Ariodaut, 1799; Épicure (with Cherubini), 1800; Bion, 1800; L'Irato, ou l'Emporté, 1801; Une Folie, 1802; Le Trésor supposé, 1802; Joanna, 1802; L'Heureux malgré lui, 1802; Héléna, 1803; Les deux Aveugles de Tolède, 1806; Uthal, 1806; Gabrielle d' Estrées, 1806; Joseph, Feb. 17, 1807; La Prince Troubadour, 1813; La Journée aux Aventures, 1816; Arminius, 1794. *Ballets:*—Le Jugement de Paris, 1793; Le Dansomania, 1800; Le Retour d' Ulysse, 1809; Persée et Andromede, 1811. Church and instrumental music.

Méthul was one of the greatest and most original of the French composers of the present century. His melody, orchestration, and command over dramatic expression were all of much merit, and in his treatment of involved operatic situations he was several generations in advance of his contemporaries.

MEIBOMIUS (Marcus). Danish writer, B. Fœnningen in Schleswig-Holstein, 1626. Prof. for a time at Upsala. D. Utrecht, 1711. Author of "Antiqua Musicæ auctores septem Græce et Latina," Amsterdam, 1652, 4to.

MEINARDUS (Ludwig Siegfried). German comp., B. Hooksiel, Oldenburg, 17 Sept., 1827. S. at Leipzig, Weimar and Berlin. Teacher at Dresden Cons., 1865. Teacher at Hamburg. Comp. *oratorios:* "Simon Petrus;" "Gideon;" "Luther in Worms," etc. Chamber music, songs, symphonies, and writings on music.

MEL (Rinaldo del). Flemish comp., B. Liège. Flourished during the latter half of the 16th century. Musician for a time to Philip II. of Portugal. Lived at Rome, 1580-90. Music director at cath. of Magliano, 1590. D. about end of 16th century.

WORKS.—Fifteen Books of Madrigals. Five Books of Motets; and other church music.

MELLON (Alfred). English comp., cond., and violinist, B. London, April 7, 1820. Violinst at Roy. Ital. Opera, Covent Garden, London. Cond.

at Haymarket Theatre; do. Adelphi; do. Pyne and Harrison opera company; do. Musical Society; do. Promenade Concerts, Covent Garden; do. Liverpool Philharmonic Society, 1865. Married to Miss Woolgar, the actress. D. London, March 27, 1867.

WORKS.—Victorine, opera, Covent Garden, 1859. Numerous Songs and Ballads. Pf. pieces, and other instrumental music.

Mellon was held in much esteem in his day as a good practical musician, and his abilities as a conductor were widely known and highly appreciated. His compositions are not so numerous nor so important as to call for much comment.

MELTON (William). English writer, Chancellor of the Duchy of York, flourished during the early part of the 16th century. Author of a treatise entitled "De Musicæ Ecclesiasticæ," preserved in MS.

MENDEL (Hermann). German writer, B. Halle, Aug. 6, 1834. D. Berlin, Oct. 26, 1876. Editor of "Musikalisches Conversations-Lexikon," Berlin, 1870-79, 11 vols. Completed by Dr. Reissman. This work is one of the most perfect books of its kind, but is very unsatisfactory, like other continental works of a similar character, as regards British musical biography.

MENDELSSOHN (Jakob Ludwig Felix Mendelssohn - Bartholdy). German comp., B. Hamburg, Feb. 3, 1809. Grandson of Moses Mendelssohn the Jewish philosopher. S. under Madame Bigot, Ludwig Berger (Pf.); Zelter (comp.); and Henning (violin), at Berlin. First appeared as a public performer, Oct. 1818; second, 1822. Alto singer at the Singakademie, Berlin, 1819. First began to compose, 1820. Acquainted with Weber, 1821; Goethe, 1821; Spohr, 1822; Moscheles, 1824. Examined in music by Cherubini, at Paris, 1825. S. at University of Berlin, 1827-29. Visited London and Edinburgh, and travelled in Highlands of Scotland, 1829. Visited Italy and Switzerland, 1830-1; and Paris again, 1831. Director of theatre at Dusseldorf, 1833. Married to Cecilie Jean Renaud, 1837. Ph.D., Leipzig University, 1841. Superintendent of sacred music in Germany, 1841. Chapel-master to King of Saxony. Musical director of Leipzig Cons., 1843. Cond. Philharmonic Concerts, London, 1844. Cond. "Elijah" at London, 1847. D. Leipzig, Nov. 4, 1847.

WORKS.—Op. 1. Quartet for Pf. and strings, in C min., 1822; op. 2. do., No. 2, in F min., 1823; op. 3. Do. in B. min., 1825; op. 4. Sonata for Pf. and violin, F min.; op. 5. Capriccio for Pf., in F sharp min., 1825; op. 6. Sonata for Pf., in E, 1826; op. 7. Seven characteristic pieces for Pf.; op. 8. Twelve songs for voice and Pf., 1829; op. 9. Twelve do., 1829; op. 10. The Wedding of Comacho (Die Hochzeit des Camacho), comic operetta in 2 acts, Aug. 10, 1825; op. 11. Symphony No. 1, in C min., 1824; op. 12. First quartet for strings, in E flat; op. 13. Second do., in A min.; op. 14. Andante and Rondo capriccioso, in E, Pf.; op. 15. Fantasia on the Last Rose of Summer, in E, Pf.; op. 16. Three Fantasias, Pf.; op. 17. Variations concertants, in D, Pf. and 'cello; op. 18. First quintet, in A, for strings; op. 19. Six songs; op. 20. Ottetto, in E flat, for strings; op. 21. Overture: Shakespeare's Midsummer Night's Dream, 1826; op. 22. Capriccio brilliant, in B min., Pf. and orch.; op. 23. In Deep Distress, Psalm 130 (Bartholomew), for solo and chorus, 2 motets; op. 24. Overture, in C, for military band; op. 25. First concerto, in G min., Pf. and orch.; op. 26. Overture: The Hebrides, in B min., 1829; op. 27. Overture in D, Die Meeresstille und Glückliche Fahrt; op. 28. Fantasia for Pf. in F sharp min.; op. 29. Rondo Brillante, for Pf. and orch., in E flat; op. 30. Sechs Lieder ohne Worte, Pf., Book 2; op. 31. Psalm 115, for solo, chorus, and orch. [1830]; op. 32. Overture, in F, Märchen von die Schöne Melusine [1833]; op. 33. Three caprices for Pf.; op. 34. Sechs Gesänge [1824]; op. 35. Sechs Präludien und 6 Fugen; op. 36. St. Paul, oratorio ("Paulus") Düsseldorf [1836]; op. 37. 3 Präludien und Fugen für Orgel; op. 38. Sechs Lieder ohne Worte; op. 39. Three motets; op. 40. Second concerto, for Pf. and orch., in D min. [1837]; op. 41. Six four-part lieder; op. 42. Psalm 42, for solo, chorus, and orch.; op. 43. Serenade und Allegro giojoso, for Pf. and orch., in D; op. 44. First, second, and third quartets, for strings, in D, E minor, and E flat [1837-8]; op. 45. Sonata for Pf. and 'cello, in B; op. 46. Psalm 95, for solo, chorus, and orch. [1838]; op. 47. Sechs lieder, voice and Pf.; op. 48. Six lieder, for 4 voices, 2nd set; op. 49. First trio for Pf., violin, and 'cello [1839]; op. 50. Six lieder for male voices ; op. 51. Psalm 114, for 8 voice choir and orch ; op. 52. Lobgesang Symphonie-cantate [1840]; op. 53. Sechs lieder ohne worte, Pf. ; op. 54. Variations (17) Sérieuses, for Pf. ; op. 55. Music for the "Antigone" of Sophocles, male choir and orch. [1841] ; op. 56. Third Symphony, in A min., "Scotch" [1843]; op. 57. Sechs Lieder ; op. 58. Sonata for Pf. and 'cello, in D ; op. 59. Sechs lieder, for 4 voices, 3rd set ; op. 60. Die erste Walpurgisnacht, Ballade von Goethe, for chorus and orch., 1832 (2nd version, 1843); op 61. Musik zu Sommernachtstraum von Shakespeare (Incidental music to "Midsummer Night's Dream"); op. 62. Lieder ohne worte, Pf. book 5 ; op. 63. Sechs lieder for 2 voices and Pf. ; op. 64. Concerto for violin and orch. in E minor [1844]; op. 65. Six Sonatas for organ ; op. 66. Second trio for Pf., violin, and 'cello, in C min. ; op. 67. Lieder ohne worte, Pf., 6th book ; op. 68. Festgesang : "An die Künstler" (Schiller), chorus and orch.; op. 69. Three motets, solo and chorus ; op. 70. Elijah, oratorio, Birmingham. Aug. 26, 1846 ; op. 71. Sechs lieder ; op. 72. Sechs Kinderstücke (children's pieces), Pf.; op. 73. Lauda Sion for chorus, solo, and orch., 1846 [op. 1. posthumous] ; op. 74. Musik zu "Athalia" von Racine [1843-5]; op. 75. Four lieder for 4 male voices, 2nd set ; op. 76. do., 3rd set ; op. 77. Three lieder for 2 voices and Pf.; op. 78. Three Psalms (2nd, 43rd, and 22nd), for solo and chorus, [1844]; op. 79. Six Sprüche (motets) for 8 part choir ; op. 80. Sixth Quartet for strings, in F min. [1847]; op. 81. Andante, scherzo, capriccio, and fugue for strings, in E, A min, E min, and E flat ; op. 82. Variation for Pf. in E flat ; op. 83. do. in B flat ; op. 83A. Andante and variation, in B, Pf. 4 hands ; op. 84. Three songs for a deep voice ; op. 85. Lieder ohne worte, Pf. book 7 ; op. 86. Six songs, voice and Pf. ; op. 87. Second quintet for strings, in B [1845] ; op. 88. Six lieder for four voices, 4th set ; op. 89. Heimkehr aus der Fremde ("Son and Stranger,") operetta or leiderspeil in 1 act [1829]; op. 90. Fourth Symphony for orch. "Italian," in A [1833] ; op. 91. Psalm 98 for 8 voice choir, solo, and orch. [1844]; op. 92. Allegro brillant, Pf. in A ; op. 93. Musik for "Oedipus in Kolonos" of Sophocles, for male chorus and orch. [1845] ; op. 94. "Concertarie (scena) for soprano, solo, and orch. ; op. 95. Overture for orch. "Ruy Blas" (Hugo) in C min. [1839]; op. 96. Hymn for alto solo, chorus and orch.; op. 97. Christus, unfinished oratorio (8 numbers); op. 98. Loreley, unfinished opera, comprising finale to act 1, Ave Maria and chorus, and Vintage chorus for male voices [1847]; op. 99. Six songs, for voice and Pf.; op. 100. Four lieder for 4 voices ; op. 101. "Trumpet" overture, for orch., in C ; op. 102. Lieder ohne worte, Pf., book 8 ; op. 103. Trauermarsch for orch. in A min.; op. 104. Three preludes and three studies for Pf.; op. 105. Sonata for Pf. in G min. [1821]; op. 106. do. in B flat [1827]; op. 107. Fifth symphony for orch., "Reformation," in D min [1832] ; op. 108. March for orch in D ; op. 109. Lieder ohne worte, for 'cello and Pf., in D ; op. 110. Sextet for Pf. and strings, in D ; op. 111. "Tu es Petrus," chorus for 5 voice choir and orch.; op. 112. Two sacred songs for solo voice and Pf.; op. 113. Concertstück for clarinet, basset-horn, and Pf., in F.; op. 114. do., in D min.; op. 115. Two sacred choruses for male voices ; op, 116. Trauergesang (funeral hymn), for mixed choir ; op. 117. Albumblatt, Pf., in E min.; op. 118. Capriccio, Pf., in E ; op. 119. Perpetuum mobile, Pf., in C ; op. 120. Four lieder for 4 male voices ; op. 121. Responsorium et Hymnus, for male voices and org. "Hear my prayer," Psalm for solo, chorus, and orch. [1844]. Numerous unnumbered works, including songs, part-songs, sacred music (hymns, anthems, etc.), and pianoforte music (studies, "gondellied," preludes, etc.)

One of the greatest and most eclectic musicians who ever lived. Brought up to music, with everything in his favour, and well endowed by nature and fortune to meet successfully all the difficulties attending the pursuit of the musical art, he encountered comparatively few of the disappointments and struggles which fell in the way of other famous composers, of whom Mozart and Schubert are familiar instances. His career was for the most part unclouded by any of those mercenary considerations which have fettered so many equally able men, and he was free to devote his whole life and study to his adopted art. That he nobly did this is a matter of musical history. Never during his too short career did he manifest any of those huckstering traits which form the most distinguishing feature of the German-Jewish character, and of which a shining example is shown in the career of Jacob Meyerbeer. He devoted himself with heart and soul to the cultivation of music, and he made it a kind of life-work and worship, as well as a mere profession.

His works are among the very finest in the whole range of musical art, and in their peculiar style, among the most original. As original creations his works are indeed marvels, when it is considered that so many great workers, each on his own lines, preceded him. His works have been criticised, discussed, and re-discussed *ad infinitum*, and it is our purpose merely to give a brief resumé of some of the more prominent characteristics of his style, and to point out what are deemed his most important works. He has been described as standing mid-way between the classical and romantic schools of musical thought, with a strong and decided leaning towards the latter. All of his works are impressed in a degree more or less strongly marked, with the emotional and highly-wrought feeling of the Romantic school, while in form, and very often in spirit, the Classical element is allowed full sway. Perhaps the best-known and most appreciated of his minor works are the Lieder ohne worte (Songs without words), in which he gave a title and an existence to one of the most refined and beautiful forms of Pianoforte music. These pieces, which are usually allowed to be his *invention*, are simply thoughts in music, admirably adapted to the capabilities of the Pianoforte. Their difference from the ordinary *pensée, impromptu, rêverie,* and other similar forms of more modern Pianoforte music, consists in the original style of their treatment, which makes them indeed Songs, as opposed to mere exercises in harmonical combination. His other works for the Pianoforte are no less distinguished for the bold and original features which they exhibit, and their constant use throughout the World, is a sufficient testimony to their worth and vitality. Coming to his larger works, the two which immediately appeal to the attention are the magnificent oratorios, "Elijah" and "St. Paul," both of which are unmatched for impressive dignity and originality. The works of Händel bear no comparison with those creations, save in a few of the choral numbers, as the styles of both masters are quite opposed to each other in every respect. The harmonies of Händel are thin and colourless beside those of Mendelssohn, and the whole structure and character of the dramatic and emotional feeling is entirely different in both. It is a matter for congratulation that the merits of such works as "Elijah" and "St. Paul" were first recognised and appreciated in Britain; a country which has been pledged to Händel and his works since the advent of that master. Mendelssohn's other works, such as the music to the plays of Sophocles, Goethe's "Walpurgisnacht," and the magnificent array of Psalms and Motets, need not be noticed in detail, as their fine harmonies, massive structure, and general impressiveness are known to every musical student. As an instrumental composer he stands nearest Beethoven of any musician of the present century. His fire, grasp of instrumental resource, clearness of design, and command of fresh combinations and beautiful forms, are all united in everything which he wrote, and his symphonies, overtures, and incidental pieces are all invested with those characteristics, together with a richness and warmth of treatment which stamp them as his own. The characteristics of Mendelssohn's music can never be mistaken by a musician of ordinary experience, and it speaks volumes to his influence that so many musicians of every nation imitated his peculiar florid and rich harmonies. It should be mentioned, however, that although much of Mendelssohn's music is characterised by his individuality and spirit, a large proportion of his works are much more conspicuous for mere formal beauty than deep feeling. This is particularly observable in the "Reformation Symphony," where the composer's imagination seems to have become jaded and mechanical long before the conclusion of the work. As a writer of part-songs and lieder he stands among the foremost of modern Germany, and, taken as a musician all in all, he is no doubt the most eclectic and original the world has yet seen. His genius shone in every department of music save opera, in which he only attempted a few fragmentary sketches, and as a man of general literary culture and fine character he has been long since acknowledged. Among the works on this gifted artist, the following is a selected list :—

Letters from Italy and Switzerland and Letters from Felix Mendelssohn-Bartholdy, from 1833 to 1847, translated by Lady Wallace, Lond., 2 vols., 8vo, 1862-63; Goethe and Mendelssohn, 1821-1831, trans. from the German of Karl Mendelssohn-Bartholdy, by M. E. von Glehn, Lond, 1872, 8vo; Barbedette. Felix Mendelssohn, sa Vie et ses Œuvres, Paris, 1869, 8vo; Devrient (E.) Meine Erinnerungen an Felix Mendelssohn-Bartholdy...Leipzig, 1869; also in English, 1869; Polko (E.) Reminiscences of F. Mendelssohn-Bartholdy, trans. by Lady Wallace, Lond., 1869, 8vo; Mendelssohn Family, 1729-1847, by Sebastian Hensel, from

Letters and Journals, trans. by Carl Klingemann, Lond. [1884], 2 vols., 8vo; Lampadius (W. A.) Life of Mendelssohn...Lond., 1876, 8vo. *Periodical Articles*: Edinburgh Review, vol. 115; British Quarterly Review, vol. 24 and 36; Fraser's Magazine, vols. 36, 37, 68, and 79; Dublin Review, vol. 52; Temple Bar, 1871 and 1874; Journal of Speculative Philosophy, vol. 7; Boston Review, vol. 5. See also the Bibliography.

MENTER (Joseph). German violoncellist and comp., B. Teysbach, Bavaria, Jan. 18, 1808. D. Munich, April 18, 1856. Comp. music for 'cello and orch. Was 'cellist at Munich opera.

MENTER (Sophie). German pianist, B. Munich, July 29, 1848. Daughter of above. S. at Munich Cons., and under Liszt. First appeared about 1863 at Stuttgart, and has since appeared at all the principal concerts in Britain and Europe. Appeared at Leipzig, 1867; London, 1881. Married to David Popper, the violoncellist, in 1872. Madame Menter is distinguished for the powerful style of her performance of works of the most advanced modern school.

MERCADANTE (Saverio). Italian comp., B. Altamura, Bari, 1797. S. at Coll. of S. Sebastian, Naples, 1809. Resided successively at Milan, Madrid, Cadiz, and Naples. Director of Naples Cons., 1840-62. Mem. of the Institute of France. D. Naples, Dec. 13, 1870.

WORKS.—*Operas:* Violenza e Costanza, 1819; Anacreonte in Samo, 1820; Il geloso ravveduto; Scipione in Cartagine; Maria Stuarda, 1821; Elisa e Claudio, 1821; L'Andronico, 1822; Adele ed Emerico, 1822; Alfonso ed Elisa, 1823; Didone, 1823; Gli Sciti, 1823; Dorolice; Il podesta di Burgos; Nitocri, 1825; Il Montanaro, 1827; La Rappresaglia, 1829; La Testa di Bronzo, 1831; I. Briganti; Le due illustré rivali, 1839. Cantatas, songs, etc.

The reputation of this composer, once brilliant and far-spread, has at the present date dwindled down to very small bulk. He is chiefly famous for a great command of fine melody, and a wide range of comic expression.

MERCY (Louis). French flute-a-bec player and comp., B. England. Flourished in first part of 18th century. Associated with Stanesby, a musical instrument-maker of London, in an endeavour to keep up an interest in the flute-a-bec, which was being superseded by the German flute. He published "Twelve Solos for the English Flute-a-bec, with a Preface;" Six do., op. 2, etc.

MERKEL (Gustav). German org. and comp., B. Oberoderwitz, Saxony, 1827; S. under Schneider, Reissiger and Schumann. Org. of Waisenkirche, Dresden, Dresden, 1853; do. Kreuzkirche, 1860; Court org., Dresden, 1864. Director of the Singakademie, Dresden, 1867-73. Prof. at Dresden Academy, etc. D. Dresden, Oct. 30, 1885.

WORKS.—*Org. and Pf. Music:* Sonata in D min., org. duet, op. 30; Introduction and double fugue, org., op. 34; Adagio, org., op. 35; Second Sonata, in G, op. 42; Variations (Beethoven), op. 45; 36 kurze und leichte Präludien, op. 47; 50 Do., op. 48; Three characterstücke, Pf., op. 50; Weihnachts pastorale, org., op. 56; Nachklänge aus schöner Zeit, romance Pf., op. 66; Three Idyllen, Pf., op. 68; Valse-impromptu, Pf., op. 69; Polonaise Pf., op. 70; Bunte Blätter, 4 kleine Tonbilder, Pf., op. 71; Stimmungsbilder, 8 lyrische stücke, Pf., op. 72; Four pieces, Pf., op. 74; Third sonata, org., C min., op. 80; Six trios, org., op. 100, 2 books; 12 Orgelstücke, op. 102; Pastorale in G, org., op. 103; Fantasia and fugue, org., op. 104; Do., op. 109; Fourth sonata, org., F, op. 115; Choralestudies, org., op. 116; Fifth Sonata, D min., op. 118; Reigen, Pf., op. 119; Lenz und Lied, Pf., op. 120; Two andantes, org., op. 122; Twelve fugues, org., op. 124; Waldbilder, Pf. op. 127; Two military marches, Pf. op. 128; 12 Präludien und Fughetten, org., op. 130, etc.

The works of Merkel are marked by great taste and brilliancy, and enjoy much favour among English and American organists, as well as on the Continent.

MERMET (Auguste). French comp., B. 1815. S. under Lesueur and Halévy. Chevalier of Legion of Hon. Comp. Le Roi David, opera, 1846. Roland à Roncevaux, do., 1864. Jeanne d'Arc, 1876, etc.

MERSENNE (Marin). French writer, B. Oizé on the Maine, Sept. 8, 1588. Ordained priest, 1611. Prof. of Philosophy, Nevers. Resided in Paris. D. Paris, Sept. 1, 1648.

WORKS.—Traité de l'harmonie universelle, 1627. Philosophical writings, etc.

MERZ (Karl). German writer and comp., B. Bensheim, Frankfort-on-the-Main, Sept. 10, 1834. S. under his father, etc. Went to America, 1854. Engaged in a music-store in Philadelphia. Org. of the Sixth Presbyterian Church, Philad. Musical director of Eden Hall Seminary, Lancaster, Pa., 1856. Teacher in South Virginia till 1861. Teacher of music at Oxford Coll., Oxford, Ohio. Editor of *Brainard's Musical World* from 1870.

WORKS.—*Operettas, etc.:* Katie Dean; Miriam's Song of Triumph, cantata; Runaway Flirt; Gipsy Girls, chorus; The last will and testament. *Theoretical works:* Modern Method for the Reed Organ (Brainard's), Cleveland, n. d. Musical Hints for the Million (Brainard's), Cleveland, n. d. Harmony and Thorough-bass. Part-music and Songs, Pf. music, etc. About 52 biographies of eminent American and other musicians in *Brainard's Musical World.*

Mr. Merz holds a high position in the Western States of America for his efforts in the cause of classical music, as well as for several didactic works which he has published.

METASTASIO (Pietro). Italian poet and dramatist, B. Rome, 1698. D. Vienna, 1782.

Metastasio gave life and form to much of the operatic work of the 18th century; his librettos having been the most widely used and popular of any poet of the period. At the same time his librettos had a decided tendency to make the musical settings stilted and lacking in variety. Metastasio was opposed to Gluck and operatic reform, and was the representative of the old classical form. His life was written by Burney, and to this reference must be made for further information.

METCALFE (Rev. Joseph Powell). English musician and writer, B. Canterbury, 1824. S. at Cambridge. B.A., 1847; M.A., 1850. Ordained, 1847. Rector of Bilbrough, Yorks., 1856.

WORKS.—School Round Book. Rules in Rhymes and Rounds. Metrical Anthems. Rounds, Catches, and Canons of England (with E. F. Rimbault), Lond., 1873. Contributions to Musical Literature, etc.

METHFESSEL (Albert Gottlieb). German comp., B. Stadtilm, Sept. 20, 1786. S. at Rudolstadt. Musician at Court of Schwarzburg. Teacher at Brunswick and Hamburg. D. Brunswick, Mar. 1869. Comp. numerous lieder, Pf. music, etc. ALBERT, his son, B. 1806, D. Berne, Nov. 19, 1878, wrote some of the most famous lieder of modern Germany.

METRA (Jules Louis Olivier). French comp., B. Rheims, June 2, 1830. S. Paris Cons., under Elwart and Thomas. Cond. etc.

WORKS.—Le Valet de chambre de Madame, 1872; Robinson Crusoe, 1857; Yedda, 1879; Ballets, etc.

METZLER & CO. English firm of music-publishers, established in London about the end of the 18th century. They publish vocal music by Abt, G. B. Allen, Balfe, Benedict, Bishop, Blumenthal, Campana, Cellier, Clay, Dick, Gabriel, Glover, Gounod, Hatton, Hullah, Linley, Lutz, Moore, Offenbach, Pinsuti, Sainton-Dolby, Smart, Sullivan, Wrighton, and numerous other living and recent composers. Their instrumental catalogue includes works by many of the modern and classic masters.

MEYER (Leopold von). Austrian comp. and pianist, B. Baden, near Vienna, Dec. 20, 1814. S. under Czerny. Visited U. S. A., 1845 and 1868. Has played in London, Paris, etc. D. Dresden, March 6, 1883. Comp. variations, fantasias, dances, studies, nocturnes, etc. for Pf. Was a performer of great ability but of eccentric manner.

MEYERBEER (Jacob), or BEER. German comp., B. Berlin, Sept. 5, 1791. S. under Vogler, Lauska, Clemenka, and Zelter. Chap.-master to King of Prussia. Cond. of Opera, Berlin. Mem. of Academy of Fine Arts, Berlin.

Comp. to Duke of Darmstadt. Visited London, 1847. Resided in Vienna, 1813. Resided at Venice and Milan; Paris from 1826. D. Paris, May 2, 1864.

WORKS.—*Operas:* Les Amours de Tevelinde, 1813; Wirth und Geist, 1813; Romilda e Costanza, 1815; Emma di Resburgo, 1819; Semiramide riconosciuta, 1819; Margherita d'Anjou, Milan, 1820; L'Esule di Granata, 1822; Almanzor; Das Brandenburger, 1823; Il Crociato in Egitto, Venice, 1824; Robert le Diable (libretto by Scribe and Delavigne),(Paris, Nov. 21, 1831 (Lond., 1831); Les Huguenots (Scribe), Paris, Feb. 21, 1836; Lond., 1842; Ein Feldlager in Schlesien, 1843; Struensée, Berlin, 1846; Le Prophete, Paris, 1849 (Lond., July, 1850); L'Etoile du Nord, Paris, Feb., 1854 (Lond., July, 1854); Le Pardon de Ploërmel, Paris, 1859 (London, as "Dinorah"); "L'Africaine," 1864. *Oratorios:* Gott und die Natur, 1811; Jephtha's Gelübde, 1811. *Cantatas, etc.:* Seven Sacred Cantatas of Klopstock, for 4 voices and accomp.; Le Génie de la Musique à la tombe de Beethoven, cantata; Cantata for the inauguration of Gutenberg's Statue at Mayence, 1836; Le Fête à le cour de Ferrare, 1843; Cantatas for the marriages of Royal personages; Ode au Sculpteur Rauch, 1851; Ninety-first Psalm for 8 voices; Stabat Mater; March for Schiller Centenary Festival, Paris, 1859; Overture for London International Exhibition, 1861; Coronation March, 1863. Numerous Pf. and lyrical pieces.

A composer of much influence on the operatic style of the present century. Basing his style upon that of Rossini, he produced a succession of brilliant and clever works, in which every artificial means of dazzling was resorted to. His works were as much spectactular as musical, and he strove to gain effects by an overwhelming quantity of tricky devices, rather than by those legitimate resources by which Weber and others maintained their renown as musicians. Meyerbeer brought the means of operatic representation to a degree of perfection far above anything achieved by his predecessors, and in this respect he has been followed by Wagner. His claim to be regarded as a true artist has been very keenly discussed on several occasions, and while on all hands his cleverness as an adapter and arranger is admitted, much doubt exists as to the existence of much originality in his works. Perhaps the term which best describes his style would be Germanised-Rossini. He has been blamed for looking too sharply after the mercenary rather than the artistic aims of a musician's career, but the explanation is easily found in his nationality.

Of his works the best known are "Robert le Diable," "Les Huguenots," "L'Etoile du Nord," and "Dinorah," and of these "Les Huguenots" is regarded as the best. It is a work containing many powerfully conceived and well worked out situations. Two works on Meyerbeer are Blaze de Bury's "Meyerbeer et son Temps," Paris, 1865; and Pougin's "Meyerbeer," Paris, 1864. There are also articles on him in the *Atlantic Monthly*, 1864 and 1879, and in nearly every musical journal.

MILANOLLO (Maria). Italian violinist, B. Sevigliano, near Turin, June 19, 1832. S. under her sister Teresa, and travelled with her, concert giving. D. Paris, Oct. 21, 1848.

MILANOLLO (Teresa). Italian violinlist, B. Sevigliano, near Turin, Aug. 28, 1827. S. under Lafont, etc. First appeared, 1839. Appeared in London with Maria, her sister. Travelled through France, Germany, Italy, and England. Married M. Parmentor. Revisited England, 1845.

MILDER-HAUPTMANN (Pauline Anna). German soprano vocalist, B. Constantinople, 1785. S. under Salieri, etc. *Début*, April 9, 1805, in Süssmayer's "Der Spiegel von Arkadien." Married Hauptmann, 1810. Appeared successively in Italy, Germany, etc. D. Berlin, May 29, 1838.

MILLARD (James Elwin). English writer. Was Headmaster of Magdalene Coll. School, Oxford. Author of "Historical Notices of the Office of Choristers, Lond., 8vo, 1848.

MILLER (Edward). English comp. and writer, B. Norwich, 1731. Bred a paviour, but absconded and S. under Burney at Lynn. Org. of Church of Doncaster, 1756-1807. Mus. Doc., Cantab., 1786. D. Doncaster, Sept. 12, 1807.

WORKS.—Six solos for German flute; Six sonatas for the harpsichord; Elegies for voice and Pf.; Twelve songs, 1773; Institutes of Music, or Easy Instructions for the Harpsichord, Lond., fo., n.d. [1771]; Elements of Thorough-bass and Composition, Lond., fo., 1787; The Psalms of David set to music, and arranged for every Sunday in the year, 1774; Treatise of Thorough-bass and Composition, Dublin, fo., n.d.; History of Doncaster, Doncaster, 1804.

MILLER (H. W.) English writer. Author of "Notes on Old English Music, a Lecture," London, 1875.

MILLER (William Mackie). Scottish teacher and cond., B. Glasgow, 1831. Cond. of Tonic Sol-fa Society, and late principal of a College of Music. He has edited a few works by Händel, in the tonic sol-fa notation, and written a "Tonic Sol-fa Flute Instructor," Edin., n.d., and other works designed for instruction in the Tonic Sol-fa notation.

MILLÖCKER (Carl). Austrian comp. and cond., B. Vienna, April 29, 1842. S. at Vienna Cons. Cond. at Gratz, and now teacher and cond. in Vienna. He has comp. a number of operas and operettas of which "Diana," 1865, "Three Pairs of Shoes," "The Enchanted Castle," Gasparone, 1884, Der Feldprediger, 1884, and "The Beggar Student" were successful. The last named was produced in London in 1885.

MILLS (S. B.) English pianist, comp., and teacher, B. Leicester, March 13, 1839. S. at Leipzig. Settled in New York, 1858. Teacher and comp. there. Has comp. numerous fanciful pieces for the Pf., and is regarded as one of the leading pianists in America.

MILTON (John). English musician, B. about end of 16th century. Scrivener in Bread Street, Cheapside, London. D. 1646. Comp. "Fayre Oriana in the Morne," madrigal, and numerous songs and motets in the principal collections of the period. His merits as a musician are celebrated in a short poem, "Ad patrem," by his son, the celebrated poet, whose works have been set by numerous composers, like Handel, Lawes, King, Nelson, and others.

MINGOTTI (Regina), *née* VALENTINI. Italian vocalist, B. Naples, 1728. S. under Porpora. Married Mingotti. Appeared in opposition to Faustina-Hasse. Sang in Spain. Appeared in London, 1755. D. at Neuburg on the Danube, 1807.

MITCHISON (William). Scottish musician and publisher in Glasgow.

WORKS.--The Psalmist's Companion, a Collection of Devotional Harmony for the use of Presbyterian Churches, selected from the works of Steven, Robertson, R. A. Smith, &c., Glasgow, 16mo, n. d: [c. 1843]. A few Remarks on the Pianoforte, giving details of the Mechanical Construction of that Instrument, etc., Glas., 8vo, 1845. Selection of Sacred Music, n. d. R. A. Smith's anthems, edited Glas., n. d.

MOLIQUE (Bernhard). German violinist and comp., B. Nuremberg, Oct. 7, 1803. S. under Spohr and Rovelli. Vnst. in theatre at Vienna. Leader of band at Munich, 1820. Do. Royal band at Stuttgart, 1829-49. Resided in London, 1849-66. Retired to Caustadt, 1866. D. Caustadt, near Stuttgart, May 10, 1869.

WORKS.--Concertos for vn. and orch., various; Quartets for strings etc.; Symphony for orch., 1837; Fantasias for vn.; Variations, concertinos, trios, etc.; Mass in B minor, op. 42. Abraham, oratorio, Norwich, 1860. Songs, etc.

A composer of much refinement, and a violinist of skill and taste. "Abraham," and selections from it, are still in use in England.

MOLINEUX (John). English writer and comp., B. about end of 18th century. Author of "The Singer's Systematic Guide to the Science of Music," Lond., fo., 1831. A Concise Collection of the Rudiments of Vocal Music, intended to assist persons who practise Glees or Church Music in the Art of Singing at sight, Lond. [1830].

MOLLESON (Alexander). Scottish minor poet, flourished at end of 18th and beginning of 19th centuries. Carried on a bookseller's business in Glasgow. Published anonymously, "Melody the Soul of Music, an Essay towards the

Improvement of the Musical Art," Glasgow, 8vo, 1798. This was reprinted in his "Miscellanies in Prose and Verse," Glasgow, 1806.

MOLLOY (James L.) Irish amateur comp. and writer, B. 1837. Eldest son of Kedo Molloy, Esq., of Cornolore, King's County. M.A. of the Catholic University of Ireland. Called to the English bar, 1864. Married Florence Baskerville, youngest daughter of Henry Baskerville, Esq., J. P. of Crowsley Park, Lord of the Manor of Shiplake, and deputy-lieutenant for the County of Oxford. Secretary to the late Sir John Holker, attorney-general. Member of the South-Eastern Circuit and Brighton Sessions. Member of the Middle Temple ; the Windham Club, etc.

WORKS.—*Operettas:* Student's frolic ; My aunt's secret ; Very catching. Irish melodies (Boosey), edited with new accomps. "Our Autumn Holiday on French Rivers" (prose work). *Songs:* Blue eyes ; Because I do ; By the river ; Bird and the cross ; Child's vision ; Clang of the wooden shoon ; Clochette ; Colleen ; Coquette ; Cragsman ; Darby and Joan ; Dreams ; Drifting boat ; Eily's reason ; Far from my native land ; Flowers that bloom ; Golden gleamed the river ; Jack's Farewell ; Jamie ; Kerry dance ; Knitting ; London Bridge ; Marching along ; My love has gone a-sailing ; My own true love ; Old Chelsea pensioner ; Our home by the sea ; Polly ; Postillion, the ; Thady O'Flinn ; Twenty-one ; Vagabond, the ; Wandering Jew ; and Will o' the wisp.

MOMIGNY (Jérome Joseph de). French comp. and writer, B. Philippeville, 1766. D. 1855. Author of "Cours Complet d'Harmonie et de Composition..." Paris, 1806, 3 v.

MONK (Edwin George). English org. and comp., B. Frome, Somerset, Dec. 13, 1819. S. under H. and G. Field ; in Hullah's classes, and under H. Phillips and Macfarren. Org. Coll. of St. Columba, Ireland, 1844. Teacher in Oxford, 1847. Org. and choir-master in Coll. of S. Peter, Radley, 1848. Mus. Bac. Oxon., 1848. Mus. Doc. Oxon., 1856. Org. York Cathedral, 1859-1883.

WORKS.—The Bard, ode for Mus. Doc. degree (Gray) 1856 ; Church Service, in A. *Anthems:* Blessed are they that fear the Lord ; Great and marvellous are Thy works ; The pains of Hell ; God so loved the world ; My soul truly waiteth upon God, etc. *Part-Songs:* Good-night, beloved ; Empress of India ; Stars of the summer night ; The beggar maid ; The miller's daughter ; A Magdalen College song ; Boating song ; Football song ; The jolly cricket-ball. Songs, hymns. The Anglican Hymn-Book (with R. C. Singleton). Descriptive account of the York Minster organs, 1863.

MONK James Jonathan). English org. and comp., B. Bolton-le-Moors, 20 Feb. 1846. Held various organ appointments, but now a teacher, and local secretary of Trinity Coll., in Liverpool. Hon. life mem. of Trinity Coll., Lond. Musical critic and writer to *Liverpool Courier, Choir, Musical Standard*, and *Liverpool Evening Express.*

WORKS.—*Songs:* Ah ! thou pale moon ; O lyric of the sea ; Among the new mown hay ; Ev'ning rest ; Home recollections ; In tranquil night ; I saw thee weep ; Oh ! give me back those kisses ; Primrose lane ; Snowflakes ; There is a maiden ; True for aye ; 'Twas but a glimpse ; Visions of the past ; Waiting but to say farewell ; What care I for the weather. Pianoforte music. I met my love, part song. O be joyful in God, anthem. Te Deum for parochial use. The Compilation of Musical Directories, a Paper read at the third meeting of the Society of Professional musicians, Liverpool, 12mo, 1883. Articles in the *Choir* on the St. George's Hall Organ ; History of the Liverpool Musical Society ; Musical Festival, etc..

MONK (William Henry). English comp. and org., B. London, 1823. S. under T. Adams, J. A. Hamilton, and G. A. Griesbach. Org. of Eaton Chapel, Pimlico, London ; do. S. George's Chap., Albemarle St. ; do. Portman Chap , Marylebone. Choir-master (1847) ; org. (1849) ; and Prof. of vocal music in King's College, London, 1874. Prof. of music at school for indigent blind, 1851. Org. of S. Matthias, Stoke Newington, 1852. Prof. in National Training Coll. for music, 1876 ; Prof. do., Bedford Coll., London, 1878.

WORKS.—Te Deums, Kyries, and other works for the church service. *Anthems:* And the angel Gabriel; Blessed are they that alway keep judgment; If ye love me keep my commandments; In God's word will I rejoice; Like as the hart; The Lord is my strength; They shall come and sing, etc. Hymns, psalms, etc. Hymns of the Church, Lond., n.d.; Fifty-two simple chants; The Canticles arranged for chanting to the ecclesiastical tones; The Book of Psalms in Metre (Church of Scotland), Harmonies revised; Scottish Hymnal (edited); The Psalter (Ch. of Scotland); Book of Anthems (Ch. of Scotland). Hymns *p. & M. 166 - times*

MONPOU (Francois L. H.) French comp., B. Paris, Jan. 12, 1804. S. under Choron, etc. D. Orleans, Aug. 10, 1841. Wrote songs to verse of Musset, Hugo, Beranger, etc.; also several operas.

MONRO (Henry). English comp. and org., B. Lincoln, 1774. Chor. in Lincoln Cath. S. under Dussek, D, Corri, etc. Org. St. Andrews, Newcastle, 1796. D. ? [after 1824]. Comp. songs, sonatas, and other Pf. music.

Another org. and comp. named GEORGE MONRO flourished during the first part of the 18th century. He competed unsuccessfully against Rosingrave for the post of org. of S. George's, Hanover Sq., London. He was afterwards org. of Ch. of S. Peter, Cornhill, and played the harpsichord in Goodman's Field's Theatre. He died in 1731. His songs appear in the "Musical Miscellany," 1731.

MONSIGNY (Pierre Alexandre). French comp., B. Fauquembergue, near St. Omer, Oct. 17, 1729. Maitre de Hotel to Duke of Orleans. S. under Gianotti. Inspector-General of Canals, Inspector of Instruction at Conservatoire de Musique, 1800. Member of the Institut, 1813. Mem. of Legion of Honour, 1816. D. Paris, Jan. 14, 1817.

WORKS.—*Operas:* Les aveux indiscrets, 1759; Le Maître en droit, 1760; Le Cadi dupé, 1761; On ne s'avise jamais de tout, 1761; Le Roi et le Fermier, 1762; Rose et Colas, 1764; Aline, Reine de Golconde, 1766; L'Ile sonnante, 1768; Le Déserteur, 1769; Le Faucon, 1772; Le Rendezvous bien employé, 1774; La belle Arsène, 1775; Félix ou l'enfant trouvé, 1777; many others in MS.

MONTAGNANA (Antonio). Italian vocalist of 18th century. Appeared in London, 1731. Sang in Handel's operas. Disappeared after 1738.

MONTAUBRY (Jean Baptiste Edouard). French vnst. and comp., B. Nivrt, Mar. 27, 1824. S. Paris Cons. Comp. operettas, songs, etc.

His brother, ACHILLE F., B. Nov. 11, 1826, is a vocalist of repute.

MONTE or MONS (Philippe de). Belgian comp., B. Mons, 1521. Resided in Antwerp, 1557. Chap.-master to Emperor Maximilian at Vienna, 1568. Do. to Rudolph II. at Prague. Treasurer and canon of the Cath. of Cambrai. D. Cambrai, July 4, 1603.

Comp. 30 books of madrigals, 2 books of masses, and 6 books of motets.

MONTEVERDE (Claudio). Italian comp., B. Cremona, 1568. Violinist in band of the Duke of Mantua. S. under Marc A. Ingegneri. Chap.-master at the Ducal Court ot Mantua, 1603. Chap.-master of S. Mark's, Venice, 1613-1643. D. Venice, 1643.

WORKS.—*Operas*: Ariadne, 1606; Orfeo, 1607; Arianne; Il Ballo delle Ingrate. Masses, motets, etc.

Monteverde was a great innovator on the harmonic methods of his time, and gained the usual amount of blame and praise by his originality. His dramatic works are in every respect superior to his sacred compositions, especially in the effective use of the instrumental forces; a department in which Monteverde surpassed all his predecessors. For the present age his music is more curious than pleasing; there being in it much of that laboured dryness peculiar to the Italian and Flemish schools of the 17th century. His influence on opera was great, and his use of the accompaniment has been often noticed as much in advance of anything achieved by his predecessors.

MONTGOMERY (R.) English writer of present time, author of "The Voice and Vocalisation," Lond., 1879.

MONTGOMERY (William H.) English comp., has produced an immense quantity of dance music, songs, etc., some of which will be found in the catalogues of almost every music-publisher. In addition to his numerous compositions he has published "The Royal Standard Tutor for the Harmonium," Lond., n. d.

MONTI (H. de). Italian music-teacher and music-seller, established in Edinburgh and Glasgow. Author of "The Self-taught Musician; a Treatise on Music," Edinburgh, 8vo, 1796. "Strictures on Mr. Logier's System of Musical Education," Glasgow, 8vo, 1817.

MONTIGNY-REMAURY (Fanny Marceline Caroline). French pianist, B. Pamiers, Jan. 22, 1843. S. under Le Couppey at Paris Cons., from 1854. Gained first prize for Pf., 1858; do. for Harmony, 1862. Married Léon Montigny, a journalist, 1866. Has performed in Paris, London (1872), and in other parts of the continent of Europe. Her repertory is large and varied, and her style of performance is brilliant but elevated.

MOODIE (William). Scottish cond. and comp., B. Bonhill, Dumbartonshire, April 19, 1833. Cond. successively of Episcopal Ch., Dumbarton; Dumbarton Choral Union; Lansdowne (Glasgow) U. P. Ch.; St. George's Choral Union; Musical Union; Barony Ch., and other Glasgow appointments.

WORKS.—*Anthems:* Blessed are the poor; Let your light so shine; Grace be to you; Now unto him; Behold how good; etc., with some in MS. *Part-Songs:* The auld man; Willie Wastle; To the woodlark: Afton water; John Barleycorn; Scroggam; and numerous arrangements of Scotch songs. Pianoforte music, miscellaneous, and Songs. *MS. works:* An oratorio; Chorus on Marriage of the Princess of Wales, "Alexandra" (Tennyson); Cantata, "Evening Pastoral"; Humorous overture for orch. on word "Cabbage"; Glees, and Songs.

MOORE (Henry Eaton). American comp. and writer, B. Andover, N. H, July 21, 1803. D. Cambridge, Mass., Oct. 23, 1841.

WORKS.—Grafton Journal, 1825-26; Musical Catechism; Merrimack Collection of Instrumental Music; New Hampshire Collection of Church Music; Supplement to do., 1834; The National Choir, Concord, 1834; Collection of Anthems; The Northern Harp.

MOORE (Jacob Bailey). American comp., B. Georgetown, Maine, Sept. 5, 1772. Descendant of a Scotch family. S. medicine, and became a surgeon in the U. S. army. D. Jan. 10, 1813.

Moore was a poet, and comp. a number of psalms in Holyoke's Collection.

MOORE (John Weeks). American writer, brother of the above, B. Andover, N. H., April 11, 1807. Teacher and writer in Boston, U. S. A.

WORKS.—Complete Encyclopædia of Music, Elementary, Technical, Historical, Biographical, etc., Boston, 1854 (with an Appendix of later date). Dictionary of Musical Information, Boston (condensed from foregoing). Vocal and Instrumental Instructor. Sacred Minstrel, 1841. Musician's Lexicon. American Collection of Instrumental Music, 1856.

The Encyclopædia, though by no means a reliable work, is one of the most important American contributions to the Literature of Music.

MOORE (Thomas). English music teacher, was resident in Glasgow in latter part of 18th century. On Nov. 22, 1756, he was appointed by the Magistrates Teacher of the Free music classes in Hutcheson's Hospital. D. Glasgow, about 1792. He compiled "Psalm-Singer's Compleat Tutor and Divine Companion," Manchester, 2 vols. [c. 1750]. "The Psalm-Singer's Pocket Companion, containing great variety of the best English Psalm-Tunes, suited to the different Metres in the Scotch Version of the Psalms of David, set in Three and Four Parts; Likewise all the Tunes that are usually sung in most Parts of Scotland. With a plain and easy Introduction to Musick...," Glasgow, 12mo, 1756. "The Psalm-Singer's Delightful Pocket Companion. Containing a Plain and Easy Introduction to Psalmody, and an Introduction explaining more at large, the grounds of Music in general. Illustrated with great variety of Tables, Scales, and Initial Lessons...," Glasgow, 12mo, n. d. [1762]. The Vocal Concert, 1761.

MOORE (Thomas). Irish poet and musician. B. Dublin, May 28, 1779. D. Feb. 25, 1852.

Connected with music through his "Irish Melodies," originally published in 1807-34, with accompaniments by Sir John Stevenson; and a few original pieces of music, as the Canadian boat song, "Row, brothers, row," in "Seven Glees," Lond., 1820. The only thing national about the "Irish Melodies" is the music, the poetry, unlike that of Burns, being only illustrative of commonplace sentiments of general application, which could as well be localized in France as in Ireland. His letters to Power, the original publisher of the melodies, were re-issued in New York in 1854, with an introductory letter by T. Crofton Croker. See his "Memoirs and Correspondence," by Lord John Russell. He wrote the words of "A Selection of Popular National Airs," 1818, 6 parts; and compiled "Evenings in Greece," Lond., 2 vols., 1831 [vocal music].

MOOREHEAD (John). Irish violinist and comp., B. about middle of 18th century. Vnst. in English provincial orchestras. Do. at Covent Garden Theatre, London. D. 1804.

Comp. music for the following plays:—The Naval Pillar, 1799; The Volcano, 1799; Harlequin's Tour; Il Bondocani (with Attwood), 1801, etc. Numerous songs and instrumental pieces.

MORALES (Cristofero). Spanish comp., B. Seville, early in 16th century. Mem. of the Papal choir, Sixtine Chapel, 1540. D. (?)

Comp. numerous masses, motets, etc., published between 1539 and 1569. Morales was the forerunner of Palestrina in the production of high-class church music, and shares with Rore, Lassus and others, the honour of having founded the noble ecclesiastical style of the 16th century.

MORALT. A family of quartet players, consisting of JOSEPH (1775-1828), first violin; JOHANN BAPTIST (1777-1825), second violin; PHILIPP (1780-1847), violoncello; and GEORG (1781-1818) viola.

This family was famed for admirable rendering of the quartets of Haydn, etc. Three of this family were members of the Court band of Munich.

MORELLI (Giovanni). Italian bass singer, who flourished about the end of last century. Appeared in opera, and sang at the Handel Commemoration in London.

MORGAN (George Washbourne). English comp. and org., B. Gloucester, April 9, 1823. Org. of Christ Church, and S. James', Gloucester. Org. of South Hackney; St. Olave, Southwark; Harmonic Union, London, etc. Settled in America, 1853. Org. successively of St. Thomas Epis. Ch., N.Y.; Grace Ch.; S. Ann's; S. Stephens; Brooklyn Tabernacle, etc.

Morgan has comp. music for the church service, miscellaneous vocal music, and some instrumental pieces.

MORGAN (J. Wilford). English comp. and tenor singer of present time, comp. of a number of songs and a cantata entitled "Christian the Pilgrim."

MORI (Nicolas). English violinist and comp., B. London, 1793. Pupil of Viotti. Principal violinist in London orchestras. Music publisher in Bond St., London. D. June 18, 1839.

MORI (Frank). English comp., son of the above, B. 1820. D. Aug. 2, 1873.

WORKS.—Fridolin, cantata; The River Sprite, operetta, words by G. Linley, Covent Garden, Feb. 9, 1865. *Songs:* Twelve Songs, by Mackay, Longfellow, Oxenford, etc.; Six Songs, by Moore, Shelley, Tennyson, Hunt, etc.; Breathe, oh! breathe that simple strain; Life's seasons; I love my love in the spring time; 'Tis only thee I love; Ruth in the corn; and Whither art thou roaming. Vocal Exercises.

MORISON (Christina W.), *neé* BOGUE. Scottish comp., B. Dublin, 1840. From an early age evinced decided talent for musical composition. S. under Glover and John Blockley. Remarkable as the first Scotchwoman who ever wrote an opera. This work, "The Uhlans," in 3 acts, written by her husband, Wm. M'Ivor Morison, was produced in Dublin in 1884, and in Glasgow, 1885, obtaining in both places considerable success. Her other works consist of Songs, Pf. pieces, and some larger pieces still in MS.

MORISON (Roderick), RORY DALL O'CAHEN. Scottish poet, harper, and comp., B. Lewis, 1646. Son of an Episcopal clergyman. Educated at Inverness. Lost sight with small-pox. Engaged as harper at Edinburgh in the family of Macleod. Visited Ireland. D. near Stornoway, Lewis. The composer of a few Gaelic airs, but best known as a poet of some ability.

MORLACCHI (Francesco). Italian comp., B. Perugia, June 14, 1784. S. under Caruso. Zingarelli, and Mattei. Cond. of Italian opera, Dresden, 1810. Mem. of Academy of Fine Arts, Florence. D. Innspruck, Oct. 28, 1841.

WORKS.—*Operas:* Il Poeta in Campagne, 1807 ; Il Ritratto, 1807 ; Cariadino, 1808 ; Oreste, 1808 ; Rinaldo d'Aste, 1809 ; La Danaïde, 1810 ; Raoul de Crequi, 1811 ; Il Nuovo Barbieri de Siviglia, 1815 ; La Semplicetta di Pirna, 1818 ; Laodicea, 1825 ; Il Colombo, 1828. *Oratorios:* La Morte d'Abele, 1820 ; Isacco, 1818. Masses, Cantatas, Misereres, and Te Deums. Sonatas and other instrumental music.

MORLEY (Thomas). English comp. and writer, B. about middle of the 16th century, circa 1550-76. S. under Byrd. Chor. S. Paul's Cath. Mus. Bac., Oxon., 1588 ; Org. S. Paul's Cath., London, 1591 ; Gent., etc., of Chapel-Royal, 1592-1602. Obtained patent for exclusive right to print music-books, 1598. D. 1604.

WORKS.—Canzonets, or Little Short Songs to three Voyces, 1593 ; Madrigalls to Foure Voyces, 1594 ; First Booke of Ballets to five Voyces, 1595 ; First Booke of Canzonets to Two Voyces, 1595 ; Canzonets, or Little Short aers to Five and Sixe Voyces, 1597 ; The First Booke of Consort Lessons, made by divers exquisite Authors for sixe instruments to play together, etc., 1599 ; The Triumphs of Oriana, to five and six voices, composed by divers several authors, newly published by Thomas Morley, London, Este, 1601 [contains madrigals by M. Este, J. Bennet, J. Hilton, J. Holmes, Wilbye, Morley, E. Johnson, T. Weelkes, Kirbye, Carlton, Cavendish, Lisley, Farmer, Milton, Jones, Croce, Hunt, Bateson, Mundy, E. Gibbons, R. Nicholson, Tomkins, Marson, F. Pilkington, Norcome, and Carbold]; Services in D min.; Evening Service in G min. (in Barnard's collection) ; Burial Service (in Boyce) ; A Preces, Psalms, etc., in Bernard's MS. coll.; Five Sets of Lessons in Queen Elizabeth's Virginal Book ; A Plaine and Easie Introduction to Practicall Musicke, set downe in forme of a dialogue. Divided into three partes. The first teacheth to sing with all things necessary for the knowledge of prickt song. The second treateth of descante and to sing two parts in one upon a plain song or ground, with other things necessary for a descanter. The third and last part entreateth of composition of three, foure, five or more parts, with many profitable rules to that effect, with new songs of 2, 3, 4, and 5 parts. Lond., fo., 1597.

Morley holds a distinguished position in the annals of English musical history, both as a didactic writer, and as a composer. In the former role he has credit by his "Plaine and Easie Introduction to Musicke," which stands foremost among all similar works of the same period, and is an admirable introduction to music as practised in the 16th and 17th centuries. As a composer, he excelled chiefly in madrigals of a light and airy cast, many of which hold their own at the present day, when " My bonny lass she smileth," " Now is the month of Maying," " April is in my mistress' face," " Dainty fine sweet nymph," " Sing we and chant it," " Fire ! fire ! my heart," " Lo ! where with flow'ry head," and several others, are stock pieces with our glee clubs and choirs. T. Oliphant considers Morley "decidedly inferior to Wilbye or Weelkes," and accuses him of wholesale thefts from F. Anerio and Gastoldi.

MORLEY (William). English comp. of the 18th century. Mus. Bac., 1713. Gent. Chap.-Royal, 1715. D. Oct. 29, 1731. Supposed to be the composer of the oldest double chant known, published in Boyce's Collection, in D minor.

MORNINGTON (Garrett Colley Wellesley, Earl of). Irish peer and comp., B. Dangan, Ireland, July 19, 1735 [1720?] Father of the Duke of Wellington, and of the Marquis of Wellesley. Mus. Doc., Dublin. Succeeded to title, 1758. Created Viscount Wellesley, 1760. Gained prizes from catch club in 1776, 1777, 1779. D. May 22, 1781.

WORKS. —Glees and Madrigals composed by the Earl of Mornington, edited by Sir H. R. Bishop. Lond., fo., 1846. Among them, the following are famous :— As it fell upon a day ; Beneath this rural shade ; By greenwood tree ; Come, fairest nymph ; Gently hear me, charming maid ; Go, happy shade ; Hail, hallowed fane ; Here in cool grot ; O bird of eve ; Rest, warrior, rest ; and, Soft sleep profoundly. To these may be added the catch, "Twas you, sir." The collection of glees, etc., made by Bishop, is the only complete one extant ; though all the glees, madrigals, and catches can be had as originally published in single parts. The cheerful pastoral character of Mornington's glees makes them highly acceptable, and such pieces as "Here in cool grot" are as popular now as when first composed. Mornington is numbered among the classic masters of the English glee.

MORTEN (A.). English author, published "Hints on the purchase of an Organ." Lond., 1877.

MOSCHELES (Ignaz). Bohemian comp. and pianist, of Jewish extraction, B. Prague, May 30, 1794. See under D. Weber, Albrechtsberger, and Salieri. Concertized in Europe, 1815-25. Appeared in London, 1822. Taught Mendelssohn the Pf., 1824. Married to Charlotte Embden at Hamburg, 1826. Settled in London, 1826-46. Director of Philharmonic Society, 1832 ; Cond. of do., 1845. Prof. of Pf. at Leipzig Cons., 1846. D. Leipzig, Mar. 10, 1870.

WORKS.—Variations and Arrangements for Pf., opp. 1, 2, 5, 6, 7, 15, 17, 20, 23, 29, 36, 39, 40, 42, 46, 50, 59, 99, 109, 128, 137, 138, 139. Polonaises for Pf., opp. 3, 19, 53. Sonatas and Sonatinas for Pf. solo, duet, and with other instruments, opp. 4, 22, 27, 41, 44, 47, 49 (melancolique), 79, 112, 121. Waltzes and Dances, opp. 8, 9, 33, 118. Marches, etc., opp. 10, 26, 31, 32, 86, 130, 141. Rondos for Pf., opp. 11, 12, 14, 18, 30, 43, 48, 52, 54, 58, 61, 63, 66, 67, 71, 74, 76, 82, 85, 94. Fantasias and Caprices for Pf., opp. 13, 25, 37, 38, 51, 55, 57, 68, 69, 72, 75, 77, 80, 83, 106, 108, 113, 114, 122, 123, 124, 129. Songs, opp. 16, 97, 116, 117, 119, 125, 131, 136. Duo concertante for Pf. and guitar, op. 20 ; Do. for Pf. and 'cello, op. 34. Divertissements for Pf., opp. 28, 78. Sextuor for Pf., violin, flute, two horns, and 'cello, op. 35. Concert de Société, Pf. and orch., op. 45. Concertos for Pf. and orch. in E, op. 56 ; G minor, op. 60 ; 4th, op. 64 ; C, op. 87 ; 6th, op. 90 ; "Pathetique," op. 92 ; "Pastoral," op. 96. Impromptus for Pf., opp. 62, 65, 89. Studies for Pf., opp. 70, 95, 98, 105, 107, 111, 126. Symphony in C, op. 81. Trio for Pf., violin and 'cello, op. 84. Septet, op. 88. Overture : "Joan of Arc" (Schiller), op. 91. Hommage à Handel, Pf. duet, op. 92 ; Do. Weber, op. 102. Ballads and Romances for Pf., opp. 100, 101, 104, 110. Vocal duets, op. 132. Miscellaneous Pf. music, as preludes, scherzos, toccatos, mazurkas, etc.

During his career Moscheles held a distinguished place among his contemporaries as a pianist. As a performer he had no equal in his peculiar style, which united the best features of legato and bravuara playing. He was for a long period one of the leading teachers and performers in London, and in his after connection with Leipzig Conservatory he did much to direct the studies of many now-famous performers. His friendship with Mendelssohn is another feature in his career which recommends him to the lasting regard of musicians. His musical works are valuable for didactic purposes, and it is chiefly as teaching pieces that any of them are used. The occasional appearance of a few of his larger pieces in concert programmes sufficiently show that he is not forgotten as a composer. He edited "The Life of Beethoven, including his Correspondence with his friends," London, 1841, 2 vols., 8vo. This work, though originally written in German by Schindler, was for some reason never acknowledged by Moscheles to be merely a translation. A work of great interest and some value is "Life of Moscheles, with Selections from his Diaries and Correspondence, by his Wife. Trans. by A. D. Coleridge," Lond., 1873, 2 vols., 8vo, with portrait. This is a most amusing work, and contains many sensible remarks on music and musicians.

MOSELEY (Rev. W. Willis). English writer, author of "The Quantity and Music of the Greek Chorus Discovered." Oxford, 8vo, 1847.

MOSZKOWSKI (Moritz). German pianist and comp., B. Breslau, Aug. 23, 1854. Here follows his own account of himself :—

"I took my first step before the public in my earliest youth, following my birth,

which occurred August 23, 1854, in Breslau. I selected this warm month in hopes of a tornado, which always plays so prominent a part in the biography of great men. This desired tempest in consequence of favourable weather did not occur, while it accompanied the birth of hundreds of men of much less importance. Embittered by this injustice, I determined to avenge myself on the world by playing the piano, which I continued in Dresden and Berlin as Kullak's pupil. In spite of the theoretical instruction of Kiel and Wüerst, a lively desire to compose was early aroused in me. I perpetrated, in time, an overture, a piano concerto, two symphonics, piano and violin pieces, songs, etc. ; in short, I have twenty works in print."
WORKS.—Op. 1. Scherzo für Pf. ; op. 2. Albumblatt, Pf., op. 4. Caprice, Pf.; op. 5. Hommage à Schumann, Fantaisie für Pf. ; op. 6. Fantaisie-Impromptu für Pf.; op. 7. 3 Moments Musicaux, Pf. ; op. 8 ; 5 Walzer für Pf., à 4 mains ; op. 9. 2 Lieder für sopran.; op. 10. Skizzen (4 kleine stücke für Pf.) ; op. 11. Drei stücke für Pf., à 4 mains; op. 12. Spanische Tanze für Pf., à 4 mains ; op. 13. Drei Lieder für baryton ; op. 14. Humoreske für Pf.; op. 15. Sechs stücke für Pf. ; op. 16. Zwei concertstücke für violine (Ballade, Bolero) ; op. 17. Drei Clavierstücke in Tanze form ; op. 18. Fünf Clavierstücke ; op. 19. Johanna d'Arc ; Symphonische Dichtung, für grosses orch (from Schiller) ; op. 20. Allegro Scherzando für Pf. ; op. 21. Album Espagnol for Pf. ; op. 22. Thränen ("Tears"), Fünf gesänge für eine singstimme mit Pf. ; op. 23. Aus Aller Herrn Länder (6 Pf. pieces, Russian, German, Spanish, Polish, Italian, Hungarian); op. 24. Drei Concert-etuden für Pf. ; op. 25. Deutsche Reigen (5 German dances) ; op. 26. Drei Leider im Volkston, Pf. accomp. ; op. 27. Barcarolle und Tarantelle für Pf.; op. 28. Miniatures (5 short Pf. pieces) ; Valse-brilliante für Pf. (unnumbered); op. 29. Concerto for Pf. and orch. (MS.)

MOTHERWELL (William). Scottish poet and ballad collector, B. Glasgow, Oct. 13, 1797. D. Glasgow, Nov. 1, 1835.
Best known in connection with music as editor of "Minstrelsy, Ancient and Modern, with an Historical Introduction and Notes," Glasgow, 1827, 4to ; A standard collection of choice ballads, to which is appended a number of ancient ballad tunes.

MOUNSEY (Elizabeth). English org. and comp., B. London, Oct., 1819. Org. of St. Peter's, Cornhill, 1834-81. Mem. of the Philharmonic Soc., 1842. Has published works for Pf., guitar, organ, and voice. Sister of Mrs. Mounsey Bartholomew. (See BARTHOLOMEW.)

MOUNT EDGCUMBE (Richard Edgcumbe, 2nd Earl). English Amateur comp. and writer, B. Sept. 13, 1764. Married Lady Sophia Hobart, daughter of the 2nd Earl of Buckinghamshire. D. Sept. 26, 1839. Comp. "Zenobia," an opera, King's Theatre, London, 1800. Author of "Musical Reminiscences of an Amateur, chiefly respecting the Italian Opera in England, for fifty years, 1773 to 1823, Lond., 1823 ; 2nd ed., 1827 ; 3rd ed., 1828 ; 4th ed., 1834.

MOUNTAIN (Sarah or Sophia), née WILKINSON. English soprano vocalist, B. 1768. First appeared in 1782. Appeared with Tate Wilkinson's Company at Hull, and there made her début in 1786. In same year sang in Leeds and Liverpool. Married Mr. Mountain, violinist, 1786. Sang at Covent Garden, and also in Dublin. Retired, 1814. D. July 3, 1841.

MOUTON (Jean). French comp., B. 1475. S. under Josquin. Teacher of Willaert, etc. Musician to Louis XII. Comp. masses, motets, etc.

MOZART (Johann Chrysostom Wolfgang Gottlieb, or Amadeus). Austrian comp., B. Salzburg, Jan. 27, 1756. Son of Leopold Mozart, sub-director of the Archbishop's chapel, Salzburg. S. under his father. Taken by his father as an infant prodigy through various European courts, along with his sister Catherine ; Munich (1762), Vienna (1762), Paris (1763), London (1764-5). Returned to Salzburg, 1766. Director of Archbishop of Salzburg's concerts, 1769. Visited Italy, Milan, Bologna, Florence, Rome, Naples, etc., 1769. Made Knight of the Golden Spur by the Pope. Member of the Philharmonic Soc. at Rome. Resided in Paris, 1778. Settled in Vienna as comp. to the Imperial Court, 1779. Married Constance Weber, Aug. 16, 1782. D. Vienna, Dec. 5, 1791.

WORKS.—*Operas:* Bastien und Bastienne, 1768 ; La Finta Simplice (comp. for the Emperor Joseph II.), Vienna, 1768; Mitridate, Milan, Dec., 1770; Ascanio in Alba (cantata), Milan, 1771; Il Sogno di Scipione, 1772; Lucio Silla, Milan, 1773; Zaïde, Venice [1773]; La Finta Giardiniera, Munich, 1774; Il Re Pastore, pastorale, Salzburg, 1775; Idomeneo, Re di Creta, Munich, 1781; Die Entführung aus dem Serail, Vienna, 1782, London, "The Seraglio," 1827; Der Schauspiel Director, 1786; Le Nozze di Figaro, Vienna, 1786; Il Dissoluto punito, ossia il Don Giovanni, Prague, 1787 (Vienna, 1787; London, King's Theatre, 1817); Cosi fan tutte, Vienna, 1790; Die Zauberflöte, Vienna, 1791; La Clemenza di Tito, Prague, 1791. Davidde Penitente, cantata for solo, chorus, and orch.; Eight vespers and litanies. *Masses*: No. 1, in C; 2, in C; 3; 4; 5; 6; 7, in B flat; 8, in F; 9, in G; 10, in C; 11; 12, in G; 13, in E flat; 14; 15, Requiem, in D minor; 16, in E flat (part of 13); 17, in C; 18, Requiem (short), in D minor; 19 and 20. Cantatas, scenas, arias, lieder, and miscellaneous vocal music. 49 Symphonies for orch.: op 7 in D: "Jupiter," in C, op. 38, 1788; G minor, op. 45, 1788; C, op. 34; D, op. 87; D, op. 88; E flat, op. 58, etc. Fifteen overtures for orch. Ten quintets for 2 violins, 2 violas, and 'cello, in C minor, C major, G minor, D, E flat, etc. Quintet for strings and horn, E flat; Quintet for Pf., oboe, clarinet, horn, and bassoon. Thirty-two quartets for 2 violins viola, and 'cello. Nine Trios for 2 violins and 'cello; Twenty-three Trios for Pf., violin, and 'cello; Twenty-seven Concertos for Pf. and orch. in C, A, F, B, E flat, C minor, D minor, G, A, B, etc.; Seven Concertos for violin and orch.; Five Concertos for flute and orch,; Concertos for clarinet and orch., and bassoon and orch.; Fortyfive Sonatas for Pf. and violin, op. 2 (6), op. 8 (3), op. 110, and in F, B, A, C, D, E minor, G, etc. Sonatas for Pf. solo: No. 1, in C; 2, in F; 3, in B flat; 4, in B flat; 5, in G; 6, in D; 7, in C; 8, in A minor; 9, in D; 10, in C; 11, in A; 12, in F; 13, in B flat; 14, in C minor; 15, in F; 16, in C; 17, in F; 18, in B flat; 19, in D; 20, in B flat; 21, in B flat; 22, in G. Concerto for 3 Pfs. and orch., 1777. Marches, serenades, and miscellaneous instrumental music. Sonatas for organ, motets, hymns, etc.

Mozart was one of the greatest operatic composers the world has seen. His works in every respect far transcend the best efforts of those composers who adopted classical subjects for musical treatment, and until the rise of the romantic departure in music, his works were the most original, fresh, and brilliant in the whole range of the lyric drama. His dramatic music is more interesting than that of Gluck, and in the power of its emotional colouring it is also considerably in advance of the works of that master. Altogether it is less formal, statuesque, and severe than that of Gluck, and vastly superior in regard to appropriate treatment than the music of any other dramatic composer during and preceding his period. His melodic faculty was great, and its originality and fecundity has served to keep certain of his works always on the stage. Of these, "Don Giovanni," "Figaro," and "Die Zauberflöte" are always in use. Though famous as a melodist Mozart is also due great credit for his method of treating the orchestral aids in his operatic works, and it is his strength in this department, together with his melodiousness, which places him so far above all the composers of his time. The works of Grétry, Paisiello, Cimarosa, Salieri, and others of his contemporaries, all lack this union of dramatic and melodious features, and while all of them were gifted with tunefulness in the highest degree, none of them could use the orchestra in a manner half so powerful and appropriate as Mozart. Until the rise of Cherubini, Beethoven, and Weber, Mozart could lay claim to be the greatest dramatic composer. Most of his works were received with the greatest enthusiasm by the public on their original production, and, as before stated, three of them still maintain a place among modern operatic works. The main characteristics of Mozart's dramatic music are their melody, and appropriate and occasionally powerful orchestral aids. Though not uniformly successful in catching the exact character of the dramatic situation, he rarely fails to excite the interest of the auditor, and whether the work is comic or tragic, there will always be found beauty combined with plenty of energy and skill in the treatment of effects.

His symphonies are still in universal use, and with those of Haydn, mark an historical epoch in Music. Some of them are much more powerful and deeply felt than those of Haydn, and though all are bright and melodious, such works as that in C, op. 38, commonly called the "Jupiter," rise to a very considerable height of dignity and grandeur, and for the period in which they were composed, must be held to stand among the greatest works of the kind. His music for stringed instruments, as the quintets and quartets, are always being performed at the present date, and with his trios and concertos for Pf. and orch., form a very considerable body of highly inspired, fresh, and agreeable compositions. His sonatas and other works for the Pf. are also in constant use, and almost any of his various pieces in this department of composition will be found in the catalogues of modern publishers; a fact which testifies at once to their vitality and popularity. In their general features his Pf. works resemble those of Haydn, and are generally very pretty, easy, and polished in style. They are not now much used for concert purposes, but are always in demand as fresh and agreeable teaching pieces. Of his other works, the best known are the masses, and of these, only one, the Requiem in D minor, can be regarded as rising in any great degree above the average of the works composed for the Roman Catholic Church service. In it will be found a larger amount of impressive dignity and the true sacred character than is contained in all the rest of his works of the same class. As a rule, the use of his masses is confined to Roman Catholic chapels, though they are also frequently given as concert-pieces by choirs and choral societies. Altogether, Mozart is one of the world's greatest composers, and for melody, grace, and clear instrumental writing, has never been surpassed by any writer of his school. His very remarkable musical faculty was developed early in life, and he travelled all over Europe with his father in the character of infant prodigy, thereby gaining a polish and ease which is impressed on nearly every one of his works, save such as have dramatic character sufficient to raise them above the gloss of the world. This is not the place in which to detail his adventures, nor the many vicissitudes which befel him, but reference can be made to the following list of works, in which will be found everything necessary for the satisfaction of readers :—

Holmes, Life of Mozart, including his correspondence, Lond., 1845. Nissen, Biographie, W. A. Mozart's...Leipzig, 1828; French trans. by Sowinski, 1869. Jahn, W. A. Mozart, Leipzig, 4 vols., 1856. Oulibicheff, Nouvelle Biographie de Mozart, Moscow, 3 vols., 1843. Nohl, Mozart, Stuttgart, 1863; Trans. by Lady Wallace, 2 vols., 1877. Schlösser, W. A. Mozart's Biographie, Augsburg, 1844. Nohl, Briefe [Letters], Salzburg, 1865; Trans. by Lady Wallace, Lond., 2 vols., 1865. Köchel, Chronologisch Thematisches Verzeichniss sammtlicher Tonwerke, ...1862. See also the *Bibliography*, and the following Periodicals :—Edinburgh Review, vol. 150; Foreign Quarterly Review, v. 4; Westminster Review, v. 32; Blackwood's Magazine, v. 58; Quarterly Review, v. 18; Fortnightly Review, v. 3; Fraser's Magazine, v. 41; Cornhill Magazine, v. 21; Dublin University Magazine, v. 27; North American Review, v. 102; London Society, v. 37; and Bentley's Magazine, v. 61.

MOZART (Johann Georg Leopold). German violinist and comp., father of the preceding, B. Augsburg, Nov. 14, 1719. Violinist in Chap. of Bishop of Salzburg. Second chap.-master at Court of Salzburg. Travelled all over Europe, and in England, with his son and daughter. D. Salzburg, May 28, 1787. He comp. much church music and operas, and wrote "Gründliche Violinschule," of which many editions were issued. It remained the standard violin-school for many years. He is now best known as W. A. Mozart's father, and remembered for the care and skill with which he trained his children as musicians. His daughter, MARIA ANNA (B. Salzburg, July 30, 1751, D. there Oct. 29, 1829), was also well skilled in music, and accompanied her brother in his artistic tours. She was married to the Baron von Berthold of Sonnenberg. She has been figured in engravings along with her brother.

MUDIE (Thomas Molleson). Scottish comp. and org., B. Chelsea, Nov. 30, 1809. S. under Crotch, Potter, etc., at R. A. M., 1823-32. Prof. Pf. R. A. M., 1832-44. Org. at Galton, Surrey, 1834-44. Teacher in Edinburgh for a time. Returned to London, 1863. D. London, July 24, 1876.

WORKS.— Symphonies in C, B flat, F, D, etc. ; Quintets, quartets, trios, etc., for strings, etc. ; Pf. music, consisting of duets, solos, fantasias, etc. ; Anthems and sacred songs ; Songs, various ; Accompaniments in Wood's "Songs of Scotland," ed. by Graham, etc.

MUFFAT (Georg). German org. and comp., B. about middle of 17th century. Org. of Strassburg Cath. till 1675 ; do. to Bishop of Passau, 1695. D. Passau, Feb. 23, 1704.

WORKS.—Suavioris Harmoniæ instrumentalis hyporchematicæ Florilegium, Augsburg, 1695. Florilegium Secundum, Passau, 1698. Apparatus Musico-Organisticus, 1690.

His son, AUGUST GOTTLIEB, B. near Weissenfels, April 17, 1683. Was org. and instructor in music to the Imperial Family at Vienna. D. Dresden, July 16, 1729. He published "Componimenti Musicali per il Cembalo;" "Parthien" Vienna, 1727; "Versets;" Toccatts, fugues, preludes, and other organ music, also much church music.

MULLEN (Alfred F.) English writer, etc., author of "Harmonium Tutor, with a Series of Easy Lessons progressively arranged, Lond., n.d.; Easy and Complete Instructions for the Pianoforte, Lond., n.d.; Catechism of Music, n.d.; Numerous transcriptions for Pf., and songs.

MULLEN (Joseph). Irish comp. and org., B. Dublin, 1826. Chor. in Christ Ch. Cath., Dublin. Org. at Tuam Cath.; Succentor of Limerick Cath.; org. of S. Mary's Ch., S. Catherine's Ch., and of Christ Ch., Leeson Park, Dublin.

MÜLLER (August Eberhardt). German org. and comp., B. Nordheim, Hanover, Dec. 13, 1767. S. for the Law. Org. at Magdeburg, 1789. Org. S. Nicholas' Ch., Leipzig, 1794. D. Weimar, 1817.

WORKS.—Sonatas for Pf., opp. 3, 5, 7, 14, 26; Sonatas for Pf. and vn., opp. 18, 36; Sonata for Pf. and 'cello, op. 17; Concerto, Pf. and orch., op. 21; Themes for Pf., opp. 8, 9, 12, 15, 32, 37; Organ sonatas, various; Organ suites; Concertos for flute, opp. 6, 10, 16, 19, 20, 22, 23, 24, 27, 30, 39; Methods for Flute and Pf.; Songs.

MÜLLER FAMILY. A celebrated family of quartet players, consisting of KARL FRIEDRICH, first violin (1797-1873); FRANZ FERDINAND GEORG, second violin (1808-1855); THEODOR HEINRICH GEORG, viola (1799-1855); and AUGUST THEODOR, violoncello (1802-1875), all natives of Brunswick. They excelled in the works of Beethoven and Haydn.

MULLINGER-HIGGINS (William). See HIGGINS (William Mullinger).

MUNDY (John). English org. and comp., B. in latter half of 16th century. S. under his father. Org. of Eton College. Org. St. George's Chapel, Windsor, 1585. Mus. Bac., Oxon., 1586; Mus. Doc., do., 1624. D. 1630.

WORKS.—Songs and Psalms, composed into three, four, and five parts, for the use of all such as either love or learn music, 1594; Anthems and other sacred music; "Lightly she tripped," madrigal for 5 voices, in "Triumphs of Oriana."

MUNDY (William). English comp. of 16th century, father of the above. Vicar-choral S. Paul's. Gent. Chap. Royal, 1563. D. 1591. Comp. anthems in Clifford's collection, etc.

MURBY (Thomas). English writer and publisher, author of "The Musical Student's Manual," Lond., 8vo, n. d.

MURIS (John). English writer and musician, who flourished during the 14th century. Doctor and Canon of the Sorbonne, or a Chanter in the Church of Notre Dame of Paris. Author of a number of musical works, preserved in MS.; among which are treatises on counterpoint, and notices, the earliest of the kind, of the time table. Nationality variously stated as Norman and French, but a concensus of opinion fixes his nativity as English.

MURRAY (James R.) American compiler of school music books, B. Andover, Mass., 1841. His publications bear fanciful titles, but are mainly collections of vocal music. Among them may be named:—School Chimes; Heavenward; Joyful Songs; Pure Diamonds; Royal Gems; The Imperial; Songs of P. P. Bliss, edited.

MURSKA (Ilma di). Hungarian soprano vocalist, B. in Croatia, 1843. S. under Marchesi at Vienna. *Début* at Florence, 1862. Appeared in London at H. M. Theatre in "Lucia di Lammermuir," 1865. Visited America, Australia, etc. Re-appeared in England, 1879, and has since sang in opera, but with much less success than formerly.

MUSARD (Philippe). French comp. and violinist, B. Paris, 1789 [1793]. S. under Reicha. Cond. at Paris opera. Cond. Promenade Concerts at Drury Lane, London, 1841. D. near Paris, Mar. 31, 1859. Comp. numerous pieces of chamber and concert music of a high degree of merit.

MYSLIWECZEK (Josef). Bohemian operatic comp., B. Prague, Mar. 9, 1737. D. Rome, Feb. 4, 1781.

N.

NACHBAUR (Franz). German tenor vocalist, B. near Friedrichshafen, Würtemberg, Mar. 25, 1835. S. at Stuttgart. Chorister at Basle. S. under Lamperti. Has sung in Germany, Italy, Austria, etc., in operas by Rossini, Meyerbeer, etc.

NÄGELI (Johann Georg). Swiss comp., writer and publisher, B. Zurich, 1768. Publisher in Zurich, and engaged in educational projects there. D. Zurich, Dec. 26, 1836. He composed much vocal music, chiefly choral, and published an amount of standard classics. He corresponded with Beethoven, Weber, and other great musicians.

NAIRNE (Caroline Oliphant, Baroness). Scottish song and ballad writer, B. Gask, Perthshire, July, 1766. D. Oct., 1845. The well-known songs "Caller Herrin," "The Rowan Tree," "Laird o' Cockpen," "Land o' the Leal," "The Auld House," "Will ye no come back again," "The Bonnie Brier Bush," are by her, and have exercised the talents of a number of composers from the time of the Gows to the present day. A collection of 45 songs is issued by Paterson of Edinburgh under the title of "Lays of Strathearn." Her works were edited by the Rev. Charles Rogers, LL.D.

NALDI (Giuseppe). Italian buffo vocalist, B. Bologna, Feb., 1770. S. at Bologna and Pavia Universities. Was a government official for a time. Appeared at Rome, 1789. Appeared successively at Naples, Venice, Turin, and Milan. Appeared in London, April, 1806. Sang in Paris, 1819. Killed at Paris by accidental bursting of a kettle, Dec. 15, 1820.

NANINI (Giovanni Bernardino). Italian comp., B. Vallerano, about middle of 16th century [1550]. S. under his brother, Giovanni Maria. Chap.-master of Ch. of S. Luigi de'Francesi; do. S. Lorenzo in Damaso. D. [Rome] after 1620.

WORKS.—Il primo libro di Madrigali a 5 voci, Venice, 1598. Il secondo libro di Madrigali, 1599. Il libro terzo di Madrigali, Rome, 1612. Mottecta J. B. Nanini singulis, binis, ternis, quaternis et quinis vocibus una cum gravi voce ad organi sonum accommodata, Rome, 1608. Book 2, do., 1611; Book 3, 1612; Book 4, 1618. Salmi a 4 voci per le domeniche solennità della Madonna ed Apostoli, con due Salmi, una a 4, l'altro a 8 voci, Rome, 1620. Numerous detached pieces of church music.

NANINI (Giovanni Maria). Italian comp., brother of the above, B. Vallerano, 1540. S. at Rome under Goudimel. Chap.-master at Vallerano; do. at S. Maria Maggiore, 1571-75. Established a music school at Rome in conjunction with his brother. Member of the Pontifical choir. D. Rome, March 11, 1607.

WORKS.—Motetti a tre voci, Venice, 1578. Motetti a 5 voci, 1579. Second (1580), third (1584), and fourth (1586) books, do. Canzonette a 3 voci, 1587. Madrigals, psalms, etc. in contemporary collections.

NANTIER-DIDIÉE (Constance Betsy Rosabella). French mezzo-soprano vocalist, B. S. Denis, Isle of Bourbon, Nov. 16, 1831. S. at Paris Cons. under Duprez, 1847-49. *Début* at Turin, 1850. Sang in London, 1853. Sang also in Paris, St. Petersburg, and generally in Europe. D. Madrid, Dec. 4, 1867.

NAPIER (William). Scottish publisher, B. 1740. Established in London as music-seller to the Royal family. Member of the King's band. D. London, 1812. He published A Selection of the most favourite Scots Songs, chiefly Pastoral, adapted for the Harpsichord, with an accompaniment for the Violin, by Eminent Masters, Lond. [1790]; A Selection of Original Scots Songs, in three parts, the harmony by Haydn, Lond. [1792]; Napier's Selection of Dances and Strathspeys, with new and appropriate Basses, adapted for the Pianoforte, Harp, etc., n.d. The "eminent masters" mentioned in No. 1 were S. Arnold, W. Shield, Carter, and Barthelemon. No. 1 contains Tytler's "Dissertation on Scottish Music."

NAPRAVNIK (Eduard). Bohemian pianist and comp., B. Bejsti, Aug. 24, 1839. S. at Prague. Director of the Imperial Opera, St. Petersburg, 1861. Chiefly known as the writer of a number of pianoforte pieces of a national character, and an opera, "Nizegorodzy," which obtained some success. His songs are good, but chiefly of Bohemian interest, and his other operas are unknown here.

NARDINI (Pietro). Italian comp., B. Fibiana, Tuscany, 1722. S. under Tartini. Court violinist at Stuttgart, 1753-68. Resided at Leghorn, 1767-70. Court violinist and musical director to the Duke of Tuscany, 1770-93. D. Florence, May 7, 1793.

WORKS.—Op. 1. Six concertos for violin; op. 2. Six sonatas for violin and bass; Six trios for flute, composed for Lord Lyndhurst, London, n.d.; Six solos for violin, op. 5; Six quartets for 2 violins, alto and bass, Florence, 1782. Other instrumental music.

NARES (James). English comp. and org., B. Stanwell, Middlesex, 1715. Chorister in Chap. Royal, under Gates. S. under Pepusch. Deputy-org. of S. George's Chap., Windsor. Org. York Cath., 1734. Org. and comp. to Chap. Royal, 1756. Mus. Doc. Cantab., 1757. Master of children of Chap. Royal, 1757-80. D. London, Feb. 10, 1783.

WORKS.—Eight Setts of Lessons for the Harpsichord, 1747; Five Harpsichord lessons, 1758; Three Easy do.; The Royal Pastoral, a Dramatic Ode; Collection of Catches, Canons, and Glees, Lond. [1772]; Twenty Anthems in Score, Lond., 1778; Morning and Evening Service, with Six Anthems in Score, 1788; Six Organ Fugues. A Treatise on Singing, n.d.; Il Principio, or, a Regular Introduction to Playing on the Harpsichord or Organ, n.d.; Concise and Easy Treatise on Singing...with a Set of English duets for Beginners; Songs and miscellaneous instrumental music.

It is as a composer for the church that Nares is now known, and his claims in this direction are considerable. His anthems unite grandeur with a large amount of able contrapuntal treatment, which, though simple, is also effective.

NATHAN (Isaac). English comp. and writer, B. Canterbury, of Jewish parents, 1792. S. at Cambridge. S. music under D. Corri. Sang at Covent Garden Theatre. Emigrated to Melbourne, Australia, Feb., 1841. Killed in Sydney, Jan. 15, 1864.

WORKS.—Hebrew Melodies (from Byron), 1822; Sweethearts and Wives, 1823; The Alcaid, opera, 1824; The Illustrious Stranger, musical farce, 1827; Musurgia-Vocalis, an Essay on the History and Theory of Music, and on the Qualities, Capabilities, and Management of the Human Voice, 4to [1823], illust.; Life of Madame Malibran de Beriot, interspersed with original anecdotes, and critical remarks on her musical powers, Lond., 1836. Miscellaneous vocal music; The King's Fool, drama. The Southern Euphrosyne and Australian Miscellany, containing Oriental Moral Tales, Original Anecdotes, Poetry and Music; an Historical Sketch, with examples, of the Native Aboriginal Melodies, etc., Sydney [1846].

Only a very few detached pieces of his compositions now exist, and the only songs which obtain currency now are those from Byron's "Hebrew Melodies."

NAU (Maria Dolores Benedicta Josefina). Spanish soprano vocalist, B. New York, Mar. 18, 1818. S. Paris Cons., 1832. Début at Paris, 1836. Sang successively in Brussels, London, 1844; Paris, 1844-48; United States, 1848-9, etc. Retired, 1850.

NAUDIN (Emilio). Italian tenor vocalist, B. Parma, Oct. 23, 1823. S. under G. Panizzi. *Début* at Cremona. Appeared in various Continental theatres, and in London, 1858, 1862, to 1872, and following years. Sings in works of Meyerbeer, Verdi, Auber, etc.

NAUMANN (Emil). German writer and musician, grandson of J. G. Naumann, B. Berlin, Sept. 8, 1827. S. under Hauptmann, etc. Music-director of St. Thomas's, Leipzig, 1880.

Naumann is best known as a historian, and as a writer of some tracts of a controversial character, such as "Musikdrama der Oper?" and "Die Moderne Musikalische Zopf," in which his Conservative leanings are set forth. His History of Music has been translated by F. Praeger, and is now publishing in parts by Messrs. Cassell, & Co., under the editorship of the Rev. Sir F. A. G. Ouseley. He has also composed oratorios, operas, cantatas and sonatas.

NAUMANN (Johann Gottlieb). German comp. and org., B. Blasewitz, near Dresden, April 17, 1741. S. at Dresden. Gave concerts in conjunction with a Swede named Weestroem, 1757. S. under Martini. Court-comp. at Vienna, 1763. Resided in Italy, 1769-72. Vice-chap.-master to the Elector at Dresden. Principal do., 1786. Married Frau Grotschilling. D. Dresden, Oct. 23, 1801.

WORKS.—*Oratorios:* La Passione de Giesu; Giuseppe riconosciuto; Zeit und Ewigkeit; Santa Elena; Davidde in Terebinto, 1796; La Morte d'Abele. *Operas:* Achille in Sciro, 1767; Alessandro nell Indie, 1768; La Clemenza di Tito; Le Nozze disturbate, 1772; Solimano, 1772; Osiride; Ipermestra; Amphion, 1776; Cora, 1780; Gustave Wasa, 1780; Orpheo et Eurydice, 1785. Eighteen symphonies for orch; Ballets, various. Instrumental music: Trios, sonatas, etc.; Psalms and Masses, 1766-1800; Vater Unser (Klopstock); Songs and miscellaneous music.

Naumann had undoubtedly originality in his style, and might have attained considerable individual fame but for an imitation of the Italian school which, though fashionable enough in its day, proved fatal to many other German writers who adopted its conventionalities.

NAVA (Franz). See RIMBAULT (E. F.).

NAVA (Gaetano). Italian singing-master and writer, B. Milan, May, 1802. S. at Milan Cons. Prof. of Singing at Milan Cons. from 1837. D. Milan, 1875.

WORKS.—A Baritone Vocal School; published in London, ed. by C. Santley. Vocal Exercises, numerous books, etc.

Nava was best known as a teacher, and has special interest for English musicians as the instructor of C. Santley, the well-known barytone vocalist.

NAYLOR (John). English comp. and org., B. Stanningley, near Leeds, June 8, 1838. S. under R. S. Burton, Leeds. Org. Parish Ch., Scarborough, 1856. Mus. Bac., Oxon., 1863. Mus. Doc., Oxon., 1872. Org. All Saints Ch., Scarborough, 1873. Org. York Minster, 1883.

WORKS.—Church oratorio, "Jeremiah," York, 1883. Church Services. *Anthems:* If ye then be risen with Christ; Sing, O daughter of Zion; My soul truly waiteth; O praise the Lord; Out of the deep; O ye that love the Lord. Hymns. *Part-Songs:* The angels breathe on flowers; O, Phœbus! etc. Songs.

NAYLOR (Sidney). English pianist, cond., and comp., B. Kensington, London, July 24, 1841. Chor. in the Temple Ch., 1849. S. org. and harmony under Dr. Hopkins. Org. successively of St. George's, Bloomsbury; St. Michael's, Bassishaw; St. Mary's, Newington, etc. Married to Miss Blanche Cole, the vocalist, 1868. Became associated with J. Sims Reeves as accompanist, etc., 1870. Partner with Mr. Carl Rosa in connection with his second opera season, 1874. Has conducted and accompanied at many of the more important concerts throughout Britain.

Mr. Naylor has composed some church music, but has published only a few pieces, among them being a Te Deum and some songs. He is best known as a most successful pianist, and as a sympathetic and refined accompanist. His merits as a conductor are also well known and widely appreciated.

NEATE (Charles). English comp. and pianist, B. London, March 28, 1784. S. under J. Field, and Woelfl. Appeared as pianist, at Covent Garden, 1800. Member of Philharmonic Soc., 1813; afterwards a director and conductor of do. Acquainted with Beethoven, 1815. S. under Winter. Played in England at principal concerts. D. Brighton, March 30, 1877.

WORKS.—Grand Sonata for Pf., op. 1, 1808; Sonata for Pf., in D. min., op. 2, 1822; Pf. rondos, and other instrumental works; Trio for Pf., violin, and 'cello, op. 22 [1831]. Essay on Fingering, chiefly as connected with Expression, with General Observations on Pianoforte Playing. Lond., fo., n. d. Songs.

Neate was best known as a performer of classical music, and as one who did much to popularize the works of contemporary German composers, at a time when musical affairs in Britain were almost stagnant. He composed much instrumental music, but none of it is now in use.

NEEDLER (Henry). English musician and violinist, B. London, 1685. D. Aug. 1760. One of the original founders of the Academy of Ancient Music, and a performer of contemporary fame.

NEEFE (Christian Gottlob). German org. and comp., B. Chemnitz, Feb. 5, 1748. Cond. orchestras in various towns in Germany. Court org. at Bonn, 1781, where Beethoven was for a time under his instruction. Afterwards theatrical cond. D. Dessau, Jan. 26, 1798.

Neefe wrote several operas and other works, but is only now remembered as the early instructor of Beethoven.

NEILSON (Laurence Cornelius). English comp., org., and pianist, B. London, 1760. Went to America, 1767. Org. at Dudley; Do. at Chesterfield. D. 1830 (?) Comp. sonatas, duets, divertissements, for Pf. Songs, psalms, flute music, etc.

NEITHARDT (August Heinrich). German comp. and cond., B. Schleiz, Reuss-Schleiz, Aug. 10, 1793. Served in Army, 1813-15. Bandmaster in Army, 1816-22. Do. of Kaiser Franz Grenadiers, 1822-40. Königliche musik-director, 1839. Founded Dom-chor. of Berlin (Cath.), 1843. Visited London with Choir, 1850. D. Berlin, April 18, 1861.

WORKS.—Manfred und Julie, opera. Band music. Arrangements of choral music, part-songs, etc.

NELSON (Sidney). English comp. and writer, B. 1800. Teacher in London. D. London, April 7, 1862.

WORKS.—*Songs*: Better Land (Hemans); Corsair's bride; Guide, the; Gipsy king; Gipsy's invitation; Home song; Hunter's horn; Mary of Argyle; Pilot, the; Rainy day; Rose of Allandale; Sweet Ellen Dale; Mountain Lays, six sacred songs; Songs of the Gipsies, Lond., 1832; etc. *Duets*: By the gentle Guadalquiver; Our happy home. *Trios*: Six Vocal [1852]; Vintager's Evening Hymn. Pf. music. Vocal School, a Series of Scales, Exercises, etc., Lond., n.d. Vocalist's Daily Practice, Lond., n.d.

NERI (San Filippo). Italian priest, and founder of the Congregation of the Oratory, B. Florence, 1515. D. Rome, 1595.

Associated with Animuccia in establishing the oratorio.

NERUDA (Wilhelmine). Austrian violinist, B. Brünn, Moravia, Mar. 21, 1840. S. under Jansa. *Début*, Vienna, 1846. Travelled in Germany. First appeared in London, 1849. Appeared in Paris, 1864. Married Ludwig Normann, a Swedish musician, 1864. Reappeared in London, 1869, and has since that date performed throughout the English Provinces and in Scotland. She is one of the best-known violinists in London, and her skill in quartet playing is widely known.

NESSLER (Victor Ernst). German comp., B. Baer, Jan. 28, 1841. Comp. operas, The Piper of Hamelin; Der Trompeter von Säkkingen, 1885; instrumental and vocal music.

NEUKOMM (Chevalier Sigismund). Austrian comp. and pianist, B. Salzburg, July 10, 1778. S. under M. and J. Haydn. Chap.-master to Emperor of Russia, at S. Petersburg, 1806. Pianist to Tallyrand, in Paris. Chevalier of Legion of Hon., 1815. Chap.-master to Dom Pedro of Brazil, Rio Janeiro, 1816-21. Appeared in London, 1829, and spent much of his time in England and Paris. D. Paris, April 3, 1858.

WORKS.—*Oratorios:* Mount Sinai; Christi Grablegung, oratorium (Klopstock); David, 1834; Absalom; Miriam; etc. *Cantatas:* Napoleon's Midnight Review; Easter Morning; etc. Fifteen masses. Ten German operas. Many Psalms and other church music. Symphonic héroique, op. 19; another one, op. 37. Overtures, op. 23, 25, 45, etc. Miscellaneous instrumental music: Fantasias; Pf. concertos; Quintets, Quartets, etc. Elementary Method for the Organ or Harmonium (Novello), n. d. Songs, and many pieces of vocal music.

NICHOLDS (Joseph). English comp., B. near Birmingham (?). D. Sedgeley, near Dudley, Feb., 1860. Wrote oratorios, psalms, and vocal music.

NICHOLSON (Charles). English flute-player and comp., B. Liverpool, 1795. Flute-player at Covent Garden, Drury Lane, Philharmonic Society, etc. D. London, March 26, 1837.

Wrote "Preceptive Lessons for the Flute," with Portrait and Appendix, Lond., n.d.; "Complete Preceptor in a style perfectly simple and easy," Lond., 2 pts. n.d.

NICHOLSON (Rev. Henry D., M.A.) English writer, author of "The Organ: its Mechanism, Stops, etc., explained, Lond., 12mo, n.d. (2 editions) Boston edit. published under the title of "Organ Manual."

NICODÉ (Jean Louis). German comp., B. Jerzye, near Posen, Aug. 12, 1853. S. under Hartkaes, Wüerst, and T. Kullak. Teacher in Kullak's Academy, Berlin. Pf. teacher at Dresden Cons. Has travelled in Europe as a pianist and concert giver.

WORKS.—Maria Stuart, symphony, op. 4; Charakteristische polonaise, Pf., op. 5; Andenken an Robert Schumann, op. 6; Zwei charakterstücke, Pf., op. 9; Introduktion und Scherzo, orch., op. 11; Zwei Etuden, Pf., op. 12; Romanze, violin und orch, op. 14; 3 Lieder, op. 15; Sonate für Pf., op. 19; Jubiläumsmarsch für orch., op. 20; Ein Liebesleben, Pf., op. 22.

NICOLAI (Carl Otto Ehrenfried). German comp. and org., B. Königsberg, June 9, 1810. Ran away from home on account of ill-treatment, 1826. S. at Berlin, under Zelter and Klein. Org. at Prussian Embassy at Rome, 1833. S. at Rome under Baini. Cond. of opera at Vienna, 1837. Resided at Rome, 1838-41. Director of Opera at Vienna, 1841-47, and afterwards at Berlin, 1848. D. Berlin, May 11, 1849.

WORKS.—*Operas:* Enrico II., 1839; Il Templario, 1840; Odoardo e Gildiffa, 1841; Il Proscritto, 1841; Die Lustigen Welber von Windsor, Berlin, 1849; London (Merry Wives of Windsor), 1864; Six Lieder, op. 6: Lieder und Gesänge, op. 16; Polonaise, Pf., op. 4; Concerto for Pf. and orch.; a mass, and much unpublished music.

NICOLAI (Wilhelm F. G.) German org. and comp., B. Leyden, 1829. S. at Leipzig, and under Schneider at Dresden. Prof. of organ at the Hague.

WORKS.—Op. 1. Four Lieder; op. 2. Four Lieder; op. 4. Sonate für Pf.; op. 10. Three Duette, Sopran und Tenor; op. 13. Three Lieder.

NICOLINI (Ernest), or NICHOLAS. French tenor vocalist, B. Tours, Feb. 23, 1834. S. Paris Cons. Sang in Paris and in Italy. First appeared in England, May, 1866. With Madam A. Patti he has appeared frequently in London, the English Provinces, the United States, Europe, etc.

NICOLINI (Nicolino Grimaldi, detto). Italian vocalist, B. Naples, 1673. Sang successively in Rome, Naples, Milan, etc. Appeared in London, 1708. Sang in operas by Handel and others till 1717, and was last heard of in 1726, after which all trace of him disappears.

NICOLSON (Richard). English org. and comp., B. in second half of 16th century. Org. and chorus-master, Magdalen Coll., Oxford, 1595. Mus. Bac. Oxon., 1596. Prof. of Music in Oxford University on Heyther's Foundation, 1626. D. Oxford, 1639.

NIECKS (Friedrich). German writer, B. Dusseldorf, Feb. 3, 1845. Best known by his writings in musical journals on æsthetical and theoretical subjects, and by "A Concise Dictionary of Musical Terms...," London [1884], 12mo.

NIEDERMAYER (Louis). Swiss pianist and comp., B. Nyon, on Lake of Geneva, April 27, 1802. S. under Moscheles, Förster, Fioravanti, and Zingarelli. Went to Paris and resided there, 1823-28. Teacher in Brussels, 1828. Established the "Ecole de Musique Religieuse," Paris, 1854. D. Paris, March 14, 1861.

WORKS.—*Operas*: Il reo per amore, 1821; Stradella, 1836; Marie Stuart, 1844; Robert Bruce (adapted from Le Donna del Lago), 1846; La Fronde, 1853. Traité théorique et pratique de l'accompagnement du Plain-chant, Paris, 8vo, 1857.

NIEMANN (Albert). German tenor vocalist, B. Erxleben, near Magdeburg, Jan. 15, 1831. Sang in theatre at Dessau, 1849. S. under F. Schneider, Nusch, and Duprez. Chamber singer to the Emperor of Germany. Has sung with much success in Germany, and has created the heroic parts in Wagner's operas.

NILSSON (Christine). Swedish soprano vocalist B. Wexiö, Wederslöf, Sweden, Aug. 20, 1843. S. under the Baroness Leuhusen (*née* Valerius), Berwald, and Wartel. *Début* at Théâtre Lyrique, Paris, Oct. 27, 1864, as *Violetta* in "La Traviata." *Début* at H. M. Theatre, London, in same part, June 8, 1867. Sang at Birmingham Festival, 1867; do. Royal Italian Opera, 1868; in London again, 1870. Sang in the United States, 1870-72. Married to M. Auguste Rouzaud, July, 1872. Has since appeared in all the principal cities.

Madam Nilsson unites the most perfect vocal powers with a large amount of dramatic instinct, and her conception of the various parts which she has filled is intelligent, powerful, and always vocally superb. Wherever she has appeared she has won an unfailing appreciation, and has been greeted with every possible degree of cordiality. She has created some of the best modern operatic parts as "Mignon" and "Ophelia." About 1869 a small biography, under the title of "Memoir of Mdlle. Christine Nilsson," (12mo, n. d.), was issued.

NISARD (Theodore). See NORMAND (Théodore E. X., Abbé).

NISSEN (Georg Nickolaus von). Danish writer, B. Hardensleben, Jan. 22, 1761. D. 1826. He married Mozart's widow in 1809, and wrote a biography of the composer, "Biographie, W. A. Mozart," 1828, best edition, Leipzig, 2 vols., 8vo, 1869.

NISSEN (Henriette), SALOMON. Swedish soprano vocalist, B. Gothenburg, 1822. D. Harzburg, Sept., 1879. She married S. Salomon, 1850, and was a successful pupil of M. Garcia's, under whom she S. at Paris. She sang in operas of Bellini, Rossini, and Verdi, and appeared in London in 1848. Her husband, SIEGFRIED SALOMON, a Danish violinist and comp., was B. Tondern in 1818. He writes operas, lieder, overtures, etc.

NIXON (Henry George). English org. and comp., B. Winchester, Feb. 20, 1796. Org. S. George's Chap., London Road, 1817-20; Do. Chap. in Warwick St., 1820-36. Org. S. Andrew's R. C. Chap., Glasgow, 1836-39. Org. S. George's Cath., London. D. London, 1849.

His sons JAMES C. (1828-1842), and HENRY COTTER (London, 1842) composed music of a miscellaneous character. The former was also a violinist; while H. C., is a Mus. Bac. Cantab., 1876.

NOBLE (Oliver). American minister, of Newbury, Mass., D. 1792. Published a "Discourse on Church Music," 1774.

NOHL (Carl Friedrich Ludwig). German writer, B. Iserlohn, Westphalia, Dec. 5, 1831. S. music under S. Dehn. Member of Prussian Civil Service. Prof. Munich University. D. Heidelberg, Dec. 16, 1885.

WORKS.—Mozart, Stuttgart, 8vo, 1863. Musikalisches Skizzenbuch, Munich, 8vo, 1866. Musiker Briefe (Gluck, P. E. Bach, Haydn, Weber, Mendelssohn), Leipzig, 8vo, 1867. Translated under title of Letters of Distinguished Musicians, by Lady Wallace, Lond., 8vo, 1867. Neue Briefe Beethovens nebst einigen ungedruckten Gelegenheite compositionen, Stuttgart, 8vo, 1867. Beethoven depicted by his Contemporaries, Trans. by E. Hill, London, 8vo, 1880 (German edition, 1877).

NORMAND (Théodule E. Xavier, Abbé), THEODORE NISARD. Belgian writer, B. Quaregnon, Jan. 27, 1812. Author of several works on musical theory and history, among which are "Du Plain-Chant Parisien...," 1846, 8vo ; "De la Notation Proportionnelle du Moyen-Age," Paris, 1847 ; "L'Accompagnement du Plain-chant sur l'orgue," Paris, 1860, 8vo.

NORRIS (Charles, or Thomas). English comp., and tenor vocalist, B. Salisbury, 1740 [? 1745]. Chor. Salisbury Cath. under Stephens. Sang at Worcester and Hereford Festivals, 1761-62; and at Drury Lane Theatre, 1762. Org. Christ Ch., Oxford, 1765. Mus. Bac. Oxon., 1765. Org. S. John's Coll., Oxford, 1765. Sang at Handel Commemoration, 1784. D. near Stourbridge, Sept. 5, 1790. Composed symphonies, anthems, and Four Glees [circa 1770].

NORTH (Francis), LORD GUILDFORD. English writer, B. 1637. D. 1685. Held several important legal appointments, but has interest in a musical sense only as the author of "A Philosophical Essay on Music," 1677. His brother ROGER (B. 1650, D. 1733), was a miscellaneous writer, who left in MS. "Memoirs of Musick,...now first printed from the original MS. and edited, with copious notes, by E. F. Rimbault," London, 1846, 4to. This is an interesting work, containing a fund of information on events in the musical history of the author's period.

NORTH (James M.) English vocal teacher and comp., B. Huddersfield, 1835. Settled in America, 1842. Vocal teacher in St. Louis. Mo. Pupil of Dr. Lowell Mason, G. F. Root, Geo. James Webb, and Bassinia. Teacher at the N. Y. State Normal School, Albany, N. Y., from 1859 to 1860. Director of music in the public schools, 1863 to 1865.
WORKS.—Vocal Exercises, 3 books, sacred songs and church services, ballads, etc., with and without orchestral instruments. Associate editor of works for church and singing-societies.

NORTON (Honourable Mrs. Caroline Elizabeth Sarah Sheridan). English poetess and musician, B. 1808. D. London, June 15, 1877.
She is best known as the writer of a number of songs, some of which obtained much popularity. Among them may be named "Love Not," "Juaneta," "Morning Star," "Arab's Farewell," "Voice of Music," "Murmur of the Shell," and "Blind Girl."

NOTTEBOHM (Martin Gustav). German comp. and writer, B. Lüdenschied, Arnsberg, Nov. 12, 1817. S. at Berlin under L. Berger, Dehn, and Sechter. Teacher and editor in Vienna. D. Gratz, Oct. 31, 1882.
WORKS.—Ein Skizzenbuch von Beethoven, Leipzig, 1855 ; Beethoveniana, Aufsätze und Mittheilungen, 1872 (Second Series, 1875-9); Beethoven's Studien, Beethoven's Unterricht bei J. Haydn, Albrechtsberger, und Salieri nach den Original Manuscripten dargestellt ; Thematic Catalogues of works of Beethoven and Schubert ; Quartets and trios for strings.

NOURRIT (Adolphe). French tenor vocalist, B. Paris, Mar. 3, 1802. S. under his father. *Début* in Paris, in Gluck's "Iphigenie en Tauride," 1821. Leading tenor at the Paris Opera for a long period, and Prof. in Paris Cons. He retired to Italy when Duprez began to rival him in Paris, and while singing at Naples received a disappointment which acted so strongly on his nervous and sensitive nature that he killed himself by leaping from the window of his abode, March 8, 1839. He had a fine light style of singing, and appeared in operas of Meyerbeer, Mozart, Cherubini, Auber, Méhul, Rossini, and Weber. His father, LOUIS, B. Montpellier, Aug. 4, 1780, D. Brunoy, Sept. 23, 1831, was for long a leading tenor singer in Paris.

NOVELLO (Clara Anastasia). English soprano vocalist, B. London, June 10, 1818. Daughter of Vincent Novello. S. at Paris Cons. and under John

Robinson of York. First appeared at Windsor, 1833. Sang at Ancient and Philharmonic Concerts. Sang at all the important Provincial Festivals, and at the Gewandhaus Concerts, Leipzig, Italy, etc. Married Count Gigliucci, 1843. Retired in 1860.

Known as one of the best and most successful English soprano vocalists. She possessed a voice of uncommon power and compass, which she used in a manner at once refined and impressive. She excelled chiefly in oratorio music, and was unrivalled in her day for the performance of the music of Handel, Mendelssohn, etc.

NOVELLO (Joseph Alfred). English publisher and musician, B. London, 1810. Eldest son of Vincent Novello. Choir-master of Lincoln's Inn Chapel. Bass vocalist at various concerts. Publisher under title of Novello & Co. in succession to the business founded by his father. Retired to Genoa in 1856. He wrote "Analysis of Vocal Rudiments by Question and Answer," Lond., n.d.; "Concise Explanations of the Gregorian Note," Lond., 1842, etc.

NOVELLO (Mary Sabilla). English writer and soprano-vocalist, daughter of Vincent Novello. Appeared as singer at various places, but now known only as writer of a "Vocal School, etc..," Lond., ob. fo., n.d.; "Voice and Vocal Art," n.d.

NOVELLO (Vincent). English org., comp., and publisher, B. London, Sept. 6, 1781. Chorister in the Sardinian Chap., Duke St., under S. Webbe. Deputy-org. to Webbe and Danby. Org. of Portuguese Chap., 1797-1822. Founded firm of Novello & Co., 1811. Pianist to Italian Opera, London, 1812. Org. R.C. Chap. in Moorfields, 1840-43. Member of Philharmonic Soc., and founder of the Classical Harmonists' Society. Retired to Nice. D. Nice, Aug. 9, 1861.

WORKS.—Collections of Church Music, consisting of selections from the writings of composers of all times. Anthems, kyries, hymns, and other church music. Cathedral Voluntaries for Organ, 8 books of selections. Short Melodies for Organ, in 6 books. Select Organ Pieces, in 18 books (containing numerous original pieces). Rosalba, cantata. Masses, various. Collection of Motets for the Offertory. Convent Music, collection of sacred pieces. Studies in Vocal Counterpoint, consisting of Rounds, etc. Surrey Chapel Music. Glees, songs, etc. The works of Purcell (sacred). The Fitzwilliam Music. Madrigalian Studies, Lond., 8 parts, 1841. A Biographical Sketch of Henry Purcell, from the best authorities, Lond., fo. [1832].

NOVELLO, EWER, & CO. English firm of music-publishers, established in London by Vincent Novello, in 1811. Their operations at the present time are world-wide, while as a publishing firm they are the foremost in Britain. Their catalogue is comprised in several volumes, each containing the titles of their various publications of different classes, as Sacred Music, Organ Music, Secular Vocal Music, Instrumental Music, etc. It would be impossible in a work of this sort to do more than enumerate a few of the works which they publish, as their catalogues embrace the names of nearly every British composer of note, and many eminent foreign names. Of theoretical works they issue a few important translations of Fétis, Albrechtsberger, Marx, Cherubini, Berlioz, etc.; to which may be added a reprint of Hawkins' "History of Music." Among their more important collections of vocal music may be named "Novello's Glee Hive," "Opera Choruses," "Part-Song Book," "Standard Glee Book," "Musical Times" series of part-music, and numberless single part-songs, madrigals, and glees, by many writers. Of sacred music they publish editions of nearly every famous British work, as also numerous oratorios and masses by foreign writers. A series of "Music Primers" embraces works by eminent specialists on all the principal branches of the musical art, edited by Dr. Stainer. The well-known journal, *The Musical Times*, is also the property of the firm, as also was another journal, which lived about six months, named the *Musical Review*.

NUNN (John Hopkins). English org., comp., and cond., B. Bury-St.-Edmunds, Nov. 10, 1827. S. at R. A. M. Org. at Penzance, 1859; since cond. of several musical societies. He is composer of anthems, songs, part-songs, etc.

ROBERT LINDLEY NUNN, who was Mus. Bac., Cantab., 1867, is also a comp. and org.

O.

OAKELEY (Sir Herbert Stanley). English comp., org., cond., and prof., B. Ealing, Middlesex, July 22, 1830. Second son of Sir Herbert Oakeley, Bart., and of Athole Murray, niece of the 4th Duke of Athole. S. at Rugby, and at Christ Church, Oxford. B.A., 1853; M.A., 1856. S. at Leipzig under Plaidy, Moscheles, and Papperitz; J. Schneider, at Dresden (organ); and Breidenstein, Bonn. Prof. of Music in Edinburgh University, 1865. Mus. Doc. Cantuar, 1871. Knighted (at the inauguration of the Scottish National Monument to the late Prince Consort, at Edinburgh), 1876. Mus. Doc. (honoris causâ), Oxon, 1879. LL.D., Aberdeen, 1881. Comp. to H.M. in Scotland.

WORKS.—Six Songs (Bagatelles), op. 2; Mazurka brillante, Pf., op. 3. Anthems: Who is this that cometh from Edom?; O God, who hast prepared, op. 5. Anthems: Whatsoever is born of God; Behold, now praise the Lord, op. 6. Four Quartets (1st set): Evening and Morning; Parting; A warning; The Glowworm, op. 7. Three duets (vocal): Time flies fast away; Meet me at even; The evening star, op. 8. Service in E flat (Morning, Communion, and Evening), op. 9. Lieder: O du mein Mond; Frühlingsabend; Sehnsucht, op. 10. Chansons: A qui pense-t'il; Marguerite, op. 11. Songs: Break, break, break; Edward Gray, op. 12. Canzonette: Sempre piu t'amo; Ad amore; Ritorno del Montanar, op. 13. Six Short Anthems: O praise the Lord; O God, our Refuge; This is the Day; O everlasting God; Come unto Me; Now unto the King eternal, op. 14. Songs: Farewell, if ever fondest prayer; 'Tis not alone that thou art fair; O my Lady's true and tender, op. 15. Three quartets (2nd set): Morgenlied; Abendlied; Nachtlied, op. 16. Six part-songs for men's voices, op. 17; National Melodies (Scottish), arranged for men's voices in chorus (5 parts of 3 numbers each), op. 18; Rondo Capriccioso, for Pf., op. 19; Sonata, in A, for Pf., op. 20; Romance, in F sharp, Pf., op. 21; Edinburgh Festal March, orch., Liverpool Musical Festival, 1874, op. 22; Funeral March, orch., op. 23. Minuet in old style, Chester Festival, 1885. Songs from Tennyson's "Princess": Bugle song; Tears, idle tears; Swallow song; Ask me no more; Home they brought her warrior dead; Shepherd's song, op. 24. Four Choral Songs for male voices, op. 25. Student's Song, "Alma Mater," for men's voices. 40 Choruses (arrangements) for male voices, with orch. accomp., for Edinburgh University Musical Society. Contributions to Periodical Literature. Hymns: Sun of my Soul; "Edina," in Hymns Ancient and Modern, and others in numerous collections. Bible Psalter (edited), Prayer-book Psalter, London, Nisbet; and other works.

Sir Herbert Oakeley has done for classical music in Scotland more real good than any other single individual. The influence which he possesses as Professor of Music in Edinburgh University is of itself sufficiently great to enable him to do good beyond the power of other musicians; but when such an influence is joined to well-directed energy, and an earnest, artistic desire to further musical art, the result is beneficial to the community, and creditable to himself. To enumerate the services he has rendered in the diffusion of knowledge of great musical works, would be to write the history of musical progress in Scotland within the last twenty years. His labours in connection with the University of Edinburgh are sufficiently well known; but so important as to require detailed mention. They include, an entirely successful solution of the "Reid Concert" problem, that commemoration having been by him developed into an annual three days "festival," which may fairly be said to have given the first impulse to advance of taste for orchestral music in Scotland; the establishment of the Edinburgh University Musical Soc., and his aid and visits to Aberdeen, St. Andrews, and Glasgow Universities, where the students have followed the example of Edinburgh; and finally, the influence of his organ recitals, which have done much to spread a love for that instrument. His works are all conceived in the purest artistic spirit, and have gained for their author much fame among modern musicians. His songs are especially worthy of attention, though not less so are his many fine anthems and part-songs. An Album, dedicated by permission to Her Majesty the Queen, and containing some twenty of his songs, is, it is understood, in the press.

OAKEY (George). English comp., writer, and teacher, B. St. Pancras, London, Oct. 14, 1841. Gained first prizes in Society of Arts Examination, under Hullah, 1869, and under Macfarren, 1873. Mus. Bac. Cantab, 1877. Examiner in Harmony and Composition to Tonic Sol-fa Coll., 1870. Lecturer on harmony, do., 1877; and counterpoint, 1878. Prof. of harmony and counterpoint, City of London Coll., 1883.

WORKS.—*Part-Songs*: The daisies peep; Pack clouds away, 1874; Stars of the summer night; Our happy harvest home, 1879; The beacon light, 1880. *Anthems*: Blessed be the Lord God; Praise the Lord of Hosts. Hymns and chants and arrangements of part-songs and glees published in various collections. Graduated Exercises in Harmony, 1877. Text-Book of Counterpoint, Lond., 1878 [3 editions]. Text-Book of Harmony, Lond., 1884 [2 editions]. Songs and glees.

OBERTHÜR (Charles). German comp. and harpist, B. Munich, Mar. 4, 1819. S. under Mrs. E. Brauchle and G. V. Röder. Harpist at theatre of Zürich on recommendation of Charlotte Birch-Pfeiffer. Solo-harpist at Court theatre Wiesbaden; also at Mannheim. Settled in London, 1844. Harpist to Italian opera, London. Latterly devoted to teaching and composition.

WORKS.—Floris de Namur, opera by C. Gollmick, Wiesbaden. The Pilgrim Queen, cantata for treble voices, by Mrs. A. Roberts. The Red Cross Knight, cantata for ladies' voices. Lady Jane Grey, cantata. *Part Songs*: Ave Maria; Breezes of Evening. *Songs*: Rose and the ring; Je voudrais etre; Babe and the sunbeams; 'Tis the gold in the heart; Golden days; Mighty spirit; Three wishes, etc. Overtures for orch., "Macbeth," Rubezahl. Loreley, a Legend for orch. with harp obligato (MS.); Prelude, Shakespeare; Concertino for harp and orch., op. 175; Trio for harp, violin, and 'cello, in F min., op. 139 (MS); Trio for harp, violin, and 'cello, in C, op. 162 (MS.); Una Lagrima sulla tomba di Parish-Alvars, Elegie, harp, op. 38; Trois études caractéristiques, harp, op. 57; Three characteristic melodies, harp, op. 106; Pensées musicales, harp, op. 110; Le Reveil des Elfes, harp, op. 181; Miranda, scena senza parole, op. 185; Le Sylphe. *Pianoforte*: Royal Academy pictures; Espagnolia; Chant d'Amour; Solitude. Missa Philipp di Neri (MS.) etc.

Oberthür is the leading harpist in Britain, and on the Continent he is held in the highest esteem. Wherever he has performed, in London, Munich, Leipzig, Zurich, Mannheim, Prague, Wiesbaden, Weimar, or Meiningen, he has been invariably greeted with enthusiasm, and he is respected as a composer no less than as a performer.

OBRECHT (J.) See HOBRECHT (Jacob).

O'CAHAN (Roderick Dall). See MORRISON (Roderick).

O'CAROLAN (Turlough), or CAROLAN. Irish comp. and harp-player, B. Baile-Nusah, or Newton, West Meath, 1670. Became blind when about 16 years old. Married, and settled on a farm at Mosshill, Leitrim. Was extravagant in his manner of living, and was forced to become an itinerant harper. Travelled about the country, and became widely known as a minstrel and boon companion. D. Alderford House, March 25, 1738.

He was a poet, and comp. a large number of popular Irish tunes, such as "Bumper Squire Jones," "Bridget Cruise," "Liquor of Life," and "Savourna Deelish." His musical works were published in 1747, and again in 1780, but it is understood that only a very small number of his tunes have been preserved or identified. Specimens of his works will be found in Hardiman, Bunting and Walker.

O'DALY (Gerald). Irish harpist and comp. of last century. The supposed composer of "Eileen a Roon," now adapted to the song, "Robin Adair."

E 2

ODIER (Ludovic). Author of "Epistola Physiologica Inauguaralis de Elementariis Musicæ Sensationibus," Edinburgh, 8vo, 1770. Treatise on the connection between Music and Medicine.

O'DONNELY (Abbé). Irish (?) writer, author of "The Academy of Elementary Music, containing a lucid Exposition of the Theory and Basis of the Practice from its Primary Notions to those of Composition," etc., Lond., 8vo, 1841; Paris, 8vo, 1842.

OESTEN (Theodor). German comp., B. Berlin, Dec. 31, 1813. S. at Berlin under Böhmer, Schneider, Rungenhagen, etc. Teacher and comp. in Berlin. D. Berlin, Mar. 16, 1870.

His works consist of transcriptions for Pf. from operas by all the famous composers, and some original works possessing merit.

OFFENBACH (Jacques). German (Jewish) comp., B. Cologne, June 21, 1819. S. at Paris Cons., 1833-4. Violinist at Opera Comique. Cond. of orch. of Théâtre Français; and of the Bouffes Parisiens, 1855. Visited United States. D. Paris, Oct. 5, 1880.

WORKS.—*Operettas, Ballets, and Comic Operas*: Pepito, 1850; Oyayaye, 1855; Une Nuit blanche, 1855; Les Deux Aveugles, 1855; Le Rêve d'une nuit d'ete, 1855; La Violoneux, 1855; Ba-Ta-Clan, 1855; Madame Papillon, 1855; Un Postillon en gage, 1856; La Rose de Saint-Fleur, 1856; Le Dragées du Baptême, 1856; Le 66, 1856; La Bonne d'enfants, 1856; Les Trois Baisers du Diable, 1857; Dragonette, 1857; Une Demoiselle en loterie, 1857; Les deux Pécheurs, 1857; Mesdames de la Halle, 1858; Orphée aux Enfers, 1858; Geneviève de Brabant, 1859; Daphnis et Chloé, 1860; Le Papillon, 1860; Le Pont des Soupirs, 1861; Le Roman Comique, 1861; Les Bavards, 1863; L'Amour Chanteur, 1864; Le Fifre enchanté, 1864; La Belle Helene, 1864; Les Bergers, 1865; Barbe-Bleue, 1866; La Vie Parisienne, 1866; La Grande Duchesse de Gérolstein, 1867; Robinson Crusoe, 1867; Le Château à Toto, 1868; Le Périchole, 1868; La Princesse de Trébizonde, 1869; Vert-Vert, 1869; Les Brigands, 1869; Le Roi Carotte, 1872; Fantasio, 1872; Le Jolie Parfumeuse, 1873; Madame L'Archiduc, 1874; Whittington et son chat, London, 1875; Le Voyage dans le Lune, 1875; La Boîte au lait, 1876; Madame Favart, 1879; Le Fille du Tambour Major, 1880. Songs.

Offenbach produced music with a prolificacy truly amazing, though the quality was by no means so apparent as the quantity. His most popular works, Orphée aux Enfers, Geneviève de Brabant, La Grande Duchesse, and Madame Favart, are also his best; though none of his compositions are destined to achieve immortality.

O'KEEFE (John). Irish dramatist and writer, B. Dublin, 1748. D. Southampton, 1833. Writer of the librettos of numerous comic operas, comedies, and farces, some of which obtained great popularity. In 1826 he published "Recollections of the Life of John O'Keefe," Lond., 2 vols., with portrait. This book contains anecdotes, gossip, etc., relative to the theatrical and musical doings of his time.

O'KELLY (Joseph). Irish (?) violinist and comp., B. Boulogne-sur-Mer, 1829. S. under Osborne, Kalkbrenner, etc. D. Paris, Jan. 1885.

WORKS.—Paraguassii, Poem Lyrique in 3 parts, 1855; Ruse contre Ruse, operetta; Cantata for Centenary of O'Connell, Dublin, 1878; Lutin de Galway, opera, 1878; La Zingarella, opera, 1879. Songs and Pf. music.

OKENHEIM (Johann), or OKEGHEM. Flemish comp., B. Termonde (Dendermonde, Belgium), early in 15th century [c. 1415-20 *Ambros*, 1430, *Fétis*]. Member of Coll. of Singers at Antwerp, 1443. Musician in service of King of France, 1444; Chap.-master, do., 1461. Treasurer at Ch. of S. Martin, Tours, 1476. D. Tours, 1513.

Okenheim's works consist of masses, motets, chansons, etc. They are distinguished by learned and artificial construction. Josquin, Pierre de la Rue, Agricola, Compère, and Brumel, may be named among a number of other pupils. He is credited with having perfected the canon form.

OLD (John). English comp. and cond., B. Totness, South Devon, 1829. S. under John and Edward Loder, 1842. S. also at R. A. M., Lond., under

Bennett; afterwards under Thalberg and Molique. Cond. of Torquay Choral Soc., 1852-55. Teacher and cond. at Reading, Berks.

WORKS.—The Seventh Seal, sacred drama, 1853. Dramatic Solo and Chorus: The Battle (on Charge at Balaklava), 1854. Herne the Hunter, opera in 3 acts, by E. Oxenford, 1879. Overture for orch., Tenth of March (on Marriage of Prince of Wales). *Pianoforte:* Etude de concert; Reveries; Impromptus; Mazurkas; Caprices; Melodie Chantante; Serenade; Tarantella in A; Romances; Legende; Valse de Concert; Gavotte in F; Characteristic Sketches, etc. Part-songs. *Songs:* I have a home in fairy land; Farewell to the Summer birds; My happiness; Where the golden sun; Gone out with the tide; Eulalie; Jack's good-bye; The vulture; Meet me at morn; When thou art near; My native vale; Winter song; Annabel Lee. Anthems. Essays contributed to the *Monthly Musical Record*, and MS. works.

"Herne the Hunter" is Mr. Old's most important published work, and has been described as an introductory preface to the published score by Joseph Bennet.

OLDMIXON (Lady), *née* GEORGE. English vocalist, B. 1768. Sang in opposition to Mrs. Billington at Dublin, 1789. Sang at Drury Lane, the Oratorio, and other concerts. Biography unknown.

O'LEARY (Arthur). Irish comp. and pianist, B. near Killarney, March 15, 1834. Early attracted attention of a member of the Dunraven Family by his Pf. playing. Educated in Dublin. S. at Leipzig Cons. under Moscheles, Hauptmann, Richter, Rietz, and Plaidy, 1847-52. S. at R. A. M., Lond., under Bennett and Potter. Prof. R. A. M. in 1856. Married to Rosetta Vinning, of Newton Abbott, Devon, 1860. Prof. at National Training School for Music.

WORKS.—Overture and Incidental Music to Longfellow's "Spanish Student," (with C. Potter); Symphony, in C; Concerto, in E. min., for Pf. and orch. *Pianoforte:* Rondo grazioso; Zwei clavierstücke; Fête rustique; Minuet, in B flat; Conte Mauresque. op. 14; Berceuse; Chant des Sirènes, op. 12; L'adieu du Conscrit; Fleurs et Pleurs; Pastorale, op. 13; Wayside Sketches; Thema in C min. Toccata in F; Stradella, fantasia and hymn; Scène de chasse. Mass of S. John (unison); Ode to the victor, part-song. *Songs:* He roamed in the forest; 'Tis Jamie's step I hear; Ask not why I love; Listening; For Rosabelle; Six songs (collection); etc.

Mr. O'Leary has edited some works of Bennett, Bach, and Hummel, in addition to the works above given. His wife was King's scholar, R. A. M., conjointly with J. F. Barnett, in 1852. She has comp. a number of songs, among which may be named "Craigie Burn," "My angel lassie," "A smile upon the shore," "She is coming down this way," "I am the angel," etc.

OLIPHANT (Thomas). English writer and musician, B. 1799. Member of Madrigal Soc., 1830; Hon. sec., do.; President, do. D. London, March 9, 1873.

WORKS.—A Brief Account of the Madrigal Society...Lond., 1834. Short Account of Madrigals from their Commencement to the Present Time. Lond., 1836. La Musa Madrigalesca, or a Collection of Madrigals, Ballets, Roundelays, etc., chiefly of the Elizabethan age; with Remarks and Annotations. Lond., 8vo, 1837. Catalogue of MS. Music in British Museum. Lond., 8vo, 1842. Ten Favourite Madrigals, arranged from the Original Part Books, with an accompaniment for the Piano. Lond., fo., n. d. Collection of Glees, Madrigals, etc. (Novello), n. d. Catches and Rounds. Lond., n. d. Ditties of the Olden Times. Arrangements of Songs, etc. Tallis' Song of Forty Parts; Responses (edited). Stay one moment, gentle river, madrigal. Poetry for various pieces of vocal music. Swedish Part-songs (1860), etc.

OLIVER (Edward B.) American writer, author of "A New Manual of Thorough-base, and Test-book of Musical Theory," Boston, 12mo, 1864. "Text-book of Music, as connected with the Art of Playing the Pianoforte,", Boston, n.d.

O'NEILL (Arthur.) Irish harper and collector, B. 1726. D. near Armagh, Oct., 1816. He was possessed of great stores of traditional melodies, etc., and was referred to by Bunting when preparing the first portion of his Irish Melodies.

ONSLOW (George). English comp., B. Clermont-Ferrand, July 27, 1784. Grandson of the First Lord Onslow. S. under Hüllmandel, Dussek, Cramer, and Reicha. Resided for a time at Vienna, 1802. Returned to Paris and received Cross of Legion of Honour. Member of the Institut (in succession to Cherubini), 1842. D. Clermont-Ferrand, Oct. 3, 1853.

WORKS.—L'Alcalde de la Vega, opera, 1824; Le Colporteur, opera, 1827; Le Duc de Guise, opera, 1837. Symphonies for orch., op. 41, 42. Quintets for 2 violins, viola, and 2 'cellos, or 'cello and bass, opp. 17, 18, 19, 23, 24, 25, 32, 33, 34, 35, 37, 38, 39, 40, 43, 44, 45, 51, 57, 58, 59, 61, 67, 68, 72, 73, 74, 78, 80, 82. Quartets for strings, opp. 4, 8, 9, 21, 36, 44, 46, 47, 48, 49, 50, 52, 53, 54, 55, 56, 62, 63, 64, 65, 66, 69. Trios for Pf., violin, and 'cello, opp. 3, 14, 20, 24, 26, 27. Duets for Pf. and violin, op. 11, 15, 21, 29, 31. Sextet, op. 30. Sonata for Pf. and 'cello, op. 16. Sonatas for Pf. solo, op. 1, 2. Sonatas for Pf. duet, op. 7, 22.

Though French by birthplace, he is English by parentage, and is usually reckoned among the foremost composers of instrumental music in the form commonly called chamber.

ORGÉNYI (Anna Maria Aglaja). Austrian soprano vocalist, B. Rima Szombat, Galicia, 1841. Daughter of an Austrian General (Görger St. Jörgen). S. under Mme. Viardot-Garcia, and Lamperti. *Début* at Berlin in "Sonnambula," 1865. Sang in London, 1866; again in 1870. Has appeared in operas of Donizetti, Weber, Mozart, and Rossini.

ORNITHOPARCUS (Andreas), or correctly, VOGELSANG. German writer, B. Meiningen about end of 15th century. D. in first half of 16th century. Author of the rare work entitled "Musicæ Activæ Micrologus libris quatuor digestus, Leipzig, 1519, 4to, translated by John Dowland in 1609, as Andreas Ornithoparcus his Micrologus, or Introduction; containing the art of Singing, and the perfect use of the Monochord according to Guido Aretinus," Lond., fo.

ORRIDGE (Ellen Amelia). English contralto vocalist, B. London, 1856. D. Guernsey, Sept. 16, 1883. She studied at the R. A. M. under Garcia, and gained the Thomas (1877), Nilsson (1878), and Parepa-Rosa (1878), prizes. She was well-known at most of the London and provincial concerts, and was a special favourite in oratorio music.

ORTIQUE (Joseph Louis D.) French writer, B. Cavaillon, May 22, 1802. D. Paris, Nov. 20, 1866. Best known by his "Dictionnaire Liturgique, Historique et Théorique de Plain Chant, et de Musique d'Eglise au Moyen Age et dans les Temps Modernes," Paris, 1854, 8vo.

OSBORNE (George Alexander). Irish pianist and comp., B. Limerick, Sept. 24, 1806. S. at Paris under Pixis and Fétis, 1826; and under Kalkbrenner. Settled in London, in 1843, from which date he has been a well-known figure in the musical world, and a most successful teacher. Member of the Musical Association, etc.

WORKS.—*Pianoforte:* Florizelle; La Zingarella; La Pluie de Perles; Rolando; La coquette; Harp of Erin; Souvenir de Sims Reeves; Victorine valse; Libiamo; La Fiorenza; Evening dew; March militaire; A Summer's eve; The elves; A moonlight walk; Transcriptions, arrangements, etc., in large numbers. Songs, various, etc.

Mr. Osborne during a long life has seen and known nearly every eminent musician the 19th century has produced. His reminiscences in this particular would accordingly form an interesting item in musical literature. His works abound in brilliant passages, and his arrangements are clever and dashing. Some of them achieved extraordinary popularity.

OSGOOD (Emma Aline). American soprano vocalist, B. Boston, Mass., 1849. First appeared in Boston, 1873. S. under Randegger, in London, 1875. Sang at Crystal Palace, 1875. Sang in English provinces, 1875-76. Sang at Brighton Festival, 1877; Leeds Festival, 1877. Appeared at Cincinnati and New York, 1878. Has since appeared repeatedly in England and America, and always with invariable success. Her voice is a rich and expressive soprano, with a magnificent low register. In oratorio music she is especially successful, and has been highly appreciated wherever she has appeared.

OSGOOD (George L.). American writer, author of "Guide to the Art of Singing," Boston, n. d.

OSWALD (James). Scottish comp. and collector, B. about beginning of 17th century. Dancing-master in Dunfermline. Settled in Edinburgh as teacher of music and dancing. Settled in London, 1742. Chamber comp. to George III., 1761. D. (?)

WORKS.—A Curious Collection of Scots Tunes, for a Violin, Bass Viol, or German Flute, with a Thorough-bass for the Harpsichord, etc. Edin., n. d. [c. 1740]. Collection of Curious Scots Tunes, for a Violin, German Flute, or Harpsichord, Lond., n. d. [c. 1742]. A Second Collection of Curious Scots Tunes, for a Violin and German Flute, with a Thorough-bass for the Harpsichord, Lond., n. d. [c. 1742]. The Caledonian Pocket Companion, containing a favourite collection of Scotch Tunes, with variations for the German Flute or Violin. Lond. [1759, etc.]. Issued in 12 parts. Six Pastoral Solos for a Violin and Violoncello, with a thorough-bass for the Organ or Harpsichord, Lond., n. d. Airs for the Spring, Summer, Autumn, and Winter, Lond., n. d. Issued separately in 4 parts. A Collection of Scots Tunes, with Variations, particularly adapted for the Violin and Harpsichord, Lond., n. d. Ten Favourite Songs, sung by Miss Formantel at Ranelagh, Lond., n. d. Fifty-five Marches for the Militia...Lond., n. d. A Collection of the best old Scotch and English Songs set for the Voice, with Accompaniments and Thorough-bass for the Harpsichord, Lond., n. d. ; etc.

Oswald was an industrious collector of Scottish tunes, but a most unscrupulous editor. He gave rise to the absurd tradition of Rizzio being the composer of certain Scottish melodies, by attaching that name to tunes in his collections, when such tunes were in reality his own composition or of an ancient date.

OTTO (Ernst Julius). German comp. and cond., B. Königstein, Sept., 1804. Cantor in Kreuzschule of Dresden, 1838. D. Dresden, March 5, 1877. He comp. oratorios, 2 operas, masses, sonatas, trios, and songs.

OTTO (Franz). German comp. and bass vocalist, B. Königstein, 1806. D. Mayence, 1842. He wrote much part-music and songs, some of which are highly popular.

OTTO (Jacob Augustus). German writer, author of "A Treatise on the Construction, Preservation, Repair, and Improvement of the Violin." Trans. by T. Fardely, Lond., 8vo, 1833. The same work, with additions, was edited by John Bishop, and published by Messrs. Cocks & Co., London, in 1833.

OULD (Charles.) English violoncellist, B. Romford, Essex, July 19, 1835. Member of H. M. Private Band. Has performed at most of the provincial concerts, and is a well-known instrumentalist in London, where he has also taken part in important concerts, etc.

OULIBICHEFF (Count Alexander von). Russian writer, B. Dresden, 1795. D. Nischni-Novgorod, Feb. 5, 1858. Author of "Nouvelle Biographie de Mozart," Moscow, 3 vols., 8vo, 1843 ; German trans., 1847, Stuttgart. "Beethoven : ses Critiques et ses Glossateurs," Leipzig, 8vo, 1857 ; etc. These are both valuable and useful works.

OURY (Anna Caroline), *née* DE BELLEVILLE. French pianist and comp., B. Landshut, Bavaria, Jan. 24, 1806. S. at Vienna under Czerny. Appeared in Paris, 1821. S. under A. Stricker at Vienna. Appeared in London, at concert given by Paganini, 1831. Married to M. Oury, violinist, 1831. Travelled with him concert-giving, in Germany, Russia, Holland, and France. Settled in London, 1839-66. D. Munich, July 22, 1880.

WORKS.—Pianoforte transcriptions, fantasias, etc., of which the following are samples : — L'Africaine (Meyerbeer), fantasia ; Per valli, per boschi, nocturne ; Plaintes de l'absence, ballade ; Souvenir d' Edimbourg ; Marche Ecossaise ; Valse brillante ; I montanari, melodies ; La chasse de Compiègne, fanfare, etc.

Madame Oury was for a time one of the most popular teachers and performers in London, while her reputation on the Continent was considerable. Her playing was distinguished by brilliancy and spirit, and was marked by careful technique.

OUSELEY (Rev. Sir Frederick Arthur Gore, Bart.) English comp., org., and writer, B. London, Aug. 12, 1825. Son of Sir William Ouseley, Bart. Succeeded his father, 1844. S. at Oxford. B.A., 1846; M.A., 1849. Ordained, 1849. Curate of St. Paul's, Knightsbridge, 1849-50. Mus. Bac. Oxon, 1850. Mus. Doc. Oxon, 1854. Prof. of Music in Oxford Univ. (in succession to Sir Henry Bishop), 1855, Precentor of Hereford Cath., 1855. M.A. and Mus. Doc., Durham, 1856. Warden of S. Michael's Coll. and Vicar of S. Michael, Tenbury, 1856. Mus. Doc. Cantab, 1862. Hon. LL.D. Cantab., 1883. Hon. LL.D., Edinburgh, 1885.

WORKS.—The Martyrdom of St. Polycarp, oratorio, 1855; Hagar, oratorio, Hereford Festival, 1873. Church Services in D, B minor, A, G, E, E flat, and D, etc. *Anthems*: And there was a pure river; Awake, thou that sleepest; Behold now praise the Lord; Christ is risen from the dead; Great is the Lord; I will give thanks; I waited patiently for the Lord; I will magnify Thee, O Lord; It came even to pass; In God's Word will I rejoice; Love not the world; O love the Lord; O sing unto God; Sing unto the Lord; The Lord is king; The Lord is my Shepherd; Thus saith the Lord; Unto Thee will I cry; Why standest Thou so far off; etc. The Psalter, arranged for chanting, with appropriate English chants (with E. G. Monk), Lond., various editions and dates. Anglican Psalter Chants, Lond. [1872]. Eighteen Preludes and Fugues for Organ; Sonata for the opening of the New Organ in the Sheldonian Theatre, Oxford; Three Andantes for organ; Preludes and Fugues, various. Cathedral Services by English masters [Farrant, Creyghton, Kempton, Child, Kelway, Aldrich, etc.], Lond., fo., n.d. [1853]; Collection of Anthems for certain Seasons and Festivals (edited), 2 vols., 1861-66; Glees; Six Songs, etc. Treatise on Harmony, Oxford, 4to, 1868; 2nd edit., 1876; 3rd ed., 1883. Treatise on Counterpoint, Canon, and Fugue, based upon that of Cherubini, Oxford, 4to, 1868; 2nd ed., 1884. Treatise on Musical Form and General Composition, Oxford, 4to, 1875; 2nd ed., 1886. Naumann's History of Music, trans. by F. Praeger (edited). Sermons, etc.

Sir F. A. G. Ouseley is one of the ablest and most widely-respected musicians in Britain. The amount of practical good which he has done is great, and his influence is no less potent than widespread. As a didactic writer, a composer, and an organist, he is equally well known; while his ability as a musical professor is great, and beneficial to the art.

OVEREND (Marmaduke). English org. and writer, B. first half of 18th century. S. under Boyce. Org. of Isleworth, Middlesex. D. 1790.

WORKS.—A Brief Account of, and an Introduction to Eight Lectures on the Science of Music, Lond., 4to, 1781; Twelve Sonatas for 2 violins and violoncello, 1779; Vocal music, etc.

OWEN (John), OWAIN ALAW PENCERDD. Welsh comp. and teacher, B. Chester, 1821. D. Chester, Jan. 30, 1883. Took a prominent part during his lifetime in furthering musical education, and was himself a prize-taker, and member of the Eisteddfod. He comp. cantatas ("The Prince of Wales," etc.), part-songs, songs, and edited a collection of Welsh melodies entitled "Gems of Welsh Melody." He left other works in MS.

OXENFORD (John). English dramatist, poet, and general writer, B. Camberwell, London, Aug. 12, 1812. Educated for the Law, but never practised. D. London, Feb. 21, 1877.

Wrote a number of lyrical and other works for music, which have been set by Macfarren, and other composers. His son EDWARD has written many librettos and lyrical pieces which have been set by many of the best living composers.

P.

PACCHIEROTTI (Gasparo). Italian soprano vocalist, B. Fabriano, near Ancona, 1744. Chorister in Forli Cath., 1757. S. privately at Venice. Appeared at Venice, 1769. Sang in Palermo, 1771. Sang successively at

Parma, Florence, Milan, Venice, Genoa, Turin, etc. Appeared in London, 1778. Returned to Italy, but afterwards re-appeared in London. D. Padua, Oct. 28, 1821.

PACHELBEL (Johann). German org. and comp., B. Nuremberg, Sept. 1, 1653. S. under H. Schemmern at Nuremberg; also at Gymnasium at Regensburg. Org. at Ch. of S. Stephen, Vienna; at Eisenach, 1675; Org. at Erfurt, 1678-90; Gotha, 1690-95; and of Ch. of S. Sebald, Nuremberg, 1695. D. Nuremberg, Mar. 3, 1706.

His works consist of church and organ music, in which is foreshadowed much of the severe contrapuntal style which is shown in the school of Bach and following composers.

PACHMANN (Vladimir de). Russian pianist and comp. of present time, B. Odessa. Has appeared on the Continent, in London (May 20, 1882), and the British Provinces, with distinguished success. He represents the most advanced style of pianoforte-playing, and is remarkable as an exponent of the music of composers of the romantic school, and especially of Chopin.

PACINI (Giovanni). Italian comp., B. Catania, Feb. 19, 1796. S. under Marchesi and Furlanetto. Taught in Music School at Viareggio. Director of Music School of Florence. Chap.-master to Empress Marie Louise, widow of Napoleon I. Married to Adelaide Castelli, 1825. D. Pescia, Tuscany, Dec. 6, 1867.

WORKS.—*Operas:* Annetta e Lucindo, 1813; Atala, 1818; La Sposa fedele, 1819; Wallace, 1820; La Schiava di Bagdad, 1820; La Vestale, 1823; Isabella ed Enrico, 1824; Amazilea, 1825; Niobe, 1826; I Cavalieri di Valenza, 1828; Il Talismano, 1829; Il Corsaro, 1831; Ivanhoe, 1832; Irene di Messina, 1833; Carlo di Borgogna, 1834; Furio Camillo, 1840; Saffo, 1840; Il Duca d'Alba, 1842; L'Ebrea, 1844; Lorenzino de' Medici, 1845; La Regina di Cipro, 1846; Allan Cameron, 1848; Zaffira, 1851; Il Cid, 1853; Belfegor, 1861; Berta di Varnol, 1867; Niccolo di Lapi, 1873. *Oratorios:* La Destruzione di Gerusalemme, 1858; Carrere Mamertino, 1867; Il Trionfo di Giuditta, etc. Cantatas and Masses. Symphony, octet, quartets, trios, etc. Corso Teorico-practico di lezioni di Armonia, cenni Storici sulla Musica, e Trattato di Contrappunto, 1864, etc.

Pacini was a voluminous and agreeable composer, his style being based on that of Rossini.

PADDON (John). English musician and writer, author of "System of Musical Education," Lond., 12mo, 1818.

PADILLA Y RAMOS (M. R.) Spanish barytone vocalist, B. 1831. Married to Madlle. Désirée Artot, 1869. Has appeared with much success in various countries as an operatic singer.

PAËR (Ferdinando). Italian comp., B. Parma, June 1, 1771. S. under Ghiretti. Chap.-master at Venice, 1791. Teacher and comp. at Venice, 1797. Opera-director at Dresden, 1801-6. Chap.-master to Napoleon I., 1807. Director of opera in succession to Spontini, at Paris, 1812-27. Member of French Academy. Director of King's chamber music, 1832. D. Paris, May 3, 1839.

WORKS.—*Operas:* La Locanda de' Vagabondi, 1789; I Pretendenti burlati, 1790; Circe, 1791; Saïd, 1792; Il Tempo fa Giustizia a tutti, 1794; Idomeneo, 1794; Matrimonio improviso, 1794; La Rossana, 1795; Tamerlano, 1796; I due Sordi, 1796; Sofonisbe, 1796; Griselda, 1796; Il Nuovo Figaro, 1797; La Sonnambule, 1797; Camilla, 1801; Il Sargino, 1803; Leonora, 1805; Cleopatra, 1808; I Baccanti, 1811; L' Agnese, 1811; Le Maître de chapelle, 1821. *Oratorios:* Il San Sepolcro, 1803; Il Trionfo della Chiesa, 1804; La Passione di Giesù-Christo, 1810. Military music; Sonatas; Fantasias; Symphonies; etc. Motets and other church music.

PAGANINI (Nicolo). Italian violinist and comp., B. Genoa, October 27, 1783. S. by himself, and under Costa, Ghiretti, and Paër. Travelled in Italy concert-giving with his father. Travelled alone after 1801. Court musician at Lucca, 1805. Appeared at Milan, 1813. Appeared at Bologna (where he made the acquaintance of Rossini), 1814. Defeated Lafont at a public contest at Milan, 1816. Appeared successively at Venice (where he met Spohr), 1816; Verona, 1817; Turin and Piacenza, 1818; Rome, Florence, Milan, 1819; Rome, 1821; Milan, 1822; Vienna, 1828; Paris, Mar. 9, 1831; London, June 3, 1831; Scotland, Ireland, and English provinces. Farewell concert, in Victoria Theatre, London, June 17, 1832. Decorated by Pope Leo XII. with Order of the Golden Spur. Chap.-master to Emperor of Prussia. Made acquaintance of Berlioz at Paris, 1833. D. Nice, May 27, 1840.

WORKS.—Op. 1. Ventiquattro capricci per Violino solo; op. 2. Sei Sonati per Violono e chittarra; op. 3. Ditto; op. 4 and 5. Tre Gran Quartetti a violono, viola, chittarra e violoncello; op. 6. Concerto in E flat, for violin and orch.; op. 7. Concerto in B minor; op. 8. Le Streghe : variations on air by S. Mayr; op. 9. Variations on "God Save the King"; op. 10. Le Carnaval de Venise : Burlesque on a popular air; op. 11. Moto perpetuo; op. 12. Variations on "Non più masta"; op. 13. Variations on "Di tanti palpiti." Other variations, etc.

His playing is said by experts to have been chiefly remarkable for the great command displayed over the technical requirements of the violin, while he was equally clever in the production of certain original effects now considered beneath the dignity of any but common music-hall performers. His doings on one string, and his duet between two strings, may be instanced as examples of his devices to mystify the public. His performance of legitimate violin music was in no way remarkable, save for its eccentricity, and was matched, if not excelled, for dignity and expression by many of his contemporaries. It is chiefly as an individual that Paganini is remembered, the fame of his performance being now less thought of than the supposed mysterious nature of his life and surroundings. The Paganini literature is large, but in addition to the works noted in the BIBLIOGRAPHY, the following PERIODICALS should be consulted :—Foreign Quarterly, v. 7; Dublin University Magazine, v. 37; Argosy, 1875, v. 21; Good Words, v. 14; Living Age, v. 33; and Hogg's Instructor, v. 7.

PAGE (John). English editor and tenor singer, B. about middle of 18th century. Lay-clerk St. George's, Windsor, 1790. Gent. of Chap. Royal. Vicar-choral, St. Paul's, 1801. D. Aug., 1812.

WORKS.—Harmonia Sacra: a Collection of Anthems in Score, selected for Cathedral and Parochial Churches from the most Eminent Masters of the 16th, 17th, and 18th Centuries, Lond., 3 vols. fo., 1800; 2nd edit. by E. F. Rimbault. Festive Harmony : a Collection of the most favourite Madrigals, Glees, and Elegies; selected from the Works of the most eminent Composers, Lond., 4 vols., 1804. Collection of Hymns, 1804. Burial Service, Evening Service, Anthems, etc., performed at the Funeral of Lord Nelson, Jan 9, 1806, fo. Four anthems (festival), etc. Responses, Anthems, and Psalms performed at St. Paul's Cathedral on the Day of the Anniversary Meeting of the Charity Children, 4to, n.d.

PAIGE (Mrs. J. B.) American writer, authoress of "New Inductive and Eclectic Method for the Pianoforte," Boston, n.d.

PAIGE (Kate). English writer, authoress of "Exercises on General Elementary Music." Part I., 1880; Part II., 1881. Lond., 8vo.

PAINE (John Knowles). American comp., org., and professor, B. Portland, Maine, Jan. 9, 1839. S. under H. Kotzschmar of Portland. First appeared as organist, 1857. S. under Haupt, Wieprecht, and Teschner, in Germany, 1858-61. Returned to United States, 1861. Instructor in Music, Harvard Univ., 1862; Prof. do., 1876.

WORKS.—Saint Peter oratorio, op. 20, Portland, 1873; Variations for org. on Austrian Hymn and The Star Spangled Banner, op. 3; Christmas Gift, for Pf., op. 7; Funeral March, Pf., op. 9; Mass, in D, for soli, chorus, and orch., op. 10; Vier Character-Stücke, Pf., op. 11; Two preludes for org., op. 19; Four characteristic pieces, Pf., op. 25; "In the Country," Ten sketches for Pf., op. 26; Centennial Hymn, by Whittier, op. 27, May, 1876; Four songs, op. 29; Symphonic-fantasie, The Tempest; Symphony in C minor, op. 23; Symphonie in A, Spring, op. 34; Sonatas, etc., for Pf.; Songs and other vocal music.

PAISIELLO (Giovanni). Italian comp., B. Tarento, May 9, 1741. S. at Jesuit School of Tarento, 1746; and under Durante and Abos at Naples.

Resided at Naples till 1776. Married Cecile Pallini, 1772. Musician to the Empress Catherine of Russia, 1776. Returned to Italy, 1784. Chapel-master to Ferdinand IV. at Naples, 1784. Director of National Music, Naples, 1799. Music director to Napoleon I. at Paris, 1801-3. D. Naples, June 9, 1816.

WORKS.—*Operas* [1763-1803]: La Pupilla, 1763; Demetrio; Artaserse; Il Negligente; Le Pescatrici; L'Imbroglio delle ragazze; Lucio Papirio; Olimpia; L'Innocente fortunato; Semiramide; Il Tamburo notturno; I Filosofi; Don Chisciotte delle Mancia; Nina; Il Demofoonte; Le due Contesse; La Serva Padrona; Il Barbiere di Siviglia; Lucinda ed Armidoro; Achille in Sciro; I Zingari in Fiera; Ginnone Lucina; La Molinara; Elvira; Proserpine, 1803; etc. La Passione di Gesu Cristo, 1784, oratorio. Over one hundred Masses. Quartets for strings, and other combinations; Concertos for Harpsichord; Twelve symphonies for orch., and other instrumental music.

The music of Paisiello is always pretty and graceful, though very often trivial and monotonous. He wrote, in all, 70 comic and other operas.

PALADILHE (Emile). French comp., B. Montpellier, June 3, 1844. S. at Paris Cons., 1853; also under Halevy. Gained first prize for Pf., 1857. Gained Prix de Rome, 1860.

WORKS.—*Operas, etc.*: La Passant, 1872; L'Amour Africain, 1875; Suzanne, 1878; Dianna, 1885; Patric. Symphony for orch., 1860. Six Mélodies Ecossaise; 20 Melodies for voice and Pf.; and numerous other vocal and instrumental works.

PALESTRINA (Giovanni Pierluigi da). Italian comp., B. Palestrina, Province of Rome, 1524 [1515, 1526 '28-'29]. S. at Rome under Goudimel, 1540. Teacher of music in the Cappella Giulia of the Vatican, 1551. Married, about 1554. Singer in the Pontifical Choir, Jan., 1555, under Pope Julius; dismissed, with compensation, by Pope Paul IV., 1555. Chap.-master of Lateran Chapel, 1555-61. Do. at Ch. of S. Maria Maggiore, 1561-71. Do. at Vatican Chap., 1571-83. Do. of Oratory S. Fifippo Neri. Master of the Pontifical Choir, 1586. D. Rome, Feb. 2, 1594.

WORKS.—Joannis Petri Aloysii Prænestini in Basilica S. Petri de Urbe cappellæ Magistri, Missarum, liber primus. Rome, 1554. Missarum, Liber secundus, Rome, 1567. Missarum, Liber III. Rome, 1570. Missarum cum quatuor et quinque vocibus, liber quartus. Rome, 1582 [2nd edit., 1582; 3rd edit., 1590]; Missarum...Liber quintus. Rome, 1590. Missæ...Liber sextus. Rome, 1590. Missæ, quinque, quatuor, etc., vocibus...Liber septimus. Rome, 1594. Missarum ...Liber VIII., 1599. Missarum...Liber nonus, 1599. Missarum...Liber X., 1600. Missarum...Liber undecimus, 1600. Missarum...Liber duodecimus, 1601. Missæ quatuor, octonis vocibus concinendæ, 1601. Motecta festorum totius anni, cum communione Sanctorum quaternis vocibus, Liber primus. Rome, 1563. Motettorum quæ partim quinis, partim senis, partim septenis vocibus concinantur. Liber primus, Rome, 1569. Motettorum...Liber II. Venice, 1572. Motettorum... Liber III. Rome, 1575. Motettorum quatuor vocibus partim plenâ voce, et partim partibus vocibus, Liber II. Venice, 1581. Motettorum quinque vocibus, Liber quartus. Rome, 1584. Motettorum...Liber V. Rome, 1584. Lamentationum, liber primus cum quatuor vocibus. Rome, 1588. Hymni totius anni, secundum S. R. E. consuetudinem quatuor vocibus concinendi nec non hymni religionum. Rome, 1589. Offertoria, Rome, 1593. Magnificat octo tonorum, Liber primus. Rome, 1591. Litaniæ Deiparæ Virginis. Rome, 1600. Madrigali Spirituali a cinque voci, liber primo, Venice, 1581. De' madrigali Spirituali a cinque voci il libro II, Rome, 1594. Sacra omnia solemn Psalmodia vespertina, 1596. Il Primo Libro di Madrigali a quattri voci. Rome, 1555. Il primo Libro di Madrigali a cinque voci, 1581. Il secondo libro di Madrigali a quattro voci. Venice, 1586; etc.

One of the greatest and most dignified ecclesiastical composers of musical history. He is famous as the regenerator of Italian church music, and as one whose influence was long felt by succeeding composers of church music, both Italian and other. A number of his works are still in use, and for concert purposes in Britain, a few of his masses, motets, and madrigals are practised. His music is somewhat learned and dry in style, but for church use is admirable.

PALMER (Charles Austin). American comp. and pianist, B. Rio Janeiro, May 6, 1840. D. 1880. Comp. of music for Pf., songs, etc.

PALMER (H. R.). American editor and teacher, B. New York State, 1835. S. under J. Piowski and Dr. Hastings.
  WORKS.—Theory of Music, Cincinnati, n. d. Rudimental Class Teaching, Cincinnati, n. d. Collections of Songs and Choruses : The Standard ; The Leader ; The Song Monarch ; Songs of Love, for Sunday-schools ; Song Herald ; Song Queen ; Song King ; Concert Choruses ; Normal Collection of Sacred Music.

PALMER (Lucas Shelton). English writer and org., author of "First Studies in Sight-Singing, for the use of Schools, Choirs, and Choral Societies," London (Novello). "A Short Catechism on Singing." Lond. *Part-songs* : Sunset ; The white rose sighed ; Phyllis.

PANNY (Josef). Austrian violinist and comp., B. Kohlmitzleur, Oct. 23, 1794. S. under Eybler. D. Mayence, Sept. 7, 1838.
  WORKS.—Op. 1. Trio for Pf., vn. and 'cello ; Quartets for strings, op. 19 ; Masses for 4 voices and orch., op. 17; etc. Songs. Das Mädchen von Rügen, opera, 1831.

PANOFKA (Heinrich). German comp., violinist, and writer, B. Breslau, Oct. 3, 1807. S. at Vienna under Mayseder and Hoffmann, 1824-27. Gave first concert, Vienna, 1827. Resided in Munich, Berlin, and Paris. Established, with Bordogni, the "Académie de Chant," Paris, 1842. Resided in England from 1844. Returned to Paris, 1852. Settled at Florence, 1866.
  WORKS.—Ballads for voice and Pf., opp. 7, 12, etc. ; Duets for Pf. and violin, opp. 10, 13, 15, 16, 27 ; L'Art de Chanter, op. 81 ; L'Ecole de Chant [English translations] ; 24 Vocalises progressives, op. 85 ; Quartets for Pf., etc., opp. 6, 11, 14, 18 ; Elegie for violin and Pf., op. 17 ; Ballade for do., op. 20.

PANORMO (Francesco). Italian flute-player and comp., B. Rome, 1764. D. London, Dec. 29, 1844. He wrote some music for his instrument, and improved the action of the pianoforte.

PANSERON (Auguste Mathieu). French writer, comp., and singing-master, B. Paris, April 26, 1796. S. at Paris Cons. under Berton, Gossec, etc. Gained Grand Prix de Rome, 1813. Prof. of Solfeggi, Paris Cons., 1826 ; Vocal Prof., 1831 : Singing Prof., 1836. D. Paris, July 29, 1859.
  WORKS.—Methode Complete de Vocalisation, Paris (English trans.), London, n. d.) Traité de l'Harmonie Pratique et de Modulation. Numerous books of Solfeggi, and Songs and Romances.

PAPE (William Barnesmore). American pianist and comp., B. Mobile, Feb. 27, 1850. Arranger and comp. of a large number of pieces for the Pf., chiefly of a light, brilliant class.

PAPINI (Guido). Italian violinist, B. Camagiore, near Florence, Aug. 1, 1847. S. under Giorgetti at Florence. *Début* at Florence, 1860. Appeared in London, 1874, and Paris, 1876. Established in London as Prof. Has appeared in the English Provinces and in Scotland. He has composed a concerto, romances, and other pieces for the violin, and has published a School for the Violin ; and "La Mécanisme du Jeune Violiniste," 1883. His performance is distinguished by much refinement.

PAPPENHEIM (Eugenie). Austrian soprano vocalist of present time. Appeared about 1874, and has since sung in Britain, Germany, and elsewhere on the Continent. Her repertory consists of operas by Weber, Beethoven, Wagner, Verdi, etc.

PAPPERITZ (Benjamin Robert). German teacher and pianist, B. Pirna, Saxony, 1826. Has been a teacher at Leipzig Cons. since 1851. He is chiefly known as a successful teacher of the Pf.

PAQUE (Guillaume). Belgian violoncellist, B. Brussels, July 24, 1825. S. Brussels Cons. Played in Paris, Madrid, etc. Appeared in London as member of Jullien's orchestra, 1851. Was afterwards Prof. of 'cello at Dr. Wylde's Academy of Music, London ; a member of the Queen's private band, etc. D. London, Mar. 2, 1876. His brother, P. J. Paque, is Queen's trumpeter.

PARADIES (Pietro Domenico). Italian comp., B. Naples, 1710. S. under Porpora. Teacher in London for a time, during which he instructed the elder Thos. Linley in harmony. D. Venice, 1792. He composed an opera, "Phaeton," 1747, and Sonatas for the Pf., etc.

PARADIS (Marie Theresa von), née ANTON. Austrian pianist and comp., B. Vienna, May 15, 1759. S. under Kotzeluch, Salieri, Righini, Vogler, etc. Blind from an early part of her career. Appeared in Paris, 1780. Appeared in London, 1780. Travelled in Germany, etc. D. Vienna, Feb. 1, 1824.

WORKS.—*Operas:* Der Schulcandidat, 1792; Ariadne und Bacchus, 1791; Rinaldo und Algina. Cantata, and other vocal works. Sonatas for Pf., and Lieder.

PAREPA-ROSA (Euphrosyne Parepa de Boyesku). Roumanian soprano vocalist, B. Edinburgh, May 7, 1839. Daughter of a native of Wallachia. Educated by her mother, Elizabeth Seguin. *Début* at Malta, 1852. Sang at Naples, Genoa, Rome, Florence, Madrid, Lisbon, etc. Appeared in London, May, 1857. Married Captain de Wolfe Carvell. Sang at Handel Festival, London, 1862-65. Married Carl Rosa (after death of her first husband, 1865), 1867. Visited America, 1867-1871. Revisited America, autumn of 1871. D. London, Jan. 21, 1874.

This vocalist sang in a wide range of opera, and was distinguished for a voice of much power and richness. She appeared in operas by Bellini, Mellon, Macfarren, Balfe, Meyerbeer, Auber, Mozart, with much success, and did much to establish the now well-known Carl Rosa Opera Company.

PARIS (Edouard de). See DE PARIS (Edouard).

PARISH-ALVARS (Elias). English harpist and comp., B. Teignmouth, Feb. 29, 1816. Jewish by parentage. S. under Dizi, Labarre, and Bochsa. Played in Germany, 1831; Italy, 1834. Appeared in London, 1836-7. Travelled in the East, 1838-42. Appeared in Germany and Italy again, 1842-44. Settled in Vienna, 1847. Chamber harpist to Emperor. D. Vienna, Jan. 25, 1849.

WORKS.—Voyage d'un Harpiste en Orient, Recueils d' airs et de melodies populaires en Turquie et dans l'Asie Mineure, Harp solo, op. 62; Concerto for harp and orch., in G min., op. 81; Concerto for 2 harps and orch., op. 81; Concerto for harp and orch., in E flat, op. 98; March for harp, op. 67; Fantasias, transcriptions, romances, and melodies, for harp and orch., and harp and Pf., etc.

Parish-Alvars was one of the greatest harp-players of his period, and probably one of the best ever known. His works are well-known to harpists generally, and abound in good points.

PARK (Rev. John, D.D.) Scottish poet, comp., and divine, B. Greenock, 1804. Educated at Greenock and Paisley, and at Glasgow and Aberdeen Universities. Licensed to preach. Assistant to Dr. Steele, West Ch., Greenock, and afterwards to Dr. Grigor of Bonhill. Minister at Liverpool. Minister at Glencairn in Dumfriesshire. Do. Collegiate Parish Ch. of St. Andrews, first charge. D. St. Andrews, April 8, 1865.

Dr. Park first became publicly known as a musician by the publication of "Songs composed and in part written by the late Rev. John Park, D.D., St. Andrews, with Introductory Notice by Principal Shairp, LL.D., St. Andrews," Leeds, 1876, 4to, portrait. This collection displays considerable merit throughout.

PARKE (John). English oboe-player and comp., B. 1745. S. under Simpson and Baumgarten. Oboist at the opera, 1768. Concerto player at Vauxhall, 1771. Principal oboist at Drury Lane, 1771. Member of King's Private Band. Chamber Musician to Prince of Wales, 1783. Principal at Concert of Ancient Music, etc. D. London, Aug. 2, 1829.

PARKE (Maria Hester), BEARDMORE. English pianist, comp., and singer, B. 1775. Daughter of John Parke. S. under her father. *Début* as vocalist at Gloucester Festival, 1790. Sang at London concerts, etc. Married Mr. Beardmore. D. 1822.

She wrote sonatas for Pf., songs, a set of six glees, and some other music.

PARKE (William Thomas). English writer, oboe-player, and comp., B. London, 1762. S. under Dance, Baumgarten, and his brother, John. Chorister at Drury Lane Theatre, 1775. Oboist at Vauxhall, 1776. Principal oboist at Covent Garden, 1783. Employed at principal concerts, Vauxhall, etc. as oboist after 1800. D. London, Aug. 26, 1847.

WORKS.—Overtures to "Netley Abbey," 1794; "Lock and Key," 1796. Concertos for oboe. Flute music. Tutor for the Hautboy; being a Familiar Introduction to the Art of Playing this Instrument. With sixteen duets for two Hautboys, n. d. Musical Memoirs; Comprising an Account of the General State of Music in England from the First Commemoration of Handel in 1784 to the year 1830, interspersed with numerous Anecdotes, Musical, Histrionic, etc., Lond., 2 vols., 8vo, 1830.

Parke was a leading performer on the oboe during his period, but is now chiefly remembered as the author of a gossipy and amusing account of music during his own time. This book gives graphic glimpses of the various musical events which transpired between 1784 and 1830, and the anecdotes and useful historical facts chronicled in the book make it a valuable and interesting authority.

PARKER (Henry). English comp., cond., and vocal instructor, B. London, Aug. 4, 1845. S. at Leipzig under Moscheles, Richter, and Plaidy, and at Paris under Lefort. Author of "The Voice: its Production and Improvement, with Practical Exercises." London, 4to (various editions). Has comp. a number of orchestral works: Pamela, gavotte, 1879; Clarissa, minuet, 1880; Dorothea, sarabande; Pavanne de Guise, 1881; Imogen, 1882; Dance of Sirens, 1885. Over 400 Songs and Pf. pieces published since 1863.

PARKER (James C. D.). American comp., pianist, org., and teacher, B. Boston, 1828. Educated at Harvard University. S. music at Leipzig Cons. under Moscheles, Hauptmann, Richter, and Rietz, etc., 1851-54. Org. of Trinity Episcopal Church, Boston. Prof. of Pf. and Harmony in New England Cons. of Music, and Boston University, Coll. of Music, from 1871.

WORKS.—Redemption Hymn, a cantata, Handel and Haydn Soc., Boston, 1877. Church Services. Seven Four-part songs, Boston, 1875. Songs. Manual of Harmony. Translation of E. F. Richter's "Manual of Harmony," Boston, n. d. Pf. music, and miscellaneous pieces for orch. and church.—*Musical Herald*, Boston, etc.

PARKER (Louis Napoleon). English comp. and pianist, B. in Department of Calvados, France, Oct. 21, 1852. Educated in Italy, France, and Germany. S. at R. A. M., London, 1870, under H. Thomas, Walworth, Banister, Steggall, Cusins, and Sir W. S. Bennett. Received first-class diploma from R. A. M., and was elected an Associate. Org., choirmaster, and senior music master at King's School, Sherborne, 1877. Mem. of Committee of United Wagner Soc., and English Representative of the *Revue Wagnérienne*.

WORKS.—The Wreck of the Hesperus, cantata; Silvia, cantata, 1880. The Lord is my Shepherd, motet. Overtures for orch. (MS.) Part-songs, songs, vn. and Pf. music.

PARKINSON (W. W.). English writer, author of "The Natural and Universal Principles of Harmony and Modulation, with Illustrative and Analyzed Extracts from the Works of Classical Composers." Lond., 1873.

PARR (Rev. Henry). English divine and musician, B. Lythwood Hall, Salop, 1815. Educated at Oxford. Ordained, 1845. Vicar of Yoxford, Suffolk, 1872. Best known as the compiler of "Church of England Psalmody: Psalm Tunes, Chants, with Responses, etc., with Memoirs of the Composers and Histories of the Pieces." London, Novello (8 editions to 1880). In this collection the author claims to have restored the tunes to their original forms; that is, he has freed them from the alterations of editors and meddlers.

PARRATT (Walter). English org., B. Huddersfield, 1841. S. under his father and G. Cooper. Org. of Armitage Bridge Ch., 1852; S. Paul's, Huddersfield, 1854; Witley, 1861; Wigan Parish Ch., 1868; Magdalen Coll., Oxford, 1872. Mus. Bac., Oxon., 1873. Org. of S. George's, Windsor, 1882. Prof. of org. at Royal Coll. of Music.

PARRY (Charles Hubert Hastings). English comp. and writer, B. Bournemouth, Feb. 27, 1848. Educated at Eton and Oxford. S. under Elvey, H. H. Pierson, G. A. Macfarren and E. Dannreuther. M.A., and Mus. Doc., Oxon. Prof. of Music at Royal Coll. of Music. Choragus of Oxford University. Mus. Doc. Cantab., 1883 (Hon. degree).

WORKS.—Scenes from Shelley's "Prometheus Unbound," for soli, chorus, and orch., Gloucester Festival, 1880; Incidental Music to "The Birds" of Aristophanes, 1883; Ode for chorus and orch.; Sonata No. 1, in F, for Pf.; Sonata No. 2, in A, for Pf.; Grosses duo for 2 Pf., in E. min.; Trio in E min., for Pf., violin, and 'cello; Quartet for strings, in G min.; Quartet for Pf. and strings, in A flat; Quintet for strings, in E flat; Fantaisie Sonate, for Pf. and violin, in B min.; Sonata for Pf. and' cello, in A min.; 2nd Trio in B min., 1885; Overture for orch., "Guillem de Cabestanh," Crystal Palace, Mar. 15, 1879; Concerto for Pf. and orch., in F sharp; Symphony, No. 1, in G, for orch., Birmingham, 1882; No. 2, in F, Cambridge, 1883; Sonata for Pf. and violoncello, 1883; Morning and Evening Service in D; Three Odes of Anacreon; Characterbilder, for Pf. Songs, etc. Cantata, O Lord thou hast. Contributions in Grove's "Dictionary of Music," and other works.

PARRY (John). Welsh harper and collector, of Rhuabon, North Wales. Was bard or harper to Sir W. W. Wynne of Wynnstey, during the middle of the 18th century. He appeared in London. D. 1782.

WORKS.—Antient British Music; or a Collection of Tunes never before published. An Historical Account of the Rise and Progress of Music among the Ancient Britons, Lond., fo., 1742 [with Williams]. Cambrian Harmony; a Collection of Ancient Welsh Airs, fo. n.d. Music for the Harpsichord.

PARRY (John). Welsh comp. and writer, B. Denbigh, Feb. 18, 1776. Member of band of Denbigh Militia, 1795. Bandmaster of same, 1797-1807. Teacher of flageolot in London, 1807. Comp. for Vauxhall from 1809. Cond. an Eisteddfod in Wales. Received degree of Master of Song (Bard Alaw), 1821. Musical critic of *Morning Post*, 1834-48. Treasurer of Royal Soc. of Musicians, 1831-49. D. London, April 8, 1851.

WORKS.—Incidental Music to "Harlequin Hoax," 1814; Oberon's Oath, 1816; High Notions, 1817; Ivanhoe, 1820; Fair Cheating. 1814; Helpless Animals, 1818; Two Wives, 1821; My Uncle Gabriel; Caswallon, etc. The Welsh Harper, being an Extensive Collection of Welsh Music, to which are prefixed observations on the Character and Antiquity of the Welsh Music, Lond, fo. n.d.; An Account of the Royal Musical Festival held in Westminster Abbey, 1834, drawn up from Official Documents, 4to, n. d.; Beauties of Caledonia, or Flowers of Scottish Song...with symphonies and accompaniments for the Pf., Lond., 4 v. fo. n.d.; Selections of Six Brazilian Melodies; The Vocal Companion; British Minstrel; Flowers of Song; London Collection of Glees, etc.; Glees, part-songs, etc. *Songs:* Jenny Jones; Apollo and the Muses; Oh, merry row the bonny bark; Maid of Toro, etc.

Parry's music was extremely popular in its day, and some of it is even now in use. Parry's songs are written in a light, pleasant style, and are agreeable effusions.

PARRY (John Orlando). Welsh comp., pianist, and barytone vocalist, son of above, B. London, Jan. 3, 1810. S. under Bochsa and his father. *Début* as harpist, 1825. Appeared as ballad vocalist, 1831. Sang in operettas and entertainments by himself and others. Org. of S. Jude's, Southsea, 1853. Reappeared at the German Reed Entertainments, 1860-69. Retired, 1877. D. East Molesey, Feb. 20, 1879.

WORKS.—Songs, of which the following is a selection:—Bridal Bells; Blue Beard; Cinderella; Country Commissions; Crotchet; Norah the pride of Kildare; Take a bumper and try; A heart to let; Wanted a wife; Fayre Rosamonde. The A B C duet, and numerous comic and sentimental pieces.

PARRY (Joseph). Welsh comp. and prof., B. Merthyr, May 21, 1841. Son of Daniel Parry. Went to America with his family, 1854, where he afterwards worked in the Ironworks. S. at a Music School in America in company with P. P. Bliss, etc. Mus. Bac. Cantab., 1871. S. at R. A. M., London, 1878, under Steggall, Garcia, Sir Wm. S. Bennett, etc. Prof. of Music at University Coll. of Wales, Aberystwith. Mus. Doc. Cantab., 1878.

Works.—Emmanuel, an oratorio. Blodwen, Welsh opera in 3 acts. Prodigal Son, prize cantata. Six Easy and Devotional Anthems, 2 parts. About 100 other anthems. *Songs:* The skylark ; The sailor's wife ; Old yew tree ; Pleasure boat of Niagara ; The train ; The nightingale ; The tolling bell ; Serenade, etc., and others to number of 150. Trios and quartets, various. *Pianoforte:* Three recollections ; Reverie ; Fantasia ; Druid's march. Three Sonatas. String Quartet. Six Overtures.

PARSONS (Albert R.). American pianist, teacher, and comp., B. Indianapolis, about 1850. Teacher in New York. He has translated Wagner's "Beethoven," and comp. Pf. and other works.

PARSONS (Robert). English comp., B. Exeter. Comp. services, anthems, madrigals. Drowned in the Trent at Newark, Jan. 25, 1570 (1569?) His son JOHN (?) was org. of S. Margaret's, Westminster, in 1616. Org., etc., Westminster Abbey, 1621. D. 1623.

PARSONS (Sir William). English musician, B. 1746. Chorister under Dr. Cooke, Westminster Abbey. S. in Italy, 1768. Master of King's Music, 1786. Mus. Bac. and Mus. Doc. Oxon, 1790. Knighted, 1795. Magistrate of Middlesex. D. July 17, 1817.

PASCAL (Florian). See WILLIAMS (Joseph).

PASCAL (Prosper). French comp. and writer, B. 1825. Comp. the following operas :—Le Roman de la Rose, 1854 ; La Nuit aux Gondoles, 1861 ; Le Cabaret des Amours, 1862 ; Fleur de Lotus, 1864. Songs, and contributions to periodical literature.

PASDELOUP (Jules Etienne). French cond. and comp., B. Paris, Sept. 15, 1819. S. Paris Cons. Gained first prize for Solfeggi, 1832 ; do. Pf., 1834. Founded the Société des jeunes artistes du Conservatoire, 1851. Established "Concerts Populaires" at Cirque d'Hiver, 1861. Director at the Orpheon. Member of Legion of Honour, etc. Pasdeloup has earned universal fame as a conductor by the production of works by eminent modern composers at his concerts. He has introduced at his Concerts Populaires works by Gounod, Lalo, Saint-Saëns, Gouvy, Schumann, Gade, Rubinstein, Raff, Guiraud, Massenet, Berlioz, Grieg, Wagner, and numerous other well-known names. He first introduced Wagner to the Parisian public by a performance of "Rienzi" in 1869.

PASQUALI (Nicolo). Italian comp. and writer. Flourished in London and Edinburgh in the first half of the 18th century. D. Edinburgh, 1757.

Works.—Thorough-bass made Easy, or Practical Rules for finding and applying its various Chords...etc., Edin., fo., 1757 ; London edition, fo., n.d. Art of Fingering the Harpsichord, Edin., fo., n.d. ; London edition, fo., n.d. Vocal and Instrumental music, various.

PASTA (Giuditta), *née* NEGRI. Italian soprano vocalist, B. Como, 1798. S. under Asioli at Milan Cons., 1813. *Début* at Brescia. Appeared successively in small Italian towns, London, Jan. 1817, and Paris, without much success. Successfully appeared at Verona, 1822, Paris, 1823, London, April 14, 1824. Afterwards appeared in London, Paris, in Italy, and elsewhere. D. Como, April 1, 1865.

Madame Pasta possessed a "finely regulated and flexible" voice, "and her style was full of expression," says Parke in his "Musical Memoirs" (1817) ; and further (1824) that she "sang and acted in a style of high perfection."

PATEY (Janet Monach), *née* WHYTOCK. Scottish contralto vocalist, B. London, May 1, 1842. Her Father was a native of Glasgow. S. under Wass, Pinsuti, and Mrs. Sims Reeves. First appeared, when young, in Town Hall of Birmingham. Afterwards member of Henry Leslie's choir. Sang in Provinces with the Lemmens' Concert Party, 1865. Married John George Patey, 1866. Sang at Worcester Festival, 1866. Appeared in America, with Wynne, Cummings, Santley, and her husband, 1871. Sang in Paris, 1875. Has since sung at all the principal British concerts.

Mrs. Patey is one of the finest British contraltos, and has held a first place among concert vocalists for many years. She created parts in a number of important works by English composers, among which may be named J. F. Barnett's "Ancient Mariner," and "Raising of Lazarus"; Macfarren's "St. John the Baptist," "Resurrection," "Joseph," and "Lady of the Lake."

PATEY (John George). English barytone vocalist, B. Stonehouse, Devon, 1835. Husband of above. S. at Paris and Milan. Début in Flotow's "Martha," London, 1858. Sang afterwards in English opera, and appeared in America in 1871. Latterly a music publisher in London.

PATEY (C. A.) English writer, author of "An Elementary Treatise on the Art of Playing the Violin, with Scales, Exercises, etc.," Lond., n. d.

PATON (Mary Ann), Wood. Scottish soprano vocalist, B. Edinburgh, Oct., 1802. Daughter of George Paton, writing-master of Edinburgh High School. Sang at the Edinburgh Concerts, 1810. S. harp and Pf. under S. Webbe, Jun. Sang in London, 1811; and Bath, 1820-1. Sang at Covent Garden Theatre, London, as Susannah in Mozart's "Figaro," 1822. Appeared in Weber's "Der Freischutz," July, 1824. Married Lord William Pitt Lennox, 1824. Created part of *Reiza* in Weber's "Oberon," April 12, 1826. Divorced from her husband (Lennox), 1830. Married Mr. Joseph Wood, tenor vocalist, 1831. Resided chiefly at Woolley Moor, Yorks, 1833-54. Visited United States, 1834-36. Appeared in London again in 1837, 1844. Embraced Roman Catholic religion, 1843. Retired, 1844. Lived abroad, 1854-63. D. Bulcliffe Hall, near Chapelthorpe, Wakefield, July 21, 1864.

Miss Paton was one of the best and most popular British singers of her period. Her voice was full and rich in quality, and she excelled in the romantic works of Weber as well as in simple ballad music. She appeared in Britain and America with the most pronounced success, and enjoyed the most unbounded popularity as long as she remained on the stage.

PATTI (Adelina Maria Clorinda). Italian soprano vocalist, B. Madrid, Feb. 10, 1843. Daughter of Salvatore Patti and Signora Barili, both vocalists. Taken to America by parents when a child. S. under Maurice Strakosch, her brother-in-law. *Début* in New York as *Lucia* in "Lucia di Lammermoor," 1859. *Début* in London as *Amina* in "La Sonnambula," May 14, 1861. Sang at Birmingham Festival and in the Provinces, Scotland, etc. Appeared successively in Brussels, Berlin, Paris, Vienna, St. Petersburg, Moscow, in Spain, Italy, etc. Married Marquis de Caux, July, 1868. Separated from him, 1877. Divorced, 1885. Travelled in United States with much success, 1883. Marin. Ernst Nicolini, 1886.

Madame Patti has created the parts of Esmeralda, Juliet, Aidä, Estella, etc., in works by various composers. Her style of vocalization is pretty and graceful, but never rises above a medium degree of dramatic ability.

PATTI (Carlotta). Italian soprano vocalist, sister of above, B. Florence, 1840. *Début* in New York as concert singer, 1861. *Début* in London, April, 1863. Has since appeared as a concert vocalist in Britain, America, and the European Continent. Married Ernst de Munck, violoncellist, 1879.

Her voice is of great upward compass, and is of uniform good quality. She appears chiefly as a concert vocalist.

PATTISON (John Nelson). American pianist and comp., B. Niagara Falls, Oct. 22, 1843. S. in Germany under Hauptmann, Reinecke, Stern, Marx, Bülow, and Henselt. Returned to America, 1860. Visited Germany again, and played in Italy, Paris, etc. Travelled on concert tours in America with Parepa-Rosa, Kellogg, Ole Bull, Albani, Lucca, etc. Comp. of "Niagara," a symphony, numerous Pf. pieces, etc.

PATTISON (Thomas Mee). English org. and comp., B. Warrington, Jan. 27, 1845. Org. Warrington Musical Soc. since 1868. Org. St. Paul's Ch., Warrington, since 1869.

WORKS.—*Cantatas:* The Ancient Mariner; Lay of the Last Minstrel, 1885. The Happy Valley, opera. *Anthems:* O how plentiful is thy goodness; I did call upon the Lord; Truly God is loving; It is a good thing to give thanks; O praise the Lord; Give ear, O Lord; Magnificat and Nunc Dimittis in A. *Organ:* Five

Introductory Voluntaries ; Five Concluding do. ; Pastorale in F ; Fifteen Introductory and Concluding Voluntaries. *Pianoforte:* Allegretto Grazioso ; Chanson des Oiseaux. Rudiments of Vocal Music, with Preparatory Exercises, etc., Lond., 8vo, n.d.

PAUER (Ernst). Austrian pianist, comp., and writer, B. Vienna, Dec. 21, 1826. S. under Dirzka ; and Sechter and Lachner, at Munich, 1845. Musical Director at Mayence, 1846. Appeared at a Philharmonic Concert, London, April, 1851. Married Miss Andreae of Frankfort. Juror for Austria at International Exhibition, London, 1862. Delivered courses of historical lectures from 1862. Prof. of Pf. at R. A. M. ; Do. at National Training School for Music, etc.

WORKS.—Don Riego, opera, 1849 ; Die Rothe Maske, opera, 1850 ; Symphony in C minor for orch., op. 50. *Pianoforte:* Sonata, op. 22 ; Caprice, op. 30 ; Nocturne, op. 32 ; Pensées fugitives, op. 33 ; Seguidille, op. 35 ; La cascade, morceau de concert, op. 37 ; Two sonatas, op. 38 ; Capriccio, op. 39 ; Passacaille, op. 40 ; Presto Scherzando, op. 42 ; Bagatelles ; New Gradus ad Parnassum, 100 Studies for Pf. ; Capriccio, in E flat ; Tarentelles, various ; Arrangements, transcriptions, and collections, various. Family Gift Book, Lond. [1878]. The Classic Companion, 2 vols. Sunday Music. Old English Composers (selections from Byrd, Bull, Gibbons, Blow, Purcell, and Arne, with notices by W. A. Barrett), London, n. d. Children's Classics, various. March Album. The Birthday Book of Musicians and Composers, for every day in the year, Lond. [1883]. Six Historical Performances of Pianoforte Music, in strictly chronological order, April and May, 1863, with Biographies of the Composers, and criticisms on their works, Lond., 8vo, n. d. Three Lectures on the History of Oratorios, 8vo, n. d. Elements of the Beautiful in Music (Music Primer), Lond. [1877]. Musical Forms (Music Primer), Lond. [1878]. The Pianoforte (Music Primer), Lond. [1877]. Contributions to periodical literature, and lectures.

PAUL (Mrs. Howard), *née* ISABELLA FEATHERSTONE. B. Dartford, Kent, 1833. Appeared in the Beggar's Opera, 1853, and in many musical and dramatic pieces. Married Mr. Henry Howard Paul, and in 1854 appeared with him in a large number of different entertainments. She had a voice of much beauty, but as she turned her attention to comedy, she never attained the position as vocalist which she easily could. She D. London, June 6, 1879.

PAUL (Oscar). German writer and teacher, B. Freiwaldau, Silesia, April 8, 1836. S. at Univ. of Leipzig ; and music under Plaidy, Richter, and Hauptmann. Graduated as Ph.D., 1860. Prof. of Musical Science at Leipzig Univ., 1866. Teacher in Cons., and critic of *Leipziger Tagblatt*. Author of theoretical and other works.

PAVESI (Stefano). Italian comp., B. Casaletto Vaprio, Jan. 22, 1779. S. at Cons. la Pietà de' Turchini, Naples. D. Crema, July 28, 1850.

WORKS.—*Operas:* L'Avvertimento ai Gelosi, 1803 ; Fingallo e Comala, 1805 ; Il Maldicenti, 1809 ; Tancredi, 1812 ; Le Celanira, 1815 ; I Pitocchi fortunati, 1819 ; Don Gusmano, 1819 ; L'Egilda di Provenza, 1823 ; Il Solitario, 1826. Oratorios. Songs and miscellaneous music.

PAXTON (Stephen). English glee-writer, B. 1735. Gained Prizes from Catch Club in 1779, 1781, 1783, 1784, and 1785. D. London, Aug. 18, 1787. He comp. numerous glees and catches, some of which were republished in "Collection of Glees, Catches, etc., for 3 and 4 voices," op. 5. London [1780], and in other collections. He also comp. a few masses and songs. His brother WILLIAM (D. 1781), was a violoncellist, and comp. " Breathe soft, ye winds," a well-known glee for 3 voices, besides other pieces contained in the collections above noted.

PAYER (Hieronymus). Austrian comp., B. Meidling, Vienna, Feb. 15, 1787. D. Wiedburg, Sept. 1845. Comp. trios for Pf., concertos, sonatas, variations, dances, etc., for Pf., motets, and operas. Best known as an instrumental composer.

PAYNE (John Howard). American poet and dramatist, B. New York, June 9, 1792. D. Tunis, April 10, 1852. Celebrated as the author of " Clari, or the Maid of Milan," in which appears the world-famous song, "Home, sweet home," set by Sir Henry Bishop. He edited, from 1826 to 1827, the *Opera Glass*, a dramatic and musical journal.

PEACE (Albert Lister). English org. and comp., B. Huddersfield, 1845. Org. of Parish Ch. of Holmfirth, 1854. Settled in Glasgow as org. of Trinity Congregational Ch., 1866. Org. of Glasgow Univ. Mus. Bac. Oxon, 1870. Mus. Doc., do., 1875. Org. at St. Andrew's Hall, 1877. Org. Glasgow Cath., 1879.

WORKS.—The 138th Psalm, 1870. The Narrative of John the Baptist, 1875. Morning, Communion, and Evening Services. *Anthems:* Awake up my glory, etc. Editor of "The Scottish Hymnal," and "Psalms and Paraphrases." Organ arrangements of "L'étoile du Nord," "William Tell," "Der Freischutz," and "Oberon," overtures, etc., etc.

Dr. Peace enjoys a wide reputation in Great Britain as an organist of extraordinary executive ability, and has appeared throughout Scotland ; at the Bow and Bromley Institution, London ; and in the Provinces, with uniform success.

PEARCE (Joseph). English writer, author of "Violins and Violin-makers : Biographical Dictionary of the Great Italian Artistes, their Followers and Imitators to the Present Time. With Essays on Important Subjects connected with the Violin," Lond., 12mo, 1866.

PEARMAN (William). English tenor vocalist, B. Manchester, 1792. Went to sea as a cabin-boy. Engaged at Battle of Copenhagen, and wounded. Appeared unsuccessfully as an actor. Sang at Sadler's Wells Theatre. S. for a short time under Addison. Sang at Newcastle, Bath, Bristol, etc. *Début* as operatic vocalist at English Opera House, July 7, 1817, in "The Cabinet." Sang at Drury Lane, Covent Garden, and principal concerts.

PEARSALL (Robert Lucas de). English comp., B. Clifton, March 14, 1795. Educated for Law. Called to the Bar, 1821. Practised till 1825. S. music under Panny at Mayence, Re-visited England, 1829. Settled at Carlsruhe, 1830. Lived at Wartensee Castle on Lake of Constance from 1832. D. Wartensee, Aug. 5, 1856.

WORKS.—Madrigals for 4, 5, 6 and 8 Voices, Lond. [1840]. Eight Glees and Madrigals, Lond. [1863]. Twenty-four Choral Songs, etc., ed. by J. Hullah [1863]. Ballet Opera Choruses [1878]. Sacred Compositions, ed. by Trimnel, n. d. Edited a Catholic Hymn Book, 1863, and comp. Psalms and Anthems. *Part-Songs :* A king there was in Thule ; Let us all a-Maying go ; O who will o'er the downs so free ; Purple glow the forest mountains ; Sing we and chaunt it ; Sir Patrick Spens (10 parts) ; Bishop of Mentz ; Hardy Norseman's house of yore ; Red wine flows ; Watchman's song ; Winter song ; Who shall win my lady fair, etc. Essay on Consecutive Fifths and Octaves in Counterpoint, Lond., n. d., 4to.

Pearsall's concerted vocal music is probably the most popular of any in use at the present time. At least this can be easily affirmed of "O who will o'er the downs so free," and "The Hardy Norseman's House of Yore," both of which are familiar to everyone. He was an artist too many-sided to attain great distinction in any one of the numerous walks he attempted, but his achievements in music will certainly keep his name in constant remembrance.

PEARSON (Martin). English comp., B. in latter half of 16th century. Master of the children, S. Paul's Cath., 1604. Mus. Bac., Oxon., 1613. D. 1650.

WORKS.—Private Musicke, or the First Booke of Ayres and Dialogues, containing Songs of 4, 5, and 6 Parts of severall sorts, etc., 1604. Mottects, or Grave Church Musique, 1630.

PEARSON (William Webster). English comp. and org., B. Bishop-Auckland, Sept. 27, 1839. Org. Parish Ch., Elmham. Teacher of the violin in Norfolk County School, Dereham.

WORKS.—*Part-Songs :* Departed joys ; Jäger chorus ; Over the mountain side ; Soul of living music ; Sweet spring (madrigal) ; The anglers ; The coral grove ; The dream of home ; The Ironfounders ; The ocean ; The river ; The stormy petrel ; The iron horse ; Three doughtie men ; Autumn ; Soldier, rest ! Sweet to live amid the mountains; Welcome, young Spring; A ryghte merrie geste. Notation of Vocal Music on the principle of the substitution of Pitch, Lond., n. d. The National Method of Vocal Music for Elementary Schools, Manchester, 1874. Church music, org. music, songs, Pf. pieces, and orch. works.

PEASE (Alfred H.). American comp. and pianist, B. Cleveland, Ohio, 1842. S. music in Berlin, under Kullak, Wüerst, and Wieprecht, and afterwards under Bülow. Gave concerts throughout America. D. S. Louis, Mo., July 13, 1882. Comp. of Songs, etc., Blow, bugle, blow; Good night; Stars of the summer night; Absence; Beautiful Emeline; Fanny Lee; May belle; Memory's refrain; Rock me to sleep, mother; Song for freedom.

PECK (James). English music-publisher and engraver, established in London. He edited "Two Hundred and Fifty Psalm Tunes in Three Parts," 1798. He was succeeded in business by his son JOHN, org. of S. Faith's, who issued in conjunction with his brother JAMES, Junr., "Peck's Pocket Arrangement or General Collection of Psalm and Hymn Tunes," Lond., 1833, 3 v., 8vo.

PEGLER (Daniel). English amateur comp. and pianist, was well known in the early part of the present century as a performer of great ability. D. Colchester, Dec. 29, 1876.

PELLEGRINI (Felice). Italian bass vocalist and comp., B. Turin, 1774. Chor. in Turin Cath. S. under Ottavi. Début at Leghorn, 1795. Sang in Rome, Milan, Naples, Venice, etc. Sang in Paris, 1819. Appeared in London, 1828-9. Prof. of Singing in Paris Cons., 1829. D. Paris. Sept. 20, 1832.

Comp. Harpsichord lessons, songs, and other vocal music. His son, GIULIO, B. Milan, Jan 1, 1806. S. Milan Cons., 1817. Début at Turin, 1821. Bass singer at Munich. D. Munich, July 12, 1858.

PENNA (Frederic). English barytone vocalist and writer, B. London, 1832. Author of "Singing, an Essay," Lond., 8vo, 1878. His wife, CATHERINE LOUISA SMITH, was a soprano vocalist of ability, and D. London, 1879. His daughter, CATHERINE, is also a soprano vocalist.

PENFIELD (Smith Newell). American org., pianist, and comp., B. Oberlin, O., April 4, 1837. B.A. and M.A. of Oberlin Coll. S. at Leipzig under Reinecke, Moscheles, Papperitz, and others, and at Paris under Delioux. Org. and teacher in New York city. Mus. Doc., Univ., N.Y., 1883. President of Music Teachers' National Assoc., 1884.

WORKS.—The 18th Psalm, for chorus and solo voices, with orch.; Eleven anthems, constituting full set of Canticles of Prot. Epis. Ch.; Concert Overture for full orchestra; Various songs; Pf. and organ pieces.

PEPUSCH (Johann Christoph). German comp. and writer, B. Berlin, 1667. S. under Klingenberg. Musician at Prussian Court, 1681-1697. Resided in Holland, 1698. Came to England, 1700. Musician in orch. of Drury Lane Theatre. Assistant to Este at Academy of Ancient Music. Org. to Duke of Chandos, 1712. Mus. Doc. Oxon, 1713. Musical director of Lincoln's Inn Fields Theatre. Married Margarite de l'Epine. Org. at Charter House, 1737. F.R.S., 1746. D. London, July 20, 1752.

WORKS.—Arranged overture and airs in "The Beggar's Opera," 1728; "Polly," etc. Edited Corelli's Sonatas. Six English Cantatas, Lond., Walsh, 1712. Odes and anthems, various. Short Treatise on Harmony, containing the chief rules for composing in 2, 3, and 4 parts, Lond., 8vo, 1730; second edit., 1731.

Pepusch was best known as a teacher and theorist, and by his arrangement of the airs in "The Beggar's Opera." The Treatise on Harmony is said to be by Lord Abercorn, or Paisley; but authorities say, in nothing more than name.

PERABO (Johann Ernst). German pianist and comp., B. Wiesbaden, Nov. 14, 1845. Went to America with his family, 1852. Resided successively at New York, Dover, N. H., and Boston. S. under his father and W. Schultze in America. Educated at Eimsbüttel, near Hamburg. S. music at Leipzig Cons. under Moscheles and E. F. Wenzel (Pf.); Papperitz, Hauptmann and Richter (harmony); and Reinecke (comp.); 1862-65. Awarded one of the Helbig Prizes. Returned to New York, Nov. 1865. Settled in Boston, 1865.

Has given concerts in Sandusky; Lafayette; Chicago; Cleveland; Boston; at the Harvard Musical Association; Boston Symphony Concerts; and in other cities in the United States.

WORKS.—Op. 1. Moment Musical, Pf.; op. 2. Scherzo, Pf.; op. 3. Prélude, Pf.; op. 4. Waltz; op. 5. Introduction and Andante; op. 6. Pensée Fugitive; op. 7. "After School," six short pieces; op. 8. Souvenir, Pf.; op. 9. Three Studies; op. 10. Petit Scherzo, Pf.; op. 11. Pensées, in G minor, Pf.; op. 12. For Amy, musical sketch, in A minor; Transcriptions of Ballads by C. Löwe, arrangements from Rubinstein, Bennett, Schubert, Beethoven, and collections of Pf. pieces for the use of pupils.

His style unites delicacy of touch and expression, with a keen poetic insight of the truest meaning of the composer, and a technical capability at once correct and vigorous. He has introduced into America many interesting pianoforte works by European composers, and has done much to spread the public knowledge of the works of Sir W. S. Bennet. Some of the works introduced by Perabo were given for the first time in America. His works are finished and poetical effusions, and have commanded admiration wherever produced.

PERCIVAL (Samuel). English org., flute-player, and comp., B. 1824. S. at R. A. M., London. Org. at School for the Blind, Liverpool. Org. of Wallasey Parish Ch. Teacher in Liverpool. D. Liverpool, Nov. 7, 1876. He composed some vocal music, songs, etc., and a cantata entitled "The Lyre."

PERCY (John). English comp., org., and tenor vocalist, B. (?) D. London, January 24, 1797. Little is known of this musician, and he is only remembered as the composer of the ballad, "Wapping Old Stairs."

PERCY (Bishop Thomas). English antiquary and divine, B. Bridgenorth, Shropshire, 1728. D. 1811. Best known by his "Reliques of Ancient English Poetry," 1765, and numerous other editions. This work contains the poetry of many old songs and ballads, and has been compared and collated in this connection by the late Dr. Rimbault, who published "Musical Illustrations of Bishop Percy's Reliques of Ancient English poetry, Lond., 8vo, 1850.

PEREZ (Davide). Spanish comp., B. Naples, 1711. Chap.-master to the King of Portugal, 1752. D. Lisbon, 1778. Comp. church and operatic music.

PERGETTI (Paolo). Italian writer and singing master, author of "A Treatise on Singing, forming a complete School of the Art," Lond., 3 parts, fo. [1857].

PERGOLESI (Giovanni Battista). Italian comp., B. Jesi, Jan. 3, 1710. S. at Cons. dei Poveri in Gesù Cristo. Naples, under Matteis, Feo, Durante, Greco, and Vinci. Chap.-master, Ch. of Loretto, 1734. D. Pozzuoli, near Naples, March 16, 1736.

WORKS.—S. Guglielmo d'Aquitania, sacred drama, 1731. *Operas:* La Sallustia, 1731; Amor fa l'uomo cieco, 1731; Recimero, 1731; La Serva Padrona, Naples, 1731 (London, 1873); Il Maestro de Musique, 1732; Il Geloso Schernito, 1732; Le Frate innamorato, 1732; Il Prigionier superbo; Adriano in Siria, 1734; Livietta e Tracolo, 1734; La Contadina astuta, 1734; Flaminio, 1735; L'Olimpiade, 1749. Masses, various; Miserere, 4 voices and orch. Stabat Mater; Salve Regina; Cantatas, songs, and other vocal music; Trios for strings.

Pergolesi's music was considered an advance on the style current in his day, inasmuch as it afforded a brilliant contrast by its refreshing, varied, and tuneful character to the formal and stilted efforts of many of his contemporaries. The production of "La Serva Padrona" in Paris is said to have helped to form the school of French opera comique.

PERI (Jacopo). Italian comp., B. Florence, about middle of 16th century. S. at Lucca under Malvezzi. Chap.-master to Fernando, Duke of Tuscany; do. to Duke Cosmo II.; do. Duke of Ferrara, 1601. Married a lady of the House of Forlini. D. after 1610.

WORKS.—Dafne (the first musical drama), by Rinuccini, Florence, 1597; Euridice, by Rinuccini (with Caccini), 1600; Le Musiche di Jacopo Peri, nobil Fiorentino sopra l'Euridice del sig, Ottavio Rinuccini, rappresentati nello sposalizio della cristianissima Maria Medici, regina di Francia e di Navarra; in Fiorenza, 1600, 4to.

Peri is usually regarded as the principal founder of the opera, and was associated with Bardi, Caccini, Corsi, and Rinuccini in the original endeavours to establish a musical drama.

PERKINS (Henry S.) American teacher and comp., B. Stockbridge, Vermont, March 20, 1833. S. at Boston. Cond. and music director. Compiler of a number of song collections, as "The Advance;" "Song Echo;" "The Nightingale;" "Glee and Chorus Book;" "College Hymn and Tune Book.",

PERKINS (Julius E.) American bass vocalist and pianist, B. Stockbridge, Vt., 1845. Brother of above. S. in Paris and Italy. Début in Italy, 1868. Joined Mapleson Opera Company, 1873. Married Marie Roze, 1874. D. Manchester, Feb. 24, 1875.

PERKINS (William O.) American comp. and Doc. Mus., B. Stockbridge, Vt., May 23, 1831. S. at Boston, and is a teacher and cond. there.

WORKS.—The Temple; Laurel Wreath; Seminary Album; Golden Robin; Mocking Bird; The Whip-poor-will; Male Voice Glee Book; Union Star (with B. F. Baker); Singing School; The Chorister; Church Welcome; Anthem Book, and numerous other collections edited by himself and in conjunction with his brother, etc.

PERNE (Francois Louis). French writer and Prof., B. Paris, 1772. Prof. of harmony, Cons., 1811. Inspector of Cons., 1816; Librarian, do., 1820. D. Paris, May 26, 1832. Comp. some church music, and wrote on ancient music and on notation.

PERRY (George). English org. and comp., B. Norwich, 1793. Chorister in Norwich Cath. S. under Beckwith. Settled in London, 1822. Director of music in Haymarket Theatre, 1822. Org. of Quebec Chap. Leader of band, Sacred Harmonic Soc., 1832-47. Cond. do., 1848. Org. Trinity Ch., Gray's Inn Road, 1846. D. March 4, 1862.

WORKS. - Overture to the Persian Hunters, 1817; Elijah and the Priests of Baal, oratorio, 1818; Morning, Noon, and Night, opera, 1822; The Fall of Jerusalem, oratorio, 1830; The Death of Abel, oratorio; Belshazzar's Feast, cantata, 1836; Hezekiah, oratorio, 1847; Anthems.

PERSIANI (Fanny), née TACCHINARDI. Italian soprano vocalist, B. Rome, Oct. 4, 1812. S. under her father. Married to Giuseppe Persiani, 1830. Début at Leghorn, 1832. Appeared successively at Milan, Florence, Vienna, Padua, Venice, and Naples. Début at Paris in Lucia di Lammermoor, Dec., 1837. Appeared in London, 1838, as Amina in "La Sonnambula." Sang thereafter in London, Paris, Holland, Germany, Russia, etc. Last appeared in London, 1858. D. Neuilly-sur-Seine, May 3, 1867.

"Never was there woman less vulgar, in physiognomy or in manner, than she; but never was there one whose appearance on the stage was less distinguished. . ." Her voice "was an acute *soprano*, mounting to E flat *altissimo*—acrid and piercing rather than sweet, penetrating rather than full, and always liable to rise in pitch."— *Chorley's Recollections.*

PERSIUS (Louis Luc L. de). French comp., B. Metz, May 21, 1769. Prof., Paris Cons., 1795-1802. Cond. of Emperor's Court Concerts, 1810-15, etc. D. Paris, Dec. 20, 1819.

WORKS.—Le Passage de la Mer Rouge, oratorio, 1787. *Operas*: Le Nuit Espagnole, 1791; Estelle, 1794; Phanor et Angela; Fanny Morna; Léonidas, 1799; Marcel, 1801.

PERTI (Jacopo Antonio), Italian comp., B. Bologna, June 6, 1661. S. under his uncle, Lorenzo Perti. Educated at the Jesuit Coll., Bologna. Chap.-master of San Petronio, Bologna, till 1756. D. Bologna, April 10, 1756.

WORKS.- *Operas:* Atide, 1679; Oreste, 1681; Marzio Coriolano, 1683; Brenno in Efeso, 1690; Furio Camillo, 1692; Nerone fatto Cesare, 1693; Laodicea e Berenice, 1695. Cantate morali e spirituali, 1688. Masses, etc.

PESCHKA-LEUTNER (Minna). Austrian soprano vocalist, B. Vienna, Oct. 25, 1839. S. under Proch. Début at Breslau as "Agatha," 1856. Sang at

Dessau, 1857-61. Married to Dr. Peschka, 1861. Sang in Vienna, 1863. S. under Mme. Bockholtz-Falconi. Sang at Leipzig, 1868-76. Sang in London, at Crystal Palace, etc., 1872. Sang at Boston, Mass., 1872. Engaged at Hamburg, 1877. Reappeared in America, 1881. Since engaged on the Continent.

PESSARD (Émile Louis Fortuné). French comp., B. Montmartre, Paris, May 29, 1843. S. Paris Cons. under Bazin and Carafa. Inspector of singing in public schools of Paris. Chevalier of Legion of Honour, 1879.

WORKS.—*Operas:* La cruche cassée, 1870; Le Char, 1878; Le Capitaine Fracasse, 1878; Tabarin, 1885. Cantata, Dalila, 1867. Joyeusetés de bonne compagnie (a collection of songs); Trios for Pf., vn., and 'cello; Marches, mazurkas, and nocturnes for Pf.

PESTALOZZI (Johann Heinrich). Swiss educationist, B. Zürich, Jan., 1745, D. Brugg, Basle, 1827.

The theories of Pestalozzi have been successfully applied to music, and is in fact the basis of all illustrative class music-teaching. A text-book specially adapted to the method has been published in America by Lowell Mason and T. F. Seward, under the title of "The Pestalozzian Music-Teacher, or Class Instructor in Elementary Music," Boston, n. d.

PETERBOROUGH (Countess of). See ROBINSON (Anastasia).

PETERS (Carl Friedrich). German music-publisher, established at Leipzig, about 1814. He bought the copyrights of Kühnel and Hoffmeister, and founded a great business in editions of classical works. The catalogue of the firm includes the principal works of all the leading composers, ancient and modern; full scores of orchestral works; and a great variety of miscellaneous works. The full scores of this firm are famed for their correctness.

PETERS (W. C.) American writer and teacher, author of "Eclectic Piano Instructor," Boston; "Elements of Thorough Base," Boston; "Art of Singing," Boston; Collections for Pf., etc.

PETERSILEA (Carlyle). American pianist and teacher, B. Boston, Mass., Jan. 18, 1848. S. at Leipzig Cons., under Plaidy and Moscheles, and also under Bülow. Pianist and teacher in Boston, where he founded the Petersilea Academy of Music, 1871. Famous throughout the United States as a pianist and teacher.

PETIT (Adrien). See COCLICUS.

PETTIT (Walter). English violoncellist, B. London, March 14, 1835. S. at R. A. M. Principal 'cellist at Philharmonic Society, H. M. Theatre, etc. D. London, Dec. 11, 1882.

PETRELLA (Enrico). Italian comp., B. Palermo, Dec. 10, 1813. S. at Naples under Zingarelli, Bellini, and Ruggi. D. Genoa, April 7, 1877.

WORKS.—Il Diavolo color di rosa, 1829; I Pirati Spagnuoli, 1837; Le Miniere di Freiberg, 1839; Galeotto Manfredi, 1843; Elena di Toloso, 1852; Marco Visconti, 1854; Il Duca di Scilla, 1859; Morosina, 1860; Virginia, 1861; I Promessi Sposi, 1866; Giovanna II. di Napoli, 1869; Manfredo, 1872; Bianca Orsini, 1874, and other operas.

PETRIE (Robert). Scottish musician, of Kirkmichael, Perthshire, flourished about end of 18th century. Published four "Collections of Strathspey Reels and Country Dances, with a Bass for the Violoncello, etc.," Edin., n.d. The titles of the succeeding vols. vary slightly from the first, which is the one here given.

PETRUCCI (Ottavio, da Fossombrone). Italian printer, B. June, 1466. D. 1524 (?) Inventor of the process of printing music by means of movable metal types, 1502. This invention did much to spread music by the multiplication of musical works, and Petrucci printed a number of the compositions of the leading writers of his day.

PEVERNAGE (Andre). Belgian comp., B. Courtrai, 1543. Chap.-master at Courtrai, and afterwards Choir-master of Antwerp Cath. D. Antwerp, July

30, 1589. Comp. masses, motets, 5 books of chansons, and madrigals contained in "Harmonia Celeste," 1593.

PFEIFFER (Georges Jean). French pianist and comp., B. Versailles, Dec. 12, 1835. S. under his Mother, Maleden, and Daincke. Appeared in London as pianist, 1862.
WORKS.—Concertos for Pf. and orch., opp. 11, 21, 58; Sonata for Pf. and 'cello, op. 28; Symphony for orch., op. 31; Jeanne d'Arc, symphonie-poem, op. 23; Le Capitaine Kock, opera comique, op. 19.

PFLUGHAUPT (Robert). German pianist and comp., B. Berlin, Aug. 4, 1833. S. under Liszt. D. Aachen, June 12, 1871. Comp. mazurkas, galops, themes, and other works for Pf.

PHILIDOR (Francois Andre), DANICAN. French comp. and chess-player, B. Dreux, Sept. 7, 1726. S. music under Campra. Went to Paris and was a teacher and chess-player. Travelled in Germany and Holland as chess-player, 1745-48. Came to England, 1748. Resided between France and England, but quitted the former on outbreak of French Revolution. D. London, Aug. 31, 1795.
WORKS.—*Operas:* Blaise le Savetier, 1759; L'Iluître et les Plaideurs, 1759; Le Soldat Magicien, 1760; Le Jardinier et son Seigneur, 1761; Sancho Pança, 1762; Le Bûcheron, 1763; Le Sorcier, 1764; Tom Jones, 1764; Zelime et Melide, 1766; Ernelinde, 1767; La Nouvelle Ecole des Femmes, 1770; Le Bon fils, 1773; Les Femmes vengées, 1774; L'Amitie au Village, 1785 Carmen Sæculare of Horace, 1779. Analyse du Jeu des Echecs, 1777 (translated into English). Ode to Harmony (Congreve).
The fame of Philidor as a musician has long since been eclipsed by his repute as a chess-player. In the latter art he enjoyed a wide contemporary reputation, which has long survived him and his musical works.

PHILIPPS (Peter), PETRUS PHILIPPUS. English comp., B. in England [1560]. Canon of Bethune in Flanders. Org. of vice-regal chapel of the Governor of Low Countries. Canon of Collegiate Ch. of S. Vincent, Soignies. D. April, 1625.
WORKS.—Melodia Olympica di diversi eccellentissimi Musici a 4, 5, 6, e 8 voci, 1591 (and other editions). Il Primo libro de' Madrigali a sei voci, 1596. Madrigali a otto voci, 1598. Il Secondo libro di Madrigali a sei voci, 1604. Cantiones Sacræ, 5 vocum, 1612. Gemmulæ Sacræ, 2 e 3 voci, 1613. Cantiones Sacræ octi vocum, 1613. Litaniæ, 1623.

PHILLIPPS (Adelaide). English contralto vocalist, B. Bristol. Sang in Boston and Philadelphia. S. in London under Garcia and W. C. Masters, 1852; also in Italy. Appeared in London, Paris, and in U. S. of America.

PHILLIPPS (Arthur). English org. and comp., B. 1605. Clerk of New Coll., Oxford, 1622. Org. of Bristol Cath., 1638. Org. of Magdalen Coll., Oxford, 1639. Prof. Music, Oxford Univ., 1639. Mus. Bac., Oxon., 1640. Org. to Queen Henrietta Maria of France. Comp. "The Requiem, or Liberty of an imprisoned Royalist," 1641; "The Resurrection," 1649; etc.

PHILLIPS (Henry). English barytone vocalist and writer, B. Bristol, Aug. 13, 1801. Sang in chorus at Drury Lane Theatre. S. under Broadhurst, and Sir G. Smart. Sang at English Opera House. Sang at Lenten Oratorios; in Arne's "Artaxerxes," 1824; "Der Freischutz," 1824. Sang at Provincial Festivals. Appeared in America, 1844. Retired, 1863. D. Dalston, Nov. 8, 1876.
WORKS.—The True Enjoyment of Angling, 1843. Hints on Musical Declamation. Lond., 8vo, 1848; Birmingham ed., n. d. Musical and Personal Recollections during Half-a-Century. London, 1864, 2 vols., 8vo. Songs and other vocal music.

PHILLIPS (Thomas). Welsh tenor vocalist, lecturer, and comp., B. Monmouthshire, 1774. Lectured and sang at concerts during his lifetime. Author of "Elementary Principles and Practices for Singing," Lond., fo. [1830].

Comp. a few songs and part-songs, and compiled "The Mentor's Harp,' moral ballads by T. H. Bayly ; " Improved Psalmody for the Church and the Chamber." Also an arrangement of Linley's "Duenna." D. Northwich, Oct. 29, 1841.

PHILLIPS (William Lovell). English comp. and pianist, B. Bristol, Dec. 26, 1816. Chor. in Bristol Cath. S. under C. Potter at R. A. M. Prof. of comp. R. A. M. S. violoncello under Lindley. Mem. of orch. of H. M. Theatre, Philharmonic Soc., and Sacred Harmonic Soc. Cond. at Olympic Theatre ; Princess' Theatre. Org. of St. Catherine's Church, Regent Park, etc. D. London, March 19, 1860.

WORKS.—Symphony in F min. ; Cantata. *Songs*: Lady mine ; The sleeping beauty ; Longings ; The old ballad ; Voice of Songs ; Christmas rose ; England's hope and pride ; Bear and forbear ; One word ; What must I sing you?

PHILLIPSON (W.) English writer, author of "Guide to Young Pianoforte Teachers and Students, with Analysis of Examples, etc., London, 8vo, n.d., 2 editions.

PHILP (Elizabeth). English vocal comp., B. Falmouth, 1827. S. under Garcia, Marchesi, and F. Hiller. D. London, Nov. 26, 1885. Comp. a number of meritorious songs, etc., of which the following is a select list :—

WORKS.—*Songs :* Bye and Bye ; Dolly ; Fisherman's story ; Forgiven ; Golden past ; Hop-pickers ; I love him more than I can say ; Love that's never told ; My head is like to rend ; Oh ! why not be happy ; Poacher's Widow ; River ran between them ; 'tis all that I can say ; 'Tis wine ; Violets of the Spring : Wrecked hope. Part-songs, various. How to sing an English Ballad, Lond., 8vo, 1883 [Reprint], etc.

PHILPOT (Lucy). See ANDERSON (Lucy).

PHIPPS (Alexander James). English org. and comp. S. under W. H. Holmes and Steggall. Org. of S. James', Swansea, 1866. Wrote an oratorio entitled "The Ten Virgins," and other works.

PHIPPS (Sireno B.) American writer, author of "Musical Mirror," Elementary instructions in Vocal Music, Boston, 8vo, n. d.

PHIPSON (Dr. T. L.) English writer, author of "Biographical Sketches and Anecdotes of Celebrated Violinists," Lond., 8vo, 1877. "Bellini and the Opera of La Sonnambula," Lond., 1880.

PIATTI (Alfredo). Italian violoncellist and comp., B. Bergamo, Jan. 8, 1822. S. under Merighi at Milan Cons., 1832. *Début* as 'cellist, 1837. Settled in England, 1844. Has since held foremost position as principal performer at Philharmonic Society, London Popular Concerts, and the Provincial and Scottish Festivals.

WORKS.—Introduction et Variations sur un theme de Lucia di Lammermoor, for 'cello, op. 2 ; Une Prière, theme, 'cello and Pf., op. 3 ; Passe-temps sentimental (Schubert), op. 4 ; Souvenirs de " La Sonnambula," op. 5 ; Mazurka sentimentale, op. 6 ; Les Fiancés, petit caprice, op. 7 ; Airs Baskyrs, scherzo, op. 8 ; Souvenir de " I Puritani," op. 9 ; Amour et Caprice, fantaisie, op. 10 ; La Suédoise, caprice, op. 11 ; Divertissement sur un Air napolitain, op. 12 ; Souvenirs de " Linda di Chamounix," op. 13 ; Bergamasca, op. 14 ; Three Russian Airs, varied, op. 16 ; Sa rentrée Italienne, op. 17 ; Siciliana, op. 19 ; Nocturne, op. 20. Songs and other works.

His playing is distinguished by much refinement, taste, and skill ; and his interpretation of whatever he undertakes is marked by much poetical feeling and careful execution. His tone is large, and his execution is correct and finely controlled. His playing and phrasing of simple melodies is exquisite, and the whole style of his performance is artistic and enjoyable.

PICCINI (Niccolo). Italian comp., B. Bari, Naples, 1728. S. under Leo and Durante at the Cons. of San Onofrio, 1742-56. Married to Vincenza Sibilla, 1756. Went to Paris, 1776. Teacher to Marie Antoinette, 1776. Director of the Italian Opera, Paris. Rivalry with Gluck commenced, 1779. D. Passy, May 7, 1800.

WORKS.—*Operas*: Le Donne dispettore, 1754; Le Gelosie, 1755; Zenobia, 1756; L'Astrologa, 1756; L'Amante ridicolo, 1757; La Schiava, 1757; Gli Uccellatore, 1758; Siroe, 1759; Le Donne vendicate, 1759; Il Re Pastore, 1760; La Contadina bizzarra, 1701; L'Olimpiade, 1761; Le Vicende della sorte, 1762; Il Demetrio, 1762; Il Barone de Torre forte, 1762; La Villegiatura, 1762; Il Mondo della Luna; Il Nuova Orlando; Il gran Cid; Berenice; La l'escatrice; Il Cavaliere per amore; Artaserse; Gli amanti mascherati; Gli Stravagante; Catone, 1770; La Finta Giardiniera, 1771; Don Chisciotto, 1771; L' Olimpiade (new version), 1771; L' Antigono, 1771; La Molinarella, 1772; Artaserse (new version), 1772; L' Ignorante astuto, 1773; I sposi persequitati; L'Americano ingentilito; Alessandro nelle Indie (new version), 1775; I Viaggiatori felice, 1776; Radamisto, 1776; Roland, Paris, Jan. 27, 1778 (Quinault): Phaon, 1778; Le Fat Méprisé, 1779; Atys, Paris, 1780; Iphigenie en Tauride, 1781; Adele de Ponthieu, 1781; Didon, 1783; Le faux Lord, 1783; Diane et Endimion, 1784; Pénélope, Nov., 1785; Clytemnestre, 1787. Jonathan, oratorio, 1792. Church music, etc.

Piccini was a composer of great natural abilities, and turned his powers to considerable advantage during his career. His melodies are flowing, warm, and tuneful; while his handling of dramatic combinations and situations displays skill and a good measure of science. His rivalry with Gluck served in a measure to dim his fame.

PICCOLOMINI (Maria). Italian soprano vocalist, B. Sienna, 1835 [given also as 1834 and 1836]. Came of a noble family. S. under Mazzarelli and Romani. *Début* as "Lucrezia Borgia" at La Pergole, in 1852. Appeared in London, at H. M. Theatre, May, 1856, in "La Traviata." Appeared in America, 1858. Re-appeared in London, 1859-60. (Farewell, April, 1860.) Married to Marchese Gaetani, and retired, 1860.

Piccolomini had a voice of great flexibility and brilliancy, though she was deficient in tone. She excelled in light, graceful, and rapid passages, and displayed a surprising volubility in many of the characters which she assumed. Among the operas in which she appeared may be named "La Figlia di Regimento," "Norma," "L'Elisir d'Amour," "Don Giovanni," "Bohemian Girl," and "Luisa Miller."

PICHEL (Wenzel). Bohemian comp. and cond., B. Bechin, Tabor, 1740. S. at Prague. Musical comp. to Archduke Ferdinand. D. Vienna, Jan. 23, 1805.

WORKS.—Symphonies (nearly 100); Concertos, duets, etc., for violin; Trios, quartets, and quintets for strings; Sonatas and smaller pieces for Pf.; Operas and other vocal music.

PICKARD (J.) English writer, author of "Modulation exemplified by a grand tabular view of the preparations of all the notes of the octaves," Lond., fo, n.d.

PIERSON (Henry Hugo), or PEARSON. English comp., B. Oxford, April 12, 1815. Educated at Harrow and Trinity Coll., Oxford. S. music under Attwood and Corfe, in England: Rink, Tomaschek, and Reissiger in Germany. Professor of Music in Edinburgh University, 1844. Married to Caroline Leonhardt. Resided mostly in Germany. D. Leipzig, Jan. 28, 1873.

WORKS.—*Oratorios:* Jerusalem, Norwich Festival, 1852; Lond., 1853. Hezeziah. Music to Second Part of Goethe's "Faust." Hamburg, 1854. *Operas:* Contarini, Hamburg, 1872; Leila, Hamburg, 1848. *Overtures:* "Macbeth"; "As You Like It"; "Romeo and Juliet"; Romantique. Salve Æternum, a Roman dirge, op. 30, 1853; Der Elfensieg. Six Romances for voice and Pf.; Six Songs for voice and Pf.; Elegies, do.; Lieder, various; Ye Mariners of England, part-song; Hurrah for Merry England; Now the bright morning star. Blessed are the dead, anthem; Ave Maria.

Pierson was a composer of great talent, and held in Germany a high position, while in England his name is only associated with a single part-song, though it is by no means the chief effort of his genius. Under the name of Edgar Mansfeldt he published a number of his minor works.

PIESENDEL. See PISENDEL.

PIGGOTT (Francis). English org. and comp., B. about middle of 17th century. Org. of Magdalen Coll., Oxford, 1686-87. Org. Temple Ch., Lond., 1688. Gent. extraordinary, Chap. Royal, 1695. Org. do., 1697. Mus. Bac., Cantab., 1698. D. May, 1704. Comp. anthems, etc.

PILATE (August). French operatic comp., B. Bouchain, Sept. 29, 1810. S. at Douai and at Paris Cons. D. Paris, Aug. 1, 1877.

WORKS.—*Operettas:* Les Etoiles, 1854; Olivier Basselin, 1838; La Modiste et le Lord, 1833; Jean le Sot, 1856.

PILKINGTON (Francis). English comp. of 16th and 17th centuries. Was a chorister in Chester Cath., and Mus. Bac., Oxon., 1595. He published First Booke of Songs or Ayres of 4 Parts, 1605; First Set of Madrigals and Pastorals of 3, 4, and 5 Parts, 1613; Second Set of Madrigals and Pastorals of 3, 4, 5, and 6 Parts, apt for Violl and Voyce, 1624.

PILKINGTON (H. W.) English writer, author of "A Musical Dictionary," Boston, 8vo, 1812.

PINSUTI (IL CAVALIERE, CIRO E.) Italian comp., B. Sinalunga, Siena, 9 May, 1829. S. under his father, in Italy. Taken to England by Henry Drummond, M.P. S. under C. Potter and Blagrove in London; and at Cons. of Bologna, 1845; pupil also of Rossini. Resided permanently in London since 1848. Prof. at R. A. M., London, 1856.

WORKS.—*Operas:* Il Mercante di Venezia, opera, 1873; Mattia Corvino, opera, 1877; Margherita, opera (MS.). Te Deum. *Part-Songs:* April time; Autumn song; A Rivederci; Bridal chorus; Crusader; Caravan, the; Fairest flowers; Fair land, we greet thee; Good-night, beloved; In this hour of softened splendour; I canta storie; Irlanda; Kings and Queens; My lady comes to me; Over woodland, over plain; Rhine-raft song; Silent-tide; Song to Pan; Spring song; Sea hath its pearls; Stradella; Tell me, Flora; Tell me where is fancy bred; Think of me; Tell me not in mournful numbers; Two angel bands; Would you ask my heart; Watchword. *Trios:* Italian trios, various; It is not always May; Kind words; Music; May morning. *Duets:* After the rain; Boating; Bygone days; Golden leav'd autumn; Heather breezes; Meeting; Separation; Sunrise; Sunset; Italian duets, various, etc., etc. *Songs:* A smile; A dream of two worlds; After long years; A maiden's love; As a flower; Afterglow; Arrow and the song; Beatrice; Bedouin love song; Before the fight; Bugler; Better than gold; Christmas; Changed; Captive skylark; Crusader's love song; Dreams, only dreams; England's dead; Excelsior; Estelle; El sereno; Eterna memoria; Flower and the hope; Fairer than thee; Free lance; Five barred gate; Ferryman; Fairer still; Farewell, dear love; Falconer; Gathered roses; Gentle heart; Good old times; Heaven's chorister; Harbour lights; In shadowland; In the spring-time; I love my love; I fear no foe; It may be so; I remember; King's minstrel; Knight's shield; Last watch; Lost and won; May-day Queen Marie; Minster windows; Miller's daughter; Moorish serenade; My lady's heart; My lass; Night; Night watch; Old comrades; Ophelia; Owl; Old cathedral; Outposts; Pilgrim song; Playmates; The raft; Roll call; Swallow; Skylark; Summer friends; Sleep on, dear love; To-morrow; Too soon; 'Twas on a market-day; Three letters; Vicar's daughter; Water lilies; Warrior; Wayside ministry. *Pianoforte Music:* Les trois graces, valses; Rosina, mazurka; Nocturne; Grand March; Serenata Spagnola, for 'cello and Pf.; Three melodies; Gran marcia; Outpost march; Transcriptions; etc. Daily Vocal Exercises, Lond., n. d. Hints to Students on Singing, written in a familiar style for all engaged in tuition, Lond., n. d.

The vocal works of Pinsuti have achieved great and deserved success in Britain. His part-songs and many of his single songs are among the standard favourites with all the principal choirs.

PINTO (George Frederick), or SAUTERS. English violinist and comp., B. Lambeth, London, Sept. 25, 1786. Grandson of Thomas Pinto. S. under Salomon. Performed at principal London and provincial concerts; and appeared in Scotland with great success, 1802. D. Little Chelsea, London, March 23, 1806.

WORKS. —Sonatas for Pf. solo ; Sonatas for violin and Pf. ; Six Canzonets for voice and Pf. ; Four Canzonets and a sonata, edited, with preface, by S. Wesley. Other vocal and instrumental works.

PINTO (Thomas). Italian violinist, B. in England, of Italian parents, early in eighteenth century. Performed at provincial festivals, and at King's Theatre, London. Resided successively in Edinburgh and Ireland. Married to Miss Brent, the vocalist. D. in Ireland, 1773.

His second wife, Miss BRENT, whom he married in 1766, was a famous soprano vocalist, and appeared as a concert vocalist for many years in London and elsewhere, from 1758. She D. London, April 10, 1802.

PISARONI (Benedetta Rosamunda). Italian contralto vocalist, B. Piacenza, Feb. 6, 1793. S. under Marchesi. *Début* as soprano in opera of Paër, 1811. Cultivated her lower voice and appeared as a contralto in Venice, Florence, Padua, Palermo, Naples, Milan, Turin, Paris, 1827, London, 1829. Retired, and resided at Piacenza. D. there, Aug. 6, 1872.

PISCHEK (Johann Baptist). Bohemian barytone vocalist and comp., B. Melnik, near Prague, Oct. 14, 1814. S. at Prague for the law, but forsook that study to appear as a vocalist, 1835. Appeared afterwards as a dramatic and concert vocalist at Pressburg and Vienna, 1837 ; Frankfort-on-Main, 1840 ; Berlin, 1843 ; London, 1845 ; Hamburg, etc. Court singer to the King of Würtemberg, Stuttgart, 1844-63. Re-appeared in London, 1846-51. D. Sigmaringen, Stuttgart, Feb. 16, 1873.

Pischek was a vocalist of much power and talent, and comp. some very meritorious songs, etc. He sang in operas of Beethoven, Spohr, Kreutzer, Mozart, Méhul, Donizetti, Hérold, etc.

PISENDEL (Johann Georg). German violinist and comp., B. Carlsburg, Franconia, Dec. 26, 1687. Chor. in Chap. of Margrave of Anspach, under Pistocchi and Corelli. Concert-meister at Dresden, 1730 ; Leader at the theatre, under Hasse, 1731. D. Dresden, Nov. 25, 1755. Comp. an amount of instrumental music existing mostly in MS.

PISTOCCHI (Francesco Antonio). Italian comp. and vocal trainer, B. Palermo, 1659. S. singing under P. Vastamigli and Monari. Chap.-master to the Margrave of Anspach. Established a Singing School at Bologna, 1700, where he trained Bernacchi, Fabri, Minelli, and many other famous vocalists. D. Bologna, 1720.

WORKS.—*Operas:* Narciso, 1697 ; Leandro, 1679 ; Il Girello, 1681. *Oratorios:* Il Martirio di S. Adriano ; Maria Virgine addolorata, 1698. *Vocal Works:* Caprici puerili variamente composti in 40 modi, sopra un basso, da un balbetto in età d'anni 8, op. 1, 1687 ; Scherzi Musicali ; Duetti e Terzetti, 1707 ; etc.

One of the most celebrated masters of singing of the olden time.

PITMAN (Ambrose). English writer, author of "The Miseries of Musick Masters. A Serio-comick dramatick Poem...," London, 4to, 1815.

PITONI (Giuseppe Ottavio). Italian comp. and writer, B. Rieti, March 18, 1657. S. at Rome under Foggia, etc. Chap.-master at Terre di Rotondo, 1673 ; Cath. of Assisi, 1674 ; S. Marks, Rome, 1677 ; S. Peters, Rome, 1719 ; D. Rome, Feb. 1, 1743.

WORKS.—Masses and other church music. Notizie dei Maestri di Cappella si di Roma che, oltramontani, ossia Notizia di contrappuntisti e compositori di musica degli anni dell' era cristiana 1500 sino al 1700 ; Title of a MS. work on the Chapelmasters of Rome, preserved in the Vatican Library.

Pitoni is noted as the teacher of Durante, Leo, and other masters. Some of his church music is still in use.

PITTMAN (Josiah). English org. and comp., B. London, Sept. 3, 1816. S. under S. S. Wesley, Moscheles, and Schnyder von Wartensee. Org. at Sydenham, 1831 ; Spitalfields, 1835-47. Org. Lincoln's Inn, 1852-64. Accompanist at H. M. Theatre, 1865-68 ; R. I. O., Covent Garden, 1868-80.

WORKS.—The People in the Church, their Rights and Duties in connection with the Poetry and Music of the Book of Common Prayer, Lond., 8vo, 1858. The People in the Cathedral ; a letter to the very Rev. Henry Hart Milman, D.D., London, 8vo, 1859. Songs of Scotland, edited (with Colin Brown). Songs from the Operas, 2 vols. (edited). Royal Edition of Operas, edited with Sir A. Sullivan (Boosey). Callcott's Grammar of Music (edited), London, n. d.

PIXIS (Friedrich Wilhelm). German violinist and comp., B. Mannheim, 1786. S. under his father, Fränzel and Viotti. Vnst. in Chap. of the Prince Palatine, Mannheim, 1804. Prof. at Prague Cons., and leader of theatre orch., 1806. D. Prague, Oct. 20, 1842. Com. variations for violin and orch., etc. His son, THEODOR, B. Prague, April 13, 1831, D. Cologne, Aug. 1, 1856, was a violinist and comp.

PIXIS (Johann Peter). German pianist and comp., B. Mannheim, 1788. Brother of preceding. S. under his father. Resided successively in Munich (1809), and Vienna. Resided in Paris from 1825. D. Baden-Baden, Dec. 20, 1874.

WORKS.—Bibiana, opera ; Die Sprache des Herzens, 1836 ; Symphony for orch., No. 1, op. 5 ; Quartet for Pf., vn., viola, and 'cello, op. 4 ; Theme for Pf. and violin, op. 105. Pf. music, consisting of variations, fantasias, rondos, caprices, etc.

Pixis adopted a young German orphan girl named FRANCILLA GÜRINGER, whom he had educated as a vocalist. She appeared under the name Pixis in Germany, Italy, etc., with much success.

PLACE (Gertrude). English writer, authoress of "A Catechism of Music for the Use of Young Children." Lond., 12mo, 1856.

PLAIDY (Louis or Ludwig). German violinist, teacher, and writer, B. Wermsdorf, Saxony, Nov. 28, 1810. S. under Agthe and Hache. Pf. teacher at Dresden for a time. Prof. of Pf. at Leipzig Cons., on invitation of Mendelssohn, 1843. D. Grimma, March 3, 1874.

WORKS.—Technische Studien für das Pianofortespiel, Eingeführt in Conservatorium der Musik in Leipzig und München. Translated into English, and published in Germany, United States, and Britain, as Technical Studies for the Pf. ; Der Klavierlehrer, translated as the "Pianoforte Teacher's Guide," by F. R. Ritter, and as the "Piano Teacher," by John S. Dwight, both American. The first named translation has been re-published in London.

Plaidy was one of the most successful Pianoforte teachers known to musical history, and his influence on the pupils whose studies he directed must have been great.

PLANCHÉ (James Robinson). English dramatist and herald, B. London, Feb. 27, 1796. Descended from a French family which settled in England in 1685. Wrote plays, etc., for Madame Vestris, early in his career. Rouge Croix Pursuivant of Arms, 1854 ; Somerset Herald, 1866. D. London, May 30, 1880.

WORKS.—Numerous writings on Costume and Heraldry ; Librettos of operas, including Weber's "Oberon," and Bishop's "Maid Marian ;" Farces, etc. ; Lays and Legends of the Rhine, music by Bishop; Contributions to Musical Annuals, etc.

Planché published, in 1872, his "Recollections" (2 vols.), a book containing much interesting matter relating to British musical history.

PLANQUETTE (Robert). French comp., B. Paris, July 31, 1850. S. under Duprato, and in Paris Cons.

WORKS.—Operas and Operettas: Méfie-toi de Pharaon, 1872 ; Le Serment de Mme. Grégoire, 1874 ; Paille d'avoine, 1874 ; Les Cloches de Corneville, Paris, 1877 (London, 1878) ; Le Chevalier Gaston, 1879 ; Les Voltigeurs de la 32 me, 1880 ; Rip Van Winkle, Lond., 1883 (Paris, 1883) ; Nell Gwynne (Farnie), 1884. Refrains du Regiment, 12 military songs ; songs and instrumental music, miscellaneous.

PLANTADE (Charles Henri). French comp., B. Pontoise, Oct. 14, 1764. S. under Duport, Langlé and Hullmandel. Singing master to Queen Hortense.

Prof. in Paris Cons., 1799. Chap.-master to Louis Napoleon, King of Holland. Music director to Queen Hortense. D. Paris, Dec. 18, 1839.

WORKS.—*Operas:* Les deux Sœurs, 1791; Les Souliers mordorés, 1793; Palma, 1798; Zoé, 1800; Bayard à la Ferté, 1811; Le Mari de circonstance, 1813. Masses and motets; Sonatas for Pf. and other instruments; Romances and songs.

PLANTÉ (Francois). French comp. and pianist, B. Orthez, March 2, 1839. S. at Paris under Mme. Saint-Aubert; and in Cons. under Marmontel, Bazin, etc., gaining various prizes while there. Chevalier of Legion of Honour. Planté is best known as a performer of great brilliancy, and by the recitals he has given in Paris in conjunction with other artists.

PLATEL (Nicolas Joseph). French violoncellist and comp., B. Versailles, 1777. S. under L. Duport and Lamare. 'Cellist in orch. of Theatre Feydeau, 1796. Prof. of 'cello in Brussels Cons., 1831. D. Brussels, Aug. 25, 1835.

Comp. concertos, sonatas, caprices, romances, etc. for his instrument.

PLATT (Edward). English comp. and horn-player, B. 1793. D. 1861. Author of an Instruction Book for the Pianoforte, and comp. of songs and Pf. music. "New, Easy, and Correct System of Vocal Music: a Practical Manual of Singing at Sight." Lond., 8vo, 1847.

PLAYFORD (John). English comp. and music-publisher, B. London, 1623 [1613]. Established a music-selling and publishing business, in the Inner Temple, London. Clerk of the Temple Church, 1653. D. London, 1693 [1694].

WORKS.—An Introduction to the Skill of Musick, in two books. To which is added the Art of Descant, by Dr. Thomas Campion, and Annotations thereon by Mr. Chr. Simpson...[? 2nd edit.]. Lond., 8vo, 1655. [An earlier edition [1654] is noted in Grove's "Dictionary of Music," as having been in the possession of Dr. Rimbault, and the only known copy]. 3rd edit., 1660; an unnumbered edit., 1662; 4th edit., with portrait, 1664; unnumbered editions in 1667, 1670; 6th edit., portrait, 1672; 7th edit., with the Order of Performing the Divine Service in Cathedrals and Collegeate Chapels, portrait, 1674; 8th edit., portrait, 1679; 9th edit. (?); 10th edit. (to which is added as a third book in place of Campion's treatise, "A brief Introduction to the Art of Descant, or Composing Music in Parts," ascribed in future editions to Henry Purcell), portrait, 1683; 11th edit., port, 1687; 12th edit., port, 1694; 13th edit., port, 1697; 14th edit., port 1700; 15th edit., port, 1703; 16th edit., port, 1713; 17th edit., port, 1718; 18th edit., port, 1724; 19th edit., port, 1730. Psalms and Hymns in Solemn Musick of four parts on the Common Tunes to the Psalms in Metre...Lond., fo., 1671. The Whole Book of Psalms, with the usual Hymns and Spiritual Songs, etc., composed in three parts, Lond., 8vo (?); other editions, 1697; 6th, 12mo, 1700; 19th edit., 1738; 20th, 1757. A Paraphrase upon the Psalms of David, by George Sandys. Set to new tunes, for private devotion, by Henry Lawes. Revised and corrected, by John Playford...Lond., 8vo, 1676. The Musical Companion in two books. The first book containing catches and rounds for three voyces, the second book containing dialogues, glees, ayres, and songs for two, three, and four voyces, Lond., 4to, 1673. A Booke of New Lessons, for the Cythern and Gittern, Lond., 4to, 1652. Musick's Recreation on the Viol, Lyra-way; being a choice collection of Lessons...etc., Lond., 2nd edit., 1682. In Locke's "Present Practice of Musick vindicated," 1673, is "A Letter from John Playford to Mr. T. Salmon," in which he espouses Locke's cause to the manifest disadvantage of Salmon. *Publications, various*: Hilton's Catch that catch can; or a choice collection of catches, rounds, and canons for 3 and 4 voyces, 1652; Select Musical Ayres and Dialogues, in three books, for one, two, and three voyces...by sundry composers (composed by Wilson, Colman, Lawes, etc.), 1653; another edition, 1659; Choice Ayres, Songs, and Dialogues to be sung to the theorbo...5 books, 1676-84; The English Dancing Master: or Plaine and Easie Rules for the Dancing of Country Dances...Lond., 4to, 1651: 2nd edit., 1657; 3rd edit., 1665, and numerous other editions till 1728; Musick's Delight on the Cithern, 1666; also published works of Lawes; Court Ayres; and most of the important music books of the period.

PLAYFORD (Henry). English publisher, second son of foregoing, B. London, May 5, 1657. Succeeded to his Father's business in 1685, which he carried on for a time in company with Robert Carr, but afterwards alone at the Temple Change, Fleet Street. D. London [1710].

His principal publications consist of the Theater of Music ; or a choice collection of the newest and best songs sung at the Court, etc. The words composed by the most ingenious wits of the age, and set to music by the greatest masters...Lond., fo., 4 books, 1685-87. Banquet of Musick; a collection of the newest and best songs sung at Court...6 books, fo., 1688-92. Pleasant Musical Companion, being a choice collection of catches for three and four voices ; published chiefly for the encouragement of the Musical Societies, which will be speedily set up in all the chief cities and towns in England, 4to, 1701 ; 5th edit., 1709. A Collection of Original Scotch Tunes (full of the Highland Humours) for the Violin: being the first of this kind yet printed: most of them being in the compass of the Flute, Lond., 4to, 1700. He also published Purcell's "Ten Sonatas, in four parts," 4 vols., 1697; Purcell's "Orpheus Britannicus," 1698-1702; Blow's "Amphion Anglicus," 1700, etc. He also published a work which went through a number of editions, viz., "Harmonia Sacra ; or Divine Hymns and Dialogues, with a Thorow-bass, etc.," Lond., fo , 1687-93 ; 3rd edit., with "four excellent hymns of the late Mr. Henry Purcell, never before printed," 1726.

His younger brother JOHN (B. 1665, D. 1686), carried on business of music printer, and reprinted some of his father's works. For some years he was in partnership with the Widow of William Godbid, a well-known London music-printer, who executed much work for John Playford, senior.

PLEYEL (Ignaz Josef), Austrian comp., B. Ruppersthal, near Vienna, June 1, 1757. S. at Vienna under Vanhall and Haydn. Chap.-master to Count Erlödy in 1772. Chap.-master at Strassburg Cath., 1783-93. Married, 1788. Appeared in London as cond. of the Professional Concerts, 1792. Left Strasburg and settled in Paris during the Revolution, 1795. Established a music-selling and publishing firm, and afterwards founded (1807) the Pianoforte-manufacturing firm now known as Pleyel, Wolff & Co. D. near Paris, Nov. 14, 1831.

WORKS.—*Symphonies:* No. 1 and 2, op. 6 ; 3, 4, and 5, op. 12 ; 6, 7, and 8, op. 14 ; 9, op. 20 ; 10, 11, and 12, op. 27 ; 13, 14, 15, 16, op. 29 ; 17, 18, 19, op. 30 ; 20, 21, op. 33 ; 22, op. 38 ; 23, op. 62 ; 24, op. 68 ; 25, op. 75, and others, up to no. 29. Septets, sextets, and quintets, various, for strings, etc. *Quartets* for strings, op. 1, 2, 3, 4, 5, 7. Trios for strings, op. 11, etc. Concertos for vn. and orch., and Pf. and orch. Sonatas for Pf. solo. Duets for Pf. and violin, and for strings. *Vocal Music:* Iphigenia in Aulide, opera ; Lieder, etc.

Pleyel, from being a pupil of Haydn, copied his style so closely, that many of his works are quite plainly mere imitations of that master. Their original merits consist in a certain easy flow, combined with much grace and an agreeable leavening of vigour.

PLEYEL (Camille). Austrian comp. and Pf. manufacturer, son of preceding, B. Strassburg, Dec. 18, 1788. S. under his father and Dussek. Succeeded to his father's business in Paris, in 1821, and carried it on in company with Kalkbrenner, from 1824. Chevalier of Legion of Honour. D. Paris, May 4, 1855.

He comp. quartets and trios for strings, sonatas, fantasias, rondos, and other Pf. music.

PLEYEL (Marie Felicité Denise), *née* MOKE. Belgian pianist, wife of foregoing, B. Paris, Sept. 4, 1811. S. under Moscheles, Kalkbrenner, etc. Performed in various parts of Europe. Appeared in London, 1846. Prof. of Pf. in Brussels Cons., 1848-72. D. near Brussels, March 30, 1875.

PLEYEL WOLFF, & Co. French firm of pianoforte manufacturers, established originally by Ignaz Pleyel in 1808, and with whom his son Camille became associated in 1821. In 1824 C. Pleyel was joined by Kalkbrenner, and was in turn succeeded by M. A. Wolff, a musician who at one time was a Prof. in Paris Cons.

POHL (Carl Ferdinand). German writer, B. Darmstadt, Sept. 6, 1819. S. under Sechter at Vienna. Org. of Protestant church at Gumpendorf, Vienna, 1849-55. Resided in London, 1863-66, searching for materials regarding Mozart and Haydn. Librarian to the Gesellschaft der Musikfreund, Vienna, 1866.

WORKS.—Mozart und Haydn in London, Vienna, 2 vols., 1867; Die Gesellschaft der Musikfreunde und ihr Conservatorium in Wien, 1871; Joseph Haydn, Berlin, 1875 (vol. 1); Some Pf. music, and many contributions to periodical literature, Grove's "Dictionary of Music," etc.

POHL (Richard). German musician and writer, B. Leipzig, Sept. 12, 1826. S. at Göttingen and Leipzig. Prof. in University of Gratz. Joint editor of the "Neue Zeitschrift für Musik." Best known as a supporter of the theories and works of Wagner.

POISE (Jean Alexandre Ferdinand). French comp., B. Nîmes, June 3, 1828. S. Paris Cons. under Adam and Zimmermann.

WORKS.—*Operas, etc.*: Bonsoir, voisin, 1853; Les Charmeurs, 1855; Le Thé de Polichinelle, 1856; Don Pèdre, 1858; Le Jardinier galant, 1861; La Surprise de l'Amour, 1878; Joli Gille, 1884. Pf. and vocal music.

POLE (William, F.R.S.) English writer and musician, B. Birmingham, 1814. Civil Engineer. Mus. Bac., Oxon., 1860. Mus. Doc., Oxon., 1867. Reporter to the Jury on Musical Instruments, International Exhibition, 1862. Examiner for Musical degrees at London University.

WORKS.—Musical Instruments in the Great Industrial Exhibition of 1851, Lond., 1851, 8vo; Diagrams and Tables to Illustrate the Nature and Construction of the Musical Scale and the various Musical Intervals, Lond., 4to, 1868; Story of Mozart's Requiem, Lond., 1879; Philosophy of Music, being the substance of a course of Lectures,...1877, Lond., 1879; The Hundredth Psalm arranged as a motet for 8 voices, etc.

POLKO (Elise), *née* VOGLER. German soprano vocalist and writer, B. Leipzig, Jan. 31, 1831. S. under Mendelssohn and Garcia at Paris.

WORKS.—Erinnerungen an Felix Mendelssohn-Bartholdy, Ein Künstler und Menschenleben, Leipzig, 1868, trans. by Lady Wallace as Reminiscences of Felix Mendelssohn-Bartholdy, Lond., 8vo, 1869; Faustina Hasse [novel], Leipzig, 3 vols., 1870; Nicolo Paganini und die Geigenbauer, Leipzig, 8vo, 1876; Musikalische Mæhrchen, Leipzig, 3 vols., trans. by M. P. Maudslay as Musical Tales, Phantasms, and Sketches, Lond., 2 vols., 1876-77. The "Musical Sketches" was trans. by Fanny Fuller, Philadelphia, 1864.

POLLEDRO (Giovanni Battista). Italian violinist and comp., B. Piova, Piedmont, June 10, 1781. S. under Pugnani. Mem. of Royal band of Turin. Appeared as vnst. successively at Milan, Moscow, S. Petersburg, Warsaw, Berlin, etc. Leader of court band, Dresden, 1814-24. Do. at Turin, 1824. D. Piova, Aug. 15, 1853.

WORKS.—Concertos for violin and orch., op. 6, 7, and 10; Airs with variations for violin and orch., op. 3, 5, 8; Trios for strings, op. 2, 4, 9; Duets and exercises for violin; Mass, miserere, etc.

POLLINI (Francesco). Italian pianist and comp., B. Laybach, Illyria, 1763. S. at Vienna under Mozart and Zingarelli. Prof. of Pf. at Milan Cons. D. Milan, Sept. 17, 1846.

WORKS.—La Casetta nei boschi, opera, 1801; Cantatas; Stabat mater. *Pianoforte Music:* Sonatas, rondos, caprices, variations, scherzos, toccatos, etc.; also a "Metodo per Pianoforte" (Ricordi).

PONCHARD (Louis Antoine Éléonore). French vocalist, B. Paris, Aug. 31, 1787. S. at Cons. under Garat. *Début* in Paris, 1812. Sang in Operas of Auber, Boildieu, Isouard, etc. Chevalier of Honour, 1845. D. Paris, Jan. 6, 1866. His wife, MARIE SOPHIE CALLAULT, B. Paris, May 30, 1792. D. there, Sept. 19, 1873. S. at Paris Cons. under Garat, and appeared in operas of Auber, Carafa, Hérold, and others. CHARLES MARIE AUGUST, son of the foregoing, B. Paris, Nov. 17, 1824, is a tenor singer of much repute, and Prof. at Paris Cons.

PONCHIELLI (Amilcare). Italian comp., B. Paderno, Fasolaro, near Cremona, Sept. 1, 1834. S. Milan Cons. under Cagnoni, etc., 1843-54. Bandmaster at Plaisance and Cremona. Married to Teresina Brambilla, vocalist. D. Milan, Jan. 16, 1886.

WORKS.—*Operas:* I promessi Sposi, Cremona, 1856; La Savojarda, Cremona, 1864; Roderico, re de' Goti, 1867; La Stella del monte, 1867; Il parlatore eterno, 1873; I Lituani, 1874; Gioconda, Milan, 1876 (London, Covent Garden, July, 1883); Il Figliuol prodigo, Milan, 1880. La Maschere, etc. (MS.) *Ballets:* Le due Gemelle, 1873; Clarina, 1873. Cantate a Gaetano Donizetti, 1875. Instrumental music, etc.

PONIATOWSKI (Prince Josef Michel Xaver Johann). Polish comp., B. Rome, Feb. 20, 1816. S. under Ceccherini, and at Florence. Sang as tenor at Florence, etc. Involved in the political affairs of Italy. Plenipotentiary at Paris, of the Grand Duke of Tuscany, 1848-1870. Resided in London from 1870. D. London, July 3, 1873.

WORKS.—*Operas:* Giovanni da Procida, 1838; Don Desiderio, 1839. Ruy Blas, 1842; Bonifazio dei Geremei, 1844; I Lambertazzi, 1845; Malck-Adel, 1846; Esmeralda, 1847; Pierre de Medicis, Paris, 1860; L'Aventurier, do., 1865; La Contessina, do., 1868; Gelmina, London, 1872. *Songs:* Farewell, the breeze blows fair; Flower girl; For a year and a day; Claude Duval; Stag hunt; Yeoman's wedding song; Love's antidote. Les Progrés de la Musique Dramatique, Paris, 8vo, 1859.

PONTE (Lorenzo da). Italian poet, B. Ceneda, Venice, Mar. 10, 1749. D. New York, Aug. 17, 1838. Author of the librettos of "Le Nozze di Figaro," "Il Dissoluto punito ossia il Don Giovanni," and "Cosi fan tutte," the three famous operas of Mozart.

POOLE (Elizabeth). English mezzo-soprano vocalist, B. London, April 5, 1820. *Début* in opera at Drury Lane, 1834. Sang in the United States, 1839. Sang in opera, at concerts, etc., in London, from 1841 to 1870. Married a Mr. Bacon.

Best remembered as a ballad vocalist, and as an actress of much original talent.

POOLE (Maria). See DICKONS (Mrs.)

POPE (Alexander). English poet, B. London, 1688. D. Twickenham, 1744. Wrote Odes: St. Cecilia's Day (" Descend, ye Nine "), set by Jackson, Busby, and Greene; Ode on solitude; Dying Christian to his soul; which with others of his works have been at various times utilized by T. Billington and different composers.

POPPER (David). Bohemian violoncellist and comp., B. Prague, June 18, 1846 [1842]. S. at Prague Cons., and was pupil of Goltermann for 'cello. Chamber musician to Prince Hohenzollern. Travelled concert-giving in Germany, Holland, Switzerland, England, Austria, etc. Was solo 'cellist at the Court Theatre, Vienna, for a time. Married to Sophie Menter, pianist, 1872.

WORKS.—Perles musicales, for 'cello and Pf., op. 3; do. op. 9; Sarabande and Gavotte, 'cello and Pf., op. 10; Drei stücke, 'cello and Pf., op. 11; Nocturne in G, op. 22; Gavotte in D, op. 23; Polonaise, op. 28; Menuetto in D, op. 48; Im Walde, suite for orch., with obbligato for 'cello, op. 50; Spinning song, concert study for 'cello and Pf., op. 56, etc.

One of the most distinguished instrumentalists of the present time. His style of performance is marked by much power of expression and great volume of tone.

PORPORA (Niccolo). Italian comp. and vocal instructor, B. Naples, 19 Aug., 1686. S. under Greco, Mancini, A. Scarlatti, etc. Chap.-master to the Portuguese Ambassador at Naples. Established a famous school for singers. Director of the Cons. of San Onofrio, Naples. Travelled about in Europe. Resided in London, where he wrote operas in opposition to Händel, 1729-36. Director of the Ospedaletto Music School, Venice. Returned to Naples 1759,

and became Chap.-master of the Cath., and director of the Cons. of San Onof
rio. D. Naples, Feb. 1767, in poverty.

WORKS.—*Operas*: Basilio, re di Oriente, 1710; Berenice, 1710; Flavio Anicio
Olibrio, 1711; Eumene, 1721; Issipile, 1723; Adelaide, 1723; Siface, 1726;
Imeneo in Atene, 1726; Meride e Selinunte, 1727; Ezio, 1728; Tamerlano,
1730; Alessandro nelle Indie; Annibale, 1731; Mitridate, 1733; Ferdinando,
London, 1734; Lucio Papirio, 1737; Temistocle, London, 1742; Il Trionfo di
Camillo, 1760; Statira; Ifigenia in Aulide; Didone: and others to number of 40
or more. *Oratorios*: Gedeone; I Martiri di S. Giovanni; Nepomucene; Davide,
London, 1735. Masses, and other church music. Cantatas. Sonatas for harpsi-
chord, and for violin and bass.

The fame of this master is now altogether traditional, and concerns as much his
pupils as himself. As a teacher he was responsible for the excellence of Farinelli,
Caffarelli, and other vocalists of repute.

PORTA (Costanzo). Italian comp., B. Cremona in first half of 16th century.
S. under Willaert. Chap.-master at Padua, Osimo, Ravenna, and at Santa
Casa, Loretto. D. Loretto, 1601.

WORKS.—Five Books of Motets, 1555-85. Missarum, Lib. I., 1578. Liber I.
Introitus Missarum, 1566; 2nd book, 1588. Madrigali a 4 e 5 voci, 1555; 2nd
book, 1573; 3rd book, 1586. Psalmodia Vespertina, 1605, etc.

PORTA (Giovanni). Italian comp., B. Venice, at end of 17th century. Visited
Lond., 1729. Chap.-master to the Elector of Bavaria, 1737. D. Munich, 1740.

Comp. a number of operas mostly produced at Venice. "Numidor," an opera,
was produced at London under direction of The Royal Academy of Music, April 2,
1720.

PORTER (R.). English writer, author of a small tract entitled "Rudiments of
Music, abridged for the use of Choirs," 8vo, n. d.

PORTER (Samuel). English org. and comp., B. Norwich, 1733. S. under M.
Greene. Org. Canterbury Cath., 1757-1803. D. Canterbury, Dec. 11, 1810.

He comp. "Four Anthems and Two Psalm Tunes"; "Cathedral Music in
Score," edited by Rev. W. J. Porter, fo., n. d. His Service in D has been reprinted by Novello & Co.

PORTER (Thomas). English writer, author of "How to choose a Violin,"
Lond. [1879].

PORTER (Walter). English comp., B. about end of 17th century. Gent. of
Chap. Royal, 1616. Master of Choristers, Westminster Abbey, 1639. D.
Nov. 1659.

WORKS.—Madrigals and Ayres of two, three, foure, and five voyces...1632.
Aires and Madrigals for two, three, four, and five voices, with a thorough-bass for
the Organ or Theorbo-lute, the Italian way, 1639. Motetts of two Voices-treble,
tenor and bass, with continued bass or score, to be performed on an organ, harp-
sychor, lute, or bass viol, 3 parts, Lond., 1657. Psalms of Mr. George Sandys
composed into Music for two Voyces, with a Thorough-bass for the Organ [1670].

PORTOGALLO (Marco Antonio), properly SIMAO. Portuguese comp., B.
Lisbon, March 24, 1762. S. under Borselli. Resided in Italy, 1787-90.
Chap.-master to King of Portugal, 1790. Accompanied Portuguese Count to
Brazil, and resided in Rio, 1807-1815. D. Lisbon, Feb. 7, 1830.

WORKS.—*Operas:* L'Eroe cinese, 1788; Il Molinaro, 1790; La Donna di genio
volubile, 1791; I due Gobbi, 1793; Demofoonte, 1794; Fernando in Messico,
Rome, 1797 (written for Mrs. Billington); Semiramide, 1802. Church music, etc.

POSTANS (Mary). See SHAW (Mrs. Alfred).

POTT (F. August). German violinist and comp., B. Nordheim, Hanover, Nov.
7, 1806. S. under Spohr at Cassel. Appeared as violinist successively at
Cassel (1824), Austria, Paris, London (1838), Belgium, etc. Chap.-master to
the Duke of Oldenburg till 1861. D. Grätz, Nov. 1883. Comp. music for
violin, songs, etc.

POTTER (John). English writer and comp. of last century, author of "Observations on the Present State of Music and Musicians, with General Rules for Studying Music," Lond., 8vo, 1762. He also comp. for Vauxhall Gardens, and published a collection entitled "New Songs, sung at the Vauxhall Gardens, 1771-1772, fo., Lond., n.d.

POTTER (Philip Cipriani Hambly). English pianist and comp., B. London, 1792. S. under his father, Callcott, Attwood, Crotch, and Woelfl. *Début* as pianist at Philharmonic Soc. Concert, 1816. S. at Vienna under Förster, and while there came in contact with Beethoven, 1817-18. Prof. of Pf. at R. A. M., Lond., 1822. Principal of R. A. M. in succession to Crotch, 1832-59. D. London, Sept. 26, 1871.

WORKS.—Symphonies for orch., in A, G minor, etc., nine in all (MS.); Four Overtures for orch.; Three Concertos for Pf. and orch.; Sextet for Pf., flute, violin, viola, 'cello, and D.-bass, op. 11; Three trios for Pf., violin, and 'cello, or clarinet and bassoon, op. 12; Sonata concertante for Pf. and horn, op. 13; Duet for two Pf., op. 7; Variations for Pf., op. 1; Sonatas for Pf., in D, op. 2; E min., op. 3; and C. Toccattas in G and B flat, for Pf. Rondeaus in C and F for Pf. Introduction and Rondo for Pf., 4 hands, op. 8. Pezzi di bravura, Pf. String Quartets. Etudes dans tous les tons majeurs et mineurs, à l'usage du Conservatoire de Musique à Londres, op. 19.

Potter was a musician of much influence in his time, and it is due to his good management that the Royal Academy of Music of London is now on such a substantial basis. His works possess many merits, and though nearly defunct, in the sense of their being now unused, deserve to be kindly remembered. As one of the few Englishmen who have attained distinction as writers of instrumental music, his works should have much wider currency than is at present accorded them. Birmingham and London concert-givers are, indeed, the only ones who condescend to perform the works of an Englishman who at one time commanded respect from the most cultured opinion on the Continent.

POUGIN (Francois Auguste Arthur). French writer, B. Chateauroux, Indre, Aug. 6, 1834. S. at Paris Cons. under Reber, etc. Violinist in various Parisian theatres. First violin in Musard's orch. Attached to staff of many journals as "Ménestrel," "L'Art Musical," "Soir," "Journal Officiel," etc.

WORKS.—Meyerbeer, notes biographiques, Paris, 1864; F. Halévy, écrivain, 1865; William-Vincent Wallace, étude biographique et critique, Paris, 8vo, 1866; Almanach illustré, chronologique, historique, critique et anecdotique de la Musique, Paris, 3 vols., 1866-8; De la Littérature Musicale en France, 1867; Leon Kreutzer, 8vo, 1868; Bellini, sa vie, ses œuvres, 1868; Albert Grisar, étude artistique, 1870; Rossini, notes, impressions, souvenirs, commentaires, Paris, 1871; Auber—ses commencements, les origines de sa carrière, 1873; Notice sur Rode, 1874; Boildieu: sa vie, ses œuvres, son caractere, sa correspondance, 1875; Rameau, 1876; Adolphe Adam, 1876; Biographie Universelle des Musiciens...par F. J. Fétis, Supplement et Complément [edited by Pougin], Paris, 2 vols, 1878-80.

The work last named contains much valuable information in regard to contemporary musical celebrities, and continues with great exactness the work of Fétis.

POVEY (Miss). English soprano vocalist, B. Birmingham, 1804. *Début* June 3, 1817. S. under T. Cooke and Bartleman. Sang at Drury Lane, 1819, English Opera House, etc. D. [?]

POWELL (Thomas). English violinist and comp., B. London, 1776. S. harp, violin, and Pf. Mem. of Royal Soc. of Musicians. Married, 1811. Resided in Dublin as teacher. Performed a violin concerto in Haymarket Theatre, London. Comp. 15 Concertos for violin and orch; Three duets for violin and 'cello, op. 1; Three duets for two 'cellos, op. 2; Capriccio for 'cello, op. 24; Introduction and Fugue for organ; Sonatas, etc., for Pf.; Overtures for orch., etc.

POWELL (Walter). English tenor vocalist, B. Oxford, 1697. Chor. and Clerk to Magdalen Coll., Oxford. Sang in Handel's oratorios. D. Oxford, Nov. 6, 1744.

PRADHER (Louis Barthelemi), or PRADÈRE. French comp., violinist, and pianist, B. Paris, Dec. 18, 1781. S. under Mme. de Montgeroult, and at Cons. under Gobert and Berton. Married a daughter of Philidor. Prof. of Pf., Paris Cons. Accompanist to Chap.-Royal, Paris. Married second time to Mlle. F. More, 1820. Retired from Cons., 1827, and settled at Toulouse as director of Cons. there. D. Gray, Oct., 1843.

WORKS.—*Operas:* Le Voisinage, 1800; Le chevalier d' industrie, 1804; Jenny la bouquetière, 1823. Concertos and sonatas for Pf. with other instruments. Sonatas for Pf. solo, etc.

His second wife, FÉLICITÉ MORE, B. Carcassone, Aude, Jan. 6, 1800, D. Gray, Nov. 12, 1876, was an actress and vocalist of great celebrity.

PRAEGER (Heinrich Aloys). Dutch comp., violinist, and guitarist, B. Amsterdam, Dec. 23, 1783.

WORKS.—Quintet for viola, 2 clarinets, flute, and bassoon, op. 12; Quintet for strings, op. 28; Quartets for strings, opp. 13, 17, 18, 19; Trios and duets for strings. Pf. music. Mehrstimmige Gesänge, op. 30, etc.

PRAEGER (Ferdinand Christian Wilhelm). Dutch violinist, pianist, and comp. Son of above. B. Leipzig, Jan. 22, 1815. Teacher at the Hague. Settled in London, 1834. Has performed at important concerts in London, Paris, Leipzig, etc. English correspondent of "Neue Zeitschrift für Musik."

WORKS.—Manfred, prelude symphonique, 1881. Leben und Lieben, symphonic poem, 1885. Sonata in G, Pf. and 'cello, Birmingham, 1883. *Pf. Music:* Danse rustique; Mazurka élégante, op. 67; Styrienne brillante, op. 68; Rêverie-nocturne, op. 69; Moment joyeux, op. 72; etc. A selection of 48 short works has been published in 2 vols. at Leipzig, entitled the "Praeger Album." 12 Pf. sonatas, 20 string quartets, a Pf. trio, and other works in MS. History of Music, by Emil Naumann, translated, 1883-6. Elementary and Practical School for the Violin, 3 parts. Lond. (Cocks), n. d. Orchestral works, various.

PRÆTORIUS (Hieronymus), or SCHULTZ. German org. and comp., B. Hamburg, 1560. Son of the org. of Church of St. James. S. under his father, and at Cologne. Cantor of Erfurt, 1580. Succeeded his father as org. of Church of St. James, Hamburg, 1582. D. Hamburg, 1629.

WORKS.—Cantiones Sacræ de præcipius festis totius anni 5, 6, 7, et 8 vocum. 1599. Magnificat octo vocum über die acht Kirchen-Tœne, 1602. Six Masses, 1616. Cantionum Sacrarum, op. 5, 1618. Ein Kindelein so lœbelich, carol for 8 voices, 1613; etc.

PRÆTORIUS (Michel), or SCHULTZ. German comp. and writer, B. Creutzberg, Thuringia, Feb. 15, 1571. Chap.-master and org. to the Duke of Brunswick, and secretary to his Consort Elizabeth. D. Wolfenbüttel, Feb. 15, 1621.

WORKS.—Syntagma musicum ex veterum et recentiorum ecclesiasticorum autorum lectione...Wittenberg, 4to, 1615 [general title-page]. The separate parts were issued in 1615, 1618, and the Appendix to part 2, consisting of plates in 1620. Sacrarum Motetarum primitiæ, 4, 5, usque ad 6 vocum, 1600. III. Polyhymnia panegyrica.. 15 vols., fo., 1602. Musarum Sioniar motectæ et psalmi Latini... Nuremberg, 8 vols., 1607. Hymnodia Sionia; continens hymnos sacros 24 anniversarios selectos...Wolfenbüttel, 6 vols., 4to, 1611. Megalynodia Sionia; continens canticum B. Mariæ Virginis magnificat, 5, 6, et 8 voc. Wolfenbüttel, 6 vols., 4to, 1611.

PRAT (Daniel). English divine and writer, was rector of Harrixham, Kent, and Chaplain to George III. Wrote "An Ode to Mr. Handel, on his playing on the Organ," Lond., fo., 1722; reprinted as "An Ode on the late celebrated Handel on his playing on the Organ," Cambridge, 4to, 1791.

PRATO. See JOSQUIN.

PRATT (John). English org. and comp., B. Cambridge, 1772 [1779]. Son of Jonas Pratt, music-seller there. Chor. in choir of King's Coll. S. under Dr. Randall, whom he succeeded as org. of King's Coll., 1799. Org. of Cambridge University, 1800. Org. S. Peter's Coll., 1813. D. Cambridge, March 9, 1855.

WORKS.—Collection of Anthems in Score, selected from the works of Handel, Haydn, Mozart, Clari, Leo, and Carissimi, with Organ or Pianoforte Accompaniment, 2 vols., fo., n. d. Selection of Ancient and Modern Psalm Tunes, arranged for Two Trebles, or Tenors, and a Bass, for the use of Parish Churches, fo., n. d. Psalmodia Cantabrigiensis...4to, 1817, with an Appendix of later date. Four Double Chants, and the Responses to the Commandments, as performed at the King's College, Cambridge, 8vo, n. d.

PRATT (Silas Gamaliel). American comp. and pianist, B. Addison, Vt., Aug. 4, 1846. S. at Chicago, and at Berlin under Wüerst, Bendel, Kullak, and Kiel. Afterwards S. under Liszt at Weimar. Played in London, 1885.

WORKS.—Zenobia, opera, 1882. Symphonies for orch., No. 1, op. 16 (1871); 2nd, Prodigal Son, op. 33 (1876); Symphonic sketch, Magdalena's Lament. *Pianoforte:* Shadow thoughts; Mazurka caprice; Mazurka dolour; Polonaises; Reveries; Fantasie-caprice, op. 24; Fantasie-impromptu, op. 28; Continuous Scales and Exercises; Mazurka-andante; Nocturne; Antique minuet; Rocking minuet; other works in MS. Songs and part-songs. Grand march, Homage to Chicago, for orch., 1873. Soul Longings, String quintet. Centennial overture, chorus and orch., 1876. Serenade for strings. Elegy to General Grant, for chorus and orch., etc.

PRATTEN (Robert Sidney). English flute-player and comp., B. Bristol, Jan. 23, 1824. Performed when a boy at concerts in Bath, Bristol, etc. First flute in orch. of Theatre Royal, Dublin; Do. at Royal Italian Opera, London, 1846; Sacred Harmonic Society; Philharmonic Society, etc. S. for a time in Germany. D. Ramsgate, Feb. 10, 1868.

WORKS.—Fantasias, arrangements, studies, solos, etc. for flute, in combination with other instruments. Complete Series of Exercises for the Siccama Flute. Complete Series of Scales and Exercises, carefully fingered for Pratten's Perfected Flute, n. d. Flute Tutors (one published by Boosey & Co., and another by Edwin Ashdown).

His wife, MADAM SIDNEY PRATTEN, is a well-known guitar-player, and writer for that instrument. Solos for the Guitar, a series of about 100 original and selected pieces; Numerous Divertimentos on original and selected themes; Guitar School, being complete Instructions for Modern Guitar Playing in the Common Key; Learning the Guitar Simplified... Also a book of Instructions for the Gigliera (wood and straw instrument).

PREINDL (Joseph). German org. and comp., B. Marbach-on-the-Danube, 1758. S. under Albrechtsberger. Org. and chap.-master of St. Stephen's, Vienna, 1809-23. D. Vienna, Oct. 23, 1823.

WORKS.—Op. 1 and 2. Concertos for Pf.; op. 3, 4 and 6. Themes for Pf.; op. 5 and 13. Fantasias for Pf. Gesanglehre (vocal method), op. 33. Wiener Tonschule (treatise on harmony), 1827. Masses, graduels, and other church music. Organ music, etc.

PRELLEUR (Pierre, or Peter). French musician and writing master. Settled in London in first part of 18th century. Writing master in Spitalfields. Org., church of St. Alban, 1728. Accompanist and comp. Goodman's Fields Theatre, till 1737. Org. of Christ Church, Spitalfields, 1735. D. probably about middle of 18th century.

WORKS.—Ballets and pantomime music. The Songs and Duets in Baucis and Philemon, as they are now perform'd at the New Wells in Goodman's Fields; to which is prefix'd, the Overture in Score, Lond., fo. [c. 1737]. The Modern Musick-master, or the Universal Musician; containing an introduction to singing, with directions for the flute, hautboy, violin, harpsichord, etc., with a brief history of Musick, and a Musical Dictionary, Lond., 8vo, 1731. Introduction to Singing, or plain rules whereby any person may in a short time learn to sing any song that is set to musick, Lond., 8vo, n. d. Divine Melody, in twenty-four choice hymns, set to music, in two parts...Lond., 8vo, 1758. This last work was written in conjunction with Moze, an organist. Another work comp. conjointly is The Harmonious

Companion, or the Psalm-singer's Magazine...in four parts, with Benjamin Smith, Lond., 1732, 8vo.

PRENDERGAST (Arthur Hugh Dalrymple). English comp. and cond., B. London, June 28, 1833. S. under James Turle. Cond. of Lombard Amateur Musical Soc. Late secretary of the Bach Choir.

WORKS.—Cantate Domino and Deus Misereatur, in F; Festival Te Deum, 1882; *Anthems*: O Lord our Governour; O God! Thou hast cast us out; Shew me thy ways. *Part Songs, etc., for male and mixed voices*: A Grace; Hark! how the cheerful birds (prize madrigal, 1880); My love is now awake; Sunshine; When weeping friends are parting; O, mistress mine; Phillis dyes her tresses black; Song of the silent land; Take, oh take those lips away; Sweet western wind; When for the world's repose; Wines, the; Although soft sleep; A garden is my lady's face; Light, wandering, murmuring wind; Imbuta. *Songs*: A birdie's life; A shady nook; I do confess thou'rt smooth and fair; Sleep! wake! live!

PRENTICE (Thomas Ridley). English pianist and comp., B. Paslow Hall, Ongar, Essex, July 6, 1842. S. at R. A. M. Gained silver medal, 1863, and Potter Exhibition. Associate R. A. M. Started the "Monthly Popular Concerts" at Brixton, 1869. Org. of Christ Church, Lee. Started Kensington "Twopenny Concerts," 1880. Prof. of Pf. Guildhall School of Music, 1880. Prof. of Pf. and harmony, Blackheath Cons. of Music. Principal of Beckenham and Wimbledon Schools of Music.

WORKS.—Cantata for ladies' voices—Linda. *Anthems*: Break forth into joy; I love the Lord. *Part Songs, etc.*: Christmas; Ye little birds; The day is done; O the summer night; The mermaid's invitation. *Songs*: The God of love my shepherd is; Love floweth on for ever; Evensong; Echoes; Broken links. *Pianoforte Music*: Gavotte in E flat; Gavotte fantastique; Elegy; Reverie, By the sea; Children's fancies; Harvest home; Maypole; Sunday musings, etc. The Musician, a Guide for Pianoforte Students: Helps towards the better understanding and enjoyment of Beautiful Music, Lond., 8vo, 1883, in 6 grades or parts. Edited cantatas by Carissimi.

PRESCOTT (Oliveria Louisa). English comp. and writer, B. London, Sept. 3, 1842. S. under Lindsay Sloper, and for 7 or 8 years at the R. A. M. under Prof. Macfarren, Jewson, Folkes, and Ralph. Associate R. A. M. Teacher of harmony at the Ch. of England High School for Girls, Upper Baker Street, London. Conducts classes for harmony, etc., in the University of Cambridge correspondence system for ladies.

WORKS.—Two symphonies, several overtures, and some shorter pieces for orch.; Concerted music for stringed instruments; Psalm XIII. for soprano solo, chorus, and orch.; Psalm CXXVI. for voices alone (sung in S. Paul's Cath.); Lord Ullin's Daughter (Campbell), for chorus, with orch.; The righteous live for evermore; Our conversation is in prayer (anthems). *Part-songs*: Ballad of Young John; Douglas raid; The Huntsman. Songs. Form, or Design, in Music: Part I. Instrumental; Part 2. Vocal. Lond., 12mo, 1882 (reprinted from the *Musical World*).

The work last named has been received with great favour by the Press and teachers, on account of its clearness of exposition, and interesting treatment of a difficult subject.

PRESSER (Theodore). American journalist and teacher, B. Pittsburg, Pa., 1848. Educated at Mount Union Coll., Ohio. S. music at Boston and at Leipzig Cons. Editor of *The Etude*, a journal for teachers and students of the pianoforte. Organizer of the Music Teacher's National Assoc.; Virginia State Assoc., etc.

Presser has translated and enlarged Urbach's Pianoforte Method; and has published Pf. studies and teaching pieces. He is widely known as a teacher and writer.

PRÉVOST (Eugene Prosper). French comp., B. Paris, Aug. 23, 1809. S. Paris Cons. under Lesueur, etc. Gained 2nd prize for comp., 1829; gained Grand Prix de Rome, 1831. Travelled for a time in Italy. Married to Éléonore Colon. Cond. at Havre Theatre. Settled in New Orleans, 1838, as cond. of the opera, and teacher. Cond. in Paris for a time about 1863. D. New Orleans, Aug. 30, 1872.

WORKS.—*Operas*: L'Hôtel des Princes, 1831; Le Grenadier de Wagram, 1831; Cosimo, 1834; Le bon Garçon, 1837; Blanche et René; Esmeralda; L' Illustre Gaspard, 1863. Bianca Capella, cantata which gained the Prix de Rome, 1831. Masses. Arrangements for orch., etc.

PREVOST (Jean Marie Michel Hippolyte). French musician and stenographer, B. Toulouse, 1808. D. Paris, Feb. 17, 1873. Author of "Stenographie musicale, ou art de suivre l' exécution musicale en écrivant," Paris, 1833, 8vo. Translated into English under title of "A System of Musical Stenography," Lond., 8vo, 1849.

PRIDHAM (John). English comp. and arranger for the Pf., B. Popsham, Devon, Oct. 1, 1818. Teacher in Taunton.

WORKS.—*Pianoforte*: Sabbath Recreations, 13 numbers of sacred pieces arranged; Spring Flowers, 6 original pieces; Early Blossoms, do.; Hills and Lakes of Scotland, 12 numbers; Hills and Lakes of Ireland and England, 6 nos. each. Songs, vocal duets, etc. New Method for the Piano, Lond., Brewer, n.d.

PRILIPP (Camille). See SCHUBERT (Camille).

PRING (Jacob Cubitt). English org. and comp., B. Lewisham, 1771. Org. of St. Botolph, Aldgate, London. Mus. Bac., Oxon., 1797. D. 1799.

WORKS.—Eight Glees, Catches, etc., Lond. [c. 1795]. Eight Anthems as performed in St. Paul's Cathedral, fo., n. d. Glees, and catches in Warren's collection.

PRING (Joseph). English org. and comp., brother of above, B. Kensington, Jan. 15, 1776. Org. of Bangor Cath., 1793. Mus. Bac. and Doc., Oxon., 1808. D. Bangor, Feb. 13, 1842.

WORKS.—Twenty Anthems in Score, for 1, 2, 3, 4, and 5 voices, fo.[[1805]. Magnificats, and other church music.

PRING (Isaac). English org. and comp., brother of above, B. Kensington, 1777. Assistant to Dr. Philip Hayes, at New Coll., Oxford, and his successor in 1797. Mus. Bac., Oxon., 1799. D. Oxford, Oct. 18, 1799. Comp. chants, anthems, etc.

PRINGLE (John). Scottish musician, resided in Edinburgh at end of last, and beginning of present century. Published "A Collection of Reels, Strathspeys, and Jigs, with a Bass for the Violoncello or Pianoforte." Edin., n. d.

PRINTZ (Wolfgang Caspar), surnamed WALDTHURN. German comp. and writer, B. Waldthurn, Upper Palatinate, Oct. 10, 1641. Educated at University of Altorff. S. under Stoeckel and Merz. Org. and court musician in service of Count Promnitz, Dresden, 1682; with whom he afterwards travelled in Germany, Austria, etc. Cantor of Triebel, and afterwards at Sorau in Upper Saxony. D. Sorau, Oct. 13, 1717.

WORKS.—Anweisung ur ... ... Dresden, 1689. Compositions for the church.

PROCH (Heinrich). Austrian comp. and violinist, B. Laybach [Vienna], July 22, 1809. S. under Benesch. Educated for the Law at Vienna University. Mem. of Imperial Chap., Vienna, 1834. Leader in orch. of Josephstadt Theatre, Vienna, 1837; do. Imperial Opera House, 1840-70. Chevalier of the Order of Franz-Joseph of Austria, etc. D. Vienna, Dec. 18, 1878.

WORKS.—*Operas*: Ring und Maske, 1844; Die Blutrache, 1847; Der Gefährlich Sprung, 1848. Overtures for orch. Quartets, trio for Pf., vn., and 'cello., op. 27, and other chamber music. Masses, graduels, offertoires, and other church music. Lieder for voice, with accomp., for Pf., 'cello and horn, opp. 1, 3, 4, 5. 6, 11, 14, 17, 18, 19, 21, 22, 28, 29, 31, 34, 38, 46, etc., of which the following are the titles of some of the best known single songs:—Das Alpenhorn; Morgengruss; Wanderlied; Der jüngling am Bache; Liebesend; An die sterne; Lebewohl; Das Erkennen Das; Blümlein; Das blinde Mädchen.

PROSKE (Carl). German ecclesiastic and collector, B. Gröbing, Upper Silesia Feb. 11, 1794. Ordained priest, 1826. Canon and Chap.-master of Ratisbon Cath., 1830. Travelling in Italy collecting and transcribing ancient pieces of MS. ecclesiastical music. Member of Order of S. Michel, and of Episcopal Council of Ratisbon. D. Ratisbon, Dec. 20, 1861.

Best known as the editor and collector of the fine work entitled, "Musica Divina, sive Thesaurus concentuum Selectissimorum omni cultui divino totius anni juxta ritum Sanctae Ecclesiæ catholicæ inservientium...," Ratisbon, 4 vols., 4to, 1853-59. This is a collection of scarce and previously unpublished church music, chiefly by early composers, and is a most valuable, accurate, and altogether monumental compilation.

PROUDMAN (Joseph). English writer and cond., B. London, Nov. 10, 1833. Identified with the Tonic Sol-fa movement, of which he is a prominent leader. He has conducted numerous large festivals, and has done much to foster the spread of popular vocal music. His works include "Musical Lectures and Sketches," Lond., 1869, and "Musical Jottings," Lond., 1872. Also numerous articles on musical education and lectures on kindred subjects.

PROUT (Ebenezer). English comp., writer, and cond., B. Oundle, Northamptonshire, March 1, 1835. Graduated B.A., London University, 1854. S. Pf. under C. K. Salaman. Org. of Union Chap., Islington, 1861-73. Gained first prizes offered by the Soc. of British Musicians, for his op. 1 and 2, 1862-65. Editor of *Monthly Musical Record*, 1871-74. Musical Critic of the *Academy*, 1874-79; do. of the *Athenæum*, 1879. Prof. of Harmony and comp. at National Training School for Music, 1876. Cond. of the Borough of Hackney Choral Assoc., 1876. Prof. at R. A. M., 1879. Prof. at Guildhall School of Music, 1884.

WORKS.—Op. 1. Quartet for strings in E flat, 1862; op. 2. Pf. quartet in C, 1865; op. 3. Pf. quintet in G, 1860; op. 4. Sonata for Org., in D, 1866; op. 5. Concerto for org. and orch., in E min., 1870; op. 6. Concertante duet for Pf. and harmonium, in A; op. 7. Magnificat for solo voices, chorus, and orch., in C, 1873; op. 8. Evening service for solo voices, chorus, and org., in E flat, 1875; op. 9. Evening service in F, for chorus and org. (written for the London Church Choir Assoc.), 1876; op. 10. Hail to the chief, chorus, with orch. (written for the reopening of the Alexandra Palace), 1877; op. 11. Happy is the man that findeth wisdom, anthem, for chorus and org.; op. 12. Hereward, cantata, written for the Borough of Hackney Choral Assoc., 1878; op. 13. Morning and communion service, in F, 1879; op. 14. Minuet and trio, in B flat, for orch., 1877; op. 15. 2nd string quartet, in B flat, 1881; op. 16. Alfred, cantata, London, 1881; op. 17. Sonata in A, for Pf. and flute, 1882; op. 18. Quartet in F, for Pf. and strings, 1881; op. 19. Evening Service in D, 1883; op. 20. "Freedom," chorus, with orch., 1885; op. 21. Queen Aimée, cantata for female voices, with Pf., 1885; op. 22. Third symphony, for Pf., 1884; op. 23. The Hundredth Psalm, for soprano solo, chorus, and orch., 1886. *Unpublished*: Romance, for viola, with Pf. accomp., 1870; First symphony, in C major, 1873; Second symphony, in G minor, 1876; Suite in D, for orch., 1878; Overture to "Twelfth Night," 1880; Sonata in D, for Pf. and clarinet, 1882; Second organ concerto, in E flat, 1883; Love and Taxation, comic opera, in 3 acts, 1883; Fourth symphony, in D major, 1886. Organ Arrangements, 2 vols., in 44 numbers, selected from the great masters. Instrumentation (Music Primer), London, 8vo, 1876; also a German trans. issued in Leipzig. Songs and some pieces of various kinds for Pf.

PRUCKNER (Dionys). German pianist, comp., and teacher, B. 1830. S. at Weimar, with Liszt. Resided in New York for a short time after 1874. Prof. of Pf. in Stuttgart Cons.

CAROLINE PRUCKNER, the soprano vocalist, was B. Vienna, 1832.

PRUDENT (Émile Beunie). French pianist and comp., B. Angoulême, Feb. 3, 1817. S. Paris Cons. under Le Couppey. Gained prizes for Pf. and harmony. Travelled in Europe, concert-giving, and appeared in London as pianist, 1848, and 1852-3. Resided chiefly in Paris as teacher. D. Paris, May 14, 1863.

WORKS.—Concerto-Symphonie, for Pf. and orch., op. 67; Trio for Pf., vn., and 'cello. *Miscellaneous Pf. Works*: Rondo, op. 3; Andante, op. 9; L'Hirondelle, étude, op. 11; La ronde de nuit, étude, op. 12; Barcarolle, op. 21; Etude de concert in F flat, op. 28; Six pieces, op. 30; Concerto—symphonie, op. 34; Le Réveil des Fées, op. 14; Les Naïades, caprice-étude, op. 45; Scherzo, op. 47; La Prairie, 2nd concerto, op. 48; 6 Etudes de Salon, op. 60; Solitude, andante, op. 65. Numerous transcriptions and arrangements.

PRUME (Francois Hubert). Belgian violinist and comp., B. Stavelot, June 3, 1816. S. at Liége Cons. and Paris Cons., under Habeneck. Prof. of violin in Liége Cons. Performed in Germany, Russia, Sweden, Belgium, etc. D. Stevelot, July 14, 1849.

WORKS.—La Mélancolie, for violin and orch., op. 2; Concerto héroique, for vn. and orch., op. 11; Caprice, op. 12; La Danse des Sorcières, scherzo, vn. and Pf., op. 13. Studies for violin, etc.

PRUMIER (Antoine). French harpist and comp., B. Paris, July 2, 1794. S. Cons. under Catel, etc. Harpist of the Theatre Italien and Opera-Comique. Prof. of Harp. at Paris Cons., 1845. Chevalier of Legion of Honour, 1845. D. Paris, Jan. 20, 1868. Comp. fantasias, rondos, transcriptions, etc., for harp. His son, ANGE CONRAD, B. Paris, Jan. 5, 1820. S. under his father, and at Paris Cons., where he gained several prizes. He succeeded Labarre as Prof. of Harp in Paris Cons., in 1870. His comps. consist mainly of harp music, with some pieces for the church. D. Paris, April 3, 1884.

PUCCITA (Vincenzo). Italian comp., B. Rome, 1778. S. at Cons. of La Pietà, Naples, under Sala. Director of Italian Opera, London, 1809. Travelled as accompanist to Catalani. Accompanist at the Paris Opera. D. Milan, Dec. 20, 1861.

WORKS.—*Operas*: L' Amor Platonico, 1800; Le Nozze senza sposa, 1800; I due Prigionieri, 1801; I Villeggiaturi bizarri, London, 1809; La Vestale, Lond., 1809; Le tre Sultane, Lond., 1812; L' Orgoglio avvilito, Paris, 1815; Adolfo e Chiara, Milan, 1833. Songs, and other vocal music.

PUGNANI (Gaetano). Italian violinist and comp., B. Turin, 1727. S. under Somis. Violinist to King of Sardinia, 1752. Appeared in Paris, 1754. Resided in London till 1770, where for a time he led the opera band. Established school at Turin, and taught Viotti, Bruni, Olivieri, Polledro, etc. D. Turin, 1803.

WORKS.—*Operas*: Tamas Koulikan, 1772; Adone e Venere, 1784; Nanetta e Lubino, 1784; Achille in Sciro, 1785; Demofoonte, 1788. Ballets and cantatas. Sonatas for violin solo, op. 1, 3, 6, 11. Duets for 2 violins, op. 2, 13. Quartets or 2 vns., alto and bass, op. 7 (London, Preston). Six Symphonies for 2 vns., viola, bass, 2 oboes, and two horns, op. 4; Do., op. 8; Quintets for 2 vns., 2 flutes, and bass. Three books of trios, etc.

One of the most famous of classical violinists, and one who did much to establish the modern school, through the agency of his pupils.

PULLEN (H. W.). English writer, author of "Our Choral Services," Lond., 1865; and "The Real Work of a Cathedral," Lond., 1869.

PUPPO (Giuseppe). Italian violinist and comp., B. Lucca, June 12, 1749. S. at Cons. of S. Onofrio, Naples. S. violin under Tartini. Appeared successively in Paris (1775), Spain, Portugal, Britain, etc. Returned to Paris, 1784, as leader at the Théâtre Feydeau, and as cond. at Théâtre Français. Wandered about in Italy, and was finally reduced to a state of complete destitution from which he was rescued by Prof. Edward Taylor, the English musician, who had him removed to an hospital in Naples, in which he D. April 19, 1827.

He comp. three duets for 2 violins, studies for violin, and fantasies for Pf., but is best known as a peripatetic fiddler who could say smart things: one of his best being that in which he aptly terms Boccherini "the wife of Haydn."

PURCELL (Daniel). English org. and comp., B. London, 1660. Youngest son of Henry Purcell the elder. Org. of Magdalen Coll., Oxford, 1688-95.

Settled in London, 1695. Comp. for various theatres. Org. of S. Andrew's Ch., Holborn, 1713-17. D. London, 1718.

WORKS.—*Music to Dramas*: Love's Last Shift (Cibber), 1696; Indian Queen, 1696; Brutus of Alba, or Augusta's Triumph, 1697; Cynthia and Endymion (D'Urfey), 1697; Phaeton, or, the Fatal Divorce, 1698; The Island Princess (Motteaux), with Clark and Leveridge, 1699; The Grove, or Love's Paradise, 1700; The Unhappy Penitent, 1701; The Inconstant (Farquhar), 1702; The Judgment of Paris, a Pastoral (Congreve). [This masque gained the third prize in competition with Weldon, Eccles, etc.], 1700. Odes, numerous; including several for "St. Cecilia's Day," by Addison and others; Songs in contemporary collections; The Psalms, set full for the organ or harpsichord, as they are plaid in churches and chappels in the maner given out; as also with their interludes of great variety, Lond., ob. fo., n.d.; Instrumental music, church music, etc.

PURCELL (Edward). English org., youngest son of Henry Purcell, the younger, B. London, 1689. Org. of St. Clement, Eastcheap, London. Org. S. Margaret's, Westminster, 1726. D. London, 1740.

PURCELL (Henry), the Elder. English musician, father of the celebrated Henry Purcell of musical history, B. in first half of 17th century. Gent. of Chap.-Royal, 1660. Master of the Choristers in Westminster Abbey. Member of Royal Band of Music, 1663. D. London, Aug. 11, 1664. Comp. three-part song in Playford's Musical Companion, 1667.

PURCELL (Henry). English org. and comp., B. Westminster, London, 1658. Second son of the preceding. S. in Chap. Royal under Cooke and Humphrey, 1664. S. under Blow. Copyist in Westminster Abbey, 1676-78. Org., Westminster Abbey, 1680. Org., Chap. Royal, 1682. Comp. in Ordinary to the King, 1683. D. Westminster, London, Nov. 21, 1695. Buried in Westminster Abbey.

WORKS.—*Dramatic Music*: Epsom Wells (Shadwell), 1676; Aurenge-Zebe (Dryden), 1676; The Libertine (Shadwell), 1676; Abdelazor (Behn), 1677; Timon of Athens (Shakspere), 1678; The Virtuous Wife (D'Urfey), 1680; Theodosius (Lee), 1680; Dido and Æneas (Tate), 1680 [Published by the Musical Antiquarian Soc., 1840]; Circe, 1685; Tyrannic Love (Dryden), 1686; A Fool's Preferment (D'Urfey), 1688; The Tempest (Shakspere), 1690; Dioclesian, 1690; Massacre of Paris (Lee), 1690; Amphitryon, 1690; Distressed Innocence (Settle), 1691; King Arthur (Dryden), 1691 [published by the Musical Antiquarian Soc., 1843]; The Gordian Knot Untyed, 1691; Sir Anthony Low (Southerne), 1691; The Fairy Queen (Shakspere's Midsummer Night's Dream), 1692; The Wife's Excuse (Southerne), 1692; The Indian Queen (Dryden), 1692; The Indian Emperour (Dryden), 1692; Œdipus, 1692; Cleomenes, 1692; The Marriage-hater Match'd (D'Urfey), 1692; The Old Bachelor (Congreve), 1693; The Richmond Heiress (D'Urfey), 1693; The Maid's Last Prayer (Southerne), 1693; Henry the Second (Bancroft), 1693; Don Quixote (D'Urfey), 1694-95; The Married Beau (Crowne), 1694; The Double Dealer (Congreve), 1694; The Fatal Marriage (Southerne), 1694; Love Triumphant (Dryden), 1694; The Canterbury Guests (Ravenscroft), 1695; The Mock Marriage (Scott), 1695; The Rival Sisters (Gould), 1695; Oroonoko (Southerne), 1695; The Knight of Malta (Beaumont and Fletcher), 1695; Bonduca (Beaumont and Fletcher), 1695. *Odes and large Vocal Works*: Elegy on Death of Matthew Locke, 1677; A Welcome Song for His Royal Highness' Return from Scotland, 1680; A Song to Welcome His Majesty home from Windsor, 1680; Swifter, Isis, swifter flow (ode), 1681; Ode for the King on his Return from Newmarket, 1682; Three Odes for St. Cecilia's Day, 1683; From Hardy Climes and Dangerous Toils of War, ode on Marriage of Prince George of Denmark with Princess Anne, 1683; Welcome to all the Pleasures, ode, published 1684; Why are all the Muses mute? ode for James I.; Ye tuneful muses, ode, 1686; Sound the trumpet, beat the drum, ode, 1687; Celestial Music, 1689; The Yorkshire Feast Song, D'Urfey, 1689 [Reprinted by the Purcell Soc., edited by W. H. Cummings, 1878]; Arise, my Muse, ode for the Queen's Birthday, 1689; Sound the Trumpet, ode, 1689; Welcome, glorious morn, Birthday ode, 1691; Love's Goddess sure was blind, ode, 1692; Hail! great Cecilia, ode, 1692; Celebrate this Festival, 1693; Come, come, ye Sons of Art, ode, 1694; Who can from joy refrain, ode, 1695. *Church Music*: Purcell's

Sacred Music, edited by Vincent Novello, Lond., fo., 6 vols. [1829-32], contains most of the master's church music, with portrait and biography, including the Te Deum and Jubilate in D (1694). Other collections in which his church music will be found are Boyce's; Tudway's; Smith's Harmonica Sacra; Page's Harmonia Sacra; and in nearly every other important general selection. The names of the anthems in current use in our churches and cathedrals will be found in Novello's catalogue of sacred music. *Instrumental Music:* Three sonatas, for two violins, violoncello, and basso-continuo, Lond., 4 vols., 1683. Lessons for the Harpsichord or Spinnet, Lond., 1696. Ten Sonatas, in four parts, 1st and 2nd violins, bassus and organ, Lond., 4 vols., fo., 1697. Collection of Ayres compos'd for the Theatre, and upon other Occasions, Lond., 1697. Orpheus Britannicus: a Collection of the Choicest Songs, for 1, 2, and 3 voices, with such Symphonies for Violins or Flutes as were by him designed for any of them, and a Thorough-bass to each Song figured for the Organ, Harpsichord, or Theorbo-Lute..book I., Lond., fo., 1698, with portrait engraved by White. Book II., 1702; Second edition (enlarged), 2 vols., 1706-1711; Third edition, 1721. The Catch Club, or Merry Companion. By Purcell, Blow, etc., 2 books, 4to, n. d. "The Art of Descant," contributed to the 10th ed. of Playford's "Introduction to the Skill of Musick," 1683. *Selections from Purcell's works:* The Beauties of Purcell: a Selection of the Favourite Songs, Duets, Trios and Choruses from his different works, arranged with Pf. accomp. by Dr. John Clarke, 2 vols., fo., n. d. Beauties of Purcell...ed. by Joseph Corfe, 2 vols., fo., n. d. The Words of Henry Purcell's Vocal Music, 8vo, n. d. (privately printed). A Selection of his Harpsichord pieces has been edited by Herr Ernst Pauer (Augener, London).

The greatest and most original English composer of his period, and one of the most influential musicians of British nativity. His works are full of fresh, vigorous and original ideas, and his whole style is powerful and masterly. To him is due that broad and dignified style of music which is always called English, and which numbers among its exponents such men as Händel, Arne, Boyce, Attwood, Bishop, and Macfarren, not to mention many minor luminaries who have been more directly under Purcell's influence. Purcell was not only the greatest composer of his country, but also of his period, and there can be no doubt that all of his foreign contemporaries are quite overshadowed, if not in science, certainly in genius, by the great Englishman. The stilted arias of Lulli and Scarlatti bear no comparison with the crisp dignity and real power with which Purcell almost invariably invests his works. His dramatic and church compositions form a body of music unmatched in variety and originality till we reach the period of Handel, when the development of musical art, and the introduction of new effects and orchestral colouring by Mozart and Haydn, created a wide difference in styles, and renders comparison out of the question. His music for the church is much more suitable for the purpose than much of the pretentious productions of recent times, British and Foreign, which require a ponderous array of instrumental accessories to bring out their dramatic meaning. In the simplicity, purity, and vigorous handling of his musical works, Purcell has never been excelled by any composer of any school or period. His music is in constant use in our churches, while many efforts have been made recently to bring forward some of his dramatic and secular works with considerable success.

PURCELL (Thomas). English comp., uncle of preceding, B. in first half of 17th century. Gent. of Chap.-royal, 1660. Lay-vicar and copyist, Westminster Abbey, 1661. Comp. in ordinary to the King, with Humphrey, 1662; and master of the royal band of music (also with Humphrey), 1672. D. London, July 31, 1682. Comp. of chants, some of which are now in common use.

PURDAY (Charles Henry). English comp. and writer, B. Folkestone, Jan. 11, 1799. Lecturer on musical topics in London and the English provinces; and at one time a vocalist of some repute. Chiefly celebrated as a reformer of the laws relating to musical copyright. D. London, April 23, 1885.

WORKS.—The Sacred Musical Offering, Lond., 1833. Copyright, a Sketch of its Rise and Progress...Lond., 8vo, 1877. Writer and composer of a considerable number of songs; joint editor with John Thomas of a large volume of Welsh airs; Various volumes of church tunes; Trios for female voices; Two volumes of children's songs, etc.

PURKIS (John). English org. and comp., B. London, 1781. D. London, 1849. Performer on the Apollonicon, and org. of some repute. Comp. a few works of no great merit for the organ.

PYE (Kellow John). English comp., B. Exeter, Feb. 9, 1812. S. at R. A. M. under C. Potter and Dr. Crotch till 1829. Resided in Exeter till about 1840. Mus. Bac., Oxon., 1842. Afterwards resided in London, where he connected himself with various musical institutions. Composer of many anthems, glees, and songs.

PYNE (James Kendrick). English org. and comp., B. London, Aug. 21, 1810. S. at R. A. M. Org. of St. Mark's, Pentonville, London, 1829-39. Org. and teacher at Bath. Comp. of church services, anthems, glees, songs, and Pf. music. Son of JAMES KENDRICK PYNE (1785-1857), a once celebrated tenor vocalist.

PYNE (James Kendrick). English org., lecturer, and comp., B. Bath, Feb. 5, 1852. S. under S. S. Wesley. Org. of Chichester Cath., 1874; St. Mark's, Philadelphia, Pa.. 1875; and Manchester Cath., 1877. Org. of Town Hall, Manchester, where his weekly recitals have been extremely popular and successful. He has lectured frequently before the Royal Manchester Institution, and other learned bodies, on musical matters, and has given much attention to the history of ancient instruments; his collection of clavichords, spinnets, harpsichords, etc., being a very celebrated one. Comp. of an orch. festival "Communion Service"; a Morning Service in D; Evening Service in F; a Mass; Te deum and jubilate in D. Pf. pieces, songs, etc.

PYNE (Louisa Fanny), or BODDA. English soprano vocalist, B. 1832. S. under Sir George Smart. First appeared in public, with her sister Susan (Mrs. Galton), 1842. Sang in Paris, 1847. Appeared at Boulogne in "La Somnambula," 1849. Début on London stage as "Zerlina" in Don Juan, Oct., 1849. Sang afterwards at the principal theatres and concerts in London. Appeared in America, with her sister and Wm. Harrison, 1854-56. Established with Wm. Harrison, the "Harrison-Pyne" English opera company, which performed with much success in Britain, and produced a number of famous English operas, 1856-62. Married Frank Bodda, a barytone vocalist, 1868, and retired from the stage. Teacher of singing in London. Her voice was a clear soprano of great compass, and possessed of much expressive power. She excelled in such works as Wallace's "Maritana" and "Lurline"; Balfe's "Bohemian Girl" and "Rose of Castile"; and it is due to her no less than to Harrison, that English opera flourished so successfully under their management. Her father, GEORGE PYNE (1790-1877), was an alto singer of some fame in his day.

Q.

QUANTZ or QUANZ (Johann Joachim). German flute-player, B. Oberscheden, Hanover, Jan. 30, 1697. S. flute under Buffardin. Travelled in Europe as flute-player, and in 1726 visited Paris, and in 1727 appeared in London. Flute-player and teacher to Frederick the Great at Berlin, and afterwards comp. to the court. D. Potsdam, July 12, 1773. Author of "Versuch einer Anweisung die Flöte traversière zu spielen..." Berlin, 1752|; and comp. of sonatas, solos, duets, and other music for flute.

QUARENGHI (Guglielmo). Italian violoncellist and comp., B. Casalmaggiore, Oct. 22, 1826. S. Milan Cons. Music-director of the Duomo, Milan. Comp. music for 'cello, etc. D. Milan. Feb. 3, 1882.

QUEISSER (Carl Traugott). German trombone player, B. Döben, near Leipzig, Jan. 11, 1800. Trombone player at the Gewandhaus and other concerts in Leipzig. D. Leipzig, June 12, 1846.

QUIDANT (Joseph). French pianist and comp., B. Lyons, Dec. 7, 1815. S. Paris Cons. Comp. of studies, valses, nocturnes, fantasias, and caprices for Pf.

QUINAULT (Jean Baptiste Maurice). French dramatist, B. Paris, 1635. D. Nov. 26, 1688. Author of the librettos of many of Lulli's operas.

R.

RAAFF (Anton). German tenor vocalist, B. Gelsdorf, 1714. S. at Jesuits' Coll. at Cologne, for the church. S. music at Cologne, and Munich, and at Bologna, under Bernacchi. Appeared successively in Italy, Germany, Spain, Portugal. Sang in Paris, 1778. Taught music school at Munich from 1779. D. Munich, May 28, 1797.

RADECKE (Louise). German soprano vocalist, B. Hanover, June 27, 1847. S. Cologne Cons., under Hiller and Marchesi. *Début* at Cologne in Der Freischutz, 1867. Appeared with success in Wagner's operas. Married Baron Brümmer and retired, 1876.

RADECKE (Robert). German org., pianist, and comp., B. Dittmannsdorf, Silesia, Oct. 31, 1830. S. under his father, an org. S. at Breslau, and under E. Köhler, Lüstner, and Brosig. S. Leipzig Cons., 1848. Second director of the Leipzig Sing-Akademie, 1852. Cond. of Opera, Berlin, 1863.

WORKS.—Op. 1. Four Stücke for Pf. and violin; L'Amazone, study for Pf., op. 4.; King John, overture for orch.; Der Liebe Huldigung, cantata; Die Mönkguter, opera; Psalms, Lieder, etc.

RADIGER (Anton). German comp., B. Chatham, 1749. D. 1817. Comp. a number of now obsolete psalm tunes, such as "Praise," "Compassion," "Denton's Green," etc. Also a few sonatas and other pieces for Pf., and "Four Setts of New Psalm and Hymn Tunes in 3 and 4 Parts," Lond., fo. n.d.

RADZIWILL (Prince Anton Heinrich.) Russian amateur comp., B. Wilna, June 13, 1775. D. Berlin, April 7, 1833.

WORKS.—Faust, compositions on the drama of Goethe, published 1835; first performed as a whole, 1833; Lieder and part-songs; instrumental music, etc.

RAFF (Anton). See RAAFF (Anton).

RAFF (Joseph Joachim). Swiss comp., B. Lachen, Lake of Zürich, May 27, 1822. Educated at the Jesuit School of Schwyz. Originally self-educated in music, but patronised at various periods by Mendelssohn, Liszt, and Bülow. Married to Doris Genast, 1859. Director of the Cons. at Frankfort, 1877. D. Frankfort-on-Main, June 25, 1882.

WORKS.—*Operas:* König Alfred, Weimar, 1850; Dame Kobold, op. 154, Weimar, 1870; Samson (MS.). *Symphonies:* An das Vaterland, op. 96, 1863; Second in C, op. 140; Im Walde, op. 153, 1869; Fourth in G minor, op. 167, 1871; Lenore, op. 177. 1872; Gelebt, gestrebt, gelitten, gestritten, gestorben, umworben, op. 189, 1876; Alpensinfonie, op. 201, 1877; Frühlingsklänge, op. 205, 1878; Im Sommerzeit, op. 208, 1880; Zur Herbstzeit, op. 213, 1882. *Orchestral works, minor:* Suite, op. 101; Jubilee overture, op. 103; Festival overture, op. 117; Concert overture, in F, op. 123; Ein'feste Burg, overture, op. 127; 2nd Suite, op. 194; Suite in B flat, op. 204. *Concertos:* Violin and orch., in B minor, op. 161; Pf. and orch., in C min., op. 185; Violoncello and orch., in D minor, op. 193; Violin and orch. (No. 2), op. 206. *Concerted Instrumental Music:* Octet for strings, op. 176; Sestet for strings, op. 178; Quintet, Pf., violins, viola and 'cello, op. 107; Quartets for strings, No. 1, op. 77; No. 2 in A, op. 90; No. 3 in E min., op. 136; No. 4 in A min., op. 137; No. 5 in G, op. 138; 3 Quartets, Nos. 6-8, op. 192; Quartets for Pf., vn., viola, and 'cello, op. 202; Trios for Pf., violin, and 'cello, No. 1, op. 102; No. 2, op. 112; No. 3, op.

155; No. 4, op. 158. Duets, numerous. *Pianoforte works:* Sonatas, Pf. and vn., No. 1, op. 73; No. 2, op. 78; No. 3, op. 128; No. 4, op. 129; No. 5, op. 145; Pf. and cello, op. 183; Serenade, op. 1; Scherzo, op. 3; Romances, op. 8; Sonata and fugue, op. 14; Fantasias (various); Morceaux de Salon; Frühlingsboten, op. 55; Salon-étuden from Wagner, op. 62; Capriccio, op. 64; Suites, opp. 69, 71, 75, 82, 91, 162, 163; Ungarische Rhapsodie, op. 113; Festival overture, Pf. duet, op. 124; Studies, marches, barcarolles, humoreskes, variations, etc. *Vocal Music:* Wachet auf (by Geibel), male chorus and orch., op. 80; Deutschlands Auferstehung, cantata, op. 100; Psalm 130, 8 voices and orch., op. 141; Morgenleid, op. 186a; Lieder, opp. 47, 48, 49, 50, 51, 52, 53, 97, 122; Sanges-Frühling, op. 98. Part-Songs, etc. The World's End, The Judgment, The New World. Oratorio, posthumous, 1883.

Raff was one of the most successful and prolific composers of recent times, and though not an original genius of the highest order, yet one who had considerable influence in promulgating and enforcing the artistic creed of the more modern development in instrumental music. He is well known in Britain by his chambermusic, which is quite as popular as that of any living continental composer, but his larger and more ambitious works have been less often heard. Some of his symphonic works have been frequently performed in various towns in Britain, and among them perhaps "Lenore" has been most popular. Excerpts from many of the others have been also given; while in London and other cities they have been performed in their entirety with considerable frequency.

Some of Raff's minor works are of the highest value, and give evidence of his possession of great culture and artistic feeling. His songs and concerted pieces for various instruments show his originality to fine advantage, and it must be conceded that his talent for melodious writing was great and refined. He possessed a wealth of beautiful and fanciful melody which he was lavish in bestowing on most of his works, but which is most appreciably felt in his shorter pieces; as those for Pf. and violin, the trios and quartets, but above all, the songs.

RAHLES (Ferdinand). German comp. and writer, B. Düren, 1812. D. London, March 19, 1878. He composed a number of part-songs and lieder, and published "Practical Hints and Observations relative to the Introduction by Government of Singing in Public Schools," Lond., n.d.

RAIMONDI (Pietro). Italian comp., B. Rome, Dec. 20, 1786. S. in Cons. of the Pietà de' Turchini, Naples. Director of the Royal Theatres, Naples, 1824-32. Prof. of comp. at Palermo Cons., 1832. Chap.-master of S. Peter's, Rome, 1850. D. Rome, Oct. 30, 1853.

WORKS.—*Operas:* Le Bizarrie d'Amore, 1807; Ero e Leandro; Il Fanatico deluso; La Lavandaja [the foregoing produced between 1807 and 1814]; Andromacca; Il Dissoluto punito [1815-19]; Le Finte Amazzoni; La Donna Colonella; Il Disertore; Argia; I Minatori Scozzesi; La Gioja pubblica [produced 1820-30]; Il Ventaglio, 1831; L' Orfana Russa; Il Trionfo dell' Amore; Rafaello d' Urbino; Il Fausto arrivo; Il Caffetiere [1831-40]. *Oratorios:* Ruth; Giuditta; Mosè al Sinai. Potiphar; Pharaoh; Jacob [1848], produced simultaneously as Joseph, Aug., 1852. Ballets. Masses, requiems, psalms fugues, etc. The whole Book of Psalms for 4, 5, 6, 7, and 8 voices; numerous minor works.

Raimondi is chiefly remarkable for his great contrapuntal skill, which enabled him to combine and have performed at the same time three separate and independent oratorios. This undertaking is unexampled in the annals of music. Many of his other works are written on the same principle, and he composed two operas, one comic and the other serious, capable of being performed together as one work, or separately if desired.

RAINFORTH (Elizabeth). English soprano vocalist, B. Nov. 23, 1814. S. under T. Cooke, and George Perry. Appeared in Arne's "Artaxerxes," at S. James's Theatre, 1836. S. under Crivelli. Sang at Philharmonic Concerts, Concert of Ancient Music, Provincial Concerts, etc. Appeared as the original Arline in Balfe's "Bohemian Girl," 1843. Sang in dramatic pieces in Dublin, etc. Resided in Edinburgh, 1852-56. Retired, and lived as a teacher at Old Windsor, from about 1858. After 1871, resided at Bristol. D. Redland, Bristol, Sept. 22, 1877.

RAMANN (Bruno). German comp., B. Erfurt [1830]. S. under Brendel, Riedel, and Hauptmann. Comp. and teacher in Dresden.
WORKS.—10 kleine Tondichtungen, for Pf., op. 2; Lob der Frauen, Poem by Walther von der Vogelweide, for male voices and Pf., op. 6; Ein Tanz-Poëm, for Pf. duet, op. 22; Three Lieder for mixed choir, op. 23; Schwert und Minne, voice and Pf., op. 25; Album fürstlicher Minnesänger und Lieder, op. 39, 40, 41, 42, 47; Miniatures for Pf., op. 53.

RAMANN (Lina). German writer, cousin of above, B. Mainstockheim, near Kitzingen, Bavaria, June 24, 1833. S. under F. Brendel's wife at Leipzig. Opened Institute for training of music mistresses at Glückstadt, Holstein, 1858-65. Do. at Nürnberg, 1865. Visited London, 1882. Writer of various works on musical education, but best known by her "Franz Liszt" (Leipzig, 1880), a work now in progress.

RAMEAU (Jean Philippe). French comp., org., and theorist, B. Dijon, Sept. 25, 1683. Son of Jean Rameau, org. of Dijon Cath. Educated at the Jesuit Coll. of Dijon. Sent to Italy by his father, 1701, which, however, he soon left to travel as first violinist to a theatrical company, and in this capacity visited the whole South of France. Resided in Paris for a time as org. of the Jesuit Convent in the Rue St. Jacques, and of the Chap. of the Pères de la Merci. Competed for place of org. of St. Paul's, Paris, 1717, but was unsuccessful. Org. of St. Etienne, Lille. Org. of Cath. of Clermont, Auvergne, which post was resigned in his favour by his brother Claude. Went to Paris and brought out his "Harmonie," 1722. Org. of Ch. of S. Croix de la Bretonnerie, Paris. Married Marie Louise Mangot, 1726. Cond. of the Opéra-Comique. Paris. Chamber Musician to the King of France, 1745. D. Paris, Sept. 12, 1764.
WORKS.—*Operas, Ballets, etc.*: Samson (Voltaire), 1732; Hippolyte et Aricie, 1733; Les Indes galantes, 1735; Castor et Pollux, 1737; Les Fêtes d' Hébée, ou les Talents lyriques, 1739; Dardanus, 1739; Les Fêtes de Polymnie, 1745; La Princesse de Navarre, 1745; Le Temple de la Gloire, 1745; Les Fêtes de l'Hymen et de l'Amour, 1748; Zaïs, 1748; Pygmalion, 1748; Naïs, 1749; Platée, 1749; Zoroastre, 1749; Acante et Cephise, 1751; La Guirlande, 1751; Daphné et Eglé, 1753; Lysis et Délie, 1753; La Naissance d'Osiris, 1754; Anacreon, 1754; Zephire, 1754; Le Retour d' Astrée, 1757; Les surprises de l'Amour, 1757; Les Sybarites, 1759; Les Paladins, 1760. *Theoretical Works:* Traité de l'harmonie réduite à ses principes naturels,...Paris, 4to, 1722, trans. into English as Treatise on Harmony, in which the Principles of Accompaniment are fully explained and illustrated by a variety of examples...Lond., n.d. [By Griffith Jones, circa 1820]; Third book trans. as A Treatise of Music, containing the Principles of Composition, Lond., 4to, 1752; Nouveau Système de Musique Théorique,...Paris, 4to, 1726; Dissertation sur les différentes méthodes d'accompagnement pour le Clavecin ou pour l'orgue,...Paris, 1732; Génération Harmonique,...Paris, 8vo, 1737; Demonstration du principe de l'harmonie,...Paris, 8vo, 1750; Nouvelles réflexions sur la Demonstration du principe de l'harmonie, Paris, 8vo, 1752; Erreurs sur la Musique dans l' Encyclopédie, Paris, 1755; Pièces de Clavécin, Paris, 3 books, 1706, 1721, 1726, etc.
Rameau was one of the greatest among the theorists and composers of the eighteenth century. His industry was remarkable, and the success of some of his works pronounced. His theoretical writings and discoveries laid the foundation of a new system of harmony, and did much to elucidate and ventilate what was erroneous or bad in the older practice. His operas were regarded as dangerous innovations, and his views on musical practice as impracticable.

RAMM (Friedrich). German oboeist, B. Mannheim, Nov. 18, 1744. S. under Stark, etc. Member of Elector of Bavaria's private band under Cannabich. Appeared in Munich, Frankfort, Vienna, Paris, London (1784), Berlin, Italy, etc. D. [?]

RAMONDON or RAYMONDON (Louis). French singer and comp., appeared in various Italian operas in London about the beginning of the 18th century. Comp. "A New Book of Songs, the Words and Musick by Mr. Raymondon," Lond., fo. [1710]. He also wrote songs in the "Merry Musician," 1716, and in other collections of the period.

RAMSAY (Allan). Scottish poet, B. Leadhills village, Lanarkshire, Oct. 15, 1686. D. Edinburgh, Jan. 7, 1758. Author of the well-known pastoral, "The Gentle Shepherd," of which an edition with the music and overtures to the songs, etc., was published. Bremner issued in Edinburgh about 1749, "Thirty Scots Songs for a Voice and Harpsichord, the Music taken from the most genuine sets extant, the words from Allan Ramsay." Another work is "Musick for Allan Ramsay's Collection of Scots Songs, set by Alex. Stuart." Edin., n. d., selected from the first volume of the Tea Table Miscellany. Ramsay did much to preserve old Scots melodies by wedding them to his verses in such collections as the "Tea Table Miscellany," 1724-27, "The Evergreen," 1724, etc. Among such may be named "The yellow hair'd Laddie," "Farewell to Lochaber," "Bessie Bell and Mary Gray," "Lass o' Patie's Mill," "Wae's my heart that we should sunder," "Through the wood, Laddie," "Mary Scott," "The Highland Laddie," "My mither's aye glowrin' owre me," "The Widow," "This is no mine ain House," "The Ewe Bughts," etc.

RAMSAY (D. C.). Scottish musician, author of "Four Diagrams illustrative of Intervals, Scales, and Chords." Glasgow, fo., 1860.

RAMSAY (Edward Bannerman Burnett). Scottish Episcopal divine and writer, B. Aberdeen, Jan. 31, 1793. Dean of Diocese of Edinburgh, 1846. D. Edinburgh, Dec. 27, 1872. Author of "Two Lectures on the Genius of Handel, and the Distinctive Character of his Sacred Compositions," Edin., 8vo, 1862. "Proposals for providing a Peal of Bells for Edinburgh," 1863, etc.

RANDALL (John). English org. and comp., B. 1715. Chorister in Chap.-Royal under B. Gates. Mus. Bac., Cantab., 1744. Org. of King's Coll., Cambridge, 1745. Prof. of Music Cambridge Univ., in succession to M. Greene, 1755. Mus. Doc., Cantab., 1756. D. Cambridge, Mar. 18, 1799. Comp. of odes, anthems, psalms, and chants, and a "Collection of Tunes, some of which are new, others by permission of the authors." Cambridge, 12mo, 1794.

RANDALL (Richard). English tenor vocalist, B. Sept. 1, 1736. S. under B. Gates. Sang principally in works of Handel. D. April 15, 1828.

RANDEGGER (Alberto). Austrian comp., teacher, and writer, B. Trieste, April 13, 1832. S. under Tivoli, Lafont, and L. Ricci. Musical director in theatres of various towns. Settled in London about 1854. Prof. of Singing at R. A. M., London, 1868. Has cond. various musical festivals. Successful teacher of singing in London.
WORKS.—*Operas*: Bianca Capello, Brescia, 1854; The Rival Beauties, Leeds, 1863. Medea, scena, 1869; Saffo, scena, 1875. Fridolin, cantata, Birmingham Festival, 1873. 150th Psalm, for solo, chorus, and orch., Boston, 1872. Funeral Anthem on death of the Prince Consort. Sacred songs for little singers, illustrated, Lond., 8vo, n. d. *Songs*: A life for old Olympians; Ben è ridicolo (Joyous life); Beneath the blue transparent sky; Bird of the springtime; Bonnie Nelly; Come hither, shepherd swain; Cupid; Freshening breeze; Friendship; Fair northern flower; Good-night; Goldbeater; The hammer; Innamorata d'una stella; King of Thule; King Solomon; La luna è bella; Live long day; May morning; Mill wheel; Marinella; My pipe; My true love hath my heart; Peacefully slumbering; Round the bottle; She loves me best of all; Spinning wheel; Starlight; Violet and the maiden; There's rest in heaven; Till we meet; Una; Well a day; Where wilt thou meet me? Singing (Novello's Music Primers), Lond., 4to, 1878.

RANDHARTINGER (Benedict). Austrian comp., B. Ruprechtshofen, July 27, 1802. S. under Salieri. Was a tenor singer for a time. Court Chap.-master at Vienna, 1862. Comp. a large number of works, including an opera, symphonies, masses and motets, part-songs and songs. Otherwise celebrated as a friend of Schubert.

RANDLES (Elizabeth). English pianist, B. Wrexham, Aug. 1, 1800. Known as the "little Cambrian prodigy." Gave very early indications of a talent for music, which was encouraged by her father [1760-1820], a blind harper and org. in Wrexham. S. under John Parry. Appeared in London and the English provinces. Teacher for a time in Liverpool. D. 1829.

RANSFORD (Edwin). English barytone vocalist and comp., B. Bourton-on-the-Water, Gloucestershire, Mar. 13, 1805. Sang in London theatres in various operas and musical dramas. Wrote various musical entertainments, and engaged in musical publishing. D. London, July 11, 1876.
He wrote a number of ballads, and was also a lyric author of popular renown.

RAPPOLDI (Eduard). Austrian violinist and comp., B. Vienna, Feb. 21, 1839. S. under Doleschall, Mittag and Jansa. Appeared in London, 1850. S. at Vienna Cons., under Patronage of the Countess Banffy, with Hellmesberger, 1851-54. S. also under Böhm, Sechter, and Hiller. Travelled as violinist from 1854. Leader of German opera, Rotterdam, 1861-66. Leader in theatres of Lübeck (1866), Stettin (1867), and Prague (1869). Teacher at the Hochschule, Berlin, with Joachim, 1870-77. Married Laura Kahrer, 1874. Leader at the Dresden Opera, and Prof. in Cons. there, 1876. Comp. instrumental music, consisting of symphonies, sonatas, quartets, solos, and a number of songs. His wife, LAURA RAPPOLDI-KAHRER, B. Wistelbach, near Vienna, 1853. S. under Dachs and Dessoff, at Vienna Cons., 1866-69; gained first prize for Pf. playing, 1867. Appeared as pianist in Prague, Dresden, Berlin, and Weimar. S. under Liszt at Weimar. Appeared afterwards at Warsaw, St. Petersburg, Moscow, etc., and with her husband in London, 1881. Pianist to the Court of Saxony at Dresden.

RASOUMOWSKY (Prince Andreas Kyrillovitsch). Russian nobleman and amateur violinlist, B. Lemeschi, in the Ukraine, Oct. 22, 1752. Russian Ambassador at Vienna. D. Sept. 23, 1836. Celebrated as the person to whom Beethoven dedicated his op. 59, three quartets in F, E minor, and C, and jointly with Prince Lobkowitz, his symphonies No. 5 and 6 (op. 67-68).

RASTRELLI (Joseph). German violinist and comp., B. Dresden, April 13, 1799. S. violin under Poland, and harmony under Feildler and Mattei. Vnst. in Chap. of King of Saxony, 1820. Second cond. at theatre, and cond. at Chap.-Royal, Dresden, 1829-30. D. Dresden, Nov. 14, 1842.
WORKS.—*Operas:* La Distruzione di Gerusalemme, 1816; La Schiava Circassa, 1820; Salvator Rosa, Dresden, 1832; Berthe de Bretagne, 1835. Church music. Violin and Pf. music.

RATCLIFFE (James). English comp., B. 1751. Lay-vicar in Durham Cath. D. 1818. Comp. of church music, including anthems, psalms, and chants.

RAUZZINI (Venanzio). Italian comp. and vocal instructor, B. Rome, 1747. S. singing in Rome. *Début* in opera at Rome, 1765. Sang afterwards at Vienna and Munich, 1767-74. Appeared in London, 1774, in an opera by Corri, and remained there till 1787. Settled at Bath as teacher and concert-giver, 1787. D. Bath, April 8, 1810.
WORKS.—*Operas:* Piramo e Tisbe, 1769; L'Ali d' Amore, 1770; L' Eroe cinese, 1770; Astarto, 1772; La Regina di Golconda, London, 1775; Armida, 1778; Creusa in Delfo, 1782; La Vestale, 1787. Requiem Mass, 1801. Quartets for strings, op. 2, 5 and 7. Sonatas for Pf., op. 8, etc. *Songs:* Adieu (the); Ah, how the hours on golden plumes; Avon side; Blithe were the hours; By all the softness of the hour; Cease to blame my melancholy; Cupids; Fair was the morning of my love; False shepherd; Go, gentle zephyr; Haymakers; If in your village; Jervis and Duncan; Maid of the Severn; Reconciliation; Rose (the); Shepherds, I have lost my love; 'Tis midnight hour; etc. Twenty-four Solfeggi, or Exercises for the Voice, Lond., fo., n. d.
Rauzzini was in his day the fashionable vocal teacher, and reigned like a little king at Bath. Among his pupils were Mara, Billington, Selina Storace, Miss Poole, Sarah Mountain, Braham, and Incledon, besides many others of less fame.

RAVENSCROFT (John). English violinist and comp., was one of the Waits of the Tower Hamlets and a violinist in Goodman's Fields Theatre. D. 1745. He published a collection of hornpipes, also sonatas for stringed instruments. —*Hawkins.*

RAVENSCROFT (Thomas). English comp., B. [1582]. Chorister of S. Paul's Cath., London, under Edward Pearce. Mus. Bac., Cantab., 1607. D. London, 1635.

WORKS.—Pammelia, Musicke's Miscellanie, or Mixed varietie of pleasant Roundelayes and delightful Catches of 3, 4, 5, 6, 7, 7, 8, 9, 10 Parts in one. Lond., 1609. 2nd edit., 1618. Deuteromelia : or the Second Part of Musick's Melodie, or melodious Musicke of pleasant Roundelais, K. H. mirth, or Freemen's Songs, and such delightfull Catches. Lond., 4to, 1609. Melismata ; musical Phansies, fitting the Court, Citie, and Country humours, to three, four, and five voyces. Lond., 4to, 1611. The Whole Booke of Psalmes, with the Hymnes Evangelicall and Songs Spiritual, Composed into 4 Parts by sundry authors, to such severall Tunes as have been and are usually sang in England, Scotland, Wales, Germany, Italy, France, and the Netherlands. Lond., 12mo, 1621. 2nd edit., 1633. Selections from the Works of Thomas Ravenscroft, a musical composer in the time of King James I. (Roxburghe Club). Lond., 4to, n. d. A Briefe Discourse of the True but neglected use of Charact'ring the Degrees by their Perfection, Imperfection, and Diminution in Mensurable Musicke, against the common practise and custome of these times. Lond., 1614.

Ravenscroft is best known by his "Booke of Psalmes," a work of much importance, containing contributions by Tallis, Dowland, Morley, Farnaby, Tomkins, Pearson, Parsons, Hooper, Kirbye, Allison, Farmer, Bennet, Milton, Cranford, Harrison, and the editor. It has been drawn upon by nearly every succeeding compiler of psalmody, and is now a somewhat rare work. It is worthy of notice that his "Pammelia" is the earliest collection of rounds and canons published in Britain.

RAVINA (Jean Henri). French comp. and pianist, B. Bordeaux, May 20, 1818. S. at Paris Cons., 1831, and gained several prizes. Prof. of Pf. at Paris Cons., 1835-37. Performed in Russia, Spain, France, etc. Chevalier of Legion of Honour, 1861.

WORKS.—*Pianoforte* : 12 Etudes de style, op. 14 ; Le mouvement perpétuel, op. 18 ; Rêverie, op. 19 ; Elégie, op. 22 ; 25 Exercises, études, op. 28 ; Pastorale, op. 29 ; Idylle, op. 46 ; 25 Etudes harmonieuses, op. 50 ; 25 Etudes mignonnes, op. 60 ; First concerto, op. 63 ; Scherzo, op. 75 ; Canzonetta, op. 77.

RAWLINGS (Thomas). English violinist, B. about 1703. S. under Pepusch. Performed at Handel's oratorios when originally produced. Org. of Chelsea Hospital, 1753. D. 1767.

RAWLINGS (Robert). English violinist, son of above, B. London, 1742. S. under his father and Barsanti. Org. of Chelsea Coll., 1759. Musical page to the Duke of York, till 1767. Member of private band of George III. D. 1814.

RAWLINGS (Thomas A.). English comp. and violinist, son of above, B. London, 1775. S. under R. Rawlings and Dittenhofer. Violinist at the Opera, the Ancient, Vocal, and Professional Concerts, etc. Teacher in London. D. about middle of present century.

WORKS.—Concerti di camera, for Pf., flute, violins, viola, and 'cello. *Pianoforte* : The bugle ; Spring ; May Day ; Le Plaisirs de la chasse ; Le Retour ; The Wreath ; The Bouquet. Duet for harp and Pf. *Songs :* Bee's wing ; Evergreen leaf ; Hither, love, hither ; Home of youth ; Lilla's a lady ; O 'twas sad ; Oh come to me ; Oh what a pity ; Sabbath bells ; Strike the guitar ; Weep not, thou lovely one ; When spring time was gay. Also in collected form, "Selection of Foreign Melodies" [1825], and "Songs to Rosa [1826], with endless contributions to the musical annuals. Rawlings is usually identified with the well-known song, "Isle of Beauty," which, however, was only arranged, not composed, by him, but by a Major Whitmore.

RAWLINS (Rev. John). English writer, was rector of Leigh. Author of "The Power of Musick, and the particular influence of Church Musick : a Sermon preached in the Cathedral Church of Worcester, at the Anniversary Meeting of the Choirs of Worcester, Hereford, and Gloucester." Ravington, 1773.

REA (William). English org., comp., and cond., B. London, March 25, 1827. S. under J. Pittman for org. Org. of Christ Church, Watney Street, 1843. S. for a time under Sir W. S. Bennett. Org. of St. Andrew, Undershaft. S.

under Moscheles and Richter at Leipzig, and under Dreyschock at Prague, 1849. Gave concerts in London, and became org. to the Harmonic Union, 1853. Established the London Polyhymnian Choir, 1856. Org. of St. Michael's, Stockwell, 1858. Org. to the Corporation of Newcastle-upon-Tyne, 1860. Cond. of various musical societies, among them the Newcastle Amateur Vocal Society, etc. Org. of St. Hilda's Ch., South Shields.

WORKS.—*Organ:* Andante cantabile; Andante con variazioni; Larghetto. Operatic fantasias for Pf. *Anthems:* O give thanks; The souls of the righteous. *Songs:* I arise from dreams of thee; Oh, thou breeze of spring; Go, happy rose; What song does the cricket sing?; Arab lover; Leaning on the path-way.

READE (Charles). English writer, author of "Cremona Violins, Four Letters descriptive of those Exhibited in 1873 at the South Kensington Museum, also giving the Data for producing the True varnishes used by the great Cremona makers, reprinted from the *Pall Mall Gazette* by George H. M. Muntz," Gloucester, 1873, 8vo.

READING (John). English org. and comp., B. probably some time before the middle of the 17th century. Lay-vicar of Lincoln Cath., 1667. Master of the choristers, do., 1670. Org. of Winchester Cath., 1675-81; and of Winchester Coll., 1681. D. Winchester, 1692. Comp. an "Election Grace" for the scholars of Winchester Coll.; "Dulce Domum," a hymn, printed in Harmonia Wiccamica; and is stated to have comp. the well known hymn, "Adeste Fideles," otherwise the "Portuguese Hymn."

READING (John). English org. and comp. (son of above?), B. 1677. Chor. in Chap.-Royal, where he S. under Dr. Blow. Org. of Dulwich Coll., 1700-1702. Lay-vicar, 1702, and Master of Choristers, Lincoln Cath., 1703. Org. of S. John's Hackney, London; St. Mary, Woolnoth; S. Dunstan in the West; S. Mary, Woolchurchaw. D. 1764. [The dates 1740 and 1766 are also given.]

He comp. "A Book of New Anthems, containing a hundred plates fairly engraved with a thorough-bass figured for the Organ or Harpsichord, with proper Ritornels," London, fo., 1742; "A Book of New Songs," etc. To him has also been attributed the composition of "Adeste Fideles." Another JOHN READING was org. of Chichester Cath. from 1674 till 1720.

READING (Rev. John, D.D.) English divine, was Prebendary of Canterbury Cath. Author of "A Sermon lately delivered in the Cathedral Church of Canterbury, concerning church-musick," London, 4to, 1663.

REAY (Samuel). English org. and comp., B. Hexham, Northumberland, Mar. 17, 1826. Son of the org. of Hexham Parish Ch. Chor. in Durham Cath., and while there S. under Rev. P. Penson; afterwards had org. lessons from James Stimpson (now of Birmingham). Org. of St. Andrew's, Newcastle, 1843 (where for the first time in any parish church in that part of the country, a surpliced choir and choral service were established); St. Peter's, Tiverton, 1847; St. John's, Hampstead, 1854; St. Saviour's, Paddington, 1850; St. Stephen's, Paddington; Org. and precentor of St. Peter's Coll., Radley, in succession to Dr. Monk, 1859. Org. of parish ch., Bury, Lancashire, 1861. Song-schoolmaster and org. of parish church, Newark-on-Trent, 1864, which post he still holds. Mus. Bac., Oxon., 1871.

WORKS.—Morning and evening service in F. *Anthems*: I will go to the altar; O Lord, why sleepest Thou?; O sing unto the Lord; Rejoice in the Lord; The Gentiles shall come; The love of God; This is the day. *Part-Songs*: As it fell upon a day; Bright hair'd morn is glowing; Clouds that wrap the setting sun; Cuckoo; Dawn of day; Fly night away; Good-night; Here let's join; Huntsman rest; I lov'd a lass; In an arbour green; It was a lover and his lass (madrigal); Love's good morrow; Merrily rolls the mill stream on; Now night her dusky mantle folds; Oh, springtime; Red o'er the forest; See the rivers flowing; Spring voices; Spring's free sunshine; Sweet is the breath of early morn; Take, oh take, those lips away; 'Tis May upon the mountain; Wake, love, day is breaking; Waken, lords and ladies gay; Way is long and weary; Ye little birds that chant. Hymns contributed to Chope's "Congregational Hymn and Tune Book"; the "Hymnary," etc. Joint musical editor with Drs. Gauntlett and Bridge, of Dobson's "Tunes New and Old." He produced at the Bow and Bromley Institute,

London, Bach's "Coffee" and "Peasants," cantatas, in 1879, which was their first performance in England. He also edited and adapted them to English words, and they have since been published.

REBEL (Francois). French comp., B. Paris, June 19, 1701. S. under his father, Jean Ferry Rebel [1669-1747], a comp. D. Paris, Nov. 7, 1775. Comp. operas, cantatas, etc.

REBER (Napoléon Henri). French comp., B. Mülhausen, Upper Rhine, Oct. 21, 1807. S. at Paris Cons. under Reicha, Jelensperger, and Lesueur, from 1828. Prof. of Harmony at Paris Cons., 1851. Member of the Institut de France in succession to Onslow, 1853. Chevalier of Legion of Honour, 1854. Prof. of comp. at Cons. in succession to Halévy, 1862. Inspector of Branches of the Cons., 1871. D. Paris, Nov. 24, 1880.

WORKS.—*Operas:* Le Diable Amoureux, ballet (with Benoist), 1840; La Nuit de Noël, 1848; Le Père Gaillard, 1852; Les Papillotes de M. Benoist, 1853; Les Dames Capitaines: 1857; Le Ménétrier à la cour (MS.); Naïm (MS.) Roland, scènes lyriques, from Quinault, 1875. Symphonies for orch., in D minor, C, E flat, and G. Quartets and trios for strings, etc. Duets for Pf. and violin. Pianoforte music. Church music, choruses, and songs. Traité d' Harmonie, Paris, 8vo, 1862.

Reber was a successful comp., and one of the best teachers ever connected with the Paris Conservatory. His work on Harmony has been received with much favour, on account of its great superiority in regard to lucidity and directness. Among his pupils may be named Godard, E. Diaz, Legouix, and Pougin.

REBLING (Gustave). German org. and comp., B. Barby, Magdeburg, July 10, 1821. S. under his father and F. Schneider. Org. of Church of S. John, Magdeburg.

WORKS.—Pf. sonatas, various, Psalms XII. (op. 13), LXXXV. (op. 13), CXXXVIII. (op. 14), LI. (op. 16), for 5 and 8 voices, and accomp.; Elegie for 'cello and orch., op. 32; Organ music, songs.

REDEKER (Louise Dorette Auguste). German contralto vocalist, B. Duingen, Hanover, Jan. 19, 1853. S. at Leipzig Cons. *Début* at Bremen, 1873. Appeared at the Gewandhaus Concerts, Leipzig, 1874. Appeared in London, 1876, and has sung with much acceptance at many of the leading concerts. She married and retired, 1879.

REDFORD (John). English org. and comp. of 16th century. Org. and almoner, and master of choristers, St. Paul's Cath., 1543. D. circa, 1546-7. Comp. the well-known anthem, "Rejoice in the Lord," as well as several similar pieces in various collections.

REDHEAD (Richard). English org. and comp., B. Harrow, 1820. Educated at Magdalen Coll., Oxford. Org. of St. Mary Magdalene's Ch., Paddington, London.

WORKS.—Laudes Diurnæ, the Psalter and Canticles in the Morning and Evening Service of the Church of England, Lond., 8vo, 1843; The Order for Morning and Evening Prayer, with Litany and Proper Psalms; Proper Psalms, appointed by the Church to be said on certain Days, together with the Gospel Canticles, set to Ancient Psalm Tunes. Metrical Litanies, for the several Seasons of the Christian Year, 2 parts. Hymns for Holy Seasons and other occasions. The Celebrant's Office Book: being the Office of Holy Communion. Church Hymn Tunes sung at All Saints', Margaret Street. Canticles at Matins and Evensong, pointed as they are to be sung in Churches, and adapted to the Ancient Psalm Chants. Music to the Divine Liturgy. The Cathedral and Church Choir Book, a Collection of Pieces, chiefly adaptations from the Latin works of the great masters, arranged for use in the English Church. Parochial Church Tune Book and Appendix. Universal Organist, a Selection of Short Classical and Modern pieces, 5 books. Several masses, and many other compositions for the church.

REED (Daniel). American comp. and psalmody collector, B. Rehoboth, Conn., Nov. 2, 1757. Lived at New Haven as teacher. D. New Haven, 1836. Compiled among other works the "American Singing Book," 1785. "The Columbian Harmony," New Haven, 1793. Comp. of the tunes "Sherbourne," "Windham," "Newport," etc.

REED (Thomas German). English musician and actor, B. Bristol, June 27, 1817. Org. of Catholic Chap., Sloane Street, London. Musical director of Haymarket Theatre, 1838-51. Chap.-master of Royal Bavarian Chapel, 1838. Married Miss Priscilla Horton, 1844. Established "Mr. and Mrs. German Reed's Entertainments," 1855, and produced pieces by Brough, Parry, Gilbert and Sullivan, Burnand, Clay, Cellier, Reed, and Macfarren.

His wife, *née* PRISCILLA HORTON (B. Birmingham, Jan. 1, 1818), a contralto singer and actress of great repute who appeared in Macready's revivals of Shakespere's plays, and afterwards in Planché's pieces at the Haymarket Theatre.

REES (David). English writer, author of "Reasons for and against singing of Psalms in Private or Public Worship." Lond., 8vo, 1737.

REEVE (William). English comp., B. 1757. S. under Richardson. Org. of Totness, Devon, 1781-83. Comp. to Astley's Circus, London. Comp. to Covent Garden Theatre, 1791. Org. of Ch. of St. Martin, Ludgate Hill, 1792. Joint-proprietor of Sadler's Wells Theatre. D. London, June 22, 1815.

WORKS.—*Music to Plays*, etc.: Oscar and Malvina, 1791; Orpheus and Eurydice, 1792; The Apparition, 1794; British Fortitude, 1794; Hercules and Omphale, 1794; The Purse, 1794; Merry Sherwood, 1795; Harlequin and Oberon, 1796; Bantry Bay, 1797; Raymond and Agnes, 1797; Harlequin Quixote, 1797; The Round Tower, 1797; Joan of Arc, 1798; Ramah Droog (with Mazzinghi), 1798; The Turnpike Gate (do.), 1799; Embarkation, 1799; Thomas and Susan, 1799; Paul and Virginia (with Mazzinghi), 1800; Harlequin's Almanac, 1801; The Blind Girl (with Mazzinghi), 1801; The Cabinet (with Braham, Moorhead, and Davy), 1802; Family Quarrels (with Braham), 1802; The Caravan, 1803; The Dash, 1804; Thirty Thousand (with Davy and Braham), 1804; Out of Place, or the Lake of Lausanne (with Braham), 1805; The White Plume, 1806; An Bratach, 1806; Kais, or Love in the Deserts (with Braham), 1808; Tricks upon Travellers, 1810; Outside Passenger, 1811; Chains of the Heart (with Mazzinghi); Jamie and Anna, Scots Pastoral. Glees. *Songs:* Cherry-cheeked Patty; Fryar of Orders Grey; Little haymaker; Live and be jolly; Margery Grinder; Rose of the Valley; Tippetywitchet, clown's songs for Grimaldi; etc. The Juvenile Preceptor, or Entertaining Instructor: a Complete and Concise Introduction to the Pianoforte, with 24 Lessons and 4 Easy Duets. Lond., n.d.

REEVES (Daniel M. G. S.) English amateur musician, author of "A Treatise on the Science of Music," Lond., 8vo, 1853; 2nd edit., 1861. Chorton Hill

REEVES (John Sims). English tenor vocalist, B. Woolwich, Oct. 21, 1822. S. originally under his father. Org. of North Cray Ch., Kent, 1836. *Début* as barytone vocalist at Newcastle-on-Tyne, June 1839, in "La Sonnambula." S. under Callcott, Hobbs, J. B. Cramer, and T. Cooke, and was engaged as tenor vocalist at Drury Lane Theatre, London. S. singing at Paris, and at Milan, under Mazzucato, where he appeared in Italian opera in "Lucia." Re-appeared at Drury Lane Theatre, London, as *Edgar* in "Lucia di Lammermoor," Dec. 1847, with great success. Sang his first original part, in Balfe's "Maid of Honour," 1847. Appeared at H. M. Theatre, 1848, in Donizetti's "Linda." Sang in oratorio at Norwich Festival, 1848; and at the Sacred Harmonic Society. Appeared at Royal Italian Opera, Covent Garden, 1849. Married to Miss Emma Lucombe, Nov. 1850. Appeared at various Handel Festivals, and has sang in the English Provinces, Scotland, and Ireland, with extraordinary success. He withdrew from public life to a considerable extent about 1881. His wife *née* EMMA LUCOMBE, was a soprano singer of considerable fame, appearing in opera and oratorio from 1839 till within recent times, when she retired, and devoted herself to tuition in singing, in which she has attained much success. Their son HERBERT (B. 1860), S. under his father, and made his *début* in June 1880, and has since appeared with some success in various parts of Britain.

Reeves has been justly regarded as the greatest tenor Britain ever produced, and as one of the most successful the world has known. He achieved equal success in oratorio, opera, and ballad vocalisation, and was invariably received with great enthusiasm by the public. Almost equally successful in whatever he undertook, it is impossible to name one part more than another in which he chiefly excelled.

His voice is of great range, strength and purity, managed with exquisite taste and skill, and equally capable of rendering with acceptance the lightest as well as the most passionate and powerful music.

REGAN (Anna). See SCHIMON.

REGGIO (Pietro). Italian lute-player and comp., B. Genoa in first part of 17th century. Member of private band of Christina, Queen of Sweden. Settled in Oxford as teacher, 1654. Teacher and performer in London. D. London, July 23, 1685. Comp. music to Cowley's "Mistress," etc., and wrote "A Treatise to Sing well any Song whatsoever," Oxford, 1677.

REGNARD (Francois). French comp., B. Douai in first half of 16th century. Chap.-master of Cath. of Tournai from 1573. Comp. Masses; Chansons, 1575; Poésies de P. de Ronsard, Paris, 4to, 1579; etc. His brother JACOB (B. Douai, 1531, D. 1600), was chap.-master to the Emperor Rudolf II. at Prague. He comp. large numbers of masses, motets, chansons, lieder, etc.

REGONDI (Giulio). Italian concertina player, guitarist, and comp., B. Geneva, 1822. Travelled as an infant prodigy. Appeared in England, 1831, and remained in London as teacher and performer till his death there, May 6, 1872.
His concertina comps. include two concertos; Morceau de fantasie; Introduction et caprice; Les Oiseaux; Le Delizie dell' Italia; Arrangements for concertina. He also wrote a "Concertina Tutor, containing Plain and Practical Instructions,..." London, n.d., of which different editions appeared.

REICHA (Anton Joseph). Bohemian comp. and writer, B. Prague, Feb. 27, 1770. S. under his uncle Joseph (B. Prague, 1746, D. Bonn, 1793). Resided in Hamburg, 1794-1799. Went to Paris, 1799, and produced a few instrumental works. Resided in Vienna, 1802-8, where he came much in contact with Beethoven, Haydn, Salieri, etc. Settled in Paris, 1808, and became Prof. of counterpoint and fugue at the Cons. Naturalised as Frenchman, 1829. Member of the Institut de France, 1835. D. Paris, May 28, 1836.

WORKS.—*Operas:* Godefroid de Montfort, 1794; Cagliostro, Paris, 1810; Natalie, 1816; Sapho, 1822. Symphonies for orch., op. 41, 42; Overture for orch., op. 24; Quintet for strings, op. 92; Twenty-four quintets for flute, oboe, clarinet, horn, and bassoon, op. 88, 91, 99, 100; Quartets for strings, op. 48, 49, 52, 58, 90, 94, 95; Trios for strings, etc.; Sonatas for Pf. and violin, op. 44, 54, 55, 62; Sonatas for Pf. solo, op. 40, 43, 46; Studies, fugues, etc., for Pf. *Theoretical:* Etudes ou Théories pour le Piano-forte, Paris, 4to, 1800; Traité de Mélodie,...Paris, 4to, 1814; Cours de Composition Musicale,...Paris, 4to [1818]; Traité de haute Composition Musicale,...Paris, 2 vols., 1824-26 (trans. from the German edition of Czerny by Arnold Merrick, and edited by John Bishop, Lond., 4to, n.d.); Art du Compositeur Dramatique,...Paris, 2 vols., 4to, 1833; Petit Traité d' Harmonie pratique, op. 84.
Reicha was famous in his day for his theoretical writings and his success as a teacher. His works on harmony, etc., have been superseded, but his fame as a teacher survives in such pupils as Dancla, Lecarpentier, Lefebvre, Elwart, etc.

REICHARDT (Alexander). Hungarian tenor vocalist and comp., B. Packs, April 17, 1825. S. under his uncle. First appeared at Lemberg, 1833. Sang at Court Opera, Vienna, where he also S. under Catalani, etc. Chamber-musician (vocalist) to Prince Esterhazy. First appeared in London, at Musical Union and Philharmonic Concerts, 1851. Sang afterwards with some regularity in London, the English provinces, and Scotland, in oratorio and opera. *Début* in Paris, 1857. Settled at Boulogne as cond. and choir organiser. D. Boulogne, May 14, 1885.
A famous and well-liked vocalist in Britain, renowned for the sweet, clear, and agreeable character of his singing. He wrote a number of songs, of which the following list is representative:—Love's request; Thou art so near and yet so far; Good night; Golden stars; Memory; Of thee I think; I love but thee; Nelly's letter; and Remembrance.

REICHARDT (Gustav). German comp. and cond., B. Stralsund, Nov. 13, 1797. S. music under B. Klein at Berlin. Director of Royal music, etc., Berlin, 1850. D. Berlin, 1884.

WORKS.—Sonatas for Pf., various. Part-songs for male voices, op. 5, 7, 8, 12. Part-songs for S. A. T. B., op. 9, 11, 13, 16. German songs for voice and Pf., op. 6, 10, etc. Lieder for voice and Pf. He composed the well-known patriotic chorus, "Where is the German's Fatherland."

REICHARDT (Johann Friedrich). German comp., cond., and writer, B. Königsberg, Nov. 25, 1752. S. under Veichtener and Richter. Travelled as an infant prodigy from 1762. Educated at Universities of Königsberg and Leipzig. Succeeded Agricola as chap.-master to Friedrich the Great, 1776. Visited Italy, 1782; London, 1785; and Paris, where some of his works were produced. Music-director to Friedrich Wilhelm II., 1786. Revisited Italy, 1790. Dismissed from the Prussian royal service on grounds of his holding revolutionary principles, 1794. Settled at Hamburg as editor of a journal entitled *Frankreich*, 1794. Inspector of salt works at Hallé, near which he settled for a time, 1796. Re-instated in his offices by Friedrich II., 1797. Chap.-Master to Jerome Buonaparte at Cassel, 1808. D. at his estate of Giebichenstein, near Halle, June 17, 1814.

WORKS.—*Operas, etc.*: Hanschen und Gretchen, 1772; Le Bûcheron, 1775; Artemisia, 1778; Andromeda, 1778; Protesilas, 1779; Ino, 1779; Procris et Céphale, 1780; Tamerlan, 1785; Panthée, 1786; Claudine von Villabella, 1788; Lilla, 1790; Erwin und Elmira, 1790; Rosamunda, 1801; Jerry and Bätely, 1790; Bradamante, 1808; La Passione, oratorio, London, 1785; La Ressurection, oratorio, 1785. Cantatas, psalms, and te deums. Numerous Lieder; Elegy for Händel cantata, Lond., 1785. Symphonies, concertos, quartets, trios, sonatas, rondos, and other instrumental music. *Literary*: Ueber die Deutsche komische Oper, Hamburg, 1774; Briefe eines aufmerksamen Reisenden, die musik betreffend, 1774-76; Vertraute Briefe aus Paris, 1802-3; do. Wien, 1810; Das Künst Magazin, Berlin, 1781-91; Georg-Friedrich Händel's Jugend, Berlin, 1785; Studien für Tonkunstler und Musikfreunde, Berlin, 1793.

REICHARDT (Louise). German comp., B. Berlin, 1778. D. Hamburg, Nov. 17, 1826. Daughter of J. F. Reichardt, She comp. songs, chansons, etc.

REID (General John). Scottish musician, and founder of the Edinburgh Professorship of music, B. Straloch, Perthshire, Feb. 13, 1721 [1720]. Son of Alexander Robertson of Straloch. S. at Edinburgh University. Lieut. in Earl of Loudon's Regiment, 1745; afterwards became a General in the Earl of Loudon's Highlanders. D. London, Feb. 6, 1807.

WORKS.—A Sett of Minuets and Marches, inscribed to the Right Hon. Lady Catharine Murray, by J— R—, Esq., London, 4to, n. d. (Bremner). [Contains the well-known air, "The Garb of Old Gaul," to verses of Sir H. Erskine of Alva]. Six Solos for a German Flute or Violin, with a Thorough-bass for the Harpsichord, by J— R—, Esq., a Member of the Temple of Apollo, Lond., fo., n. d. (Oswald). There have also been ascribed to him "Three Grand Marches, and Three Quicksteps for a Full Military Band, by an Eminent Master," Lond., 4to, n. d.

General Reid directed in his will that, subject to the life-rent of his daughter, the sum of £52,000 should be applied to founding a Chair of Music in Edinburgh University, and that an annual concert (to include a full military band) should be given on his birthday, at which was to be performed some specimens of his own compositions, to show the style of music that prevailed about the middle of last century. The chair was instituted in 1839, when a sum of between £70,000 and £80,000 became available. The succession of Professors has been John Thomson, 1839; Sir Henry Bishop, 1842; Henry Hugo Pierson, 1844; John Donaldson, 1845; and Sir Herbert Stanley Oakeley, 1865.

REINAGLE (Joseph). Austrian violoncellist, comp., and writer, B. Portsmouth, 1762. Intended for the navy, but afterwards apprenticed to an Edinburgh jeweller. S. 'cello under Schetkey, who married his sister. S. violin under Aragoni and Pinto, and became leader at the Edinburgh Theatre. Performed 'cello in London, etc. Resided in Dublin, 1784-86. Played at Salomon's Concerts in London, and in Oxford, where he latterly resided. D. Oxford, 1836.

WORKS.—Twenty-four Progressive Lessons for the Pianoforte, London, 1796. Twelve Duets for the violoncello, op. 2; 3 Sets of 6 do., op. 3, 4, 5. Six Quartets for strings. Concertos for violin and violoncello, with accomp. Concise Introduction to the Art of Playing the Violoncello, Lond., n. d. This work has reached 4 editions.

His son, ALEXANDER ROBERT, B. Brighton, Aug. 21, 1799, was org. of S. Peter's-in-the-East, Oxford. D. Kidlington, near Oxford, April 6, 1877. Comp. "Preparatory Exercises for the Violin"; "Selection of Popular Airs, varied, for Violin"; "Violinist's Portfolio, for Amateurs"; "Seven Easy Studies for Violoncello"; "First Lessons for Beginners on Violoncello, to which are added a Selection of Psalm Tunes and Chants"; "Ten Airs for Organ or Harmonium"; "Four Introits for Organ"; "Processional March," do. Twelve songs without words, Pf.; Two Sets of Bagatelles, Pf. Comp. also a number of Psalm and hymn tunes.

Another musician named CAROLINE REINAGLE wrote "A Few Words on Pianoforte Playing," Lond., n. d., which has reached at least two editions.

REINCKE. See REINKEN.

REINECKE (Carl). German comp., cond., and pianist, B. Altona, June 23, 1824. S. under his father J. P. R. Reinecke, a piano-teacher and writer. Travelled as a violinist concert-giving, and visited Copenhagen, Stockholm, Cologne, and Leipzig, in which he settled about 1843. Travelled with Wasielewski to Riga, etc. Court pianist to King of Denmark. Prof. of Pf. and counterpoint at Cologne Cons., 1851. Cond. at Barmen, 1854; and music-director at Breslau University, 1859. Cond. of Gewandhaus Concerts, and Prof. at Leipzig Cons., 1860. Appeared in London, 1869-72, with much success. Ph. D., Leipzig Univ., *honoris causâ*, 1884.

WORKS.—Op. 5. Six Lieder, voice and Pf.; op. 12. Four Lieder, for 2 sopranos and Pf.; op. 14. Five Lieder, for S. A. T. B.; op. 15. Fantasia, in sonata form, for Pf.; op. 20. Ballade for Pf.; op. 27. Six Lieder, for barytone or bass; op. 37. Eight Kinderlieder, voice and Pf.; op. 38. Trio for Pf., violin, and 'cello; op. 43. Three Phantasiestücke, for Pf. and viola, or violin; op. 45. Der Vierjährige Posten, operetta; op. 46. Music to Hoffman's nursery tale of "Nussknacker und Mausekönig," for Pf., 2 hands; op. 47. Three Sonatinas, for Pf.; op. 51. Overture to Calderon's "Dame Kobold," for orch.; op. 56. Schlachtlied by Klopstock, for 2 male choirs and orch.; op. 57. Alte und neue Tänze, for Pf.; op. 63. Nine Kinderlieder, for voice and Pf.; op. 66. Impromptu, for 2 Pf., on motive from Schumann's "Manfred"; op. 72. Concerto, for Pf. and orch., in F sharp minor; op. 74. Miriam's Song of Triumph, for soprano and orch.; op. 75. Ten Kinderlieder, voice and Pf.; op. 78. Te Deum laudamus; op. 79. Symphony, for orch., in A; op. 81. Eine Novelle in Liedern, cyclus of 8 songs for tenor and Pf.; op. 83. Quintet for Pf. and strings; op. 87. Cadenzen zu classischen Pianoforte-concerten (17 selected pieces); op. 89. Sonata for Pf. and 'cello, in D; op. 91. Eight Kinderlieder, for 2 voices and Pf.; op. 92. Overture 'to Goethe's "Das Jahrmarkts-Fest zu Plundersweilern," Pf., 4 hands; op. 93. König Manfred, opera in 5 acts, by F. Röber; op. 94. La belle Griselidis, improvista for 2 Pf.; op. 98. Three sonatinas, for Pf.; op. 102. Music to Schiller's "Wilhelm Tell"; op. 109. Six lieder, for 2 female voices and Pf.; op. 110. Deutscher Triumph-marsch, for orch.; op. 116. Sonata for Pf. and violin; op. 124. Almansor, Heine, for barytone voice and orch.; Concerto for violin and orch., in G minor, op. 141; Three pieces for 'cello and Pf., op. 146; Festival overture in C, op. 148; Sieben Ländler, Pf., op. 152; Ein mährchen ohne worte, Pf. duet, op. 165; Bethlehem, cantata, op. 170; Glückskind und Pechvogel, fairy opera, op. 177; Ein Abenteuer Händel's, operetta; Belsazar, oratorio; Hakon Jarl, cantata; "Aladin" and "Friedensfeier," overtures. Masses, etc.

REINHOLD (Hugo). Austrian comp., B. Vienna, March 3, 1854. Chor. in Imperial Chap. S. Vienna Cons. under Bruckner, Epstein and Dessoff. Gained silver medal, 1874. Comp. orch music, string quartets, Pf. music, choruses for male voices, lieder, etc.

REINHOLD (Thomas). German bass vocalist, B. Dresden [1690]. Son or nephew of Archbishop Reinhold of Dresden. Became acquainted with Handel in Germany, and followed him to London, where he appeared at the

Haymarket Theatre in 1731. Appeared in many of Handel's works on their original production, among others "Samson," "Susanna," "Joshua," "Judas Maccabeus," "Solomon," etc. D. London, 1751.

His son CHARLES FREDERICK, B. London, 1737, was a chor. in S. Paul's Cath. and Chap. Royal. Appeared at Drury Lane Theatre in J. C. Smith's "Fairies," opera, 1755. Org. of St. George the Martyr, Bloomsbury. Sang at Marylebone Gardens, in the Provinces, and at the Handel Commemoration of 1784. D. London, Sept. 29, 1815. He had a bass voice of much power and good compass.

REINKEN (Johann Adam), or REINCKE. Dutch org. and comp., B. Deventer, Overyssel, April 27, 1623. S. under Swelinck at Amsterdam. Succeeded H. Scheidmann as org. of S. Catharine's Ch., Hamburg, 1654, a post he retained till his death. D. Hamburg, Nov. 24, 1722. He comp. "Hortus Musicus: Sonaten, concertanten, allemanden, couranten, sarabanden und chiquen, auf zwei violinen und dem cembalo," Hamburg, 1704.

REINTHALER (Carl Martin). German comp. and cond., B. Erfurt, Oct. 13, 1822. S. under Ritter for a time. S. under A. B. Marx. S. in Italy through bounty of Friedrich Wilhelm IV. S. singing under Géraldy and Bordogni. Prof. of singing at Cologne Cons., 1853. Org. of Bremen Cath., 1858, and director of Singing Academy there.

WORKS.—Jephtha und Seine Tochter, oratorio (produced London, 1856), Edda, opera, 1875. Das Mädchen von Kola, op. 16, elegy for chorus and orch. In der Wüste, cantata. Symphony for orch. in D, op. 12. Overtures for orch. Bismarkhymne, prize comp., for chorus. Six Male Quartets, op. 11. Six Lieder for voice and Pf., op. 10. Gesänge und Lieder zu einer hohen Feier der heiligen Taufe, 1837. Die heilige Passion unsers Herrn, 1837.

REISSIGER (Carl Gottlieb). German comp. and prof., B. Belzig, near Wittemberg, Jan. 31, 1798. S. under Schicht at S. Thomas School, Leipzig. S. at Vienna, and Munich under Winter. Prof. at the Sing-Academie, Berlin, under Zelter. Organized the Hague Cons., 1826. Chap.-master to the King of Saxony, 1827. Cond. of German opera at Dresden, 1827. D. Dresden, Nov. 7, 1859.

WORKS.—*Operas:* Das Rockenweibchen, Vienna, 1821; Nero (incidental music), 1822; Didone, 1823; Der Ahnenschätz, 1825; Yelva, 1827; Libella, 1828; Die Felsenmühle zu Etalieres, 1829; Turandot, 1835; Adele von Foix; Der Schiffbruch der Medusa, 1846. Masses, psalms, and hymns. Symphony in E flat for orch., op. 120; Overture for orch., op. 128; Quintet for strings, op. 90; Quartets for strings, etc., op. 29, 70, 108, 135, 141; Trios, Pf., violin, and 'cello, op. 25, 33, 40, 56, 75, 77, 85, 97, 103, 115, 125; Duets for Pf. and violin; Sonatas for Pf., op. 22, 41; Sonata, violin and 'cello, op. 147; Rondos for Pf., op. 21, 30, 31, 36, 37, 39, 47, 51, 55, 57, 58, 59, 64, 78, 83. Lieder for voice and Pf., op. 13, 16, etc.

REISSMANN (August). German writer and comp., B. Frankenstein, Silesia, Nov. 14, 1825. S. at Breslau under Mosewius, Lüstner, and Richter. Employed as writer in Leipzig.

WORKS.—*Operas:* Gudrun, 1871; Das Gralspiel; Le Bourgmestere de Schondorf. Oratorio, Wittekind, 1877; Concertos; Sonatas for Pf. and violin; Lieder, Pf. music, etc. *Literary:* Von Bach bis Wagner, Berlin, 1861; Das Lied in seiner historischen Entwickelung, 1861, re-issued as Geschichte des Deutschen Liedes, 1874; Allgemeine Musikgeschichte,...Leipzig, 3 vols., 8vo, 1863-4; Lehrbuch der Musikalischen Composition, Berlin, 3 vols., 1866-70; Felix Mendelssohn-Bartholdy, 1872; Franz Schubert, 1874; and monographs upon Schumann (1865) and Haydn (1879), etc.; Handlexikon der Tonkünst, Berlin, 8vo, 1882. Edited the "Musik Conversations Lexikon" in succession to Hermann Mendel, 1871.

RELFE (John). English comp. and writer, B. Greenwich, 1763. Son of Lupton Relfe, who was org. of Greenwich Hospital, under whom he studied. S. also under Keeble. Member of King's Band of Music, 1810. Teacher of harmony and Pf. in London. D. there, *circa* 1837.

WORKS.—Guida Armonica, or Introduction to the General Knowledge of Music, theoretical and practical, Lond., 3 parts, fo. [1798]; reprinted as "The Principles of Harmony, containing a complete and compendious Illustration of the Theory of Music," Lond., 1817; Remarks on the Present State of Musical Instruction, with a Prospectus of a new order of Thoroughbass designation, and a demonstrative view of the defective nature of the customary mode,...Lond., 8vo, 1819. Lucidus ordo; comprising an Analytical Course of Studies on the several branches of Musical Science...London, 4to, 1821. *Songs:* Come, thou laughter-loving power; Mary's dream. Duets.

Relfe's "Guida Armonica" anticipated in a large measure the method of Logier in regard to instruction by exercises.

RELLSTAB (Johann Carl Friedrich). German comp., printer and writer, B. Berlin, Feb. 27, 1759. S. under Agricola and Fasch. Established a musical lending library, 1783. D. Berlin, Aug. 19, 1813.

WORKS.—Versuch über die Vereinigung der Musikalischen und Oratorisch Declamation, Berlin, 1789. Oratorios; Cantatas; Symphonies and overtures; Organ sonatas; Songs, etc.

RELLSTAB (Heinrich Friedrich Ludwig). German writer and musician, son of preceding. B. Berlin, April 13, 1799. S. under his father. Engaged as soldier in the war, till 1816. S. under L. Berger and Klein. Devoted himself afterwards to literature. D. Berlin, Nov. 28, 1860.

WORKS.—Henrietta, ou la belle cantatrice [Satire on Sontag, for which he was imprisoned], 1825. Ueber die Theater-verwaltung Spontini's. Ueber mein Verhältniss als kritiker zu Herrn Spontini. A collected edition of his essays, novels, and other writings, appeared in 24 vols., with title, "Gesammelte-Schriften," Leipzig. His sister CAROLINE, B. Berlin, April 18, 1794, D. Berlin, Feb. 17, 1814, was a soprano vocalist of much promise, famed for the extraordinary upward compass of her voice.

RÉMAURY. See MONTIGNY-RÉMAURY.

REMÉNYI (Eduard). Hungarian violinist, B. Hewes, 1830. S. at Vienna Cons. under Böhm, 1842-45. Took part in Hungarian revolutionary troubles, 1848, and was exiled. Settled in the United States, where he occupied himself with concert-giving. Returned to Europe, 1853, and was made solo-violinist to Queen Victoria, 1854. Was made solo-violinist to the Emperor of Austria, King of Hungary, after obtaining his pardon for political offences, 1860. Appeared successively at London (1854), Paris (1865), in Germany, Holland, and Belgium. Settled at Paris, 1875. Appeared in London, 1877-78, with some success. Resident in the United States as violinist and concert-giver. Famous for the wild and almost whimsical characteristics of his performance. His works consist of transcriptions of Field's nocturnes; Chopin's mazurkas and polonaises; Mendelssohn's songs without words, etc., for violin.

RÉMUSAT (Jean.) French flute-player and comp., B. Bordeaux, Gironde, May 11, 1815. S. at Paris Cons. under Tulou. Gained first prize for flute-playing, 1832. Flute-player for a time in Queen's Theatre, London, and solo-flute at the Théâtre-Lyrique, Paris. Settled at Shanghai as flute-player, and D. there, Sept. 1, 1880.

Comp. cavatinas, fantasias, and transcriptions from operas for flute and Pf.

RENDANO (Alfonso). Italian pianist and comp., B. Carolei, Cosenza, April 5, 1853. S. at Naples Cons., under Thalberg, and at Leipzig Cons. Appeared at the Gewandhaus Concerts, Leipzig; the Musical Union, London (1872); Philharmonic and Crystal Palace Concerts, etc. Resident in Italy. Comp. gavottes, valses, sonatinas, marches, "chant der paysan," and other Pf. pieces.

REUTTER (Georg). Austrian org. and comp., B. Vienna, 1656. Org. of S. Stephen's Ch., Vienna, 1686. Court org., 1700. Chap.-master of St. Stephen's, 1715. D. Vienna, Aug. 29, 1738. Comp. masses, misereres, and other church music. His son, GEORG CARL, B. Vienna, April 6. 1708. S. under his father. Court comp., 1731. Married Theresia Holzhauser, a vocalist, 1731. Chap.-master of St. Stephen's, 1738. Court chap.-master in succession to Predieri, 1751. D. Vienna, Mar. 12, 1772. Comp. "Forza dell'Amicizia," opera (with Caldara); "La divina Providenza in Ismael," oratorio, 1732; "Il ritorno di Tobio," and "Betulia liberata;" also oratorios; and some cantatas and church music. Best remembered for his maltreatment of Haydn, who was a chorister under him in St. Stephen's.

RÉVIAL (Marie Pauline Francois Benoit Alphonse). French tenor vocalist and Prof., B. Toulouse, May 29, 1810. S. under Kuhn and Henry at Paris Cons. *Début* at Opera Comique, Paris, 1833. Prof. of singing at Paris Cons., 1846. D. Paris, Oct. 13, 1871.

REY (Jean Baptiste). French comp., B. Lauzerte, Tarn-et-Garonne, Dec. 18, 1734. Chap.-master to Louis XVI., 1779. Prof. of harmony in Paris Cons. for a time. Chap.-master to Napoleon I., 1804. D. Paris, July 15, 1810.

Comp. "Apollon et Coronis," 1781; "Diane et Endymion," 1791, and other operas, etc., and an "Exposition Elémentaire de l'Harmonie," 1807. His brother LOUIS CHARLES JOSEPH, B. Lauzerte, Oct. 26, 1738, was a violinist and comp. D. Paris, May 12, 1811.

REYER (Louis Étienne Ernest), or REY. French comp., B. Marseilles, Dec. 1, 1823. S. at Barsotti's Free Music School, Marseilles; and under his aunt Louise Farrenc. Held Government appointment in Algiers, 1839-48. Resides in Paris as writer, comp., and librarian at the opera. Member of the Institut, 1876.

WORKS.—*Operas, ballets, etc.*: Le Selam, symphonic-poem (Gautier), 1850; Maître Wolfram, 1854; Sacountala (Gautier), 1858; La Statue, 1861; Erostrate, 1862; Sigurd, Brussels, 1884, London, 1884. Victoire, cantata, 1859. Recueil de 10 Melodies, for voice and Pf. Pf. music, scenas, songs, etc.

REYNOLDS (John). English comp. of 18th century. Was Gent. of Chap.-Royal, 1765-1770. D. Lambeth, 1770 [Nov. 1778?]. Comp. the well-known anthem, "My God, my God, look upon me."

RHAW (Georg), or RHAU. German comp. and writer, B. Eisfeld, Franconia, 1488. Director and cantor at Leipzig, and latterly printer at Wittenberg. D. Wittenberg, Aug. 6, 1548.

WORKS.—Enchiridion utruisque Musical practical ex variis Musicorum...Wittenberg, 8vo, 1530 [7 editions to 1553]. Enchiridion Musicæ mensuralis...Leipzig, 12mo, 1520. Opus decem missarum quatuor vocum collectum, Wittenberg, 4to, 1541.

RHEINBERGER (Joseph). German pianist, org., and comp., B, Vadutz, Lichtenstein, March 17, 1839. Org. at Vadutz, 1846. S. at Munich Cons. under F. Hauser, Léonhard, Herzog, and Meier, 1851-58. Pf. teacher in Munich Cons., 1859, and org. of the Hof-kirche of S. Michael. Cond. of Munich Oratorio Society. Prof. in Royal School of Music, and Cond. of Bavarian Court Band, Munich.

WORKS.—*Operas:* Magnus; Crown of Misfortune; Die Sieben Raben, 1869; Thürmer's Tochterlein, 1873. Three Latin Hymns, female voices and org., op. 96. Wittekind, ballad for chorus and orch. Das Thal des Espingo, do. Christoforus, legend, op. 120. Wallenstein, symphony, op. 10. Florentinische Sinfonie. *Overtures:* Taming of the Shrew; Demetrius (Schiller), op. 110; and to a Play by Shakespeare, op. 17; Fantasia for orch., op. 79; Requiem Mass for chorus, solo, and orch., 1871; Stabat Mater, op, 138; Quintet for strings, op. 82: Quintet for Pf., 2 violins, viola, and 'cello, op. 114; Quartet for strings, in C min., op. 89; Quartet for Pf., violins, and 'cello, in E flat, op. 38; Trio, Pf., violin, and 'cello, op. 34; 2nd Trio for Pf., violin, and 'cello, op. 112; Concerto in A flat for Pf. and orch., op. 94; Sonata in E flat for Pf. and violin, op. 77; Do. in E min., op. 105. *Pianoforte:* Sonata symphonique, op. 47; Sonata in D flat, op. 99; Humoresques, op. 28; Toccatas, opp. 12, 104, 115; 3 Kleine concertstücke, op. 5; 3 Klaviervorträge, op. 53; Zum Abschied, study, op. 59; Drei vortrags studien, op. 101; 3 Studies for left hand, op. 113. *Organ:* Sonata, No. 1 in C min., op. 27; No. 2 in A flat, op. 65; No. 3 in G, op. 88; No. 4 in A min., op. 98; No. 5 in F sharp, op. 111; No. 8 in E min., op. 132; Sonata pastorale in G.

RICCI (Federico). Italian comp., B. Naples, Oct. 22, 1809. S. at Cons. of S. Sebastiano, under Zingarelli, Raimondi, etc. Resided with his brother till 1844. D. Conegliano, Dec. 10, 1877.
WORKS.—*Operas:* Il Colonello, 1835; Il Desertore per Amore, 1836 (comp. in association with his brother Luigi); La Prigione d' Edimburgo, 1837; Michel Angelo e Rolla, 1841; Vallombra, 1842; Isabella de' Medici, 1844; Estella, 1846; Griselda, 1847; Crispino e la comare, 1850 (with Luigi); I due Ritratti, 1850; Il Paniere d' amore, 1853; Una Follia a Roma, 1869. Masses, cantatas, duets, songs, etc.

RICCI (Luigi). Italian comp., brother of preceding, B. Naples, June 8, 1805. S. Naples Cons. under Zingarelli, Furno, and afterwards under Generali. Married Lidia Stoltz, 1844. Chap.-master at Trieste Cath., and cond. of the opera. D. insane, at Prague, Dec. 31, 1859.
WORKS.—*Operas:* L'Impresario in angustie, 1823; La Cena frastornata, 1824; Il Diavolo condamnato, 1826; La Lucerna di Epitteto, 1827; Ulisse, 1828; Il Colombo, 1829; Il Sonnambulo, 1829; La Neve, 1831; Il Nuovo Figaro, 1832; I due Sergenti, 1833; Chi dura vince, 1834; Il Colonello (with Federico), 1835; Chiara di Montalbano, 1835; Il Disertore per amore (with Federico), 1836; Le Nozze di Figaro, 1838; La Solitaria delle Asturie, 1844; L'Amante di richiamo (with Federico), 1846; Il Birrajo di Preston, 1850; Crispino e la comare, Venice, 1850 (with Federico); La Festa di Piedigrotta, 1852; Il Diavolo a quattro, 1859. Songs, church music, etc.
A number of the above operas were produced with much success in Italy, and "Crispino e la Comare" is still in use. His son LUIGI, B. Trieste, is resident in London as teacher and comp. He has written Frosina, 1870; Un Curioso accidente, 1871; Donna Ines, Milan, 1885. Masses, songs, etc.

RICE (Fenelon B.) American musician. Director of Oberlin Conservatory of Music, Ohio. Past President of the Music Teachers' National Association. Author of many valuable papers on musical subjects read at the meetings of the M. T. Nat. Assoc. and elsewhere.

RICE (Philip). American writer, D. 1857. Author of "Method for the Banjo, with or without music," Boston, n.d. Rice was a negro minstrel.

RICHARDS (Henry Brinley). Welsh comp., pianist, and teacher, B. Carmarthen, Nov. 13, 1817. Son of H. Richards, org. of S. Peter's, Carmarthen. Intended for medical profession, but abandoned it in favour of music. Entered R. A. M. as student, with assistance of the Duke of Newcastle. Gained King's Scholarship, 1835 and 1837. Member R. A. M. Resided in London as teacher and pianist. D. London, May 2, 1885.
WORKS.—*Orchestral:* Overture in F minor, Paris, 1840, Lond., 1841; The "Albert Edward," march (military band), 1862; The Carmarthen march. *Pianoforte:* Andante Pastorale; The angel's song; Picciola Estelle; Fête de la Reine (1849); La Reine Blanche, scherzo; Recollections of Wales (1852); Warblings at eve (1856); Marie, nocturne (1857); Book of Octave Studies; Andante cantabile (1858); Fantasias on Welsh airs (1861); Tarantelle (1864); Evening, nocturne (1877); Autrefois (1880). *Part Songs:* Up quit thy bower, trio (1846); In the hour of my distress, solo and choir (1856); There's not a heath (1857); The boat song; Ye little birds madrigal (1863); Sun of my soul (1868); The Cambrian plume (1869); Let the hills resound (1873); The men of Wales (1877); Nobody cares for thee (1878). *Duets:* How beautiful is night; The old church chimes; Home, etc. *Songs:* In the hour of my distress; Cambrian war-song (1859); The harp of Wales (1862); God bless the Prince of Wales (Dec. 1862); As o'er the past (1868); The harper's grave (1869); The Black Watch (1874); Men of Wales (1877), etc. Songs of Wales, edited, London, 8vo, 1873 (other editions).

RICHARDSON (John E.) English org., comp., and writer. S. at Salisbury Cath., under A. T. Corfe. Org. and master of the choristers, Salisbury Cath., 1863. Comp. Service in F. *Anthems:* I will give thanks; Turn Thee, O Lord; Praise to Thee, O God; Short anthems for Whitsuntide and Trinity. Organ music. "The Tour of a Cathedral Organist," Salisbury, 8vo, 1870.

RICHARDSON (Joseph). English flute-player and comp., B. 1814. Member of Jullien's orch., and latterly principal flutist in Queen's private band. D. London, March 22, 1862.
Comp. fantasias, variations, original pieces and arrangements for flute; Songs, etc.

RICHARDSON (Nathan). American comp. and pianist, B. Gloucester, Mass., 1827. S. under Dreyschock at Prague, etc. Established music-publishing firm of Russell and Richardson at Boston. D. Paris, Nov. 19, 1859. Author of "Modern School for the Pianoforte..." Boston, 4to, 1859. "New Method for the Pianoforte," 1859, with American or Foreign Fingering.

RICHARDSON (Vaughan). English org. and comp., B. in latter half of the 17th century. S. under Blow, in Chap.-Royal. Org. of Winchester Cath., 1695. D. 1729.
WORKS.—A Collection of Songs for one, two, and three voices, accompany'd with Instruments, Lond., 1701. Odes, cantatas, etc. Anthems and songs.

RICHARDSON (William). English org. and comp., was org. of Deptford, London, early in last century. Published "The Pious Recreation..." Lond., 8vo, 1729. A collection of psalms.

RICHAULT (Charles Simon). French music-publisher, B. Chartres, May 10, 1780. Established famous publishing business at Paris, 1805. D. Paris, Feb. 20, 1866. His son, GUILLAUME SIMON, B. Paris, Nov. 2, 1806, carried on the business in succession to his father, till his death at Paris, Feb. 7, 1877. In his turn he was succeeded by his son, LEON, B. Paris, Aug. 6, 1839, who has greatly increased the business and the number of works issued. The catalogue of this celebrated firm contains good editions of the works of Schubert, Mozart, Handel, Bach, Beethoven, Cherubini, Méhul, Meyerbeer, Onslow, Spontini, Marschner, Rossini, Cimarosa, Hummel, Pacini, Balfe, Paër, Gretry, Joachim, Piatti, Thomas, Berlioz, Reber, Gounod, Gouvy, Guilmant, Massé, etc.

RICHMOND (Rev. Legh). English divine and musician, B. Liverpool, 1772. D. May 8, 1827. Author of "The Dairyman's Daughter" in the "Annals of the Poor," and other religious works. Known to musicians by some good glees, contained in Hague's collections.

RICHMOND (William Henry). English org. and comp. S. under Jas. Rhodes and T. A. Marsh. Org. successively at Knaresborough and Dundee. Comp. church services and anthems, marches and other music for organ, etc.

RICHTER (Ernst Friedrich Eduard). German writer, comp., and teacher, B. Gross-Schönau, Zittau, Oct. 24, 1808. Educated at the School of Zittau, and afterwards at Leipzig University. S. music under Weinlig. Prof. of harmony and counterpoint at Leipzig Cons., 1843. Music-director at Leipzig University, 1843. Cond. the Singakademie till 1847. Org. of S. Peters, Leipzig, 1851, and afterwards of St. Nicholas. Cantor of St. Thomas School, 1851. D. Leipzig, April 9, 1879.
WORKS.—*Oratorio:* Christus der Erlöser, 1849. Cantatas, etc. Op. 7. 3 Romanzen für Pf.; op. 8. Hymne, chorus and orch.; op. 9. Four lieder; op. 10. The 126th Psalm; op. 11. Six lieder; op. 12. Four 4-part lieder; op. 14. Six 4-part lieder; op. 16. The 116th Psalm, for solo, chorus, and orch.; op. 17. The 137th Psalm; op. 18. Six 4-part lieder; op. 19. Fantasia and fugue, for org.; op. 20. Six pieces for org.; op. 21. Three preludes and fugues, org.; op. 25. Quartet for strings, in E minor; op. 26. Sonata for Pf. and violin, A minor; op. 27. Sonata for Pf.; op. 35. Two poems for female chorus, with solo; op. 37. Sonata for 'cello; op. 44, 46. Masses for solo, chorus, and orch., etc. *Didactic:* Lehrbuch der Harmonie Praktische anleitung zu den Studien in derselben, zunächst für das Conservatorium der Musik in Leipzig, Leipzig, 8vo, 1860 (numerous editions), trans. as Treatise on Harmony, by Franklin Taylor, London, 8vo, 1864; American trans. by J. P. Morgan, and J. C. D. Parker, in numerous editions. Morgan's trans. was reprinted in London, 1880. Lehrbuch des einfachen und doppelten Contrapunkts, Leipzig, 8vo, 1872, English trans. by Franklin Taylor, Lond., 8vo, 1874. Lehrbuch der Fuge...Leipzig, 8vo, 1872, trans. by Franklin Taylor, London, 8vo, 1878, American edition by Arthur W. Foote, Boston.

Richter attained great fame as a teacher, and his influence in this respect is still maintained through his excellent theoretical hand-books.

RICHTER (Ernst Heinrich Leopold). German comp., B. Thiergarten, Glogau, Nov. 15, 1805. S. under Ernst, Berner, Klein and Zelter. Prof. of music at Normal School of Breslau, 1826. Music-director at Görlitz, 1845.
Comp. an opera, symphonies, psalms, motets, masses, org.-music, part-songs, lieder, etc.

RICHTER (Hans). Hungarian cond., B. Raab, April 4, 1843. Son of the Chap.-master of Raab Cath. Chorister in Court Chap., Vienna. S. at Vienna Cons. under Kleinicke (horn), Sechter, and Hellmesberger, 1859. Horn-player in Kärnthnerthor orch. Associated with Wagner in the production of his operas from 1866. Cond. at Hof-und-National Theatre, Munich. Cond. at National Theatre, Pesth, 1871. Cond. at Court Opera Theatre, Vienna, 1875. First appeared in London, 1877. Court Chap.-master at Vienna, 1878. Cond. series of orchestral concerts in London which attracted much attention, 1879-1885. Mus. Doc. Cantab., *honoris causâ*, 1885. Cond. the Birmingham Musical Festival, 1885, at which were produced original works by Gounod, Dvorák, Stanford, Mackenzie, etc.
Richter is regarded as the greatest master of orchestral conducting presently before the public. His great grasp of his art is evidenced by the fact that his intimate knowledge of the works of many great masters, including Beethoven and Wagner, enables him to conduct with ease and in unsurpassable style without score. It is chiefly as a conductor of Wagner's operas that he is most favourably known, and he is understood to have enjoyed the advantage of the practical advice of the composer himself, imparted during many years of personal communion.

RICORDI (Giovanni). Italian music-publisher, B. Milan, 1785. Became famous as a publisher early in the present century, and issued an enormous quantity of operatic music, as well as Pf. music, songs, and other works from about 1808. He D. Milan, March 15, 1853. Succeeded by his son TITO, who added much to the number of publications. In his turn Tito was succeeded by GIULIO DI TITO (B. 1835), who relieved his Father from the cares of the business consequent on his withdrawal through illness. The firm is now one of the most extensive in the world, their publications numbering upwards of 50,000 items. They have branch establishments in Rome, Naples, Florence, London, and Paris. Among their periodical publications may be named the *Gazzetta Musicale di Milano*, which, under the editorship of Mazzucato, has attained great success. In addition to works in musical literature, including Paloschi's well-known "Annuario Musicale," the firm issues works by the following composers:—Asioli, Auber, Basily, Bellini, Boïto, Bottesini, Cagnoni, Carafa, Cimarosa, Donizetti, Dussek, Fioravanti, Gomes, Jommelli, Marchetti, Mayr, Mercadante, Meyerbeer, Morlacchi, Mosca, Mozart, Orlandi, Pacini, Paër, Peri, Ponchielli, Raimondi, Ricci, Rossini, Spontini, Tosti, Vaccaj, Verdi, Weber, Weigl, and Zingarelli.

RIDDELL (Captain Robert). Of Glenriddell, Dumfriesshire, Scottish antiquary and musician, best known as the friend of Burns the poet. He published "A Collection of Scotch, Galwegian, and Border Tunes, for the Violin and Pianoforte, with a Bass for the Violoncello or Harpsichord," Edinburgh, 1794, fo. "New Music for the Pianoforte or Harpsichord, composed by a Gentleman. Consisting of a Collection of Reels, Minuets, Hornpipes, Marches, and two Songs in the Old Scotch taste, with variations to five favourite tunes," Edinburgh, n. d., fo. Also music to some of Burns' songs. He D. Friar's Carse, near Dumfries, April 21, 1794.

RIEDEL (Carl). German org. and comp., B. Kronenberg, near Elberfeld, Oct. 6, 1827. S. under Carl Wilhelm, and at Leipzig Cons. under Moscheles, Hauptmann, Plaidy, etc. Established at Leipzig the "Riedelsche Verein," a society for the cultivation and performance of choral music, famous throughout Germany for the number of new works brought forward at its concerts. Riedel has comp. a number of pieces of concerted vocal music, and has edited and republished a few works of the older German masters.

RIEDT (Friedrich Wilhelm). German flute-player and comp., B. Berlin, Jan. 5, 1710. S. flute under Graun and Schaffrath. Chamber musician and flutist to King of Prussia, 1741. D. Berlin, Jan. 5, 1783. Comp. sonatas, concertos, and trios for flute, and theoretical works.

RIEM (Wilhelm Friedrich). German org. and comp., B. Cölleda, Thuringia, Feb. 17, 1779. S. under J. A. Hiller at Leipzig. Org. of the Cath., and director of the Singing School, Bremen, 1822. D. Bremen, April 20, 1837. WORKS.—Op. 1-5. Sonatas for Pf.; op. 6. Quintet for strings in G minor; op. 7. Two sonatas, Pf.; op. 8. Quartet for Pf., 2 violas, and 'cello; op. 19. Three quartets for strings; Songs, lieder, etc.; Sammtliche Orgel-Compositionen; Cantatas.

RIEPEL (Joseph). German theorist and writer, B. in Saxony in first half of 18th century. S. at Dresden. Musical director at Ratisbon. D. Ratisbon, Oct. 23, 1782.

RIES (Ferdinand). German pianist, comp., and cond., B. Bonn, Nov. 28, 1784. Son of Franz Ries (B. Bonn, 1755, D. 1846), who was court musician at Bonn. S. under his father and Bernhard Romberg. Blind of an eye, which he lost after an attack of smallpox. Resided successively at Munich (where he S. under Winter), and Vienna, where he S. under Beethoven, and was greatly befriended by him. Visited Paris, Cassel, and travelled via Hamburg and Copenhagen to Russia, where he gave concerts in conjunction with B. Romberg. Appeared in London, 1813, became a member of the Philharmonic Soc., and resided there as a fashionable pianist and teacher till 1824. Retired to Godesberg, near Bonn, 1824. Cond. Lower Rhine Festivals for a few years. Cond. of the Cecilian Soc., Frankfort. Revisited London, 1831, and produced his opera, "Liska." D. Frankfort-on-Main, Jan. 13, 1838.
WORKS.—*Operas*: Die Räuberbraut, Frankfort, 1829 (London, 1829); Liska, 1831, London (The Sorcerer, 1831). *Oratorios*: Der Sieg des Glaubens, 1835; Die Könige Israels, 1837. *String quintets*: op. 37, 68, 107, 167, 171, 183. *String quartets*: op. 70, 126, 145, 150, 166. *Concertos for Pf.*: op. 24, 42, 55, 115, 120, 123, 132, 151, 177. *Trios for Pf., violin, and 'cello*: op. 2, 28, 35, 63, 143. *Duets, Pf. and violin*: op. 3, 8, 10, 16, 18, 19, 20, 21, 29, 30, 38, 45, 69, 71, 76, 81, 83, 86, 87, 169. *Sonatas, Pf. solo*: op. 1, 5, 9, 11, 26, 49, 114, 141, 175. Sonata for Pf. and horn, op. 5. Rondos, marches, variations, fantasias, and transcriptions for Pf. solo. Songs, etc. Biographische Notizen über Ludwig van Beethoven [with Wegeler], Coblentz, 8vo, 1838. Trans. into French by M. A. F. Legentil, Paris, 1862.
Ries is best remembered by his connection with Beethoven, and the interesting biographical notice relative to him which he has left us. His works are permeated with the style and essence of Beethoven, but lack the necessary fire and originality.

RIES (Hubert). German violinist and comp., brother of the preceding, B. Bonn, April 1, 1802. S. under his father and Spohr. Member of Royal Band, Berlin. Director of the Philharmonic Society, Berlin, 1835. Author of a Standard Method for the Violin, and concertos, quartets, duets, etc.

RIES (Louis). German violinist and teacher, son of the preceding, B. Berlin, Jan. 30, 1830. S. under his father and Vieuxtemps. Visited Brussels and Paris. Settled in London, 1852. Engaged there as member of the Musical Union, and second violin at the Monday Popular Concerts. His brothers ADOLPH, B. Berlin, 1837, is a pianist and comp. S. under Kullak and Böhmer. Teacher and comp. in London. FRANZ, B. Berlin, April 7, 1846, violinist and comp. S. under Kiel and at Paris Cons. Performed in Paris, London, etc. Now engaged as music publisher in Dresden. Comp. overtures, concertos, Pf. music, lieder, etc.

RIETZ (Julius). German comp., cond., and violoncellist, B. Berlin, Dec. 28, 1812. S. under Zelter, Schmidt, and B. Romberg. 'Cellist in Royal Theatre, Berlin, 1828. Sub.-cond. at Düsseldorf Opera, 1834; and chief director, 1835. Director of the royal music, and cond. of Choral Soc., Düsseldorf, 1836-1847. Cond. of the opera, and director of the Singing School, Leipzig, 1847. Cond. of the Gewandhaus Concerts, and Prof. of comp. at the Cons., 1848. Cond. of royal opera, Dresden, and chap.-master to the King of Saxony in succession to Reissiger, 1860. Director of Dresden Cons. D. Dresden, Oct. 1, 1877.

WORKS.—*Operas, etc.*: Lorbeerbaum und Bettelstab, 1833; Das Mädchen aus der Fremde, 1839; Jery und Bätely; Der Corsar, Leipzig, 1850; Georg Neumark und die Gambe, 1859. *Symphonies*: No. 1, in G minor, op. 13; No. 2, op. 23; No. 3, in E flat, op. 31. *Overtures*: Military, op. 3; Concert, in A, op. 7; Hero und Leander, op. 11; Lustspiel, op. 18; Shakspeare's "Tempest." Quartet for strings, op. 1; Fantasia, for 'cello and orch., op. 2; Scherzo capriccioso, Pf., op. 5; Concertos, for 'cello and orch., op. 16, 32; Sonatas, for Pf. solo, op. 17, 21; Concerto for clarinet and orch., op. 29; Concerto for violin and orch., op. 31; Concertstücke for oboe and orch., op. 33; Arioso for violin and org., etc. *Vocal*: 13 Gesänge for voice and Pf., op. 6; Altdeutscher schlachtgesang, chorus and orch., op. 12; 7 Lieder, voice and Pf., op. 27; 6 Geistliche lieder, for 4-part choir, op. 37; Das Grosse Deutsche Vaterland, hymn by Pabst, op. 51; Dithyrambe, chorus and orch.; Mass, in F; Psalms; Cantatas; Te deums; Motets; duets, etc. Editions of Mozart, Beethoven, Handel, and Mendelssohn.

Rietz will be best remembered as an editor and teacher. His pupils were many, and among them it will be sufficient to mention Radecke, Bargiel, Dessoff, and Nicolaï. His brother EDUARD, B. Berlin, 1801, D. there, 1832, was a violinist and cond. of great merit.

RIGBY (George Vernon). English tenor vocalist, B. Birmingham, Jan. 21, 1840. Chor. in St. Chad's Cath., Birmingham. Sang in Birmingham, and in 1861 appeared in London. Sang as tenor in Corri's Opera Company, 1865. S. under San Giovanni at Milan, where he also sang in opera. Sang afterwards at Berlin and the North of Europe. Sang at the Gloucester Festival, 1868, and at the Sacred Harmonic Society, London, in the same year. Has sung in London and the provinces with great success as an oratorio and operatic vocalist.

RIGEL (Heinrich Josef), or RIEGEL. German comp. and cond., B. Wertheim, Franconia, Feb. 9, 1741. S. under Jommelli and Richter. Resided in Paris as cond. of the Concerts Spirituals, Concert Olympique, and Prof. at Cons. D. Paris, May, 1799. Comp. oratorios, operas, quartets, Pf. sonatas, etc.

His son, HENRI JEAN, B. Paris, May 11, 1772. S. under his father. Director of music at Cairo, and member of the Egyptian Institute. Pianist to Napoleon I. D. Abbeville, Dec. 16, 1852. He comp. sonatas and concertos for Pf., etc.

RIGHINI (Vincenzo). Italian comp. and cond., B. Bologna, Jan. 22, 1756. S. under Martini. Actor and buffo vocalist at Prague. Director and comp. at Italian Opera, Vienna, 1779. Singing-master to Princess Elizabeth of Würtemberg. Court music-director at Mayence, 1788. Married to Henriette Kneisel (1761-1801), a vocalist. Cond. to Friedrich Wilhelm II. at Italian Opera, Berlin, 1793 till 1806. Re-visited Italy, 1804. D. Bologna, Aug. 19, 1812.

WORKS.—*Operas*: La Vedova scaltra, Prague, 1778; La Bottega del Café; Don Giovanni; Antigono, 1788; Alcide al Bivio, 1789; Enea nel Lazio, 1793; Il Trionfo d'Ariane, 1795; Atalante e Meleagro, 1797; Armida, 1799; Tigrane, 1799; Gerusalemme liberata, 1802; La Selva incantata, 1803, etc. Masses and other church music, cantatas, ariettas, lieder, solfeggi; Concertos for various instruments, etc.

Best known in his day as a conductor and teacher, Righini still holds a considerable degree of attention as a composer of vocal exercises.

RILEY (William). English musician and writer, was "principal teacher of psalmody to the Charity Schools in London, Westminster, and Parts adjacent." Author of "Parochial Musick Corrected, containing Remarks on Psalmody in Country Churches; on the ridiculous and profane manner of singing by Methodists; on the bad performance of Psalmody in London and Westminster, with hints for its Improvement...To which is added a Scarce and Valuable Collection of Psalm Tunes,..." Lond., 1762, 4to. "Parochial Harmony, in three and four Parts, by some of the most Eminent Ancient and Modern Composers, and others," London, 4to, n.d.

RIMBAULT (Stephen Francis). English org., pianist, and comp., B. London, 1773. S. under Dittenhofer, Hook, and Possin. Org. of St. Giles in the Fields. D. London, 1837. Published numerous adaptations for Pf. from Haydn, Mozart, Beethoven, Rossini, Winter, etc. Comp. three grand sonatas for Pf., with Flute accomp., etc.

RIMBAULT (Edward Francis). English writer and comp., son of preceding, B. Soho, London, June 13, 1816. S. under his father and Samuel Wesley. Org. of the Swiss Ch., Soho, 1832, and subsequently of several other London churches. Lectured at the Royal Institution and elsewhere on English musical history. One of the founders of the Percy and Musical Antiquarian Societies. Editor to Motett Society, 1841. F.S.A., 1842 ; Mem. of Academy of Music, and Ph.D., Stockholm, 1842. Hon. Degree of LL.D., Harvard Univ., U.S.A., 1848. D. Regent's Park, London, Sept. 26, 1876.

WORKS.—Who was Jack Wilson, the Singer of Shakespeare's Stage ? an attempt to prove the identity of this person with John Wilson, Doctor of Music in the University of Oxford, A.D. 1644, Lond., 8vo, 1846. Bibliotheca Madrigaliana ; a Bibliographical Account of Musical and Poetical Works published in England during the reigns of Elizabeth and James I....London, 8vo, 1847. The First Book of the Pianoforte, being a Plain and Easy Introduction to the Study of Music, Lond., 12mo, 1848. The Organ : its History and Construction (with E. J. Hopkins), Lond., 8vo, 1855 (various editions). The Pianoforte : its Origin, Progress, and Construction : with some Account of Instruments of the same class which preceded it, viz.: the Clavichord, the Virginals, the Spinet, the Harpsichord, etc., Lond., 4to, 1860. The Early English Organ-Builders and their Works, from the Fifteenth Century to the period of the Great Rebellion,...Lond., 12mo [1864]. J. S. Bach : his Life and Writings, compiled from Hilgenfeldt and Forkel, Lond., 8vo, 1869. A Guide to the Use of the New Alexandre Church Harmonium with two rows of Keys,...Lond., n.d. The Harmonium : it Uses and Capabilities for the Drawing Room as well as the Church, 8vo, 1857. Rimbault's Harmonium Tutor, a Concise and Easy Book of Instruction,...Lond., n.d. Rimbault's New Singing Tutor, adapted from the valuable work of Lablache, Lond., n.d. *Edited, secular*. Little Book of Songs and Ballads, gathered from Ancient Musick Books, MS. and Printed,...Lond., 8vo, 1840 (2nd ed., 1851). The Ancient Vocal Music of England, Lond., 2 v. [1846-49. Little Lays for Little Learners, set to Easy Songs, Lond., 4to, n.d, Nursery Rhymes, with the Tunes to which they are sung in the Nursery of England, obtained principally from Oral Tradition, Lond., 4to, 1847 ; 2nd edit., 1863; 3rd edit., 1867 (other edits.). Musical Illustrations of Bishop Percy's Reliques of Ancient English Poetry, a Collection of Old Ballad Tunes, etc....Lond., 8vo, 1850. The Rounds, Catches, and Canons of England...16, 17, and 18 Centuries (with the Rev. J. Powell Metcalfe), Lond., 4to, n.d. The Old Cheque-Book, or Book of Remembrance of the Chapel Royal from 1561 to 1744, Lond. (Camden Soc.), 4to, 1872. Memoirs of Musick by the Hon. Roger North, Attorney-General to James II....Edited, with copious notes, Lond., 4to, 1846. Thomas Morley's First Book of Ballets for 5 voices (Mus. Antiq. Soc.) Thomas Bateson's First Set of Madrigals (Mus. Ant. Soc.) Orlando Gibbons' Fantasies of 3 parts for viols (Mus. Ant. Soc.) Purcell's Bonduca, a tragedy...to which is added a History of the Rise and Progress of Dramatic Music in England (Mus. Ant. Soc.) Byrd, Bull and Gibbons' " Parthenia " (Mus. Ant. Soc.) Purcell's Ode for St. Cecilia's Day (Mus. Ant. Soc.) *Edited, Sacred:* Cathedral Chants of the xvi., xvii., and xviii. centuries...Biographical Notices of the Composers, Lond., 4to, 1844. The Order of Daily Service...as used in the Abbey Church of Saint Peter, Westminster...Lond., 1844. A Collection of Anthems by Composers of the Madrigalian Era, Lond. (Mus. Antiq. Soc.), 1845. Cathedral Music, consisting of Services and Anthems...Lond., fo., n. d. [Vol. I. all published]. Collection of Services and Anthems, chiefly adapted from the works of Palestrina, Orlando di Lasso, Vittoria, Colonna, etc., Lond. (Motett Society), 3 vols., fo. The Hand-Book for the Parish Choir, a Collection of Psalm Tunes, Services, Anthems, Chants, etc., Lond., n. d. The Order of Morning and Evening Prayer, with the Harmony in 4 parts...Lond., n. d. Vocal Part Music, Sacred and Secular, a Collection of Anthems, Motetti, Madrigals, Part-Songs, etc., Lond., n.d. A Little Book of Christmas Carols, with the Ancient Melodies to which they are sung in various parts of the Country...Lond., 4to [1847]. Old English Carols and Two Hymns, Lond., 4to, 1865. The Full Cathedral Service composed by Thomas Tallis...with an Historical Preface, and a Biography of the Composer, Lond., fo.,

n. d. The Order of Daily Service with the Musical Notation as adapted and composed by Thomas Tallis, Lond., fo., n. d. Edward Lowe's Order of Chanting the Cathedral Service, Lond., n. d. The Whole Book of Psalms, with the Tunes in four parts as printed by Thomas Este, 1592...historical and biographical notice, Lond. (Mus. Ant. Soc.), n.d. The Booke of Common Prayer with Musical Notes, as used in the Chapel Royal of Edward VI., 1550. Compiled by John Merbecke... Reprinted in Facsimile, Lond., n. d. *Vocal:* Country Life, cantata; Fair Maid of Islington, operetta, 1838. Part-songs and numerous single songs. *Organ:* Organist's Handbook, a Collection of Voluntaries...arranged from Composers of the German School, Lond., n. d. The Organist's Portfolio, a Series of Voluntaries from the works of Ancient and Modern Composers, Lond., 4to, 1866 (Boston edition, 1867). Some original pieces. *Pianoforte:* An enormous quantity of Albums, Arrangements, Selections, Transcriptions and other pieces for solo and duet, with a few original pieces. In addition to all the foregoing it should be mentioned that Rimbault edited many works for the Percy Society; an edition of Sir Thomas Overbury's Works; several of Handel's oratorios; Operas by various composers; and contributed many articles biographical and otherwise to the "Imperial Dictionary of Biography," Grove's "Dictionary of Music," and to periodical literature.

Much of the work done by Rimbault has high value for practical musicians as well as for the mere antiquary. His labours in reviving some of the older works, and the light which his researches threw on many important subjects connected with English music, entitle him to the respect of all succeeding students of Music. He was especially successful in rescuing from oblivion some of the best productions of the early English composers.

RINALDO DA CAPUA. Italian comp., B. Capua, Naples, 1715. His biography has not been preserved, nor is it known when or where he died. He composed the following operas:—Farnace, 1739; La Donna Vendicativa, 1740; La Libertà novica, 1744; L'Ambizione delusa, 1745; La Commedia in Commedia, 1749; La Zingara, 1753; etc.

RINCK (Johann Christian Heinrich), or RINK. German org. and comp., B. Elgersburg, Gotha, Feb. 18, 1770. S. under Kirschner, Kittel, and Forkel. Org. at Giessen, 1789, and afterwards Prof. at the Music School there, 1805. Org. and Prof. at University, Darmstadt, 1806; Court org. at Darmstadt, 1813; Chamber musician to Ludwig I. Ph.D., Giessen Univ., 1840. Travelled in Germany as concert-giver and org. D. Darmstadt, Aug. 7, 1846.

WORKS.—*Church Music*: Masses, motets, chorales, hymns, etc. *Organ*: Preludes, op. 2, 25, 37, 47, 49, 52, 53, 58, 63, 74, 95, 103, 116, etc.; Themes with variations, op. 56, 57, 70, 84, 89, 108; Twenty pieces, various, op. 33; Chorales, op. 40, 64, 77, 78, 109. Practical Organ School, op. 55; English editions by J. Bishop, W. T. Best, and J. A. Hamilton. Ecole pratique de la Modulation...op. 99. Der choralfreund, oder Studien für das Choralspielen, 7 vols., op. 101, 104, 110, 115, 117, 119, 122, etc. Pianoforte sonatas, variations. Three sonatas for Pf. violin and 'cello, op. 1, etc.

Rinck's Organ School, the work by which he is now known in Britain, is a standard practical authority on the subject of which it treats, illustrated by many examples of various styles of performance which renders it valuable both in a didactic and artistic sense.

RING (John). English writer, B. 1751. D. 1821. Author of "The Commemoration of Handel, and other Poems," Lond., 8vo, 1786; second edition, Lond., 8vo, 1819.

RINUCCINI (Ottavio). Italian poet, flourished at end of 15th and beginning of 16th centuries. B. at Florence. Wrote the pastorals "Daphne" and "Eurydice," 1600, both composed by Peri, and supposed to have been the originals of modern opera.

RIOTTE (Philipp Jacob). German comp., B. Trier, Rhenish Prussia, Aug. 16, 1776. S. under André. Music-director at Gotha, 1806. Resided at Vienna as cond. and teacher. D. Vienna, Aug. 20, 1856.

WORKS.—*Operas, etc.*; Das Grenzstädtchen, 1803; Mozart's Zauberflöte, 1820; Liebe auf dem Lande, 1833; Noureddin; Die Lieb 'in der Stadt, 1834. Symphonies, op. 25, etc.; Concertos for Pf., clarinet, and flute and orch.; Quartets for strings; Sonatas for Pf. and violin, op. 13, 35, 44, 45, 50, 55; Sonatas for Pf. solo, op. 2, 3, 11, 20, 32, 37, 38, 41, 52. Fantasias, variations, etc., for Pf. solo.

RISELEY (George). English cond. and org., B. Bristol, Aug. 28, 1845. Chor. Bristol Cath., 1852. Articled to John D. Corfe, of Bristol Cath. Deputy-org., Bristol Cath., and in 1876 he succeeded to the full post. Established a series of Orchestral Concerts at Bristol in 1877, which have now become most important and influential in the west of England. Mr. Riseley is known as an organist throughout England, and as a conductor and organiser he is widely celebrated.

RITSON (Joseph). English antiquary and writer, B. Stockton, 1752. D. London, 1803. Compiled, among other valuable and interesting works, "Ancient Songs, from the Time of King Henry the Third to the Revolution. Prefixed are observations on the Ancient English Minstrels, and Dissertation on Ancient Songs and Music." Lond., 1790, 8vo. "Scottish Songs, with the Music, and Historical Essay..." Lond., 2 vols., 1794, 12mo. Reprinted, Glasgow, 2 vols., 1869. Also an English Anthology, Ballad Collections, and a Bibliographia Poetica, etc.

RITTER (August Gottfried). German org. and comp., B. Erfurt, Aug. 23, 1811. S. under Müller and L. Berger. Org. at Erfurt, and afterwards of Magdeburg Cath., 1843. D. Magdeburg, Aug. 27, 1885.

WORKS.—Die kunst der Orgelspiels, Erfurt, n. d.; Concerto for Pf. and orch.; Sonatas for Pf., op. 20, 21, etc. Preludes, fugues, sonatas, variations, etc., for org. Songs, etc.

RITTER (Frederick Louis). French writer and comp., B. Strasburg, 1834. Descended from a Spanish family of name Caballero. S. under Hauser, Schletterer, and G. Kastner. Prof. of music in Protestant seminary of Fénéstrange. Went to the United States, and was a cond. and teacher in Cincinnati, New York, etc, directing Sacred Harmonic Soc., N. Y., Arion Choral Soc., etc. Prof. of music in Vassar Coll., Poughkeepsie, 1867. Mus. Doc., New York, 1878.

WORKS.—Symphonies for orch, in A, E min., and E flat; Overture for orch., Othello; Concerto for Pf. and orch.; Stella, symphonic poem; op. 1. Hafis, Persian songs; op. 2. Scherzo, Pf.; op. 3. Ten children's songs; op. 5. Eight Pf. pieces; op. 6. Six songs; op. 7. Five choruses for male voices; op. 8. Psalm xxiii. for female voices; op. 11. Organ fantasia. History of Music, in the form of Lectures, Boston, 2 vols., 1870-74, 8vo. Reprinted as History of Music, from the Christian Era to the Present Time, Lond., 8vo, 1878. 2nd edit., 1880. Music in England, New York, 8vo, 1883. Music in America, N. Y., 8vo, 1883. London reprint 2 vols. 1884. Practical Method for the Instruction of Chorus-Classes, etc.

Ritter's History of Music is the best and most comprehensive work in English coming down to recent times.. His other literary works also possess some value. His wife, *née* FANNY RAYMOND, B. Philadelphia, 1840, is an accomplished musician and writer, and has published "Letters on Music to a Lady, by L. Ehlert," trans., London, 8vo, 1877. "Woman as a Musician, an Art Historical Study," Lond., 8vo, 1877. "Some Famous Songs, an Art Historical Sketch," Lond., 8vo, 1878. She also translated Schumann's Music and Musicians, Essays and Criticisms ...2 series, 8vo, 1878-1880.

RIVIÈRE (Jules Prudence). French comp. and music-publisher. Partner in the music-publishing firm of Rivière and Hawkes, London. Comp. "Babil and Bijou," opera, containing "Spring, gentle spring," chorus, which was greatly popular. He also composes much music for military band, and many dances, Pf. music, and songs. He is also celebrated as a cond., and in this capacity has directed some large series of promenade concerts.

RIZZIO (Davide), or Riccio. Italian musician, B. Turin, early in the 16th century. Son of a dancing-master. Musician in service of Court of Savoy, and in suite of Ambassador of the Grand Duke to Scotland, 1564. French Secretary to Mary Queen of Scots. In this position Rizzio made himself very distasteful to the Protestant party in Scotland and also to Darnley, husband of the Queen, and on March 9, 1566, as the outcome of a joint conspiracy, he was assassinated in Holyrood Palace by Lord Ruthven, George Douglas, and others. He receives mention here on account of the very absurd notion which has got abroad that to him is due the invention of the Scottish style of music. Oswald encouraged this belief by affixing Rizzio's name to several tunes in his collections, which are now supposed to have been Oswald's own. Among the tunes said to have been composed by Rizzio are "Gala Water," "Bush aboon Traquair," and others. Rizzio had some skill on the lute, but seems otherwise to have been an artful Italian, more bent on self-advancement than on improving the national music of a turbulent country.

ROBBERECHTS (André). Belgian violinist and comp., B. Brussels, Dec. 16, 1797. S. Paris Cons., and under Baillot and Viotti. Solo violinist to the King of Belgium. D. Paris, May 23, 1860. Comp. music for the violin, etc.

ROBERTI (Giulio). Italian comp. and singing master, B. Barga, Saluzzo, Nov. 14, 1823. S. under Rossi. Director of singing school at Florence, 1869, etc.

WORKS.—Pier de' Medici, opera, 1849; Petrarca, opera, 1858. Masses. Corso elementare di Musica Vocale, Pagine di buona fede a proposito di Musica, Florence, 1876. Solfeggi, Songs, etc.

ROBERTS (John Varley). English org. and comp., B. Stanningley, near Leeds, Sept. 25, 1841. At an early age became org. of S. John's Ch., Farsley, near Leeds. Org. of S. Bartholomew's Ch., Armley, Leeds. Org. and choir-master, Parish Church, Halifax, 1867 (of this church Sir John Herschell was at one time organist. The organ, originally built by Snetzler, was in 1870-1879 enlarged and improved on the suggestion and under the direction of Dr. Roberts, at a cost of about £4000, and it is now one of the finest instruments in the English provinces). Org. Magdalen Coll., Oxford, 1882. Bac. Mus. Oxon., 1871. Doc. Mus. Oxon., 1876. F. C. O., 1876.

WORKS.—Jonah, a sacred cantata, 1876; Appendix and Supplement to Cheetham's Psalmody; Full Morning and Evening Service in D; Evening Service in F, 1880. *Anthems:* Lord, we pray Thee; Seek ye the Lord, etc. *Songs:* I'm thinking of the past; My World; Happy moments I remember; Opposite; Home and Friends; Maiden with the Merry Eye, etc. *Organ:* Andantes in F and G; Postlude in F; Siciliano in F; Fugues, etc. The 103rd Psalm, for chorus and orch. (MS.)

ROBERTSON (Alexander). Scottish musician and teacher of first part of present century. He taught the Pf. on the Logierian system, and was in company with Penson, a violinist, as musicseller in Edinburgh. He afterwards carried on a music-publishing business in partnership with his brother John. Robertson published Marshall's Reels and Strathspeys, and many other Scottish musical works.

ROBERTSON (James Stewart, of Edradynate). Scottish collector, published "The Athole Collection of the Dance Music of Scotland,"...Edinr., 1884, 2 v., fo.

ROBERTSON (Rev. Thomas, D.D.). Scottish divine and writer, was minister at Dalmeny, Linlithgowshire. D. Edinburgh, Nov. 15, 1799. Author of "An Inquiry into the Fine Arts...." Vol. I. London, 1784, 4to. This vol., all that was published of the work, contains the "History and Theory of Ancient and Modern Music."

ROBINSON (Anastasia), COUNTESS OF PETERBOROUGH, English contralto vocalist, B. London, about end of 17th century [1698]. Daughter of a portrait painter. S. under Croft and Sandoni. *Début* in "Creso," 1714. Appeared afterwards in operas by Handel, Scarlatti, and Buononcini. Privately married to the Earl of Peterborough, 1724, at which time she quitted the stage. She is supposed to have lived with him, and to have been considered as his "mistress" till 1735, when, a short time previous to his death in that year, the Earl acknowledged the marriage. D. Bevis Mount, Southampton, 1750.

ROBINSON (Charles S.). American musician, published the following collections:—"Songs for the Sanctuary : or, Hymns and Tunes for Christian Worship," New York, 8vo, 1865 (other editions) ; " Songs for Christian Worship in the Chapel and Family..." 1869 [selected from the foregoing]; "Short Studies for Sunday School Teachers." 1868 ; etc.

ROBINSON (Daniel). English writer, author of "An Essay upon Vocal Musick," Nottingham, 12mo, 1715.

ROBINSON (John). English org. and comp., B. 1682. S. in Chap. Roy. under Dr. Blow. Org. of St. Lawrence, Jewry, and St. Magnus. Org. Westminster Abbey, 1727. D. London, April 30, 1762. Comp. chants, psalms, etc. His wife, ANN TURNER ROBERTSON, whom he married in 1716, was a vocalist of some fame in her day, and sang in the works of Handel. She D. Jan. 5, 1741.

ROBINSON (Joseph). Irish cond and comp., B. Dublin, Aug. 1816. Son of Francis Robinson, a musician. Chor. in St. Patrick's Cath. Established and cond. the Antient Society from 1834. Cond. of University Choral Soc., 1837. Married to Miss Fanny Arthur, 1849. Cond. at the Exhibitions of Cork (1852), and Dublin (1853). Prof. at Irish Academy of Music, 1856. Established the Dublin Musical Soc., 1876. Best known for his enterprise in producing new and large works in Ireland. He comp. anthems, songs, and Pf. music. His wife, FANNY ARTHUR ROBINSON, B. Sept., 1831, was a comp. and pianist. She appeared in London, Paris, and Ireland with great success. D. Dublin, Oct. 31, 1879. Among her comps. should be named "God is Love," cantata ; a number of Pf. pieces, such as "Song of the Mill-wheel," "Elf Land," "The Hunt," "Village Fête," and a few songs,

ROBINSON (Thomas). English musician and writer. Flourished in the 16th and 17th centuries. Published "The Schoole of Musicke : wherein is taught the perfect method of the true Fingering of the Lute, Pandora, Orpharion, and Viol de Gamba..." London, 1603, fo.

ROCHLITZ (Friedrich Johann). German writer and musician, B. Leipzig, Feb. 12, 1769. S. at St. Thomas School, under Doles. Founder and editor of the *Allgemeine Musikalische Zeitung*, 1798-1818. Councillor of Court of Saxe-Weimar. D. Leipzig, Dec. 16, 1842.

WORKS.—Für Freunde der Tonkunst, 1824-32, 4 v. 8vo [Essays on musical subjects reprinted from the *Musikalische Zeitung*] ; Sammlung vorzüglicher Gesangstücke...Mayence, 1838-40, 3 vols., 4to [Collection of vocal music from the works of all the composers who aided in the progress of music to the time of Haydn]. He comp. also masses, cantatas, and hymns.

ROCK (Michael). English comp. and org., B. in latter part of 18th century. S. under Dr. B. Cooke. Org. of Margaret's, Westminster, 1802. D. Lond., March, 1809. Comp. glees, "Let the sparkling wine go round" (prize, 1794), etc. Another musician named WILLIAM ROCK, was org. of St. Margaret's, Westminster, 1774-1802. He comp. glees, songs, and some instrumental music.

ROCKSTRO (William Smyth). English musician and writer, B. about 1830. Pupil of Mendelssohn. Precentor of All Saints, Babbicombe, Devon. Author of the following

WORKS.—Harmonies for Additional Chants and the Ambrosian Te Deum, Lond., 1870, 4to ; History of Music for the Use of Young Students,...Lond., n.d. ; The Rules of Counterpoint, Lond. ; Practical Harmony for Young Students, Lond., 1881 ; Life of G. F. Handel, London, 1883, 8vo ; A General History of Music from the Infancy of the Greek Drama to the Present Period, Lond., 1886, 8vo. Numerous important contributions to Sir George Grove's "Dictionary of Music." He has also comp. and edited numerous Pf. pieces, and published several tales.

RODE (Jacques Pierre Joseph). French violinist and comp., B. Bordeaux, Feb. 16, 1774. S. under Dacosta, Gervais and Viotti. *Début* as violinist at

Paris, in Viotti's 13th Concerto, 1790. Appeared in Berlin and Hamburg. Shipwrecked on the English coast when on his way from Hamburg, 1794. Played at concert in London, 1794. Performed again in Germany, with great success. Returned to Paris and became Prof. of violin in the Cons. Appeared in Spain, 1799. Solo violinist to Napoleon I., 1800. Went to St. Petersburg with Boieldieu, 1803, where he became solo violinist to the Emperor Alexander. Returned to Paris, 1808, and afterwards travelled in Germany, concert-giving, 1811-14. Retired to Bordeaux, and after an unsuccessful re-appearance at Paris in 1825, finally quitted public life and D. Château de Bourbon, Tonneins, near Bordeaux, Nov. 26, 1830.

WORKS.—Concertos for violin and orch., No. 1 in D minor; No. 2 in E; No. 3 in G minor; No. 4 in A; No. 5 in D; No. 6 in B flat; No. 7 in A minor; No. 8 in E minor; No. 9 in C; No. 10 in B minor; No. 11 in D; No. 12 in E. Quartets for strings, opp. 11, 14, 15, 18, 24, 25. Themes with variations, for violin and orch., opp. 10, 13, 19, 21, 26. Cavatina and rondo, violin and orch., op. 28. Duets for 2 violins. Caprices, op. 22. Romances, Exercises, etc. Songs.

With Kreutzer and Baillot, he compiled the violin school adopted for use in Paris Cons. Rode was one of the greatest performers of his time, and did much by example to improve the style of playing current during the period of his public appearances. His works are still in use, especially for didactic purposes.

RODOLPHE (Jean Joseph), or RUDOLPHE. French horn-player and comp., B. Strasburg, Oct. 14, 1730. S. horn under his Father. S. under Leclair. Horn-player in service of Duke of Parma, 1754; Duke of Würtemburg; and in band of Prince de Conti, at Paris. Prof. of Horn in Paris Cons. D. Paris, Aug. 1812. Comp. operas, horn music, etc.

RODWELL (Ann). English writer, authoress of "The Juvenile Pianist," Lond., 4to [1838]; several editions.

RODWELL (George Herbert Bonaparte). English comp. and dramatist, B. London, Nov. 15, 1800. Son of Thomas Rodwell, part-proprietor of the Adelphi Theatre, on whose death in March, 1825, he succeeded to his share in the theatre. Music-director of Covent Garden, 1836. Married to Miss Liston, daughter of John Liston, the comedian. D. Pimlico, London, Jan. 22, 1852.

WORKS.—*Operettas, etc.:* The Bottle Imp, 1828; The Mason of Buda, 1828; The Spring Lock, 1829; The Earthquake, 1829; The Devil's Elixir, 1829; My Own Lover, 1832; The Evil Eye, 1832; The Lord of the Isles, 1834; Paul Clifford, 1835; The Sexton of Cologne, 1836; Jack Sheppard, 1839; Grace Darling; Die Hexen am Rhien; Sathanus; Don Quixote; The Bronze Horse; Quasimodo (from Weber's "Preciosa"); The Last Days of Pompeii. Songs of the Sabbath Eve, poetry by E. Fitzball. Songs of the Birds, by Fitzball; Six Rounds, two Books, Lond., 8vo, n. d. The Royal Serenades, 3 part-songs. *Songs:* A cup of nectar; Awake ye gallant sons of Greece; Banks of the Blue Moselle; Beautiful blue violets; Blind flower-girl's song; Flower of Ellerslie; Hurrah! for the road; Here's a health to thee, Mary; Land of the free; Muleteer; Nix, my dolly, pals fake away; Poor Louise; Song of Night; Up, brothers, up; Who cares, etc. The First Rudiments of Harmony, with an Account of all Instruments employed in an Orchestra, Lond., 1830, 8vo. A Catechism on Harmony, Lond., n. d. The Guitar, Lond., n. d. A Letter to the Musicians of Great Britain, Lond., 1833. Also a few novels, of which "Old London Bridge" ran through several editions, and was reprinted in America. "The Memoirs of an Umbrella," and "Woman's Love," are two others. Also farces and dramatic pieces.

Rodwell was a favourite lyric composer in his day, and was very popular among all classes. He was associated with Barnett, Bishop, and others, in the attempt to get a National English Opera established.

ROE (Richard). Irish vocalist and writer. D. London, April, 1853. He wrote "The Principles of Rhythm, both in Speech and Music, especially in the mechanism of English verse," Dublin, 1823, 4to.

ROECKEL (Joseph Augustus). German cond. and tenor vocalist, B. Neumburg, Upper Palatinate, Aug. 28, 1783. Employed as secretary to the Bavarian chargé d' Affaires, at Salzburg. Tenor singer in opera at Vienna,

1804. Prof. of singing at the Imperial Opera, Vienna, 1823. Opera director at Aix-la-Chapelle, 1828. Introduced German opera into Paris, 1829-32. D. Anhalt-Köthen, Sept. 19, 1870. His eldest son, AUGUSTUS (B. Gratz, Dec. 1, 1814, D. Buda Pesth, June 18, 1876), was a music director at Dresden. His second son, EDUARD, B. Trèves, Nov. 20, 1816, S. under Hummel. Appeared in London, 1835, and gave concerts till 1848, when he settled at Bath as a teacher and pianist. He has published caprices, nocturnes, scherzos, marches, mazurkas, etc., for Pf.

ROECKEL (Joseph Leopold). Youngest son of Joseph Augustus Roeckel, B. London, April 11, 1838. S. under Eisenhofer and Götze. Teacher and pianist at Clifton.

WORKS.—*Cantatas:* Fair Rosamond, 1871 ; The Ten Virgins ; Ruth ; Father Christmas ; The Sea Maidens ; Westward Ho ; Heather Belles ; Mary Stuart. *Songs:* Two sets of five songs, op. 12, 13 ; Angus Macdonald ; Arise, sweet maiden, mine ; Beside the sea ; Bride bells ; Children in the wood ; Elsie's dream ; I cannot say good-bye ; Nellie's good-night ; Sea story ; Sun dial ; Storm fiend ; Sun dial ; The river and the rose ; The tryst, etc. *Pianoforte:* Air du Dauphin ; Allegretto pastorale ; Bella Napoli! ; Fête Roumaine ; Impromptu caprices, 2 books ; Morgenlieder, 4 nos. ; Three musical sketches ; Sylphentanz, etc.

ROEDER (Martin). German comp. and violinist, B. Berlin, April 7, 1851. S. under Joachim and Kiel. Chorus-director at Teatro dal Vermio, Milan, 1873. Cond. Italian opera company in Spain and Azores, 1875-76. Resident in Berlin.

WORKS.—*Operas:* Pietro Candiano IV. Giuditta ; Vera. Maria Magdalena, oratorio ; Two symphonic poems ; Lieder, op. 11, 12 ; Gavotte for Pf., op 7 ; 5 Gesänge, voice and Pf., op. 3 ; Trio for Pf., vn., and 'cello, op. 14 ; Italienische wanderbilder, Pf. duet, op. 24. Various literary works, and contributions to periodical literature.

ROFFE (Alfred). English writer, author of "The Handbook of Shakespeare Music, being an Account of Three Hundred and Fifty Pieces of Music set to words taken from the Plays and Poems of Shakespeare, the Compositions ranging from the Elizabethan Age to the Present Time," Lond., 1878, 4to ; "Ghost Belief of Shakespeare," London, 1851, privately printed ; etc.

ROGEL (José). Spanish comp., cond., and violinist, B. Orihuela, Alicante, Dec. 24, 1829. S. under Cascales, Gil, and P. Perez. Cond. in Spain. Comp. operas, operettas, etc.

ROGER (Gustave Hippolyte). French tenor vocalist, B. Chapelle-Saint-Denis, Paris, Dec. 17, 1815. Educated for the law. S. music at Paris Cons., under Martin, 1836 ; gained prizes for singing. *Début* at the Opéra Comique, Paris, Feb. 1838. Appeared afterwards in operas by Thomas, Halévy, Auber, Meyerbeer, David, and Boieldieu. Appeared in London, 1847, and afterwards sang in the English provinces, 1848. Sang in Germany in 1850, and afterwards. Lost his right arm through the accidental bursting of a rifle. Prof. of singing in Paris Cons., 1868. D. Paris, September 12, 1879.

One of the most famous of French tenor vocalists. For him parts were specially written by various composers, and he was uniformly successful in all of his representations. He was a very good actor, and was best adapted for light parts. After his death, was published "Le Carnet d'un Ténor," Paris, 1880, a book of reminiscences.

ROGERS (Benjamin). English comp. and org., B. Windsor, 1614. Son of Peter Rogers, lay-clerk of S. George's Chap. Chor. under Dr. Giles, and lay-clerk. S. George's Chap., Windsor. Org. Christ Church Cath., Dublin, 1639. Gent. of S. George's Chap., Windsor, 1641. Music-teacher in Windsor. Mus. Bac. Cantab., 1658. Org. Eton Coll., circa 1662. Reappointed lay-clerk, Windsor, 1662. Org. Magdalen Coll., Oxford, 1664-85. Mus. Doc., Oxon., 1669. D. Oxford, June, 1698.

WORKS.—A Set of Airs in Four Parts, for Violins, 1653. Hymnus Eucharisticus, 1660. Evening Service in G. Services in D, A minor, E minor, and F.

Anthems: Behold now, praise the Lord ; Lord, who shall dwell ; O pray for the peace of Jerusalem ; Teach me, O Lord ; etc., contained in the collections of Boyce, Page, Ouseley, and Rimbault. Hymns, songs, and instrumental pieces.

ROGERS (Edmund). English comp. and org., B. Salisbury, 1851. Chor. Salisbury Cath., 1860-65. Org. of Church of S. Thomas, Portman Sq., Lond.

WORKS.—*Cantatas:* The Bridal Lay, 1871 ; Jack and the Beanstack, 1879 ; Blue Beard, 1881 ; Beauty and the Beast, 1882 ; John Gilpin ; or, the Ride to Ware, 1883 ; The Pilgrim's Progress, 1883 ; The Forty Thieves, 1884. Mass in D. Offertory Sentences. *Part-Songs:* Sleep on, my babe ; Softly falls the moonlight. *Songs:* The Huguenot ; My Pet ; When we two parted ; Timothy Tym. Twenty-five Nursery Rhymes. Organ voluntaries, Pf. music, hymns, etc.

ROGERS (Frederick F.) English comp. and org., B. Cheltenham, 1846. Org. and choir-master Parish Ch., Highworth, 1863-65. Assistant org. Parish Ch., Great Malvern ; and org. at College Chap., 1865-69. Org. and choirmaster, St. Peter's, Malvern Wells.

WORKS.—Festival Setting of Te Deum, in F ; Te Deum in G, for Parish Choirs. 69th Psalm for solo, chorus and organ (MS.) Offertory Sentences. Numerous Chants and Kyries. Deborah, sacred cantata for solo voices, chorus, and orch. *Pianoforte:* Valse Sentimentale ; Minuet Sentimentale ; In the Gloaming ; Minuet, in A. Songs and Part-songs.

ROGERS (Sir John Leman, Bart.) English amateur comp., B. April 18, 1780. Succeeded to the baronetcy, 1797. Mem. of the Madrigal Soc., 1819. President of Madrigal Soc., 1820-41. D. Dec. 10, 1847.

WORKS.—Sixteen Glees, for three, four, five, and six voices, Lond., n. d., fo. Church Service in F ; anthems, chants, and other sacred music.

ROGERS (Roland). English comp. and org., B. West Bromwich, Staffordshire, Nov. 17, 1847. Commenced study of music at the age of 11. Org. of S. John's, Wolverhampton, 1861. Org. Tettenhall Parish Ch., 1867. Mus. Bac. Oxon., 1870. Org. Bangor Cath., after competition, before George Cooper, 1872. Mus. Doc. Oxon., 1875.

WORKS.—Prayer and Praise, a Cantata. Symphony for orch. in A minor (MS.) Quintet for strings (MS.) Anthems, Part-songs, Songs, Organ music.

ROHNER (Georg Wilhelm). German writer and comp., B. Saxe-Coburg, 1806. Mus. Doc. Dublin, 1870. D. Liverpool, Feb. 26, 1884. Author of "A Practical Treatise on Musical Composition, in three Parts," Lond., 1849-54, 4to. "Art of Singing," Lond., 1856, fo. "Art of Piano Playing," Lond., n. d., fo. "Moses," an Oratorio ; Foxglove, or the Quaker's Will, opera, 1883 ; a Stabat Mater ; and Vocal and Pf. music.

ROKITANSKY (Victor, Freiherr von). Austrian bass vocalist and teacher, B. Vienna, July 9, 1834. S. at Bologna and Milan. Appeared in England, 1856. *Début* at Prague, 1862. Re-appeared in London, 1865, and again in 1876-77. Prof. of singing in Vienna Cons., 1871-80, and teacher there.

ROLLA (Alessandro). Italian violinist and comp., B. Pavia, April 22, 1757. S. under Renzi and Conti. Leader in band at Parma, where Paganini was his pupil. Cond. of the Opera at La Scala, Milan, 1802. Prof. Milan Cons., etc. D. Milan, Sept. 15, 1841. Comp. ballets, serenades, concertos ; quartets, trios, and duets for stringed instruments. His son ANTONIO, B. Parma, April 18, 1798. D. Dresden, May 19, 1837, was a violinist and comp. for that instrument.

ROLLE (Johann Heinrich). German comp. and org., B. Quedlinburg, Dec. 23, 1718. S. under his father, a musician. Court musician in chapel of Frederick the Great. Org. of church of St. John, Madgeburg. D. Madgeburg, Dec. 29, 1785.

WORKS.—*Oratorios, etc.*: Der tod Abels, 1771 ; La Victoire de David, 1776 ; Saul, 1776 ; Abraham auf Moria, 1777 ; Lazarus, 1777 ; David und Jonathan, 1773 ; Samson ; Thirza und ihre Söhne, 1784 ; Oreste et Pylade ; Idamant, 1782 ;

Melida, 1785; Mehala; La Tempête, 1802. Odes of Anacreon. Passion music. Church cantatas. Lieder. Pf. music, etc.

ROMAINE (Rev. William). English divine and writer, 1714-1795. Author of "An Essay on Psalmody, by W. R.," Lond., 1775, 12mo.

ROMANI (Felice). Italian librettist, B. Genoa, Jan. 31, 1788. D. Moneglia, Riviera, Jan. 28, 1865. Author of many opera librettos, among which may be specified "La Sonnambula," "Norma," and "L'Elisir d'Amore." He wrote numerous other opera books for composers like Rossini, Mercadante, Donizetti, and Ricci.

ROMANO. See CACCINI (GIULIO).

ROMBERG (Andreas). German comp. and violinist, B. Vechte, Osnabruck, April 27, 1767. S. music under his father, a clarinet player. Appeared as violinist when only seven years old. *Début* at Paris, 1784. Violinist in band of the Elector at Bonn. Appeared in Italy, 1793-96. Travelled in North Europe as a violinist. Resided at Hamburg, where he was married. Chap.-master at Gotha. D. Gotha, Nov. 10, 1821.

WORKS.—*Operas and Operettas:* Das Graue Ungeheuer, 1790; Der Rabe, 1791; Die Macht der Musik, 1791; Don Mendoce, 1800. *Cantatas*: Die Ruinen von Paluzzi; Die Grossmuth des Scipio; Die Glocke, Schiller (The Lay of the Bell), op. 25, 1808; Harmony of the Spheres, op. 45 (Kosegarten); The Transient and the Eternal (Kosegarten); The Power of Song (Schiller); Die Kindesmörderin, op. 27; Psalms; Te Deums, etc. Symphonies for orch., op. 6, 22, 33, and 51. Concertos for violin and orch., op. 3, 8, 46, 50. Quintets for strings, op. 23, 58. Quartets for strings, op. 1, 2, 5, 7, 11, 16, 30, 58, 59. Rondos for violin and orch., duets for violins, studies for violin, etc. Psalmodie...Offenbach, n. d., 4to. Lieder. Sonatas for violin and Pf. and other works.

Best known by his cantata, the "Song of the Bell," and his symphony for toy instruments. His style is formed on that of Mozart, and is careful and unaffected.

ROMBERG (Bernhard). German violoncellist and comp., B. Dinklage, Nov. 11, 1767. Cousin of the foregoing. S. under his father. Played in band of the Elector of Cologne at Bonn. Travelled as 'cellist in Italy, Spain, and Austria. Resided at Hamburg. Prof. of 'cello in Paris Cons., 1801-3. 'Cellist in Royal band at Berlin till 1806, and Court music-director till 1817. Travelled as a virtuoso till about 1840. D. Hamburg, Aug. 13, 1841.

WORKS. —*Operas:* Die wiedergefundene Statue, 1790; Der Schiffbruch, 1791; Don Mendoce (with Andreas Romberg), Paris, 1800; Ulysses und Circe, op. 26, 1827; Rittertreue, 1817. Concertos for violoncello and orch., op. 2, 3 in D, 7 in E, 30, 31 (military), 44 in C, 48 in A, 56 in B minor; Overtures for orch., op. 11 and 14; Concertino for 2 'cellos and orch., op. 72; Quartets for strings, op. 1, 12, 25, 39, etc ; Trios for strings, op, 8, 38, etc. Sonatas, fantasias, duets, caprices, rondos, etc., for 'cello and Pf. Music written in association with his cousin Andreas. Method for the Violoncello, Berlin, 1840.

Famous as a performer more than as a composer. His concertos are still in the repertoires of the best players, and some of his music for the violoncello is in use at the present time for teaching purposes.

ROMER (Emma). English soprano vocalist, B. 1814. S. under Sir George Smart. *Début* at Covent Garden Theatre, London, 1830. Sang in English Opera House, etc. Appeared chiefly in English operas, which she produced at the Surrey Theatre, London. D. Margate, April 11, 1868.

ROMER (Frank). English writer and comp., B. London, Aug. 5, 1810. Member of the music-publishing firm of Hutchings and Romer. Comp. Fridolin, opera, 1840; The Pacha's Bride, opera. *Songs*: Day dreams, Fair Chloris, I joyfully carol, I've watched with thee, Maiden of the sunny clime, Now smiling comes the joyous spring, O mother hear thy poor blind child, The lay of the chimes; Part-music for three and four voices, etc. "The Physiology of the Human Voice," London, 1850, 8vo (2 editions).

RONCONI (Domenico). Italian tenor vocalist, B. Lendinara-di-Pollesine, Venetia, July 11, 1772. S. under Pacchierotti and Babini. Singing master at

Conegliano and Venice. *Début* as tenor at the San Benedetto Theatre, Venice, 1796. Afterwards appeared in various parts of Italy, and in St. Petersburg. Court vocalist to the King of Bavaria at Munich, 1819-29. Teacher in Milan. D. Milan, April 13, 1839. He comp. ariettas and other vocal pieces. His sons were all distinguished vocalists. GIORGIO, barytone, B. Milan, Aug. 6, 1810, S. under his father, and made his *début* in 1831 at Pavia. He subsequently sang in various parts of Italy, and found much favour in Rome, Florence and Naples. Married Giovannina Giannoni, 1837. Appeared at H. M. Theatre, London, 1842, in Donizetti's "Lucia di Lammermoor." Sang also in the provinces same year. Sang in Paris, 1842, and in succeeding years appeared successfully in Austria, Spain, and Italy. He sang in London again, in 1847, and continued to appear there till 1866. He had in 1863 established a singing school at Granada. He afterwards appeared in America, and on his return to Europe, in 1874, became Prof. of singing at Madrid Cons. He has comp. some fine songs, and published "Il Baritono moderno, 12 vocalizzi per voce di baritono," Milan, n.d. His brother FELICE, B. Venice, 1811, D. St. Petersburg, Sept. 10, 1875, wrote songs and a vocal method. He had some fame as a teacher. Finally, SEBASTIANO, the youngest son of Domenico, B. at Venice, 1814. S. under his father, and appeared with much success as a barytone singer in Italy, Spain, Austria, and America. He sang in London in 1860. Now a teacher of singing at Milan.

RONDINELLA (Pasquale). Italian writer and vocal teacher, B. Naples, March 16, 1825. S. Naples Cons. under Lanza, Ruggi, Mercadante, etc. Settled in Philadelphia, U.S.A., as teacher of singing, 1852. Author of ("Preparatory Lessons in the Art of Singing,..." Philadelphia, 1864, 2 parts; 65 Progressive Exercises; 50 Vocalises; 12 Vocalising Melodies; Fundamental Rules for the study of Harmony, Boston, n.d.

RÖNTGEN (Julius). German comp. and pianist, B. Leipzig, May 9, 1855. Son of Engelbert (B. Deventer, Holland, 1829), a violinist and prof. in Leipzig Cons. S. under his father, and Hauptmann, Richter, and Plaidy. Afterwards S. under F. Lachner at Munich. Travelled in Germany with Julius Stockhausen, the vocalist, concert-giving, 1873. Teacher at Amsterdam.

WORKS.—Op. 1. Sonata for Pf. and violin; op. 2. Sonata for Pf.; op. 3. Sonata for Pf. and 'cello; op. 4. Aus der Jugendzeit, Pf. pieces; op. 5. Ballade, Pf.; op. 6. Cyclus of Pf. pieces; op. 7. Suite for Pf.; op. 8. Phantasie, Pf.; op. 9. Toskanische Rispetti, operetta; op. 10. Sonata for Pf.; op. 11. Neckens Polska, variations for Pf.; op. 14. Serenade for wind instruments; op. 15. Lieder for voice and Pf.; op. 18. Concerto for Pf. and orch.; op. 20. Sonata for Pf. and violin in F sharp minor; op. 21. Nordisches Volkslied, Pf. and violin, etc.

RONZI (Claudine). See BEGNIS (Claudine Ronzi de).

ROOKE (William Michael), or ROURKE. Irish comp., B. Dublin, Sept. 29, 1794. Self-taught, with the exception of a few lessons from Dr. Cogan. Chorus-master and deputy-leader at Crow St. Theatre, Dublin, 1817. Settled in England. Chorus-master at Drury Lane Theatre, London, and teacher of singing. D. London, Oct. 14, 1847.

WORKS.—*Operas:* Amilie, or the Love Test, Lond., 1837; Henrique, or, the Love Pilgrim, Lond., 1839; Cagliostro (MS.) *Songs,* Pf. music, etc.

ROOT (George Frederick). American comp. and writer, B. Sheffield, Mass., Aug. 30, 1820. Removed with his parents to New Reading, 1826. Partner with A. N. Johnson, as teacher of singing and org. at Boston, 1834-43. Music teacher in New York, where he established a school for the training of music teachers, 1844-55. Removed to Chicago, and founded the firm of Root & Cady, 1860-80.

WORKS.—*Cantatas:* The Flower Queen; Daniel (with Bradbury); The Haymakers, 1865; Pilgrim Fathers; Belshazzar's Feast; The Song Tournament. *Collections:* Church Music, 1849; Academy Vocalist, 1852; Young Ladies' Choir; Musical Album; Young Men's Singing-book (with L. Mason), 1855; Sabbath Bell, 1856; Festival Glee-book, 1857; The Shawm; The Diapason, 1860; The Bugle-call, 1863; The Cornet, 1865; Silver Lute; The Forest Choir; The

Triumph, 1868; The Choir and Congregation. *Theoretical:* Singer's Manual, 18mo, 1849; School for the Melodeon, Harmonium, and Cabinet Organ, 4to, 1863; The Musical Curriculum for Solid and Symmetrical acquirement in Pianoforte playing, etc., 4to, 1865 (numerous editions); Guide for the Pianoforte, Cincinnati, n. d.; School of Singing, n. d.; Normal Musical Hand-book, n. d. *Songs:* Away on the prairie alone; Battle-cry of freedom; Beyond; Boy at the fountain; Dearest spot on Earth to me is home; Hazel Dell; Honeysuckle glen; Jenny Lyle; Just before the battle, Mother; Kiss me Mother, kiss your Darling; Lilly Brook; Rosalie the prairie flower; There is music in the air, etc. Numerous vocal quartets, and many Pf. pieces.

Some of Root's productions have been received with extraordinary popular favour, especially such as are in the same vein as S. C. Foster's contributions to American negro minstrelsy. A number of Root's songs, etc. were issued under the *nom de plume* of G. F. *Wurzel,* the German for *root.*

ROOTSEY (S., F.L.S.) English writer, author of "An attempt to simplify the Notation of Music, together with an account of that now in use,"...London, 1811, 4to.

RORE (Cipriano di). Flemish comp., B. Mechlin, 1516. S. at Venice under Adrien Willaert. Musician in service of the Duke of Ferrara. Returned to Venice and became second chap.-master of St. Marks, 1559; succeeded Willaert in full post, 1563. Went to Court of Parma shortly after. D. Parma, 1565.

WORKS.—Il Primo Libro de' Madrigali à quattro voci, Venice, 1542, 4to; Il secondo Libro de' Madrigali a quattro e cinque voci, 1543; Madrigali a cinque voci, 1544; Mottetti a quattro, cinque, sei et otto voci, 1544; Il secondo libro de' Mottetti a quattro e cinque voci, 1547; Il terzo libro di Mottetti,..1569; Fantasie e Ricercari à 3 voci,...Venice, 1549, Madrigali Cromatici à 5 voci, 5 books, 1560-68; Liber Missarum 4, 5, et 6 vocum, 1566; Cantiones sacrae, 1573; Salmi e Vespere, 1593; Tutti i Madrigali di Cipriano di Rore,...Venice, 1577, fo., etc.

This famous and learned musician is still remembered by a few of his madrigals. He is commonly named along with Lassus as a reformer of the musical style current in the 16th century, and as one of the first to employ chromatic progressions with ease and skill.

ROSA (Carl August Nicolas), or ROSE. German cond., violinist, and opera manager, B. Hamburg, March 22, 1842. S. under Lindenau, and at Leipzig Cons., 1859, under David, Dreyschock, Hauptmann, and Richter. *Début* as violinist in a concerto by Jansa, 1850. Appeared as violinist at Crystal Palace, London, 1866. Travelled with Mdlle. Parepa, etc., on a concert-tour in the United States. Married Mdlle. Parepa at New York, Feb. 26, 1867. About this period he established the Carl Rosa Opera Company, and with it gave performances in London and throughout Britain from 1875. Among the operas introduced to the British public by Rosa may be named Gounod's "Faust," Cherubini's "Water Carrier," Adam's "Giralda," Wagner's "Flying Dutchman," Cowen's "Pauline," Brüll's "Golden Cross," Wagner's "Rienzi," Bizet's "Carmen," Thomas' "Mignon," Wagner's "Lohengrin," Verdi's "Aida," Stanford's "Veiled Prophet of Khorassan," Goring Thomas' "Esmeralda," Mackenzie's "Colomba," Stanford's "Canterbury Pilgrims," and G. Thomas' "Nadeshda." In addition to all those works originally presented by the Rosa Company, there is included in the repertory of the company many standard works of Balfe, Wallace, Benedict, Auber, Flotow, Verdi, Mozart, Bellini, Hérold, and Meyerbeer.

ROSA (Salvator). Italian painter, poet, and musician, B. Benella, near Naples, June 20, 1615. D. Rome, March 15, 1673. Was a performer on the lute, and comp. numerous madrigals and cantatas. Burney possessed an MS. collection of music by Italian musicians, in which appeared several of Rosa's compositions, and of these specimens are contained in Burney's History.

ROSE (John), or ROSS. English musician of reign of Elizabeth. Invented a musical instrument of the guitar kind, which he called the bandore. It differed in the method of tuning from the lute or orpharion. His son, JOHN, of the Bridewell, London, was famous during his period as a maker of viols.

ROSE (Mrs. H. R.). See SAMUELL (Clara).

ROSEINGRAVE. See ROSINGRAVE.

ROSELLEN (Henri). French pianist and comp., B. Paris, Oct. 13, 1811. Son of a Pf. manufacturer there. S. at Paris Cons. under Pradher, Zimmerman, Halévy, and Herz, from 1823. Teacher of Pf. in Paris. D. Paris, March 20, 1876.

WORKS.—*Pianoforte*: Op. 1. Perles d'Italie, 2 rondos ; op. 28. Three reveries ; op. 37. 2 Fantasias ; op. 55. Décameron des jeunes pianistes ; op. 57. Follette, rondo-valse ; op. 69. Etudes ; op. 83. 3 Divertissements Espagnols ; op. 92. Nocturne, tarentelle, etc.; op. 112. La Rosée, valse ; op. 129. Promenade en mer, barcarolle ; op. 132. Ballade ; op. 138. Pensées ; Numerous fantasias, transcriptions, etc., on airs from popular operas. Méthode de Piano, op. 116 (English edition also); Manual du Pianiste, exercises, etc., op. 116a.

ROSENHAIN (Jacob). German comp. and pianist, B. Mannheim, Dec. 2, 1813, S. under J. Schmitt. Appeared as pianist at Mannheim, 1824, and at Stuttgart, 1825. Afterwards he resided at Frankfort. S. under Schnyder von Wartensee. Appeared in London, 1837, and about the same period settled in Paris.

WORKS.—*Operas, etc.:* Der Besuch in Irrenhause, 1834 ; Liswenna, Frankfort, 1835 ; Le Démon de la Nuit ("Liswenna," rewritten), Paris, 1851 ; Volage et Jaloux, 1863. *Symphonies:* Op. 42. in G minor ; F minor, op. 43 ; F minor " Im Frühling," op. 61. Concerto for Pf. Cantata, for solo voices, chorus, and orch. Quartets and trios for Pf. and strings. *Pianoforte :* Op. 14. Four romances ; op. 15. Romance ; op. 20. 24 Etudes mélodiques ; op. 24. Poëme ; op. 25, 31, 37, Romances. Transcriptions, etc. Lieder, op. 21, 23, etc.

His brother, EDUARD, B. Mannheim, Nov. 18, 1818, D. Frankfort-on-Main, Sept. 6, 1861, was a pupil of Schnyder von Wartensee, and comp. works for the Pf. as follows :—Sicilienne, op. 8 ; Nocturnes, op. 6 and 9 ; Sonata, op. 12 ; Sarmatienne, op. 15 ; Elegie, op. 18 ; A Serenade for Pf. and 'cello, and other works.

ROSENMÜLLER (Johann). German comp. and org., B. in Saxony, 1615. S. at St. Thomas School, Leipzig, of which he afterwards became joint cantor in association with Tobias Michaelis. Resided at Hamburg for a time, but afterwards went to Italy, where he gained much fame as an organist. Chap.-master to Duke of Brunswick at Wolfenbüttel. D. Wolfenbüttel, 1686.

WORKS.—Maximes de l'Ancien et du Nouveau Testament à 3, 4, 5, 6, et 7 voix, 1648-52. XII. Sonata da Camera a 5 stromenti, 1667 ; etc.

Famous for his chorales, and other sacred pieces, some of which appear in modern collections.

ROSETTI (Franz Anton), or DLABACZ. Bohemian comp., B. Leitmeritz, 1750. Educated at Prague. Chap.-master to Count Wallerstein, and at Court of Mecklenburg-Schwerin, 1789. D. Ludwigslust, June 30, 1792. Comp. oratorios, masses, symphonies, quartets, concertos for flute and orch., and sonatas for Pf. His brother, GOTTFRIED JOHANN, B. Prague, July 17, 1758. D. Prague, Feb. 4, 1820. Was a writer, and held musical appointments in Prague.

ROSINGRAVE (Daniel), or ROSEINGRAVE. English org., was chorister in Chap. Royal, and S. with Purcell, etc., under Blow. Org. Winchester Cath., 1681. Org. Salisbury Cath., 1693-98. Org. and vicar choral St. Patrick's Cath., Dublin, June 9, 1698-1727. Org. and stipendiary of Christ Church, Dublin, Nov. 11, 1698. D. Dublin, May, 1727. His son RALPH, became vicar-choral of S. Patrick's Cath., 1719 ; org. do., and of Christ Church, 1727, which post he held till his D. at Dublin, Oct. 1747. THOMAS, another son, B. Dublin, was educated by his father. S. at Rome, at expense of the Dean and Chapter of S. Patrick's Cath., 1710. Comp. at the King's Theatre, London. 1720. Org. of St. George's, Hanover Square, 1725-37. D. insane, London [1750]. He published "Voluntarys and Fugues made on purpose for the Organ or Harpsichord," Lond., n. d., 4to. "Twelve Solos for the German Flute, with a Thorough-bass for the Harpsichord," n. d. ; "Eight Suits of Les-

sons for the Harpsichord or Spinnet in most of the Keys," Lond., fo., n. d. ;
"Six Cantatas, with accompaniments..." Lond., fo., n. d. ; "Narcissus,"
opera by D. Scarlatti, adapted for the English stage, with additional songs,
1720; "A Collection of 42 Suits of Lessons, by D. Scarlatti, with an introduction." Also some anthems, Italian songs, etc. He had some fame as an
organist in his day.

ROSS (John). English org. and comp., B. Newcastle-upon-Tyne, Oct. 12,
1763. S. under Hawden. Org. of S. Paul's Ch., Aberdeen, 1783. D.
Craigie Park, Aberdeen, July 28, 1837.

WORKS.—Six concertos, for Pf. and orch.; Seven sets of 3 sonatas, for Pf., op.
31, etc.; Three sonatas, for Pf. and flute or violin, op. 16; Four sets of six waltzes,
for Pf. ; Duets for Pf., op. 26, etc. Ode to Charity, for solo, chorus, and org.; Six
hymns, for 3 voices and org.; Two books of 6 canzonets, for voice and Pf.;
Numerous songs, in sets and single. A Select Collection of Ancient and Modern
Scottish Airs, adapted for the Voice, with Introductory and Concluding Symphonies
and accompaniments for the Pianoforte, Edin., n. d., fo. Sacred Music, consisting
of Chants, Psalms, and Hymns, Lond., n. d., 4to. A Complete Book of Instructions for Beginners on the Harpsichord or Pianoforte, to which is added a select set
of Airs, Scots Songs, and Lessons, Lond., 1820, fo.

Ross was a musician of great local fame. A number of his songs are well known,
and some of them appeared in R. A. Smith's "Scottish Minstrel."

ROSSETOR (Philip). English lute-player and comp., of first part of 17th century. Published "A Booke of Ayres, set foorth to be song to the Lute,
Orpherian, and Base Violl," Lond., 1601, 4to ; "Lessons for Consort, made
by sundry excellent authors, and set to sixe severall instruments, namely the
Treble lute, Treble violl, Base violl, Bandora, Citterne, and the Flute," Lond.,
1609.

ROSSI (Lauro). Italian comp., B. Macerata, Feb. 20, 1812. S. Naples Cons.
under Crescentini, Furno, and Zingarelli. Leader and comp. at the Teatro
Valle, Rome, 1832. Resided for a time in Milan. Travelled as operatic cond.
in Mexico, Havannah, New Orleans, etc. Married, 1841. Returned to Italy,
1843. Director of Milan Cons., 1870-78. D. Cremona, May 6, 1885.

WORKS.--*Operas*: Le Contesse Villane, 1829 ; Costanzo ed Oringaldo, 1830 ; Il
Disertore Svizzero, 1832 ; I falsi Monetari, 1834 ; Amelia, 1834 ; Leocadia, 1835 ;
Giovanna Shore, 1836 ; Il Borgomestro di Schiedam, 1844 ; Cellini a Parigi, Turin,
1845 ; Azema di Granata, 1846 ; Bianca Contarini, 1847 ; Il Domino nero, Milan ;
Le Sabine, 1852 ; L'Alchimista, 1853 ; Gli Artisti alla fiera, 1868 ; La Contessa
di Mons, 1874 ; Cleopatra, 1874 ; Biorn, 1877 ; La Figlia di Figaro. Saul, ora-
torio, 1833. Cantatas, elegies, songs, and vocal exercises. Guida di Armonia
Pratica Orale, Milan, 1858, and other works.

ROSSI (Luigi). Italian comp. of end of 16th and beginning of 17th centuries.
B. Naples. Comp. operas, cantatas for solo voice, with accomp. Some of
the cantatas have been republished in modern collections.

ROSSI (Luigi Felice). Italian comp. and writer, B. Brandizzo, Chivasso,
Piedmont, July 7, 1805. D. Turin, June 20, 1863. Comp. masses, psalms,
and other sacred music. Also author of some literary works and translations.

ROSSINI (Gioacchino Antonio). Italian comp., B. Pesaro, Feb. 29, 1792.
Son of Giuseppe Rossini, a horn-player, attached to various travelling theatrical companies, and at one time town-trumpeter of Pesaro. S. at Bologna,
under Tesei and Padre Mattei, 1807-8. Travelled about from town to town
in Italy as comp. and cond., 1810-1814. Director of the Concordi Society of
Bologna. Cond. of the San Carlo and Del Fondo theatres at Naples, 1815.
Married Isabella Colbran, the singer, Bologna, 1822. Appeared at Vienna,
1822. Visited London, Dec., 1823. Musical director of the Théâtre Italien,
Paris, 1824. Comp. to the King of France, etc., 1826. Returned to Bologna,
1829. His first wife died, 1845. Grand Officer of the Legion of Honour.
Married Olympe Pelissier, 1847. (She D. Passey, Mar. 22, 1878.) Resided
in Italy till 1855. Returned to Paris, 1855, and resided thereafter always
there, when his home at Passy became the centre of great musical, literary,

and artistic circles. D. Passy, near Paris, Nov. 1, 1868. Established a prize for composition at Paris, and endowed a Cons. of Music at Pesaro.

WORKS.—*Operas*: La cambiale di matrimonio, Venice, 1810; L'Equivoco Stravagante, Bologna, 1811; Demetrio et Polibio, 1812; L'Inganno felice, Venice, 1812 (London, 1819); La scala di seta, Venice, 1812; La Pietra del Paragone, Milan, 1812; L'Occasione fa il ladro, Venice, 1812; Il Figlio per azzardo, 1813; Tancredi, Venice, 1813 (Lond., May, 1820); I due Bruschini, Venice, 1813; L'Italiana in Algeri, Venice, 1813 (Lond., 1819), Aureliano in Palmira, Milan, 1813 (Lond., 1826); Il Turco in Italia, Milan, 1814 (Lond., 1821); Elisabetta, regina d'Inghilterra, Naples, 1815 (Lond., 1818); Sigismundo, Venice, 1815; Torvaldo e Dorliska, Rome, 1815; Il Barbiere di Siviglia, Rome, Feb. 5, 1816 (London, 1818; Paris, 1824); La Gazzetta, Naples, 1816; Otello, Naples, 1816 (London, 1822; Paris, 1844); La Cenerentola, Rome, 1817 (London, 1820); La Gazza ladra, Milan, 1817 (London, 1821); Armida, Naples, 1817; Adelaide di Borgogna, Rome, 1818; Adina, o il Califfo di Bagdad, 1818; Mosè in Egitto, Naples, 1818 (London as "Pietro l'Ermita," 1822; Paris, 1827); Ricciardo e Zoraide, Naples, 1818 (London, 1823); Ermione, Naples, 1819; Eduardo e Cristina, Venice, 1819; La Donna del Lago, Naples, Oct. 4, 1819 (London, 1823; Paris. 1825); Bianca e Faliero, Milan, 1819; Maometto Secondo, Naples, 1820; Matilde di Shabran, Rome, 1821 (London, 1823; Paris, 1857); Zelmira, Naples, 1821 (London, 1824); La Pie Voleuse, Paris, 1822; Semiramide, Venice, 1823 (London, 1824; Paris, 1860); Il Viaggio a Reims, Paris, 1825; Le Siège de Corinthe (a revision of Maometto II.), Paris, 1826 (London, as "L'Assedio di Corinto); Le Comte Ory, Paris, 1828 (London, 1829); Guillaume Tell, Paris, Aug. 3, 1829 (London, in Italian, July, 1839); Robert Bruce (pasticcio by Niedermeyer, from "La Donna del Lago," "Zelmira," and "Armida"), Paris, 1846. Ciro in Babilonia, oratorio, Ferrara, 1812. *Cantatas and occasional pieces*: Il Pianto d'Armonia, 1808; Didone abbandonata, Bologna, 1810; Irene e Egle; Teti e Peleo, 1816; Partenope, 1819; La Riconoscenza, 1821; Il Vero Omaggio, Verona, 1823; L'Augurio felice, 1823; Il Bardo, 1822; La Sacra Alleanza, 1823; Il Pianto delle Muse, London, 1823; Il Ritorno, 1823; I Pastori, 1825; Il Serto votivo, 1829; La Foi, l'Espérance et la Charité, for female voices, 1844; Cantata for the Paris Exhibition, 1867. *Sacred*: Stabat Mater, 1832-41; Petite Messe Solennelle, 1864; Tantum ergo; O Salutaris. Les Soirées musicales, ariettas and duets (these have been transcribed for Pf.); Gorgheggi e Solfeggio, exercises and solfeggios, Lond., fo., n. d. (trans. by Sabilla Novello). *Instrumental*: Mariage de S. A. R. le Duc d' Orléans, 3 marches pour musique militaire (Pf. arrangement also): Quartet for flute, clarinet, horn, and bassoon, in F; Le Rendez-vous de Chasse, fanfare for 4 trumpets (1828); Serenade for orch., in E flat; 5 Sonatinas for Pf. (arranged from string quartets), in G, A, B, E flat, and D; Variations for clarinet and orch., in B. Numerous pieces for Pf., mostly in MS., and consisting of short sketches with whimsical titles.

One of the most famous and popular composers of the 19th century. Many of his operas attained extraordinary contemporary fame, and on all hands his influence on the dramatic music of Italy is allowed to have been great. He did much to strengthen the orchestral department of Italian operatic music, and although he composed very few pieces of transcendent power, his example must be held to have influenced every succeeding Italian musician down to recent times. His music is almost invariably florid in character, and his melodies are not lacking in the excessive ornamentation common to the Italian school. The instrumental accompaniments to his operas are too frequently noisy, and he not uncommonly resorted to the cheap expedient of covering harmonical defects in his concerted vocal music with an overloading crash of brass-and-drum. Notwithstanding, it must be stated that with capable vocalists, no Italian composer can be placed alongside of Rossini for brilliancy, dash, and melody. It is partly due to the trying vocal difficulties of Rossini's works that so few of them now keep the stage; and to this may be added the gradually awakening taste of the musical public for works showing stronger dramatic continuity, and less of the effect got by mere vocal ornament. Some of his overtures, and especially that to "William Tell," continue to be used in Britain for concert purposes, and his Stabat Mater is of constant appearance in the programmes of our choral societies. His operatic works have of recent years been declining in popular esteem, and few of his operas obtain a hearing out of Italy. Of

Rossini literature there is abundance, and the following section may prove useful to the student desirous of a detailed account of his career :—Carpani, "Le Rossiniane..." Padua, 1824; Beyle (Stendhal), "Vie de Rossini," Paris, 1823 (trans. into English, London, 1824); Escudier, "Rossini, sa vie et ses œuvres..." Paris, 1854; Azevedo, "G. Rossini, sa vie et ses œuvres..." Paris, 1865; Edwards, "Life of Rossini..." London, 1869; Pougin, "Rossini..." Paris, 1870; Edwards, "Rossini and his School" (Great Musicians), London, 1881. See also the following Periodicals :—Blackwood's Magazine, vol. 12 ; Cornhill, 1863 (vol. 19); Eclectic Magazine, 1868 (vol. 72); Englishwoman's Domestic Magazine, 1867 (vol. 3); Colburn's New Monthly Magazine, 1828-29 (vols. 26 and 28); Once a Week (by F. Hiller), 1868 (vols. 19 and 20); Edinburgh Review, 1870 (vol. 133); British Quarterly Review, 1869 (vol. 50); London Magazine, 1823 (vol. 9); Musical Journals, *passim*.

ROTA (Andrea). Italian comp., B. Bologna, 1553. Chap.-master of the Basilica of San Petronio. D. Bologna, June, 1597. Comp. "Madrigali a cinque voci," 1579, 2 books ; "Madrigali a 4 voci," 1792 ; " Motetti a 5, 6, 7 voci," 1584 ; "Missarum," 1595.

ROUGET DE LISLE (Claude Joseph). French poet and musician, B. Montaigu, Lons-le-Saulnier, May 10, 1760. D. Choisy-le-Roi, near Paris, June 27, 1836. Was engaged as an officer in the army during the French Revolutionary period. On April 24, 1792, during the excitement occasioned by the declaration of war by the King of Bohemia and Hungary against France, he wrote and set to music a "Chant de Guerre aux Armées " ; afterwards successively known as " Marche des Marseillais," " Hymne des Marseillaise," and " La Marseillaise." This chant is now known all over the world, and as the " Marseillaise Hymn " is used as a national anthem by the French, and as a song of liberty by every other nation.

He wrote also " Essais en vers et en prose," Paris, 1796 ; "Cinquante Chants Français, Paris, 1825 ; and the librettos of " Jacquot, ou l' Ecole des Mères," comic opera by Dellamaria, 1798 ; " Macbeth," opera, Chelard, 1827 ; and many battle chants in the style of the " Marseillaise," none of which attained more than local fame.

ROUSSEAU (Jean Jacques). French writer and musician, B. Geneva, June 28, 1712. Educated in and near Geneva. Lived a strange wandering life, during which he occupied a few appointments. D. Ermenonville, near Paris, July 2, 1778.

WORKS.—*Operas, etc.*: Les muses galantes, 1745 ; Le Devin du Village, Paris, Oct., 1752 ; Pygmalion, scene lyrique, Paris, 1775 ; Daphnis et Chloé (fragment), published at Paris, 1779. Les Consolations des Misères de ma Vie, ou Recueil d'Airs, Romances, et Duos, Paris, 1781, fo. *Literary :* Dissertation Sur la musique Françoise, Paris, 1753, 8vo ; Lettre d'un symphoniste de l'Académie Royale de Musique à ses camarades de l'orchestre, Paris, 1753, 8vo ; Dictionnaire de Musique, Geneva, 1767, 4to ; Paris, 1768, 8vo, and many other editions to that of Paris, 1821-22, 2 vols. English translation as "The Complete Dictionary of Music, consisting of a copious explanation of all words necessary to a true knowledge and understanding of Music, translated from the original French of J. J. Rousseau by William Waring," Lond., 1771, 8vo (2nd edit., 1779). Projet concernant de nouveaux signes pour la Musique, Geneva, 1781, 12mo. The articles on music in Diderot's "Encyclopédie." Numerous letters and pamphlets on the controversies in which he became involved.

Rousseau is much more famous in connection with literature than with music, though his achievements as a musician created no small stir in his day. His only musical works now known are his " Dictionary of Music," and the melody called " Rousseau's Dream," which has been attributed to him, and is now constantly used as a hymn tune.

ROUSSELOIS (Marie Wilhelmine). Austrian soprano vocalist, B. Vienna, Feb. 26, 1765. D. Brussels, Nov. 8, 1850.
Sang with much acceptance in operas by Gluck and other composers.

ROUSSELOT (Scipion). French comp. and violoncellist, B. in early years of present century. S. Paris Cons, under Baudiot, and gained first 'cello prize in 1823. S. harmony under Reicha. Went to London as 'cellist, and took part in the Musical Union Concerts of 1845. He continued to reside in London as a concert-giver, teacher, and music-publisher till 1849, when he retired to Paris.

WORKS.—Symphony for orch., 1834; Sextet for oboe, clarinet, horn, bassoon, 'cello, and d.-bass; Quintets for strings. op. 14, 16, 21, 23, 26; Quartets for strings, op. 10, 25; Trio for Pf., violin and 'cello, op. 7; 3 Sonatinas for 'cello and d.-bass, op. 2; Variations and solos for 'cello, and music for Pf. and violin. His brother JOSEPH FRANCOIS, B. Feb. 6, 1803. S. horn under Dauprat. Horn-player in Paris. D. Argenteuil, near Paris, Sept., 1880.

ROVEDINO (Carlo). Italian bass-singer, B. 1751. Appeared chiefly in England. Sang in London from 1778. D. London, Oct. 6, 1822. Another musician of the same name, TOMMASO, published some vocal music, including a "Descriptive Cantata for Seven Voices," Lond., fo. n.d.

ROVELLI (Pietro). Italian violinist, B. Bergamo, Feb. 6, 1793. S. under G. B. Rovelli, and afterwards under Molique. Appeared with success in Paris, Weimar, Munich, and Vienna. Married Micheline Förster, a pianist. Vnst. in Church of S. Maria Maggiore, Bergamo, 1819. D. Bergamo, Sept. 8, 1838. His grandfather, GIOVANNI BATTISTA, his uncle, GIUSEPPE (B. Bergamo, 1753, D. Parma, 1806), and his father, ALESSANDRO, were all musicians of note.

ROVETTA (Giovanni). Italian comp. of 17th century. Chap.-master of S. Mark's, Venice, in succession to Monteverde, 1643. D. Venice, Oct. 23, 1668. He composed masses, motets, psalms, and madrigals, also operas. His nephew, GIOVANNI BATTISTA, comp. operas during 1649-1664.

ROWBOTHAM (John Frederick). English writer, author of "A History of Music," London, Vol. 1., 1885, 8vo. To be issued in 3 vols.

ROWLAND (Alexander Campbell). English double-bass player, violinist, and comp., B. Trinidad, Jan. 1, 1826. S. under his father, a bandmaster, and in London. Violinist in orch. of Queen's Theatre, 1833, and afterwards at many of the best London and provincial concerts and festivals. Performer on the drum, etc., in Jullien's orch., 1842-46. Double-bass player in orch. of Royal Italian Opera, the Philharmonic Soc., Sacred Harmonic Soc., and H. M. Theatre. Since 1866, has resided at Southampton as teacher.

WORKS.—70th Psalm, for solo, chorus, and orch.; Overture for orch.; Waltzes and other dance pieces, for orch. and Pf.; Fantasias, etc, for double-bass and Pf. *Songs:* Blessed be the Lord; Moonrise; Look out upon the stars, my love; Morning thoughts; The statue over the cathedral door; The white dove; etc. Tutor for the Double-bass, Lond., n. d.

ROXAS (Emanuele de). Spanish comp., B. Reggio, Calabria, Jan. 1, 1827. S. Naples Cons. under Crescentini, Ruggi, etc. Prof. of singing, Naples Cons. Comp. *Operas:* La Figlia del Sergente, 1847; Gisella, 1852; Rita, 1857. Masses, songs, and other works.

ROY. See LEROY.

ROYER (Jean Nicolas Pancrace). French org. and comp., B. Burgundy, 1705 [1700]. Resident in Paris from 1725. Music master to Royal Family of France, and Director of the Concert Spirituels, 1747. Comp. to the King, 1754. D. Paris, Jan., 1755. Famous as an org. and performer on the harpsichord. He comp. operas and music for the harpsichord.

ROZE (Marie), PONSIN. French soprano vocalist, B. Paris, March 2, 1846. S. at Paris Cons., under Molker, and gained prizes for vocalization. *Début* in Hérold's "Marie," at Paris, 1865; and appeared there in works of Méhul, Boieldieu, Auber, Gounod, and Flotow. The original Djalma in Auber's "Le Premier jour de Bonheur." On the outbreak of the Franco-Prussian War, she served as a nurse in the ambulance, and received the Geneva Cross and a diploma of thanks for her services. Appeared in London, April 30,

1872, in Gounod's "Faust," and from then till 1877 remained in England as an operatic and concert vocalist. Married Julius Perkins, the American bass singer, 1874. Travelled in the United States as an operatic singer, 1877-79, visiting New York, Boston, Chicago, St. Louis, New Orleans, San Francisco, etc. Married to Mr. Henry Mapleson, 1877. Has since appeared chiefly in Britain as an opera, oratorio, and concert singer. She sings in operas of Mozart, Weber, Thomas, Verdi, Bizet, Beethoven, Mackenzie, etc., and occupies the position of prima donna of the Carl Rosa Opera Company. Her voice is a powerful soprano, brilliant and clear in tone, and her abilities as a dramatic singer are of the highest order. She excels equally as an exponent of sacred and ballad music, and has been everywhere received with marked favour and enthusiasm.

RUBINELLI (Giovanni Maria). Italian contralto vocalist, B. Brescia, 1793. Chorister in service of Duke of Würtemberg, at Stuttgart, 1772. Sang in Italy with success, from 1774; appearing successively at Milan, 1778, Florence, 1782. Naples, 1784. Appeared in London, May 4, 1786, in "Virginia." Sang also in works by Handel. Returned to Italy about 1790, and appeared in Rome, Verona, etc. Retired to Brescia, 1800, and D. there 1829.

RUBINI (Giovanni Battista). Italian tenor vocalist, B. Romano, Bergamo, April 7, 1795. Son of a music-teacher, under whom he studied. Appeared at Romano theatre in small parts. Sang as a chorister at Bergamo, and afterwards became a tenor-singer with a strolling company. Sang with varying success till 1815, when he was engaged for Brescia and Venice, and afterwards for Naples, by Barbaja. Sang in Rome, Palermo, and Naples, till 1825. Married ADELAIDE CHOMEL (1794, D. Milan, Jan. 30, 1874), a mezzo-soprano vocalist of some renown. Appeared at Paris, Oct. 6, 1825, in Rossini's "Cenerentola," and afterwards in other works by the same master, both in Paris, Naples, and Vienna. Appeared in London, 1831, and sang alternately there and in Paris till 1843. Went with Liszt to Berlin, via Holland and Germany, and afterwards alone to St. Petersburg, where he achieved extraordinary success, and where he was much patronised by the nobility and decorated by Royalty. Sang afterwards occasionally in Italy, Vienna, and again in St. Petersburg, 1844, but retired soon afterwards to his native place. D. Romano, March 3, 1854.

Famous for his fine voice, and original style of using it. Chorley says of him:— "As a singer, and nothing beyond a singer, he is the only man of his class who deserves to be named in these pages as an artist of genius. No one, in my experience, so merely and exclusively a singer as he was, so entirely enchanted our public, so long as a shred of voice was left to him : no one is more affectionately remembered...." Certain features in his style of performance by no means unpleasing in Rubini, became in the hands of many inferior imitators, a caricature and outrage upon good taste, and hurtful to the progress and cultivation of operatic singing.

RUBINSTEIN (Anton Gregor). Russian pianist and comp., B. Wechwotynetz in Russian Bessarabia, near Jassy, Nov. 30, 1829. Son of Jewish parents. S. under his mother, and afterwards at St. Petersburg under Villoing. Made concert-tour in Europe, and reached Paris, where he S. for a time. Came to England, 1842, and afterwards played in Germany and North Europe. S. comp. under Dehn at Berlin, 1845. Resided in Vienna and Pressburg till 1848. Chamber pianist to the Grand Duchess Helen at St. Petersburg, 1848. Gave concerts in North Germany, and was received with great acclamation, 1856. Appeared in London at a Philharmonic Concert, May 18, 1857. Imperial concert-director at St. Petersburg, 1858. Founded the St. Petersburg Cons., in conjunction with C. Schuberth and his brother Nicholas, 1862. Principal of this Cons. till 1867. Since then he has appeared as a pianist all over Europe and America (1872-3), and has been many times a concert-giver in Britain. The Russian decoration of Vladimir, carrying with it a patent of nobility, was conferred on him in 1869.

WORKS.—*Operas:* Dimitri Donskoï, 1852; The Children of the Heath, 1861; Feramors, 1863; The Demon, 1875 (London, 1881); Die Rebe (ballet); The Maccabees, 1875; Der Papagei (comic); Nero. *Oratorios, Cantatas, etc.:* Tower of Babel, op. 80, 1872 (London, 1881); Paradise Lost (Milton), op. 54, 1876; Der Morgen, cantata, op. 74; Songs and Requiem for Mignon (Goethe), op. 91. *Symphonies:* No. 1, in F, op. 40; No. 2, "The Ocean," in C, op. 42 (London, 1861, since enlarged); No. 3, in A, op. 56; No. 4, "Dramatic," in D minor, op. 95; No. 5, in G minor, op. 107. *Overtures and large orchestral pieces:* Triumphal overture, op. 43; Concert overture, B flat, op. 60; Faust, musical portrait, op. 68; Ivan the Terrible, mus. port., op. 79; Don Quixote, op. 87; Eroica, fantasia, op. 110. *Concertos:* First, Pf., in E, op. 25; Second, Pf., in F, op. 35; Third, Pf., in G, op. 45; Fourth, Pf., in D minor, op. 70; Fifth, Pf., in E flat, op. 94; First, violin, in G, op. 46; First, 'cello, in A minor, op. 65; Second, 'cello, op. 96. *Concerted Instrumental, various:* Octet, in D, op. 9; Three pieces, Pf. and vn., op. 11; First sonata, Pf. and vn., op. 13; Two trios, Pf., vn. and 'cello, op. 15; Three string quartets, op. 17; First sonata, Pf. and 'cello, in D, op. 18; Second sonata, Pf. and vn., op. 19; Second sonata, Pf. and 'cello, in G, op. 39; Three string quartets, op. 47; Sonata for Pf. and viola, op. 49; Third trio, Pf. and strings, op. 52; Quintet for Pf. and wind insts., in F, op. 55; String quintet in F, op. 59; Quartet, Pf. and strings, op. 66; Fantasia, Pf. and orch., in C, op. 84; Fourth trio, Pf. and strings, in A, op. 85; Romance and caprice, vn. and orch., op. 86; Two string quartets, op. 90; Sextet for strings, in D, op. 97; Third sonata, Pf. and vn., op. 98; Quintet, Pf. and strings, op. 99; Caprice Russe, Pf. and orch., op. 102; Two string quartets, op. 106; Trio, Pf., vn. ,and 'cello, C minor, op. 108. *Pianoforte:* Fantasias on Russian themes, op. 2; Two melodies, op. 3; Mazurka fantasia, in G, op. 4; Polonaise, Cracovienne and mazurka, op. 5; Tarantelle, op. 6; Hommage à Jenny Lind, impromptu-caprice, op. 7; Kamennoi-Ostrow, 24 portraits, op. 10; First sonata, in E, op. 12; The Ball, fantasia, op. 14; Impromptu, berceuse, and serenade, op. 16; Second sonata, in C minor, op. 20; Three caprices, op. 21; Three serenades, op. 22; Six études, op. 23; Six Preludes, op. 24; Romance and Impromptu, op. 26; Nocturne and caprice, op. 28; Two funeral marches, op. 29; Barcarolle, etc., op. 30; Akrostichon, op. 37; Suite, op. 38; Third sonata, in F, op. 41; Soirées à St. Petersbourg, op. 44; Six charakter-Bilder, op. 50; Six Morceaux, op. 51; Six preludes and fugues, op. 53; Five morceaux, op. 69; Three morceaux, op. 71; Fantasia, for 2 Pfs., op. 73; Album de Peterhof, op. 75; Fantasia, in E. minor, op. 77; Six études, op. 81; Album of National dances, op. 82; Theme with variations, op. 88; Sonata, Pf. duet, op. 89; Nine books of Pieces, op. 93; Fourth sonata, in A minor, op. 100; Bal Costumé, 20 characteristic pieces, 4 hands, op. 103; Elegie, etude, etc, op. 104. *Vocal:* Six songs, op. 1; Six Songs (Russian), op. 8; Nine Songs (Russian), op. 27; Six four-part songs, male voices, op. 31; Six Songs (Heine), op. 32; Six songs, op. 33; Twelve Persian songs, op. 34; Twelve songs (Russian), op. 36; Twelve duets (Russian), op. 48; Six songs, op. 57; 'E dunque vero? scena, op. 58; Three part-songs, male voices, op. 61; Six part-songs, op. 62; "Die Nixe," for solo, female chorus, and orch., op. 63; Five fables (Kriloff), op. 64; Six duets, op. 67; Six songs, op. 72; Six songs, op. 76; Twelve songs (Russian), op. 78; Ten songs, op. 83; Two scenas for contralto voice and orch., op. 92; Twelve songs, op. 101; Russian songs, op. 105.

Although he occupies a high place in music as a composer, Rubinstein is perhaps best appreciated and most lauded as a pianist. With one notable exception, he stands unrivalled as a performer on the piano. Younger, equally vigorous, and with as high and enthusiastic an artistic conception, he holds his own with Liszt, the one notable exception named. He is a virtuoso of the most extraordinary stamp; extremely impassioned, and carrying into his music and performance a vigour and variety of expression hitherto unequalled by any of his younger contemporaries.

Rubinstein is best known in Britain by his Pianoforte works and some of his songs. Occasionally a few of his orchestral works have been given, either entire or as excerpts, but their merits have not yet been recognised as being greatly beyond the common. None of his dramatic music can be noted as having achieved more than temporary and ordinary success.

RUBINSTEIN (Nicolaus). Russian pianist, and comp., B. Moscow, 1835. Brother of preceding. Gave early indications of a disposition for music. S. at Berlin under Kullak and Dehn, 1845-6. S. Law at Moscow University for a

short time. Travelled in Germany and Russia as pianist. Founded the Russian Musical Society, Moscow, 1859; also, conjointly with his brother, etc., he founded Moscow Cons., 1864, and became its director. Appeared in London, at Musical Union Concerts, 1861. Organised and gave orchestral concerts at the Paris Exhibition, 1878. D. Paris, March 23, 1881.
Comp. some interesting Pf. and vocal music.

RUCKERS or **RUYCKERS (Hans)**. Flemish harpsichord-maker, B. Mechlin, about middle of 16th century [1555]. Established at Antwerp as a musical instrument maker, his speciality being harpsichords and spinets. Engaged in the same manufacture were his sons, HANS (1578-1642), and ANDRIES (B. 1579), and their successors. The instruments of this firm, now excessively rare, are usually decorated with paintings, and date between 1579 and 1667.

RUDERSDORFF (Herminie) [EMILIA]. Soprano vocalist and teacher, B. Ivanowsky, Ukraine, Dec. 12, 1822. Daughter of Joseph Rudersdorff, violinist, with whom she went to Hamburg, in 1825. S. under Sessi, Bandeiali, and Bordogni, at Paris. Appeared as concert vocalist in Germany. Sang in opera at Carlsruhe, 1841. Married Dr. Kuchenmeister, mathematician, at Frankfort-on-Main, 1844. Renounced the stage for a time, but re-appeared at Breslau in 1846. Sang at Berlin, 1852-54, in operas by Lortzing, Bellini, Auber, Boieldieu, Hérold, Thomas, etc. Removed to London in May, 1854, and appeared there in operas by Mozart, Weber, Auber, Meyerbeer, Loder, and Beethoven. Became famous as a teacher, and renowned as a concert and oratorio vocalist. Sang at Birmingham Festival, 1861; Handel Festivals, etc. Settled in Boston, U.S.A., 1867. Sang there in concert music, but latterly employed in tuition. D. Boston, Feb. 26, 1882.

RUDHALL (Abraham). English bell-founder, B. Gloucester, 1657. D. Gloucester, Jan. 25, 1736. The most famous of a family of Gloucester bell-founders, established in the 17th century by Abraham Rudhall, the elder. This family supplied bells for innumerable churches in London and the English provinces. Abraham, junr., greatly improved the art of bell-founding, and bells of his workmanship are said to be distinguished by fine tone.

RUDORFF (Ernst). German comp., B. Berlin, Jan. 18, 1840. S. under Bargiel, L. Ries, Hauptmann, and Reinecke. Prof. at Cologne Cons. Prof. at High School, Berlin, and cond. of the Stern Singing Soc.
WORKS.—Op. 1. Variations for 2 Pf.; op. 2. Six songs; op. 5. Sextet for strings; op. 6. Four part-songs; op. 8. Overture, Der blonde Ekbert; op. 10. Eight fantasie-stücke, Pf.; op. 12. Overture, Otto der Schütz; op. 15. Ballade for orch.; op. 18. Der Aufzug der Romanze (Tieck), soli, chorus, and orch.; op. 25. Four 6-part songs; Studies for Pf., songs, etc.

RUE (Pierre de la), or LA RUE. French comp., B. Picardy. Flourished in second half of 15th and beginning of 16th centuries. S. under Okenheim. Musician in court service in Germany, and chap.-master at Antwerp. Comp. masses, motets, and madrigals, mostly existing in MS.

RUFFO (Vincenzo). Italian comp. of 16th century, B. Verona. Chap.-master of Milan Cath., and afterwards at cath. of Verona, 1554. Comp. Motetti a 5 voci, 1551; Motetti a 6 voci, 1583; Il Libro Primo di Madrigali a 5 voci, 1550; Armonia Celeste. 1563; Madrigali Cromatici, 1554; Salmi, 1574.

RUGGIERI (Francesco). Italian violin-maker of end of 17th and beginning of 18th century. The founder of the family of noted violin-makers of Cremona, known as Ruggierius. The instruments of Francesco bear dates ranging between 1668 and 1720. Other members of the family, notably GIOVANNI BATTISTA (1700-25), PIETRO (1700-20), GUIDO, and VICENZO, were all more or less celebrated. The general character of their instruments is closely akin to those of the Amati family, and they are noted for a smooth, soft tone, and good model.

RUMMEL (Christian Franz Ludwig Friedrich Alexander). German pianist, violinist, clarinet-player, and comp., B. Brichsenstadt, Bavaria, Nov. 27, 1787. S. under Ritter and Vogler. Chap.-master to Duke of Nassau, D. Wiesbaden, Feb. 13, 1849.

K 2

Comp. much music for military bands, Pf. music, and songs. See catalogue of Schott, etc. His daughters JOSEPHINE, B. Manzanarès, Spain, May 12, 1812, was court-pianist at Wiesbaden. D. Wiesbaden, Dec. 19, 1877. FRANCISCA, B. Wiesbaden, Feb. 4, 1821. S. singing under Bordogni and Lamperti. Married P. Schott, the music-publisher. Famous as a singer. His son JOSEPH, B. Wiesbaden, Oct. 6, 1818. S. under his father. Chap.-master to Prince of Oldenburg. Resided in Paris and London alternately, from 1842. D. London, March 25, 1880. Comp. for Pf., 3 mazurkas, op. 20; Boléro, op. 25; Mélodie originale, op. 29; Cardonia, romance, op. 52; Etude de concert, op. 57; Perles Enfantines; Bonbonnière des Pianistes; Echos de l' Opéra; Impromptus, fantasias, and an immense quantity of transcriptions of every class.

RUMMEL (Franz). Grandson of Christian Rummel, B. London, Jan. 11, 1853. S. Brussels under Brassin, and in Cons. Gained first prize for Pf. playing, 1872. Employed there as a teacher, 1872-76. First appeared as pianist at Antwerp, 1872; London, 1873. Travelled afterwards in Germany, France, England, and the U. S. of America, 1878-81. Has appeared in various parts of Britain, and very frequently in London.

RUNGENHAGEN (Carl Friedrich). German comp. and cond., B. Berlin, Sept. 27, 1778. S. under Benda and Zelter. Succeeded Zelter as director of the Singakademie of Berlin, 1832. D. Berlin, Dec. 21, 1851. He comp. "Caecilia," an oratorio; Cantatas, motets, hymns, songs, etc.

RUPPE (Christian Friedrich). German comp. and writer, B. Salzungen, Saxe-Meiningen, 1765. S. for the law at Leyden University. Music-director at Leyden University, at which town he was living in 1812. Comp. Trios for Pf., vn. and 'cello, opp. 1, 3, 6, 7, 14, 25, 26, 27; Sonatas for Pf., and Pf. and violin; Theoretical works, etc. His brother, FRIEDRICH CHRISTIAN, B. Salzungen, Feb. 18, 1771. D. Meiningen, Aug. 14, 1834, was a pianist, and comp. oratorios, cantatas, quartets, and sonatas, rondos, etc. for Pf.

RUSH (James). American physician and writer, B. 1790. Practised in Philadelphia. Author of "The Philosophy of the Human Voice, embracing its Physiological History, together with a System of Principles by which Criticism of the Art of Elocution may be rendered intelligible," Philadelphia, 1827, 8vo. This work has gone through many editions to the present time; an incontestable proof of its value and popularity.

RUSSELL (Henry). English comp. and barytone vocalist, B. Sheerness, Kent, Dec. 24, 1815. S. under P. King. Left England in 1825, and became an outdoor scholar at Bologna Cons. Went to New York, 1833, and began his career of concert-giver and comp. Returned to England, 1840, and from that time travelled in Britain as a singer and comp., attaining a most extraordinary popularity. Retired from public life some years ago.

WORKS.—*Songs and Ballads:* Ballad singer; Bandit's song; Brave old oak; Birds of passage; Blind girl!; Cheer! boys cheer; Columbia's the pride of the ocean; Come fill the cup; Chieftian's daughter; Canadian song; Chase, the; Dream of the reveller; Dance of death; Exile, the; Far, far upon the sea: Feast of the Despots; Fanny Mavourneen; Felon, the; Fishman, the; Founding of the bell; Gambler's wife; I'm afloat!; I love, I love the free!; Ivy green; Life on the ocean wave; Long parted have we been; Land ho!; Land! land! land!; Last tree of the forest; Maniac, the; Man the Life-boat; Mad girl's song; Midnight watch; Old arm chair; Old water mill; Old clock; Old Sexton; Over the waters; Patriot's farewell; Phantom ship; Ship on fire; Spider and the fly; Song of the scaffold; Slave ship; Sea diver; Sky-lark; Song of the silent night; Song of the Indian; Song of the raft; Signal gun; There's a good time coming boys; To the West!; to the West! Tubal Cain; Woodman spare that tree; Where there's a will there's a way; Wine cup; Wreck of the Hesperus; Wind of the Winter night; Weaver; A series of songs from Scott's "Lady of the Lake"; Scripture Melodies; A few glees and part-songs. Songs, Dramatic Scenes, Cantatas, etc., with a Memoir, Lond., 1846. Copyright Songs, 1860, 2 vols., 4to. L'Amico dei Cantanti, the Singer's Friend, a treatise on the art of Singing. Lond., fo., n. d.

Some of Russell's songs had a most extraordinary run some forty years ago. In an entertainment written by Charles Mackay, entitled "The Emigrant's Progress, or

Life in the Far West," many of them originally appeared. At the present day only a small number are in use, and among them may be named "Cheer, boys, cheer!" "I'm afloat," "Ivy green," "Old Sexton," "To the west! to the west!" and "Woodman, spare that tree." A number of his songs possess very powerful dramatic feeling. The number of songs composed by Russell is estimated by himself to amount to 675.

RUSSELL (William). English org. and comp., B. London, 1777. Son of an organ-builder. S. under Shrubsole, Arnold, etc. Deputy Org. St. Mary, Aldermanbury, 1789-93; Chap. of Great Queen Street, Lincoln's Inn Fields, 1793-98; St. Ann's Limehouse, 1798; Foundling Hospital, 1801. Pianist at Sadler's Wells Theatre, 1800, and held similar post at Covent Garden, 1801. Mus. Bac., Oxon., 1808. D. London, Nov. 21, 1813.
WORKS.—*Oratorios:* Job, with org. accomps. by S. Wesley (1826); The Deliverance of Israel; The Redemption. Mass in C minor for 4 voices. *Odes:* To music; Genius of Handel; St. Cecilia's Day (Smart); To Harmony. Glees and Songs. Psalms, Hymns, and Anthems for the Foundling Chapel, London, 1809. Six Anthems, adapted from the works of Haydn, etc.,...and a morning and evening service composed by the late William Russell,...arranged by William Patten. Several books of organ voluntaries. Services and anthems. Theatre and pantomime music, songs, etc.

RUST (Friedrich Wilhelm). German comp., B. Wörlitz, near Dessau, July 6, 1739. S. under F. and E. Bach, F. Benda, and Tartini. Music-director of Dessau Theatre. Married Henriette Niedhart. Court Musician of Dessau. D. Dessau, Feb. 28, 1796. He comp. operas, cantatas, sonatas, and concertos, for Pf.; choruses and songs, and some violin music. His son, WILHELM CARL, B. Dessau, April 29, 1787. S. under Türk. Org. in Protestant ch. of Vienna for a time, where he became acquainted with Beethoven. D. Dessau, April 18, 1855. Comp. Pf. music and lieder.

RUST (Wilhelm). German comp. and cond., B. Dessau, Aug. 15, 1822. S. under W. C. Rust and F. Schneider. Org., teacher, and cond., in Berlin. Prof. in Stern's Cons., Berlin, 1870. Cantor of S. Thomas School, Leipzig, 1879.
WORKS.—Op. 1. Cäcilia, songs for voice and Pf.; op. 4. Eighty-fourth Psalm, for voices and org.; op. 5. Fantasia for Pf.; op. 9. Sonata for Pf.; op. 10. Ave Maria, voices and Pf. Lieder and Pf. pieces. Also edited several of Bach's works for the Leipzig Bach Society.

RUTHERFORD (D......). English musician of 18th century. Author of "Art of Playing on the Violin, showing how to stop every note exactly..." Lond., 8vo, n. d.; Gentleman's Pocket Guide for the German Flute, with some agreeable Lessons..." 8vo; "Ladies' Pocket Guide for the Guitar..." 8vo.

RUYCKERS. See RUCKERS.

RYAN (Michael Desmond). Irish dramatic and musical writer, B. Kilkenny, March 3, 1816. Educated at Edinburgh University. Engaged as musical and dramatic critic on staff of *The Morning Post, Morning Herald*, and *Standard*. Sub.-editor of *Musical World*. D. London, Dec. 8, 1868.
Author of the libretto of Macfarren's "Charles II.," and words for various musical works by Crouch, Loder, Mori, etc. His son, DESMOND L. RYAN, is a composer and writer of various works in poetry and prose.

RYBA (Jacob Johann). Bohemian comp., B. Przesstiez, October 26, 1765. S. at Prague. D. Roczmittal, 1788. Comp. masses, stabat mater, duets, quartets, etc.

S.

SABBATINI (Galeazzo). Italian comp. and writer, B. Pisaro, at end of 16th century. D. in first half of 17th century.

WORKS.—Il primo libro de'Madrigali, op. 1, 1627; Second do., op. 2, 1636; Sacræ laudes, op. 3, 1642; Madrigali, op. 4, 1636, etc.

SABBATINI (Luigi Antonio). Italian ecclesiastic, writer, and comp., B. Albano, Rome, 1739. S. under Martini and Valotti. Chap.-master at Rome, 1780, and Padua. D. Padua, Jan. 29, 1809.
WORKS.—Gli elementi teorici della musica, colla pratica de' medesimi in duetti e terzetti a canone, Rome, 1789, 2nd ed., 1795. Trattato sopra le fughe musicali, Venice, 4to, 1802. Edition of Marcello's Psalms, and miscellaneous comps.

SACCHINI (Antonio Maria Gasparo). Italian comp., B. Pozzuoli, near Naples, July 23, 1734. S. under Durante at Cons. of S. Onofrio, Naples. Comp. to Argentina Theatre, Rome, etc., 1762-69. Director of Cons. of L'Ospedaletto, Venice, 1768-1771. Resided in London as comp., April 1772-1782 [?1784]. Resided afterwards in Paris as comp. D. Paris, Oct. 7, 1786.
WORKS.—*Operas:* Fra Donato, 1756; L'Olimpia tradita, 1758; I due Fratelli beffati, 1760; I due Baroni, 1762; Semiramide, 1762; Eumene, 1763; Andromacca, 1763; Il gran Cid, 1764; Lucio Vero, 1764; La Contadina in Corte, 1765; L'Isola d'Amore, 1766, Paris, 1781; L'Olimpiade, 1767; Artaserse, 1768; Alessandro nell' Indie, 1768; Armida, 1772; Il gran Cid (revised from Rome version of 1764), London, 1773; Tamerlano, Lond., 1773; Nitetti, Lond., 1774; Perseo, Lond., 1774; Montesuma, Lond., 1775; Il Creso, do., 1775; Erifile, do., 1776; L'Amor Soldata, do., 1777; Il Calandrino, do., 1778; Enea a Lavinia, 1779; Renaud (Rinaldo), Paris, 1783; Dardanus, Paris, 1784; Œdipe à Colone, 1787; Evelina, etc. *Oratorios:* Esther; St. Philippe; Jefte, etc. Misereres, masses, motets, and sacred solos. Six trios for 2 violins and bass, op. 1, Lond.; Six quartets for 2 violins, viola and bass, Lond.; Six sonatas for clavecin and violin, op. 3; Six do., op. 4.

A composer of much power and originality. His best work was "Œdipe à Colonne," which remained popular in France for many years after his death.

SACHS (Hans). German poet and musician, B. Nuremberg, Nov. 5, 1494. D. Nuremberg, Jan. 25, 1576. He wrote an immense number of poetical works, comedies, tragedies, psalms, songs, etc., and to a large number of the last named he comp. music. His career forms the subject of Wagner's opera, "Die Meistersinger von Nürnberg," 1868.

SACHS (Julius). German comp. and pianist, B. Meiningen, 1830. S. under Kessler and Rosenhain. Comp. much Pf. music, as rondos, caprices, etc., and lieder for voice and Pf.

SAINT-AUBIN (Jeanne Charlotte), *née* SCHRÖDER. French actress and singer, B. Paris, Dec. 9, 1764. D. Paris, Sept. 11, 1850. Celebrated as an actress and burlesque singer, in which capacities she attained much renown in Paris. She married an actor named Saint-Aubin, by whom she had two daughters, CECILE and ALEXANDRINE, who were singers of some local fame.

SAINT-GEORGES (Chevalier de). French violinist and comp., B. Gaudeloupe, Dec. 25, 1745. S. under Leclair and Gossec. Violinist in Paris, and engaged in connection with the French Revolution. D. Paris, June 12, 1799. Comp. Ernestine, opera, 1777; Le Marchand de Marrons, opera, 1788; Concertos, sonatas, and other violin music.

SAINT-GEORGES (Jules Henri Vernoy, Marquis de). French novelist and opera-librettist, B. Paris, 1801. D. Paris, 1875. Wrote librettos for the most popular operas of Halévy, Adam, Auber, Donizetti, etc.

SAINT-HUBERTY (Antoinette Cecile), or CLAVEL. French soprano vocalist, B. Toul, 1756. Sang in operas by Piccinni, Gluck, Gossec, Grétry, Sacchini, and others. Married Count d'Entraigues, in whose political schemes she became involved, 1790. Settled at Barnes, near Richmond, with her husband, and was assassinated along with him on July 22, 1812, by a servant in the pay of the French Government.

SAINT-SAËNS (Charles Camille). French comp. and pianist, B. Paris, Oct. 9, 1835. S. Pf. under Stamaty, and harmony under Maleden. S. at Cons.

under Benoist, and gained 2nd org. prize in 1849, and the first in 1851. Org. of Ch. of S. Méry, Paris, 1853. Prof. in Niedermayer's School of Religious Music. Org. of the Madeleine, Paris, 1858-1877. Appeared in London as pianist, 1871, and has since appeared there often. Member of the Institute of France, 1881.

WORKS.—*Operas:* La Princesse Jaune, op. 30, 1872; Le Timbre d'Argent, 1877; Samson et Dalila, sacred drama, op. 47, Weimar, 1877; Etienne Marcel, Lyons, 1879; Henry VIII., Paris, March 5, 1883. *Cantatas and large choral works:* Les Noces de Prométhée, 1867; Le Déluge, poëme biblique, op. 45, 1876; La Lyre et la Harpe, Birmingham Festival, 1879; Oratorio de Noël, op. 12; Psalm XVIII., op. 42; Ode à Sainte Cécile, solo, chorus, and orch.; Mass, 4 voices, orch. and 2 orgs.; Requiem Mass, op. 54, etc.; Hymn to Victor Hugo, op. 69, 1885; Scènes d'Horace (Corneille), op. 10, etc.; Les Soldats de Gédéon, double chorus for male voices, op. 46. *Symphonic and large orchestral works:* Symphony No. 1, in E flat; No. 2, in F, 1856; No. 3, in A minor; No. 4, in D, 1863; Le Rouet d'Omphale, poëme symphonique, op. 31; Marche héroïque, op. 34; Phaëton, op. 39; Danse Macabre, op. 40; Suite for orch. (prelude, saraband, gavotte, romance, and finale), op. 49; La Jeunesse d'Hercule, op. 50; Suite Algérienne; Overture, Spartacus, 1863. *Concerted Instrumental Music:* Op. 6. Tarentelle for flute and clarinet; op. 14. Quintet for Pf., 2 violins, viola, and 'cello, in A minor; op. 15. Serenade for Pf., org., vn., viola, and 'cello; op. 16. Suite for Pf. and 'cello; op. 17. First Concerto for Pf. and orch, in D; op. 18. Trio in F, Pf., vn., and 'cello; op. 22. Second do., in G minor; op. 27. Romance, Pf., org., and vn.; op. 28. Introduction and rondo, vn. and Pf.; op. 29. Third concerto, Pf. and orch., in E flat; op. 32. Sonata, Pf. and 'cello, in C min.; op. 33. Concerto, 'cello and orch., in A minor; op. 36. Romance for horn or 'cello and Pf. in F; op. 37. Romance, flute or vn., and Pf., in D flat; op. 38. Berceuse, Pf. and vn., in B flat; op. 41. Quartet for Pf. and strings, in B flat; op. 43. Allegro appassionata, 'cello and Pf.; op. 44. Fourth Concerto, Pf. and orch., in C minor; op. 48. Romance, vn. and Pf., in C; op. 51. Romance, 'cello and Pf., in D. *Pianoforte:* op. 11. Duettino, Pf. duet, in G; op. 21. Mazurka; op. 23. Gavotte; op. 24. Mazurka; op. 25. Occident et Orient, duet; op. 35. Variations, Pf. duet (Beethoven); op. 52. Six studies; op. 56. Minuet and valse; op. 59. Ballade, duet; op. 72. Album of six pieces; op. 73. Rhapsodie d'Auvergne. Transcriptions from Bach, Beethoven, Gluck, Wagner, etc. *Vocal:* op. 26. Mélodies Persanes; op. 53. Chansons; also numerous songs in collections and detached.

Saint-Saëns is one of the most prominent French instrumental composers of the present time. His works have been heard in Europe, Britain, and America, and some of them have achieved distinguished success. His style is original, but the formality and occasional uninteresting character of his music militates against its continued popularity. A number of his Pf. works are, however, among the adopted classics of recent times.

SAINTON (Prosper Philippe Catherine). French violinist and comp., B. Toulouse, June 5, 1813. Originally educated for the law. S. at Paris Cons., under Habeneck, from 1831. Gained second violin prize, 1833, and the first, 1834. Member of orch. of the opera, etc. Made concert tour in Italy, Germany, Austria, Russia, Denmark, and Spain. Violin prof. at Toulouse Cons 1840-44. First visited London, 1844, and settled there, 1845. Prof. of violin, R. A. M., 1845. Leader at Musical Union, Sacred Harmonic, Monday Popular, and other concerts; and of Philharmonic Orch., 1846-54. Leader at Covent Garden Theatre, 1847-71; and at H.M. Theatre, 1871-80. Also leader at several provincial festivals. Married Miss Charlotte Dolby, 1860. Cond. of Royal Band of Music, 1848-55. Retired from professional life in June, 1883.

WORKS.—First concerto for violin and orch., op. 9; Thème Italien, varied, vn. and orch., op. 10; Fantasia (Lindpaintner), op. 11; Fantasias (Donizetti), op. 12, 13; Air Montagnard, vn. and Pf., op. 14; Solo de Concert, vn. and orch., op. 16; Rondo-mazurka, vn. and orch, op. 17; Three romances, vn. and Pf., op. 18; Tarentelle, vn. and Pf., op. 20.

SAINTON - DOLBY (Charlotte Helen), *née* DOLBY. English contralto vocalist and comp., B. London, May 17, 1821. S. at R. A. M., from 1832, under J. Bennett, Elliott, and Crivelli. Gained the King's Scholarship, 1837. Member of R. A. M. First appeared as a public singer about 1840, and sang at Philharmonic Concert, 1841. Sang in oratorio and ballad music till 1846, when she appeared at a Gewandhaus concert in Leipzig, in Mendelssohn's "Elijah"; the contralto part of which was specially written for her voice. Made concert tours in France and Holland. Married M. Prosper Sainton, 1860. From thence onwards to 1870, when she retired, she appeared at all the most important concerts in Britain, and became the most popular and successful contralto of her period. Established in London a Vocal Academy, 1872, in which many promising vocalists have been trained. Made her last public appearance as a vocalist at her husband's farewell concert, in June, 1883. D. London, Feb. 18, 1885.

WORKS.—*Cantatas*: The Legend of St. Dorothea, London, 1876; The Story of the Faithful Soul, 1879; Florimel, female voices, 1885. *Songs*: A stream of golden sunshine; A-sailing we will go; Bonnie Dundee; Coming home; Charlie yet; Come forth, my love; Drummer's song; The G.L.O.V.E.; Heigho! Janet; In August; Is it for ever?; I love her; Lady's yes; My Donald; Marjorie's almanack; My love he stands upon the quay; Never again; Watching and waiting; While I listen to thy voice. Tutor for English Singers, a Complete Course of Practical Instructions in Singing, Lond., n. d., 8vo.

Madam Dolby was a vocalist of great culture and taste, and excelled in ballad singing. She had a voice of much power, and of a full, round tone, which was highly effective and telling in oratorio music. Some of her songs and cantatas attained much popularity.

SALA (Nicolo). Italian comp. and writer, B. near Naples [1701]. S. at Cons. of La Pietà de' Turchini, Naples, under Abos and Leo. Succeeded Cafaro as Director of the Cons. of La Pietà, 1787. D. Naples, 1800.

WORKS.—*Operas*: Vologese, 1737; Zenobia, 1761; Mérope, 1769. Oratorio, odes, masses, etc. "Regole del Contrappunto prattico...," Naples, 1794, 3 vols., fo. A work of very considerable importance in the literature of harmony and fugue.

SALAMAN (Charles Kensington). English comp., pianist, lecturer, and writer, B. London, March 3, 1814. Gave early indications of a disposition for music. Was elected a student of R. A. M., 1824, but never availed himself of the election. S. Pf. under Charles Neate, 1826-1831; and harmony under Dr. Crotch, and Ely, with whom he also S. the 'cello. Had Pf. lessons from H. Herz, in Paris, 1828, in which year he first appeared as a pianist and comp. Commenced series of annual orch. and vocal concerts, 1833, at the second of which Grisi first appeared in London as a concert singer. Elected Mem. of Royal Soc. of Musicians, 1837. Associate of Philharmonic Soc., 1837-55, when he withdrew from the Soc. Visited Continent in 1838, and gave Pf. performances in Vienna, Munich, etc. Resided at Rome, 1846-48. Made Hon. Mem. of Academy of S. Cecilia, Rome, 1846, and of the Royal Philharmonic Soc., 1847. Founded the first private Amateur Choral Soc. in London, 1849, and appeared at a Philharmonic Concert, 1850. Lectured on musical subjects from 1855. One of the founders of the Musical Society of London, 1858, and was its secretary till 1865. Assumed the additional surname, Kensington, on death of his father, in 1867. Aided in establishing the Musical Association, 1874.

WORKS.—Cantata for Shakespeare Jubilee at Stratford-upon-Avon, April 30, 1830. *Anthems and Part-Songs*: A voiceless sigh; Fair is the swan; Give to the Lord (double choir); Have mercy; How lovely are Thy habitations; Preserve me O God; There is an hour. Many Hebrew choral works for the service of the synagogue. *Musical Settings of the Ancient Lyrics*: Ad Chloen (Horace, Ode 23, Bk. 1); Donec gratus, duet soprano and tenor (Horace, Ode 9, Bk. 3); To Neæra, "Non erat" (Horace, 15 Epode); Luctus in morte passeris (Catullus, Ode 3); Para ten skien, duet for soprano and contralto (Anacreon, Ode 22); Hebrew Love-song (Halevi, circa 1200). *Songs in English, German, French, Italian, and Spanish*: A leave-taking; Al Salir; Are other eyes; As I did walk; A toi, toujours a toi (Hugo); A voiceless sigh; Away with sorrow; Biondina's song; Celia; Come dry those tears; Come quel fior; Cradle song; Dost thou love the blue to see?; Du Süsses mädchen; Eva Tual; Farewell! if ever fondest prayer;

Fare thee well; Già la notte; Good-bye; Home; How lonely; I arise from dreams of Thee (Shelley), 1836; I would tell her; I cannot part from Thee; I dare not ask; I ever think of Thee; Io lo so; Io sento che in petto; Katie; Leila; Linger not long; Lov'd one; Love's legacy; Love's philosophy; Medora's song; Memory; My sweetheart; No, I never was in love; No, non vedrete mai; Oh, if thou wert mine own; Oh! I have lov'd thee; Oh! linger on the oar; Perdita's song; Placido zefiretto; Pyrrha; Song of welcome; Sweet, have the roses; The farewell; The sun has set; There is beauty; There's not an accent; Think'st thou on me?; This Rose; Thought (sonnet by Shakespeare); Tu di saper; What shall I send to thee, sweet?; Where is my lov'd one?; Why didst thou ever; Without thine ear; Zahra; Zuleika. *Pianoforte*: Atalanta; Birthday valse; Clœlia; Egeria; Hesperus; Habanera; Hilda; Il riposo è l'agitazione; Iris; Joy; La barchetta sul fiume; La notte serena; Lullaby; Mazurka; Medora; Pavan; Pegasus; Prelude and Gavotte; Remembrance; Rondo nel tempo della giga; Saltarello; Serenata; Spanish caprice; Syrian bride; Toccato, op. 44; Tranquility; Twilight thoughts; Un fantasma, op. 21; Zephyrus. *Orchestral*: Overture in D; Fantasia orchestrale, in G min.; Rondo al capriccio, Pf. and orch. Grand Funeral March, in honour of Victor Hugo, for orch. and military band, 1885. Grand Parade March for military band. Twelve Voluntaries for org., harmonium, or American org., 1885. *Lectures*: The History of the Pianoforte, and the ancient keyed instruments, the immediate precursors of the Pianoforte, 1855-6; Music in connection with the dance; Handel and his Contemporaries; Beethoven and his works; Carl Maria von Weber, his Dramatic compositions; History of Italian, German, and English Opera. Papers in Proceedings of Musical Association—Musical Criticism (republished, 1876); The English Language as a Language for Music; On Music as a Profession in England (republished, 1880). Contributions to Musical Journals— Musical Recollections (*Concordia*); History of English Opera; Music in connection with Dancing; Classical Music (in *Musical Times*). Jews as they Are. Lond., 1884, 8vo.

One of the best of modern English composers, and as a song-writer one of the most refined and original of his period. Certain of his lyrical compositions are not matched for taste, skill, or melody, in the anthology of any nation in Europe. "I arise from dreams of Thee," the classical lyrics, and many others which considerations of space must prevent us from re-enumerating, are unequalled for beauty of melody, fine sympathy with the feeling of the poet, and warmth of musical imagery. His pianoforte music and choral works are likewise marked by similar evidences of poetic and scholarly treatment. His son, MALCOLM CHARLES, a lyric poet and dramatist, was B. Lond., Sept. 6, 1855. He is author of "Ivan's Love-Quest and other Poems," Lond., 1879, 8vo, and the verses of many of his father's best songs, as "Biondina's song," "Love's Legacy," "Zahra," and others; also of words for compositions by Sir G. A. Macfarren and G. A. Osborne, etc. As a dramatic author and librettist he has produced "Deceivers Ever," a farcical comedy, Strand Theatre, Nov. 26, 1883; and "Boycotted," a comedietta in one act, with music by Eugene Barnett. Other two of his plays, "Dimity's Dilemma," and "Only Sympathy," have been accepted for production at London theatres. Edited, 1879-80, *Replies, a Weekly Journal of Questions and Answers*.

SALDONI (Baltasar). Spanish comp., B. Barcelona, Jan. 4, 1807. S. at Barcelona, and under Andrevi. Org. of S. Maria del Mar, Barcelona. Prof. of Singing Madrid Cons. from 1830. Comp. Ipermestra, 1838; Boabdil; La Porte de Monaco, 1857, and other operas. Also masses, motets, cantatas, and orch. music.

SALE (John). English bass vocalist and comp., B. London, 1758. Son of John Sale (B. Gainsborough, 1734, D. Windsor, 1802), a lay-clerk of S. George's Chap., Windsor. Chor. Chap. Roy., Windsor, and in Eton Coll., under W. Webb, 1767-1775. Lay-vicar Chap.-Roy., Windsor, and Eton Coll., 1777-96. Gent. of Chap.-Roy., London, 1783. Vicar-choral, S. Paul's Cath., 1794. Lay-vicar Westminster Abbey, 1796. Almoner and master of choristers, S. Paul's Cath., 1800-1812. Secretary of the Catch Club, 1812. Cond. of the Glee Club, and bass at Concert of Ancient Music, the Ladies Concerts, and in many parts of England at festivals and concerts. D. London, Nov. 11, 1827.

Works.—A Collection of New Glees, composed by John Sale...Lond., ob. fo., n. d. Also some issued in a collection, with others comp. by Lord Mornington, Callcott, etc.

SALE (John Bernard). English comp. and bass vocalist, B. Windsor, 1779. Chor. in St. George's Chap., Windsor, and in Eton Coll., 1785. Lay-vicar Westminster Abbey, 1800. Gent. of Chap.-Roy., 1803. Org. S. Margaret's, Westminster, 1809. Musical instructor to Queen Victoria. Org. of the Chap.-Roy., 1838. D. London, Sept. 16, 1836.

Works.—Psalms and Hymns for the Service of the Church, Lond., 1837, 4to. S. Webbe's Solfegios as Exercising Duetts, newly arranged by J. B. Sale, Lond., fo., n. d. The Butterfly, duet, and other vocal pieces.

His daughters, MARY ANNE, and SOPHIA (D. May 3, 1869), were also musicians. Another daughter, LAURA, married W. J. Thoms the writer. His brother, GEORGE CHARLES, B. Windsor, 1796. Chor. S. Paul's Cath., 1803. Org. S. Mary's, Newington, in succession to Dr. T. Busby, 1817; St. George's, Hanover Square, 1826. D. London, Jan. 23, 1869. Both JOHN and J. B. SALE were very remarkable bass singers, and were famous throughout Britain during their careers.

SALES (Pietro Pompeo). Italian comp., B. Brescia, 1729. Travelled in Germany. Appeared in London, 1763-68. Chap.-master to the Elector at Coblentz, 1768. Re-visited London, 1777, with his wife, who was a singer. D. Hanau, 1797. Comp. operas and oratorios.

SALIERI (Antonio). Italian comp., B. Legnano, Venice, Aug. 19, 1750. S. under his brother, Pescetti, Passini, and Gassmann. Accompanied Gassmann to Vienna, 1766, and he S. under him till 1774. Court comp., and director of opera at Vienna, 1774. Court Chap.-master, 1788. D. Vienna, May 12, 1825.

Works.—Operas: Le Donne letterate, 1770; Armida, 1771; Il Don Chisciotte, 1771; Europa riconosciuta, 1776; Il Talismanno, 1779; Der Rauchfangkehrer, 1781; Semiramide, 1784; Il Ricco d'un Giorno, 1784; Les Danaïdes, Paris, 1785; La Grotto di Trofonio, 1785; Les Horaces, 1786; Tarare, 1787 (reproduced as Axur, re d'Ormus, 1788); Chimène et Rodrigue, 1788 (never produced); Il Pastor Fido, 1789; Falstaff, 1798; Die Neger, 1804. Oratorios, La Passione di Gesù Cristo, 1776, etc. Masses, cantatas, ballets, and other vocal music. Concertos for Pf. and org.

Salieri occupied a very influential position in Vienna, and associated with the best musicians of the age, among them being Gluck, Beethoven, Haydn, Schubert, and Mozart. He professed to be a follower of Gluck in the style of his operatic works, but no traces of the powerful dramatic characteristics of Gluck are apparent in his compositions. He trained many first-class musicians, and was instrumental, in many ways, in forwarding the musical culture of his time.

SALINAS (Francesco). Spanish writer and comp., B. Burgos, 1512. Blind from his birth. S. at Salamanca, and in Italy. Abbot of S. Pancratio della Rocca Salegna, Naples. D. Salamanca, Feb. 1590. He wrote "De Musica libri septem..." [Salamanca], 1577. Comp. church and org. music.

SALMON (Eliza), née MUNDAY. English soprano vocalist, B. Oxford, 1787. S. under John Ashley. Début at Lenten Oratorio Concerts, Covent Garden, London, 1803. Married James Salmon, a singer, 1805. Sang at the principal London and provincial concerts till 1824, when her voice was lost, through a break down of her nervous system, caused by intemperance. Married the Rev. Mr. Hinde, after Salmon's death. Became quite destitute on death of her second husband, and after various ineffectual attempts to regain a position D. Chelsea, June 5, 1849. Her husband, JAMES SALMON, was org. of S. Peter's, Liverpool, 1805. He was latterly in very embarrassed circumstances, and went to the West Indies as a soldier, where he died. His brother WILLIAM, B. 1789, D. Windsor, Jan. 26, 1858, was a singer and teacher.

SALMON (Rev. Thomas). English writer of 17th century, was educated at Oxford University, of which he was M.A., and became Rector of Mepsall, Bedfordshire. He wrote "An Essay to the Advancement of Musick by casting away the perplexity of different cliffs, and uniting all sorts of Musick, lute, viol, violins, organ, harpsichord, voice, etc., in one universal character," Lond., 1672, 8vo. This was answered by Matthew Locke in his "Observations," and elicited "A Vindication of an Essay to the Advancement of Musick, from Mr. Matthew Lock's Observations, enquiring into the real nature and most convenient practice of that science," Lond., 1673. To this, Lock replied conclusively in his "Present Practice of Music vindicated," in which is a letter by John Playford. His other works are "A Proposal to perform Music in perfect and mathematical proportions," Lond., 1688, 4to ; "The Theory of Music reduced to Arithmetical and Geometrical Proportions " (Philosophical Transactions, 1705). His sons, Nathaniel and Thomas, were both writers.

SALO (Gasparo di). Italian violin-maker, B. Salo, on Lake of Garda, in latter part of 16th century. His biography is unknown. His instruments include violins, violas, and double-basses, and on the good quality of the last-named, his fame chiefly rests. His double-basses are of excellent tone and model, and one was in the possession of Dragonetti, the celebrated contrabassist.

SALOMÉ (Theodore César). French comp. and org., B. Paris, Jan. 20, 1834. S. Paris Cons. under Bazin, Thomas, and Benoist. Gained various prizes between 1855-59, and the second grand Prix de Rome in 1861. Org. of Ch. of the Trinity, Paris. Comp. symphonies, chamber music, org. music, and vocal works.

SALOMON (Johann Peter). German violinist, cond., and comp., B. Bonn, Feb. 1745. Originally educated for the Law, but relinquished it in favour of music, and became famous as a violinist when quite young. Violinist in court band of the Elector, at Bonn, 1758. Travelled in Germany and France as violinist and concert-giver. Appeared in Paris, 1781, and arrived in London in March of the same year. Appeared at the Theatres, the Professional Concerts, Academy of Ancient Music, and at Concerts organised by himself, which he gave between 1781 and 1790. In 1791 he gave a series of concerts at which the twelve symphonies of Haydn, known as the Salomon set, were produced. He afterwards gave other concerts, and engaged the Haymarket Theatre with Arnold for oratorio performances, 1801, and took an active part in the musical doings of his time, aiding among other things with the establishment of the Philharmonic Society. D. London, May 28, 1815. Buried in Westminster Abbey.

He comp. Windsor Castle, an opera ; The Marriage of Peleus and Thetis, a masque ; Two sets of canzonets ; Violin concertos and concertos ; Glees and songs. Chiefly celebrated as a violinist, and as the one who introduced Haydn and his works to the English public.

SALOMON (Henriette and Siegfried). See NISSEN (Henriette).

SALVAYRE (Gervais Bernard). French comp., B. Toulouse, June 23, 1847. S. at Toulouse for a time, but afterwards entered Paris Cons. as a pupil of Thomas, Benoist, and Bazin. Gained various prizes for org., and the Grand Prix de Rome, in 1872, with "Calypso," a cantata.

WORKS.—Le Bravo, opera, 1877 ; Le Fandango, ballet, 1877. Le Résurrection, symphonie biblique (Le Jugement dernier), 1876. Psalm CXIII. for soli, chorus and orch. Stabat Mater. Les Bacchantes, scene instrumentale. Songs and Pf. music.

SAMUEL (Adolph). Belgian comp., B. Liége, July 11, 1824. S. at Liége, and in Brussels Cons., 1832-40. Prof. of Harmony, Brussels Cons., 1860. Comp. Operas, symphonies, overtures, cantatas, masses, motets, theoretical works and songs.

SAMUELL (Clara), ROSE. English soprano vocalist, B. Manchester, August 29, 1857. S. in Milan, and at R. A. M., and gained the Parepa-Rosa Scholarship in 1876 and 1880. Married Mr. Henry Robert Rose, org. and comp., Dec., 1880. Associate of R. A. M., 1881. She has appeared at most of the Principal Festivals in England and Scotland, and has sang in London with distinguished success. Chiefly celebrated as a concert vocalist.

SANDERSON (James). English violinist and comp., B. Workington, Cumberland, 1769. Self-taught in music and on the violin. Violinist in Sunderland

Theatre. Teacher in South Shields, 1784-87. Leader of theatre orch., Newcastle-on-Tyne, 1787. Vnst. in orch. of Astley's Amphitheatre, 1788. Music-director at the Surrey Theatre, Was violinist in Philharmonic Orch., and comp. for Vauxhall Gardens. D. London, 1841.

WORKS.—*Music to Dramas, etc.*: Harlequin in Ireland, 1792 ; Blackbeard, 1798 ; Cora, 1799 ; Sir Francis Drake, 1800 (containing the once-famous song, "Bound 'Prentice to a Waterman") ; The Magic Pipe ; and many melo-dramas, burlettas, and pantomimes to the number of over 150. Collins' Ode on the Passions, 1789. Overtures, violin music, and songs.

SANDONI (Francesa), *née* CUZZONI. Italian contralto vocalist, B. Parma, 1700. S. under Lanzi. Sang in Italy with much success, and in Venice, 1719. Appeared in London about 1722. Sang in Handel's operas, etc., as the rival of Faustina Bordoni, till 1729, when she quitted England. Returned, 1734, and again 1750, but each time with less success. She went to Holland, where she was imprisoned for debt, and afterwards returned to Italy, and D. at Bologna, 1770.

SANDYS (George). English poet. B. 1577. D. 1643. He wrote "A Paraphrase upon the Psalms of David...set to new tunes for private devotion by Henry Lawes," of which there are several editions, one of which was revised by John Playford.

SANDYS (William). English writer, B. 1792. Member of the legal profession in London ; an F.S.A., etc. D. London, Feb. 18, 1874.

WORKS.—Christmas Carols, Ancient and Modern, including the most Popular in the West of England, and the Airs to which they are sung, also specimens of French Provincial Carols, with an Introduction and Notes, Lond., 1833. Christmas Tide, its History, Festivities, and Carols, with their Music, Lond., 1852, 8vo (various editions); History of the Violin and other Instruments played on with the Bow, from the Remotest times to the Present. Also an account of the Principal Makers, English and and Foreign," Lond., 1864, 8vo.

SANGSTER (Walter Hay). English org. and comp., B. London, 1835. Educated at City of London School. Chor. in Temple Ch., London. S. org. under E. J. Hopkins, and Pf. under W. Rea. S. also in Berlin, 1855. Org. successively of Christ Church, Ealing ; English Ambassador's Chap., Berlin, 1855 ; St. Michael's, Chester Sq. ; All Saints, St. John's Wood ; St. James', Weybridge; St. Michael's, Star St., Paddington ; and St. Saviour's, Eastbourne. Mus. Bac., Oxon. F.C.O.

WORKS.—The Lord is my Light, cantata ; The Knight of Elle, cantata (MS.) Anthems, songs, organ and Pf. music.

SANKEY (Ira David). American comp. and barytone vocalist, B. in Pennsylvania, Aug. 13, 1840. Chiefly known as the coadjutor of Mr. D. L. Moody in a series of meetings held in connection with religious revivals throughout Britain and America. Comp. of a large number of hymn tunes which have attained much favour in some circles, and among which are the vigorous tunes named "Hold the Fort," "Come to the Saviour," "Jesus of Nazareth passeth by," "More to Follow," "Safe in the arms of Jesus," "The Life-Boat," etc.

SANTINI (Abbe Fortunato). Italian musician, B. Rome, July 5, 1778. S. music under Jannaconi. Educated at the Collegio Salviati, Rome, and was ordained priest in 1801. Hon. member of the Singakademie of Berlin. D. (?) Best known as an assiduous collector of church music, and celebrated as one who did much to make known in Italy the works of German and other masters. He issued a "Catalogo della Musica esistente presso Fortunato Santini in Roma," 1820.

SANTLEY (Charles). English barytone vocalist, B. Liverpool, Feb. 28, 1834. S. at Milan under Gaetano Nava, 1855-1857, and in London under Garcia. *Début* in London as Adam in Haydn's "Creation," Nov. 16, 1857. Appeared in English opera as Hoel in Meyerbeer's "Dinorah," 1859 ; and in Italian opera in 1862. Married Miss Gertrude Kemble, 1859. First sang at Handel Festival, Crystal Palace, 1862 ; Birmingham Festival, 1864. Appeared in the U. S. of America, 1871. Has appeared in all the principal towns of Britain as a concert vocalist. Celebrated as one of the finest barytone vocalists of the present time. He has comp. a few songs, and has edited "Nava's Method of Instruction for a Baritone Voice..." Lond., n. d.

SAPIO. An Italian vocalist of this name was a professor of singing in Paris, and the vocal instructor of the Empress Maria Antoinette. He emigrated to England during the French Revolution. His son, A. SAPIO, B. London, 1792, held a commission in the army for a short time. Afterwards became a tenor vocalist, and made his *début* in the "Messiah" in 1822. He sang also at York and Edinburgh, and sang on the stage from 1824. Appeared at Drury Lane Theatre, London, 1824, and afterwards sang chiefly in opera. D (?).

SARASATE (Martin Meliton). Spanish violinist and comp., B. Pampeluna, Navarre, March 10, 1844. S. at Paris Cons. from 1856, under Alard and Reber, and gained several prizes. Travelled in France, Spain, Norway, America, etc. First appeared in London, 1874. Travelled in Austria and Germany, 1876-77; in Belgium and Russia, 1878. Has appeared in London several times since, and also in the provinces.

WORKS.— Op. 7. Confidence, romance; op. 8. Souvenir de Domont, valse; op. 11. Le Sommeil; op. 12. Moscovienne; op. 15. Mosaïque sur Zampa; op. Prière et Berceuse; Spanish Dances, for vn. and Pf., 6 books, op. 26, etc.; Serenade Andalouse, vn. and Pf., op. 28; Fantasias on Don Juan; Faust; Spanish airs; Scottish airs, etc.

One of the greatest of living violinists, and distinguished as much by the fire and brilliancy of his performance, as by his refinement and technique. He has travelled over most of the world, and has everywhere met with success.

SARONI (Hermann S.) German writer and comp., resident in the United States of America. Author of "Musical Vade Mecum, a Manual of the Science of Music," New York, 1852, 8vo. "Marx's Musical Composition, translated from the Third German edition, with Appendix by E. Girac," New York, 8vo, n. d. "Theory of Harmony," Boston, n. d. He also comp. "Twin Sisters," an operetta, and some vocal music.

SARRIA (Enrico). Italian comp., B. Naples, Feb. 19, 1836. S. under Vitale and Fornasini. Comp., among others, the following operas, "Carmosina," 1853; "Estella," 1858; "Babbeo e l'Intrigante," 1872; "Giudetta," 1875; "Gli Equivoci," 1878, etc.

SARTI (Giuseppe). Italian comp., B. Faenza, Dec. 28 [Dec. 1], 1729. S. music originally in Cath. of Faenza, and afterwards under Martini at Bologna. Music-director of Faenza Theatre, and org. of Cath., 1748-50. Court chap.-master at Copenhagen, 1756; and cond. of court theatre, 1770-1775. Visited London, 1769. Prof. in Cons. of l'Ospedaletto, Venice, 1770. Chap.-master of the Duomo, Milan, 1779. Chap.-master to the Empress Catherine II. of Russia, 1785. Director of the Cons. at Katorinoslaw. D. Berlin, July 28, 1802.

WORKS.—*Operas*: Pompeo in Armenia, 1751; Il Rè Pastore, 1753; Medonte; Demofoonte; L'Olimpiade; Ciro riconosciuto, Copenhagen, 1756; La Figlia ricuperata; La Giardiniera brilliante, 1758; Mitridate, 1765; Il Vologeso, 1765; La Nitetti, 1765; Ipermnestra, 1766; Didone, 1767; Semiramide, 1768; Cléomène, 1770; La Clemenza di Tito, 1771; Le Gelosie villane, 1776; Farnace, 1776; Ifigenia in Aulide, 1777; Epponina, 1777; Achille in Sciro, 1779; Scipione, 1780; Giulio Sabino, 1781; Le Nozze de Dorina, 1782; Siroe, 1783; Armida e Rinaldo, 1785; La gloire du Nord, 1794; I rivali delusi, London. Masses, misereres, cantatas, and sonatas for harpsichord.

SARTORIS (Mrs.) See KEMBLE (Adelaide).

SARTORIUS (Erasmus), or SCHNEIDER. German poet and writer, B. Schleswig, 1577. Chap.-master and vicar of Hamburg Cath. D. Hamburg, Oct. 17, 1637. Wrote "Institutionum Musicarum.." Hamburg, 1635, and other works.

SASS or SAX (Marie Constance). Belgian soprano vocalist, B. Ghent, Jan. 26, 1838. S. Ghent Cons. Sang in Paris, in opera, 1859. Married to M.

Castan, 1864, and separated from him in 1867. Has appeared in operas of Gounod, Meyerbeer, Halévy, Verdi, Spontini, Wagner, etc.

SATTER (Gustav). Austrian pianist and comp., B. Vienna, Feb. 12, 1832. S. at Vienna and Paris. Made concert tours in America and Europe. Cond. at Hanover.
WORKS.—Washington, symphony for orch. Overtures for orch., Loreley, Julius Cæsar, etc. Iolanthe, opera. *Pianoforte:* Niagara, op. 52; Scherzo, op. 54; Impromptu, op. 71; Sonatas, fantasias, etc.

SAUNDERS (George). American writer, author of "Self-Instructing School for the Violin," Boston, 1857, 3 parts.

SAURET (Emile). French violinist and comp., B. Dun-le-Roi, Cher, May 22, 1852. S. under Beriot. Travelled as a violinist in France and Italy, and appeared in London, 1866. Played in the United States, 1872, and 1874-76. Played at the Gewandhaus Concerts, Leipzig, 1876. Reappeared in the U.S., 1877, and in London, 1880. Has also played in Scotland. Prof. of violin in Kullak's Academy of Music, Berlin, since 1879.

He has comp. a concerto for vn. and orch., in G minor, op. 26; A Serenade; Ballade, and Legende; Caprices, and many transcriptions for violin and orch. Eighteen Studies for violin, 3 books. Cavatina and aubade mauresque, op. 25; Fantasia on Spanish airs, op. 27; Pensées Fugitives, vn. and Pf., op. 29; Romance and Tarantelle, op. 31.

SAUZAY (Charles Emile). French violinist and comp., B. Paris, July 14, 1809. S. under Vidal, and in Cons. under Baillot, Guerin, and Reicha. Gained several prizes. Was a member of Baillot's quartet party, and married his daughter. Violinist to Louis Philippe, 1840, and leader of second violins to Napoleon III. Prof. of violin, Paris Cons., 1860. Chevalier of the Legion of Honour.
WORKS.—Op. 1. Fantasia on "Zampa," vn. and Pf.; op. 12. Symphonie rustique, Pf. duet; op. 13. Etudes harmoniques pour Violon; Music for "Georges Dandin," and " Le Sicilien " (Molière). Haydn, Mozart, Beethoven, étude sur le quatuor, Paris, 1861. L' Ecole de l'Accompagnement...Paris, 1869, 8vo; etc.

SAVAGE (William). English org., comp., and bass vocalist, B. [1720]. S. under Dr. Pepusch. Gent. of Chap.-Roy., 1744. Almoner, vicar-choral, and master of choristers, S. Paul's Cath., 1748. D. London, July 27, 1789. Comp. chants and other church music.

SAVARD (Marie Gabriel Augustin). French writer and teacher, B. Paris, Aug. 21, 1814. S. Cons. under Bazin, etc. Prof. of harmony, Paris Cons. Author of "Cours complet d'Harmonie," Paris, 1853, 2 vols.; "Manuel d' Harmonie"; "Principes de la Musique..." Paris, 1865; " Recueil de Plain chant d'Eglise," Paris; "Etudes d'Harmonie pratique," Paris, n. d., 2 vols, 8vo. Comp. motets, and other vocal pieces.

SAVART (Felix). French scientist, B. Mézières, June 30, 1791. D. Paris, March, 1841. Author of "Mémoire sur la Construction des Instruments à cordes et à archet..." Paris, 1819, but best known for his valuable discoveries in acoustical science. Inventor of Savart's wheel, for measuring the vibrations in sounds.

SAVILE (Jeremy). English comp. of 17th century. Now known as comp. of "The Waits," a four-part song sung at the meetings of Glee societies. He also published songs in contemporary collections (*circa*, 1650-60).

SAWERTHAL (Joseph Rudolf). Bohemian violinist, comp. and cond., B. Polep, Leitmeritz, Nov. 5, 1819. S. at Prague Cons., from 1830 to 1837. Bandmaster of 6th Kurassier Regiment (Austrian), 1840. Correspondent of the Viennese "Allgemeine Musik-Zeitung," 1842. Married, 1844. Bandmaster of 53rd Infantry regiment. Established the Pension Soc. for Bandmasters of the Austrian Army (1846), the statutes of which were confirmed by the Emperor in 1859. Bandmaster of Imperial Marines, 1850-64. Director of Military Music to Emperor Maximilian of Mexico, 1864. Bandmaster of the 4th (British) "King's Own" regiment, 1868. Bandmaster of the

Royal Engineers, 1871. He has comp. "Pastyrka," a Serbian opera, 1847; Numerous pieces of military music; Marches and dance music; Songs, choruses, and operatic selections for military band. It is almost needless to say the band of the Royal Engineers, under Sawerthal, is one of the finest military bands in existence. [See also ZAVERTAL].

SAX (Charles Joseph). Belgian musical-instrument maker, B. Dinant, Meuse, Feb. 1, 1791. Established a manufactory for the production of brass instruments at Brussels. Gained several decorations and prizes at various Exhibitions for improvements in the manufacture of wood and brass wind instruments. D. Paris, April 26, 1865.
His eldest son ANTOINE JOSEPH, or ADOLPHE, B. Dinant, Nov. 6, 1814. S. music in Brussels Cons. Devoted himself to the improvement of brass instruments, and invented the whole family of Sax instruments, including Sax horns (1845), Saxophones (1846), and other varieties. Exhibited in various Exhibitions, and was highly rewarded. Became bankrupt in 1852. Reconstructed his business afterwards, but it declined to nothing. His saxophones have been adopted in military bands all over the world. He wrote "Méthode complète pour Sax-Horn et Saxotromba...," Paris, n. d.

SAX (Marie C.) See SASS.

SCALCHI (Sofia). Italian vocalist, B. Turin, Nov. 29, 1850. S. under Boccabadati. *Début* at Mantua, 1866. Sang afterwards in various parts of Italy, and in 1868 appeared in London, and has since sang there with success. Married Signor Lolli, of Ferrara, 1875. Has sang since 1868 in English provinces, Ireland, Scotland, St. Petersburg, Moscow, Warsaw, Vienna, Madrid, Rio Janeiro, 1883, and New York, 1883. She sings both mezzo-soprano and contralto parts, and usually appears in works by Verdi, Donizetti, Meyerbeer, Cimarosa, Massé, and Nicolai.

SCARIA (Emil). Austrian bass vocalist, B. Grätz, Styria, 1838. S. at Vienna Cons., but principally under Garcia in London, 1860. Appeared at Dessau, 1862; Leipzig; and from 1865 to 1872 at Dresden. Singer in opera at Vienna, from 1872, but has also appeared in other parts of Europe. Successful in operas of Wagner. Has also appeared in operas by Mozart, Weber, Lortzing, Cimarosa, Cherubini, and Boieldieu.

SCARISBRICK (Thomas). English org. and comp., B. Prescot, Lancashire, Mar. 24, 1805. D. Kendal, Feb. 26, 1869, where he was org. Comp. anthems and other church music. His wife, *née* WHITNALL (B. 1829, D. 1874), was a contralto singer.

SCARLATTI (Alessandro). Italian comp. B. Trapani, Sicily, 1659. S. under Carissimi at Rome. Musician in service of Queen Christina of Sweden, 1680-88 (?). Chap.-master to the Viceroy of Naples, 1694. Second chap.-master at S. Maria Maggiore, Rome, 1703; chief do., 1707-9. Also master of the private music of Cardinal Ottoboni. Retired to Naples, 1709. D. Naples, Oct. 24, 1725.

WORKS.—*Operas:* L'Onesta nell' amore, Rome, 1680; Pompeo, Naples, 1684; Teodora, 1693; Odoacre, 1694; Pirro e Demetrio, 1697; Il Prigioniero fortunato, 1698; Il Prigioniero superbo, 1699; Gli equivochi nel sembiante, 1700; Eraclea, 1700; Laodicea e Berenice, 1701; Il Figlio delle selve, 1702; La caduta de' decemviri, 1706; Il trionfo della libertà, 1707; Il Medo, 1708; Il martirio di Santa Cecila, 1709; Cirò riconosciuto, 1712; Scipione nelle Spagne, 1714; Arminio, 1714; Il Tigrane, 1715; Il Trionfo dell' Onore, 1718; Il Telemacco, 1718; Attilio Regolo, 1719; Tito Sempronio Gracco, 1720; La Principessa fedele, 1721; Griselda, 1721; Didone abbandonata, and others to number of 115. *Oratorios*: I dolori di Maria sempre Vergine, 1693; Il Sacrifizio d'Abramo, 1703; Il Martirio di Santa Teodosia, 1705; San Filippo Neri, 1718, etc. Masses (about 200), motets, and psalms. Serenata a quattro voci...1723. Madrigals. Duets. Tocattas for harpsichord or organ, etc.

Scarlatti was one of the greatest lights of the Italian school of the 17th century. His influence on operatic music was considerable, and much of his church music is highly original and impressive. His name and style were further spread by many celebrated pupils, among whom may be named Porpora, Feo, Durante, Leo, Hasse, Logroscino, Abos, Gizzi, and Sarri.

SCARLATTI (Domenico). Italian comp., son of above, B. Naples, 1683. S. under his father, Gasparini, and Pasquini. Became acquainted with Händel at Venice, 1708. Succeeded T. Baj as chap.-master of S. Peter's, Rome, 1715-19. Comp. and accompanist at the opera, London, 1719. Proceeded to Lisbon, and became a musician at court, 1721. Afterwards became music-master at court of Madrid. Returned to Naples, 1754, and D. there, 1757.

WORKS.—*Operas*: Irène, 1704; La Silvia, 1710; L'Orlando, 1711; Tolomeo ed Alessandro, 1711; Tetide in Sciro, 1712; Ifigenia in Aulide, 1713; Ifigenia in Tauri, 1713; Amor d'un' ombra e gelosia d'un' aura, 1714; Il Narciso, 1714 (London, under T. Rosingrave, 1720); L'Amleto, 1715; Telemacco, 1718. Pièces pour le Clavecin, composées par Domenico Scarlatti...2 vols. Harpsichord pieces in Farrenc's "Tresor des Pianistes," etc.

Chiefly famous as a performer, who did much to found the modern style of playing keyed instruments. Some of his instrumental works are very quaint and pretty, and others of them are stiff and dry. His operas are never now heard.

SCARLATTI (Giuseppe). Italian comp., grandson of Alessandro, B. Naples, 1711. D. Vienna, Aug. 17, 1777. Comp. operas, among which may be named "Pompeo in Armenia," 1747; "Adriano in Siria," 1752; Ezio, 1754; Merope, 1755; L'Isola disabitata, 1757; La Clemenza di Tito, 1760; La moglie padrona, 1768, etc.

SCHACHNER (Joseph Rudolf). German comp. and pianist, B. Munich, Dec. 31, 1821. Comp. of "Israel's Return from Babylon," an oratorio which has achieved considerable popularity in Britain. His other works are chiefly choral pieces and Pf. music.

SCHAD (Joseph). German pianist and comp., B. Steinach, Bavaria, May 6, 1812. S. under Frölich and A. Schmitt. Travelled as a concert-giver, and was successively prof. of Pf. in Geneva Cons., and in Bordeaux from 1847. D. Bordeaux, July 4, 1879.

WORKS.- -Frantzia, ballet, 1864. *Pianoforte:* op. 6. Three nocturnes; Etudes, Pf. duet, op. 31; Amour à Jésus Christ, in 3 parts, op. 40, 42, 43. Concert studies. Concerto for Pf. and orch., op. 62. Transcriptions and dances, numbering in all about op. 100.

SCHAEFFER (August). German comp., B. Rheinsberg, Aug. 23, 1814. S. under Koch, Böttcher, and Birnbach. D. Berlin, 1879. Comp. operas, Pf. music, lieder and choral music.

SCHARWENKA (Philipp). German pianist and comp., B. Samter, Posen, Feb. 25, 1847. S. in Kullak's Academy, Berlin, 1865. Teacher of composition there.

WORKS.—*Pianoforte*: op. 6. Scenes de Danse; op. 10. Romance et Scherzo (Pf. and vn.); op. 11. Fantaisiestücke; op. 13. Humoresque; op. 18. Miscellanées; op. 25. Caprice; op. 27. Albumblatter; op. 33. Album polonais; Three morceaux de Concert, Pf. and 'cello, op. 17; Serenade for orch., op. 19. Two polonaises, orch., op. 20; Cavatina, Pf. and 'cello, op. 22; Menuet et Mouvement perpétuel, vn. and Pf., op. 24; Four pieces, vn. and Pf., op. 53; Lieder und Tanzweisen, Pf. duet, op. 54; Seestücke, Pf., op. 60. Symphonies, overtures, and suite for orch. Lieder.

SCHARWENKA (Xaver). German pianist and comp., B. Samter, Posen, Jan. 6, 1850. S. at Kullak's Academy, Berlin. First appeared as pianist at Berlin, 1869. Travelled in Europe as a performer, and in 1879 appeared in London. He has since appeared in London several times.

WORKS.—Op. 1. Trio for Pf., vn., and 'cello; op. 2. Sonata for Pf. and vn; op. 3. Polnische nationaltänze, Pf.; op. 4. Scherzo, Pf.; op. 5. Zwei erzählungen, Pf.; op. 6. Sonata, Pf., C sharp minor; op. 7. Polonaise, Pf.; op. 8. Ballade, Pf.; op. 9. Polnische nationaltänze, Pf.; op. 10. Four lieder, voice and Pf.; op. 15. Three lieder, voice and Pf.; op. 16. Polonaise and mazurka, Pf.; op. 17. Impromptu, Pf.; op 22. Novelette et melodie, Pf.; op. 23. Wanderbilder, Pf.; op. 24. Four danses, Pf. duet; op. 25. Two romances, Pf.; op. 28. Six valses; op. 29. Two

Polish dances; op. 30. Valse-impromptu; op. 32. Concerto, Pf. and orch.; op. 33.
Romance, Pf.; op. 36. Second sonata; op. 37. Quartet for Pf. and strings, in F;
Sonata, Pf. and vn., in D min; Trio for Pfs., op. 45.; Sonata for Pf. and 'cello,
op. 46; Symphony for orch., in C minor, op. 60.

One of the most gifted instrumental composers of the present time. His Pf. works abound in original features, and all are marked by much that is graceful and clever.

SCHEBEK (Edmond). Austrian writer and amateur musician, B. Petersdorf, Oct. 22, 1819. Imperial counsellor, and secretary to Chamber of Commerce, Prague. Author of "La Fabrication des Violons en Italie et son origine Allemande," Prague, 1874. Trans. as "Violin Manufacture in Italy, and its German Origin, an Historical Sketch," by Walter E. Lawson, Lond., 8vo, 1877.

SCHEBST or SCHEBEST (Agnes). Austrian mezzo-soprano vocalist, B. Vienna, Feb. 15, 1813. Singer in court theatre of Dresden. S. under Madame Werdy. *Début* at Dresden in Méhul's Joseph. Sang at Pesth, Vienna, Carlsruhe, and elsewhere in Germany, and in France and Italy. Married Dr. David F. Strauss, the author of a Life of Jesus, 1841, and quitted the stage. D. Stuttgart, Dec. 22, 1869. She published an autobiography with title, "Aus dem Leben einer Künstlerin," Stuttgart, 8vo, 1857.

SCHECHNER-WAAGEN (Nanette). German soprano vocalist, B. Munich, 1806. S. under Grassini and Ronconi. *Début* at Munich. Sang in Vienna (1826), Berlin (1827); and in 1831 married Herr Waagen, a painter. Retired from the stage in 1835. D. Munich, April 30, 1860. Sang in operas of Weigl, Cimarosa, Mozart, Gluck, Weber, and Beethoven.

SCHEIBLER (Johnn Heinrich). German musician, B. Montjoie, Aix-la-Chapelle, Nov. 11, 1777. Silk manufacturer at Crefeld. D. Crefeld, Nov. 20, 1837. Inventor of a tonometer, for measuring sound, and various other devices in acoustical science. His discoveries are contained in "Der Physikalische und Musikalische Tonmesser,"...Essen, 1834; "Anleitung die Orgel vermittelst der Strœsse und des Metronoms," Crefeld, 1834.

SCHEIN (Johann Hermann). German comp., B. Grünhain, Saxony, Jan. 29, 1586. Chor. in Elector's Chap., at Dresden. Chap.-master to Duke of Saxe-Weimar, 1613. Cantor at Leipzig, in succession to Calvisius, 1615. D. Leipzig, 1630.

WORKS.—Venus Krænzlein, oder weltliche lieder mit 5 stimmen...1609; Cymbalum Sionium, 1615; Banchetto Musicale, 1617; Israels Brünlein, 1623. Some of Schein's chorales are now in use as psalm tunes.

SCHELBLE (Johann Nepomuk). German tenor vocalist, teacher and comp., B. Höffingen, in the Black Forest, May 16, 1789. S. under Vogler and Krebs. Director of the Musical Academy of Frankfort-on-Main, 1817. Established the "Cæcilian Society" of Frankfort, 1818. D. Frankfort, Aug. 7, 1837. Celebrated as a cond. and for his connection with Beethoven, Mendelssohn, Spohr, and others. He comp. operas and some choral music.

SCHELLER (Jacob). Bohemian violinist and comp., B. Schettal, Rakonitz, May 12, 1759. Educated at Prague. S. music under Vogler. Violinist in orchs. in Vienna, and court orch. of Mannheim. Leader in court-band at Stuttgart till 1792. Travelled over Europe as a violinist, and became reduced by intemperate habits to the lowest possible straits. D. in a village in Frisia, 1800. Comp. violin music.

SCHENCK (Johann). Austrian comp., B. Neustadt, Vienna, Nov. 30, 1753. S. under Stall and Wagenseil. Instructed Beethoven in harmony. Music-director to Prince of Auersberg. D. Vienna, Dec. 29, 1836.

WORKS.—*Operas, etc.*: Dis singspiel ohne Titel, 1790; Im Finstern ist nich gut tappen, 1791; Die Weinlese, 1791; Der Aerntekranz, 1791; Die Weihnacht auf dem Lande, 1792; Der Bettelstudent, 1796; Der Dorfbarbier, 1796; Der Jagd, 1798; Der Fassbinder, 1802. Symphonies, masses, quartets, lieder, and other music.

SCHETKY (Johann Georg Christoph). German comp. and violoncellist, B. Darmstadt, 1740. Educated at Jena University. S. music under Filtz.

'Cellist at Court of Hesse. Travelled in Italy, France, etc., as 'cellist. 'Cellist at Darmstadt and Frankfort, 1772. Engaged by Bremner as principal 'cellist for the S. Cecilia Concerts in Edinburgh, 1773. Married Maria Anna Theresa Reinagle, 1774. D. Edinburgh, Nov. 30, 1824.

WORKS.—Op. 1. Six trios for 2 vns. and 'cello; op. 2. Six duets for vn. and 'cello; op. 3. Six trios for harpsichord, vn., and 'cello; op. 4. Six sonatas for 'cello and bass; op. 5. Six duets for two flutes; op. 6. Six string quartets; op. 7. Twelve duets for 2 'cellos; op. 13. Six sonatas for 'cello and bass; op. 24. Three duets for vn. and 'cello. Concertos for 'cello and orch.; symphonies; and vocal music. Practical and Progressive Lessons for the Violoncello, dedicated to J. Crosdill, Esq. Lond., n. d., fo.

Schetky was a great power in musical Edinburgh in his day, and held a high place as a teacher. His son, JOHN CHRISTIAN, was a painter of some celebrity. The melody of "Mary's Dream" has been attributed to him, but is now known not to have been his composition. See Wood's Songs of Scotland, edited by Graham, first edition.

SCHICHT (Johann Gottfried). German comp., B. Reichnau, Zittau, Sept. 29, 1753. Educ. at Leipzig University. S. music under Trier. Married Mdlle. Valdestrula, a singer (D. 1809), in 1786. Succeeded J. A. Hiller as Cantor of S. Thomas Schule, Leipzig, 1810. D. Leipzig, Feb. 16, 1823.

WORKS.—Das ende der Gerechten, oratorio. Motets and Psalms. Allgemeine Choralbuch für Kirchen Schulen...Leipzig, n. d., 3 vols. Grundregeln der Harmonie...Leipzig, n. d. An edition of Bach's Motets, and some other works.

SCHICK (Margaret Louise), *née* HAMEL. German soprano vocalist, B. Mayence, April 26, 1773. S. under Hellmuth and Righini. Married Ernst Schick, violinist (B. the Hague, 1756. D. Berlin, 1813), 1791. Travelled in Germany, and appeared in operas of Salieri, Gluck, Mozart, Martini, and others.

SCHIEDMAYER & SONS. German firm of Pianoforte makers, established in Stuttgart, 1809. Celebrated on the Continent for the superior make of their instruments. Another firm bearing the same name, but known as J. & P. SCHIEDMAYER, have been established in Stuttgart since 1854. Both firms have gained prizes at various Exhibitions for the good quality of their manufactures. JOHANN DAVID SCHIEDMAYER, B. Erlangen, April, 1753, D. Nuremberg, Mar. 20, 1805, was the original founder of both families. His son, JOHANN LORENZ, B. Erlangen, 1786, established the firm of Schiedmayer & Sons, at Stuttgart, as above noted. He D. Stuttgart, April, 1860.

SCHIKANEDER (Johann Emmanuel). German actor and singer, B. Ratisbon, 1751. Played throughout Europe. D. Vienna, Sept. 21, 1812. Of note as the author of the libretto of Mozart's "Zauberflöte."

SCHILLER (Johann Christoph Friedrich von). German poet and writer, B. Marbach, Würtemberg, Nov. 11, 1759. D. Weimar, May 9, 1805. Many of Schiller's dramatic works have been utilized by different composers for musical treatment, among them are "The Robbers," "Don Carlos," "Wallenstein," "Jeanne d'Arc," and "Bride of Messina." His lyrical works have inspired Beethoven, Mendelssohn, Löwe, Reichardt, Romberg, Brahms, and many other musicians.

SCHILLING (Gustav). German writer and teacher, B. Schwiegershausen, Hanover, Nov. 3, 1805. Son of the Protestant pastor there. Educated at Göttingen and Halle universities. Director of a music school in Stuttgart, 1830. Settled in New York, and became director of a music-school there, 1857. Resident in Montreal for a time. D. Nebraska, May, 1880.

WORKS.—Musikalische Handwörterbuch,...Stuttgart, 1830; Encyclopædie der gesammten Musikalischen Weissenschaften, oder Universal Lexikon der Tonkunst, Stuttgart, 1835-40, 7 vols., 8vo; Versuch einer Philosophie des Schœnen in der Musik, oder Æsthetik der Tonkunst, Mayence, 1838; Allgemeine generalbasslehre,...Darmstadt, 1839; Geschichte der heutigen oder Modernen Musik,...Carlsruhe, 1841; Das Musikalische Europa, ..Stuttgart, 1840; Musikalische Didaktik,... 1851.

SCHIMON (Anna), *née* REGAN. Bohemian soprano vocalist, B. Aich, near Carlsbad, Sept. 18, 1841. S. under Mme. Sabatier-Ungher, 1860-64. Appeared in Italy, Hanover, and St. Petersburg. Visited London, 1869, and again sang in England, 1869-75. Sang in Vienna, 1870. Married Adolf Schimon, 1872. Chiefly famous as a concert vocalist. Her husband, ADOLF SCHIMON, B. Vienna, Feb. 29, 1820. S. at Paris Cons. under Halévy. Appeared in England, 1850. Prof. of singing successively at Leipzig and Munich. Comp. operas, songs, etc.

SCHINDELMEISSER (Ludwig). German comp. and cond., B. Königsberg, Dec. 8, 1811. Son of Fanny Schindelmeisser, a pianist (D. Berlin, Feb 28, 1846). S. violin and became cond. in various theatres. Chap.-master to Grand Duke of Hesse-Darmstadt. D. Darmstadt, Mar. 20, 1864. Comp. oratorios; operas—Mathilde; Die Zehn Glücklicher Tage; Peter von Szapary, 1839; Die Rächer, 1844; Overtures, Pf. music, and lieder.

SCHINDLER (Anton). Austrian writer, B. Modl, Neustadt, 1796. Educated at Vienna University, and cond. at the Josephstadt theatre there. Became intimately acquainted with Beethoven, 1814, and on his death became possessed of his papers. Music-director at Münster Cath., and afterwards at Aix-la-Chapelle, 1835. D. Bockenheim, near Frankfort-on-Main, Jan. 16, 1864.

WORKS.—Biographie von Ludwig van Beethoven,...Münster, 1840, 8vo, with portrait, 3 editions to 1860; Beethoven in Paris,...Münster, 1842, 8vo. The first of these two works was edited and translated by Moscheles as "The Life of Beethoven, including his correspondence with his Friends," Lond., 1841, 2 vols., 8vo.

SCHIRA (Francesco). Italian comp. and teacher of singing, B. Malta, Sept. 19, 1815. Descended from a family of Milanese origin. S. at Milan Cons., under Basily, till about 1832. Cond. of theatre of Santo Carlos, Lisbon, and Prof. at the Cons. there. Went to Paris, 1842, and was there engaged as cond. of the Princess's Theatre, London. Cond. at Drury Lane, 1844-47 and 1852; and of Covent Garden Theatre, 1848. Teacher of singing in London. Officer of Order of the Crown of Italy. D. London, Oct. 15, 1883.

WORKS.—*Operas:* Elena e Malvina, Milan, 1832; I cavalieri di Valenza, 1837; Il Fanatico per la Musica, Lisbon; Kenilworth (never produced); Mina, London, 1849; Theresa, or the Orphan of Geneva, 1850; Nicolo de' Lappi, Lond., 1863; Selvaggia, Naples, 1865; Lia, Venice, 1866. The Ear-ring, operetta. Cantata, The Lord of Burleigh, Birmingham Festival, 1873. Numerous songs, and other vocal music.

His brother VINCENZO (B. Madrid, D. Lisbon, 1857), was educated at Milan Cons., and became cond. of Santo Carlos Theatre at Lisbon. He comp. ballets and operas. MARGHERITA, sister of the preceding, was also a pupil of Milan Cons., and became celebrated in Italy as an operatic vocalist, and afterwards as a teacher. D. Milan, April, 1885.

SCHIRMACHER (Dora). Pianist, B. Liverpool, Sept. 1, 1857. S. at Leipzig Cons. from 1872. Appeared at Crystal Palace, London, 1877. Has since appeared with much success in the English provinces, and on the Continent.

SCHIRMER (Gustav). German music-publisher, B. Thuringia, 1830. Went to New York, 1840, and in 1853 entered into the music-publishing business there. Firm known for a time as Beer and Schirmer, but now as Schirmer of Broadway, New York. The firm act as American agents for Peters, Breitkopf and Hartel, and Augener and Co., and publish numerous works of every kind. The catalogue of the firm includes titles of many works of Abt, Arditi, Bassford, Buck, Damrosch, Gounod, Gumbert, Kücken, Liszt, Millard, Pease, Schumann, S. P. Warren, and other American and European composers. The *Musical Review*, a weekly magazine on musical topics, was established about 1879, and has since been published by the firm.

SCHLESINGER (Martin Adolph). German music-publisher, established a large business in Berlin in 1795, and issued many important musical works, as well as a musical periodical. He D. 1839, and was succeeded by his second son HEINRICH (1807-1879), who continued the business. The firm still exists.

His eldest son, MORITZ ADOLPH (B. Berlin, Oct. 30, 1798. D. Baden-Baden,

Feb. 1871), was bred to business in Paris, and about 1823 he established a large music-publishing firm, which existed in his name till 1846, when he sold out and retired. The Business is now in the hands of Messrs. BRANDUS and DUFOUR. Among the composers of importance whose works in whole or in part the firm issues, may be named Beethoven, Mozart, Meyerbeer, Weber, Hummel, Moscheles, Halévy and Berlioz. The other publications of Schlesinger included the now defunct "Gazette Musicale de Paris," 1843-1881, and many important theoretical works.

SCHLETTERER (Hans Michel). German writer, violinist, and comp., B. Anspach, May 29, 1824. S. violin under J. Durrner, Spohr, and David. Prof. of music at Heidelberg, Augsberg, etc. Married Hortensia Zirges (B. 1830), a singer. Author of "Histoire de la Musique d'Eglise...." "Das Deutsch Singspiel von seinen ersten Anfangen, etc," 1863, 8vo. Comp. Psalms, and other vocal music.

SCHLÖSSER (Ludwig). German comp. and cond., B. Darmstadt, 1800. S. at Vienna under Mayseder, Rinck, Seyfried, and Salieri; also at Paris Cons. under Kreutzer and Lesueur. Cond. of Court Band of Darmstadt.

WORKS.—*Operas:* Granada; Das Leben ist ein Traum, 1839; Kapitæn Hector; Die jugend Karls II. von Spanien. String quartets, op. 1, 4, 6, 15 Concertino for horn and orch., op. 16. Themes varied, for vn. and orch., op. 2, 5, 9, and 11. Sonatas for Pf., op. 17, 20, etc.

His son CARL WILHELM ADOLPH, was B. Darmstadt, Feb. 1, 1830. Educated in music by his father, and appeared as pianist in Germany and France. He settled in London in 1854 as teacher, and is one of the Pf. teachers at the R. A. M. His works include op. 3. L'Attente; op. 6. Impromptu; op. 7. Fantasiestuck; op. 8. Allegro capriccioso; op. 9. Le Papillon; op. 16. Idylle. Caprices, and other Pf. works.

SCHLÜTER (Joseph). German writer, author of "Allgemeine Geschichte der Musik in übersichtlicher Darstellung," Leipzig, 1863, 8vo. Trans. as "A General History of Music," by Mrs. Tubbs, London, 1865, 8vo.

SCHMIDT (Bernard). "Father Smith," German organ-builder, B. in Germany about 1630. Learned business under Christian Former. Came to England about 1660, with his nephews Gerard and Bernard, and in the same year secured the erection of the organ in the Chapel Royal, Whitehall. Made organ-maker in ordinary to Charles II. Involved in dispute with Renatus Harris regarding the erection of an organ for the Temple Chapel, London, which was subsequently decided by the organ which Schmidt submitted on trial being accepted, 1683-84. D. London, 1799.

The principal organs built by Schmidt or his nephews are as follows :—Westminster Abbey, 1660; St. Giles-in-the-Fields, 1671; St. Margaret's, Westminster, 1675; Durham Cath., 1683; St. Paul's Cath., London, 1694-97; Trinity Coll., Cambridge, 1708; Wells Cath., 1664; Christ Church Cath., Oxford, 1680; Ripon Cath.; St. George's Chap., Windsor; Southwell Collegiate Church; Manchester Cathedral, and Chester Cathedral.

SCHMIDT (Gustav). German comp., B. Weimar, Sept. 1, 1816. S. under Toepfer. Music-director at Brünn, Würzburg Frankfort-on-Main, and Mayence. D. Darmstadt, Feb. 11, 1882. Comp. operas. Lieder and Pf. music.

SCHMIDT (Johann Philipp Samuel). German comp., B. Königsberg, Sept. 3, 1779. D. 1850. Comp. "Alfred der Grosse," opera; Overtures; Lieder for single voice and Pf; Choral music, etc.

SCHMITT (Aloys). German comp. and pianist, B. Erlenbach-on-Main, 1789. S. under his father and André. Prof. of Pf. at Frankfort, 1816, and afterwards at Berlin. Court org. at Hanover. Resided afterwards successively at Frankfort, Brussels, and Paris. D. Frankfort-on-Main. July 25, 1866.

WORKS.—Tongemälde, symphony for orch.; Overtures for orch., op. 36, 46; Quartets for strings, op. 70, 80, 81; Concertos for Pf. and orch., op. 14, 34, 60; Concertinos, Pf. and orch., op. 75, 76; Sonatas, Pf. and vn., op. 27, 66; Sonatas, Pf. duet, op. 31, 39, 46; Sonatas, Pf. solo, op. 6, 7, 8, 10, 11, 14, 78, 83, 84.

Exercises and studies for Pf., including a famous teaching series of five-finger exercises.
Schmitt was a successful teacher, and numbered among his pupils the late Ferdinand Hiller.

SCHMITT (Jacob). German comp. and pianist, brother of preceding, B. Obernburg, Nov. 2, 1803. S. under Aloys. Prof. of Pf. at Hamburg. D. Hamburg, June, 1853.
His works include Variations for Pf. duet, op. 27, 28, 30, 45, 48, 58, 60, 65; Sonatas, Pf. duet, op. 31, 39, 46; Sonatas, Pf. solo, op. 24, 25, 29, 50-55; also exercises, rondos, studies and transcriptions.

SCHNEIDER (Georg, or Gottleib Abraham). German comp. and cond., B. Darmstadt, April 19, 1770. Oboe-player in the army. Music-director in service of Duke of Mecklenburg, 1790. Member of Royal Chap., Berlin. Leader at the opera, 1825, and bandmaster of the Royal Guard. D. Berlin, Jan. 19, 1839. Comp. masses and sacred cantatas, music for wind instruments, a symphony, and overtures for orch.

SCHNEIDER (Friedrich Johann Christian). German comp., writer, org., and teacher, B. Alt-Waltersdorf, near Zittau, Jan. 3, 1786. S. under his father, org. of Gersdorf. Educated at Zittau, and at Leipzig Univ., and S. music under Schönfelder and Unger. Org. of Univ. Ch., S. Paul's, Leipzig, 1807. Cond. of an opera company which performed in Leipzig and Dresden alternately, 1810. Org. of S. Thomas's Ch., Leipzig, 1812-21. Chap.-master to the Duke of Anhalt-Dessau, 1821. Established a music school at Dessau, and cond. choral festivals there, and in other German towns. D. Dessau, Nov. 23, 1853.
WORKS.—*Oratorios:* Die Sündfluth (The Deluge, trans. by E. Taylor); Das Weltgericht (Last Judgment), 1819; Das Verlorne Paradies (Paradise Lost), op. 75, 1824; Pharaon, op. 74, 1828; Christus der Meister; Absalon; Christus das Kind, op. 83, 1829; Gideon, op. 88, 1829; Gethsemane und Golgotha, op. 96, 1838; Das befreiete Jerusalem; Salomonis Tempelbau; Bonifacius; Christus der Erlöser; Jehova, hymn, op. 94. Alwins Entzauberung, opera, 1809. Mass, op. 55. Psalm xxiv. (Herder), op. 72; Vater Unser, for double male choir, orch., and org., op. 103. Songs and lieder, op. 16, 24, 28, 44, 53, 60, 64, and 69. *Overtures for orch.:* Op. 11; Die Braut von Messina, op. 42; On theme of God save the King, op. 43; Tragic, in C minor, op. 45; opp. 50, 60, 67; Gaudeamus Igitur, op. 84. Polonaise for orch., op. 48. Concertos for Pf. and orch., op. 18 and 22. Quartets for strings, opp. 24, 34, 36. Trio for Pf., clarinet, and bassoon, op. 10. Duets for Pf. and violin, or flute, opp. 19, 31, 33, 35, 61. Sonatas for Pf. duet, op. 2, 8, 13, 29. Sonatas, Pf. solo, opp. 1, 3, 5, 6, 14, 20, 21, 26, 27, 30, 37, 40. *Theoretical:* Elementarbuch der Harmonie und Tonsetzkunst, Leipzig, 1820, 4to, Trans. as The Elements of Musical Harmony and Composition...Lond., 1828, fo., also as Treatise on Thorough Bass and Harmony, by Edward L. White, Lond., 1856, 8vo. Vorschule der Musik, Leipzig, 1827. Handbuch des Organisten, Halberstadt, 1829-30, 4 parts, Trans. as Complete Theoretical and Practical Organ School...Lond. (Novello), n. d.
Famous as a teacher and learned musician. His pupils were numerous, and include some of the best modern men, among them Robert Franz. His compositions are of the same school as those of Haydn and Mozart, and only a few lieder and sacred pieces are now in use. His life was issued as Friedrich Schneider als Mensch und Künstler, von F. Kempe, Dessau, 1859, 8vo, with portrait.

SCHNEIDER (Johann Gottlob). German comp. and org. B. Alt-Gersdorf, Oct. 28, 1789. S. under his father and Unger. Org. to University of Leipzig, 1811. Gave organ recitals in Görlitz, Dresden, and Zittau, 1816-17, and in Freiberg, Leipzig, Weimar, Gotha, and Dresden, from 1820. Court org. at Dresden, 1825. D. Dresden, April 13, 1864.
WORKS.—Op. 1. Fantasia and Fugue, org.; op. 2. Religiöse Chorgesänge für 3 soprane, oder 2 tenöre u. Bass; op. 3. Fantasia and Fugue, org.; op. 4. Twelve easy organ pieces; op. 5-6. Six sacred choruses.
Teacher of Van Eyken, Faisst, Herzog, Merkel, A. G. Ritter, Naumann, E. F. Richter, Oakeley, and others. In 1861 his pupils presented him with a "Jubel-Album für die Orgel," consisting of compositions by themselves.

SCHNEIDER (Wilhelm). German org. and comp., B. Neudorf, July 21, 1783, Org. Merseburg Cath. D. Merseburg, Oct. 9, 1843. Comp. overtures, org. and Pf. music, lieder, and theoretical works.

SCHNORR VON CAROLSFELD (Ludwig). German tenor vocalist, B. Munich, 1836. S. at Leipzig Cons. from 1853. Sang in Wagner's operas at Carlsruhe, 1858, and also in Dresden. D. Dresden, 1865.

SCHNYDER VON WARTENSEE (Xaver). German comp. and writer, B. Lucerne, April 18, 1786. Of noble German family. S. under Kienlen. Entered army and served against the French. Afterwards settled at Frankfort-on-Main, and became celebrated as a teacher. D. Frankfort-on-Main, Aug. 30, 1868.

WORKS.—Fortunat mit den Söckel und Wundschütsein, opera, 1829; Zeit und Ewigkeit, oratorio, 1838; Symphonies; Geistliche Lieder; Sonatas for Pf.; Choruses, songs, and cantatas.

More famous as a teacher than as a composer. He was one of the teachers of Pearsall, John Thomson, and John Barnett. His writings were chiefly contributed to periodical literature.

SCHOBERLECHNER (Franz). Austrian pianist and comp., B. Vienna, July 21, 1797. S. under Grüner, a pupil of Hummel. Patronised by Prince Esterhazy, and at his instance placed under Förster for tuition. Appeared at Grätz, Trieste, and Florence as pianist. Chap.-master at Lucca. Appeared in Vienna, 1820, and in 1823 went to St. Petersburg. Married there to Sophie Dall' Occa, 1824. Travelled in Europe, but latterly retired to Florence, where he chiefly resided. D. Berlin, Jan. 7, 1843.

WORKS.—*Operas*: I virtuosi teatrali; Gli Arabi nelle Gallie; Le jeune Oncle; Il Barone di Dolzheim, 1827; Rossane, 1839. Themes, varied, Pf. and orch., op. 46-47. Trios for Pf., vn., and 'cello. Sonatas for Pf., rondos, fantasias, variations, etc.

His wife, *née* SOPHIE DALL.' OCCA (B. St. Petersburg, 1807; D. Florence, 1863), was a soprano vocalist, and appeared with success in operas by her husband and others.

SCHOBERT or **SCHUBART.** German comp. and harpsichord-player, B. Strassburg. Christian name unknown. Musician in service of the Prince de Conti at Paris, 1760. D. Paris, Aug., 1767, from effects of eating poisonous mushrooms. Famous in his day as a performer, and held in considerable esteem for his compositions, which consist of "Sonatas for Clavecin and Violin, op. 1, 2, 3. Sonatas for Clavecin solo, op. 4, 5, 16, 17. Trios for Clavecin, violin, and bass, op. 6, 8. Quartets for clavecin and strings. Concertos for Clavecin, op. 9, 10, 11, 12, 13, and 18. Symphonies for Harpsichord, violin, and 2 horns, op. 14, 15.

SCHŒLCHER (Victor). French writer, B. Paris, July 21, 1804. Expelled from France for political reasons, 1851, and took up residence in London. Returned to France, 1870, and became member of the National Assembly. Made collection of publications relating to Handel, and presented it to Paris Conservatory. Author of "The Life of Handel," Lond., 1857, 8vo.

SCHOLTZ (Herrmann). German pianist and comp., B. Breslau, June 9, 1845. S. under Brosig, at Leipzig; under Plaidy and Riedel; and afterwards under Liszt, Bulow, and Rheinberger. Teacher and comp. in Dresden. Court pianist there. Has travelled as a concert giver. Comp. sonatas, variations, elegies, fantasias, and other pieces for Pf. solo; Trio for Pf., violin, and 'cello, op. 51; Concerto for Pf. and orch., etc.

SCHOLZ (Bernard). German comp. and cond., B. Mayence, March 30, 1835. S. under Pauer and Dehn. Prof. in Munich Cons., 1856-58. Chap.-master to King of Hanover, and cond. at theatre, 1859. Teacher in Florence, Berlin, and Breslau. Comp. operas, Carlo Rosa, Morgiana, 1870, Golo, 1875; Die vornehmen Wirthe, 1883; Pf. music; Symphony in B flat; concerted vocal music, etc. Edited Dehn's "Die Lehre vom Contrapunkt, dem Canon und der Fuge," Berlin, 1858.

SCHÖNFELD (Henry). American comp., B. Milwaukee, Oct. 4, 1856. S. at Leipzig Cons., and under Lassen. Has written "The Easter Idyll," cantata; Pf. music, songs, and choral music.

SCHOP or SCHOPP (Johann). German comp. of 17th century, B. Hamburg. Music-director in Hamburg and Luneburg. He published "Neues Paduanen, Galliarden, Allemanden, Balletten, Couranten und canzonen, mit 3, 4, 5, und 6 Stemmen," Hamburg, 1633-1644. "Geistlicher Concerten," 1644. "Ristii Frommer Christen Alltegliche Haus-Musik," 1654, etc. A number of Schop's chorales are in use as psalm-tunes in Britain.

SCHOTT (Anton). German tenor vocalist, B. Staufeneck, Swabia, June 25, 1846. S. under Agnes Schebest. *Début* at Frankfort in "Der Freischütz," 1870. Served in army through Franco-Prussian War. Sang in London, 1879, and appeared in Wagner's operas, 1880. Has since appeared in opera in Germany.

SCHOTT'S SÖHNE. German firm of music-publishers, established in Mayence in 1773, by Bernhard Schott (D. 1817). He was succeeded by his son JOHANN JOSEPH (1782-1855), and the business in time passed on to the grandson, FRANZ PHILIPPE (B. 1811, D. Milan, 1874), being now mainly in the hands of Peter Schott and Dr. L. Strecker. The firm has branches in Brussels, Paris, London, Leipzig, Rotterdam, and New York. Their catalogue of Pianoforte music alone extends to about 200 pp., and it contains the name of nearly every prominent composer for that instrument, as Ascher, Beethoven, Bertini, Beyer, Clementi, Cramer, Czerny, Dupont, Gottschalk, Herz, Hünten, Liszt, Osborne, Prudent, Rummel, Schubert, and Wallace. Their other catalogues are equally representative, and among the large vocal works issued by the firm are those of Auber, Wagner, Rossini, and Donizetti. They also issue a considerable number of theoretical and didactic works of all kinds.

SCHRÖDER-DEVRIENT (Wilhelmine). German soprano vocalist, B. Hamburg, Dec. 6, 1804. Daughter of Antoinette Sophie Schröder, *née* Bürger, a celebrated actress. Appeared originally as a ballet-girl at Hamburg theatre. Afterwards appeared as a tragic actress in plays by Racine and Schiller. *Début* as vocalist in Mozart's "Zauberflöte," Vienna, 1821; where she had S. singing under Mazatti. Sang in Berlin from 1823, in works of Beethoven, Spontini, and Weber. Married Devrient, the actor, 1823, and separated from him in 1828. Appeared in Paris, 1829-30. Sang in London, 1832-3, and again in 1837. Afterwards sang in Dresden, where she married an officer named Döring, but soon separated from him. Travelled afterwards in North Europe, and made her last appearance at Riga, 1847. Married Herr von Bock, 1850. D. Coburg, Jan. 26, 1860.

Famous for her powers as a dramatic singer, and especially for the earnestness and energy of her singing and acting in Beethoven's "Fidelio." She had a voice of much strength and richness of tone, which she used to best advantage in exciting and passionate operatic scenes. In many respects she excelled most of her contemporaries, but in the matters of execution and training she was deficient, as the early deterioration of her voice sufficiently proved.

SCHRÖTER (Christoph Gottlieb). German writer and inventor, B. Hohenstein, near Dresden, Aug. 10, 1699. S. under Schmidt at Dresden. Lecturer and org. at Jena, Nordhausen, etc. D. Nordhausen, Saxony, Nov. 1782. Wrote much on Harmony and musical theory. Attributed with the invention of the Pianofore, which later authorities have fixed with certainty on Cristofori.

SCHRÖTER (Johann Samuel). German pianist and comp., B. Warsaw, 1750. Travelled as a pianist in Holland, and in 1772 settled in London as teacher. Org. in German chap., and music-master to the Queen. Married clandestinely to one of his pupils, who was highly connected; but obliged by her friends to consent to a separation and a settlement of £500 per annum. D. Pimlico, London, Nov. 2, 1788.

He comp. Six Sonatas for harpsichord, op. 1; Three quintets for Pf., 2 vns., viola, and bass; Three trios for harpsichord, violin, and 'cello, op. 2; Six concertos for harpsichord, op. 3; 3 do., op. 4; 3 do., op. 5; and 6 do., op. 6. His brother, JOHANN HEINRICH (B. Warsaw, 1762), resided in London from 1782, was a violinist and comp. His sister, CORONA ELISABETH WILHELMINE (B. Warsaw, 1748. D. Weimar, 1802), was a singer at the court of Weimar.

SCHUBERT (Camille), *mon de plume* of CAMILLE PRILIPP. French comp. and music-publisher, B. 1810. In business in Paris. Chiefly known by his Pf. works, which number over 400, and include nocturnes, fantasias, serenades, transcriptions, and nearly every form of light Pf. music.

SCHUBERT (Franz Peter). Austrian comp., B. Vienna, Jan. 31, 1797. Son of Franz Schubert, a schoolmaster. S. music under M. Holzer. Chor. in Lichtenhal Choir, Vienna. Chor. and pupil in the Imperial Convict, Vienna, 1808, and afterwards first violin there. Pupil-teacher in his father's school for three years. S. under Salieri. Teacher of music in family of Count Johann Esterhazy, 1818. His songs first publicly performed, 1821. Member of the Musical Society of Vienna, 1827. He never held any musical appointments, though he often acted as a conductor, and twice unsuccessfully applied for musical directorships in Laybach and Vienna. D. Vienna, Nov. 19, 1828.

WORKS.—*Operas, operettas, etc.*: Der Teufels Lustschloss, 1814; Die Vierjahrige Posten, 1815; Fernando, 1815; Der Spiegelritter, 1815; Die Freunde von Salamanka, 1815; Die Zwillingsbrüder, 1819; Die Zauberharfe, 1820; Alfonso und Estrella, 1822; Die Verschworenen, 1823; Fierabras, 1823; Rosamunde, op. 26, 1823. Miriam's Siegesgesang, oratorio, op. 136. *Symphonies:* No. 1, in D, 1813; No. 2, in B flat, 1815; No. 3, in D, 1815; No. 4 (tragic), in C minor, 1816; No. 5, in B flat, 1816; No. 6, in C, 1818; No. 7, in E, 1821; No. 8 (unfinished), in B minor; No. 9; No. 10, in C, 1828. *Overtures:* Italian, op. 170, others in MS., and arrangements for Pf. Octet for 2 vns., viola, 'cello, D-bass, horn, bassoon, and clarinet, op. 166. Quintet for Pf. and strings, op. 114. *String Quartets:* Twenty, of which numbers 9; 12, op. 168; 13; 16-17, op. 125; 18, op. 29; 19; and 20, op. 161, are published. Trios for Pf., violin, and 'cello, op. 99, 100. Notturno for Pf., violin, and 'cello, op. 148. Rondo for Pf. and violin, op. 70; Phantasie, do., op. 159; Duo, do., op. 162. *Pianoforte:* Sonatas, twenty-four in all, op. 30, 40, 42, 53, 78, 120, 143, 147, 162, 164, and others published; op. 9. Originaltänze; op. 10. Variations (4 hands); op. 15. Phantasie; op. 18. Walzer, Ländler, etc.; op. 27. Marches (4 hands); op. 33. Deutsche Tänze; op. 35. Variations (4 hands); op. 40. 6 marches (4 hands); op. 49. Galopp und Ecossaises; op. 50. Valses sentimentales; op. 51. Three marches militaires (4 hands); op. 54. Divertissement à la Hongroise (4 hands); op. 55. Funeral march of Alexander I. (4 hands); op. 61. Polonaises (4 hands); op. 62. Divertissement (4 hands); op. 63. March héroique; op. 64. Wiener Damen-Ländler; op. 75. Four Polonaises; op. 77. Valses; op. 78. Phantasie; op. 82. Variations (4 hands); op. 84. Andantino and Rondo (4 hands); op. 90. Four impromptus; op. 91. Grätzer Walzer; op. 94. Moments musicals (also arranged for orch.); op. 103. Phantasie (4 hands); op. 107. Rondo (4 hands); op. 121. Two marches (4 hands); op. 127. Letzte Walzer; op. 138. Rondo (4 hands); op. 140. Grando Duo (4 hands); op. 142. Impromptus; op. 144. Lebensstürme, allegro (4 hands); op. 152. Fugue; op. 171. Twelve Ländler; etc. *Masses:* No. 1 in F, 1814; No. 2, in G, 1815; No. 3, in B flat, op. 141, 1815; No. 4, in C, op. 48, 1818; No. 5, in A flat, 1822; No. 6, in E flat, 1828. Cantatas; Salve Regina, op. 47; Stabat Mater; and other large vocal works. *Lieder*, originally issued in collections of 3 or more, or singly, and including Erlkönig, op. 1; Das Wirthshaus; Ave maria; Am meer; Adieu; Hark! hark! the lark at heaven's gate sings; Serenade; Der Fischer; The Fishermaiden; The Post; Wanderer; Nur wer die Sehnsucht kennt; Das Wandern; Der König von Thule; Memnon; Gretchen am Spinnrade; Ganymed; Der Sänger; Der Jäger; Sehnsucht; Des Mädchen's Klage; Thekla; Schlummerlied; Der Kampf; Der Pilgrim; Die Rose; Schwanengesang (collection), etc. Four-part songs for various combinations of voices, trios, and other vocal works.

At the present time Schubert is widely known, and the merits of his compositions have been long since recognised. This was not so in his own time; as, save by a select circle of Austrians, his compositions were almost entirely neglected. Posterity has thought proper to reverse this state of matters, and now Schubert is placed along with Beethoven, Mendelssohn, and Mozart, in the forefront of musical art. His works are all in use in Britain, with the exception of those which are purely dramatic, and are daily receiving more attention. The lieder are perhaps the works by which he is best known among amateurs, though some of the symphonies, overtures, and other concerted pieces, are popular and familiar among all grades of musicians. None of his operatic works have achieved success, and he is best known in Britain as a dramatic composer, by the incidental music to "Rosamunde." His symphonies and quartets are also familiar, and very often appear in concert programmes. His Pf. music also receives a large share of attention. The character of his genius is in a measure identical with that of Beethoven, with less strength, and a somewhat less laboured style. The rapidity with which he composed, induced careless writing, and there are apparent in most of his works a diffuseness and want of attention to the ordinary rules, which detracts from their value both practically and æsthetically. These faults are especially conspicuous in his instrumental works. The German lied as a song form is practically his, as it was he who first invested it with a dramatic character, and sought to make the union of the music and verse absolutely perfect. He very rarely fails to accomplish this, and his songs form one of the most unique and splendid monuments to musical genius ever reared by a single hand. The Schubert literature is very considerable, but mostly exists in the German language. The best English works are Coleridge's translation of Kreissle von Hellborn's "Life," London, 2 vols., 1866; Wilberforce s version of the same, Lond., 1866; and the small "Schubert" handbook of H. F. Frost, in Low's "Great Musicians" series.

SCHUBERT (Ferdinand). Austrian comp., B. Vienna, Oct. 19, 1794. D. Vienna, Feb. 28, 1859. Elder brother of the preceding, and a comp. of church and Pf. music

SCHUBERTH (Edward Charles). German cond., violoncellist, and comp., B. St. Petersburg. Educated in Germany, and in 1864 settled in London. Founded the Schubert Society, 1866; and the Mozart and Beethoven Society, 1870. These Societies are both under Herr Schuberth's directorship, and at them have been produced many works by eminent composers, not hitherto performed in Britain. Herr Schuberth has composed many songs, and pieces for the violoncello.

SCHUBERTH (Julius Ferdinand Georg). German writer and publisher, B. Magdeburg, July 14, 1804. Established firm of Schuberth & Co., of Leipzig and New York. He was employed in business successively in Hamburg, Leipzig, and New York. He also accompanied H. Vieuxtemps on an artistic tour in Mexico. D. Leipzig, June 9, 1875. He published works by Chopin, Liszt, Mendelssohn, Wallace, Schumann, and Rubinstein, and compiled a "Kleines Musikalisches Conversations Lexikon für Tonkunstler und Musikfreunde," of which numerous editions have been issued. Its English title is " Musical Hand-book for Musicians and Amateurs," Hamburg, n. d., also New York.

His brother CARL (B. Magdeburg, Feb. 25, 1811. D. Zürich, July 22, 1863), S. under Hesse and Dotzauer. He appeared as a violoncellist in Germany, France, Holland, and London (1835), and latterly became cond. at St. Petersburg.

SCHULHOFF (Julius). Bohemian pianist and comp., B. Prague, Aug. 2, 1825. S. under Tomaschek. Appeared as pianist in Paris, 1845. Afterwards appeared in Spain, England, Germany, and Russia.

WORKS.—Op. 1. Allegro, Pf.; op. 2. Des pieces, Pf.; op. 3. Andante and Study; op. 5. Two Suites of mazurkas; op. 7. Two Scherzos; op. 11. Nocturne; op. 17. Galop di bravura; op. 37. Sonata; op. 53. Six Morceaux; etc.

SCHULZ. See PRÆTORIUS.

SCHULZ (Johann Abraham Peter). German comp. and cond., B. Lüneburg, March 31, 1747. S. under Kirnberger at Berlin. Music-director at Berlin. Chap.-master to King of Denmark at Copenhagen, 1787. D. Schwedt, June 10, 1800. He comp. Clarissa, 1783; Minora, 1786; Höstgilde, 1790; and other operas, oratorios, hymns, and instrumental music, but is chiefly celebrated as a composer of lieder, many of which are now current in Germany.

SCHUMANN (Gustav). German comp. and pianist, B. Holdenstedt, March 15, 1815. Teacher and pianist in Berlin. Comp. of works for Pf. and voice.

SCHUMANN (Robert Alexander). German comp. and pianist, B. Zwickau, Saxony, June 8, 1810. Son of F. A. G. Schumann, a Bookseller. S. music under Kuntzsch, org. of Zwickau. S. for the Law at Leipzig and Heidelberg Universities. S. Pf. under F. Wieck, and harmony under H. Dorn, at Leipzig. Established the "Neue Zeitschrift für Musik," 1834. Resided in Vienna, 1838-39. Ph.D., Jena, 1840. Married to Clara Wieck, 1840. Travelled with his wife as a concert-giver in Austria, Russia, and North Germany. Prof. of Pf. in Leipzig Cons. for a time. Settled at Dresden, 1844, where he became cond. of a Choral Soc., in succession to F. Hiller. Director of music at Düsseldorf, 1850. D. Enderich, near Bonn., July 29, 1856 (Insane).

WORKS.—Op. 1. Variations, Pf.; op. 2. Papillons, Pf.; op. 3. Studies (Paganini), Pf.; op. 4. Intermezzi, Pf.; op. 5. Impromptus, Pf.; op. 6. Davidsbündlertänze, Pf.; op. 7. Toccata, Pf.; op. 8. Allegro, Pf.; op. 9. Carnaval, Pf.; op. 10. Six studies (Paganini), Pf.; op. 11. Sonata in F sharp minor, Pf.; op. 12. Fantasiestücke, Pf.; op. 13. Studies, Pf.; op. 14. Sonata in F minor, Pf.; op. 15. Kinderscenen, Pf.; op. 16. Kreisleriana, Pf.; op. 17. Fantasia, Pf.; op. 18. Arabeske, Pf.; op. 19. Blumenstück, Pf.; op. 20. Humoreske, Pf.; op. 21. Novelletten, Pf.; op. 22. Sonata in G min., Pf.; op. 23. Nachtstücke, Pf.; op. 24. Liederkreis, voice and Pf.; op. 25. Myrthen (26 songs); op. 26. Faschingsschwank aus Wien, Pf.; op. 27. Five Lieder; op. 28. Three romances, Pf.; op. 29. Three songs, of Geibel; op. 30. Three do.; op. 31. Three songs, by Chamisso ; op. 32. Four pieces for Pf.; op. 33. Six four-part songs for male voices; op. 34. Four vocal duets; op. 35. Twelve songs, by Körner ; op. 36. Six do., by Reinick; op. 37. Rückert's 'Liebesfrühling' (songs); op. 38. Symphony for orch., in B flat [1840]; op. 39. Liederkreis (12 songs); op. 40. Five songs; op. 41. Three string quartets [1842]; op. 42. Songs by Chamisso ; op. 43. Three 2-part songs; op. 44. Quintet for Pf. and strings, in E flat; op. 45. Three romances (vocal); op. 46. Andante and variations, Pf. (4 hands); op. 47. Quartet for Pf. and strings ; op. 48. Sixteen songs by Heine; op. 50. Das Paradies und die Peri, for soli, chorus, and orch. (T. Moore's Lalla Rookh), 1843 ; op. 52. Overture, scherzo, and finale, for orch. ; op. 53. Three romances (vocal) ; op. 54. Concerto for Pf. and orch., in A min ; op. 55. Five part-songs, by Burns ; op. 56. Studies for the Pedal Pf.; op. 57. Belsatzar, ballad (Heine); op. 58. Sketches for Pedal Pf.; op. 59. Four part-songs; op. 60. Six Fugues on name B A C H ; op. 61. Symphony for orch., in C, 1846 ; op. 62. Three part-songs for male voices; op. 63. Trio for Pf., vn., and 'cello, in D min.; op. 64. Three romances (vocal); op. 65. Ritornelle von Rückert, in canon form, for male voices ; op. 66. Bilder aus Osten, Pf. duet; op. 67. Five romances for chorus; op. 68. Album of 40 Pf. pieces ; op. 69. Romances for female voices ; op. 70. Adagio and Allegro, Pf. and horn ; op. 71. Adventlied, Rückert, for solo, chorus, and orch.; op 72. Four fugues, Pf.; op 73. Fantasiestücke for Pf. and clarinet ; op. 74. Spanisches Liederspiel (songs); op. 75. Five romances for chorus ; op. 76. Four marches for Pf.; op. 77. Lieder and Songs ; op. 78. Four vocal duets; op. 79. Lieder-Album für die jugend ; op. 80. Trio for Pf., vn., and 'cello, in F ; op. 81. Genoveva, opera in 4 acts, Leipzig, 1850 ; op. 82. Waldscenen, Pf.; op. 83. Three songs ; op. 84. Parting song, for solo, chorus, and orch.; op. 85. Twelve pieces for Pf. duet ; op. 86. Concertstück for 4 horns and orch.; op. 87. Der Handschuh, ballad ; op. 88. Phantasiestücke for Pf., vn., and 'cello ; op. 89. Six Songs (Nenn); op. 90. Six Songs (Lenau) ; op. 91. Romances for female voices ; op. 92. Concertstück for Pf. and orch. (Introduction and Allegro appassionato), in G ; op. 93. Motet for double male chorus ; op. 94. Three Romances, Pf. and oboe ; op. 95. Three Songs (Byron); op. 96. Five Lieder ; op. 97. Symphony in E flat, for orch., 1850 ; op. 98a. Nine Lieder (Goethe); op. 98b. Requiem for Mignon, solo, chorus and orch. ; op. 99. Bunte Blätter, Pf.; op. 100. Overture to Schiller's "Braut von Messina," 1851 ; op. 101. Minnespiel (Rückert), voices and Pf. ; op. 102. Five pieces for Pf. and 'cello ; op. 103. Mädchenlieder, for 2 soprano voices ; op. 104. Seven Songs ; op 105. Sonata, Pf. and vn.; op. 106. Schön Hedwig, ballad by Hebbel, voice and Pf. ; op. 107. Six Songs; op. 108. Nachtlied (Hebbel), solo, chorus, and orch. ; op. 109. Ballscenen, Pf. duet; op. 110. Trio for Pf., vn., and 'cello. in G min. ; op. 111. Three Fantasiestücke, Pf.; op. 112. Der Rose Pilgerfahrt (Pilgrimage of the Rose), for solo, chorus, and orch., 1851 ; op. 113. Märchenbilder, for Pf. and viola; op. 114. Three trios for female voices; op. 115. Music for Byron's "Manfred," Weimar, 1852; op. 116. Der Königssohn, ballad by Uhland, solo, chorus, and orch.; op. 117. Four Lieder (Lenau); op. 118. Three Sonatas, Pf.; op. 119. Three Songs; op. 120. Symphony in D min., for orch., 1851; op. 121. Sonata for Pf. and vn., in D min.; op. 122. Ballad in "Haideknabe" (Hebbel); op. 123. Festival overture, on the "Rheinweinlied," with chorus, 1853; op. 124. Albumblätter, Pf.; op. 125. Five Songs; op. 126. Seven Pf. pieces in fughetta form; op. 127. Five Lieder; op. 128. Overture to Shakespeare's "Julius Cæsar"; op. 129. Concerto for 'cello and orch., in A min.; op. 130. Kinderball, 6 dances, Pf. duet; op. 131. Phantasie for vn. and orch.; op. 132. Märchenerzählungen, 4 pieces for Pf., clarinet, and viola; op. 133. Morning Songs, Pf.; op. 134. Concert allegro, Pf. and orch.; op. 135. Five Songs of Mary Stuart; op. 136. Overture to Goethe's "Hermann und Dorothea"; op. 137. Five hunting songs, male voices and horn accomp.; op. 139. Des Sängers Fluch, ballad (Uhland); op. 140. Vom Pagen und der Königstochter, ballads; op. 141. Four Part-songs for double chorus; op. 142. Four Songs; op. 143. Der Gluck von Edenhall, ballad; op. 144. New Year's Song (Rückert), solo, chorus, and orch.; op. 145. Romances for chorus; op. 146. Do.; op. 147. Mass for solo, chorus, and orch. (1852); op. 148. Requiem Mass, do., 1852. Scenes from Goethe's "Faust." Edition of Bach's violin suites, etc. Other works unpublished. He wrote many critical notices on music, and these were issued as "Gesammelte Schriften über Musik und Musiker," Leipzig, 1854, 4 vols. Trans. by F. R. Ritter as "Music and Musicians, Essays and Criticisms," Lond., 1st series, 1878, 8vo; 2nd series, 1880.

Schumann's life is given with much fullness in "Robert Schumann eine Biographie," by J. W. von Wasielewski, Dresden, 1858, and it is only needful to refer students to that work for all other information regarding him. A translation of this work entitled "Life and Letters of Robert Schumann," trans. by A. L. Alger, was issued in London, 8vo, 1878. Schumann was one of the most thoroughly romantic composers of the century, his works being completely invested with the characteristics of the poetical leaders of the movement, whose aims and ideas he sought to convey in his works, so far as is possible in music. His best and most original works are those for the pianoforte and the voice. None of his large works have ever been popular, and though his symphonies are remarkable in many respects, they are not sufficiently interesting, and too involved and obscure, to meet with general acceptance. His chamber music is much cultivated, and forms on the whole the most representative outcome of his genius. His critical works have received much attention and praise for the delicacy and appreciative kindness of the style.

SCHUMANN (Clara Josephine), *née* WIECK. German pianist and comp., B. Leipzig, Sept. 13, 1819. S. under her father, a musician. *Début* Leipzig, 1828. Appeared afterwards with success in Weimar, Cassel, Frankfort, and Paris, 1831. Appeared at the Gewandhaus Concerts, Leipzig, 1832, and in Vienna, 1836. Married to Robert Schumann, 1840. Travelled with her husband in North Germany and Denmark, 1842. Appeared with other artists at numerous concerts in various parts of Europe. Appeared in London, at the Philharmonic Soc., and Musical Union Concerts, April-June, 1856. Resided afterwards at Baden-Baden till 1874. Re-appeared afterwards at the Philharmonic and Musical Union Concerts, in April, May, and June, 1865, and has since appeared frequently. Principal Pf. teacher at Dr. Hoch's Cons. at Frankfort, 1878.

Madame Schumann is celebrated as the greatest living female pianist, and especially for her rendition of her husband's works. It is due to her that so much is now known of them, as her introduction and interpretation of all of his more recent pianoforte works contributed greatly in extending the public knowledge of them. She has composed a number of Pf. works and songs, including 4 Polonaises, op. 1; Concerto, op. 7; Three songs, op. 12 (in her husband's op. 37, nos. 2, 4, 11); Trio, for Pf. and strings, G minor, op. 17, etc.

SCHUNKE (Ludwig). German pianist and comp., B. Cassel, Dec. 21, 1810. S. under his father. Appeared at Darmstadt, Cassel, Hanover, Leipzig, Munich and Vienna. Visited Paris, and S. under Kalkbrenner and Reicha. Friend and associate of R. Schumann. D. Leipzig, Dec. 7, 1834. Comp. sonata for Pf., op. 3; Caprices, op. 9, 10, 11; Rondo, op. 15; Variations, etc.

SCHUPPANZIGH (Ignaz), Austrian violinist and comp., B. Vienna, 1776. S. under Mayseder. Teacher of Beethoven for a time. Cond. in Vienna. Estab. Rasoumoffsky quartet party at Vienna. Married Fräulein Kilitzky. Travelled in Germany, Poland, Russia. Chap.-master and director of court opera, Dresden, 1828. D. Vienna, March 2, 1830. Comp. variations and other solos for violin. Chiefly remembered as the friend of Beethoven and Schubert.

SCHÜTZ (Heinrich). German comp., B. Kösteritz, Voigtland, Oct. 8, 1585. Educated at Court of Hesse-Cassel. S. law at Marburg. S. music under Gabrielli at Venice, till 1612. Held appointments in Dresden, and in 1642 was made Director of Royal Music at Copenhagen. D. Copenhagen, Nov. 6, 1672.
WORKS.—Madrigali a cinque voci, 1611; Psalmen Davids,...1619, 3 parts; Geistreiches Gesangbuch,...1619; Symphoniæ Sacrae,...1625-58; Kleinen Geistlicher Concerten,...1636; Daphné, opera, 1627.

SCHWEIZER (Otto). Swiss pianist and comp., B. Zürich, May 26, 1846. S. at Leipzig Cons. under Moscheles, Plaidy, Reinecke, etc. Settled in Edinburgh, 1870, as teacher. Comp. of the following works for Pf.:—Polonaise brillante; Village tales; Three Romantic Studies; Suite in 4 movements; Valsette, op. 3; Berceuse, op. 6; Pf. duets. Trios, songs, and other vocal music; also cantatas and large works in MS.

SCOTT (Sir Walter). Scottish poet and general writer, B. Edinburgh, Aug. 15, 1771. D. Abbotsford, Sept. 21, 1832.
Although not himself possessing the slightest musical faculty, Scott inspired more musicians than any other modern writer. Among the operas founded on dramatised versions of his novels and poems may be mentioned "La jolie fille de Perth," Bizet; "Quentin Durward," Gevaërt; "Ivanhoe," Rossini, Pacini, and J. Parry; "Dame Blanche" (on Guy Mannering and the Monastery), Boieldieu; "Guy Mannering," Bishop; "Donna Bianca d'Avenello" (on the "Monastery"), Pavesi and Galliero; "Il Talismano," Balfe; "Prison de Edimbourg" (Heart of Midlothian), Carafa; "Rob Roy," Davy and Flotow; "Antiquary," Bishop; "Leicester" (Kenilworth), Auber; "Montrose" (Legend of Montrose), Bishop; "Lucia di Lammermoor" (Bride of Lammermoor), Donizetti; "Il Donna del Lago" (Lady of the Lake), Rossini; "Robert Bruce" (from the History of Scotland), Rossini; "Lord of the Isles" (Gadsby), cantata; "Lady of the Lake" (Macfarren), cantata; and "Waverley" (Berlioz), symphony. Of composers who have set his lyrical pieces the number is immense, nearly every musician of eminence having at some period made use of his verses. The following may be specially named, however, as being both prominent and successful:—Schubert, Sullivan, Macfarren. Callcott, Alex. Lee, John Thomson, Sir H. Bishop, Attwood, Rimbault, Loder, Graham, Wilson, Pearsall, Prout, Hatton, Leslie, Oakeley, Smart, Reay, Schumann, Mendelssohn, etc.

SCRIBE (Eugene). French dramatist, B. Paris, Dec. 25, 1791. D. Paris, Feb. 21, 1861. Author of the librettos of Auber's "Masaniello" (La Muette de Portici); "Fra Diavolo;" "Lestocq;" "Domino Noir;" Meyerbeer's "L'Africaine;" "Robert le Diable;" "Les Huguenots;" "Le Prophète," etc. Also librettos for Boieldieu "Dame Blanche;" Hérold; Adam; Halévy, and Verdi. Some of his librettos are among the most brilliant and clever in the whole range of opera.

SCUDO (Pietro). Italian writer and comp., B. Venice, June 6, 1806. D. (insane), Blois, Oct. 14, 1864. Author of many critical works, among which are "L'Anné Musicale," 1860-63, 4 vols; "La Musique Ancienne et Moderne," 1854; "Critique et Littérature Musicale," 1850; etc., being mostly republications of articles contributed to periodical literature. Comp. songs, and other vocal music.

SECHTER (Simon). Bohemian comp., org., and teacher, B. Friedberg, Oct. 11, 1788. S. under Kotzeluch and Hartmann, at Vienna, from 1804. Music master in Institute for the Blind, and attached to the Imperial Chap., by influence of Stadler. Court org., 1824, and Prof. of comp. in Vienna Cons., 1850. D. Vienna, Sept. 10, 1867.

Works.—Ali Hitsch Hatsch, opera, 1844 (under name of Ernst Heiter). Fugues for Pf. or org., opp. 1, 2, 4, 5, 9, 20, 55 and 61 Versets for org., opp. 3, 12, 22. Preludes for org., opp. 8, 13, 14, 21, 52, 56. Masses, Songs, and Pf. music. Die Grundsätze der Musikalischen Komposition, Leipzig, 1853-54, 3 vols., etc.

Chiefly celebrated as a teacher. Among his pupils were Thalberg, Pauer, Döhler, Henselt, Vieuxtemps, Preyer, Bibl, Schachner, Bagge and Pohl.

SECOND (Mary), née MAHON. English soprano vocalist, B. Oxford, about 1771. Daughter of Mahon, a celebrated clarinet player. Début in "The Woodman," Covent Garden, London, Sept. 17, 1796. Married to a Mr. Second. 1800. Afterwards retired from the stage. She appeared at the principal concerts of her time.

SEDGWICK (Alfred B.) Author of the following works:—Complete Method for the French Accordeon; Complete Method for the German Accordeon; Complete Method for the English Concertina; also for German Concertina; Complete Method for the Cornet, etc.

SEDIE (Enrico delle). Italian barytone vocalist, B. Leghorn, 1826. S. under Galassi. Appeared in Pistoja, 1851; Florence, 1854; Rome, Vienna, Paris, and London. Prof. of Singing in Paris Cons. Author of "L'Art Lyrique," Paris, 1874, a treatise on Singing.

SEELING (Hans). Bohemian pianist and comp., B. Prague, 1828. S. Leipzig Cons. D. Prague, May 26, 1862. Comp. many Pf. pieces of which "Loreley," op. 2; 12 Concert studies; and numerous nocturnes, idylls, etc. are well known.

SEGUIN (Arthur Edward Shelden). English bass vocalist, B. London, April 7, 1809. S. at R. A. M. Sang at Exeter Festival, 1829; and in 1831 appeared on the stage in London. Sang at the Concert of Ancient Music and on the stage till 1838. Appeared in New York in Rooke's "Amilie," Oct. 1838, and from that date travelled in the States with an opera company to which he gave his name. D. New York, Dec. 9 [11], 1852.

His wife, née ANN CHILDE, was a soprano vocalist, and sang with her husband at all the principal British concerts, and on the stage from 1837. Sang in the United States. His sister ELIZABETH SEGUIN (B. London, 1815, D. London, 1870), was the mother of Madame Parepa-Rosa, and his brother, WILLIAM HENRY (1814-1850), was a bass-singer known in London.

SEIDEL (Friedrich Ludwig). German org. and comp., B. Treuenbriezen, June 1, 1765. S. under Reichardt. D. Charlottenburg, May 5, 1831. Comp. operas, oratorios, masses, Pf. music, and songs.

SEIDEL (Johann Julius). German writer, B. Breslau, July 14, 1810. D. 1837. Author of a work on the organ, trans. as "The Organ and its Construction," Lond., 1852, 8vo.

SEILER (Emma). German teacher and writer, now resident in the United States. Authoress of "The Voice in Singing," Philadelphia, 1869, 12mo. "Exercises for Training the Voice," Boston, n. d.

SÉJAN (Nicolas). French org. and comp., B. Paris, March 19, 1745. S. under Bordier. Joint-org. Notre Dame Cath., 1772; Org. S. Sulpice, 1783; Court org., 1789; and org. Ch. of the Invalides. Prof. org., Paris Cons. D. Paris, Mar. 16, 1819. Comp. fugues, sonatas, etc. for org., Pf. and vn. music, etc.

SELIGMANN (Hippolyte Prosper). French violoncellist and comp., B. Paris, July 28, 1817. S. at Paris Cons. under Alkan, Norblin, and Halévy. Travelled in France, Italy, Algeria, and Spain as violoncellist. D. Monte Carlo, 1882. Comp. Album Algérien, op. 60; Concerto, op. 70; Caprices, fantasias, studies and other music for 'cello; Songs, etc.

SELIGMANN (Julius). German violinist, cond., and comp., B. Hamburg, Nov. 2, 1817. Settled in Glasgow as teacher, and became cond. of the Choral Union; a post which he held till 1860. Comp. "Victory," a cantata for female voices; Pf. music, songs, and part-songs.

SELLE (Thomas). German comp., B. Zörbig, Saxony, Mar. 23, 1599. Cantor and music-director of S. Catherine's Cath., Hamburg. D. Hamburg, July 2, 1663. Comp. psalms, motets, and wrote theoretical works.

SEMBRICH (Marzella). Austrian soprano vocalist, B. Lemberg, Galicia, 1858. S. Pf. and violin, but afterwards S. singing at Milan under Lamperti. *Début* at Athens in "I Puritani," 1877. Appeared at Vienna, Dresden, and in London in 1880, in "Lucia di Lammermoor." Has since appeared in England, Russia, Poland, Austria, and Italy.

SEMET (Théophile Aimé Emile). French comp. and cond., B. Lille, Sept. 6, 1824. S. at Lille and at Paris Cons. under Halévy. Music-director in Paris, and played drums in orch. of the opera, Paris. Comp. La petite Fadette, 2 acts, 1850; rewritten, 3 acts, 1869; Gil Blas, 1860; Ondine, 1863, and other operas. Also cantatas, songs, and ballet music.

SEMPLE (Armand, M.B,) English physician and writer, author of "The Voice Musically and Medically Considered," Lond., 1885. (Reprinted from the *Musical Standard*.)

SENESINO (Francesco Bernardi detto). Italian soprano vocalist, B. Sienna, about 1680. S. under Bernacchi. Singer at Dresden in 1719. Engaged by Handel for the London opera, and first appeared there in Buononcini's "Astarto," Nov., 1720. Afterwards sang in operas by Handel till 1726, when he returned to Italy. He re-appeared in London, in 1727, under Handel's direction, until the break up of the company. Noted for his quarrels and disputes with Handel and the Italian singers. He afterwards sang in Handel's oratorio, "Esther," and sang in opposition to Handel at Lincoln's Inn Fields Theatre, at the opera founded by the nobility, till 1735. Retired to Sienna, and D. about 1750.

SENFL or SENFEL (Ludwig). Swiss comp., B. Basle about end of 15th century. S. under Heinrich Isaac. Chap.-master to Maximilian I., Duke of Bavaria, at Munich. D. Munich [1555]. Comp. motets, chorales, graduels, masses, etc. Also "Quinque Salutationes Domini nostri Hiesu Christi,"... 1526; "Magnificat," 1537; "Melodiæ in Odas Horatii," 1557; "Harmoniæ Poeticæ,"...1539, etc.

SERAFIN. Italian violin-maker of 18th century. GIORGIO and SANTO worked between 1710 and 1740, and produced instruments of fair quality and some value.

SEROFF (Alexander Nikolàvitch). Russian comp., B. St. Petersburg, May 11, 1818. S. under Carl Schuberth and Hunke. Was for some time engaged in profession of the law. D. St. Petersburg, Feb. 1, 1871.

Comp. Judith, 1863; Rogneida, 1863; Taras Bulba, 1866; Wakula, 1867; Wrajia Siela, 1872, operas and ballets; Stabat Mater; Songs, etc. Also many writings in periodicals. A follower of Richard Wagner in style, and popular in Russia as a composer.

SERPETTE (Henri Charles Antoine Gaston). French comp., B. Nantes, Nov. 4, 1846. S. Paris Cons. under Thomas, etc., 1868. Gained Grand Prix de Rome, 1871. Comp. La Branche cassée, 1874; Le Manior de Pic-Tordu, 1875; Le Moulin du Vert galant, 1876; La petite Muette, 1877; La Nuit de St. Germain, 1880; Madame le Diable, 1882, and other operas.

SERVAIS (Adrien Francois). Belgian violoncellist and comp., B. Hal, near Brussels. June 7, 1807. S. Brussels Cons. under Platel. 'Cellist in orch. of Brussels Theatre. Appeared in Paris, and in London, 1835, at l'hilharmonic Concert. Travelled afterwards as 'cellist in Germany, France, Norway, Russia, etc. Married, 1842. 'Cellist to King of the Belgians. Prof. of 'cello, Brussels Cons. from 1848. D. Hal, Nov. 26, 1866.

WORKS. --Op. 1. Fantasia, 'cello, and Pf. ; op. 5. Concerto, 'cello and orch., in B minor ; op. 7. Andante cantabile, 'cello and orch. ; op. 18. Concerto Militaire, 'cello and orch. ; other concertos, fantasias, studies, duets, etc., for 'cello and Pf., or orch.

His eldest son, JOSEPH (B. Hal, Nov. 23, 1850; D. Hal, Aug. 28, 1885), S. under his father, and in 1872 became Prof. of 'cello at Brussels Cons. Appeared at Paris and in Germany. Both father and son were remarkable performers, and formed many now famous pupils.

SESSI (Marianna). Italian soprano vocalist and comp., B. Rome 1776. D. Vienna, Mar. 10, 1847. Sang in France, Germany, London, etc.

SEVERN (Thomas Henry). English vocal comp., B. Lond., Nov. 5, 1801. D. Wandsworth, April 15, 1881. Comp. songs and part-songs.

SEWARD (Theodore Frelinghausen). American comp., B. Florida, N.Y., Jan. 25, 1835. Editor of "The Sunnyside Glee Book, a Collection of Secular Music," New York, 1866; "The Temple Choir" (with Mason and Bradbury), N.Y., 1867; and comp. of part-songs, songs, etc.

SEWELL (John). English org. and comp. Org. at Bridgnorth, and Mus. Bac., Oxon., 1848; Mus. Doc., Oxon., 1856. Comp. of anthems, "Break forth into joy," "They that wait upon the Lord," etc.

SEXTON (William). English comp. and org., B. 1764. Chor. S. George's Chap., Windsor, and Eton Coll., 1773. S. under Edward Webb. Org., sub-precentor, and master of choristers S. George's Chap., Windsor, 1801. D. about 1824. Comp. anthems, glees, and songs; and edited Handel's Chandos Anthem, 1808.

SEYFRIED (Ignaz Xaver, Ritter von). Austrian comp., B. Vienna, Aug. 15, 1776. Educated at Prague. S. under Kotzeluch and Haydn. Musical director in Vienna. Intimate with Beethoven, Mozart, and other eminent musicians. D. Vienna, Aug. 27, 1841. He comp. Der Löwenbrunnen, 1797; Der Wundermann am Rheinfall, 1799; Saul, 1810; Abraham, 1817; Die Ochsenmennette, 1823; and many other operas. He wrote some theoretical works, and trained a large number of eminent musicians, among whom are Suppé, Parish-Alvars, Ernst, Krebs, Schlösser, Kessler, Sulzer, and Fischhof.

SGAMBATI (Giovanni). Italian pianist and comp., B. Rome, May 28, 1843. S. under Natalucci. Settled in Rome in 1860, as pianist and comp., and S. there for a time under Liszt. Cond. numerous concerts in Rome, and introduced much high class instrumental music. Appeared as pianist in London, at Philharmonic Concert, May 11, 1882, when he performed his own Pf. concerto, op. 15. Prof. of Pf. in S. Cecilia Academy, at Rome.

WORKS.—Op. 1. Album of 5 songs; op. 2. Album of 10 songs; op. 3. Notturno, Pf.; op. 4. Quintet for Pf. and strings; op. 5. Quintet for Pf. and strings, in G min.; op. 6. Prelude and Fugue, in E flat min., Pf.; op. 10. Two studies, Pf.; op. 14. Gavotte, Pf.; op. 15. Concerto for Pf. and orch., in G min.; op. 16. Symphony in D; op. 17. String quartet; Festival overture for orch.; Second Symphony for orch., in E flat.

SHAKESPEARE (William). English dramatic poet, B. Stratford-on-Avon, 1564. D. Stratford-on-Avon, April 23, 1616. A poet of much influence on musical art all over the world. To versions of his plays music has been set by many composers, while the number of times his lyrical pieces have been set by different composers cannot be computed. A work on the subject of Shakespeare Music was written by Alfred Roffe [see that name], and from it and other sources the following list of composers who have set his poetry is compiled:—

Arne, J. Addison, S. Arnold, T. Aylward, Bishop, Braham, Balfe, Banister, Beethoven, Carey, Chilcot, B. Cooke, Curschmann, T. Cooke, Clifton, Dignum, Dibdin, Duggan, Fisin, Gabriel, Galliard, W. Gardiner, H. Glover, Greene, Hilton, Hatton, Horn, Hobbs, Hook, P. Humphry, C. Horsley, Haydn, Hime, Harrington, Jackson, Johnson, Kemp, Knyvett, Kelly, M. P. King, Locke, E. J. Loder, T. and W. Linley, Leveridge, Leslie, Lampe, Levey, Laniere, G. A. Macfarren, Mellon, Morehead, Macirone, Percy, Parry, Purcell, Reay, W. Russell, Reinhold, Shield, Stevens, J. S. Smith, Schubert, Stevenson, Sullivan, Webbe, Dr. John Wilson, Weldon, S. Wesley, and A. Zimmerman. Collections of Shakespeare music are:—Caulfield (John), "A Collection of the Vocal Music in Shakespeare's Plays..." Lond., n. d.; Linley (Wm.), "The Dramatic Songs of Shakespeare," Lond., n. d. More recently a selection has been issued as the "Shakespeare Album," by Augener of London, containing 62 songs. The principal operas founded on his plays are.—"Macbeth," by Chelard, André, Reichardt, Rastrelli, Taubert, and Verdi; "Hamlet," by Thomas, Mareczek, and Vogler; "Othello," by Rossini; "Romeo and Juliet," by Steibelt, Zingarelli, Gounod, d'Ivry, Vaccaj, and Bellini (Capuletti ed i Montecchi); "Henry IV.," and "Merry Wives of Windsor," by Nicolaï, Balfe, Adam, and Salieri, as "Falstaff"; "Taming of the Shrew," by Goëtz; "King Lear," by André; "Richard III.," by Meiners; "Timon of Athens," by Purcell; "Anthony and Cleopatra," by Kafka; "Merchant of Venice," by J. A. Just; "Midsummer Night's Dream," by Mendelssohn; "Much ado about Nothing," by Berlioz (Beatrice et Benedict); "Winter's Tale," by Flotow (Conte d' Hiver); "Tempest," by Halévy and Winter. The amount of illustrative orchestral music is also very large, and includes Berlioz's "Romeo and Juliet," symphony; numerous overtures, symphonies, and other pieces.

SHAKESPEARE (William). English tenor vocalist, pianist, comp., and cond., B. Croydon, June 16, 1849. Played org. when only 13 years old. S. under Molique, 1862; and at R. A. M., where he gained the King's Scholarship, 1866. S. Pf. under Sir W. S. Bennett. Elected Mendelssohn Scholar, R. A. M., 1871, and afterwards S. at Leipzig Cons. under Reinecke. S. singing under Lamperti at Milan. Sang in oratorio and concert music in Britain from 1875. Prof. of singing, 1878, and cond. of concerts, R. A. M., 1880-86. Has comp. symphonies, overtures, a Pf. concerto, and much Pf. music and songs.

SHARP (Granville). English writer, B. 1734. D. 1813. Author of "A Short Introduction to Vocal Musick," Lond., 4to, 1767; another edition, 1777.

SHARP (Richard). English writer, author of "New Guida di Musica, being a Complete Book of Instructions for Beginners of the Pianoforte..." Lond., 4to, 1794. Pub. Pf. sonatas, etc.

SHARP (Simeon). English writer, author of "Music, a Satire," London, 12mo, 1824.

SHARPE (Charles Kirkpatrick). Scottish amateur musician, poet, etc., B. 1781. D. Edinburgh, Mar. 18, 1851. He comp. music, and contributed to Stenhouse's Lyric Poetry of Scotland. He also edited and published the Earl of Kellie's "Minuets and Songs," 1839.

SHAW (Mrs. Alfred), née MARY POSTANS. English contralto vocalist, B. London, 1814. S. at R. A. M., and under Sir George Smart. Sang as Miss Postans in 1834-35 at the Concert of Ancient Music, and at York Festival. Married Alfred Shaw, artist, 1835. Sang afterwards at all the principal festivals, and sang the contralto part in Mendelssohn's "St. Paul," on its first production in England. Sang at Leipzig, 1838; in Italy, 1839, and afterwards in England. She was married a second time to J. F. Robinson. Her voice failed owing to the shock which the appearance of insanity in her first husband caused, and she retired from public life soon after. D. Hadleigh Hall, Suffolk, Sept. 9, 1876.

SHAW (James). English org. and comp., B. Leeds, 1842. S. under R. Burton. Org. of S. John's Episcopal Chap., Edinburgh; and afterwards of St. Paul's there. Cond. of Edinburgh Choral Union, 1862-63. Org. and choirmaster of Parish Ch., Hampstead; and of the Collegiate Chap. of St. John, Clapham.

WORKS.—*Church Music:* Evening Service, comp. for London Church Choir Assoc., 1874; Evening Service in F, 1881; Communion Service, 1881; The Lord is my Shepherd; I will magnify Thee; and many other anthems. An Ode of Thanksgiving, for solo, chorus and orch., 1880. *Pf. Music:* Gavotte in A, minuett, Bourée; Gavotte in G; Introduction and Polonaise, 'La Belle France,' 1872; Grand concert valse, 1870; Three sketches, 1870; Introduction and fugue; Two grand studies, etc. *Songs:* Break, break (Tennyson), 1868; Angel's welcome; Mary's lament; Morning greeting; A wet sheet and a flowing sea; Constancy, etc. Also part songs.

SHAW (Oliver). American comp., B. 1778. D. Providence, R.I., Dec. 1848. Wrote an "Instruction Book for the Pianoforte," and comp. songs, hymns, etc.

SHENTON (Rev. Robert). English musician, was B. A., Oxon., 1750; M.A. Cantab., 1757. Vicar-choral Hereford Cath.; Dean's-vicar at Christ Church, 1757, and vicar of St. Patrick's Cathedral, Dublin, 1758. Dean's-vicar at St. Patrick's, 1783. D. Dublin, 1798. Comp. anthems and music for the church service.

SHEPHERD (William). Scottish teacher and violinist, was music-teacher in partnership with Nathaniel Gow, 1796. D. Edinburgh, Jan. 19, 1812. Comp. "A Collection of Strathspey Reels, etc., with a Bass for the Violoncello or Harpsichord," Edin., fo.; "A Second Collection...for the Pf., violin, and violoncello," Edin., fo., n. d.

SHEPHERDSON (William). English writer, D. Oct. 12, 1884. Author of "The Organ, Hints on its Construction, Purchase, and Preservation," London, 8vo, 1873.

SHEPPARD (Elizabeth Sara). English novelist and writer, B. Blackheath, 1830. D. Brixton, London, March 13, 1862. Authoress of "Charles Auchester," 1853, 3 vols; "Rumour," 1858, 3 vols., musical novels, in the former of which Mendelssohn is depicted as Seraphael.

SHEPPARD or SHEPHERD (John). English comp., B. early in 16th century. Chorister in S. Paul's, London. Instructor of the choristers and org., Magdalen Coll., Oxford, 1542-47. D. (?). Comp. numerous anthems, masses, motets, and other pieces of church music, mostly preserved in MS. in English libraries.

SHERINGHAM (J. W.) English writer, author of "Our Choir Festivals, can they be Reformed without Abolition?" Gloucester, 1874.

SHERRINGTON (Helena), Lemmens-Sherrington). English soprano vocalist, B. Preston, Oct. 4, 1834. Went to Rotterdam with her family, 1838. S. there under Verhulst; and at Brussels Cons. Gained prizes for singing while there. First appeared in London, April 7, 1856, and at once took a position as a prominent soprano vocalist. She has appeared at all the principal concerts and festivals in Britain, and has sung with success in operas of Wallace, Auber, Macfarren, Meyerbeer, Flotow, and Mozart. She is undoubtedly the greatest English soprano singer of recent times, and her success as an oratorio singer has never been excelled. She has composed some songs.

SHERRINGTON (Jose). English soprano vocalist, younger sister of preceding, B. Rotterdam, Oct. 27, 1850. S. at Brussels under Meyer-Boulard and Chiriamonte. Appeared in London, 1871, and afterwards travelled in Britain with her sister. Travelled in Holland, concert-giving, 1873, but has appeared chiefly in Britain as a singer.

SHERWIN (William Fisk). American comp., B. Buckland, Mass., March 14, 1826. Publishes collections of vocal music, and comp. part-songs, songs, and sacred music.

SHERWOOD (William H.) American pianist, comp., and teacher, B. Lyons, N. Y., Jan. 31, 1854. S. at first under his father and W. Mason. S. in Berlin under Kullak and Weitzmann, 1871; in Stuttgart under C. Doppler; and in London under F. Scotson Clark. Was also for a time under L. Deppe and Richter. Married to Miss Mary Fay, a pianist of great ability. Performed successfully in Germany, and in 1876 returned to America, and appeared at the Centennial Exhibition at Philadelphia. Has performed in the principal American cities. Teacher in Boston, and Fellow of the American Coll. of Musicians. He has comp. a number of Pf. pieces, but is chiefly celebrated in America as one of the leading pianists and teachers.

SHIELD (William). English comp. and writer, B. Swallwell, Durham, 1748. S. under his father, a singing-master, and practised violin and harpsichord. Apprenticed to a boat-builder at North Shields, on the death of his father,

Became leader at Newcastle Subscription Concerts, and S. music under Avison. Went to Scarborough as leader of the theatre orch., and of subscription concerts. Violin-player in orch. of the Opera, London, 1772; and in 1773 he was made principal viola-player. Composer to Covent Garden Theatre, 1778-91 and 1792-97. Visited France and Italy with Ritson the Antiquary, 1791. Master of the Royal Music on death of Parsons, 1817. Original member of Philharmonic Soc. D. Berners Street, London, Jan. 25, 1829.

WORKS.—*Music to Dramas, Operas, etc.:* The Flitch of Bacon, 1778; Lord Mayor's Day, 1782; Rosina, 1783; The Poor Soldier, 1783; Harlequin Friar Bacon, 1783; Robin Hood, 1784; The Noble Peasant, 1784; Fontainbleau, 1784; The Magic Cavern, 1784; The Nunnery, 1785; Love in a camp, 1785; The Choleric Fathers, 1785; Omai, 1785; Richard Cœur de Lion, 1786; The Enchanted Castle, 1786; Marian, 1788; The Prophet, 1788; The Highland Reel, 1788; Aladdin, 1788; The Crusade, 1790; The Picture of Paris, 1790; Oscar and Malvina (with Reeve), 1791; The Woodman, 1792; Hartford Bridge, 1792; Harlequin's Museum, 1793; The Deaf Lover, 1793; Midnight Wanderers, 1793; Sprigs of Laurel, 1793; Travellers in Switzerland, 1794; Arrived at Portsmouth, 1794; Netley Abbey, 1794; Mysteries of the Castle, 1795; Lock and Key, 1796; Abroad and at Home, 1796; Italian Villagers, 1797; The Farmer, 1798; Two Faces under a Hood, 1807; The Wicklow Mountains. A Cento, consisting of Ballads, Rounds, Glees, and a Roundelay; Cavatinas, Canzonettas, etc., Lond., fo. [1809]. Collection of Six Canzonets and an Elegy, Lond., n. d. Collection of Favourite Songs, etc., Lond., n. d. Six Trios for violin, tenor, and violoncello, Lond., n. d., 3 vols. Six Duos for two violins. An Introduction to Harmony, Lond., 1800, 4to; 2nd ed., 1817. Rudiments of Thorough-Bass for Young Harmonists, Lond., 1815, 4to. Numerous Songs, of which the best known are The Wolf; The Thorn; Old Towler; The Heaving of the Lead; The Post Captain; The Plough-boy; Death of Tom Moody; The Arethusa; Last whistle; Lovely Jane; My own native village; The bud of the rose; Sailor's epitaph; On by the spur of valour goaded; and Violet nurs'd in woodlands wild.

Shield was one of the most famous of English ballad composers, and shares with Storace, Arne, Linley, and Jackson the honour of giving a form and character to the English song as bequeathed by Purcell and the older composers. His concerted music is melodious and pretty, and most of his music is composed in a quiet and beautiful pastoral vein. His dramatic works are now forgotten, save for the songs they contain. His theoretical works are well written, and though now disused served a valuable purpose in their day.

SHIRREFF (Jane). English soprano vocalist, B. 1811. S. under Thomas Welsh. *Début* Covent Garden Theatre, London, in Arne's "Artaxerxes," 1831. Sang at the Philharmonic Concerts, the Concerts of Ancient Music, and at Provincial Festivals. Sang also at Drury Lane Theatre, and in 1838 appeared in America with Seguin's company. Married Mr. J. Walcott, Secretary of the Army and Navy Club, and retired. D. Kensington, London, Dec. 23, 1883.

SHORE (John). English trumpeter, B. in latter part of 17th century. Succeeded his brother WILLIAM in office of sergeant trumpeter. Trumpeter in the Queen's band. D. Nov. 20, 1750. Credited with the invention of the tuning-fork. The most celebrated trumpet-player of his time. He was succeeded in his office by Valentine Snow. His sister CATHERINE, B. 1668, S. under H. Purcell. Married Colley Cibber, 1693. Appeared as a singer in operas by Purcell and others. D. 1730. The founder of the Shore family was MATTHIAS (D. 1700), who was King's trumpeter in 1685, and was succeeded by his son WILLIAM (D. 1707).

SHORE (William). English amateur comp., B. Manchester, 1792. D. Buxton, Jan. 16, 1877. Was Founder and Musical Director of the Manchester Madrigal Soc.; and Hon. Secretary of the Gentlemen's Glee Club. He edited "Sacred Music, selected and arranged from the works of the most eminent composers...," Lond., fo., n.d., and comp. glees and songs, and the well-known trio, "O Willie brew'd a peck o' Maut."

SHRUBSOLE (William). English comp., B. Sheerness, 1758. Chorister in Canterbury Cath. Was org. in Spa Fields Chap., 1784-1806. D. 1806. Comp. hymns and other sacred music.

SHUDI (Burkhardt), properly TSCHUDI. Swiss harpsichord-maker, B. March 13, 1702. Came to London, 1718. Established a manufactory in Great Pulteney Street. Entered into partnership with his son-in-law, JOHN BROADWOOD, 1769. D. London, Aug. 19, 1773. A famous harpsichord-maker, and original founder of the great firm of Broadwood & Sons.

SHUTTLEWORTH (Obadiah). English org., violinist, and comp., B. Spitalfields, London, 1675. Vnst. at Swan Tavern Concerts, Cornhill, 1728. Org. successively of S. Michael's, Cornhill, and of the Temple Church. Comp concertos and sonatas for violin. D. 1735.

SIBBALD (James). Scottish publisher and bookseller in Edinburgh (D. 1803.) Edited "The Vocal Magazine, containing a selection of the most esteemed English, Scots, and Irish Songs, Ancient and Modern, adapted for the Harpsichord and Violin," Edin., 1797-99. 3 vols., issued in 19 parts. A second series only reached a few parts. "Collection of Catches, Canons, Glees, etc., in score, from the works of the most eminent Composers, Ancient and Modern," Edin., 3 vols., 4to, n.d.

SIBONI (Giuseppe). Italian tenor vocalist, B. Forli, Jan. 27, 1780. *Début* at Florence, 1797. Appeared in London, 1806. Appeared at Vienna, Prague, etc., and in 1818 settled at Copenhagen, where he became Director of the Opera and Cons. D. Copenhagen, March 29, 1839.

His son, ERIK ANTON WALDEMAR, B. Copenhagen, Aug. 26, 1828. S. under Goetze, Vogel, J. P. E. Hartmann, Moscheles, and Hauptmann, Org. and Prof. of Music at Royal Academy of Music, Sorö, Seeland. He has comp. "Loreley," opera ; "Carl den Andens Flugt," opera ; Stabat Mater ; Cantatas, overtures, quartets, sonatas, and org. and Pf. music. He married in 1866 JOHANNA FREDERIKA CRULL, B. Rostock, Jan. 30, 1839, a pianist of great ability, who S. under Marschner and Moscheles.

SICOAMA (A.) Author of "The New Diatonic Flute," Lond., 1847, 4to.

SIFACE (Giovanni Francesco Grossi, detto). Italian soprano vocalist, B. Pescia, Tuscany [1666]. S. under T. Redi. Chorister in the Pope's Chapel, 1675. Sang in Italy, and about 1686-7 was in England, in service of James II. Murdered in Italy [1699].

SIGHICELLI (Filippo). Italian violinist, B. San Cesario, Modena, 1686. D. Modena, April 14, 1773. His son and descendants, GIUSEPPE, B. Modena, 1737, D. Modena, Nov. 8, 1826 ; CARLO, B. Modena, 1772, D. there, April 7, 1806 ; ANTONIO, B. Modena, July 1, 1802—D. Modena, 1883; and VINCENZO, B. Cento, July 30, 1830, form a most remarkable family of violinists, in which son succeeded father for four generations.

SILAS (Edward). German pianist and comp., B. Amsterdam, Aug. 22, 1827. S. under Kalkbrenner, Benoist, and Halévy, at Paris. Gained first prize for organ, Paris Cons., 1849. Settled in London as pianist and teacher. Org. of Catholic Chap., Kingston-on-Thames. Prof. in Guildhall School of Music, London.

WORKS.—Joash, oratorio, Norwich Festival, 1863. Nitocris, tragic opera, in 3 acts, words by E. Fitzball. Overture and incidental music to Fanchette, a drama. Kyrie eleison, for 4 voices and orch. Symphony for orch., in A, 1850 ; Symphony in C ; Overtures : in E, and to Olivier Brusson, and Don Quixote. Concertos for Pf. and orch., in D, C minor, and D minor. Nonetto in F min., for flute, oboe, clarinet, bassoon, horn, violin, viola, 'cello, and double-bass. Two quintets. Quartets for Pf. and strings, and for other combinations. Trios for Pf., vn., and 'cello, in C min., A, C, D, etc. *Pianoforte* : Two books of romances; Mazurkas; Nocturnes; Sonata in F ; La Gentilezza, op. 14 ; Caprices ; Allegretto, op. 20 ; Pastorale in F ; Gavottes in F and D ; Tarantelle, op. 51 : Idylle, op. 63 ; Barcarolle in G min., op. 54 ; Six esquisses, op. 67 ; Impromptus ; Bourée in G min.; Bolero in C ; Sonatina in D ; Pf. duets, etc. *Church music*: Mass for 4 voices and org. (prize gold medal and 1000 fcs. at Belgian International Exhibition, 1866) ; Ave Verum ; Tantum ergo ; Ave Regina ; O Salutaris ; Four Litanies ; Offertorium ; Magnificat ; Responses, etc. *Part-Songs:* Christmas Carol, for 6 voices ; Softly fall the shades of evening ; The Owl ; Song for Spring. *Songs:* Treue Liebe ; The life chase ; Entsagen ; O thou pale orb ;

M 2

Stars of the summer night ; The dying child ; The Curfew ; Orange blossoms ; I think of thee ; Polly Vanderdecken ; etc. Numerous comic and humoristic pieces for voices and instruments. *Organ*: Andantes in C, D, A flat, etc.; Fugues in D and C min.; Preludes in D and F min.; March in B flat ; Sonata in F ; Menuet in F ; Fantasias in E min., on S. Ann's tune, etc.; Melodies in C, and E. min.; Allegro in F ; Canzonetta ; Pastorales ; Six pieces ded. to J. Lemmens ; and many other works.

SILBERMANN (Gottfried), German organ and clavichord maker, B. Kleinbobritzsch, 1683. D. Aug. 4, 1753. Descended from a celebrated family of organ builders, of whom ANDREAS (1678-1733), and his sons, JOHANN ANDREAS (1712-1783), JOHANN DANIEL (1678-1766), and JOHANN HEINRICH (1727-c1792), were eminent. Gottfried built many organs in Saxony, and is equally celebrated for his pianofortes, some of which he made for Frederick the Great.

SILCHER (Friedrich). German comp. and writer, B. Schnaith, in Würtemberg, Jan. 27, 1789. S. under Auberlen. Teacher at Stuttgart, and cond. in Tübingen University. D. Tübingen, Aug. 26, 1860. Comp. choral music, songs, and hymns, and wrote "Harmonie und Composition Lehre..." 1851. One of his books was translated by Sabilla Novello as "Succinct Instructions for the Guidance of Singing-Schools and Choral Societies," Lond., 8vo, 1857.

SIMAO. See PORTOGALLO.

SIMPSON (Christopher), or SYMPSON. English violinist and writer, B. [about 1610]. Was a soldier in the army raised by the Duke of Newcastle for service of Charles I. He was a Roman Catholic, and was patronized by Sir Robert Bolles of Leicestershire, whose son he taught the viol. D. Turnstile, Holborn [?].

WORKS.—The Division-Violist, or an Introduction to the Playing upon a Ground, divided in two parts, the first directing the hand, with other preparative instructions ; the second laying open the manner and method of playing, or composing division to a ground, Lond., fo., 1659 ; 2nd edit. as "Chelys Minuritionum artificio exornata, sive Minuritiones ad Basin, etiam extempore modulandi ratio...or The Division Viol," etc., Lond., 1667 ; Third edition, with portrait, 1712. The Principles of Practical Musick, Lond., 1665 ; 2nd ed. A Compendium of Practical Music, in 5 parts : 1. The Rudiments of Song ; 2. The Principles of Composition ; 3. The Use of Discords ; 4. The Form of Figurate Descant ; 5. The Contrivance of Canon ...Lond., 12mo, 1667. Of this work there are many editions dated and undated to about 1760. Art of Discant, or Composing Musick in Parts, by Dr. Thomas Campion, with Annotations thereon by Mr. Christopher Simpson, Lond., 8vo, 1655. Also contained in Playford's "Introduction."

Simpson was a viol-player of great renown in his day. His works are becoming scarce in the earlier editions.

SIMPSON (Robert). Scottish comp., B. Glasgow about 1792. He was a weaver to trade, and led the singing in Dr. Wardlaw's church, Glasgow, for a time. Precentor and session-clerk of East Parish Ch., Greenock, from 1823. D. Greenock, June or July, 1832. Known as comp. of the well known psalm-tune, "Ballerma."

SIMPSON (Thomas). English violinist, who in 1615 was vnst. in Chap. of Prince of Holstein-Schaumburg. Comp. "Opusculum neuer Pavanen, Galliarden, Couranten, und Volten..." Frankfort, 1610. "Pavanen, Volten und Galliarden," Frankfort, 4to, 1611. "Tafel-Consort, allerhand lustige Lieder von 4 Instrumenten und Generalbass," Hamburg, 1621.

SIMPSON (T.) English writer, author of "The Norma Virium, or Musical Accentuator, a Disquisitory Essay on the Obstructions Students meet with in becoming good timeists..." Lond., 4to, n. d.

SIMROCK (Nikolaus). German music-publisher, B. Bonn, 1755. Established at Bonn, 1790. Famous as the publisher of Beethoven's works. The Berlin branch of the firm publish the works of Brahms and other modern composers.

SINCLAIR (John). Scottish tenor vocalist, B. near Edinburgh, 1790. Clarinet player in band of Campbell of Shawfield's Regiment. Teacher of music in Aberdeen. First appeared as a singer in London, Haymarket Theatre, as *Cheerly* in "Lock and Key," 1810. S. for a time under Thomas Welsh. Engaged for Covent Garden Theatre, and appeared in Linley's "Duenna," 1811. Married Miss Norton, daughter of Captain Norton, 1816. Appeared in London, and in English Provinces till 1819; when he visited Paris, and S. for a time under Pellegrini, and under Banderali at Milan. Visited Rossini at Naples, 1821. Sang in Pisa, Bologna (where he was made a mem. of the Philharmonic Academy), Modena, Florence, Venice (where Rossini wrote for him the part of *Idreno* in "Semiramide"), and Genoa, 1822-23. Re-appeared in London, Covent Garden, Nov. 19, 1823, and at other theatres till 1830. Sang in America, and appeared in opera, 1830. Retired about same time. D. Margate, Sept. 23, 1857.

Sinclair was one of the most popular singers of his day, and was the creator of the tenor *rôles* in Bishop's "Guy Mannering," "The Slave," "Noble Outlaw," and Davy's "Roy Roy." He comp. the well-known songs "Hey, the bonnie breast-knots," "Johnnie Sands," and others in the Scotch style.

SINGELÉE (Jean Baptiste). Belgian violinist and comp., B. Brussels, Sept. 25, 1812. S. in Brussels under Wéry. Violinist in Paris for a time. Violinist and cond. at Brussels and Ghent, and travelled as a virtuoso. D. Ostend, Sept. 29, 1875. Comp. Arsène, ballet, 1845. Concerto for vn. and orch., op. 10. Fantasias for vn. and Pf. on operas of Bellini, Auber, Hérold, Verdi, Donizetti, Rossini, Meyerbeer, Weber, etc. Fantasia Pastorale, op. 56; Fantasia élégante, op. 98, etc.

SINGER (Edmond). Hungarian violinist and comp., B. Totis, Oct. 14, 1830. S. Pesth Cons., and under Böhm. Travelled as violinist in Hungary, Germany, France, etc. Solo-violinist at Court of Weimar, and Prof. at Stuttgart. Comp. Adieux à la Patrie, op. 4; La Sentimentale, op. 13; Caprice-étude, op. 14; Le Carnaval Hongrois, vn. and orch., op. 15; and many other violin pieces.

SINGER (Otto). German pianist, comp., and teacher, B. 1833. Established in Cincinnati as Prof. of the Coll. of Music. Comp. variations and other works for Pf. solo and duet; Festival Ode, for chorus and orch., and other choral music.

SIRMEN (Maddalena), *née* LOMBARDINI. Italian violinist, B. Venice, 1735. S. at Cons. de' Mendicanti, and under Tartini at Padua. Appeared in Italy. Married Luigi de Sirmen. Played in Paris, 1761, and appeared in London, 1768. Afterwards a singer at Dresden, 1782. D. about end of last century. She comp. Trios for 2 vns. and 'cello, op. 1; Concertos for violin, op. 2, 3.

SIVORI (Ernesto Camillo). Italian violinist, B. Genoa, Oct. 25, 1815. Early displayed talent for violin. S. under Paganini, and received general musical education from Costa and Serra. Appeared in Paris and London, 1827. Travelled in France. Appeared in America, 1846, and again in London. Chevalier of Order of S.S. Maurice and Lazare, 1855; of Order of Charles II. of Spain, 1856, etc.

WORKS.—Concertos in E flat and A, vn. and orch.; La Génoise, caprice, op. 1; Fantasia-étude, op. 10; Carnavals de Cuba, Chili, Americain, etc.; Les Folies Espagnoles; Tarentella Napolitan; Duets, etc.

SKEAF (Joseph). English comp. and pianist, B. Liverpool, Nov. 10, 1836. Cond. of Apollo Glee Club, and Grand Org. to Freemasons of West Lancashire. Comp. part-songs and songs. D. Liverpool, Nov. 1, 1884.

SKEATS (Highmore). English comp. and org., B. 1787. Son of Highmore Skeats, org. of Canterbury Cath. (D. 1831.) Org. of S. George's Chap., Windsor, 1830. D. Jan. 24, 1835. Comp. church music. His father published a "Collection of Songs," Lond., 1784, fo.

SKEFFINGTON (Hon. and. Rev. T. C.). English writer, author of "Handy-

Book of Musical Art, with some Practical Hints to Students," Lond., 1858, 12mo; "The Flute in its Transition State, a Review of its Changes during the past Fifty Years," Lond., 1862, 8vo.

SKENE (John) of Halyards. Scottish collector of 16th and 17th centuries. The supposed compiler of the "Skene Manuscript," 1614-1620, a collection of vocal and dance music which was edited and published by Dauney and Graham for the Bannatyne Club, in 1838. It contains, among other melodies, the old set of the "Flowers of the Forest."

SKRAUP (Franz). Bohemian cond. and comp., B. Vosic, June 3, 1801. D. Rotterdam, Feb. 7, 1862. Comp. operas, songs, etc. His brother, JOHANN NEPOMUK, B. Vosic, Sept. 15, 1811, D. Prague, Nov. 18, 1865, comp. operas, lieder, etc.

SLAVIK or **SLAWJIK (Josef).** Bohemian violinist and comp., B. Ginetz, March 1, 1806. D. Pesth, May 30, 1833. Comp. violin music.

SLOMAN (Robert). English org. and comp., B. Gloucester. S. under Amott, Wesley, and C. Lucas. Private org. to Earl of Powis, 1852. Org. of Parish Ch., Welshpool. Org. S. Martin's, Scarborough, 1869; West Dulwich, Lond., 1877. Mus. Bac., Oxon., 1861. Mus. Doc., Oxon., 1867. Comp. "Supplication and Praise," a sacred cantata; anthems, part-songs, songs, and Pf. music.

SLOPER (E. H. Lindsay). English pianist and comp., B. London, June 14, 1826. S. under Moscheles, at Frankfort under A. Schmitt, at Heidelberg under Vollweiler, and at Paris under Rousselot, 1841-46. Appeared in London at Musical Union, 1846. Teacher and pianist in London.

WORKS.—Op. 1. Czartoryska, 3 mazurkas, Pf.; op. 2. Henriette, valse, Pf.; op. 3. 24 Studies, Pf.; op. 8. Six songs; op. 12. Serenade and canzonette, Pf.; op. 13. 12 Studies, Pf.; Sonata for Pf. and vn.; op. 15. Pensée fugitive, Pf.; Transcriptions and arrangements for Pf. *Songs:* Medora, Song to May, Child and the skylark, Fairy's reproach, The Violet, To-night, etc. Tutor and Technical Guide for the Pianoforte.

SMALLWOOD (William). English org. and comp., B. Kendal, 1831. Org. S. George's Ch., Kendal. Comp. of a large number of teaching pieces for Pf., chiefly in collections, like "Home Treasures," "Classics at Home," "Flowers of Melody," "Youthful Pleasures," and some original pieces, as "Hawthorn Blossoms," "Elfin Bower," "Clarissa," etc. He is also author of a "Tutor for the Pianoforte."

SMART (Christopher). English writer. D. May 18, 1770. Published a "Collection of Melodies for the Psalms of David, according to the Version of Christopher Smart, A.M. By the most Eminent Composers of Church Music." Lond., Walsh, 1765, 4to.

SMART (Sir George Thomas). English cond. and teacher, B. London, May 10, 1776. Chor. in Chap. Royal under Ayrton. S. org. under Dupuis, and comp. under Arnold. Org. S. James's Chap., Hampstead Road. Knighted at Dublin by Lord Lieutenant, after cond. a successful series of concerts, 1811. Original mem. of Philharmonic Soc., 1813. Cond. concerts of Philharmonic Soc., 1813-44. Cond. Lenten oratorios. One of org. of Chap. Roy., 1822. Connected with Weber, who died at his house in 1826. Cond. Mendelssohn's "St. Paul," at Liverpool, 1836. Comp. to Chap. Royal, 1838. Cond. all the principal provincial festivals of his time. Cond. music at coronations of William IV. and Victoria. D. Bedford Square, London, Feb. 23, 1867. One of the greatest English conductors. He was a successful vocal teacher, and gave instruction to Jenny Lind and Sontag. His works include anthems, chants, glees, and songs; and he edited Gibbon's "First set of Madrigals," for the Musical Antiquarian Soc.

SMART (Henry). English violinist, B. London, 1778. Brother of the preceding. S. under W. Cramer. Leader in various theatre orchs., the Philharmonic Soc., English Opera House, etc. Became part-proprietor of a brewery, which did not succeed. Established a Pf. manufactory. D. Dublin, Nov. 23, 1823.

SMART (Henry). English org. and comp., son of above, B. London, Oct. 26, 1813. S. under his father and W. H. Kearns; and self-taught. Articled to a solicitor. Org. of Parish Ch. of Blackburn, 1831-36. Org. S. Philip's, Regent St., London, 1836. Married, July, 1840. Org. S. Luke's, Old St., City, London, 1844 64. Org. S. Pancras, Euston Road, 1864. His sight failed him in 1864. Granted pension of £100 per annum by the Government, in 1879. D. London, July 6, 1879, and is buried in Hampstead Cemetery, Finchley Road, London.

WORKS.—*Operas:* Bertha, or the Gnome of Hartzberg, Haymarket Theatre, Lond., 1855; Undine (unfinished); Surrender of Calais, by Planché (unfinished). *Cantatas:* The Bride of Dunkerron, Birmingham Festival, 1864; King René's Daughter (by F. Enoch), 1871; The Fishermaidens, 1871; Jacob, sacred, Glasgow Choral Union, Nov. 10, 1873. Full Morning and Evening Services in F and G, 1871. *Anthems:* O God, the King of Glory; Sing to the Lord; The Angel Gabriel; Be glad, O ye righteous; The Lord is my strength; The Lord hath done great things; Lord Thou hast been our refuge. *Part-Songs:* Ave Maria (1859); Behold where laughing Spring (1859); Cradle Song; Evening Hymn; Queen of the night; The shepherd's farewell; The waves' reproof; Stars of the Summer night; Lady, rise, sweet Morn's awaking; Six four-part songs (1869); Four-part songs comp. for Leslie's choir. Trios for female voices, and many Vocal duets. *Songs:* The Lady of the Lea; The Spinning wheel; Near thee, still near thee; Vineta; The Lady Isoline; Autumn song; Come again Spring; I dream of thee at morn; Rose of May; The gleaner maiden; The midnight ride; The talisman; The fairy's whisper; Blue eyes; Go, whispering breeze; Wake, Mary, wake; Echo of the lake; Sir Roland; The bird's love song; The lark's song; etc. *Organ:* Fifty Preludes and Interludes (1862); Andantes in G, A, and E min.; Eighteen short easy pieces; Postludes in C, D, E flat, etc.; Twelve short interludes; Grand solemn march; March in G; Festive march in D; Minuet in C; Choral, with variations; The Organ Student, 12 pieces. Chamber Duets and Trios, by G. F. Handel, edited by Smart for the English Handel Soc., 1852. The Presbyterian Hymnal, 1877 (edited). Report on the Organ of Christ Church Cathedral, Dublin, 1878.

Smart was one of the most gifted and original of recent English organists and composers. His songs, part-songs, and organ-music enjoy a wide popularity, while his cantatas are very frequently performed. His most striking work is the "Bride of Dunkerron," which contains many powerful and highly dramatic passages. He was an authority on the organ, and the very large and beautiful instruments at Leeds Town Hall, and in St. Andrew's Hall, Glasgow, were erected from his specifications. As a performer he possessed several original points. Some books on him are "Henry Smart: His Life and Works," by Wm. Spark, London, 1881, 8vo, with portrait. "Henry Smart," by W. D. Seymour [Leeds, 1881]. "Henry Smart's Compositions for the Organ, analysed by John Broadhouse," Lond., 1880.

SMETANA (Friedrich). Bohemian comp., B. Leitomèschel, near Prague, March 2, 1824. S. under Proksch at Prague from 1843; under R. Schumann, 1846; and under Liszt. Married Katharina Kolàr, 1848, and taught in Music School at Prague. Gave Concerts at Prague in conjunction with Liszt. Cond. of Philharmonic Soc. at Gothenburg, Sweden, 1856. Cond. of National Theatre at Prague, 1866-74. Retired on account of his deafness. Teacher of Dvorák. D. Prague, May, 1884.

WORKS.—*Operas:* The Brandenburger in Bohemia; Married for Money, 1866; Dalibar, 1868; The Kiss; etc. *Symphonic Poems:* Mein Vaterland; Ultava; Libussa; Vyschrad. Quartets, Pf. music, and Songs.

SMETHERGELL (William). English org., comp., and writer, flourished in London in last century. Was org. of St. Margaret-on-the-Hill, Southwark, and of Allhallows, Barking. Author of "A Treatise on Thoroughbass," Lond., 1794, 4to. "Rules for Thoroughbass, to which are annexed three sonatas," Lond., n. d., fo. Comp. Six Overtures; Lessons for Pf.; Sonatas for Pf., etc.

SMITH (Alfred Mor. tem). English tenor vocalist and comp., was, chor. in S. George's Chap., Windsor. Lay-vicar Westminster Abbey, and Gent. of

Chap.-Royal (1858). Prof. of Singing at R. A. M., and Guildhall School of Music. A concert vocalist of much repute. Has comp. songs and glees.

SMITH (Alice Mary), Mrs. MEADOWS WHITE. English comp., B. London, May 19. 1839. S. under Sir W. S. Bennett and Sir G. A. Macfarren. Married to Mr. Frederick Meadows White, Q.C., 1867. Associate of Philharmonic Soc., 1867. D. London, Dec. 4, 1884.

WORKS.—*Cantatas:* Rüdesheim, Cambridge, 1865 ; Ode to the North-east Wind, Hackney Choral Assoc., 1880; Ode, The Passions (Collins), Hereford Festival, 1882 ; Song of the Little Baltung (Kingsley), Lombard Amateur Assoc., 1883 ; The Red King (Kingsley). Symphony in C minor, Mus. Soc. of Lond., 1863. *Overtures:* Endymion, 1864 (re-written, Crystal Palace, 1871); Lalla Rookh, 1865 ; Masque of Pandora, 1878 ; Jason, or the Argonauts and Sirens, 1879. Quartets for Pf. and strings, B flat, 1861 ; D, 1864; Quartet for strings in D, 1862 ; another, 1870 ; Concerto for clarinet and orch., Norwich Festival, 1872 ; Introduction and Allegro, Pf. and orch, 1865 ; Two Intermezzi from the "Masque of Pandora," 1879. Part-songs, songs, etc.—*Musical Times.*

SMITH (Bernard). See SCHMIDT (Bernard).

SMITH (Boyton). English comp. and pianist, B. Dorchester, Feb. 23, 1837. S. under S. S. Wesley.

WORKS.—Te Deums, anthems, and other music for the church service ; Organ pieces for church use, 6 sets ; Andante con moto for org., etc. *Pianoforte:* Fern leaves, melody, op. 45 ; La Fête de la Reine, op. 50 ; La Fée coquette, op. 64 ; La bayadere ; La Napolitaine ; La sirène ; La vivandière ; Maidenhair; Sur le lac; Numerous transcriptions. *Songs:* Bird of the Wilderness ; For ever and a day ; I think of thee ; Remembrance ; Sweet Leonora ; Old Millstream ; The Parting ; Violets of Spring, etc.

SMITH (Charles). English vocalist and comp., B. London, 1786. S. under Costellow. Chor. in Chap.-Royal under Ayrton. S. under John Ashley. Sang as a soprano from 1799 at Ranelagh, in Scotland, etc., till his voice broke in 1803. Org. Croydon Ch. ; org. Welbeck Chap., 1807. Sang as a bass in oratorio, 1813. Married Miss Both of Norwich. Resided in Liverpool from 1816. D. Crediton, Devon, Nov. 22, 1856. Comp. music to the dramatic pieces, Yes or No, 1809 ; The Tourist Friend ; Hit or Miss ; Anything New, etc.; and many songs, Far o'er the Sea, The Battle of Hohenlinden, and others.

SMITH (Catherine Louisa). See PENNA.

SMITH (Rev. George). English writer, author of "Church Music, Two Lectures," Lond., 1860, 8vo.

SMITH (George Townshend). English comp. and teacher, B. Windsor, Nov. 14, 1813. Chor. in St. George's Chap., Windsor. S. under Highmore Skeats and S. Wesley. Org. of Old Parish Ch., Eastbourne. S. Margaret's Lynn. Org. Hereford Cath., 1843. Cond. and Hon. Sec. of the Three Choir Festival. D. Hereford, Aug. 3, 1877. Comp. of anthems, songs, and other vocal music.

SMITH (Isaac). English comp., B. about middle of 18th century. Was precentor of Alie Street Meeting House, London. D. London, about 1800. Published "A Collection of Psalm Tunes in Three Parts," Lond., n.d., 8vo. Comp. of the well-known psalm tune "Irish."

SMITH (John). English org. and comp., B. Cambridge, 1795. Stipendiary Choirman of Christ Church Cath., Dublin, 1815. Vicar-choral of St. Patrick's Cath., 1816. Org. of the Chap., Dublin Castle, 1833-35. Prof. of Music in University of Dublin. Mus. Doc., Dublin. D. near Dublin, Nov. 12, 1861.

WORKS.—The Revelation, oratorio ; Cathedral Music, fo., n.d.; Lyra Masonica, collection of masonic songs, Lond., 1847 ; Glees, songs, and other vocal music. Treatise on the Theory and Practise of Music, with the Principles of Harmony and Composition, Dublin, 1853, 2 v., 4to; A Selection of Original Melodies of Erin, with characteristic words by Edward Fitzsimons; symphonies by J. Smith, 1814, fo.

SMITH (John Christopher). German comp. and cond. B. Anspach, 1712. Originally Johann Christoph Schmidt. His father was Händel's treasurer. He got lessons in music from Pepusch, Rosingrave, and Handel. Org. of Foundling Hospital. Händel's amanuensis when that comp. became blind. Cond. several series of concerts, including Händel's oratorios, 1732-74. D. Bath, Oct. 3, 1795.

WORKS.—*Operas*: Teraminta, 1732; Ulysses, 1733; Rosalinda, 1739; Dario, 1746; Issipile, 1746; The Fairies, 1754; The Tempest, 1756; Medea; Il Ciro riconosciuto; The Enchanter, 1760. *Oratorios*: The Lamentation of David, or the Death of Saul and Jonathan, 1738; Paradise Lost, 1758; Rebecca; Nabal (from Händel), 1764; Gideon (from Händel), 1769; Judith; Jehosaphat; The Redemption. The Seasons. Daphne, pastoral by Pope. Thamesis; Isis and Proteus, cantatas. Six Sets of Lessons for the Harpsichord, op. 3, 4, etc. Anecdotes of George Frederick Handel and John Christopher Smith...Lond., fo., 1799.

SMITH (John Stafford). English org. and comp., B. Gloucester, 1750. Son of Martin Smith, the Cath. org., from 1743 to 1782. S. under his father and Dr. Boyce. Chor. in Chap.-Royal under Nares. Gent. of Chap.-Royal, 1784. Lay-vicar Westminster Abbey, 1785. Org. of Chap.-Royal, 1802; and from 1805-1817 master of the children, do. Gained many prizes for glees, 1773-1780, etc. D. London, Sept. 20, 1836.

WORKS.—Musica Antiqua, a Selection of Music of this and other Countries, from the commencement of the Twelfth to the beginning of the Eighteenth Century, comprising some of the earliest and most curious Motettes, Madrigals, etc., Lond., 2 vols., fo., 1812. A Collection of English Songs in Score, for 3 and 4 voices, composed about the year 1500, taken from MSS. of the same age, Lond., fo., 1779. Anthems Composed for the Choir Service of the Church of England, Lond., fo., n. d. Twelve Chants composed for the Use of the Choirs of the Church of England, Lond., ob. 4to, n. d. A Collection of Songs of Various Kinds for Different Voices, Lond., fo., 1785. A Collection of Glees, for 3, 4, 5, and 6 Voices, Lond., n. d.

A most industrious compiler, whose "Musica Antiqua" is one of the best English collections of ancient vocal music. He aided Sir John Hawkins with the compilation of his "History of Music." Many of his glees are among the standard favourites in this class of music.

SMITH (Montague). English org. and comp., B. Norwich, July, 1843. Org. Glasgow University; St. Silas Episcopal Ch. Cond. University Choral Soc. Local Examiner in Music, Glasgow University. Prof. of Harmony in Queen Margaret College, Glasgow. Comp. of "Blessed is the Man," and "By the Waters of Babylon," cantatas; The Killabag Shootings, opera; Concert overture, Gloucester Festival, 1877; Songs, part-songs, and instrumental music.

SMITH (Robert). English writer and professor, B. Cambridge, 1689. Plumian Prof. of Astronomy, Cambridge. Master of Trinity Coll., 1742. D. Cambridge, 1768. Author of "Harmonics, or the Philosophy of Musical Sounds," Cambridge, 8vo, 1749; 2nd ed., enlarged, Lond., 8vo, 1759. A Postscript upon the Changeable Harpsichord, a Perfect Instrument, Lond., 1762, 8vo. A learned and able work.

SMITH (Robert Archibald). Scottish comp., B. Reading, Berks, Nov. 16, 1780. Son of Robert Smith, silk weaver, a native of East Kilbride, who settled at Reading in 1774, during a heavy depression of trade in Paisley. Gave very early indications of musical ability. Apprenticed to the weaving trade, which he followed in Reading, and in Paisley, from 1800, where he became intimate with Tannahill, Motherwell, etc. Married Mary MacNicol, 1802. Teacher of music, and precentor in the Abbey Church, Paisley, 1807. Musical director of S. George's, Edinburgh, Aug. 1823. D. Edinburgh, Jan. 3, 1829 (buried in S. Cuthbert's churchyard).

WORKS.--The Scotish Minstrel, a Selection from the Vocal Melodies of Scotland, Ancient and Modern, arranged for the Pianoforte, Edin. [c. 1821-24], 6 vols., large 8vo. The Irish Minstrel, a Selection from the Vocal Melodies of Ireland, Ancient and Modern, Edin., n. d. [1825]. Flowers of Scottish Song, Glasgow, n. d., fo. Select Melodies, with appropriate words, chiefly original, collected and arranged with Symphonies and Accompaniments for the Pianoforte, Edin., n. d. [1827]. Devotional Music, original and selected, arranged mostly in four parts, with a Thorough-bass for the Organ or Pianoforte, 1810; New ed. by John Turnbull, Glas., n. d., 8vo. Anthems in Four Vocal Parts, with an Accompaniment for the Organ or Pianoforte...1819. Sacred Harmony, for the use of S. George's Church, Edinburgh, being a Collection of Psalm and Hymn Tunes.....Edin. [1820], 12mo (with Rev. A. Thomson); other editions, and a modern one edited by Jas. S. Geikie, Edin., n.d., 8vo. Sacred Music, consisting of the Tunes, Sanctusses, Doxologies, Thanksgivings, etc., sung in St. George's Church, Edinburgh, Edin., 1825, 8vo. Edinburgh Sacred Harmony for the Use of Churches and Families, arranged for Four Voices, Edin., 1829, 2 vols., fo. The Sacred Harmony of the Church of Scotland, n. d. [1828], 8vo. *Songs*: Jessie, the Flow'r o' Dunblane (1808); Bonnie Mary Hay; O wha's at the window? The lass o' Arranteenie; The Harper of Mull; Loudon's bonnie woods and braes; On wi' the tartan; Maid of the sea; Highlander's farewell; The willow. *Duets*: Row weel, my boatie, row weel; etc. *Psalm tunes*: Morven, St. Mirren, Invocation, St. Lawrence, Kelburn, Irvine, Paisley, Abbey, and many others, all published in his collections. *Anthems*: How beautiful upon the mountains; The earth is the Lord's; etc. An Introduction to Singing, comprising various examples, with scales, exercises, and songs, etc., Edin. [1826], fo.

Smith was one of the best musicians whom Scotland produced in the first part of this century. His works are now as much used as ever they were, and his songs and psalms will always remain in use in Scotland. He composed many fine Scottish melodies, and did not scruple occasionally to pass a number of them off as genuine antiques. His anthems are of no particular merit judged by present standards, but considering the state of music in Scotland during his period, are very creditable works.

SMITH (Sydney). English pianist and comp., B. Dorchester, July 14, 1839. S. at Leipzig Cons. under Moscheles, Plaidy, Hauptmann, Richter, Papperitz, and Rietz, from 1855. Settled in London as pianist and comp., 1859.

WORKS.—*Pianoforte*: Arcadia; Barcarolle; Bolero; Chant des oiseaux; Chant der savoyard; Coquetterie; Danse Napolitaine; Etudes de concert; Eventide; Fairy realms; Fairy whispers; Fandango; Fête champêtre; Fête Hongroise; Fête militaire; Gavotte; La harpe Eolienne; Le jet d'eau; Les trompettes de la guerre; Marche Hongroise; Maypole dance; Pas de sabots; Rêve angélique; Rhapsodie; Saltarello; Tarentelles; The spinning wheel; Titania; Tyrolienne; Fantasias on Operas, and Transcriptions, numerous.

SMITH (Thomas). English org., comp., and writer, B. Arnold, Notts., Feb. 20, 1832. Org. at Bury St. Edmunds. Author of several didactic treatises; Short Practical Method for teaching Singing, Lond., n.d., etc.; and comp. of anthems.

SMITH (T. R.) English writer, author of "The Violoncello Preceptor, containing the Rudiments of Music, with Scales, etc." Lond., n. d.

SMITH (Dr. William). Scottish amateur musician and divine, B. in Scotland, 1754. Settled in New York, 1783. D. New York, April 6, 1821. Author of "The Reasonableness of Setting forth the Praises of God, according to the Use of the Primitive Church; with Historical Views of Metre Psalmody," New York, 1814. Chants for Publick Worship, 1814.

SNETZLER (Johann). German organ-builder, B. Passau, 1710. Settled in England, and built a number of fine organs, among which may be named those at Lynn Regis (1754), Halifax (1766), and St. Martin's, Leicester (1774). D. London about end of 18th century.

SNOW (Valentine). English trumpet-player, of 18th century. Serjeant-trumpeter to the King, in succession to John Shore, 1753. Played in Handel's oratorios, the trumpet parts in which were specially written for him. D. London, Dec. 1770.

SOAPER (John). English comp., B. about middle of 18th century. Gent. of Chap.-Royal, and Vicar-choral S. Paul's. D. London, June 5, 1794. Comp. psalms and chants.

SOBOLEWSKI (Eduard). German violinist and comp., B. Königsberg, Oct.

1, 1808. S. under C. Gollmick. D. St. Louis, U.S., May 23, 1872. Comp.
Velleda, 1836; Salvator, Rosa, 1848, and other operas; oratorios; hymns,
and choral music.

SÖDERMANN (Johan August). Swedish comp., B. Stockholm, July 17,
1832. S. at Leipzig under Richter and Hauptmann. Chorus-master of
Royal Opera, Stockholm. Mem. of Swedish Academy of Music. D. Stockholm, Feb. 10, 1876.
WORKS.—Hinandes första lärospons; Wedding at Ulfasa; Regina von Emmeritz,
operettas. Overture, Joan of Arc (Schiller). Masses. Trios for male voices.
Hymns, Songs, etc.

SOLA (Charles Michel Alexis). Italian guitar-player and comp., B. Turin,
June 6, 1786. Settled in London about 1829. D. London [?]. Comp.
music for guitar and harp. Method for the Guitar, etc.

SOLDENE (Emily). English soprano vocalist and actress, B. Islington, London. *Début* at Drury Lane in "Il Trovatore." First appeared in Opera
bouffe in "The Grand Duchess," 1869. Sang at the Crystal Palace, Lyceum
Theatre, etc. Visited the United States, 1874, and 1876-77. Sang in New
Zealand and Australia. Has sang throughout the Provinces of England and
in Scotland (since 1878) with great success.

SOLIÉ. See SOULIER.

SOLOMON (Edward). English comp. of present time, has written the following
popular operas and operettas:—Billee Taylor, Oct. 1880; Claude Duval, or
Love and Larceny, Aug., 1881; Quite an Adventure, 1881; Lord Bateman;
or, Picotee's Pledge, April, 1882; Through the Looking Glass (farce), 1882;
Vicar of Bray, 1882; Paul and Virginia, 1883; Polly, 1884; Pocahontas,
1885. Comp. also songs, and other pieces.

SOMIS (Giovanni Battista). Italian violinist and comp., B. in Piedmont,
1676. S. at Rome under Corelli, and at Venice under Vivaldi. Settled at
Turin as leader of the Royal music. D. Turin, Aug. 14, 1763. Comp.
Opera Prima di Sonate a violino e violoncello e cembalo, Rome, 1722.
XII Sonate da Camera. Amsterdam, n. d.

SONNLEITHNER (Christoph). Hungarian comp., B. Szegedin, May 28,
1734. D. Vienna, Dec. 25, 1786. Comp. symphonies, music for the church,
organ pieces, etc. Founder of a Family intimately connected with the musical
life of Vienna.

SONTAG (Henriette Gertrude Walpurgis, Countess Rossi). German
soprano vocalist, B. Coblentz, Jan. 3, 1806. Appeared in an opera at Darmstadt, 1811. S. at Prague Cons., 1815, and appeared there in Boieldieu's
"Jean de Paris," 1820. S. at Vienna under Mdme. Fodor-Mainville. Engaged for opera of Leipzig, 1824; Berlin, 1825; Paris, June 15, 1826; London, April, 19, 1828, at King's Theatre. Married to Count Rossi and retired,
1830. Re-appeared in London and Paris, 1849-51. Visited the United States,
1852. D. Mexico, June 17, 1854.
A popular soprano, famed alike for the beauty of her voice and person. She
created the utmost enthusiasm wherever she appeared, and in Germany and Paris
was all but worshipped. She sang in operas of Weber, Donizetti, Rossini, Mozart,
Halévy, etc.

SORIA (Jules Diaz de). Portuguese barytone vocalist, B. Bordeaux, April 28,
1843. Has sang in Vienna, Paris, St. Petersburg, and London, 1867, 1872,
with great success.

SORIANO (Francesco). Italian comp., B. Rome, 1549. S. under Nanini and
Palestrina. Chap.-master of St. Peter's, Rome, 1603. D. Rome, Jan. 1620.
Comp. madrigals, masses, psalms, motets and canons.

SOULIER (Jean Pierre), or SOLIE. French comp., B. Nimes, 1755. D.
Paris, Aug. 6, 1812. Comp. Le Jockey, 1795; Azeline, 1796; Le Diable à
quatre, 1806; Les Ménestrels, 1811, and other operas.

SOWINSKI (Albert). Polish writer and comp., B. Ladyzyn, Ukraine, 1803. S. at Vienna under Czerny, Seyfried and Gyrowetz. Travelled in Italy, and settled in Paris. D. Paris, March 5, 1880. Comp. St. Adalbert, oratorio, op. 66; La Reine Hedwige, Mazeppa, op. 75, overtures; Symphony in E min. op. 62; and Pf. music. Author of "Les Musiciens Polonais et Slaves, Anciens et Modernes, Dictionnaire Biographique des Compositeurs, Chanteurs, Instrumentalistes, etc.," Paris, 8vo, 1857. Edited a collection of Polish national music.

SOUTHARD (L. H.) American writer and comp., author of "Thorough Base and Harmony," Boston, n. d.; The Organist (with G. E. Whiting); and editor of The Bouquet, a Collection of Vocal Music, New York, 1856; The Offering, a Collection of New Church Music, 1866.

SPAGNOLETTI (Pietro). Italian violoncello player and comp., B. Cremona, 1768. D. 1834. Appeared in England, and played with success. Teacher of a number of violinists and other musicians.

SPARK (William). English org., comp., and writer, B. Exeter, Oct. 28, 1825. Chor. Exeter Cath., and articled pupil to Dr. S. S. Wesley, 1834. Org. of St. Laurence's, Exeter, 1840; deputy-org. Leeds Parish Ch., 1842; Chapeltown; and St. Paul's, Leeds. Org. successively at Tiverton, Daventry, Northampton, and St. George's Ch., Leeds, 1850. Org. of Leeds Town Hall, 1859. Mus. Doc. Dublin, 1861. Has appeared as an org. throughout Britain. Established the Leeds Madrigal and Motet Soc., and a series of People's Concerts.

WORKS.—Trust and Triumph, cantata; Ode to Labour; Magnificat and Nunc dimittis in D. *Anthems:* All we like sheep; O God, have mercy upon me; Christ being raised from the dead; etc. The Practical Choirmaster (12 parts), edited; Sacred Harmony, selected and arranged, Lond., 1862, 4to; The Organist's Quarterly Journal, containing Original Compositions (edited), 1869, and now being published. Grand Organ Sonata, op. 21. Short Pieces for the Organ, original and selected (12 books). Part-songs, glees and songs, various. Handy Book for the Organ, Instructions for use of Manuals and Pedals, fo., n. d. Lecture on Church Music, more particularly the Choral Service of the Church of England, as applied to Parochial Worship, Leeds, 1851, 8vo. Choirs and Organs, Lond., 1852. A Few Words to Musical Conductors, by a Musician, 1853. Musical Tour in North Germany, Lond., 1871. Handy Book of Choral Singing. Henry Smart, his Life and Works, Lond., 1881, 8vo, etc.

SPEIDEL (Wilhelm). German comp. and cond., B. Ulm, Sept. 3, 1826. S. under I. Lachner. Musical-director at Ulm and Stuttgart. Comp. of choral and Pf. music, etc. His brother LUDWIG, B. Ulm, April 11, 1830, is a writer on music, and is noted for his anti-Wagnerian views.

SPENCE (Mrs. Sarah). English writer, authoress of "An Introduction to the Science of Harmony," Lond., 1810, 8vo.

SPENCER (Charles Child). English writer and comp., B. London, 1797. Was Mus. Doc. and org. and choir-master of St. James' Chap., Clapton. Author of "Elements of Practical Music," Lond., 1829, 8vo; "Elements of Musical Composition," Lond., 1840, 8vo; "The Pianoforte, the Rudiments of the Art of Playing," Lond., n. d.; "Rudimentary and Practical Treatise on Music," Lond., 1850, 2 vols., 12mo; "A Concise Explanation of the Church Modes, with Remarks on the Mutations they have undergone since the Inventions of the Hexachord and the Modern Tonal System of Music...," Lond., 1846. Some of the foregoing works have gone through several editions. He comp. many glees and songs, and other vocal music.

SPEYER (Wilhelm). German violinist and comp., B. Frankfort-on-Main, June 21, 1790. D. there, April 5, 1878. Comp. music for stringed instruments, violin music, lieder and choral music.

SPINDLER (Fritz). German pianist and comp., B. Wurzbach, Lobenstein, Nov. 24, 1817. S. under F. Schneider. Teacher in Dresden. Comp. numerous Pf. works, among which are Schneeglöcklein, op. 19; Fisherlied, op. 35 ; Reiterlied, op. 38 ; Unter dem Lindenbaum, op. 39 ; Tonblitthen, op. 43 ; Scherzo, op. 46 ; Romance, op. 52 ; Silberquell, op. 74 ; Tannhäuser, transcribed, op. 94 ; Flying Dutchman (Wagner), transcribed, op. 122. He has also comp. symphonies for orch., concerto for Pf. and orch., trios for Pf. and strings, etc.

SPINOLA (J. J. De Virués y). Author of "An Original and Condensed Grammar of Harmony, Counterpoint, and Musical Composition ; or the Generation of Euphony reduced to Natural Truth, preceded by the Elements of Music..." Lond., 1850, 8vo. With F. T. A. Chaluz de Vernevil.

SPITTA (Julius August Philipp). German writer, B. Wechold, Hanover, Dec. 27, 1841. S. at Göttingen Univ. Prof. of Musical History in Berlin Univ. Director of Berlin High School for Music. Author of "Johann Sebastian Bach," Leipzig, 1873-80, 2 vols., 8vo, and other works.

SPOFFORTH (Reginald). English comp., B. Southwell, Notts, 1768 [1767?] S. under his uncle, Thomas Spofforth, org. of Southwell Collegiate Ch. ; and Dr. B. Cooke. Gained two prizes given by Nobleman's Catch Club. D. Kensington, London, Sept. 8, 1827.

WORKS.—Set of Six Glees, Lond. [1799] ; A Collection of Glees, compiled from the Unpublished Manuscripts of the late Mr. Spofforth, carefully collated with the Originals, by W. Hawes, Lond., fo., n. d. ; The Christmas Box, a variety of Bagatelles for 1, 2, and 3 voices, with Pf. accompaniment, 2 books, Lond., n. d. *Single Glees:* Hail, smiling morn (in No. 1), 1799 ; Come bounteous May ; How calm the evening ; Fill high the grape's exulting stream (prize), 1810 ; Health to my dear ; My dear mistress ; The Spring, the pleasant spring ; While the madly raging nations ; Where are those hours ; See, smiling from the rosy east ; Lightly o'er the village green. Canzonets.
A composer whose name is kept in remembrance by his ever fresh glee, "Hail, smiling morn." His brother, SAMUEL, B. 1780, S. under his uncle, and in 1798 became org. of Peterborough Cath., and in 1807 org. of Lichfield Cath. D. Lichfield, June 6, 1864. Comp. chants and other church music.

SPOHR (Louis or Ludwig). German comp. and violinist, B. Brunswick, April 25, 1784. Son of a physician. S. under Dufour, Kunisch, Maucourt, and Franz Eck. Early appeared as a violinist. Went on concert tour with Franz Eck in 1802, and visited Russia, France, and Germany. Leader in band of Duke of Gotha, 1805. Married to Dorette Scheidler. Cond. first musical festival in Germany, 1809. Appeared in Vienna, 1812, and became leader of the Theatre-an-der-Wien till 1815. Made concert-tour in Germany, Italy, etc. 1816-17. Cond. of the opera at Frankfort-on-Main, 1817-19. First appeared in London, at Philharmonic Soc., March 6, 1820. Court chap.-master to the Elector of Hesse-Cassel, 1822. Revisited London, 1839, and cond. at the Norwich Festival. Cond. his "Faust" opera at London, 1852. Pensioned by Elector of Hesse-Cassel, 1857. D. Cassel, Oct. 16, 1859.

WORKS.—*Operas:* Der Zweikampf mit der Geliebten, Hamburg, 1809 ; Faust, op. 60, Frankfort, 1818 (Lond., 1852) ; Zemire und Azor, Frankfort, 1819 (in English as Azor and Zemira, by Sir Geo. Smart) ; Jessonda, op. 63, Cassel, 1822 (Lond., 1823) ; Der Berggeist, op. 73, Cassel, 1825 ; Pietro von Albano, op. 76, Cassel, 1834 ; Der Alchymist, Cassel, 1832 (Lond., 1832); Der Kreuzfahrer (the Crusaders), Cassel, 1844. *Oratorios:* Das jüngste Gericht, 1812 ; Die letzten Dinge (The Last Judgment), Düsseldorf, 1826 ; Des Heiland's letzte Stunden (Calvary), Cassel, 1835 (Norwich, 1839) ; The Fall of Babylon, Norwich, 1842 ; Vater Unser (The Lord's Prayer), by Klopstock. *Choral Works, other:* Mass, op. 54 ; Three Psalms for soli and double choir, op. 85 ; Six four-part songs for male voices, op. 90; Hymn, St. Cæcilia, op. 97 ; God, thou art Great, hymn, op. 98 ; Six four-part songs, op. 120 ; Psalm 128, for soli and chorus, op. 122 ; Psalm 84, for soli and chorus, op. 84 ; Six four-part songs, op. 151. *Symphonies:* First, in E flat, op. 20 ; Second, in D min., op. 49 ; Third, in C min., op. 78 ; Fourth, "The Consecration of Sound," op. 86 ; Fifth, in C min., op. 102 ; Sixth, "Historical," in G, op. 116 ; Seventh, for double orch., op. 121 ; Eighth, in G min., op. 137 ; Ninth, "The Seasons," op. 143. *Overtures:* No. 1 in C min., op. 12 ; "Die Prüfung" (to an unpublished opera), op. 15 a ; "Alruna" (unpub. opera), op. 21 ;

"Macbeth," in B min., op. 75; "Im ernsten styl," in D, op. 126. Concertante for 2 vns. and orch., op. 48, in A minor, and op. 88. Concertos for violin and orch., op. 1, in A min.; op. 2, in D min.; op. 7, in C min.; op. 10, in B min.; op. 17, in E flat; op. 28, in G min; op. 38, in E min.; op. 47, in A min.; op. 55, in D min.; op. 62, in A min.; op. 70, in G; op. 128, in E min.; also several concertinos, op. 79, 92, 110, etc.; Concertos for clarinet and orch., op. 26, 57; Nonetto, in F, for vn., viola, 'cello, d-bass, flute, oboe, clarinet, bassoon, and horn, op. 31; Octet, in E, for strings, clarinet, and 2 horns, op. 32; Septet for Pf., strings, flute, etc., op. 147; Sextet for strings, op. 140; Quintets for strings, op. 33, 69, 91, 106, 129, 144; also for wind insts. and Pf. and strings, op. 52 and 130; Quartets for strings, op. 4, 11, 15, 27, 29, 30, 43, 45, 58, 61, 68, 74, 82, 83, 84, 93, 141, 146, 152 (in all, about 34 single quartets); Double Quartets for strings, op. 65, in D minor; op. 77, in E flat; op. 87, in E minor, and op. 136, in B flat; Quartet concert. for 2 violins, viola, 'cello, and orch., op. 131; Trios for Pf., vn., and 'cello. Numerous potpourris, variations, duets, fantasias, rondos, etc., for vn., and orch. or Pf. and other combinations. *Songs*: op. 25, 37, 41, 72, 94, 101, 103, 105, 139, and op. 154, with accomp. for vn. and Pf. Vocal duets, and other pieces. Violin-Schule, 1831; trans. into English by John Bishop, Lond., n.d., fo., etc. Louis Spohr's Selbstbiographie, Cassel, 1860, 2 v. port.; trans. as "Autobiography of Louis Spohr," Lond., 1865, 2 v., 8vo.

Spohr was a composer of great originality and refinement, and his works are now enjoying a large amount of popularity. As a violinist he was one of the greatest who ever lived, and his Violin School is the standard instruction book everywhere. His oratorios and operas are still in use, but none of them are powerful works, though they all bear the impress of the composer's individuality, and no less so of his mannered and self-repeating style. Probably his orchestral and violin music will outlive all his other works.

SPONTINI (Luigi Gasparo Pacifico). Italian comp. and cond., B. Majolati, near Jesi, Nov. 14, 1774. S. at Cons. de' Turchini, Naples, 1791, under Salo and Tritto. Comp. to Italian court at Palermo, 1798-1800. Visited Paris, and comp. several operas, 1803. Comp. to the Empress Josephine, 1806. Cond. of the Italian opera, Paris, 1810. Cond. of Opera, and Director of Royal Music at Berlin from 1820 to 1842. Member of the Institut of France, 1838. Retired to Italy and Paris, 1843. D. Majolati, Jan. 14, 1851.

WORKS.—*Operas:* I puntigli delle donne, Rome, 1796; L'Eroismo ridicolo, Rome, 1797; Il finto Pittore, 1798; La fuga in maschera, 1800; Julie, ou le pot de fleurs, Paris, 1804; La petite maison, 1804; Milton, Paris, 1804; La Vestale, Paris, 1807; Fernand Cortez, Paris, 1809; Pélage ou le Roi de la Paix, Paris, 1814; Les Dieux rivaux, ballet (with Persius, Berton, and Kreutzer), 1816; Olympia, Paris, 1819; Nurmahal, Berlin, 1822; Alcidor, Berlin, 1825; Agnes von Hohenstaufen, Berlin, 1827. Cantatas, church music, and songs.

Spontini is chiefly known as a composer, in whose works are united the utmost measure of pompous dignity and brilliancy. All his operatic works are written in a heroic style, and very often attain a pitch of grandeur unequalled in musical art. His operas are, however, so vast in conception, and so difficult and expensive to mount successfully for the stage, that little if any attention has been accorded them in recent years.

SPORLE (Nathan James), properly BURNETT. English tenor vocalist and comp., B. Ipswich, 1812. S. under Thomas Welsh. D. March 2, 1853. Comp. many popular songs and ballads, such as—Merrie England; I dwell amid the beautiful; A calm is o'er the sea; In the days when we went gipsying; Country Life; The Lugger; and The Union Standard.

STADLER (Maximilian, Abbé). Austrian org. and comp., B. Melk, Aug. 4, 1748. Joined Benedictine order, 1766, and in 1786 was made Abbot of Lilienfeld, and in 1789, of Kremsmünster. Settled in Vienna, where he D. Nov. 8, 1833. Comp. Pf. and org. music; masses, psalms, and other church music, and the oratorio "Die Befreiung von Jerusalem," 1816. He also contributed in various ways to musical literature.

STAFFORD (William Cooke). English writer, B. York, 1793. D. Norwich, Dec. 23, 1876. Author of "A History of Music," Edinburgh, 1830, 12mo

(Constable's Miscellany, v. 52). Trans. into French, Paris, 1832, and into German, Weimar, 1835. A work of no authority, and now very generally condemned.

STAGGINS (Nicholas). English comp., was made master of the Royal music, 1682; and Mus. Doc. Cantab. First Prof. of Music in Cambridge University, 1684. Comp. Odes, Songs, etc. D. 1705.

STAINER (Jacob), or STEINER. German violin-maker, B. Absam, near Innsbrück, July 14, 1621. D. (insane), 1683.

One of the most famous German makers, and one whose instruments are held in very high repute. He worked in or near his native place, and was patronized by the Archbishop of Salzburg, the Archduke Ferdinand Charles, and others. His instruments follow the Italian or Cremona model, and are celebrated for tone and finish.

STAINER (John). English comp., org., and writer, B. London, June 6, 1840. Chorister in S. Paul's Cath., 1847-1856. Org. and choir-master of St. Benedict and St. Peter, Paul's Wharf, 1854. S. under Bayley, Steggall, and Geo. Cooper. Org. at S. Michael's Coll., Tenbury, 1856. Mus. Bac. Oxon., 1859. Org. Magdalen Coll., Oxford. B.A., Oxford, 1863. Org. to University of Oxford. Mus. Doc., 1865, and M.A., Oxon., 1866. Org. S. Paul's Cath., London, 1872. Examiner for musical degrees for various institutions. Mem. of R. A. M., and Vice-president of Coll. of Organists. Government Inspector of Music in Schools in succession to Dr. Hullah, 1882. Hon. Mus. Doc., Durham, 1885.

WORKS.—Gideon, oratorio. The Daughter of Jairus, cantata, Worcester Festival, 1878. S. Mary Magdalen, cantata, Gloucester Festival, 1883. Church Services in E flat, A and D. Communion Service. Magnificat and Nunc Dimittis, in A. Canticles of the Church arranged to Gregorian Tones. Choir Book of the Office of Holy Communion. *Anthems:* Awake, awake, put on Thy strength; Deliver me, O Lord; Drop down, ye heavens; Hosanna in the highest; I am Alpha and Omega; I saw the Lord; Lead, kindly light; O clap your hands; The Lord is in His holy temple; The morning stars sang together; The righteous live for evermore; They have taken away my Lord; They were lovely and pleasant in their lives; etc. Arrangements and other works for Exercises for Students, Lond., 1871, 8vo (3rd. ed., 1876). Dictionary of Musical org. A Theory of Harmony founded on the Tempered Scale, with Questions and Terms, Lond., 1876, la. 8vo (with W. A. Barrett); abbreviated edition, 1880. Harmony (Music Primer), Lond., 1877, 8vo. The Organ (Music Primer), Lond., 1877, 4to. The Music of the Bible, with an Account of the Development of Modern Musical Instruments from Ancient Types, Lond. [1879]. 12mo. Composition (Music Primer), Lond., 1880, 8vo. Tutor for the American Organ, Lond., 1883, 4to.

STAINS (V. D. de). Author of "Phonography, or the Writing of Sounds, in Two Parts, viz., Logography and Musicography," Lond., 1842, 8vo.

STAMATY (Camille Marie). Italian pianist and comp., B. Rome, March 23, 1811. S. under Kalkbrenner, Fessy, and Mendelssohn. Married, 1848. Chev. of Legion of Hon., 1862. D. Paris, April 19, 1870. Comp. concertos, variations, and studies for Pf., and a number of didactic works for Pianoforte. Teacher of Saint-Saëns.

STAMITZ (Johann Karl). Bohemian violinist and comp., B. Deutschbrod, 1719. D. Mannheim, 1761. Comp. sonatas, concertos, and violin music. His son KARL, B. Mannheim, May 7, 1746. D. Jena, 1801. Comp. an opera, symphonies, concertos, and other instrumental pieces.

STANFORD (Charles Villiers). Irish comp. and cond., B. Dublin, Sept. 30, 1852. Son of the late John Stanford, Esq., Examiner in the Court of Chancery, Dublin. S. under Arthur O'Leary and Sir Robert Stewart of Dublin, and in 1874-76, under Reinecke at Leipzig, and Kiel at Berlin. Org. Trinity Coll., Cambridge, 1873. Cond. of University Musical Soc. Graduated in Classical honours, Cambridge, 1874. M.A., Cambridge, 1877. Prof. of comp. and orch. playing at Royal Coll. of Music, London. Hon. Mus. Doc. Oxon., 1883. Cond. of the Bach Choir, 1885.

574 STA — STA

WORKS.—Op. 1. Set of Songs from George Eliot's "Spanish Gypsy"; op. 2. Courante, Sarabande and Gavotte for Pf.; op. 3. Toccata for Pf.; op. 4. Six Songs of Heine; op. 5. The Resurrection, cantata, poem by Klopstock, for tenor solo, chorus and orch., Cambridge, May, 1875; op. 6. Overture, Songs, and Entr'actes to Tennyson's drama "Queen Mary," Gentlemen's Concerts, Manchester, March, 1880; op. 7. Six Songs of Heine, 2nd set; op. 8. The 46th Psalm for soli, chorus and orch., Cambridge, 1877; op. 9. Sonata for Pf. and 'cello; op. 10. Morning, Communion and Evening Service in B flat; op. 11. Sonata for Pf. and violin; op. 12. Festival Evening Service in A, for chorus, orch. and org., Festival of Sons of the Clergy, St. Paul's Cath., Lond., 1880; op. 13. Three Intermezzi for Pf. and violin, clarinet, or 'cello; op. 14. Songs; op. 15. Quartet for Pf. and strings in F (1879); op. 16. Awake my Heart. choral hymn (Klopstock); op. 17. Serenade for orch., in five movements, Birmingham Festival, 1882; op. 18. Cavalier Songs; op. 19. Six Songs; op. 20. Pf. Sonata, in D flat, 1884; op. 21. Elegiac Ode, Norwich Fest., 1884; op. 22. The Three Holy Children, oratorio, Birmingham Fest., 1885; op. 23. Choruses and incidental music to "Eumenides" of Œschylus, Cambridge, 1885; op. 24. The Revenge, ballad for chorus and orch., Leeds Fest., 1886. *Operas*: The Veiled Prophet of Khorassan, Hanover, Feb. 6, 1881; Savonarola, Hamburg, 1884; The Canterbury Pilgrims, London, 1884. Symphony for orch., in B flat, Crystal Palace, 1879; Elegiac symphony for orch., Cambridge, 1882, Gloucester Festival, 1883. Festival overture for orch., Gloucester Festival, 1877. Concerto for 'cello and orch. Quintet for Pf. and strings. Fifty Irish Melodies, arranged and edited, 1883. Song Book for Schools, 1884. Songs and other works.

STANHOPE (Charles, Third Earl). English peer and scientist, author of "Principles of the Science of Tuning Instruments with Fixed Tones," Lond., 1806, 8vo.

STANISLAUS (F.) Comp. of present time, has published "The Lancashire Witches...," an opera. Numerous Songs, Part-songs, and other music.

STANISTREET (Henry Dawson). English org. and comp., was a chorister in York Cath. Mus. Bac. Oxon., 1862. Mus. Doc., Dublin, 1872. Org. at Bandon, Cork. Comp. anthems and other music. D. Dublin, Aug. 1, 1883.

STANLEY (Albert Augustus). American comp. and org., B. Manville, R.I., May 25, 1851. S. at Leipzig Cons. under Wenzel, Papperitz, Paul, and E. F. Richter, 1871-75. Org. of Grace Ch. (Episcopal), Providence, Rhode Island. Comp. org. fugues; a suite for vn. and Pf.; Psalm of Victory, solo, chorus and orch.; Part-songs, and songs. Has given organ recitals in various parts of America.

STANLEY (John). English org. and comp., B. London, Jan. 17, 1713. Blind from infancy. S. under J. Reading and Greene. Org. of All Hallows, Bread St., Lond., 1724; St. Andrews, Holborn, 1726. Mus. Bac. Oxon., 1729. Org. of the Temple Ch., 1734. Master of the King's Band of Music, 1779. D. London, May 19. 1786.
WORKS.—*Oratorios*: Jephthah, 1757; Zimri, 1760; The Fall of Egypt, 1774. Arcadia, or the Shepherd's Wedding, 1761. Twelve Cantatas for a Voice, harpsichord and violin [1742]. Three Cantatas and Three Songs for a Voice and Instruments. Three Sets of Organ Voluntaries. Eight Solos for a Flute, Violin, or Harpsichord, op. 1. Six do., op. 4.

STANLEY (Samuel). English comp., B. Birmingham, 1797. D. 1822. Precentor in Carr's Lane Congregational Chap., Birmingham. Comp. a number of melodious hymn tunes, of which the best known is probably "Warwick." "Twenty-four Tunes, in Four Parts," Birmingham, n. d. "Nineteen Psalm, Hymn, and Charity Hymn Tunes," Birmingham, n. d.

STARCK. See BRONSART.

STARK (Humphrey John). English comp. and org., B. May 22, 1854. Mus. Bac. Oxon., 1875. Org. and choir-master Holy Trinity Ch., Tulse Hill, London, 1875. One of the founders of Trinity Coll, London, and Hon. Registrar and Visiting Examiner of same. Comp. Festival Setting of the Magnificat and Nunc Dimittis in D; Evening Service, with orch. accomp.; anthems; Organ music and songs.

STARK (Ludwig). German teacher, comp., and writer, B. Munich, June 19, 1831. Founded, in association with Lebert and others, the Stuttgart Cons. of

Music. He has written a number of didactic works for Pf., including a "Pianoforte School," with Lebert, and has comp. a number of original songs, Pf. pieces, etc. D. Stuttgart, Mar. 22, 1884.

STAUDIGL (Joseph). Austrian bass vocalist, B. Wöllersdorf, April 14, 1807. Chorister in Karnthnerthor Theatre, Vienna. Chor. in Court Chapel, 1831. Appeared at all the principal concerts in Vienna, as leading bass. Appeared in England, and in 1846 he sang in Mendelssohn's "Elijah" at Birmingham. Became insane latterly, and was confined in an Asylum in Vienna, where he D. March 28, 1861. He was one of the most famous bass singers of his time, and was great in oratorio music, and in the lieder of Schubert.

STEED (Albert Orlando). English comp. and writer, B. 1839. D. Oct. 25, 1881. Author of "Music in Play, and Music in Earnest," Lond., 1873; and comp. of anthems, songs, etc.

STEENKISTE. See GRAS.

STEETZ (William). German writer, author of "Treatise on the Elements of Music in a Series of Letters to a Lady," Tiverton, 1812, 4to.

STEFFANI (Agostino). Italian comp., B. Castelfranco, Venice, 1655. S. music under Bernabei. Chamber musician at Munich. Took holy orders, 1680, and became Abbot of Lipsing. Chap.-master at court of Hanover, and director of opera there. Much engaged in the political life of his time. Made Bishop of Spigna. President of Academy of Ancient Music, London. D. Frankfort-on-Main, 1730.

WORKS.—*Operas*: Marco Aurelio, 1681; Il Solone, 1685; Servio Tullio, 1686; Alarico in Baltha, 1687; Niobe, 1688; Enrico detto il Leone, 1689; Alcide, 1692; Alexandre l'Orgueilleux, 1695; Roland, 1696; Alcibiade, 1697; Atalante, 1698; Il Trionfo del Fato, 1699. Psalmodia Vespertina...1674; Janus Quadrifons tribus vocibus...1685; Sonata da camera a due violini, alto e continuo, 1679; Duetti da Camera a Soprana e Contralto, 1683.

STEGGALL (Charles). English org. and comp., B. London, June 3, 1826. S. at R. A. M. under Sterndale, Bennett, etc. Org. of Christ Chap., Maida Hill, 1847; Christ Church, Paddington, 1855; and Lincoln's Inn, 1864. Prof. of Harmony and org. at R. A. M., 1851. Mus. Bac. and Doc., Cantab., 1851. Comp. church services in F and G. *Anthems*: God came from Teman; Hear ye and give ear; Have mercy upon me; He was as the morning star; O clap your hands; Praised be the Lord; Remember now thy Creator; Turn Thy face from my sins. Sacred cantata, Rejoice in the Lord, for voices and orchestra. Orchestral service in C. Instruction Book for the Organ, and numerous compositions and arrangements for that instrument. Editor of Bach's Motetts, and composer of about 100 Hymn Tunes, Carols, etc., contributed to various Collections.

STEIBELT (Daniel). German pianist and comp., B. 1755 or 1764-5. Son of a Pf. manufacturer. Patronised by William III. of Prussia, who had him educated under Kirnberger. Resided in Paris and London, from 1796, and made concert tours in various parts of Europe. Chap.-master to the Emperor Alex. of Russia. D. St. Petersburg, Sept. 20, 1823.

WORKS.—*Operas and ballets*: Romeo et Juliette, 1793; Albert and Adelaide, London, 1799; Le Retour de Zephyr, 1802; Le Jugement du berger Paris, Lond., 1804. La belle Laitière, 1805; La Fête de Mars, 1806; Condrillon; Sargines, etc. *Pianoforte*: Concertos, sonatas, rondos, variations, fantasias, and numerous other single pieces in large numbers. Quartets, trios, duets, and other concerted pieces of all kinds for various combinations. Overtures for orch., etc.

Steibelt is a composer whose once brilliant reputation has completely faded. Scarcely a single piece of his composition is now ever used, save for teaching purposes. Most of his works were written for merely temporary purposes, but among them are many numbers of great brilliancy and some originality.

STEINER (Jacob). See STAINER (Jacob).

STEINWAY & SONS. American firm of pianoforte manufacturers, established in New York, 1853. The founder of the firm was HENRY ENGELHARDT STEINWAY, B. Wolfshagen, Brunswick, Feb. 15, 1797. Settled in America, 1849, and established the now-famous firm of Steinway & Sons, in company with his sons. Originators of the "Iron Frame" system of Pf. manufacture, for which the firm has gained prizes in Exhibitions all over the world. In 1875 they established a branch in London. The instruments of the firm are noted for the power and beauty of their tone, and for the solidity and perfection of the workmanship.

STENDHAL. See BEYLE.

STENHOUSE (William). Scottish writer and collector, B. Roxburghshire, 1773. Accountant in Edinburgh. D. Edinburgh, Nov. 10, 1827. Published "Illustrations of the Lyric Poetry and Music of Scotland..." Edin., 1853, 8vo, (edited by David Laing, LL.D.)

STEPHENS (Catherine), Countess of Essex. English soprano vocalist, B. London, Dec. 18, 1791. S. under Lanza and Thomas Welsh. Appeared in Italian opera, 1812. Appeared in Arne's "Artaxerxes," 1813. From then on till 1835 she appeared at all the principal concerts in London, and at the Provincial Concerts. She also appeared in English opera at Covent Garden and Drury Lane Theatres. Retired, 1835. Married to the Earl of Essex, 1838. D. London, Feb. 22, 1882. Well-known in her day as "Kitty Stephens," and famed as an admirable exponent of English ballad music.

STEPHENS (Charles Edward). English comp., pianist, and teacher, B. London, March 18, 1821. Nephew of the preceding. S. under C. Potter, J. A. Hamilton, and Henry Blagrove. Org. S. Mark's, Myddleton Sq., 1843; Trinity Ch., Paddington, 1846; St. John, Hampstead, 1856; St. Mark's, St. John's Wood, 1862-63; S. Clement Danes, Strand, 1864-69; S. Saviour's, Paddington, 1872-75. Mem. of Roy. Soc. of Musicians, 1843. Associate, 1850, and Mem., 1857, of Philharmonic Soc.; Hon. Treasurer since 1880. F. C. O., 1865. Hon. mem. of R. A. M., 1870. Original Mem. of Musical Assoc., 1874. Hon. Licentiate in Music, Trin. Coll., London, 1877. Mem. and Hon. Treas. South Eastern Section, National Soc. of Professional Musicians, 1886.

WORKS.—Op. 1. Trio for Pf., vn., and 'cello, 1851; op. 2. Quartet for Pf. and strings, 1853; op. 3. Two movements for org., 1857; op. 4. Duo concertant for 2 Pfs., 1859; op. 5. Mathilde, valse, Pf.; op. 6. Sehnsucht, nocturne, Pf.; op. 7. Two movements for org., 1863; op. 8. First Pf. sonata, 1866; op. 9. Allegro-rhapsodie, Pf.; op. 10. Idylle Rustique, Pf.; op. 11. Fantasia for org.; op. 12. O Praise the Lord all ye nations, anthem, 1868; op. 13. Impromptu, Pf.; op. 14. Romance, Pf.; op. 15. Two movements for org., 1869; op. 16. Offertoire for org., 1870; op. 17. Reverie, Pf.; op. 18. Marche guerrière, Pf., 1872; op. 19. Duo brillant, Pf., 4 hands, 1875; op. 20. Printemps, Pf. piece, 1882; op. 21. Prize string quartet in G, 1880; op. 22. Prize string quartet, in F, 1880 (both Trinity Coll. prizes); op. 23. Magnificat and Nunc Dimittis, in F, comp. for 8th festival of Lond. Church Choir Assoc., S. Paul's Cath., 1880; op. 24. Fantasia for org., 1882; op. 25. Sonata Pincevole, Pf. and flute, 1883. Symphony for orch., concert overtures (A Dream of Happiness, 1873, etc.), and chamber music in MS. Complete Services for the Church, 1847 and 1853. Part-song, Come, fill ye right merrily (gained prize offered by Leslie's choir, 1858); Glees, songs, and Pf. pieces, unnumbered. "Bemrose's Choral Chant Book," edited and enlarged with biographical notices of composers, Lond., 1882.

STERKEL (Johann Franz Xaver, Abbé). German comp., B. Würzburg, Dec. 3, 1750. Took holy orders, and became org. and chaplain at Aschaffenburg. Chap.-master to Elector of Mayence, and afterwards at Ratisbon. D. Ratisbon, Oct. 21, 1817. Comp. an opera; Symphonies for orch., op. 7, 11, 35, etc.; overtures; concertos; quintet and trios for strings; Sonatas and variations for Pf.; Songs, canzonets, and choral music.

STERLING (Antoinette). American contralto vocalist, B. Sterlingville, N.Y., Jan. 23, 1850. S. under Marchesi, Viardot, and Garcia in Europe. Returned to America, 1871, and became widely known as a concert singer. Appeared in London, 1873, and since then has resided in England. Married to Mr. John MacKinlay, 1875. She has appeared with brilliant success in London, and at the principal provincial festivals.

STERN (Julius). German cond. and comp., B. Breslau, Aug. 8, 1820. S. under Rungenhagen and Maurer. Founder of the Stern Choral Society, 1847; and in conjunction with Kullak and Marx, of the Stern Cons. of Music, Berlin, 1850. D. Berlin, Feb. 27, 1883. Comp. of songs, vocal exercises, and choral music.

STEVEN (James). Scottish musician and psalm-collector, was a music-seller in Glasgow early in the present century. He compiled "A Selection of Psalm and Hymn Tunes in Four Parts...to which is added a compendious Introduction...," Glasgow [1801], Vol. I.; "A Selection of Sacred Music...," Vol. II., Glasgow, n. d.; "A Selection of Sacred Music...," Vol. III., n. d.; Vols. IV. and V., same title. "Selection of Original Sacred Music...," Vol. VI., edited by John Turnbull, Glasgow [1833]. "Harmonia Sacra, a Selection of the most approved Psalm and Hymn Tunes," Glasgow, 2 vols., n. d. Flute duets, etc.

STEVENS (Charles Isaac). English writer, author of "An Essay on the Theory of Music," Gottingen, 1863, 8vo.

STEVENS (Richard John Samuel). English comp. and org., B. London, 1757. Chor. S. Paul's Cath. under Savage. Org. of the Temple Church, 1786; and of the Charter House, 1796. Gained prizes from Catch Club, 1782 and 1786. Prof. of Music Gresham Coll., 1801. D. Peckham, London, Sept. 23, 1837.

Works.—Eight Glees for 4 and 5 voices, op. 3, Lond. [1790]; Eight Glees, op. 4, Lond. [1792]; Ten Glees for 3, 4, 5 and 6 voices, op. 5, Lond. [1800]; Seven Glees, op. 6, Lond. [1808]. Eight Glees, expressly composed for Ladies. Sacred Music for 1, 2, 3 and 4 voices, consisting of Selections from the works of the most esteemed composers, Italian and English, Lond., n. d., 3 vols., fo. Ten Songs, with an accomp. for two violins, Lond., n. d.

One of the most popular of English glee composers. Some of his works are in constant use at the present time. Among his best known glees are "From Oberon in Fairy Land," "Sigh no more Ladies," "Ye spotted snakes," "The cloud-capt towers," "Crabbed age and Youth," etc.

STEVENS (William S.) English pianist and comp., B. Westminster, 1778. S. under R. J. S. Steven, Dr. Cooke, and T. Smart. Author of "Treatise on Pianoforte Expression, containing the Principles of Fine Playing on that Instrument,"...Lond., 1811, fo. He comp. Pf. music and songs.

STEVENSON (Sir John Andrew). Irish comp., B. Dublin, 1761-62. S. under Dr. Murphy. Chor. in S. Patrick's Cath., 1775-80. Vicar-choral, do., 1783. Mus. Doc., Dublin, 1791. Vicar-choral Christ Church Cath., Dublin, 1800; and chorister in Trinity Coll., Dublin. Married to daughter of Mr. Morton of the Custom House, Dublin. Knighted, 1803. D. Dublin, Sept. 14, 1833.

Works.—Music to The Son-in-Law; The Patriot; Border Feuds; The Bedouins; Spanish Patriots; The Agreeable Surprise; The Contract, 1783; and Love in a Blaze, 1800, etc. Thanksgiving, an oratorio. Morning and Evening Services and Anthems for the Use of the Church of England,...Lond., 2 vols., fo. [1825]. *Glees:* See our oars with feathered spray; Welcome friends of harmony; To thy lover, dear, discover; Hail! to the mighty pow'r of song; Dublin Cries (round), etc. Canons, catches, and Glees (collected), Lond., fo. Duets and songs. Moore's Irish Melodies, with symphonies and accompaniments by Sir John Stevenson and Henry R. Bishop, 10 parts and supplement, 1807-34; reissued, harmonized, 1858. A Series of Sacred Songs, Duets, and Trios, the words by Thomas Moore... London, n.d. A Selection of Popular National Airs, with symphonies and accompaniments by Sir John Stevenson...Lond., 1818, 2 v., 4to, illust.

STEWART (Mrs. Colonel). Authoress of "Critical Remarks on the Art of Singing," Lond., 1836, 4to.

STEWART (Charles). Scottish collector, B. Glenlyon House, Fortingall, Dec. 24, 1823. Published "The Killin Collection of Gaelic Songs, with Music and Translations," Edin., 1884, 4to.

N 2

STEWART (Charles). Scottish dance-music comp., published "A Collection of Strathspeys, Reels, Giggs, etc., with a Bass for the Violoncello or Harpsichord," n.d., fo.

STEWART (Neill). Scottish comp. and editor, flourished in Edinburgh in latter half of last century. Published A New Collection of Scots and English Tunes, adapted to the Guitar...Edin. [1760]. A Collection of the Newest and Best Minuets...[1770]. A Second Collection of Airs and Marches for Two Violins, German flutes, and Hautboys, all of which have Basses for the Violoncello or Harpsichord, Edin. A Collection of Scots Songs adapted for a Voice or Harpsichord, Edin. [1790]. A Collection of Catches, Canons, Glees, Duettos, &c., selected from the Works of the most Eminent Composers, Antient and Modern, Edin. [1780].

STEWART (Robert B.) Scottish violinist of present century. Long connected with all the concerts and musical assemblies in Edinburgh. He D. Edinburgh, in 1884. He published in Edinr. "A New Set of Military Quadrilles, arranged for the Pianoforte," 1826, 4to.

STEWART (Sir Robert Prescott). Irish comp. and prof., B. Dublin, Dec. 16, 1825. Son of C. F. Stewart, librarian of the King's Inns, Dublin. Chor. Christ Church Cath., Dublin; Org. of do., 1844. Org. of Chap. of Trinity Coll., 1844. Cond. of University of Dublin Choral Soc., 1846. Mus. Doc., Dublin, 1851. Org. and vicar-choral, S. Patrick's Cath., 1852. Prof. of Music in Dublin University, 1861. Knighted, 1872. Cond. of Dublin Philharmonic Soc., 1873.

WORKS.—A Winter Night's Wake, cantata; The Eve of S. John, cantata; Ode on Shakespeare, Birmingham Festival, 1870; Ode for the opening of Cork Exhibition, 1852. Service in G. *Anthems*: In the Lord put I my trust; If ye love Me, keep My commandments; Thou, O God, art praised in Zion. Glees and Partsongs, including a number of prize compositions. Church Hymnal. Music, a Lecture, 1863; also papers read before Social Science Assoc. Contributions to periodical literature, and Grove's Dictionary of Music.

STIASTNÝ (Johann). Bohemian violoncellist and comp., B. Prague, 1774. Musical director at Nuremberg. Appeared in London and Paris. D. (?) Comp. sonatas, concertos, duets, trios, and other pieces, for violoncello, all of great originality and merit.

STIEHL (Heinrich F. D.). German org. and comp., B. Lübeck, Aug. 5, 1829. S. under Moscheles, Gade, and Hauptmann. Resided in Vienna, London (1872-73), Belfast (1874-77), and now org. and cond. in Revel. Comp. Jerry and Bateley, operetta; Trios for Pf.; Sonatas for Pf., and Pf. and violin; Numerous single pieces for Pf., numbering about 200 in all.

STIELER (J.). German writer, author of "Great German Composers, Biographical Notices, with some Account of their several Works, adapted for the Young," Lond., 1879, 8vo. Trans. by C. P. S.

STILLIE (Thomas Logan). Scottish amateur musician and writer, B. Maybole, Ayrshire, 1832. D. Glasgow, June 6, 1883. Was musical critic of *Glasgow Herald* for a long period. He left a valuable musical library to the University of Glasgow.

STILLINGFLEET (Benjamin). English poet and naturalist, B. 1702. D. 1771. Wrote words of five oratorios, and a "Treatise on the Principles and Power of Harmony," Lond., 1771, a commentary on Tartini's "Trattato di Musica."

STILLINGFLEET (Henry Anthony). English divine, author of "The Antiquity and Advantages of Church Music, a Sermon," 1803, 8vo.

STIMPSON (James). English org. and writer, B. Lincoln, Feb. 29, 1820. Chor. Durham Cath., 1827. Articled to Mr. Ingham, org. of Carlisle Cath., 1834. Org. of S. Andrew's Newcastle, 1836; and of Carlisle Cath., 1841. Org. of Town Hall, Birmingham, 1842, and of S. Paul's Ch. there. Founded the Birmingham Festival Choral Soc., 1843, and was cond. of it till 1855.

Prof. of Music at the Birmingham Institution for the Blind. Has given important organ recitals in Birmingham, and was the org. on the production of Mendelssohn's "Elijah." Editor of "The Organist's Standard Library." His brother, ORLANDO, J., music master at the Durham Diocesan Training Coll. for Masters, was Mus. Bac., Oxon., 1871. He is author of a "Singing Class Book for Use in Elementary Schools," Glasgow, 1877, 12mo.

STIRLING (Elizabeth), MRS. F. A. BRIDGE. English comp. and org., B. Greenwich, Feb. 26, 1819. S. under W. B. Wilson, Edward Holmes, J. A. Hamilton, and Macfarren. Org. of All Saints, Poplar, 1839-58. Org. S. Andrew's, Undershaft, 1858-80. Married to Mr. Frederick A. Bridge, May, 16, 1863.

WORKS.—*Part-Songs:* Nine Choral Songs: All among the barley, The dream, War song, The hermit, The early settlers, Red leaves, An emigrant's song, Friendship, love, and truth, Parted friends ; Buttercups and daisies ; Disdain returned ; Sleeping, why now sleeping ; The forester ; Song of the poppies ; Now autumn strews on every plain ; Faded flowers ; The portrait ; Vernal showers ; Oh! the merry day ; The warrior, etc., in all about 50 pieces. Two grand voluntaries for org. ; Six pedal fugues and eight slow movements for the org. Songs, Pf. music, etc.

STOCKHAUSEN (Julius). German barytone vocalist, B. Paris, July 22, 1826. S. under Stamaty and E. Garcia. Sang in London, 1849, 1851, 1870, etc. Music-director at Hamburg, 1862. Director of Stern's Vocal Society in Berlin, 1874. Prof. of Singing in Frankfort Cons. He appeared in opera, and was famous for his singing of German lieder. His brother, FRANZ, B. Gebweiler, Jan. 30, 1839. S. under Alkan, and is a cond. at Stuttgart. Both sons of MARGARET STOCKHAUSEN, *née* SCHMUCK, a German soprano vocalist who sang in London and Paris with success in 1828-40. B. Gebweiler, 1803. D. Colmar, Oct. 6, 1877.

STOKES (Charles). English org. and comp., B. 1784. Chor. S. Paul's Cath., Lond. Org. at Croydon, etc. D. London, April 14, 1839. Comp. anthems, glees, songs, and organ music.

STOLTZ (Rosine). French mezzo-soprano vocalist, B. Paris, Feb. 13, 1815. Appeared in operas of Weber, Halévy, Donizetti, Rossini, etc.

STONARD (William). English org. and comp. Org. of Christ Church Cath., Oxford. Mus. Doc. Oxon., 1608. D. 1630. Comp. anthems in Clifford's Coll., and in MS. in Music School of Oxford.

STONE (William H.) English writer, author of "Sound and Music," Lond., 1876 ; "Elementary Lessons on Sound," Lond., 1879 ; "Scientific Basis of Music" (Music Primer), Lond., n. d., 8vo.

STORACE (Anna Selina). Italian soprano vocalist, B. London, 1766. S. under her father and Rauzzini. Appeared as a concert vocalist in London, 1774-1778. S. at Venice under Sacchini. Sang at Florence, 1780 ; Parma, 1781 ; Milan, 1782 ; and Vienna, 1784. Married to J. A. Fisher, 1784, and separated from him soon afterwards. Appeared in Mozart's "Figaro," at Vienna, 1786. Returned to London and appeared in English and Italian opera from 1787. Sang at Handel Festival, 1791. Retired, 1808. D. Dulwich, Aug. 24, 1817.

STORACE (Stephen). Italian comp., B. London, 1763. Son of Stefano Storace, an Italian double-bass player. S. under his father, and at Naples in Cons. of S. Onofrio. Resided in London as comp. to the principal theatres. D. London, March 19, 1796.

WORKS.—*Musical Dramas:* Gli sposi malcontenti, 1785 ; Gli Equivoci, Vienna, 1786 ; The Doctor and Apothecary, Lond., 1788 ; The Haunted Tower, 1789 ; No Song no Supper, 1790 ; The Siege of Belgrade, 1791 ; Cave of Trophonius, 1791 ; The Pirates, 1792 ; Dido, 1792 ; The Prize, 1793 ; My Grandmother, 1793 ; The Glorious First of June, 1794 ; Lodoiska, 1794 ; The Cherokee, 1794 ; The Iron Chest (Colman), 1796 ; Mahmoud, 1796 ; Three and the Deuce. His other works are mostly songs, published singly.

Storace is a composer of the same school as Shield. His melodies are remarkable for their agreeable and fluent character, and his concerted music for its sweetness and freshness. He was thoroughly English in his style, and is reckoned among the best of our national ballad composers. Of his works, "No Song no Supper" has been reprinted.

STORER (John). English org. and comp., B. Hulland, near Derby, May 18, 1858. S. under Dr. John Naylor. Org. and choir-master of S. Michael's, Whitby, 1879; Do., Scarborough Parish Church. Comp. anthems, glees, songs, and Pf. music.

STRADELLA (Alessandro). Italian comp., B. Naples, 1645. D. about 1679-81. Celebrated chiefly on account of a romantic episode in his career, which will be found in any book of musical anecdotes. He comp. operas, oratorios, cantatas, and other vocal works.

He is a musician of no weight or importance in music, and save for the fact that his career has been made the subject of several operas, and that his deliverance from assassins is frequently cited as an instance of the power of music, it would not be necessary to do more than mention his name. The air, "Pietà! Signor!" attributed to Stradella, is supposed to be of modern composition.

STRADIVARI (Antonio), ANTONIUS STRADIVARIUS. Italian violin-maker, B. [Cremona], about 1650. Supposed to have worked with Niccolo Amati till 1648, when he established himself as a violin-maker on his own account, and turned out a very large number of instruments till his death at Cremona, in December, 1737.

Stradivarius improved the model of the violin, and increased its tone-power, and his instruments, when genuine, are preferred above all others. He made violins, violas, and violoncellos, and those made in the later part of his career are most sought after by collectors. They are the instruments chiefly used by all great solo violinists, and as a rule fetch, when in good condition, prices ranging from £80 to £800. His sons FRANCESCO and ORTOBONE, also made violins.

STRAKOSCH (Maurice). Hungarian pianist, comp., and impresario, B. Lemberg, 1825. S. under Sechter at Vienna. Organised and directed in the United States, from 1855, numerous operatic and concert companies which travelled all over the country. Most of the best European singers have been engaged by him, or his brother MAX, who joined in his management in 1860. Maurice Strakosch has comp. some Pf. and vocal works. He is married to Amalia Patti, an elder sister of the famous vocalist.

STRATTON (Stephen Samuel). English comp., writer, and lecturer, B. London, Dec. 19, 1840. First S. Pf. under Miss Elizabeth Chamberlaine (Mrs. H. von Höff). S. org. under Chas. Gardner, and comp. under Charles Lucas. Prof. of music at Totteridge Park School, Herts, 1864-6. Original member of Coll. of Organists, 1864. Settled in Birmingham as teacher and org., 1866. Org. of Edgbaston Parish Ch. for a number of years. Established the Popular Chamber Concerts in Birmingham, 1879, and at them brought forward many new works by British and Foreign composers for the first time, including Anderton, Bache, Bennett, Carrodus, Cowen, Griesbach, Heap, King, Kjerulf, Lucas, Mackenzie, Mellon, Onslow, Parry, Praeger, Prout, Sharp, Stanford, Stephens, Ward, and Westrop. Assoc. of Philharmonic Soc., London, 1882. Associate musical critic of *Birmingham Daily Post*. Has lectured in Birmingham, and other towns in the Midlands, on musical topics. Has lectured on "Woman in relation to Musical Art," and on other subjects, before the Musical Association, London.

WORKS.—Church Music, a collection of Hymn Tunes, Chants, etc., Lond., n.d. The Nicene Creed. Te Deum. *Part Songs*: Christabel; Hark, the nightingale is singing; Merrily every bosom boundeth; May Day; Monarch Winter; Summer is but fleeting. Two-part songs for the use of schools, several numbers. *Songs*: Arise, my love; Cricketer's song; Dreaming in the shadow; Hark! sweet bells are ringing; Lover's star; Little rosebud; Magic harp; Sun and the flower; That smile of thine; Winter and spring; The woodman; etc. *Pianoforte*: The ride; Musings (rondoletto); The merry heart; Evening by the sea; Gondolier's song (barcarolle); etc.

STRAUSS (Johann). Austrian comp. and cond., B. Vienna, March 14, 1804. S. under Seyfried. Organised an orch. and appeared with it in various parts of Germany, Belgium, France, and Britain, 1833-38, and afterwards in Europe. Cond. of Court Balls, Vienna. D. Vienna, Sept. 25, 1849. Comp. a large number of waltzes, quadrilles, galops, polkas, marches, etc., most of which had great success on publication. His three sons are noted below.

STRAUSS (Johann). Austrian comp., B. Vienna, Oct. 25, 1825. Organised a band of his own, and on his father's death, combined the two bands and travelled with it in Europe. Married Jetty Treffz, singer, 1862. Cond. of the Court Balls, 1863. Comp. of numerous operettas, Indigo und die vierzig Räuber, 1871; Die Fledermaus, 1874; Cagliostro, 1875; Mathusalem, 1877; Blinde Kuh, 1878; Die lustige Krieg, etc. His dances are innumerable, and consist chiefly of waltzes, some of which became extremely popular. His brother JOSEPH, B. Vienna, Aug. 22, 1827. D. there, July 22, 1870. He also had his band, but is best known by his dance music, which is of a very high class. The youngest brother, EDUARD, B. Vienna, Feb. 14, 1835. S. under Preyer. Cond. at St. Petersburg. Organised a band and travelled with it in Germany. In 1885, he appeared with his band at the Inventions Exhibition, London. His works consist of dance pieces of various kinds.

STREABBOG. See GOBBAERTS.

STREETER (Dr. H.). American writer, author of "Voice-Building," Boston, n.d. "Primary Elements of Music," Boston, n.d. Vocal Exercises.

STRUNGK (Nicolas Adam). German violinist and comp., B. Zell, 1640. D. Leipzig, Sept. 20, 1700. Comp. operas, violin music, etc.

SUCH (Edwin Charles). English comp., B. London, Aug. 11, 1840. Educ. at Merchant Taylor's school, and at London University Coll. B.A., London University Coll. S. at Cologne under Dr. F. Hiller, from 1861. Mus. Bac., Cantab., 1877. Comp. "Narcissus and Echo," a dramatic cantata; "The Watersprite," cantata; "God is our Refuge," 46th Psalm for solo, chorus, and orch.; Anthems, part-songs, songs, and Pf. pieces.

SUCHER (Josef). Hungarian cond. and comp., B. Döbör, Eisenburg, Nov. 23, 1844. S. under Sechter at Vienna. Cond. at Vienna and Leipzig. Married Rosa Hasselbeck, 1877, who has appeared in London (1882), in opera, with great success. Cond. at Hamburg, where his wife is prima donna. Comp. orchestral works, lieder, etc.

SULLIVAN (Sir Arthur Seymour). Comp. and cond., B. London, May 13, 1842. Son of Thomas Sullivan, prof. at Kneller Hall. Chor. in Chap.-Royal under Helmore. Elected Mendelssohn Scholar, R.A.M., 1856. S. at R. A. M. under Goss and Bennett till 1858. S. Leipzig Cons. under Plaidy, Moscheles, Richter, Rietz, Hauptmann, 1858-61. Cond. of Leeds Festivals; Promenade Concerts, London; Glasgow Musical Festivals, etc. Principal of National Training School of Music, 1876-1881. Mem. of Council of Royal Coll. of Music. Hon. Mus. Doc., Cantab., 1876; do., Oxon., 1879. Knighted, May 15, 1883.

WORKS.—*Operas and Operettas:* The Contrabandista, 1868; Cox and Box, 1869; Trial by Jury (Gilbert), Lond., 1875; The Sorcerer, 1877; H. M. S. Pinafore, or the Lass that Loves a Sailor, 1878; The Pirates of Penzance, 1880; Patience, or Bunthorn's Bride, 1881; Iolanthe, 1882; Princess Ida, 1884; The Mikado, or the Town of Titipu, 1885. *Oratorios:* The Prodigal Son, 1869; The Light of the World, Birmingham, 1873; The Martyr of Antioch, Leeds, 1880. *Cantatas:* Kenilworth, Birmingham, 1864; On Shore and Sea, Albert Hall, London, 1871. *Orchestral and Dramatic:* Music for the Tempest (op. 1), Crystal Palace, 1862; The Merchant of Venice, 1871; The Merry Wives of Windsor, 1874; Henry VIII., 1878; Symphony in E, 1866; In Memoriam, overture, 1866; Marmion, overture, 1867; Overture di Ballo, 1870; Procession March, 1863; Concerto for 'cello and orch., 1866; Festival Te Deum and Domine salvum fac Reginam, in commemoration of the recovery of H. R. H. the Prince of Wales, 1872; Te Deum, jubilate, and kyrie, in D. *Anthems:* Hearken unto Me, My people; I will mention the loving kindnesses; I will worship; I will sing of Thy power; O taste and see; O love the Lord; O God, thou art worthy to be praised; Rejoice in the Lord; Sing, O Heavens; Turn Thee again; Turn Thy face from sin; We have heard with our ears. *Part-songs:* Echoes; Evening; Joy to the Victors; O hush thee, my babie; Parting gleams; Song of Peace; The long day closes; The beleagured; The last night of the year. *Songs:* The Window, or the Loves of the Wrens (Tennyson), 1871; A life that lives for you; Ah! county Guy; A weary lot is thine; Arabian love song; Christmas bells at sea; Distant shore; Dove song; Guinevere; If doughty deeds; In the summers long ago; Let me dream again, 1875; Lost chord, 1877; Love that Loves me not, 1875; Looking back; Mary Morison, 1874; Maiden's story; Mother's dream; My dear and only love; My dearest heart; Orpheus with his lute; O ma charmant; O mistress mine; O sweet and fair; Once again; Old love letters; Rosalind; St. Agnes Eve; Sweet day so cool; Snow lies white; Sailor's grave; Sweet dreamer; Sometimes; Sweethearts, 1875; Tender and True; Thou'rt passing hence; Troubadour; Willow song, etc. Hymns in various collections, of which "Onward, Christian Soldiers" is best known.

The popularity of Sir Arthur Sullivan's operatic works has never been equalled in Britain nor America. "The Sorcerer" and "H. M. S. Pinafore" were the forerunners of a series of the most brilliant and lasting successes ever obtained on the stage. In America especially, the run after "Pinafore" was for a time most tremendous, and the merry tunes of the opera were in everybody's mind. Others of the Series which gained much favour were "The Pirates of Penzance" and "Patience." "The Mikado" has equalled "Pinafore" in popularity. The music of Sir Arthur Sullivan is always that of a scholar, however trifling may be the piece on which his talents are exercised. His orchestral music is clever and effective, and his dramatic works are always appropriately and prettily treated in the matter of accompaniments. His songs and concerted vocal music have also been successful, and he no doubt holds the highest position in Britain as a popular composer at the present time. His brother FREDRICK, B. London, 1838. D. London, Jan. 18, 1877. A popular vocalist, whose clever impersonation of the Judge, in the "Trial by Jury," did much to aid its original success.

SUPPE (Franz von). Austrian comp., B. Spalato, Dalmatia, April 18, 1820. Descended from a Belgian family. Educated at University of Padua. S. at Vienna under Sechter and Seyfried. Cond. at Pressburg and Vienna. Comp. numerous operatic works, of which the following are best known:—Das Mädchen vom Lande, 1847; Die Müllerin von Burgos, 1849; Paragraph III., 1858; Zehn Mädchen und kein Mann, 1862; Franz Schubert, 1864; Schöne Galathea, 1865; Leichte Cavalerie, 1866; Freija, 1866; Isabella, 1869; Die Jungfrau von Dragant, 1870; Cannebas, 1873; Fatinitza, 1876 (Lond., 1878); Boccaccio, 1879 (Lond., 1882); Donna Juanita, 1880. Also symphonies, overtures (Dichter und Bauer), etc., masses, quartets, songs, etc. He is best known in Britain by his "Poet and Peasant" (Dichter und Bauer) overture.

SURENNE (John Thomas). English org. and comp., B. London, March 4, 1814. Org. S. George's Episcopal Chap., Edinburgh. D. Edinburgh, Feb. 3, 1878. He compiled "The Dance Music of Scotland, a Collection of all the best Reels and Strathspeys, both of the Highlands and Lowlands, for the Pianoforte," Edin. [1851], fo., 5 editions. "Songs of Scotland without Words," 1852, 8vo, and 1854 8vo. "Songs of Ireland," 1855, 8vo. A Collection of Church Music (with H. E. Dibdin), 2 vols., 4to, n. d. Psalm Tunes; Hymns; Part-songs, and songs. Students' Manual of Classical Extracts for Pf., and other instrumental compositions.

SURMAN (Joseph). English cond. and writer, B. at Chesham, 1794 [1803]. Cond. of Sacred Harmonic Soc., 1832-48. Music publisher in London. Cond. Worcester Festival. D. London, Jan. 20, 1871. He wrote "The Sacred Harmonic Society, a Statement in Reply to Charges preferred against the Conductor of the Society," London, 1848, 8vo. He had been removed from the conductorship of the Society on certain charges against his management being proved.

SÜSSMAYER (Franz Xaver). Austrian comp. and cond., B. Steyer, 1766. S. under Salieri and Mozart. Cond. of the Kärnthnerthor Court Theatre,

Vienna, 1795. D. Vienna, Sept. 17, 1803. Comp. Moses, 1792; Der Spiegel von Arkadien, 1794; Die edle Rache, 1795; Der Wildfang, 1797; Soliman der Zweite, 1799, and other operas. He is chiefly remembered as the friend and last companion of Mozart, whose death-bed he attended, and for his share in completing that composer's requiem.

SUTHERLAND (G.). Author of "A Manuel of the Theory of Music," Lond., 8vo, 2 editions to 1871.

SUTTON (Alfred James). English comp. and cond., B. Droitwich, May 1, 1827. Accompanist to Birmingham Festival Choir, 1855, and cond. of Birmingham Amateur Harmonic Assoc. Cond. of choir in Birmingham. Cond. of Edgbaston Amateur Musical Union, 1883. Comp. Serenade on Marriage of H. R. H. the Prince of Wales; Songs, Part-songs, and Pf. music. His wife is well known as an excellent soprano vocalist.

SUTTON (F. H.). Author of "Some Account of the Mediæval Organ Case still existing at Old Radnor," London, 1866.

SUTTON (R.). Author of "Elements of the Theory of Music," Lond., n. d. (Cocks).

SVENDSEN (Johan Severin). Norwegian comp., B. Christiania, Sept. 30, 1840. S. Leipzig Cons. under Hauptmann, Richter, and F. David, 1863-67, and gained the honorary medal of the Cons. Travelled as violinist in Denmark, Scotland, Ireland, and in England. Vnst. in Paris, 1868-70. Leader of the Euterpe Concerts in Leipzig. Cond. in Christiania. Visited Italy, 1877-78. Appeared in London, 1878. Now teacher and cond. in Christiania.

WORKS.—Op. 1. String quartet in A min.; op. 2. Songs; op. 3. Octet for strings in A min.; op. 4. Symphony in D; op. 5. String quartet in C; op. 6. Concerto for vn. and orch. in A; op. 7. Concerto for 'cello and orch. in D. min.; op. 8. Overture, Sigurd Slembe, 1871; op. 9. Carnaval à Paris, orch.; op. 10. Funeral March for Charles XV.; op. 11. Zorahayde, legend for orch.: op. 12. Polonaise for orch.; op. 13. Coronation March for Oscar II.; op. 14. Marriage cantata; op. 15. Symphony in B flat; op. 16. Carnaval; op. 17. Norwegian rhapsody, for orch.; op. 18. Overture, Romeo and Juliet; op. 19. Norwegian rhapsody, No. 2; op. 20. Scandinavian airs, for string quartet; op. 21-22. Norwegian rhapsodies, Nos. 3 and 4; op. 23. Five songs; op. 24. Four songs; op. 25. Romance for 'cello and Pf. (from Popper); op. 26. Romance for vn. and orch. in G; Marche humoristique for orch.

SVENDSEN (Oluf). Norwegian flute-player, B. Christiania, April 19, 1832. S. Brussels Cons. Appeared at Jullien's Concerts in London. Flute-player in Crystal Palace band; Philharmonic orch.; H. M. Theatre orch. First flute in the Queen's Private Band, 1861. Prof. of Flute at R.A.M., 1867.

SWAINE (N.). Author of "The Young Musician, or the Science of Music familiarly explained," Stroudport, n.d., 12mo.

SWELINCK or SWEELINCK (Jan Peter). Dutch org. and comp., B. Deventer, 1562. S. at Venice under Zarlino (?). Org. of the Old Church, Amsterdam. D. Amsterdam, Oct. 9, 1621. Comp. Chansons, Rimes Françaises, Psalms, and much organ music. Celebrated as the most famous Dutch organist of his period.

SWERT. See DE SWERT (JULES).

SYMMERS (James). Scottish writer, Rector of Alloa Academy. Author of "The Sol-fa Method of Singing at Sight from the Common Musical Notation," Glasgow, 1858-59, 2 parts, 8vo.

SYMMES (Thomas). English writer, B. 1678. D. 1725. Author of "Utile Dulci, or a joco-serious dialogue concerning regular singing," Boston, 1723.

SYMONDS (Henry). English comp. and org. One of the King's Band of Music. Org. of S. Martin's, Ludgate, and of the Church of S. John. D. 1730. Comp. Six Sets of Lessons for the Harpsichord, etc.

SZARVADY (Wilhelmina), *née* CLAUS. Bohemian pianist, B. Prague, Dec.

13, 1834. First appeared as pianist, 1849. Married F. Szarvady, author (D. Paris, 1882), 1856. Has performed in France, Germany, and England. Resident in Paris as teacher and pianist.

SZEKELY (Emerik). Hungarian comp. and pianist, B. Matyfalva, May 8, 1823. Appeared in Paris and London, 1846. Prof. in Buda-Pesth. Comp. music for Pf., etc.

T.

TACCHINARDI (Niccolo). Italian tenor vocalist, B. Florence, Sept. 3, 1772. Sang in churches and at concerts from 1798, and first appeared in public, 1804. Sang in Milan, 1804, and in Rome till 1811. Appeared in Paris, 1811, in an opera by Zingarelli, and afterwards in other works. Returned to Italy, 1814. Solo vocalist to Grand Duke of Tuscany, 1822. Sang in Spain, etc. D. Florence, March 14, 1859. Comp. a few vocal exercises, etc. His daughter FANNY is noticed under PERSIANI.

TADOLINI (Giovanni). Italian comp., B. Bologna, 1793. S. under Mattei and Babbini. Accompanist at Paris Opera. D. Bologna, Nov. 29, 1872. Comp. operas, canzonets, rondos, etc.

TAGLIAFICO (Joseph Dieudonné). Italian barytone vocalist and comp., B. Toulon, Jan. 1, 1821. S. under Lablache and Piermarini. Appeared in Paris, 1844, and in London from 1847 till 1876. Stage manager at Italian opera, London, 1877-82. Appeared in America and Russia. Comp. of songs, etc., and writer of articles in musical journals.

TÄGLICHSBECK (Thomas). German comp., B. Ansbach, Bavaria, Dec. 31, 1799. D. Baden Baden, Oct. 4, 1867. Comp. symphonies, operas, Pf. music, and lieder.

TALEXY (Adrien). French pianist and comp., B. 1820, D. Paris, 1881. Comp. operettas, Un Garçon de Cabinet, 1872; La Fête des Lanternes, 1872; Le Secret de Rose, 1875, etc. Also author of a method for the Pf., and comp. of a large number of Pf. works, studies, fantasias, valses, nocturnes, and other pieces, numbering over op. 100.

TALLIS (Thomas). English comp. and org., B. [c. 1520-1529]. Chor. in Chap. Royal (?). Org. of Waltham Abbey till 1540. Gent. of Chap. Royal during reigns of Henry VIII., Edward VI., Mary, and Elizabeth. Joint org. with Byrd, of Chap. Roy., and joint patentee with him in the exclusive right to print music. D. Nov. 23, 1585, and was buried in Parish Church of Greenwich.

WORKS.—Cantiones quæ ab argumento Sacræ vocantur, quinque et sex partium, Lond., 1575. The Preces, Chants, Te Deum, Benedictus, Responses, Litany, Kyrie, Creed, Sanctus, Gloria, Magnificat and Nunc Dimittis (Church of England Service), first printed in Barnard's Collection, 1641, and since reprinted many times by Novello, Rimbault, Jebb, etc. Song of Forty Parts, for 8 choirs of 5 voices each, "Spem in alium non habui." The Order of the Daily Service of the United Church of England and Ireland, Ed. by John Bishop, Lond., 1843, 8vo. *Anthems:* All people that on earth do dwell; Come, Holy Ghost; Hear the voice and Prayer; I call and cry; If ye love Me; Hear my prayer; Blessed are those; Salvator Mundi (motet); and many others in MS. contained in the British Museum, Music School of Oxford, Fitzwilliam Museum, Cambridge, and elsewhere.

Tallis was one of the greatest contrapuntists of the English school. His works are invested with great learning and much dignity, and are highly calculated to impress by their solemnity and power. His cathedral service is sufficiently well-known to require no comment.

TAMBERLIK (Enrico). Italian tenor vocalist, B. Rome, March 16, 1820. S. under Guglielmi. *Début* at Naples in Bellini's "Giulietta," 1841. Appeared successively in Lisbon, Madrid, London (1850, 1864, and 1877), St. Petersburg, Europe, and America. Appeared in Paris, 1858. Retired to Madrid, but re-appeared in 1884 for a time.

TAMBURINI (Antonio). Italian barytone vocalist, B. Faenza, March 28, 1800. S. under Rossi. Appeared at Bologna in opera by Generali, 1818. Sang in principal Italian cities till 1832. Appeared in London, 1832, and afterwards sang there and in Paris till 1852. Sang. in St. Petersburg, etc. Reappeared in London, 1852 and 1859. D. Nice, Nov. 9, 1876.

TANS'UR (William). English comp. and writer, B. Barnes, Surrey, 1699 [Dunchurch, Warwickshire, 1700]. Was org. at Barnes, Ewell, Leicester, and S. Neot's, and a bookseller in Leicester. D. S. Neot's, Oct. 7, 1783.
WORKS.—The Melody of the Heart, 1730, 1735, 1737. A Compleat Melody, or the Harmony of Zion... Lond. [1724?], 1735 and 1736. Heaven on Earth, or the Beauty of Holiness, 1738. Sacred Mirth, or the Pious Soul's Daily Delight, 1739. Poetical Meditations on the Four Last Things, with a Variety of Poems on other Divine Subjects, 1740. The Universal Harmony, containing the whole Book of Psalms, 1743, 1746. The Royal Melody Compleat, or the New Harmony of Zion, Lond., 1754, 1755 and 1764. The Royal Psalmodist Compleat, Lond., n.d. The Psalm-Singer's Jewel, or, Useful Companion, Lond., 1760, 8vo. Melodia Sacra, or, The Devout Psalmist's New Musical Companion, 1771, 1772. A New Musical Grammar, or the Harmonical Spectator, Lond., 1746, 12mo, 1753. New Musical Grammar and Dictionary... (3rd ed.), Lond., 1756; 7th ed., Lond., 1829, 8vo. The Elements of Musick Displayed; or its Grammar or Ground-work made Easy, Lond., 1772. He comp. some Psalm Tunes, contained in his works above named.

TAPPERT (Wilhelm). German writer, B. Ober-Thomaswaldau, Feb. 19, 1830. S. at Berlin under Dehn. Journalist and Teacher in Berlin. Author of "Musikalische Studien." "Ein Wagner-Lexikon, Wörterbuch der Unhöflichkeit," Leipzig, 1878, etc.

TAROHI (Angelo). Italian comp., B. Naples, 1760. D. Paris, Aug. 19, 1814, Produced numerous operas at Naples, Rome, London, Milan and Paris. Comp. "Isaaco" and "Ester," oratorios; Masses, and vocal music.

TARTINI (Giuseppe). Italian violinist and comp., B. Pirano, Istria, April 12, 1692. Educated at Padua for the Law. Solo violinist in Chap. of S. Antonio, Padua, 1721. Established himself at Padua as teacher of the violin, from about 1728, and there he instructed Nardini, Lahoussaye, Graun, Manfredi, and Pasqualino. D. Padua, Feb. 16, 1770.
WORKS.—Op. I. Sei Concerti; op. 2. Six Sonatas for vn., 'cello, and harpsichord, 1745; op. 3. XII Sonate a violino e basso; op. 4. Sei Concerti; op. 8. Sei Sonate, etc. Trattato di Musica..., Padua, 1754. De' Principii dell' Armonia Musicale..., 1767. Lettera sur Signora Maddalena Lombardini..., 1770, trans. by Burney as A Letter from the late Signor Tartini to Signora Maddalena Lombardini (afterwards Signora Syrmen), published as an important Lesson to Performers on the Violin..., 1779.

TATE (Nahum). Irish poet and writer, B. Dublin, 1652. D. London, 1715. Author of "An Essay for Promoting Psalmody," Lond., 1710.

TATTERSALL (William de Chair). English divine and musician, B. 1752. Rector of Westbourne, Sussex, 1778, and of Wotten-under-Edge, 1779. D. 1829. Published "Improved Psalmody, with New Music," Lond., 1794, 4to; Improved Psalmody, in Three Parts, 1795, 3 vols., 8vo.

TAUBERT (Carl Gottfried Wilhelm). German comp., B. Berlin, March 23, 1811. S. under Neithardt, L. Berger, and B. Klein. Appeared as pianist, 1825, and visited England and Scotland, 1836. Cond. of Royal opera, Berlin, 1841. Court Kapellmeister, 1845-69. Mem. of Council of Royal Academy of Fine Arts, Berlin, 1875.
WORKS.—Operas: Der Kermesse, op. 7, 1832; Der Ziegeuner, 1834; Marquis und Dieb, 1842; Joggeli, op. 100, 1852; Macbeth, 1857; Phedra, 1868; Cesario, 1874. Symphonies for orch., No. 1 in C, op. 31; No. 3 in F, op. 69; No. 4 in

B min., op. 113. Concertos for Pf. and orch., op. 18 and 189. Quartet for Pf. strings, op. 19. String Quartets, op. 73, 93, 130, etc. Trios for Pf., vn., and 'cello, op. 32, 38. Sonatas for Pf. and vn., op. 1, 15, 104. Sonatas for Pf. solo, op. 4, 20, 21, 35, 44, 114. Cantatas, Lieder, and Psalms.

TAUSCH (Julius). German comp. and cond., B. Dessau, April 15, 1827. S. under Schneider, etc., and at Leipzig Cons. Teacher and cond. in Düsseldorf. Cond. Glasgow Musical Festival of 1878. Comp. overtures, lieder, and Pf. music.

TAUSIG (Carl). Polish pianist and comp., B. Warsaw, Nov. 4, 1841. S. under Liszt at Weimar. First appeared at Berlin, 1858. Teacher and comp. in Berlin, where he was married in 1865. D. Leipzig, July 17, 1871. Best known as a remarkable performer, and as a successful teacher. His works consist of arrangements for Pf., with a few studies and other original pieces.

TAVERNER (John). English org. and comp. of 16th century. Org. of Boston, Lincolnshire, and of Christ Church Coll., Oxford. He was involved in the Reformation struggle, and narrowly escaped martyrdom. He comp. masses, motets, and anthems, now existing in MS.

TAVERNER (John). English musician, B. 1584. Prof. of Music at Gresham College, 1610. Was Vicar of Stoke Newington. D. there 1638.

TAYLOR (Edward). English writer and musician, B. Norwich, Jan. 22, 1784. Son of John Taylor, a Unitarian preacher there. S. under Charles Smyth and Dr. Beckwith. Bass singer at the Norwich Concerts. Established, with others, the Norwich Musical Festival, 1824. Settled in London, 1825, and became bass singer, teacher, and musical critic of the *Spectator*, and a writer in the *Harmonicon*. Prof. of Music, Gresham Coll. in succession to Stevens, 1837. Cond. Norwich Festivals of 1839 and 1842. Founded the Purcell Club, and with Rimbault and Chappell, the Musical Antiquarian Soc. Secretary of the Vocal Society. D. Brentwood, March 12, 1863.

WORKS.—Three Inaugural Lectures (Gresham College), Lond., 1838, 8vo.; An Address from the Gresham Professor of Music to the Patrons and Lovers of Art,... Lond., 1838; The Vocal School of Italy in the Sixteenth Century, Madrigals, full Anthems, Motets, and Villanellas, adapted to English Words, Lond. [1839], fo.; The People's Music Book (with J. Turle), Lond., 1844; The English Cathedral Service: its Glory, its Decline, and its Destined Extinction, Lond., 1845, 8vo (Reprinted from the *British and Foreign Review*); The Art of Singing at Sight (with Turle), Lond., 1846, 2nd ed., 1855; Airs of the Rhine, edited. Edited Purcell's "King Arthur" for the Musical Antiquarian Soc. Trans. librettos of Mozart's Requiem, Haydn's Seasons, Graun's Death of Jesus, Spohr's Last Judgment and Fall of Babylon, etc.

TAYLOR (Franklin). English pianist and teacher, B. Birmingham, Feb. 5, 1843. S. under Flavell and Bedsmore. S. at Leipzig Cons. under Plaidy, Moscheles, Hauptmann, Richter, and Papperitz; and in Paris under Madame Schumann. Teacher in London, where he has performed at all the principal concerts. Prof. at National Training School for Music, and the Royal Coll. of Music, 1882. Author of "Primer of Pianoforte Playing," Lond., 1877; "Pianoforte Tutor," Lond., n. d.; Trans. of Richter's Harmony, Lond., 1864; Counterpoint, Lond., 1874; and Canon and Fugue, Lond., 1878. Arrangements for Pf., etc.

TAYLOR (James). English writer, author of "A Course of Preceptive Lessons for the Spanish Guitar, designed for the assistance of Master and Pupil," Lond. [1827].

TAYLOR (John). English writer, author of "A Manual of Vocal Music," Lond., 1872; "Music and the Sol-fa Systems in Elementary Schools," Lond., 1873; "A Few Words on the Anglican Chant," Lond., n.d.; "Student's Text-Book on the Science of Music," Lond., 1876, 8vo.

TAYLOR (John). English divine and writer, B. Lancaster, 1694. D. Warrington, 1761. Author of "The Music Speech at the Public Commencement at Cambridge," Lond., 1730; "A Collection of Tunes in various Airs, with a

Scheme for supporting the spirit and practice of Psalmody in Congregations," Lond., 1750, 8vo.

TAYLOR (John Bianchi). English comp. and cond., B. Bath, 1801. D Bath, April, 1876. Comp. "A Set of Seven Glees," Bath [1840]; and a number of single part-songs and songs.

TAYLOR (Richard). English comp. and writer, B. Chester, 1758. D. Chester, Feb., 1813. Author of "The Principles of Music at One View," Lond., 1791, 8vo; "Beauties of Sacred Verse," Lond., 1795, 3 vols. National Songs. *Glees:* Now Winter with her hoary train; The gloomy season's past; Summer now upholds her scenes; Clad in her brown vesture; Gently as the breathing gale. Songs, etc. His son, THOMAS, B. Chester, 1787, was org. of S. John's, Liverpool. He published "A Book of Original Chants," songs, etc.

TAYLOR (Sedley). English writer, author of "Sound and Music, a Non-Mathematical Treatise on the Physical Constitution of Musical Sounds and Harmony..." Lond., 1873, 8vo.

TAYLOR (Silas). English comp., B. Harley, 1624. D. 1678. Published "Court Ayres, or Pavins, Almaines, Corants, and Sarabands," Lond., 1655, 8vo.

TAYLOR (Mrs. Tom), *née* LAURA W. BARKER. Third daughter of the Rev. Thomas Barker, vicar of Thirkleby, Yorks. Married Mr. Tom Taylor, June, 1855. Comp. Sonata for Pf. and vn., the Country Walk, 1860. "Ballads and Songs of Brittany...Trans. by Tom Taylor, with some of the Original Melodies harmonized by Mrs. Tom Taylor," Lond., 1865. "Enone," cantata; Glees, Songs, etc. Music to "As You Like It," 1880.

TAYLOR (William Frederick). English pianist and comp., B. Bristol, 1833. Comp. of a large number of Pf. pieces, songs, and part-songs.

TEDESCO (Ignaz Amadeus). Bohemian comp. and pianist, B. Prague, 1817. S. under Tomaschek. Resided in London from 1856. Comp. a large number of pieces for the Pf. in various styles. D. Odessa, Nov. 13, 1882.

TEETGEN (Alexander). German writer, author of "Beethoven's Symphonies critically and sympathetically discussed," Lond., 1879, 8vo.

TELEMANN (Georg Philipp). German org. and comp., B. Magdeburg, March 14, 1681. Org. of the Neukirche, Leipzig. Chap.-master to Prince Promnitz at Sorau, 1704. Do. at Eisenach, 1708. Org. of S. Catherine's, Frankfort. Music-director of the Church of St. John, Hamburg, 1721. D. Hamburg, June 25, 1767. Comp. oratorios, operas, overtures, cantatas and other large works, now obsolete. Fugues and other works for org. Violin sonatas, trios, and works for flute, etc.

TELLEFSEN (Thomas Dyke Acland). Norwegian pianist and comp., B. Drontheim, Nov. 26, 1823. S. at Paris under Chopin. Appeared in London, 1848. D. Paris, Oct., 1874. Comp. Pf. music, and edited Chopin's works.

TEMPLETON (John). Scottish tenor vocalist, B. Riccarton, Kilmarnock, July 30, 1802. One of a family of which other members were singers. Precentor in Dr. Brown's Church, Edinburgh. Went to London, and S. under Blewitt, Welsh, and T. Cooke. *Début* on stage at Worthing, 1828. First appeared in London as Belville in Shield's "Rosina," Oct. 13, 1831. Became associated with Malibran in 1833, and sang with her in opera in London with great success. Sang in Scotland, 1836. Appeared in the United States as lecturer and vocalist, 1845-6, and published his lecture as "A Musical Entertainment," Boston, 1845, 8vo. He retired from public life in 1852. He sang in operas of Meyerbeer, Spohr, Mozart, Auber, Barnett, Balfe, Benedict, and Rossini, and was one of the most popular and refined ballad vocalists ever reared in Britain. See Templeton and Malibran, Reminiscences of these Renowned Singers, with Original Letters and Anecdotes, by W. H. H., Lond., 1880, 8vo, 3 portraits. He comp. a few songs, "Put off! put off!" (Queen Mary's Escape from Lochleven), etc.

TENDUCCI (Giusto Ferdinando). Italian soprano vocalist, B. Siena, 1736.

Appeared in London in a pasticcio called "Attalio,", 1758, and afterwards in Cocchi's "Ciro riconosciuto," 1759. Travelled as singer in Scotland and Ireland, with Dr. Arne, 1765. Left England on account of his debts, 1776, but returned and sang till 1790. Returned to Italy, and died there early in the present century. Author of a "Treatise on Singing," Lond., n. d. Songs, an overture, etc.

TENNYSON (Alfred, Lord). English poet, B. Somersby, Lincolnshire, 1809. One of the most popular modern poets, in a musical aspect. Author of many fine lyrics, which have been set by the best living musicians. One work of surpassing interest is "Songs from the Published Writings of Alfred Tennyson. Set to Music by Various Composers, and Edited by W. G. Cusins." This volume contains contributions by Barnby, Cowen, Cummings, Cusins, Gounod, Hatton, Hullah, Joachim, Liszt, Pinsuti, Raff, Saint-Saëns, Stanford, Sullivan, and Tours. His works have also been set by Balfe, Anderton, Blockley, Macfarren, Claribel, Glover, J. C. D. Parker, Lindsay, Wallace, Blumenthal, Oakeley, Linley, etc., etc.

TERRADELLAS (Domenico M.B.), or TERRADEGLIAS. Spanish comp., B. Barcelona, 1701 [or 1711]. S. under Durante. Visited England, 1746. Chap.-master at Rome. D. Rome, 1751. Comp. Astarte, 1739; Romolo, 1740; Mitridate, Lond., 1746; Bellerophon, London, and other operas. Twelve Italian Airs and Duets, Lond., n.d.

TERSCHAK (Adolf.) German flute-player and comp., B. Hermannstadt, 1832. S. Vienna Cons. Appeared in Berlin, London, Scotland, Ireland, France, etc. Teacher and comp. in Vienna. Comp. works for flute.

TESI-TRAMONTINI (Vittoria). Italian soprano vocalist, B. Florence, 1690. S. under Redi and Bernacchi. Sang in Bologna, Venice, Dresden, Milan, Naples, Vienna, etc. D. 1775.

TESSARINI (Carlo). Italian violinist and writer, B. Rimini, 1690. S. under Corelli. Appeared in Italy, and in 1752 went to Amsterdam. D. 1762. Comp. sonatas, concertos, etc., for vn., and wrote "Grammatica di Musica ;" trans. as "A Musical Grammar, which teaches an easy and short method of learning to play to perfection the Violin in parts," Edin., n.d., fo. [? a London edition.]

THALBERG (Sigismund). Swiss pianist and comp., B. Geneva, Jan. 7 [Feb. 7], 1812. Natural son of Prince Maurice Dietrichstein and the Baroness de Wetzlar. S. under Sechter, Hummel, and Mittag. Appeared as pianist at Vienna, Paris, London, 1830, etc. Appeared in London, 1839; Russia, 1839; Spain, 1845. Married Madame Boucher, 1845. Pianist to the Emperor of Austria. Travelled in Brazil and the United States, 1855-56. Appeared in London again in 1863. D. Naples, April 27, 1871.
WORKS.—*Pianoforte:* Fantasias, op. 1, 2, 6, 9, 10, 12, 20, 27 (God save the Queen), 33, 37, 40, 42, 43, 50, 51, 52, 53, 63, 67, 68, etc.; Concerto, in F min., op. 5; Sonata in C min., op. 56; Impromptus, Divertissements, Variations (Home, sweet home, and Last Rose of Summer), Ballades, Valses, Marches, Caprices, Nocturnes, Romances, and other works for the Pf. ; "L'Art du Chant appliqué au Piano," op. 70; trans. as "The Art of Singing applied to the Pianoforte," Lond., 1853. Boston edition, n.d.
Thalberg was one of the most famous pianists of the brilliant school, who ever lived. His performance was marked by great power and dexterity, and was renowned for its accuracy and spirit. His works are showy and difficult pieces, mostly all containing novel ideas, and well worked out. His natural daughter, ZARA (by Madame d'Angri, an Italian vocalist), B. New York, April 16, 1858, was for a time a soprano vocalist in the Italian opera, and appeared in London and elsewhere from 1874. She married the Marquis Doria and retired in 1881.

THAYER (Eugene). American musician and writer, author of "The Organist's Reliance," Boston, n. d.; and comp. of a "Festival Cantata "; Part-songs, songs, and other works.

THAYER (Alexander Wheelock). American writer, B. South Natick, near Boston, Mass., Oct. 22, 1817. Educated at Harvard University. Travelled in Germany collecting materials for his Life of Beethoven from 1854. U. S. Consul at Trieste. Autor of "Signor Masoni, and other Papers of the late J. Brown," Berlin, 1862; "Ludwig van Beethoven's Leben," Berlin, 1866, etc., 3 vols published, but work not yet completed.

THEILE (Johann). German comp., B. Naumburg, July 29, 1646. S. under H. Schütz. Chap.-master at Gottorp, Wolfenbüttel, and Merseburg. D. Naumburg, 1724. He comp. a Passion oratorio, 1675; The Birth of Jesus, oratorio, 1681. Noviter Inventum opus Musicalis Compositionis 4 et 5 vocum. Novæ Sonatæ. Adam and Eve, opera, 1678. Masses, etc.

THIBAUT (Anton Friedrich Justus). German writer, B. Hameln, Hanover, Jan. 4, 1772. Prof. of law at Heidelberg. D. Heidelberg, March 28, 1840. Author of "Ueber Reinheit der Tonkünst," Heidelberg, 1825. Third ed., 1853. Trans. by Mr. W. H. Gladstone, as "Purity in Musical Art," Lond., 1877; and by John Broadhouse as "Purity in Music," Lond., 1882, 8vo.

THILLON (Anna), née HUNT. English soprano vocalist, B. Calcutta, 1819. Educated in London. Married M. Thillon, cond. of Philharmonic Soc. of Havre. Sang in opera in France, and made début at Paris, 1838. Sang in London, 1844-47; in California, 1850; and now retired.

THIRLWALL (John Wade). English comp. and violinist. B. Shilbottle, Northumberland, Jan. 11, 1809. D. London, June 15, 1876. Comp. "A Book of Ballads," 1843; songs, violin music, etc.

THOMAS (Arthur Goring). English comp., B. Ratton, near Eastbourne, Sussex, Nov. 21, 1851. Educated at Haileybury Coll. S. under Durand of Paris Cons., 1874-76. S. at R. A. M., London, under Sullivan and Prout. Gained "Charles Lucas" prize, 1879-80.

WORKS.—*Operas*: The Light of the Harem (MS.); Esmeralda, 1883; Nadeshda, 1885. The Sun-Worshippers, cantata, Norwich Festival, Feb., 1881. Four dramatic scenas, "Hero and Leander," etc. Psalm for solo, chorus, and orch., 1878. Ballet Music. *Songs*: Chanson d'Avril; Chanson de Mai; The Girl to her bird; Sous les etoiles; Gentle sleep; The veiled Bayadère; etc.

THOMAS (Charles Louis Ambroise). French comp., B. Metz, Aug. 5, 1811. S. under his father at Metz, and at Paris Cons. from 1828 under Zimmerman, Lesueur, and Kalkbrenner. Gained various prizes, and in 1832 carried off the Grand Prix de Rome. Mem. of Académie des Beux Arts, 1851. Commander of Legion of Honour, 1868, and decorated with Grand Cross of same, 1880. Director of Paris Cons., 1871.

WORKS.—*Operas:* La Double échelle, 1837; Le Perruquier de la Régence, 1838; Le Panier fleuri, 1839; La Gipsy (ballet), with Benoist, 1839; Carline, 1840; Le Comte de Carmagnola, 1841; Le Guerillero, 1842; Angélique et Médor, 1843; Mina, ou le Ménage à trois, 1843; Betty (ballet), 1846; Le Caïd, 1849; Le Songe d'une nuit d'été, 1850; Raymond, ou le Secret de la Reine, 1851; La Tonelli, 1853; La Cour de Célimène, 1855; Psyche, 1857; Le Carnaval de Venise, 1857; Le Roman d'Elvire, 1860; Mignon, 1866; Hamlet, 1868; Gille et Gillotin, 1874; Françoise de Rimini, 1882. Masses, Cantatas, Part-Songs, Songs, etc. Contributions to periodical literature.

THOMAS (Harold). English pianist and comp., B. Cheltenham, July 8, 1834. S. at R. A. M. under Bennett, Potter, and Blagrove. Appeared as pianist at London concerts, from 1850. Prof. of Pf. at R. A. M., and Guildhall School of Music. D. London, July 29, 1885.

WORKS.—Mountain, Lake, and Moorland, overture for orch., 1880; overture to "As You Like It," 1864. *Pianoforte*: Ave Maria (from Arcadelt); Nocturne; Fantasias; Et Bondebryllup, Danish wedding song; The Waits, 2 pieces, and numerous transcriptions; Songs, etc.

THOMAS (John), PENCERDD GWALIA. Welsh harpist and comp., B. Bridgend, Glamorganshire, March 1, 1826. S. at R. A. M., under J. B. Chatterton for harp, Potter and Read. Assoc., Mem., and Prof. of Harp at R. A. M., in which he has endowed a "John Thomas" Scholarship. Travelled as harpist in France, Germany, Russia, Austria, and Italy. Gave Welsh concerts in London from 1862. Harpist to the Queen, 1872. Prof. of harp at Royal Coll. of Music.

WORKS.—Llewelyn, cantata, Swansea Eisteddfod, 1863; The Bride of Neath Valley, a Welsh scene, Chester Eisteddfod, 1866; Welsh Melodies (collection), 1862-76; Concertos for harp; Olivia valse, harp and Pf.; La Gassier valse, do.; Transcriptions, various, for harp; Six songs, with accomp. for harp; Guardian Spirit, song; The Minstrel, song, etc.

THOMAS (John R.) Welsh comp., B. Newport, Monmouth, 1830. Teacher and editor in America, where he published "Church Music, a Selection of Gems from the Best Masters," N. Y., 1863, 8vo. Comp. "The Pic-nic," cantata; "Diamond cut Diamond," operetta, and many songs, including Beautiful Isle of the Sea, In the moonlight, 'Tis but a little faded flower, Evangeline, Pretty Nelly, The return, Thine alone, I dream of thy sweet smile, etc.

THOMAS (Lewis William). Welsh bass vocalist, B. Bath, 1826. S. under J. Bianchi Taylor, and Randegger. Lay-clerk Worcester Cath., 1850. Master of Choristers Worcester Cath., 1852. Sang at Provincial Festivals till 1854, when he appeared in London with much success. Bass singer in St. Paul's Cath., Temple Church, etc. Gent. of Chap. Royal, 1857. Famous as a concert vocalist of much ability.

THOMAS (Theodore). German cond. and comp., B. Esens, Hanover, Oct. 11, 1835. S. violin under his father. Settled with his family in America, 1845. Violinist at concerts with Sontag, Jenny Lind, Grisi, Mario, etc. Vnst. and cond. of various Italian opera companies. Established a quartet soirée in conjunction with W. Mason, etc., at New York. Established symphony concerts in New York, 1864. Travelled in the United States from 1869, with his orch. Cond. of New York Philharmonic Soc., Philharmonic Society of Brooklyn, and New York Chorus Soc. He has done everything to introduce high-class orchestral music to American audiences, and has produced at his concerts many novelties of all kinds.

THOMPSON (General Thomas Perronet). English political writer and musician, B. Hull, 1783. D. London, Sept. 6, 1869. Author of "Instructions to my Daughter, for Playing on the Enharmonic Guitar, being an Attempt to effect the Execution of Correct Harmony, on Principles analogous to those of the Ancient Euharmonic," Lond., 1829. "Enharmonic Theory of Music," Lond., 1829; Second edition issued as "Theory and Practice of Just Intonation," Lond., 1850; Third ed.: "Principles and Practice of Just Intonation, with a view to Embodying the Results of the Sol-fa Associations, as Illustrated on the Enharmonic Organ..." Lond., 1859, 8vo.

THOMSON (Rev. Andrew). Scottish divine and musician, B. Sanquhar, Dumfriesshire, June, 1778 [July 11, 1779]. Pastor of S. George's Ch., Edinburgh. D. Edinburgh, Feb. 9, 1831. Famous for his patronage of R. A. Smith, and for his efforts to promote good psalmody in the Church of Scotland. Edited "Sacred Harmony for the use of S. George's Church, Edinburgh," 1820. He comp. "St. George's, Edinburgh," and other well-known psalm tunes, and some other pieces for the musical service of the church.

THOMSON (George). Scottish collector and editor, B. Limekilns, Fife, March 4, 1759. Secretary to the Board of Trustees for the Encouragement of Arts and Manufactures in Scotland, 1780. D. Leith, Feb. 18, 1851. Published "A Select Collection of Original Scottish Airs for the Voice, to each of which are added Introductory and Concluding Symphonies and Accompanyments for the Pianoforte, Violin, and Violoncello" [by Pleyel, Kozeluch, Haydn, and Beethoven, vol. titles differ], with select and characteristic verses by the most admired Scottish Poets...London [1792-1841], 6 vols., fo. Collection of the Songs of Burns, Sir Walter Scott, and other eminent Lyric Poets, Ancient and Modern, united to the Select Melodies of Scotland, and of Ireland and Wales, with Symphonies and Accompaniments for the Pianoforte, by Pleyel, Haydn, Beethoven, etc....Lond., 1822, 6 vols., 8vo. Select Collection of Original Welsh Airs, adapted for the Voice, united to Characteristic English Poetry, with Introductory and Concluding Symphonies [by Haydn, Beethoven, etc.], Lond., 1809, 3 vols., fo. Select Collection of Original Irish Airs, united to Characteristic English Poetry, with Symphonies and Accompaniments for the Pianoforte, Violin, and Violoncello, composed by Beethoven, Lond., 1814-16, 2 vols., fo.

THOMSON (James). Scottish writer, author of " Rudiments of Music, with a Collection of Tunes, Hymns, etc.," Edin., 1778, 16mo.

THOMSON (John). Scottish comp., cond., and professor, B. Sprouston, Roxburgh, Oct. 28, 1805. Son of the Rev. Dr. Andrew Thomson. Became acquainted with Mendelssohn in Edinburgh, and renewed his acquaintance at Leipzig, where he S. under Schnyder von Wartensee. Returned to Edinburgh, and in 1839 became first Reid Professor of Music at the University. Cond. the first Reid Concert, Feb. 12, 1841, at which for the first time analytical programmes were used. D. Edinburgh, May 6, 1841.

WORKS.—*Operas*: Hermann, or the Broken Spear, London, 1834 ; The House of Aspen, London, 1834 ; The Shadow on the Wall, London, 1835. Vocal Melodies of Scotland, with Symphonies and Accompaniments by John Thomson and Finlay Dun, Edin., n. d., 4to ; New edition, 1880. Minuetto for Pf. and flute ; Capriccio for Pf. and violin. Bagatelle, 1831 ; Divertimento (duet) ; Polonaises ; and waltzes for Pf. *Songs:* Arab to his steed ; Blow light, thou balmy air ; Cleveland's farewell to Minna ; Die tanti mei tormenti ; Farewell, my love ; Love, art thou waking or sleeping? ; The merry moonlight ; Midnight dream ; O ! sweet be your slumbers ; The pirate's serenade ; Poor Camille ; Song of Harold Harfager ; Song of the Rhenish peasant ; Song of the Spanish maid ; The Savoyard's return ; Where art thou? ; Zara ! art thou sleeping ? etc.

THOMSON (William). Scottish musician, son of Daniel Thomson, King's Trumpeter in Edinburgh. Went to London, and became known as a singer. Published " Orpheus Caledonius, or a Collection of the best Scotch Songs set to Musick by W. Thomson," Lond. [1725], fo. Second edit., Lond, 1733, 2 vols., 8vo.

THORNE (Edward Henry). English org. and comp., B. Cranbourne, Dorset, May 9, 1834. Articled to Sir George Elvey, Chap. Royal, Windsor, under whom he studied. Org. successively of Henley-on-Thames, 1853 ; Chichester Cath., 1863 ; St. Patrick's, Brighton, 1871 ; St. Peter's, Cranley Gardens, 1873 ; and St. Michael's, Cornhill, London, 1875.

WORKS.—Sacred Music for the Home Circle, 1859. A Selection of Psalm and Hymn Tunes, Lond., n. d. Church Services in E flat, B flat, and C. *Anthems:* All Thy works praise Thee ; Behold the Lord the Ruler is come ; I was glad when they said unto me ; O cast thy burden upon the Lord ; The Lord is in His holy temple. Part-songs, Songs, and Pf. music. Two Trios for Pf., vn., and 'cello ; Sonata for Pf. and vn. ; Sonata and romance for Pf. and violoncello : Suite for Pf. and clarinet. Psalm LVII. for tenor solo, chorus and orch.

THUNDER (Henry G.) Irish pianist and comp., B. near Dublin, Feb. 10, 10, 1832. S. under Thalberg. Settled in New York, and was org. of S. Augustine's, S. Clement's, and S. Stephen's R. C. Churches. D. New York, Dec. 14, 1881. Successful as a teacher. He comp. much church music, songs, etc.

THURSBY (Emma). American soprano vocalist, B. Brooklyn, Long Island, Nov. 17, 1857. S. under Julius Meyer, in Italy, and under Madame Rudersdorff. Was originally a church choir singer. Made a concert tour in the U. S., 1875. Appeared in London at the Philharmonic Soc., May, 1878. Sang in Paris, and in other parts of France, Germany, Austria, Belgium, Spain, and Norway, 1879-1882. Since then has appeared chiefly in the United States. She is best known as a concert vocalist. Her voice is a powerful soprano, which she uses with great ease and skill.

THYS (Alphonse). French comp., B. Paris, March 8, 1807. S. Paris Cons. under Bienaimé and Berton. D. Bois-Guillaume, near Rouen, Aug., 1879. Comp. operas, cantatas, songs, and much Pf. music. His daughter, PAULINE THYS-SEBAULT, B. 1836, comp. operas and vocal music.

TICHATSCHEK (Josef Alois). Bohemian tenor vocalist, B. Ober-Weckelsdorf, July 11, 1807. Chor. in S. Michael's, Vienna. *Début* Dresden, 1837. Appeared in London, 1841. Has sung in operas of Weber, Méhul, Spohr, Meyerbeer, Beethoven, etc., in all parts of Germany. Teacher in Dresden. D. Jan. 19, 1885.

TIETJENS, or TITIENS (Theresa Caroline Johanna). Hungarian soprano vocalist, B. Hamburg, July 17, 1833 [1831]. *Début* in "Lucrezia Borgia," at Hamburg, 1849. Sang in Frankfort and Vienna till 1856. Appeared at H. M. Theatre, London, as Valentine in "The Huguenots," April 13, 1858. Sang throughout Britain from that date, and appeared in London every season. She sang in America in 1876. Last appeared in London, May, 1877. D. London, Oct. 3, 1877.

A vocalist of great popularity in Britain, where she was greatly admired for the extraordinary power and sweetness of her voice. She sang in operas of Verdi, Donizetti, Bellini, Cherubini, Meyerbeer, Flotow, Weber, Gluck, and Wagner.

TILLEARD (James). English comp. and editor, B. 1827. D. 1876. Published Sacred Music for Schools, Lond., 1853; Secular Music for Schools, 1853; People's Chant Book, 1853. Te Deums, anthems, and other church music. Patriotic Part Songs, 19 numbers, Lond. [1864]. Original part-songs, songs, etc.

TILLMAN (S. D.) American writer, author of "A Treatise on Musical Sounds, and an Explanation of the Tonometer," New York, 1860.

TIMANOFF (Vera). Russian pianist, B. 1858. S. under Liszt. Appeared in London at the Promenade Concerts, Covent Garden, 1880. Has since appeared in London, and in various parts of the continent.

TINCTOR (Joannes). Belgian comp. and theorist, B. Nivelle, Brabant, 1434. Chaplain to Ferdinand of Arragon, King of Naples, and established a music school there. D. Nivelle, 1520. He wrote a number of most important theoretical works, of which "Terminorum Musicæ Diffinitorium," n. d., 4to (a musical dictionary, and the first of the kind); reprinted by John Bishop as a supplement to his edition of Hamilton's Dictionary of Musical Terms; "Liber de Arti Contrapuncti;" "Proportionale Musices," etc.

TITIENS. See TIETJENS.

TODI (Maria Francesca). Portuguese contralto vocalist, B. Portugal, 1748. S. under Perez. *Début* in London, at King's Theatre, 1772. Sang in Paris, Berlin, and St. Petersburg, Hanover, etc. At St. Petersburg she became highly intimate with the Empress Catherine, and acquired much court influence. D. Lisbon, June, 1793.

TOEPFER (Johann Gottlob). German writer and teacher, B. Niederrossla, near Weimar, Dec. 4, 1791. D. Weimar, May 8, 1870. Comp. org. and choral music, and wrote on musical theory.

TOFTS (Catherine). English soprano vocalist of 18th century. She was the first English vocalist who attempted Italian opera, and appeared in "Arsinoe," "Camilla," "Rosamond," and "Love's Triumph." She is said to have been very avaricious, and was continually mixed up in the broils and rivalry which early beset the Italian opera. Latterly she married Mr. Joseph Smith, British Consul at Venice, and is supposed to have become insane. She was living in Venice in 1735.

TOLHURST (George). English comp. and org., B. 1827. D. Barnstaple, Jan. 18, 1877. He comp. "Ruth," an oratorio, which went through two editions; org. music, church music, and songs.

TOLLET (Thomas). English musician, author of "Directions to Play the French Flageolet"; and comp., with John Lenton, of "A Consort of Musick in Three Parts," 1694.

TOMASCHEK (Wenzel Johann). Bohemian comp. and pianist, B. Skatsch, April 17, 1774. Chiefly self-taught in music. Comp. to Count Bucquoy von

Longueval. D. Prague, April 3, 1850. Chiefly famous as a teacher. He numbers among his pupils Dessau, Kittl, Kuhe, Dreyschock, Schulhoff, Bocklet, etc. His works consist of Masses, Hymns, and other church music; "Seraphine," opera, 1811; Leonore, ballad by Bürger, 1808; Symphonies, quartets, trios, and a large quantity of pieces for the Pf.

TOMKINS (Thomas). English org. and comp., B. Gloucester in latter part of 16th century. Chor. in Gloucester Cath. Educated at Magdalen Coll., Oxford. Mus. Bac. Oxon., 1607. S. under Byrd. Gent. of Chap. Royal, 1621, and org. do., 1621. Org. of Worcester Cath. D. Worcester, 1656.

He comp. "Songs of 3, 4, 5 and 6 Parts," 1622, 4to; "Musica Deo Sacra et Ecclesiæ Anglicanæ, or Musick dedicated to the Honor and Service of God...," Lond., 1664, 4to (issued in 10 parts). His father THOMAS, comp. "The Faunes and Satirs Tripping," madrigal in the "Triumphs of Oriana." His brother JOHN (D. London, Sept. 27, 1638), was org. of King's Coll., Cambridge, and afterwards of S. Paul's Cath., London. Another brother, GILES, was org. successively of King's Coll., Cambridge, and Salisbury Cath., till his death in 1668.

TOMLINS (William L.) English cond. and comp., B. London, Feb. 4, 1844. Settled in the U. S., 1869. S. under Sir G. A. Macfarren, and E. Silas. Cond. of the "Apollo Musical Club," Chicago, from 1875, and became associated with Theodore Thomas, as chorus master, at the Festivals given at Chicago under his direction. Mem. of American Coll. of Musicians. Comp. vocal music, and author of papers on Choral Training.

TOPLIFF (Robert). English musician, editor of "Selection of the most Popular Melodies of the Tyne and the Wear, harmonised, with appropriate words, symphonies, etc.," n. d., fo. "Scripture Melodies, the Words from Holy Writ," Lond., 2 vols., n. d., fo. Some of his sacred songs, "Consider the Lilies," etc., are still popular.

TORRANCE (Rev. George William). Irish comp. and writer, B. Rathmines, Dublin, 1835. Ordained, 1866. Incumbent of Holy Trinity Church, Balaclava, near Melbourne. Mus. Bac. and Doc., Dublin, 1879. Has comp. "Abraham," "The Captivity," and "The Revelation," oratorios. Author of "Music and its Relation to Religion, a Lecture," Dublin, 1861; etc.

TOSI (Pietro Francesco). Italian sopranist and comp., B. Bologna, 1650. Travelled in Europe as vocalist, and resided in London as teacher during the reign of Charles I. D. London. Author of "Opinioni de' Cantori Antichi e Moderni...," 1723. Trans. by Galliard as "Observations on the Florid Song, or Sentiments of the Ancient and Modern Singers," Lond., 1742, 2nd edit., 1743. He comp. songs and other vocal works. D. London, [1730].

TOSTI (Francesco Paolo). Italian comp., B. Ortona, in the Abruzzi, April 9, 1846. S. under Pinto, Conti, and Mercadante. Teacher of Singing to the Queen of Italy. Visited London, 1875. Teacher of Singing to the Royal Family of Britain. Comp. of many fine Songs, of which the most popular are:—At Vespers; For ever and for ever; Good-bye; Mother; Non m' ama più; Lamento d'amore; Aprile; also a number of vocal duets, etc.

TOURJÉE (Eben). American musician, B. Warwick, R. I., June 1, 1834. Self-taught in music. Org. in Old Trinity Ch., Newport. Established a Musical Institute at East Greenwich, R. I. S. in Berlin under Haupt, 1863. Established in Boston the New England Conservatory of Music, 1867, one of the largest music schools in the world. He aided in the organisation and direction of the Peace Jubilee, in 1869. He aided "The Centennial Old Folks' Collection " (church music), and has written papers on musical subjects. The teachers in the New England Cons. are the best known musicians in America, and include Bendix, Chadwick, Daniell, Elson, Emery, Howard, Maas, Parker, Whitney, Whiting, and Zerrahn.

TOURS (Berthold). French comp. and writer, B. Rotterdam, Dec. 17, 1838. S. at Cons. of Brussels and Leipzig. Settled in London, 1861, and in 1878 became musical editor to Messrs. Novello, Ewer, & Co.

WORKS.—Church Service in F. *Anthems:* Blessed are they that dwell in thy house ; Blessing, glory, wisdom, and thanks ; God be merciful ; God hath appointed a day; In Thee, O Lord ; O saving victim ; Praise God in His holiness ; etc. Magnificat and Nunc Dimittis in F, with orch. accomp. Part-songs. *Songs*: Angel at the window ; Because of thee ; Fisherman's wife ; Gate of Heaven ; How shall I picture thee ; Ivy tower ; Little chair ; Myrrha ; Name in the sand ; New kingdom ; O mother dear, good-night ; Solitude ; Stars of the summer night ; Tears of childhood ; Sea hath its pearls ; etc. Pf. music. The Violin (Music Primer), London, n. d., 4to. He has also edited a number of large choral works.

TOURTE (Francois). French violin-bow maker, B. Paris, 1747. D. Paris, April, 1835. Invented the violin-bow now in use. These bows are famous for their fine workmanship and extreme lightness and elasticity. They invariably fetch good prices, and have been valued at all prices between £30 and £3.

TOWERS (John). English cond. and writer, B. Salford, Feb. 18, 1836. Chor. in Manchester Cath. S. at R. A. M., 1856, and at Berlin under Marx, 1857. Org. of S. Stephen's Conell, Manchester, and cond. of Rochdale, Fallowfield, and other Glee Societies. Author of "Beethoven, a Centenary Memoir ;" "The Mortality of Musicians," etc.

TOWERSON (Rev. Gabriel, D.D.) English divine and writer, B. 1635. Rector of S. Andrew Undershaft. D. 1697. Author of "A Sermon concerning concerning Vocal and Instrumental Musick in the Church," Lond., 1696, 4to.

TOWNSEND (Mrs.) Authoress of a "Floral Music Book for Young Learners," Lond., 1862, 8vo.

TOWNSEND (Horace). Author of "An Account of the Visit of Handel to Dublin," Dublin, 1852 ; "The Moral Uses of Music, Lecture," Dublin, 1862.

TOWNSEND (John). English flute-player, B. Yorkshire. S. under Müller and Ware. Author of a "New and Complete Flute Preceptor," Lond., n.d.

TRAETTA (Tommaso). Italian comp., B. Bitonto, Naples, March 30, 1727. S. under Durante. Chap.-master to Duke of Parma. Director of Cons. dell' Ospedaletto, Venice. Comp. at Court of Catherine II. of Russia. Visited London, 1776. D. Venice, April 6, 1779.

WORKS.—*Operas*: Farnace, 1751 ; Ezio, 1754 ; Stordilano, 1760 ; Armida, 1760 ; Sofonisba, 1761 ; Semiramide, 1765 ; L'Olimpiade, 1770 ; Antigone, 1772 ; Germondo, Lond., 1776 ; Artenice, Venice, 1778. Oratorios, and much vocal music.

TRAVERS (John). English comp. and org., B. about 1703. Chor. in S. George's Chap., Windsor. S. under Greene and Pepusch. Org. of S. Paul's Covent Garden, 1725, and afterwards became org. at Fulham. Org. of Chap. Royal, May 10, 1737. D. 1758. Published "The Whole Book of Psalms for one, two, three, four, and five voices, with a Thorough Bass for the Harpsichord," Lond., 1746, 2 vols., fo. "Eighteen Canzonets for two and three Voices, the words chiefly by Matthew Prior." *Anthems*: Ascribe unto the Lord ; Ponder my words ; Keep, we beseech Thee, O Lord.

TRAVIS. See KNYVETT (Deborah).

TREBELLI or GILLBERT (Zelia), BETTINI. French contralto vocalist, B. Paris, 1838. S. under Wartel. *Début* at Madrid, 1859. Sang afterwards in Germany and Holland. Appeared in London, May, 1862. Married Signor Bettini 1863, and soon afterwards separated from him. Has sang in St. Petersburg, Berlin, Vienna, and in 1875 and 1881 appeared in Norway and Sweden. Appeared in the United States, 1884. Has since sang principally in Britain. She sings in operas by Rossini, Donizetti, Weber, Bizet, Bellini, Gounod, Verdi, Meyerbeer, Flotow, Mozart, etc.

TRITTA or TRITTO (Giacomo). Italian comp. and writer, B. Altamura, Bari, 1732. S. under Cafaro. D. Naples, Sept. 16, 1824. Comp. Il Principe riconosciuto, 1780 ; Don Procopio, 1782 ; La Molinarella, 1789 ; Ginevra di Scozia, 1800 ; Masses, Theoretical works, etc.

TROUTBECK (Rev. John). English writer, B. Blencowe, Cumberland, Nov. 12, 1832. Educated at Oxford, and graduated B.A., 1856; M.A., 1858. Precentor of Manchester, 1865-69; Canon of Westminster, 1869. Author of Manchester Psalter, 1868; Manchester Chant Book, 1871; "A Music Primer for Schools," Lond., 1873, 8vo; 2nd ed., 1876 (with Reginald F. Dale). "Church Choir Training" (Music Primer), Lond. [1879], 8vo. Hymn Book in Use in Westminster Abbey. English librettos for Beethoven's "Mount of Olives"; Gade's "Crusaders," etc.; Hiller's "Song of Victory;" Wagner's "Flying Dutchman," etc.

TROYTE (Arthur Henry Dyke), or ACLAND. English amateur comp., B. May 3, 1811. Son of Sir J. D. Acland. Assumed name of Troyte in 1852. D. June 19, 1857. Comp. the chants known by his name.

TRÜHN (Friedrich Hieronymus). German comp., B. Elbing, Oct. 14, 1811. S. under Klein, Mendelssohn, and Dehn. Comp. operas and choral music, and known in Britain by his part-song "The Three Chafers."

TRYDELL (Rev. John). Irish writer, author of "Two Essays on the Theory and Practice of Music," Dublin, 1766, 8vo.

TSCHAIKOWSKY (Peter Iljitsch.) Russian comp., B. Wotkinsk, Ural District. April 25, 1840. S. at St. Petersburg Cons. under A. Rubinstein, etc. Prof. of Harmony at Moscow Cons., 1866. Comp. resident in St. Petersburg, etc.

WORKS.—*Operas:* Voievode, 1869; Opritschnik, St. Petersburg, 1874; Vakoul le Forgeron, 1876; Schwanensee, ballet; Snegourotska; Eugeny Onegin; Mazeppa, 1884. *Overtures:* Romeo and Juliet; Triumphal, op. 15; 1812, Solennella, op. 49. *Symphonies:* No. 1, op. 13; No. 2; No. 3, op. 29; No. 4, op. 36. Suites, fantasias, etc., for orch.; String quartets, op. 11, 22, 30, etc.; Symphonic poem for orch., "Francesca da Rimini," op. 32; Concerto for violin and orch., op. 35; Concertos for Pf. and orch., op. 23 and 44. Pf. music, lieder, and concerted vocal music.

TSCHIRCHE (Wilhelm). German org. and comp., B. Lichtenau, Lauban, June 8, 1818. S. under Rungenhagen, Grell, and Marx. Cantor and org. at Liegnitz. Comp. music for church, orch. and org. music, lieder, etc. His brothers ERNST (1819-1854), JULIUS (1820-1867), RUDOLF (1825-1872), and ADOLF (D. 1875), were also musicians.

TSCHUDI. See SHUDI.

TUA (Maria Felicita, or Teresina). Italian violinist, B. Turin, May 22, 1867. S. at Paris Cons. under Massart, and gained first prize for violin, 1880. Travelled as violinist on Continent, and appeared at the Crystal Palace, London, May 5, 1883. Has appeared elsewhere in London, and again on the Continent with great and increasing success.

TUBBS (Mrs. F. Cecilia). Translator of Dr. Joseph Schlüter's "General History of Music," London, 1865.

TUCKER (Isaac). English comp., of Westbury, Leigh, Wilts, B. 1761. D. 1825. Comp. psalms and hymns.

TUCKER (Rev. William). English comp. of 17th century. Was Gent. of Chap. Royal. Minor canon and precentor of Westminster Abbey, 1660. D. London, Feb. 28, 1678. Comp. anthems and other church music.

TUCKERMAN (Samuel Parkman). American comp. and org., B. Boston, Mass., Feb. 17, 1819. S. under C. Zeuner. Org. S. Paul's Ch., Boston, 1840. S. in London, and resided in various cathedral towns, studying the Ch. service. Mus. Doc., Cantuar, 1853. Returned to England, 1856, and remained till about 1860. Now resident in Switzerland.

WORKS.—The Episcopal Harp, Boston, n. d. The National Lyre, a Collection of Psalm and Hymn Tunes (with Bancroft and Oliver), Boston. Cathedral Chants, a Collection of Psalm and Hymn Tunes, Anthems, Chants, etc. The Trinity Collection of Church Music...New York, 1864. Church Services in C, G, F, and

E flat. *Anthems:* Thou shalt shew me the path; Come unto Him; God so loved the world; Lighten our darkness; And they rest not; Their sun shall no more go down; Come unto Me; I looked, and behold a door was opened in heaven; I was glad when they said unto me; Hear my prayer; etc. Hymns, part-songs, and other works.

TUDWAY (Thomas). English comp. and org. of 17th century. Chor. in Chap. Royal under Dr. Blow, from 1660. Lay-vicar St. George's Chap., Windsor, 1664. Org. of King's Coll., Cambridge, 1670. Instructor of Choristers, King's Coll., 1679-80. Org. of Pembroke Coll. Mus. Bac. Cantab., 1681. Prof. of Music in Cambridge University, 1704. Mus. Doc. Cantab. Suspended from his University offices, 1706-7. Resigned his organ at King's Coll., 1726, and retired to London, where he employed himself in forming a collection of Music for Edward (Lord Harley), Earl of Oxford. D. 1730.

WORKS.—A Collection of the most celebrated Services and Anthems used in the Church of England, from the Reformation to the Restoration of K. Charles II., composed by the best masters and collected by Thomas Tudway...," 6 vols. [1715-1720], now preserved in MS. in the British Museum, London. Of this collection a list will be found in the British Museum Catalogue of MS. Music. From it a number of services and anthems have been printed at various times. Tudway comp. various anthems, motets, services, and songs.

TUFTS (Rev. John). American musician, was minister of the second church in Newbury, Mass. D. 1750. Published "A Very Plain and Easy Introduction to the Art of Singing Psalm Tunes, with a Collection of Tunes in Three Parts," 1710, 16mo; 8 editions to 1731.

TULLY (James Howard). English comp. and cond., B. 1815. Cond. opera at Drury Lane Theatre and elsewhere. D. London, Jan. 28, 1868. Comp. "I'm a light bright water sprite," "Summer Hours," and a large number of other songs. He also comp. operatic works.

TULOU (Jean Louis). French flute-player and comp., B. Paris, Sept. 12, 1786. S. at Paris Cons. Prof. of Flute in Paris Cons. Afterwards flute manufacturer at Nantes. D. Nantes, July 23, 1865. Comp. concertos, solos, fantasias, variations, etc. for flute; and a symphonic concertante, for flute, oboe, and bassoon.

TUNSTED (Simon). English Franciscan monk and Doctor of Theology. B. at Norwich early in 14th century. D Bruzard, Suffolk, 1369. Author of "De Musica Continua et Discreta cum Diagrammatibus," and "De Quatuor Principalibus in quibus totius Musicæ Radices Consistunt," two works preserved in MS. in the Bodleian Library. Oxford.

TÜRK (Daniel Gottlieb). German comp. and writer, B. Claussnitz, near Chemnitz, Aug. 10, 1756. S. under Homilius. Music-director of Halle University, 1779; and org. of ch. of Notre Dame, Halle, 1787. D. Halle, Aug. 26, 1813. Author of a "Clavierschule..." 1789, 4to, of which an English translation exists as "A Treatise on the Pianoforte, from the German of D. G. Türk, by C. G. Vaunberger, Lond., 1804, 8vo. Comp. cantatas, sonatas for Pf., and a large number of songs.

TURLE (James). English org., comp., and writer, B. Taunton, March 5, 1802. Chor. in Well's Cath., 1810-13. Org. of Christ Ch., Surrey, 1819-29, and of St. James', Bermondsey, 1829-31. Assistant org. to Greatorex at Westminster Abbey till 1831, and succeeded him as org. and master of the choristers, 1831. Music-master at the School for the Indigent Blind, 1829-56. D. London, June 28, 1882.

WORKS.—Art of Singing at Sight (with E. Taylor), Lond., 1846, 8vo. Psalms and Hymns, 1855. Psalms and Hymns for Public Worship, Lond., 1863, 1864, 1869. Hymns for Public Worship, revised, 1863. Psalter and Canticles, with Chants, Lond., 1865. Child's Own Tune Book, 1865. The People's Music Book (with E. Taylor), Lond., n. d. Edited Wilbye's First Set of Madrigals, for the Musical Antiquarian Soc., 1841. Single and Double Chants, composed for the use of the Choral Service of Westminster Abbey. The Westminster Abbey Chant Book, with Dr. J. F. Bridge, n. d. Church Services in D, E flat, etc. *Anthems:* Almighty and most merciful God ; Hear my crying, O God ; The Lord that made heaven and earth ; This is the day which the Lord hath made ; Arise, and help, etc.

TURNBULL (John). Scottish musician, B. Paisley, Jan. 12, 1804. Precentor in St. George's Ch., Glasgow. D. Glasgow, 1845. Published "A Selection of Original Sacred Music in Four Parts," adapted to the various metres used in Presbyterian churches and chapels...Glasgow, 1833, 8vo. The Garland of Scotia, a Musical Wreath of Scottish Songs, with Descriptive and Historical Notes, Glasgow, 1841, 8vo (with Patrick Buchan). Easy and Progressive Exercises in Singing and in Reading Music, Glasgow, n. d., 8vo. Six Glees, for three and four voices, Glasgow, n. d., fo. An edition of R. A. Smith's Devotional Music, and a number of anthems, psalms, and songs.

TURNER (John). English writer, author of "Manual of Instruction in Vocal Music, chiefly with a view to Psalmody..." Lond., 1833, 2nd ed. 1835, Boston ed. 1836 ; "Class Singing Book for Schools," 1844, 2 parts, 8vo.

TURNER (William). English comp., B. 1651. Chor. of Christ Ch., Oxford, under Lowe, and chor. Chap. Royal under Cooke. Chorister in Lincoln Cath., and Gent. of the Chap. Royal, 1669. Vicar-choral of S. Paul's, and lay-vicar Westminster Abbey. Mus. Doc., Cantab., 1696. D. Westminster, Jan. 13, 1740. Comp. music for " Presumptuous Love," 1716 ; Services, anthems, and other church music. Another WILLIAM TURNER wrote " A Philosophical Essay of Musick directed to a Friend," Lond. [1677], 4to ; "Sound Anatomized in a Philosophical Essay on Music, wherein is explained the Nature of Sound, both in its Essence and Regulation," Lond., 1724, 4to (3 editions).

TURPIN (Edmund Hart). English org., comp., and writer, B. Nottingham, May 4, 1835. S. org. under C. Noble, and in London under Hullah and Pauer. Org. of Ch. of S. Barnabas, Nottingham, 1850. Appeared as an org. in London, at the Exhibition of 1851, and performed at the Crystal Palace, Royal Albert Hall, Bow and Bromley Institute, etc. F. C. O., 1869. Org. S. George, Bloomsbury, 1869. S. music Trinity Coll., London, 1874. Cond. and Secretary of Coll. of Organists, 1875. Musical Examiner for Coll. of Preceptors, and Prof. of Form and Instrumentation at Trinity Coll., London. Editor of the *Musical Standard* since 1880.
WORKS.—*Cantatas* : A Song of Faith, 1867 ; Jerusalem. *Oratorios:* S John the Baptist, and Hezekiah (MS). Symphony, The Monastery (MS.). A Festival Mass, in D (with orch.) ; Motets, etc. Overtures for orch., quartets, etc. Hymn Tunes, edited, 1872. *Anthems* : Trust ye in the Lord ; The Offertory Sentences ; Blessed be the Lord God of Israel ; etc. *Organ* : Overtura pastorale ; Musette ; Adagio and Allegro ; Andante ; Allegro maestoso ; Gavotte moderne ; Short Voluntaries from unpublished scores ; Impromptu in C ; Prelude and Fugue in F ; Postlude alla Marcia. Students' Edition of Classical Composers (36 numbers), Pf. Songs, duets, and other vocal music.

TWINING (Rev. Thomas). English musician and writer, B. London, 1734. Rector of S. Mary's Colchester, 1770. D. Colchester, Aug. 6, 1804. Published "Aristotle's Treatise on Poetry, translated with Notes.. and Two Dissertations on Poetical and Musical Imitation," Oxford, 1789, 4to ; London, 1812, 2 v., 2nd ed.

TYE (Christopher). English org., comp., and verse-writer, B. Westminster early in the 16th century. Chor. and Gent. of Chap. Royal. Mus. Bac., Cantab., 1536. Org. of Ely Cath., 1541-1562. Mus. Doc., Cantab., 1545, and Oxon. (*ad eundem*), 1548. D. March, 1572 [? 1580].
WORKS.—The Actes of the Apostles, translated into Englyshe meter, and dedicated to the Kynge's moste excellannte Maiestye...wyth notes to eche chapter, to synge and also to play upon the Lute,...London, 1553, 4to ; A Notable Historve of Nastagio and Traversari, no less Pitiefull than Pleasaunt, out of Italian, Lond., 1569, 12mo ; Service in G min. *Anthems*: I will exalt Thee ; Sing unto the Lord ; This is the day which the Lord hath made ; Arise, and help us. Masses, anthems, and other works in MS.

TYNDALL (John). Irish scientist and writer, B. Leighlin Bridge, near Carlow, 1820. Author of "Sound: a Course of Eight Lectures delivered at the Royal Institution of Great Britain," London, 1867, 8vo; other editions.

TYTLER (Sarah). See KEDDIE (Henrietta).

TYTLER (William), of WOODHOUSELEE. Scottish antiquary and writer, B. Edinburgh, Oct. 12, 1711. D. Woodhouselee, Sept. 12, 1792. Member of the Musical Society of Edinburgh, and author of "A Dissertation on the Scottish Music," which has been printed along with Arnot's "History of Edinburgh;" Napier's "Selection of Favourite Scots Songs;" and in "The Poetical Remains of James I. of Scotland." "An Account of the Fashionable Amusements and Entertainments of Edinburgh in the Last Century, with the Plan of a Grand Concert of Music performed there on St. Cecilia's Day, 1695," in the "Transactions of the Society of Antiquaries of Scotland." His advice to persons seeking health and contentment was, "Short, but cheerful meals, *Music,* and a good conscience."

U.

UBER (Friedrich Christian Hermann). German violinist and comp., B. Breslau, April 22, 1781. D. Dresden, March 2, 1822. Comp. operas, oratorios, symphonies, concertos, overtures, etc.

UGALDE (Delphine), *née* BEUCÉ. French soprano vocalist, B. Paris, Dec. 3, 1829. S. under Madame Moreau-Santi. *Début* at Opéra Comique, 1848. Appeared in London, June, 1852. Afterwards sang in Paris in operas of Auber, Thomas, Rossini, Mozart, Massé, etc. Retired, and now employed as a vocal teacher.

UGOLINI (Vincenzo). Italian comp., B. in 2nd half of 16th century, at Perouse. S. under B. Nanini. D. 1626. Comp. masses, motets, and psalms.

ULRICH (Hugo). German comp., B. Oppeln, Silesia, Nov. 26, 1827. S. under Dehn and Brosig. Prof. for a time in Berlin Cons. D. Berlin, May 22, 1872. Comp. an opera, three symphonies, overtures, string quartets, Pf. music, and lieder.

UMBREIT (Carl Gottlieb). German comp. and org., B. Rehstedt, Gotha, June 9, 1763. S. under Kittel. D. Rehstedt, April 27, 1829. Published organ and vocal music, and "Allgemeines Choral-Buch," 1811.

UMLAUF (Ignaz). Austrian comp., B. Vienna, 1756. D. Vienna, June 8, 1796. Comp. "Bergknappen," "Die Schöne Schustern," "Das Irrlicht," "Die Glücklichen Jäger," and other operettas or singspiele. His son MICHAEL, B. Vienna, 1781. D. Baden, near Vienna, June 20, 1842, was a violinist and comp.

UNGER or UNGHER (Caroline). Hungarian contralto vocalist, B. Stuhlweissenburg, near Pesth, Oct. 28, 1805 [1800]. S. under Vogl. etc. *Début* at Vienna, 1821. Sang in Italy and in Paris, 1833. Married M. Sabatier, and retired, 1840. D. Florence, March 23, 1877. Sang in operas of Rossini, Donizetti, Mercadante, and Bellini.

URBANI (Pietro). Italian comp., B. Milan [1749]. S. at Milan. Resided in Edinburgh from 1776; and was latterly a teacher and cond. in Dublin. D. Dublin, 1816.

WORKS.—*Operas*: Farnace, Dublin, 1784; Il Trionfo di Clelia, Dublin, 1785. A Selection of Scots Songs, harmonised and improved, with simple and adapted graces...Edinburgh [1792-99], Books 1 to 4. A Select Collection of Original Scotch Airs, with Verses, the most part of which were written by the celebrated Robert Burns...1804, Books 5 and 6. A Favourite Selection of Scots Tunes, properly arranged as Duettos for Two German Flutes or Two Violins, Edinburgh, n. d., 2 vols.

URFEY (Thomas D'). See D'URFEY (THOMAS).

URQUHART (Thomas). Scottish violin-maker of 17th century. Established in London in reign of Charles II., and made instruments of considerable value. These are now rarely met with. Noted for good varnishing.

USIGLIO (Emilio). Italian comp., B. Parma, Jan. 8, 1841. S. under Mabellini. Cond. in various Italian towns, and of Théâtre Italien, Paris, from 1877. Comp. "La Locandiera," "La Secchia rapita," "Le Donne Curiose," and other operas.

V.

VACOAJ (Nicola). Italian comp., B. Tolentino, March 15, 1790. S. under Jannaconi and Paisiello. Teacher at Trieste and Vienna, and in Paris and London, 1829-30. Principal of Milan Cons., 1838. D. Pesaro, Aug. 5, 1848. Comp. I solitari di Scozia, 1814; Giulietta e Romeo, Naples, 1825 (London, 1832); Marco Visconti, 1831 ; Giovanna d'Arco ; Giovanna Grey ; Zadig ed Astartea ; Virginia ; and other operatic works. Melodo pratico di canto Italiano, London, n.d., fo. Arias, and other vocal works.

VAET (Jacob). Flemish comp. of 16th century. Chap.-master at Imperial Chap. of Vienna. D. Vienna, Jan. 8, 1567. Comp. chansons, Te Deums, motets, and much church music.

VALENTINE (John). English writer, author of " Elements of Practical Harmony," Lond., n.d., 8vo.

VALENTINE (Thomas). English comp. and writer, B. 1790. D. near Birmingham, Jan. 11, 1878. Author of "Instructions for the Pianoforte, to which is added a Selection of Favourite Airs,..." Lond. [1826]; "A Dictionary of Terms used in Music," Lond., 1833, 8vo. Comp. and arranged music for the Pf.

VALLERIA (Alwina), or LOHMANN. American soprano vocalist, B. Baltimore, Maryland, Oct. 12, 1848. S. at R. A. M., London, under W. H. Holmes and Wallworth. Gained Westmoreland Scholarship, 1869. S. also under Arditi. *Début,* 1871. Appeared at St. Petersburg, 1871 ; in Germany, Milan, and at H. M. Theatre, London, May, 1873. Sang at Italian opera, till 1882, and from then onwards with the Carl Rosa company in English opera. Married Mr. R. H. F. Hutchinson, 1877. Sings in operas of Meyerbeer, Verdi, Mozart, Bizet, Mackenzie, Wagner, etc. She has also appeared with much success throughout Britain as a concert vocalist.

VAN BREE. See BREE (J. B. Van).

VAN DYK (Harry Stoe). English lyric author and librettist, B. 1798. D. 1828. Author of "Theatrical Portraits, and other Poems," "Selection of Russian Melodies," and songs set to music by Barnett, Bishop, Rodwell, Rawlings, Crouch, and other contemporary composers.

VAN EYKEN. See EYKEN.

VANHALL or **WANHAL (Johann Baptist).** Dutch comp., B. Nechanicz, Bohemia, May 12, 1739. S. under Dittersdorf at Vienna. Violinist and comp. there. D. Vienna, Aug. 26, 1813.

Comp. 100 symphonies, 100 string quartets, masses, an oratorio, operas, and Pf. sonatas. Some of his Pf. works and overtures were republished in England.

VAUCORBEIL (Auguste Emmanuel). French operatic manager and comp., B. Rouen, Dec. 15, 1821. S. Paris Cons. Became director of the Paris

Opéra, 1879, and managed it till he D. at Paris, Nov. 2, 1884. He comp. operas, string quartets, sonatas for vn. and Pf., songs, and other works.

VAUGHAN (Thomas). English tenor vocalist, B. Norwich, 1782. Chorister in Norwich Cath. under Beckwith. Lay clerk St. George's Chap., Windsor, 1799. Gent. of the Chap. Royal, 1803. Vicar-choral St. Paul's, London, and lay-vicar Westminster Abbey. Married Miss Tennant, a soprano singer. Singer at Concert of Ancient Music, and at the principal London and provincial concerts. D. Birmingham, Jan. 9, 1843.

VECCHI (Orazio). Italian comp., B. Modena, 1551. Chap.-master of Modena Cath., 1596. Director of music to court of Modena, 1598. D. Modena, Sept. 19, 1605. He comp. "Canzonette," 1580, 1585, 1590, and 1611; "Madrigali," 1589, 1591, etc. Motets, masses, and other church music.

VELLUTI (Giovanni Battista). Italian soprano vocalist, B. Monterone, Ancona, 1781. S. under Calpi. *Début* at Forli, 1800. Appeared at Rome, 1805; Naples, 1807, Milan, 1809, Vienna, 1812, London, 1825 and 1829. D. Padua, Feb. 1861.

VENOSA (Prince of). See GESUALDO.

VERACINI (Francesco Maria). Italian comp. and violinist, B. Florence, 1685. Leader of the opera orch. in London, 1714-20. Soloist at Court of Dresden, 1720. Comp. in London, 1735. D. Pisa, 1750. Comp. "Adriano," 1735; "Roselinda," 1744; and "L'Errore di Salomone," 1744, operas produced at London; Violin sonatas, concertos, and other instrumental music.

VERDI (Giuseppe). Italian comp., B. Roncole, near Busseto, Oct. 10, 1813. S. under Provesi, at Busseto, and at Milan, under Lavigna. Married to Margherita Barezzi, 1836, and in 1838 settled in Milan. Married again to Mme. Strepponi. Comp. for various Italian cities, London, 1847, etc. Has resided for a number of years at St. Agata, near Busseto.
WORKS.—*Operas:* Oberto Conte di S. Bonifacio, Milan, Nov. 1839; Un giorno di Regno, 1840; Nabucodonosor, Milan, 1842; I Lombardi, Milan, 1843; Ernani, Venice, March, 1844; I due Foscari, Rome, 1844; Giovanna d'Arco, Milan, 1845; Alzira, Naples, 1845; Attila, Venice, 1846; Macbeth, Florence, 1847; I Masnadieri, London, July 22, 1847; Jerusalem, Paris, 1847; Il Corsaro, Trieste, 1848; La Battaglia di Legnano, Rome, 1849; Luisa Miller, Naples, 1849; Stifellio, Trieste, 1850; Rigoletto, Venice, March, 1851 (London, 1853); Il Trovatore, Rome, Jan. 19, 1853 (London, May, 1855); La Traviata, Venice, March 6, 1853 (London, May, 1856); Les Vêpres Siciliennes, Paris, 1855; Simon Boccanegra, Venice, 1857; Aroldo, Rimini, 1857; Un Ballo in Maschera, Rome, 1857; La forza del Destino, St. Petersburg, 1862; Don Carlos, Paris, 1867; Aïda, Cairo, 1871; Requiem mass, Milan, 1874. Some miscellaneous church and chamber music.
One of the most popular operatic composers of the present century. His works abound in fine melody, and it is due to this more than to anything else that they have taken such a prominent place in the affections of the people. Notwithstanding, they are now declining in popular esteem in Britain, and his earlier works have long since lost place everywhere. His most powerful work, and that possessing the greatest kinship to the recent development in operatic writing, is Aïda, in which he has followed in a measure the leading of Wagner. "Il Trovatore" achieved most extraordinary popularity, and is still a leading favourite in Britain, where an English version has been performed for a number of years by various opera companies. His music is an advance on that of Donizetti and Bellini in its dramatic colouring, and in some respects equals and transcends that of Rossini. In his recent works he takes rank above all other Italian composers of the present time.

VERHULST (Johannes Josephus Herman). Dutch comp. and cond., B. at the Hague, March 19, 1816. S. under J. Klein, and at Leipzig. Cond. of Euterpe Concerts at Leipzig (resigned 1882). Cond. at the Hague, Rotterdam, and Amsterdam. Comp. symphonies, overtures, quartets, and other instrumental works, and music for the church and voice.

VERNON (Joseph). English tenor vocalist, B. Coventry [1738]. S. under W. Savage. Appeared at Drury Lane Theatre, London, 1751, and from 1756 sang at Vauxhall and other London Concerts, and appeared on the stage in various musical dramas. D. Lambeth, London, March 19, 1782. Comp. songs and ballads.

VERNON (M.). English writer. Author of "Analogy of the Laws of Musical Temperament to the Natural Dissonance of Creation," London, 1867, 8vo.

VERRINDER (Charles Garland). English org. and comp., B. Blakeney, Gloucestershire. S. under Sir G. J. Elvey. Org. successively of S. Giles'-in-the-fields; Christ Ch., Lancaster Gate; and S. Michael's, Chester Square, Lond. Org. of the Reformed Synagogue, Lond. Mus. Bac., Oxon, 1862; Mus. Doc., Cantuar. 1873. Comp. of "Israel," a cantata; Church Service in E. *Anthems*: Seek ye the Lord; The light hath shined upon us; Remember, Lord. Thy loving kindness; Blessed is he that considereth the poor; Grant to us, Lord, we beseech Thee; O Lord, raise up, we pray Thee; etc. Hebrew Music and Psalms, 3 vols. Organ music, etc.

VESTRIS (Lucia Elizabeth), *née* BARTOLOZZI. English contralto vocalist and actress, B. London, 1797. S. under Corri. Married Armand Vestris, a ballet-master, 1813. Appeared in opera, 1815. Appeared in Paris, 1816, and again sang in London from 1820, appearing in operas and in numerous theatrical pieces. She became manager successively of the Olympic, Covent Garden, and Lyceum Theatres, and produced a large succession of dramatic pieces, in many of which she appeared. Married to Charles Mathews the younger, 1838. D. Fulham, London, Aug. 8, 1856. Famous for her beauty, and her charming style of acting and singing.

VIADANA (Ludovico). Italian comp., B. Lodi, 1565. Chap.-master at Fano in Urbino, Mantua, etc. He was living in Mantua in 1644. Comp. church music, madrigals, and "Cento concerti ecclesiastici a 1, 2, 3, e 4 voci, con il basso continuo per sonar nell' organo..." Venice, 1603, 5 vols. Famous as the first to write solos with organ accompaniments.

VIARD-LOUIS (Jenny), *née* MARTIN. French pianist and writer, B. Carcassonne, Sept. 29, 1831. S. at Paris Cons., and under Madame Pleyel. Married Nicolas Louis (D. 1857), a comp., 1853. Married M. Viard, a merchant, 1859. Performed as pianist in Germany and Paris. Appeared in London, 1876, and since then has given numerous concerts of Pf. music. Authoress of "Music and the Piano," Lond., 1884, 8vo.

VIARDOT-GARCIA (Michelle Ferdinande Pauline). Spanish mezzo-soprano vocalist and comp., B. Paris, July 18, 1821. S. under her father, Manuel Garcia, the celebrated vocal trainer. S. Pf. under Meysenberg and Liszt, and comp. under Reicha. *Début* as a vocalist at Brussels, 1837. Appeared at H. M. Theatre, London, May, 1839. Married M. Louis Viardot, 1840. Travelled as a vocalist in Italy, Spain. Germany, Russia, and England, and in 1849 sang again in Paris. Sang in London and Paris from 1849. Has resided since 1871 in Paris, where she is a teacher, and Prof. of singing at the Cons. Her husband died in 1883. She has comp. a number of operettas, chamber and Pf. music, songs, etc. Among her pupils are Artot, Brandt, and Antoinette Sterling.

VIDAL (Louis Antoine). French writer, B. Rouen, July 10, 1820. Author of "Les Instruments a Archet, les Fesseurs, les Joueurs d'Instruments leur Histoire sur le continent Européen suivi d'un Catalogue general de la Musique de Chambre," Paris, 1876, 3 vols., 4to; A monumental and beautifully illustrated work on musical instruments played by the bow.

VIERLING (Georg). German org. and comp., B. Frankenthal, Bavaria, Sept. 15, 1820. S. under Rinck and Marx. Org. of the Oberkirch, Frankfort-on-Main, 1847, Founded a Bach Society at Berlin. Retired from the musical profession. Comp. a symphony, overtures, vocal quartets, lieder, and several large choral works.

VIERLING (Johann Gottfried). German org. and comp., B. Metzels, Saxony, Jan. 25, 1750. D. Schmalkalden, Nov. 22, 1813. Comp. Choralvorspiele for the org., sonatas for org. and Pf., preludes, fugues, and interludes for org. Writer on theory.

VIEUXTEMPS (Henri). Belgian violinist and comp., B. Verviers, Feb. 17, 1820. S. originally under Lecloux, a musician of Verviers; afterwards under De Beriot, Sechter, and Reicha. Travelled as a violinist in Germany, and performed in Vienna. Appeared in London at a Philharmonic Concert, June, 1834. Visited Russia, Germany, and in 1841 appeared again in London. Visited the United States, 1844. Married Josephine Eder, a pianist, 1845. Solo violinist to the Emperor of Russia, and Prof. at the Cons, 1846-52. Appeared again in America, 1857, and in 1870. Prof. of violin at Brussels Cons., 1871. D. Mustapha-lez-Alger, Algiers, June 6, 1881.

WORKS.—Concertos for violin and orch., in E, op. 10; F sharp minor, op. 19; A, op. 25; D minor, op. 31; A minor, op. 37; G, op. 47; Hommage à Paganini, caprice, op. 9; Fantaisie-caprice, op. 11; Sonata for Pf. and vn., op. 12; Duo brillant for vn. or 'cello and orch., op. 39; Feuilles d'Album, op. 40; Ballade and Polonaise, vn. and orch., and many other violin pieces.

A great and brilliant performer of the French school, famed for his command over the technique of the instrument, and the breadth and originality of his interpretation of the more modern masters. His works are clever, difficult, and possess much originality and dash.

VILBAC (Alphonse Charls Renaud de). French comp., org., and pianist, B. Montpellier, June 3, 1829. S. Paris Cons. D. Brussels, March 19, 1884. Comp. operettas, cantatas, and much Pf. music of a brilliant and effective character.

VILLOTEAU (Guillaume André). French writer, B. Bellême, Sept. 6, 1759. D. Tours, April 27, 1839. Author of several works on musical theory, and of the musical portion of "La Description de l'Egypte," 1809-26, published in 20 vols., fo. and 8vo.

VINCENT (Marvin R.) Author of "Church Music," New York [1880], 8vo.

VINCENT (Rev. William, D.D.) English writer, author of "Considerations on Parochial Music," Lond., 1790, 8vo.

VINCI (Leonardo). Italian comp., B. Strongoli, Calabria, 1690. S. under Greco. D. 1732. Comp. operas, and much vocal music for solo and duet. His "Six Arie," issued by Walsh, London, in folio, is scarce.

VINNING. See O'LEARY.

VIOTTI (Giovanni Battista). Italian vnst. and comp., B. Fontanetto, Piedmont, Mar. 23, 1753. D. Mar. 3, 1824. S. under Pugnani. Travelled with Pugnani in Germany and Russia, and about 1780 appeared in London. He performed in Paris, 1782, and afterwards resided there as a teacher, and director of the Italian opera till 1793. Resided in London from about 1793, and became manager of Italian opera. Resided between London and Paris till his death at London, March 10, 1824.

His works consist of Concertos for violin and orch.; Quartets for strings; Trios for strings, opp. 16, 17, 19, 20, etc.; Sonatas for violin and bass; Duets for two violins; Serenades for Pf. and vn., op. 23; and other instrumental pieces, only a small proportion of which is now in use. He was celebrated as a teacher and performer, and as the former was one of the most influential instructors who ever lived. His works are melodious and agreeable, without exhibiting much that is powerful or original.

VITTORIA (Tommaso Ludovico da). Spanish comp., B. Avila, 1540. S. at Rome. Choir-master of Ch. of S. Appollinare, Rome, 1575-89. Chap.-master at Royal Chap., Madrid. D. Madrid [1606-8]. Comp. masses, motets, hymns, psalms, and other works for the Roman Catholic church service, some of which are still in use.

VIVALDI (Antonio). Italian comp. and violinist, B. Venice, in latter part of 17th century. Violinist in service of the Court of Hesse-Darmstadt. Leader at the Ospitale della Pietà, Venice. D. Venice, 1743. Comp. many operas and other vocal music, and numerous concertos, trios, sonatas, and other works for stringed instruments.

VOGL (Heinrich). German tenor vocalist, B. Au, near Munich, Jan. 15, 1845. S. under F. Lachner. *Début* in Der Freischütz. 1865. at Munich. Married Therese Thoma. 1868. Has appeared chiefly in Wagner's operas in Germany, and in 1882 sang at H. M. Theatre, London. His wife, *née* THOMA, B. Tutzing, Bavaria, Nov 12, 1846. S. under Hauser at Munich Cons. Sang in Wagner's operas with her husband, and appeared with him in London, in 1882.

VOGL (Johann Michael). Austrian barytone vocalist. B. Steyer. Aug. 10, 1768. Sang at Court opera in Vienna in operas of Gluck, Mozart, Méhul, etc. D. Vienna, Nov. 19, 1840. Celebrated as an exponent of the music of Schubert.

VOGLER Georg Joseph, Abbé). German comp., org. and writer, B. Würzburg. June 15, 1749. S. under Valotti and Mysliweczek, and in 1773 was ordained priest. Spent most of his life travelling about Europe, and in 1784 was in London. Chap.-master to the King of Sweden at Stockholm, and held other appointments. Chap.-master and director of a music school at Darmstadt, 1807. D. Darmstadt. May 6. 1814.

WORKS.—*Operas:* Albert III. von Baiern, 1780; La Kermesse, 1783; Castor und Pollux, 1784; Egle, 1787; Gustav Adolf, 1792; Samori, 1804, etc. Masses, motets, hymns. Instrumental music, consisting of trios for Pf. and strings: Concertos for Pf. and org.; Preludes, fugues, and other works for organ. An Organ School, 1797: A Choral System, 1800; Handbuch zur Harmonielehre, etc., 1802; and many other theoretical works.

Famous as a teacher of influence, and as a composer and performer of great note in his day. He was the teacher of C. M. von Weber, Winter, Meyerbeer, Danzi, and Gänsbacher.

VOGT (Gustave). French oboe-player and comp., B. Strasburg, March 18, 1781. S. Paris Cons. Solo oboist at the opera. and Prof. at the Cons. Played at the Philarmonic Soc., London. 1825-28. D. Paris, May 30, 1870. Author of an Oboe Method, and comp. ot arrangements and original pieces for oboe.

VOLCKMAR (A. B. Wilhelm). German org. and comp., B. Herzfeld, Dec. 26, 1812. S. under his father, and became org. and teacher at Brunswick and Homberg. Author of "Hülfsbuch für Organisten"; a "School for the Organ." op. 50; and many fantasias, fugues, preludes, and other pieces for org. Comp. also quartets for strings, and vocal music.

VOLKMANN (Friedrich Robert). German comp., B. Lommatzsch, Saxony, April 6, 1815. D. Oct. 29. 1883. S. under Anacker, and in Leipzig from 1836. Resided successively in Vienna and Pesth as comp. and teacher. Comp. symphonies for orch., op. 44. 53. Overtures for orch. Concertos for 'cello, Pf., etc., and orch. Quartets for strings, op. 9, 14, 34, 35, and 37. Pf. music, and masses. Part-songs and lieder. Member of Berlin Academy of Arts, 1883.

VOSS (Carl). German pianist, B. Schmarsow, Sept. 20, 1815. D. Verona, Aug. 29, 1882. Comp. Rhapsodies; Etudes; Fantasias, op. 59, 101, etc.; Melodies; Polka; Transcriptions, etc.

VUILLAUME (Jean Baptiste). French violin-maker, B. Mirecourt, Oct. 7, 1798. Learned under Chanot. Established himself at Paris, and became the most famous modern violin-maker. Gained various medals at Exhibitions of Paris and London. D. Paris. Feb. 19, 1875. His instruments are the most celebrated and highly valued among those of modern manufacture. They are finely toned and beautifully modelled instruments, and some of the best specimens are now scarce and valuable.

W.

WACHTEL (Theodor). German tenor vocalist, B. Hamburg, March 10, 1823. Son of a stable-keeper. S. at Hamburg. Appeared at Court Theatre of

Schwerin; afterwards at Dresden, Hanover, Cassel, Vienna, Berlin, etc. Appeared in London, June, 1862; Paris, 1869; America, etc. He had a voice of much power and compass, and appeared in works by Rossini ("William Tell"); Mozart ("Don Giovanni"); Meyerbeer, Verdi, Adam, Boieldieu, Donizetti, etc.

WACKERBARTH (F. D.) German (?) writer, author of "History of the Church of the Reformation," New York, 8vo, 1834, "Music of the Anglo-Saxons; being some account of the Anglo-Saxon orchestra; with remarks on the Church Music of the 19th Century," Lond., 8vo, 1837. "Lyra Ecclesiastica," 1842-43, 2 parts, etc.

WADDEL (William). Scottish violinist and cond., B. Edinburgh, 1842. S. under David at Leipzig. Originated the choir named after him, producing by its means for the first time in Scotland Schumann's "Faust," "Requiem," "Pilgrimage of the Rose," and "Requiem for Mignon"; Brahm's "German Requiem" and "Song of the Fates"; Bruch's "Odysseus" and "Lay of the Bell," etc. Formed the Edinburgh Ladies Orch., and successfully carried on chamber concerts. Gave Free Musical Evenings for the People. He has also exhibited at the R. S. A. for many years as a painter in oil colours.

WADE (Joseph Augustine). Irish comp. and writer, B. Dublin [1796]. Married Miss Kelly of Garnavilla, and was a surgeon for a time. Went to London, and worked for the theatres and publishers. D. London, July 15, 1845.

WORKS.—The Two Houses of Granada, opera, 1826; The Pupil of Da Vinci, operetta; The Prophecy, oratorio, 1824. Polish Melodies, Lond., 1831. Songs of the Flowers, 2 books. Many duets, "I've wandered in dreams," etc. *Songs*: Meet me by moonlight alone; Love was once a little boy; A Woodland life; and others.

WADE (Richard). English pianist and writer, flourished in London about middle of 18th century. Author of "The Harpsichord illustrated and improved, wherein is shewn the Italian manner of Fingering..." Lond., 4to, n. d., anon.

WAELRANT (Hubert). Flemish comp., B. Antwerp, 1517. S. at Venice under Willaert. Returned to Belgium in 1547. D. Antwerp, Nov. 19, 1595.

WORKS.—Liber nonus Cantionum sacrarum vulgo motetta vocant, quinque et sex vocum, 1557; Madrigali e Canzoni Francesi à 5 voci, Antwerp, 1558; Canzoni alla Napoletana, a 3 et 4 voci, Venice, 1565; Symphonia Angelica di diversi eccellentissimi musici a 4, 5, et 6 voci, Antwerp, 1565; Canzoni scelti di diversi eccellentissimi musici a 4 voci, Antwerp, 1587.

WAGENSEIL (Georg Christoph). Austrian comp. and pianist, B. Vienna, Jan. 15, 1715. Music teacher to Maria Therese. D. Vienna, March 1, 1779.

WORKS.—Op. 1. Sei Divertimenti di Cembalo; op. 2. Six do.; op. 3. Do. do.; op. 4. Quatre Symphonies pour le Clavecin, avec 2 violons et bass; op. 5. Three Divertissements; op. 6. Six sonatas for harpsichord and violin; op. 7. Four symphonies for harpsichord, 2 violins, and bass; op. 8. Two do. Trios, concertos, symphonies, sonatas, etc., in MS.

WAGNER (Johanna). German soprano vocalist, B. Hanover, Oct. 13, 1828. Niece of W. R. Wagner. S. under her parents, and M. Garcia at Paris. Appeared at Dresden, Bernburg, etc., in small parts, and in 1847 made her *début* at Dresden. Sang at Hamburg, 1849, Vienna and Berlin, 1850, where she was afterwards engaged as leading soprano at the opera, and became court singer. Appeared in London, 1856. Married Councillor Jachmann, 1859, and on the loss of her voice, became a very successful actress. Afterwards sang in Wagner's operas, and in 1883 became Prof. of dramatic singing at the Royal School of Music, Dresden. She appeared in works of Wagner, Rossini, Verdi, Weber, Boieldieu, Bellini, etc.

WAGNER (Wilhelm Richard). German comp. and writer, B. Leipzig, May 22, 1813. Educated at Kreuz-Schule of Dresden, and matriculated at Leipzig University, 1830. S. music under Weinlig. Chorus-master at Würzburg theatre, 1833. Music director at Magdeburg theatre, 1834. Married Frauient Pianer at Konigsberg, 1836. Music director at Riga, 1838. Went to Paris, 1839, and endeavoured to get his " Rienzi " produced, but without success. Cond. of the Royal Opera at Dresden, 1842-49. Exiled for his share in the Dresden revolutionary movements, 1849, and took up his residence at Zürich. Cond. a series of Philharmonic Concerts at London, 1855. Gave concerts in Germany and Russia, 1863. Established in Munich under the patronage of Ludwig II. of Bavaria, 1864. Married to Cosima von Bülow, née Liszt, 1870. Settled at Bayreuth, 1872, and there carried out his plan of a theatre, and had performed all his large works. Cond. a Wagner Festival in London, 1877. D. Venice, Feb. 13, 1883.

WORKS.—*Operas:* Die Feen, 1833 (MS.); Das Liebesverbot, 1836 (MS.); Rienzi, der letzte der Tribunen, 5 acts, Dresden, 1842 (London, 1879); Der fliegende Holländer, 3 acts, Dresden, 1843 (London, 1870); Tannhäuser, und der Sängerkrieg auf Wartburg, Dresden, 1845 (London, 1876); Lohengrin, Weimar, 1850 (London, 1875); *Der Ring des Nibelungen* (London, 1882)—Part 1, Das Rheingold, Munich, 1869; Part 2, Die Walküre, Munich, 1870; Part 3, Siegfried, Bayreuth, 1876; Part 4, Götterdämmerung, Bayreuth, 1876. Tristran und Isolde, 3 acts, Munich, 1865 (London, 1882); Die Meistersinger von Nürnberg, 3 acts, Munich, 1868; Parsifal, eine Bühnenweihfestspiel, 3 acts, Bayreuth, 1882. Das Liebesmahl der Apostel, eine Biblische scene, Dresden, 1847. Symphony in C (1832); MS. overtures in D min., 1831; C, 1833; "Polonia," in C, 1832; "Columbus," 1835; Eine Faust Overture, 1855. Huldigungsmarsch, orch., 1864; Siegfried Idyll, orch., 1870; Kaisermarsch, orch., 1871; Grosser Festsmarsch (Philadelphia Exhibition), 1876. Sonatas, albumblatt, and other Pf. pieces. Songs, and arrangements for Pf. *Literary:* A collected edition was issued at Leipzig, 1871-85, 10 vols., as "Gesammelte Schriften und Dichtungen." The separate publication of some of the principal is as follows:—Die Kunst und die Revolution, 1849; Das Kunstwerke der Zukunft, 1850; Kunst und Klima, 1850; Oper und Drama, 1852; Das Judenthum in der Musik, 1852; Ueber Staat und Religion, 1864; Ueber das Dirigiren [1870]; Beethoven, 1870 (trans. by A. R. Parsons, Indianapolis, 1873; also, London, trans. by Dannreuther, 1880); Deutsch Kunst und Deutsch Politik, 1868; Uber Schauspieler und Sänger, 1882, etc. Translations exist of "The Nibelung's Ring" (Forman), "Die Meistersinger," "Tristran und Isolde," and "Parsifal" (Corder).

The most famous musician of modern times. Celebrated alike for his reforms in every department of the musical drama, and for his boldness and energy in getting them carried into practice. His principal reform consists of the close union which he effected between his music and poetry, and generally the balance one part with another which in his operas is so conspicuous. In this respect they stand apart from the operas of every other master. His work has been the completion of that inaugurated by Gluck, but applied to the romantic instead of the classic drama. Wagner's operas are drawn largely from what we might call ballad literature, and are in some respects more suited for musical treatment and the attainment of magnificent stage effects than the usual run of hackneyed opera libretti. His music is highly original and bold in general style, but very often disappoints and displeases by too apparent an effort to produce startling and new effects. The straining after originality is very conspicuous in his instrumental music, and frequently conveys the impression that the composer is unable to express in music the full extent of his meaning. In recent times his influence has been great, and most of the younger composers are adopting in a measure his reforms. The slipshod Italian opera which held universal sway till within the last ten years is fast dying out, and it is to be expected and hoped that the unique musical dramas of Wagner will form the starting point and example for every future composer. We say nothing of the taste or morality of certain of Wagner's librettos, which have been generally condemned on their artistic and moral merits alike.

WAINWRIGHT (Jonathan Mayhew). English comp., B. Liverpool, 1792. D. New York, Sept. 21, 1854. Comp. Chants, Psalms, and other church music, in collections.

WAINWRIGHT (John). English comp. and org., B. Stockport. Org. of Manchester Cath. D. Manchester, Jan., 1768. Comp. Psalms, anthems, etc. His sons, ROBERT (B. 1748, D. July 15, 1782) and RICHARD (B. 1758, D.

Aug. 20, 1825) were both organists and composers. Robert is known as the comp. of "The Fall of Egypt," an oratorio, and the Psalm tunes "St. Gregory" and "Manchester."

WALDAUER (A.) Violinist and teacher, B. in Germany. Director of the Beethoven Cons., St. Louis, Mo. Pupil of Molique. Went to America when young, and was one of the pioneers in orchestral work. Travelled as solo violinist during the triumphal tour of Jenny Lind through the States. Member of American Coll. of Musicians, and trans. of many plays, etc.

WALEY (Simon Waley). English amateur comp. and pianist, B. London, 1827, S. under Moscheles, Bennett, etc. D. London, Dec. 30, 1875. Comp. services for the Jewish church service, Pf. music, a Pf. concerto, and much vocal music.

WALKER (James). Scottish amateur musician, author of "On Just Intonation in Song and Speech," Aberdeen, 1876, 4to, privately printed.

WALKER (Joseph Cooper). Irish writer and musician, B. Dublin, Nov. 1760. D. St. Valery, near Bray, April 12, 1810. Author of "Historical Memoirs of the Irish Bards, interspersed with Anecdotes and Occasional Observations on the Music of Ireland .." Dublin, 1786, 4to. "An Historical Account and Critical Essay on the Opera, and on the Revival of the Drama in Italy," Edin. 1805, 8vo. "Memoirs of Alessandro Tassoni, edited by S. Walker," 1815, 8v. Other works chiefly on Irish antiquities.

WALLACE (Lady Maxwell), *née* GRACE STEIN. Scottish writer, B. at Edinburgh. D. 1878. Translated "Letters from Italy and Switzerland, by Felix Mendelssohn-Bartholdy," Lond., 1862 (2 editions); "Letters of Felix Mendelssohn-Bartholdy, from 1833 to 1847..." 1863, 8vo; "Letters of Wolfgang Amadeus Mozart, 1769-1791 .." Lond., 1865, 2vo; "Beethoven's Letters, 1790-1826," Lond., 1866, 2 vol.; "Letters of Distinguished Musicians, Gluck, Haydn, P. E. Bach, Weber, Mendelssohn," Lond., 1867, 8vo; "Reminiscences of Felix Mendelssohn-Bartholdy, by Elise Polko," Lond., 1869.

WALLACE (William Vincent). Scottish comp. and violinist, B. Waterford, Ireland, June 1, 1814. Son of Scottish parents, his father being an army bandmaster. Played violin in various orchestras for a time, and about 1836 went to Australia. He afterwards travelled about in New Zealand, India and South America, and in 1845 appeared in London. He afterwards gave concerts in America, and after another visit to London, D. at the Château de Bagen, Haute Garonne, France, Oct. 12, 1865.

WORKS.—*Operas:* Maritana, London (Drury Lane), Nov. 15, 1845; Matilda of Hungary, London, 1847; Lurline, London (Covent Garden), Feb. 1860; The Amber Witch, Lond., Feb. 1861; Love's Triumph, London, Nov. 1862; The Desert Flower, London, Oct. 1863; The Maid of Zurich (never performed); Estrella (unfinished); Gulnare, operetta; Olga, operetta. *Pianoforte*: La Gondola, op. 18; Three nocturnes, op. 20; Chant d'Amour, op. 26; Tarentellas; Numerous transcriptions of popular airs and arrangements from operas. *Songs:* If doughty deeds; Silent love; The bellringer; Coming of the flowers; Gipsy maid; Leaves are turning red (Autumn song); Star of love; Wood-nymph; etc.

One of the most successful British composers, and with Balfe, the only one of the British school whose works keep the stage. "Maritana" is no doubt the most popular opera we have, and is also one of the best excepting the same composer's "Lurline," which is of very high merit. His works are written in the style common to nearly every British composer up to quite recent times, and as we have already spoken at length on the main characteristics of the school, reference need only be made to the articles BALFE and BARNETT in this work. The musical merits of Wallace's works are in general much higher than are common to those of Balfe, and there can be no doubt that his works unite a greater degree of richness and fine melody than any other English writer. His Pf. music is refined and graceful. See "William-Vincent Wallace, étude biographique et critique, par A. Pougin," Paris, 1866, 8vo.

WALLBRIDGE (Arthur). See LUNN (William A. B.)

WALLIS (John). English mathematician and writer, B. Ashford, Kent, Nov. 23, 1616. D. London, Oct. 28, 1703. Author of "Observations concerning the swiftness of sound," Lond., 1672, fo. "Claudii Ptolemæi Harmonicorum..." Oxford, 1680, 4to. Also numerous papers on musical subjects in Philosophical Transactions.

WALLWORTH (Thomas Adlington). English comp., teacher, and writer. B. Liverpool, Jan. 18, 1831. S. at R. A. M., where he is now Prof. of singing. Prof. at Guildhall School of Music. Sang as a barytone vocalist at London concerts, and in opera. Comp. "Kevin's Choice," opera, part-songs, and songs. Author of "The Art of Singing," Lond., n. d. "A Course of Study and Practice for the Voice," etc.

WALMISLEY (Thomas Forbes). English comp. and org., B. London, 1783. Chor. in Westminster Abbey. S. under Attwood. Married eldest daughter of Wm. Capon, 1810. Org. of S. Martin's-in-the-Fields, 1812. D. London, July 23, 1866.
WORKS.—Six Glees for 3, 4, 5 and 6 Voices, Lond., 1814 ; A Collection of Glees, Trios, Rounds, and Canons, Lond., 1826 ; Six Glees, dedicated to the Catch Club, Lond., 1830, fo. Six Glees for 4 Voices, 3rd collection, Lond., 1830, fo. ; Six Glees, 4th collection, Lond., fo. Many single glees, including prize glees, etc. Six Anthems and a Short Morning and Evening Service, Lond., n. d., fo. Sacred Songs, Lond., 1841. Songs.

WALMISLEY (Thomas Attwood). English org. and comp., B. London, Jan. 21, 1814. S. under Attwood. Org. of Croydon Ch., 1830 ; Trinity and S. John's Colls., Cambridge, 1833. Mus. Bac. Cantab., 1833. Prof. of Music at Cambridge, 1836. B.A., 1838 ; M.A., 1841. Mus. Doc. Cantab., 1846. D. Hastings, Jan. 17, 1856.
WORKS.—Cathedral Music, a Collection of Services and Anthems, Lond., 1857, fo., Edited by T. F. Walmisley. Anthems, odes, trios, songs, and concerted vocal music.

WALSHE (Walter Hayle). Irish writer, B. Dublin, 1816. Author of "Dramatic Singing Physiologically estimated," Lond., 1881, 8vo.

WALTER (Thomas). American writer, B. Roxbury, Mass., 1696. D. 1728. Author of the "Grounds and Rules of Musick Explained, or an Introduction to the Art of Singing by Note..." 1721 ; other eds., 1740, 1746, 1760.

WALTHER (Johann Gottfried). German writer, B. Erfurt, Sept. 18, 1684. Org. at Erfurt and Weimar. D. Weimar, Mar. 23, 1748. Author of "Musikalisches Lexikon, oder Musikalisches Bibliothek, darinnen nicht allein die Musici, welche so wol in alten als neuen Zeiten..." Leipzig, 1732. A combined biographical and technological dictionary.

WANHAL. See VANHALL.

WARD (Frederick). English violinist and comp., B. Birmingham, Dec. 26, 1845. Soloist and leader at the principal Birmingham and Midland concerts. Comp. a concert overture for orch. ; Concerto for clarinet and orch. ; Ten string quartets ; Songs, etc.

WARD (John). English comp. of 16th and 17th centuries. D. circa 1640. Comp. "The First Set of English Madrigals, to 3, 4, 5, and 6 parts, apt both for viols and voyces ; with a Mourning Song in Memory of Prince Henry..." London, 1613, 4to. Songs in Leighton's "Teares," and service and anthem in Barnard's collection.

WARE (George). English comp. and writer, B. 1762. D. Liverpool, 1850. Son of George Ware (B. 1723, D. London, Mar. 7, 1814), a vocal comp. Author of "A Dictionary of Musical Chords, arranged so as to find any Modulation, by various methods, through the twelve half tones..." Lond., n.d., fo. His brother, WILLIAM HENRY, was leader at Covent Garden Theatre, and comp. "Mother Goose," and other musical pieces.

WAREING (Herbert Walter). See BAPTIE. English comp., B. Birmingham, April 5, 1857. S. under Dr. C. S. Heap, and at Leipzig Cons. Mus. Doc., 1886.

WARING (William). See ROUSSEAU (J. J.).

WARMAN (John Watson). English org. and writer, B. Canterbury, Aug. 12, 1842. Author of a work on "The Organ," originally contributed to the *English Mechanic*, and now being republished in book form.

WARNER (James F.). American writer. Author of "A Universal Dictionary of Musical Terms," Boston, 1842, 8vo ; "Primary Note Reader, or First Steps in Singing at Sight," New York, n. d., 12mo ; " Rudimental Lessons on Music," New York, 1845, 18mo. Trans. Gottfried Weber's "General Music Teacher, adapted for Self-Instruction," Boston, 1842, 8vo ; and "Theory of Musical Composition," 1842, 8vo. Lond. ed. by John Bishop, 1851, 2 vols., 8vo.

WARNOTS (Henri). Belgian comp. and tenor vocalist, B. Brussels, July 11, 1832. S. at Brussels Cons., and now Prof. of Singing there. Comp. operas, etc. His daughter, ELLY, B. Liége, 1857, has sung in Brussels, and in 1881 appeared in London, where she has since frequently sung.

WARREN (Ambrose). English writer, author of "The Tonometer, explaining and demonstrating by an easy method in Numbers and Proportions, all the 32 Distinct and Different Notes, adjuncts, or supplements contained in each of four octives..." London, 1725, 4to.

WARREN (Edmund Thomas). English music-publisher, B. [1730]. D. 1794. Was Secretary of the Catch Club. Edited "Reliques of Ancient Music," and issued in monthly and annual parts the collection of catches and glees known as "Vocal Harmony."

WARREN (Joseph). English writer and org., B. London, March 20, 1804. S. under J. Stone. Org. and choir-master of S. Mary's R. C. Chapel, Chelsea, 1843. D. Bexley, Kent, March 8, 1881.

WORKS.—Hints to Young Organists, Lond., 1844. Biographical Dictionary of Deceased Musicians, Lond., 1845. Chanter's Hand Guide, Lond., 1845. Hints to Young Composers, Lond., 1846. Instruction Book for the Organ, Lond., n. d. Instructions for the Harmonium, Lond., 1852, fo. Introduction and Observations on the Mode of Singing Catches, Rounds, Canons, Glees, and Madrigals...Lond., n. d., fo. Selection of One Hundred Chants, 1845. Repertorium Musicæ Antiquæ, Lond., 1848, fo. (with John Bishop). Collection of Psalm and Hymn Tunes, 1850-53, 4 vols., 8vo. Hymns and Canticles, 1852, 12mo. Burial Service, as performed at the Funeral of the Duke of Wellington, 1853, 4to Edited Hymns of Joh. Sebastian Bach, Lond., n. d. ; Hamilton's Writing for the Orch., 1846 ; etc.

WARREN (Samuel P.) Canadian pianist and comp., B. Montreal, Feb. 18, 1841. Son of S. R. Warren, org.-builder. S. Pf. originally at home, and org. under G. F. Graham. Org. in a Ch. at Montreal, 1853-1861. S. at Berlin under Haupt (org., harmony, etc.), G. Schumann (Pf.), Wieprecht, and others, 1861-64. Returned to Montreal, 1864, and in 1865 became org. of All Soul's Ch., New York, till 1868. Afterwards org. of Grace Ch., and for a time, 1874-76, org. of Ch. of the Holy Trinity. Comp. Church services, anthems, and songs. Known as one of the most distinguished pianists of the United States.

WARTENSEE. See SCHNYDER VON WARTENSEE.

WASIELEWSKI (Joseph W. von). German violinist and writer, B. Gross-Leesen, near Dantzig, June 17, 1822. S. at Leipzig Cons. under Mendelssohn. Cond. at Bonn. Author of "Die Violine in XVI. Jahrhundert," Leipzig, 1869 ; "Geschichte der Instrumentalmusik in XVI. Jahrhundert," Berlin, 1878 ; A Life of Schumann, and other works. Resigned post of Town Conductor, Bonn, 1883, in order to devote more time to musico-literary labours.

WATSON (Thomas). English poet and comp. of 16th century. D. 1592. Comp. "The First Sett of Italian Madrigals Englished, not to the Sense of the Original Dittie, but after the Affection of the Noate," Lond., 1590, 4to.

WATSON (William Michal). English comp. and poet, B. Newcastle-on-Tyne, July 31, 1840. Best known as a very successful comp. of songs and Pf. music. Among his songs may be named :—Far o'er the mountains ; Little birdie, mine; Phœbe's trust; the blush rose; Talisman; Powder monkey; Mariner's song; Valiant knight; Two summer days; There's a bower of roses; Thoughts of home; My country calls; Gallant Vaquero, etc. Part-songs, and numerous Pf. pieces, original and arrangements.

WAYLETT (Mrs.), *née* COOKE. English soprano vocalist, B. Bath, Feb. 7, 1800. S. under Loder. *Début* at Bath, 1816. Married Mr. Waylett, 1819; separated from him, 1822. Afterwards married to G. Alex. Lee. Appeared in London, 1820; Dublin, 1826. Sang at principal London and provincial concerts. D. London, April 19, 1851.

WEATHERLY (Frederic E.) English poet, B. Portishead, 1848. Educated at Oxford, and became B.A., 1871; M.A., 1874. Tutor in Oxford. One of the most popular lyric authors of the present day. Author of "Muriel and other Poems;" "Verses for Children;" "Told in the Twilight;" "Sixes and Sevens;" "Dresden China," and other volumes of poetry. Librettos of many cantatas and oratorios, but best known by his popular songs, "Angus Macdonald" (Roeckel), "Nancy Lee" (Adams), "Polly" (Molloy), "London Bridge" (Molloy); "Midshipmite" (Adams); "When we are old and gray" (Sainton-Dolby); "The Worker" (Gounod); "The Chorister" (Sullivan); "Jack's Yarn" (Diehl); "Darby and Joan" (Molloy); "Old Lock" (Wellings); "At the Ferry" (Wellings); "Children's Dream" (Cowen), etc.

WEBB (Daniel). English writer, B. Taunton, 1735. D. Bath, Aug. 2, 1815. Author of "Observations on the Correspondence between Poetry and Music," Lond., 1769, 8vo (Anon.) Reprinted in his "Miscellanies," 1802.

WEBB (Francis). English writer, author of "Panharmonicon, an Illustration of an Engraved Plate, in which is attempted to be proved that the principles of Harmony more or less prevail throughout the whole System of Nature, but more especially in the Human Frame," Lond. [1815], 4to.

WEBB (George James). English org. and comp., B. near Salisbury, June 24, 1803. Org. and teacher in Boston, Mass., U. S. A. Author of "Vocal Technics," Boston, n. d.; and editor of "Young Ladies' Vocal Class Book," Boston, 1853; Glee Hive (with L. Mason); New Odeon (with L. Mason); Cantica Laudis (with Mason) N. Y., 1850.

WEBB (Rev. Richard, M.A.) English musician. Was minor Canon of S. Paul's, London. D. near Windsor, April 13, 1829. Published "A Collection of Madrigals for 3, 4, 5, and 6 voices, selected from the Works of the most eminent composers of the 15th and 16th Centuries," Lond., 1808, fo. Comp. a "Set of Four Glees for 3 Voices," Lond., n. d.

WEBBE (Samuel). English comp. and org., B. Minorca, 1740. S. under Charles Barbandt. Married 1763. Chap.-master in Portuguese Chap., London, 1776. Secretary to Noblemen and Gentlemen's Catch Club, 1794. D. London, May 25, 1816.

WORKS.—A Collection of Sacred Music, as used in the Chapel of the King of Sardinia in London, Lond., fo., n.d. A Collection of Masses, with an Accompaniment for the Organ...Lond., 1792, 12mo. Eight Anthems by Samuel Webbe, the Organ Parts by V. Novello, Lond., n.d. A Collection of Original Psalm Tunes for 3 and 4 Voices, by S. Webbe, Senr. and Junr., Lond., fo. *Glees:* A Selection of Glees, Duets, Canzonets, etc., published at different periods from the year 1764, to which are added many new glees and canzonets never before published, Lond., 3 vols., fo. A Collection of Catches, Canons and Glees, Lond., 9 vols. Six Original Glees, Lond., 1840, fo. *Single Glees*: Breathe soft, ye winds; Cecilia, more than all the muses skilled; Come live with me; Come, rosy health; Discord, dire sister, 1771; Glorious Apollo; Great Apollo, strike the lyre; Great Bacchus, O aid us; Fierce, all ye vain delights; Hail, star of Brunswick; Mighty conqueror of hearts, 1715; Swiftly from the mountain's brow (1788); Thy voice, O harmony; When winds breathe soft. Those dated are prize glees. Duets, songs. Concerto for harps. Pf. music, and other works.

Webbe was one of the most celebrated glee composers of England. With Callcott, Horsley, and Cooke, he stands foremost among British composers of concerted vocal music. He is best known by his glees, "When winds breathe soft," and "Swiftly from the mountain's brow.

WEBBE (Samuel, Junr.) English comp., writer, and org., B. London, 1770. S. under his father and Clementi. Org. successively of Unitarian Ch., Paradise St., Liverpool; Spanish Ambassador's Chap., Lond.; S. Nicholas Ch., and S. Patrick's R. C. Chap., Liverpool. D. Hammersmith, London, Nov. 25, 1843.

WORKS.—Collection of Motetts or Antiphons for 1, 2, 3, and 4 Voices, Lond., n.d., 4to. Collection of Psalm Tunes, intermixed with Airs adapted as such, for four Voices, Lond., 1808, 4to. Glees, duets, etc. Convito Armonico, a Collection of Madrigals, elegies, glees, canons, catches, and duets, selected from the works of the most eminent Composers, Lond., 4 vols., n.d. L'Amico del Principiante, being 28 short Solfaing Exercises for a Single Voice, Lond., n.d., 4to; 2nd edit. ed. by J. B. Sale. 42 Vocal Exercises...n.d. Short Exercises for Young Singers ...n.d. Harmony Epitomised, or Elements of the Thoroughbass, Lond., n.d., 4to.

WEBER (Carl Maria Friedrich Ernst, Baron von). German comp. and cond., B. Eutin, Holstein, Dec. 18, 1786. Son of Baron Franz Anton Weber and Genovefa Brenner. S. under Michael Haydn and J. W. Kalcher, and at Vienna under Vogler. Cond. to Duke Eugen Friedrich of Würtemberg, at Carlsruhe. Private Secretary to Duke Louis of Würtemberg, 1806. Travelled in Germany and Switzerland with Barmann the clarinet-player, 1811. Opera director at Prague, 1813-16. Married to Caroline Brandt, Dec., 1817. Cond. of German opera at Dresden. D. London, June 5, 1826 (in house of Sir George Smart). Buried at Dresden.

WORKS.—*Operas:* Das Waldmädchen, 1800; Peter Schmoll und seine Nachbarn, 1801; Silvana, 3 acts (new version of Das Waldmädchen), 1810; Abu Hassan, 1 act, Munich, 1811 (London, 1825); Der Freischütz, 3 acts, by Friedrich Kind, Berlin, June 18, 1821 (London, July, 1824); Preciosa, 4 acts, by P. A. Wolff, Dresden, 1822; Euryanthe, 3 acts, by Helmina von Chezy, Vienna, 1823 (London, 1833); Oberon, 3 acts, by J. R. Planché, London, 1826; Die drei Pintos, 3 acts (unfinished); Rübezahl (MS.) Op. 1. Six fugues, Pf., 1798; op. 2. Six variations, Pf.; op. 4. 12 Allemandes; op. 6. Six variations, Pf. and 'cello; op. 8. Overture, Peter Schmoll, 1807; op. 10. Six pieces, Pf. duet; op. 11. I. Concerto, Pf. and orch., in C, 1810; op. 12. Momento Capriccioso, Pf., 1808; op. 13. 6 Lieder; op. 14. Der erste Ton, poem by Rochlitz, 1808; op. 15. 6 Songs; op. 16. Concert aria, Il momento s'avoicina; op. 17. Six sonatas, Pf. and vn.; op. 18. Quartet, Pf. and strings; op. 19. Symphony, No. 1 in C, 1807, No. 2 in C, 1807; op. 23. 6 Songs; op. 24. I. Sonata, Pf., in C, 1812; op. 25. Five songs; op. 26. Concertino for clarinet, 1811; op. 27. Overture, Beherrschen der Geister (Ruler of the Spirits), 1811; op. 30. Six lieder; op. 32. II. Concerto, Pf. and orch., in E flat, 1812; op. 34. Quintet for clarinet and strings, 1815; op. 36. Hymn, In seinen ordnung schafft der Herr, 1812; op. 37. Music to "Turandot," a play; op. 39. II. Sonata for Pf. in A flat; op. 42. Six songs (including "Lützow's Wild Hunt); op. 44. Kampf und Sieg, cantata, 1815; op. 45. Concertino, horn and orch.; op. 49. III. Sonata, Pf., in D min., 1816; op. 50-53 Scenas, "Misera me!" "Non paventar," etc.; op. 54. Seven songs; op. 58. Jubel cantata, 1818; op. 59. Jubel overture, 1818; op. 61. Natur und Liebe, cantata, 1818; op. 62. Rondo, "La Gaite," Pf., 1819; op. 63. Trio, Pf., flute, and 'cello; op. 65. Aufforderung zum Tanze (Invitation à la valse), rondo for Pf., also for orch. by Berlioz; op. 66. Six songs; op. 70. IV. Sonata, Pf., in E min.; op. 71. Six songs; op. 72. Polacca, "L'hilarité," Pf.; op. 73. Concerto for clarinet and orch. in F min., 1811; op. 74. Do., in E flat; op. 75. Concerto for Bassoon, 1811; op. 75a. Missa Sancta, in E flat; op. 76. Mass, in G, No. 2; op. 79. Concertstück for Pf. and orch., 1821; op. 80. Six lieder; op. 81. Les Adieux, for Pf. in G min. Accompaniments for 10 Scottish Melodies, for Pf., flute, vn., and 'cello. Detached songs and Pf. pieces.

Weber was the most remarkable composer of the early days of romantic opera. To him is due the development of the romantic movement in music, and his operas mark the commencement of a long series of musical dramas founded on incidents which centre round supernatural events. His works are the musical complement of the corresponding romantic element in German literature which was forming and flourishing in Weber's time. His instrumental music is in general very rich and varied in character, and much of it remains in present use. His operas "Der Freischütz" and "Oberon," are, however, those works on which his fame will hereafter rest. See "Carl Maria von Weber, ein lebensbild," von Max Maria von Weber, Leipzig, 1864-68, 3 vols. Trans. as "Carl Maria von Weber, the Life of an Artist," by J. P. Simpson, Lond., 1865, 2 vols. Carl M. von Weber in seinen Werken, F. W. Jähns, 1871. Weber (Great Musicians), by Sir J. Benedict, Lond., 1881.

WEBER (Bernhard Anselm). German comp., B. Mannheim, April 18, 1766. S. under Vogler, etc. Chap.-master to the King of Prussia at Berlin, 1804. D. Berlin, March 23, 1821. Comp. operas, lieder, and instrumental music.

WEBER (Friedrich Dionysius). Bohemian teacher and writer, B. Welchau, 1771. Founder and director of Prague Cons. D. Prague, Dec. 26, 1842. Author of numerous theoretical works, and comp. operas, cantatas, masses, and much instrumental music.

WEBER (Gottfried). German writer, B. Freinsheim, Bavaria, Mar. 1, 1779. Educated at Heidelberg and Göttingen universities. Counsellor of Justice at Darmstadt. D. Kreuznach, Sept. 12, 1839. Author of "Versuch einer geordneten Theorie der Tonsetzkunst zum selbstunterricht, mit Anmerkungen für Gelehrtere..." Mayence, 1817-21, 3 vols. New edit., 1830-32, 4 vols. Trans. as "The Theory of Musical Composition treated with a View to a Naturally Consecutive Arrangement of Topics," by Jas. F. Warner, Boston, Mass., n.d., 8vo ; and another edition edited by John Bishop, Lond., 1851, 2 vols, 8vo. Numerous other writings on music.

WECKERLIN (Jean Baptist Theodor). French comp., B. Guebwiller, Alsace, Nov. 9, 1821. S. at Paris Cons. under Elwart and Halévy. Cond. in Paris, and was librarian at Cons. Comp. operas "L'Organiste," 1853, etc. Symphonies, choral music, songs, and writings on music.

WEELKES (Thomas). English comp. and org., B. [1575]. Org. of Winchester Coll. in 1600 ; and of Chichester Cath., 1608. D. [?]
WORKS.—Madrigals to 3, 4, 5, and 6 voyces, Lond., 1597, 4to ; Ed. by E. J. Hopkins for the Musical Antiquarian Soc., 1843. Ballets and Madrigals to five Voyces, with one to six voyces, 1598, 4to. Madrigals of Five and Six Parts, apt for Viols and Voices, 1600. Madrigals of Six Parts, apt for the Viols and Voices, Lond., 1600, 4to. Ayres or Phantasticke Spirites for 3 Voices, with a Song, a Remembrance of my Friend Mr. Thomas Morley, for 6 voices, Lond., 1608, 3 parts, 4to. Anthems and church music in collections of Clifford and Rimbault.

WEHLE (Charles). Bohemian pianist and comp., B. Prague, Mar. 17, 1825. S. under Thalberg, Moscheles, and Richter. Travelled in Europe, America, and Australia, and has appeared in London. D. Paris, June 2, 1883. Comp. Sonata in C min., op. 38 ; Marche Cosaque, op. 37. Tarentelles, ballades, serenades, valses, and numerous transcriptions for Pf.

WEIGL (Josef). Hungarian comp., B. Eisenstadt, Mar. 28, 1766. S. under Albrechtsberger and Salieri. Second chap.-master of Imperial Chap., Vienna. D. Vienna, Feb. 3, 1846. Comp. Cleopatra, 1807 ; Swiss Family, 1816 ; Eduard und Caroline. 1825 ; Ostade, 1806 ; Waldemar, 1824 ; and other operas and ballets. He comp. also oratorios, cantatas, overtures, and songs.

WEISS (Willoughby Hunter). English bass vocalist and comp., B. Liverpool, April 2, 1820. D. London, Oct. 24, 1867. A well-known vocalist, who appeared at the principal London and provincial concerts. Known also as comp. of the popular songs "The Village Blacksmith," "Bowmen of Old England," "Knight's Vigil," "Wreck of the homeward bound," etc.

WEITZMANN (Carl Friedrich). German writer and comp., B. Berlin, Aug. 10, 1808. S. under Klein, Spohr, etc. Prof. in Berlin Cons. D. Berlin, Nov. 7, 1880. Author of "Geschichte der Griechischen Musik," Berlin, 1855 ; "Geschichte der Harmonie und ihrer Lehre"; "Harmonic System," etc.

WELDON (Georgina), *née* TREHERNE. English soprano vocalist and writer, B. London, May 24, 1837. S. under her mother and Jules de Glimes. Gave concerts in Canada, and appeared in London as a vocalist. Organised a training school for vocalists, 1871. Authoress of "Musical Reform," Lond., 1872; "Hints for Pronunciation in Singing, with Proposals for a Self-supporting Academy," Lond., 1872. Autobiographie de Ch. Gounod...Lond., etc.

WELDON (John). English comp. and org., B. Chichester, about 1680. S. under John Walter of Eton Coll., and H. Purcell. Org. of New Coll., Oxford. Gent. extraordinary of Chap. Royal, June 6, 1701. Org. of Chap. Royal, 1708. Second comp. to Chap. Roy., 1715. Org. of S. Bride's and of S. Martin-in-the-Fields, London. D. London, May 7, 1736.

WORKS.—Divine Harmony, six select anthems for a voice alone, with a thorough-bass for the organ, Lond., n. d., fo. ; Hear my crying; In Thee, O Lord ; O God, Thou hast cast us out ; Who can tell how oft he offendeth, anthems   The Judgment of Paris, masque. Many songs in contemporary collections, such as "Let ambition fire thy mind," etc.

WELLER (S.) American writer, author of numerous practical handbooks, published in Boston, among which are—"Piano without a Master," "Reed Organ or Melodeon," "Violin without a Master," "Flute without a Master," "Fife without a Master," "Clarionet without a Master," and "Flageolet without a Master."

WELSH (Thomas). English bass vocalist, teacher, and comp., B. Wells, Somersetshire, 1770. Chor. in Wells Cath. S. under J. B. Cramer and Baumgarten. First appeared in opera in Attwood's "Prisoner," 1792. Engaged by Linley to sing in oratorio at Haymarket Theatre, London, 1796. Gent. of Chap. Royal. Celebrated as a vocal teacher in London, and numbered among his pupils John Sinclair, Charles Horn, Miss Stephens, and Miss Wilson (*Début*, 1821, sang in opera, D. 1867), who became his second wife. D. Brighton, Jan. 31, 1848.

WORKS.—Music to The Green Eyed Monster ; Twenty Years Ago ; Kamschatka, and other dramatic pieces. Sonatas for Pf. Part-songs, glees. and duets, numerous songs, etc. Vocal Instructor, or the Art of Singing exemplified in Fifteen Lessons leading to Forty progressive Exercises, Lond., n. d., fo.

WERCKMEISTER (Andreas). German org. and comp., B. Benneckenstein, Thuringia, Nov. 30, 1645. Org. at Halberstadt. D. Halberstadt, Oct. 26, 1706. Comp. org. and violin music, and wrote works on theory.

WÉRY (Nicolas Lambert). Belgian violinist and comp., B. Huy, Liége, May 9, 1789. S. under Gaillard. Prof. of vn. at Liége Cons. till 1860. D. Bande, Luxembourg, Oct. 6, 1867. Comp. concertos for vn. and orch., rondos, polonaises, and other vn. music, songs, etc. His pupils include Singelée, Colyns, Dubois, Massct, etc.

WESLEY (Charles). English org. and comp., B. Bristol, Dec. 11, 1757. Son of the Rev. Charles Wesley, and nephew of John Wesley, the Methodist leader. S. under Rooke, Kelway, and Boyce. Teacher in London. Org. of S. George's, Hanover Sq. Org. in ordinary to George IV. Gave subscription concerts at his house in London. D. London, 1834. Comp. "A Set of Eight Songs," 1784 ; "A Set of Six Concertos for the Organ or Harpsichord ;" Anthems in Page's "Harmonia Sacra."

WESLEY (Samuel). English org. and comp., B. Bristol, Feb. 24, 1766. Brother of the preceding. Gave very early indications of a disposition for music. S. under his brother Charles, and from an early age excited great interest among musicians by his extraordinary genius for music. He became the greatest organist of his time, and was the first Englishman to make known the music of Bach. D. London, Oct. 11, 1837.

WORKS.—Church Service in F. *Anthems and Motets:* My soul hath patiently ; Thou, O God, art praised in Sion ; I said I will take heed to my ways ; Dixit Dominus ; Exultate Deo ; In exitu Israel ; and other church music. Original Hymn Tunes adapted to every Metre in the Collection of the Rev. J. Wesley, Lond., n.d. Sonatas for Pf. Organ voluntaries, fugues. etc. "O, synge unto my roundelaie," madrigal, etc. The Misanthrope, opera (MS.) Letters of Samuel Wesley to Mr. Jacobs, relating to the Introduction into this Country of the Works of Bach, edited by E. Wesley," Lond., 1878, 8vo. See also "An Account of the Remarkable Musical Talents of several Members of the Wesley Family, collected from Original MSS., with Memorial Introduction and Notes by W. Winters," Lond., 1874, 8vo.

WESLEY (Samuel Sebastian). English org. and comp., B. London, Aug. 14, 1810. Son of the preceding. Chor. in Chap. Royal. Org. Hereford Cath., 1832; Exeter Cath., 1835. Mus. Bac. and Doc., Oxon., 1839. Org. Leeds Parish Ch., 1842; Winchester Cath., 1849; Gloucester Cath., 1865. D. Gloucester, April 19, 1876.

WORKS.—Church Services in E (1845), F, F (chant), and G. *Anthems:* Ascribe unto the Lord; All go unto one place; Blessed be the Lord; Blessed be the God and Father; Cast me not away; Give the King Thy judgments; Glory be to God on high; God be merciful; I am Thine; I will arise; Let us lift up our heart; Man that is born of a woman; O give thanks; O God, whose nature; O Lord, my God; O Lord, Thou art my God; Praise the Lord; The face of the Lord; The Wilderness; Thou wilt keep him in perfect peace; Wash me thoroughly; etc. The Psalter, with Chants, arranged for Daily Morning and Evening Service, Lond., 1843, 4to. *Glees and Part-songs:* At that Dread Hour; I wish to tune my quiv'ring lyre; Shall I tell you whom I love?; When fierce conflicting passions; etc. *Songs:* The Butterfly; Orphan hours the year is dead; There be none of beauty's daughters; Wert thou like me; etc. *Organ:* A Studio for the Organ, exemplified in a Series of Exercises; Air composed for the Holsworthy Church Bells; Andantes in G, A, E min., etc. Two sets (6 pieces) of Organ Pieces, etc. Melodia Sacra, Händel's airs arranged for Pf. The English Cathedral Service, its Glory, its Decline, and its designed Extinction, Lond., 1845. A Few Words on Cathedral Music and the Musical System of the Church, with a Plan of Reform, Lond., 1849, 8vo.

WEST (George Frederick). English writer, comp. and teacher, B. Bath. Author of "Questions relating to the Theory of Music," Lond., 1864, 12mo; and comp. of a very large number of Pf. pieces.

WEST (H.) English writer, author of "Singing Preceptor," Lond., 1846. "Accordian Preceptor," 1846.

WESTBROOKE (William Joseph). English comp., org. and writer, B. London, Jan. 1, 1831. Org. of S. Bartholomew, Bethnal Green, 1849; S. Bartholomew, Sydenham, 1851-84; Co-org., Crystal Palace, 1860. Cond. of South Norwood Musical Soc., 1865-78. Musical Examiner to the Coll. of Preceptors, London. Mus. Bac., Cantab., 1876: Mus. Doc., 1878. Established with A. W. Hammond and John Crowdy, the *Musical Standard*, 1862.

WORKS.—Jesus, oratorio, 1877. The Lord is my Shepherd, cantata, 1875. Services in G, D, etc. *Anthems:* Let them give thanks; Holy, holy!; Set up Thyself, O God; O God, Thou art my God; Now is Christ risen; O God, who by the leading of a star; With hearts renewed; I saw the Lord, etc., Bristol prize madrigal, 1865, "All is not gold." *Part-songs, and Trios for Ladies' Voices:* Holly berries; Fall on us, O night; Lines to the Evening Star; Sigh no more, Ladies; Burly Winter; Hurrah for Father Christmas; Consider the Lilies (trio); Dream, baby, dream; The little voice; Sing merrily all! *Songs:* Gather me smiles; The snow; On the water; Bonnie Bessie; Minnie mine; Shelley's Good Night; Watching; Christmas songs. *Organ:* Sonata in E flat, 1882; Three pieces, 1883; Voluntaries, 3 vols.; The Young Organist, 2 vols.; The Organist, 2 vols.; Haydn's Last Seven Words (complete); The Practical Organist, 5 nos.; The Organ Journal; Ancient and Modern Fugues, 3 books; The March Album, etc. Harmonium Music, The Hundred Composers, English, French, Italian, and German, 4 vols. Pianoforte pieces, The Young Artist, 12 sonatas, 1883. *Literary:* Elementary Music, a Primer, London, 1879; A Practical Organ Tutor, n.d.; Translations of De Beriot's, Dancla's, and Alard's Violin School's, etc.

WESTMORELAND (John Fane, Earl of), Lord BURGHERSH. English comp., B. London, Feb. 3, 1784. Entered army, 1803. Envoy at Court of Florence, 1814. S. music under Hague, Mayseder, Portogallo, and Bianchi.

Succeeded to title, 1841. British Minister at Berlin, 1841-51. Established the Royal Academy of Music, London, in which a scholarship was founded in his memory, 1861. D. Apthorpe House, Oct. 16, 1859.

WORKS.—*Operas*: Bajazet, Florence, 1821 (Lond., 1822); L'Eroe di Lancastre, R. A. M. Pupils, 1826; Lo Scompiglio teatrale, Florence, 1830 (published 1846); Catarina, ossia l'assedio di Belgrade, Lond., 1830 (in English as Catherine the Austrian Captive); Fedra, Florence, 1828 (pub. Berlin, 1848); Il Torneo, Florence, 1829 (Lond., 1838); Il Ratto di Proserpina, 1845. Cathedral Service, 1841; Messa Solenne, 1858; Requiem to the Memory of Samuel Webbe (with others); Six Canons, for three voices; Six Cantatas of Metastasio, for solo voice and Pf., 1831. Madrigals, glees, and numerous single songs. Three symphonies for orch., quartets, and Pf. music.

WESTROP (East J.). English comp., B. Lavenham, Suffolk, 1804. D. London, 1856. Comp. "Carmina Sacra," Lond., 1857, 8vo; 100 Little Songs for Little Singers, 1857; Normal Singer, 1857; 200 Psalms and Hymns, with Wade, 1859; etc.

WESTROP (Henry). English comp., violinist, org. and cond., B. Lavenham, Suffolk, July 22, 1812. Org. of S. Stephen's, Norwich; Little Stanmore, 1831; Fitzroy Chap., London, 1833; S. Edmund the King and Martyr, Lombard St., London, 1834. Vnst. at Italian opera and Philharmonic Soc. Cond. the Choral Harmonist's Soc. Mem. of Philharmonic Soc., and of Royal Soc. of Musicians. D. London, Sept. 23, 1879.

WORKS.—Maid of Bremen, opera (E. Fitzball), in MS. (was preparing for production by the Pyne and Harrison Company when that undertaking ceased). Anthem, O taste and see, in E flat. Symphony for orch., 1838. Quintets for Pf. and strings, in E flat, 1843, and C min. 1844; Quartet for Pf. and strings, in A flat, op. 2; Trio, for Pf. and strings, in F, 1841. Sonata, Pf. and violin, in F, 1844; Sonata, Pf. and flute, in F, op. 6; Sonata for Pf. and viola, E flat. Quartets for strings, in E, and E flat. *Pianoforte*: Allegro, in E flat; Parting; Greeting; A summer eve. Winter, descriptive cantata for bass voice and orch.

A musician much respected in London. His daughter, KATE, is a pianist and org. of ability. His brother, THOMAS, B. 1816, D. 1881, was a writer and comp. He published "120 Selected Short Anthems," Lond., 1861; "Psalms, Hymns, etc.," 1862, 4to; "18 Selected Vocal Duets," 1863; "Sacred Songs," 1863; "Universal Violin Tutor," 1862, 8vo; "Complete Organ Tutor," 1863, 4to.

WEYMAN (David). Irish collector, was vicar-choral of S. Patrick's, Dublin, early in 19th century. Published "Melodia Sacra, or, the Psalms of David, arranged for 1, 2, 3, or 4 Voices," Dublin, 1812-14, fo. Sequel in 3 vols., 1840-52, 4to.

WEYSE (Christoph Ernst Friedrich). German comp., B. Altona, Mar. 5, 1774. Prof. of music in Copenhagen. D. Copenhagen, Oct. 4, 1842. Comp. "Ludlam's Höhle," opera, 1809. Symphonies, overtures, sonatas and other Pf. works.

WHEALL (William). English org. and comp., was org. of St. Paul's, Bedford. Mus. Bac. Cantab., 1719. D. 1745. Comp. the psalm-tune, "Bedford," etc.

WHEELER (Lyman Warren). American tenor vocalist and teacher, B. Swampscott, Mass, April 7, 1835. S. under C. A. Adams, and in 1860 went to London, where he S. under Garcia. He afterwards continued his studies under Prati and San Giovanni, of Milan; Skafati, of Naples; and again in London under Garcia, Perrin, and Smith. Sang in America as a concert vocalist, but best known there as a successful teacher. His pupils include the well-known vocalists Miss Annie Louise Cary, and Miss Jennie Sargent.

WHICHELLO (Abiell). Org. and comp., was deputy org. to Philip Hart. Org. of Ch. of S. Edmund the King. Played at Britton's concerts. D. about 1745. Comp. songs, and a "Collection of Lessons for the Harpsichord or Spinnet."

WHITAKER (John). English comp., B. 1776. D. London, Dec. 4, 1848. His biography is obscure. Known as the comp. of the popular songs, "Oh! say not woman's heart is bought;" "Thine am I, my faithful fair;" and a number of glees, "Winds gently whisper," and other works.

WHITE (Mrs. F. Meadows). See SMITH (Alice Mary).

WHITE (Maude Valerie). English comp., B. Dieppe, June 23, 1855. S. under Sir G. A. Macfarren at R. A. M., and in 1879 gained the Mendelssohn Scholarship. Comp. part-songs. *Songs*: Ave Maria; The lassie I lo'e best; To Daffodils; There was a king of Thule; My ain kind dearie, O; To Blossoms; Loving and true; Montrose's Love Song, etc. Also comp. Pf. music, a mass, and other works.

WHITE (Richard Grant). American writer on musical and philological topics, B. New York, May 23, 1822. D. there April 8, 1885.

WHITE (Robert). English comp. and org. of 16th century. Org. of Ely Cath., 1562. D. about 1581. The Library of Christ Church Coll., Oxford, contains a number of his comps. in MS.

WHITFIELD. See CLARKE-WHITFIELD.

WHITING (George E.) American comp. and org., B. Holliston, Mass, 1842. S. under W. T. Best and R. Radecke. Org. at Hartford, Conn.; King's Chap., Boston; Pro Cath.; Music Hall Soc.; Ch. of the Immaculate Conception, Boston. Org. of Cincinnati Music Hall for five years. Now head of the org. department in New England Cons. of Music, Boston.

WORKS.—Op. 1. The organist, 12 pieces; op. 2. Three preludes, org.; op. 3. 25 Studies; op. 4. Mass in C; op. 10. Six songs; op. 11. Prologue to Longfellow's "Golden Legend"; op. 12. Set of Part-songs; op. 13-18. Church services; op. 21. Festival Te Deum; op. 22. Fantasia, org.; op. 23. Registration fantasia, org.; op. 24. Storm fantasia, org.; op. 25. Magnificat; op. 26. Preludes for Grand Mass; op. 31. Bethlehem, female voices; op. 32. Suite, 'cello and Pf.; op. 33. Hymns and Offertory Pieces; op. 34. Psalm; op. 35. Grand Sonata; op. 36. Preludes; op. 37. 2nd Mass, F min.; op. 40. Tale of the Viking; op. 41. March of the Monks of Bangor; op. 42. Leonore, cantata; op. 43. Midnight cantata; op. 44. Overture to Tennyson's "Princess," etc.

WHITNEY (Samuel B.) American comp. and org., B. Woodstock, Vermont, June 4, 1842. Org. of Christ Ch., Montpelier, Vt.; S. Peter's, Albany, N.Y.; S. Paul's, Burlington, Vt.; Old Ch. of the Advent; and now of New Ch. of the Advent, Boston. Prof. in New England Cons. of Music, and in Boston University. Comp. Two full Communion Services; Five Te Deums; and numerous other pieces for the church service; Organ music; Trio for Pf. and strings; Pf. music, and songs.

WHITTINGHAM (Alfred). English org. and writer, author of "The Major and Minor Scales, in Octaves, Sixths, and Thirds..." Lond., n. d. "Life and Works of Mozart," 1880, 8vo. "Life and Works of Handel," Lond., 1881, and other works.

WHYTHORNE or WHITHORNE (Thomas). English comp., B. 1531. Comp. "Songes of Three, Fower and Five Voyces..." Lond., 1571, 4to. "Bassavo, Duos, or Songs for Two Voices," 1590.

WIDOR (Charles Marie). French comp., org., and pianist, B. Lyons, Feb. 22, 1845. S. at Brussels under Lemmens and Fétis. Org. of S. Francis, Lyons, 1860; S. Sulpice, Paris, 1869.

WORKS.—La Nuit de Walpurgis, symphonic poem. Concerto for Pf. and orch., 1876. Concerto for 'cello and orch.; Quintet in D min. for Pf. and strings, op. 7; Six Symphonies for org.; Ballet Airs, Pf., op. 4; Psalm CXII., for chorus, 2 orgs., and orch. Songs, duets, and other vocal music.

WIECK (Friedrich). German pianist, comp., and writer, B. Pretsch, Wittemberg, Aug. 18, 1785. Teacher in Leipzig and Dresden. D. Loschwitz, Dresden, Oct. 6, 1873. His daughter, CLARA, married Robert Schumann (see that name). His second daughter, MARIE, is also a pianist of note. His "Piano and Singing" was translated *for* Clara and Marie by H. Krueger.

WIENIAWSKI (Henri). Polish violinist and comp., B. Lublin, July 10, 1835. S. under Massart at Paris Cons., 1844. Gained first violin prize, 1846. Appeared as violinist in Russia, 1848. Solo vnst. to Emperor of Russia. Prof. of violin at Brussels Cons., 1874-77. D. Moscow, April 2, 1880. Comp. Fantasias, polonaises, legends, airs, and transcriptions for the violin. His brother, JOSEPH, B. Lublin, May 23, 1837. S. at Paris Cons. under Alkan, Marmontel, and Le Couppey. Gained first prize for Pf. playing, 1849. Appeared with his brother in Poland, Germany, Belgium, and Holland. Comp. op. 1. Two Idylles, Pf.; op. 3. Valse; op. 4. Tarantelle; Duets, transcriptions, etc., for Pf.

WIEPRECHT (Wilhelm Friedrich). German comp. and teacher, B. Aschersleben, Aug. 9, 1800. Director of military music in Prussia. D. Berlin, Aug. 4, 1872. Comp. much military music, and was noted as a teacher.

WIGAN (Arthur Cleveland). English writer and comp., B. London, 1815. Author of "Modulating Dictionary, consisting of 552 Modulations with the Returns," Lond., 1852, 8vo. Comp. also many good songs.

WILBYE (John). English comp. of 16th century. His biography is very obscure. In 1598 he was a teacher of music in Austin Friars, London. Comp. "Madrigals to 3, 4, 5, and 6 Voices..." London, Este, 1598. Reprinted by Musical Antiquarian Soc., edit. by James Turle, 1841. "The Second Set of Madrigals, to 3, 4, 5, and 6 parts, apt both for Voyals and Voyces," Lond., 1609. Reprinted by Mus. Antiq. Soc., edit. by G. W. Budd, 1846. "The Lady Oriana," madrigal is in the "Triumphs of Oriana." Among his best known madrigals are "Flora gave me fairest flowers," "Sweet honey-sucking bee," "Die, hapless man," "When Cloris heard," "Stay, Corydon," "Lady, when I behold," "Why dost thou shoot," etc. These madrigals are the sweetest, most appropriate, and fanciful pieces of pastoral music ever composed. There can be no hesitation in accepting Oliphant's verdict, which places him above all other madrigal composers as a writer of pretty pastoral music.

WILHELM (Carl). German comp., B. Schmalkalden, Sept. 5, 1815. S. under Spohr, etc. Cond. at Crefeld. D. Schmalkalden, Aug. 25, 1873. Comp. many fine lieder, but only remembered now as the composer of the "Watch on the Rhine" (Die Wacht am Rhein).

WILHELMJ (Auguste Emil Daniel Friedrich Victor). German violinist and comp. B. Usingen, Nassau, Sept. 21, 1845. S. originally under Fischer. Appeared first in public, 1854. Patronised by Liszt. S. at Leipzig Cons. under Hauptmann, Richter, and David, 1861-64. Appeared in Switzerland, Holland, London, 1865-66; Paris, 1867, Denmark, Sweden, and the United States. Has appeared frequently in London, and is esteemed one of the greatest living violinists. Has comp. a number of transcriptions for violin.

WILHEM (Guillaume Louis Bocquillon-). French writer and teacher, B. Paris, Dec. 18, 1781. D. Paris, April 26, 1842. A strenuous advocate of the fixed Doh principle, which was adopted by the late Dr. Hullah, in connection with which he compiled a number of instruction books, "Methode. Manuel Musicale," 1840, etc. Some of his books have been translated.

WILLAERT (Adrien). Belgian comp., B. Bruges [1490]. Educ. at Paris Univ. S. under Mouton, Okenheim, and Josquin. Resided at Paris for a time. Chap.-master, S. Mark's, Venice, 1527. D. Venice, Dec. 7, 1562. He comp. Il Primo Libro de Motetti, 1542; Canzone Villanesche, 1545; Libro primo de Madrigali, a cinque voci, 1548. Fantasie, 1549. Psalmi Vespertini, 1550, and other books of sacred and secular music.

WILLIAMS (Anna). English soprano vocalist. S. in London under H. Deacon and J. B. Welch, and at Naples under Scapati. *Début* at Crystal Palace, 1874. Has appeared at most of the principal London and provincial concerts, and is a leading soprano in oratorio.

WILLIAMS (George Ebenezer). English comp. and org., B. 1783. Chor. in S. Paul's Cath. under R. Bellamy. Deputy Org. Westminster Abbey, 1814. D. London, April 17, 1819. Comp. "Sixty Chants, Single and Double," and other vocal music.

WILLIAMS (Joseph), FLORIAN PASCAL. English comp., son of the late Joseph Williams, music-publisher. B. London, 1850. S. at Zurich and Stuttgart. Comp. an opera, overtures, orch. suites, Pf. music, and songs.

WILLIS (Richard Storrs). American writer, B. Boston, Feb. 10, 1819. Editor of the *New York Musical Times*. Compiled "Church Chorales and Choir Studies," N. Y., n. d. Author of "Our Church Music, a Book for Pastors and People," 1855, 12mo.

WILLMERS (Heinrich Rudolf). German pianist and comp., B. Berlin, Oct. 31, 1821. S. under Hummel and F. Schneider. D. Vienna, Aug. 24, 1878. Comp. Rêverie, op. 8; Sonata héroique, op. 33; Jugendtraume, op. 80; Scènes champêtres, op. 84; Impressions du Rhin, op. 86; and numerous Pf. studies, transcriptions, and other works.

WILSON (Hugh). Scottish comp., B. 1764. Comp. of the well-known psalm tune, "Martyrdom."

WILSON (John). English comp. and lute player, B. Feversham, Kent, 1594. Doc. Mus., Oxon., 1644. Resided with family of Sir Wm. Walter of Sarsden, Oxfordshire, 1646. Prof. of Music, Oxford, 1656. Gent. of Chap. Royal, 1662. D. Westminster, Feb. 22, 1673. Identified by Rimbault as the Jack Wilson who sang in Shakespeare's plays. Comp. "Psalterium Carolinum, the Devotions of his Sacred Majestie in his Solitudes and Sufferings, rendered in Verse, set to Music for Three Voices, and an Organ or Theorbo," 1657; "Cheerful Airs or Ballads, first composed for one single voice, and since set for three voices," Oxford, 1660; "Aires for a Voice alone to a Theorbo or Bass Viol. Divine Services and Anthems," 1663; "Fantasias for Viols."

WILSON (John). Scottish tenor vocalist, B. in the Canongate, Edinburgh, Dec. 25, 1800. Married about 1820. Reader for the Press in Ballantyne's Printing Office, Edinburgh. S. under Finlay Dun. Choir-singer in Duddingston Parish Ch., where the Rev. John Thomson was pastor. Precentor of Relief Ch., Roxburgh Place, Edin. ; do. S. Mary's, 1826. Sang at concerts in Edinburgh. S. singing in London under Lanza, 1827, and Crivelli, 1830. S. harmony under Aspull. First appeared in opera in "Guy Mannering," as Harry Bertram, Edinburgh, March, 1830. Sang in opera in London, from 1830, and became highly successful in English opera at Covent Garden, Drury Lane, and other theatres. Travelled in Britain giving his Songs of Scotland entertainment, and appeared as concert and opera singer till 1838. Appeared in the United States, 1838. Visited Canada, 1849. D. Quebec, July 8, 1849. One of the most successful Scottish singers. His entertainments consisted of Nights with Burns, Jacobite Songs, etc., and were very well patronised wherever he appeared. He published "Wilson's Edition of the Songs of Scotland, as Sung by him at his Entertainments on Scottish Music and Song," Lond., 1842, 3 books.

WILSON (Miss). See WELSH.

WILSON (William). Author of "A New Dictionary of Music" (with Grier), Lond., n.d. 12mo.

WILT (Marie). Austrian soprano vocalist, B. Vienna, 1838. S. under Gänsbacher. *Début* Gratz, 1865. Appeared in London, 1866, Vienna, etc. Sang in operas of Meyerbeer, Thomas, Weber, Mozart, etc.

WILTON. See LABLACHE (Fanny).

WILTON (Thomas Egerton, Second Earl of). English comp., B. 1799. D. 1882. Comp. "O Praise the Lord," anthem; "Hymn to Eros," chants, and other vocal music.

WINGHAM (Thomas.) English comp., B. London, Jan. 5, 1846. S. at R. A. M. under Bennett. Prof. of Pf. at R. A. M. Comp. six overtures, symphonies, Mass in D, anthems, songs, and other works.

WINN (William). English bass vocalist and comp., B. Bramham, Yorks., May 8, 1828. Gent. of Chap. Royal, 1864. Vicar-choral of S. Paul's, London, 1867. Comp. glees and part-songs; Songs—The Old Ice-king, Evening Thoughts, A kiss and nothing more; and other vocal works. Well known as a bass singer of great power and culture.

WINNER (Septimus). American writer, author of New School for the Violin, 1870; Easy System for the Pianoforte; New School for the Piano; New School for the Cabinet Organ; Easy System for the Melodeon; Guitar Primer; Perfect Guide for the Violin; New School for the Flute; Easy System for the Violoncello; Perfect Guide for the Accordeon; New School for the Banjo; Perfect Guide for the German Concertina; New School for the Clarionet; New School for the Flageolet; New School for the Cornet; and Singing Method. All these, with many others, are issued by Ditson of Boston, Mass.

WINTER (Peter von). German comp., B. Mannheim, 1754. S. under Vogler. Cond. Court Theatre, Munich. Visited Paris, 1802; London, 1803-5. D. Munich, Oct. 17, 1825.

WORKS.—*Operas*: Der Bettelstudent; Psyche, 1793; Der Sturm, 1793; Das Unterbrochene Opferfest (Interrupted Sacrifice), Munich, 1795; Die Thomasnacht, 1795; Calypso, Lond., 1803; Castor and Pollux, Lond., 1803; Proserpina, do., 1804; Zaira, do., 1805; Der Sanger und der Schneider. Ballets—Colman, 1809, etc. Cantatas, church music, symphonies, overtures, etc.

WISE (Michael). English comp., B. Salisbury, 1638. Educated in Chap. Royal under Cook. Org. and choirmaster, Salisbury Cath., 1668. Gent. of Chap. Royal, 1675. Almoner and master of the choristers, S. Paul's, Lond., 1686-7. Killed at Salisbury in a midnight brawl with the Watch, Aug. 1687. Comp. Magnificat in E flat. *Anthems*: Prepare ye the way of the Lord; Awake, put on Thy strength; Blessed is he; Awake up, my glory; The Ways of Zion do mourn; Thy beauty, O Israel; etc.

WOAKES (W. H.) English writer and comp., was org. at Hereford. Author of "A Catechism of Thorough-bass, Catechism on Music, and Dictionary," Hereford, 1820, 12mo. Comp. also glees, songs, and anthems.

WOHLFAHRT (Heinrich). German writer and comp., B. Kossnitz, Dec. 16, 1797. D. May 7, 1883. Best known by his instruction books in theory and for the Pf., and by numerous pieces for that instrument. His "Guide to Musical Composition" was trans. by J. S. Dwight, Boston, n.d.

WÖLFFL (Joseph). Austrian comp. and pianist, B. Salzburg, 1772. S. under L. Mozart and M. Haydn. Appeared at Warsaw, Vienna, etc. Married Therese Klemm, 1798. Appeared in London and Paris till 1801. Resided in London as teacher from 1805. D. London, May 22, 1814.

WORKS.—Concertos for Pf. and orch., op. 20, 26, 32, 49, etc.; Quartets for strings, op. 4, 10, 30; Trios for strings, op. 6, 19, 25, 33; Sonatas, Pf. and vn., op. 7, 9, 13, 18, 24; Sonatas, Pf. solo, op. 1, 15, 19, 22, 36, 38, 41, 45, 47, 50, 54, 55, 58, 62, etc.; School for the pianoforte, op. 56. Rondos and arrangements for Pf. "The Surprise of Diana," and other works.

WOLLENHAUPT (Hermann Adolph). German pianist and comp., B. Schkenditz, Dusseldorf, Sept. 27, 1827. S. under Hauptmann. Teacher in New York from 1845. D. New York, Sept. 18, 1863. Comp. Polkas, op. 8; Nocturne, op. 15; La campanella, op. 16; Five pieces, op. 22; Galop, op. 24; Andante, op. 45; Valse gracieuse, op. 70; and numerous Pf. transcriptions and arrangements.

WOOD (Anthony a). English antiquary and writer, B. Oxford, Dec. 17, 1632. D. Oxford, Nov. 29, 1695. From his writings many biographies of the older musicians have been taken. His "Athenæ Oxonienses...," Lond., 1691-92, 2 v. fo., contains notices of musicians who were educated at Oxford, and there exists in MS. in the Ashmolean Museum a work entitled "Some Materials towards a History of the Lives and Compositions of all English Musicians." "A Wood," as he styles himself, was a great amateur musician.

WOOD. See PATON.

WOOD (John Muir). Scottish music-publisher, B. early in the present century. Established music-publishing businesses in Edinburgh and Glasgow. He was associated with Chopin and other great artists who visited Scotland on concert-giving enterprizes. His firm published for a time the *Scottish Monthly Musical Times*, a journal which lived only for a short time 1876-78. He edited a new edition of the "Songs of Scotland" (1884), and has contributed important Scottish matter to Grove's "Dictionary of Music."

WOODBURY (Isaac B.) American writer and comp., B. Beverly, Mass., Oct. 18, 1819. S. in Europe for one year, and was chiefly engaged as teacher and cond. in various American towns. D. Colombia, S.C., Oct. 26, 1858.

WORKS.—The Dulcimer, collection of church music, N. Y., 1850. Liber Musicus, 1851. The Cythara. Cultivation of the Voice without a Master, N. Y., n. d. Self-Instruction in Musical Composition and Thorough-Bass, n. d. Singing School and Music Teacher's Companion, n. d. Melodeon and Seraphine Instruction-Book, n. d. Edited and established the *Musical Review*, 1850; and the *Musical Pioneer*.

WOODMAN (Rev. W.) Author of "Singing at Sight made Easy, complete course of Instruction," Lond., 1860, 8vo.

WOODWARD (Richard). Irish org. and comp., B. Dublin, about 1744. Bac. Mus., Dublin, 1768; Doc. Mus., 1771. Vicar-choral, S. Patrick's Cath., 1772. Org. of Christ Ch. Cath., 1765. Master of Choristers, S. Patrick's and Christ Ch. Cathedrals. D. Dublin, 1777-78. Comp. "Cathedral Music in Score," op. 3. Anthems. "Songs, Catches, and Canons," n. d., etc.

WOOLHOUSE (W. S. B.) English writer, author of "A Catechism of Music," Lond., 1843, 18mo. "A Treatise on Singing," Lond., n. d., fo.

WORGAN (John). English org. and comp., B. London, 1724. S. under Rosingrave and Geminiani. Org. and comp. to Vauxhall Gardens, 1751-74. Org. of S. Botolph's, Aldgate, London, 1753; S. Mary Axe; and S. John's, Bedford Row. Mus. Bac., Cantab., 1748. Mus. Doc., 1775. D. London, Aug. 24, 1790.

WORKS.—*Oratorios*: Hannah, 1764; Manasseh. Anthems, various. Canzonets; The Agreeable Choice, a collection of Songs; Pieces for the Harpsichord; Six Sonatas for the Harpsichord, 1769; Org. music, etc.

Celebrated as an organist. His son, THOMAS DANVERS WORGAN, was author of "Rouge et Noine de Musique, or Harmonic Pastimes, being games of cards constructed on the principles of Music," Lond., 1807, 12mo. "The Musical Reformer, comprising an Apology for Intellectual Music...," Lond., 1829, 8vo. He was brother-in-law of Sir Wm. Parsons.

WRAGG. English flute-player, comp., and writer, of early part of present century. Author of "Wragg's Improved Flute Preceptor," Lond., n. d., which went through many editions. He comp. solos for the flute.

WRIGHT (Henry S.). English writer, author of "An Introduction to the Study of Music, with Historical and other References," London, n. d., 8vo.

WRIGHT (Thomas). English org. and comp., B. Stockton-on-Tees, 1763. Assistant org. to Garth, and Ebdon of Durham. Org. at Sedgefield, 1785-97; afterwards at Stockton. D. at Wycliffe Rectory, near Barnard Castle, Nov. 24, 1829. Comp. Pf. concerto; "Rusticity," an operetta, 1860; Anthems, songs, and Psalm tunes, "Stockton," etc.

WRIGHT (T. H.). English writer, author of "New Preceptor for the Harp, including a Series of Exercises, and succeeded by Preludes, and Progressive Lessons..." London, 1825.

WRIGHTON (W. T.). English comp., B. 1816. D. Tunbridge Wells, July 13, 1880. Comp. of numerous popular songs, among which may be named "Her bright smile haunts me still," "Approach of Spring," "A wish."

"Days gone by," "Ever with thee," "Memories," "My mother's name," "Our English rose," "Postman's knock," "You need na come courting o' me"; Duets, etc.

WÜERST (Richard). German comp. and teacher, B. Berlin, Feb. 22., 1824. S. under H. Ries and Mendelssohn. Prof. in Kullak's Cons., Berlin. Director of Royal Music. Berlin. D. Berlin, Oct. 9. 1881. Comp. Rothmandel, opera, 1848; Der Stern von Turan, 1864; Vineta, 1864; Faublas, 1873. Cantatas, lieder, chamber music. Writings on music, etc.

WÜLLNER (Franz). German comp. and cond., B. Münster, 1832. S. under Schindler. Cond. at Aix-la-Chapelle and Munich. Chap.-master at Dresden. Comp. choral music, songs, Pf. music, and wrote a "Chorgesangschule." Succeeded Dr. Hiller at Cologne, 1884.

WYLDE (Henry). English comp. and writer, B. Hertfordshire, 1822. Mus. Doc., Cantab., 1851 (accumulated degrees). Gresham Prof. of music in succession to Prof. E. Taylor, 1863. Assoc. R. A. M., etc. Author of "Harmony and the Science of Music," Lond., 1865, 8vo, and 1872; "Music in its Art Mysteries," Lond., 1867, 8vo; "Modern Counterpoint in Major Keys," Lond., 1873; "Occult Principles of Music..." 1881, 8vo; "Music as an Educator..." 1882, 8vo.

WYVILL (Zerubbabel). English comp., B. Maidenhead, Berks., 1762. Teacher at Maidenhead. D. there, 1837. Comp. "A Collection of Psalms and Hymns for four voices," Lond., n. d.; "A Collection of Catches and Glees, for 3 and 4 voices,..." Lond., n.d., fo. Now remembered as the composer of "Eaton" and other hymns.

Y.

YANIEWICZ. See JANIEWICZ.

YONGE (Nicholas). English musician, published "Musica Transalpina, Madrigales translated, of 4, 5, and 6 parts, chosen out of divers excellent authors..." Lond., 1588, 4to; "Musica Transalpina, the Second Book of Madrigalles, to 5 and 6 voices, translated out of sundry Italian authors .." Lond., 1597, 4to; Contents set out in Oliphant's "Musa Madrigalesca."

YOUNG (Anne). See GUNN (Anne).

YOUNG (Rev. Edward). English writer on art and music, author of "The Harp of God, Twelve Lectures on Liturgical Music, its Import, History, Present State, and Reformation," Lond., 1861, 8vo.

YOUNG (John Matthew Wilson). English org. and comp., B. Durham, Dec. 17, 1822. S. under Henshaw. Prof. of music at York Training Coll. Org. Lincoln Cath. from 1850. Comp. "The Return of Israel to Palestine," cantata; O Lord, Thou art great and glorious; I will extol my God; O Lord, God of my salvation, anthems, etc.

YOUNG (William James). English comp. and org., brother of preceding. B. Durham, April 18, 1835. S. under his brother. Assistant org. Lincoln Cath., 1857-8. Org. at S. John's, Longsight, Manchester, 1858-71; St. Peters, Levenshulme; and S. James's, Birch-in-Rusholme, 1880. Composed 27 good part-songs—I love the merry spring time; Gaily through the greenwood; Welcome, merry May; Fairy revels; The merry bird; The streamlet; Coming of Spring, etc.

YOUNG (Rev. Matthew, D.D.). Irish writer, B. Roscommon, 1750. D. 1800. Author of "Inquiry into the Principal Phenomena of Sounds and Musical Strings," Lond., 1784, 8vo.

YRIARTE (Tomas de). Spanish poet, author of "La Musica Poema," Madrid, 1784. Trans. as "Music, a Didactic Poem, in five cantos," by John Belfour, Lond., 1807, 8vo.

Z.

ZACCONI (Lodovico). Italian theorist of 16-17th centuries. Author of "Pratica di Musica...," Venice, 1596, fo.

ZACHAU (Friedrich Wilhelm). German org. and comp., B. Leipzig, Nov. 19, 1663. D. Halle, Aug. 14, 1717. Comp. music for the church service, org. pieces, etc., but now remembered only as the teacher of Handel.

ZARLINO (Gioseffo). Italian writer and comp., B. Chioggia, 1519. Chap.-master of St. Mark's, Venice. D. Venice, Feb. 16, 1590. His didactic works were collected under the general title "Di Tutti l'Opere," Venice, 1589, 4 v. fo., containing his most famous works, "L'Istituzioni harmoniche"; "Le Dimostrationi harmoniche," "Sopplimenti Musicali," etc.

ZAVERTHAL (J. R.). See SAVARTHAL (J. R.).

ZAVERTHAL (Wenceslas Hugo). Bohemian comp., B. Polep, Aug. 31, 1821. Brother of Johann Rudolf Saverthal. Clarinet-player and bandmaster. Married Carlotta Maironi, 1847. Cond. at Modena, etc. Resident at Helensburgh, on the Clyde, since 1875. Comp. orchestral music, church music, part-songs, and songs. His second son, LADISLAO, B. Milan, Sept. 29, 1849, was appointed bandmaster of the Royal Artillery, at Woolwich, in 1882. Comp. operas, dance music, etc.

ZELTER (Carl Friedrich). German comp. and writer, B. Berlin, Dec. 11, 1758. S. under Fasch. Director of the Sing-Akademie in succession to Fasch. Prof. of music at the Academy of Arts, Berlin, 1809. Founded the Liedertafel, Berlin, 1809. D. Berlin, May 15, 1832.

He comp. cantatas for voice and Pf., songs, and numerous part-songs, all of great merit. He was a friend and correspondent of Goethe, and their letters to each other fill several volumes. Mendelssohn was also closely connected with Zelter, who was a most influential musician in Berlin.

ZERRAHN (Carl). German cond., B. Malchow, Mecklenburg-Schwerin, July, 1826. Settled in New York, 1848. Cond. of the Handel and Haydn Soc. of Boston, 1854. Cond. of the Harvard Symphony Assoc., 1866. Celebrated in America as a cond. of musical festivals.

ZEUNER (Charles). German comp., B. 1797. Settled in U. S., and became org. of Park Street Ch., Boston, and of Handel and Haydn Soc. Comp. "The Feast of the Tabernacles," oratorio, 1832; American Harp, 1839; Ancient Lyre, 1848; Musical Manual, n.d.; etc. D. Philadelphia, Nov. 1857.

ZIEGFELD (F.). German pianist and teacher, B. Jever, 1841. Founder of the Chicago Coll. of Music. S. under Moscheles, Plaidy, Richter, etc. Well known in America as a teacher and performer.

ZIMMERMANN (Agnes). German pianist and comp., B. Cologne, July 5, 1847. Resided in London from 1851. S. at R. A. M. under Potter, Steggall, and Macfarren. Gained King's Scholarship, 1860, and re-elected, 1862. Gained silver medal. *Début* at Crystal Palace, London. Appeared in Germany at Gewandhaus Concerts, 1879-80, 1882-83. Has performed in Britain, and very frequently in London. Comp. much Pf. music, arrangements, and original works. *Part-Songs:* Come follow, follow me; Flowers; Gone for ever; Good morrow; Good night; To daffodils. *Songs:* Der Verbannte; Lebewohl; After war; Blow, blow, thou winter wind; My heart is sair for somebody; O! that we two were maying; The Exile; The ringlet; Stars are with the voyager, etc.

ZINGARELLI (Niccolo Antonio). Italian comp., B. Naples, April 4, 1752. S. at Cons. of Loretto under Feneroli and Speranza. Chap.-master of Milan Cath. Chap.-master of S. Peter's, Rome, in succession to Guglielmi, 1804. Comp. "Cantata Sacra," the first work directly commissioned for the Birmingham Festival, 1829. D. Naples, May 5, 1837.

WORKS.—*Operas:* Montezuma, 1781; Il Telemacco, 1785; Armida, 1786; Annibale, 1787; Antigone, 1789; Artaserse, 1794; Romeo e Giulietta, 1796; Il Ritratto, 1799; Inès de Castro, 1803; Baldovino, 1810. *Oratorios:* La Distruzzione di Gerusalemme, 1810; Saulle; La Passione. Vocal music, and other works. Celebrated as a teacher.

ZISKA (Leopoldine). Authoress of "Handbook of the Four Elements of Vocalization, edited by Leopold Wray," Lond., 1850, 8vo.

ZOELLER (Carli). German comp., writer, and cond., B. Berlin, March 28, 1840. S. at Royal Academy of Arts there. Settled in England, 1873. Bandmaster of the 7th (Queen's Own Hussars), 1879. Mem. of Academy of S. Cecilia, Rome, 1884. Corresponding Mem. of Royal Academy of Music, Florence, 1885.

WORKS.—Mary Stuart, Queen of Scots, in her Prison at Fotheringay, lyrical monodrama, with male voice chorus; Qui sedes Domine, cantata, with viola d' amour solo; The Missing Heir, operetta in one act; Suite for flute, clarinet and bassoon; Trio for Pf., vn., and 'cello; Quartet for strings; Quintet for wind instruments; Concerto dramatique for violin and orch.; Bless the Lord, O my Soul, anthem, 1875; Ave Maria for 8 voices; 3 Masses; and Songs, Pf. music, etc.

Well known as a virtuoso on the viola d'amour, which instrument he has made a special study, and has comp. for it a Concertino: Two Introductions and Rondos in D minor and D major; Adagio religioso, for 2 violas d'amour; Offertorium for viola d'amour and org.; Fantasias, transcriptions, etc. Author of "Art of Modulation, a Handbook showing at a glance the Modulation from one key to any other in the octave.. " Lond., 1880; The Viole d'Amour, its Origin, History, and Method of Playing it," Lond., 1885.

ZÖLLNER (Christian Heinrich). German comp., B. Oels, Silesia, May 5, 1792. D. Hamburg, July 12, 1836. Org. and cond. at Dresden, Hamburg, etc. Comp. " Kunz de Kanfungen," opera; psalms, sonatas for Pf., songs, etc.

ZOTTI (Carlo). See CROAL (George).

ZUMSTEEG (Johann Rudolf). German comp. and violoncellist, B. Sachsenflur, Odenwald, Jan. 10, 1760. S. under Poli, Mazzanti, etc. Cond. at Stuttgart. D. Stuttgart, Jan. 27, 1802. Comp. cantatas for solo voice and Pf., Ballads and Lieder; Tamira, 1791; El Bondokani, 1792; Schuss von Sänsewitz, 1792; Die Geisterinsel, 1793; Das Pfauenfest, 1796; and other operatic works.

ZUNDEL (Johann). German writer and comp., B. Erslingen, 1815. Settled in America, and became org. of St. George's Ch., N. Y., and of Plymouth Ch., Brooklyn. D. Cannstadt, July 1882. Published Book of Easy Voluntaries for the Organ, N. Y., 1851; Complete Melodeon Instruction Book, Boston, 1853; Model Melodeon Instructor, 1854, 4to; Amateur Organist, 1854; Modern Organ School, Boston, 1860; Psalms, etc.

APPENDIX OF ADDITIONS AND CORRECTIONS.

The matter shewn in *Italics* is additional or correctory.

ABINGDON, p. 3. Third line from top, read *A Representation*, etc. (new title.)
ABT, p. 3. *D. Wiesbaden, April 2, 1885.*
ALLEN (H. R.), p. 15. Comp. *Maid of Athens and other popular songs.*
ALLON, p. 16. For B. 1881 read *B. 1818.*
APRILE (*Giuseppe*) not (GUISEPPE).
Archilochus, p. 24, not ARCHILACHUA.
ASHTON (HUGH), p. 30, or *Aston*, not ASHTAN.
ATTWOOD, p. 32. B. London, *Nov.* 23, 1767.
BÄRMANN (HEINRICH), p. 50. (B. 1820, *D. Munich, June* 1885.
BARR (JAMES), p. 56. *D. Govan (Buried at Kilbarchan),* Feb. 21, 1860. *Comp. " Thou Bonnie Wood o' Craigielea," and other melodies.*
BASEVI (ABRAMO). p. 60. *D. Florence, Dec. 1885.*
BECKER (JOHANN), p. 67. B. Mannheim, *May* 11, 1836. *D. Mannheim, Oct. 10, 1884.*
Bedsmore (Thomas), English org. and comp., B. Lichfield, 1833, D. Lichfield, June 9, 1881. Org. of Lichfield Cath. from 1864. Comp. Anthems, etc.
BENEDICT (SIR JULIUS), p. 77. *D. London, June* 5, 1885.
BEST (W. T.), p. 89, top line, "Arrangements *from*," not "for."
BICKNELL (JOHN L.), p. 91. six lines from bottom, "Redivivus, an entirely *new* edition," etc.
BITTER (C. H.), p. 97. *D. Berlin, Sept.* 13, 1885.
Blumner, p. 101, not BLUMMER.
BRAHMS, p. 112, fourteen lines from top, for "imitate" read *initiate*.
BUCHANNAN, p. 124. Physiological Illustra-*tions*.
BUTLER (CHARLES), p. 132. The four lines of note under THOMAS HAMLY BUTLER beginning "The first work is a curious production," and ending "described in his Grammar," belong to the notice of Charles Butler, *not* to Thomas H. Butler.
Cecilia (Saint), p. 151, not CECELIA (SAINT).
CHILMEAD, p. 158. Authority quoted is *Hearne* not Herue.
CHOUQUET (A. G.), p. 161. *D. Paris, Jan. 30, 1886.*
CLARKE (JOHN), *Clarke*-WHITFIELD, p. 166.
CUMMINGS (W. H.), p. 191. B. *Aug.* 22, 1831. *F.S.A.,* 1883. *Gent. of Chap. Royal. Prof. in R.A.M., and Guildhall School of Music. Hon. Treasurer of Royal Soc. of Musicians. Cond. of Sacred Harmonic Soc.*

DIBDIN (CHARLES), p. 209. A correspondent in the "Musical Times," April, 1886, states that Dibdin was *Baptised on March 4, 1745*, thus making the birth date, March 15, wrong.

HOYTE (W. S.), p. 334. *B. Sidmouth, Devon, Sept.* 22, 1844. *Org. of All Saints, Margaret St., London. Comp. a Communion Service in D, Anthems, etc.*

KÖHLER (LUDWIG) p. 363. *D. Königsberg, Feb.* 16, 1886.

Lamond (Frederic). Scottish Pianist, B. Glasgow, 1868. *S. Violin under H. C. Cooper, in Glasgow, and from* 1882 *S. Pf. in Germany under Bülow and Liszt. Played with great success in Berlin and Vienna, and in* 1886 *appeared in Glasgow and London, obtaining at both places the most complete triumphs. He has comp. a few studies and other works for Pf.*

LESLIE (H. D.) p. 384. Oratorio "Judith," 1857 not 1858. *A Biblical Pastoral, The First Christmas Morn,* 1880. *Symphony in D, " Chivalry,"* 1880. *Quartet for strings in C min.,* 1842 ; *Do. in A,* 1843 ; *Quintet for strings in D,* 1846 ; *Quintet in G. min, for Pf., oboe, clarinet, bassoon and horn,* 1851.

MACFARREN (SIR G. A.) p. 404. *M. A. Cantab., and Mus. Doc. Oxon.* Principal of R.A.M. *Feb.* 8, 1875, not 1876. Opera *Jessy* not Jenny Lea.

MACFARREN (NATALIA), *née Andrae,* not Novello. *B. at Lübeck.*

Marzials (T.), p. 417, not MARZIELS.

Mirrlees (Alexander). Scottish organ-builder. In 1844, *in company with his brother John, succeeded his father Robert Mirrlees in the business, which was established in Glasgow in* 1811. *For many years the only organ-builders in Glasgow. Besides many chamber-organs the firm have erected church organs in St. Andrew's R. C. Pro-Cath. ; St. John's Episcopal Church. ; St. Andrew's Parish Ch. ; Parkhead Parish Ch. : Woodside R. C. Church, all in Glasgow, as well as other important instruments in Greenock, etc.*

MONK (E. G.) p. 430. *S. with J. Hullah,* not in his classes. *An Oxford Univ. Examiner for musical Degrees,* 1872-1884. Works—*" The Anglican Chant Book," " The Psalter Pointed," and " Anglican Psalter Chants, with Sir F. Ouseley.*

MONK (W. H.), p. 430. Add to biography—*Vice-President of the Musical Assoc. of Lond., and of North-East London Soc. of Musicians. Mem. of London Diocesan Conference.* Add to works—*Hymns Ancient and Modern, with tunes (edited),* 1861, *(numerous editions). The Psalter and Canticles, Ancient and Modern (with Rev. Sir H. W. Baker). The Congregational Psalmist (edited),* 1886.

PACHMANN (V. DE). p. 455. *B. Odessa, July* 27, 1848. *S. under his father, and Prof. Dachs at Vienna Cons. Gained the gold medal for Pf. playing. Gave a series of concerts in Russia,* 1869, *with great success. Appeared in Vienna, after many years hard private study,* 1882, *and was received with acclamation. Appeared next in Paris and London. Has appeared in nearly every large continental city of musical repute, and in* 1885 *was decorated by the King of Denmark, and made Chevalier of the Order of Danebrog. He married in* 1884, *his only pupil Miss Maggie Okey.*

PATTISON (T. M.) p. 463. Now *Org. of S. Mary's, Ealing, London.*

REEVES (JOHN SIMS). *B. Shooters Hill.* Début, *December* 1839. *S.* singing at Paris *under Bordogni.* Sang his first original part in Balfe's Maid of Honour, 1848. Appeared also with great success in Paris, at the Italian Opera, 1851. *Mr. Reeves made strenuous efforts to effect the lowering of the present high pitch used in England.*

ROCKSTRO (WILLIAM *Smith). Formerly Hon.* Precentor of All Saints, Babbicombe, Works—*The Standard Lyric Drama,* Lond., 1847-1853, 12 *vols. Mendelssohn,* Lond., 1884. *The Good Shepherd,* oratorio, *comp. for Gloucester Festival,* 1886.

BIBLIOGRAPHICAL SUBJECT-INDEX:

A TENTATIVE INDEX OF THE PRINCIPAL SUBJECTS AND WORKS IN THE ENGLISH LITERATURE OF MUSIC.

As the titles of most of the works indexed have already been given in full under Authors' or Editors' names, the titles in this index are only repeated in brief. When subject words occur in titles, the initials of such words only are given : M. = music.

ACCORDEON.
Cruikshank, J. A., teacher, 1851.
Howe, E. A., preceptor, n. d.
Sedgwick, A. B., Methods, n. d.

ACOUSTICS.
Airy, Sir G. B , Sound, 1868.
Blaserna, P., Theory of Sound, 1876.
Broadhouse, J., Musical A., 1881.
Donkin, W. F., Acoustics, 1870.
Griesbach, J. H., Musical sounds, n. d.
Helmholtz. Sensations of Tone, 1875 and 1885.
Marsh, J., Harmonics, 1809.
Smith, R., Harmonics, 1749.
Stone, W. H., Sound and M., 1876.
— Lessons on Sound, 1879.
— Scientific Basis of M., n. d.
Taylor, S., Sound and M., 1873.
Tyndall, J., Sound, 1867.

ÆSTHETICS.
Avison, Charles, Musical Expression, 1752.
Banister, H. C., Musical Ethics, 1884.
Banister, H. J., Domestic M., 1843.
Barry, W. V., Emotional Nature of Musical Art and its Media of Operation, Lond., 1863.
Beattie, J., Poetry and M., 1776.
Eaton, T. D., Musical Criticism, 1872.
Ehlert, L., Letters, 1877.
— Tone-World, 1885.
Gurney, E., Power of Sound, 1880.
Hand, F. G., A. of Musical Art, 1880.
Hastings, T., Musical Taste, 1822 and 1853.
Pauer, E., Beautiful in M. [1877].
Hullah, J., M. in the House, 1877.
Steed, A. O., Music in Play, 1873.
Thibaut, A. F. J., Purity in M., 1877. 1882.

AMERICA.
Gould, N. D., Church M. in A., 1853.
Hood, G., M. in New England, 1846.
Ritter, F. L., Music in A., 1883.
American Organ. See Reed Organ.

ANECDOTES.
Burgh, A., Anecdotes, 1814, 3 v.
Busby, T., Concert Room, 1825. 3 v.
Crowest, F. J., Musical A., 1878, 2 v.
Anthems. See Church Music Collections.

BACH.
Barnard, C., Bach, 1871.
Forkel, J. N., Life of J. S. B., 1820.
Rimbault, E. F., ed. Life, 1869.
Spitta, J. A. P., J. S. Bach, 1884, 3 v.

BAG-PIPE.
Glen, D., Highland B.-P. M., 1876.
Macdonald, D., Martial M. of Caledonia, n. d.
Mackay, A., Ancient Piobaireachd, 1838.
Mackay, W., Tutor for Highland B., 1840.
Macleod, N., Piobaireachd, 1828.

BANJO.
Briggs, T. F., Instructor, n. d.
Buckley, J., B. Guide, n. d.
— B. Method, n. d.
Dobson, G. C., New System, n. d.
Rice, P., Method, n. d.
Winner, S., New School, n. d.

BASSOON.
Bassoon Tutor (Williams), n. d.
Kappey, J. A., Tutor, n. d.
Tamplini, G., Instruction Book, n. d.

BEETHOVEN.
Barnard, C., Beethoven, 1871.
Graeme, E., Memoir, 1870.
Nohl, L., B. depicted, 1880.
Schindler, Life, 1841, 2 v.
Teetgen, A., B. Symphonies, 1879.
Towers, J., B. a Memoir, n. d.
Wagner, R., Beethoven, 1880.

BELLS.
Campanalogia, ringing made easy, 1733.
Ellacombe, H. T., Belfries and Ringers, 1871.
Gatty, A., The Bell, 1848.

Hubbard, H., Campanologia, 1876.
Jones. W., Art of Ringing, n. d.
Lewis, T., Bell Founding, 1878.
Lukis, W. C., Church Bells, 1857.
Troyte, C. A. W., Change Ringing, 1869.
Wigram, W., Change Ringing, 1880.

BERLIOZ.
Bennett, J., Berlioz, 1883.
Berlioz, H., Autobiography, 1884, 2 v.
Bernard, D., Life, 1882, 2 v.

BIOGRAPHY.
Baptie, D., Musical B. [1883].
Barret, W. A., English Church Composers, n. d.
— Glee and Madrigal Writers, 1877.
Bingley, W., Musical B., 1814. 1834.
Bourne, C. E., Great Composers, 1884.
Burney, C., History of M....1776-89, 4 v.
Busby, T., History of M....1819, 2 v.
Charlton, R., Sketches of Musicians, 1836.
Clayton, E. C., Queens of Song, 1863, 2 v.
Crowest, F. J., Great Tone Poets, 1874 (7 eds.)
Dictionary of Musicians, from the earliest ages to the present time, Lond., 1824, 2 v., 8vo.
Dictionary of Musicians, 1878 (Cocks).
Ferris, G. T., Great Singers, 1880, 2 v.
Grove, Sir G., Dictionary of Musicians, 1879—4 v.
Keddie, H., *Tytler*. Musical Composers, 1875.
Mathews, W. S. B., Dictionary, 1880.
Pauer, E., Birthday Book [1883].
Phipson, T. L., Celebrated Violinists, 1877.
Schuberth, J. F. G., Musical hand-book, n.d.
Stieler, J., German Composers, 1879.
Universal Dictionary of Music [A – M, all published], Lond., n. d.
Warren, J., Deceased Musicians, 1845.

CAROLS.
Chope, R. R., Carols, 1868-76.
Husk, W. H., Songs of Nativity [1866].
Rimbault, E. F., Little Book [1847].
— Old English Carols, 1865.
Sandys, W., Christmas C., 1833.
— Christmas Tide, 1852.
Sylvester, J., Garland, 1833.

CHANTS.
Acland, T. G., Chanting Simplified, 1843.
Allon, H., Book of C., 1860.
Beckwith, J. C., First Verse of every Psalm ...1808.
Bemrose's Choir C. Book, 1882.
Clarke-Whitfield, J., Chants, 2 v., n. d.
Clare, E., Guide n. d.
Cleland, G., Selection [1824].
Goss, Sir J., Chants, 1841.
Helmore, T., St. Marks' C. Book, n. d.
Holloway, H. R., Manual, 1850.
Joule, B., Collection, 1860.

Ouseley, Sir F., Anglican Psalter C. [1872].
Rimbault, E. F., Cathedral C., 1844.
Troutbeck, J., Manchester C. Book, 1871.
Turle, J., Single and Double C., n. d.
— Westminster Abbey C. Book, n. d.
Warren, J., 100 Chants, 1845.
Chants See also Psalmody.

CHOIR-TRAINING.
Atkyns, B. K., Choir-master's Manual...n. d.
Barrett, W. A., Chorister's Guide, 1874.
Concone, G., Part-Singing, n. d.
Fétis, F. J., Choir Singing, 1854.
Hamilton, J. A., Choral Singing, n. d.
Helmore, F., Church Choirs, 1874.
Hiles, J., Part-Singing, n. d.
Jackson, W., Singing-class Manual, n. d.
Johnson, A. N., Choir Instruction, 1847.
— Method for Singing Classes, n. d.
Mann, R., Manual of Singing, 1866.
Molineux, J., Vocal Music [1830].
Silcher, F., Instructions, 1857.
Troutbeck, J., Church Choir Training [1879].
Warren, J., Singing Catches, etc., n. d.

CHOPIN.
Bennett, J., Chopin, 1884.
Davison, J. W., Essay [1849].
Habicht, E., Recollections, n. d.
Karasowski, M., Life, 1879, 2 v.
Liszt, F., Life, 1877.

CHURCH MUSIC: COLLECTIONS.
Arnold, S., Cathedral M....1790.
Ayrton, W., Sacred Minstrelsy...1835, 2 v.
Barnard, J., Church Music, 1641.
Bishop and Warren. Repertorium Musicæ Antiquæ...1848.
Boyce, W., Cathedral M....1760, 3 v.
Clifford, J., Services and Anthems, 1664.
Jebb, J., Choral Responses, 1847-57, 2 v.
Joule, B. St. J. B., Directorium Chori Anglicanum, 1849.
Latrobe, C. J., Sacred Music, 1806-25, 6 v.
Novello, V., Collections, v. d.
— Fitzwilliam M., n. d.
Ouseley, Sir F., Anthems, 1861-66, 2 v.
— Cathedral Services [1853].
Page, J., Harmonia Sacra, 1800, 3 v.
Pratt, J., Anthems, n. d., 2 v.
Rimbault, E. F., ed. Anthems, 1845.
— Cathedral M., n. d. [v. 1].
— Services and Anthems, n. d., 3 v.
Stevens, R. J. S., Sacred M., 3 v.
Turle and Taylor. People's M. Book, 1848, 2 v.
Church Music Collections. See also Psalmody.

CHURCH MUSIC: LITERATURE.
Abbot, H., Use and Benefit, 1724.
Allen, R., Singing of Psalms, 1696.
Allon, H., Church Song, 1862.

Allon, H., Psalmody of Reformation, n. d.
Anderson, W., Apology for Organ, 1829.
Anderson W., Congregational Psalmody, 1855.
Bayly, A., Sacred Singer...1771.
Bedford, A., Temple of M., 1706.
— Great Abuse of M., 1711.
Begg, J., Use of Organs, 1808.
— Use of Organs, 1866.
Belcher, J., Ecclesiastical M., 1872.
Biggs, Rev. L. C., English Hymnology, n. d.
Binney, T., Service of Song, 1849.
Bishop, J., Degraded State of M., 1860.
Box, C. C. M. in Metropolis, 1884.
Brady, N., C. M. vindicated, 1697.
Brookbanck, J., Well-tuned Organ...1660.
— Organ's Echo, 1641.
— Organ's Funereal, 1642.
— Gospel-Musick...1644.
Bruce, T., Common Tunes; or, Scotland's C. M. made Plain, 1726.
Candlish, R. S., Organ Question, 1856.
Carnie, W., Psalmody in Scotland, 1854.
Cromar, A., Vindication of Organ, 1856.
Curwen, J. S., Worship M., 1880.
Dodwell, H., Instrumental M., 1700.
Druitt, R., Church M., 1845.
— Choral Service, 1853.
Engel, C., Reflections, 1856.
Hall, C. C., Education in C. M. [1878].
Hicks, E., Church M., 1881.
Hirst, T., Music of the Ch., 1841.
Hodges, E., Cultivation of C. M., 1841.
Horne, T. H., Notices of Psalmody, 1847.
Kilner, T., Choral Services, 1872.
Latrobe, J. A., M. of the Ch., 1831.
Riley, W., Parochial M., 1762.
Young, E., Harp of God, 1861.

CLARINET.

Howe, E., Instructor, n. d.
Kappy, J. A., Tutor, n. d.
Lazarus, H., Method, n. d.
Tyller, G., Instruction Bk., n. d.
Weller, S., C. without a Master, n. d.
Willman. Instruction Book, n. d.

COLOUR AND MUSIC.

Allen, G. B., Scales in Music and Colours, n. d.
Hughes, F. J., Harmonies of Tones and Colours, 1883.
Jameson, D.D., Colour M., 1844.
Macdonald, J. D., Sound and Colour, 1869.

COMPOSITION.

Albrechtsberger, J. G., Methods, 1834. 2 v.
Crotch, W., Elements, 1812, 1833, 1856.
— Questions on do. [1830].
Czerny, K., Practical C. [1840], 3 v.
Dawson, C., Analysis of C., 1845.
Fux, J. J., Practical Rules, n. d.
Graham, G. F., Theory and Practice, 1838.

Hamilton, J. A., Musical Ideas, 1838.
Jones, W., Art of Music, 1784.
Kollmann, A. F., Musical C., 1799.
Marsh, J., Hints to Young Composers.
Marx, A. B., School, 1852-53, 54.
Reicha, A. J., Course of C., n. d.
Röhner, G. W., Treatise, 1849-54.
Spencer, C. C., Elements, 1840.
Stainer, J., Composition, 1880.
Weber, G., Musical C., 1842, 1851, 2 v.

CONCERTINA.

Case, G., Instructions, n. d.
Chisney, E., Instructor, 1853.
Haskins, J. F., Preceptor, 1852.
Regondi, G., Tutor, n. d.
Sedgwick, A. B., Methods, n. d.

CORNET.

Arban, Method, n. d.
Arbuckle, M., Method, n. d.
Eaton, E. K., New Method, n. d.
Howe, E., Instructor, n. d.
Jones, S., Tutor, n. d.
Levy, I., Tutor, n. d.
Sedgwick, A. B., Method, n. d.

COUNTERPOINT.

Bridge, J. F., Counterpoint [1880].
— Double C., 1881.
Cherubini, M. L., Course, 1837-41, 1854, 2 v.
Hamilton, J. A., Catechism, n. d.
Hiles, H., Part Writing, 1884.
Hullah, J. Grammar, n. d.
Jones, J. H., Guide, 1855.
Macfarren, Sir G. A., Counterpoint, 1879.
Mangold, C. G., Counterpoint, 1885.
Oakey, G., Text-Book, 1878.
Ouseley, Sir F., Treatise, 1868.
Richter, E. F., Counterpoint, 1874.
Rockstro, W. S., Rules, n. d.

DANCE MUSIC.

Bremner, R., Scots Reels.
Davie, J., Caledonian Repository, 1829-30, 6 v.
Gow, Nath., Collection of Reels, etc., n. d.
Gow, Neil, Collection of Reels, 1784-1822, v. d.
M'Gibbon, W., Scots Tunes, 1742-55, 3 v.
M'Glashan, A., Strathspey Reels, 1778; Scots Measures [1778].
Mackenzie, A., Dance M. of Scotland, n. d.
Napier, W, Dances and Strathspeys, n. d.
Robertson, J. S., Athole Collection, 1884, 2 v.
Surenne, J. T., D. M. of Scotland [1851].

DICTIONARIES, TECHNOLOGICAL.

Adams, J. S., 5000 Terms, 1861.
Bottomley, I., Dictionary, 1816.
Buck, D., Musical terms, n. d.
Busby, T., Dictionary of Music, 1786.
Danneley, J. F., Encyclopædia, 1825.

Grassineau, J., Musical Dictionary, 1740.
Grove, Sir G., D. of Music, 1879—in progress, 4 v.
Hamilton, J. A., D. of 3500 terms, 1849.
Hiles, J., D. of 12,500 terms, 1871.
Hoyle, J., Dictionarium Musicæ, 1770.
Jackson, S., Complete D., n. d.
Jousse, J., D. of Italian terms, 1829.
Lott, E. M., D. of Terms, n. d.
Ludden, W., Pronouncing D., n. d.
Mathews, W. S. B., Pronouncing D., 1880.
Moore, J. W., Encyclopædia, 1854.
Niecks, F., Concise D. [1884].
Pilkington, H. W., Musical D., 1812.
Rousseau, J. J., Complete D., 1771. 79.
Schuberth, J. F. G., Musical Hand-book, n. d.
Stainer and Barrett, Dicty., 1876.
Universal Dictionary of Music [A.M., all published], Lond., n. d.
Valentine, H., Dictionary, 1833.
Warner, J. F., Universal D., 1842.

DOUBLE-BASS.

Bottesini, G., Complete Method, n. d.
Friedheim, J., Instructor, n. d.
Hamilton, J. A., Method, 1833.
Rowland, A. C., Tutor, n. d.

DRUM.

Hart's Instructor, n. d.
Keach, O. W., Modern School, n. d.
— Drum and Fife Book, n. d.
Tamplini, G., Drum Major, n. d.
Winner, S., Drum Book, n. d.

EDUCATION.

Fay, A., M. Study in Germany, 1881.
Geary, E. M., Musical E., 1851.
Harris, J. J., Musical Exposition, 1845.
Mainzer, J., M. and Education, 1848.
Paddon, J., Musical E., 1818.

Elements of Music. See Principles.

FLAGEOLET.

Colinet, A., Tutor, n. d.
Green, J., Complete Preceptor, n. d.
Greeting, T., Pleasant Companion, 1660.
Howe, E., Instructor, n. d.
Tollet, T., Directions, n. d.
Weller, S., F. without a Master, n. d.

FLUTE.

Arthur, J., F. Playing, 1827.
Beale, J., German F., n. d.
Boehm, T., Construction...1882.
Challoner, N. B., Method, n. d.
Clinton, J., Equisonant F., n. d.
— Mechanism and Principles, n. d.
— School for Boehm F., n. d.
— F. Tutor, n. d.
Coggins, J., Instructions, 1830.
Howe, E., F. without a master, n. d.

Howe, E., School for F., n. d.
James, W. N., Word or two on the F., 1826.
— Flutist's Catechism, 1829.
— Flutist's Magazine, n. d.
Keith, R. W., Tutor. n. d.
Lindsay, T., Flute Playing, 1828.
Nicholson, C., Lessons, n. d.
— Preceptor, n. d.
Pratten, R. S., Siccama Flute, n. d.
— Tutors, n. d.
Rockstro, W. S., School, n. d.
Siccama, A., Diatonic F., 1847.
Skeffington, T. C., The Flute, 1862.
Welch, C., Boehm F., 1883.

FORM.

Barrett, W. A., Form, 1879.
Goddard, J., Musical Development, n. d.
Mathews, W. S. B., Musical F., 1868.
Ouseley, Sir F., Treatise, 1875.
Pauer, E., Musical Forms [1878].
Prentice, T. R., Musician, 1883.
Prescott, O. L., Form in M., 1882.

FUGUE.

Cherubini, M. L., Course, 1837-41-54, 2 v.
Flowers, G. F., Construction, 1846.
Higgs, J., Fugue [1878].
Richter, E. F., Fugue, 1878.
Gage, Rev. W. L., Trans. of Mendelssohn's Life by Lampadius, and other musical works.

GLEES.

Barrett, W. A., English Glee Writers, 1877.
Bellamy, T. L., Lyric Poetry, 1840.
Clark, R., First Volume of Poetry revised, 1824; Continuation, 1833.
Clark, R., Words of Favourite Pieces, 1814.

See also Part-Music.

GUITAR.

Bremner, R., Instructions, n. d.
Burnet, A., Spanish G., 1829.
Carcassi, M., Method, n. d.
Carulli, F., Method, n. d.
Challoner, N. B., Method, n. d.
Culver, R., American Guitarist, n. d.
— G. Instructor, n. d.
Curtiss, N. P. B., Method, n. d.
Duvernay, E., Instruction Book, 1829.
Green, J., Spanish G. [1830].
Hayden, W. L., Method, n. d.
Holland, J., Method, n. d.
— Modern Method [1874].
Light, E., Art of Playing, 1795.
Pratten, Mrs. S., School, n. d.
Rodwell, G. H., The Guitar, n. d.
Sola, C. M. A., Method, n. d.
Taylor, J., Lessons [1827].

HANDEL.

Barnard, C., Handel, 1871.
Bishop, J., Memoir, 1856.

Bowley, R. K., Handel Festival, in 1857.
Bray, A. E., Handel, 1857.
Burney, C., Musical Performances in Commemoration of Handel, 1785.
Callcott, W. H., Life of Handel, 1859.
Chorley, H. F., Handel Studies, 1859, 2 pts.
Kyte, F., Portrait of Handel, 1829.
Mainwaring, J., Memoirs, 1760.
Marshall, Mrs. J., Handel, 1883.
Prat, D., Ode to Mr. Handel, 1722.
Ramsay, E. B. B., Genius of Handel, 1862.
Ring, J., Commemoration of H., 1786.
Rockstro, W. S., Life, 1883.
Schoelcher, V., Life, 1857.
Smith, J. C., Anecdotes, 1799.
Townsend, H., Visit of H. to Dublin, 1852.

HARMONIUM.

Clark, F. S., First Steps, n. d.
Grieve, J. C., Harmonium, n. d.
Hall, C. K., School [1874].
— H. Primer, n. d.
Montgomery, W. H., Tutor, n. d.
Mullen, A. F., Tutor, n. d.
Rimbault, E. F., Harmonium, 1857.
— Tutor, n. d.

HARMONY.

Albrechtsberger, J. G., Collected Writings, 1855, 3 v.
— Methods...1834, 2 v.
Baker, B. F., Theoretical H.
Barnhill, J., Statics, 1865.
Barr, S., Theory, 1861.
Becker, C. J., Treatise, 1845.
Bowman, E. M., Harmony, n. d.
Brown, R., Rudiments, 1863.
Burns, D. J., Practical Notes [1883].
Carleton, H., Genesis, 1882.
Catel, C., Treatise, 1832-75.
Clifton, J. C., Theory, 1816.
Corfe, A. T., Principles, n. d.
Curwen, J., How to observe, n. d.
Czerny, K., Exercises [1846].
Dana, W. H., Practical H., 1884.
Day, A., Treatise, 1845.
Done, J., Short Treatise, n. d.
Emery, S. A., Element, n. d.
Fétis, F. J., Method, n. d.
Frike, P. F., Guide, 1793.
Gadsby, H. R., Harmony, 1884.
Geminiani, F., Guida Armonica, 1742.
Gilbert, E. B., School H., n. d.
Goss, Sir J., Introduction, 1833.
Hiles, H., H. of Sounds, 1871.
Hiles, J., Catechism, 2 v., n. d.
Holder, W., Natural Grounds, 1731.
Horsley, C. E., Text-Book, n. d.
Horsley, W., Introduction, 1847.
Hullah, J., Musical H., 1853.
Johnson, A. N., Instruction, 1854.
Jousse, J., Guida Armonica, 1808.
King, M. P., General Treatise, 1800.

Kirkman, J., Principles, 1845.
Kollmann, A. F., Musical H., 1796.
Macfarren, Sir G. A., Rudiments, 1860.
— Six Lectures, 1867.
— 80 Musical Sentences, Chords, 1875.
Mangold, C. G., Harmony, 1884.
Merz, K., Harmony, n. d.
Oakey, G., Graduated Services, 1877.
— Text-Book, 1884.
Ouseley, Sir F., Treatise, 1868.
Parker, J. C. D., Manual, n. d.
Pepusch, J. C., Treatise, 1730.
Richter, E. F., Treatise, 1864-80.
Rockstro, W. S., Practical H., 1881.
Rodwell, G. H., First Rudiments, 1830.
— Catechism, n. d.
Saroni, H. S., Theory, n. d.
Schneider, F. J. C., Elements, 1828; Treatise, 1856.
Shield, W., Introduction, 1800-1817.
Stainer, J., Theory, 1871.
— Harmony, 1877.
Wigan, A. C., Modulating Dictionary, 1852.
Harmony. See also *Principles and Thorough-Bass.*

HARP.

Bochsa, R. N. C., Method, n. d.
Challoner, N. B., Method, n. d.
Dizi, F. J., Ecole de Harpe, 1827.
Egan, C., Harp Primer, 1822.
Erard, P., The Harp, 1821.
Gunn, J., H. in Highlands of Scotland, 1807.
Meyer, F. C., New Treatise, n. d.
Wright, T. H., New Preceptor, 1825.

HARPSICHORD.

Bemetzrieder, New Lessons, 1783.
Falkner, R., Instructions, 1762.
Nares, J., Il Principio, n. d.
Pasquali, N., Art of Fingering, n. d.
Ross, J., Instructions, 1820.
Wade, R., The H., n. d.

HISTORY.

Backus, A., History of M., 1839.
Bird, J., Gleanings from H., 1850.
Burney, C., General H. of M., 1776-89, 4 v.
Busby, T., General H. of M., 1819, 2 v.
Challoner, R., Art of M., 1880.
Chappell, W., H. of Music...v. 1, Lond, 1874.
Crowest, F. J., Musical H., 1883.
Eastcott, R., Origin of M., 1793.
Gaskin, J. J., H. of Vocal Music, 1860.
Hawkins, Sir J., General History, 1776, 5 v.
Hogarth, G., Musical H., etc., 2 v., 1835 and 1838.
Hooper, R., Music and Musicians, 1855.
Hullah, J., H. of Modern M., 1862.
— Transition Period of, 1865.
Hunt, G. B., Concise H., 1878, etc.

Jones, G., Rise and Progress of M., 1818.
Kiesewetter, R., M. of Western Europe, 1848.
Macfarren, Sir G. A., Musical H., 1885.
Marx, A. B., M. of 19th Century, 1856-58.
Music in England, Ireland, Wales, and Scotland, 1845.
Naumann, E., History of M., n. d.
North, R., Memoirs of Musick, 1846.
Parke, W. T., Musical Memoirs [1784-1830], 1830, 2 v.
Ritter, F. L., History of M., 1870-74, 2 v., 1878, 1880.
— Music in England and America, 2 v., 1883, 1884.
Rockstro, W. S., H. of Music, n. d.
— General H. of M., 1886.
Rowbotham, J. F., H. of Music, 1885 (v. 1).
Schlüter, J., General H. of M., 1865.
Stafford, W. C., History, 1830.
Hymns. See Church Music and Psalmody.

INSTRUMENTATION.

Barrett, W. A., Instrumentation, 1879.
Clarke, J., Wind Instruments, n. d.
Dana, W. H., Orchestration, 1875.
— Military Band I., 1876.
Hamilton, J. A., Writing for an orch., 1844.
Mandel, C., Military Bands, n. d.
Prout, E., Instrumentation, 1876.

IRISH MUSIC.

Walker, J. C., Irish Bards, 1786.
See also Songs.

LUTE.

Alford, J., Introduction (Le Roy), 1568.
Light, E., Instructions, n. d.
Mace, T., Musik's Monument, 1676.
Robinson, T., Schoole of Musicke, 1603.

MADRIGALS.

Barrett, W. A., English Writers, 1877.
Bellamy, T. L., Poetry...1840.
Clark, R., Derivation, etc., of "Madrigale," 1852.
Oliphant, T., Account of M., 1836.
— La Musa Madrigalesca, 1837.
Rimbault, E. F., Bibliotheca Madrigaliana, 1847.
Madrigals. See also Part Music.

MEDICAL MUSIC.

Brocklesby, R., M., Application to Cure of Diseases, 1749.
Browne, R., Medicina Musica...1729.
Lilley, G. H., Therapeutics of M., 1880.

MENDELSSOHN.

Barnard, C., Mendelssohn, 1870.
Devrient, E., Recollections, 1869.
Glehn, M. E., Goethe and Mendelssohn, 1872.
Hensel, S., M. family, 1884, 2 v.
Lampadius, W. A., Life, 1876.
Letters from Italy, etc., 1862-3.

Polko, E., Reminiscences, 1869.
Rockstro, W. S., Mendelssohn.

MOZART.

Barnard, C., Mozart, 1870.
Beyle, M. H., *Bombet*, Lives of Haydn and Mozart, 1817, 1818.
Gehring, F., Mozart, 1883.
Holmes, E., Life, 1845.
Jahn, O., Mozart, 1883, 3 v.
Nohl, L., *ed.*, Letters, 1865, 2 v.
— Mozart, 1877, 2 v.
Pole, W., Mozart's Requiem, 1879.

NATIONAL MUSIC.

Chorley, H. F., N. M. of the World, 1880.
Crotch, W., Specimens.
Elson, L. C., Curiosities of Music, n. d.
Engel, C., Study of N. M., 1866.
Jones, E., Lyric Airs, 1804.
Moore and Stevenson, National Airs, 1818.
National Music See also Songs.

NOTATION.

Acland, A. H. D., Musical N., 1841.
Griesbach, J. H., Musical N., n. d.
Lunn, W. A. B., Sequential system, 1844.
Macdonald, A., N. simplified, 1826.
Rootsey, S., N. of Music, 1811.
Notation. See also Principles.

OBOE.

Kappey, J. A., Tutor, n. d.
Oboe Tutor (Williams), n. d.
Tamplini, G., Instruction Book, n. d.

OPERA.

Algarotti, F., Essay on the O., 1768.
Armstrong, W. G., O. in Philadelphia, 1884.
Austin, W. F., O. for England, 1883.
Brown, J., M. of Italian O., 1789.
Chorley, H. F., Recollections, 1862, 2 v.
Edwards, H. S., History, 1862, 2 v.
— Lyric Drama, 1881, 2 v.
Egestorff, G., Lecture...German Opera, 1840.
Ella, J., Dramatic Music, 1872.
Grunéisen, C. L., O. and the Press, 1869.
Hogarth, G., Musical drama, 1838, 2 v.
— Memoirs of the O., 1851.
Lumley, B., Reminiscences, 1864.
Lyric Muse revived in Europe, Lond., 1768.
Mount Edgcumbe, Reminiscences, 1823.
Walker, J. C., Historical Account, 1805.

ORGAN.

André, P. F. J., Use of Pedals, n. d.
Archer, F., Collegiate O. Tutor, n. d.
— The Organ, n. d.
Beckel, J. C., Amateur's O. School, n. d.
Best, W. T., O. Playing, n. d.
— Modern School [1855].
Blew, W. C. A., Handbook of law, 1878.
Blewitt, J., Treatise, n. d.
Buck, D., Influence, 1882.
Casson, T., Modern O. [1883].

Cheese, G. J., Rules for Playing, n. d.
Clagget, C., O. made without Pipes,...1793.
Clark, F. S., First Steps, n. d.
Clarke, H. A., School for Parlor O., n. d.
Clarke, W. H., Instructor, n. d.
— Harmonic School, n. d.
— Structure, 1877.
Cooper, G., Introduction, n. d.
Dickson, W. E., Organ Building, 1881.
Done, J., Treatise, 1837.
Edwards, C. A., Organs and O. Building, 1881.
Faulkner, T., O. builder's assistant, 1826.
— Designs for Organs, 1838.
Getze, J. A., Young Organist, n. d.
Gladstone, F. E., O. Student's Guide, n. d.
Glover, J. H. L., O. Tutor, n. d.
Hamilton, J. A., Catechism, n. d.
Hemstock, A., Tuning [1876].
Hiles, J., Introduction, n. d.
— Handbook, n. d.
— Catechism, 1878.
Hill, A. G., Organ Cases [1882].
Hinton, J. W., Facts about Organs, n. d.
Hopkins and Rimbault, The O., 1855, 1870, 1877.
Lewis, T., O. Building, 1878.
Loud. T., O. School, n. d.
Macrory, E., Temple Org. [1859].
Mathews, W. S. B., School, 1870.
Morten, A., Purchase, 1877.
Neukomm, S., Method, n. d.
Nicholson, H., The Organ, n. d.
Rimbault, E. F., English O. builders [1864].
Schneider, F. J. C., O. School, n. d.
Seidel, J. J., Construction, 1852.
Shepherdson, W., The Organ, 1873.
Spark, W., Handy-Book, n. d.
Stainer, J., Organ, 1877.
Steggall, C., Instruction Book, n. d.
Warman, J. W., Organ, n. d.
Warren, J., Instruction Book, n. d.
Organ question. See Church Music.

PART MUSIC.

Alcock, J., Harmonia Festi, 1791.
Appollonian Harmony, Glees, Madrigals, etc., n. d., 6 vols.
Arnold, J., Essex Harmony, 1767-74, 2 v.
Bland, J., Ladies Collection of Catches [1720].
— Gentleman's Collection, n. d.
Bremner, R., Vocal Harmonist's Magazine, n.d.
Gwilt, J., Madrigals, 1815.
Hilton, J., Catch that Catch can, 1652.
Hullah, J., Singer's Library, 6 v., n. d.
Metcalfe, J. P., Rounds, etc., of England, 1873.
Novello, V., Madrigalian Studies, 1841.
Novello's Glee Hive, Lond., 3 v., n. d.
— Standard Glee Book, v. d.
— Part-Song Book, in progress.
Oliphant, T., Collection (Glees), n. d.
Orpheus, the, Glees and Part-songs (Novello), in progress.
Page, J., Festive Harmony, 1804, 4 v.
Playford, J., Musical Companion, 1673.
Pleasant Musical Companion, catches, 1701 (Playford).
Rimbault, E. F., Vocal Part Music, n. d.
Smith, J. S., Musica Antiqua, 1812, 2 v.
— English Songs in Score, 1779.
Taylor, E., Vocal School of Italy [1839]
Triumphs of Oriana, ed. by T. Morley, 1601.
Warren, E. T., Vocal Harmony, v. d.
Vonge, N., Musica Transalpina, 1588-97, 2 v.

PERIODICALS.

American Art Journal, New York, 1846—
Apollo, Boston, U.S., 1882—
Apollonicon, or Musical Album, London, 1832.
Athenæum, Journal of Literature, Science, the Fine Arts, Music, and the Drama, London, 1828—
Benham's Musical Review, Indianapolis—monthly.
Birmingham and Midlands Musical Journal, 1884.
Birmingham Musical Examiner, Sept. 1, 1845, Jan. 3, 1846 (19 no's.)—weekly.
Brainard's Musical World, Cleveland, 1863—monthly.
British Minstrel, and Musical and Literary Miscellany, 1842-44.
Choir and Musical Record, London, July, 1863—
Church's Musical Visitor, Cincinnati, 1871—monthly.
Concordia, A Journal of Music and the Sister Arts, London, 1875-76.
Dramatic and Musical Review, London, April 1842, Dec. 1851—weekly and monthly.
Dwight's Journal of Music, Boston, 1852-1880.
English Musical Gazette, or Monthly Intelligence, London, 1819.
Euterpean, The, A Critical Review of Music and the Drama, London, Aug., Nov., 1849—weekly.
Euterpeiad, The, A Musical Review, and Tablet of the Fine Arts, New York, 1830.
Gem, and Musical Herald, London, 1884.
Goldbeck's Journal of Music, Chicago—monthly.
Grafton Journal, 1825-26 (H. E. Moore).
Harmonicon, London, 1823-33 — monthly. Edit. by W. Ayrton.
Howe's Musical Monthly, Boston.
London and Provincial Music Trades Review, 1877—
London Figaro, May 1870—
London Literary and Musical Observer, Mar., Sept., 1848—weekly.
Loomis' Musical and Masonic Journal, New Haven, Conn.—monthly.

Lute, The, A Monthly Journal of Musical News, London, 1883—.
Magazine of Music, and Journal of the Musical Reform Association, London, 1884—
Monthly Musical and Literary Magazine, London, 1830.
Monthly Musical Record, London, 1870 —
Music, A Weekly Newspaper for Musicians and Amateurs, London, April to Aug. 1880
Music Publishers' Circular and Monthly Trade List, London, 1853.
Music Trade Review, New York, 1871—
Musical Album, Montreal, 1882.
Musical Amateur, a Monthly Chronicle, Liverpool, 1861.
Musical American, New York, 1882.
Musical and Dramatic Courier, New York, 1880.
Musical and Dramatic World, Liverpool, 1881-83.
Musical Athenæum (Mainzer), London, 1842.
Musical Echo, Milwaukee—monthly.
Musical Education, a Monthly Review, London, 1883.
Musical Examiner, London, Nov. 1842, Dec. 1844.
Musical Gazette and Review, London, 1878.
Musical Globe. New York—monthly.
Musical Herald, a Journal of Music and Musical Literature, London, May 1846, May 1847—weekly.
Musical Herald, Boston, U.S., 1880—
Musical Library, Supplement, London, April 1834, July 1836—monthly.
Musical Magazine. London, 1835, 12 nos.
Musical Monitor, New York—quarterly.
Musical Notes, London, 1883—monthly.
Musical Observer, Boston, Mass., 1883.
Musical Opinion, London, 1873—monthly.
Musical Pioneer, New York.
Musical Reporter, Boston, Mass., Jan., Aug., 1841.
Musical Review, or Guide to the Musical World, London, 1863.
Musical Review, New York, 1850.
Musical Review, New York, 1879—
Musical Review, London, 1884.
Musical Society, London, 1886.
Musical Standard, a Newspaper for Musicians, London, 1862—
Musical Times and Singing Class Circular, London, 1842—
Musical World, London, 1836—
Musician and Artist, Boston.
New Musical and Universal Magazine, London, Sept. 1774, Dec. 1775, 4 v.
New York Musical Times, edited by Willis.
New York Philharmonic Journal.
Orchestra, the, London, Oct. 1863, Mar. 1874 — weekly; 1874-1882 — monthly; from 1882 combined with the "Choir" and "Musical Educator."
Organist, the, a monthly musical journal, Apr.-Dec., 1866; changed to Church Choir Master and Organist, Jan., 1867-Dec., 1868; The Choir Master, 1869, etc.; ended Dec., 1869.
Orpheonist, the, New York, ed. by E. Jerome Hopkins.
Psalmodist, a monthly magazine, Paisley, 1874.
Psalmodist and Magazine of Sacred Music, Edinburgh, 1856.
Quarterly Musical Magazine and Review, London, 1818-29.
Quarterly Musical Register, London, 1812.
S. Cecilia Magazine, Edinburgh, 1883-84, monthly.
Scottish Monthly Musical Times, Edinburgh, Oct. 1876, Dec. 1878.
Sherman and Hydes Musical Review, San Francisco, monthly.
Tonic Sol-Fa Reporter, London, 1853; enlarged, 1883—
Whitney's Musical Guest and Literary Journal, Toledo, Ohio, monthly.

PIANOFORTE.

Aguilar, E., Learning the Pf. [1866].
Allen, G. B., New Tutor, n. d.
Benedict, Sir J., Art of Playing, n. d.
Bennett, A., Instructions [1825].
Bottomley, J., System [1847].
Brainard, G. W., New Method, n. d.
Brinsmead, E., History, n. d.; 2nd ed. 1879.
Burrowes, J. F., Primer, 1822.
Challoner, N. B., Guida di Musica, n. d.
Clark, F. S., First Steps, n. d.
Clark, R., Playing from Score, 1838.
Clarke, H. A., New Method, n. d.
Clarke, J., Instruction Book, n. d.
Clementi, M., Art of Playing, n. d., 2 v.
    — Gradus ad Parnassum, n. d., 2 v.
Clifton, J. C., Instructions, n. d.
Coggins, J., Musical Assistant, 1815.
    — Companion to do., 1824.
Corri, D., Art of Fingering, 1799.
Cramer, J. B., Method, 1846, 5 parts.
Czerny, C., Art of Playing, n. d.
    — Primer, n. d.
    — School, n. d., 4 vols.
Dixon, E. S., Primer, n. d.
Done, J., Tuner's Companion, n. d.
Eavestaff, W., Instructions, 1830.
Engel, C., Handbook, 1853.
Fillmore, J. C., Music, 1883-85.
Gilbert, E. B., Natural Method, n. d.
Goddard, J., Graduated Method, n. d.
Hallé, C., Practical School, n. d.
Hamilton, J. A., Modern Instructions, many eds.
Hiles, J., Catechism, n. d.
Howe, E., Instructor, n. d.
Hughes, G. A., Instruction Book for Blind, 1848.
Keith, P. W., Instructions [1833].

Lott, E. M., Catechism, 1879.
MacHardy, R., Progressive Playing, n. d.
Macmurdie, J., Juvenile Preceptor, 1828.
Mason, W., and Mathews, Pf. Technics, n. d.
Mason, W., Method, n. d.
— System for Beginners, n. d.
May, A., Piano School, n. d., 3 pts.
Neate, C., Essay on Fingering, n. d.
Pauer, E., The Pianoforte [1877].
Peters, W. C., Eclectic Instructor, n. d.
Plaidy, L., Technical Studies, n. d.
— Pf. Teacher's Guide, n. d.
Prentice, T. R., The Musician, 1883.
Richardson, N., Modern School, 1859.
— New Method, 1859.
Rimbault, E. F., First Book, 1848.
— Pianoforte, its origin, etc., 1860.
Rodwell, A., Juvenile pianist [1838].
Röhner, G. W., Piano Playing, n. d.
Root, G. F., Musical Curriculum, 1865.
— Guide for the Pf., n. d.
Rosellen, H., Method, n. d.
Sloper, L., Tutor, n. d.
Smallwood, W., Tutor, n. d.
Spencer, C. C., The Pianoforte, n. d.
Taylor, F., Primer, 1877.
— Tutor, n. d.
Thalberg, S., Singing applied to Pf., 1853.
Wade, J. A., Handbook, 1806.

PRINCIPLES OF MUSIC.

Adcock, James, Rudiments, n. d.
Antoniotti, G., L'Artê Armonica, 1760, 2 v.
Arne [T. A.] Compleat Musician...1760.
Asioli, B., Musical Grammar, 1825.
Backus, A., Analysis of M., 1839.
Baker, B. F., Elementary M. Book, n. d.
Banister, H. C., Text-book, 1872, etc.
Bathe, W., True Arte of M., 1584, 2nd. edit., n. d.
Bemetzrieder, Music made easy, 1778.
Betts, E., Skill of M., n. d.
Bremner, R., Rudiments of M., 1756 ; 2nd ed., Edin; 3rd ed., London, 1763.
Brown, R., Musical Science, 1860.
Busby, T., Grammar, 1818.
Busby, T., Musical Manual...1828.
Callcott, J. W., Grammar, 1806 ; other ed.
Camidge, M., Instruction, n. d.
Clarke, J., Catechism, n. d.
Corri, D., Grammar, n. d.
Culwick, J. C., Rudiments, 1881.
Cummings, W. H., Rudiments [1877].
Currie, J., First Musical Grammar [1873].
Danneley, J. F., Musical Grammar, 1826.
Davenport, F. W., Elements, n. d.
Dawson, C., Elements, 1844.
D'Esté, J., Music made easy, 1849.
Dibdin, C., Music epitomized, n. d.
Fairbairn, J., Elements, 2 pts., 1832.
Fétis, F. J., Music explained, 1842, 1844.
Fontana, B., Musical Manual, 1847.

Gauntlett, H. J., 156 Questions, 1864.
Goodban, T., Rudiments, 1825, 1836.
Goss, Sir J., Catechism, 1835.
Groome, W., Concise Treatise, 1870.
Gunn, A., Introduction, 1803.
Hewitt, D. C., New Analysis, 1828.
— True Science, 1860.
Hiles, H., Grammar, 2 v., n. d.
Hullah, J., Musical Grammar, n. d.
Jousse, J., Music epitomized, n. d.
Keith, R. W., Musical Vade Mecum, 1820, 2 v.
Lampe, J. F., Art of Music, 1740.
Law, A., Rudiments, 1783.
— Musical Primer, 1803.
Lobe, J. C., Catechism, 1885.
Logier, J. B., Manual, 1828.
— System, 1827.
Lunn, H. C., Elements, 1849.
Macmurdie, J., Elements, n. d.
Mainzer, J., Grammar, 1843.
Malcolm, A., Treatise, 1721.
Mandel, C., System, 1869.
Mason, L., Pestalozzian Teacher, n. d.
Mathews, W. S. B., How to Understand M. 1880.
Merz, K., Musical Hints, n. d.
Morley, T., Introduction, 1597.
Murby, T., Student's Manual, n. d.
O'Donnely, Elementary M., 1841.
Playford, J., Skill of Musick, 1655.
Prelleur, P., Musick-master, 1731.
Relfe, J., Guida Armonica [1798].
— Lucidus ordo, 1821.
— Musical Instruction, 1819.
Saroni, H. S., Musical vade mecum, 1852.
Simpson, C., Principles, 1665.
Skeffington, T. C., Musical Art, 1858.
Smith, J., Treatise, 1853, 2 v.
Spencer, C. C., Elements, 1829.
— Treatise, 1850, 2 v.
Spinola, J. J., Grammar, 1850.
Tans'ur, W., Musical Grammar, 1746, etc.
— Elements of M., 1772.
Taylor, J., Text-book, 1876.
Troutbeck and Dale, M. Primer, 1873.
Weitzman, C. F., Musical Theory, n. d.

PSALMODY : COLLECTIONS.

Ainsworth, Henry, Booke of Psalmes, Amsterdam, 1612.
Alcock, J., Harmony of Sion, 1802.
Allon and Gauntlett, Congregational Psalmist, 1868.
Billings, W., New England Psalm Singer, 1770.
Brown-Borthwick, R., Supplemental Tune Book, n. d.
Carnie, W., Northern Psalter [1870].
Chetham, J., Book of Psalmody, 1718.
— Revised by Houldsworth, 1832.
Chope, R. R., Hymn Book, 1857-62.
Daniel, J., P. of Church of Scotland [1837].
Davie, J., M. of Church of Scotland, n. d.

Dibdin, H. E., Standard Psalm Tune Book [1851].
Este, T., Whole Booke of Psalmes, 1592.
Gauntlett, H. J., Comprehensive Tune Book, 1846-7.
— Congregational Psalmist, 1851.
Goss, Sir J., Parochial P., 1827.
Hamilton's Psalm and Hymn Tunes, 1868.
Hart, A., CL. Psalmes of Dauid, 1611.
Hately, T. L., National Psalmody [1847].
— Scottish P., 1852.
Havergal, W. H., Old Church P., 1849.
Holden, O., American Harmony, 1793.
— Worcester Collection, 1797.
Mason, L., Handel and Haydn Coll., 1822.
— Modern Psalmist, 1839.
Ives, E., American P., 1829.
Jacob, B., National P. [1819].
Livingston, N., Scottish Psalter, 1635, 1864.
Monk, E. G., Anglican Hymn Book, n. d.
Monk, W. H., Hymns of the Church, n. d.
Parr, H., Church of England P., v. d.
Playford, J., Whole Book of Psalms, 1697.
Pratt, J., Selection, 1817.
Ravenscroft, T., Whole Booke of Psalmes, 1621.
Redhead, R. Cathedral Choir Book, n. d.
— Parochial Ch. Tune Book, n. d.
Reed, D., Columbian Harmony, 1793.
Robinson, C. S., Songs for the Sanctuary, 1865.
Smith, R. A., Devotional Music, 1810.
— Sacred Harmony, 1829.
Tans'ur, W., Sacred Mirth, 1739.
— Psalm-singer's Jewel, 1760, etc.
Turle, J., Psalms and Hymns, 1863.
Warren, J., Collection, 1850-53, 4 v.
Psalm-singing. See Church Music.

PURCELL.

Cummings, W. H., Purcell, 1882.
Holmes, E., Life of P., n. d.
Novello, V., Biographical Sketch [1832].

REED ORGAN.

Beckel, J. C., School, n. d.
Clarke, W. H., New Method, n. d.
— R. O. Companion, n. d.
Emerson, L. O., Method, n. d.
Gurney, T. E., American School, n. d.
Kimball, H. E., New Method, n. d.
Merz, K., Modern Method, n. d.
Root, G. F., Guide, 1863.
Stainer, J., Tutor, 1883.
Rudiments of Music. See Principles.

SCALE.

Biddle, H. P., Musical S., n. d.
Capes, J. M., Growth of Musical S., 1879.
Clark, R., High Pitch of S., 1845.
Jackson, F., Musical S., n. d.
Pole, W., Diagrams, 1868.

SCHUBERT.

Austin, G. L., Life, 1873.
Frost, H. F., Schubert, 1881.
Hellborn, H., Life, 1869, 2 v.

SCHUMANN.

Maitland, J. A. F., Schumann, 1884.
Wasielewski, J. W. von, Life, 1878.

SCOTTISH MUSIC.

Coutts, W. G., Scottish *versus* Classic M., 1877.
Dalyell, Sir J. G., Musical Memoirs, 1849.
Dauney, W., Ancient S. Melodies, 1838.
Stenhouse, W., Lyric M. of Scotland, 1853.
Tytler, W., Dissertation, n. d.
See also Songs.

SHORTHAND MUSIC.

Austin, J., Stenographic M., n. d.
Hutchison, G. B., S. Music, n. d.

SINGERS.

Chorley, H. F., Musical Recollections, 1862, 2 v.
Clayton, E. C., Queens of Song, 1863, 2 v.
Ferris, G. T., Great Singers, 1880, 2 v.

SINGING.

Addison, J., S. practically treated...[1836].
Aprile, G., Italian Method (Cooke), n. d.
Arnold, C., Art of S., 1828.
Bach, A. B., Musical Education, 1880.
Bacon, R. M., Improving the Voice, 1825.
— Vocal Science, 1824.
... Vocal Ornament, n. d.
Balfe, M. W., Method of S., n. d.
Barnett, John, School [1860].
Barr, S., S. at Sight, 1859.
Bassini, C., Art of S., 1857.
— Method for the Barytone, 1868.
— Method for the Tenor, 1866.
Behnke, E., Mechanism of Human Voice, 1880.
Bennett, J., Cultivation of Voice, n. d.
Blockley, J., Singer's Companion, n. d.
Browne, L., Science and Singing, 1884.
— Throat and its Diseases, 1878.
— Medical Hints, 1876.
— Voice Use and Stimulants, 1885.
Browne and Behnke, Voice, Song, and Speech, 1883.
Camus, J. P. le, Art of S., 1833.
Carnaby, W., S. Primer, 1827.
Cazalet, W. W., Voice, or the Art of S., 1861.
Concone, G., Fifty Lessons in S., n. d.
— School of Sight-S., n. d.
Cooke, T. S., S. exemplified, n. d.
Corri, D., Singer's Preceptor, 1810, 2 v.
Curwen, J., Tonic Sol-fa Method, 1854.
— Grammar of Vocal Music, n. d.
— Standard Course, n. d.
Daniell, W. H., The Voice, 1873.

Day, H. W., Vocal School, 1844.
Dixon, W., Introduction, 1795.
Duggan, J. F., Singing-master's Assistant, n.d.
Ellis, A. J., Pronunciation, 1877.
— Speech in song, 1878.
Emerson, L. O., Method, n.d.
Ferrari, A. A. G., Formation of Voice, 1857.
Ferrari, G. G., Italian Singing [1815].
— Instructions, 1827.
Forde, W., New Method, n. d.
— Principles [1830], etc.
— Singing at Sight, n. d.
Goodban, T., Introduction, 1829.
Hamilton, J. A., Modern Instructions, n. d.
Harker, W., Elements, 1845.
Henry, P. C., S. Preceptor. n. d.
Hiles, H., Vocal Tutor, n. d.
Horncastle, J. H., S. at Sight, 1829.
Howard, J., Vocal Reform, n. d.
Huckel, W., Art of S., 1845.
— Cultivation of Voice, n. d.
Hullah, J., Vocal Music, 1843.
Jousse, J., Art of Sol-fa-ing, n. d.
King, M. P., S. at First Sight, 1806.
Kitchiner, W., Vocal Music, 1821.
Lablache, L. Vocal Method, n. d.
Lanza, G., Elements of S., 1809, 3 v.
— S. Familiarly Exemplified, 1817.
Lee, G., The Voice, 1870.
Lee, G. A., Vocal Tutor, n. d.
Loder, E. J., Instructions, n. d.
Lunn, C., Philosophy of Voice, n. d.
— Vox Populi, 1880.
— Vocal Expression, 1878.
— Conservation and Restoration, 1882.
— Artistic Voice, 1884.
Mason, L., Vocal Music, 1834.
Nava, G., Baritone School, n. d.
Nelson, S., Vocal School, n. d.
Novello, J. A., Vocal Rudiments, n. d.
Novello, M. S., Vocal School, n. d.
— Voice and Vocal Art, n. d.
Parker, H., The Voice, n. d.
Penna, F., Singing, 1878.
Pergetti, P., Treatise [1857], 3 pts.
Phillips, H., Musical Declamation, 1848.
Phillips, T., Principles [1830].
Philp, E., How to Sing an English Ballad, 1883.
Pinsuti, C. E., Hints to Students, n. d.
Randegger, A., Singing [1878].
Rauzzini, V., Solfeggi, n. d.
Rimbault, E. F., Tutor, n. d.
Röhner, G. W., Art of S., 1856.
Romer, F., Physiology of Voice, 1850.
Root, G. F., Singer's Manual, 1849.
— School of S., n. d.
Rush, J., Philosophy of the Human Voice, 1827.
Sainton-Dolby, C. H., Tutor, n. d.
Seiler, E., Voice in S., 1869.
Semple, A., The Voice, 1885.
Smith, R. A., Introduction [1826].

Taylor and Turle, S. at Sight, 1846.
Tenducci, G. F., Treatise, n. d.
Tosi, P. F., Florid Song, 1742.
Wallworth, T. A., Art of S., n. d.
Walshe, W. H., Dramatic S., 1881.
Welsh, T., Vocal Instructor, n. d.
Wilhelm-Hullah, Method, 1842 and 1850.
Sound. See Acoustics.

SONGS.

Aird, J., Selection of Airs, 6 v., n. d.
American Musical Miscellany, 1798.
Arnold, J., Essex Harmony...1767-74, 2 v.
Banquet of Musick, 1688-92, 6 books (Playford).
Barsanti, F., Old Scots Tunes, 1742.
Bickham, G., Musical Entertainer [1750], 2 v.
Bishop, Sir H. R., National Melodies, n. d.
Bremner, R., Thirty Scots Songs, 1749.
— Twelve Scots Songs, 1760.
— Curious Scots Tunes, 1759.
British Musical Miscellany, 1733, 4 v.
Bunting, E., Ancient Irish Music, 1796-1840, 3 v.
Calliope, or English Harmony, 1739, 2 v.
Campbell, A., Albyn's Anthology...1816-18, 2 v.
Campbell, D., Music of Highland Clans, 1862.
Carey, H., Musical Century, 100 E. Ballads, 1737-40, 2 v.
Chappell, W., National Airs, 3 pts., 1838-40.
— Old English Ditties, n. d., 2 v.
— Popular M. of Olden Time... [1845-59], 2 v.
Choice Ayres, Songs, and Dialogues, Lond., 1676-84, 5 books.
Christie, W., Traditional Ballad Airs, 1876-81, 2 v.
Clio and Euterpe, 1759-62, 3 v.
Comes Amoris, or Companion of Love, n. d., 5 v.
Conran, M., Music of Ireland, 1850.
Corri, D., Favourite Scots Songs, 1788, 2 v.
Deliciæ Musicæ, newest and best songs, 1695-6, 4 books.
Dun, F., Orain na'h Albain, 1848.
D'Urfey, T., Wit and Mirth, 1719, 6 v.
Fraser, S., Airs and Melodies, 1815 and 1874.
Gow, Nath., Vocal Melodies of Scotland, n.d.
Graham, G. F., Songs of Scotland, 1848-49, 3 v.
Grier, W., Musical Encyclopædia, 1835.
Hamilton, W., Select Songs of Scotland, 1848.
Hardiman, J., Irish Minstrelsy, 1831, 2 v.
Hodges, C. L., Peninsular Melodies [1830].
Hogg, J., Jacobite Relics, 1819-21, 2 v.
Horncastle, F. W., Music of Ireland, 1844, 3 parts.
Hullah, J., Ed. 58 English Songs, 17th and 18th Century, n. d.
Johnson, J., Scots Musical Museum [1787], 5 vols.
Jones, E., Musical Relicks, 1784-94.

www.ingramcontent.com/pod-product-compliance
Lightning Source LLC
Chambersburg PA
CBHW021223300426
44111CB00007B/404